SOCIAL DISORGANIZATION

HARPER'S SOCIAL SCIENCE SERIES

F. Stuart Chapin, Editor

SOCIAL
DISORGANIZATION
FOURTH EDITION

MABEL A. ELLIOTT, PH.D.

PROFESSOR OF SOCIOLOGY
CHATHAM COLLEGE

and

FRANCIS E. MERRILL, PH.D

PROFESSOR OF SOCIOLOGY
DARTMOUTH COLLEGE

HARPER & BROTHERS, PUBLISHERS, NEW YORK

TO OUR FELLOW SOCIOLOGISTS

Contents

Contents

PART FOUR. COMMUNITY AND NATIONAL DISORGANIZATION

PART FIVE. INTERNATIONAL DISORGANIZATION

Preface to the First Edition

American sociologists have traditionally presumed an interest in the practical considerations of social welfare. Courses in "Social Problems" or "Social Pathology" have been among the most popular offerings of academic sociology, yet there has seldom been any attempt to integrate the subject matter within a scheme of systematic sociology. For the most part, the approach to the conglomerate topics listed under these headings has been on a strictly common-sense level. Little or no consideration has been given to the social processes involved in these objective manifestations of disordered social relationships.

Social Disorganization, as the name implies, is an attempt to study these problems from the standpoint of the social processes which bring them about. It is in a sense a study of the genesis of anti-social attitudes in the individual, the family, and the community, and of the conflict between these attitudes and those held by the larger defining group. The specific manifestations of disorganization, whether they take the form of individual sex behavior, tensions between husband and wife, or the failure to obey the laws of a given community, are incidental to an underlying conflict of attitudes.

The wide variety of problems of individual, family, and community disorganization considered below are related, as far as possible, to the sociological concepts which they exemplify. The authors have attempted to integrate the most significant conclusions of contemporary sociology on these subjects. The disorganization of the homeless man, for instance, is not treated as an isolated phenomenon; rather, he is discussed as an unfortunate victim of the larger process of human mobility. Divorce is not considered simply as an alarming symptom of the decay of marriage; rather is it treated as a significant index of a number of converging social movements which have resulted in drastic changes in the structure and function of the family. Political corruption is not held to be the result of the sinister machinations of a group of vicious and unprincipled politicians; rather is it viewed as a phase of disorganization that is the natural result of certain social forces operating in the community.

The authors have consciously avoided the use of the term, "social pathology," and the biological implications of the organic nature of society that such a concept embodies. We have spoken of a *disorganized,* rather than a *pathological,* individual, family, or community. We realize that this may seem merely to be substituting one norm for another, a standard of social organization for that of social health. But the implications of this distinction go farther than this. In recent years, students of the nature of society have gradually abandoned the quasi-biological organic concepts that were so popular at the turn of the century. Society has been conceived in terms peculiar to itself, rather than in terms of a hypothetical superorganism. As must be apparent from any perusal of our book, we believe that any fruitful study of the nature of social disorganization must be based upon an analysis of social organization and social processes.

In our exposition of the specific manifestations of social disorganization we hope to make some claim to logical arrangement. The division of the subject matter into individual (or personal), family, and community disorganization is the first step in this direction. This order might, of course, be reversed with equal logic, inasmuch as the disorganization of the individual and that of the community are essentially but two aspects of the same whole. Each of the major divisions is prefaced by discussion of the conceptual nature of the social processes involved in the particular type of disorganization under consideration. Similarly, this arrangement has been applied to the individual chapters wherever feasible. Each division is concluded by a discussion of those types of acute disorganization which represent the tragic dénouement of the particular crisis that is under investigation. Thus suicide is presented as the final outcome of the process of individual disorganization, the last and irrevocable step in a series of minor crises. Desertion and divorce are the twin issues of family disorganization; personal demoralization following divorce is a possible aftermath. Revolution is considered as the violent breakdown of a traditional organization of both the local and the national community. Thus we have attempted to develop a certain conceptual unity to problems that have heretofore been considered in a somewhat random fashion.

While our book represents a conscious effort to reorganize the approach to the academic study of social problems, we recognize our side debt to all previous contributions in the field from which we have drawn so liberally for illustrative material. A survey of European literature in the field indicates that the French have made the most notable contribution. Since so little of the French sociological theory is available in contemporary American publications, we are including a summary statement, "Social Disorganization in Contemporary French Thought," in the Appendix.

In the preparation of the manuscript we wish particularly to acknowledge our indebtedness to Professor Winnifred D. Lowrance of the University of Kansas who read the proof, and to Mrs. Dorothy Grauerholz Wright who gave so much time and care to the preparation of the index.

Mabel A. Elliott
Francis E. Merrill

December, 1933

Preface to the Fourth Edition

The fourth edition of *Social Disorganization* is a completely new book. It is still organized, however, about the same general theoretical framework as the first edition published in 1934. While a number of books on social problems have appeared in the intervening years, we are still convinced that the social disorganization approach is better. In our judgment, such an approach affords greater sociological insight and gives the student a better tool for analyzing the tensions and conflicts which disturb modern society. Social disorganization, furthermore, is truly concerned with sociology, for it is the process by which the relationships binding persons together in groups are strained, loosened, or broken completely. When the patterns of interaction which hold the group together are impaired or disrupted, social disorganization results.

Some books on social problems contain comparatively little sociology. A social problem by definition involves value judgments which define a particular situation as undesirable. The concept of undesirability is, however, difficult to measure, whereas social disorganization is concerned more directly with objectively measurable phenomena. At the same time we recognize that much of the material covered in the present text is also primary data to a social problems approach. On the other hand, all social problems do not result in social disorganization. Only the social problems which are related to social disorganization are treated in our text.

There have been many additions to scientific sociology during the decade since 1950 when the third edition of this book appeared. The present book is much richer for this fact. There has been much research, for example, with reference to: class, status and role, small groups, juvenile delinquency and adult criminality, factors in mental deficiency, mental illness, divorce and desertion, alcoholism, the place of women in industry, and matters concerning racial and religious prejudice—to mention some of the most important. Developments in agriculture and the mechanization of agricultural production have produced unparalleled shifts in population with consequent disorganization to rural economic and social institutions. Considerable sociological research in the rural community has reflected this trend. Most of the above research data concern problems which have always existed but of which we are at present more aware. In some cases, however, the problems themselves are more acute, as for example racial segregation and world revolution.

On the international scene, revolution has been on the march in Asia and Africa as well as in Eastern Europe and the Near East. The treatment of this theme has therefore been pointed up. Meanwhile, several intensive analyses of totalitarianism by European and American scholars have given us new perspectives and fresh insights into this phenomenon. War as the most disruptive of all social disorganization has temporarily, at least, been replaced by the "Cold War." International tensions are so patent, however, that sociological research in the reduction of these tensions deserves greater political and scientific support than has thus far been available. Nevertheless, there have been a number of trenchant studies of war costs and problems of adjustment to a nonmilitary economy.

Social change is one of the most significant factors in social disorganization and is thus an important focus of the present book. We have tried to incorporate most of the significant new research in the various subjects covered in the text. By so doing we hope to give the student a comprehensive picture of scholarly sociological research, as well as that of related disciplines which bear directly upon the different aspects of social disorganization. If we have stretched the students' minds a bit in the process we shall be satisfied.

In order to incorporate the new research data in other fields, we have somewhat condensed the treatment of family disorganization. Present day courses in the Family now cover much of the material formerly treated in our section on family disorganization. In the chapters on the juvenile delinquent and the adult offender, material from several heretofore unpublished research projects supervised by Miss Elliott are incorporated. These and other recent researches give some provocative insights into delinquency and crime. We have added two entirely new chapters on the rural community which throw additional light on community disorganization. In order to keep the size of the book within reason, we have reduced or eliminated less significant materials in the community disorganization section. All of the chapters are completely rewritten, but certain chapters, for example those on alcoholism, migration, racial minorities, and totalitarianism, contain almost wholly new materials.

We are, first of all, primarily indebted to the authors whose research has been summarized and cited in this book. Certain persons, however, should be given special recognition for their assistance. Professor Otis Durant Duncan of the University of Oklahoma made detailed suggestions with reference to current aspects of social disorganization in the rural community. One of his many valuable suggestions was to include a discussion of the closing of country banks. This we were able to trace through the help of the Federal Deposit Insurance Corporation which supplied important materials.

As always, we have found the various federal governmental agencies very cooperative. Mrs. Alice K. Leopold, assistant to the Secretary of Labor, supplied important research data on women and children in industry. Mr. A. W. Motley of the Bureau of Labor Standards organized unpublished data on current standards for child labor laws and compulsory school legislation. Dr. Halbert S. Dunn and his assistants at the National Office of Vital Statistics furnished unpublished materials on marriage and divorce and illegitimacy as well as information on venereal disease. Dr. Mapheus Smith of the United States Office of Education furnished us with the prepublication study of schools in 101 most rural counties. Dr. Margaret Hagood of the Bureau of Agricultural Economics of the United States Department of Agriculture supplied us with important studies in rural health institutions and rural levels of living. Dr. Howard Brunsman and Dr. Paul C. Glick of the Census Bureau supplied special information on unemployment, racial populations, and marriage and family data. Dr. Glick and his publishers, John Wiley and Sons, also gave us permission to quote from a table in his book, *American Families*. Dr. Richard Perlman of the Children's Bureau has supplied statistical data on juvenile delinquency and Dr. James V. Bennett of the Federal Prison Bureau and Mr. J. Edgar Hoover of the F.B.I. have supplied data on prisoners and adult criminals. The Bureau of Public Assistance of the United States Department of Health, Education and Welfare has supplied special studies on desertion and old age security.

Dr. August B. Hollingshead and John Wiley and Sons permitted us to quote from tables in *Social Class and Mental Illness*. We are also grateful to Dr. Thomas P. Monahan and *Marriage and Family Living* for permission to quote from tables in his study on divorce rates among various occupational levels. Dr. Austin L. Porterfield likewise granted permission to quote from his tables in *Youth in Trouble*. We also wish to thank Professor Albert J. Ossman, Jr., of Chatham College for his suggestions on bibliographical materials on totalitarianism.

The librarians at Baker Library of Dartmouth College, James Laughlin Library of Chatham College, Carnegie Library in Pittsburgh, and the libraries of the University of Pittsburgh and the University of Georgia have likewise given valuable assistance in locating special materials. We are also grateful to Mr. Herbert E. Hodges, Mr. Joseph G. Winders, and to Mrs. Emily Archibald Merrill for help in the proofreading, and to Mrs. Merrill for her generous contribution in making the author index.

Needless to say, we have been gratified at the reception of the previous editions of *Social Disorganization*. The sociologists who have used this book as a text have made helpful suggestions, many of which we have incorporated in the fourth edition. To these colleagues we also express our hearty appreciation.

MABEL A. ELLIOTT
FRANCIS E. MERRILL

November, 1960
Pittsburgh, Pennsylvania
Hanover, New Hampshire

Suggestions to the Teacher

Part of the problem of everyone who teaches this or any book dealing with social disorganization is the matter of keeping statistics up to date. If the teachers will correspond with the Census Bureau and the various federal agencies dealing with the various problems covered in the text, statistical materials can be obtained, usually without fee. Likewise, state and city governments will often provide statistical data for classroom use.

PART ONE

Introduction

CHAPTER 1

Social Organization

Social Organization in a Dynamic Society

Life is dynamic. Life is continuous and often bewildering change. Modern man must adjust to situations for which no precedents exist, no rules are formulated, and no laws are written. The individual, the family, the community, the nation, and the world of nations are all involved, in varying degrees, in changing situations. This process tends to make old truths inapplicable and new ones uncertain. We are moving toward an unpredictable future and one for which previously established patterns are no longer adequate. New patterns of belief and behavior have not yet evolved to take the place of the old. The group relationships that held a former society together are undergoing stresses and strains. The groups range in size from the married pair to the family of nations. The process by which group relationships are broken is called social disorganization.

Social change has occurred since the dawn of history. The *fact* of change is therefore by no means new, but the *rate* of change is unprecedented. Long before the industrial revolution ushered in modern times, men were forced to adjust to new technological and material developments. Each advance, from the stone ax to the hydrogen bomb, produced modifications in individual reactions that eventually altered group patterns of conduct. The Western world has survived several disruptions so intense that the very pillars of society seemed on the verge of permanent dissolution. We are not the first to face the necessity of adapting to social change or collapsing before the inexorable march of events. Only the time element is no longer the same. Social change is now more accelerated than at any period hitherto faced by the human race. Society is becoming increasingly dynamic.[1]

Every society has ways of thinking and acting that grow out of common experience and crystallize into systems of social control. These normative patterns include the folkways, mores, laws, institutions, and (more recently) many elements of the mass culture. Group life thus assumes a comparative orderliness which the average person seldom questions. When minor adjust-

[1] Hornell Hart, "Technological Acceleration and the Atomic Bomb," *American Sociological Review*, 11:277–293 (June, 1946); Hornell Hart, "Some Cultural-Lag Problems Which Social Science Has Solved," American Sociological Review, 16:223–227 (April, 1951).

3

ments are required, the individual can usually make them by employing the conventional procedures which society has established. When these patterns prove inadequate to the new situation, however, the old equilibrium breaks down. The group becomes disorganized, and its relationships disintegrate. Since change continually threatens the social equilibrium, social disorganization is a normal characteristic of a dynamic society.[2]

This book is primarily concerned with social disorganization in its various aspects. An adequate understanding of social *disorganization,* however, depends upon an understanding of social *organization.* We are using each of these terms, in a sense, as the opposite of the other. Social organization implies the reverse of social disorganization. Social organization is characterized by the harmonious operation of the different elements of a social system. When a group functions harmoniously, it is (relatively) organized. We may thus speak of the organization of a family, community, political unit, or nation. Social organization depends upon common definitions of social goals and an accepted program for their achievement.[3]

Social organization is, however, a relative concept. No society has ever functioned with complete efficiency, each member playing his part in harmonious coordination with every other member according to accepted group patterns. Different degrees of social organization are known to the historian and cultural anthropologist. The feudal society of the late Middle Ages was a relatively highly organized society, despite minor local struggles. A small, preliterate, isolated, contemporary society is another.

Even in the latter case, however, social organization is not completely effective. As Malinowski discovered in his researches among the Trobriand Islands, many of the more burdensome group customs in a primitive society are evaded when the person believes that he can get away with it.[4] There is no society in modern Western civilization in which perfect social organization exists, for such a situation implies a unanimity and a stability that are inconceivable in a rapidly changing world. Nevertheless, the concept of an organized society is an abstraction useful for comparative and analytical purposes, even though it does not depict complete "reality" in the world in which we live.[5]

Meanwhile our contemporary dynamic society exhibits a confusing dualism toward social change. In the process of daily living, the individual faces a succession of new situations which require new physical adjustments, new definitions of behavior, and new ways of thinking. At the same time, social controls tend to become fixed, formalized, and invested with moral sanctions. Experience is continually changing, but the ways of thinking about experience

[2] Ralph Kramer, "The Conceptual Status of Social Disorganization," *American Journal of Sociology, 48:*466–474 (January, 1943).

[3] We are departing somewhat from the traditional usage in this respect. Cf. Charles Horton Cooley, *Social Process,* Charles Scribner's Sons, New York, 1922.

[4] Bronislaw Malinowski, *Crime and Custom in Savage Society,* Routledge and Kegan Paul, London, 1926, part II, chap. 1.

[5] Lawrence K. Frank, "What Is Social Order?" *American Journal of Sociology, 49:* 470–477 (March, 1944).

remain relatively static. The impact of change upon what society regards as sacred norms leads to stress and maladjustment. The norms may involve churchgoing, compulsory school attendance, marriage ceremonies, respect for private property, or the place of women in the home. In an earlier society, these norms helped to hold the group together. When such normative practices break down, the group relationship is impaired. This process is known as social disorganization.[6]

Social Interaction in a Dynamic Society

The basic unit of society is the group. The group may be provisionally defined as two or more persons who *interact* with each other over an appreciable period of time. Social interaction is the process in which persons participate in reciprocal actions. That is, one person acts in response to the real or anticipated action of the other. In social interaction, as Blumer has aptly stated, one takes the other into account and governs himself accordingly.[7] Interaction is the very stuff of social behavior, for without interaction there would be no society. The concept of social interaction was more formally defined by Homans as follows: "When we refer to the fact that some unit of activity of one man follows or . . . is stimulated by some unit of activity of another . . . we are referring to interaction."[8] Social interaction is the way in which social relationships take place.

Social interaction may be analyzed in terms of social processes. Park and Burgess classified social processes in terms of communication, conflict, competition, accommodation, and assimilation. To these a sixth process, cooperation may be added. In other words, when people interact they do something. They communicate, conflict, compete, accommodate, assimilate, or cooperate.[9] They also interact in more than one way at the same time, as a nation at war accommodates its internal differences to fight more effectively. In a dynamic society, social processes are also in a constantly shifting state of equilibrium; large numbers of persons influence one another in roughly similar ways over appreciable intervals of time. Social processes are thus closely related to social organization and social disorganization since they are involved in both. A short clarification of these processes is therefore in order.

1. *Communication.* Communication is basic to social interaction. Indeed, as John Dewey has pointed out, "society not only continues to exist *by* transmission, *by* communication, but it may fairly be said to exist *in* transmission, *in* communication."[10] Communication is the process of transmitting and receiving symbolic stimuli by conversation, gestures, and other signs. Com-

[6] Talcott Parsons, *The Social System,* The Free Press, Glencoe, Ill., 1951, pp. 96–101.

[7] Herbert Blumer, "Psychological Import of the Human Group," chap. 8 in Muzafer Sherif and M. O. Wilson (eds.), *Group Relations at the Crossroads,* Harper & Brothers, New York, 1953.

[8] George C. Homans, *The Human Group,* Harcourt, Brace and Company, New York, 1950, p. 36.

[9] Robert E. Park and Ernest W. Burgess, *Introduction to the Science of Sociology,* University of Chicago Press, Chicago, 1924, p. 51.

[10] John Dewey, *Democracy and Education,* The Macmillan Company, New York, 1916, p. 5.

munication involves common understandings and definitions of the situation. These understandings may differ from one social class to another, and members of the lower and middle classes in our society may have difficulty in communicating even though they speak the same language. Words often do not mean the same thing to them.[11] Complete understanding is seldom reached for any length of time. Communication is often incomplete and fragmentary in a dynamic society. The conveying of ideas must continue, however, for the individual or the group to function.[12]

2. *Conflict.* Communication between persons or groups is necessary for social organization. Communication may also result in social disorganization, however. When the contact between persons or groups is acrimonious, the process has been defined as conflict.[13] Although conflict may occasionally produce constructive ends, it is generally injurious to social organization.[14] In many social situations some degree of conflict is inevitable. In labor-management relations, for example, both sides are struggling for limited goals. Each side tries to increase its share of money or power. The desires of men are unlimited, and hence conflict is bound to arise from time to time.[15] In the family, continued conflict is injurious to marital solidarity and indicates underlying differences in attitudes and values. Such general conflict situations as feuds, class struggles, and strikes break down the relationships that hold other groups together. War and violent revolution are two of the most destructive forms of conflict. Under conditions of modern technology the organization of society itself is threatened by revolution and total war.[16]

3. *Competition.* When impersonal forces are in opposition, the process is called competition. When competition takes place, the members of society interact without personal antagonism. They are, indeed, often unconscious that they are competing; the wheat growers in Canada and Kansas may be unaware that they are vying in the world market. Competition has other attributes. As Park and Burgess expressed it, competition is the process which "determines the distribution of population territorially and vocationally."[17] Rural and urban population densities, interaction between the individuals in rural and urban areas, and the economic interdependence between classes and nations—these are all more or less determined by competitive processes. In contrast to those in a static and closed society, many of the statuses and goals in a dynamic society are open to competitive interaction.[18]

[11] Leonard Schatzman and Anselm Strauss, "Social Class and Modes of Communication," *American Journal of Sociology, 60*:329–338 (January, 1955).

[12] Jurgen Ruesch, "Synopsis of the Theory of Human Communication," *Psychiatry, 16*:215–243 (August, 1953).

[13] Park and Burgess, *op. cit.,* p. 574.

[14] Georg Simmel, *Conflict* and *The Web of Group-Affiliations* (translated by Kurt H. Wolff and Reinhard Bendix), The Free Press, Glencoe, Ill., 1955, chap. 3.

[15] Clark Kerr, "Industrial Conflict and Its Mediation," *American Journal of Sociology, 60*:230–245 (November, 1954).

[16] Raymond Aron, *The Century of Total War,* Doubleday and Company, Inc., New York, 1954.

[17] Park and Burgess, *op. cit.,* p. 508.

[18] Mark A. May and Leonard W. Doob, *Competition and Cooperation,* Social Science Research Council, New York, 1937.

4. *Accommodation.* Men in conflict eventually come to terms, if only through mutual exhaustion. Competitive and conflicting groups in modern society make various mutual, if impermanent, adjustments in order to carry on their various activities with a minimum of friction. In the mass industries —automobile, steel, coal, and the like—the powerful labor organizations and the giant corporations often submit their differences to mediation. In this way, they virtually acknowledge the impossibility of continued conflict and the necessity for accommodation.[19] If the conflicting forces are evenly matched, the exhaustion of both sides may come before any cessation of hostilities. When they vary in power, subordination of the weaker group often results. Whatever the type of accommodation, however, the stability of the society is affected. The resulting equilibrium may be prolonged, or it may be only a prelude to further conflict. Dynamic forces are still operative in the form of intergroup tensions, even though their potentialities for social disorganization may not be apparent.[20]

5. *Assimilation.* Assimilation is the process by which people of divergent cultures are absorbed into a new cultural synthesis. Since it is impossible for persons to divest themselves wholly of their old culture patterns, this synthesis is never complete. Various ethnic groups in the United States have contributed their own traits to the common culture which they have accepted and shared. The integration of millions of immigrants into a new and dynamic pattern has made this country the most impressive example of assimilation the world has ever known. Assimilation is a gradual process and depends upon intimate communication between the members of the larger group. It is true that assimilation has not operated with complete effectiveness in our society, but in general it has contributed to social organization.[21]

6. *Cooperation.* This social process is perhaps the most important of all. Cooperation is a form of interaction whereby two or more persons come together for the purpose(s) of performing tasks or evoking emotions which cannot take place without such shared activity. Cooperation is a type of interaction in which two or more persons work together for a common end. Despite the emphasis upon competition in the development of modern society, the importance of cooperation is infinitely greater. We are dependent upon others for almost everything, from food to affection. From the prehistoric family to the modern nation, cooperation has brought people together and holds them together in durable group relationships. In this sense, cooperation is basic to social organization. When cooperation breaks down, part of the organization of the group goes with it.

All processes of social interaction are characteristic of every society. The emphasis upon one or another process, however, varies greatly from one society to another. In recent centuries, our society has tended to encourage

[19] Kerr, *op. cit.*

[20] Robin M. Williams, Jr., *The Reduction of Intergroup Tensions,* Social Science Research Council, New York, 1947.

[21] Francis J. Brown and Joseph S. Roucek (eds.), *One America,* Prentice-Hall, Inc., New York, 1945.

competition and discourage cooperation, at least in the "practical" activities of everyday life. In economic behavior, athletics, education, and love, the individual has, by various devices, been encouraged to compete rather than cooperate. In other societies cooperation is encouraged to the virtual exclusion of competition or conflict. The warlike virtues are highly esteemed in some societies, whereas others develop personalities that are friendly, peaceable, and cooperative.[22]

Social Interaction in the Small Group

In their earlier analyses of social interaction, sociologists dealt in broad generalities in isolating the general processes which we have just considered. More recently, there have been investigations of social interaction between members of small, intimate, face-to-face groups whose size and composition lend themselves to experimental study.[23] Under laboratory conditions, the behavioral scientist has been able to observe and, to a certain extent, control social interaction in small groups. Quantitative methods have been applied in these studies, and a measure of controlled experimentation has thus been introduced into the observation of group behavior.[24] In this context, the small group has been defined as "any number of persons engaged in interaction with each other in a single face-to-face meeting or a series of such meetings, in which each member receives some impression or perception of each other member distinct enough so that he can . . . give some reaction to each of the others as an individual person."[25]

The reasons for the formation of the small group have been studied in terms pertinent to the larger subject of social organization. These appear to be (1) *personal attraction*—individuals join with others to form groups because they enjoy the company of other persons; (2) *group prestige*—they also form groups because of the prestige attached to such membership; (3) *task performance*—they may come together in groups because they want to do a job that cannot be done by individuals working alone.[26] In many cases these reasons overlap; the undergraduate joins a fraternity because he likes the members and also wishes to gain prestige. Men and women marry because they are romantically in love, because of the prestige of marriage, and because they want to start a home and rear a family.

The principles that govern interaction in the small group are, in many respects, the same as those in larger social systems. In the small group, however, the behavior of each individual can often be observed and measured more readily than in groups with a more complicated structure. The unit of

---

[22] Ruth Benedict, *Patterns of Culture*, Penguin Books, Inc., New York, 1946.

[23] Fred L. Strodtbeck, "The Case for the Study of Small Groups," *American Sociological Review, 19*:651–657 (December, 1954).

[24] G. E. Swanson, "Some Problems of Laboratory Experiments with Small Populations," *American Sociological Review, 16*:349–358 (June, 1951).

[25] Robert F. Bales, *Interaction Process Analysis,* Addison-Wesley Publishing Company, Inc., Reading, Mass., 1950, p. 33.

[26] Kurt W. Back, "Influence Through Social Communication," *Journal of Abnormal and Social Psychology, 46*:9–23 (January, 1951).

behavior in these investigations is *the meaningful act,* which refers to any form of communication, whether consciously carried on or not.[27] The organization of the group reflects the adequacy of communication. Without a minimum of effective communication, group agreement can never be reached.[28]

The cohesiveness of the small group is therefore directly related to the degree and efficiency of communication. Cohesiveness may be defined as the "forces which are acting on the members to stay in a group . . . the attraction of membership in a group for its members."[29] The forces that give rise to cohesiveness are important in group behavior, inasmuch as the group is effective only as long as it continues to function as such. A family group, a church group, or a friendship group is useful only as it continues to act toward its common goal(s). The forces that hold the group together are therefore basic to social organization. In the small social system we can see many of these forces at work.

The small group of the conjugal family in our society is a highly personal relationship, established by two persons with complex emotional and psychological needs. In the past, the conventional definition of family success was based upon its permanence—i.e., whether the spouses remained married throughout their lives. At the present time, the criteria of success have partially changed. Marriage is supposed to add to the personal happiness of the participants. When this satisfaction is not forthcoming, some persons believe that the marriage group should be broken and that the spouses should try again. Cohesiveness per se, therefore, is no longer the sole definition of the success in marriage.[30]

Social Structure in a Dynamic Society

"Social structure" is the term applied to the arrangement of the interrelated institutions, social patterns, and statuses and roles of individuals making up a given society.[31] *Status* is the position which the individual occupies in the group by virtue of his sex, age, family, class, occupation, marriage, and achievement. *Role* is the part he plays as a result of each status. In other words, the role is "the classification of the social position given to the individual who performs an activity differentiated in terms of the social structure. These roles involve obligations, rights, and expected performances of the individuals who hold them."[32] The status is "the sum total of an individual's (or group's) institutionalized positions in a social structure. . . ."[33]

[27] Robert F. Bales *et al.,* "Channels of Communication in Small Groups," *American Sociological Review, 16:*461–468 (August, 1951).

[28] Frederick F. Stephan, "The Relative Rate of Communication Between Members of Small Groups," *American Sociological Review, 17:*482–486 (August, 1952).

[29] Back, *op. cit.,* p. 9.

[30] William L. Kolb, "Sociologically Established Family Norms and Democratic Values," *Social Forces, 26:*451–456 (May, 1948).

[31] Talcott Parsons, "Age and Sex in the Social Structure of the United States," *American Sociological Review, 7:*604–616 (October, 1942).

[32] Marion J. Levy, Jr., *The Structure of Society,* Princeton University Press, Princeton, 1952, p. 159.

[33] *Ibid.,* p. 160.

Every person has a status because he is the child of his parents, because of his sex, because he is young or old, married or unmarried, an obscure or well-known person, a leader or a follower, educated or illiterate, articulate or inarticulate. Men and women are assigned different statuses and play different roles in every society.[34] Certain statuses are *ascribed* to each person by society, which defines the class position of the parents and the importance attached to the age group, the sex group, the marriage group, and the economic group. Other statuses are *achieved* by the person acting in various competitive situations. The poor boy may become a leader of industry with high position in society or he may become a scholar with high rank in a small academic group. Each achieved status is the result of individual effort, with an added element of good luck. The status of man or woman, however, is largely derived from the accident of birth in a particular society at a particular time. The person can do little about status ascribed on the basis of sex except play his part as best he can. He must, in general, act the way a man is *supposed* to act.[35]

Modern society is marked by a comparatively large number of achieved, as compared to ascribed, statuses, however. In primitive and static societies, the majority of persons remain in the position assigned to them at birth. The United States is the outstanding example of a society which is more or less dominated by achieved status. The individual has theoretically been free to rise as high in the social scale as his ability or good fortune permitted. In certain respects, the opportunity for attaining great wealth has decreased in recent decades. Nevertheless, the comparative chances for the average man to achieve higher status are still probably greater here than in any other society.[36]

The group, as we have said, assigns a particular role to each status. Little girls are expected to play with dolls and take an early interest in domestic activities. Boys are expected to devote themselves to pursuits virtually defined as masculine, such as baseball and fishing. Children are not expected to act like adults and vice versa. Persons who depart significantly and consistently from the roles which society considers appropriate to their statuses interfere with social organization. Social behavior must have a minimum of predictability. Members of each group must act as they are supposed to act (i.e., in terms of their appropriate statuses and roles) or the stability of social life is threatened. The behavior attached to the various statuses and roles represents an important aspect of social organization.[37]

The success with which an individual accepts his various roles depends in some cases upon his genetic abilities and in others upon the social situation.

[34] Margaret Mead, *Male and Female,* William Morrow and Company, Inc., New York, 1949.

[35] Ralph Linton, *The Cultural Background of Personality,* Appleton-Century-Crofts, Inc., New York, 1945, pp. 76–77.

[36] Cf. Ely Chinoy, "Social Mobility Trends in the United States," *American Sociological Review, 20:*180–186 (April, 1955).

[37] Kingsley Davis, "A Conceptual Analysis of Stratification," *American Sociological Review, 7:*309–321 (June, 1942).

In a dynamic society, there are often difficulties involved in carrying out the expected roles so that many persons, through no fault of their own, are unable to perform their social duties. Large-scale unemployment may cause a husband to fail as a breadwinner, for example. A dynamic society is characterized by a great deal of role conflict, which means "the exposure of the actor to conflicting sets of legitimized role expectations such that complete fulfillment of both is realistically impossible."[38] In a static society, on the other hand, status and role are more secure, and adjustment is proportionately easier. In terms of social structure, therefore, a dynamic society is marked by (1) complexity of status and role, (2) high rate of change in these expectations, and (3) attendant difficulty of personal adjustment.

American society inherited a system of statuses and roles that evolved in an agrarian and homogeneous society. This system no longer operates effectively in an industrial and heterogeneous society. In consequence, many persons are not sure of their positions. The continuity between the generations in the performance of many roles has been broken by the rapidity of social change. The role of the husband as the sole economic head of the family has changed. The role of the wife in homemaking and child training has correspondingly changed, with millions of married women employed outside the home. For many persons, such a widespread change is a desirable modification of an obsolete system. By others it is regarded as a catastrophic decay of vital social relationships. Whatever the definition, these changes in family patterns represent the disorganization of traditional group relationships.[39]

In a dynamic society, a person has many choices as to what his lifework shall be, whom he shall marry, and where he shall live. The very fact of choice in these fields tends to complicate life, for the individual must make personal decisions on questions which a static society would decide for him. A decision in one area may involve role conflict in another decision and produce a certain amount of strain and frustration. The individual is also forced to improvise new roles to meet the unprecedented situations with which he is faced. Such improvisation may be difficult and uncomfortable, and many persons are unable to achieve it effectively. Faced with a degree of freedom which is probably unique in the history of organized society, they are often unequal to their new-found opportunities.[40]

Social Change in a Dynamic Society

The rate of social change is another factor in social organization. In earlier periods when society was relatively static, social change was correspondingly slow. It has been said that the era of George Washington resembled that of the Roman emperors more than modern industrial society.

---

[38] Parsons, *The Social System*, p. 280.

[39] Talcott Parsons, "The Social Structure of the Family," chap. 13 in Ruth N. Anshen (ed.), *The Family: Its Function and Destiny*, Harper & Brothers, New York, 1959 (rev. ed.).

[40] Roland L. Warren, "Social Disorganization and the Interrelationship of Cultural Roles," *American Sociological Review, 14*:83–87 (February, 1949).

The impact of technology and industry has altered the way of life in America so completely that many of its characteristic aspects would be incomprehensible to the father of our country.[41] The railroad, the automobile, the airplane, the radio, television, nuclear fission, intercontinental ballistic missiles, and man-made planets have immeasurably modified the world since this country became an independent nation. These technological innovations have produced the need for other changes in the social structure. Old patterns have crumbled and new ones have arisen to take their place. The interrelationships in technological, social, and cultural change produce a dynamic society.[42]

As a concept, social change was hitherto both vague and relative. Through quantitative measurements of mass changes in status, we have now begun to objectify this concept.[43] Social change occurs for many reasons—technological, industrial, economic, religious, and ideological. Discussion has arisen as to which, if any, of these factors has priority in "causing" changes in social structure. The Marxists maintain that changes in the ownership of the instruments of economic production are the prime movers in social change. Others are equally certain that religious and spiritual factors (e.g., the introduction of Christianity) set all the rest of the changes in motion. Still others point to ideological elements, such as the capitalistic ethic or the belief in the rights of man, as basic to all alterations in the social structure. Some attach great importance to science and invention as the chief factors which have modified the social structure.

All of these factors—and many others—have had an influence upon social change. There is no *single* cause, no *basic* prime mover, no *unique* instrument. The question of what *causes* social change therefore has no simple answer. Society is so complex, with technological, ideological, cultural, and structural elements involved in reciprocal relationships, that one factor influences every other and vice versa. The steam engine, for example, has been used for a variety of social purposes, from providing power for factories to moving a man-of-war. But the steam engine did not *create* the factory or the battleship, let alone the system of industrial production or the institution of government.[44]

In the world of science, however, the problem cannot be left at this point. The scientist must simplify his universe and then isolate the factors in a relationship of cause and effect. In the study of society, this approach has been used in estimating the role of technological innovation in social change. The sociologist tacitly admits that social change is a product of a variety of fac-

[41] William F. Ogburn, "Stationary and Changing Societies," *American Journal of Sociology*, 42:16–31 (July, 1936).

[42] Cf. S. C. Gilfillan, "Social Implications of Technical Advance," *Current Sociology*, 1:191–207 (Published by UNESCO, Paris, 1953).

[43] Donald J. Bogue, "The Quantitative Study of Social Dynamics and Social Change," *American Journal of Sociology*, 57:565–568 (May, 1952).

[44] Gilfillan, *op. cit.*, pp. 202–203.

tors, but at the same time he attempts to isolate the technological from the political, religious, economic, and ideological factors. In this sense, therefore, social change has been linked to technological innovation, which in turn transforms many of the other elements in the social structure. If the process of technological accumulation is slow, the society remains comparatively stable. As the culture base increases in size and complexity with the introduction of new technological traits, the stability of the society is threatened. The material and nonmaterial elements of the culture become maladjusted. A situation of "cultural lag" appears.[45]

In terms of the technological approach to social change, this sequence has been viewed as follows:

1. *Technological Innovations.* An innovation is "any thought, behavior, or thing that is new because it is qualitatively different from existing forms." An invention is "a technological innovation, a new thing."[46] The techniques by which the members of a society make a living are often the first to change. During the long millennia of preindustrial development, this process was infinitely slow. In recent decades the introduction of new techniques has occurred with geometric progression. New productive machinery and improvements on the old are constantly taking place as man seeks to better his material circumstances. In the United States these improvements in technology have brought about the highest standard of living in history.[47]

2. *Economic Institutions.* The economic relationships and institutions growing out of the underlying technological processes are the next to follow in this process of social change. Business units grow larger as the cost of specialized machinery increases. Entirely new industries, such as the automobile, petroleum, rubber, glass, and electronics industries, follow the new inventions in other fields. New social classes are created by the different productive functions in an industrial society. Large industrial unions occasion new power relations in the economy and provide careers for a new generation of labor leaders.[48]

3. *Social Institutions.* The institutions of the family, the school, the church, and the state are in turn affected by changes in the economic and social world. Members of these institutions participate in all the other institutions; hence the influence of institution upon institution is reciprocal. In the family alone the impact of technological change has been revolutionary, and in many respects family relationships will never be the same again. Future discoveries and inventions in the behavioral sciences may involve the family even more directly than have past innovations in industry. The social and

[45] William F. Ogburn, *Social Change,* The Viking Press, Inc., New York, 1950 (rev. ed.).
[46] H. G. Barnett, *Innovation: The Basis of Cultural Change,* McGraw-Hill Book Company, Inc., New York, 1953, pp. 7–8.
[47] William F. Ogburn, "Technology and the Standard of Living in the United States," *American Journal of Sociology,* 60:380–386 (January, 1955).
[48] Nelson N. Foote, "The Professionalization of Labor in Detroit," *American Journal of Sociology,* 58:371–380 (January, 1953).

biological sciences will doubtless bring about more radical changes in human relationships in the future than the physical and technological sciences have done in the past.[49]

4. *Ideological Elements.* The folkways, mores, myths, and ideologies tend to persist long after the situations which produced them have disappeared. These ideological elements are incorporated in the basic institutions through the personalities of their members. The lag between institutional practices and ideological sanctions is the cause for much of the instability of modern society. We shall discuss the implications of cultural lag for social disorganization in the next chapter. We merely wish to indicate here that the parts of a dynamic society change at a differential rate.[50]

Consensus in a Dynamic Society

In the process of social interaction, members of a group learn to expect certain behavior from one another. These expectations are reciprocal and they involve the behavior of the individual toward others, as well as their behavior toward him. Some of the aspects of these expectations have been discussed in connection with social roles, which are patterned conceptions of behavior appropriate to a certain status. Expectations also take on aspects of right and wrong, of what the person should and should not do. Some (but not all) of the group expectations become *norms*.

"The term 'social norm,'" says Sherif, "is a sociological designation referring . . . to all products of group interaction which regulate members' behavior in terms of the expected or even the ideal behavior. . . . A norm denotes not only expected behavior but a *range of tolerable behavior,* the limits of which define deviate acts."[51] Behavior thus has meaning largely in normative terms. Social organization depends upon the maintenance of group norms most of the time by most of the people. When the members act in accordance with the norms, their behavior is predictable and the group functions adequately. When the norms are not observed, social disorganization is imminent.

In social interaction, members of the group receive certain "benefits" from agreement upon norms and conforming to them. Paramount among these benefits is the basic one of being accepted. Society (and smaller groups) tends to accept persons who agree with its norms and reject those who are unwilling or unable to behave in accordance with the norms. Social organization is fostered by this feeling of identification with the group, whether in a boys' gang, labor union, or national state. In short, "if an individual desires to attain, or maintain, an intimate relationship with others, if he wants to 'get somewhere' either within a group or via a group, he must identify himself

---

[49] Meyer F. Nimkoff, "Technology, Biology, and the Changing Family," *American Journal of Sociology, 57:*20–26 (July, 1951).

[50] William F. Ogburn, "How Technology Changes Society," *Annals of the American Academy of Political and Social Science, 249:*81–88 (January, 1947).

[51] Muzafer Sherif, "Integrating Field Work and Laboratory in Small Group Research," *American Sociological Review, 19:*759–771 (December, 1954), p. 763.

with [their] opinions and values."[52] This identification and agreement within a society is known as consensus.

Social organization is thus in final analysis a matter of consensus. Without a general agreement on basic norms, society cannot exist. As Wirth has pointed out, "There is no society without an ethos, i.e., without shared values, objectives, preferences, and the well-founded anticipation of the members that all the others recognize the rules of the society and will abide by them."[53] When men fail to concur in these purposes, machine guns and police are impotent to maintain the *status quo*. Consensus involves a fund of common understandings and expectations on such vital matters as religion, government, economic relationships, and family systems. When the members of a society begin to lose faith in the normative definitions, group ties are loosened and social disorganization exists.

Consensus may be understood in terms of its literal derivation—namely, as a process of "feeling together" by the members of a society on the important norms of their common life. Consensus is thus a spontaneous product and cannot be enforced by fiat or force. In a sense, consensus is the intangible expression of the inner life of a society. It is difficult to define but it is important to understand, if one is to grasp the essential element of social organization. Park and Burgess have expressed the basic importance of consensus as follows: "Society is . . . a complex of organized habits, sentiments, and social attitudes—in short, consensus."[54]

Consensus arises from the common definition of situations of vital importance. When these definitions are in essential agreement, when common understandings remain concerning the basic institutional relationships, consensus may be said to exist. In a heterogeneous society, consensus can never be absolute. Some norms that are acceptable to one class are not acceptable to another. Premarital chastity, for example, is important to the middle-class male in our society but is not considered important to the lower-class male.[55] Nevertheless, a substantial degree of consensus *is* evident in all classes on such matters as monogamous marriage, the Christian faith, and the democratic form of government. Divergent definitions on a few items do not indicate that social disorganization is imminent. A comparative lack of consensus on many matters may exist as long as agreement is present on the basic issues.

Social norms are affirmed and re-created through the definitions of recurrent situations.[56] Every marriage ceremony is a reaffirmation of belief in the

---

[52] Elihu Katz and Paul F. Lazarsfeld, *Personal Influence: The Part Played by People in the Flow of Mass Communications,* The Free Press, Glencoe, Ill., 1955, pp. 52–53.

[53] Louis Wirth, "Ideological Aspects of Social Disorganization," *American Sociological Review,* 5:472–482 (August, 1940), p. 472.

[54] Park and Burgess, *op. cit.,* p. 163.

[55] Alfred C. Kinsey *et al., Sexual Behavior in the Human Male,* W. B. Saunders Company, Philadelphia, 1948, pp. 331–335.

[56] William I. Thomas, *The Unadjusted Girl,* Little, Brown and Company, Boston, 1923, pp. 42–43.

monogamous family. Every violent criminal apprehended gives tacit recognition to the belief in the inherent worth of the person. Every time an individual votes in a national election he confirms his belief in the institutions of representative government. Group consensus must be continually strengthened in connection with these fundamental social values if the society is to remain in a state of relative organization. Moral codes are patterns of normative behavior established by generations of persons who have learned to define the same situation in the same way. By affirming these definitions on appropriate occasions society maintains its consensus.[57]

When the members of a society are in substantial agreement on the definitions of fundamental and recurrent situations, society is thus characterized by social organization. This condition is highly relative and ranges from the virtual consensus of an isolated folk society[58] to the murderous conflict of interests in a nation in the throes of revolution.[59] Modern societies ordinarily fall between these extremes. England, for example, has had close and continuous interaction through a common culture for many centuries. A powerful consensus has evolved among Englishmen of all classes and walks of life. They are in substantial agreement on the monarchy, individual freedom, and the Church of England. Language, culture, and history combine to render the consensus of the English people proverbially strong.

In many other modern nations such consensus is impossible because of differences in ethnic background, racial composition, or religious affiliation. Our own society illustrates this situation in many respects. Ethnic groupings are complex and the many cultural diversities have not yet blended perfectly into a completely homogeneous pattern. The caste status of the Negro is an indication that consensus is likewise still far from a reality. Democracy is not extended to the Negro except to a limited degree. Religious unity is by no means complete, with conflicts between religious groups playing a part in social disorganization within local communities, states, and the nation. Social change itself is so rapid in our society that a stable culture pattern has not yet had time to evolve from so many disparate units. Consensus is difficult to achieve or maintain under the impact of so much individualism.[60]

Mass Media in a Dynamic Society

The mass media of communication have an important function in maintaining consensus in a dynamic society. Before social organization can arise, communication must be present. At the United Nations, for example, science has made it possible to provide simultaneous translation devices, with a selective apparatus on earphones which enables the different language

---

[57] Cf. Frank E. Hartung, "Common and Discrete Group Values," *Journal of Social Psychology, 38:*3–22 (August, 1953).

[58] Howard W. Odum, "Folk Sociology," *Social Forces, 31:*193–223 (March, 1953).

[59] Philip Selznick, *The Organizational Weapon,* McGraw-Hill Book Company, Inc., New York, 1952.

[60] Cf. Matilda White Riley, John W. Riley, Jr., and Marcia L. Toby, "The Measurement of Consensus," *Social Forces, 31:*97–106 (December, 1952).

groups to comprehend the same speeches. Without such communication devices an international and multilingual organization could not function effectively. Similarly, individuals must be able to "take each other into account" before they can form any effective group, whether play group, family, or nation. Language, gestures, and signs are forms of symbolic communication by which human beings understand each other and maintain group patterns. Communication is thus "the cement which gives cohesion to social groups."[61]

Mass communication provides cohesion to large and complex societies. In this sense, mass communication is "any communication produced at a single source which is capable of being transmitted to an infinitely large audience."[62] Radio and television are literally mass communications, as they transmit messages to increasingly larger audience with no technological difficulty. Movies, mass-circulation magazines, and newspapers are also mass communications, although additional copies must be provided for each extension of the audience. Government is dependent upon mass media, not only for the election of officials, but for public announcements, information on legislation, and circulation of the many regulations of a complex society. Business depends upon mass media for commercial advertising, and education has begun to make serious use of television in the classroom. All of these forms of the mass media increase social organization, since they channel the same ideas to large numbers of people.

The mass media also transmit a group of behavior patterns known as the mass culture. The latter is "a set of patterns of thought and action which are common to the subcultures of a heterogeneous society. These patterns have common meanings and value for all or most of the members of the society and serve as points of mutual identification and recognition for these members."[63] The mass culture constitutes a kind of least common denominator for our society and provides its members with common definitions of many situations, ranging from democracy to baseball. Practically all of the people of the United States participate in one or more of the mass media, and they receive many of their ideas from this source. A certain degree of consensus as a national group is thus derived from the mass media.[64]

The mass media also present working definitions of many roles. Adolescents learn how to talk, dance, and dress from the movies. The mass culture is thus replacing many of the traditional norms. Courtship customs that grew up in a rural community, for example, no longer apply in the large city. As

[61] Fred S. Siebert, "The Role of Mass Communication in American Society," chap. 2 in *Mass Media and Education*, Fifty-third Yearbook of the National Society for the Study of Education, University of Chicago Press, Chicago, 1954, p. 13.

[62] Franklin Fearing, "Social Impact of the Mass Media of Communication," chap. 8 in *ibid.*, p. 166.

[63] John W. Bennett and Melvin M. Tumin, *Social Life: Structure and Function*, Alfred A. Knopf, Inc., New York, 1948, p. 609.

[64] Philip Selznick, "Institutional Vulnerability in Mass Society," *American Journal of Sociology*, 56:320–331 (January, 1951).

Wirth points out, "It is upon these mass media . . . that to an ever-increasing degree the human race depends to hold it together. Mass communication is rapidly becoming, if it is not already, the main framework of the web of social life."[65]

The most extensive implementation of the mass media is found in the United States. Several factors brought about this situation: (1) the sheer size of the country, (2) the heterogeneity of the population, (3) the importance of technological change, (4) the prevalence of social mobility, and (5) the lack of a deeply embedded traditional culture because of our cultural heterogeneity. No other nation has all these characteristics, nor do the media play as important a part in any other country. This does not mean, of course, that the mass culture has completely supplanted the older Anglo-Saxon culture. The unifying values of democracy, our concepts of equal justice before the law, individual initiative, and fair play remain basic to our culture. But the mass media provide many patterns that supplement the traditional culture.

Through the mass media important ideas are daily transmitted to millions of viewers, listeners, and readers. Among these are "the political and social symbols of a society, the images of its leaders, its angels and its demons, and the patterns of mythology. . . ."[66] The social norms are thus handed on through the media and the people learn what behavior is expected, what actions will be tolerated, and what the ideal forms of personality and performance are.[67] Behavior is made predictable through social norms, as each person learns what is expected of him in his family, school, play group, and business. By transmitting and reinforcing these norms, the mass media are agencies of social organization.

The media also confer status on norms, issues, individuals, and social movements. A person whose picture is in a mass-circulation magazine may have his status appreciably increased. An organization that is presented on a national television program likewise receives added status. Nothing succeeds like success, and the mere fact that a person, party, or group is recognized by the mass media is an indication to many people that it is worthy of such attention. When many persons see, hear, or read about these so-called "famous" people or institutions, they tend to accept them as important, and in this sense they *are* important. The norms of an earlier, primary society derived their status from word of mouth affirmation and example. The norms of our present-day "secondary" society are increasingly established by the mass media.[68]

In their periodic crusades against prostitution, white slavery, alcoholism, drug addiction, political corruption, white-collar crime, and juvenile delin-

[65] Louis Wirth, "Consensus and Mass Communication," *American Sociological Review,* 13:1–15 (February, 1948), p. 10.
[66] Fearing, *op. cit.,* pp. 166–167.
[67] Sherif, *op. cit.*
[68] Paul F. Lazarsfeld and Robert K. Merton, "Mass Communication, Popular Taste, and Organized Social Action," in Wilbur Schramm (ed.), *Mass Communications,* University of Illinois Press, Urbana, 1949, pp. 464–469.

quency, the mass media further support the norms by reminding people of their (the norms') existence. Readers of the mass-circulation magazines are reminded that this society is opposed to corrupt, vicious, and criminal actions and that retribution often comes to those who violate the norms. By holding up immoral or antisocial activities to the light of publicity, the mass media strengthen the norms.[69] The media thus serve somewhat the same function as the storyteller in primitive society; they remind people that some activities are approved and some are not.[70]

The commercial nature of the media also contributes to their conservative function. Advertising is the principal source of revenue of newspapers, magazines, television and radio corporations, and the sponsor is anxious not to offend any large section of his audience by demonstrating, sanctioning, or even suggesting drastic departures from the norms. The media tend thus to be conservative influences, in that they literally "conserve" the accepted culture patterns. The media seldom contribute to "progress" or "change," but they *do* contribute to the cohesion (i.e., organization) of society. In such fields as religion, politics, race relations, sex behavior, marriage, and the family, the media follow the norms as they (the media) conceive them.[71]

This conservative function may be illustrated by the daytime radio serial, often designated "soap opera" because its commercial purpose is to sell soap to housewives. These women are consciously seeking entertainment and also (perhaps unconsciously) a justification for their social role. The soap opera stresses the norms that define the status of the wife in the middle-class American family. She is expected to remain in the home, care for the children, and be a companion to her husband. Compared to the real or imagined role of the woman in business, the arts, or the professions, the lot of the housewife often lacks glamour and appeal.[72]

The soap opera helps to strengthen the norms that keep the wife in the home. The drama constantly assures listeners that the heroine's marriage is fundamentally sound, no matter how much she may appear to be threatened by the "other woman." In the radio (and television) serial, virtue triumphs in the end, and wives who accept their traditional lot always win over those who do not. The listener is assured that her role is important in the scheme of things. If she continues to be a dutiful wife and mother, she will be happier than those women who work in offices, factories, and department stores. The function of the radio serial is therefore "very much like a folk tale, expressing the hopes and fears of the feminine audience and on the whole [contributing] to the integration of their lives into the world in which they live."[73]

---

[69] *Ibid.*

[70] W. Lloyd Warner and William E. Henry, "The Daytime Radio Serial: A Symbolic Analysis," *Genetic Psychology Monographs, 37*:3–71 (February, 1948).

[71] W. Lloyd Warner, *American Life: Dream and Reality,* University of Chicago Press, Chicago, 1953, chap. 10.

[72] Rudolph Arnheim, "The World of the Daytime Serial," in Schramm, *op. cit.,* pp. 360–380.

[73] Warner and Henry, *op. cit.,* p. 7.

Value Judgments in a Dynamic Society

Social organization and disorganization are often thought of in terms of "normality" and "abnormality" and the corresponding value judgments. In fact, an organized society has usually been considered normal and a disorganized one abnormal. This conception in turn carries strong moral implications, with the "normal" conceived of as the suitable and ethical and the "abnormal" as the unethical. Such an attitude obscures a realistic understanding of social organization and disorganization. Situations which are approved are thus considered "normal" and those which are disapproved as "abnormal." This point of view has some validity in a static society, where social organization *is* the norm and social disorganization the departure from the norm. In a dynamic society, however, no such simple and comforting conclusion is possible.

Some psychiatrists would have us believe that modern society itself is "sick" or "abnormal" and that it is therefore impossible for the average person to be completely "well" or "normal" under these circumstances. Their criteria of normality are those of mental health, which is characterized by "the ability to love and to create, . . . by a sense of identity based on one's experience of self as the subject and agent of one's powers, and by the grasp of reality inside and outside of ourselves, that is, by the development of objectivity and reason."[74]

While the emphasis upon love and creativity is an important element in mental health, these criteria do not apply to modern "normal" or organized society. Our own society contains many aspects that are frustrating, alienating, and disorganizing to the individuals and groups which comprise it. But it would be unrealistic to contend that the very structure of society itself is pathological.[75] Critics of modern society may well find much that is lacking or undesirable in the dynamic, secular, and anxiety-producing world in which we live. Our society and the social interaction of its members are as "normal," however, as life itself.

The individual may also define the normal in terms of his own values. Family organization and permanent monogamy are conditions that agree with the traditional values of our society.[76] The degree of social organization in a society, indeed, reflects the consensus concerning these value systems. Throughout our discussion of social organization and disorganization we shall refer to social values as constituting some of our most important data. "Social science research," as Kolb has said, "is a human activity carried on within and responsible to the moral values which govern human life, and it is of necessity governed by the norms to which those ultimate values give rise."[77]

The presence of these value systems should not, however, confuse the issue.

[74] Erich Fromm, *The Sane Society,* Rinehart and Company, Inc., New York, 1955, p. 69.

[75] *Ibid.,* chap. 2, "Can a Society Be Sick?—The Pathology of Normalcy."

[76] Ernest W. Burgess, "Values and Sociological Research," *Social Problems,* 2:16–20 (July, 1954).

[77] William L. Kolb, "The Impingement of Moral Values on Sociology," *Social Problems,* 2:66–70 (October, 1954), p. 68.

Values are basic to social organization. Social disorganization is the dissolution of the relationships that bind the society together. At the same time, the theory of social disorganization does not employ the term "social values" as a basis for determining the "goodness" or "badness" of a given situation. Social organization and disorganization are analytical, rather than normative, concepts. They attempt to define what *is,* rather than what *should be.*

Social disorganization in modern society is therefore not an "abnormal" phenomenon. It is the natural result of the breakdown of group interaction under the impact of social change. Persons who consider social organization as the normal (i.e., usual) situation are thinking in much the same terms as those who believe economic booms are normal and depressions are abnormal states in the economy. By the very nature of social interaction, social disorganization is as "normal" as social organization and change is as "normal" as stability. It is difficult for many students to adjust their wishful thinking to this reality. We must make this adjustment, however, if we are to think intelligently about society. In a time of world crisis, the facts of social change and social disorganization must be faced.

The "natural" character of social disorganization is illustrated in such activities as crime, prostitution, and political corruption, which are the natural products of the existing social structure. Crimes against property grow out of the violation of the mores of private property. Prostitution is a violation of the taboos against extramarital sexual relationships. Political corruption results from trying to hold to principles of democracy in a laissez-faire economy, where money is often more important than honesty. These are, of course, only partial explanations of complex social situations. The important consideration here is that the breakdown of institutional relationships is the *natural* result of a social system in a state of rapid change.[78]

Social disorganization may eventually be viewed in the same impersonal terms as sickness and death. Sickness is no longer considered evidence of moral turpitude. Mental derangement is likewise viewed as a form of illness, rather than a result of demoniacal possession. It is possible that crime may be viewed as the natural result of social forces and not as evidence of deliberate moral depravity. Any acceptance of the "natural" aspects of social disorganization is complicated, however, by the value judgments that classify this behavior. Such value judgments are themselves social products which have grown out of group interaction, and the definitions vital to one period often lose their validity for another. Conditions that originally gave rise to the norms have drastically changed. The norms themselves persist as vestigial remains of a vanished age.

SELECTED BIBLIOGRAPHY

Bales, Robert F., *Interaction Process Analysis,* Addison-Wesley Publishing Company, Inc., Reading, Mass., 1950. In this book quantitative methods are applied

[78] Lawrence K. Frank, "Society as the Patient," *American Journal of Sociology, 42*:335–344 (November, 1936).

for the first time on a systematic scale to the measurement of social interaction. This is an important contribution to the theory of small-group interaction.

Barnett, H. G., *Innovation: The Basis of Cultural Change*, McGraw-Hill Book Company, Inc., New York, 1953. An extensive theoretical analysis of the nature of innovation and its role in cultural and social change is offered in this volume. In the author's frame of reference, invention is a technological innovation.

Blumer, Herbert, "Psychological Import of the Human Group," chap. 8 in Muzafer Sherif and M. O. Wilson (eds.), *Group Relations at the Crossroads*, Harper & Brothers, New York, 1953. An eminent social psychologist offers some stimulating insights into the nature of social interaction, whereby two or more persons take each other into account and act accordingly.

Burgess, Ernest W., "Values and Sociological Research," *Social Problems*, 2:16–20 (July, 1954). Social values are the heart of social problems and hence constitute valid subjects for teaching and research. In this brief article, a senior statesman of sociology explores some of the implications of this position.

Cooley, Charles Horton, *Social Organization*, Charles Scribner's Sons, New York, 1909. Also *Social Process*, Charles Scribner's Sons, New York, 1922. In these two pioneer studies, the psychological forces that integrate society in a dynamic equilibrium are explored by one of the great figures in American sociology. These books are vital to an understanding of the antecedents of the contemporary work in social organization, social processes, and small-group interaction.

Fromm, Erich, *The Sane Society*, Rinehart and Company, Inc., New York, 1955. A leading social psychiatrist surveys contemporary society in terms of his criteria of mental health and finds it wanting. His central thesis is that modern society is itself "sick," in that it cannot provide the background for the development of adequate human beings.

Homans, George C., *The Human Group*, Harcourt, Brace and Company, New York, 1950. This book combines an examination of several leading empirical studies of the small group with a theoretical analysis of the role of the small group in society. As such, it is an important contribution to the theory of social organization.

Ogburn, William F., *Social Change*, The Viking Press, Inc., New York, 1950 (rev. ed.). This well-known essay is a discussion of social organization and disorganization in terms of social change and cultural lag. In introducing the latter concept, this book (originally published in 1922) has been influential both in professional sociological circles and among the general public.

Parsons, Talcott, *The Social System*, The Free Press, Glencoe, Ill., 1951. The author is the leading sociological theorist in the field of social structure, and his analysis has been important in stimulating a variety of empirical studies in this area.

Strodtbeck, Fred L., "The Case for the Study of Small Groups," *American Sociological Review*, 19:651–657 (December, 1954). The title of this article is self-explanatory, in that it deals with the general subject of small-group study and comments briefly upon some of the insights and methods of this burgeoning field.

CHAPTER 2

Social Disorganization

Social Disorganization in a Dynamic Society

Social disorganization is, in a sense, the reverse of social organization. When the orderly processes of social interaction and effective functioning of a group break down there is social disorganization. Social disorganization may thus be defined as the process by which group relationships are broken.[1] A group in turn is a number of people between whom vital relationships exist with some degree of permanence. This is true whether we are talking of the family, the community, or the nation. Our concern in this book is with the social forces or processes which disturb or break the relationships between groups.[2] One section of the book is devoted to personal or individual disorganization, but even here it is the relationship of the individual to the group that measures his social disorganization. Much personal disorganization is likewise a result of social disorganization. Social disorganization, as Leighton says, is "evident in societies that have been disrupted by forced migration, wars, economic disaster, individual revolution and extremely rapid acceleration." As a consequence, "defects in communication, leadership, followership and cooperation" appear.[3] As we have indicated in Chapter 1, these and other processes of social interaction are vital to the organization and maintenance of the group. By the same token, any substantial interference with them is equivalent to group disorganization. The regularity and predictability of human relationships depend upon the continuance of ordered patterns of interaction.

"Social organization" and "social disorganization" are relative terms. There are all degrees of social organization, just as there are all degrees of social disorganization. These concepts represent reverse aspects of the same functioning social system. Social disorganization occurs when there is a change in the equilibrium of forces, so that many former expectations no longer apply and many forms of social control no longer function effectively. In a dynamic society, social change dissolves institutional relationships and behavior patterns. The

[1] Ralph Kramer, "The Conceptual Status of Social Disorganization," *American Journal of Sociology, 48:*466–474 (January, 1943).

[2] Robert E. L. Faris, "Contemporary and Prospective Social Disorganization," *Sociology and Social Research, 32:*679–684 (January–February, 1948).

[3] Alexander H. Leighton, "Psychiatric Disorder and Social Environment," *Psychiatry, 18:*367–383 (November, 1955).

rapidity of change makes it difficult to establish new patterns. Contemporary society is, meanwhile, controlled by norms that arose under conditions that are gone, never to return. Men are still legally responsible for the support of their wives, for example, even though the latter earn an adequate income.

A society is a functioning whole. Individual and society are different aspects of the same process of interaction. This organic unity of society makes impossible any rigid division into the constituent elements of individual, family, community, and nation. The individual is a product of the group, and the group cannot exist without individuals and their patterned relationships. Long ago Cooley eloquently pointed out that, when we refer to the individual and the group, we are not considering two distinct phenomena but the same phenomenon from different angles.[4] Half a century later, the fundamental unity of the individual and the group was reaffirmed by such men as Harry Stack Sullivan in the light of modern psychiatry. As he points out, the individual suffering from mental illness should therefore be treated not as an isolated person but as a member of several groups.[5]

Social disorganization is a complex process. The breakdown of the group is caused by the same combination of factors that produces it. In his study of the human group, Homans calls this process social disintegration, but it is similar to the concept of social disorganization as advanced by the present authors. Social disintegration (disorganization), Homans says, is a conditon "marked by a decline in the number of activities in which the members of a group collaborate, by a decrease in the frequency of interaction between these members, and by a weakening of the control exercised by the group over the behavior of individuals."[6] The healthy functioning of the group demands the active participation of its members. Without this participation, the group (by definition) declines and eventually ceases to exist.

The reverse of the above statement is equally true, although it is not so obvious. That is to say, the healthy functioning of the *individual* requires his active and continued participation in the *group*. This relationship is discussed in detail in connection with the concept of individual disorganization. Here we wish merely to indicate that the individual needs the group as much as the group needs the individual. As Homans states, if an individual's "group is shattered around him, if he leaves a group in which he was a valued member, and if, above all, he finds no new group to which he can relate himself, he will, under stress, develop disorders of thought, feeling, and behavior."[7] The individual who is isolated from *one* group becomes poorer. The individual who is isolated from *all* groups eventually becomes completely disorganized.

[4] Charles Horton Cooley, *Human Nature and the Social Order,* Charles Scribner's Sons, New York, 1902.

[5] Harry Stack Sullivan, "The Illusion of Personal Individuality," *Psychiatry, 13:*317–332 (August, 1950); Harry Stack Sullivan, *The Interpersonal Theory of Psychiatry,* W. W. Norton and Company, Inc., New York, 1953.

[6] George C. Homans, *The Human Group,* Harcourt, Brace and Company, New York, 1950, p. 369.

[7] *Ibid.,* p. 457.

Society is made up of groups, both large and small, and social organization depends upon their effective interrelationships and adequate functioning. The simplest unit of society is the small group, and its state of organization and disorganization has important implications for society as a whole. The small group has always been the central unit of society, whether it be a "primitive" or "civilized," "preliterate" or "advanced" society. Throughout most of human history the principal small group has been the family, irrespective of what pattern it may have assumed under varying social conditions.[8] Everyone ordinarily belongs to several other small groups, ranging from the childhood play group to the adult friendship group.

Social interaction within the small group is the very stuff of social existence. Social organization means group organization, and most interaction has been in small and face-to-face (primary) groups. Today with mass communication, this situation is partially (although by no means wholly) changing. The orbit of social interaction is increasing in size and extent as the press, radio, and television add their influence to each individual's experience. At the same time, the primary group continues to play a vital role, even in the process of mass communication.[9]

As Katz and Lazarsfeld indicate, there is a "two-step flow of communication" from the mass media to the individual. Certain members of small groups read the papers, listen to the radio, view television and *then* transmit this information to others in their immediate group who are, themselves, not so active. In this sense, the primary group has been "rediscovered" and its intimate relationships have been restored. Mass communication is no longer viewed solely as a large and impersonal process, in which communicators in radio, television, and the press merely transmit information to an amorphous public. The small group is an important "communications network" of its own.[10]

Social Structure and Social Disorganization

In a dynamic society, the social structure is in process of rapid change. Status and role are not clearly defined, and many persons find themselves in situations where no established role patterns exist. They are often forced to improvise new roles. This is difficult for the individual and often dangerous to the society. A dynamic society thus carries within itself, as it were, the forces of its own disorganization. The same elements that make the social structure dynamic bring about its disorganization. We may indicate some of the characteristics of the social structure of a disorganized society.

Status and role are the products of social interaction. Society assigns the statuses which the individual occupies and the roles which he assumes. In his analysis of social structure, Cottrell develops the concept of role "to refer to an

[8] Carle C. Zimmerman, *Family and Civilization*, Harper & Brothers, New York, 1947.

[9] Eliot Freidson, "Communications Research and the Concept of the Mass," *American Sociological Review, 18:*313–317 (June, 1953).

[10] Elihu Katz and Paul F. Lazarsfeld, *Personal Influence: The Part Played by People in the Flow of Mass Communications,* The Free Press, Glencoe, Ill., 1955, chap. 14, "The Two-Step Flow of Communication."

internally consistent series of conditioned responses by one member of a social situation which represents the stimulus pattern for a similarly internally consistent series of conditioned responses of the other(s) in that situation."[11] The leader must thus be recognized as such by his followers, who in turn respond to him. When the statuses and roles are clear and well defined, a society is relatively organized. When the reverse is true, social disorganization is present. Our own society is marked by a widespread ambiguity of status and role. Husbands, wives, teachers, students, workers, and managers often are not sure of their roles.

This ambiguity results in lack of agreement concerning the demands imposed by different positions in the social structure. In a dynamic society, the individual has many choices open to him as to what his lifework shall be, whom he shall marry, and where he shall live. The majority of careers, in theory at least, are open to talent. At the same time, the very possibility (indeed, the necessity) of choice complicates the life of the average person, for he must make personal decisions on a variety of questions which are decided by the group in a less dynamic society. These qualities of a secular society are at once the hope of democracy and a basic cause of social disorganization. Whether of a wife or a career, choice involves a certain amount of instability.

In a disorganized society, furthermore, there is inconsistency between the expectations embodied in the social roles and the extent to which these expectations can be realized. In every field of social relationships the individual is presented with aspirations which he cannot possibly attain. His chances of becoming a millionaire or marrying the most beautiful girl in the world are slight indeed, no matter how passionately he may wish to carry out these expectations. Many persons try to satisfy the role aspirations of society by engaging in behavior contrary to the mores and/or the law. The most obvious example is the individual who attempts to rise in the socioeconomic scale by theft, embezzlement, fraud, or in some other illegal or antisocial manner.[12] A society in which a significant number of persons attempt to reach goals by unorthodox methods is in a state of (relative) disorganization.[13]

In static and organized societies, status and role are defined by custom, and the individual has little occasion to depart from the patterns laid down by the group. If he behaves in a manner appropriate to his ascribed status and passes from childhood to maturity in much the same way as his ancestors before him, he fulfills expectations. The rapidity of social change in modern society has disrupted the old patterns, however, and the changing social situation has forced the individual to depart from conventional roles. Men and women live under different social conditions, earn their living in different ways, and raise

---

[11] Leonard S. Cottrell, Jr., "The Adjustment of the Individual to His Age and Sex Roles," *American Sociological Review*, 7:617–620 (October, 1942), p. 617.

[12] Robert K. Merton, "Social Structures and Anomie: Revisions and Extensions," chap. 14 in Ruth N. Anshen (ed.), *The Family: Its Function and Destiny*, Harper & Brothers, New York, 1959 (rev. ed.).

[13] Roland L. Warren, "Social Disorganization and the Interrelationship of Cultural Roles," *American Sociological Review*, 14:83–87 (February, 1949).

their families in different environments from those of their forefathers. The old roles cannot be retained intact in the face of the new situations.[14]

Many members of a disorganized society therefore do not act the way they are "supposed" to act. The wife no longer remains in the home, the married pair no longer has several children, and the family no longer stays in the same place. Such role failures do not embody deliberate disobedience of the individuals concerned. Most persons like to conform to the group and play the roles expected of them. The demands of the immediate social situation, however, are often so incompatible with former expectations that the individuals *cannot* conform. They must fashion their lives from new and untried responses, even if the latter have not been accepted. When large numbers of persons face these unexpected situations, the society is partially disorganized.[15]

Attempts to redefine basic roles may also involve varying degrees of social disorganization. The majority do not act completely contrary to the traditional expectations, even though they are unable to play all their roles as ideally conceived. Most men do not become criminals when they fail to become rich, but instead adjust to their status in other ways.[16] Most married women do not become neurotic because they cannot assume the whole galaxy of roles expected of them, ranging from glamour girl to practical nurse. Some persons, however, are unable to make the adjustment between the ideal role as culturally defined and the actual role which they are obliged to play. These people may become disorganized.[17]

The process by which the individual rises in the social scale is called social mobility. In our society, the belief in the possibility of attaining a higher status is part of the cultural tradition which middle- and lower-class individuals absorb during their formative years. Those who are successful in this competition for status have a sense of accomplishment at filling the preferred roles held out by society. Even the successful ones, however, may gain their status at the cost of unsatisfactory primary group relationships. In one study of unmarried career women, for example, upward mobility was accompanied by a disproportionate incidence of emotional and psychosomatic difficulties, which suggests that their intimate family relationships left something to be desired.[18]

A society with a high degree of upward mobility is characterized by social disorganization in another sense. A large number of statuses are open to achievement in a mobile society. This means that many persons ultimately reach positions for which they have had no previous special training. They may not completely understand their roles because they have gained them only after a long and bitter struggle. Such self-made men may also be success-

[14] Cf. Annabelle B. Motz, "The Role Conception Inventory: A Tool for Research in Social Psychology," *American Sociological Review,* 17:465–471 (August, 1952).

[15] Talcott Parsons, *The Social System,* The Free Press, Glencoe, Ill., 1951, pp. 280–283.

[16] Ely Chinoy, "The Tradition of Opportunity and the Aspirations of Automobile Workers," *American Journal of Sociology,* 57:453–459 (March, 1952).

[17] Cottrell, *op. cit.,* p. 618.

[18] Evelyn Ellis, "Social Psychological Correlates of Upward Social Mobility Among Unmarried Career Women," *American Sociological Review,* 17:558–563 (October, 1952).

ful in business but strikingly unsuccessful in other roles, such as those of husband and father. The qualities which made them successful as competitors in business do not necessarily make them good husbands and fathers. Hence the families of many self-made men are torn with conflict, alcoholism, and divorce.[19]

Warren, in fact, maintains that "social disorganization varies directly with the proportion of important roles which are achieved rather than ascribed."[20] In a comparatively stable society, each individual occupies a series of ascribed statuses for which he has been trained from infancy. In a feudal society, the average individual knows in general which statuses he will occupy throughout his life and learns the roles he is expected to play accordingly. The democratic concept of achieved status inevitably means that some men will be trained for statuses which they will never occupy and for roles which they will never assume.

The majority of persons who fail to achieve their goals may have an even stronger sense of frustration and failure. The relationship between "status striving, anxiety, and mental health" was analyzed in a study of mental disorder in New Haven. An apparent factor in the illness of those observed was their failure to rise in social and occupational status as far or as rapidly as they desired. Many of the patients in the lower economic group seemed to think that their jobs carried no hope of advancement, that there was not enough status connected with their employment, and that there was no possibility of upward mobility.[21]

Social Change and Social Disorganization

Social change is therefore closely related to social structure. Social change refers to "whatever may happen in the course of time to the roles, the institutions, or the orders comprising a social structure: their emergence, growth, and decline."[22] A changing society is one in which large numbers of people occupy different statuses and play different roles over a period of time. When we consider society in terms of its structure, we are viewing it at one moment of time, when the statuses and roles have assumed a certain pattern. This pattern, however, is always subject to change. Social structure and social change are therefore functions of time.[23]

A changing society also tends to be a disorganized society because of the disparity in the rate of change between the various elements. The structural

[19] August B. Hollingshead, "Class Differences in Family Stability," *Annals of the American Academy of Political and Social Science, 172:*39–46 (November, 1950).

[20] Warren, *op. cit.,* p. 86.

[21] August B. Hollingshead, R. Ellis, and E. Kirby, "Social Mobility and Mental Illness," *American Sociological Review, 19:*577–591 (October, 1954); cf. also August B. Hollingshead and Frederick C. Redlich, "Social Stratification and Schizophrenia," *American Sociological Review, 19:*302–306 (June, 1954).

[22] Hans Gerth and C. Wright Mills, *Character and Social Structure,* Harcourt, Brace and Company, New York, 1953, p. 398.

[23] Bernard Barber, "Structural-Functional Analysis: Some Problems and Misunderstandings," *American Sociological Review, 21:*129–135 (April, 1956).

and other nonmaterial elements of the society are incorporated in the personalities of the members, where they assume normative qualities. The male role of economic provider thus continues to be the norm, even though in practice it is modified by (1) unemployment and (2) employment of the wife. The female role of mother and housekeeper likewise remains the norm, even though these activities have also been modified by the rush of events. In these and many other instances the *form* of the role remains long after the *function* has changed.

This situation further illustrates the complex (and contradictory) character of social organization and disorganization. The structures (i.e., roles) which lend stability to social interaction may actually contribute to social disorganization by their fixity and resistance to change, as illustrated by the roles based on segregation in the South. In order to survive in a society which is rapidly changing, an institution (which involves a pattern of roles) must be sufficiently elastic to adjust to new needs and functions. Yet countless institutional anachronisms persist until they eventually break down under their own inertia and thereby augment the very disorganization they are presumed to prevent. In the local community, many political practices illustrate this situation. The formalism of creeds, myths, and norms may lead to the breakdown of the institutional patterns and may also contribute to the disorganization of the larger society.

Social and cultural change are related but not synonymous. Society is made up of human beings in symbolic interaction; culture is the product of this interaction. Changes in culture bring about changes in society and vice versa. A change in culture—such as a new scientific theory, technological development, or religious doctrine—produces changes in the forms of interaction—i.e., in society. Changes in the social structure likewise bring about changes in cultural values, beliefs, and ideologies. The industrial revolution was essentially a technological (i.e., cultural) change, but it ushered in a series of modifications in social interaction which are still in progress.[24] Society and culture are parts of the same functioning whole, but they are different parts.

Cultural changes occur through *invention*[25] and *diffusion*.[26] We have discussed this process in the preceding chapter with particular reference to technological invention. Hence we need only point out the role of cultural change in social disorganization. The addition of new culture patterns alters the statuses and roles of the members of the society. These structural changes are followed by changes in social values. The latter incorporate the basic meanings of the society. When culture changes rapidly, a conflict arises between the established habits and patterns and the demands of the new situation. Social disorganization is thus part of the price of social change.

[24] George A. Theodorson, "Acceptance of Industrialization and Its Attendant Consequences for the Social Patterns of Non-Western Societies," *American Sociological Review*, 18:477–484 (October, 1953).

[25] H. G. Barnett, *Innovation: The Basis of Cultural Change*, McGraw-Hill Book Company, Inc., New York, 1953.

[26] Ralph Linton, *The Tree of Culture*, Alfred A. Knopf, Inc., New York, 1955.

The failure of nonmaterial culture to keep abreast of material culture accounts for part of this disruption. Nothing changes as slowly as an idea, especially one invested with values of what is right and wrong. Men will therefore shed their blood to protect their belief in what is right, especially when such beliefs involve religious ideas, political philosophies, or economic theories. Changes in material culture occur with less opposition because the advantages of new inventions are more easily recognized. An electric refrigerator is a clear improvement over an icebox. The advantages of changes in governmental philosophy, in religious dogma, or in the role of women are not so clearly demonstrable.

The classic statement of this general hypothesis was made by William F. Ogburn in his analysis of *cultural lag*. According to his thesis, "the various parts of modern culture are not changing at the same rate . . . and . . . since there is a correlation and interdependence of parts, a rapid change in one part of our culture requires readjustments through other changes in the various correlated parts of culture."[27] Changes in material culture cause adaptations in nonmaterial culture, which latter often lag far behind the original material modification. Social roles which arose under one set of circumstances are inadequate to meet the exigencies of another set. Women's place is no longer in the home, but in the office, store, and factory as well. Social values which embodied the judgments of one era are unsuitable to another. In the South, the educated Negro is no longer content to remain "in his place."

The differential rate of change between the various elements of culture gives rise to other maladjustments. Modern means of transportation and communication have so altered the matter of distance that new problems of social control have arisen. A stronger central government is necessary when social interaction takes place over the wide area of modern society. With airplanes and intercontinental guided missiles winging their way through stellar space, relationships between nations in a nuclear age cry out for drastic change in the form of stronger international organizations. Policies of isolation which once had great validity lose their significance in a closely interrelated world, where Europe is only a few hours away by plane and a few minutes by missile.

Scientific achievements in agriculture and industry have similarly altered the economic structure.[28] Monetary theories based upon scarcity have lost much of their validity in an economy of abundance. Changes of this kind, however, always bring disruptions on the nonmaterial level of ideas, attitudes, and values. Social attitudes in economics, politics, the family, religion, education, social welfare, and sexual morality have all experienced the direct or indirect impact of changes in material culture. Modifications on the ideological level come slowly and grudgingly. We are always in a sense "governed by

[27] William F. Ogburn, *Social Change*, B. W. Huebsch, Inc., New York, 1922, pp. 200–201. A revised edition was published by The Viking Press, Inc., New York, 1950.
[28] William F. Ogburn, "Technology and the Standard of Living in the United States," *American Journal of Sociology*, 60:380–386 (January, 1955).

dead men's bones." In a static and "conservative" society, control over the future by the past assures continuity and stability. In a dynamic and "radical" society, cultural lag may bring social disorganization.[29]

Social Attitudes and Social Disorganization

Social disorganization arises (in part) from the disparity in the rate of change between related elements of a dynamic society, as we have mentioned. When new forms of behavior threaten accepted patterns, social disorganization in some form may result. Desegregation thus causes widespread community disorganization in the deep South. The components of the social structure are out of accord and the members of the society are no longer able to behave as formerly. Disparities between behavior and its definition result, and social attitudes become confused and contradictory. In one sense, therefore, the heart of the matter is the relationship between attitudes and values.

A social attitude has been briefly defined as a tendency to act. More completely, an attitude is an entire psychological complex including "an individual's experience of a certain object or class of objects, a feeling which accompanies this experience, and a disposition or tendency to act in a certain way in dealing with this object or class of objects."[30] Thomas and Znaniecki formulated an earlier and similar conception of social attitudes in connection with their theory of social disorganization. The essential characteristic of their concept is the actual or potential activity of an individual or group with reference to some social fact. The nature of the attitude can be approximated from the activity which it calls forth. A social attitude is thus "a process of individual consciousness which determines real or possible activity of the individual in the social world."[31]

Attitudes are not isolated patterns of tendencies to act. They have reference to specific objects or situations. The tendency to act is always directed toward some goal or situation. The object of the attitude, the end result of the tendency to act, is the social value. Any material or nonmaterial object may become a value when an attitude refers to it. Because of the attitude, the object acquires a social meaning. That is to say, the real or potential action incorporated in the attitude gives meaning to objects, persons, and ideas.

These meanings may be varied, since a given object may inspire different potential actions in various persons. The hydrogen bomb has different meanings for the scientist, the politician, and the survivor in Hiroshima. The American flag inspires a variety of reactions from the Chinese, the Argentinian, and the German. The concept of Communism evokes one meaning from the devoted Russian and another from the American. In each of these

---

[29] S. C. Gilfillan, "Social Implications of Technical Advance," *Current Sociology, 4*:191–207 (published by UNESCO, Paris, 1953).

[30] Florian Znaniecki, *Cultural Sciences: Their Origin and Development,* University of Illinois Press, Urbana, 1952, pp. 237–238.

[31] William I. Thomas and Florian Znaniecki, *The Polish Peasant in Europe and America,* Alfred A. Knopf, Inc., New York, 1927, Vol. I, p. 22.

relationships the attitude is directed toward a social object (material object, symbolic object, or concept) which is given meaning.[32]

A social attitude is thus a state of mind. The state of mind is a product of a way of life, an outgrowth of previous experience with objects and situations. Hence a social attitude is a *psychocultural* (i.e., *both* psychological *and* cultural) product. In Znaniecki's words, "The definition of a situation is a cultural phenomenon. . . . The situation as defined includes common data of human experience, observed present facts and anticipated future facts; the definer's selection and evaluation of these data, his observation and anticipation of facts, and his judgment of their desirability or undesirability are culturally conditioned and may be shared by others."[33] Social attitudes are learned in the course of culturally defined experience. As the child gradually learns his social roles, he learns the appropriate attitudes that go with them.[34]

The Southern white child thus learns the prevalent social attitude toward the Negro. The schoolboy in the Soviet Union learns the Communist attitude toward capitalism. The child in America also learns the attitudes of his particular subculture or social class, and these may be at variance with those of the larger society. The child in the delinquency area learns the gang's attitudes toward property and the police. His antisocial attitudes are generated by experiences which endow a given object, concept, or ideal with a meaning for the gang although the larger society holds them unacceptable. Attitudes thus bring about social disorganization by motivating the individual to activities that the larger group opposes.

An attitude is therefore much more than a simple tendency to act, in which a previously organized tendency is released and then carried through to a preordained conclusion. In the course of his behavior, the person reacts to his own tendency (attitude) and modifies it as he goes along. In fitting his tendency into the developing act, he may, as Blumer says, "organize it, transform it, hold it in suspense, block it, or sternly cast it aside as a basis of action."[35] In any social interaction, furthermore, each individual takes into account both his own attitudes and those of others. In so doing, he modifies his tendencies. In short, "the tendency to act cannot be taken as moulding or controlling the act. At the best the tendency or preparation to act is merely an element that enters into the developing act—no more than an initial bid for a possible line of action."[36]

The concept of the social attitude thus entails the process of interaction in which the tendency to act has been built up, and the process that takes place once the act has been set in motion. In other words, everyone's attitudes must

[32] Cf. William Buchanan and Hadley Cantril, *How Nations See Each Other,* University of Illinois Press, Urbana, 1953.

[33] Znaniecki, *op. cit.,* p. 247.

[34] Meyer Rabban, "Sex-Role Identification in Young Children in Two Diverse Social Groups," *Genetic Psychology Monographs, 42:*81–158 (August, 1950).

[35] Herbert Blumer, "Attitudes and the Social Act," *Social Problems, 3:*59–65 (October, 1955), p. 62.

[36] *Ibid.,* p. 63.

also take into account the attitudes of others, both toward themselves and toward outside objects.[37] Thus an individual delinquent may hesitate to steal if he thinks the police are watching. But several members of a gang may wish to express their contempt for middle-class values and steal a car although they know they are relatively sure to be caught. If the gang rejects the social values of the larger group they obviously will not be controlled by it.

Social disorganization has been defined by Thomas and Znaniecki in terms of the decreasing influence of established norms upon the members of various groups. This decline in the influence of "existing social rules of behavior" reflects an increase in antisocial attitudes, as the individual acquires tendencies to act in a deviant fashion. Today many situations exist which were not anticipated by earlier generations, as for example the employment of women, the unemployment of men, and the increased freedom of children. Institutions are organized ways of doing and behaving that evolved under different conditions. In departing from these established practices, the individual breaks the group relationships based upon them. The study of social disorganization deals with "the appearance of such attitudes as impair the efficiency of existing rules of behavior and thus lead to the decay of social institutions."[38]

Social Values and Social Disorganization

Social values are objects which have a meaning for us and which we consider important in our life scheme. The essential element in the value is the social meaning. Social values range in content from a piece of money to a religious dogma, from a choice steak to a political ideal. Certain values are especially important in the organization and disorganization of society. Among these values of "infinite worth" are the following: (1) human life itself, (2) the creative achievements of man in the arts and in human relations, (3) cooperation with others for a happier life, (4) worship of a power that is greater than we are, (5) the fullest development of moral character, and (6) the highest development of human intelligence and abilities.[39] In addition, our society has such basic values as (7) nationalism or love of country, (8) economic success, and (9) love as the basis for marriage.

All societies have patterns of values. Important social behavior is oriented with reference to them. The form and content of these patterns vary from one society to another, and the emphasis placed upon each value is likewise a function of cultural definition. Some meaningful pattern of social values, however, is a fundamental part of the heritage of every society. It determines what the society considers important and what its members will strive for and defend. Values thus are part of the province of the sociologist, and to ignore them is to ignore the heart of the subject. As Burgess has said, "Both groups and persons have values. The values of the group are primary since all of us are born into a world of values. Those of the person are therefore derivative. The study

---

[37] *Ibid.*
[38] Thomas and Znaniecki, *op. cit.*, Vol. II, p. 1131.
[39] William R. Catton, Jr., "Exploring Techniques for Measuring Human Values," *American Sociological Review,* 19:49–55 (February, 1954), p. 53.

of values is essential to understanding the motivations of human action."[40] Without social values, neither social organization nor social disorganization would exist.

When common value definitions break down, some degree of social disorganization is therefore present. A lack of consensus is apparent in modern society and reflects the impact of social change. Social action is inconsistent and often contradictory when values conflict. The particular aspects of social disorganization—e.g., the decline in organized religion, the instability of the family, and the rise of conflicting political ideologies—reflect this situation rather than cause it. Social disorganization may therefore be conceived "as a state of conflict among social values."[41]

This conflict in values was dramatically illustrated during the cold war by the widespread pressure toward conformity and the unwillingness to grant elementary civil rights to persons suspected of unorthodoxy in religious, political, or economic opinions. The basic value in the American culture pattern has traditionally been individual freedom; each person has been free to vote, worship, and trade as he saw fit, so long as he did not endanger the public welfare. The tensions and anxieties of the cold war became so pervasive that large numbers of persons believed that those whose religious beliefs were unorthodox were also unreliable and (perhaps) treasonable in political affairs.[42]

The tolerance of nonconformity during the decade of the 1950's varied between groups and regions. (1) The less educated were less tolerant than the more educated; (2) those who lived in rural areas than those from urban areas; (3) the older age groups than the younger (a factor that may be related to the level of education, which has been steadily increasing in recent years). (4) The West was, generally speaking, the most tolerant region and the South was the least; (5) persons who were mobile and had moved about a good deal were more tolerant than those who were less mobile. Social interaction and communication appear, therefore, to be productive of tolerance, whereas lack of communication tends to give rise to intolerance.[43]

In a disorganized society many persons are unable to achieve certain social values (e.g., financial status) without violating certain other values (e.g., those relating to property). Crimes against property, both those involving actions against persons (robbery) and those involving betrayal of financial trust (embezzlement), illustrate this value conflict. Persons in many walks of life are impelled to steal in order to attain monetary gain.[44] In other cases, social values may conflict because they are mutually incompatible. The value

---

[40] Ernest W. Burgess, "Values and Sociological Research," *Social Problems*, 2:16–20 (July, 1954), p. 16.

[41] Ralph H. Turner, "Value-Conflict in Social Disorganization," *Sociology and Social Research*, 38:301–308 (May–June, 1954), p. 302.

[42] Samuel A. Stouffer, *Communism, Conformity, and Civil Liberties*, Doubleday and Company, Inc., New York, 1955.

[43] *Ibid.*, pp. 222–223.

[44] Edwin H. Sutherland, "White-Collar Criminality," *American Sociological Review*, 5:1–12 (February, 1940).

of individual competition for limited rewards may conflict with the Christian value of humility.[45] Such value conflicts are rare in stable societies, but they are increasingly characteristic of those in a relative state of social disorganization.[46]

Not all social values are equally important. A large number of common values exist in any complex society, and it is a matter of comparative unimportance whether there is working unanimity among some of them. But certain values are "infinite" in character and are fundamentally important to the effective functioning of society. Christianity, monogamy, and private enterprise are among these "infinite" values for our own society, and its effective functioning requires a certain unanimity among the members concerning them. Disagreement on these levels threatens the social organization based upon these value patterns.[47]

Social disorganization is a gradual process. The decline in consensus that marks contemporary society began many years ago. In one sense, this decline may be traced to the early discoveries in physical science which first began to alter the classical conception of man's place in the universe. The discoveries in biological science during the nineteenth century further changed the previous notions of man's nature. Changing value judgments on divorce have come still more recently to modify the organization of society in another field. Definitions of sexual relationships have changed even more recently, as contraception and the so-called miracle drugs have altered the possibilities of pregnancy and venereal disease. In each of these areas of human experience traditional norms have weakened or dissolved.

The material changes in American society which accompanied urbanism and industrialism have likewise given rise to conflicts in the values of a village and agricultural society. The prolonged depression of the 1930's caused many persons to change their values with reference to the welfare functions of the federal government. Threats to national survival during World War II increased national consensus in some respects and produced further value conflicts in other directions.[48] Since World War II there has been an increase in ideological conflict between nations and a corresponding decrease in consensus in world society.[49] The disparity in social values will doubtless increase if this society becomes more dynamic.

The Crisis and Social Disorganization

Crises also produce social disorganization. A crisis is a serious interruption in the customary activities of a group, which requires adjustments in pat-

[45] Karen Horney, *The Neurotic Personality of Our Time,* W. W. Norton and Company, Inc., New York, 1937.
[46] Cf. David F. Aberle, "Shared Values in Complex Societies," *American Sociological Review,* 15:495–502 (August, 1950).
[47] Turner, *op. cit.,* p. 303.
[48] Francis E. Merrill, *Social Problems on the Home Front,* Harper & Brothers, New York, 1948.
[49] Arthur K. Davis, "Conflict Between Major Social Systems: The Soviet-American Case," *Social Forces,* 30:29–36 (October, 1951); Byron L. Fox, "The Cold War and American Domestic Problems," *Social Problems,* 1:10–12 (June, 1953).

terns of behavior. In modern society, both the individual and the group are faced with a variety of actual or potential interruptions in their regular activities. Among these situations are "wartime bombing attacks, large-scale natural disasters, and a variety of personal disasters in which individuals undergo threats of injury, near-miss accidents, or some form of profound personal loss."[50] The threat of nuclear warfare hangs over modern man and constitutes the potential crisis of complete destruction.

The generally hazardous character of modern life has prompted the National Research Council to undertake a comprehensive program of disaster (i.e., crisis) studies. The Committee on Disaster Studies has been established with the purpose of understanding (1) disasters as overall phenomena, (2) the reactions of the American people to disaster, and (3) the available resources for dealing with such situations when, as, and if they arise.[51] This acceptance of the role of crisis in modern society is itself a significant development. Crisis has become a recognized part of the life of modern man and a subject for scientific study.[52]

Crisis has been analyzed in terms of three types of situations, which occur in successive stages: (1) *threat situations*—involving the preliminary condition before the danger actually strikes, but when it is known to be approaching; thus a hurricane is coming or the war has started; (2) *danger impact situations*—when the danger has actually struck; the hurricane has arrived and the individuals must save themselves from injury or death; (3) *danger victimization situations*—when the impact of the danger has passed and the victims are left to view their immediate losses and other impending losses to themselves, their families, and the community. The *group* may react to crisis in different ways, depending upon the personalities involved, prior experience with the situation, and the cultural expectations toward such situations. *Individual* reactions may include avoidance of the situation, frozen immobility, extreme apathy, childlike dependency, or aggression against others in the immediate environment.[53]

Psychological reactions to the crisis are often marked by a loss of mental efficiency in the individual and a corresponding impairment in the group's efficiency. As the relationships holding the group together are broken, social disorganization arises. The disorganization may be mild or acute, depending upon the extent of the disaster and the degree to which the group is destroyed. Communication temporarily breaks down, as the members are too stunned, apathetic, or emotionally disturbed to carry on their ordinary functioning.[54] Consequently, the group structure is threatened because it is no

[50] Irving L. Janis, "Problems of Theory in the Analysis of Stress Behavior," *Journal of Social Issues, 10:*12–25 (1954), p. 18.

[51] Harry B. Williams, "Fewer Disasters, Better Studied," *Journal of Social Issues, 10:* 5–11 (1954).

[52] The entire issue of the *Journal of Social Issues (10:*1–76, 1954) is devoted to this subject. The issue is entitled *Human Behavior in Disaster: A New Field of Social Research.*

[53] Janis, *op. cit.,* pp. 18–20. The terms are his.

[54] For an analysis of communication *after* a disaster, see Leonard Schatzman and Anselm Strauss, "Social Class and Modes of Communication," *American Journal of Sociology, 60:*329–338 (January, 1955).

longer adequate to meet the new situation. Unfamiliar adjustments are required, and the members of the group suffer from extreme anxiety in the face of the new situation.[55]

Social disorganization imposed by crisis situations has been all too common for modern man. The people in the bombed cities of England had to carry on as best they could in the rubble which remained. Residents of Berlin at the end of World War II were obliged to dig their streets out from the mass of fallen brick and stone. The survivors of Hiroshima had to bury their dead before they could start to rebuild their devastated city. The inhabitants of flooded towns and cities in the United States have had to clean out the mud and water before they could begin life again. Whole communities have been temporarily overcome by anxiety and despair.

Crises may involve an entire society. The Great Depression of the 1930's affected everyone in the United States although the impact was more severe on certain groups than on others. The weakening of group relationships during this period was indicated in the increase in "suicide, burglary, bastardy, manic depressive psychosis, drug addiction, and pre-adult delinquency (boys' court cases)."[56] The same crisis, however, had less effect upon aspects of group life that were not directly related to economic status.[57]

Total war is another crisis situation affecting a whole society. This situation was illustrated in the United States during World War II. Within a few months after the attack on Pearl Harbor a sizable fraction of the population was forced to change jobs, move from their homes, or enter the armed forces. Each change required an adjustment, whether to the customs of a strange city or to the threat of death in battle. The old and accustomed patterns of behavior were, to a greater or lesser degree, inadequate to meet the new situations. Most persons made the necessary transition to new forms of group relationships. In a significant number of cases, however, such adjustment was not possible. The male juvenile delinquents, the abandoned children, the members of broken homes, and the sexually delinquent girls were among the civilian casualties of the crisis of total war.[58]

These sudden interruptions in the activities of the group are called *precipitate crises*. A rapid and unexpected break in the group's pattern of behavior forces the members to improvise new roles and reactions. Social crises may also be *cumulative*, in the sense that they develop through a long succession of events. The latter are ordinarily not as spectacular as the precipitate crises, but they may in the long run cause even more drastic breaks in the traditional patterns. The assimilation of new ethnic groups is a cumulative crisis. Out of the progressive impact of successive waves of immigrants, serious problems of adjustment have emerged in American society. The new arrivals have unwittingly provided support for corrupt political machines in the large cities.

[55] Bradford B. Hudson, "Anxiety in Response to the Unfamiliar," *Journal of Social Issues, 10*:53–60 (1954).

[56] Ernest R. Mowrer, "Social Crises and Social Disorganization," *American Sociological Review, 15*:60–66 (February, 1950), p. 65.

[57] *Ibid.*, p. 66.

[58] Merrill, *op. cit.*, chap. 1.

The clash of cultures between immigrants and their children has accentuated juvenile delinquency. In these and many other ways an earlier and comparatively well-organized culture pattern has been strained by the arrival of millions of persons bearing new cultures.[59]

The socioeconomic system of western Europe and America has likewise suffered from the effects of cumulative stresses and strains. The patterns of an agrarian economy were shattered by the change from agriculture to industry, as an increased number of persons moved to the city and worked outside the home. The former social structures were undesirable in terms of modern value judgments, since they were marked by feudal property relations, poverty, ignorance, and endemic disease. Similar large-scale changes are now visible in the industrialization of many "backward" areas. In the long run, these changes are "desirable," but they bring temporary social disorganization in their wake.[60]

Measurement of Social Disorganization

The study of social disorganization has both theoretical and practical implications. In the theoretical sense, the processes by which the group is broken are an important part of the overall interaction of society. In the practical sense, the reorganization of the individual and the group must rest upon a solid foundation of scientific knowledge. The study of social disorganization is therefore a link between "pure" and "applied" science. The "pure" scientist is interested in conceptual schemes, their development, testing, and extension. The "applied" scientist is interested in the application of the conceptual schemes to some human purpose.[61]

Social disorganization as developed in this text deals with both of these goals. In the preliminary chapters we present a conceptual approach to social disorganization in a dynamic society. In subsequent chapters we examine such specific examples as delinquency, crime, alcoholism, suicide, divorce, political corruption, racial prejudice, revolution, and war in the light of this conceptual approach. The applied scientist who attempts to treat these situations must understand them as recurrent natural phenomena and not as isolated examples of individual perversity. This book is thus a scientific treatise, in the sense of presenting, correlating, and conceptualizing the existing scientific knowledge of social disorganization. The applied scientist must base his therapy upon the regularities set forth by the pure scientist.

One of the basic functions of social science is measurement.[62] In one sense, the problem involves an attempt to measure social values, since social disorganization finds expression in value conflicts.[63] Although some sociologists

[59] Cf. Clyde V. Kiser, "Cultural Pluralism," Annals of the American Academy of Political and Social Science, 262:117–130 (March, 1949).

[60] Theodorson, op. cit.

[61] Bernard Barber, Science and the Social Order, The Free Press, Glencoe, Ill., 1952, p. 95.

[62] Cf. Leon Festinger and Daniel Katz, Research Methods in the Behavioral Sciences, The Dryden Press, Inc., New York, 1953.

[63] Turner, op. cit.

believe that social values neither can nor should be measured, the need for their measurement is obvious. Preliminary attempts have therefore been made. In one attempt, the scientist has taken such "infinite" values as the creative achievements of man and has measured these (and other values) in relation to each other. The methodological problem is difficult but not impossible. The experimenter must devise techniques for obtaining responses that discriminate between one value and another and establish their relative importance.[64] The criterion of the importance of a value is the meaningful activity directed toward it. When large numbers of persons direct *different* forms of meaningful activity toward such values as the state or the church, social disorganization is a reality.

The traditional method of attempting to measure social disorganization is by the index. An index is a simple and measurable aspect of behavior that indicates the extent to which more complex aspects of behavior are present. An index is thus a relatively simple phenomenon showing the presence of a more complicated phenomenon. Otherwise stated, an index is an "indirect, quantitative measure of a characteristic that is not itself directly measurable." The index may be used "when satisfactory techniques for directly measuring the characteristic have not been invented or if the cost of direct measurement is excessive."[65]

The relation between the index and the situation is not always simple or obvious. There are complicating factors in every example of social disorganization. Group relationships are complex and an attempt to simplify them artificially serves no good purpose. It is difficult to separate a social phenomenon from the social matrix in which it arises. Juvenile delinquency, for example, is the product of a variety of factors, ranging from emotional problems of the home to the frontier disrespect for law in American society. An index to one of the factors in delinquent behavior does not necessarily indicate the presence of the other causal factors. In general, however, indices of social disorganization are fairly reliable indicators of the comparative lack of consensus in a social system.

Indices of individual disorganization include statistics of juvenile delinquency, crime in all its manifestations, first admissions to mental hospitals, arrests for prostitution, public and private patients under treatment for alcoholism, suicides and attempted suicides, and the like.[66] An index to family disorganization is given by rates of divorce and estimates of desertion, as well as by the rate of illegitimate births, persons under treatment for venereal disease, and children of broken homes brought before the juvenile courts.

Community disorganization may be indicated by the literacy rate of the population, figures for irregular school attendance, rates of social mobility

---

[64] Catton, *op. cit.*, p. 55.

[65] Edward J. Baur, "Statistical Indexes of the Social Aspects of Communities," *Social Forces, 33*:64–75 (October, 1954), p. 64.

[66] Cf. Austin L. Porterfield, "Suicide and Crime in Folk and in Secular Society," *American Journal of Sociology, 57*:331–338 (January, 1952).

and transiency, political corruption, suicide, vice, and crime.[67] Indices for personal and social disorganization may thus overlap. In an ingenious attempt to establish relative degrees of social organization as between the various states, one investigator found that the per capita expenses for education, the percentage of Negroes in the general population, and the literacy rate of Negroes and whites were among the indices that established social organization and disorganization.[68]

On the international level, disorganization may be measured by data on war, both hot and cold: the number of persons killed, wounded, or systematically exterminated in recent wars; the number of men under arms in peacetime; the proportion of the national budget spent on past, present, and future wars; and the symbolic expression of hostile attitudes in newspapers, radio and television programs, and other agencies of mass communication.[69]

In the present volume, these various aspects of social disorganization are presented separately. The authors recognize, however, that any complete separation of individual, family, community, national, and international disorganization is both impossible and unrealistic. Consideration of the above indices makes this apparent. Many of the statistics are indicative of all types of social disorganization. The rate of venereal disease, for example, is at once a measure of the breakdown of family control, of disregard for the law, and of various emotional and physical difficulties of the individual. The infected person has defined the situation as hedonistic, rather than traditionally moral, which in itself is a further indication of social disorganization. A high rate of venereal disease, on the other hand, is an index of community disorganization.

An index therefore indicates more implications for social disorganization than appear in the single phenomenon which it purports to measure. Crime, unemployment, alcoholism, venereal disease, divorce, vertical and horizontal mobility, mental disease, suicide, illiteracy, graft, and wartime casualties are all indices of different aspects of a disorganized society. Some of these indices pertain primarily to the individual, others to the family, and still others to the local community. But they seldom involve these items separately. Every person lives in a complex web of group relationships, which constitute his social life.[70] Each of these patterns is in turn a part of the larger complex of patterned relationships which constitute the society. The adequate functioning of each group requires the maintenance of consensus in social interaction. Society as a whole rests upon an acceptance of similar basic norms and values. The group depends upon the individual and the individual depends upon the

[67] Cf. Robert C. Angell, *The Moral Integration of American Cities*, Special Supplement, *American Journal of Sociology, 57*:1–140 (July, 1951).

[68] P. R. Hofstaetter, "A Factorial Study of Cultural Patterns in the U.S.," *Journal of Psychology, 32*:99–113 (July, 1951).

[69] Harold D. Lasswell *et al.*, *The Comparative Study of Symbols*, Hoover Institute Studies, Stanford University Press, Stanford, 1952.

[70] Georg Simmel, *Conflict* and *The Web of Group-Affiliations* (translated by Kurt H. Wolff and Reinhard Bendix), The Free Press, Glencoe, Ill., 1955, p. 140.

group. In a dynamic society, these vital relationships are continually building up and breaking down.[71]

SELECTED BIBLIOGRAPHY

Barber, Bernard, "Structural-Functional Analysis: Some Problems and Misunderstandings," *American Sociological Review, 21:*129–135 (April, 1956). The rationale of structural-functional analysis is outlined in this article, which also deals with the relationships of this approach to social change. Structure and change are both functions of time; the first represents society at any one moment and the second takes the same society at a later time.

Blumer, Herbert, "Attitudes and the Social Act," *Social Problems, 3:*59–65 (October, 1955). A social attitude is more than a "mere" tendency to act. Human behavior, furthermore, cannot be understood simply in terms of attitudes. In the course of action, the individual "acts back" upon his attitude and changes it as he goes along. In this brief article, we have some penetrating suggestions for a revision of the traditional concept of social attitude.

Gerth, Hans, and Mills, C. Wright, *Character and Social Structure,* Harcourt, Brace and Company, New York, 1953. This is a thoughtful and closely reasoned analysis of contemporary society, with particular reference to the relationships between social character, structure, and change. The book is especially noteworthy in its emphasis upon the historical antecedents of contemporary social structures.

*Journal of Social Issues, 10:*1–76 (1954). The concept of disaster as a social crisis is here exhaustively explored by a number of social psychologists. In the years of the cold war, the ultimate disaster of attack by nuclear weapons has also become a subject of serious study.

Leighton, Alexander H., "Psychiatric Disorder and Social Environment," *Psychiatry, 18:*367–383 (November, 1955). Although the central interest of this study is in psychiatric difficulties, the frame of reference is that of social disorganization. The overall study, of which this article is a preliminary report, is expected to document thoroughly the relationship between individual and social disorganization.

Merrill, Francis E., "The Study of Social Problems," *American Sociological Review, 13:*251–262 (June, 1948). This article is an exposition of the theory of social problems. The conceptual approach based upon social problems is related to, but not synonymous with, that based upon social disorganization. Problem situations thus may or may not involve social disorganization—and vice versa.

Porterfield, Austin L., "Suicide and Crime in Folk and in Secular Society," *American Journal of Sociology, 57:*331–338 (January, 1952). Social disorganization and its meaning in different types of society are explored in this article. Such indices of social disorganization as suicide and crime have different meanings in different social settings.

Stouffer, Samuel A., *Communism, Conformity, and Civil Liberties,* Doubleday and Company, Inc., New York, 1955. This important study presents a variety of data on contemporary social issues, with particular emphasis upon intolerance

[71] Homans, *op. cit.,* p. 369.

of nonconformity. In the context of social disorganization, the study illustrates the conflict in basic values in our society.

Thomas, William I., and Znaniecki, Florian, *The Polish Peasant in Europe and America*, Alfred A. Knopf, Inc., New York, 1927 (2 vols.). This study was the first complete analysis of personal, family, and community disorganization in the sociological literature. Many of the conceptual tools have been subsequently modified (e.g., social attitude, social value), but it nevertheless remains a landmark in the field.

Turner, Ralph H., "Value-Conflict in Social Disorganization," *Sociology and Social Research, 38:*301–308 (May–June, 1954). The author of this article has extended the analysis of Thomas and Znaniecki (above) and explored the implications of the attitude-value approach through empirical research. In the present essay, social disorganization is conceived as a "state of conflict among social values."

PART TWO

Individual Disorganization

CHAPTER 3

Individual Disorganization

Individual Disorganization in a Dynamic Society

The individual and society are, in a sense, different aspects of the same process of social interaction. A society exists when a number of persons interact regularly and continuously on the basis of behavior patterns whose meanings have been previously established. Social interaction takes place between socialized individuals, whose social selves have been acquired by contact with other similarly developed individuals. In this development, the individual learns to "take the role of the other" and put himself in the place of the person with whom he is interacting. Social interaction involves the communication of one person with another, as well as that of the individual with himself.[1]

This identification of the individual with society is basic to understanding our analysis of individual disorganization. On one level, we are viewing the breakdown of the group and the consequent disorganization of the individuals comprising it. On another level, we are concerned with the impact upon the individuals of the disorganization of the interpersonal relationships which bind them together in the group.

The essential inseparability of the individual and society was indicated long ago by Charles Horton Cooley, George Herbert Mead, and Ellsworth Faris. More recently, this premise has been stated even more categorically by the psychiatrist Harry Stack Sullivan, who bases his theory of psychiatry upon it. In an essay entitled "The Illusion of Personal Individuality" Sullivan said that, for purposes of either understanding or therapy, "it makes no sense to think of ourselves as 'individual,' 'separate,' capable of anything like definitive description in isolation. . . . No great progress in this field of study can be made until it is realized that the field of observation is what people do with each other, what they can communicate to each other about what they do with each other. When this is done, no such thing as the durable, unique, individual personality is ever clearly justified."[2]

The essence of personality is thus based upon interpersonal relations, both

---

[1] Herbert Blumer, "Psychological Import of the Human Group," chap. 8 in Muzafer Sherif and M. O. Wilson (eds.), *Group Relations at the Crossroads,* Harper & Brothers, New York, 1953.

[2] Harry Stack Sullivan, "The Illusion of Personal Individuality," *Psychiatry, 13*:317–332 (August, 1950), p. 329.

those to which the child is exposed and those which the adult continues as long as he lives. The same dynamic forces that produce social disorganization produce the disorganization of the individual. Social disorganization is the impairment or dissolution of the network of patterned relationships binding individuals together in a series of functioning groups. The individuals are the actors in the drama and their relationships are the ties holding them in the group. Each individual is only as strong as his group relationships; in this sense, no man lives unto himself alone. Although social disorganization is the dissolution of group relationships, individuals are also inevitably involved in the process.[3]

A disorganized society is composed of individuals who are also more or less disorganized. For a large number of perfectly adjusted individuals to exist in a society whose structure is seriously disorganized is difficult, if not impossible. A confused, disorganized, and disoriented society tends to produce confused, disorganized, and disoriented personalities. The individual's personality develops by learning the approved patterns and roles from other members of the group. When these patterns are confused, he cannot know exactly what is expected of him. Under such conditions, his chances for developing a completely integrated personality are slim indeed.

In analyzing individual disorganization, therefore, the sociologist emphasizes the group rather than the individual. The primary data of the sociologist are *interpersonal relations*, which are the very stuff of society and which produce both the organization and the disorganization of personality. Delinquency, crime, prostitution, and suicide (to name only a few forms of individual disorganization) are thus viewed as group phenomena. The psychiatrist, clinical psychologist, and pathologist are concerned with the individual *qua individual*, and they direct their various forms of therapy to reorganizing or healing him. The sociologist, however, is primarily concerned with the *patterned relationships* between persons.[4]

"Sociocultural situations," suggests an eminent social psychiatrist, "which interfere with the orientation of the individual in regard to his place in society and the place of others foster psychiatric disorder."[5] These situations are numerous in contemporary society, judging by such indices of individual disorganization as alcoholism, neurosis, and psychosis. The difficulties individuals encounter are relative, and the majority of persons manage to make a relatively workable adjustment to a changing world. Making such an adjustment is a tribute to the adaptability of the human being, who is obliged to make his way in a society where many of the former primary ties no longer exist.[6]

---

[3] Ralph Kramer, "The Conceptual Status of Social Disorganization," *American Journal of Sociology, 48:*466–474 (January, 1943).

[4] Herbert Blumer, "Social and Individual Disorganization," *American Journal of Sociology, 42:*871–877 (May, 1937).

[5] Alexander H. Leighton, "Psychiatric Disorder and Social Environment," *Psychiatry, 18:*367–383 (November, 1955), p. 383.

[6] Erich Fromm, *The Sane Society,* Rinehart and Company, Inc., New York, 1955, chap. 2.

Individual and social disorganization also operate in reciprocal fashion. The maladjusted individual, in other words, produces further maladjustment to the degree that his behavior affects others. No one lives in a social vacuum and each person influences many others. ("No man," said the seventeenth-century poet John Donne, "is an *Iland,* intire of it selfe; every man is a peece of the *Continent,* a part of the maine. . . .") The person who is unable to assume his roles properly sets up a chain reaction of social disorganization. Each person interacts with others, notably with the members of his family and his immediate associates. The neurotic wife who is unable to function adequately as wife and mother helps to disorganize the personalities of her husband and children. A social role involves a reciprocal pattern of relationships and thus requires the adequate functioning of at least two persons. When one group member fails to do his part, the relationship itself suffers.[7]

Personal disorganization reflects a disorganized society in varying degrees. Individuals who are inadequately endowed either mentally or physically may be unable to meet their normal social responsibilities. The feeble-minded individual lacks the mental equipment to live up to many of the expectations of his group. Those who are deaf, dumb, or blind suffer equally obvious impairments in communication and social interaction. Our concern, however, is primarily with those who are products of a disorganized society, rather than those whose difficulties arise from physical disabilities or deficiencies. Social disorganization is much more important as a source of individual disorganization than are personal inadequacies per se.

Individual Life Organization

The individual is the microcosm of the social macrocosm—a small part of a much larger whole. Within his own personality, nature and nurture are inextricably related, but for sociological purposes he is the product of social interaction. The individual is socialized in the course of his growing up, and in the process achieves the status of a person. As Park and Burgess concluded, "The person is an individual who has status. We come into the world as individuals. We acquire status and become persons. Status means position in society."[8] One of the aspects of this position in society is the life organization of each person.

The individual's life organization may be defined as that pattern of attitudes, values, purposes, goals, statuses, and roles which grow out of his social experience and through which, consciously or unconsciously, he hopes to make his life meaningful. His life organization is his own set of rules for guidance in the spheres of morality, law, social relationships, religion, business, recreation, love, and marriage. These rules are the embodiment of a given person's norms and values, by which he attempts to define each particular situation. They constitute his code of behavior, the things he will and will not do, whether he is a gambler, politician, clergyman, or stockbroker. Within a wide

---

[7] Leland H. Stott, "The Problem of Evaluating Family Success," *Marriage and Family Living,* 13:149–153 (Fall, 1951).

[8] Robert E. Park and Ernest W. Burgess, *Introduction to the Science of Sociology,* University of Chicago Press, Chicago, 1924, p. 55.

range of individual variations, each person sets up a life organization, based upon what he is and what he wants to be.[9]

Each society has its own conception of the ideal life organization and its own methods of imposing such organization upon each successive generation. In a general sense, this conception is known as the "social character" of a given society. According to Fromm, "the social character . . . is the nucleus of the character structure which is shared by most members of the same culture in contradistinction to the individual character in which people belonging to the same culture differ from each other."[10] The agreement on the social character helps each individual to fit into the ongoing activities of the society with a minimum of friction. The social character is inculcated by the process which has been variously described as transmitting the group values, educating the young, or imparting the cultural heritage. In short, it is the process of socialization.

This process is not uniform, nor does it turn out uniform personalities. Each member of a particular society has certain elements of the social character in his life organization, and these elements set him off from the members of other societies. Americans and Frenchmen thus have different traits because they participate in different cultures. At the same time, each American absorbs the culture patterns of his society slightly differently from the way every other American absorbs them.

The interaction between each individual and his sociocultural world is unique. This fact, coupled with the unique biological heritage of every human being (except in the case of identical twins), insures the individuality of the life organization of every person. In the words of Mead, "every individual self has its own peculiar individuality, its own unique pattern, because each individual self . . . reflects in its organized structure a different aspect or perspective of this whole social behavior pattern from that which is reflected in the organized structure of *any individual self* within that process."[11] Each person interacts with others who have certain general similarities in cultural background. The ultimate product of this interaction, however, is a unique human being with a life organization of his own.

It follows that everyone's life organization is not necessarily in harmony with the organization and purposes of the larger society. Wide variations in this harmony exist as between societies, as well as within a single society. In general, working harmony between the individual and the group is easier to achieve in a simple society than in a complex one. In simple societies the major statuses and roles comprisng the life organization are socially ascribed. Primitive people are not, of course, in any sense automatons, nor does the culture place a completely uniform stamp upon them. Among the Trobriand

---

[9] William I. Thomas and Florian Znaniecki, *The Polish Peasant in Europe and America*, Alfred A. Knopf, Inc., New York, 1927, Vol. II.

[10] Fromm, *op. cit.*, p. 78.

[11] George Herbert Mead, *Mind, Self, and Society*, University of Chicago Press, Chicago, 1934, p. 201. (Our italics.)

Islanders, for example, Malinowski found striking differences between personalities, as well as a tendency to deviate from the norms if the individual believed he could do so without incurring punishment.[12]

In a complex and dynamic society the inconsistencies between any life organization and the norms of the larger society are much greater. The presence of different racial, cultural, ethnic, religious, and class groups means that the variety of possible life organizations is very great. A child growing up in a lower-class environment will have a different set of norms from those of a middle-class child. The subcultural differences between the classes include such matters as sex behavior, personal aggression, conceptions of the self, ideas of saving, beliefs in vertical mobility, and ability to take the other person's point of view. Because of these differences, it is impossible to have any complete conformity or any rigidly defined group of behavior patterns for society as a whole.

The degree of conformity that exists (or is reputed to exist) in primitive societies would also be repugnant to the average person in our own society. Uniformity of outlook and behavior is contrary to the freedom which modern man accepts as his birthright. Social disorganization is thus the price of change and diversity. As a society becomes more dynamic, the difficulty of maintaining harmonious relationships between the individual and the group increases proportionately. A stable (or stagnant) society is comparatively free of social change and social disorganization. A dynamic society (by definition) is characterized by the constant building up and breaking down of group relationships, as each individual strives to adjust to changing situations.

Individual Attitudes and Social Values

Motivation is also important in individual disorganization. In a strict sense, motivation is the province of the psychologist, who has developed both the conceptual schemes and the methodology to explore this phase of human behavior. A complete understanding of motivation, in psychological terms, would involve a knowledge of the entire personality and how it came to be what it is. Among the elements in such a conception are "(1) external appearance and superficial attractiveness, (2) the bodily self, (3) self-conceptions, (4) memory, (5) self-control, (6) reason and rationality, (7) traits determining status, (8) individual uniqueness, (9) reputation, (10) sum total of all innate and acquired traits, impulses, dispositions, etc., (11) style of life, (12) character, (13) temperament, (14) adjustment to environment, (15) hierarchic organization, (16) subjective aspect of culture."[13]

Such an extensive consideration in the present context of individual and social disorganization is manifestly impossible. Some of the above elements are clearly individual and genetic (e.g., external appearance, temperament), whereas others are largely social (e.g., self-conceptions, subjective aspect of

---

[12] Bronislaw Malinowski, *Crime and Custom in Savage Society*, Routledge and Kegan Paul, London, 1926, part II, chap. 1.

[13] Alfred R. Lindesmith and Anselm L. Strauss, *Social Psychology*, The Dryden Press, Inc., New York, 1956 (rev. ed.), p. 485.

culture). We are primarily interested here in those factors that cause the individual to violate social norms. This behavior is a reflection of the social environment; the individual either learns and tries to conform to the norms of his society or deliberately acts in ways contrary to them.

The related concepts of attitudes and values offer considerable insight into this learning process. Each individual has his own interpretation of social situations, and hence his own adjustments are to a certain extent unique. Out of his past experience, each person builds a life organization which, as we have indicated, is both similar to and different from that of every other person. To understand the disorganized person, we must see him through his subjective interpretation of his own experience and that of others. It is in this very general sense, therefore, that we are employing the concepts of attitudes and values.[14]

Whether "normal" or "abnormal," "organized" or "disorganized," human behavior is a complex process. The mere tendency to act in a particular way when confronted with a certain stimulus is not sufficient to explain behavior. The social act is a central consideration, and the individual changes his behavior in the course of his act by adjusting to the acts of other persons. "In this process," as Blumer says, "the individual indicates things to himself, defines them, judges them, prepares plans of action, chooses between them, and makes decisions."[15] In this continuous and dynamic process of social action, some persons deviate from the established norms and values of the group and contribute both to social disorganization and to their own individual disorganization.

This general process of social action is apparent whether we are dealing with juvenile delinquency, sexual maladjustment, alcoholism, mental disorder, or suicide. In each type of disorganized behavior the individual performs a series of acts which are opposed to existing group values. He may or may not understand his own motivations. His interpretation of his behavior is often rationalized, in order to convince himself that he has good and sufficient (i.e., "rational") reasons for behaving as he has learned to behave. On the other hand, he may be completely unaware of his motivations. In certain cases, his "real" reasons may be revealed only through the techniques of psychoanalysis.

Overt behavior may also veil motivations rather than reveal them. A deserting father may not behave as he does so much out of lack of concern for his family as because of anxiety brought about by conflicting emotions. A boy may steal because he is ashamed of his mother rather than because he wants a given object. By performing an antisocial act, he feels obscurely that he is getting even with her. In his study of the maladjustment of interpersonal relations, Harry Stack Sullivan holds that anxiety is very important. In many such difficulties, he points out, the individual's ability to communicate is

---

[14] *Ibid.*, pp. 493–495.
[15] Herbert Blumer, "Attitudes and the Social Act," *Social Problems, 3:*59–65 (October, 1955), p. 63.

disturbed by anxiety. Anxiety itself is the result of personal inadequacies, insecurities, and frustrations of which the individual may not be aware.[16] Some deviant behavior, e.g., juvenile delinquency, is related to growing up and seems to be characteristic of adolescence itself.

To understand individual behavior, whether normal or deviant, it is important to take the role of the other person and attempt to see the world as he sees it. The ability to do this is similar to what the psychologists call "empathy," which means the emotional identification of one person with another. A certain amount of empathy is necessary to all social interaction, inasmuch as each individual must have some emotional identification with the person with whom he is interacting.[17] Individuals vary in their ability to take the role of the other. Some are warm, outgoing, and expressive and have this empathic quality to a high degree. Others are cold, rigid, and diffident and are largely lacking in empathic ability. The student who seeks to understand individual disorganization should have a certain amount of empathic ability in order to understand the behavior of others.

Individual Deviation and Social Norms

In the process of socialization, some persons do not conform to the norms of the group. This lack of conformity is called *deviation* and the individuals are known as *deviants*. In deviating from the expected group behavior, the deviant may weaken the group ties and thus contribute to social disorganization. The person who consistently deviates from many group norms becomes disorganized himself, so close is the relationship between the individual and society. Effective functioning of the group depends upon the relationships which bind the members together as a functioning whole. The deviant usually (although not always) weakens these group ties and himself at the same time.[18]

Social norms arise from group interaction and are transmitted in the same way. Since they reflect the interaction of the group, norms often appear to benefit the group more than the individual. Many persons therefore find it disagreeable, inconvenient, boring, or otherwise unsatisfactory to follow these norms and are tempted to depart from them when they can do so unobserved. Even in primitive societies, where conformity is high, individuals may evade norms against sexual relationships between close relatives, interfering with one another's property, and using magic to obtain other illicit gains.[19]

In our own society, the systematic evasion of (or deviation from) social norms is even more common. Members may proclaim the importance of various norms and at the same time avoid abiding by them as systematically

[16] Harry Stack Sullivan, *The Interpersonal Theory of Psychiatry*, W. W. Norton and Company, Inc., New York, 1953, p. xii.

[17] Leonard S. Cottrell, Jr., and Rosalind F. Dymond, "The Empathic Responses," *Psychiatry, 12:*355–359 (November, 1949).

[18] George C. Homans, *The Human Group*, Harcourt, Brace and Company, New York, 1950, p. 457.

[19] Malinowski, *op. cit.*, pp. 81–82.

as they can. Among these hypocritical practices are (1) the public affirmation of traditional sexual morality and the widespread practice of premarital and extramarital relationships; (2) the formal statement of a belief in the democratic creed and the prevalence of discrimination on ethnic, religious, and racial grounds; (3) the concept of honesty in government and the practice of political corruption; and (4) the emphasis upon the Christian virtues of love and humility and the indulgence in chicanery and sharp practice in business. In these and many other ways the norms of modern society are systematically evaded.[20]

Just as social norms differ in importance, so do the violations assume various degrees of importance to the group. Persons evade some norms because they do not consider them important. The traffic violator is a case in point. Others deviate because they do not understand why the norms are the standards for behavior. Lower-class males thus deviate widely, persistently, and enthusiastically from the sexual norms of the middle class, which are the formal basis for sexual behavior in our society. Lower-class males may be well aware that they are violating the middle-class norms against premarital sexual relationships, but they (the lower-class males) do not appear to be greatly concerned.[21]

On the other hand, some deviations are tacitly accepted, even though the behavior is formally condemned. Individuals can therefore act in different ways without conflicting drastically with the norms. The latter are flexible and the range of permitted behavior is correspondingly wide. A study of student cheating in examinations, for example, disclosed that the cheaters approved (or at least accepted) a variety of such activities, depending upon the circumstances. In a complex and dynamic society some flexibility in defining norms is necessary, or social interaction could not continue at all.[22]

Deviation should also be considered in its social setting. We have been using the term to describe the individual who violates the norms of the larger society, on matters ranging from mild breaches of etiquette to murder. The individual may also belong to a group whose norms are opposed to those of the larger society. The juvenile delinquent may follow the norms of his gang and thus conforms on one normative level. He will lie to and steal from persons not in the gang. In so doing, he is conforming to the norms of his immediate group, although he is deviating from the norms of the larger society.

In a complex and heterogeneous society such as our own, these deviant groups include criminals, drug addicts, homosexuals, hoboes, and prostitutes.[23] If the members were able to carry on all their activities wholly within their

[20] Robin M. Williams, Jr., *American Society: A Sociological Interpretation,* Alfred A. Knopf, Inc., New York, 1951, pp. 357–366.

[21] Alfred C. Kinsey *et al., Sexual Behavior in the Human Male,* W. B. Saunders Company, Philadelphia, 1948; Alfred C. Kinsey *et al., Sexual Behavior in the Human Female,* W. B. Saunders Company, Philadelphia, 1953.

[22] Samuel A. Stouffer, "An Analysis of Conflicting Social Norms," *American Sociological Review, 14:*707–717 (December, 1949).

[23] Lindesmith and Strauss, *op. cit.,* chap. 21, "Deviant Subsocieties."

subsocieties, their behavior might be considered neither deviant nor disorganized, since they would be following the systematic behavior patterns of an organized group. All persons must interact with persons in the larger society, however, and their behavior is deviant because they violate the expectations of the larger defining group.

The larger group may react to deviant behavior in a number of ways. It may try to bring the deviant back into the group by informing him of the error of his ways. In some experimental groups there has been considerable effort expended in trying to help the deviant understand the need for conforming. After a while the efforts tended to drop off sharply. No group can permit the indefinite flouting of its norms and values, and ultimately the wayward member is excluded.[24]

On a more drastic level, the group may actively punish the deviant for endangering its norms and behavior patterns. Among the possible penalties in addition to expulsion are avoidance, restriction of relations to those of a less intimate character, ridicule, slight gestures of disapproval, and the threat of such possibilities.[25] Penalties themselves are contingent upon the nature of the norms which the deviant person threatens. Society is obviously less concerned with violations of rules of etiquette than with murder; the eccentric ordinarily incurs less drastic penalties than the criminal. The criteria for such penalties are based upon the real or supposed welfare of the group.[26]

Individual Disorganization and Social Structure

The average individual has a strong emotional need to participate in a number of groups. From infancy on, he is continually striving to attain the security that comes from such status. His position in the family, his adjustments to his peer groups, his heterosexual development, and his marriage all reflect the desire to belong to different groups and occupy a desirable status in each. Any situation threatening his position in a *system of interpersonal relations* brings about anxiety, which in turn produces individual disorganization. In Leighton's words, "Sociocultural situations which interfere with the individual's membership in a definite human group foster psychiatric disorder."[27]

These situations begin in infancy. During the child's early years, his sense of security is derived from the love of his parents and his status in the family. As he grows older, his status is determined by other interpersonal relations. In the peer group, from childhood through adolescence, the attitudes of his

[24] Stanley Schachter, "Deviation, Rejection, and Communication," *Journal of Abnormal and Social Psychology*, 46:190–207 (April, 1951).

[25] Robert E. L. Faris, "Development of the Small-Group Research Movement," in Sherif and Wilson *op. cit.*, p. 175.

[26] Cf. Leon Festinger and John Thibaut, "Interpersonal Communication in Small Groups," *Journal of Abnormal and Social Psychology*, 46:92–99 (January, 1951). For a further discussion of deviation, see Robert Dubin, "Deviant Behavior and Social Structure: Continuities in Social Theory," *American Sociological Review*, 24:147–164 (April, 1959).

[27] Leighton, *op. cit.*, p. 383.

contemporaries mean a great deal to him, and he tries in every possible way to make his status secure with them.[28]

In one study of adolescent peer groups, the boys and girls did everything they could to participate in the teen-age world of the group, embrace its norms, and gain acceptance. The teen-age world in general is marked by "the irresponsible desire to 'have a good time,' with the accent on humor, comedy, fads and crazes, popular music and 'teen-age stuff'; in terms of social activities in company with the opposite sex; in athletic prowess for boys and glamor for girls; and in the stereotype of the all-around 'swell guy.' . . ."[29] When the members of the group were asked to picture their conception of the ideal life, they could think of nothing better than to be surrounded by their present companions.

The adolescent who can bask in the warmth of group approval is an "adjusted" person in this sense, despite any other personal problems. Even these conformists, however, often have a niggling sense of insecurity lest they do something which will threaten their position. For many other persons of all ages insecurity becomes a real feeling of anxiety, which Sullivan characterizes as an "anticipated unfavorable appraisal of one's current activity by someone whose opinion is significant."[30] When personal disorganization has become intensified, this anxiety is often so acute that the individual escapes it only in the compulsions of alcoholism or the hallucinations of mental disorder, or by ending it all in suicide.

Anxiety also reflects the conscious or unconscious fear that the individual will be unable to play his social role (or roles) in a fashion approved by society. Social roles are very much a part of the self, and self-feeling depends largely upon one's ability to fulfill his role in a way society expects. The male role carries the strong expectation that the husband will be a "good provider." The female role carries the obligation to bear and rear children. In either case, the person identifies himself with his basic role as male or female and may have a strong sense of anxiety lest he fail to meet the requirements.[31]

The self-feeling related to the adequate assumption of expected responsibilities operates in a circular fashion. The person who is chronically anxious about his role tends to be inadequate in its performance, which further increases his anxiety. The individual's conception of his role and his sense of adequacy in it come from other persons. The boy learns what is socially expected of the male member of society in childhood and continues learning through adolescence into maturity. He does not invent these expectations but learns them in his family and other primary groups. As he becomes an adult and actually assumes the obligations of husband, father, and provider, he

[28] August B. Hollingshead, *Elmtown's Youth,* John Wiley and Sons, Inc., New York, 1949.

[29] Matilda W. Riley and Samuel H. Flowerman, "Group Relations as a Variable in Communications Research," *American Sociological Review, 16*:174–180 (April, 1951), p. 175.

[30] Sullivan, *The Interpersonal Theory of Psychiatry,* p. 113.

[31] Margaret Mead, *Male and Female,* W. W. Norton and Company, Inc., New York, 1949.

judges himself in terms of the expectations which he has learned and the appraisals of the people around him. Throughout this process, he looks at himself through the eyes of others and experiences satisfaction or anxiety as a result.[32]

In a stable and organized society, the average individual is usually able to accept responsibilities in accordance with the organized expectations of others with a minimum of anxiety. In a disorganized society, anxiety is greater. The individual's responsibilities as an executive may conflict with his role as a father. When this happens, it may be difficult to develop a stable life organization, which itself is so dependent upon the (real or imagined) attitudes of other people. The individual may come to distrust his status, his roles, his motives, and (hence) his own personal integrity. Many forms of individual disorganization, from alcoholism to psychosis, are a result of such anxiety.

Social roles are not static and bloodless abstractions but are active elements in personality. They carry *demands* upon the individual to act or *prohibitions* not to act. Roles are normative elements of personality that come from the groups with which the individual interacts: his family, peer group, adolescent clique, professional group, and religious group.[33] In a simple and stable society, most of these roles are compatible and make demands which are all of a piece, as it were. Family, religion, government, economic activity, education, and the rest of the institutional role patterns tend to be consistent in a closely knit society and do not present demands that are contradictory or incompatible.[34]

This is not true in modern society. The complexity of modern society is so great that many persons are called upon to play roles which are mutually irreconcilable. These role patterns were developed and handed down from a simpler structure in which they bore some relationship to the actual situation. The individual today is faced, however, with new and often totally different situations, for which there are no accepted roles. Business roles call for an impersonal attitude toward persons in need, while one's belief as a Christian demands lenient treatment of the man behind in his mortgage. Social opinion moreover does not conform with reality. The person is told that he can make himself what he wishes, but at the same time he is limited by his class status. Men from lower-class families do not have the same opportunities for success as do men from upper-class families.[35]

Social roles are also difficult for older persons. In a traditional society, the aged have definite tasks to perform and they also act as guides and mentors for younger persons. Under modern conditions, especially in the United States, the aged have no such vital place in the social structure. They are, in-

[32] S. Frank Miyamoto and Sanford M. Dornbusch, "A Test of Interactionist Hypotheses of Self-Conception," *American Journal of Sociology, 61*:399–403 (March, 1956).

[33] Jackson Toby, "Some Variables in Role Conflict Analysis," *Social Forces, 30*:323–327 (March, 1952).

[34] Ruth Benedict, *Patterns of Culture*, Penguin Books, Inc., New York, 1946.

[35] W. Lloyd Warner and James C. Abegglen, *Big Business Leaders in America,* Harper & Brothers, New York, 1955, p. 14.

stead, deprived of their jobs through involuntary retirement and made to feel that they are a drain upon the society. Today the average young couple even hesitates to provide a home for a widowed parent. Greater life expectancy has meant that there are larger numbers of persons in the older age brackets, who are almost completely frustrated by a youth-centered society. The retired person often feels useless and becomes a prey to apathy and melancholy, while his relationships with others progressively deteriorate.

Interruptions in the plans for a lifetime, frustrations, and discontinuities in social roles are all crises to the individuals concerned. We have previously discussed the concept of group crisis and the disorganization that results from the serious interruption of the group's activities. A disruption in the group's interpersonal relations is also a crisis for the members. In some cases, these interruptions are *precipitate* and come like a bolt from the blue. The sudden death of a member of the family is such a crisis. A crisis is *cumulative* when the individual gradually loses his ability to assume his normal responsibilities. Such a crisis is evidenced in the slow development of alcoholism or in a clinical neurosis.

A close relationship exists between the particular organization of the society and the prevalence of individual crises. In an organized society the average person can go through life without making drastic adjustments in his social relationships.[36] In a disorganized society such continuity of role may be more difficult. The possibility of interpersonal change is so great that virtually everyone must make a series of role adjustments of varying degrees of severity, for which they have had little or no preparation. In his analysis of the relationship between social disorganization and cultural roles, Warren has proposed a tentative hypothesis. "Social disorganization," he suggests, "varies inversely with the degree of continuity in normal role sequences."[37]

In a dynamic and democratic society, this role continuity is therefore considerably less than in a stabler society. Continuity implies stability, and stability in turn means that the great majority of persons remain in the same social class in which they are born. In our own society, class lines are presumed to be fluid and the individual is able to rise in the social scale. The son of a poor immigrant who becomes a doctor thus benefits from the open social structure. Strong and creative persons will find the adjustments to a new status stimulating and, instead of being crushed and bewildered by the demands of their new role, will adjust triumphantly to these demands. Less competent people cannot do this and may become the victims of individual disorganization, because of their anxiety over assuming a new role.

Isolation and Individual Disorganization

Individuals in the modern world are often isolated in their social contacts. The disorganization of the traditional way of life has destroyed many of the ties which formerly bound them to groups. They are living under conditions

[36] Ruth Benedict, "Continuities and Discontinuities in Cultural Conditioning," *Psychiatry, 1:*161–167 (1938).

[37] Roland L. Warren, "Social Disorganization and the Interrelationship of Cultural Roles," *American Sociological Review, 14:*83–87 (February, 1949), p. 85.

which, in Leighton's words, "interfere with a sense of belonging to a moral order and of being right in what one does. . . ."[38] Status in the family, the neighborhood, and the work group are important, and for many the possibility of achieving or maintaining such status is impaired. The sense of isolation is especially apparent among the urban middle classes, who lead mobile and secular lives. This segment of our population provides most of the members of the voluntary associations that have sprung up in urban areas, the professed functions of which vary from stamp collecting to poll watching.[39]

The individual feels isolated if he is not a part of things. This isolation reflects social disorganization that has taken place in the past and is still going on. The extended rural family no longer maintains its close ties. The bonds of the early church have likewise suffered impairment before a growing secularization. Not all people view these social changes alike. Some believe they are desirable, since they liberate the individual from many of the restraints of an earlier period. Others regard the same changes as highly undesirable, since they have destroyed a way of life still widely regarded as ideal. Whatever the definition, these processes represent social disorganization in its literal sense.[40]

The isolated person suffers from a lack of those relationships which are at once primary, personal, and emotional. Secondary, impersonal, and rational relationships exist on every hand, but these apparently fail to provide the satisfactions so necessary for personal stability. Modern bureaucratic society is characterized by a proliferation of secondary group relationships, which the individual enters as means to his own ends, rather than as ends in themselves. The group relationships that in the past have "automatically" satisfied many emotional needs are either weakened or destroyed. The isolated man lacks friendship and love and seeks both.[41]

The relationships between isolation and individual disorganization have been documented in several studies. In one study of mental disorder, the concentration of schizophrenia was found to be closely correlated with such indices of isolation as "knowing the names of fewer neighbors; fewer personal friends, fewer acquaintances; more renting than owning of homes; less membership in lodges or fraternal organizations; [and] greater unemployment. . . ."[42] In another study, members of the lowest class in a large industrial city had a rate of schizophrenia that was *eleven times* that of members living in upper-class areas in the same city.[43] One of the differences between these two groups is presumably the relative degree of social isolation.

Social isolation and individual disorganization operate in an augmenting

[38] Leighton, *op. cit.*, p. 383.

[39] John M. Foskett, "Social Structure and Social Participation," *American Sociological Review*, 20:431–438 (August, 1955).

[40] Margaret M. Wood, *Paths of Loneliness*, Columbia University Press, New York, 1953, chap. 1.

[41] William C. Menninger, "Men, Machines, and Mental Health," *Mental Hygiene*, 36:184–196 (April, 1952).

[42] E. Gartly Jaco, "The Social Isolation Hypothesis and Schizophrenia," *American Sociological Review*, 19:567–577 (October, 1954), pp. 575–576.

[43] August B. Hollingshead and F. C. Redlich, "Social Stratification and Psychiatric Disorder," *American Sociological Review*, 18:163–169 (April, 1953).

and reciprocal fashion. That is, each acts on the other and in the process both become more pronounced. The lonely and introverted child may develop a rich fantasy life to compensate for his lack of intimate contact with his parents and playmates. Less sensitive members of his peer group may ridicule his fantasies and force him still further back upon himself. As he grows older, his shyness may continue to alienate him from the group and increase his anxiety at meeting other persons. The latter become, in Sullivan's words, "unpredictable sources of humiliation, anxiety, and punishment,"[44] and the isolation is further intensified. In short, "social isolation is . . . a sign that the individual's interpersonal difficulties have become so great that he is no longer capable of functioning in interpersonal relationships."[45]

Contemporary social isolation is a subject much discussed by philosophers, psychiatrists, and social psychologists. In his book *Escape from Freedom,* Erich Fromm holds that man has succeeded in freeing himself from many of the physical limitations and restraints that marked human society from its earliest beginnings. These emerging freedoms are especially apparent in technology and industrial production. Advances in technology have liberated many a man from hunger and physical want. Advances in scientific knowledge have freed him from ignorance and superstition (at least in theory) by providing him with tested knowledge of the universe and man's place in it.[46]

But these new freedoms, as Fromm says, have not brought the Utopia that was so optimistically expected. Something is lacking in the emancipation of modern man, and he is not happy about it. He has no sense of participation in a number of warm, intimate, human relationships. Fromm maintains that "modern man, freed from the bonds of pre-individualistic society, which simultaneously gave him security and limited him, has not gained freedom in the positive sense of the realization of his individual self. . . . Freedom, though it has brought him independence and rationality, has made him isolated and, thereby, anxious and powerless."[47]

The same social changes that dissolved the restraints of a traditional society have disorganized many of the group relationships that formerly embodied unity and security. The individual is indeed free from hunger, want, and ignorance, but he is also free of the comforting of the large family, the church, the local community, and the stratified social system. The free individual is thus isolated from his fellows in a spiritual and emotional sense. Often he finds this isolation intolerable.

Modern man has tried by a variety of ways to escape from this unbearable situation. Some of these attempts have been conscious and others have been unconsciously motivated. One such attempt to "escape from freedom" is through authoritarian political organization. Here the individual gives up his

---

[44] Sullivan, *The Interpersonal Theory of Psychiatry,* p. 225.
[45] Melvin L. Kohn and John A. Clausen, "Social Isolation and Schizophrenia," *American Sociological Review, 20*:265–273 (June, 1955), p. 273.
[46] Erich Fromm, *Escape from Freedom,* Rinehart and Company, Inc., New York, 1941.
[47] *Ibid.,* p. viii.

independence and seeks to identify himself with persons or organizations stronger than himself. In this way, the isolated individual turns away from his newly found freedom, with its mingled rationalism and isolation, and embraces authoritarian social movements. In recent decades, scores of millions of persons in western Europe have accepted Communist and Fascist authoritarianism. Such a desire for emotional security is not the only reason for the rise of modern authoritarianism. But social isolation is undoubtedly one factor in this situation.[48]

The plight of the isolated individual has been most effectively explored by David Riesman, in his book *The Lonely Crowd*.[49] His basic thesis is that the urban individual is socially isolated even in the midst of the crowds with which he is daily obliged to associate. The member of the "lonely" crowd is in constant interaction with many persons, but his relationships lack the warmth and intimacy which he apparently needs. Today, permanent status is no longer ascribed at birth. The breakdown of the traditional class structure has increased the amount and intensity of status striving.[50]

The member of the lonely crowd is continually afraid that he will not secure and maintain the approval of others. The trend toward "groupism" and conformity apparently is an indication of this need for belonging. In an unconscious effort to gain approval and avoid anxiety, the individual gladly sacrifices his individuality on the altar of group approbation. The paradox lies in the fact that the "other-directed" person continually seeks the approval of the group but at the same time is overanxious about the possibility of failing to gain this approval. The appreciation of others thus becomes so important that the possibility of failure is almost unbearable.

The concept of isolation has direct implications for several forms of personality disorganization. Among these specific manifestations are (1) *alcoholism*—the alcoholic often has a case history of isolation reaching far back into his childhood; the compulsive nature of his drinking intensifies his later isolation, as he progressively loses contact with family, friends, and fellow workers; (2) *mental disorder*—the mentally ill person is typically an isolated individual, as we have suggested; the most important psychosis (schizophrenia) is characterized by a gradual withdrawal from the world of others until isolation becomes virtually complete; (3) *suicide*—the suicide has so completely broken with the group that further existence is meaningless. His is the final isolation of death.

On the other hand, the delinquent, the adult criminal, and the sex offender tend to isolate themselves from the group by their conduct even though they are largely products of social disorganization, as we shall discuss in detail. The

[48] The relationships between authoritarianism and social disorganization are discussed at length in Chapter 30.

[49] David Riesman, *et al.*, *The Lonely Crowd*, Yale University Press, New Haven, 1950. A somewhat abridged edition was published by Doubleday Anchor Books, New York, 1953.

[50] Talcott Parsons, "Certain Primary Sources and Patterns of Aggression in the Social Structure of the Western World," *Psychiatry*, 10:167–181 (May, 1947).

problems of the industrial male worker and those of women and children in industry have arisen for a variety of reasons. They exist in a special sense, however, because of the personal problems of the individuals. Modern industrial production and distribution has become so impersonal that the laborer as a human being is often ignored. Large-scale industry thus provides a very special isolation for the individual at the same time that it is relatively disinterested in the plight of individual workers. This disinterest has been partially offset by social legislation, but impersonality of the modern economic organization is an underlying factor in many of the problems.

SELECTED BIBLIOGRAPHY

Cooley, Charles Horton, *Human Nature and the Social Order,* Charles Scribner's Sons, New York, 1922. Cooley was one of the first sociologists to call attention to the close and reciprocal relationship between the individual and the society. In an interactional sense, they may be viewed as two aspects of the same process.

Kohn, Melvin L., and Clausen, John A., "Social Isolation and Schizophrenia," *American Sociological Review, 20:*265–273 (June, 1955). Social isolation and individual disorganization are closely related, in that proper mental functioning requires constant intimate contact with others. When this participation is impaired or broken, the individual suffers accordingly.

Leighton, Alexander H., "Psychiatric Disorder and Social Environment," *Psychiatry, 18:*367–383 (November, 1955). This article is a careful theoretical exposition of the relationship between the individual and society, with particular reference to psychiatric disturbance. The social environment is seen as the network of interpersonal relationships in which the individual functions.

Mead, George Herbert, *Mind, Self, and Society* (edited by Charles W. Morris), University of Chicago Press, Chicago, 1934. In this collection of the edited lectures of George Herbert Mead, the relationship between the social self and society is explored in detail. The self is a product of social interaction and arises in the process of taking the role of the other.

Riesman, David, *Individualism Reconsidered,* Doubleday and Company, Inc., New York, 1955. This is a group of essays by the author of *The Lonely Crowd,* in which the role of the individual in modern society is viewed in different contexts. The title essay examines some of the implications of the "identity" of the individual and the society.

Sherif, Muzafer, and Cantril, Hadley, *The Psychology of Ego-Involvements,* John Wiley and Sons, Inc., New York, 1947. This is an analysis of the ego and its role in personality. Chap. 7 is entitled "Breakdown of the Ego" and deals with personal disorganization in terms of the disintegration of the ego.

Sullivan, Harry Stack, "The Illusion of Personal Individuality," *Psychiatry, 13:*317–332 (August, 1950). This noted psychiatrist based his theoretical and therapeutic position on the identity of the individual and the society. As the title indicates, Sullivan believed that separate, unique, individual personality is an illusion and that the individual cannot be understood or treated apart from the group.

Thomas, William I., and Znaniecki, Florian, *The Polish Peasant in Europe and America,* Alfred A. Knopf, Inc., New York, 1927 (2 vols.). In Vol. II, part IV, the concept of the individual life organization is set forth in connection with the analysis of personality. This is followed by the complete life history of an immigrant, whose experience illustrates many aspects of the conceptual scheme.

Warren, Roland L., "Social Disorganization and the Interrelationship of Cultural Roles," *American Sociological Review, 14:*83–87 (February, 1949). This article contains some significant insights into the structural aspects of individual and social disorganization. In a disorganized society many important role sequences are interrupted and broken.

Wood, Margaret M., *Paths of Loneliness,* Columbia University Press, New York, 1953. This book examines the status of the isolated and lonely individual in the modern world and indicates some of the factors responsible for this isolation. When group relationships are broken, the individual loses a vital element in his personality.

CHAPTER 4

The Juvenile Delinquent

Current Alarm over Juvenile Delinquency

In recent years juvenile delinquency has been one of the most widely discussed domestic problems in the United States. An undue percentage of young persons are allegedly coming into conflict with the law. Newspapers, women's magazines, and literary and religious journals all give prominent space to news and analyses of the current problem of young offenders. Meanwhile women's clubs, chambers of commerce, school boards, educational associations, legislators, the Congress of the United States, and local communities have held forums, conducted inquiries, issued reports, and demanded social action in their attempts to understand and deal with the problem.

In the midst of this current concern adults appear to take a more hostile attitude toward the juvenile delinquencies than they do toward their own serious crimes. Juvenile delinquency seems to be increasing but so too does adult crime. Much juvenile misbehavior is unquestionably related to youth itself, to adolescent revolt against adult authority. Logically adults because they are older should be even more condemned for breaking the law. They are old enough to know better, but the public seldom gets half so aroused over adult crime.

Part of the present-day awareness concerning juvenile delinquency stems from the activities of the Special Juvenile Delinquency Project, established by the United States Children's Bureau on July 1, 1952. This project, financed by private foundations and other private resources, made its basic purpose that of creating a national awareness of the problem. This was achieved by calling national meetings to discuss both the extent of delinquency and ways and means of developing preventive programs. The project came to an end on June 30, 1955, but its essential service has been continued under the Division of the Juvenile Delinquency Service of the Children's Bureau.[1]

Awareness of the nature and extent of a problem is always desirable, but the unprecedented publicity about juvenile delinquency stimulated by the various meetings and activities of the project has undoubtedly made many people believe that young persons have taken a sudden change for the worse. In fact the publicity has probably convinced the young people themselves that

[1] *News Notes on Juvenile Delinquency,* Children's Bureau, U.S. Department of Health, Education, and Welfare, Washington, June 3, 1955, p. 2.

they are inevitably going to be mixed up, and a problem to themselves, their parents, and the community. Robert L. Lamborn, in an article in the *New York Times Magazine,* tells of a twelve-year-old boy who said to his mother: "You know I don't like looking forward to the next six or eight years, considering how mixed up I am going to be and how hard I'm going to be to get along with."[2]

The belief that one is "mixed up" and difficult to handle in itself is not conducive to social adjustment. And if a juvenile becomes a delinquent a headlined article about his offensive conduct amounts to labeling him. This is true whether he feels like a hero because his name is in the papers or is chagrined because he has behaved in a way which society has condemned. Young people tend to behave as they are expected to behave. If they are convinced that older persons reject them as a bad lot the effect is bound to be disastrous.

On the other hand, young persons in conflict with the law present an especially distressing problem of individual disorganization. Experience has shown that many youthful offenders disposed by our courts are not deterred by the courts' action but become recidivists, committing three, four, five, or more offenses before they show any tendency to conform to the law.

At a time when the individual should be achieving an increased awareness of the importance of accepting the common ethical values, as incorporated in our laws and codes of behavior, the juvenile delinquent is setting himself in opposition to the restraints which society is presumably imposing for purposes of group welfare. Moreover, society through its various institutions often has not given young persons any adequate understanding of the importance or merit underlying the rules and regulations. But this sad fact does not alter the stigma placed upon the young offender by designating him a juvenile delinquent. And this same stigma makes it difficult for the young person so labeled to re-establish himself in the community. The social values of the community which are aligned with law enforcement are thus sometimes conducive to the very disorganization they are attempting to overcome.

A major aspect of religion is that it teaches the value of forgiveness. Forgiveness, as we all know, is an important (and necessary) aspect of life whether in the family, the office, the classroom, or the market place. Life would be relatively unendurable if we refused to forgive our friends, if husbands and wives failed to forgive their spouses, if parents never overlooked the aberrations of their children, or if children continually condemned the errors of their parents. Christian teaching has stressed forgiveness as a central doctrine. Western society has been greatly affected by Christian doctrine and the various attempts to rehabilitate the offender are directly related to this Christian belief. But Western society has never in any complete or genuine sense divested itself of a vindictive attitude toward those who have failed to conform to its dictates and particularly toward lower-class offenders. At the same time we have large reason for believing that the condemnation heaped

[2] Robert L. Lamborn, "Must They Be 'Crazy, Mixed-up Kids'?" *New York Times Magazine,* June 26, 1955, p. 20 (quoted by permission).

upon juvenile offenders is a factor in their continued misconduct. We make it hard for the child to overcome his court record.

Who Is the Juvenile Delinquent?

From the point of view of most parents, teachers, and others who deal extensively with young persons, virtually all children are in a sense behavior problems. All children have to be taught to curb selfish and aggressive tendencies, to respect other people's property, to differentiate between what is true and what is imaginary, and in general to behave decently in the eyes of the group. All societies recognize, however, that very young children cannot be held accountable for their early behavior. Roman law, for example, held (1) that a child under seven years was in no sense accountable for its acts, (2) that those from seven to puberty were accountable only if they understood the nature of their acts, and (3) that the punishment of those under twenty-five years of age should take their youthfulness into account. These principles were incorporated into the eighteenth-century English law, which likewise made it impossible to assess guilt against the child under seven and ordinarily presumed the child between eight and fourteen to be incapable of guilt.[3]

For those fourteen and over the English law was less lenient, and the tendency to exact punishment from puberty on was relatively common in pre-colonial England and the United States (whose law is so largely based on the English common law). Even so, the youthfulness of the offender was rather generally taken into account by American judges in passing sentence. During our Federal period institutions for incarcerating young sentenced offenders, so as to separate them from older convicts, were established. New York City thus opened a House of Refuge for young offenders in 1825, Boston in 1826, and Philadelphia in 1828.

A Definition of Juvenile Delinquency

Current concepts of juvenile delinquency in the United States have evolved through the development of the juvenile court. Juvenile delinquency today is thus legally defined, but curiously enough much so-called juvenile delinquency does not involve any commission of a legal crime on the part of the child or young person considered a juvenile delinquent. Rather, a juvenile delinquent in most jurisdictions is technically speaking a child or young person (in most states under 16, 17, or 18, in two states under 21) who has committed an offense for which he may be referred to juvenile court authorities. (California through the Youth Authority has jurisdiction over all young persons under 23.) What constitutes such offenses varies markedly according to the laws of the various states and territorial jurisdictions. All states hold conduct which is criminal if committed by adults to be juvenile delinquency if committed by those in the age group referred to the jurisdiction of the juvenile court, except where such offenses are restricted to the jurisdiction of the

[3] Sir William Blackstone, *Commentaries on the Law of England,* London, 1795 (12th ed.), Book IV, chap. II, pp. 21–24. Quoted by Milton L. Barron, *The Juvenile in Delinquent Society,* Alfred A. Knopf, Inc., New York, 1954, p. 12.

criminal court, as we shall discuss later. California places all young offenders irrespective of offense under the California Youth Authority. But juveniles in all states are referred to the various juvenile courts for violating codes of socially accepted behavior which could not become a matter of criminal court action if committed by an adult. That is, if a child stays out late at night, runs away from home or plays truant from school, is alleged by his parents to be incorrigible, knowingly visits a "policy shop," or smokes cigarettes, he may be defined as a delinquent in certain states. Children may also be brought into court for knowingly associating with vicious persons (despite the fact that the vicious people may be their parents), for loitering in stores or lobbies (when a crowded, dirty, tension-torn home may be the last place anyone would choose to go), patronizing gambling joints, consuming alcoholic beverages, and in general behaving like the adults who live in their particular communities.[4] A large share of children, moreover, are referred to court as much for displeasing adults, be they teachers, social workers, policemen, or parents, as for offenses technically criminal. This fact the alarmists often ignore!

The legal fact that parents are generally assessed with the responsibility for bringing up and supporting their children has been accompanied by the vested authority for disciplining their children except where they exercise undue severity or neglect them. This authority has been legally construed as giving the parents the right to seek the courts' aid when they (the parents) are unable to control their children. This tendency is well illustrated in a recent analysis of parent-referred and police-referred cases in the Allegheny County Juvenile Court which will be discussed later.[5] The significant fact is that the parents themselves are permitted to define delinquency whereas the child's basic problem often is that the parents are incompetent.

The Juvenile Delinquent's Dilemma

Part of the juvenile offender's problem arises from the confusion underlying the definition of his status in modern society. Technically speaking, children have few rights, except when they are actually cruelly treated or shamefully neglected. Even then they may receive little but stigma in any attempt to secure relief or redress for their grievances through the juvenile court.

Most children have problems or difficulties in connection with growing up, but the children who become charges of the juvenile court are generally *victims of bad bringing up*. Although the court purports to act as a wise parent it usually acts too late to give the child any basic advantage of wise counseling. Society meanwhile presents two conflicting sets of philosophies for dealing

[4] Cf. *Comparative Survey on Juvenile Delinquency: Part I, North America,* United Nations Department of Social Affairs, Division of Social Welfare, New York, 1952, p. 3. Barron, *op. cit.,* pp. 22–24, also discusses this aspect of juvenile delinquency very effectively. Cf. also Frederic B. Sussman, *Law of Juvenile Delinquency,* Oceana Publications, New York, 1950.

[5] Cf. Marcia Glazer and Barbara Wietrzynski, "Comparative Study of Parent-Referred and Police-Referred Cases of the Allegheny County Juvenile Court, Disposed January 1 through June 30, 1954," unpublished MS., Chatham College Library, 1955, pp. 48–109. (Tutorial project supervised by Mabel A. Elliott.)

with the child who is in the clutches of the law or in difficulty with the elders who seek to discipline him. The juvenile court is theoretically committed to helping the child, but the judge and the probation officer often exact severe penalties of the offender instead of treating him or her with a view to rehabilitation. Furthermore, the stigma of being designated as delinquent produces bitter resentment on the part of the youngster who knows many other children who have escaped such treatment. Society, which likewise purports to help the child by providing probationary and other services, usually refuses any such help to the child or youthful offender who has been most aggressive or most violent. A seventeen-year-old offender who killed his great-aunt in a sudden rage received a twenty-two-year sentence for second-degree murder in Pittsburgh in 1955. This was scarcely "helping him." No adult would have been likely to receive a sterner sentence. In fact many adults committing second-degree murder in Pennsylvania have received a two- to five-year sentence.

Meanwhile most juvenile court judges and probation officers recognize that the majority of their charges or wards are victims of unfortunate home situations and neighborhood influences. As the wag says, "These youngsters didn't choose their parents wisely." Even where the youngsters are technically absolved from responsibility for their own misbehavior, the misbehavior rather than the factors producing it is usually the basis of the plans for "disposing" the child's case.

Many elements contribute to this dilemma. The legal training of the judges is based essentially upon a retributory concept of justice. This is undoubtedly a major factor in the juvenile court's failure to divest itself of a confused set of values. No one supposes that all delinquents can be directed into ways of conduct which will be socially accepted and that they will all become well adjusted. But any intelligent planning for juvenile offenders must be concerned with understanding the motivating factors in their misconduct and with aiming to develop a situation in which socially accepted behavior is motivated within the child. Such an achievement would seem to require a team of psychologists, sociologists, social workers, and psychiatrists rather than judges per se.

The disorganized child who is a juvenile delinquent is thus not only the victim of his environment and his aggressions toward society arising out of his internal reactions. He is likewise a continually produced result of an inconsistent society which holds that as a child he is not responsible but which puts him in a category of needing help and then persistently invokes shame and guilt upon him by giving him the ascribed status of a delinquent.

The Juvenile Court and Its Philosophy

We cannot give a detailed account in this book of the organization and function of the juvenile court. We should mention, however, that the philosophy underlying the initial development of the juvenile court was distinctly *protective* rather than *punitive*.

The Chicago juvenile court was the first juvenile court authorized by law in the United States and was created by legislative enactment in 1899.[6] Other states had previously tried to devise noncriminal methods of dealing with juvenile offenders but too many technicalities arose to make the laws function effectively. The Illinois law was in a true sense a social invention combining the notion of equity or chancery procedure with the probationary type of treatment which had been legally adopted in Boston in 1878.[7] Chancery or equity procedure, however, was of long standing. It had developed in England during the thirteenth century as a means of helping widows, children, and others in need of special protection which could not be assured through ordinary civil courts. The word "chancery" itself is derived from the word "Chancellor," who was the King's representative or Chancellor who presided over this court. The King, through his Chancellor, acted as *parens patriae,* or "father of the country." In adopting the chancery principle in this country the parental power was transferred to the state. Thus the philosophy underlying the chancery court was held to be that of acting in the capacity of a wise parent, as mentioned above. Another feature of the chancery court was the informal nonjury trial. This in general characterizes most juvenile court hearings today. Certain states, it is true, have adopted permissory provisions for jury trials on the insistence of the child's parents or next friends, but even in these states such provision is seldom called for. Most parents accept the principle that the juvenile court is aiming to help the child—as laid down in the famous *Commonwealth* vs. *Fisher* decision of the Pennsylvania Supreme Court in 1905:

To save a child from becoming a criminal, or from continuing in a career of crime, to end in mature years in public punishment and disgrace, the legislature surely may provide for the salvation of such a child, if its parents or guardian be unable or unwilling to do so, by bringing it into one of the courts of the state without any process at all, for the purpose of subjecting it to the state's guardianship and protection. The natural parent needs no process to temporarily deprive his child of its liberty by confining it in his own home, to save it, and to shield it from consequences of persistence in a career of waywardness; nor is the state, when compelled, as *parens patriae* to take the place of the father for the same purpose required to adopt any process as a means of placing its bonds upon the child to lead it into one of its courts.[8]

Because the juvenile courts are equity or chancery courts rather than criminal courts, many extend their protective function to cover non-delinquents in need of help. This was true of the first juvenile court in Chicago. The Illinois law authorized jurisdiction over dependent and neglected, as well as delinquent, children.[9] The 502 courts making report as to the nature of the cases in 1957 handled 603,000 delinquency cases. In addition about 123,000 or 17 percent of the total cases brought to court were referred for neglect, abandon-

---

[6] Cf. *Illinois Laws* (1899), pp. 301–307.

[7] Cf. Mabel A. Elliott, *Conflicting Penal Theories in Statutory Criminal Law,* University of Chicago Press, Chicago, 1931, chap. III, "Juvenile Delinquency and the Law."

[8] *Commonwealth* vs. *Fisher,* 213 Pa. 48, 62. Atl. 198 (1905).

[9] Cf. *Illinois Laws* (1899), pp. 131–137.

ment, or cruelty on the part of their parents or because they were mentally defective or up for adoption.[10] Authorities disagree as to whether these children should be under the same jurisdiction as delinquent children. Some say the fact that juvenile delinquents constitute the major reason for the juvenile court's existence *ipso facto* makes for stigma and that non-delinquents should therefore be referred to another type of court or agency. Others maintain that the state should eliminate the stigma associated with the court—since theoretically none exists. In any event, a juvenile court record tends to stigmatize the child despite any reasoning to the contrary. This in itself is a factor in his continued disorganization.

The juvenile delinquent does not lose his citizenship rights, and his juvenile court record is not "held against him" in any later criminal court proceedings. Nevertheless juveniles with a court record are far more apt to become recidivists than youngsters who committed similar offenses but were never brought into court or regarded as unofficial cases. Class status and home neighborhoods, as we discuss later, are often significant factors in differentiating the status of the juvenile brought into court from one who is undetected or whose parents assume responsibility in the matter. The official designation of the juvenile as a delinquent appears to be decisive in his long-trend behavior.

Differences in Juvenile Court Jurisdictions

As we mentioned, the juvenile courts differ in the age categories for which they have original jurisdiction. This fact affects the rates of delinquency in the various states. The number of cases referred to the juvenile court thus depends upon the age limits prescribed by the law. At the present time most states have original jurisdiction over young persons under 18 years of age, whereas previously most courts had jurisdiction over cases under 16. Most states, however, permit concurrent jurisdiction with criminal courts for certain types of offenses. In two states, Arkansas and California, the juvenile court has original jurisdiction for all persons under 21, and the jurisdiction of the California Youth Authority extends until 23. Since California includes "young adults" under the juvenile classification, the rate in that populous state significantly affects the total of reported juvenile court cases. In 1955, for example, there were 54,682 delinquency cases reported by California out of the total of 324,469 reported by 1549 courts throughout the United States. This was 16.9 percent, or more than a sixth of the total cases of juvenile delinquency reported in the United States. Obviously no one would believe that California has one-sixth of the cases of delinquency in the United States were we to consider only those under 18. The variation in the jurisdiction of the various courts thus distorts the total picture of delinquency.[11]

The age for original jurisdiction for juveniles varies considerably not only

[10] *Juvenile Court Statistics, 1957*, Children's Bureau Statistical Series, No. 52, U.S. Department of Health, Education, and Welfare, Washington, 1959, p. 5.

[11] Estimation derived from Table 1, *Juvenile Court Statistics, 1953*, Children's Bureau Statistical Series, No. 28, U.S. Department of Health, Education, and Welfare, Washington, 1955, p. 7. These data for California are not available for later years.

among the several states but also within certain states. Delaware, Illinois, Kentucky, and Texas extend the protection of the juvenile court to boys under 17 and girls under 18. The juvenile court in Oklahoma has original jurisdiction for boys up to 16 and girls up to 18, while Wyoming extends such jurisdiction to boys up to 19 and girls up to 21. Complicating the variations in age coverage, the juvenile courts have exclusive jurisdiction over cases within their respective states in only 23 states. In 3 states, Indiana, New Hampshire, and Rhode Island, traffic law violations of juveniles are under the jurisdiction of the criminal court, and New Hampshire, along with 22 other states, places all juvenile capital offenses under the criminal court. Maine places all infamous crimes of juveniles under the criminal court.[12]

These facts illustrate the confused philosophy of the juvenile court. If a juvenile is not to be held responsible for petty thieving but is held accountable in case of murder, the whole logic of his needing protection breaks down. Strictly speaking, the worse a juvenile behaves the more he probably needs treatment, but society is more willing for the juvenile court to have jurisdiction over petty offenders than over those guilty of major offenses.

Statistics on Juvenile Delinquency

No exact figures for the country as a whole are available, but in the next few years the Children's Bureau hopes to develop a reliable estimate of the total delinquent group. Statistics gave a 16 percent increase in 1957[13] over the year before and a 70 percent increase from 1948 to 1955, while the number of young persons 10 to 17 increased only 16 percent during the latter period.[14] However, in many states the jurisdiction of the juvenile court has changed with reference to age, and the number of delinquents who are 18 or above may be an important factor in the rate since serious delinquency tends to go up with older boys. The largest five-year classification for adult offenders is also for the young offender falling in the 19-to-24 group. This group is wholly outside the juvenile classification except in 3 states.

Actually a 16 percent increase should not be regarded as especially alarming; it may reflect, in part at least, better reporting of delinquency rather than any significant increase in actual cases. Certainly it does not necessarily mean that more serious offenses are committed. In fact, since 1946 all unofficial as well as official cases of delinquency have been included in the totals (which makes them greater, *ipso facto*). The increased awareness of the problem of juvenile delinquency has also produced a higher percentage of referrals on the part of police officers (as a presumed method of controlling the problem). In recent years police have been instructed that the juvenile court is to help young persons. Some young persons recognize this, too. In Pittsburgh in 1958, forty children came on their own initiative to the juvenile court for help. The general interpretation of statistics by agencies and news-

[12] *Comparative Survey on Juvenile Delinquency: Part I, North America,* United Nations Department of Social Affairs, Division of Social Welfare, New York, 1952, pp. 6–7.
[13] *Juvenile Court Statistics, 1957,* p. 8.
[14] *News Notes on Juvenile Delinquency,* p. 1.

paper articles to the effect that delinquency is getting worse is thus to be discounted against the fact that many more cases are reported than formerly.

The Federal Bureau of Investigation's annual report for 1958 shows that the arrests for juveniles under eighteen increased 8.1 percent for 1958 over 1957.[15] The increasing trend in the number of juvenile delinquents during 1940–1957 as shown in Chart 4.1 therefore should be viewed with more per-

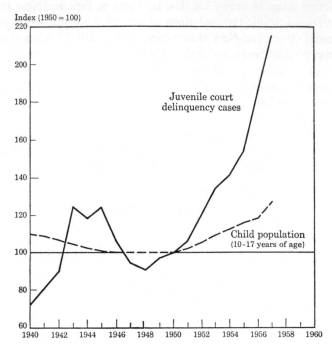

CHART 4.1. Trend in Juvenile Court Delinquency Cases and Child Population 10–17 Years of Age, 1940–1957. (From *Juvenile Court Statistics, 1957,* Children's Bureau, U.S. Department of Health, Education, and Welfare, 1959, p. 9.)

spective than some alarmists are indicating. According to this chart there was a sharp increase from 1940 to 1945, a marked decline from 1945 to 1948, and a subsequent sharp increase from 1948 to 1956. It is obvious, however, that rates were not significantly higher in 1953 than in 1942–1944 if the increase is considered in relation to the child population from ten to seventeen years. The confused and tense world conditions during and since the Korean War have been doubly confusing to the teen-agers who started to school during or after World War II. These youngsters have never known a truly peaceful world. It is small wonder that many young persons rebel against a social order which offers so little stability or opportunity for planning one's future.

[15] *Uniform Crime Reports, 1958,* Federal Bureau of Investigation, U.S. Department of Justice, Washington, 1959, pp. 110–111.

World conditions are of course only one explanation for delinquency but we should remember that the confusion during the twenties following World War I also seemed to produce youthful revolt, the "Lost Generation" of F. Scott Fitzgerald. Delinquency showed a marked increase during the 1920's, reaching a peak in most cities in 1929. Furthermore, the present disturbed world conditions appear to be affecting the delinquency rate in other countries too. At least we hear of alarm over delinquency in England, in Germany, in Russia, and even in Korea.

Long-trend statistics in the United States are available only for the larger cities, but these show a general increase in delinquency during the postwar twenties[16] and a decline of delinquency during the onset of the depression in 1930 for every major city except New York, where the decrease did not occur until 1932–1933.[17] Chart 4.2 shows delinquency rates for the United

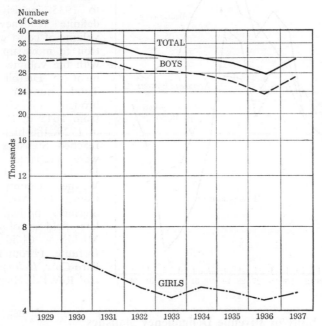

CHART 4.2. Number of Boys' and Girls' Delinquency Cases Disposed of by 28 Courts, 1929–1937. (From *Social Statistics,* Children's Bureau, Supplement No. 4 to *The Child, 3*:3 [June, 1939].)

States as a whole. Chart 4.3 shows the same trend in Detroit. Some people interpret the decline during the depression to mean that the increased supervision of the families of the lower economic classes by social workers was

[16] Cf. Lowell J. Carr, *Delinquency Control,* Harper & Brothers, New York, 1950 (rev. ed.) pp. 87–88.
[17] J. B. Maller, "Juvenile Delinquency in New York City," *Journal of Psychology, 3*:1–25 (January, 1937).

responsible for lowered delinquency. It is likely that less spending money and more supervision of children by parents who were forced to stay at home were both important factors. Economic pressures were so widespread that it became "smart to be thrifty." In any event juvenile delinquency decreased although crime waves for adults appeared to increase. Prosperity and high employment appear to be correlated with a higher delinquency rate and part of the increase after 1950 may very well be related to the high prevailing prosperity.

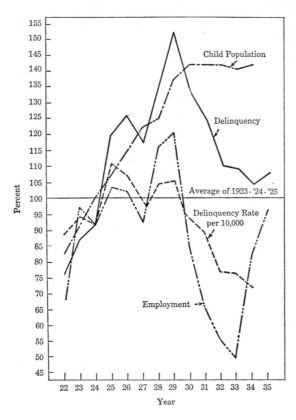

CHART 4.3. 34,000 Wayne Cases Follow Employment Curve: Court Cases Move with Industrial Activity. Statistics covering 34,821 alleged delinquents from 1922 to 1935 inclusive show a definite tendency for the volume of court cases in Detroit to move up and down with the volume of employment in Detroit industries. Total number of cases brought to court ranged from 1645 in 1922 to 3318 in 1929, the highest number reached. Statistics and graph were prepared for Judge D. J. Healy, Jr., of the Wayne County Juvenile Court, by Mr. James E. Stermer, probation officer, later field sociologist for the Michigan Child Guidance Institute. (From Lowell Julliard Carr, *Delinquency Control,* Rev. Ed., Harper, 1950.)

The Unreliability of Juvenile Delinquency Statistics

Although statistics for delinquency appear to indicate trends they do not furnish any accurate picture of juvenile delinquency as a whole. The reasons for this may be stated briefly:

1. First of all, the statistics gathered vary from year to year. In 1957, 502 courts reported 603,000 cases to the United States Children's Bureau. Since the larger courts were included here, the statistics probably give a fairly accurate picture. In 1956, 1549 of the 3000 juvenile courts reported. In 1954 only 66 reported. Initially only the larger cities made any report—and the first published statistics were for only 28 courts, as Chart 4.2 shows. The figures gathered today indicate trends chiefly in our larger cities and larger county seat towns where the better courts are located, but statisticians have

worked out techniques for comparison. Modern sampling methods make it clear, however, that these figures are a fairly reliable index of reported delinquencies in the larger cities so far as reported cases are concerned. They are no index to the serious behavior problems in rural areas.

TABLE 4.1. Reasons for Reference to Juvenile Court—Boys' and Girls' Cases Referred in 1945[a] and in 1957[b]

| | Juvenile Delinquency Cases | | | | | |
| | 1945 (percent) | | | 1957 (percent) | | |
Reason for Referral to Court	Total	Boys	Girls	Total	Boys	Girls
Total	100	100	100	100	100	100
Stealing	37	42	12	42	48	15
Act of carelessness or mischief	17	19	8	12	14	9
Traffic violation	9	10	1	c	c	c
Truancy	8	7	13	6	4	11
Running away	8	6	19	11	7	23
Being ungovernable	9	6	22	8	6	19
Sex offense	5	3	18	4	3	10
Injury to person	3	3	2	3	3	2
Other reason	4	4	5	14	15	14

[a] Cases disposed of by 374 courts.
[b] Cases disposed of by courts in 15 states.
[c] Traffic violations not counted in 1957.

SOURCES: *Juvenile Court Statistics, 1944–1945*, Social Statistics Supplement to Vol. 11 of *The Child*, November, 1946, Children's Bureau, Federal Security Agency, p. 11, and *Juvenile Court Statistics, 1957*, Children's Bureau Statistical Series, No. 52, U.S. Department of Health, Education, and Welfare, 1959, p. 7.

2. The statistics do not measure the true extent of delinquency. There is much hidden delinquency because middle- and upper-class family status keeps many children out of the courts. We simply cannot estimate their hidden delinquencies or those of children referred to court.

3. The varying age of original jurisdiction of the juvenile courts in the different states means that offenses of certain persons are defined as juvenile delinquency in some states and as crimes in others.

4. Capital and other serious offenses which are referred to juvenile courts in some states are referred to criminal courts in others.

5. Police vary markedly in reporting youngsters who are in trouble. Some police invariably take such children to their parents. Others refer the child to the juvenile court. Personal prejudices and biases of police may affect reporting. As Dr. Herman N. Adler used to say, an Irish policeman on an Italian beat will arrest more children than an Irish policeman on an Irish beat!

6. In large cities many cases of delinquency are handled by social agencies and are never referred to the juvenile court.

7. Statistics for certain types of juvenile misconduct are also misleading. Girls commit most of the heterosexual offenses reported to the juvenile court despite the fact that boys are involved. Boys are not likely to be reported for sex offenses other than rape or homosexual offenses. Even where an older man

is involved in a sex offense it is usually only the girl who is reported to the juvenile court.

8. Statistics as to the disposition of juvenile offenders are likewise misleading because judges' practices vary so widely. Some judges will give "any first offender a chance" even if it means the child is returned to a vicious or immoral home. Other judges place very few children on probation and contend that reformatory experience is what every delinquent needs.

As must be clear from this discussion statistics are misleading. Some of the items summarized warrant further analysis, in particular on the instances of unreported and hidden delinquencies. These in fact make delinquency appear to be rather normal, as we will discuss more fully later.

Offenses for Which Delinquents Are Referred to Court

The actual statistics for cases referred to the court are misleading because they were not analyzed according to offenses in recent years. The report covering 1953 cases merely stated that they ranged from the most serious to the most trivial acts.[18] Yet great alarm over the increase involves alarm over these trivial offenses. Beginning in 1956 statistics were gathered in more detail and we shall have better statistics for comparative trends within a few years. There is no reason to believe that the categories for major offenses will be very different, however.

Offenses committed by boys and girls brought before the juvenile courts were not classified after 1945 until 1957. Stealing was the major category of offenses for boys in both years as Table 4.1 shows. Despite the increase in cases there has not been much change in offenses except for girls. A smaller percentage of girls (10 percent) were brought to court for sex offenses in 1957 than in 1945 (when the number was 18 percent), as shown in the table. In both years running away and being ungovernable were the two highest offenses for girls, but these are nearly always euphemistic terms for sex offenses. While only 3 percent of the boys were referred to court in 1957 for sex offenses, there was a much larger number of boys than girls. Actually the violation of sex codes by boys is much greater than among girls, especially in the lower economic groups as measured by educational achievements, as the Kinsey report makes clear.[19]

Boys, on the other hand, are apparently more likely than girls to be guilty of aggressive mischief and careless damage to property. We may presume this is because boys' play is often unsupervised. Boys tend to roam the streets at will, whereas girls (even in the lower classes) seldom spend much time on street corners or play in alleys. Boys are also more aggressive by nature than girls, and Dr. von Hentig maintains that much of the delinquency of boys is in response to an adolescent male urge to throw off bonds of parental control.[20]

[18] *Juvenile Court Statistics, 1953*, p. 1. Cf. also *Juvenile Court Statistics, 1957*.
[19] Cf. Chapter 6 for a discussion of the Kinsey report.
[20] Hans von Hentig, *Crime: Causes and Conditions*, McGraw-Hill Book Company, Inc., New York, 1947, pp. 140–145.

Most delinquents are referred to the juvenile court by the police. Detailed data on referral have not been gathered since 1945, but in that year 71 percent of the children reported to 374 courts were police-referred.[21] Cities vary markedly in the degree to which social agencies report children, but wherever there are well-organized agencies dealing with family problems, such agencies report a sizable number of the cases. In Allegheny County (Pittsburgh) Juvenile Court police referred 59 percent of the cases in a recent year, parents referred 5 percent, and probation officers, schools, other courts, individuals, and miscellaneous sources including social agencies referred the other 36 percent.[22] In general, parents do not refer their own children unless there is conflict between the parents and child. When police refer the children there is usually a conflict between the community and the child.

Characteristics of Juvenile Court Cases

Most of what we know about juvenile offenders is limited to the cases reported to the juvenile court. Of the 324,369 juvenile delinquency cases reported in 1955, over half (51 percent) were handled unofficially—that is, they did not become cases of official record.[23] This does not mean the official cases were necessarily worse cases, but rather that certain factors mitigated the charge in unofficial cases. Children from good families are less likely to be treated as official cases and many judges hesitate to make girls' cases official.

SEX

Slightly more than five-sixths of the delinquents reported to the courts in 1957 were boys. That year boys' cases increased less than girls, 15 percent in contrast to 20 percent.[24] While boys in court greatly outnumber girls, the ratio has dropped significantly during the history of the juvenile court. In New York City in 1902, for example, the ratio of boys to girls was 60 to 1. By 1932 it had dropped to 8 to 1. Girls have been exposed to more nearly the same environment as boys with the passing years.[25] Even so, girls are obviously much better protected than boys from influences which get them in trouble.

AGE

The age of juvenile offenders was analyzed for 1957 statistics. The median age for boys was 15.5 years, while the median age for girls was 15.4.[26] As Table 4.2 shows, relatively few delinquents are referred under 10, the bulk of cases are referred after 14 years, and the modal group is from 15 to 18 for both groups if both official and unofficial cases are included. The tendency for

[21] *Social Statistics*, Supplement to Vol. 4, *The Child*, Children's Bureau, Washington, 1945.

[22] Glazer and Wietrzynski, *op. cit.*, p. 14.

[23] *Juvenile Court Statistics, 1957*, Children's Bureau Statistical Series, No. 52, U.S. Department of Health, Education, and Welfare, Washington, 1959, p. 5.

[24] *Ibid.*

[25] J. B. Maller, "The Trend of Juvenile Delinquency in New York City," *Journal of Juvenile Research*, 17:10–18 (1933).

[26] *Juvenile Court Statistics, 1957*, p. 6.

TABLE 4.2. Age of Children in Delinquency Cases (Excluding Traffic Offenses) Disposed of by a Selected Group of Courts, 1957[a]
(percentage distribution)

Age of Child When Referred	All Courts		Age Jurisdiction of Court							
			Under 16		Under 17		Under 18		Under 21[b]	
	Boys	Girls	Boys	Girls	Boys	Girls	Boys	Girls	Boys	Girls
Total	100	100	100	100	100	100	100	100	100	100
Under 10	3	2	7	5	4	3	2	1	1	c
10	2	1	5	3	3	2	2	1	1	1
11	3	2	6	3	4	2	3	1	2	1
12	5	4	10	8	6	7	5	4	3	2
13	10	11	15	18	12	14	9	12	6	7
14	16	21	23	29	19	24	16	22	12	17
15	21	25	28	30	24	26	20	25	18	24
16	22	20	4	3	27	21	24	21	21	23
17	13	11	2	1	1	1	19	13	23	17
18 and over	5	3	—	—	c	c	c	c	13	8
Median age	15.5	15.4	14.3	14.4	15.1	14.9	15.7	15.4	16.3	15.9

[a] Data are from 15 state publications of juvenile court statistics.
[b] Data for one state only.
[c] Less than 0.5 percent.

SOURCE: *Juvenile Court Statistics, 1957*, Series No. 52, Children's Bureau, U.S. Department of Health, Education, and Welfare, 1959, p. 6.

more delinquents to fall in the age group 15 to 18 is of course conditioned by the increased number of courts extending jurisdiction from 16 to 18.

ADOLESCENCE AND DELINQUENCY

For both boys and girls, delinquency is significantly a phenomenon of adolescence. Moreover, as the Gluecks' studies have shown, many adolescent delinquents outgrow their tendency to get into trouble as they grow older. Five years after Sheldon and Eleanor Glueck made their study of 1000 delinquents they conducted a follow-up study. They found that approximately one-third of the delinquents were arrested (while only 26.8 percent had actually committed no offense) during a second five-year span.[27] Equally important, 65.6 percent spent no time in penal institutions because many were able to pay fines for their misconduct.[28] Five years later a second checkup was undertaken. This time the Gluecks discovered that there had been both a further decline in criminality and a decrease in the seriousness of offenses.[29] If as the evidence indicates delinquency decreases with greater maturity we may assume that part of the reason for delinquency is the matter of youth itself.

[27] Sheldon and Eleanor Glueck, *Juvenile Delinquents Grown Up*, The Commonwealth Fund, New York, 1940, p. 58.
[28] *Ibid.*, p. 49.
[29] *Ibid.*, p. 89.

CULTURAL ORIGINS

Miss Elliott's study in Chicago showed a significant correlation between cultural and racial heterogeneity and juvenile delinquency.[30] As late as 1930 statistics for juvenile delinquency indicated that children of the foreign born were more likely to be referred to the juvenile court than children with native-born parents. Following the reduction of immigration under the quota laws of the 1920's delinquent children with immigrant backgrounds decreased sharply by 1937. By 1944 such data were no longer gathered because there were so few foreign-born parents.

RACIAL BACKGROUND

Racial data with reference to juvenile delinquency cases are no longer published for the country as a whole, but local studies indicate that Negro children are referred to court far oftener than white children in proportion to their numbers. For example, 35 percent of the cases disposed by the Allegheny County (Pittsburgh) Juvenile Court in 1954 were Negro. In 1950 the non-white population (almost entirely Negro) in Pittsburgh was only 7.5 percent of the total. The referral of Negro delinquents was thus about five times as high as the white rate.[31] A study of the Negro delinquency rate in New York City also showed it to be five times as high as the white rate. Negro children are more frequently handicapped by poverty. More also live in slum neighborhoods and come from broken homes than is true for white children. These three factors, as we analyze later, are apparently major factors in all juvenile delinquency. Negro children are also more likely to be referred to court when they commit an offense than are white children. In general Negro children have fewer wholesome opportunities for play than white children. Nevertheless where Negroes constitute the whole or major population in an area their delinquency rates tend to be much lower than where they live in a mixed neighborhood. Negroes often live in a subculture, and the Negro delinquency rate stems essentially from conflict with the dominant values of the white group.[32]

Bernard Lander's recent study in Baltimore showed that Negroes were contributing to delinquency at a very high rate. (During the years 1939–1942 Negroes constituted 49 percent of the delinquents in Baltimore.) When the census tracts with large Negro populations were studied in greater detail, however, it was found that the Negro rate went up from 8 percent in areas where the Negro population was less than 10 percent of the total population to 14 percent where the Negro population was 10–29.9 percent and 30 to 49.9 percent. When Negroes amounted to over 50 percent of the population

[30] Mabel A. Elliott, *A Correlation Between Rate of Juvenile Delinquency and Racial Heterogeneity,* Institute for Juvenile Research, published by Department of Public Welfare, Springfield, Illinois, 1926, especially pp. 14–25.

[31] Glazer and Wietrzynski, *op. cit.,* p. 35. Today Negroes total approximately 16 percent of the population.

[32] Cf. Negley K. Teeters and John O. Reinemann, *The Challenge of Delinquency,* Prentice-Hall, Inc., New York, 1950, pp. 115–124.

there was a decrease in Negro delinquency rate and when Negroes constituted 90 percent or more of the population delinquency decreased to 7 percent.[33]

In other words, the fact of racial heterogeneity apparently contributes to delinquency. Dr. Lander holds that where the population is solidly Negro there is greater social stability and the delinquency rate goes down. His conclusion is that the differential delinquency rate may be explained in terms of *anomie* or normlessness.[34] Miss Elliott's study in Chicago indicated much the same thing. Where there was marked ethnic heterogeneity in Chicago—that is, where the ethnic group varied most significantly from the native-born Nordic population—the delinquency rate was higher than where the foreign-born group was also Nordic.[35]

Bad housing and low economic status unquestionably characterize many of the Negro neighborhoods, but delinquency is not a product of these so much as it is of normlessness. The Negroes do not accept the white population's values nor are they bound with the whites into a cohesive group. Where Negroes constitute the dominant group there is less deviation and Lander believes they create a norm of their own.

There are relatively few Orientals and American Indians in our population and these groups constitute a very small problem so far as juvenile courts are concerned, partly because they live in rather isolated solidarity. The Chinese tend to solve their own problems through their own quasi courts, while the agencies of the Bureau of Indian Affairs generally look after the small number of Indian delinquents.

The Multiple Handicaps of Delinquents

Virtually all research concerning juvenile delinquents show them to be an especially handicapped group. In Cyril Burt's study of 197 British delinquents and 400 non-delinquents from the same neighborhoods, each delinquent suffered from four or five unfortunate factors in his background or physical or mental make-up.[36] Healy and Bronner's famous analysis of delinquents in Chicago and Boston came to a similar conclusion,[37] which Miss Elliott's investigation in Pennsylvania also confirmed.[38] In fact all subsequent studies have shown that children brought into court are socially and economically handicapped. A sizable number are also mentally and physically below normal. The recent findings of Austin L. Porterfield's study with reference to the unreported delinquencies of the middle and upper economic classes (discussed later in this chapter) give us basis for thinking that children are

---

[33] Bernard Lander, *Towards an Understanding of Juvenile Delinquency,* Columbia University Press, New York, 1954, p. 82.

[34] *Ibid.,* p. 89.

[35] Elliott, *A Correlation Between Rate of Juvenile Delinquency and Racial Heterogeneity,* pp. 24–25.

[36] Cyril Burt, *The Young Delinquent,* Appleton-Century-Crofts, Inc., New York, 1925.

[37] William Healy and Augusta F. Bronner, *Delinquents and Criminals, Their Making and Unmaking,* The Macmillan Company, New York, 1926.

[38] Mabel A. Elliott, *Correctional Education and the Delinquent Girl,* Commonwealth of Pennsylvania, Harrisburg, 1929.

probably referred to court because of their differential economic and social handicaps. Unfortunately the boys and girls referred to court tend to persist in delinquencies whereas the unreported cases make a better social adjustment. The middle and upper classes "believe in the law" and try to enforce standards of good behavior upon their children even when their children break the law, whereas many lower-class families have no great respect for the law or regard it as something that "they" (the middle class) enforce.

The many studies made with reference to delinquents' characteristics and backgrounds shed light on the influences which have conditioned them in their persistent habits of delinquency. These influences also may be regarded as factors which have conditioned society to regard children as delinquent and in need of differential treatment since most court workers and officials belong to the middle class. The middle class is particularly rigid about trying to enforce moral standards and social values, as we have discussed in Chapter 1.

The Family Aspects of Delinquency

The poor family background of the delinquent in court tends to be a significant factor which militates against his growing up successfully and in favor of his coming into conflict with the law. Good family background on the other hand helps the child come to quick conformity if he has broken the law. When the delinquent's parents are not able to provide him with suitable home surroundings—whether because of ignorance, poverty, or unfortunate moral attitudes—the child may be forced to grow up in a neighborhood unsuited for him to live in. Parents may be unable to supply him with sufficient economic goods. They may fail to provide him with what many authorities regard as even more important, namely, emotional security. They may give him little or no training in meeting problems of sex. They may fail entirely in educating him to the importance of honesty and the value which our society attaches to property. The family gives every child his start socially as well as biologically, and many parents are obviously not suited to the task of parenthood. The various aspects of the family's relation to delinquency may be considered in brief detail.

1. *Physical Heredity.* The child's biological heritage is important to his health and general well-being and his physical and social functioning. Modern criminology has rather generally discarded the notion of the inheritance of delinquency but recognizes that physical defects and handicaps may cause bitterness and resentment, which may result in behavior problems. Earlier studies tracing the "biological" trail of degeneracy and crime through families ignored the fact that such families had bad influence on their children and were not transmitting the delinquency through the germ plasm.[39] Today most psychologists disavow the inheritance of overt behavior traits.[40]

[39] Cf. Richard L. Dugdale, *The Jukes,* G. P. Putnam's Sons, New York, 1877; Arthur H. Estabrook, *The Jukes in 1915,* Carnegie Institution, Washington, 1916; and Henry H. Goddard, *The Kallikak Family,* The Macmillan Company, New York, 1912, pp. 18–19.

[40] Edwin H. Sutherland and Donald R. Cressey, *Principles of Criminology,* J. B. Lippincott Company, Philadelphia, 1955 (5th ed.), chap. 10 and pp. 171–180.

Sheldon and Eleanor Glueck's recent research in bodily types and delinquency gives some credence to this point of view, however. Stimulated by Hooton and by W. H. Sheldon's studies, *The Varieties of Human Physique* and *Atlas of Men*[41] (as well as by earlier European researches), they explored the physical data on the 500 delinquents they had previously studied in *Unraveling Juvenile Delinquency*. These delinquents had been compared with 500 non-delinquents who were matched with reference to age, intelligence, and ethnic, social, and economic background in the Boston public schools. From intensive study of the physical, psychiatric, and other data the Gluecks concluded that the somatypes correlated significantly with delinquency. Their major body classifications were (a) ectomorphs (thin, fragile type), (b) endomorphs (round, soft type), (c) mesomorphs (heavy bone, muscle, and tissue type), and (d) balanced (with no dominance of type although many were mixed types). All the delinquents and non-delinquents either were classified as to dominant type or were considered "balanced."

The Gluecks found that the majority of the delinquents (298 of 498 for whom there were data) were dominantly mesomorphs whereas the largest group of the non-delinquents (191 to 482 for whom there were data) were ectomorphs. That is, 60.1 percent of the delinquents were mesomorphs while 39.6 percent of the non-delinquents were ectomorphs. Only 14.4 percent of the delinquents were ectomorphs. The number of endomorphs in both groups did not vary significantly; 15 percent of the non-delinquents were endomorphs, as were 11.5 percent of the delinquents. Balanced types were also approximately the same for each group, as shown in Table 4.3.[42] Actually there was no great preponderance of any bodily type in the non-delinquent group.

The Gluecks attach great significance to these findings and believe that the active, muscular, well-built type is more apt to become delinquent because of greater energy. Nevertheless 30 percent of the non-delinquents were mesomorphs. When boys are of the vigorous, active type the Gluecks conclude there is more reason to expect them to get into trouble unless their activities are directed into socially accepted patterns of behavior. It takes a certain amount of energy to commit some types of delinquency, obviously. We need to know the percentage of each bodily type in the general population of teenagers, however, before we can attach great importance to constitutional factors in delinquency. If there are more mesomorphs than other somatypes, there will inevitably be more mesomorphs among delinquents. Meanwhile we know the Gluecks' data indicated that balanced types were approximately the same for both the delinquent and the non-delinquent groups.

2. *The Broken Home.* Virtually every study made of the home conditions of delinquents reveals that broken homes are far more frequent among de-

[41] W. H. Sheldon, *The Varieties of Human Physique,* Harper & Brothers, New York, 1940, and W. H. Sheldon, *Atlas of Men,* Harper & Brothers, New York, 1954.

[42] Sheldon and Eleanor Glueck, *Physique and Delinquency,* Harper & Brothers, New York, 1956, p. 9. (Students should read the entire book to make a fair appraisal of this research.)

TABLE 4.3.   Incidence of Somatotype Dominance Among Delinquents and Non-delinquents in Boston

Endomorphic Component Dominance	496 Delinquents No.	Percent	482 Nondelinquents No.	Percent
Extreme endomorphs	6	1.2	24	5.0
Endomorphs	14	2.8	23	4.8
Mesomorphic endomorphs	16	3.2	7	1.5
Ectomorphic endomorphs	23	4.6	18	3.7
Subtotal	59	11.8	72	15.0
Mesomorphic component dominance				
Extreme mesomorphs	115	23.2	34	7.1
Mesomorphs	84	16.9	59	12.2
Endomorphic mesomorphs	66	13.3	15	3.1
Ectomorphic mesomorphs	33	6.7	40	8.3
Subtotal	298	60.1	148	30.7
Ectomorphic component dominance				
Extreme ectomorphs	9	1.8	70	14.5
Ectomorphs	25	5.0	71	14.7
Endomorphic ectomorphs	21	4.2	15	3.1
Mesomorphic ectomorphs	17	3.4	35	7.3
Subtotal	72	14.4	191	39.6
No component dominance				
Balanced types	67	13.5	71	14.7

SOURCE: Sheldon and Eleanor Glueck, *Physique and Delinquency*, Harper & Brothers, New York, 1956, p. 9.

linquents than non-delinquents, although a broken home per se is not always serious. Evidence suggests that homes broken by death are not as likely to result in delinquency as homes where there has been divorce, separation, or desertion or where the disruptive factors producing the voluntary break are great. A study in New York City showed that 52 percent of the children who had conduct difficulties in Public School No. 11 were from broken homes, in contrast to 25 percent of the non-delinquents.[43] Healy and Bronner found that almost one-half of 4000 delinquents in Chicago and Boston were from broken homes.[44] Approximately 31 percent of the Pennsylvania girls studied at Sleighton Farm were from broken homes[45] (but non-delinquent girls from comparable economic backgrounds in Philadelphia also had a high rate).[46] However, delinquent girls come from broken homes more frequently than de-

[43] Eleanor H. Johnson, "The Relation of Conduct Difficulties of a Group of Public School Boys to Their Mental Status and Home Environment," *Journal of Delinquency*, 6:557 ff. (November, 1921).
[44] Healy and Bronner, *op. cit.,* pp. 121–125.
[45] Elliott, *Correctional Education and the Delinquent Girl,* pp. 26–27.
[46] Hazel Grant Ormsbee, *The Young Employed Girl,* Woman's Press, New York, 1927.

linquent boys,[47] and younger delinquent white boys and Negro boys are more likely to be from broken homes than are older white delinquent boys.[48] A study made by the U.S. Children's Bureau in 1931 showed 37 percent of the boys and 53 percent of the girls brought before reporting juvenile courts to be from homes broken for various reasons.[49] The study of parent-referred and police-referred cases in Pittsburgh in 1955 showed 43 percent of the former and 38 percent of the latter came from broken homes. Furthermore, 11 percent of the parent-referred and 5 percent of the police-referred cases were children of common-law marriages.[50] In 1949 broken homes characterized 65 percent of all the girls referred to the Philadelphia Municipal Court (which is also the Philadelphia Juvenile Court) and 46 percent of all the boys.[51]

Delinquency among girls is apparently more frequently related to broken homes than boys' delinquency because of the differences in types of behavior represented. H. Ashley Weeks' analysis of 94 cases of delinquent girls and 413 cases of delinquent boys in Spokane, Washington, showed that ungovernability, running away, and truancy were the types of offenses more closely associated with broken homes for both sexes than other types of delinquency. In fact, 88.5 percent of the 94 girls and 77.8 percent of the 413 boys who were ungovernable were from broken homes, as were 69.5 percent of the girls and 57.2 percent of the boys who were runaways. Weeks also found that where cases were referred to the court by parents, a very high proportion (87 percent of the boys and 63.2 percent of the girls) came from broken homes, where the remaining parent was unable to cope with the abnormal family situation. Where police referred the cases to the court, the number of broken homes was much less (36.3 percent for males and 50 percent for females). Neighbors and friends referred proportionately far more cases of girls than boys, however (86.7 percent in contrast to 30.4 percent).[52] Meanwhile there is some reason to believe that the high rate of broken families is itself a symptom of the low economic and social status of the delinquent's family.[53]

3. *Delinquent Siblings.* If the home were the only factor in producing delinquency it would presumably affect the behavior of all children in the same family similarly. But we know this is not true. Each child has a separate home environment, a different place in his parents' affection, and a particular status in the family which he as an individual achieves or has ascribed to him. The second child always has to strive for status with the first-born, for example. Sibling studies thus have shown widely varying rates of delinquency in fami-

[47] Cf. Healy and Bronner, *op. cit.*

[48] Clifford R. Shaw and Henry D. McKay, "Social Factors in Juvenile Delinquency," National Commission on Law Observance and Enforcement, *Report on the Causes of Crime*, No. 13, Vol. II, Washington, 1931, p. 266.

[49] Sutherland and Cressey, *op. cit.*, p. 160.

[50] Glazer and Wietrzynski, *op. cit.*, p. 71.

[51] *Thirty-Sixth Annual Report of the Municipal Court of Philadelphia*, 1949, p. 42, quoted in Teeters and Reinemann, *op. cit.*, p. 151.

[52] H. Ashley Weeks, "Male and Female Broken Home Rates by Types of Delinquency," *American Sociological Review*, 5:601–609 (August, 1940).

[53] Sutherland and Cressey, *op. cit.*, p. 166.

lies. Healy and Bronner state that among 372 delinquents from two-child families the second child was delinquent in only 20 percent of the cases, with the behavior of 2 percent unknown. In 333 six-child families only 12 percent were known delinquents, with 6 percent unknown.[54] In the Allegheny County Juvenile Court study information on whether or not siblings were in court was recorded in 109 of the 170 cases. Of the 109 there were 43 siblings with records or 39 percent. However, this 43 was only 25 percent of the total group of 170.[55] Obviously siblings may be too young to be delinquent, and this fact may account for part of the difference in conduct.

4. *Parental Rejection of Child.* Austin L. Porterfield's data need to be confirmed by additional studies, but his study of delinquents in Texas seems to indicate that the social and parental rejection of children by the persons who refer them to court is important to the whole problem of delinquency. Where parents and the neighbors are really interested in helping and protecting the child, there tend to be few children reported to the courts in the first place.[56] Any type of unhappy home life may upset the emotional equilibrium to the extent of producing behavior difficulties. Where families are in constant tension and there is continual quarreling or bickering, the unbroken family may be as serious a source of unstable behavior in the child as the worst broken home.

5. *The Immoral Home.* The pattern of delinquency so far as girls are concerned is often found in the home, especially among female delinquents from broken homes. In Miss Elliott's study of the Sleighton Farm girls, in 67 percent of the broken homes both parents were immoral. This was also true for 44 percent of the unbroken homes.[57] Similarly, Miss Lumpkin found that 82 percent of the broken homes of Wisconsin delinquents were socially defective, as was also true of 61 percent of the unbroken homes.[58] In the Allegheny County Court study information was recorded for 135 of the 170 mothers and for 115 of the 170 fathers. For the cases for which there was information, 70 of the fathers or 63 percent had personality deviations. The most frequent of these deviations were excessive drinking (23 fathers) and "irresponsibility" (25 fathers). Other fathers rejected their children, were jealous, had illicit sex habits, etc. In the case of the mothers, 50 percent of the 135 for whom information was recorded were regarded as normal. The two deviations most characteristic of the other 50 percent were illicit sex relations and irresponsibility. Interestingly enough, most of the mothers indulging in illicit sex relations were in the group who referred their children to court.[59] The immoral home is more conducive to delinquency than is the merely broken home where

[54] Healy and Bronner, *op. cit.*, p. 104.

[55] Glazer and Wietrzynski, *op. cit.*, p. 97.

[56] Austin L. Porterfield, *Youth in Trouble*, Leo Potishman Foundation, Fort Worth, 1946.

[57] Elliott, *Correctional Education and the Delinquent Girl*, pp. 26–28.

[58] Katharine D. Lumpkin, "Factors in the Commitment of Correctional School Girls in Wisconsin," *American Journal of Sociology*, 37:225–226 (September, 1931).

[59] Glazer and Wietrzynski, *op. cit.*, pp. 83–89.

high standards prevail. Few children can be expected to conform to the values of the group if they are taught by precept and example to accept sex immorality, lying, and stealing.

Parental training in the importance of property values is evidently lacking among many delinquent boys. Somehow parents do not make children understand the importance which society attaches to the sanctity of personal property. If property holds so large a place in social values, parents are equally immoral who do not interpret this importance to their children. Such parents err as seriously, so far as the outcome is concerned, as the parent who instructs the child to steal. Certain Old World parents in times past have accepted petty pilfering by children as more or less synonymous with "gleaning" on the great estates. Such variances between New World and Old World mores are sometimes factors in delinquent behavior.[60]

6. *Social Training and Delinquency.* The patterns of behavior which are set in the family, the degree of courtesy, honesty, and general consideration for the rights of others, are very important in affecting attitudes and behavior outside the home. In his adjustments to members of his family the child builds many attitudes which will condition his adjustments in the world outside. Similarly, discipline and training in what the larger community accepts as desirable conduct constitute the most significant preparation the family can give the child.[61]

7. *The Economic Status of the Home.* Earlier studies of delinquency have shown that delinquents come from homes of low economic status. This was especially true before World War II.[62] A number of studies also have shown that the father of the delinquent tends to be a low-skilled or unskilled laborer. In consequence many youngsters have been industrially employed at an early age and subjected to all sorts of temptation in their daily contacts with persons both at work and going to and from work.[63] With the advent of widespread aid to dependent children under federal social security legislation, higher wages, and compulsory school attendance, the economic differential should now be less serious than it was. Even so, the low social status assigned to unskilled labor still prevails and thus creates a sense of inferiority in the child. Where the mother must work children often lack supervision.

Seventy percent of the Allegheny County Court cases studied had a social agency record, which indicates the relatively low social strata represented. Information as to the fathers' present employment status was recorded for only 117 or 71 percent of the cases. Of these 109 or 94 percent were employed

---

[60] Cf. Clifford R. Shaw, *The Jack Roller,* University of Chicago Press, Chicago, 1930.

[61] Cf. Jessie Bernard, *The American Family,* Harper & Brothers, New York, 1942, especially chaps. 5, 10, and 11.

[62] Cf. Elliott, *Correctional Education and the Delinquent Girl,* p. 29, and Clifford R. Shaw and Henry D. McKay, *Juvenile Delinquency and Urban Areas,* University of Chicago Press, Chicago, 1942, pp. 141 ff.

[63] Cf. Sheldon and Eleanor Glueck, *One Thousand Juvenile Delinquents,* Harvard University Press, Cambridge, 1934, pp. 89–90. Cf. also Chapter 9 "Women in Industry," pp. 232–233.

regularly.[64] This gives further credence to the theory that when employment and wages go up delinquency may increase where judgment in expenditures is not wise.

Personal Characteristics of the Delinquent

1. *Physical Factors in Delinquency.* Most authorities believe that heredity is not basic to the problem of delinquency, but there are nevertheless protagonists for the belief that physical characteristics are important factors in criminality.[65]

2. *Mental Factors in Delinquency.* Many delinquents were formerly thought to be mentally defective. The low mental rating of delinquents (as shown in the earlier studies) stemmed from the earlier practice of giving intelligence tests shortly after the children were referred to a court or committed to an institution. Their emotionally upset state was undoubtedly a factor in their low scores. Later studies show a higher percentage of the mentally normal among delinquents. Leslie D. Zeleny concluded from a number of studies, in fact, that the ratio of mental deficiency among delinquents to that among the general population was 1.2 to 1—not greatly different.[66]

The study cited above of children referred to Allegheny County Juvenile Court showed that 73 percent rated dull normal or above and that 50 percent were normal or above, as Table 4.4 shows. Harry M. Shulman believes that

TABLE 4.4.   Mental Ability of 170 Parent-Referred and
Police-Referred Cases by Percentages[a]

Mental Ability	Total Number	Percent
Total	170	100
Moron (50–69 IQ)	12	7
Borderline (70–79 IQ)	19	11
Dull normal (80–89 IQ)	33	19
Normal (90–109 IQ)	59	35
Superior (110–119 IQ)	6	4
Very superior (120–140 IQ)	2	1
Not recorded	39	23

[a] There was no significant difference by type of referral.

SOURCE: Marcia Glazer and Barbara Wietrzynski, "Comparative Study of Parent-Referred and Police-Referred Cases of the Allegheny County Juvenile Court, Disposed January 1 through June 30, 1954," unpublished ms., Chatham College Library, 1955, p. 128.

perhaps greater importance may be attached to the comparative intellectual ability of delinquents and their non-delinquent siblings. Healy and Bronner found that the non-delinquent siblings rated somewhat better than delin-

[64] Glazer and Wietrzynski, *op. cit.*, p. 63.

[65] Cf. also Chapter 5, "The Adult Offender."

[66] Leslie D. Zeleny, "Feeblemindedness and Criminal Conduct," *American Journal of Sociology,* 38:564–578 (January, 1933).

quents.[67] Shulman in a smaller study found markedly higher mental ability in the delinquents than among delinquents' families.[68] It seems obvious that unfavorable comparisons by parents and siblings might produce aggressive and resentful conduct on the part of the less gifted children, although this factor has never been analyzed in connection with delinquency.

High mental ability, however, is no index to the capacity to make a successful adjustment to the rules and regulations society imposes. Delinquents who possess unusual ability do not necessarily make a better subsequent adjustment than delinquents with low intelligence. Miss Elliott's study[69] of the after-careers of Sleighton Farm girls and Healy and Bronner's analysis of cases receiving rehabilitative treatment in Detroit, New Haven, and Boston both indicated that a high IQ was no key to a favorable outcome. In Healy and Bronner's study, in fact, those with an IQ above 110 did not do so well as the group as a whole.[70]

3. *Emotional Instability and "Mental Conflicts."* Emotional stability is a much better index to satisfactory adjustment. Burt's research indicated that marked emotionality was the most frequent and most influential of all the psychological characteristics of delinquents. He found 48.1 percent of the delinquents to be characterized by "general innate emotional instability," in constrast to 11.7 percent of the non-delinquent control group.[71]

Healy and Bronner made a comparative study of 105 delinquents and 105 non-delinquent siblings in an effort to determine why the delinquents became delinquent and their brothers and sisters did not. They found that the delinquents were in general characterized by foreign-born parents, broken homes, illegitimacy, large number of siblings, etc., and most of the parents had no generally prevalent high social ideals. Nineteen of the children, however, came from homes where conditions were relatively good. They became delinquent, according to Healy and Bronner, because of deep-seated emotionalized attitudes. In seventeen out of the nineteen cases there was a sense of emotional insecurity, of not being wanted. In the remaining eighty-six cases there were many unfortunate circumstances, but in general these too indicated serious emotional disturbances. All told, 96 of the 105 delinquents indicated such stresses, in contrast to only 13 of the non-delinquents.

Of the 96, the emotional disturbances were classified by types and incidence as follows (the disturbances obviously were complex and overlapped):

(a) Feeling keenly either rejected, deprived, insecure, not understood in affectional relationships, unloved, or that love has been withdrawn—46 cases.

[67] William Healy and Augusta F. Bronner, *New Light on Delinquency and Its Treatment,* Yale University Press, New Haven, 1936, p. 75.
[68] Harry Manuel Shulman, *A Study of Problem Boys and Their Brothers,* New York State Crime Commission, Albany, 1929, p. 61, quoted in Harry M. Shulman, "Intelligence and Delinquency," *Journal of Criminal Law, Criminology and Police Science,* 41:763–781 (March–April, 1951).
[69] *Correctional Education and the Delinquent Girl,* pp. 53–56.
[70] *New Light on Delinquency,* p. 190.
[71] *Op. cit.,* pp. 491–492.

(b) Deep feeling of being thwarted other than affectionally; either (1) in normal impulses or desires for self-expression or other self-satisfactions, (2) in unusual desires because earlier spoiled, or (3) in adolescent urges and desires—even when (as in 5 cases) desire for emancipation had been blocked only by the individual's counteractive pleasure in remaining childishly attached—28 cases.

(c) Feeling strongly either real or fancied inadequacies or inferiorities in the home life, in school, or in relation to companionship or to sports—46 cases.

(d) Intense feelings of discomfort about family disharmonies, parental misconduct, the conditions of family life, or parental errors in management and discipline —34 cases.

(e) Bitter feelings of jealousy toward one or more siblings, or feelings of being markedly discriminated against because another in the family circle more favored —31 cases.

(f) Feelings of confused unhappiness due to some deep-seated, often repressed, internal mental conflict—expressed in various kinds of delinquent acts which often are seemingly unreasonable—17 cases.

(g) Conscious or unconscious sense of guilt about earlier delinquencies or about behavior which technically was not delinquency; the guilt sense directly or indirectly activating delinquency through the individual's feeling of the need of punishment (in nearly every instance this overlaps with the last category)—9 cases.[72]

Healy and Bronner, in fact, became so convinced of the importance of emotional attitudes in the delinquent from this study that they would not say there were no such emotional discomforts for the nine for whom no discontents were uncovered. For this group, they conceded that social pressures probably played the most important role.

Most delinquents probably experience some mental conflict because of their dislike for school, feelings of discrimination, and grudges against siblings or playmates. Their conduct may not seem to bear much relation to the particular difficulty, but that fact in itself is a characteristic of delinquency. A child thus steals to compensate for emotional insecurity, or may be a truant from school because he is not allowed the family car. He may set fire to the house as a release to sex urges or run away from home to escape the tyranny of a parent. The emotional strivings of adolescence are in themselves an explanation for much delinquency—a part of the awkwardness and misunderstanding of youth. Who has not seen a child who has sadly misbehaved under mental stress and emotional disturbance? Yet such behavior may be the result of thwarted sex feelings, and the truancy, staying out late, and running away are less socially reprehensible than the overt sex delinquency would be.

Information was available with reference to family tensions for 128 out of 170 cases in the Pittsburgh study. Of these 128 cases 75 or 59 percent had definite tensions. Fifty of these were among the parent-referred cases and only 25 were in the group referred to court by the police. Since parents often referred their children for being ungovernable, it might be assumed that family tensions would be greater than in police-referred cases. On the other hand,

---

[72] Healy and Bronner, *New Light on Delinquency*, pp. 128–129, quoted by permission of the Yale University Press.

most of the conflicts in the parent-referred cases were between child and parent or child and step-parent and not between the parents themselves. There were in fact more conflicts (eleven) between the parents in the police-referred group than between the parents in the parent-referred group (where there were nine). Obviously these numbers are too small to be significant. The main point is that serious emotional tensions characterized more parent-referred than police-referred delinquents although 59 percent of both groups had such tensions.[73] But 41 percent had no such tensions, and this too is important. Further studies with reference to emotional tensions should be made. Psychiatrists have perhaps exaggerated the emotional factor in delinquency because they seldom see the cases where no such tensions exist. Juveniles may also be in an emotional state in consequence of being referred to court, and such emotionality is in a sense a result, not a cause, of delinquency. There are many difficulties involved in measuring emotionality objectively. But psychologists and psychiatrists often draw conclusions from hunches rather than from scientifically established facts.

Community Factors in Delinquency

The school and other community facilities (or lack of them) may engender conflict and tensions, as Miriam Van Waters pointed out in her significant book *Youth in Conflict,* although she too relied on her own convictions rather than objective proof.[74]

1. *Housing.* Much nonsense has been spoken and written to the effect that bad housing is a cause of delinquency. Poor housing is a symptom of social and economic inadequacy and is likely, therefore, to characterize the background of a child brought before the juvenile court. A poor family usually cannot pay the rent prevalent in a good neighborhood. Overcrowding may result in lack of privacy and thus contribute to cases of sex delinquency. If there is no room to play in the house, if laundry is always drying in the kitchen, and if the whole place is so congested and sordid that the child goes out on the street to escape the clutter and confusion, the house in this sense may contribute to delinquency. Children need adequate living space, and it is psychologically important to live in attractive surroundings. But even so, it is the lack of family and community resources, the poor family standards, the absence of supervised playgrounds, and the poor community patterns of conduct that are much more directly factors in the child's delinquency than the house itself. As Bertram M. Beck points out, the slum area is a segregated area isolated from the values of the larger community. The majority of slum dwellers are unable to compete socially or economically with those who live in better neighborhoods. Often slum residents develop a sense of failure and rejection which gives rise to aggressive and delinquent conduct. The child reared in the slums absorbs the attitudes of his community, which often oppose the cultural values of the larger society. Only the strongly knit family

---

[73] Glazer and Wietrzynski, *op. cit.,* pp. 104–107. (Information was lacking for 42 cases.)

[74] Miriam Van Waters, *Youth in Conflict,* New Republic, Inc., New York, 1925.

can induce adherence to more widely accepted social values when the children are exposed to so many antisocial values within their segregated community.[75]

On the other hand, an important reduction of delinquency is likely to occur in places where a housing project with play space and better living standards has supplanted a slum area. In New Haven, Connecticut, the rate of juvenile delinquency in 317 families (mostly Negroes) who were residents of a new development was compared with their previous rate; it was found to be nearly twice as great during the slum period as during the period in the new development. Furthermore, this decrease took place during the years 1940–1944 when there was a general increase in delinquency.[76]

2. *Recreation.* The improved recreational facilities in connection with the above project must have been important in reducing delinquency. Good housing must be in a good neighborhood for the child to feel the importance of cooperating with the social values of the larger community.[77] Actually, the *whole* standard of living goes up in an area where there are attractive surroundings and where adequate play space supplants a deteriorated neighborhood.

Because delinquents usually get into trouble when they are not occupied in school or in wholesome play or quasi-vocational activities, some have regarded juvenile delinquency as a leisure-time activity. In fact, Thurston concluded that the 2587 cases of delinquents he analyzed in Cleveland were so because of habitual misuse of their leisure.[78] Children may become delinquent, however, in order to spend their leisure normally. For example, in so many cities they have sold stolen milk bottles in order to obtain money to go to the movies that milk bottles cannot now be sold in many communities. Frederick M. Thrasher's classic study of boys' gangs in Chicago established their major *raison d'être* in the spontaneous play groups from which they developed. In consequence, much momentum has been given to group recreational projects—boys' clubs, girls' clubs, and settlement recreational projects —on the ground that they prevent delinquency.

Nevertheless, later projects have shown that recreation alone will not prevent delinquency where delinquent habits are well established. In New York City it was found that athletic clubs were no deterrent to the delinquency of the boys participating in their program. On the contrary, there were more delinquencies in the clubs than among other boys in the neighborhood who were not members of these organized recreational groups.[79]

The recreational survey later conducted in Chicago showed that delin-

[75] Bertram M. Beck, "The Exiled Delinquent," *Children*, 2:208–212 (November–December, 1955).

[76] Naomi Barer, "Delinquency Before, After Admission to New Haven Housing Development," *Journal of Housing* (December, 1945–January, 1946), p. 27, quoted by Sidney Maslen, "Housing and Juvenile Delinquency," *Federal Probation*, 12:40–44 (June, 1948).

[77] *Ibid.*

[78] Cf. H. W. Thurston, *Delinquency and Spare Time*, Cleveland Recreational Survey, Cleveland, 1918, pp. 105–118.

[79] Frederick M. Thrasher, "The Boys' Club and Juvenile Delinquency," *American Journal of Sociology*, 42:66–80 (July, 1936).

quents participated extensively in the neighborhood recreational programs in parks and settlements. Furthermore, delinquents who attended recreational programs committed fewer delinquencies than delinquents who did not participate in such activities. Out of a total of 2062 delinquents living in the areas covered by the survey, 999 participated in recreational programs, and of these, 106 or 10.6 percent became recidivists. Of the remaining 1063 who did not participate in the recreational facilities, 15.7 percent or 168 became recidivists. That is, 30 percent more of those not participating in recreation became recidivists than of those participating. But the survey also disclosed that delinquents spent more time in recreational projects than non-delinquents. A sizable number of the non-delinquents became delinquent during the period they were participating in recreational programs, but it was generally true that those who became delinquents were not as well supervised as the non-delinquents. If a park is used as a hangout for a gang, the constructive recreational work accomplished obviously may be negligible.[80] The problem of the relation of recreation to delinquency has many tangents. Recreation needs to be well organized and highly supervised if it is to become a therapeutic agent in areas where delinquency patterns already prevail.

3. *Movies and Comic Books.* Movies and comic books have both been roundly denounced for motivating children to behave in delinquent ways. Crime and gangster movies and movies glamorizing illicit love have undoubtedly stimulated some young persons to act in similar fashion. Playing "cops and robbers" has been one type of play activity among boys for hundreds of years, chiefly because it provides thrills and excitement of the make-believe world in which children re-enact adult behavior. Crime scenes in movies have unquestionably stimulated some children to real-world delinquencies, particularly lower-class children whose fantasies are seldom shaped by good literature. Children who have plenty of wholesome stimulation apparently are not so extensively affected.[81]

Comic books purchased at newsstands and drug and grocery stores formerly totaled some 50,000,000 or more a year, and the majority of them used to be full of murder, mayhem, and other violence. Frederic Wertham, New York City psychiatrist, spearheaded an attack on these books for their vicious influence and contended that a large share of the increase in violence on the part of youngsters stems from such influence, along with television, which has copied crime comics.[82] Meanwhile various civic groups and the PTA have demanded that such books be withdrawn from circulation and the worst variety has virtually disappeared.

That children are thrilled and excited by violence and thoughts of bloodshed and murder there can be no doubt. The number of toy pistols, swords,

[80] Ethel Shanas, *Recreation and Delinquency,* Chicago Recreation Commission, Chicago, 1942, pp. 238–244.

[81] Herbert Blumer, *Movies and Conduct,* The Macmillan Company, New York, 1933, pp. 198–199.

[82] Frederic Wertham, *Seduction of the Innocent,* Rinehart and Company, Inc., New York, 1954.

and rubber daggers sold is tacit evidence. The fact that all children wish to copy what they see other children doing, playing, or wearing merely quickens the demand. On the other hand, there is little evidence to support the charges that comic books were ever a major factor in juvenile delinquency.

4. *The School's Role in Delinquency.* The school has often been blamed for its failure to arouse the enthusiasm and interest of the child, and some persons have laid the blame for delinquency squarely on the school's doorstep. Most schools until recently have indeed ignored both training for citizenship and the fact that growing up effectively requires training. Although we must not suppose that the school alone can make up for all the inadequacies of the home and the wider community, it is certainly in a position to do much more than it previously has to prepare the child for effective social living. The National Education Association has recently accepted the responsibility for helping teachers deal with the problem.[83]

The school's chief task is obviously education in subject matter. Nevertheless the school has the child under its supervision a major part of the waking day. It therefore is in a position to detect behavior problems and to cooperate with other agencies in the community such as the church, the YMCA, and child guidance clinics where advisable. More important, the school should adjust the curriculum and learning process to the special needs of the children —with tutoring help for the retarded child. It is equally important that the school provide an enjoyable social climate. Many of the children who come into conflict with authorities are those who drop out of school because they dislike it or who have no encouragement at home. This is a special problem in which curricular adjustments and teachers' attitudes are of particular influence. Unfortunately the PTA is usually dominated by middle-class parents.[84] If greater tact and skill were employed in dealing with lower-class parents they too might be brought into the organization. Parents will not participate when they feel out of place, and since they have much more influence over the child's behavior than the school does, securing their cooperation is imperative in any school prevention-of-delinquency program.

In certain cities, notably New York, enraged and upset students have terrified teachers by their conduct. A few schools, including those in the Jersey City school system, meanwhile have attempted to help belligerent and discouraged children instead of referring them to the juvenile court. Dislike for school ranks fourth as the alleged reason which delinquents have given for their misconduct.[85] The dislike may be for the teacher, the course of study, the principal, or other classmates. Often the basic reason for disliking school

[83] Cf. the reports of the National Education Association juvenile delinquency project: (1) William C. Kvaraceus and Walter B. Miller, *Delinquent Behavior, Culture and the Individual,* and (2) William C. Kvaraceus and William E. Ulrich, *Delinquent Behavior Principles and Practices,* both published by the National Education Association, Washington, 1959.

[84] Kvaraceus and Ulrich, *op. cit.,* pp. 29–30.

[85] William C. Kvaraceus, *Juvenile Delinquency and the School,* World Book Company, Yonkers, 1947, p. 150.

grows out of a home situation: the mother's illness, the parents' divorce, or the father's unemployment. The major reasons children leave school are that they fail, receive very low marks, or are otherwise markedly retarded. Low marks or failures are often due to emotional causes rather than to sheer lack of mental ability. Children may fail because they are ashamed of their clothes, or because they are taunted about their father's police record or their mother's notorious conduct. Children stay away from school for any reason which makes them conspicuously different or unhappy in the group. Sometimes it is the best-dressed child who is condemned as a "sissy," or the child who has had exceptional training or travel opportunities is rejected because "he thinks he's smart." Teachers sometimes nag a child to recite when he is unable to do so or criticize a child's untidy clothes when there is no one at home to launder them. Teachers have failed to realize that a child sometimes cannot read the blackboard because of defective eyesight.[86]

Revising the curriculum so that it will view the task of education through the child's eyes is an important step in educational procedure. But schools must do more. They must also educate children to the importance of social values, of obeying laws, of becoming responsible citizens, of being practicing members of a democratic society. There has been a general failure of schools to make the child feel a part of the educational process. Children as well as adults can be made to feel responsible for their role in the group if there is proper presentation of the subject.[87]

This means teaching children habits of emotional control, consideration for the rights of others, and responsibility for tasks assigned. It also means helping the individual child to work out his own personality problems. Lack of effective guidance and counseling programs is thus the key to many of the failures of education. Part of this may be attributed to teachers' lack of interest in their students. On the other hand, the overworked and underpaid teacher in many of our communities can scarcely be expected to assume additional duties. If our schools are to accept a larger responsibility, they must be provided with far more adequate staffs.

5. *Unemployment Among Those Not in School.* Part of the problem of delinquency among 16- to 17-year-olds is unquestionably related to the number of young persons in this age group who are neither in school nor employed. Altogether 97.1 percent of the group 14 to 15 years of age and 80.5 percent of those 16 to 17 were in school in 1957. Those not in school in these age groups totaled 967,000. Of these 15 percent or 145,050 were not employed, but were unquestionably clamoring for activity.[88] It is a well-known

[86] Cf. National Society for the Study of Education, *Juvenile Delinquency and the School,* University of Chicago Press, Chicago, 1948, especially chap. XII, and Kvaraceus, *op. cit.,* chap. 12, "Frustrating Factors in the School."

[87] John M. Brewer, *Education as Guidance,* The Macmillan Company, New York, 1938, pp. 1–2.

[88] Data computed from census material on school enrollment: October, 1957, *Population Characteristics, Current Population Reports,* Series P-50, No. 80, Washington, February 13, 1958, p. 8, and *Employment of Students and Other Persons: 1957 Current Population Reports,* Series P-50, No. 83, Washington, April, 1958, p. 3.

fact that young persons in this age group who have left school and are not working contribute a disproportionate number of the juvenile delinquency cases. Many of these youngsters wanted jobs. One can readily understand how relatively easy it might be for this group to get into trouble.

6. *Delinquency Areas.* As Shaw and McKay[89] have conclusively shown, some communities are not safe places for children to live in. A study of juvenile delinquency in Chicago; Greater Boston; Omaha; Richmond, Virginia; Birmingham, Alabama; Columbus, Ohio; Denver; and five cities of the Pacific Northwest showed that a direct relationship existed between local conditions in various neighborhoods and the differential rates of delinquency. Male delinquency, Shaw and McKay concluded, has dynamic roots in the community, and the rate depends upon the differences in social values, norms, and attitudes to which children are exposed. Within every city they found delinquency rates to be astonishingly uniform. The highest rates were in the area surrounding the business section, the lowest were in the outer zones, and for all but three cities there was a progressive decline in rates from the center to the outskirts. The rates were highest in the areas where social disorganization in its other manifestations was also highest.[90]

Shaw and McKay hold that social traditions in the low-income and deteriorated areas enforce patterns of delinquency and these tend to be preserved through various delinquent groups or gangs. Within the local community the delinquent child may thus conform to the social values of his elders. It is only with reference to the larger social group which enforces the laws that his conduct is defined as illegal and antisocial. The higher-income-level neighborhoods tend to accept the conventional values. Even where the individual child from the upper-income groups offends the law, the group in which he lives favors it. The child therefore usually develops a "natural" wish to conform.[91] Moreover, teachers and other persons who try to induce lower-class children to accept middle-class values may meet with hostile response because adolescent boys resent the imputation that they represent a lower status or a degraded set of values.[92] This is very important for teachers to recognize.

At the same time, Shaw and McKay maintain that the luxury values of the larger society are those which the child would emulate. The larger regulating community in which the child lives and his economic status combine to frustrate his achieving these values unless he resorts to stealing. Hence, although Shaw and McKay recognize that multiple factors may lead this particular child to misconduct, they hold that the delinquency tradition in the local area is a powerful factor in inducing the slum child's delinquent conduct. As Healy and Bronner insist, the prevailing pattern of delinquent behavior is an important force motivating children to behave like the other members of the play group.

[89] Clifford R. Shaw and Henry D. McKay, *Juvenile Delinquency and Urban Areas,* University of Chicago Press, Chicago, 1942, chap. 20.

[90] *Ibid.,* pp. ix, xi.

[91] *Ibid.,* p. 442.

[92] Solomon Kobrin, "The Conflict of Values in Delinquency Areas," *American Sociological Review, 16:*653–661 (October, 1951).

War and Juvenile Delinquency

War seems to produce a marked increase in delinquency. During World War II in Europe the child's school work was interrupted, his parents were often both engaged in wartime activities (with the husband at the front, the mother in a factory), and he lived in a world that had little place for normal care of children. Where there was bombing it was easy enough to break into stores and warehouses and run off with loot.[93] Girls were exposed to far more sex advances and consequent sex delinquencies than in peacetime.[94] In the United States there was also a wartime increase in delinquency—in some instances allegedly as much as 50 percent.[95] Women's clubs, churches, educators, and newspapers indicated much concern. Actually, the greatest increase in delinquency during the war years was in the large cities and war-industry areas, where working mothers left their children unsupervised and community resources were inadequate to meet the call for additional services.

Immediately following World War II Great Britain, for example, had a far more serious delinquency situation than the United States because life was still disrupted on many counts. Poverty was particularly serious, housing difficult, food scanty, and prices high. Children had an especially hard time readjusting to the prewar moral standards. Educators complained that cheating and lying had become familiar problems in the schools because it is difficult to implant in the young person's mind any reason for disavowing the obvious advantages to be obtained by hoodwinking someone else.[96] With the advent of the Korean War, however, delinquency in the United States took an upturn. Most adolescents, particularly boys, were discouraged about world tensions during the Korean conflict and the increased antagonism of the Communist-dominated countries and the Western democratic countries. Some believe that these disturbed conditions are enough to induce greater hostility on the part of young persons.

Religious Values and Delinquency

The emphasis upon ability to consume material goods without any accompanying emphasis upon the ethical and spiritual values of our culture may be the whirlwind of our generation. Thus far there has been no satisfactory check-up on the effectiveness of religious and spiritual values as a prophylaxis against delinquency. The Cambridge-Somerville study set out to gauge the impact of such values, but as the project was finally carried out, only one of the adult leaders paid any significant attention to emphasizing religious values, although all leaders unquestionably tried to promote good citizenship and

[93] Basil Henriques, "Britain's Young Offenders," *Atlantic Monthly, 183*:45–49 (June, 1949).

[94] Elsa Castendyck, "Juvenile Delinquency in Wartime," *Federal Probation, 6*:45–48 (July–September, 1942).

[95] Cf. Victor H. Evjen, "Delinquency and Crime in Wartime," *Journal of Criminal Law and Criminology, 33*:136–146 (July–August, 1942).

[96] Sophia Ramondt, well-known Dutch educator, has so described the moral aftermath of war in a letter to the authors.

law-abiding conduct.[97] A truly scientific study in this area would be enlightening.

How Delinquents Differ from Non-Delinquents

General social opinion, the law-enforcing agencies, the various welfare agencies, and the courts have combined to build up the notion of a rising tide of delinquency. Many public leaders have demanded that a national plan for reducing delinquency be put into operation. But in all this manifest interest in young persons in distress and society in danger there has been a general failure to recognize that there is nothing especially unique about the behavior of children brought before the courts. Practically all children do things which are socially disapproved. All children have to be taught to be honest, to tell the truth, to respect other people's property, to curb tendencies to strike at other persons, to observe socially accepted patterns of decency, modesty, and sex conduct. Often urges to behave in antisocial or condemned ways occur before the child has received sufficient training to understand that such behavior is frowned upon or punished by the group. Sometimes children disobey rules merely to see what will happen. Or young persons may understand vaguely that a certain mode of conduct is contrary to adult values but still have very little comprehension of *why* society opposes such conduct.

Antisocial behavior is in a sense natural and virtually all children commit some delinquencies. Middle-class and upper-class parents usually try to make their children see wherein they have erred and help them to overcome any damage they have done to society or to themselves. The extent of delinquency among the comfortably fixed and well-to-do has been strikingly illustrated by Austin L. Porterfield's study of delinquent conduct past and present among college students. He therefore holds delinquent conduct to be relatively common among all young persons. He maintains, however, that the children of the poor suffer for their ignorance, their unfortunate background, and the failure (or inadequacy) of their parents in helping them over the rough spots in growing up. Children of the middle and upper economic and social classes, on the other hand, are seldom if ever officially punished or brought before a juvenile court. Professor Porterfield analyzed 2049 cases brought before the Fort Worth Juvenile Court and compared their record with the admitted delinquencies of 337 Texas college students, composed of 200 men and 137 women. The court cases had been charged with fifty-five types of offenses ranging from "shooting spit-wads at a wrestling match" to murder. Offenses of college students were obtained in answer to a questionnaire presented personally and returned anonymously; 100 percent of both college men and women admitted pre-college offenses.[98] These students represented a cross section of all college classes from freshmen through seniors and comprised

---

[97] Edwin Powers and Helen Leland Witmer, *An Experiment in the Prevention of Delinquency* (the Cambridge-Somerville Youth Study) Columbia University Press, New York, 1951, p. 154.

[98] Austin L. Porterfield, *Youth in Trouble*, Leo Potishman Foundation, Fort Worth, 1946, chap. 2.

graduate students, athletes, class officers, honor students, and theological students from all economic groups, as Table 4.5 shows.

TABLE 4.5. Average Number of Offenses Reported by Texas College Students Among 100 Men and 137 Women in Pre-College Days, and the Percentage Reporting One or More of the Offenses

Group	Percentage Reporting One or More of the Offenses		Number of Persons		Total Offenses		Offense Average	
	Male	Fe-male	Male	Fe-male	Male	Fe-male	Male	Fe-male
Freshmen	100.0	100.0	25	56	479	203	19.2	3.6
Sophomores	100.0	100.0	17	22	307	97	18.1	4.4
Juniors	100.0	100.0	28	33	496	229	17.7	6.9
Seniors	100.0	100.0	26	26	432	124	16.5	4.8
Graduates	100.0	....	4	..	45	...	11.2	..
Athletes	100.0	100.0	43	23	954	124	23.3	5.4
Class officers[a]	100.0	100.0	48	77	723	427	17.0	5.5
Honor students[b]	100.0	100.0	41	91	717	418	18.0	4.6
Musicians	100.0	100.0	9	18	151	88	16.8	4.9
Ministerial students	100.0	—	31	—	412	—	13.4	—
Family income:								
Below $500	100.0	100.0	3	2	45	6	15.0	3.0
$500–$999	100.0	100.0	15	10	247	39	16.5	3.9
$1,000–$1,499	100.0	100.0	21	29	345	134	16.4	4.6
$1,500–$1,999	100.0	100.0	17	27	293	79	17.2	2.9
$2,000–$2,499	100.0	100.0	21	25	398	123	19.0	4.7
$2,500 and over	100.0	100.0	19	41	328	300	17.0	7.3

[a] In high school and/or college.

[b] In high school and/or college. Observe that a student may be an athlete, a class officer, and a musician at the same time.

SOURCE: Austin L. Porterfield, *Youth in Trouble*, Leo Potishman Foundation, Fort Worth, 1946, p. 39. Reprinted by permission of the author.

The Class Differential in Defining Delinquent Conduct

Upper- and middle-class parents are constrained to protect their child and the family reputation from the stigma of court experience and social disapproval. Upper- and middle-class merchants, on the other hand, apparently feel no compunction about reporting the delinquencies of an annoying child whose parents are of a lower class. This is not a new conclusion. Victor Hugo's memorable novel *Les Miserables* made it clear that Jean Valjean was punished by law chiefly because he was a poor hungry child who stole a loaf of bread.

Some years ago the students at two high schools in the best residential section of Kansas City raided drug stores and destroyed considerable property in their enthusiasm following the winning of a football game. No young person in this group was brought into court. Their fathers paid the bill and one school was initially penalized by being denied the right to participate in interscholastic football the next year; after protest this penalty was revoked. Had the students been from a poorer section the ringleaders, at least, probably would have been punished as examples. Only when offenses on the part of members of the upper and middle class are so serious as to arouse wide condemnation are they likely to be punished. As we have earlier indicated, the upper middle class is the defining group and constitutes the ruling class in our particular variety of democracy. Social consensus thus favors the overlooking of all offenses by the ruling class unless the community is outraged.

This class differential in stigmatizing and penalizing juvenile delinquents needs to be more fully understood. Upper- and middle-class children who get into trouble tend to become well-adjusted individuals in later life. Part of their effective adjustment is due to the status to which the community assigns them. Community opinion expects some children to make good, and even the local officials help them to achieve this status. The average child brought before the court, however, feels the impact of social isolation and rejection in the stigma attached to his behavior. Furthermore, all studies indicate that the child once referred to the court tends to become a recidivist. The fact that society sets him apart—if he is committed to an institution for juvenile delinquents—results in his becoming schooled in the delinquent practices of his contemporaries, and he is released to further condemnation and conviction. The social stigma heaped upon the delinquent is thus contributory to his further delinquency. If society could protect the child against the inadequacies of his home environment and help him over his mistakes instead of penalizing him for them, many of the juvenile court cases might turn out as well as the college students who admitted their earlier delinquencies.

The offenses themselves were as serious as those committed by the cases referred to the court, but apparently were not so numerous. Traffic violations were the only charges brought against college students more frequently than against the juvenile court cases. For other types of delinquency, no college woman was ever called into court.

Some of the college students had a long career of delinquency but nevertheless became successful and well-adjusted personalities. One theological student reported twenty-seven delinquencies; another student who was already a minister reported twenty-eight! Some of the offenses reported were extremely serious and included several cases of attempt to rape and one case of murder, none of which was ever brought to court. Six percent of the students reported had been in jail before enrolling in college and 7 percent afterward, but in all but one of these cases the offense was a traffic violation.[99] These data indicate conclusively that Texas college students and juvenile court cases have similar behavior problems, but society has not seen fit to bring the former into court.

Hidden Delinquencies

A special project of the Cambridge-Somerville study in Massachusetts likewise disclosed many hidden delinquencies. The study covered ma-

[99] *Ibid.*, pp. 45–46.

terial secured through case workers in a delinquency prevention project. The social workers had contacts with sixty-one boys who never were brought to court and forty whose complaints were registered with the court. These boys had committed 6416 offenses, only 95 (1.5 percent) of which had ever received official court action. Approximately 1400 were infractions of city ordinances, none of which resulted in a court complaint, 4400 were minor offenses, and only 27 or .6 percent were prosecuted. Of 616 serious offenses, 68 (11 percent) were punished. Most juvenile offenses thus apparently tend to be hidden. Many of these youngsters revealed their delinquencies years after they were committed, and the offenses were not known to social agencies or the court at the time they occurred.[100]

We have little reason to suppose that the young persons in Texas and Massachusetts are much different from those in Illinois, New York, or the rest of the states. The point is that there is much hidden delinquency, and delinquency seems to be characteristic of all groups. Underprivileged children are reported by the police, social workers, clerks, and neighbors, but even in this group there are many unreported cases. Among the college students we have no way of knowing how well their offenses were hidden, but in any event their parents were more important socially than the group reported to court. Few social workers would think of investigating the home life of a child in the country club area or the well-to-do section. So far as the Texas students were concerned, their family organization was also much stronger than that of the juvenile court cases. Only 16 percent of the college students came from broken homes, in contrast to 50.6 percent of the court cases.[101]

Association and Group Experience and Delinquency

Sociologists have long emphasized the importance of association and group experience in fostering all behavior, both criminal and noncriminal. Sutherland maintained that *criminal behavior varies with the frequency, intensity, priority, and continuousness of association with deviant norms of behavior.* Wherever the group with which the individual associates fosters delinquent attitudes, he is likely to become a delinquent, whether the group be a play group, a deteriorated community, or a gang within a community.[102] We need further research on this, as Marshall Clinard insists, but it is nevertheless obvious that most of the techniques of delinquency are learned behavior, whether they involve how to jimmy a lock, "roll" a drunk, or dispose of stolen goods.[103]

Certainly we cannot assume that delinquent behavior is the automatic result of emotional instability or feelings of guilt on the one hand, or of bad housing, poverty, prosperity, feeble-mindedness, motion pictures, radio and

---

[100] Fred J. Murphy, Mary M. Shirley, and Helen L. Witmer, "The Incidence of Hidden Delinquency," *American Journal of Orthopsychiatry, 16*:686–696 (October, 1946).

[101] Porterfield, *op. cit.,* p. 47.

[102] Sutherland and Cressey, *op. cit.,* p. 78.

[103] Marshall Clinard, "Criminal Behavior Is Human Behavior," *Federal Probation, 13*:21–27 (March, 1949).

television, or comic books on the other. As we have previously shown, there is considerable misbehavior and disobedience to law in all groups. Much delinquency springs from the prevalent attitudes in the groups within which the youth has immediate contacts. Even the much maligned family of the delinquent is not directly responsible for a major share of the delinquent contacts in the community.[104] Clifford Shaw and his associates in the Chicago Area Project attacked the problem of delinquency on the theory that delinquency is a product of community forces. Any therapy directed toward delinquent behavior in their estimation should therefore be directed at the community. Out of this conviction the Chicago Area Project was developed.[105] This project has been singularly successful in reducing delinquency by promoting leadership among local residents toward creating attitudes and behavior patterns acceptable to the larger community. Local businessmen, labor leaders, clergymen, and teachers have been organized to an awareness of how delinquency has been furthered previously by the sanction of the community. The leaders in the project are convinced that the low-income areas have fostered a setting for delinquency, and that this can be overcome only by modifying the setting in which patterns of behavior are established.[106]

Herein is probably the major explanation for the difference in delinquency patterning in various parts of a city. All young persons have to be instructed in the values of non-delinquent conduct, in the importance attached to obeying the laws, and in respecting the property and person of other people. In this respect the upper and middle class do a better job of training children because they themselves define the cultural norms and have more effective facilities for interpreting them. Most persons living in slum areas are financially depressed. Many belong to cultural minorities and virtually all are inarticulate nonparticipants in the larger social groups. For these reasons the families living in most low-income areas have developed very little community consensus. Only as they have learned to participate in group activities and build up strong local group pressures to provide adequate recreation, summer camps, and community centers has there been a significant decrease in delinquency and crime. Local residents have to cooperate in making their community a suitable environment for their children.[107]

SELECTED BIBLIOGRAPHY

Barron, Milton, *The Juvenile in Delinquent Society,* Alfred A. Knopf, Inc., New York, 1954. As the title indicates, society is held responsible for the delinquents' conduct.

[104] *Ibid.*

[105] Shaw and McKay, *Juvenile Delinquency and Urban Areas,* pp. 442–445.

[106] We cannot go into detail on this important preventive project here. Interested students are referred to E. W. Burgess, J. D. Lohman, and Clifford R. Shaw, "The Chicago Area Project," *Yearbook of the National Probation Association,* 1937, pp. 8–28, and the mimeographed report, "The Chicago Area Project," 1940.

[107] *Ibid.*

Burt, Cyril, *The Young Delinquent,* Appleton-Century-Crofts, Inc., New York, 1925. This study, in London, was one of the first in which there was a control group. A group of school children from the same economic and social backgrounds were compared with the delinquent children.

Elliott, Mabel A., *Correctional Education and the Delinquent Girl,* Commonwealth of Pennsylvania, Harrisburg, 1929. This follow-up study of delinquent girls was one of the first studies to show that emotional stability is a more important factor in socially acceptable conduct than intelligence per se.

Glueck, Sheldon and Eleanor, *Juvenile Delinquents Grown Up,* the Commonwealth Fund, New York, 1940. This is a follow-up of the one thousand juvenile delinquents in the earlier study. The authors conclude that lack of maturity is important in delinquency.

Glueck, Sheldon and Eleanor, *One Thousand Juvenile Delinquents,* Harvard University Press, Cambridge, 1934. The first notable contribution of the Glueck team to understanding juvenile delinquency. This research showed that a large percentage of juvenile court clients failed to make a satisfactory adjustment.

Glueck, Sheldon and Eleanor, *Physique and Delinquency,* Harper & Brothers, New York, 1956. The physical data on the 500 children in the preceding study and on 500 non-delinquents in a control group are analyzed with the conclusion that far more delinquents than non-delinquents are of a muscular, heavy-boned (mesomorphic) type.

Glueck, Sheldon and Eleanor, *Unraveling Juvenile Delinquency,* Harvard University Press, Cambridge, 1950. The authors conclude that social factors (and especially the family) are of major importance in determining delinquency of 500 Boston children.

Healy, William, and Bronner, Augusta F., *Delinquents and Criminals, Their Making and Unmaking,* The Macmillan Company, New York, 1926. A classic in delinquency studies.

Healy, William, and Bronner, Augusta F., *New Light on Delinquency,* Yale University Press, New Haven, 1936. Delinquents with non-delinquent siblings are shown to have much more serious emotional problems than the non-delinquents.

Kvaraceus, William C., *Juvenile Delinquency and the School,* World Book Company, Yonkers, 1947. A detailed analysis of the school with reference both to school situations which produce delinquency and to the school's role in the treatment of delinquency.

Lander, Bernard, *Towards an Understanding of Juvenile Delinquency,* Columbia University Press, New York, 1954. This is an important ecological study of white and Negro delinquency rates in Baltimore. Negro rates were found to decrease in communities where Negroes constitute the bulk of the population. Where they are less than half, the Negro rate goes up with each successive 10 percent of population. Lander holds social disorganization or *anomie* responsible.

Porterfield, Austin L., *Youth in Trouble,* Leo Potishman Foundation, Fort Worth, 1946. Delinquent conduct is shown to be relatively common among young persons in the middle and upper classes, but such behavior is seldom referred to court. Lower-class parents, on the other hand, often report their children to the court.

CHAPTER 5

The Adult Offender

Despite the alarm concerning juvenile delinquency the public generally has evidenced no similar anxiety over the rise in adult crimes. Adult society wants its younger generation to conform. Yet from a social point of view adult crime should be recognized as an even greater danger. Much juvenile delinquency is related to adolescence itself, whereas adults are presumably "old enough to know better."

Adult criminals are subverting the purposes of their own adult group to their own selfish ends and promoting social disorganization in our communities, states, and nation. They themselves are major examples of disorganized individuals for whom some of the important moral values of the community as exemplified in the law have no significant meaning. Society condemns and rejects their conduct—yet somehow society is much more alarmed about the conduct of juvenile offenders. Since it is the adult criminals who set the patterns for juvenile offenses, there should be greater concern for adults who flout the law, not only to discern the reasons for their behavior but to discover better methods for rehabilitating them. This is just as important as the need for understanding and better treatment of juveniles.

Who Is an Adult Criminal?

There is considerable disparity among the various states as to which offenders are juvenile and which are adult. The trend in juvenile court legislation is toward making 18 years of age the upper limit of juvenile court legislation, unless a capital offense has been committed. In many states it is still 16 or 17, and in only two, California and Arkansas, is the jurisdiction extended to 21 years of age. Since all biologists, psychologists, and educators recognize that adolescence extends to 22 or 24, it would be much more intelligent to have this fact recognized by our courts. It *is* more or less recognized in our voting requirements.

Slightly more young persons 18 to 21 years of age inclusive (living in places of 2500 or more) were arrested in 1958 than was true for those 22 through 24 although these were not figured in ratio to the population group in each age category, as Table 5.1 shows. There was a slight drop for the years 25 to 29, but a perceptible increase for those 30 to 34 and those 35 to 39. Summarized on a cumulative basis, persons under 18 committed 12.1

TABLE 5.1. Arrests by Age Groups, 1958; 1,586 Cities

Offense Charged	Total	Age					
		Under 15	15	16	17	18	19
Total	**2,340,004**	**106,892**	**52,776**	**62,240**	**62,307**	**63,109**	**58,424**
Criminal homicide:							
(a) Murder and nonnegligent manslaughter	2,303	17	19	44	50	57	59
(b) Manslaughter by negligence	1,166	12	7	29	30	45	46
Robbery	14,968	980	637	836	962	1,080	1,060
Aggravated assault	25,824	670	393	599	678	767	732
Other assaults	82,454	2,050	1,153	1,556	1,762	2,299	2,358
Burglary—breaking or entering	61,045	13,768	5,765	6,023	4,904	3,923	2,985
Larceny—theft	118,325	28,584	9,988	10,576	8,241	6,468	4,647
Auto theft	30,240	5,018	5,666	5,368	3,334	2,053	1,491
Embezzlement and fraud	19,489	186	75	76	140	274	352
Stolen property; buying, receiving, etc.	5,504	685	287	370	358	303	286
Forgery and counterfeiting	11,317	121	128	235	283	375	396
Forcible rape	3,680	108	123	214	237	297	289
Prostitution and commercialized vice	17,482	27	25	46	97	261	483
Other sex offenses (includes statutory rape)	24,517	1,618	867	923	859	861	852
Narcotic drug laws	9,863	43	44	106	183	290	347
Weapons; carrying, possessing, etc.	18,611	726	640	849	857	886	838
Offenses against family and children	23,701	101	36	59	95	422	513
Liquor laws	52,707	711	1,337	2,955	4,491	4,544	4,174
Driving while intoxicated	102,219	11	18	186	403	857	1,274
Disorderly conduct	281,997	9,158	4,923	6,368	7,316	10,614	10,019
Drunkenness	908,957	655	998	2,240	3,855	6,652	7,812
Vagrancy	88,351	765	675	1,409	1,739	2,762	2,382
Gambling	61,546	94	107	129	245	481	611
Suspicion	96,740	3,669	2,770	4,131	7,019	7,099	5,720
All other offenses	276,998	37,115	16,095	16,913	14,169	9,439	8,698

SOURCE: *Uniform Crime Reports, 1958*, Federal Bureau of Investigation, U.S. Department of Justice, 1959, p. 93.

percent of the crimes, those under 21, 19.7 percent, and those under 25, 29.3 percent. This means that adults 25 and over were arrested for 70.7 percent of the crimes.

It is generally presumed that these arrests indicate fairly accurately the proportion of the crimes. Though many crimes are solved by arrest we have no means of being certain that the unsolved crimes were committed in the same proportions by the different age groups. The statistical likelihood that they were is great, but certain factors may make it easier to locate young persons.

The adults set the standards in the community. They vote and are elected to civic office. And adults past twenty-five constitute most of the parents and

Over 2,500, Total Population 52,329,497

						Age					
20	21	22	23	24	25–29	30–34	35–39	40–44	45–49	50 and Over	Not Known
54,267	58,762	56,691	54,576	55,610	260,117	279,461	275,803	239,538	211,998	387,049	384
71	70	74	68	64	369	363	291	231	158	297	1
33	34	49	42	31	189	165	145	95	62	152	—
941	864	744	696	629	2,403	1,537	796	389	197	215	2
760	819	847	867	884	4,259	3,878	3,390	2,283	1,676	2,322	—
2,400	2,810	2,989	2,966	3,200	14,616	13,423	10,782	7,236	4,792	6,054	8
2,341	2,135	1,807	1,680	1,435	5,452	3,710	2,203	1,307	787	814	6
3,547	3,008	2,784	2,350	2,225	9,003	7,500	5,735	4,233	3,312	6,094	30
1,052	795	665	495	432	1,485	1,018	638	341	184	193	12
426	495	601	643	656	3,545	3,884	3,085	2,051	1,380	1,620	—
221	202	193	149	141	609	518	411	289	219	263	—
412	467	506	483	434	2,068	1,988	1,442	843	506	630	—
241	213	204	180	143	536	351	239	124	85	96	—
492	790	946	940	997	3,892	2,939	2,142	1,342	933	1,128	2
846	901	966	855	816	3,696	3,001	2,484	1,729	1,161	2,078	4
434	446	480	525	561	2,595	1,776	892	445	312	384	—
726	812	790	712	658	2,784	2,217	1,832	1,155	896	1,233	—
573	780	877	963	926	4,953	4,599	3,556	2,361	1,384	1,501	2
3,353	1,099	964	928	981	4,180	4,502	4,591	4,059	3,620	6,216	2
1,685	2,446	2,648	2,651	2,865	13,795	15,490	15,613	13,900	11,298	17,077	2
9,455	10,572	9,803	8,924	8,884	40,295	38,443	33,103	25,111	19,331	29,649	29
8,855	12,855	13,174	13,616	14,693	80,088	110,696	131,874	129,001	125,630	246,014	249
1,979	2,219	1,942	1,909	1,890	8,250	9,550	10,295	9,912	9,484	21,182	7
779	1,115	1,202	1,349	1,419	8,018	9,686	9,204	7,849	6,767	12,485	6
4,798	4,735	4,119	3,574	3,538	13,450	10,298	7,297	5,068	3,847	5,597	11
7,847	8,080	7,317	7,011	7,108	29,587	27,929	23,763	18,184	13,977	23,755	11

teachers and are presumably bringing up the next generation. It is true that young persons are arrested most frequently for theft of automobiles but most of these are taken for a joy ride, and police only arrest the "takers" in 25 percent of the cases. Adults do not approve of having their automobiles "borrowed without leave," but in many instances this a fairly accurate description of what has been done, at least in the minds of the boys who steal cars. Gangsters, on the other hand, steal cars for a quick getaway or they strip them of parts to be sold. Most cars are recovered by the police, chiefly because they are abandoned. Young adults 21 to 25 years old took less than 3000 of the 30,240 automobiles stolen in 1958.

But adults past 25 (who presumably should know better) commit some very serious crimes. They were in fact arrested for 74.3 percent of the murders and 69.1 percent of the manslaughter cases. They constituted 42 percent of those arrested for receiving stolen goods, 79.1 percent of those arrested for forgery and fraud, 66.1 percent of those arrested for counterfeiting. Those over 25 also scored heavily in arrests for sex and narcotic offenses and for drunkenness. They constituted 70.7 percent of the prostitution cases and 67.7 percent of arrests for other sex offenses. They were arrested for 64.9 percent of the narcotic cases and 85.3 percent of the cases for driving while intoxicated. Young persons are seldom arrested for being drunk. In fact 90.6 percent of such arrests were for persons past 25.[1]

So far as brutality and scheming crimes are concerned, adults make up a very significant group. They also probably constitute virtually all of the swindlers, racketeers, confidence men, and manipulators of "shady deals" who evade arrest. Why community leaders become so wrought up about juvenile offenders and indicate so little worry over adult crime is a topic which deserves detailed sociological research.

Criminal Law and the Offender

A crime is an act forbidden and punishable by law, but the fundamental tenets of criminal law are closely reasoned. Thus the legalist regards the criminal as one who has flouted the moral values of the group by doing something which is wrong. Because his act is wrong the person committing such, to be adjudged guilty, must (theoretically, at least) *know* he has done wrong. By the same token, if he does not know he has done wrong (and does not know the difference between right and wrong) he is not guilty. Thereby hangs the whole theory of criminal responsibility. The child who does not comprehend what he has done is not guilty. Likewise the person adjudged insane is not guilty, nor is the person ordinarily held responsible who commits an act by mistake. Thus a Long Island socialite was freed from blame when she shot her husband in the mistaken belief that he was a burglar. And a man who takes a hat not his own by mistake at the checkstand has not committed a crime.

Conflict Between Criminal Law and Psychiatry

The legal theory of criminality presumes that a criminal knowingly and willfully performs a forbidden act. With this theory many psychiatrists take issue, maintaining that men are often under compulsion to commit acts even when they know they are wrong. The English and American common law still holds in many jurisdictions to the "right and wrong" test laid down in the famous McNaghten case in England in 1843.[2] Dr. Roche has attempted to resolve the disparity between the legal reasoning and modern psychiatric

---

[1] These percentages were all computed by Miss Elliott from Table 18 in *Uniform Crime Reports, 1958,* Federal Bureau of Investigation, U.S. Department of Justice, Washington, 1959, p. 94.

[2] F. H. Bradley, "Anglo-American Philosophies of Penal Law," *Journal of Criminal Law and Criminology, 2:*186–198 (July, 1911).

theory by stressing the matter of responsibility. He maintains that psychiatrists cannot say whether a man knows the difference between right and wrong. They *can* differentiate between the normal person, who can exercise judgment and accept the dictates of common sense, and the mentally ill, for whom any "freedom of the will" is impossible. Nevertheless Dr. Roche holds that criminals are different from mental cases only in our attitude toward them.[3] Since the psychiatric viewpoint is widely accepted, such a belief constitutes an attitude in direct opposition to the social values incorporated in our criminal law. The lack of consensus toward criminals creates many problems in the administration of criminal law. There is grave need for all courts to alter their practice in line with modern psychology.

The psychiatrist who specializes in mental illness cannot harmonize his conception of mental disturbances with notions of right and wrong. He insists a person may know what is considered right but still be under a compulsion to commit a crime. Dr. Roche holds that psychiatrists should be asked to testify whether the accused is responsible for his behavior in the sense that he is susceptible to legal sanctions.[4] If he needs treatment, that too comes within the scope of the testimony.

Crime as a Situation

Human behavior is not a simple matter to analyze. It cannot be thrown on a screen or separated into its component parts in test tubes. When a man behaves acceptably in the eyes of his fellows he is played upon by many different impelling urges to activity. This we know. It is almost miraculous that he is so often courteous, kindly, and intelligent. When a man's conduct is adjudged "antisocial," his behavior differs from acceptable behavior chiefly in the group's definition of the situation. Technically, the criminal is one guilty of a criminal offense, but the nature and genesis of a given crime are more difficult to explain. In modern civilized society, a crime is an act forbidden by law which may be punished by death or by fine or by imprisonment in jail, workhouse, reformatory, or prison. Popular conception of a criminal is a mental construct of either a person whose entire behavior is subversive to group interests or one who is "guilty of moral turpitude." There are many offenses, however, for which heavy fines or imprisonment are exacted that are merely violations of city ordinances involving technical rather than willful misconduct.

At the same time, a general principal in law considers the intent of the offender and holds that any violation of the law must involve both an overt act and a culpable intent to commit such an act.[5] However, this principle is not universally in effect, as any motorist may testify who absent-mindedly ignores a stop sign and is dragged into court. Science, in the meantime, has provided

---

[3] Philip Q. Roche, *The Criminal Mind*, Farrar, Straus and Cudahy, Inc., New York, 1958, p. 29. Some courts have recently accepted this point of view.

[4] *Ibid.*, p. 273.

[5] Cf. William A. White, *Insanity and the Criminal Law*, The Macmillan Company, New York, 1923, pp. 17–19.

us with no very scientific techniques for determining motivations. In final analysis, every crime involves a situation and a social definition of that situation. A crime *ipso facto* implies a disturbance in a social relationship and a social definition as to what such a disturbance is. The nature of criminal or noncriminal conduct is determined by the social values which the larger defining group considers important. The attitudes of those who reject these values or who actively oppose their maintenance are defined as criminal. Agitators guilty of criminal syndicalism, men who have stolen a loaf of bread or absconded with funds, murderers, white slavers have all rejected social values in some degree. Since the criminal endangers the social values, steps are taken to coerce him into conformity by punishing him according to established rules or principles. These same principles likewise entail additional values on the part of the group—that is, some general consensus as to the reprehensibility of the person and the degree of seriousness of the offense.

The Criminal and Society

The criminal is in conflict with society by definition. Yet he may be very well adjusted to his own group, with which he has identified his own values and habit patterns. Within the intimate group of his associates the norm of conduct is set up. As a matter of fact, everyone tends to judge and justify his behavior by the standards of his own group. This is true of children, but it is equally true of adults and especially of criminals. Thus we have the basis for "honor among thieves," for the gangster's loyalty to his group. Contrary to popular opinion, criminals are not completely at odds with their culture. The vast majority of laws are accepted by criminal and noncriminal populations alike. Most criminals observe social regulations of modesty, obey the traffic laws, and conform to a thousand-odd restrictions which the group imposes on human conduct. Usually it is only in one particular respect that the criminal is a serious offender, viz., in his respect for private property.

Most of the criminal's conduct is learned conduct, as we shall discuss later. Not all groups within a body politic define conduct similarly. Conflicts within the culture bring conflicts as to acceptable conduct. In case of disparity in social definition, the enforced social values are the values of the dominant group. Some social values are almost universally accepted. Out of human experience, certain of these values and the rules and regulations pertaining to them have come to be regarded as more important than others. For example, murder, rape, burglary, and counterfeiting are all rather generally regarded as serious offenses. Other offenses vary with cultures. Social change alters conceptions of right and wrong. Social opinions change. The Volstead Act made the sale of liquor a penal offense. Its repeal made it a legal business pursuit. The increased regulation of banking has put bankers behind bars for conduct which was accepted thirty years ago. Political ideologies also affect crime. In the USSR, persons who oppose the existing regime are criminals of the worst sort. If their activities are detected there has usually been no recourse from the firing squad. In America, criticism of the governmental authorities has been a by-product of our freedom of press and freedom of speech.

Statistics in Crime

Trends in crime in the United States are based upon offenses known to the police in 2703 cities over 2500 in population. In 1958 the number of offenses increased over the estimated average for 1953–1957 by 26.2 per-cent.[6] This increase does not reflect the rise in population hence is propor-tionately distorted.[7] Between January 1, 1950, and November 1, 1958, the population in the United States increased by approximately 24,003,000 people, which is an increase of 15.9 percent over the 1950 census.[8] Hence viewed at its worst the growth of criminal offenses is not so great if related to the population increase. A 10 or 15 percent increase in crimes known to the police is at least partly attributable to better police methods.

Although many public officials speak dramatically about the rise in our crime rates, this may be an indication that crimes are better reported. Sta-tistics on crime are not very reliable for a number of reasons: (1) There are a great many crimes which are never reported, and no one knows how many are not reported. Certain crimes like auto theft and murder are fairly accurately reported, but a large number of major and minor crimes are not. It is true also that some crimes are reported which are never committed. People often imagine they have been robbed when they have misplaced or lost articles and later discover them. (2) There is no reason to suppose that the crimes reported bear a constant ratio to the crimes committed. Police reports are, however, generally regarded as more accurate evidence of the crime rate than arrests or convictions. (3) Prison statistics are an inaccurate basis for indicating crime rates in the various states, because some states have a well-developed probation program, and certain judges are more inclined to exact fines than to sentence a man for minor offenses. (4) Crime statistics until 1958 were not computed with reference to population ratios except for census years; hence an increase in the number of arrests or prisoners received may not indicate an increase in rate but an increase in numbers. (5) Legal definitions of crime change, and thus certain types of conduct become crimi-nal which were previously considered legal. All arrests and convictions at-tributable to the implementation of a new law can scarcely be evaluated as a great increase in the crime rate, but rather as a change in the definition of conduct. (6) Similarly, different states vary in their definitions of the same type of conduct. Some states classify as murder what other states call negligent manslaughter, and states which have prohibition laws make the selling of

[6] *Uniform Crime Reports, 1958,* p. 71.
[7] *Ibid.*
[8] Bureau of the Census, *Provisional Estimates of the Population of the United States, January 1, 1950, to November 1, 1958, Current Population Reports,* Series P-25, No. 191 (December 11, 1958), p. 1.

liquor a crime.[9] (7) Rural crime rates have been notoriously inaccurate and are not included in the 1958 rates for this reason. Better data will be available for later years.[10] Federal crimes likewise are not all reported in the same document and are hard to estimate.[11]

Uniform Crime Reports

Police statistics on crimes reported and arrests made have been gathered by the Federal Bureau of Investigation since 1930.[12] Since 1948 they have covered more than half the nation and have given a fairly accurate picture of the crime situation. But whether or not the police are alert may affect the rates two ways. They may report a greater percentage of the total crimes. They may also keep down the rate by their activity.

Beginning in 1958 crime indexes for the United States were computed for the first time according to population estimates for the particular year. The 1958 rates did not include Hawaii and Alaska, but Hawaii is included in the 1959 estimates and both are included in 1960 rates. In 1958 the crime index was also changed to include only the following categories: murder, forcible rape, robbery, aggravated assault, burglary, larceny over $50, and auto theft. The crime index thus does not consider the lesser offenses for which most persons are arrested but is limited to the more serious crimes.

As Table 5.2 shows, there was a percentage change of +7.4 in the crime

TABLE 5.2.   Crime Indexes According to Seven Major
Crimes for 1957 and 1958

Crime Index Classification	Number of Crimes per 100,000 Inhabitants		Percent Change
	1957	1958	
Total	835.2	896.9	+7.4
Murder	4.7	4.7	—
Forcible rape	7.6	8.4	+10.5
Robbery	39.3	43.5	+10.7
Aggravated assault	65.0	65.5	+0.8
Burglary	354.5	392.4	+10.7
Larceny over $50	208.4	226.0	+8.4
Auto theft	155.7	156.4	+0.4

SOURCE: *Uniform Crime Reports, 1958*, Federal Bureau of Investigation, U.S. Department of Justice, 1959, p. 3.

index classification in 1958 over that of 1957 when the population was corrected. In murder there was no increase and in auto thefts only a very small increase. Actually the 7.4 percent increase is not a significant increase and

[9] Thorsten Sellin, *Status and Prospects of Criminal Statistics in the United States,* Sartryck ur Svensk Juristtidning Fest Krift fir Karl Schlyter, Stockholm, 1949, pp. 295–302.

[10] *Uniform Crime Reports, 1958,* p. 16.

[11] Sellin, *op. cit.*

[12] Cf. *10 Years of Uniform Crime Reporting, 1930–1939*, Federal Bureau of Investigation, U.S. Department of Justice, Washington, 1939.

may be due to better reporting. There were 1,867,287 cases of crimes known to the police in 1958 in 2808 cities with a population of 89,921,615 persons. (These crimes included larcenies both for $50 and over and for under $50, however.) We may presume that a large number of offenses are not included in the figure cited because approximately half the population is not included. We cannot have an accurate picture of crime until there is some sort of legislation requiring all police officers to report all crimes known to them to a central agency.

Statistics on Prisoners

Statistics on prisoners show an uneven rise in number of persons confined to penal institutions during the last twenty years except for the temporary drop during 1942 to 1945 (see Table 5.3). This decline was chiefly a result of releasing men under sentence to army service. Since 1945 fewer men have been drafted and men under sentence have not been released to army duty.

The rate of commitment per 100,000 civilian population did not increase markedly after the war. (Presumably this circumstance is related to the generally good employment conditions.) The rate began to climb in 1953 but stayed more or less constant from 1953 to 1958, and has not equaled the rate in 1940.

The commitment-to-prison rate is of course no complete index to crime. It is a partial index to serious crimes, since ordinarily lesser offenses are released on warning, fine, and probation. Some serious crimes are released on probation if the offender has a good previous record. The practices with reference to prison commitment vary markedly depending upon the law, social attitudes, and the judge himself.

As Chart 5.1 shows, the number of persons sentenced to prison in 1958 ranged from 25 per 100,000 population in New Hampshire to 257 in the District of Columbia. Georgia has the highest rate of commitment of any state. Crime rates in the different states varied decidedly. New Hampshire had a relatively low crime rate (so far as the most serious offenses are concerned), with 405.5 offenses per 100,000 population in 1958. North Dakota had a lower rate (with 325.1 offenses per 100,000 population). California had the highest rate—1775.9 offenses per 100,000. Rhode Island had the relatively high rate of 1064.7 per 100,000. Only eleven states had a higher rate, in fact, but Rhode Island ranked next to New Hampshire in low commitments.[13] Obviously commitment to prison is determined by other factors than the crime rate. Nevertheless our crime rates are disturbing and warrant careful analysis.

The only crime statistics which have any degree of accuracy are those pertaining to cities. Figures for cities show considerable variation in the rate of increase when they were classified according to population. In the larger cities (over 250,000 population) the rates had the greatest increase in those

[13] *Uniform Crime Reports, 1958,* pp. 64 and 66.

TABLE 5.3. Sentenced Prisoners Received from Court and Present at End of Year, by Type of Institution, for the United States: 1939 to 1958

Year	Present at End of Year			Received from Court		
	All Institutions	Federal Institutions	State Institutions	All Institutions	Federal Institutions	State Institutions
	Number					
1958	205,643	21,549	184,094	88,780	13,803	74,977
1957	195,414	20,420	174,994	80,409	13,305	67,104
1956	189,565	20,134	169,431	77,869	13,454	64,415
1955	185,915	20,088	165,827	78,349	15,286	63,063
1954	182,901	20,003	162,898	80,796	16,685	64,111
1953	173,579	19,363	154,216	74,149	16,376	57,773
1952	168,233	18,014	150,219	70,845	15,305	55,540
1951	165,680	17,395	148,285	67,164	14,120	53,044
1950	166,165	17,134	149,031	69,515	14,237	55,278
1949	163,749	16,868	146,881	68,836	13,130	55,706
1948	155,977	16,328	139,649	63,696	12,430	51,266
1947	151,304	17,146	134,158	64,735	12,948	51,787
1946	140,079	17,622	122,457	61,302	14,950	46,352
1945	133,649	18,638	115,011	53,212	14,171	39,041
1944	132,356	18,139	114,217	50,162	14,047	36,115
1943	137,220	16,113	121,107	50,082	12,203	37,879
1942	150,384	16,623	133,761	58,858	13,725	45,133
1941	165,439	18,465	146,974	68,700	15,350	53,350
1940	173,706	19,260	154,446	73,104	15,109	57,995
1939	179,818	19,730	160,088	a	a	a
	Rate per 100,000 of the estimated civilian population[b]					
1958	120.0	12.6	107.4	51.8	8.1	43.7
1957	116.1	12.1	103.9	47.8	7.9	39.9
1956	114.7	12.2	102.5	47.1	8.1	39.0
1955	114.5	12.4	102.2	48.3	9.4	38.9
1954	115.0	12.6	102.4	50.8	10.5	40.3
1953	111.2	12.4	98.8	47.5	10.5	37.0
1952	109.7	11.7	97.9	46.2	10.0	36.2
1951	109.7	11.5	98.1	44.5	9.3	35.1
1950	110.6	11.4	99.2	46.3	9.5	36.8
1949	111.0	11.4	99.5	46.6	8.9	37.7
1948	107.4	11.2	96.2	43.9	8.6	35.3
1947	106.1	12.0	94.1	45.4	9.1	36.3
1946	101.2	12.7	88.5	44.3	10.8	33.5
1945	104.8	14.6	90.2	41.7	11.1	30.6
1944	104.5	14.3	90.1	39.6	11.1	28.5
1943	107.6	12.6	95.0	39.3	9.6	29.7
1942	114.8	12.7	102.2	44.9	10.5	34.5
1941	125.7	14.0	111.7	52.2	11.7	40.5
1940	131.9	14.6	117.3	55.5	11.5	44.0
1939	137.6	15.1	122.5	a	a	a

a Comparable data not available.

b Based on estimates of the civilian population for July 1 appearing in the Bureau of the Census publications: *Statistical Abstract of the United States: 1958*, table 2 for 1939, and *Current Population Reports*, P–25, No. 72, 1940–49; No. 165, 1950–55; No. 186, 1956–57; and No. 189 (provisional), 1958.

SOURCE: *Prisoners in State and Federal Institutions, 1958, National Prisoner Statistics,* Federal Bureau of Prisons, 1959, p. 4.

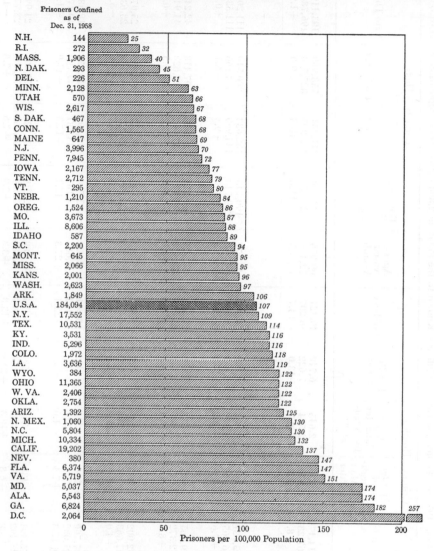

Prisoners Confined
as of
Dec. 31, 1958

State	Prisoners	per 100,000
N.H.	144	25
R.I.	272	32
MASS.	1,906	40
N. DAK.	293	45
DEL.	226	51
MINN.	2,128	63
UTAH	570	66
WIS.	2,617	67
S. DAK.	467	68
CONN.	1,565	68
MAINE	647	69
N.J.	3,996	70
PENN.	7,945	72
IOWA	2,167	77
TENN.	2,712	79
VT.	295	80
NEBR.	1,210	84
OREG.	1,524	86
MO.	3,673	87
ILL.	8,606	88
IDAHO	587	89
S.C.	2,200	94
MONT.	645	95
MISS.	2,066	95
KANS.	2,001	96
WASH.	2,623	97
ARK.	1,849	106
U.S.A.	184,094	107
N.Y.	17,552	109
TEX.	10,531	114
KY.	3,531	116
IND.	5,296	116
COLO.	1,972	118
LA.	3,636	119
WYO.	384	122
OHIO	11,365	122
W. VA.	2,406	122
OKLA.	2,754	122
ARIZ.	1,392	125
N. MEX.	1,060	130
N.C.	5,804	130
MICH.	10,334	132
CALIF.	19,202	137
NEV.	380	147
FLA.	6,374	147
VA.	5,719	151
MD.	5,037	174
ALA.	5,543	174
GA.	6,824	182
D.C.	2,064	257

Prisoners per 100,000 Population

CHART 5.1. Sentenced Prisoners Confined in State Institutions per 100,000 of the Civilian Population, December 31, 1958. (From *Prisoners in State and Federal Institutions, 1958, National Prisoner Statistics,* Federal Bureau of Prisons, 1959, p. 12.)

from 250,000 to 750,000, as Table 5.4 shows, and were lowest for those from 750,000 to 1,000,000 population. In five cities over 1,000,000 the rate was less than for those from 750,000 to a million in population, but the rate in these cities was higher than for all of the cities of 250,000 to 750,000.

The greatest increase in crime was in the places under 10,000 (12.5 percent) while the increase in places 10,000 to 25,000 was nearly as great (12.1 percent). It seems likely that crimes were better known to the police

TABLE 5.4. City Crime Trends, 1957–1958, by Population Groups (Offenses Known to the Police in 2,808 Cities, Total Population 89,921,615)

Population Group	Total	Criminal Homicide		Forcible Rape	Robbery	Aggravated Assault	Burglary, Breaking or Entering	Larceny—Theft		Auto Theft
		Murder and Nonnegligent Manslaughter	Manslaughter by Negligence					$50 and Over	Under $50	
Total:										
1957	1,714,179	3,750	2,645	6,748	49,421	69,976	382,320	247,231	758,969	193,119
1958	1,867,287	3,870	2,574	7,622	56,207	72,460	427,457	272,805	827,508	196,784
Percent change	**+8.9**	**+3.2**	**−2.7**	**+13.0**	**+13.7**	**+3.5**	**+11.8**	**+10.3**	**+9.0**	**+1.9**
GROUP I										
39 cities over 250,000; population, 35,436,745:										
1957	805,121	2,111	1,461	4,592	36,291	45,571	190,745	132,633	280,510	111,207
1958	866,565	2,216	1,370	5,069	40,956	47,540	209,748	144,969	303,166	111,531
Percent change	+7.6	+5.0	−6.2	+10.4	+12.9	+4.3	+10.0	+9.3	+8.1	+0.3
5 cities over 1,000,000; population, 17,909,957:										
1957	379,965	983	554	2,805[a]	20,836	27,425	97,171	80,528	107,418	42,245
1958	412,372	1,022	463	3,078	23,688	28,411	105,171	87,962	117,628	44,949
Percent change	+8.5	+4.0	−16.4	+9.7	+13.7	+3.6	+8.2	+9.2	+9.5	+6.4
6 cities 750,000 to 1,000,000; population, 5,133,258:										
1957	142,002	390	245	621[a]	6,600	9,379	25,849	15,387	58,453	25,078
1958	147,663	404	206	639	6,877	9,380[b]	29,131	16,257	61,139	23,630
Percent change	+4.0	+3.6	−15.9	+2.9	+4.2		+12.7	+5.7	+4.6	−5.8
9 cities 500,000 to 750,000; population, 5,311,311:										
1957	107,760	299	313	462[a]	3,661	2,878	25,706	12,497	43,056	18,888
1958	121,032	321	316	494	4,482	3,665	30,107	14,681	47,790	19,176
Percent change	+12.3	+7.4	+1.0	+6.9	+22.4	+27.3	+17.1	+17.5	+11.0	+1.5
19 cities 250,000 to 500,000; population, 7,082,219:										
1957	175,394	439	349	704[a]	5,194	5,889	42,019	24,221	71,583	24,996
1958	185,498	469	385	858	5,909	6,084	45,339	26,069	75,609	23,776
Percent change	+5.8	+6.8	+10.3	+21.9	+13.8	+3.3	+7.9	+7.6	+7.0	−4.9

GROUP II 78 cities, 100,000 to 250,000; population, 11,654,735:										
1957	258,869	524	395	625[a]	4,900	8,364	56,710	33,349	126,870	27,132
1958	284,709	533	422	737	5,733	8,705	63,971	36,594	139,046	28,968
Percent change	+10.0	+1.7	+6.8	+17.9	+17.0	+4.1	+12.8	+9.7	+9.6	+6.8
GROUP III 165 cities, 50,000 to 100,000; population, 11,227,353:										
1957	210,232	354	327	512[a]	3,398	6,181	45,225	29,640	104,383	20,212
1958	228,276	388	330	619	3,981	6,506	51,148	33,375	110,643	21,286
Percent change	+8.6	+9.6	+0.9	+20.9	+17.2	+5.3	+13.1	+12.6	+6.0	+5.3
GROUP IV 337 cities, 25,000 to 50,000; population, 11,823,796:										
1957	191,687	321	231	400[a]	2,223	4,246	38,346	24,460	105,422	16,038
1958	209,024	319	225	456	2,504	4,012	43,145	27,415	114,653	16,295
Percent change	+9.0	−0.6	−2.6	+14.0	+12.6	−5.5	+12.5	+12.1	+8.8	+1.6
GROUP V 741 cities, 10,000 to 25,000; population, 11,694,040:										
1957	162,911	293	137	351[a]	1,624	3,708	32,159	17,808	94,769	12,062
1958	182,645	240	127	425	1,960	3,764	37,632	19,615	106,666	12,216
Percent change	+12.1	−18.1	−7.3	+21.1	+20.7	+1.5	+17.0	+10.1	+12.6	+1.3
GROUP VI 1,448 cities under 10,000; population, 8,084,946:										
1957	85,359	147	94	268[a]	985	1,906	19,135	9,341	47,015	6,468
1958	96,068	174	100	316	1,073	1,933	21,813	10,837	53,334	6,488
Percent change	+12.5	+18.4	+6.4	+17.9	+8.9	+1.4	+14.0	+16.0	+13.4	+0.3

[a] Beginning in 1958 the rape category was limited to forcible offenses. Prior to 1958 statutory cases were also included. The 1957 rape figures shown are 50 percent of those reported since a special offense analysis furnished by 422 cities (total population 55,700,000) showed approximately half the reported rapes were forcible in 1957.

[b] Increase of less than one-tenth of 1 percent.

SOURCE: *Uniform Crime Reports, 1958*, Federal Bureau of Investigation, U.S. Department of Justice, 1959, pp. 69–70.

in smaller cities rather than that the rate was highest there. In large cities many corporations employ private police and try to keep down crime without reporting it to the authorities. Department stores, for example, budget their expenses to cover theft losses and seldom report minor thefts to the police.

Criminal Types

Classifications of criminals have been developed by various theorists. On the basis of his theory of the born criminal,[14] Lombroso advanced a classification in which the innate character of criminality was emphasized. He divided offenders into the born criminal (who he believed constituted the most important group), the insane and the epileptic, who were variations of the born type, the criminaloids or occasional criminals, and the criminals by passion. The occasional criminal was not marked by fate and morphology to a life of crime but because of circumstances developed criminal habits. Lombroso's theory of criminality has been completely disproved and his classification is no longer accepted.[15] Ferri made a similar classification except that he considered the habitual criminal a distinct type.[16] Garofalo held that such classifications ignored the psychological basis of human conduct and devised what he believed to be a more adequate classification, which included (1) typical criminals or murderers, (2) violent criminals, (3) criminals deficient in probity, and (4) lascivious criminals.[17]

Since these classifications appeared, numerous other attempts have been made to categorize criminals,[18] but none has been successful. More recent research and detailed study of the case histories of criminals and delinquents have convinced scientists that there is no validity in any such classification.[19] Every criminal is a unique person with unique roles in his group contacts. Intensive study of his background makes plain the individual character of his behavior. The only way we can safely classify criminals is on the basis of the offenses they have committed or the seriousness of the offenses. We can say that a man is a murderer, a thief, a burglar, a pickpocket, or a "confidence" man, or that he has committed a felony or a misdemeanor. Such classifications are logical but innocuous, and they afford no explanation whatsoever as to why men commit particular crimes. Only by analyzing all factors which might seem to have some bearing on criminal conduct can we reconstruct the motivations and stimuli to such behavior. Criminals have all broken the law. That is the significant fact which characterizes them as a group.

[14] Cf. Cesare Lombroso, *L'homme Criminel,* Paris, 1895.

[15] Cf. Lombroso, *Crime, Its Causes and Remedies* (translated by Henry P. Horton), Little, Brown and Company, Boston, 1911.

[16] Cf. Enrico Ferri, *Criminal Sociology,* Little, Brown and Company, Boston, 1917, part I, chap. 3.

[17] Raffaele Garofalo, *Criminology* (translated by Robert W. Millar), Little, Brown and Company, Boston, 1914, part II, chap. 1.

[18] Cf. Maurice Parmalee, *Criminology,* The Macmillan Company, New York, 1918, p. 198.

[19] Cf. William A. Healy, *The Individual Delinquent,* Little, Brown and Company, Boston, 1915.

The Differentiation of Prisoners by Type of Offense

A survey of Wisconsin prisoners conducted by Dr. Gillin and his graduate students classified the prisoners into three types: (1) sex offenders, (2) murderers, and (3) property offenders. Their study of 486 of a prison population of approximately 1700 has supplied us with some important information. The survey covered (1) all of the 128 sex offenders convicted of sodomy and rape, (2) 92 of the 108 men convicted of murder, and (3) 266 of the 933 property offenders. These prisoners were studied in detail and the recorded data in the files were supplemented by interviews and life histories written by the men.[20] In order to supplement these data they decided to interview law-abiding brothers of the prisoners and found 172 instances in which their brothers were available. From the material secured from all sources they concluded that there were fourteen significant differences between the two groups, as we summarize below. Some of these differences apply to persons committing specific types of offenses.[21] Certain of the conclusions verify other data discussed later in the chapter.

1. A significantly larger proportion of murderers left school at an early age than did their brothers.
2. Twenty-five percent of all prisoners went to work at an earlier age than their brothers; in case of murderers, 40.7 percent went to work earlier.
3. Prisoners thought they were their mother's favorites in 33.3 percent of the cases, in contrast to 9.9 percent of their brothers. However, in case of sex offenders there was no such disparity.[22]
4. Prisoners consistently had greater appreciation for their mothers than was true of their brothers. In the case of murderers, 87.5 percent had greater appreciation for their mothers than did their brothers.[23]
5. All prisoners held jobs for shorter times than their brothers; 75.1 percent of the brothers held jobs for longer than a year, whereas only 56 percent of the prisoners had done so. Sex offenders, however, had no such difficulties holding jobs.[24]
6. Fewer prisoners (15.8 percent) were farmers, in contrast to 26.4 percent of their brothers. However, the percentage of farmers for both murderers and their brothers was higher. Property offenders tended to be from the skilled trades more frequently than their brothers.[25]
7. Property offenders had more job turnovers than their brothers.[26]
8. A large percentage of prisoners (46.3 percent) had never married, in contrast to 27.3 percent of their non-prisoner brothers.[27]

[20] John L. Gillin, *The Wisconsin Prisoner,* University of Wisconsin Press, Madison, 1946, pp. 4–5.
[21] *Ibid.,* pp. 21–25.
[22] *Ibid.;* cf. also Table 49 in *The Wisconsin Prisoner.*
[23] *Ibid.;* cf. also Table 50 in this reference.
[24] *Ibid.;* cf. also Table 51 in this reference.
[25] *Ibid.;* cf. also Table 52 in this reference.
[26] *Ibid.,* and Tables 53 and 54 in this reference.
[27] *Ibid.,* and Table 55 in this reference.

9. Divorce and separation rates were much higher for prisoners (27.5 percent), in contrast to 4 percent of the non-prisoner brothers. Marital conflict was thought to be a factor in the prisoners' criminal conduct.[28]

10. Marital discord characterized 54 percent of the prisoners and only 8.9 percent of their brothers. Eighteen of the ninety-two murderers had killed their wives.[29]

11. Greater educational disparities existed between prisoners and their wives than was true of the brothers and their brothers' wives. This was thought to be a further factor in disharmony.[30]

12. A larger proportion of prisoners (40.9 percent) than their brothers (24 percent) married women of different nationalities. Cultural differences were regarded as possible sources of friction.[31]

13. Religious differences between prisoners and their wives existed in 40.5 percent of the cases, in contrast to 11.9 percent of the brothers and their spouses. This was also regarded as a source of emotional conflict.[32]

14. In the case of property offenders, prisoners married women from a higher economic status than their own in 23.2 percent of the cases, in contrast to 4.9 percent of their brothers. Gillin holds that this may have been a factor in marital disharmony.[33] It seems more likely that it was a factor in inducing prisoners to keep up to the economic standards of their wives.

From all this information Gillin and his assistants concluded that the brothers of prisoners had seldom had their economic security, their emotional satisfaction, or their personal safety thwarted or threatened to the same extent as had the prisoners. The prisoners had been participants in situations which undermined their egos and destroyed their self-esteem far oftener than the non-prisoner brothers. The authors believe that persons dealing with young delinquents—teachers and others responsible for developing youthful personalities—should recognize their important role in helping individuals to make an acceptable place for themselves.[34]

White-Collar Criminals

Most of what we know about criminals applies to a small part of the criminal group, i.e., the criminals who are serving sentence for crimes committed. These are the only offenders whose personal characteristics have been available for detailed study and whose record of lawlessness has been open to inspection. Most thoughtful persons concerned about crime have known for a long time that so-called law-abiding and respected citizens also commit offenses which the law defines as criminal. All have known of both peccadilloes and serious offenses which were never reported or punished, but only recently

---

[28] *Ibid.*, and Table 56 in this reference.
[29] *Ibid.*, and Table 57 in this reference.
[30] *Ibid.*, and Table 58 in this reference.
[31] *Ibid.*, and Table 59 in this reference.
[32] *Ibid.*, and Table 60 in this reference.
[33] *Ibid.*, and Table 61 in this reference.
[34] *Ibid.*, pp. 198–199.

have there been any reliable data to indicate the extent of these hidden and unpunished offenses.

In 1939 Dr. Sutherland held that there were two types of criminals: (1) the lower-class criminals derived chiefly from the underprivileged economic and social classes, whose behavior is condemned and punished by law; (2) the "white-collar" criminals who have broken laws so extensively and of such a nature as to indicate they are serious offenders. The latter have even manipulated laws and subverted the purposes of government to their own advantage, but their behavior has seldom resulted in prison sentences or social rejection. In fact, they have often been elevated to high places and have dictated or influenced the policies of governments. These criminals he called "white-collar criminals" because they are for the most part in the upper socioeconomic class.[35] "White-collar crime" Sutherland defined as "a crime committed by a person of respectability and high social status in the course of his occupation."

Following this Sutherland conducted a detailed and extensive study of the problem as represented in the illegal activities of seventy of the largest manufacturing, mining, and mercantile corporations in America.[36] He also conducted a special study of fifteen power and light corporations. His published material does not expose the corporations by name but refers to each by number because he was constrained to be fair and objective in his analysis of their illegal activities.[37] The record of each corporation was checked to determine the number of violations of laws with reference to: (1) restraint of trade; (2) misrepresentation in advertising; (3) infringement of patents, trademarks, and copyrights; (4) unfair labor practices (as defined by the National Labor Relations Act and other laws); (5) financial fraud and violation of trust; and (6) violations of war regulations and other offenses.[38]

Sutherland discovered that 980 decisions were made by the courts and commissions against the corporations, in which they were held guilty of violating these various laws. Each corporation averaged fourteen violations. Two corporations were guilty of fifty violations, and in eighteen of them the verdicts were rendered by criminal courts. In the other instances the verdicts were rendered by civil courts or by commissions.[39] All told, 158 or approximately 16 percent of the verdicts were rendered by criminal courts. Sutherland maintained, however, that in all of the 980 cases the corporations were tried for behavior considered socially harmful by the state and for which it may require penalties. He made a detailed analysis of the character of the laws violated and the penalties attached and concludes that the behavior prohibited is es-

[35] Edwin H. Sutherland, "White Collar Criminality," *American Sociological Review,* 5:1–12 (February, 1940). This was Dr. Sutherland's presidential address to the American Sociological Society in December, 1939.

[36] Edwin H. Sutherland, *White Collar Crime,* The Dryden Press, Inc., New York, 1949.

[37] *Ibid.,* chap. 2.

[38] *Ibid.*

[39] *Ibid.*

sentially criminal in nature.[40] Executives of corporations may thus appropriate huge bonuses for themselves while the stockholders receive no dividends. Financial affairs may be publicly misrepresented in annual reports.[41] False statements may be made in advertising.[42]

Many corporations violated war regulations by tax evasion, restraint of trade in war material, and violation of embargoes. One concern was convicted of fraud in securing scarce materials for an air-conditioning apparatus, allegedly for a company hospital but actually for an exclusive country club. There is documentary evidence to the effect that many corporations traded in the war primarily for extraordinary profits, even though they wanted to win the war at the same time.[43]

The fifteen public utilities investigated were also found guilty on many counts. There were twenty adverse decisions by criminal and civil courts against these corporations and eighteen settlements without decision. In addition, 386 orders were made by public utility commissions because of presumed attempted fraud or false pretenses. A frequent device of public utility companies is to establish holding companies with subsidiary operating companies in order to increase costs to consumers and earnings for the holding companies. By establishing a series of fictitious costs, they can often raise utility rates, thus defrauding consumers. As a group, the utility companies have spent great sums in advertising in an attempt to create a favorable opinion of themselves. Since 1935, according to Sutherland, utility corporations have been forced to operate on a much higher plane than previously. Nevertheless, the public interest is by no means safe, in Sutherland's estimation.[44]

"Our Law Abiding Law Breakers"

We have already mentioned the research of Porterfield and Murphy with reference to the hidden delinquencies of juveniles and young persons. Impressed by these findings, James S. Wallerstein and Clement J. Wyle of the Randen Foundation in New York City devised a questionnaire listing forty-nine offenses covered by the categories given below. It was submitted to a cross section of the population representing a balanced proportion of racial and religious groups. These persons were asked to indicate whether they had committed any of the offenses in the following categories.[45]

Malicious mischief
Disorderly conduct
Assault
Auto misdemeanors
Health law violations

[40] *Ibid.,* chap. 3.
[41] *Ibid.,* chap. 9.
[42] *Ibid.,* chap. 7.
[43] *Ibid.,* chap. 10.
[44] *Ibid.,* chap. 12.
[45] James S. Wallerstein and Clement J. Wyle, *Our Law Abiding Law Breakers,* reprint from *Probation,* April, 1947, p. 4.

Indecency
Gambling
Larceny
Burglary and possession of burglar's tools
Robbery and illegal possession of firearms
Bribery
Perjury
Falsification and fraud
Election frauds
Tax evasion
Coercion and extortion
Conspiracy and compounding a crime
Criminal libel
(Murder was not included in the categories.)

Answers to the questionnaire were received from 1698 persons (1020 men and 678 women). Of these, 91 percent admitted that they had committed offenses after they were sixteen years old (under this age all offenses in New York are regarded as juvenile delinquencies). A partial list of the offenses as given in the summary showed the respective percentages of men and women committing them to be as shown in Table 5.5.

The people answering the questionnaire were businessmen, lawyers, teachers, social workers, scientists, physicians, clergymen, sales and office workers,

TABLE 5.5.   Percentage of 1020 Men and 678 Women
Committing Specific Offenses

	Percent Men	Percent Women
Malicious mischief	84	81
Disorderly conduct	85	76
Assault	49	5
Auto misdemeanors	61	39
Indecency	77	74
Gambling	74	54
Larceny	89	83
Grand larceny (except auto)	13	11
Auto theft	26	8
Burglary	17	4
Robbery	11	1
Concealed weapons	35	3
Perjury	23	17
Falsification and fraud	46	34
Election frauds	7	4
Tax evasion	57	40
Coercion	16	6
Conspiracy	23	7
Criminal libel	36	29

SOURCE: James S. Wallerstein and Clement J. Wyle, *Our Law Abiding Law Breakers*, reprint from *Probation*, April, 1947, p. 4.

military and government employees, mechanics and technicians, farmers, laborers, housewives, and students. As analyzed, businessmen and lawyers committed the highest number of offenses involving perjury, falsification, fraud, and tax evasion. Teachers and social workers ranked highest in malicious mischief; writers and artists were highest in indecency, criminal libel, and gambling; military and government employees had the highest rate of simple larceny; mechanics and technicians were most frequently guilty of disorderly conduct, presumably involving sex offenses; farmers most frequently admitted illegal possession of weapons; laborers ranked highest in larceny, burglary, and robbery; and students most frequently committed auto misdemeanors, presumably involving traffic violations.

These persons reported circumstances which seemed to them to justify their conduct, but we must remember that most convicted criminals believe they "had to" commit the offense which led to their punishment. In the instances covered by the questionnaire survey the offenders were not punished. These people were respectable members of society who committed lawless acts and yet became prominent scientists, leading teachers, social workers, and physicians. The authors conclude it was sheer accident that the persons did not suffer arrest and conviction, although it is more likely that their status in the group kept them from being reported, arrested, and convicted. What is even more important is that they are now leading worthy lives in the community, whereas the persons condemned by society have usually been seriously damaged by the stigma of court and prison experience.[46] The question we must face is: How would the lower-class criminals turn out if they were not convicted? Would there be any organizing force in their lives which would make them respected members of the group?

Social Disorganization and Crime

From his detailed analysis of white-collar crime, Sutherland concluded that most of the factors which seem to characterize the criminal are not the factors basic to his criminality. Sutherland maintained that from a personal point of view criminals are criminals because of their differential association with others so that they become initiated into criminal activities. From the point of view of society, however, he felt that it is social disorganization which explains crime. Social disorganization, as we have suggested in Chapter 2, occurs because of (1) lack of standards, or *anomie* as Durkheim expressed it, and (2) organized attempts on the part of certain groups to oppose specific rules or practices.[47]

In American industrial and economic organization, free, unregulated business enterprise has been the traditional "folklore of capitalism," although we are advancing further and further into a controlled economy. There is, however, no consensus that this is the desirable direction. The highly organized nature of modern business makes it possible for businessmen to violate regu-

[46] *Ibid.*
[47] Cf. Sutherland, *White Collar Crime,* chap. 14.

lations without loss of prestige, because the state is not effectively organized to promote the acceptability of the new laws and to create favorable public opinion toward their enforcement.[48] Part of the difficulty stems from the relatively few able people in key positions in government, the lack of funds for propagandizing the new directions of our legislation, and the fact that business owns virtually all of the media for communication.

Although society tends to wink at white-collar crimes, it is important for students to recognize that all types of crimes, upper class and lower class alike, are evidences of social disorganization, of attitudes basically antisocial, of definitions of the situation which are concerned exclusively with the financial emolument of individuals rather than with social well-being.

Dr. Harry Elmer Barnes says that need and greed explain most crimes.[49] One can find good arguments for his point of view. Since material success forms so large a part of prestige in the modern world, both white-collar and lower-class criminals generally have a distinct desire to gratify their economic wants or desires. For the poverty-stricken youngster who lives in a "delinquency area," the gang to which he belongs provides the educational process by which he becomes familiar with the techniques of crime. For the college graduate who becomes the white-collar criminal, business and professional associates are the mentors. The rewards for unethical behavior afford many temptations. Such men build homes in the best neighborhoods and acquire a comfortable fortune through shoddy merchandise, illegal operations, and legal assistance to criminals. Chances of detection are not great. By and large, criminals who get caught are only a small share of the criminal group.

Yet even here there is confusion in values. Certain offenses are condemned irrespective of who commits them. If a banker murders his wife, he will probably suffer the full penalty. If a doctor commits an unsuccessful abortion and the unwilling mother dies, he may go to prison. The gradations between respectability and condemnability are ill defined and often distort social conceptions of crime. All offenders come to accept the values of the group with which they are associated and to look upon their behavior as a necessary means to a desired end. The crime becomes the only possible way of getting what they want. The techniques of criminality are taught them by their associates. *Economic behavior is learned behavior*. The young man who first enters a business or profession may have ethical scruples against evasions of the law or dubious practices. Eventually, however, his desire for financial gain and social prestige may influence him to accept the philosophy of his associates. Business is business. The average person is actively interested in promoting social welfare only when there is extreme pressure to do so, or when he has had some consistent education in social values. Attitudes of cooperation must also be learned.

On the other hand, social prestige and cultural advantage have become so

[48] *Ibid.*

[49] Harry Elmer Barnes, *Society in Transition*, Prentice-Hall, Inc., New York, 1939, p. 677.

closely identified with wealth that wealth is more or less assumed to be necessary to social rank. It then follows that the illegal economic activities of the
upper social classes are not likely to be severely condemned by society as a
whole or by law-enforcing bodies. This is easily explained. The upper social
groups have prestige. They are articulate, the leaders and the creators of public opinion. We thus have far too few public records of the white-collar criminals. Our detailed analysis of criminals must be restricted to one group, the
convicted prisoners. But we must continually keep in mind that the social disorganization in the upper classes is at least partially responsible for the social
disorganization among the lower group.

Legal Classifications of Crime

On the basis of offense, criminals are classified as felons or misde-
meanants. In general a misdemeanant is one who has committed a petty
offense which is punishable by fine or by imprisonment in a local jail. The
term "felon," on the other hand, has been applied to those guilty of the more
serious offenses punishable by death or by imprisonment in a state or federal
penitentiary. However, analysis of the criminal codes of the various states
indicates no unanimity as to the definition of felonious conduct. Murder, it is
true, is universally regarded as a serious offense. But many acts are classified
as misdemeanors in some states and as felonies in others. States occasionally
pass laws changing an act from one classification to another for the purpose
of repressing such conduct. Likewise, the recent wave of habitual-offender
laws has made the third or fourth misdemeanor felonious. All in all, much confusion exists as to what is and what is not a serious crime. Social definitions
vary in different states and nations. New political ideologies have created
new categories of crime, as the Communist-dominated countries now witness.
The same was true of the Fascist countries before World War II. Today the
South has made opposition to segregation laws a crime in several states!

Selective Factors in Criminality

Although Sutherland concluded that personality traits do not explain
crime satisfactorily, there are nevertheless certain factors which seem to characterize persons convicted of crime. It also seems likely that many of these
factors, personal and otherwise, may have led to the differential association
which in turn induced them to engage in criminal activities. This is probably
especially true of those who become repeaters. Differential association may
even be a factor in preventing our "law abiding law breakers" from becoming
confirmed criminals.

It would be impossible to enumerate all the topics which have been studied
with reference to their relation to crime. Students have sought for a single
cause, without regard for the diverse and varied motivations of human behavior.

Prima facie it is a little absurd to think all criminality is due to one specific
cause. Nevertheless criminologists, sociologists, psychologists, anthropologists,
biologists, theologians, and philosophers have often tried to establish the im-

portant one cause of crime. Thus willful opposition to the law of the land, a disorganizing environment, emotional disturbances, cultural conditioning, biological characteristics, sin, "natural law," and many other single alleged causes of crime have been advanced. Any cause which purports to offer an all-embracing but simple explanation is in a sense no explanation. It is either so broad that it requires further explanation or so specific that it does not cover many of the cases. Life is complex and so is behavior. The specific reasons that cause a man to snatch a woman's purse, another to fail to list all his income on his income tax report, and another to shoot his wife arise out of different motivations. A narcotic addict may steal a purse to obtain heroin, a small businessman may not report all of his income because he resents the high tax rate, a man may shoot his wife because he thinks she has a lover. Yet all in a sense reflect social disorganization in their conduct. The addict may have been introduced to the habit by a person whose aim it is to secure enormous returns on the illicit drug traffic (thus there is disorganization at the heart of the situation). Similarly there is disorganization when a sizable share of men believe they can suitably refrain from reporting all their income. And the murderer may have little regard for the moral value that life is sacred and to be protected. In this sense there is an overall cause. But even so, social disorganization is too broad a category to explain all crimes.

But to search for an explanation of crime in a single bodily type or mental, emotional, educational, or class characteristic is on the surface ridiculous. Some murderers are thin, others are fat. Some thieves are stupid, others are crafty. Some criminals are emotionally disturbed, others are cool and collected. A few criminals are highly educated, although most are not. Some criminals are wealthy, but not many. A few criminals are upper class; most are not. The fact that some men are criminals who do not have low economic status, bad family background, and low mental ability makes it evident that these are not the *sine qua non* of criminal conduct, even though all three have high incidence among criminals. These three characteristics seem to be important in affecting the crimes which make up the crime index. Certain criminals do not fit into these categories, notably those whom Sutherland called white-collar criminals, as discussed above.

The research of Healy and Bronner,[50] Cyril Burt,[51] and others has established the complex source of delinquent behavior patterns. Significant as their findings are, they stop short of considering the total situation or the factors in interrelationship. The factors in relation to the whole, rather than the sum of the single isolated factors, must be considered in any satisfactory analysis. Concretely, a bad home plus a bad neighborhood plus a poor educational background plus bad companions do not produce delinquency. Rather, from the bad home situated in a bad neighborhood a handicapped child goes forth into the crowded city streets for his recreational activities, meets up with bad

[50] *Delinquents and Criminals, Their Making and Unmaking,* The Macmillan Company, New York, 1928.
[51] *The Young Delinquent,* Appleton-Century-Crofts, Inc., New York, 1925.

companions, and is educated in a particular variety of misconduct. All have affected his differential association.

The behavior is thus a resultant of all the forces impinging upon the individual plus the characteristics of his personality. Consequently, in our analysis of the selective factors in adult criminality we shall have to bear in mind continually that the various categories—age, sex, marital status, intelligence, residence, etc.—are not important as single items. The peculiar complications which each factor lends to the whole establishes its particular role in the life organization of the individual. No one knows to what degree each factor operates. There are many imponderables in human behavior which do not lend themselves to precise measurement.

For purposes of abstract analysis, we shall separate these factors into (1) physical and developmental, (2) psychological, and (3) environmental factors. By the very nature of human existence, each is affected by the others and cannot be effectively isolated. With these limitations in mind, we may consider the various factors.[52]

PHYSICAL AND DEVELOPMENTAL FACTORS

Age

As we have already said, persons under 21 commit a sizable number of offenses. Nevertheless, as Table 5.6 shows, persons under 21 commit less than one-sixth of the crimes. *Most serious offenders are under 40, however.*

TABLE 5.6. Number and Percentage of Arrests of Persons Under 18, Under 21, and Under 25 Years of Age, 1958; 1,586 Cities over 2,500, Total Population 52,329,497

Offense Charged	Number of Persons Arrested				Percentage		
	Total	Under 18	Under 21	Under 25	Under 18	Under 21	Under 25
Total	2,340,004	284,215	460,015	685,654	12.1	19.7	29.3
Criminal homicide:							
(a) Murder and nonnegligent manslaughter	2,303	130	317	593	5.6	13.8	25.7
(b) Manslaughter by negligence	1,166	78	202	358	6.7	17.3	30.7
Robbery	14,968	3,415	6,496	9,429	22.8	43.4	63.0
Aggravated assault	25,824	2,340	4,599	8,016	9.1	17.8	31.0
Other assaults	82,454	6,521	13,578	25,543	7.9	16.5	31.0
Burglary—breaking or entering	61,045	30,460	39,709	46,766	49.9	65.0	76.6
Larceny—theft	118,325	57,389	72,051	82,418	48.5	60.9	69.7
Auto theft	30,240	19,386	23,982	26,369	64.1	79.3	87.2
Embezzlement and fraud	19,489	477	1,529	3,924	2.4	7.8	20.1
Stolen property; buying, receiving, etc.	5,504	1,700	2,510	3,195	30.9	45.6	58.0

[52] We purposely refrain from speaking of these factors as "causal," since the theory of causation involves establishing definite antecedence.

TABLE 5.6 (*Continued*)

Offense Charged	Number of Persons Arrested				Percentage		
	Total	Under 18	Under 21	Under 25	Under 18	Under 21	Under 25
Forgery and counterfeiting	11,317	767	1,950	3,840	6.8	17.2	33.9
Forcible rape	3,680	682	1,509	2,249	18.5	41.0	61.1
Prostitution and commercialized vice	17,482	195	1,431	5,104	1.1	8.2	29.2
Other sex offenses (includes statutory rape)	24,517	4,267	6,826	10,364	17.4	27.8	42.3
Narcotic drug laws	9,863	376	1,447	3,459	3.8	14.7	35.1
Weapons; carrying, possessing, etc.	18,611	3,072	5,522	8,494	16.5	29.7	45.6
Offenses against family and children	23,701	291	1,799	5,345	1.2	7.6	22.6
Liquor laws	52,707	9,494	21,565	25,537	18.0	40.9	48.5
Driving while intoxicated	102,219	618	4,434	15,044	.6	4.3	14.7
Disorderly conduct	281,997	27,765	57,853	96,036	9.8	20.5	34.1
Drunkenness	908,957	7,748	31,067	85,405	.9	3.4	9.4
Vagrancy	88,351	4,588	11,711	19,671	5.2	13.3	22.3
Gambling	61,546	575	2,446	7,531	.9	4.0	12.2
Suspicion	96,740	17,589	35,206	51,172	18.2	36.4	52.9
All other offenses	276,998	84,292	110,276	139,792	30.4	39.8	50.5

SOURCE: *Uniform Crime Reports, 1958*, Federal Bureau of Investigation, U.S. Department of Justice, 1959, p. 94.

As Table 5.7 shows, prisoners tend to be concentrated in the group 20 to 39 years old, but decline significantly with age 25 and each successive five-year group. As Chart 5.2 shows, the median age of prisoners for 1950 was 27.3 years. Criminals tend to taper off in criminal activity with middle age.

TABLE 5.7. Male Felons Received from Court in All State and Federal Institutions Except Georgia and Michigan in 1950

Age	Number
14 and under 15	15
15–19	7,085
20–24	15,426
25–29	11,299
30–34	7,205
35–39	5,234
40–44	3,752
45–54	4,016
55–64	1,244
65 and over	349

Median age: 27.3

SOURCE: Derived from Table 32, *Prisoners in State and Federal Institutions, 1950, National Prisoner Statistics*, Federal Bureau of Prisons, 1954, p. 64.

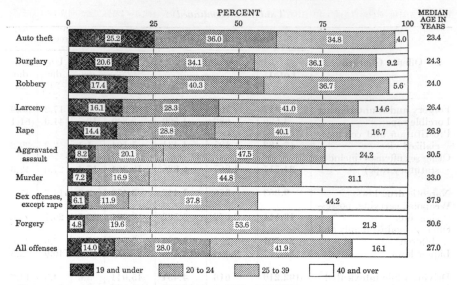

CHART 5.2. Percent by Age Groups of Male Felony Prisoners Received from Court in State Institutions for Selected Offenses, 1950. (From *Prisoners in State and Federal Institutions, 1950, National Prisoner Statistics,* Federal Bureau of Prisons, 1954, p. 23.)

This the Gluecks attribute to maturation. Their follow-up studies show that the criminal activities of 510 offenders declined during three successive five-year periods, and that many turned from serious to lesser offenses.[53]

Dr. von Hentig believes that the aggressive criminality of youth grows out of the strong primitive instinct to rid oneself of parental controls at puberty. This von Hentig attributes to a deep-seated demand of nature that all incestuous relations be avoided. The organic repulsion which the young persons manifest toward their parents they also direct toward all organized groupings. In the process, they establish new groupings for mutual protection, which are often lawless ones like the gang.[54]

An important survey of the role of youth in crime was made earlier by Dorothy Williams Burke and published by the United States government in 1930. Very little other detailed material concerning older minors is available. We know that a surprising number of youthful prisoners are under twenty-one, but actually little is known of the nether world between juvenile delinquency and adult criminality. The methods of dealing with this group vary so much from state to state that no accurate information is available. Data for the number of prisoners over eighteen in the United States were published at irregular intervals between 1904 and 1923, and since that time all data for

[53] Sheldon and Eleanor Glueck, *Criminal Careers in Retrospect,* The Commonwealth Fund, New York, 1943, pp. 118–119 and 121–122.

[54] Hans von Hentig, *Crime: Causes and Conditions,* McGraw-Hill Book Company, Inc., New York, 1947, pp. 140–145.

age groups are for commitments rather than for total prison population.[55]

Chicago was a pioneer not only in developing the juvenile court but also in establishing a Boys' Court for post-juvenile offenders between seventeen and twenty years of age in 1914. Miss Burke analyzed records of 909 boys brought before this court for the years 1915 to 1925 and found that three-fifths of the cases were under nineteen. Sixty-seven percent of these were repeaters but only 20 percent had been official juvenile court cases. Since the unofficial cases are technically not cases with a record, we have no way of knowing how many belonged to this category. In any event, 48 percent of those with juvenile court records had been committed to juvenile institutions,[56] which are notoriously unsuccessful in dealing with delinquents.

Many of these boys came from backgrounds of poverty and broken homes, had unsympathetic parents, had been members of gangs, were mentally dull or emotionally unstable. On the other hand, a large number were from good homes, with fair education and a promising vocational adjustment. Their difficulties could be ascribed essentially to adolescence. The boys convicted of felonious charges and sentenced to prisons and reformatories were with few exceptions, however, young men with long records of petty delinquencies.[57] A socialized program for dealing with such offenders would seemingly entail greater emphasis upon the need for breaking down established habit patterns and treating the boy in the light of his personality problems.

Clifford R. Shaw's research covers several noteworthy illustrations of the cumulative development of antisocial habit patterns which begin in minor behavior problems of socially handicapped boys and end behind the bars of the prison cell.

In his *Natural History of a Delinquent Career,* the life story of a nineteen-year-old prisoner is presented.[58] Sidney Blotzman, at the age of sixteen years and eight months, was arrested on the charge of rape and sentenced to the state reformatory for twenty years. This incident marked the culmination of a long series of offenses; his delinquent career started at the age of seven when he first began pilfering fruit from neighborhood stands. Sidney *learned how* to steal from older boys who attended the same school. In his own words, "between going to school and stealing, I chose stealing," and at the age of eight and a half he was sent to the Chicago Parental School. Released, he again fell in with the boy gangsters of his neighborhood. The home situation was far from happy. Both parents were Polish Jews. The father was continually drunk, deserted his family periodically, shirked his financial responsibilities. He had been arrested on separate charges of nonsupport, desertion, and beating his wife and children. The mother was industrious but timid, nervous, and worried. She tried to abide by the traditions of the Orthodox Jewish religion. The

[55] Cf. Dorothy Williams Burke, *Youth and Crime,* Children's Bureau Publication No. 196, U.S. Department of Labor, Washington, 1930, p. 1.

[56] *Ibid.*

[57] *Ibid.,* p. 28.

[58] Clifford R. Shaw, *The Natural History of a Delinquent Career,* University of Chicago Press, Chicago, 1931.

specific neighborhood in which Sidney lived is generally regarded as one of the worst in Chicago and it has also had one of the worst delinquency rates in the city.

Sidney was sent again to the Parental School, was released, and ran off to New York. His subsequent career was one of repeated instances of stealing. With the other boys he began to steal things which were the natural possessions of boys in better circumstances—articles of clothing, watches, bicycles. Eventually he was sentenced to St. Charles, and when he was again released he established contacts with an older and more highly organized boys' gang. His conduct became bolder and bolder. Finally, in company with another, he attacked and raped a girl. His companion, who was equally guilty, escaped. Sidney was found guilty of a heinous offense. Society must recognize, however, that his behavior traits developed in an undesirable social and cultural milieu. His criminal behavior was the natural development of the successive life situations in which he found himself. In his small social world his behavior conformed adequately. The conflict arose between the values of his group and those of society.

Sex

Most criminals, both those arrested and those serving sentences, are men. This is illustrated strikingly in the figures for arrest, as shown in Table 5.9, and in the number of persons in state and federal penal institutions, as given in Table 5.8. Men are arrested over sixty-four times as often as women (women constitute about 16 percent of the arrests) and are sentenced to state and federal penal institutions approximately twenty-five times as often. This is chiefly because women commit relatively few of the very serious offenses.

TABLE 5.8.   Comparative Number of Male and Female Prisoners Confined in State and Federal Prisons

Prisoners Present	Total	Male	Female
	All Institutions		
January 1, 1958	195,414	188,113	7,301
December 31, 1958	205,643	198,208	7,435
	Federal Institutions		
January 1, 1958	20,420	19,678	742
December 31, 1958	21,549	20,774	775
	State Institutions		
January 1, 1958	174,994	168,435	6,559
December 31, 1958	184,094	177,434	6,660

SOURCE: *Prisoners in State and Federal Institutions, 1958, National Prisoner Statistics,* No. 20, Federal Bureau of Prisons, July, 1959, Table 2.

What is the reason for women's lower propensity for crime? Many have believed it was due to the fact that women did not enter into the economic and competitive world. Now, however, a large number of women are in the labor market but women's crime rates have not gone up noticeably. Women

TABLE 5.9. Distribution of Arrests by Sex, 1958; 1,586 Cities Over 2,500, Total Population 52,329,497

Offense Charged	Number			Percent		
	Total	Male	Female	Total	Male	Female
Total	2,340,004	2,091,565	248,439	100.0	100.0	100.0[a]
Criminal homicide:						
(a) Murder and nonnegligent manslaughter	2,303	1,844	459	.1	.1	.2
(b) Manslaughter by negligence	1,166	1,055	111	[b]	.1	
Robbery	14,968	14,296	672	.6	.7	.3
Aggravated assault	25,824	21,769	4,055	1.1	1.0	1.6
Other assaults	82,454	74,562	7,892	3.5	3.6	3.2
Burglary—breaking or entering	61,045	59,572	1,473	2.6	2.8	.6
Larceny—theft	118,325	101,346	16,979	5.1	4.8	6.8
Auto theft	30,240	29,282	958	1.3	1.4	.4
Embezzlement and fraud	19,489	16,709	2,780	.8	.8	1.1
Stolen property; buying, receiving, etc	5,504	5,078	426	.2	.2	.2
Forgery and counterfeiting	11,317	9,612	1,705	.5	.5	.7
Forcible rape	3,680	3,680	—	.2	.2	—
Prostitution and commercialized vice	17,482	5,412	12,070	.7	.3	4.9
Other sex offenses (includes statutory rape)	24,517	19,595	4,922	1.0	.9	2.0
Narcotic drug laws	9,863	8,249	1,614	.4	.4	.6
Weapons; carrying, possessing, etc.	18,611	17,675	936	.8	.8	.4
Offenses against family and children	23,701	21,671	2,030	1.0	1.0	.8
Liquor laws	52,707	44,654	8,053	2.3	2.1	3.2
Driving while intoxicated	102,219	96,782	5,437	4.4	4.6	2.2
Disorderly conduct	281,997	239,582	42,415	12.1	11.5	17.1
Drunkenness	908,957	841,440	67,517	38.8	40.2	27.2
Vagrancy	88,351	81,637	6,714	3.8	3.9	2.7
Gambling	61,546	55,459	6,087	2.6	2.7	2.5
Suspicion	96,740	86,730	10,010	4.1	4.1	4.0
All other offenses	276,998	233,874	43,124	11.8	11.2	17.4

[a] Because of rounding, the sum of the individual classifications may not add to precisely 100.0 percent.

[b] Less than one-tenth of 1 percent.

SOURCE: *Uniform Crime Reports, 1958,* Federal Bureau of Investigation, U.S. Department of Justice, 1959, p. 96.

as a rule do not receive as high economic rewards as men, but their low wages should increase their crimes, if low wages promote thefts.

There are undoubtedly countless petty thefts on the part of women in the service industries which are not reported (since they cannot be proved). But even so this does not account for the great disparity in crime rates. Some people hold that greater leniency is shown to women in the courts. This is only partly true. The fact that most female offenses are sex crimes or drunkenness or disorderly conduct (a euphemistic term for prostitution) means that many receive light sentences. On the other hand, judges often deal harshly with women who neglect their children.

Woman's role in modern society probably has something to do with her low crime rate. The average woman is a success if she is a successful wife and mother. She usually does not strive for economic success. Her goals are more often emotional than economic. In fact it is when her emotional life is upset that she is most likely to become a criminal—as the analysis of marital status and crime indicates. In any event women do not commit as many crimes as men, apparently because they have less motivation to commit crimes. Most women are vitally concerned with rearing children. Their role as mothers may be important in their greater conformity to the moral values inherent in our criminal law.[59]

Physiological Characteristics

There have been a number of attempts to relate physiological characteristics to crime, of which Lombroso's *Criminal Man* was the most notable. Lombroso held that the true criminal was the born criminal, as we mentioned. The born criminal, Lombroso held, was an atavistic creature, a throwback to a more primitive type of man. As such he had certain stigmata —cauliflower ears, a projecting nose, a low forehead, a receding chin, too many fingers, etc. As a prison physician Lombroso carefully measured the prisoners and even made pronouncements about the relation of particular defects to specific crimes. Later he recognized that there were additional types of criminals and added the epileptic, the criminaloid, and the habitual criminal to the list. He believed the true criminal was halfway between the lunatic and primitive man.[60]

Endocrinologists, often dubbed "neo-Lombrosionists," have also come to some startling conclusions with reference to criminals. Schlapp and Smith, for example, have made statements as to the chemical aspects of glandular disturbances and the resultant effect upon human behavior. Conduct is a function of the relative irritability of the human protoplasm and is therefore directly related to the chemical balance. "Curing crime," from their point of view, is essentially a matter of regulating glandular secretions. Berman's re-

---

[59] Cf. Mabel A. Elliott, *Crime in Modern Society,* Harper & Brothers, New York, 1952, chap. VIII, "The Woman Offender," for a detailed discussion on this point.

[60] Cesare Lombroso, *L'Uomo Delinquente* (1889). This book and other works were translated into English in 1911. In Lombroso, *Crime, Its Causes and Remedies,* consult pp. 369–374.

search into glandular secretions gives further confirmation to this point of view.[61] Although criminologists cannot ignore their findings, the claims made by the endocrine enthusiasts have not been sufficiently established for us to place too much faith in their conclusions. Crime is more than irritability—and must always involve a situation.[62]

The most significant return to the Lombrosian doctrine is that of Earnest A. Hooton, Harvard anthropologist, who conducted a voluminous anthropometric study of American criminals. By this research he claimed to have established a causal relation between physical characteristics and crime. A series of 10,-953 male prisoners in ten widely separated states were given intensive anthropological measurements and compared to a check sample of normal persons, 909 white civilians and 1067 Negro or Negroid civilians. In addition, there were 1227 insane from several states. The sane check sample included Nashville firemen, patients in the Massachusetts General Hospital, a few from a public bathhouse, Negro adults from Tennessee and North Carolina, and militiamen in Massachusetts. The civil sane group was considered comparable socially and economically to the classes from which criminals are drawn. Many criminologists have, however, questioned both the methods and the conclusions. Hooton and his assistants made a detailed comparison of the physical measurements of these criminals and noncriminals.[63] In one respect these data confirm other studies which have shown criminals to be both shorter and lighter than the ordinary population.[64]

Research in physique and delinquency has recently been done by the Gluecks. W. H. Sheldon's book *Varieties of Delinquent Youth* stimulated the Gluecks to analyze delinquency in terms of body type: endomorphs, ectomorphs, and mesomorphs.[65] After detailed measurement of 500 delinquent boys according to Sheldon's prescriptions, the Gluecks concluded that mesomorphs (that is, boys of an athletic build) were most likely to become delinquents. The endomorphs (the fat round type) and the ectomorphs (the thin frail type) were less prone to become delinquents.[66] This judgment is discussed in Chapter 4. Since a delinquent has to be involved in a situation which precipitates the offense, this study is not very sound, sociologically speaking. It obviously requires a certain amount of energy to carry out delinquent projects, but energy is not the whole explanation.

[61] Max A. Schlapp and Edward H. Smith, *The New Criminology,* Boni and Liveright, New York, 1928.

[62] E. Kretschmer in his *Physique and Character,* Harcourt, Brace and Company, New York, 1925, and S. J. Morris in "The Relation of Persistent Thymus Gland to Criminology," *Medical Record,* 99:438 (March, 1921), are among others who make strong statements in support of the endocrine theory.

[63] Earnest A. Hooton, *The American Criminal,* Harvard University Press, Cambridge, 1939, Vol. I, pp. 32–35.

[64] *Ibid.*

[65] William H. Sheldon *et al., Varieties of Delinquent Youth,* Harper & Brothers, New York, 1949.

[66] Sheldon and Eleanor Glueck, *Physique and Delinquency,* Harper & Brothers, New York, 1956.

Race and Nativity

1. *The Foreign Born.* Earlier studies showed a high crime rate among young men who were foreign born. Most criminals today are native born. No figures are now compiled on the number of foreign born arrested, but the number is low. Formerly, as discussed later in Chapter 23, "Crime and the Community," persons of Southern and Eastern European origin had a very high crime rate. It seems likely that the children of the foreign born may constitute a sizable number of our older adult criminals today, but no study on this topic has ever been made. In 1950 only 1853 or 3.2 percent of the 40,057 white prisoners for whom there was information were foreign born. As long as the various foreign-born groups adhere to their national culture, cultural conflict will probably persist to complicate the adjustment of their native-born children. Where foreign-born groups have achieved middle-class status and their children have received good education cultural conflict is virtually nonexistent today.

2. *Race.* Race, however, is significantly related to crime, as Tables 5.10 and 5.11 show. Negro arrests totaled 696,209 of the 2,340,004 arrests in 1958 or over 30 percent of the total arrests. Since Negroes represent about 10 percent of the population, this means that they are arrested three times as often as white persons. The number of Indians arrested is small, only 43,126, but proportionately this means that more than one-tenth of the Indians (who number around 400,000) are arrested. Of course in all cases there is some duplication of arrest and over three-fourths of the arrests of Indians are for drunkenness (the highest for any racial group). Chinese and Japanese constitute a very small crime problem, and their number in the population is low. The majority of the "other" arrests are of Mexicans.

Many people have argued that racial discrimination is the main reason for the high Negro crime rate. This is only partially true. Negroes are arrested disproportionately for very serious crimes which ordinarily require a warrant. Negroes were arrested in 1958 for 62 percent of the murders, over half of the robberies, over 70 percent of the aggravated assaults, nearly half the forcible rape cases, nearly 60 percent of the narcotic cases, and approximately 75 percent of the gambling cases. In virtually all of the other categories they had a much higher than proportionate number of arrests.

There is no reason to believe these were "trumped-up" cases. Negroes actually break the law at an alarming rate in the United States. Even so, discrimination may enter the picture. The segregated status of Negroes, their economic disadvantages, the bad neighborhoods in which so many are forced to live—all these are factors which frustrate the Negro and make him unwilling to abide by the laws.[67]

In certain instances Negroes may be punished more severely than white persons, particularly in case of the murder or rape of a white person. But police also overlook many petty offenses of Negroes. Most Negro murders are com-

[67] Mabel A. Elliott, "Perspective on the American Crime Problem," *Social Problems,* 5:184–193 (Winter, 1957–1958).

TABLE 5.10. Race, Nativity, and Sex, by Type of Institution, of Felony Prisoners Received from Court: 5190[a]

Race and nativity	All Institutions			Federal Institutions			State Institutions		
	Total	Male	Female	Total	Male	Female	Total	Male	Female
All classes	**57,988**	**55,625**	**2,363**	**11,492**	**11,040**	**452**	**46,496**	**44,585**	**1,911**
White	40,057	38,680	1,377	8,090	7,823	267	31,967	30,857	1,110
Native	38,204	36,866	1,338	6,925	6,671	254	31,279	30,195	1,084
Foreign born	1,853	1,814	39	1,165	1,152	13	688	662	26
Negro	17,211	16,256	955	3,214	3,030	184	13,997	13,226	771
Other races	720	689	31	188	187	1	532	502	30
Indian	597	568	29	128	127	1	469	441	28
Chinese	63	63	–	44	44	–	19	19	–
Japanese	19	18	1	4	4	–	15	14	1
Filipino	23	23	–	4	4	–	19	19	–
All other	18	17	1	8	8	–	10	9	1
Percent Distribution									
All classes	**100.0**	**100.0**	**100.0**	**100.0**	**100.0**	**100.0**	**100.0**	**100.0**	**100.0**
White	69.1	69.6	58.3	70.4	70.8	59.1	68.8	69.2	58.1
Native	65.9	66.3	56.6	60.3	60.4	56.2	67.3	67.7	56.7
Foreign born	3.2	3.3	1.7	10.1	10.4	2.9	1.5	1.5	1.4
Negro	29.7	29.2	40.4	28.0	27.5	40.7	30.1	29.7	40.3
Other races	1.2	1.2	1.3	1.6	1.7	0.2	1.1	1.1	1.6

[a] Excludes statistics for state institutions in Georgia and Michigan.

SOURCE: *Prisoners in State and Federal Institutions, 1950, National Prisoner Statistics,* Federal Bureau of Prisons, 1954, p. 54, Table 20.

TABLE 5.11. Arrests by Race, 1958, 1,586 Cities Over 2,500, Total Population 52,329,497

Offense Charged	Total	Race					
		White	Negro	Indian	Chinese	Japanese	All Others
Total	**2,340,004**	**1,583,070**	**696,209**	**43,126**	**1,252**	**296**	**16,051**
Criminal homicide:							
(a) Murder and nonnegligent manslaughter	**2,303**	840	1,427	8	2	2	24
(b) Manslaughter by negligence	**1,166**	904	245	7	2	—	8
Robbery	**14,968**	6,732	8,034	72	7	—	123
Aggravated assault	**25,824**	9,073	16,389	75	5	2	280
Other assaults	**82,454**	45,840	35,733	311	26	4	540
Burglary—breaking or entering	**61,045**	41,754	18,623	343	27	1	297
Larceny—theft	**118,325**	80,292	36,642	678	57	13	643
Auto theft	**30,240**	23,691	6,135	227	31	7	149
Embezzlement and fraud	**19,489**	15,618	3,782	48	1	2	38
Stolen property; buying, receiving, etc.	**5,504**	3,666	1,765	23	1	—	49
Forgery and counterfeiting	**11,317**	9,580	1,653	52	9	3	20
Forcible rape	**3,680**	1,821	1,797	9	—	—	53
Prostitution and commercialized vice	**17,482**	9,194	7,885	110	20	7	266
Other sex offenses (includes statutory rape)	**24,517**	17,079	7,058	105	14	8	253
Narcotic drug laws	**9,863**	3,807	5,740	17	34	4	261
Weapons, carrying, possessing, etc.	**18,611**	8,678	9,693	56	13	4	167
Offenses against family and children	**23,701**	15,118	8,378	71	7	—	127
Liquor laws	**52,707**	34,158	17,877	453	21	10	188
Driving while intoxicated	**102,219**	84,640	16,068	1,008	16	16	471
Disorderly conduct	**281,997**	161,721	115,171	2,301	83	17	2,704
Drunkenness	**908,957**	673,894	195,051	33,017	297	128	6,570
Vagrancy	**88,351**	64,665	20,950	1,929	97	24	686
Gambling	**61,546**	13,820	46,767	3	341	8	607
Suspicion	**96,740**	63,231	32,711	579	42	10	167
All other offenses	**276,998**	193,254	80,635	1,624	99	26	1,360

SOURCE: *Uniform Crime Reports, 1958*, Federal Bureau of Investigation, U.S. Department of Justice, 1959, p. 97.

mitted against their own racial group and these are called to the law's attention by Negroes. Where Negroes commit crimes against Negroes they often are not punished as severely as whites, however, as a study in Houston of 100 white and 100 Negro offenders showed.[68] Some Negroes insist that white Southerners object to having Negroes cluttering their courts. The high Negro crime rate in the North is evidenced in Pennsylvania, where about 40 percent of the commitments to penal institutions are Negro. A great many of our Negroes are personally disorganized, so far as the crime rate is concerned and contribute very seriously to the crime rate. Negroes themselves can help this problem by facing the need for leadership among their own group. But Negro crime is largely the result of the Negro's being forced to live in a subculture. He is excluded from the white man's world and thus feels no constraint to abide by the white man's law. Segregation is probably a major reason for the high Negro crime rate.[69] For the United States as a whole, Negroes constituted 13,977 of the total of 46,496 persons incarcerated in 1950 or slightly over 30 percent. Thus the number of Negroes committed to institutions is proportionate to the number of Negro arrests.[70]

Recidivism—A Habit Pattern

At the present time statistics on arrest include persons who are not fingerprinted; hence recidivism is not recorded. Figures for an earlier period, however, indicated that about 60.2 percent were persons previously arrested.[71] Special research indicates that recidivism is even higher than this. According to the Gluecks' follow-up study, 88.2 percent of the 1000 delinquents became recidivists (although in many cases the recidivism was not "officially known").[72] The Gluecks also made a later follow-up study of 510 criminal men showing 62.1 percent to be total failures and 16.8 percent "partial failures." Of these groups 70.7 percent had been arrested.[73] Subsequent follow-up studies of both the juvenile and the adult criminals showed further recidivism. Criminality obviously becomes habitual with many criminals.

PSYCHOLOGICAL AND EDUCATIONAL FACTORS

Mental Deficiency and Crime

In 1914 Dr. Goddard made a solemn statement to the effect that feeble-mindedness was the greatest single cause of delinquency and crime.[74]

---

[68] John D. Bowles, "Comparative Analysis of 100 Negro Offenders and 100 White Offenders Brought Before the Court of Harris County, State of Texas," Master's thesis, University of Kansas Library, 1933.

[69] Cf. *Time*, April 21, 1958, p. 16.

[70] *Prisoners in State and Federal Institutions, 1950, National Prisoner Statistics*, Federal Bureau of Prisons, Washington, 1954, p. 55.

[71] *Uniform Crime Reports, 1950*, Federal Bureau of Investigation, U.S. Department of Justice, Washington, 1951, p. 111.

[72] Sheldon and Eleanor Glueck, *One Thousand Juvenile Delinquents*, Harvard University Press, Cambridge, 1934, p. 151.

[73] Sheldon and Eleanor Glueck, *Later Criminal Careers*, The Commonwealth Fund, New York, 1937, pp. 63–64.

[74] Henry H. Goddard, *Juvenile Delinquency*, The Macmillan Company, New York, 1914, p. 22.

His findings, as we point out elsewhere, have since been successfully refuted. In a survey of the Illinois prisoners Dr. Adler found that the criminal population of the state surpassed the men in the United States Army in intelligence. Ordinarily, prisoners are no more lacking in general intelligence than are the rank and file of the population.[75] At the same time, it is still impossible to make a satisfactory statement concerning the relation between behavior and intelligence, because there is no certainty that intelligence tests measure intelligence. Meantime Simon H. Tulchin has further verified Dr. Adler's conclusions by comparing the inmates in Illinois prisons and reformatories with the men in the Illinois army draft for World War I. Tulchin found that they ranked more or less the same in intelligence.[76] Zeleny in 1933 had concluded that there was slightly more mental deficiency in the criminal and delinquent population than in the general population in the approximate ratio of 1.2 to 1.[77] Sutherland meanwhile had made a detailed analysis of various studies dealing with feeble-mindedness and crime and came to the conclusion that there was too great a disparity between them to be conclusive. In 350 studies feeble-mindedness allegedly ranged from 1 to 89 percent among prisoners.[78] Apparently some psychologists felt they had to find Dr. Goddard's pronouncement to be true. In a large study of 9958 prisoners in New York during 1932–1935 only 2.4 percent were found to have a serious mental defect while 82.3 percent were normal.[79] Sex offenders appear to have a lower intelligence than other offenders, however.[80]

Mental Illness and Crime

Earlier studies in mental illness likewise indicated widespread mental disease among prisoners. In 1922, for example, the National Committee for Mental Hygiene surveyed thirty-four county jails and prisons in New York and concluded that 77 percent of the inmates were psychopathic in varying degrees.[81] Bowers' study of 2500 prisoners in Michigan City, Indiana, judged that 1585 of them were abnormal. According to his analysis, 675 were feeble-minded, 250 were insane, 200 were epileptic, and 450 were psychopathics.[82]

[75] Herman M. Adler and Myrtle R. Worthington, "The Scope of the Problem of Delinquency and Crime as Related to Mental Deficiency," *Journal of Psycho-Asthenics,* 30:47–57 (1925).

[76] Simon H. Tulchin, *Intelligence and Crime,* University of Chicago Press, Chicago, 1939, p. 12.

[77] Leslie D. Zeleny, "Feeblemindedness and Criminal Conduct," *American Journal of Sociology, 38:*564–578 (January, 1933).

[78] Edwin H. Sutherland, in *Social Attitudes* (edited by Kimball Young), Henry Holt and Company, Inc., New York, 1931, p. 374.

[79] Walter Bromberg and Charles B. Thompson, "The Relation of Psychosis, Mental Defect and Personality Types to Crime," *Journal of Criminal Law and Criminology, 28:*70–89 (May–June, 1937).

[80] Sutherland, *Social Attitudes,* p. 374.

[81] Cf. *Mental Diagnoses of the Prisoners in 34 County Jails and Penitentiaries in New York State,* National Committee for Mental Hygiene, New York, 1923.

[82] Cf. Paul E. Bowers, *Clinical Studies in the Relationship of Insanity to Crime,* Alexander Publishing Company, Michigan City, Ind., 1915. Cf. also Ernest B. Hoag and Edward H. Williams, *Crime, Abnormal Minds and the Law,* The Bobbs-Merrill Company, Inc., Indianapolis, 1923.

Epilepsy was held to be particularly conducive to criminal behavior because of the violent nature of the seizures characteristic of the disease.[83] Glueck's study of 608 admissions to Sing Sing showed 59 percent to be either mentally diseased, intellectually defective, or psychopathic. Only twelve were considered insane.[84] Surveys in other institutions showed a marked disparity in the number of mentally disordered. According to Ploscowe, the data include such diverse figures as 3 percent in Georgia, 9 percent in South Carolina, and 45.3 percent in Kentucky.[85] Meanwhile we have no very good reason for believing most prisoners to be mentally ill.

Emotional Disturbances and Crime

Mental illnesses, as we discuss in Chapter 12, are of two distinct types: (1) those which are due to trauma and (2) those which are psychogenic and presumably due to emotional disturbances. Mental illnesses associated with crime are usually presumed to be those of emotional origin, as Zilborg, Abrahamsen, and others insist.[86]

William Alanson White held that the major emotions are love, hate, and guilt.[87] According to his definition, love subsumes the whole range of tender emotions and friendship, as well as those social relationships which make it possible for two persons to be associated for their mutual well-being. Hate, as the ambivalence of love, represents the aggressive, predatory tendencies of man to advance himself at the expense of others, to be cruel to his associates. Hate in its manifold forms is responsible not only for killing with a knife but for malicious gossip, using the power of position to injure a person, and vicious intrigue. Guilt, the third great emotion, is the reaction resulting from hate. Thus a person loves an object, is repulsed by it, or is envious of it and the love turns to hate—with resultant attempts at injuring the former love object. This in turn leads to guilt. Some psychoanalysts insist that all love objects incite hate—that there is no true hate without love. The consequent sense of guilt may lead to sadistic conduct and injury, either social or physical, to the beloved object because the individual feels the need of punishment. By the suffering incurred by such conduct he unconsciously hopes to relieve himself of the sense of guilt.

From an objective point of view it is impossible to establish the validity of this interpretation. The basis of diagnosing the mental ills of prisoners also makes any scientific conclusions extremely dubious at the present time, inas-

[83] Cf. Robert H. Gault, *Criminology*, D. C. Heath and Company, Boston, 1932, pp. 182 ff.

[84] Bernard Glueck, "A Study of 608 Admissions to Sing Sing Prison," *Mental Hygiene*, 2:92 ff. (January, 1918).

[85] Morris Ploscowe, "Some Causative Factors in Criminality," *Report on the Causes of Crime*, National Commission on Law Observance and Enforcement, Washington, 1931, Vol. I, No. 13, p. 56.

[86] Franz Alexander and Hugo Staub, *The Criminal, the Judge, and the Public* (translated by Gregory Zilborg), The Macmillan Company, New York, 1931. Cf. David Abrahamsen, *Crime and the Human Mind*, Columbia University Press, New York, 1945.

[87] William A. White, *Crime and Criminals*, Rinehart and Company, Inc., New York, 1933, chap. VI.

much as some psychiatrists are prone to consider the fact of criminal conduct as *ipso facto* evidence of mental instability.[88] Even if criminals are mentally disordered, this is not in itself proof that their behavior was the result of their instability. Obviously not all mentally disordered persons commit crimes.[89] As is true of mental disease, crime may afford an escape from an intolerable situation. Likewise, some crimes and mental disorders may be the natural consequences of conflicts in moral standards and the detachment of individuals from the group as a whole.[90] In view of all this, Michael Hakeem maintains in fact that psychiatric opinion on this subject is vague, confused, and completely unscientific.[91]

William and Joan McCord believe, however, that there is a strong emotional factor in criminality. Dissatisfied with the findings in the Cambridge-Somerville study (described in the preceding chapter) the McCords explored the data further. They found that where the relationship between the parents was "quarrelsome and neglecting" 61 percent of the boys in the experiment were disposed by the court as juvenile delinquents.[92] They also found that absence of parental love led to adult criminality even when these grownups had no juvenile record. Forty-three percent of those whose parents were not loving were convicted of adult criminality, in comparison with only 15 percent of those who had one or two loving parents.[93]

Personality Profiles of Criminals

John M. Stanton's analysis of the personality profiles of 100 Negro and 100 white prisoners in Sing Sing indicated no major deviation between the two groups. They were then equated on a social and economic basis, including similarity in school achievement. When they were given the Army General Classification Test the whites scored significantly higher in intelligence. On the Minnesota Multiphasic Personality Inventory very little difference was found between the two groups. The MMPI includes twelve scales, L for Lie, F for Validity, H for Hypochondriasis, D for Depression, Hy for Hysteria, Pd for Psychopathic deviate, Mf for Masculinity-femininity, Pa for Paranoia, Pt for Psychasthenia, Sc for Schizophrenia, Ma for Hypomania, and Si for Social inversion. This test was administered within each prisoner's first two weeks in prison.[94]

[88] Ploscowe, *op. cit.*, p. 57.

[89] Edwin H. Sutherland and Donald R. Cressey, *Principles of Criminology*, J. B. Lippincott Company, Philadelphia, 1955 (5th ed.), pp. 121–123.

[90] *Ibid.*, p. 117.

[91] Michael Hakeem, "A Critique of the Psychiatric Approach," in Joseph S. Roucek (ed.), *Juvenile Delinquency*, Philosophical Library, Inc., New York, 1958, chap. 4, pp. 79–112; also footnotes, pp. 345–351.

[92] William and Joan McCord, *Origins of Crime*, Columbia University Press, New York, 1959, p. 164. (The McCords say these youngsters were "convicted" of juvenile delinquency, but the term "convicted" is not ordinarily applied to young persons brought before the juvenile court.)

[93] *Ibid.*, p. 165.

[94] John M. Stanton, "Group Personality Profile Related to Aspects of Anti-Social Behavior," *Journal of Criminal Law, Criminology, and Police Science*, 47:340–349 (September–October, 1956).

Since the tests showed such similar profiles for both groups, the whites and blacks were thrown together and compared with 200 normal males. Very significant differences were found between the criminal and the normal groups. The inventory from Hy through Ma (hysteria through hypomania) is considered a clinical scale to measure deviations from normal. In these scales there were significant differences between the 200 criminals and the normals. The greatest differences between prisoners and normal males were in the scores in the psychopathic deviate scale and in the hypomania scale.[95] The prisoners were then analyzed according to social data. Those known to be alcoholic addicts had a significantly higher Pd rating than those who were narcotic addicts or non-addicts. Narcotic addicts had no significantly higher rating than non-addicts. Prisoners with poor work records had a higher schizophrenia and a higher hypomania rating than those with a good work record. Those with poor family relationships had higher ratings on the hypomania and schizophrenia scales than those with good familial relationship. The backgrounds of the prisoners were thus related to their ratings on the MMPI scales.[96]

Morris Caldwell's comparative analysis of 228 Negro and 231 young adult white male offenders (16 to 23 years of age) in Alabama throws further light on personality factors of the two groups.[97] There was no significant statistical difference in the educational achievement of the Alabama prisoners although the Negro men ranked slightly higher in education. Negroes on the average had completed 8.6 grades in contrast with the whites, who had completed a mean of 8.3 grades. The mean IQ rating of the white criminals was considerably higher, 92.8 in contrast to 80.2 for the Negroes. This is a significant difference of 12.8 points and means that the average white offender was normal in intelligence, the average Negro was dull normal.[98]

Whites and Negroes were compared in intelligence and education and it was found that Negroes who were convicted for the major crimes of murder and manslaughter, assault, robbery, burglary, larceny, and auto theft ranked markedly lower than the white offenders in intelligence in the same offense categories. On the other hand (in every category of offense except auto theft) the Negroes had higher educational achievements than the white. Eighty percent of the Negroes who committed forgery had an education above the eighth grade, whereas only 52.2 percent of the white forgers had gone beyond the eighth grade. Even so, the differences were not great.[99] For the minor offenses the educational status was more nearly the same.

When the Minnesota Multiphasic Personality Inventory was given to the two groups important differences between Negro and white offenders were

[95] *Ibid.*

[96] *Ibid.*

[97] Morris G. Caldwell, "Personality Trends in the Youthful Offender," *Journal of Criminal Law, Criminology, and Police Science,* 49:405–416 (January–February, 1959).

[98] An IQ of 90 to 110 is rated "normal." Cf. Chapter 11, "The Mentally Deficient" for a discussion on this point.

[99] *Ibid.*

disclosed (in contrast to Stanton's findings). The Negro offenders scored significantly higher in hypochondriacal symptoms, moods of mental depression, feminine interests, patterns of behavior, paranoid trends, and hypomania. Whites scored higher on psychopathic deviation.[100]

Other important differences appeared among the Alabama criminals when classified as to offense. (1) Among murderers the whites ranked higher in intelligence than the Negroes. The Negroes were more often feminine and schizoid according to the test. (2) For assaulters, whites had the highest IQ while Negroes ranked highest as schizophrenic and hypomanic. (3) Among rapists whites and Negroes were both low in intelligence, but the Negro was also more often characterized by tendencies to paranoia and mental depression. (4) For robbers, whites were superior in intelligence to Negroes. Negroes were high in feminine interests and inclined toward mental depression. (5) For burglars, whites were intellectually superior and had a greater tendency to psychopathic behavior. Negroes had a higher tendency to mental depression and feminine interests. (6) For forgers there was no important difference except that Negroes had a higher educational achievement. (7) The white grand larcenist was superior in intelligence to the Negro grand larcenist and had greater tendency to psychopathic behavior. (8) The auto thief in both groups ranked the same except for intelligence. The white group was superior in intelligence. (9) For other offenses the Negro was definitely higher in scores on hypochondria, masculinity-femininity, and schizophrenia. The white was again higher in intelligence.[101]

When Caldwell's findings are compared with Stanton's it is obvious that the Negro prisoners in Alabama apparently have far more clinical symptoms than those in New York. A detailed analysis and comparison of the two groups of offenders might make an important contribution. If emotional symptoms are related to frustration the southern Negro's greater tendency to clinical reactions may be due to environmental factors. Merton, meanwhile, maintains that criminals probably have normal motivations to secure what they cannot obtain legally and hence use other means.[102] The Stanton study indicates that their motivations may be distorted.[103]

How prisoners became distorted is another question, of course, and for many reasons. For one thing, much of psychiatry is still in a prescientific stage in the sense that verifiable data are not obtained. Psychiatrists frequently deal only with the most serious offenders and so form opinions on the basis of small selected groups. Control groups of non-prisoners are seldom employed to indicate the extent of disorders in the general population. Successive studies are seldom made to confirm psychiatric conclusions, which are themselves

[100] *Ibid.*
[101] *Ibid.*
[102] Robert Merton, *Social Theory and Social Structure*, The Free Press, Glencoe, Ill., 1949, p. 136.
[103] *Op. cit.*

often vague and difficult to classify. Nevertheless psychiatrists are rather given to authoritative statements about crime.

Many psychiatrists believe that the important difference between the mentally diseased and the normal person is one of consciousness of motive. The mentally ill are unconscious of their motives, the normal are conscious, although these disparities shade into each other.[104] The psychiatrist feels that the consciously motivated normal person can be redirected through common sense. The mentally ill need conscious control from without, i.e., custodial or directed care.[105] Roche, in fact, thinks criminals and the mentally ill are different only because we choose to deal with them differently.[106]

Educational Status

The only extensive data we have on prisoners' educational achievements were gathered in connection with a study of the antecedents of those committed in 1923. This showed 89.3 percent able to read and write, whereas 10.7 percent were illiterate. More than two-thirds (67.5 percent) of the prisoners, however, had had only elementary training, whereas 14.4 percent had had some high school training, 1 percent had attended trade school, and 3.4 percent had had some college or professional training. In other words, only a very small share of the prison population had anything resembling a good education.[107]

These data were confirmed by Hooton's latter analysis of 10,953 prisoners in ten states, which number represented between 11 and 12 percent of the male prison population in 1927–1928.[108] Of these, 10.16 percent were illiterate and 4.21 percent could read and write but had no formal education. However, 7.72 percent of Dr. Hooton's sample had completed high school or had had some college training.[109]

The criminal's lack of education has been associated with his background of poverty and lack of privilege. Since compulsory education standards have increased, we may expect the educational level of prisoners to rise. The group profile studies of 200 men committed to Sing Sing in the early 1950's, and the 459 Alabama prisoners referred to earlier, indicated that they had completed from 8.3 to 8.6 years of schooling on the average.[110] There is no group of offenses, however, for which a college education appears to be essential, if we except illegal operations or abortions. Certain types of crime tend to be characteristic of better-educated prisoners, viz., embezzling, income tax evasion, fraud, and forgery. Certain types of offenses can be committed only by per-

[104] Cf. Karl A. Menninger, *Man Against Himself,* Harcourt, Brace and Company, New York, 1938, part II, chap. IV, "Anti-Social Behavior." Cf. also Roche, *op. cit.,* pp. 25–27.

[105] Roche, *op. cit.*

[106] *Ibid.,* p. 29.

[107] *The Prisoner's Antecedents, 1923,* U.S. Bureau of the Census, Washington, 1929, p. 21.

[108] Hooton, *op. cit.,* Vol. I, p. 71.

[109] *Ibid.,* pp. 85–87.

[110] Stanton, *op. cit.,* and Caldwell, *op. cit.*

sons in positions of trust, and these positions usually require higher than average education. Education at the same time diminishes the chance of reaching prison. In the survey of prisoners' antecedents, the crime rate was 42.8 per 100,000 adult population, but only 14.3 among those who had some college study. We should like to think that college improves the ethical behavior of men; the Kinsey report indicates that college men have higher standards of sex behavior, as we discuss in Chapter 6. Even so, the higher social and economic status of college students also augurs in favor of their not being arrested or convicted for certain offenses.

Whatever his other characteristics, the criminal does not accept adult responsibility. He is a person "who failed to grow up"[111] irrespective of whether or not he is mentally ill. While we no longer give credence to Lombroso's notion that criminals are a distinct biological type, criminals are a distinct sociological type—they are grown men and women who do not think or act like adults. They reject important social values of the adult world and are in turn condemned and rejected by the group.

CULTURAL AND ENVIRONMENTAL FACTORS

Unfortunately certain aspects of the cultural milieu seem to be important in producing criminality. Children appear to be particularly affected by the slum area. There are no important studies of recent date of the effect of neighborhood influence on adult criminals. Our analysis will be limited therefore to marital status and economic and seasonal factors, all of which affect the everyday life and associations of individuals.

Marital Status of Prisoners

1. *Male Prisoners.* The increasing trend toward early marriage is slightly reflected in prison statistics. In 1945, for example, 49.8 percent of all male felony prisoners received from court in the United States (for whom there was information) were single, 42.2 percent were married, and 8 percent were widowed or divorced.[112] In 1950 (when postwar prosperity appeared to affect the marriage rate slightly) 45.6 percent of the male felony prisoners received from court were single, 42.8 percent were married, and 11 percent were divorced.[113] Data with reference to marital status for prisoners for all states are not available since 1950. Marital data are published annually for federal prisoners, however. The figures for 1953, 1957, and 1958 given in Table 5.12 indicate that the percentage of single offenders among federal prisoners stays relatively constant although there appears to be a slight increase in the widowed and divorced group. Divorce may or may not be related to personal disorganization but there is presumptive evidence to that effect. Family maladjustments appear to be especially important in the case of criminal women.

---

[111] Roche, *op. cit.*, p. 243.
[112] *Prisoners in State and Federal Prisons and Reformatories, 1945,* Federal Bureau of Prisons, Washington, 1946, pp. 47, 50.
[113] *Prisoners in State and Federal Institutions, 1950,* p. 66.

TABLE 5.12.   Marital Status of Male Federal Prisoners

Marital Status	1953		1957		1958	
	Number	Percent	Number	Percent	Number	Percent
Total	**15,645**	**100**	**14,265**	**100**	**14,211**	**100**
Single	7,104	45.4	6,130	43	6,439	45.3
Married	6,119	39.1	5,210	36.5	5,098	35.9
Widowed	206	1.3	218	1.4	183	1.3
Divorced	1,231	7.9	1,556	10.9	2,491[a]	17.5
Separated	985	6.3	1,175	8.2		

[a] Divorced or separated are given in one category for 1958.

SOURCES: *Federal Prisons, 1957*, Federal Bureau of Prisons, 1958, p. 71, and *Federal Prisons, 1958*, Federal Bureau of Prisons, 1959, p. 91. (1958 percentages computed by Miss Elliott.)

The figures seem to indicate that divorce and separation rates are increasing among both state and federal prisoners. The divorce rates probably reflect the present trend in many states to grant a divorce to one whose spouse has been convicted and sentenced to prison, as discussed in Chapter 16. A significant percentage of the men in all groups were not married, and only slightly more than a third appeared to have stable marriages. The federal offenders tend to be persons who have had positions of trust, to a greater extent than is true of state prisoners, and hence are somewhat older. This fact probably affects the marriage rate.

2. *Female Prisoners.*   The marriages of women prisoners appear to be even less successful than those of the men, but the number of women is very small, as we have said. In 1946 all felony women prisoners received by state and federal prisons and reformatories numbered 2489. Of these 30.1 percent were single, 53.8 percent married, and 16.1 percent widowed or divorced.[114] In 1950 only 25.3 percent of the women felony prisoners of the total 2344 received in state and federal institutions were single. Those married constituted 54.2 percent and the widowed or divorced 20.5 percent.[115]

Unfortunate or unhappy marriages appear to contribute directly to women's offenses. That is, many women prisoners are convicted for being involved in their husbands' offenses. Divorced (and unhappy) women often commit offenses which seem to be related to their perturbed emotional state. Divorce upsets the focus of the married woman's activities, which have previously been dominated by the home. When the marriage is broken her whole way of life is disturbed, whereas the husband's occupation may go on with relatively little change. As Mrs. Browning said in *Aurora Leigh,* "marriage is to man's life a thing apart, a woman's whole existence." Since this is to a marked degree still true, any break in the marriage, especially when the husband asks for the divorce, means that the woman's aims and goals are shattered. The fact that women's motivations are so largely emotional goes far to explain why their crimes are so often associated with crimes of violence

[114] *Prisoners in State and Federal Prisons and Reformatories, 1945.*
[115] *Prisoners in State and Federal Institutions, 1950,* p. 69.

or the "personal disorganization" type of crime, including sex offenses and drunkenness.[116]

Figures for federal female offenders for the years 1953, 1957, and 1958 show somewhat different marital trends, but women federal offenders are a selected group and do not include women sentenced for personal sex offenses or drunkenness.

TABLE 5.13.   Marital Status of Federal Women Prisoners

Marital Status	1953		1957		1958	
	Number	Percent	Number	Percent	Number	Percent
Total	521	100	660	100	646	100
Single	133	25.5	237	36	242	37.5
Married	174	33.4	229	34.7	225	34.9
Widowed	29	5.6	24	3.6	26	4.0
Divorced	64	12.3	63	9.5	152[a]	23.6
Separated	121	23.2	107	16.2		

[a] Includes divorced and separated for 1958.

SOURCES: *Federal Prisons, 1953,* Federal Bureau of Prisons, 1954, p. 79, *Federal Prisons, 1957,* Federal Bureau of Prisons, 1958, p. 71, and *Federal Prisons, 1958,* Federal Bureau of Prisons, 1959, p. 91. (Percentages for 1958 computed by Miss Elliott.)

There are no clear explanations for the increasing number of single offenders among the federal female prisoners unless this is related to an increase in female employees of the federal government who are likely to be single. In any event single female prisoners increased slightly more than 10 percent between 1953 and 1958. The number married remained almost constant while those divorced and separated decreased over 10 percent.

Economic Conditions and Crime

Juvenile delinquency rates went down during the depression in the United States, as we stated in the preceding chapter. On the other hand, many studies of economic conditions and crime show a correlation between periods of economic stress and higher crime rates. Because of the apparent "conflicting evidence" George B. Vold concludes that economic influences are not "determining" influences.[117] Dr. Vold's conclusion ignores an important consideration which affected the economic well-being of juveniles, however. During the Great Depression of the thirties most people in need were on relief. Families were allotted assistance on the basis of the number of people in the family. Most such families received some supervision on the part of the welfare workers, who tried to help them plan for health, recreation, and other needs. Plant suggests that the decline in delinquency rates may have been

[116] Elliott, *Crime in Modern Society,* chap. VIII, "The Woman Offender."
[117] George B. Vold, *Theoretical Criminology,* Oxford University Press, New York, 1958, pp. 181–182.

affected by the father's greater leisure and greater opportunity to be a companion to his children.[118] This may be true although the fact of organized social welfare cannot be wholly discounted. Children were probably taken into family discussion in budgeting and told just what funds the relief agency made available for what purposes. It seems likely that children learned to cooperate in the family economic problems better than in normal times.

Daniel Glazer and Kent Rice have challenged Vold's conclusions that economic factors are probably not a significant determinant of crime by two studies. One involved the correlation of unemployment rates with arrests for property offenses in the United States from 1932 to 1950, the other a correlation of male arrests in Boston, Cincinnati, and Chicago by type of offense with unemployment rates for the United States from 1930 to 1956. In the first study Glazer and Rice found an inverse or negative correlation for those under 18 years of age and the number unemployed. On the other hand, there was a significant correlation between unemployment and arrests after the age of 20. Between ages 25 and 34 the coefficient of correlation was $+.72$ (a very significant correlation) but this dropped significantly after 35 years of age. The correlation was $-.26$ for the years 35 to 44 and $-.64$ for 45 and older.[119]

Although Glazer and Rice do not say so, the group 35 to 44 and older are those who are fathers of children of juvenile court age. Perhaps family responsibility alters the behavior. We cannot say. In any event it is well known that arrest rates *always* drop significantly after age 35 irrespective of economic need.[120]

When the specific type of offenses were studied in Boston, Cincinnati, and Chicago, unemployment appeared to be positively related to property crimes for the middle age group in all three cities, with high correlations in all groups 21 through 45. After 45 property offenses dropped significantly in Boston.[121]

When crimes against person and misdemeanors of a personal disorganization variety were analyzed, high positive correlations were found with unemployment rates in Boston for those over 25 and in Cincinnati for those 21 and over. In Chicago there was a low correlation between both crimes against persons and personal disorganization, misdemeanors, and unemployment for persons 21 to 34 and a negative correlation for those older. The fact that Chicago figures did not confirm those of the other two cities leads Glazer and Rice to suspect their validity.[122] It may be of course that patterns of youthful conduct in Chicago involved less drunkenness, disorderly conduct, and vagrancy. In any case this study gives strong evidence that adverse economic conditions increase the adult crime rate but seem to affect juvenile rates

[118] James S. Plant, *Personality and the Cultural Pattern,* The Commonwealth Fund, New York, 1937, p. 141.

[119] Daniel Glazer and Kent Rice, "Crime, Age and Employment," *American Sociological Review,* 24:679–686 (October, 1959).

[120] *Ibid.*

[121] *Ibid.*

[122] *Ibid.*

inversely. Glazer and Rice's research makes clear that there is still reason to hold that economic conditions promote crime.

No student in the social sciences should discount the severity which often characterizes the economic struggle for existence. There is grave danger, however, of interpreting an omnipresent condition as a factor uniquely responsible. There are those who hold, for example, that prostitution is an economic crime, ignoring altogether that sex conduct is also biological in its motivations. Certain types of criminal conduct might be expected, however, to be related directly to economic conditions. Social values again determine what is considered crime. To steal is a crime, but to go bankrupt, to manipulate the stock market, or to crush out competitors is not. Anything which tends to reduce economic security, on the other hand, may well be an urge to unsanctioned economic activity.

Poverty is no crime, but despite our advances in social welfare legislation it is still something like an offense to be destitute. For although theoretically we have abolished imprisonment for debt in America, the inability to pay fines is frequently the basis for determining whether a man becomes a jailbird or not. The payment of a fine, no matter how large it may be, never entails the opprobrium that goes with a short sentence behind bars.

Bonger, the Dutch criminologist, adhered strictly to the theory of economic causation of a major share of crimes against property. In this connection he tried to verify his position by correlating the price of wheat with crimes against property in England, Wales, and France. Similarly, he studied the price of rye and the number of thefts in Germany. In both cases he found an inverse ratio to exist between the cost of the cereals and the crime rate.[123] Bonger himself recognizes, however, that many economic crimes are motivated more by a desire to achieve a standard of luxury than by absolute poverty. The sight of the well-to-do and their conspicuous consumption tends to set a goal which the poor cannot achieve legally.[124]

Seasonal Aspects of Crime

Crimes vary with the seasons. Because economic need is generally more serious in winter and more people are apt to be unemployed, more economic offenses are committed. The cost of living goes up. Winter clothing is more expensive than summer apparel and fuel is a necessity. Consequently there are reasonable explanations for the increase in crimes against property during the colder months. The highest number of robberies always occurs in December and the burglary peak is in February and March. The low month for robbery is June, and for burglary, September or October. Larceny is highest during April.[125] These variations have occurred with striking similarity for years. There are apparently seasonal needs connected with winter eco-

---

[123] Cf. William A. Bonger, *Criminality and Economic Conditions,* Little, Brown and Company, Boston, 1916, pp. 564–571.
[124] *Ibid.*
[125] *Uniform Crime Reports, 1958,* pp. 5–6.

nomic crimes. The fact that there is more darkness in winter aids and abets the robber and burglar.

Offenses against the person, including murder, rape, and aggravated assault, are most frequent during the summer months.[126] More people are thrown together physically in summer; hence there are more opportunities for friction. Murders appear to concentrate in months with national holidays, which perhaps give more reason for family quarrels. Greater opportunities for sex offenses also occur in summer, when outdoor life permits more opportunities for clandestine behavior. So far as crimes of violence are concerned, some authorities have maintained that warm weather itself is conducive to irritability.[127]

Crime and the Business Cycle

The ups and downs of the business cycle show certain relations between general economic conditions and crime. Dorothy S. Thomas computed the coefficients of correlation between "all indictable crimes" and the business cycle in England for the period 1857–1913, attaining a negative correlation of .25.[128] This indicated a slight inverse ratio between increase in prosperity and the crime rate. Since "all indictable crimes" include crimes of violence, murder, and malicious injury, as well as crimes against property, separate correlations were established for the different categories. For crimes against property with violence during the whole period 1857–1913, a maximum coefficient of .44 occurred when the crime rate and business cycle were related synchronously. There was a slightly smaller coefficient of .37 when a lag of one year between business conditions and the crime rate was allowed. Dr. Thomas therefore concluded that there is a very evident relation between property crimes and the business cycle. That is, such offenses as burglary, house and shop breaking, and robbery showed a marked tendency to increase in times of economic depression and decrease when times were good.[129] Malicious injuries and crimes against the person or the morals, on the other hand, showed little connection with the business cycle. Crimes against the person, particularly those involving lascivious conduct and sex offenses,[130] showed a slight tendency to decrease during periods of depression. Sex crimes thus seem to increase in periods of prosperity. Rape, in fact, seems to be definitely correlated with the business index. Marriage rates also increase in boom times and Dr. von Hentig thinks both are stimulated by good living.[131]

Unemployment, an inevitable concomitant of business depression, has been studied as a causal factor. Detailed analyses of fluctuations in employment and in crime in both Massachusetts and New York State came to substantially

[126] *Ibid.*
[127] Cf. Parmalee, *op. cit.,* p. 45.
[128] Dorothy S. Thomas, *Social Aspects of the Business Cycle,* George Routledge and Sons, Ltd., London, 1925, p. 138.
[129] *Ibid.,* p. 139.
[130] *Ibid.,* pp. 141–142.
[131] Von Hentig, *op. cit.,* p. 223.

the same conclusions—viz., that unemployment is an important factor in vagrancy and crimes against property.[132]

The demoralization of the labor market inevitably means that certain marginal workers are deprived of the last vestige of economic security. Rather than face the humiliation of being supported by charitable agencies, they voice the sentiment frequently expressed, "I would rather steal than beg." The fact of dependents at home may be a further impetus driving the person to mercenary crime. He may burn with resentment at the thought of inequalities of opportunity and advantage. The community itself may offer many incentives to a life of crime.[133]

In summarizing the various studies of crime in the depression, Sellin pointed out the difficulty of making any sweeping generalizations on the basis of the available information. A variety of indices both of business conditions and of crime rates were employed in the various researches and because of this disparity in criteria no precise relationships were established. There is no question that certain offenses against property increase during times of acute economic stringency—particularly offenses against property with violence, which were found to increase both in England and in the United States in periods of depression.[134]

Work History

The Gluecks' study *Five Hundred Criminal Careers*[135] gives further evidence that poor work history and temporary jobs are related to crime. Information was available on work history for 381 of the 510 men in the study. Of these the majority had begun work before they were sixteen. Only 13.8 percent were skilled workers; 54.1 percent were unskilled and 32.1 were semiskilled. Only one-fifth (19.8 percent) were regarded as industrious, reliable workers. Over half (52.5 percent) were rated as definitely poor. Both personal work habits and unemployment thus appear to be factors in crime.

Today unemployment insurance takes much of the strain out of unemployment even though the benefits are not great. The relation between unemployment and crime presumably should be reduced, but no study has been made on this topic.

Social Values and the Adult Offender

We have already spoken of the concern which society has expressed for the juvenile delinquent. In a vague, groping, and usually ineffective fash-

---

[132] Cf. Emma A. Winslow, "Relationships Between Employment and Crime Fluctuations as Shown by Massachusetts Statistics," *Report on the Causes of Crime,* Vol. I, pp. 257–312; and Mary Van Kleeck, "Notes on Fluctuations in Employment and Crime in New York State," *ibid.,* pp. 315–333.

[133] Cf. Martin H. Bickham, "Unemployment and Mercenary Crime," in Ernest D. MacDougall (ed.), *Crime for Profit,* Stratford Company, Boston, 1933, pp. 55–72.

[134] Sellin, *op. cit.,* pp. 60–62.

[135] Sheldon and Eleanor Glueck, *Five Hundred Criminal Careers,* Alfred A. Knopf, Inc., New York, 1930, p. 117.

ion, society has sought to "treat" rather than to punish the child. Even though they have failed miserably, the various institutions devoted to the delinquent are at least nominally committed to "reforming" and re-educating the child. When we consider the adult offender, a completely different situation confronts us. Despite the reformatory motive which prompted the founders of present-day penitentiaries, California is the only state which has attempted a thoroughgoing attack on the behavior problems of the adult criminal. Several prison systems have made great improvements—for example, Louisiana and Pennsylvania. But few officials are willing to recognize that an adult may be a victim of circumstances and needs help in overcoming his criminal habits. Some states have tried to provide more modern facilities for youthful and first offenders. In actual practice, however, there is little to distinguish these institutions from the sad, somber cells of the older and "hardened" criminals. Actually, there is no scientific reason for assuming that adult offenders should be dealt with according to methods markedly different from those suitable for juvenile offenders. The adult may be as much the victim of circumstances as the child. At the same time he may need even greater help in overcoming long-established habit patterns.

What does this survey of the adult offender show? Simply this: The adult offender who is a member of the lower economic and social group is more likely to be apprehended, convicted, and sentenced than middle-class and upper-class offenders. The convicted offender has failed to be concerned about the welfare of society in pursuing his egoistic ends, it is true. But he usually has also been the victim of a series of unfortunate handicaps and disabilities. On the other hand, the materialistic standards of the upper economic classes have stimulated many crimes. Men steal, not merely for bread, but because they wish to acquire fine cars, beautiful houses, good clothes. The emphasis upon conspicuous consumption and the acceptance of wealth as a basis for achieved status is an index to the distorted social values which elicit criminal conduct in our society. If Sutherland and others are right about the high rate of criminal behavior among all classes of society, the rejection and punishment of the lower-class criminal by the white-collar judges who sit in authority are tantamount to group prejudice. The status of the upper and middle class is constantly threatened by the rising lower class. This fear is probably an unconscious factor in the differential punishment of criminals and in the protection of the upper-class group.

SELECTED BIBLIOGRAPHY

Alexander, Franz, and Healy, William, *The Roots of Crime,* Alfred A. Knopf, Inc., New York, 1935. One of the best psychoanalytical treatments of crime, this book places emphasis upon the emotions of love, hate, and guilt in their relation to antisocial behavior.

Barnes, Harry E., and Teeters, Negley K., *New Horizons in Criminology,* Prentice-Hall, Inc., New York, 1959. In this comprehensive analysis of crime, its causes and treatment, there is an especially good analysis of modern "racketeering" and the newer perspectives on crime problems.

Elliott, Mabel A., *Crime in Modern Society,* Harper & Brothers, New York, 1952. This contains several chapters on the adult offender including original data in two chapters on the woman offender.

Gillin, John L., *The Wisconsin Prisoner,* University of Wisconsin Press, Madison, 1946. Surveying sex offenders, murderers, and property offenders who were inmates of the Wisconsin state prison, this volume contains some of the most interesting data available with reference to prisoners.

Glueck, Sheldon and Eleanor T., *Criminal Careers in Retrospect,* The Commonwealth Fund, New York, 1943. This is one of the most important follow-up studies on adult criminals.

Glueck, Sheldon and Eleanor, *Five Hundred Criminal Careers,* Alfred A. Knopf, Inc., New York, 1930. This is the classic study of the pre-institutional and after careers of 510 men paroled from the Massachusetts Reformatory.

Prisoners in State and Federal Institutions, National Prisoner Statistics, Federal Bureau of Prisons, Washington. Short reports are issued annually and larger detailed reports at intervals which enable the student to keep alert to characteristics of prisoners and changes in rates of commitment to prison.

Roche, Philip Q., *The Criminal Mind,* Farrar, Straus and Cudahy, Inc., New York, 1958. This is one of the most lucid books on criminality and its relation to mental illness from a psychiatric point of view.

Sutherland, Edwin H., *White Collar Crime,* The Dryden Press, Inc., New York, 1949. This is a startling study of the crimes committed by seventy major corporations.

Tulchin, Simon H., *Intelligence and Crime,* University of Chicago Press, Chicago, 1939. In this study a comparison is made of the intelligence of Illinois prisoners with that of Illinois soldiers in the army draft for World War I.

Uniform Crime Reports for the United States, Federal Bureau of Investigation, U.S. Department of Justice, Washington. These reports were formerly issued semiannually and now annually. Students and instructors can keep up to date on statistics for arrest by consulting them.

Von Hentig, Hans, *Crime: Causes and Conditions,* McGraw-Hill Book Company, Inc., New York, 1947. This book, which covers the sociological aspects of crime, surveys a wide variety of research projects including many of von Hentig's own studies. It contains some especially valuable material on age, sex, and race.

Von Hentig, Hans, *The Criminal and His Victim,* Yale University Press, New Haven, 1948. This volume covers much research (including the author's) on the sociology of crime, dealing with prenatal conditions, heredity, physical traits, psychological variables, and their relation to crime.

Wallerstein, James S., and Wyle, Clement T., *Our Law Abiding Law Breakers,* reprint from *Probation,* April, 1947. This reprint summarizes the extent to which a wide variety of professional men, businessmen, teachers, housewives, *et al.* admitted they had committed crimes for which they were never punished.

CHAPTER 6

The Sex Offender

Sex and Personal Disorganization

As Jacques Barzun and many others have pointed out, there is a great deal of chaos in contemporary attitudes toward sex. Rigid notions of sex conduct incorporated in our moral values and laws do not conform to the state of our language and literature, our present-day advertising, or our public entertainment. All of the latter tend to incite sexual thoughts and to be geared to sexual appeals.[1] Current research seems to indicate that relatively few men and only half of the women conform to the concept of premarital chastity as written in the laws and embodied in our moral ideals.

Perhaps this discrepancy should not be surprising. Any deep-seated in-stinctive drive is bound to be hard for many people to control. Even more important, the unprecedented changes in political ideas, scientific advance, and military weapons have induced tremendous international tensions and great insecurity in every area of life. Times of widespread social change and consequent social and political disorganization have always been marked by an attempt to throw off rigid sex restraints. Wars, revolutions, and general social upheavals are upsetting to human life schemes and social values and many people apparently seek security through sex fulfillment. This, of course, is not a total explanation for there has always been a sizable amount of illicit sex conduct even in relatively stable periods.

No aspect of human behavior is fraught with greater possibility of personal disorganization than unconventional and illicit sex relations. The premium on illicit sex conduct is secrecy, at least for most persons in the middle and upper classes. If such conduct is discovered, married men may be sued for divorce on grounds of adultery in every state in the Union. If a man forces his atten-tions, he may be condemned as a rapist. Young girls (chiefly lower-class) known to be involved in sex delinquency are brought before the juvenile court. Prostitutes who cater for hire to illicit sex desires are considered the most degraded of women. "Respectable" women caught on the losing side of an illicit affair figure significantly among those who suffer nervous breakdowns or mental derangement. Society still wreaks vengeance upon the unmarried mother and her illegitimate child in their middle-class and upper-class roles,

[1] Cf. Jacques Barzun, *The House of Intellect,* Harper & Brothers, New York, 1959, pp. 255–257.

and in many states the child is deprived of all inheritance rights. But despite all the problems and dangers attached to illicit relations, illegitimacy is apparently on the increase.

In addition to the impact of social disorganization and world tensions, there are other explanations for much sex experimentation. One is the nature of the sex urge itself. Since it is just as "natural" for a woman to yield to the sex importunings of men as it is for men to take the initiative in such relations, obviously some women are bound to respond to such urges. Only when women have been disciplined in restraint and trained to defend themselves against sex advances are they likely to preserve premarital virginity. For certain educated and intellectual and bohemian groups, other influences have been conspicuous in producing greater willingness to violate the norms of premarital chastity. These include the widely disseminated ideas of the sexologists, notably Havelock Ellis, and the published personal opinions of the great philosopher Bertrand Russell and other elite intellectuals. These men maintain that happiness should be the criterion of sex expression and that there is no reason for confining sex experience to marriage.[2] Probably even more important has been the tremendous impact of the teachings of Dr. Sigmund Freud, who maintained that many of the serious ills of mankind are rooted in the rigid Christian doctrine of no sex experience outside of marriage. Communist propaganda with reference to sex gained rather widespread acceptance during the twenties and thirties. This doctrine held that sex should be satisfied with no more ado than drinking water when one is thirsty. These are some of the intellectual rationalizations which gave the post-World War I and present generations a basis for extensive sex experimentation. When this widespread experimentation became obvious, it was natural that there should be some scientific attempts to survey the extent of change of current sex habits.

Studies of Sex Conduct

There have been a large number of studies of sex behavior. The most important include those of Dickinson and Beam, Katherine Bement Davis, and Lewis M. Terman *et al.* during the late twenties and thirties. All of these studies showed that some women in the educated middle and upper classes were indulging in sexual intercourse before marriage. As Terman expresses it, the majority of men and women were earlier taught to believe that sexual intercourse before marriage was the most shameful and unforgivable of sins, especially for women.[3] Dr. Davis' study in 1929 showed that 71 out of 1000 women college graduates admitted premarital sex relations. This was only 7.1 percent, but it was considered shocking that *any* college woman should admit such a fact. For criminal women, on the other hand, Dr. Davis

---

[2] Cf. Bertrand Russell, *Marriage and Morals,* Liveright Publishing Corporation, New York, 1929.

[3] Lewis M. Terman *et al., Psychological Factors in Marital Happiness,* McGraw-Hill Book Company, Inc., New York, 1938, p. 319.

found such experience to be the rule. All but 1.8 percent of these women had been sexually immoral.[4]

Terman's study in 1938 included 792 married couples largely of the professional classes, of whom 760 husbands and 777 wives gave information. Terman found that date of birth was important in the premarital sex experience of both the men and the women in his group. Both men and women had a rising percentage of premarital experience with each successive decade. For men born in the decade prior to 1890, 50.6 percent were virgins at the time of marriage; for those born from 1890 to 1899, 41.9 percent; between 1900 and 1909, 32.6 percent; and after 1910, only 13.6 percent. (The latter percentage was based on only twenty-two cases, however.) For women the percentages were smaller, but they rose in a similar fashion. For the women born after 1910, only 31.7 were virgins at the time of marriage. The women were, however, much less promiscuous than the men; 45.5 percent of those with premarital experience had such experience only with their subsequent husbands.[5]

The Kinsey Reports

The most extensive studies on human sex behavior to date are those of Dr. Alfred C. Kinsey and his associates, Wardell B. Pomeroy, Clyde E. Martin, and Paul H. Gebhard. This group conducted two extensive research surveys on the sex behavior of the human male and the human female which were published in 1948 and 1953 respectively. The studies gave conclusive evidence (at least insofar as the samples were representative) that illicit sex experience was rather common, although much higher among men than among women.[6] We cannot go into the mass of detail in either of these two researches but will merely summarize the most important facts. Both studies have been questioned as to their representative character as well as their conclusions.

1. *The Human Male.* In order to study the sexual habits of the human male, Kinsey and his associates interviewed 12,214 white men. They based their initial analysis, however, on 5300 cases. One of the most significant facts they discovered was that the sexual habits of men varied markedly according to educational achievement (which Kinsey believed to be the *real* index to class in the United States). The cases were therefore classified in three groups: (1) those who did not go beyond grammar school, (2) those who went to high school, and (3) those who had some college training or completed college. Kinsey found that 98 percent of men who had not gone beyond the eighth grade had premarital sex experience, many in early ado-

---

[4] Cf. Katherine Bement Davis, *Factors in the Sex Life of Twenty-Two Hundred Women,* Harper & Brothers, New York, 1929.

[5] Terman *et al., op. cit.,* pp. 319–321.

[6] Cf. Alfred C. Kinsey, Wardell B. Pomeroy, and Clyde E. Martin, *Sexual Behavior in the Human Male,* W. B. Saunders Company, Philadelphia, 1948, and Alfred C. Kinsey, Wardell B. Pomeroy, Clyde E. Martin, and Paul H. Gebhard, *Sexual Behavior in the Human Female,* W. B. Saunders Company, Philadelphia, 1953.

lescence; that 84 percent of those who attended high school but had no further training had such experience; and that 67 percent of those who went to college had some premarital sex experience.[7]

Equally significant, he found that the extent and frequency of such experience varied markedly for the three educational levels. For the lowest educational level there was earlier and more frequent premarital intercourse in the late teens (3 times a week on the average); for those attaining the high school level, the average was 1.5 times a week; and such experience averaged *once in three weeks* for men on the college level. Moreover, some of the college group had only *one* premarital sex experience. The relative infrequency of illicit premarital sex experience in this group seemed to indicate they were more influenced by moral scruples than were the other two levels,[8] although farm boys (many of whom never went to college) as a whole had less premarital sex experience than any other group.[9]

So far as the extramarital sex experience of married men was concerned, Kinsey and his associates had greater difficulty in securing information. This was attributed to the fact that any admission of infidelity might serve as grounds for divorce. Even so, approximately 40 percent of the men on both high school and college levels admitted extramarital relations whereas only 19 percent of the grade school level admitted such infidelities. These figures are surprising when one considers the much greater sexual activity prior to marriage in the lower level. Kinsey holds that it may be the wives of the upper-level group were more restrained. Since only 60 percent of the male population are married at any one time and there is a tendency to frequent sex outlets among the unmarried, Kinsey claims that over half the sex outlets among men are non-marital outlets.

2. *The Human Female.* The Kinsey report on *Sexual Behavior in the Human Female* was based on 7789 female histories, but the major analysis was limited to 5940 cases. Because the researchers believed they would have some difficulty in finding individual women willing to respond to their detailed questions with reference to premarital and extramarital sex behavior, the women interviewed were secured chiefly from organized groups. Kinsey or one of his assistants discussed the problem before a particular organization in which members were asked to cooperate. All told, thirty-five types of groups furnished interviewees. These ranged from women in the armed forces (WAC, WAVES, and Army Nurses) to those in church congregations, clinical groups, college and high school students and student organizations, women in homes for unmarried mothers, parent-teacher groups, women's clubs, professional organizations, and YWCA groups. Occupations were as various as that of acrobat, dean of women, housewife, laundress, receptionist, taxi dancer, prostitute, riveter, and practical nurse (to choose a few). Their

---

[7] Kinsey *et al., Sexual Behavior in the Human Male,* p. 347.
[8] *Ibid.,* pp. 550–553.
[9] *Ibid.,* p. 568.

husbands' occupations (for those married) were equally various.[10] Unlike the men, the women interviewed by Kinsey and his researchers indicated no significant difference in sex experience when analyzed according to educational level. Such experience was slightly higher among the high school and college level women, in fact, than for the group that had not attended school beyond the eighth grade.

For the total group of women interviewed 50 percent admitted premarital experience. The frequency of experiences was, however, much less among the college women than those on other educational levels. At least on this score the women were more restrained in the higher educational level than were the less-educated women. So far as married women were concerned, 26 percent of the women 40 years of age or over admitted extramarital infidelities. Only 16 percent of these women had so indulged by the age of 30 and a bare 6 percent by the age of 20. After 25 years of age more women with higher education indulged in extramarital relations than was true for those younger. This would seem to indicate that the so-called "sexually-emancipated" woman is most often found in the better-educated groups. Infidelities were less common among the educated religiously devout than for the educated less devout. But where the devout were involved in illicit sex relations there was no decrease in the frequency of such relations.[11]

There were very significant differences in the number of premarital partners of the women in contrast to the men. Fifty-three percent of the women who had premarital sex relations had them with only one person and 46 percent with their fiancés only. Another 41 percent had them with their fiancés and others. There was in fact nothing resembling the promiscuity among women which was apparent in the Kinsey study of the male.[12] Only 13 percent of the women had premarital relations with six or more persons. On the other hand, 1230 women who had premarital sex experience had less than ten experiences all told. Some of the women had only one experience. The average frequency for all women having premarital intercourse ranged from once every ten weeks for the group 15 years of age and under, to once every three weeks for persons for all age groups except for those 36 to 40. For these the average was once in two and a half weeks.[13]

Male teen-agers of the lower educational level had the highest number of illicit sex outlets and averaged two to four times a week. Some had much higher. Between the age of adolescence and 25 some were having intercourse as often as twenty-five times a week.[14] While some females had had sex relations several times a week (or oftener) for a week or so, they often went for weeks, months, or even years without any further indulgence. For men as

[10] Kinsey *et al., Sexual Behavior in the Human Female,* pp. 37–43.
[11] *Ibid.,* p. 437. Very few lower-lower class women were studied.
[12] *Ibid.,* p. 336.
[13] *Ibid.,* p. 334.
[14] Kinsey *et al., Sexual Behavior in the Human Male,* p. 553.

well as women rates were much lower for the devoutly religious Protestant and Catholics. Curiously the rate was higher for men among Orthodox Jews than among inactive Jews. Devout Jewish women had a far lower rate than the inactive group.[15]

The response to the monumental data in the two Kinsey reports has varied. Some scholars denounced the whole project; others picked flaws in some of the analyses; others accepted the data cautiously; still others believed the reports a valid argument for removing all moral restraints on sex.[16] Kinsey and his associates held that their data indicated that social control which aims to punish sex offenses, especially homosexuality and other widely condemned sex practices, is unfair and absurd. In the report on female sex behavior they went further and stated that certain advantages apparently accrue from premarital sex expression.

Any detailed study of the unsavory by-products of premarital relations, however, points up many reasons why illicit relationships may be disorganizing both to personality and to physical health. Even if human sex experience frequently does not conform to the Judeo-Christian ideal, this does not mean the ideal is wrong. It seems likely that there are actual rewards for "virtuous" sex conduct. Nor does the fact that illicit sex experience is relatively common mean that it is therefore desirable. Many people have told lies, but that does not mean that perjury is desirable. One would not argue that because many people commit crimes we should therefore abolish all legal and social controls over behavior antithetical to the common welfare. Nor is it safe to argue that because few of the many sex offenders are punished there should be no social control over sexual relations.

Modern morals are obviously shot through with hypocrisy. A double standard has arisen because men allegedly have more insistent sex urges than women. It patently requires self-restraint for human beings (male or female) to observe moral rules, just as it requires restraint to be law-abiding citizens. Sexual restraint also involves consideration for the rights and privileges of others. "No man is an *Island*" in the field of sex behavior. Restraint is important to public and private health, to personality development, to sound family life and the welfare of children. Despite any arguments for sexual laxity, there are obvious dangers in illicit sex expression.

The foregoing does not mean that our present penal treatment of sex offenders is intelligent. What it does make clear is the fact that our society has made little progress in educating its citizens in the realm of sex. We have attempted to confine sex experience within monogamous marriage while tacitly permitting a double standard. This plainly does not work. If men are to be permitted sex license, they must have female partners. There will inevi-

---

[15] *Ibid.*, and Kinsey *et al.*, *Sexual Behavior in the Human Female*, pp. 306–307.

[16] Cf. Jerome Himelhoch and Sylvia Fava, *Sexual Behavior in American Society*, W. W Norton and Company, Inc., New York, 1955. This book gives the reactions of 38 sociologists, anthropologists, lawyers, clergymen, *et. al.*, to the Kinsey reports.

tably be all the problems of unmarried motherhood, illegitimacy, incest, rape, prostitution, and venereal disease. The sex problem is a challenge to a better coordination of biology, psychology, sociology, medicine, and moral values.

Sex Delinquency Among Girls

Studies of women and girls who were inmates of correctional institutions have shown a large share to be sex offenders, whether or not they were committed on that charge. Apparently judges are more apt to sentence women with a record of sex delinquency, irrespective of their current offense. No detailed institutional studies of women and girls have been published recently, but three earlier studies of delinquent girls (one by Miss Elliott, one of the authors of this text, one by Katherine DuPre Lumpkin, and a study of women criminals made by Sheldon and Eleanor Glueck) substantiate this statement.[17] More recent analysis of women serving for federal offenses at the U.S. Reformatory for Women at Alderson, West Virginia, also bears out this conclusion. Even though none of the women in the Federal Reformatory are committed for sex offenses, about 75 percent apparently have some record of prostitution.[18]

In the run-of-the-mill juvenile court cases, illicit sex behavior is apparently not so frequent. The 1958 figures for the Allegheny County Juvenile Court (Pittsburgh) girls' cases showed that 93 (or 15.3 percent) of the 604 white girls brought up during the year for hearing and disposition were referred on sex charges; and 91 (or 34 percent) of the 267 Negro girls were referred on sex delinquency. A total of 352 girls (both colored and white) were referred for "ungovernable" and "running away" (which was more than half of the group). Both of the latter classifications would indicate that these girls were in danger of becoming sex delinquents but no such charges were brought against them. More boys than girls were brought to court on sex charges. There were 304 boys in contrast to the 184 girls, but the boys' cases were only 8.9 percent of the total. The girls brought on sex charges, however, were 21 percent of the total. Some of the boys were involved in homosexual practices. There is, of course, no reason to suppose that such court cases represent more than a fraction of the total juvenile sex offenders of juvenile court age in Allegheny County.[19]

Most delinquent girls and women brought to court come from underprivileged and rather sordid home backgrounds. Negro girls and women come from much worse homes than white girls. One study of 100 unselected cases of

[17] Cf. Mabel A. Elliott, *Correctional Education and the Delinquent Girl,* Commonwealth of Pennsylvania, Harrisburg, 1929. Katherine DuPre Lumpkin, "Factors in Commitment of Correctional School Girls in Wisconsin," *American Journal of Sociology, 37:222–230* (September, 1931), and same author, "Parental Conditions of Wisconsin Girl Delinquents," *American Journal of Sociology, 38:232–239* (September, 1932); also Sheldon and Eleanor Glueck, *Five Hundred Criminal Women,* Alfred A. Knopf, Inc., New York, 1934.

[18] Statement made by the former acting warden, Margaret C. Jones, to Miss Elliott.

[19] Data obtained from unpublished annual (1958) statistical report at the Allegheny County Juvenile Court.

Negro girls and another of 100 unselected cases of white girls brought before the Allegheny County Juvenile Court in 1957 showed the percentage of economic, social, and moral handicaps to be far more serious for the Negro girls than for the white girls. This was reflected in the number of sex offenses. Only 13 of the 100 white girls were sex delinquents, whereas 46 of the 100 Negro girls were so charged.

Sixty-three percent of the Negro girls came from broken homes, and in 10 percent the parents' marriage was of the common-law variety. Such marriages are legal in Pennsylvania but socially taboo. Thirty-two of the Negro mothers and 20 of the fathers were known to be immoral, but nearly as many of the immoral charges against Negro girls occurred in families held to be relatively moral. Twenty-one of the Negro sexual offenders came from moral homes, whereas 25 came from immoral homes.[20] Eight were illegitimate. Of the 15 white sex offenders 7 came from homes considered moral, 7 from immoral homes, and in one case the morality at home was not recorded.[21] Sex morality of children is obviously as much affected by community patterns as that of the family itself.

The Unmarried Mother

The unmarried white mother has a very difficult time in American society because of the stigma attached to her status. For lower-class Negroes the stigma is not so great. If the father of the white girl's child is able and willing to marry her before the child is born or if the girl's irate father forces the man to marry his daughter, the stigma may be removed. But forced marriages are often unhappy even though the child is legitimatized.

Although Kinsey and his associates argued that illegitimate pregnancies were not an important reason for refraining from illicit relationships, their statement can scarcely be taken seriously. They found that over a fifth or 469 of the 2094 single women who had illicit relationship became pregnant.[22] Only 16 married women admitted such illegitimate pregnancies, and these 16 had 18 illegitimate pregnancies.[23] There may well have been more, but there is no way of checking the validity of these numbers.

At any rate, everyone who has ever worked with unmarried mothers knows that they face many complicated problems and have little of the joy of the married mother. In the first place, the unmarried mother from a good family background tends to suffer guilt as well as stigma. Her child shares the stigma (as discussed later on) unless he is fortunate enough to be adopted. The whole problem of securing adequate medical care and clothes, is often complicated by lack of money. In relatively few cases the father of her child (if

[20] Syada Greiss, "The Social, Economic, and Personality Factors in the Backgrounds of 100 Negro Girls Brought Before the Allegheny Juvenile Court in 1957," unpublished MS., Chatham College Library. (Tutorial project directed by Mabel A. Elliott.)

[21] Sally Head, "The Social, Economic, and Personality Factors in the Backgrounds of 100 White Girls Brought Before the Allegheny Juvenile Court in 1957," unpublished MS., Chatham College Library. (Tutorial project directed by Mabel A. Elliott.)

[22] Kinsey et al., Sexual Behavior in the Human Female, p. 327.

[23] Ibid., p. 434.

she is a white woman) helps with either medical expenses or support of the child. The mother must often face financial problems alone (if her parents do not help) as well as the difficult decision whether or not to give up her child. Social agencies generally hold that it is to the child's best interest to be given up. After the child is born, many unmarried mothers have trouble in securing employment. This is especially true if they keep their child.[24] Some unmarried mothers enter prostitution because of the stigma and shame they experience.

Unmarried mothers come from all age groups and all social and economic levels. A greater percentage fall in the group under twenty years of age, however, than in any other age group as Table 6.2 shows. A very high proportion come from homes of low economic and social backgrounds. Some unmarried mothers are repeaters and have two, three, or more illegitimate children. Such cases are usually well known to welfare agencies. Illegitimate children constitute nearly one-fourth of the relief load for dependent children in Pennsylvania,[25] and presumably this is true for other states. Apparently the unmarried girls and women from the middle and upper classes resort to abortion in case of pregnancy more often than is true in the lower classes.

Unmarried mothers fall into six main types: (1) the mentally subnormal girls who are an easy prey to sex advances, who tend to become repeatedly pregnant unless sterilized because of their lack of ability to inhibit their sex impulses; (2) the young and unprotected girls who get into trouble because they do not know what sex is all about, or because they are forced into sex relations; (3) the older girls of good character who yield to sudden impulses or false promises; (4) the girls from certain lower-class Negro families where the stigma of illegitimacy is not so great as among white persons (nearly two-thirds of illegitimacy cases are in the colored population); (5) the "really" delinquent girls whose illegitimacies are incidental to repeated illicit adventures—unmarried mothers whose babies are born in correctional institutions and who may have lost all desire to conform to social codes because of their disorganized status; (6) the small group of women who want a child but do not wish to marry the father. (7) There is also a small number of married women who have a child by men other than their husbands.

According to a study made of unmarried mothers in Delaware, the girl and her family usually have to solve the train of problems confronting her without help from the child's father. Many try to hide their problem by seeking help in another community. Some wait until they are virtually in labor before getting in touch with an agency. The ratio of unmarried nonwhite mothers (chiefly Negro) is much higher than of the white mothers, and most Negroes tend to remain in the same community. Less stigma is attached to bearing children out of wedlock among lower-class Negroes. Nevertheless the

[24] Sheila Ferguson and Hilde Fitzgerald, *Studies in the Social Services,* His Majesty's Stationer's Office, London, 1954, pp. 124–126.

[25] Data furnished by the Pennsylvania Department of Welfare, Bureau of Public Assistance, May 5, 1959. Cf. Also *State of Wisconsin Services to Unmarried Mothers,* Division for Children and Youth, State Department of Public Welfare, Madison, December, 1957, appendices No. 7 and No. 9.

unmarried colored girl still has serious problems. In many cases homes for un-married mothers are not open to her. She may not have suitable prenatal care or care at childbirth, although the majority now seek such care. Often unmarried colored mothers are also infected with venereal disease.[26] In Dela-ware nearly a third of the colored unmarried mothers had venereal disease.

In her recent book *Out of Wedlock,* Leontine Young maintains that the unmarried mother has an unconscious purpose in becoming pregnant: she *wants* an out-of-wedlock baby or she would have avoided having a child. Miss Young maintains that most of the unmarried mothers had only casual or temporary relations with the father and were generally disinterested in the father as such.[27] Some unmarried mothers come from mother-ridden or mother-dominated homes. Others come from father-ridden homes, and the illegitimate child is an expression of hostility toward the father. The rest, ac-cording to Miss Young, come from homes without any moral, emotional, or financial security. Some are illegitimate themselves, others have grown up in institutions, and still others have passed from foster family to foster family.[28]

Some of the above argument seems far-fetched. It is unquestionably true that illegitimately pregnant girls yield to deep-seated biological urges. The same may be said of the fathers. If it were not for these urges, there would be no such thing as sex attraction. But to say that these girls *wanted* a child or they would have taken precautions to avoid it is to ignore the strength of the sex impulse and the circumstances of their sexual encounters, in which the whole appeal was more or less non-rational. Yielding to sexual stimuli probably is as natural to women as to men. Girls are more rigidly brought up to restrain such impulses. Where the social controls are lacking and there is no self-restraint, illicit sex relationships are bound to increase. Many young women want children, it is true. But the sex impulse is probably stronger than the desire for a child. When confronted with pregnancy, the unmarried mother may still plausibly maintain, "I had to do this." At least she ap-parently had no great compulsion at the time to avoid the situation.

The Unmarried Father

The unmarried father, although he is often the forgotten man in the illegitimacy situation, also suffers from stigma and mental conflict. If he is a sensitive person, he feels extremely guilty for having caused the young woman so much distress. Particularly if he is from the upper educational level, he is likely to be fond of the girl. If he is in a position to marry her, their mutual conflicts may be eased by the social acceptance of their marriage. If he cannot marry her for financial reasons or because he is already married, he faces a difficult problem. In every state the law can compel him to support the child, but if he already has a family that may be virtually impossible. If he is wealthy

[26] Cf. Anonymous, *Unmarried Mothers in Delaware,* Report of the Committee on Un-married Mothers, Welfare Council of Delaware, Inc., November, 1954, pp. 29–34.

[27] Leontine Young, *Out of Wedlock,* McGraw-Hill Book Company, Inc., New York, 1954, chap. 2.

[28] *Ibid.,* chaps. 3–5.

and the girl is from a poor family, he may pay her expenses or a certain sum as a price for the suffering entailed. This was formerly a common practice and still prevails extralegally in rural communities. At an earlier period the father of the offending young man sometimes paid a lump sum to the father of the girl. In other situations, as is well known, there may be a "shotgun" marriage. Sometimes the father or brother avenges the honor of his daughter or sister by killing her accomplice. Even in recent times there have been a number of instances in which the court refused to convict the girl's avenger in such a case.

Legislators often become aroused over the tax burden created by illegitimate children. All states in the continental United States have adopted a law (1) requiring fathers to support their children and (2) providing for returning them to do so if they have gone to another state. These "deserting Pappy laws" (as they are popularly called) have not succeeded in reducing the relief load for either legitimate or illegitimate children. It is very hard to enforce support on an unwilling father, whether married or unmarried.

A federal study made of this problem in early 1956 showed that it cost more to locate and return the fathers than to support the child. Even if returned, such fathers tend to desert again. This is very likely more true of unmarried fathers than of married fathers. A higher percentage of illegitimate than legitimate children quite naturally receive relief. Of the families receiving aid to dependent children in the United States in 1956, 22.7 percent of the fathers were not married to the mothers.[29] A study three years later (in 1959) in Pennsylvania showed that 23 percent of the children receiving aid were illegitimate. There is no reason to suppose that unmarried mothers deliberately have babies in order to receive additional relief, however, as is occasionally alleged. Only 200 cases of unmarried mothers in the state became pregnant while on relief.[30]

A study made of unmarried mothers in Delaware covered cases reported by agencies during a three-month period in 1951. Information was received for 257 cases, 62 (or 24 percent) of whom were white and 195 (or 76 percent) were nonwhite. Of the 195 nonwhite, 193 were native Negro and 2 were Moors.[31] Social data furnished by the agencies regarding these cases were too incomplete to give a very accurate picture of the group. More extensive data were, however, provided with reference to the mother's relationship with the father and the father's marital status than for most items. The type of relationship of the father to the mother was reported in 214 of the 257 cases. In 52 percent of the 214, the father was the regular boy friend.

[29] Cf. Chapter 16 for a further discussion of this.

[30] Mimeographed bulletin, "Characteristics of Aid to Dependent Children Families, Early 1956," Bureau of Public Assistance, U.S. Department of Health, Education, and Welfare, August 23, 1957, p. 5, and mimeographed bulletin, "Children of Illegitimate Birth Receiving Assistance under the Pennsylvania Aid to Dependent Children Program and Birthrate on the Rolls," Commonwealth of Pennsylvania, Department of Public Welfare, April 24, 1959, p. 1.

[31] *Unmarried Mothers in Delaware,* p. 4.

In 14 percent of the white cases and 35 percent of the non-white, the mother was living with the father. In only 15 percent of the 214 cases (28 percent of the whites and 10 percent of the nonwhites) was the pregnancy the result of a casual relationship.[32]

These data appear to contradict Leontine Young's statement that unmarried mothers generally have had only casual contacts with the father and that their primary interest in the man was the urge to have a child. The fathers were generally characterized as irresponsible. Information as to marital status was available for 187 cases (42 white, 145 nonwhite). Of these, 77 percent were single, 13 percent either separated or divorced, and 9 percent married. The nonwhite fathers were unmarried in 86 percent of the cases and the white in 42 percent.[33]

Many unmarried mothers refuse to tell the father's name, but in the Delaware study 181 alleged fathers were named. Of these, 77 percent admitted paternity. The 181 men included 48 white men, 64 percent of whom admitted paternity, and 133 nonwhite, of whom 81 percent admitted paternity.[34] What is surprising in view of widespread irresponsibility on the part of unmarried fathers is that 44 percent of the alleged fathers contributed to the support of the child.[35]

The Extent of Illegitimacy

Figures for illegitimacy in the continental United States are estimates based upon projections of the illegitimacy rates in the thirty-five states which record legitimacy and illegitimacy. These estimations do not include children

TABLE 6.1.   Estimated Illegitimate Live Births by Color:
United States, 1950–1958[a]

Year	Total	White	Nonwhite
1958	208,700	74,600	134,100
1957	201,700	70,800	130,900
1956	193,500	67,500	126,000
1955	183,300	64,200	119,200
1954	176,600	62,700	113,900
1953	160,800	56,600	104,200
1952	150,300	54,100	96,200
1951	146,500	52,600	93,900
1950	141,600	53,500	88,100

[a] Estimates were rounded to the nearest hundred without being adjusted to group totals, which were independently rounded.

SOURCE: National Office of Vital Statistics, U.S. Department of Health, Education, and Welfare, April 15, 1960.

of common-law marriages where such marriages are legal. In thirteen states illegitimacy is not recorded, in order to protect children from the stigma of

[32] *Ibid.*, p. 17.
[33] *Ibid.*, p. 18.
[34] *Ibid.*, p. 19.
[35] *Ibid.*, p. 37.

having their birth certificate so stamped. The estimated illegitimate live births for 1958 were 208,700, as Table 6.1 shows, of which number 74,600 were white and 134,100 were nonwhite and chiefly Negro.

Rates have gone up significantly since World War II. The total illegitimacy rate was 39.8 per 1000 in 1950 and 49.6 per 1000 live births in 1958. The rates have gone up for both white and nonwhite populations but much more in the nonwhite. Nonwhite illegitimacy is over ten times higher than white: the nonwhite rate was 212.3 per 1000 live births in 1958, the white rate 20.9 per 1000 live births. Sexual laxity is much more common among the Negro population than among the white, as is evidenced in the illegitimacy rates. Part of this disparity is a survival of the sexual promiscuity prevalent under slavery.

In recent years there has been an effort to educate Negroes with reference to the dangers of venereal disease which may have some impact later on Negro illegitimacy rates. A much higher percentage of Negroes are in the lower economic and social classes. A larger percentage are educationally underprivileged, especially in the South. A much greater number of Negro married women are employed than is true for white women. Hence Negro girls are often unprotected. And girls at 15 years of age need protecting more than at any other period in their lives. There were 1100 white and 3300 nonwhite unmarried mothers under 15 in 1958, as Table 6.2 shows. Illegitimacy rates

TABLE 6.2. Estimated Number and Ratio of Illegitimate Live Births, by Age of Mother and Color: United States, 1958[a]

Age of Mother	Number			Ratio		
	Total	White	Nonwhite	Total	White	Nonwhite
Total	**208,700**	**74,600**	**134,100**	**49.6**	**20.9**	**212.3**
Under 15 years	4,400	1,200	3,300	661.9	453.2	825.0
15–19	79,400	28,500	50,900	143.3	65.9	419.0
15–17	40,100	13,200	26,900	233.5	108.5	537.3
18 and 19	39,300	15,300	24,000	102.8	49.2	336.0
20–24	62,800	24,100	38,600	45.9	20.6	194.2
25–29	30,800	10,000	20,800	27.8	10.4	141.6
30–34	18,700	6,100	12,600	26.3	9.9	130.9
35–39	9,900	3,500	6,300	27.6	11.3	127.1
40 and over	2,700	1,100	1,600	28.8	13.7	119.7

[a] Estimates were rounded to the nearest hundred without being adjusted to group totals, which were independently rounded. Ratios are per 1000 total live births in specified group.

SOURCE: National Office of Vital Statistics, U.S. Department of Health, Education, and Welfare, April 15, 1960.

in all age groups for the unmarried female population 15 to 44 years of age have nearly tripled since 1940. For those 20 to 24, the rate was nearly four times as high and for those 25 to 29 and over it was five times as high. Even though the rates for older groups declined, they were still proportionately three to four times as high as in 1940.

Age is a factor in illegitimacy for all racial groups. Where the unmarried mothers were under 15, the white illegitimacy rate was 453.2 per 1000 and the nonwhite rate was 825. Similarly, the greatest incidence of illegitimacy for any later five-year age span occurred in the 15- to 19-years group, and for both groups the rate was much higher for the 15- to 17- than for the 18- to 19-year-old mothers. Nevertheless the nonwhite rate was over five times as high as the white for the 15- to 17-year-olds and about seven times as high for the 18- to 19-year-olds. For 20- to 24-year-old mothers the Negro rate was ten times as high as that of whites, and for those 25 to 29 years of age it was over fourteen times as high.

For all births in all age groups, the *nonwhite* illegitimate birth rate is over ten times the white rate. The Negro population, which constitutes around 10 percent of the total population, contributes nearly *twice* as many illegitimate children as the white race (since nearly all nonwhites are Negro). After 35, rates dropped markedly, and only 28.8 per 1000 births were illegitimate after 40. Most of the unmarried mothers who have been studied tend to be very young, since they are apt to be wards of the juvenile court or other institutions where records are available. Older unmarried mothers often try to work out their own problems although many fail to find any very acceptable solution. Though youth is a factor in yielding to sex impulses, race is even more important in illegitimacy. The nonwhite group had higher incidence of illegitimacy for mothers over forty than was true for white girls in the fifteen- to nineteen-year-old group.

Figures for illegitimacy compiled for various cities based on place of residence show some interesting differences. The nation's capital has the highest rate in the United States for illegitimate white births. The white illegitimacy rate in Washington, D.C., is, in fact, slightly more than three times the national estimated rate for illegitimate white births. The female white population in Washington is much higher percentage-wise than for most cities because of the large number of typists and secretaries who are employed in government offices. Undoubtedly some of the illegitimacies occur among this group.

The major source of illegitimacy in Washington, however, is among Negroes. The nonwhite illegitimacy rate is 265.3 per 1000 registered births or more than one-fourth of the total. The highest nonwhite rate recorded for any city was for Atlanta, Georgia, and was 292.9 per 1000. The next highest nonwhite rate (278.8 per 1000) was in St. Louis, followed by Cincinnati (with a nonwhite rate of 275.8). The actual number of illegitimate births which occur in urban centers is often higher than the rates given on the basis of residence because many young women seek the anonymity of the city when confronted with pregnancy.

The Outcome of Illegitimacy

The serious stigma attached to white unmarried mothers undoubtedly leads a sizable number to seek an induced abortion. There are no reliable figures with reference to the extent of such abortions, but it is generally agreed that there is a large number and that more abortions are performed

TABLE 6.3. Number and Ratio of Illegitimate Live Births, by Color:
Specified Urban Places, 1957[a]

Area	Number			Ratio		
	Total	White	Nonwhite	Total	White	Nonwhite
Akron, Ohio	340	176	164	44.9	27.4	143.1
Atlanta, Ga.	1,820	146	1,674	144.6	21.3	292.9
Birmingham, Ala.	1,076	66	1,010	114.2	12.5	243.5
Chicago, Ill.	8,788	1,662	7,126	95.0	26.0	248.3
Cincinnati, Ohio	1,290	340	950	85.9	29.4	275.8
Cleveland, Ohio	1,926	368	1,558	75.4	21.1	192.3
Columbus, Ohio	686	300	386	52.6	27.8	172.0
Dallas, Texas	1,224	268	956	71.0	20.6	224.4
Detroit, Mich.	3,126	708	2,418	69.8	24.1	157.7
Fort Worth, Texas	548	140	408	54.9	17.2	220.8
Houston, Texas	1,602	392	1,210	75.7	26.0	199.1
Indianapolis, Ind.	944	334	610	67.0	30.8	187.7
Jersey City, N.J.	332	156	176	51.1	29.7	139.9
Kansas City, Mo.	904	226	678	79.8	26.3	248.5
Louisville, Ky.	732	182	550	66.1	20.9	230.5
Memphis, Tenn.	1,832	120	1,712	140.5	17.5	276.1
Milwaukee, Wis.	766	424	342	38.6	24.5	135.1
Minneapolis, Minn.	630	524	106	50.1	[b]	[b]
Newark, N.J.	928	198	730	87.6	32.0	165.8
New Orleans, La.	1,406	298	1,108	82.1	32.7	138.1
Philadelphia, Penn.	3,914	618	3,296	84.1	20.1	208.0
Pittsburgh, Penn.	794	322	472	41.2	19.6	164.9
Portland, Ore.	432	316	116	57.9	46.0	196.6
St. Louis, Mo.	2,156	276	1,880	105.7	20.2	278.8
St. Paul, Minn.	324	266	58	36.7	[b]	[b]
San Antonio, Texas	742	526	216	39.6	30.4	150.0
Seattle, Wash.	492	338	154	37.3	28.7	108.0
Toledo, Ohio	414	168	246	53.1	25.9	188.4
Washington, D.C.	3,844	450	3,394	188.1	58.8	265.3

[a] By place of residence. Based on a 50 percent sample. Urban places are cities with corporate population of 250,000 or more in 1950, which are located in the thirty-five states reporting legitimacy. Ratios are per 1000 live births in each specified group.

[b] Data not available.

SOURCE: National Office of Vital Statistics, U.S. Department of Health, Education, and Welfare, May 1, 1959.

on married women than upon single women.[36] A recent analysis of 5210 abortions which had been performed by one abortionist in Baltimore showed that 1830 were performed on single women, 2773 on married, and 607 on women widowed, divorced, or separated.[37]

[36] Norman Himes, "Birth Control and Social Work," *The Survey Midmonthly,* 75:74–75 (March 15, 1939).

[37] Mary Steichen Calderone (ed.), *Abortion in the United States,* Harper & Brothers, 1958, p. 60.

Adoption and Illegitimacy

We have no way of determining the total number of illegitimate children who are adopted. Adoption records are not generally correlated with the individual cases of illegitimacy. Records are kept in much greater detail in Wisconsin than in most states, and it is estimated that from 40 to 60 percent of white unmarried mothers there keep their children. Nonwhite unmarried mothers keep their children in 80 to 99 percent of the cases.[38] White unmarried mothers use social agencies to a greater extent than the others. Very few foster or adoptive homes accept Negroes.[39]

Where children are placed for adoption, policies vary. Social workers are generally agreed that great care in placing children is important. Adoptive parents should be assured a physically and a mentally normal child. Where possible, children should be matched with reference to complexion, hair color and other physical resemblance to their adoptive parents. In Wisconsin, all but 14 percent of the child placements in 1955 were made by social agencies. (Elsewhere we have information on only seventeen states with reference to adoption practices.) Where children were not adopted by relatives, 48 percent were placed by parents, friends, relatives, physicians, or lawyers in 1951.[40]

Some adopted children are not illegitimate, but the great majority are. Children not placed by social agencies are subjected to many hazards. They may later be rejected by their foster or adoptive parents because they turn out badly, or on legal grounds. The illegitimate child's parents may marry, decide they want the child, and bring suit to secure him or her. The mother may subsequently marry another man and persuade her husband to help her secure the child. Where the adoptive parents and the child have become strongly attached to each other, it is obvious that the child would be far better off undisturbed. But where no legal papers have been signed by the mother, such adoptions often have been declared null and void. The subsequent uprooting of the child may be a very upsetting emotional experience.

The Homosexual

The homosexual is a person erotically attracted by members of his or her own sex and with whom he usually (but not always) has perverted sexual contacts. Homosexuality is sometimes known by other names, including sodomy, pederasty, and crime against nature. Homosexuality is socially and legally condemned in the United States as indecent and immoral. Nevertheless there seems to be a widespread tendency of males to experiment in homosexual activities, although most do not become true homosexuals.

The extent of true homosexuality has been variously estimated at from 2 to 5 percent. Many were startled by Kinsey's research, which indicated

---

[38] *Services to Unmarried Mothers,* Report of the Program Committee of the Advisory Committee of the Division of Children and Youth, State Department of Public Welfare, Madison, Wis., December, 1957, p. 6.

[39] *Ibid.,* p. 7.

[40] *Ibid.,* p. 10.

(1) that 37 percent of the men interviewed (including those from the age of adolescence on) had engaged in some form of homosexual activity and (2) that 50 percent of the single men had had such relations by the age of thirty-five. Kinsey and his associates also maintained that 13 percent of the male population between sixteen and fifty-five had more homosexual than heterosexual experience for at least three years. They estimated that 8 percent of the population were exclusively homosexual for periods of at least three years and that 4 percent were permanently so.[41]

Despite the apparent prevalence of homosexual activities among men, society is outraged when forced homosexual activities come to public notice, particularly when involving an older man and a small boy. Many homosexuals apparently conduct their relationships in secret and are never detected. Such activities are nevertheless, as Kinsey says, "an affront to social conventions," and persons who are detected may be pitilessly condemned.[42] The latter undermine social conventions and make it more difficult for both sexes to develop normal heterosexual relations. They are also an indication of the need for more effective sex education.

Laws restricting homosexuality in the United States are derived from British church law (as is true in Great Britain). This in turn is largely based upon Hebrew concepts as embodied in the Old Testament. To the Hebrews homosexuality was "an abomination unto the Lord." Homosexuality was a common practice among the ancient Greeks and Chaldeans, but the Egyptians and Assyrians had stern laws against it. Homosexual practices are found among many primitive tribes.[43]

There are many theories on homosexuality. One is that homosexuals have an "inborn" trait, another that they are physiologically differentiated. Neither of these theories can be supported, except in rare instances. The majority of homosexuals are generally recognized to be psychologically conditioned. According to Berg and Allen, they are the result of either (1) hostility or (2) excessive affection for the mother or (3) hostility or (4) too great affection for the father. In some cases homosexuality is due to excessive isolation such as may occur in boys' schools or in the army.[44] In 1955 there were 6644 homosexual offenses known to the police in England and Wales; 2504 of the cases were brought to trial and 2288 (slightly more than one-third) were found guilty.[45] The penalty for homosexuality in England is fairly severe and was not changed essentially by the recent recommendations of the Wolfenden report on prostitution and homosexuality.

Where persons are definitely homosexual and indulge in homosexual re-

[41] Kinsey *et al.*, *Sexual Behavior in the Human Male*, pp. 650–651.

[42] *Ibid.*, p. 655.

[43] Cf. Charles Berg and Clifford Allen, *The Problem of Homosexuality*, Citadel Press, New York, 1958, pp. 16–22.

[44] *Ibid.*, pp. 46–52.

[45] Sir John Wolfenden, Chairman, *Report of the Committee on Homosexual Offences and Prostitution*, Her Majesty's Printing Office, London, 1957, Appendix, Tables I, II, and III, pp. 130–132.

lations over a long period of time, they tend to be recognized as such and known to each other. For this reason, a number of homosexuals may be employed within the same organization or business. During the Truman administration the Senate Foreign Relations Committee raised an issue about dismissals in the State Department and it was revealed that a sizable number of persons dismissed were homosexuals. Homosexuals in positions of trust are particularly subject to blackmail and may become involved in treasonous activities because they may be threatened with exposure if they do not cooperate with the blackmailer. Homosexuals with money may be similarly threatened unless they pay the racketeers large sums.[46]

So far as women are concerned, Kinsey found that 72 percent had no homosexual experience, whereas 28 percent admitted they had at some time engaged in homosexual relations of some sort. For most of these women the homosexual experience was not overt but was limited to kissing and other non-genital contacts. For many of the women the relationship was of very short duration, sometimes occurring only once or twice. Between 2 and 6 percent of the unmarried women and less than 1 percent of the married were estimated to be entirely homosexual. Previously married females who had been divorced, separated, or widowed were also rated wholly homosexual in 1 to 6 percent of the cases.[47] Some prostitutes are also homosexual.[48]

Rape
     Statutory rape is usually defined as enticing a female under the age of consent to have sex relations. In some states it is punished as a misdemeanor. Judges often regard such behavior with revulsion and define virtually all cases as forced rape. According to Ploscowe, there is great variation in the attitudes of officials. Laws covering statutory rape are considered a protection to young unmarried girls, although many men think such laws deal unduly harshly with men and boys. Rape is one of the few instances in which law and public opinion tend to consider the man's offense worse than that of his female partner.[49] Rape carries a connotation of brutal assault and men in general are disgusted by such conduct. Even in prisons, where the average convict has probably been sexually promiscuous, other prisoners regard rapists as the lowest of all offenders.

Because so much stigma is attached to rape, many cases are probably not reported because of the publicity to the women or girls involved. According to official estimates, there were 21,080 rape cases in the United States in 1957 and 20,300 in 1956.[50] Precise information on the number of cases of forcible and statutory rape is not available for the country as a whole. For 445 cities over 25,000 population, 10,677 rape cases (of which 6045 were

---

[46] Morris Ploscowe, *Sex and the Law*, Prentice-Hall, Inc., New York, 1951, pp. 206–215.
[47] Kinsey *et al.*, *Sexual Behavior in the Human Female*, pp. 453–454 and 473–476
[48] Berg and Allen, *op. cit.*, p. 61.
[49] Ploscowe, *op. cit.*, chap. VI, "Rape."
[50] *Uniform Crime Reports, 1957*, Federal Bureau of Investigation, U.S. Department of Justice, Washington, 1958, p. 71.

forcible and 4632 statutory) were reported in 1957 and 10,395 in 1956
(6004 forcible and 4391 statutory).[51] For 1958 and after, statutory rape cases
are not included in major crime trends.

Incest

Of all types of sex crimes brought before the court those involving
incest tend to represent the most depraved and disorganized home backgrounds. Incest is defined as sex relations within prohibited degrees of kinship
and between persons whose marriage is illegal. Usually such cases are in the
primary family. The most common type of incest brought to court is that in
which a father forces his attentions upon a daughter. Brother and sister cases
are less frequent, and rarer still are mother-son cases. There are, of course,
other incest cases. In twenty-one states, marriage (or intercourse) between
first cousins is considered incest. In addition, uncle-niece, aunt-nephew, and
grandparent-grandchild sex relationships are defined as incest. The old
Jewish code forbade marriage within seven degrees of relationship. In England
until fairly recently in-laws were not allowed to marry following the death
of a spouse. In fact according to the Catholic Church even godchild-godparent
marriage was taboo. At various times the church has extended the prohibition of marriage to fourth cousins, to sixth cousins, and at one time to those
related in any degree.[52]

Some psychiatrists seem to think that incestuous tendencies are widespread,
but Kinsey maintains that this is because they judge the total population by
the disturbed or problem cases which they meet professionally. Kinsey holds
that most incestuous relationships take place among preadolescent children.
These apparently seldom, if ever, come to court.[53] Statistics on incest are not
available for the country as a whole, but every urban juvenile court in the
country has an occasional case in which the father has forced his daughter
into sexual relations.

Weinberg's analysis of 203 incest cases in Illinois in and around the
Chicago area is one of the few studies available on the subject. His study
included 159 cases of father-daughter incest, 37 brother-sister, 2 mother-son,
and 5 in which there was a *combination* of father-daughter and brother-
sister incest. No other types were involved in Weinberg's study. In some of
the families the father was involved with 3 daughters, and there were some
families in which 2 sisters had relations with more than 1 brother.[54] In all cases
the aggressor in the incest had a prior career of personal disorganization.

The girls had a little more schooling on the average than their brothers
when involved with them. The girls averaged seven years of schooling, their
brothers six. Five of the girls (13.5 percent) had gone to high school and one
had had one year at college. Only two of the brothers reached the tenth grade

---

[51] *Ibid.*, p. 110.
[52] S. Kirson Weinberg, *Incest Behavior,* Citadel Press, New York, 1955, chap. I, "Incest Taboo."
[53] Kinsey *et al., Sexual Behavior in the Human Male,* p. 558.
[54] Weinberg, *op. cit.*, pp. 41–42.

—their highest achievement. The fathers involved were mostly dull normal.[55]

Certain social characteristics of the incest cases stand out. Sisters involved with brothers were more promiscuous than daughters involved with fathers. In general, however, the family setting of all the incest cases was one of promiscuity. In father-daughter incest 40.3 percent of the fathers were widowed or separated. The fathers averaged 43.5 years of age. There was usually a pattern of excessive drinking on the father's part and this often seemed to initiate incestuous relations. Homes were overcrowded and children of both sexes often slept together, sometimes in the same room with their parents. Lack of privacy was unquestionably a factor in many cases. According to Weinberg the siblings involved in incest usually did not consider their behavior wrong.[56]

The Prostitute

Prostitutes are at once among the most condemned and among the most tolerated of sex offenders. Prostitution is defined as illicit sex relations on a promiscuous and mercenary basis with accompanying emotional indifference. The mistress who receives monetary blandishments from her lover is not a prostitute. Her status, while legally and socially disapproved, has many of the aspects of marriage. The prostitute exploits sex relations for financial gain. The patron of the prostitute pays for the sex satisfaction which he receives and ordinarily has no affection or personal interest in the prostitute. In fact, he may have great contempt for her because she is antithetical to his ideals for women. Nevertheless, he patronizes her and is her excuse for being. There would be no prostitution if there were no demand for the prostitute's services.

A number of states have laws which make it a crime for a man to enter a house of prostitution or to meet with a woman for such a purpose. None of these laws has apparently discouraged men from patronizing prostitutes. If the judges were women in such cases, the decisions might be different. Male judges are seemingly everywhere reluctant to punish men for being customers of prostitutes.[57] Where prostitutes resort to open solicitation or seek out men openly in bars, taverns, hotel lobbies, or elsewhere, they are likely to be picked up by the police. When they are "careful and discreet," they are not usually caught unless they solicit a policeman in plain clothes.[58]

Prostitutes tend to ally themselves with other criminal groups. Prostitution is often controlled by gangsters and racketeers. Where this is not true, virtually all houses of prostitution depend upon strong-arm gangsters or "mobs" for protection. Law enforcement officers who are known to have plans for cleaning up a notorious house or district are often subject to blackmail. Every possible device is employed to escape the padlock, fine, and imprisonment. Prostitutes also commit other crimes in the form of larceny of

[55] *Ibid.,* p. 49.
[56] *Ibid.,* chap. VI, "The Family Setting."
[57] Ploscowe, *op. cit.,* p. 250.
[58] *Ibid.,* p. 265.

their patrons and then use blackmail to defend themselves against accusation.

The close link between the criminal underworld and prostitution is evidenced in the following case. A woman attorney posing as a would-be prostitute gained entrance to a well-known house on South Prairie Avenue, Chicago. She was actually working for the government. Shortly after her visit she reported to the U.S. Attorney's office evidence of illicit narcotic distribution by the hostess of this house. While she was standing in the office she was shot by a "mobster" from the skyscraper office building across the street. The hostess was later convicted on a narcotic charge and served a sentence in the Federal Women's Reformatory.[59]

Prostitutes are usually arrested after they have solicited an officer or an officer has observed them soliciting on the street or in a doorway. Sometimes police actually get involved in illicit relations before arresting them although this is not "in line of duty." Anyone who has observed the rank and file of prostitutes appearing on a typical day at the Morals Court can testify to the sorry, dreary picture.[60]

No one knows how many prostitutes there are in the United States—very possibly at least half a million, probably more. There were 3906 men (presumably pimps or panderers who supervise or control groups of prostitutes) and 8788 women arrested in cities of 2500 or over in 1957 for prostitution or commercialized vice. In addition, 39,605 women were arrested for "disorderly conduct" and 6737 for "vagrancy," both of which are euphemistic terms for prostitution. The women in these groups totaled 55,130 or approximately 25 percent of all women arrested. Undoubtedly some of the 1134 women arrested on narcotic charges were also prostitutes, and it is likely that the 8033 women arrested on "suspicion" were arrested on suspicion of prostitution.

We know that only a fraction of prostitutes are arrested, but we have no accurate basis for estimating the exact number so engaged. The ones arrested are largely those apprehended for streetwalking. Many prostitutes are arrested several times a year. Sometimes police arrest such women illegally simply because they recognize them on the street and presume they are "up to no good." The woman with a record may get in trouble if she merely goes out to buy a toothbrush after dark. Social workers at the House of Detention in New York say that judges are inclined to sentence a woman picked up without any real evidence if she already has a record.

It is against the law to operate a house of prostitution in forty-six states and the District of Columbia. In Nevada and Arizona such places may not exist near a school or church or on a principal street. A large share of the attempt to control prostitution has been in the abatement laws, which declare houses

[59] Material obtained from a prisoner interviewed at the Federal Women's Reformatory at Alderson by Miss Elliott.

[60] We cannot go into the history of prostitution here. Cf. Willoughby C. Waterman, *Prostitution and Its Repression in New York City (1900–1931)*, Columbia University Press, New York, 1932, and Howard B. Woolston, *Prostitution in the United States*, Appleton-Century Crofts, Inc., New York, 1921.

of prostitution public nuisances. Iowa probably has the most famous law. Adopted in 1909, it gave any citizen as well as any county attorney, group, or incorporated body the right to apply to a judge for an injunction to restrain the owner from operating such a house. All personal property in the house may be ordered sold and the house closed for one year unless the owner pays certain costs and gives his bond for good behavior. Special taxes were levied against the houses, and the owner is fined or imprisoned for failure to comply. Forty-three states now permit citizens to participate in closing such houses, although the laws vary in other details. In 1952 it was stated that only one red-light district operated in the United States, although many houses operate in rural areas or unincorporated areas outside of cities.[61]

Why Women Become Prostitutes

Most prostitutes come from the lower economic and social levels, but in general it may be said that an immoral environment is more important than poverty per se. A few prostitutes are recruited from higher social levels. In times past the early induction into industry was an important factor. Young girls aged fourteen and fifteen working in a factory met many pressures that they were not sophisticated enough to either understand or resist. Some unscrupulous men lure unsuspecting girls into opportunities to make money through street pickups or in cheap dance halls and elsewhere. Some are products of the incestuous homes previously mentioned. If a girl has been assaulted in childhood, she may drift into prostitution.

Some girls are partially intoxicated when they have their first sex experience. Some women have unusual sexual urges which they seek to satisfy in prostitution. Many have been seduced and abandoned by lovers and feel there is no other way out. Others are lured by pimps and panderers who promise a life of luxury. These girls often come from the same background as delinquents who are not promiscuous. The desire for luxury is unquestionably a factor in luring girls into prostitution. The luxury, however, is not for long. Prostitutes fade, and panderers are always searching for new recruits. Many superannuated prostitutes become scrubwomen or enter other lowly pursuits.

Some unmarried mothers become prostitutes because of their loss of status. Some women are induced to enter prostitution by their husbands or parents. Some are persuaded by other prostitutes. Women prostitutes in prison often recruit younger prisoners to become prostitutes when their time is finished.[62]

[61] Bascom Johnson, *Injunctions and Abatements Versus Houses of Prostitution,* reprint from *Journal of Social Hygiene,* May, 1952, pp. 1–6. A "red-light" district is a place where houses operate unmolested by the police within a restricted area. They are so called because they formerly advertised by placing red lights in the windows.

[62] There is extensive literature on the causes of prostitution. Courtney Ryley Cooper, *Designs in Scarlet,* Little, Brown and Company, Boston, 1939; Herbert Asbury, *Gem of the Prairie* (An Informal History of the Chicago Underworld), Alfred A. Knopf, Inc., New York, 1940; Gladys Mary Hall, *Prostitution, A Survey and a Challenge,* Williams and Norgate, Ltd., London, 1933, chap. III; Havelock Ellis, *Studies in the Psychology of Sex,* F. A. Davis Company, Philadelphia, 1910; Walter C. Reckless, "Prostitution in the

One of the unpleasant chapters in human history is the traffic in women on a local, national, and international scale. In the United States, the Mann Act makes taking a woman across a state line for immoral purposes a federal offense, and international codes and immigration laws forbid the importation of foreign women for prostitution, but these laws are often evaded.

Types of Prostitutes

There are many class distinctions among prostitutes. The lowest ranking are the streetwalkers, who solicit men on the street. Some prostitutes live in houses of ill fame; their destiny is presided over by a "madam," who pays the women a percentage of the price charged the patrons. These houses may be the low-class "crib" variety. Middle-class and well-to-do parlor houses or "massage parlors" cater to men with more money, while truly luxurious places cater to men in the upper income groups. The latter places require considerable organization in order to protect their well-known patrons and thrive because the police are bribed. Some prostitutes are call girls and either operate on their own or have a manager (madam or pimp) who makes appointments. Some meet men at cheap hotels. "Higher-class" call girls with large incomes may receive their customers at their own apartments or in expensive hotels.

Call girls derive a considerable amount of patronage from out-of-town businessmen of the upper economic echelon. Early in 1959 Edward R. Murrow presented a nation-wide documentary radio broadcast in which unidentified call girls testified that they were kept on corporation payrolls to "entertain" out-of-town customers. Mr. Murrow was attacked by corporations who said they "never heard of such practices." But he stood his ground and maintained that his evidence was correct. How extensive this practice is no one knows. Hubert I. Teitelbaum, U.S. District Attorney in Pittsburgh, says there are indications that it exists there.[63] The late Ray Sprigle, ace reporter of the *Pittsburgh Post-Gazette,* earlier made a private investigation of call girls who catered to important businessmen. His material was never published.[64]

Prostitution and World War II

Prostitution declined in most communities in the United States during World War II. It increased considerably, however, in areas near army camps and near the front in the various theaters of war. During the war there was a concerted campaign to eliminate prostitution by both the army and the navy. In this effort they had the assistance of the U.S. Public Health Service, the FBI, the Federal Security Agency, the International Association of Chiefs of Police, the National Probation Association, the National Association of Taxi Cab Owners, the American Social Hygiene Association, and many civic or-

United States," part V, chap. 2 in Morris Fishbein and Ernest W. Burgess (eds.), *Successful Marriage,* Doubleday and Company, Inc., New York, 1947, all give important insights into causes of prostitution.

[63] Eve Merriam, "Sex as a Selling Aid," *The Nation, 188*:239–242 (March 21, 1959).

[64] Interview with the authors.

ganizations. Red-light districts were closed in 650 communities, and on the whole the situation appeared to be materially improved.[65] The May Act was passed to prohibit solicitation in military areas. However, it is generally believed that much prostitution went underground.

In the military outposts in Hawaii and Europe, control was virtually nonexistent, although the army initially penalized men who lost time because of venereal disease. This rule was lifted after the invasion of France and Germany, and the disease rate (and presumably the prostitution rate) went up markedly. After World War II was over in 1945, there was a letdown in prostitution control at home, although conditions were better than after World War I.[66]

At home, meanwhile, the discovery that penicillin afforded a very effective and short treatment for curing venereal disease led to a renewed attack by the U.S. Public Health Service. Some medical leaders declared venereal disease to be a health and not a moral issue and by so doing hoped to bring unreported cases to light. A considerable number of cured persons have been reinfected, as the later discussion shows. There seems to be no way to prevent veneral disease from either spreading or recurring without moral restraint and the repression of prostitution.

Venereal Disease

Prostitution is the major source of venereal disease infection. This is one of the major reasons for the campaigns against prostitution which have been conducted by local, state, and national public health services as well as by civic organizations. Promiscuity, whether or not for hire, is the important factor in spreading the disease. The two most important venereal diseases are *syphilis* and *gonorrhea,* although chancroid and other less common venereal diseases exist.

Syphilis is the most serious venereal disease because, if untreated, it invades the tissues, nervous system, and bones and gives rise to ailments which imitate nearly every disease to which human beings are liable. If it is not arrested, it may cause insanity. A sizable percentage of mental patients are victims of late syphilis. Syphilis exacts a heavier toll among men than women and has been more virulent in the United States among Negroes than among white people.[67] The incidence of gonorrhea has always been higher than the incidence of syphilis, but it often is not regarded as serious. Women suffer more seriously from it than men because it invades the female genital organs. Many surgical operations on women are necessitated because of this disease.

Syphilis is caused by a microorganism, *spirocheta pallida,* which nearly

---

[65] "Social Protection—A Summing Up," *Journal of Social Hygiene, 21:*303–307 (May, 1945). Cf. also Francis E. Merrill, *Social Problems on the Home Front,* Harper & Brothers, 1948, chap. 6, "War and Prostitution."

[66] Editorial, "A Progress Report in Case of the People vs. the Prostitution Racket," *Journal of Social Hygiene, 35:*51–74 (February, 1949).

[67] Thomas A. Parran, *Shadow on the Land—Syphilis,* Reynal and Hitchcock, New York, 1937, p. 29.

always invades the body through genital contact, although it occasionally enters through breaks in the skin, cuts or sores. The mucous membrane, eyes, and genital tracts are particularly susceptible to syphilitic infection. Syphilis has been classified as a disease of four stages, but most modern medical authorities now differentiate the major stages as "early" and "late" syphilis.

A hard sore or chancre appears at the point of penetration (sometimes not until twelve to forty days after infection). A second early stage (not always present) is characterized by a skin rash or eruption, which may be mild or severe. In the third stage numerous growths appear, and in the fourth stage the bones, liver, lungs, eyes, and nervous system are invaded. In this final stage insanity (general paresis), locomotor ataxia, or arteriosclerosis may appear as manifestations of the disease. Congenital syphilis, passed from the infected mother to her child, is even more serious than primary syphilis. Many syphilitic fetuses are born dead. Of those born alive, many are blind or have defective hearing or some loathsome physical defects.[68]

Gonorrhea is caused by the *gonococcus bacterium*. Because it is milder than syphilis, many cases go untreated among men, who spread the disease to their wives. Surgical operations among women have often been occasioned by this disease, as stated above. Gonorrhea has also been an important source of arthritis, endocarditis, and blindness among babies. This disease may be spread in families of diseased persons if members use a common towel or fail to scrub the bathtub well. Young girls are particularly likely to contract the disease from such careless exposure.

When the antibiotic penicillin came into active use during World War II, it was soon found to have remarkable effectiveness in treating both syphilis and gonorrhea. One injection has usually been sufficient to cure gonorrhea. An estimated 90 percent of syphilis cases apparently yield to penicillin treatment, although several injections may be necessary for stubborn cases. In certain instances the antibiotic alone is not enough and metallic drugs and fever therapy may supplement the treatment. Prior to the advent of antibiotics, mercurial compounds were used for syphilis and the treatment was both long drawn out (usually eighteen months to two years) and dangerous. The new antibiotic treatments have not proved successful with late syphilis or neurosyphilis.

Venereal Disease Control

The present-day control of venereal disease has been made possible by the combination of (1) bacteriological, chemical, and antibiotic discoveries, (2) aroused public opinion, (3) legislative provisions for control, and (4) the energy and determination of public health experts. Much of the fight to overcome venereal disease stems from the initial effort of Dr. Thomas A. Parran. Appointed Chief of the Division of Venereal Disease of the Public Health Service in 1926, he immediately began a vigorous attack on venereal

[68] Harold N. Cole and Philip C. Jeans *et al., Syphilis in Mother and Child,* U.S. Public Health Service, Venereal Disease Information Supplement No. 7.

diseases. In 1930 he became U.S. Assistant Surgeon General and helped develop a policy of cooperation with state health departments. When he became Surgeon General in 1936, he was responsible for a full-scale one-man attack on venereal disease.

It is hard to realize now that Dr. Parran had to fight ignorance, public apathy, and taboo. At that time, radio authorities would not even permit him to use the word "syphilis" in a broadcast. But Dr. Parran was not discouraged and public opinion soon came to his rescue. He wrote vigorously for magazines and his book *Shadow on the Land* made the public aware of the dangers inherent in the disease. Dr. Parran insisted that every case of syphilis must be located, reported, and have its source ascertained, and that money for drugs and doctors must be made available to treat all cases. He further insisted that all public health agencies and private physicians should unite to fight the disease, and that the public must be informed about both treatment and the necessity for protection. Since Dr. Parran's early efforts clinical treatment, mass blood tests in locating cases, and improvement and general use of antibiotics in treatment have all paid off.[69]

Trends in Venereal Disease

It was not until 1939 that all states were required to report venereal diseases to the U.S. Public Health Service; hence statistics gathered before that time are not very meaningful. In 1939, as Table 6.4 shows, there were 478,738 reported cases of syphilis and 182,314 of gonorrhea. Since a great many people suffering with gonorrhea do not seek medical attention, the gonorrhea figures were unquestionably much too low. With better understanding of gonorrhea, recent figures are probably much more accurate.

For both diseases there was marked rise during World War II, although from 1940 on all military cases were excluded from both syphilis and gonorrhea figures. In 1943 a peak of 575,593 cases of syphilis were reported. Since 1944 syphilis cases have declined sharply (chiefly because of the use of penicillin). For gonorrhea, reported cases went up to 400,639 in 1947. Both syphilis and gonorrhea have since declined but, of the two, syphilis cases have been much more drastically reduced. Syphilis cases reported in 1958 were approximately one-third of the number reported in 1947, whereas the gonorrhea cases numbered 220,191 (over half of the 1947 rate). There was a slight upsurge of syphilis cases in 1957, accounted for by cases among Mexican agricultural laborers.

Many cases still exist, even though the means of eliminating venereal disease are at hand. Some of the cases are repeaters, that is, persons who have been cured and subsequently became reinfected. The highest percentage of infection has always been in the lower class and particularly among Negroes. A special study was therefore made of nonwhite syphilitic patients in Missis-

[69] *Milestones in Venereal Disease Control,* Venereal Disease Branch, Communicable Disease Center, Atlanta, Georgia, U.S. Public Health Center, 1959, pp. 1–9.

sippi in order to find out what type of education was most needed to fight the disease among the population with the highest incidence.

Several facts emerged from the survey: One was that women are less willing to recognize the disease than men. A second was that the unmarried were inclined to recognize the symptoms earlier than the married. Apparently men

TABLE 6.4. Cases of Syphilis and Gonorrhea Reported to the Public Health Service by State Health Departments, and Rates per 100,000 Population (all reporting areas in continental U.S., 1939–1958)

Fiscal Year	Syphilis		Gonorrhea	
	Cases	Rates per 100,000	Cases	Rates per 100,000
1939	478,738	367.1	182,314	139.8
1940	472,900	359.7	175,841	133.8
1941	485,560	368.2	193,468	146.7
1942	479,601	363.4	212,403	160.9
1943	575,593	447.0	275,070	213.6
1944	467,755	367.9	300,676	236.5
1945	359,114	282.3	287,181	225.8
1946	363,647	271.7	368,020	275.0
1947	372,963	264.6	400,639	284.2
1948	338,141	234.7	363,014	252.0
1949	288,736	197.3	331,661	226.7
1950	229,723	154.2	303,992	204.0
1951	198,640	131.8	270,459	179.5
1952	168,734	110.8	245,633	161.3
1953	156,099	100.8	243,857	157.4
1954	137,876	87.5	239,661	152.0
1955	122,075	76.0	239,787	149.2
1956	126,219	77.1	233,333	142.4
1957	135,542[a]	81.2	216,476	129.8
1958	126,072[a]	74.0	220,191	129.3

NOTE: Beginning in 1939, all states were included in the reporting area. Military cases were excluded after 1940. Rates are based on population estimates by the Bureau of the Census.

[a] Includes 7159 cases in 1957 and 9442 cases in 1958 among Mexican agricultural workers diagnosed in the United States.

SOURCE: Taken from Table 4, *V.D. Fact Sheet* (15th revision), Public Health Service, U.S. Department of Health, Education, and Welfare, January, 1959, p. 8.

were afraid that they would be rejected by their wives if the latter knew their husbands had syphilis. As for the question why people who were cured became reinfected, the answer seems to be that the temporary satisfactions of sex outweighed the personal and social hazards.[70] Such persons have some-

[70] Robert O. Carlson, *Case Finding and Patient Management Through an Understanding of Known Syphilitic Patients,* Cooperative Study of Mississippi State Board of Health and U.S. Public Health Service, 1950, Vol. I, pp. 78–79.

thing in common with recidivists in the criminal population. They lack self-discipline and take risks which will inevitably endanger their own well-being. Social values have no important meaning for them.

Decline in Mortality from Syphilis

Along with the reduction in the incidence of the disease, there has been a gradual decrease in syphilis mortality in the last two decades. The decline in the overall rate was from 10.7 per 100,000 population in 1940 to an estimated 2.2 in 1957. Percentage-wise the decrease has been about the same in both racial groups, but the great decline in cases has been among the Negro population. Here the rate was 40.2 per 100,000 in 1940 and declined to 7.0 in 1957—still over four times the 1957 white rate.[71] There are almost no cases of death directly due to gonorrhea although it may cause some deaths indirectly. Insanity due to syphilis has also decreased. The rate of first admissions to civilian mental hospitals was 6.1 per 100,000 in 1940. In 1956 it was .8 per 100,000.[72]

Venereal Disease Among Teen-Agers

A discouraging aspect of the current venereal disease problem is the incidence of syphilis and gonorrhea among teen-agers. A survey made by the U.S. Bureau of Public Health in 1953 (based upon mass serological tests) showed that there was a sharp increase in syphilis and gonorrhea in the 15- to 19-year-old group with the highest incidence for all in the ages 20 to 24. There was some decline after 25, and beginning with the 30- to 34-year-olds the rate of infection declined rapidly for each age group, as shown in Table 6.5.[73] The venereal disease rates for teen-agers thus coincided with what Kinsey found to be the period of highest sexual activity for males. Girls, however, had a much greater incidence of venereal disease before 17 than did boys, despite Kinsey's contention of a lower rate of illicit relations among girls generally.[74] The male rate of venereal disease exceeded that of girls at 17 years, however, and was markedly higher at 19[75] and thereafter.

The distribution of venereal disease cases among teen-agers was much higher in southern states than in the North, with the exception of Iowa. In Oklahoma, Arkansas, Mississippi, Alabama, Georgia, South Carolina, North Carolina, Delaware, Maryland, and Iowa 30 percent or more of the patients with venereal disease were under 20. And in all of the southeastern states, as well as Kansas, Missouri, Texas, and Louisiana, teen-agers comprised 25 to 29 percent of those infected. Poverty and racial factors are important

---

[71] Cf. Table 3, "Reported Mortality and Insanity Due to Syphilis in Continental U.S. 1940–1958," in *V.D. Fact Sheet* (15th revision), Public Health Service, U.S. Department of Health, Education, and Welfare, Washington, January, 1959, p. 6.

[72] *Ibid.*

[73] James F. Donahue, Geraldine A. Gleeson, Kenneth H. Jenkins, and Eleanor V. Price, "Venereal Disease Among Teen-Agers," *Public Health Reports,* 70:453–461 (May, 1955).

[74] Kinsey *et al., Sexual Behavior in the Human Male,* pp. 219–223.

[75] Donahue *et al., op. cit.*

TABLE 6.5. Cases of Primary and Secondary Syphilis and Gonorrhea and Total Syphilis and Gonorrhea Cases Reported in Continental United States, Calendar Year 1953, by Age

Age	Total Syphilis[a] and Gonorrhea			Primary and Secondary Syphilis and Gonorrhea			Percent Primary and Secondary Syphilis and Gonorrhea of Total Syphilis and Gonorrhea
	Number	Percent	Cumulative Percent	Number	Percent	Cumulative Percent	
Less than 1	514	0.13	0.13	206	0.08	0.08	40.08
1	192	.05	.18	51	.02	.10	26.56
2	225	.06	.24	138	.06	.16	61.33
3	196	.05	.29	137	.06	.22	69.90
4	235	.06	.35	162	.07	.28	68.94
5	271	.07	.42	158	.06	.34	58.30
6	313	.08	.50	159	.06	.40	50.80
7	321	.08	.58	136	.06	.46	42.37
8	312	.08	.66	114	.05	.51	36.54
9	340	.09	.75	114	.05	.56	33.53
10	381	.10	.85	100	.04	.60	26.25
11	356	.09	.94	73	.03	.63	20.51
12	586	.15	1.09	200	.08	.71	34.13
13	1,085	.28	1.37	619	.25	.96	57.05
14	2,242	.58	1.95	1,612	.65	1.61	71.90
15	4,174	1.08	3.03	3,322	1.35	2.96	79.59
16	7,369	1.90	4.93	6,208	2.51	5.47	84.24
17	11,710	3.03	7.96	10,312	4.18	9.65	88.06
18	17,504	4.52	12.49	15,483	6.27	15.91	88.45
19	18,499	4.78	17.27	16,072	6.51	22.42	86.88
20–24	93,390	24.14	41.41	80,306	32.52	54.94	85.99
25–29	72,935	18.85	60.26	56,729	22.97	77.91	77.78
30–34	44,553	11.51	71.77	28,349	11.48	89.39	63.63
35–39	28,411	7.34	79.11	13,072	5.29	94.68	46.01
40–44	21,922	5.68	84.78	6,774	2.74	97.42	30.90
45–49	16,112	4.16	88.94	3,201	1.30	98.72	19.87
50–54	13,569	3.51	92.45	1,698	.69	99.40	12.51
55–59	9,924	2.56	95.02	753	.30	99.70	7.59
60–64	8,020	2.07	97.09	383	.16	99.86	4.78
65–69	6,045	1.56	98.65	216	.09	99.95	3.57
70–74	3,008	.78	99.43	86	.03	99.98	2.86
75–79	1,398	.36	99.79	27	.01	99.99	1.93
80+	801	.21	100.00	7	.00	100.00	.87
Total	386,913	100.00	—	246,977	100.00	—	63.83

[a] Total syphilis includes early latent, late latent, and congenital as well as primary and secondary.

SOURCE: *Public Health Reports, 70:* 455 (May, 1955).

correlated factors in all of these states but Iowa. Iowa is a wealthy state with but few Negroes and has a low venereal disease rate. Of those having the disease a disproportionate share are juveniles. South Dakota is the only other state with a comparable rate. There 25 to 29 percent of the infections were among teen-agers.[76]

[76] *Ibid.*

TABLE 6.6.   Percentage of All Gonorrhea and Primary and Secondary Syphilis
Cases Reported Among Persons Under 20 Years of Age by State

State	Male	Female	Total	State	Male	Female	Total
Connecticut	6.0	25.4	9.6	Wisconsin	8.8	25.2	13.6
Maine	13.3	48.8	23.7	Iowa	16.2	51.2	32.7
Massachusetts	5.7	25.1	10.9	Kansas	17.6	39.8	27.4
New Hampshire	0	42.1	20.0	Minnesota	7.2	20.9	11.2
Rhode Island	10.4	36.7	16.7	Missouri	20.1	37.3	25.8
Vermont	13.5	21.1	16.1	Nebraska	10.7	24.5	17.2
Delaware	26.5	50.0	33.9	North Dakota	a	a	18.5
New Jersey	12.3	29.6	17.3	South Dakota	27.0	42.2	28.1
New York	9.4	24.6	11.6				
Pennsylvania	14.3	31.2	19.4	Arkansas	25.3	41.1	33.2
				Louisiana	22.1	35.7	26.7
District of				New Mexico	15.0	27.3	19.1
Columbia	a	a	a	Oklahoma	24.0	40.0	31.7
Kentucky	21.0	33.8	25.3	Texas	22.2	36.6	27.9
Maryland	24.2	48.6	31.6	Colorado	9.2	24.1	15.6
North Carolina	24.4	42.2	31.3	Idaho	12.4	35.9	22.3
Virginia	22.1	32.2	27.9	Montana	3.4	25.0	11.3
West Virginia	17.6	38.9	29.4	Utah	11.5	32.3	18.5
Alabama	27.8	45.7	33.5	Wyoming	a	a	a
Florida	22.8	34.7	26.3				
Georgia	27.1	38.6	31.5	Arizona	15.3	32.6	19.1
Mississippi	24.4	39.2	30.0	California	9.8	25.1	14.1
South Carolina	25.2	42.2	30.5	Nevada	14.6	33.3	19.3
Tennessee	19.5	32.9	25.8	Oregon	6.0	31.5	12.7
				Washington	6.1	20.0	11.8
Illinois	10.6	25.3	14.3				
Indiana	15.7	38.8	23.0				
Michigan	16.3	24.5	19.7				
Ohio	10.0	23.5	14.1				

a No data.

SOURCE: *Public Health Reports*, 70:456 (May, 1955).

TABLE 6.7.   Infectious[a] Venereal Disease Cases
per 100,000 Population

Age	Iowa		United States	
	1957	1958	1957	1958
0–9	1.17	1.71	4.5	3.1
10–14	7.05	6.95	16.3	17.9
15–19	68.25	89.95	395.8	415.9
20–24	128.10	214.74	762.1	803.0
25–29	58.62	104.73	418.5	449.6
30–34	34.92	50.00	225.4	245.4
35–39	20.00	25.13	117.1	124.1
40–44	8.47	17.62	55.1	62.2
45–49	3.95	2.79	30.8	34.4
50 and over	.70	.97	8.1	8.5
Total	20.77	31.99	131.3	139.7

a Gonorrhea, primary and secondary syphilis cases.

SOURCE: Data furnished by the National Office of Vital Statistics, Public Health Service, U.S. Department of Health, Education, and Welfare.

The cases of infectious venereal disease were also correlated with the illegitimacy rates in thirty-two states with a coefficient of correlation of +.383. Some states show no apparent connection with illegitimacy rates. Certainly there is no such correlation in Iowa, where the ratio of illegitimate births is

TABLE 6.8. Percentage of All Gonorrhea and Primary and
Secondary Syphilis Cases Reported Among Persons
Under 20 Years of Age

| | Iowa | | | United States | | |
Year	Male	Female	Total	Male	Female	Total
1956	18.46	34.46	26.82	15.76	33.48	21.26
1957	14.02	41.98	26.35	16.79	34.43	22.15
1958	13.56	34.56	23.02	16.70	35.20	22.49

SOURCE: Data furnished by the National Office of Vital Statistics, Public Health Service, U.S. Department of Health, Education, and Welfare.

lowest of the thirty-five states registering legitimacy and illegitimacy. The correlation with figures for juvenile delinquency rates according to offenses in forty-seven states was much more significant (+.631).[77] Since venereal disease among juveniles is in itself an evidence of delinquent sex behavior, this correlation is not surprising.

Present Status of Venereal Disease

In 1956, 12,500,000 serological tests for syphilis were made by the Syphilis Control Program. Of these, 121,763 or 1.1 percent were positive— a very low proportion indeed. For the nation as a whole there were 78.8 reported cases per 100,000.[78] Many cases are not reported. The death rate for syphilis and its sequelae was 2.2 per 100,000 in 1957, as mentioned. Analyzing this we find a white death rate of 1.7 per 100,000 (with the rate for white males 2.5 per 100,000 and for white females 0.9) and a nonwhite death rate of 6.9 per 100,000 (with the rate for nonwhite males 9.8 per 100,000 and for nonwhite females 4.1).

In the upper age groups the nonwhite death rate from syphilis for persons 65–69 years old was 43.1 per 100,000; for nonwhite males it was 71.1 and for nonwhite females 22.6. The nonwhite male rate was over five and a half times the white male rate, and nonwhite female rate was a little over four times that of white females. For younger groups death rates from syphilis were much lower, but the comparative nonwhite rate was six to ten times as high as the white in the various age groups.[79] The most serious problem of syphilis, by percentage, is obviously in the Negro group, but in actual numbers there are more white persons with syphilis.

[77] *Ibid.*

[78] *Summary of Four Year Report on Health Conditions in the Americas,* Regional Office of the World Health Organization, Washington, June, 1958, pp. 58–61.

[79] *Mortality from Selected Causes, by Age and Race and Sex: United States, 1957,* Public Health Service, U.S. Department of Health, Education, and Welfare, Washington, April 24, 1959, pp. 140–141.

Venereal Disease in the Army Today

Disease rates in the army are not published in our official public health reports; nevertheless the incidence of venereal disease infection is a continual problem in the army. It has, however, been much reduced since the general use of penicillin in case of infection and prophylactic treatment has been in effect. Army men on leave have been issued prophylactics on a regular basis in recent years. The 1955–1959 average rate for the army has been 2 per year per 1000, which is not greatly higher than the civilian rate for men and women aged 20 to 24.[80] In two areas, the Caribbean and the Eighth Army (stationed in Alaska and Europe), the rate has been higher than for other army men. In March, 1959, the rate in the Eighth Army was 12.5 per 1000 —the highest for any area since 1956, when it was 13.2 per 1000 in the Japanese-Korean area.[81]

Conclusion

Sex promiscuity is thus an important problem of personal disorganization. Difficult problems of personal maladjustment plague sex offenders, especially women and girls, despite the fact that there is a great deal of moral laxity today. Venereal disease, on the other hand, is decreasing because of successful medical treatment. The problem of recurrent infections is, however, an especially difficult one.

SELECTED BIBLIOGRAPHY

Berg, Charles, and Allen, Clifford, *The Problem of Homosexuality*, Citadel Press, New York, 1958. Two British physicians analyze the problem of homosexuality.

Calderone, Mary Steichen (ed.), *Abortion in the United States*, Harper & Brothers, New York, 1958. Extensive data are presented relating to abortion studies in this country.

Elliott, Mabel A., *Correctional Education and the Delinquent Girl*, Commonwealth of Pennsylvania, Harrisburg, 1929. This remains one of the few detailed published studies of young female sex delinquents.

Ellis, Havelock, *Studies in the Psychology of Sex*, Random House, New York, 1936. This is the classic pioneer study of human sex relations.

Hall, Gladys Mary, *Prostitution, A Survey and a Challenge*, Williams and Norgate, Ltd., London, 1933. An especially good analysis is made of the causes of prostitution.

Himelhoch, Jerome, and Fava, Sylvia, *Sexual Behavior in American Society*, W. W. Norton and Company, Inc., New York, 1955. This book is an appraisal of the two Kinsey reports listed below by a large number of sociologists who present widely varying reactions and some very pertinent criticisms of the Kinsey research.

Kinsey, Alfred C., Pomeroy, Wardell B., Martin, Clyde E., and Gebhard, Paul H., *Sexual Behavior in the Human Female*, W. B. Saunders Company, Philadelphia,

---

[80] *V.D. Fact Sheet*, p. 14.

[81] *Health of the Army*, Report of the Office of the Surgeon General, U.S. Army, April, 1959, p. 13.

1953. This is the second of the famous reports. The sex habits of nearly 8000 women interviewed by the research team are analyzed.

Kinsey, Alfred C., Pomeroy, Wardell B., and Martin, Clyde E., *Sexual Behavior in the Human Male*, W. B. Saunders Company, Philadelphia, 1948. This is the first of the "Kinsey reports" on the sex habits of single, married, widowed, and separated men with revelations that astounded many people.

Merrill, Francis E., *Social Problems on the Home Front,* Harper & Brothers. New York, 1948, chap. VI. An analysis of the wartime problem of prostitution is made.

Murtagh, John M., and Harris, Sara, *Cast the First Stone*, McGraw-Hill Book Company, Inc., New York, 1957. The Chief Magistrate of New York City and a well-known author of sociological material collaborate in presenting a vivid picture of prostitution and prostitutes in New York City. They give a dismal picture of the penal treatment for prostitutes.

Parran, Thomas A., *Shadow on the Land—Syphilis,* Reynal and Hitchcock, New York, 1937. This is the classic attack on syphilis made by one of the most distinguished medical men in the field of public health.

Ploscowe, Morris, *Sex and the Law,* Prentice-Hall, Inc., New York, 1951. A well-known New York jurist discusses sex offenses and the law.

Service to Unmarried Mothers, Report of the Program Committee of the Advisory Committee of the Division of Children and Youth, State Department of Public Welfare, Madison, Wis., December, 1957. This brochure presents a comprehensive analysis of illegitimacy and the treatment of the unmarried mother in Wisconsin.

V.D. Fact Sheet, Public Health Service, U.S. Department of Health Education, and Welfare, Washington. Statistical data on venereal disease are issued annually in this publication.

Weinberg, S. Kirson, *Incest Behavior,* Citadel Press, New York, 1955. A psychiatrist's insight into incest cases in the Chicago area is combined with statistical analysis.

Wolfenden, Sir John, Chairman, *Report of the Committee of Homosexual Offences and Prostitution,* London, 1957. This is the famous report of the committee appointed by Parliament to study prostitution and homosexuality in England.

Young, Leontine, *Out of Wedlock,* McGraw-Hill Book Company, Inc., New York, 1954. A social worker analyzes the factors which are conducive to unmarried motherhood.

CHAPTER 7

The Alcoholic

The Extent and Significance of Alcoholism

Alcoholics make up one of the most significant groups of disorganized persons in the United States. These unhappy individuals are unable to carry on their occupational and family roles because of their addiction. Alcoholics are not preponderantly those in the lowest walks of life but occupy all social levels. (Their personal disorganization may involve loss of job, breakup of marriage, and economic burden on the community.) Recent research in problems of alcoholism has inquired into "the customs of drinking, the relationship between these customs and other customs, the way in which drinking habits are learned, the social control of this sort of behavior . . . , the social categories in which . . . drinking occurs . . . , the societal functions served by . . . drinking . . . , the changing patterns of drinking and their relation to other changes in the society . . . , [and] the effect of no drinking, some drinking, or excessive drinking on groups, attitudes, and behavior."[1] As a people, Americans have been traditionally intemperate, and the tensions of modern life have not improved this situation.[2] Our main concern is with the personal disorganization initiated or intensified by over indulgence in alcohol.

Not all persons who use alcohol are in danger of personal disorganization. Data on the use of alcohol in the United States are not complete, but such information as we have indicates that approximately 65 percent of the adult population use alcohol in some form at some time. Obviously many of these people suffer no ill effects from their drinking. The male population tends to indulge more frequently than the female, with 75 percent of the men and 56 percent of the women listed as either "occasional" or "regular" drinkers. The proportion of women who use alcohol, both occasionally and to excess, seems to be increasing, as a by-product of their emancipation.

Drinking is primarily an urban phenomenon; 46 percent of those in farm areas and 77 percent of those in cities of more than a million population admit that they use alcohol. The culture of rural America, which has traditionally been Protestant and Puritan, has had a stronger accompanying disapproval of alcohol. As the nation has become more urbanized, both in resi-

[1] Selden D. Bacon, "Sociology and the Problems of Alcohol," *Quarterly Journal of Studies on Alcohol, 4:*402–445 (December, 1943), pp. 407–408.
[2] Robert Straus and Selden D. Bacon, *Drinking in College,* Yale University Press, New Haven, 1953, chap. 2.

dence and in attitudes, this prejudice has apparently been breaking down. There is still a wide disparity in drinking behavior between the open country and the metropolitan area, however.[3]

These percentages deal with drinking, not with excessive drinking or clinical alcoholic cases. Data on the incidence of clinical alcoholism indicate that there are approximately five million alcoholics in the United States.[4] They are "those excessive drinkers whose dependence upon alcohol has attained such a degree that it shows a noticeable mental disturbance or an interference with their bodily or mental health, their interpersonal relations and their smooth social and economic functioning; or who show . . . signs of such developments."[5]

The estimated total of five million alcoholics includes approximately 4,250,-000 men and 750,000 women, or a sex ratio of roughly 5.8 men to 1 woman. The rate of alcoholism is based upon the number of adult males and females aged 20 years and over in the population. In these terms, the male rate for 1956 was 8270 per 100,000 of the population and the female rate was 1430.[6] The sex ratio has been approximately the same for nearly fifty years, although there was a slight acceleration of the female, as compared to the male, rate between 1953 and 1956. The United States has the highest rate of any country in the world for alcoholism "with and without complications." The rate in this country is almost twice that of the next country (France), where the condition is admittedly serious.[7]

Drink and Personal Disorganization

Drink is not so much a cause of personal disorganization as it is the expression of the personal disorganization of a large (and apparently increasing) number of American people. Most of those who drink to such an extent as to disrupt their lives have some personal inadequacy or insecurity before they take their first drink. For such people, drink is merely the means that combines with their already insecure personalities to produce the compulsive drinker. Some men and women, it is true, are seemingly "normal" in every way before they begin to drink to excess. For them, alcohol is apparently the direct agency that changes their personalities and produces a progressive deterioration in their primary group relationships. But most of those who become alcoholics are patently inadequate to their social environment before they start to drink.[8]

Millions of men and women are thus in such a state of actual or potential

---

[3] John W. Riley and Charles F. Marden, "The Social Pattern of Alcoholic Drinking," *Quarterly Journal of Studies on Alcohol,* 8:265–273 (September, 1947).

[4] Mark Keller and Vera Efron, "The Rate of Alcoholism in the U.S.A., 1954–1956," *Quarterly Journal of Studies on Alcohol,* 19:316–319 (June, 1958), Table 1.

[5] E. M. Jellinek and Mark Keller, "Rates of Alcoholism in the United States of America, 1940–1948," *Quarterly Journal of Studies on Alcohol,* 13:49–59 (March, 1952).

[6] Keller and Efron, *op. cit.,* Table 2.

[7] Mark Keller and Vera Efron, "The Prevalence of Alcoholism," *Quarterly Journal of Studies on Alcohol,* 16:619–644 (December, 1955), Table 2.

[8] Selden D. Bacon, "Alcoholism: Nature of the Problem," *Federal Probation, 11:*3–7 (January–March, 1947).

personal disorganization that alcohol has become a virtual necessity. Their definitions of the social situation have become so conditioned by their way of life that they cannot reconcile themselves to a a day or an evening without one or more drinks. Alcohol has become a crutch for millions of persons and an indispensable necessity for hundreds of thousands of others. We shall first consider the social conditions that give rise to the personal disorganization of the person who drinks to excess. We shall then consider the effects of such indulgence upon his attitudes, values, status, and role. In thus dealing first with the social trends and then with the individual manifestations, we are re-emphasizing the sociological axiom that the individual and society are but different aspects of the same functioning whole.

Alcoholism as a social problem is an expression of a complex society. A small minority of individuals in a simple society, it is true, stand out as individual problems because of their overindulgence in the grape or the malt. Simple (and especially primitive) societies engage in socially sanctioned periods of mass drunkenness at harvest time or spring planting, wherein the adult members emancipate themselves temporarily from the constraints of the mores and do things they normally would not do.[9] Neither of these expressions of drunkenness, however, is primarily the outgrowth of a disorganized society, wherein the individual has become isolated from his fellows and his personal maladjustment expresses the insecurity of a complex and secular social order. In the latter society, excessive drinking is a symptom of the breakdown of the primary group relationships that have maintained mental and social health since the earliest social intercourse.

A complex society produces tensions, inhibitions, anxieties, and aggressions in the individual which may be temporarily depressed by the use of alcohol. The very complexity of the society also renders the control of alcohol more difficult, since no single institution has jurisdiction over the loosely organized group of personal activities involved in drinking. The excessive use of alcohol in a complex society tends to deteriorate group relationships, which are neither as intimate nor as binding as those of a simpler society. The individual in our society depends for many of his contacts upon secondary groups, which by their very nature are more subject to deterioration through the use of alcohol than are the primary relationships of a simpler social structure. The complexity of our society therefore "enhances the uses of alcohol for man . . . increases the dangers of alcohol for man . . . [adds] new forces and motivations for the production and distribution of alcohol . . . [takes] away the power from agencies of control. . . ."[10]

Social disorganization takes many forms. One of the most important is the decline in the influence of the primary group and the increase in the casual contacts of the secondary group. This decline is apparent in the changing func-

[9] Donald Horton, "The Functions of Alcohol in Primitive Societies," Lecture 13 in *Alcohol, Science and Society,* published by *Quarterly Journal of Studies on Alcohol,* New Haven, 1945, pp. 153–177.

[10] Selden D. Bacon, "Alcohol and Complex Society," Lecture 14 in *Alcohol, Science and Society,* p. 195.

tions of the family, the increasing secularization of religion, the complexity of economic activity, the commercialization of recreation, and numerous other aspects of contemporary life. Such changes often cause a progressive isolation of the individual from the primary contacts of the family, the neighborhood, and the friendship group. Alcohol is frequently employed by socially isolated persons as a substitute for the warm and friendly relationships of those intimate groups. Drink often seems the only way the individual can regain (even temporarily) some of the emotional satisfactions that formerly accrued from the primary group.[11]

The role of drinking in personal and social disorganization may be summarized in terms of the immediacy of the problem—i.e., the directness of the effect upon the individual actually consuming the alcohol.[12]

1. *Immediate Personal Disorganization.* The first and most obvious aspect of personal disorganization arising from excessive consumption of alcohol is immediate. The individual finds that his drinking both expresses and causes the disorganization of the social self, as his behavior tends to lack control or discrimination.[13] In this personal category are the occasional but excessive drinker, the drunken driver, the chronic drinker, and the compulsive alcoholic, whose behavior indicates clinical neurotic symptoms.

2. *Related Personal Disorganization.* This category includes the persons whose lives are directly or indirectly affected by the excessive consumption of alcohol of one of the types mentioned above. The driver or pedestrian who is killed by a drunken driver suffers complete personal extinction. The family of the excessive or compulsive drinker may have its group functions impaired or may undergo total disorganization. The college or university whose students are involved in a drinking scandal may suffer from adverse public opinion.

3. *Social Disorganization.* The third type of problem directly or indirectly stemming from alcohol is related to the broader question of social disorganization. Every society requires a minimum of social control over its members if it is to function effectively. Large-scale behavior that is uncontrolled, uncontrollable, deviant, inadequate, or insensitive endangers the organization of the society. Excessive drinking clearly constitutes one of these situations. A complex urban society carries with it the individual's obligation to control his behavior; otherwise the society may be obliged to control it for him. This latter action may threaten the very rights which the individual considers precious.[14]

Drink and Social Patterns

A complex society contains many groups that are distinguished from one another by education, occupation, religion, ethnic origin, nationality, race,

---

[11] Selden D. Bacon, "Alcoholism and Social Isolation," *1944 Yearbook, National Probation Association,* New York, 1945, pp. 222–223.

[12] The following is adapted from Straus and Bacon, *op. cit.,* pp. 12–13.

[13] Chandler Washburne, "Alcohol, Self, and the Group," *Quarterly Journal of Studies on Alcohol, 17:*108–123 (March, 1956).

[14] Straus and Bacon, *op. cit.,* pp. 12–13.

and social status. The use and abuse of alcohol varies widely within these different groups. The degree of personal insecurity is not the same in one group as compared to another. The neurosis predisposing to excessive indulgence therefore varies considerably between groups. The acceptance of alcohol as an indispensable adjunct to recreation, for example, differs widely between urban and rural groups and between subgroups within these larger categories.

Certain nationalities have accepted the copious use of strong drink in their mores as an indication of manhood and virility, whereas others use light wines and beer as a temperate beverage. The economic folkways of business and agricultural groups embody other differences concerning the use of alcohol, with drink used as an adjunct to business dealings in one group and not in the other. Groups performing heavy physical labor have different reactions to drink from those of white-collar groups. In these and many other ways, the specific social milieu (as contrasted to the society as a whole) sets patterns for the consumption of alcoholic beverages.[15]

There is a certain ambivalence concerning drinking in American society, a duality that itself contributes to the sense of guilt among some groups following overindulgence. One pattern tends to encourage heavy drinking for recreation, for business entertainment, or to escape the boredom or physical fatigue of economic activity. Another pattern regards drinking as evil, immoral, disreputable, irreligious, and otherwise undesirable. In our urban, worldly, secular, and heterogeneous society, the patterns operating against excessive drinking appear to be losing ground as the nation as a whole develops a greater tolerance to alcohol. This is especially apparent among large groups not hitherto associated with alcohol—namely, women and adolescents. This confusion in social definition enhances the disorganization of which alcoholism is one visible expression.

Among the upper classes, drinking is not a moral issue. Both men and women drink, and there is no attendant implication of immorality. Members of the upper class who fight, commit marital infidelities, or otherwise flagrantly misbehave when under the influence of alcohol are often punished or frowned upon. But it is their antisocial behavior, not the drinking as such, that is considered reprehensible.[16] The attitudes of the upper class toward drinking have gradually pervaded those immediately below it in the social scale. The upper-class tolerance is slowly sifting downward into the middle class, that vast and amorphous group comprising a majority of the urban population.

The upper middle class has absorbed many of the attitudes of the upper class, whereas the lower middle class still maintains a comparatively strong taboo upon drinking, especially for women. Members of the lower middle

---

[15] Cf. Robert E. Clark, "The Relationship of Alcoholic Psychoses Commitment Rates to Occupational Income and Occupational Prestige," *American Sociological Review,* 14:539–543 (August, 1949).

[16] John Dollard, "Drinking Mores of the Social Classes," Lecture 8 in *Alcohol, Science and Society,* pp. 99–101.

class, furthermore, adhere strongly to certain notions of "respectability" which (in their own minds, at least) distinguish them from persons lower down in the social scale. Persons of this group also tend to retain many of the traditional religious controls, with the accompanying prejudice against excessive indulgence. From this class the major strength of the organized prohibition movement has come.[17]

The drinking mores exhibit other differences as we move down the socioeconomic scale. The phenomenon of "misery drinking" long has been common among the proletariat and has been especially evident since the industrial revolution. Long hours, insufficient food, economic insecurity, heavy work, bad housing conditions, and ignorance have been among the factors contributing to the heavy drinking among those city dwellers who work with their hands. The peasant who came to this country from Europe, furthermore, had to adjust to a new way of making a living, as well as to the other phases of a new culture. Alcohol thus served as an anodyne for the humiliations and frustrations of these European peasants turned American factory workers, as well as for the backbreaking character of their work.

The saloon has long constituted the only "club" available to the average urban dweller of modest circumstances, whether he is an industrial worker or a white-collar employee. In recent years the saloon has been supplanted by the more euphemistically titled "tavern," of which there are an estimated 200,000 in the United States. Many communities, in fact, have more taverns than they do churches, theaters, and dance halls combined. This popularity suggests that the tavern is performing a function which the family, the church, and the other formal institutions of an urbanized society are failing to perform. The impersonality, secondary social contacts, social mobility, and extreme individualism of the urban community tend to deprive the individual of recognition, response, and many of the emotional satisfactions that are necessary to his well-being. The tavern appears to fill this need in contemporary society.[18]

The process of urbanization itself is thus apparently related to the use of alcohol. Social interaction in the urban community seems to generate needs for alcohol to a greater extent than in rural areas. This rural-urban differential is complicated by class, ethnic, and religious differences. Many large cultural groups in the metropolitan areas have behavior patterns receptive to alcohol, both as a food and as a beverage. It is impossible to isolate all the factors in the relationship between urbanism and drink, but the relationship itself seems to be clear.

A study of alcoholism as a clinical condition in the large cities of the United States showed a connection between the size of the city and this form of personal disorganization. The figure of 100,000 population was taken as the

---

[17] Cf. Harrison M. Trice and David J. Pittman, "Social Organization and Alcoholism," *Social Problems*, 5:294–307 (Spring, 1958), p. 304.

[18] Boyd E. Macrory, "The Tavern and the Community," *Quarterly Journal of Studies on Alcohol*, 13:609–637 (December, 1952).

lower limit of the "large" city, with the great metropolitan communities such as New York and Chicago at the upper end of the continuum. Although a direct correlation between the size of the city and alcoholism did not apply in all cases, it was generally true that the larger the city the higher the rate. In fact, the rates in the twelve largest cities were on the average almost twice the rates in the twelve smallest big cities.[19]

Ethnic differences are also apparent in the reactions of different segments of the population to alcohol. Among Americans of Irish extraction, for example, a strong cultural tradition persists that drink and conviviality are inseparable companions and that hard liquor offers the fastest road to a pleasant euphoria. The Jewish people, on the other hand, use alcohol in moderation for religious and symbolic reasons, but they rarely drink to excess. The taboos against inebriety among Jewish-Americans are very strong, and their number of alcoholics is small.[20] Italian-Americans have a tradition of serving alcoholic beverages (principally wine) with meals and exhibit no such pronounced tendency as the Irish-Americans to overindulgence. The tendency to drink to excess is in no sense a biological trait. The factors that produce a high rate of alcoholism in different ethnic groups reflect cultural, not biological, differences.[21]

Drink and the Reduction of Anxiety

Psychological factors appear to be important in alcoholism with a close causal relationship between alcoholism and anxiety.[22] In fact, a primary motivation for the use of alcohol in all societies, primitive or civilized, is the elimination (or at least the reduction) of anxiety. This emotion may be either (1) "conscious," in the sense that the individual is aware of his anxiety and can verbally formulate his symptoms, or (2) "unconscious," in the sense that he may not be aware that he is worried, even though his drinking is unconsciously motivated by the desire to reduce the disturbing effects of anxiety. Alcohol acts as a depressant (not a stimulant, as is widely supposed) and thus brings about reduced speed of reaction, impaired ability to discriminate, and, above all, a decline in control of learned behavior.

The individual of whatever society who has "learned" from childhood that there are hostile forces in the universe, that life is short and dangerous, or that he himself is inadequate, inferior, or unloved may therefore use alco-

---

[19] Mark Keller and Vera Efron, "Alcoholism in the Big Cities of the United States," *Quarterly Journal of Studies on Alcohol, 17:*63–72 (March, 1956), p. 71.

[20] Cf. Selden D. Bacon, "Studies of Drinking in Jewish Culture. I: General Introduction," *Quarterly Journal of Studies on Alcohol, 12:*444–450 (September, 1951); Charles R. Snyder and Ruth H. Landman, "Studies of Drinking in Jewish Culture. II: Prospectus for Sociological Research on Jewish Drinking Patterns," *Quarterly Journal of Studies on Alcohol, 12:*451–474 (September, 1951).

[21] Donald D. Glad, "Attitudes and Experiences of American-Jewish and American-Irish Male Youths as Related to Differences in Adult Rates of Inebriety," *Quarterly Journal of Studies on Alcohol, 8:*406–472 (December, 1947).

[22] For a critical survey of the literature on alcohol and anxiety, see Edwin M. Lemert, "Alcoholism and the Sociocultural Situation," *Quarterly Journal of Studies on Alcohol, 17:*306–317 (June, 1956).

hol to reduce the anxiety which plagues him. Many of the controls which normally restrain him are temporarily loosened through drinking. In other words, "Shyness, caution, modesty, reserve, sharing, giving way to others, and restraining aggressive impulses are temporarily subjected to unlearning under alcohol."[23]

The reduction of anxiety is thus the important consideration, whether or not the drinker is conscious of the nature of his anxiety. Freud distinguished between what he called "real" or "objective" anxiety and "unreal" or "neurotic" anxiety. Real anxiety is aroused by the imminence of danger or pain that exists because of some outside threat to the ego; unreal anxiety arises from the fear of one's own impulses (e.g., sexual drives), whose free expression is forbidden by society.[24] Whether "conscious" or "unconscious," "real" or "neurotic," the individual experiences some degree of anxiety in all societies and some attempt to reduce this emotion by the use of alcohol.[25]

The source of anxiety varies in different societies. Among many primitive peoples, anxiety is occasioned by tangible dangers—hunger, disease, and premature death. Primitives also are concerned about such intangible but equally "real" dangers as invisible enemies, spirits, ghosts, and other forces of the nonmaterial world. Among more advanced peoples, many of the dangers of starvation and epidemic disease are minimized as sources of anxiety. They have other fears, however, which are related to interpersonal relationships: failure to gain affection, fear of loss of affection, insecurity because of the deprivation of emotional support, and similar emotional uncertainties. These interpersonal fears appear to be especially prevalent in the middle class. For example, the middle-class child is taught to expect affection from his parents, and his self-confidence is shattered by the threat to withdraw this affection.[26] In these and many other ways, the culture (and subculture) defines the forms of anxiety which some individuals attempt to reduce by drinking.

Anxiety does not necessarily indicate any disorganization in group relationships. A certain amount of anxiety is everyone's normal lot. Even the process of socialization, during which the child becomes an adult, necessitates some frustration, inhibition, and anxiety. Every society exerts certain forms of social control over its members, particularly with reference to sexual expression and physical aggression. The nature of the controls varies, and conduct permitted in one society may be prohibited in another. Each society has its own norms of behavior that become internalized in the personality and carry with them the possibility of free-floating anxiety.[27] Persons in every

---

[23] Straus and Bacon, *op. cit.*, p. 10.

[24] Sigmund Freud, *The Problem of Anxiety*, Psychoanalytic Quarterly Press, New York, 1936.

[25] Donald Horton, "The Functions of Alcohol in Primitive Societies: A Cross-Cultural Study," *Quarterly Journal of Studies on Alcohol, 4*:199–320 (September, 1943), pp. 217–230.

[26] Arnold W. Green, "The Middle-Class Male Child and Neurosis," *American Sociological Review, 11*:31–41 (February, 1946).

[27] Margaret Mead, *Coming of Age in Samoa*, William Morrow and Company, Inc., New York, 1928.

society drink to reduce anxiety, even though the reasons for this emotion reflect very different cultural situations.[28]

The use of alcohol to reduce anxiety does not always (or even necessarily) bring about this desired end. In many cases the anxiety is actually intensified, rather than reduced, by drinking. Consumption of alcohol tends to bring about two general responses (among others) in the drinker: (1) intensified sexual activity and (2) increased personal aggression. Since both of these activities are, in varying degree, condemned by organized societies, the act of drinking to relieve anxiety may actually give rise to more anxiety because the drinker is subject to punishment or the fear of punishment. He is thus a prey to conflicting anxieties: (1) those which initially stimulated the drinking and (2) those reflecting the possible loss of status or other form of punishment.

In our society, where the Puritan tradition is still strong in the mores, the anxieties connected with drinking may more than counterbalance its anxiety-relieving functions. Personal and social disorganization is augmented by the social disapproval evoked by the forbidden behavior. The ambivalent effects of drinking are thus evident. In short, "the punishments suffered as a result of release of inhibited behavior, the painful sequels to narcosis . . . , and the actualization of other dangers, may serve to attach anxiety (anticipatory pain reactions) to drinking behavior."[29]

The motivation for drinking must be considered in cultural terms. The *primary* function of drinking in all societies, as noted, appears to be the desire to reduce psychological tensions arising from anxiety.[30] The cultural definition of the accompanying behavior, however, is subject to wide variations. In one society, sexual restraint is important, and any relaxation of sex inhibitions under the influence of drink may bring severe social reprisals, with consequent feelings of anxiety for those involved. In another society, sexual behavior may be defined tolerantly, but physical aggression may be severely penalized. The cultural variables must therefore be considered if the role of drinking in any society is to be understood. This general thesis has been stated by Horton thus: ". . . The function of drinking is the reduction of anxiety (the chief psychologic variable), but any actual pattern of drinking is determined by the relationship between this and related psychologic variables, and the cultural conditions of drinking behavior."[31]

The presence of anxiety obviously does not necessarily lead to drinking and drunkenness. Other reactions to basic insecurity in interpersonal relationships may occur, either among isolated individuals or in large numbers of persons in given societies. These alternative reactions include "gambling, sexual

[28] Horton, *op. cit.*, pp. 222–223.

[29] *Ibid.*, p. 226.

[30] Other motivations for drinking are also present, such as the desire for nutrition, for sociability, for mystical religious experience, but the desire to reduce anxiety seems to be found in all societies.

[31] Horton, *op. cit.*, p. 229.

misbehavior, religious ritual, and mental disease."[32] The entire sociocultural situation has a bearing upon the extent to which anxiety is resolved by alcohol. The individual responds to his whole interpersonal and cultural environment, rather than to the simple psychological factor of anxiety. His behavior is determined in large part by the prevalent modes of anxiety release.

The Physical Effects of Alcohol

The physical effects of alcohol upon the human organism are many and varied.[33] Taken in moderation, in the form of light wines and beer, there is no conclusive evidence of harmful effects. Nor has it been clearly demonstrated that even a periodic spree is *permanently* injurious to the physical mechanism, no matter how temporarily unpleasant the effect may be. Acute alcoholism, however, is as toxic as any other form of poisoning and carries a long train of ill effects. Chronic gastritis, cirrhosis of the liver, multiple or peripheral neuritis, gout, pellagra, and delirium tremens are among the pathologies initiated or intensified by alcohol.[34] In addition to the maladies directly connected with alcoholism, the individual resistance to other diseases is appreciably lowered by excessive and extended consumption. Life insurance companies are hesitant about insuring a person known to be an alcoholic, because his life expectancy is considerably shortened by his overindulgence.[35]

Physiologically, alcohol acts as a depressant, as we have mentioned above. It therefore is not a stimulant but an anesthetic, which exerts a progressively depressant effect upon the central nervous system. The first depressant effect of increasing amounts of alcohol taken in sequence begins in the cortex of the cerebrum (the "highest" part of the brain). This center controls individual and social judgments, inhibitions, and certain nervous tensions. The depressant effect thence spreads to a "lower" level of the brain, which controls muscular coordination. The centers regulating sleep are next to be depressed, and finally the center of respiration is affected, so that breathing becomes increasingly labored. Continued concentration of alcohol thus depresses the organism so extensively that the individual may die.[36] The man who speaks of absorbing a "slight stimulant" in the form of one or more drinks does not understand the precise physiological effects of alcohol.

If alcohol is actually a depressant, why does the ordinary drinker feel stimulated, refreshed, gayer, happier, less inhibited, more sociable, and generally more able to cope with the complexities and frustrations of life? The explanation for this seemingly paradoxical reaction is that the depressant action of the alcohol upon the central nervous system tends to release inhibitions, re-

[32] Lemert, *op. cit.*, p. 313.

[33] Howard W. Haggard, "The Physiological Effects of Large and Small Amounts of Alcohol," Lecture 5 in *Alcohol, Science and Society*, pp. 59–72.

[34] Norman Jolliffe, "Alcohol and Nutrition: The Diseases of Chronic Alcoholism," Lecture 6 in *Alcohol, Science and Society*, pp. 73–82.

[35] Raymond Pearl, "Alcohol, Biological Aspects," *Encyclopaedia of the Social Sciences,* The Macmillan Company, New York, 1930.

[36] Haggard, *op. cit.*, pp. 62–64.

lax tensions, and deaden the reactions from nerves that initially produced the tired feeling. The individual who has one or more drinks *is* temporarily relieved of the sensation of fatigue and consequently "feels" stimulated. In reality, he is just as tired as before, but he does not realize it. The popular expression "feeling no pain" thus graphically expresses the anesthetic influence of alcohol upon the central nervous system.[37]

Alcohol does more than depress the nerve centers that cause the person to feel fatigued. It also depresses the control centers of the brain that normally inhibit some forms of behavior, whether speech, physical conduct, or both. According to Bacon, therefore, "Alcohol, even in small quantities, lowers sensitivity, relieves tension, allows the forgetting of difficult and unpleasant conceptions and memories . . . reduces accuracy of judgment and discrimination, especially about the self."[38] The drinker is thereby enabled to escape temporarily from some of the anxieties that beset him, and to entertain the fleeting illusion that he is more witty, attractive, or otherwise better adjusted to society than he really is. Alcohol permits the delusion that the individual has attained various goals that can actually be gained only by hard work and real ability, if at all. Alcohol furthermore gives the individual a spurious sense of control over himself and his environment. It is small wonder that many persons in a complex and frustrating society come to depend increasingly upon this attractive but specious device.

The Stages of Intoxication

The reactions of the individual from the first drink to complete oblivion indicate the progressive physical effects of alcohol taken consecutively. The depressant effect is evidenced by the increasing concentration of alcohol in the blood. When a certain point of concentration has been reached, the drinker is so depressed that he may go to sleep. He may even die. Herewith is Bogen's statement of the physical stages of intoxication from the first drink in the evening to the last one in the small hours of the next morning. These stages shade imperceptibly into one another in any given case, but there is nevertheless a rough correlation in all persons between the amount of alcohol ingested and the general condition of the drinker.[39]

1. *Subclinical Stage.* The early stage is brought about by moderate doses of alcohol: the alcoholic content of the blood remains less than one-tenth of one percent. The first effects of drink are apparent in the higher centers of the brain, in which are centered the subtler faculties of "judgment, reflection, observation, and attention." These faculties are slightly blunted even by a small quantity of alcohol. A state of euphoria, of good feeling and companionship, often accompanies this initial stage of drinking.

[37] *Ibid.*
[38] Bacon, "Alcoholism: Nature of the Problem," p. 5.
[39] The following is adapted from Emil Bogen, "The Human Toxicology of Alcohol," in Haven Emerson (ed.), *Alcohol and Man,* The Macmillan Company, New York, 1932, chap. 6.

2. *"Stimulation."* In the second stage, the alcoholic concentration of the blood is somewhere between one-tenth and two-tenths of one percent. The drinker begins to lose his self-consciousness and his self-control. He is often unable to retain control of his emotions and his moods. Some persons become hilariously jovial, others abysmally depressed. Some become pugnacious, others merely sleepy. In still others, a vague feeling of depression is often evident at this stage of intoxication. Such persons may brood while their fellows laugh.

3. *Confusion.* The alcoholic content of the blood at the third stage is approximately three-tenths of one percent. The drinker experiences a definite reduction in the previous symptoms of stimulation. The decrease in social inhibitions which characterized the earlier stages begins to disappear. It is succeeded by an increasing difficulty in physical coordination. The hearing is dulled, the speech is incoherent, and the muscular coordination necessary for walking becomes more and more difficult. At this stage, the drinker cannot stand erect. Neither can he walk a straight line.

4. *Stupor.* At this period in the drunkard's progress he has absorbed enough liquor to raise the alcoholic content of the blood to four-tenths of one percent. The patient reacts only on a very rudimentary level to the external environment. He becomes less and less able to coordinate, even in an elementary manner. He is unable to stand up. Soon he cannot even sit up. He is continually on the verge of unconsciousness and can be roused only by very strong stimulation.

5. *Coma.* When the concentration of alcohol in the blood reaches five-tenths of one percent, the drinker becomes completely unconscious. He is now dead drunk. He breathes slowly and with difficulty, his temperature is subnormal, and his pulse can be barely discerned. In this condition he is perilously close to death, for the lethal concentration of alcohol varies between six-tenths of one percent and one percent. Under such circumstances, the phrase "dead drunk" takes on a certain grim truth.

The actual amount of alcohol which will bring about this fatal concentration in the blood varies from person to person and even in the same person from time to time. Such matters as health, fatigue, and the amount of food in the stomach make a given person susceptible to alcohol in varying degrees at different times. Some have succumbed from taking one to two pints of whisky or brandy in a short time. Others have taken much larger doses of alcohol and survived. The important and incontrovertible fact, however, is that alcohol taken in large quantities is a poison which may cause the death of the drinker.[40]

During the course of a drinking bout, the individual may recapitulate his entire personal development in reverse. The first drink depresses the sections

[40] Cf. Leon A. Greenberg, "The Definition of an Intoxicating Beverage," *Quarterly Journal of Studies on Alcohol*, 16:316–325 (June, 1955). See also Leon A. Greenberg, "Intoxication and Alcoholism: Physiological Factors," *Annals of the American Academy of Political and Social Science*, 315:22–30 (January, 1958).

of the brain dealing with the complex and subtle relationships between himself and other persons. Many of the inhibitions that ordinarily produce shyness and personal insecurity are temporarily removed as he reduces the social controls that he learned last in his development. Control over emotional expression is the next partial casualty of increasing alcoholic concentration, for the individual may be unable to restrain his anger or his affection, as the case may be. Emotional control is also introduced relatively late in one's social development, but not so late as the delicate nuances of social intercourse.

With the progressive depression of the brain centers that control physical coordination, the individual begins to lose complete direction of his physical behavior. He is thereby regressing another step down the line of his own chronological development, for he was taught comparatively early in life to inhibit his physical aggressions toward others. The bodily functions of urination and defecation are next, as the now extremely drunken person approaches the stage of the infant in the cradle who has not yet been taught to control his elemental urges. When he has reached this stage of reverse recapitulation, the drunken man has, in the space of a few hours, taken a long (if temporary) step toward the destruction of his adult personality.

Drink and Personal Disorganization

Drink is both a symptom and a cause of personal disorganization. It is a *symptom* in the sense that most alcoholics are sick, neurotic people whose troubles began long before they took their first drink. It is a *cause* of disorganization in the sense that, if alcohol were not consumed, there would clearly be no alcoholics. The frustrations, insecurities, and anxieties of the individual, however, would probably take some other expression if alcoholic beverages had never been discovered. Drug addiction would be one obvious form of fleeing reality, even though the effects of many drugs differ from those of alcohol. But as long as alcohol is available, it provides a handy and comparatively inexpensive medium of temporary release for the harassed individual. Alcohol is thus not the principal "cause" of alcoholism.[41]

There is a wide difference between drunkenness and alcoholism. Many of those who use alcohol may drink too much occasionally, or even periodically.[42] On such sprees, these overenthusiastic imbibers may drink away their money, fight with their friends or strangers, jeopardize their jobs by appearing at work with hangovers, neglect their children, beat their wives, engage in sexual infidelities, or otherwise give evidence of personal disorganization. Not all who become drunk on occasion are necessarily alcoholics. Alcoholism and drunkenness are essentially different phenomena. Without a realization of this distinction, the role of drink in personal and social disorganization cannot be clearly understood.

The essential difference between drunkenness and alcoholism is the mo-

[41] Bacon, "Alcoholism: Nature of the Problem," p. 3.
[42] Cf. Peter J. Hampton, "A Descriptive Portrait of the Drinker: I. The Normal Drinker," *Journal of Social Psychology,* 25:69–81 (February, 1947).

tive in drinking. The nonalcoholic drinks because he likes to; the alcoholic drinks because he must. The former drinks for various stated reasons—to relax, to forget, to make friends, to make money, to celebrate, to quench his thirst, to warm (or cool) himself, or to show his virility.[43] The principal distinguishing characteristic of the nonalcoholic is the voluntary character of his reasons for drinking. Most of the occasional users of alcohol in this country can thus take it or leave it alone, and when they do decide to have a cocktail or go on a spree the decision is a voluntary one. They drink because they believe (rightly or wrongly) that they will derive some pleasant or profitable result.

The alcoholic makes no such pleasant decision. He drinks because he can do nothing else. The chief characteristic of the true alcoholic is therefore the *compulsive* nature of his drinking. He may have started to drink for convivial reasons or because he was a neurotic and insecure person who needed artificial aid to adjust to the demands of normal life. Whatever his initial reasons, he presently finds himself obliged to drink in order to keep going. He is driven to a course of conduct that destroys him. And he knows it. But he still can do nothing about his problem without outside aid. His drinking is symptomatic of some basic personality difficulty which he cannot understand, although he is horribly aware of its existence.[44]

"Most alcoholics," comments Bacon, "hate liquor, hate drinking, hate the taste, hate the results, hate themselves for succumbing, but they can't stop."[45] Their drinking is completely compulsive. They are driven to drink by some impulse more powerful than their conscious will. Alcohol has changed for them from a beverage that once pleasantly depressed their central nervous system to a value whose importance transcends all other values. The frantic and pathetic efforts of the compulsive drinker to secure and then hide his liquor indicate the terrible force of his desire. It does no good to tell him to brace up and be a man. He has already tried that. The individual who merely drinks to excess occasionally can indeed "reform" by moral precept and rational decision. Such a man often never takes another drink. But the alcoholic cannot do this. He is a sick man.

His illness is largely mental (or psychological), although chronic physical difficulties may arise from the excessive use of alcohol.[46] We are primarily concerned here with the social role of the alcoholic, with the personal maladjustments that have led to his present condition and the personal disorganization that attends and follows it. The alcoholic is a person who has failed to make an adequate social adjustment. Most persons do not develop an uncontrolla-

[43] George E. C. Catlin, "Alcoholism," *Encyclopaedia of the Social Sciences*, The Macmillan Company, New York, 1930.

[44] Bacon, "Alcoholism: Nature of the Problem," p. 3.

[45] *Ibid.*

[46] Cf. Peter J. Hampton, "A Descriptive Portrait of the Drinker: II. The Symptomatic Drinker," *Journal of Social Psychology*, 25:83–99 (February, 1947); Peter J. Hampton, "A Descriptive Portrait of the Drinker: III. The Psychotic Drinker," *Journal of Social Psychology*, 25:101–117 (February, 1947).

ble craving for drink. Hence the situation of the individual who does develop such a craving represents a departure from the norm. The original maladjustment may have developed early in life; the individual became overly shy, reclusive, socially insecure, unable to compete with his fellows, abnormally attached to the parent of the opposite sex; or he otherwise departed strongly and consistently from the norm.

The maladjustment of the alcoholic takes the form of increasing isolation from the primary group. Relationships within this group are all-important in the formation of personality and its maintenance in a healthy state. In the various forms of the primary group—the family, the play group, the friendship group, and the like—the individual is usually at his ease. He is ordinarily not subjected to the tensions of a competitive world, although some competition between siblings is by no means lacking. The members of the primary group are interested in him as an individual, since he represents something unique to them. Our family and friends stimulate our conduct and bestow praise lavishly for our good behavior. Their affection rewards us and their love comforts us in adversity. Friends and family give most of us whatever feeling of importance we may possess. The average person needs this continual assurance, and when he is deprived of it his personality suffers.[47]

The alcoholic may lack many of these primary group contacts. He often has few close friends, merely casual acquaintances. Friendship may be denied him either because he has never had any friends or because he has alienated those he had by his consistently antisocial behavior. Selden D. Bacon holds that the lack of primary contacts among alcoholics grows out of certain characteristics: "(1) more residential mobility . . . ; (2) rapid change of jobs; (3) failure to continue in school or in college; (4) less visiting, less club or lodge attendance, less attendance at the movies or social dancing; (5) not only much less marriage, but . . . more separation and divorce."[48]

In a sense, alcohol dissolves interpersonal contacts. Group ties are washed away by alcohol and many of the subtle bonds binding the individual in permanent and ordered group relationships are weakened. The social self is the product of continuous interaction with other persons and of the reflected self-appraisals arising from this process. Each individual takes every other individual in the group into account and thereby develops and maintains his own self-image.[49] The attitudes of others are important to the self, and to know these attitudes the individual must be psychologically in touch with others. The compulsive indulgence of the clinical alcoholic makes this contact difficult. Social disorganization is literally in process, as the alcoholic gradually severs his ties with one group, then another.[50]

Alcoholic disorganization takes place in both men and women. Most sci-

[47] Cf. Alan D. Button, "The Genesis and Development of Alcoholism: An Empirically Based Schema," *Quarterly Journal of Studies on Alcohol, 17*:671–675 (December, 1956).

[48] Bacon, "Alcoholism and Social Isolation," pp. 216–219.

[49] Harry Stack Sullivan, *The Interpersonal Theory of Psychiatry,* W. W. Norton and Company, Inc., New York, 1953.

[50] Washburne, *op. cit.,* p. 115.

entific investigations have been directed at the male alcoholic, rather than his female counterpart. That there are an estimated 750,000 female clinical alcoholics, however, suggests that they are an important social problem which may become greater as a larger segment of the female population is progressively exposed to alcohol. Clinical alcoholism among women, as already mentioned, occurs at an approximate ratio of 1 to 5.8 as compared to men, but the neurosis producing the behavior in women may be more severe than in men. This differential may reflect the greater social repressions to which women are still subject in our society. As one psychiatrist puts it, women "must seek outlets that are still within the limits of conventional social acceptance of their sex. When, therefore, the pressure becomes so great as to make it beyond control, and the usual means fail of their intended purpose, it may break out in the form of alcoholism which naturally must be more vehemently expressed, being in proportion to the tension behind it."[51]

Alcoholic women exhibit several characteristic behavior patterns, which are dependent upon their personality structures and interpersonal relations. Some neuroses take the form "simply" of excessive and compulsive drinking, which progressively continues until the woman is unable to function normally in group relationships. In other instances, alcoholism may be accompanied by sexual promiscuity. The woman may first become an alcoholic and then sexually promiscuous or may first become sexually promiscuous and then attempt to overcome her persistent guilt feelings with alcohol. In either pattern, the alcoholism is presumably the symptom of a deep-seated neurosis, which was present before the alcoholic behavior became apparent.[52]

Drink and Family Disorganization

Drink is also an important factor in family disorganization. The alcoholic is seldom a good family man, and a pathological craving for drink permits little affection for a wife and children. The man who periodically drinks to excess but who is still not an alcoholic is also handicapped in his family relationships. He may spend so much time, money, and energy in the tavern that he has little left for his family. Many heavy drinkers and most true alcoholics find drink so absorbing that it transcends all other values. The family is figuratively (and sometimes literally) left out in the cold.

The role of drink in family disorganization is apparent even before there is any family. The type of man who engages in excessive drinking (or is strongly predisposed thereto) often does not marry at all. Family disorganization may, strictly speaking, never take place because such men are so selfish, aggressive, antisocial, or otherwise unfitted for marriage that they successfully avoid it in the first place. The catalogue of personality traits of the actual or potential alcoholic—"dreamers, immature, frightened of the opposite sex, aggressive, asocial, without close friends, suspicious, impossibly idealistic,

[51] Benjamin Karpman, *The Alcoholic Woman*, The Linacre Press, Washington, 1948, p. vii.

[52] *Ibid.* See also Jacob Levine, "The Sexual Adjustment of Alcoholics," *Quarterly Journal of Studies on Alcohol*, 16:674–680 (December, 1955).

generally introverted, escapist, emotionally childish"[53]—hardly designates persons who are suited for marriage. When the tendency to alcoholism becomes an actuality, these traits are enhanced and the unhappy individual becomes less and less fitted for marriage. The bottle is often the substitute for a wife.

Once the marriage is instituted, alcohol may loosen its bonds or interfere with the forging of any strong bonds. The situation often evolves into a contest between drink and the family, with the drinker as the unhappy battleground. The personality of the drinker is such that he injures his family in various ways, either consciously or unconsciously. He may use his drinking "to attack his family, to gain attention and mothering, to test their love for him, to excuse his not being a responsible husband or father."[54] Shameful as they are, these motives may be held less reprehensible in his conscious or unconscious mind than being considered a weak, immature individual, unable to face the obligations of an adult role.

When alcohol is publicly stated as an extenuating factor in his personal disorganization, the alcoholic may experience less guilt than if the real weakness of his personality became known to the world, his family, and himself. He would rather be known as a drunkard than a coward. Drink may therefore serve as a convenient scapegoat for weakness and personal insecurity which the individual hesitates to admit even to himself. In such cases alcohol is comfortably (but erroneously) defined as the active agent rather than the symptom of personal inadequacy and disorganization.[55]

Excessive drinking also tends to deteriorate the social roles of husband and wife. In our society, the mutual demands made upon the spouses are strong and inclusive. Husbands and wives are expected to be many things to each other, ranging from glamorous companions to efficient housekeepers. The alcoholic is unable to play his role in the manner which society expects. Conjugal affection, with its network of obligations and expectations, is difficult for the individual whose interest is centered upon the bottle. The alcoholic becomes increasingly selfish, aggressive, and demanding, qualities which are accentuated by the demands of drink. His inability to play the role expected by society produces further anxiety and guilt feelings, which he temporarily dulls through more drink. The vicious circle of alcoholism is thus established.[56]

Marriage itself appears to be a curb to excessive drinking, according to a study of persons arrested for drunkenness in Connecticut. The disparities in respect to marriage between this group and the rest of the population are striking. Only 47 percent of the arrested inebriates were ever married, as compared to 80 percent of all urban Connecticut males in the same age range.

[53] Selden D. Bacon, "Excessive Drinking and the Institution of the Family," Lecture 16 in *Alcohol, Science and Society,* p. 228.

[54] *Ibid.,* p. 231.

[55] *Ibid.,* pp. 231–232.

[56] *Ibid.,* pp. 232–233. Cf. also Selden D. Bacon, "Alcoholics Do Not Drink," *Annals of the American Academy of Political and Social Science, 315:55–64* (January, 1958).

The normal expectancy for these age groups is for 73 percent to be married and living with their wives, but only 23 percent of the arrested drinkers fell in this category. Some 25 percent of the married inebriates were separated from their wives, whereas the normal expectancy is 4 percent. An additional 16 percent of those who had ever married were divorced, as compared to 1.4 of the general male population of comparable age and urban residence. The mobility of excessive drinkers is also very high. The integration of the excessive drinker with the group, notably his family, is weakened by the various forms of personality disorganization symbolized by alcoholism.[57]

Family relationships influence the alcoholic as well as vice versa, however. Popular conceptions emphasize the role of the spouse (usually the husband) in relation to the other family members (especially the wife). In such circumstances, the wife is regarded as the innocent victim of a weak and/or vicious husband, whose defects of personality threaten the solidarity of the family. Some such pattern does, of course, operate in many cases of family disorganization through alcoholism. But marriage is a reciprocal relationship, and the wife is an active participant in the interpersonal contacts that cause or intensify the alcoholism of the husband. The marriage was originally instituted by both parties in a conscious or unconscious effort to fulfill certain deep emotional needs, of whose nature each was only dimly aware. These needs are not confined to the conventional ones for affection, home, and children. They may also include the need to dominate and be dominated, to control and be controlled, and to suffer and seek suffering from others.[58]

When a woman marries she has a role in the marriage that is at least equal to that of her husband. Her role, indeed, is often stronger than his. She may be the dominant figure and her dominance may drive the husband to seek refuge from his inferiority feelings in drink. The wife may, on the other hand, be a chronic sufferer, who derives real but unconscious satisfaction from the opportunities for suffering which her alcoholic husband provides. Sometimes a wife has a strong need for the dependence which can come only from a husband who is weaker than she is. Alcoholism increases this dependence and hence the wife may not "truly" wish her husband to be permanently cured.[59]

A study of the wives of alcoholics who (the wives) were admitted to a state mental hospital throws light on this. A comparatively small sample of wives was involved (eighteen), but the majority of cases (eleven) showed a pronounced similarity in behavior. The author states that, of the eighteen female patients, "all . . . had been married to alcoholics, and in 11 . . .

---

[57] Selden D. Bacon, "Inebriety, Social Integration, and Marriage," *Quarterly Journal of Studies on Alcohol,* 5:86–125 (June, 1944). Also Joan K. Jackson, "Alcoholism and the Family," *Annals of the American Academy of Political and Social Science, 315:*90–98 (January, 1958).

[58] Robert F. Winch, *Mate Selection: A Study of Complementary Needs,* Harper & Brothers, New York, 1958.

[59] Thelma Whalen, "Wives of Alcoholics," *Quarterly Journal of Studies on Alcohol, 14:*632–641 (December, 1953).

the mental disorder became manifest following a *decrease* in the husband's drinking."[60] These wives apparently retained their own mental health as long as their husbands continued to drink and they (the wives) could continue to dominate their spouses. When the husbands began to recover, the wives were deprived of this ability to dominate and became mentally disorganized.[61]

Whether or not this interpretation is correct, the interpersonal relationships of marriage are clearly related to individual disorganization through alcoholism. In this respect, dominant wives may "choose" husbands with personality characteristics complementary to their own. Husbands may likewise be attracted to wives who will either dominate them or smother them in the affection which they have been vainly seeking since childhood. Neither party bears the whole blame for the resulting personality and family disorganization. Marital interaction involves two persons.

Drinking in College

In recent decades drinking has become more and more prevalent among adolescents. Drinking in high school is a commonplace, and drunken driving by teen-agers is increasing. Nevertheless most drunken driving is among adults, as we discuss in Chapter 5, "The Adult Offender." In certain instances, however, the groundwork is laid early for behavior that will subsequently become clinically neurotic. This does not mean that every high school boy or girl who drinks an occasional glass of beer is a candidate for Alcoholics Anonymous. It *does* mean that alcohol is currently being consumed by an increasing group of young persons.[62]

Drinking in high school is partially a symbolic act, indicating the attempted emancipation of the adolescent from childhood and the beginning of his adult roles. It is also a social custom, learned from other persons. The latter may include both the peer group and the parents. The adolescent tends to follow the example of his mother and father with respect to drinking. In one study approximately the same proportion of high school students drank as were aware that their parents did likewise. The role of the parents is more important than that of the church or the school. Even the "horrible example" of a parent who drinks excessively does not seem to discourage the drinking behavior of the children.[63]

Drinking in college, in contrast to that in high school, has recently been the subject of an intensive sociological study. The Center of Alcohol Studies at Yale University directed the investigation, which involved a sample numbering approximately 16,000 students at 27 colleges and universities. The institutions represented a variety of types, namely, "public, private, and sectarian

[60] Donald E. Macdonald, "Mental Disorders in Wives of Alcoholics," *Quarterly Journal of Studies on Alcohol,* 17:282–287 (June, 1956), p. 286. (Our italics.)

[61] *Ibid.*

[62] Cf. Arthur D. Slater, "A Study of the Use of Alcoholic Beverages Among High-School Students in Utah," *Quarterly Journal of Studies on Alcohol, 13:*78–86 (March, 1952). Also E. Jackson Baur and Marston M. McCluggage, "Drinking Patterns of Kansas High School Students," *Social Problems, 5:*317–326 (Spring, 1958).

[63] Slater, *op. cit.*

institutions; coeducational, men's, and women's; white and Negro; urban and rural; with large and small enrollments, and in different regions of the country."[64] This is a subject upon which there has traditionally been more heat than light. Inasmuch as the bulk of our readers are college students, we may examine in more detail the nature, incidence, and implications of drinking at the college and university level.

1. *Extent of Drinking.* According to the students' own reports, 74 percent used alcoholic beverages "to some extent" and 26 percent were total abstainers. These data represent only the institutions in the study and not necessarily the entire college population. Neither do they represent the percentages of drinkers and abstainers in any one institution. Women reported twice as many abstainers (39 percent) as men (20 percent), although these figures also varied between types of institution.[65]

2. *Economic Level and Drinking.* Behavior tends to vary with economic and class status, and drinking is no exception. In general, students from upper-income families show a higher percentage of drinkers among both men and women than do those from lower-income families. Furthermore, certain private institutions in the eastern part of the United States draw a larger proportion of their student bodies from wealthy families than do the public and sectarian institutions. Students with family incomes of $10,000 or more show 86 percent of the men and 79 percent of the women using alcohol to some extent, whereas those with family incomes below $2500 show only 66 percent of the men and 30 percent of the women with some experience in drinking.[66]

3. *Development of Drinking Customs.* The incidence of drinking increases progressively from the freshman through the senior year. An estimated 69 percent of the men and 46 percent of the women drink in their freshman year, as compared to 87 percent and 77 percent, respectively, in the senior year. At first glance, this would appear to prove conclusively that drinking customs are "learned" in college and that the college has a definite responsibility in the development of this behavior. On the other hand, the years in college represent a progression toward adult status. Hence the increase in drinking from freshman to senior year may merely indicate the process of growing up. The majority of college students would probably learn to use alcohol if they never attended college.[67]

4. *College Drinking and Parental Example.* In our discussion of drinking in high school we indicated the importance of the family in setting the pattern for adolescent drinking. This factor is even more striking at the college level. More than nine out of ten college men whose parents use alcohol drink, whereas only 58 percent of the college men whose parents are both abstainers report the use of alcohol. This relationship between family example and student behavior is more marked with the women. In families where

[64] Straus and Bacon, *op. cit.*, p. 2.
[65] *Ibid.*, p. 47.
[66] *Ibid.*, pp. 48–50.
[67] *Ibid.*, p. 55.

both parents drink, 83 percent of the female students do likewise, whereas in families where the parents are both abstainers only 23 percent of the women drink. Negative sanctions are thus apparently more powerful with respect to women than to men.[68]

5. *Reasons for College Drinking.* In the Straus and Bacon study college students enumerated their reasons for drinking as wanting to comply with custom, to get along well on dates, to be gay, to meet difficult situations, to get "high," and to reduce shyness. There was a striking difference between the sexes, with 47 percent of the men and only 17 percent of the women saying that they drank to get "high."[69] These verbalizations may or may not coincide with the "real" reasons, which may be unknown to the drinker.

6. *Attitudes on Drinking.* In general, college students who drink themselves are more tolerant of such behavior in others than are the total abstainers. Students are not ordinarily concerned actively with the welfare of the community, since they are neither parents nor religious or business leaders. Hence they appear to be more tolerant of drinking both in themselves and in others than the adult population is. There is also a double standard in students' attitudes toward drinking, with both sexes tending to condone drunkenness in men and condemn it in women.[70]

7. *Drinking and Sexual Behavior.* There is a widespread opinion that alcohol stimulates sexual behavior and that drinking is therefore directly related to illicit sexual activity among the college generation. The Straus and Bacon study gives no *information* on this subject; it gathered only the students' *opinions* on the matter. But the majority of students of both sexes *believe* that drinking stimulates petting, necking, and sexual intercourse, although they do not state whether or not they themselves have engaged in such behavior in connection with drinking. The belief is especially strong that women's vulnerability to sexual advances is increased by drinking; 69 percent of the men and 62 percent of the women believe that drinking is related to undesirable sexual behavior. The authors maintain that the college students' belief that drinking increases illicit sex behavior tends to increase it.[71]

8. *Potential Problem Drinkers.* A further question is the extent to which drinking in college may be the prelude to later problem drinking. Alcoholism in the clinical sense is almost completely unknown in college, since it ordinarily takes from ten to twenty years to become apparent. College students are simply not old enough to become full-fledged clinical alcoholics. There are, nevertheless, certain warning signs that may indicate serious behavior disorders in the future.

Among these signs are (a) anticipatory drinking *before* going to a party so that one may be sufficiently "relaxed" to enjoy it; (b) surreptitious drink-

---

[68] *Ibid.*, pp. 56–57. Cf. Albert D. Ullman, "Sex Differences in the First Drinking Experience," *Quarterly Journal of Studies on Alcohol, 18*:229–239 (June, 1957).

[69] Straus and Bacon, *op. cit.*, pp. 72–73.

[70] *Ibid.*, pp. 182–184.

[71] *Ibid.*, chap. 14.

ing and getting drunk alone, without the excuse of a social gathering; (c) buying and consuming liquor even if it means forgoing other things; (d) blacking out, that is, temporary amnesia (loss of memory) when drinking, even though the drinker stays on his feet and does not "pass out"; (e) drinking before breakfast or instead of breakfast, because the individual needs the depressant effect of alcohol either to recover from a hangover or to face the day; (f) drinking that leads to unusually aggressive, destructive, or wanton behavior. The number of students exhibiting such warning signs of future alcoholism is not large. Straus and Bacon tentatively estimate that perhaps 6 percent of the males and 1 percent of the females show positive signs of becoming problem drinkers.[72]

We have been basically concerned in this chapter with the personal disorganization arising from the excessive use of alcohol. The vast majority of men and women who drink do not suffer any significant disorganization as a result. Most of the millions of Americans who drink do so in moderation. The college boy may engage in an occasional conspicuous spree, in which he irritates his elders and makes a fool of himself. In all probability, he would do very much the same thing if he had never gone to college. But such lapses from the folkways (and on occasion the mores) do not have any permanent effect upon his life organization.

At the same time, we should not minimize the role of alcohol as both a cause and a symptom of individual disorganization in contemporary America. The clinical alcoholic is a disorganized person. His personal maladjustment may have preceded his drinking or his drinking may have changed him from an apparently well-adjusted person to his present sorry state. His excessive use of alcohol may or may not, as the Freudians suggest, represent an unconscious and comparatively inefficient method of suicide.[73] But his behavior is indubitably an expression of acute personal disorganization. He is no longer able to function adequately in the many interpersonal relationships of a normal human being. He is one of the millions of men and women in modern society who lead lives of quiet desperation.

SELECTED BIBLIOGRAPHY

Bacon, Selden D., "Alcoholism, 1941–1951: A Survey of Activities in Research, Education and Therapy: IV, Social Science Research," *Quarterly Journal of Studies on Alcohol, 13:*453–460 (September, 1952). The author is the foremost sociological authority on problems of alcohol. In this article, he surveys the activities of a decade which saw the first systematic study of these problems in a sociological frame of reference.

Bacon, Selden D. (ed.), "Understanding Alcoholism," Special Issue, *Annals of the American Academy of Political and Social Science, 315:*1–200 (January, 1958). This is a significant and wide-ranging analysis of alcoholism by a group of

[72] *Ibid.*, chap. 12.
[73] Karl A. Menninger, *Man Against Himself,* Harcourt, Brace and Company, New York, 1938, part III, chap. 3, "Alcohol Addiction."

experts in this emerging field. Alcoholism is seen as a medical, psychological, and (above all) sociological problem.

Horton, Donald, "The Functions of Alcohol in Primitive Societies: A Cross-Cultural Study," *Quarterly Journal of Studies on Alcohol,* 4:199–320 (September, 1943). This monograph is an extensive study of the use of alcohol in a variety of primitive societies. The role of anxiety in this connection is thoroughly explored on a cross-cultural basis.

Keller, Mark, and Efron, Vera, "Alcoholism in the Big Cities of the United States," *Quarterly Journal of Studies on Alcohol,* 17:63–72 (March, 1956). This article indicates that there is a direct, although not perfect, correlation between the prevalence of alcoholism and the size of the urban community. In general, large cities have higher rates than medium-sized cities.

Keller, Mark, and Efron, Vera, "The Prevalence of Alcoholism," *Quarterly Journal of Studies on Alcohol,* 16:619–644 (December, 1955). This is the most authoritative estimate of the prevalence and trends of clinical alcoholism in the United States.

Lemert, Edwin M., "Alcoholism and the Sociocultural Situation," *Quarterly Journal of Studies on Alcohol,* 17:306–317 (June, 1956). Drinking takes place in a particular sociocultural setting, and the drinker is subject to the norms and culture patterns of his society. Hence any purely psychological explanation (e.g., anxiety) for drinking is incomplete in itself unless it takes into account the social environment.

Lester, David, and Greenberg, Leon A., "Alcoholism, 1941–1951: A Survey of Activities in Research, Education, and Therapy: III, The Status of Physiological Knowledge," *Quarterly Journal of Studies on Alcohol,* 13:444–452 (September, 1952). The physiological effects of alcohol upon the human organism are discussed in this article.

Menninger, Karl A., *Man Against Himself,* Harcourt, Brace and Company, New York, 1938, part III, chap. 3, "Alcohol Addiction." This book presents the Freudian position that alcoholism is a form of self-destruction by an individual suffering from an unconscious feeling of guilt.

Riley, John W., and Marden, Charles F., "The Social Pattern of Alcoholic Drinking," *Quarterly Journal of Studies on Alcohol,* 8:265–273 (September, 1947). Like any other form of social behavior, the use of alcohol reflects the social milieu in which it occurs. Some of the aspects of this milieu are indicated in the present article.

Straus, Robert, and Bacon, Selden D., *Drinking in College,* Yale University Press, New Haven, 1953. This is a sober account of drinking behavior in the institutions of higher learning in the United States. The college student is a maturing individual in a society where the majority of the people use alcohol in some form. Hence the authors submit that the college student probably drinks no more than he would if he had not gone to college.

"Symposium on Alcoholism," Special Issue, *Social Problems,* 5:292–338 (Spring, 1958). The articles in this symposium approach the subject of alcoholism in the framework of social problems. Included in the topics discussed are: social organization and disorganization in relation to alcoholism, the Skid Row "wino," patterns of drinking in high school, and some of the ecological correlates of alcoholism.

CHAPTER 8

The Industrial Worker

Individual Disorganization and the Worker

The way a man makes his living is an important aspect of his life. Many important group relationships occur on the job or in direct connection with it. In an industrial society, millions of men (and women) work long hours in the factory, and their personalities are subjected to tensions that are unique both in kind and in intensity. Individual disorganization may thus come to the man in the factory, either in the form of physical disability or, more often, through boredom, dissatisfaction, and apathy.

The basic source of individual disorganization in our society is no longer overwork and underpayment. The American worker is, on balance, the highest paid in the world. Nor is it a question primarily of insufficient goods and services in a society where millions of industrial workers own their own automobiles, television sets, and other material symbols of the good life. The problem is rather one of status, of attitude toward the self, of hope for the future. An estimated one out of every five urban factory workers, for example, is downwardly mobile in the sense of losing status during his lifetime.[1] These figures show how such intangibles as status and self-respect may perhaps comprise the difference between personal organization and disorganization.

Formerly an individual took pride in work and pleasure in the completed job. Today all this is changed. The ties uniting members of the family to one another, to their jobs, and to the local community have likewise undergone drastic changes. In many cases, no new group ties have arisen to take their place. The individual is living in a highly segmental world with respect to the norms which formerly controlled his behavior. His work and its relationships have become means to an end, rather than ends in themselves. Factory workers often find that their significant group contacts occur away from the job rather than in connection with it.[2]

In an important study of factory workers, Dubin has further indicated the extent of this separation of work and "life." For approximately three out of

[1] Harold L. Wilensky and Hugh Edwards, "The Skidder: Ideological Adjustments of Downward Mobile Workers," *American Sociological Review*, 24:215–231 (April, 1959).
[2] Nancy C. Morse and Robert S. Weiss, "The Function and Meaning of Work and the Job," *American Sociological Review*, 20:191–198 (April, 1955).

four industrial workers in his study, the job and place of work were not "central life interests." Only about 10 percent of the workers believed that their "important primary social relationships" took place at work; the other 90 percent enjoyed their most meaningful contacts away from the job. Work was vital to economic support, but it was instrumental rather than central in the individual's scheme of life. The job, in short, was mandatory but not intrinsically important.[3]

Harvey Swados went to work on an automobile assembly line several years ago and found to his surprise that virtually all the men, irrespective of their education, ethnic background, or personal ambition, hated their work.[4] Perhaps this should not seem surprising. Virtually all young factory or assembly line workers today have had some high school education. They are exposed to the values of middle-class society. They know that despite the high wages in industry factory workers are assigned to the lower class in our social structure. This fact may have significant impact upon the workers' attitudes.

According to Dubin, "The factory and factory work as sources of personal satisfaction, pride, satisfying human associations, perhaps even of pleasure in expressing what Veblen called 'the instinct of workmanship' seem clearly subordinated in the American scene."[5] Thus, factory work is not highly valued for its own sake, nor does it appear to be a "way of life." The home, family, friends, and recreation are more important to the factory worker than what he does to earn his living. We do not, of course, have any comparable study of an earlier and handicraft society. The assumption is that in such a society the job was the center of more meaningful social interaction than is the modern factory.

This general alienation of the worker from his job is a further aspect of social disorganization. The concept is not applied here in any invidious sense, as indicating an undesirable state of affairs. On the contrary, most persons regard technological and industrial changes as (on balance) desirable, even though they may disapprove of certain accompaniments.[6] Technical efficiency, for example, is obviously increased by technological innovations, and the productivity per worker is greatly augmented by the substitution of the factory for the handicraft system. Nevertheless, in the structural sense we are facing one of the most massive processes of social disorganization the world has ever seen.[7]

Many of the elements of social disorganization appear in accentuated form

[3] Robert Dubin, "Industrial Workers' Worlds: A Study of the 'Central Life Interests' of Industrial Workers," *Social Problems, 3:*131–142 (January, 1956).

[4] Harvey Swados, "Work as a Public Issue," *Saturday Review, 42:*13–15 and 45 (December 12, 1959).

[5] Dubin, *op. cit.,* p. 135. Cf. Gladys L. Palmer, "Attitudes Toward Work in an Industrial Community," *American Journal of Sociology, 63:*17–26 (July, 1957).

[6] Francis E. Merrill, "The Study of Social Problems," *American Sociological Review, 13:*251–262 (June, 1948).

[7] Neil W. Chamberlain, *Social Responsibility and Strikes,* Harper & Brothers, New York, 1953, chap. 1.

when traditional social systems are invaded by modern industrialism.[8] In such instances, underdeveloped nations or regions undergo in a decade the disorganizing processes that took a century and a half in the Western world. Social change is caused by technology and industry, with disastrous effects to the structure of societies that were formerly stable.[9] This does not mean that such societies were desirable from the Western standpoint. Indeed, in terms of democratic value judgments, social problems abound in "backward" countries. Poverty, illiteracy, endemic disease, child labor, ignorance, and superstition mark the societies which are currently undergoing invasion by the industrial system.

The process of social change may be discerned in this country on the community scene, when a system of social relationships built up about a given factory undergoes rapid change and corresponding disorganization. In Yankee City, for example, the network of community relationships built about a group of shoe factories was disrupted by a series of technological changes. These relationships were formerly in a state of comparative equilibrium, and the corresponding system of status was adequate to meet the desires of workers and management alike. The disruption of the status system generated aggressions which took the form of a long and bitter strike. Effective cooperation between members of the community was interrupted.[10] A strong union organization, with a new set of statuses, produced a new equilibrium about a new set of values. The worker now seeks many of the satisfactions in the union which he formerly found in the status system of the factory.[11]

Industrial Change and Social Structure

Industrial disorganization is not primarily a result of the personality traits of the individuals comprising the system. One worker may be aggressive, another uncooperative, and a third without ambition. But this is not the whole story. The personality of the industrial worker reflects his way of life, and he acquires his goals from his social milieu. The entire system of human relationships that formerly made up the productive system has undergone social disorganization. The question is not one merely of adjusting the individual to his job. It is one of recognizing that substantial changes have occurred in the entire social system.[12]

The adjustment of the worker to his job is therefore more than a matter of technical skills and aptitudes. It is an exercise in human relations, between

---

[8] George A. Theodorson, "Acceptance of Industrialization and Its Attendant Consequences for the Social Patterns of Non-Western Societies," *American Sociological Review,* 18:477–484 (October, 1953).

[9] Cf. Bert H. Hoselitz (ed.), *The Progress of Underdeveloped Areas,* University of Chicago Press, Chicago, 1952.

[10] W. Lloyd Warner and J. O. Low, *The Social System of the Modern Factory: The Strike,* Yale University Press, New Haven, 1947.

[11] Mark Starr, "Role of Union Organization," chap. VIII in William F. Whyte (ed.), *Industry and Society,* McGraw-Hill Book Company, Inc., 1946.

[12] Frederick H. Harbison, "The Basis of Industrial Conflict," chap. IX in Whyte, *op. cit.,* pp. 184–185.

the worker and his fellows on the one hand and the worker and his superiors on the other. It has been stated that "from 60 to 80 percent of all dismissals in industry are due to social incompetence and only about from 20 to 40 percent to technical incompetence."[13] Social incompetence in this sense means the inability to get along with other people both on and off the job. Numbered among this group are the person who is constantly making trouble, the person who is suspicious of the motives of others, the chronic absentee, the undependable worker, and the emotionally maladjusted person. Inability to adjust, in turn, results to some degree from changes in the socioeconomic structure.

Social disorganization is a partial function of breakdown in communication. The dissolution of the traditional handicraft system, with its close communication between workers, employers, and managers, has been accompanied by disorganization in the communicative process. Workers and management often define their interests as incompatible and are unable to communicate. The cure for this breakdown of communication would seem to be the establishment of channels through which the two sides could talk things over to their mutual benefit.[14]

The solution, however, is not as simple as this. The breakdown of communication between workers and management is real enough, but it is a *symbol* of social disorganization, not a fundamental cause of it. The cleavage lies deeper than the failure of communication. Often in actual situations where communication was maintained, industrial conflict was found to be *intensified,* rather than mitigated, by organized conferences between workers and management. In many of these instances, the management had "officially" recognized the union but wished to cooperate with it as little as possible.[15]

The disorganization of the traditional economic system has taken several forms. In a sense, indeed, many of the problems treated under different headings throughout this book have directly or indirectly reflected the breakdown of the old way of life and the rise of the new. We are referring to such representative situations as (1) changes in the status system in industry; (2) changes in the motivation of the industrial worker; and (3) changes in consensus between workers and management, culminating in the strike. Each of these situations is the result (or the symbol) of the disorganization of group patterns that arose about a former way of life. In the process of social change, a new consensus has not yet arisen.

Technology and Social Change

Before we consider these related aspects of social disorganization, we may examine the prime mover in the sequence of social change—namely, technology. The connections between science, technology, and industry have

---

[13] William C. Menninger, "Men, Machines, and Mental Health," *Mental Hygiene, 36:* 184–196 (April, 1952).

[14] Paul Pigors, "Communication in Industry: A Cure of Conflict?" *Industrial and Labor Relations Review, 6:*497–509 (July, 1953).

[15] *Ibid.,* p. 497.

been described as follows: "Technology is to be defined as the body of knowledge established by science and available for use in the processes of production. Industry may be described as the organization of production. The processes of industry are changed and shaped by the growing body of knowledge known as technology. Thus it is in the field of industry that science exerts its far-reaching influence upon society."[16] The following discussion does not profess to examine the growing field of industrial sociology.[17] We are merely exploring some of the ways in which the social change introduced by technology brings about or accelerates social disorganization.[18]

A machine is an extension or elaboration of the human faculties. Stuart Chase defines the machine as "any non-living contrivance to extend or modify the power of the body or to refine the perception of the senses."[19] The machine is an element in the disorganization of a traditional social order. The use, however, not the implement, is the important consideration. The causes of the social disorganization lie in the factory system, which is an impersonal social process.

An innovation in technology sets in motion a long chain of social problems and cultural lags.[20] As Veblen wisely remarked, "Invention is the mother of necessity."[21] The inventor continually strives to improve his product, often without reference to its effects upon the society. He does not wish to break down the status patterns and social structure of an established way of life. Instead he is interested in such mundane considerations as increasing output and lowering unit costs of production.

The factory system includes far more than the mere technical organization of labor. The factory system is a point of view, a philosophy of life, and a set of standards and norms. It includes the entire synthesis of systematic production, standardization, and division of labor.[22] Just as it would be impossible to describe modern society without describing the factory system, so it would be impossible to describe the factory system without describing modern society. The factory system includes a complex pattern of human relationships, formal and informal organizations, and statuses and roles.[23]

The human being is a basic component of the factory system, but he is

[16] Mary Van Kleeck, "Towards an Industrial Sociology," *American Sociological Review, 11*:501–505 (October, 1946).

[17] Wilbert E. Moore, "Industrial Sociology: Status and Prospects," *American Sociological Review, 13*:383–400 (August, 1948); Wilbert E. Moore, "Current Issues in Industrial Sociology," *American Sociological Review, 12*:651–657 (December, 1947).

[18] Cf. *Social Implications of Technical Change, International Social Science Bulletin,* Vol. 4, No. 2 (published by UNESCO, Paris, Summer, 1952).

[19] Stuart Chase, *Men and Machines,* The Macmillan Company, New York, 1929, p. 24.

[20] William F. Ogburn, *Social Change,* The Viking Press, Inc., New York, 1950 (rev. ed.).

[21] Thorstein Veblen, *The Instinct of Workmanship and the State of the Industrial Arts,* The Macmillan Company, New York, 1914, p. 314.

[22] Georges Friedmann, *Industrial Society,* (translated by Harold L. Sheppard), The Free Press, Glencoe, Ill., 1955.

[23] For a sociological description of a unit in the factory system, see John S. Ellsworth, *Factory Folkways,* Yale University Press, New Haven, 1952.

not a machine. Men cannot perform constant and monotonous toil for indefinite periods without rest. The human apparatus has its own fuel and cooling requirements, fatigue, specialized demands based upon sex differentiation, occupational age limits, and industrial and occupational diseases. This combination of physical and mental potentialities has apparently changed little since the last ice age.[24] Man's physical heritage is presumably better suited to other tasks than those which he now performs in the modern factory.

In addition to his physical inadequacies, man also has feelings, emotions, hopes, aspirations, ideals, attitudes, values, and symbols, all of which complicate industrial relations. Motivation is basic to the system of rewards and incentives. Status considerations bulk large on the job. The worker desires status and prestige as well as economic security, and many industrial conflicts reflect his failure to gain these intangible but important values. Social disorganization in industry arises from psychological and cultural factors, as well as from purely physical limitations.[25]

The individual must also make a variety of long-range group adjustments to the factory system. He must spend most of his waking hours away from his family. He must develop new skills and disciplines. His work is based upon greater regularity and continuity, and he must work certain hours every day rather than when the spirit moves him. His relationships with his fellow workers are more impersonal. He becomes part of a large industrial process, with competitive relationships all over the world. The values of this new and impersonal world are monetary, and his behavior becomes increasingly judged in these terms.[26]

Changes in the Status System

The status system is the organized pattern of social positions in a given social structure. It implies a hierarchical organization, whereby some persons occupy higher positions (i.e., statuses) than others. The status system further implies that the relative position of the individual is important to him. People need status, which will establish their position in the social structure, provide a sense of belonging, and give them group recognition. The organization of statuses may be formal, with an organization chart showing the president at the top and the rest of the officers and workers below, or informal, with a complex network of positions established by informal agreement. Informal status designations are often more important than the formal.[27]

Changes in technology may disorganize a status system based upon an earlier social organization. The worker in a skilled trade acquired status with his job, and this symbolic expression was as important as the rate of pay and

---

[24] Richard T. Dana, *The Human Machine in Industry,* Codex Book Company, New York, 1927, p. 7.

[25] Paul Meadows, "Culture Theory and Industrial Analysis," *Annals of the American Academy of Political and Social Science,* 274:9–16 (March, 1951).

[26] Theodorson, *op. cit.,* pp. 481–484.

[27] Burleigh B. Gardner, "The Factory as a Social System," chap. II in Whyte, *op. cit.,* pp. 5–8.

the physical conditions of labor. The skilled worker was given high status because of his skill, and he occupied a prominent position in the factory and the community because of this reflected status. When new machinery replaced the skilled hand worker with a series of mechanical operations, the old way of life was disorganized. A complicated and status-laden pattern of social relationships was broken.[28]

This process has been dramatically entitled by Warner "the break in the skill hierarchy." In an earlier day the life of the skilled craftsman was organized about a hierarchy of age blended with skill. Young men enrolled as apprentices in a skilled trade and for many years worked with a master craftsman and thereby learned their trade. Along with technical skills, the apprentice also learned the folklore of the trade and a pride in skilled craftsmanship.

The apprentice was willing to undergo a long probation because of the virtual certainty that he would become a craftsman himself, with all the status symbols pertaining thereto. These intangible aspects of his trade were important to him as he followed the slow (but reasonably sure) progression into the upper ranks of his craft. He had the assurance that comes with participation in a common enterprise with a common set of values. In short, "In learning to respect the skill of the master craftsman, the apprentice learned to respect himself. He had security in his job, but he had even greater personal security because he had learned how to respect it."[29]

The introduction of modern machinery disrupted the skill hierarchy in many industries, along with the way of life that went with it. A system of social organization was broken, and with this break personal incentives tended to become meaningless. The motivation that formerly caused the apprentice to devote years to the patient acquisition of skills has largely vanished as the machine has taken the place of the skilled craftsman. In many manufacturing communities the degeneration of a former way of life has become increasingly evident. As a result, "There was no longer a period for young men to learn to respect those in the age grade above them and in so doing to become self-respecting workers. The 'ladder to the skies' was gone and with it much of the fabric of the 'American dream.' "[30]

Changes in Motivation

The disorganization of the traditional social structure has brought about corresponding changes in motivation. Workers are increasingly interchangeable, and each man is a quantitatively determinable unit of energy in an impersonal process. The more interchangeable the units become, the more perfectly integrated is the industrial system. From top to bottom, there are no irreplaceable men. The very nature of the modern industrial process

[28] Cf. Dubin, *op. cit.,* pp. 54–58.
[29] W. Lloyd Warner and J. O. Low, "The Factory in the Community," chap. III in Whyte, *op. cit.,* p. 33.
[30] *Ibid.,* p. 33. Cf. also Robert G. Stone, "Factory Organization and Vertical Mobility," *American Sociological Review, 18:*28–35 (February, 1953).

thus makes a high degree of impersonality inevitable. The motivation of the individual worker has altered correspondingly.[31]

By changing the world in which man lives and works, the machine has changed man himself and the attitudes that motivate his behavior. The social changes introduced by the machine increase the difficulty of social adaptation, which in turn increases the degree and severity of social disorganization. One result of this situation is the dissatisfied worker, whose problems have been summarized as follows: "He is productively dependent on some one else; the dependence is called a job; for it he receives a wage; for it his day is clocked, his routine predetermined, his operations segmented, his creativity fragmented."[32] From these dissatisfactions may come frustration, aggression, prejudice, and industrial conflict.

The changing motivation of the worker has been explored in terms of the aspirations of those who work on the assembly lines of the great mass production industries. Many of the above changes are reflected in the self-attitudes of these men who make up the elite of the industrial workers. They are highly paid, enjoy comparative job security, and are substantial members of the community. They drive their own cars, own their own homes, and hope to send their children to college. They are persons for whom the American Dream still appears to hold out a strong hope of realization. The possibilities of advancement in the factory seem good. Vertical mobility would appear to be one of the basic factors in the motivation of these men.

The evidence indicates that this is not the case. Two major studies have been made of men on the automobile assembly line.[33] The purpose of both studies was to discover the goals of the men who sense the disparity between the promises of American culture and the realities of their own situation. The workers in both studies were assured through job seniority of well-paying employment as long as they were physically able. At the same time, they had gradually realized that they would probably never rise from the assembly line into more responsible executive positions. Under these conditions, they were obliged to face the fact that "they are confined to their working-class status despite the promises of the culture."[34]

The evidence suggests that this adjustment occurs on two levels—fact and fantasy. The men seek (and ordinarily find) a considerable enjoyment of material goods on the level of *fact*. Thanks to the union and the personnel policies of the corporation, they are virtually assured of job security. Their high rate of hourly pay means that they can purchase (often on installment)

---

[31] Thorstein Veblen, *The Theory of Business Enterprise*, Charles Scribner's Sons, New York, 1904, chap. 9, "The Cultural Incidence of the Machine Process."

[32] Paul Meadows, "The Worker: Archetype of Industrial Man," *Social Forces*, 25:441–445 (May, 1947), p. 443.

[33] Ely Chinoy, "The Tradition of Opportunity and the Aspirations of Automobile Workers," *American Journal of Sociology*, 57:453–459 (March, 1952); Robert H. Guest, "Work Careers and Aspirations of Automobile Workers," *American Sociological Review*, 19:155–163 (April, 1954).

[34] Chinoy, *op. cit.*, p. 459.

many of the consumer durable goods that are important symbols of status in our society. The shiny new automobile, the television set, the electric refrigerator, the deep freeze, and the rest of the tangible signs of the good life are available to them. On the level of fact, therefore, they can aspire to material possessions and security of employment and thus reconcile themselves to their permanent working-class status.

The motivations may also extend into the realm of *fantasy*. The men on the assembly line dream of leaving the line and starting a little business of their own. Most of them realize, however, that their dreams will never come true and that they will remain on the line as long as they are physically able to work. Furthermore, leaving the line and starting a business means a step into the unknown and the abandonment of the security and high wages they have worked so hard to attain. Some of the men hope that their children can get an education and thus be qualified for professional and managerial roles which they (the parents) have missed. In many cases the parents have neither the money nor the background to help their children reach these goals. The men on the assembly line nevertheless continue to hope that their children will move up the social and economic ladder.[35]

These men are, as noted, the aristocracy of factory workers. The motivations of another and larger segment of the working population are very different. These are the underprivileged workers, the men who are last hired and first fired, who perform the most unpleasant and unskilled jobs, and whose family life (if any) is marked by insecurity, inadequate food, and submarginal housing. Their status does not carry the "normal" expectations of the middle-class society, and their motivations are not those of the middle-class culture. The latter motivations are learned by people who have a reasonable hope for security, status, and advancement—all goals that are not open to many underprivileged workers.[36]

These workers lead very different lives from those of the majority of persons in our society. Their families are larger and the burden of support is heavy and continuous. The struggle for sheer physical survival is intensified. Their working efficiency is lowered by malnutrition, illness, lack of sleep, and periodic unemployment. Formal education is often wasted on their children because it is conducted in middle-class terms, with middle-class teachers, methods, and standards. The teachers often cannot understand the way of life of the underprivileged children (and vice versa), and the conventional motivations of industry, application, and advancement have little meaning for the pupils.[37]

The way of life of the underprivileged worker and his children thus often produces motivations contrary to those of the larger society. In the underprivileged culture, emphasis is placed upon the emotional satisfactions found

[35] *Ibid.*
[36] Allison Davis, "The Motivation of the Underprivileged Worker," chap. V in Whyte, *op. cit.*
[37] *Ibid.*, p. 99.

in leisure-time activities—drinking, gambling, sexual exploration, and pure physical laziness. These pleasures are considered undesirable by middle-class, ascetic, moralistic, and hard-working persons. For the underprivileged worker, however, they are both available and satisfactory. He sees no reason for working hard, staying sober, and saving his money because, in all probability, he will soon be unemployed, broke, and homeless again no matter what he does.[38]

Industrial Conflict and Social Disorganization

Industrial conflict is the symbolic culmination of social disorganization in industry. It is a collective expression of the cumulative aspects of social disorganization. The breakdown in the network of personal relationships that formerly bound the community together is one of the background factors in industrial conflict. The obsolescence of old economic roles and the emergence of new roles is another. The changes introduced by the factory system into the economic, family, and community institutions further contribute to the frustration that culminates in industrial conflict. The modifications in the status system, both inside and outside the factory, are elements. Finally, changes in motivation and the growing realization that vertical mobility is impossible for the great majority of workers are additional sociological factors in this complex situation.[39]

Industrial conflict is, then, the collective expression of dissatisfaction with the relationships in a given factory or industry. In earlier analyses, industrial conflict was often depicted as the result of disgruntled workers, striking for higher wages, shorter hours, union recognition, and welfare benefits. These are merely the immediate or precipitating causes of industrial unrest. Over and above these specific factors are more general elements of social change and social disorganization. The worker may be dissatisfied because he can no longer control his conditions of employment. He may be unhappy because of his inability to engage in creative activity. He may lack the status in the group and community which he desires. He may, in sum, wish to be captain of his fate and master of his soul. In an industrial society, this control is difficult.[40]

Industrial conflict thus "reveals either an inadequate institutional system or, what is nearly the same thing, an inadequate acceptance of the existing industrial system."[41] Each group in the industrial system has its own standards, arising from its particular status. The patterns of an earlier society have dissolved and consensus has partially broken down. A strike may therefore be "caused" either by the failure of the society to provide adequate safeguards for labor to organize or by the efforts of organized labor to seize rights tradi-

[38] *Ibid.,* pp. 102–104.

[39] Cf. Chamberlain, *op. cit.,* chap. 1, "The Meaning of Social Responsibility."

[40] Florence Peterson, "Cause of Industrial Unrest," *Annals of the American Academy of Political and Social Science,* 274:25–31 (March, 1951).

[41] Wilbert E. Moore, *Industrial Relations and the Social Order,* The Macmillan Company, New York, 1946, p. 402.

tionally belonging to the employer. Industrial conflict reflects a difference in traditional role expectations, in which labor assumes a role that conflicts with the expectations of management.

Power and status are clearly involved, for the employer is unwilling to relinquish power in a situation where he has traditionally held it. Organized labor does not behave as management expects it to behave. Industrial conflict is thus literally subversive (i.e., disorganizing) to the employer, who has hitherto taken for granted that he can run his business to suit himself. The owners of the shoe factories of Yankee City could not understand the deep-seated motives that prompted the workers to go out on strike.[42]

A certain minimum of conflict is indeed inherent between management and organized labor. Among the factors responsible are the following:[43]

1. *Unlimited Desires and Limited Satisfactions.* When the desires of two parties are unlimited and the means of satisfaction are limited, conflict is inevitable. Workers always want more wages and management always wants more profits, although the available money is necessarily limited.

2. *Subordinate and Superordinate Relationships.* In any industrial relationship, some persons are managers and others are managed. Decisions of management are important to the workers, and there is always a proportionate conflict of interests. In large industrial units this conflict of interest is often intense.

3. *Dynamic Aspects of Industrial Society.* Even when agreements are made between management and organized labor, the changes inherent in a dynamic society quickly make them obsolete and introduce a new conflict situation. Among these dynamic factors are "new regulations by the state, changed expenditure patterns of consumers, higher costs of raw materials, a reduced value of the monetary unit, [and] increased real income for a comparable group elsewhere. . . ."[44]

4. *Institutional Demands and Identities.* Both management and unions need a certain amount of conflict to justify their institutional roles and keep their groups cohesive. Unions that *always* agreed with management would eventually cease to function. Part of their role as unions is to criticize, compete, and conflict.

Conflict is, finally, not always a disorganizing force in industrial society. Out of aggressive conflict come agreement and the resolution of disputes. In view of the inherent conflict factors, the disputes could not be resolved by mediation. Conflict often reduces tensions and clears the air, provided it is not too prolonged or acrimonious. In a flexible social system, occasional conflicts can be taken in stride. As management and unions compete for the loyalty of the workers, the interests of the latter are often advanced. A dy-

[42] Warner and Low, *The Social System of the Modern Factory: The Strike, op. cit.*
[43] The following is adapted from Clark Kerr, "Industrial Conflict and Its Mediation," *American Journal of Sociology*, 60:230–245 (November, 1954).
[44] *Ibid.,* p. 231.

namic society contains all forms of social interaction between individuals and groups.[45]

In a conflict situation, organized groups develop weapons and tactics which they habitually use to gain their ends. The weapons of the employer have traditionally been more varied than those of the worker. Until recently, the balance of power has rested with management. The means used by management in the struggle for power have changed in recent decades, as the social setting has changed. Union recognition has become widely accepted and unions themselves have become stronger. Some of the more aggressive tactics formerly used by the employer have been largely abandoned, notably the use of organized violence.

Industrial Conflict and the Employer

The weapons of the employer in industrial conflict include the following:

1. *Force.* Force or the threat of force has always been an important element in the employer's arsenal. Company police, special guards, and armed watchmen have been hired to protect property against alleged violence by the workers. Such uses of force were documented by the report of the La Follette Committee of the United States Senate, published shortly before World War II.[46] Many of them have been eliminated by recent legislation, changing public opinion, and modifications in the attitudes of management and workers. Even so, the threat of force is still an important weapon in industrial conflict.

2. *Discrimination.* The La Follette Committee also unearthed widespread practices of spying on legitimate labor organizations by persons in the service of the employer. On the basis of such knowledge, the employer can discriminate in various ways against the militant worker. He can discharge men on different pretexts, transfer them to less desirable jobs, reduce their pay, and otherwise indicate that the way to advancement is through "cooperation" and not conflict. Recent legislation has likewise minimized this type of practice, as has the growing power of organized labor. When the union becomes sufficiently powerful, the employer no longer dares to take such drastic action.

3. *Communication.* An important device in industrial conflict is the dissemination of information (or propaganda) by employers or employers' groups. This communication discredits the purposes, leadership, and activities of labor organizations in general and the local organization in particular. The major agencies of communication are ordinarily more open to the employer than to the union. The former may make full use of the press, radio, and television to promote the impression that labor organizations are unpatriotic, destructive of property, and generally subversive of American institutions. The role of such informational efforts is that of (a) enlisting

[45] Robert C. Sorenson, "The Concept of Conflict in Industrial Sociology," *Social Forces,* 29:263–267 (March, 1951).

[46] United States Senate, Committee on Education and Labor, *Violations of Free Speech and Rights of Labor,* Washington, 1937–1941.

neutral (i.e., public) opinion; (b) strengthening the in-group (i.e., the employer's) forces; and (c) weakening the out-group (i.e., the workers) and causing them to abandon the conflict and return to work. Especially in smaller communities, "public opinion" is often instrumental in getting the men back to work, thereby breaking the strike.

4. *Law Enforcement.* The employer has usually been able to mobilize the forces of law enforcement against the strikers in an industrial conflict. The traditional norms of our society support private property, and these controls have been employed against striking workers. The local police, the state militia, and even federal troops have been used in this role. The courts have similarly been enlisted in the conflict, often by the use of the injunction, whereby the strikers were enjoined against continuing the strike at the risk of being held in contempt of court. Recent social trends have likewise militated against the use of the machinery of law enforcement, although the law continues (for the most part) to be on the side of the employers.

5. *Industrial Organization.* Certain programs developed by industrial management such as efficiency training, job simplification, new machinery, time studies, personnel work, merit rating, recreational programs, welfare activities, company unions, and increased communication with the workers have also helped to mitigate conflict.[47] Many of these devices, indeed, are not conflict agencies but the means of accommodation and competition. In some instances the conflict has merely changed from an overt to a covert form, whereas in other cases the emphasis has shifted to less divisive social processes. In the continued struggle for scarce goals, both labor and management hold potentially hostile attitudes, but the trend is toward a reduction of overt conflict.

Industrial Conflict and the Worker

Labor lacks many of the tactical and strategic devices of industrial management, although the increasing power of organized labor is tending to equalize the situation. Labor continues to be a challenger to the *status quo* in a particular factory or industry and hence is usually forced into taking the offensive. The union is placed in the unfavorable position of challenging existing statuses, norms, and values thus causing (or threatening to cause) social disorganization. Such considerations often make industrial conflict unequal, except in instances where the labor organization (e.g., the United Mine Workers) is as powerful as the employer group.[48]

Social disorganization is the process by which the functional equilibrium of the group is upset, and many individuals suffer corresponding impairment in their interpersonal relations. The group aspects of industrial conflict have become increasingly important in recent decades, as the interaction involves both companies and unions acting in their organizational capacities. In short,

[47] Ross Stagner, *Psychology of Industrial Conflict,* John Wiley and Sons, Inc., New York, 1956, chap. 10, "Tactics: Management."
[48] *Ibid.,* chap. 11, "Tactics: The Union."

"Individual employers and employees do, of course, interact, fight, or co-operate, but, in western civilization, the major problems of industrial relations have become group problems."[49] The individual worker or employer is strongly identified with the goals, norms, and values of his own group.

We have considered some of the tactics used by management in industrial conflict. The union has the same general goals, which are to "maintain the unity of the group, channel aggression against the employer, prevent the employer from operating, and maximize the chances of achieving important goals by the union."[50] These goals can be gained only through collective action—the main and, indeed, virtually the only weapon of the workers.

1. *Industrial Conflict and the Strike.*[51] The principal form of industrial conflict is the strike. This action has been defined as "a concerted and tem-porary suspension of function, designed to exert pressure upon others within the same social unit—industrial, political, or cultural."[52] As a public gesture, the strike is an indication that the workers have reached the end of their powers of restraint and collective bargaining. The strike is, in effect, a delib-erate casting of the die, a throwing-down of the gauntlet to the employer. In many industrial enterprises where the public is directly affected (e.g., rail-roads, public utilities), the strike also involves a deliberate appeal to public opinion by the strikers.[53]

The *cumulative* causes of the strike, as noted, involve such long-range factors as loss of status by the workers, dissatisfaction with new methods of production that threaten the skill hierarchy, and the progressive dehumani-zation of the workers in a mechanized industry. The *immediate* causes involve such tangible considerations as union recognition, hours and conditions of work, wages, welfare funds, pensions, and "fringe" benefits. In other countries strikes also involve political considerations; labor organizations are controlled by political parties and take collective action for political reasons. In the United States, political strikes are comparatively rare, and most actions reflect differences in the socioeconomic field.

The strike often brings about community and social disorganization. Local institutions are endangered and consensus is threatened. In an industrial or mining town the struggle may disrupt the normal community functions. It is difficult to remain neutral, and most persons are involved on one side or the other. Each side defines the situation differently, and social disorganization becomes a reality. Many of the group patterns that have previously held the community together are broken.[54] In the collective struggle the worker must sacrifice his only source of income. He may have to stand by and watch the faces of his children grow pinched and gaunt under the ravages of under-

[49] *Ibid.*, p. 197.

[50] *Ibid.*, p. 432.

[51] Moore, *Industrial Relations and the Social Order,* chap. 19, "Industrial Conflict."

[52] E. T. Hiller, *The Strike,* University of Chicago Press, Chicago, 1928, p. 12.

[53] Chamberlain, *op. cit.,* chap. 3, "Public Opinion on Labor-Management Relations."

[54] Paul F. Cressey, "Social Disorganization and Reorganization in Harlan County, Kentucky," *American Sociological Review, 14:*389–394 (June, 1949).

nourishment. With only his labor power to sell, he may suffer corresponding impairment in all of his institutional relationships.[55]

In 1958 there were 3694 strikes or work stoppages involving 2,060,000 workers who lost 23,900,000 man-days. This amounted to .22 percent of the total working time for the year. For the year 1959 through September there were 3125 work stoppages. The man-days lost were even more serious because of the steel strike. This strike lasted 116 days before the Taft-Hartley Act was invoked for an eighty-day "cooling off" period in which the men went back to work under an injunction. During September of this period 400 strikes were called in which 14,000,000 man-days were lost—an estimated 1.5 percent of the total working time for the month.[56] In terms of total working hours of the nation, the loss during a strike is negligible, but for the men who are out of work it means a total loss for the time being. Men often become very discouraged and their families experience serious need.[57]

The issues involved in strikes have reflected the changing times. The National Industrial Recovery Act of 1933 stipulated that workers had the specific right to organize in unions of their own choosing. Labor seized upon this right and formed unions in industries that had never before been fully organized, such as the automobile, steel, rubber, and textile industries. Many corporations contested this right and a wave of strikes followed, involving collective bargaining, union recognition, the closed shop, and related questions. This trend continued up to the outbreak of World War II.[58]

During World War II there was close cooperation between management and labor, marred only by stoppages in certain isolated industries (e.g., coal). The great mass of industrial workers respected the no-strike pledge made by their leaders and responded to the wartime emergency. The immediate post-war years, however, saw a rapid increase in strikes, arising chiefly from the desire of organized labor to keep pace with the rising cost of living. Inflation made higher wages imperative, which in turn contributed to the upward movement of prices. The trends in work stoppages from 1945 to 1958 are shown in Table 8.1.

In 1957, about three-quarters (70.3 percent) of the lost man-days involved disputes over wages and related matters. This figure compares with 73.5 percent of the lost man-days in 1956 arising from the same issues. Questions of union organization, which bulked so large in labor disputes two decades before, accounted for less than 10 percent of the man-days lost in 1957. Industry has largely accepted the right of labor to organize and present-day work stoppages involve other considerations.[59]

2. *Picketing.* The strike is the major weapon of the worker in industrial conflict. The other principal form of direct action is picketing. *Individual*

[55] Cf. Chamberlain, *op. cit.,* pp. 153–154.
[56] *Monthly Labor Review, 82:*1302 (November, 1959).
[57] Ann J. Herlihy and Harry F. Bonfils, "Analysis of Work Stoppages During 1957," *Monthly Labor Review, 81:*488–491 (May, 1958), Table 1.
[58] *Ibid.*
[59] *Ibid.,* Table 4.

picketing is intended to persuade the prospective customer or nonstriking worker that the employer is unfair to organized labor and should not be patronized or worked for. In *mass* picketing, the tactics change from persuasion to coercion, and nonstriking workers are clearly informed that their best interests (and perhaps their physical safety) lie in refraining from entering the plant. Large numbers of pickets marching back and forth in front of a factory give a convincing indication of mass solidarity.[60]

TABLE 8.1.   Work Stoppages in the United States, 1945–1957

| | | | Man-Days Idle During Year | |
Year	Work Stoppages	Workers Involved (thousands)	Number (thousands)	Percent of Estimated Working Time of All Workers
1945	4,750	3,470	38,000	0.47
1946	4,985	4,600	116,000	1.43
1947	3,693	2,170	34,600	.41
1948	3,419	1,960	34,100	.37
1949	3,606	3,030	50,500	.59
1950	4,843	2,410	38,800	.44
1951	4,737	2,220	22,900	.23
1952	5,117	3,540	59,100	.57
1953	5,091	2,400	28,300	.26
1954	3,468	1,530	22,600	.21
1955	4,320	2,650	28,200	.26
1956	3,825	1,900	33,100	.29
1957	3,673	1,390	16,500	.14
1958	3,694	2,060	23,900	.22

SOURCES: Ann J. Herlihy and Harry F. Bonfils, "Analysis of Work Stoppages During 1957," *Monthly Labor Review,* 81:488–491 (May, 1958), Table 1, and "Work Stoppages," *Monthly Labor Review,* 82:1302 (November, 1959).

Picketing has another psychological effect upon the strikers. It serves as an outlet for their accumulated aggressions, as it provides a way to demonstrate their emotions. Picketing also generates group solidarity by the gesture of defiance against the employer and possible strikebreakers. Picketing may make the strikers feel that they are advancing their cause and hence bringing about a positive good for the group. Such sentiments are aroused and maintained more effectively in a short than in a long strike. If the strike drags on, many of these psychological benefits are dissipated and the union may suffer group disorganization.[61]

3. *Boycott.*   The boycott is "a withdrawal of patronage or other business dealings in order to cause a loss to the individual or company boycotted."[62] The legal history of the boycott as employed by labor unions has been con-

[60] Moore, *Industrial Relations and the Social Order,* pp. 430–431.
[61] Stagner, *op. cit.,* p. 434.
[62] Moore, *Industrial Relations and the Social Order,* p. 436.

fused, and its effectiveness is dubious. Whether a union member or not, the individual usually organizes his buying habits about other stimuli than those of the union. He has learned to buy on the basis of price, brand names, physical proximity, and other considerations largely unrelated to unionism as such.[63] As a positive incentive, the union label carries the implied hope that the purchaser will support union labor and refrain from buying competing goods with no such label. This device also has mixed success, especially among persons not sympathetic to labor organizations.

4. *Communication.* Labor organizations also attempt to communicate with the general public and tell their side of the story. In these educational (or propagandistic) efforts, labor attempts to identify its opponents with "big business" and thereby enlist possible latent public sympathy with small business and individual enterprise. These efforts have not been notably successful. The American ideology remains sympathetic to business, whether small or large, and comparatively unsympathetic to many aspects of organized labor, especially those involving strikes. The norms and values of American society reflect a strong identification with the rights of property.[64]

Public opinion polls show that people in general tend to oppose strikes. A recent summary of such polls indicated: (a) that substantial majorities favor rigorous control of wartime strikes and those that occur under "emergency" conditions in peacetime; (b) that smaller majorities would subject all peacetime strikes to restraint, especially those in the public services and the "essential" industries; (c) that large minorities would outlaw *all* strikes under *any* conditions.[65] Most persons identify themselves with property ownership and are suspicious of all social organizations which appear to limit ownership. At the bar of public opinion, labor stands at a disadvantage in industrial conflict.

5. *Force.* Labor unions may resort to force in a desperate attempt to keep a strike from breaking up or prevent nonstriking workers from entering a plant. Responsible union leaders try to avoid force because it is self-defeating. The general public is quick to condemn any violence in connection with a strike and to blame labor for it. Despite the efforts of union leaders, however, tensions may get out of hand as strikers and nonstrikers clash before the factory gates or as the police attempt to break mass picket lines. The strike is a conflict situation and each side has much at stake. The La Follette Committee found a much greater propensity to violence by employers than by striking workmen. "Resort to arms by workmen," it reported, "is a rare occurrence, whereas the practice of industrial munitioning on the part of employers is widespread and commonplace."[66] Force on either side, however, has abated in recent years.

[63] Stagner, *op. cit.,* p. 358.
[64] *Ibid.,* pp. 434–439.
[65] Chamberlain, *op. cit.,* pp. 65–66.
[66] United States Senate, Committee on Education and Labor, *Violations of Free Speech and Rights of Labor, Report, Industrial Munitions,* Senate Report 6, part 3, Washington, 1939, p. 4, quoted by Moore, *Industrial Relations and the Social Order,* p. 434.

6. *Political Action.* The ballot is a major weapon of labor. Organized labor often cannot match industry in funds, public opinion, or campaign contributions; its principal source of power is in numbers. Approximately 15,000,000 members of organized labor, together with their families, make a formidable potential political force if mobilized for a particular purpose. Nevertheless, American labor is not traditionally politically-minded, and there is still strong opposition by some union members to any direct participation in political action.[67]

In the broad field of industrial conflict, however, the goals of labor have changed and broadened. Questions of welfare, pensions, guaranteed annual wages, vacations, sick benefits, and the like have become important considerations in collective bargaining. Organized labor is fighting for a way of life and, in a day of increasing governmental responsibility, this way of life depends in large measure upon governmental action. Future generations will doubtless see the efforts of labor gradually shift from the picket line to the halls of Congress.[68]

In industrial conflict, finally, the union is placed in the position of threatening the traditional system of property relationships and causing social disorganization. In a structural sense, this allegation is true, for organized labor *is* threatening many existing statuses, roles, and values. These patterns have come down from an earlier day when they represented the right of the individual property owner to deal with his property as he wished. The industrial system has changed, but many of the norms have not changed with comparable rapidity. Industrial conflict arises over problems of status, profits, and control.[69]

SELECTED BIBLIOGRAPHY

Chamberlain, Neil W., *Social Responsibility and Strikes,* Harper & Brothers, New York, 1953. This is a broadly conceived study of the strike, with particular stress upon its implications for the public welfare.

Dubin, Robert, *The World of Work,* Prentice-Hall, Inc., Englewood Cliffs, N.J., 1958. This is an analysis of work in American society, in which the author deals with an imposing mass of empirical knowledge in a new and meaningful theoretical framework. Work is viewed as a form of interpersonal and intergroup relationship and hence the world of work is one of related social systems.

Ellsworth, John S., *Factory Folkways,* Yale University Press, New Haven, 1952. A modern factory is here viewed as a social institution, with emphasis upon the structural aspects of this organized cluster of social patterns.

Friedmann, Georges, *Industrial Society* (translated by Harold L. Sheppard), The Free Press, Glencoe, Ill., 1955. The author of this study of man in an industrial

---

[67] Ruth A. Hudson and Hjalmar Rosen, "Union Political Action: the Member Speaks," *Industrial and Labor Relations Review,* 7:404–418 (1954).

[68] Jack Kroll, "Labor's Political Role," *Annals of the American Academy of Political and Social Science,* 274:118–122 (March, 1951).

[69] Stagner, *op. cit.,* p. 197.

society is perhaps the leading European authority on this vast subject. He views the individual in a technological and industrial civilization in a humanistic, psychological, and philosophical—as well as sociological—perspective.

Kornhauser, Arthur, Dubin, Robert, and Ross, Arthur M. (eds.), *Industrial Conflict,* McGraw-Hill Book Company, Inc., New York, 1954. This is a symposium prepared under the auspices of the Society for the Psychological Study of Social Issues. The variety of the backgrounds of the contributors and their eminence in their respective fields make it perhaps the most authoritative treatise on industrial conflict available at present.

Mayo, Elton, *The Social Problems of an Industrial Civilization,* Harvard University Press, Cambridge, 1945. This and the earlier study by the same author (*The Human Problems of an Industrial Civilization,* 1933), constitute some of the most thoughtful work that has been done in a most important sector.

Stagner, Ross, *Psychology of Industrial Conflict,* John Wiley and Sons, Inc., New York, 1956. The author places the problem of industrial conflict in a broad framework of individual and social psychology and views it as one of the several forms of conflict (along with racial and international conflict) which are currently threatening the organization of modern society.

Veblen, Thorstein, *The Theory of Business Enterprise,* Charles Scribner's Sons, New York, 1904. Written more than half a century ago, this essay by one of America's most original social philosophers offers a penetrating analysis of the cultural implications of the machine and its impact upon the lives of the workers.

Warner, W. Lloyd, and Low, J. O., *The Social System of the Modern Factory: The Strike,* Yale University Press, New Haven, 1947. This volume is one of a series of monographs describing the social structure of "Yankee City." In the present study, the forces leading to, and the events characterizing, a strike in the community are exhaustively analyzed.

Whyte, William F. (ed.), *Industry and Society,* McGraw-Hill Book Company, Inc., New York, 1946. This is a symposium dealing with various aspects of group relations in industry.

CHAPTER 9

Women in Industry

Social Change and the Employment of Women

Women have invaded the labor market in increasing numbers in recent years, many of them in the middle-class and professional occupations. There seems to be no question that women now form a vital part of the total labor force and contribute significantly to our economic output.

The role of women in society is, however, still defined largely in their functions as wife and mother. Since women must bear the children, care for them, and create a home for the family their traditional role must still go on. And our high marriage and birth rate indicates no tendency on the part of women to escape these functions. Yet many women wish to be recognized as persons as well as members of their sex. Nevertheless, anything which interferes with women's biological and sex roles produces a certain amount of social disorganization. Society expects women to look after the children and manage the home. Thus far no completely satisfactory solution to the problem of married women who work has been found. There are still more than the usual stresses and strains in families where the wife and mother works outside the home, and divorce rates seem to be higher for working women than for those not employed, as we discuss later.[1]

Women workers have, however, come to stay. The structure of business and industry is so completely geared to their presence that it could not operate without them. In October, 1959, there were 23,552,000 American women (married and unmarried) in the labor force, of which 22,287,000 were employed. As Table 9.1 shows, this was the highest number of women actually employed since the peak of World War II, when an estimated 20,500,000 were working. During the war approximately three million of the employed women came from families in which the husband had a comfortable income. Most of this group returned to their domestic pursuits after the war, and their places were taken by others from the growing number of women in the country.

A basic reason for the employment of women outside the home is, as Lorinne Pruette pointed out a good many years ago, that the industrial revolution threw women out of a job. What was formerly women's province in the

[1] Chapter 17, p. 427.

realm of baking, brewing, canning, weaving, sewing, and the like was transferred to factories where man assumed responsibility for the labor processes involved. Women were deprived of an important part of their creative work and given unparalleled leisure. Those in the upper-middle and upper classes had no suitable release for their energy and began to consume their spare time with useless or frivolous activities.[2] Those in lower economic groups, however, were virtually forced into the industrial market.

TABLE 9.1.   Employment of Women in the United States: October, 1959

Employment Status	Total[a]	Number of Women	Per-cent Distribution	Per-cent of Total	Change from September, 1959 October, 1958			
					Number	%	Number	%
Total	121,259,000	63,474,000	100	52	+69	+0.1	+808	+1.3
Civilian labor force	70,013,000	23,552,000	37	34	+585	+2.5	+596	+2.6
Employed	66,831,000	22,287,000	35	33	+528	+2.4	+682	+3.2
Agriculture	6,124,000	1,343,000	2	22	—75	—5.3	—53	—3.3
Nonagriculture	60,707,000	20,945,000	33	35	+604	—3.0	+736	—3.6
Unemployed[b]	3,272,000	1,265,000	2	39	+56	+4.6	—86	—6.4
Not in the labor force	51,155,000	39,922,000	63	78	—515	—1.3	+211	+05

[a] Noninstitutional population 14 years and over.
[b] Seasonally adjusted rate—total 6.0 percent; women 6.4 percent.
SOURCE: U.S. Department of Labor, Bureau of Labor Statistics, prepared by Division of Program Planning, Statistics, November, 1959.

Before women were deprived of their work, no man could be rightly thought of as "supporting his wife." Both husband and wife contributed to the social-economic arrangement which the family entailed. Together they supported their children, their servants, and any others making up their household.[3] In this arrangement man was undoubtedly dominant. He controlled the money and was vested with legal authority. His position in the economic world determined the family's economic well-being or lack of it. Part of his measure as a man, culturally, has been determined by *his ability as a provider*. This has often placed an undue burden on the husband, but it has also been the source of much masculine prestige. In modern times most married women have been content to be *dependent,* for if they sought a position in the economic world it has been at the expense of their husbands' egos. The accepted culture pattern in urban society has been for women to run the household, bear the children, and look after them while the father absented himself from the

[2] Cf. Lorinne Pruette, *Women and Leisure,* E. P. Dutton and Company, Inc., New York, 1924, p. 4.
[3] Cf. Mary R. Beard, *On Understanding Women,* Longmans, Green and Company, Inc., New York, 1931, p. 503.

family to earn enough money to keep them all in comfort, if possible, from want in any event.

Despite the general reluctance of men to "permit" their wives to work, women have long since invaded the industrial world. Initially, the women who worked in industry were chiefly young women earning spending money against the happy day they married. A hundred years ago, few fathers of comfortable means would consider letting their daughters work, except at some refined occupation like teaching. Even then, the daughters lived at home and employers kept their wages low in consequence.

All of the aspects of our economic system disruptive to men make a special impact upon women. In addition, women's role in society is greatly affected by employment since, if they work outside the home, they must transfer a large share of their interest and thought to concern with the job activities. This in turn must affect the role of men since they are both subjected to competition with women and required to assume greater concern for domestic affairs if any of the values of a home and a family are to be maintained. Men have been reluctant to accept these changes. The employment of women thus has created disruptive impacts upon the family by altering the traditional division of labor and sex roles within it. These problems are discussed in more detail below, but they are specifically part of the disorganizing stresses and strains which the employed woman faces.

Our basic concern here is the disorganizing aspect of paid work upon women themselves. On this topic countless tomes have been written pro and con. On the one hand, the arguments have supported the traditional contention that women's place is in the home, and on the other they have urged full economic emancipation with complete freedom of choice in job opportunities for women. Actually the contention that the proper role of women is to be found in "*Kirche, Küche und Kinder*" is as outmoded as the assertion that women have neither the intelligence nor the strength to pursue academic studies. Such an argument does not mesh with the facts. Certain other facts, however, are germane to our discussion.

The important stresses and strains which being a member of the labor force imposes upon women may be resolved briefly into:

1. Emotional stresses occasioned by the limits which wage earning imposes upon women by affecting their biological functions and traditional roles.
2. The special physical and moral hazards which paid jobs impose upon women:
   a. Hazards from night work and long hours.
   b. The dual or triple strains which holding paid jobs while functioning as homemakers and mothers impose.
3. The temporary or interim aspects of many women's employment which affect both their working skills and their employability.
4. The lower bargaining power of women, which definitely affects their economic status.
5. Wage discrimination against women.

6. Discriminations which women face by reason of male attitudes in the labor force and in professional groups.

7. There are also certain problems which relate specifically to the care of the home, the husband, and children. These also involve the wife and her attitudes toward home, husband, and children.

Emotional Maladjustments of Working Women

When women postpone or evade their traditional biological and social roles they face personal problems of emotional frustration. These are primarily the frustrations which unmarried women face. The personal unadjustment of women or their unadjustment because of sex is only partly related to whether or not they seek a career or work for wages. Most working women do not become sex offenders. Some do not marry, however. Here, too, there are many factors in sex selection, including whether or not women's work involves contact with men. When women work where they have an opportunity to meet eligible men, marriage rates are much higher than where they work in association with their own sex or with married men.

The emotional stress of deciding the question of career versus marriage appears to be chiefly a conflict for the middle-class woman who has gone to college and has achieved some of the satisfactions of working in an interesting profession or job. The average industrially employed woman in the lower economic brackets does not find her work any serious interference to her opportunity for marriage. This is even more true of Negro women than of white women. In 1957, 54 percent of the women working for wages were married and living with their husbands, as Table 9.2 shows. Twenty-five percent were single and 21 percent were widowed, divorced, or separated. Thirty

TABLE 9.2. Marital Status of Women in the Population and Labor Force: March, 1957 and 1940
(women 14 years of age and over)

Marital Status	Number of Women 1957	Percent Distribution		Change 1940–1957	
		1957	1940	Number	Percent
	Population				
Total	**61,863,000**	**100**	**100**	**+11,314,000**	**+22**
Single	11,487,000	19	28	−2,449,000	−18
Married, husband present	38,940,000	63	56	+10,423,000	+37
Other[a]	11,436,000	18	16	+3,339,000	+41
	Labor Force				
Total	**21,524,000**	**100**	**100**	**+7,684,000**	**+56**
Single	5,378,000	25	49	−1,332,000	−20
Married, husband present	11,529,000	54	30	+7,329,000	+175
Other[a]	4,617,000	21	21	+1,687,000	+58

[a] Includes women who are widowed, divorced, or married with husband absent.

SOURCE: *1958 Handbook on Women Workers*, Bulletin No. 266, Women's Bureau, U.S. Department of Labor, 1958, p. 31.

percent of the married women with husbands present were working for wages, while 49 percent of single women were working but this is because there were more married women than single women working.

It is thus chiefly the college-trained and professional women who have been the basis for so much discussion. Until relatively recently, more than half of the college-trained women did not marry, and higher education was widely accused of educating women away from marriage. Today a much larger percentage of college women are marrying, but the emotional frustrations of those professional women who pursue a career at the expense of marriage and those who curtail their home activities and childbearing when they marry still exist. Many psychiatrists, psychologists, and sociologists have maintained that women have achieved professional success by paying a high price emotionally.

Much of the emotional conflict of the working woman who does not marry is obviously related to sex. Women have inescapable roles imposed by the immutable facts of biology, both as sexual mates for their husbands and as childbearers for the human race. But they also have traditional roles as homemakers and general caretakers for husbands and children alike, special roles in the protective physical care they give the children in their upbringing. As mothers they are teachers and counselers of their children. For many middle- and upper-class women, this involves the most acceptable status, and unmarried women often feel they have been assigned an unimportant status because they have not married.

In any event, women's role is largely conceived in terms of the detailed physical care which children receive in infancy and childhood. Most children learn basic concepts of language, ethics, hygiene, manners, and religion more or less at their mother's knee. The teaching and supervising role of the mother is one of her socially defined and primary tasks in Western culture. Fathers also assume certain duties in the care and teaching of their children, but the role of most fathers is chiefly economic and primarily supplementary to that of the mother.

When women with small children are employed outside the home they are often under a serious nervous strain because of their concern for the health and safety of their children while they are on the job. Employed women with small children inevitably have more absence from work because of (1) the need for staying home when children are ill and (2) worry over the dangers to which children are exposed in their absence.

No one has made a detailed series of case histories of unmarried professional women from which a statistical study of their emotional problems could be analyzed in detail. Evelyn Ellis' analysis of upward social mobility among twenty-seven mobile and thirty-three nonmobile unmarried career women indicated, however, that successful careers were major goals for women who rose to a higher occupational level than that of their fathers. This was not so often true for the nonmobile. Fifty-two percent of the mobile women and only 27 percent of the nonmobile wished to continue their careers after marriage. The average educational level was the same for both groups. Dr. Ellis concluded that women who were striving to improve their social and occupational status were more likely to be neurotic than career women who were not so motivated.[4] Karen Horney maintains that drive toward upward mobility stems from the individual's having been humiliated.[5] This appeared to be true in 20 percent of the upwardly mobile women in Miss Ellis' study and in none of the nonmobile. However, 80 percent of the upwardly mobile were apparently not thus affected.

On the other hand many educated women have reacted against having their role defined in terms of biological function. Such women maintain that women have a right to be considered persons—apart from any biological role. Most men do not think of themselves primarily as husbands or fathers, but rather as writers, statesmen, bricklayers, or what have you. The way men have made their contribution to society has been chiefly in their occupation. The fact that women's role in the home has often been considered an inferior one has probably been a stimulus to sharing in the "superior" role. It is unfortunate that so important a task as rearing children should ever be considered a lesser role, but two items contribute to this attitude. One is that the wife and mother is an unpaid worker. The other is that motherhood depends upon biological condition rather than native intelligence or education. Practically any woman can be a mother.

Many unmarried professional women seem to be relatively well adjusted and apparently have no great conflict over their single estate. They may be dubbed the "modern nuns," but they have found great satisfaction in their chosen work. On the other hand, the high divorce rate does not speak too well for marriage as the solution to women's emotional problems. Both the unmarried and the married status thus seem to produce certain types of personal maladjustments. Until fairly recently many employers of professional women, particularly of teachers, have insisted that they be unmarried. This requirement has obviously augmented the emotional problems of working women.

In today's world many professional women have been able to combine the duties of wife and mother with a successful career. The professionally trained married woman is usually childless or has a small family, if she has any children at all, because of professional demands upon her time and strength. Lillian D. Gilbreth, with her twelve children, is a notable exception, for she has combined a significant career with a very large family.[6] Many career-minded professional wives have but a single child. Of thirteen married women members of the faculty of a certain women's college, for example, one woman has three children, two have two children, three have one child, and the re-

[4] Evelyn Ellis, "Social Psychological Correlates of Upward Social Mobility Among Unmarried Career Women," *American Sociological Review*, 17:558–563 (October, 1952).

[5] Karen Horney, *The Neurotic Personality of Our Time*, W. W. Norton and Company, Inc., New York, 1937, pp. 80–82 and 178–179 (cited by Evelyn Ellis, *op. cit.*).

[6] Frank B. Gilbreth and Ernestine Gilbreth Carey, *Cheaper by the Dozen*, Thomas Y. Crowell Company, New York, 1948.

maining seven have none. Of the twenty-one married men who are members of the same faculty, one has five children, two have four children, six have three children, five have two children, two have one child, and five have none. Approximately half of the faculty is unmarried. If this college is typical (and it probably is), there is a tendency for professional married women faculty members to have much smaller families than is true of married men on the faculty.

The professional woman's work cannot be mechanized. Success at her job requires her best thinking and she is almost bound "to take her work home with her" if she is to perform her professional services well. Her special contribution in creating a home to develop an atmosphere and a background for her family is more or less bound to suffer. Countless problems arise if her home is to be any sort of haven for its members. How to run the household, budget the income, supervise the children, entertain guests—all must be worked out differently from the way things are done in the type of home where the husband is the sole provider. Often the children feel they are left to shift for themselves while their mother pursues her career.

From a sociological point of view the working mother whose values have been distorted by wage earning and the necessity for wage earning is a matter for greater concern since so many more women are involved. The statistics available on working mothers are incomplete, however. They do not show the widowed and divorced group. Data are collected only for married women living with husbands. In 1957 there were 7,000,000 married women working whose children were under 18 years of age—most were from 6 to 17. The other 2,500,000 married working women had children under 6 years of age. Another 1,300,000 widowed, divorced, and separated women with children were also in the labor force,[7] but the number and age of their children are not available. Most working mothers' children are in school, but this does not mean that the child has no need for supervision. Many children get into trouble because there is no one at home to direct their activities when they return from school.

Working mothers who cannot afford to have someone look after their children after school hours often have to reckon with their children's delinquent behavior.[8] Children need the security of a stable home life. The fear of the disorganization of the mother's role through industrial employment is one of the most difficult aspects of child rearing faced by working mothers. Such mothers are usually working to provide income to meet the family's needs; if not, they are the sole support of families. How they can help the family financially without harming their children socially and morally presents a serious conflict for many mothers. Tommy may get into trouble because his mother is never at home when he returns from school. There is no one to say "No,

[7] *1958 Handbook on Women Workers*, Bulletin No. 266, Women's Bureau, U.S. Department of Labor, Washington, 1958, pp. 38–39.
[8] Cf. Chapter 4, "The Juvenile Delinquent," p. 84.

Tommy, you must not do that," and he resents the loneliness of the empty house.

A study of parent-referred cases in the Allegheny County Juvenile Court showed that some of the most serious delinquency problems brought to that court were from the homes with working mothers.[9] The inability to fulfill their socializing and supervising role is often a very frustrating situation to women who would like to bring their children up to be good citizens. Often working mothers themselves refer their children to guidance clinics and juvenile courts because they recognize their own inability to meet the problems.

When working mothers are separated from their husbands, they are sometimes too proud to accept public assistance or the aid to their dependent children which the state and federal governments provide. The mothers can often earn far more than the pittances which children receive through public assistance funds. The failure of welfare agencies and the community in general to provide more adequate funds or adequate facilities to enable mothers to maintain their roles is deplorable. Greater social provision for nursery care and after-school care for the children of employed mothers might lessen the emotional strain under which the working mother labors. Since 1954 working mothers have been allowed to deduct wages paid to supervisors of their children from their income tax, which helps them financially.

The Special Hazards for Women Workers

1. *Special Physical and Moral Hazards.* Women are especially susceptible physically to certain dangers inherent in industrial processes. They are more liable than men to sensitive reactions in the manufacture of certain poisonous chemicals; they are more prone to fatigue from long hours on their feet. In addition, women suffer special hazards from working too long hours and from night work.

Working long hours particularly when they are on their feet all day is often a health hazard to women. Consequently, forty-three states and the District of Columbia now have maximum hours per day or week during which a woman can be industrially employed. Five states—Alabama, Florida, Indiana, Iowa, and West Virginia—do not protect women at all, and nine of the states limiting hours have a maximum of from fifty to sixty hours a week. Georgia, Maryland, and Mississippi permit women to work sixty hours.[10] Twenty-two states and the District of Columiba limit women's work in some or all industries to a maximum of six days a week, while eight other states specifically forbid both men and women to work on Sunday. Eleven states also require a rest period.[11]

---

[9] Marcia Glazer and Barbara Wietrzynski, "Comparative Study of Parent-Referred and Police-Referred Cases of the Allegheny County Juvenile Court, Disposed January 1 through June 30, 1954," unpublished MS., Chatham College Library, 1955, p. 67. (This study was directed by Miss Elliott in cooperation with the Juvenile Court.)

[10] *1958 Handbook on Women Workers,* pp. 119–120.

[11] *Ibid.,* p. 122.

Night work is generally regarded as hazardous for women because of dangers of sex attacks in returning home late at night. Twenty states prohibit or regulate night work.[12]

Regulations with reference to employment before and after childbirth are in effect in six states and Puerto Rico. The state of Washington prohibits women from working four months before and six weeks after childbirth. The other states prohibit pregnant women from working two to four weeks before delivery and three to four weeks afterwards. Rhode Island does not prohibit employment but provides temporary disability benefits for maternity leave for six weeks before and after a child is born.[13]

Some women are distressed because certain occupations are legally closed to them. For example, the law forbids women to work in mining, logging, and heavy industry. Night work is also widely prohibited for women. Most women have no desire to be employed at heavy manual labor and hence do not resent their inability to secure work as miners. Many of them believe it wise for women to have this protection. Some women resent their exclusion from night work, however, and believe the state should protect them at such jobs rather than prohibit their employment.

2. *Dual and Triple Aspects of Married Women's Jobs.* At the present time more than half of the women employees are married, as we have stated, and so have important housekeeping duties. A sizable share of these also have young children whose physical, social, and emotional needs must be met if they are to grow up to be healthy, well-adjusted adults. Consequently, married women in industry also have major domestic responsibilities which involve labor, planning, and nervous strain after their hours at factory, store, office, or classroom are over. Shopping for groceries, clothing, and house furnishings must be crowded into noon hours, or done after work. Running the vacuum, doing the household laundry, and mending often stretch the working woman's day until 10 or 11 P.M. Mothers whose earnings are low must frequently neglect their children, and though the children may develop independence, they sometimes suffer seriously from lack of supervision after school hours. Working mothers themselves may be so harried that they are unduly irritated by relatively normal conduct on the part of teen-agers. It is not surprising that the working mother is often among those parents who turn their problem children over to the juvenile court.[14] The working wife is making a significant economic contribution, but the smoothly run home which affords so much emotional benefit to the family is difficult to achieve unless she is a well-paid executive or a professional woman.

A significant percentage of career women achieve success in the business or professional world, marry, and have a relatively happy domestic life, thus

[12] *Ibid.*

[13] *Ibid.*, pp. 122–123.

[14] Katherine Brownell Oettinger, "Maternal Employment and Children," in Erwin D. Canham (ed.), *Work in the Lives of Married Women,* Columbia University Press, New York, 1958, pp. 132–149. Cf. also Mirra Komarovsky, *Women in the Modern World,* Little, Brown and Company, Boston, 1953, chap. V, "Home Plus a Job."

combining the roles of wife and mother with their employment outside the home. In the years ahead the number who are able to do this will probably increase, since the domestic pattern for women as graduate students and in professional study has markedly altered. Although comparatively few women enter graduate schools, a significant percentage of those who do are married and are pursuing their study at the same time their husbands do. This is true both for women candidates for the Ph.D. degree and for women in law and medicine. Women graduate and professional students tend to marry fellow students, which augurs well for their later careers since they often open offices with their husbands.

Thirty or forty years ago a large share of college women did not marry. Nowadays the majority of college women marry, and in many colleges from 10 to 15 percent marry while still in college. This group is perhaps taking seriously some of the recriminations hurled against college-trained women who were failing in their biological role. Psychiatrists, sociologists, and psychologists have accused the highly educated women of "denying their biological heritage," and of being the "lost sex."[15] The reversal in marriage trends seems to indicate that this problem is no longer so serious.

Many young women who marry during their college careers are assuming serious responsibilities. Some have the first baby before they receive a sheepskin. Often their husbands are G.I.s who have not completed their own education. The wives expect to work while their husbands finish college. The stresses confronting this new group of working wives and mothers have never been subjected to detailed study, but their experiences would afford some interesting insight as to how higher education affects the problems of young working mothers.

The Temporary Aspect of Women's Employment

A major reason for the exploitation of women is directly related to the temporary aspect of the employment of so many women. The average woman tends to work a few years and then marry. After marriage a large number of women do not work at all. Others work until shortly before the first baby comes, after which they devote their full time to domestic duties. Later they may return to industry to eke out the family wage, or because of deep-seated career or professional interests. The interim aspect of women's jobs is one reason for the exploitation of women in the past. It is also true that a person who is not interested in long-time employment is *ipso facto* less valuable to the employer. Women have paid an economic price for their temporary affiliation with the labor force.

The Lower Bargaining Power of Women

The bargaining power of women is thus lower than that of men because they move in and out of the labor market. They are not as wage conscious as men and are much less effectively organized. One reason, of course,

[15] Ferdinand Lundberg and Marynia Farnham, *Modern Woman, The Lost Sex,* Harper & Brothers, New York, 1947. This book voices a labored lament over the modern woman.

is that they do not expect to stay in the labor market long. But many labor organizations prior to World War II were openly hostile to women, which fact has also militated against their organization. During the war women performed such important services that the attitudes of male workers became less inimical. Approximately 3,400,000 women were estimated to be members of labor unions in 1956 out of a total of 27,948,000 women employed during that year. This constituted slightly over one-seventh of the total women workers.[16] Until women themselves have developed strong leadership and wide membership in labor organizations which strengthen their bargaining position, the need for protective legislation will remain because they cannot force employers to recognize their claims to better conditions and pay.

Women's wages have been low traditionally because most women have worked both in the community and at home without pay. So few women worked for wages before the industrial revolution (save as teachers, seamstresses, and domestics) that their work was considered relatively unimportant. The majority of women were engaged in domestic tasks performed at home where no monetary reward was given. Whatever food, clothing, and shelter they received depended upon the bounty and the economic position of their male providers. When women first came into the labor market, any wage was more than they previously had received. Hence, low wages were accepted as a great improvement over what they had in their previous status as dependents.

Wage Discrimination Against Women

Most women who work outside the home contribute to the family support or support themselves. In a study made in 1952, practically all women who worked (whether married or single) contributed to family support. Most married women were contributing to essential family expenses or were working to pay the expense of children at college. Very few were working for professional satisfactions.[17] Where their husbands are in higher income brackets relatively few married women work. Yet discriminatory wage scales often have been enforced against women because it is alleged that men have to support families and must have the added income.

One of the perennial frustrations of women is thus that they earn so much less than men. Men not only earn more than women but are paid more for doing exactly the same work. This is justified by the contentions that men have families to support, women lack job seniority, etc. Sometimes women lack experience, but part of the reason for unequal pay for the same work is unquestionably prejudice.

In general women's incomes are lower because of lack of skill or because they do part-time work. A much larger percentage of women are in low-paid types of work, including domestic service. As Table 9.3 shows, 42 percent of the women but only 16 percent of the men received less than $1000 income in

---

[16] *1958 Handbook on Women Workers,* pp. 47–49.
[17] Study cited in *ibid.,* p. 26.

TABLE 9.3.   Income of Women and Men, 1956

Item	Total Money Income Women	Men	Wage and Salary Income Women	Men
	Total Income Recipients			
Number (in thousands)	31,823	52,016	23,517	40,900
Percent of population	52	92	38	72
Median income	$1,146	$3,608	$1,405	$3,811
Range of Income	*Percent Distribution*			
	100	100	100	100
Under $1,000	47	17	42	16
$1,000–$1,999	19	12	19	9
$2,000–$2,999	16	12	19	12
$3,000–$3,999	11	15	13	17
$4,000–$4,999	4	16	5	18
$5,000 and over	3	28	2	29
	Year-Round Full-Time Workers			
Percent of total income recipients	29	62	38	67
Median income	$2,828	$4,462	$2,827	$4,466

SOURCE: *1958 Handbook on Women Workers*, Bulletin No. 266, Women's Bureau, U.S. Department of Labor, 1958, p. 53, Table 1.

1956.[18] When incomes are classified according to occupational level women also receive much less than men. Women professional workers received on the average very little more than men service workers in 1956, as Table 9.4

TABLE 9.4.   Wage or Salary Income for Selected Occupations: 1956 and 1939

Occupational Group	Year-Round Full-Time Workers Women 1956	1939	Men 1956	1939
Professional workers	$3,650	$1,277	$5,847	$2,100
Managers, officials, proprietors	3,525	1,218	5,967	2,254
Clerical workers	3,145	1,072	4,388	1,564
Operatives	2,632	742	4,235	1,268
Sales workers	2,090	745	5,005	1,451
Service workers (except household)	1,950	607	3,521	1,019
Private-household workers	879	339	—	549

SOURCE: *1958 Handbook on Women Workers*, Bulletin No. 266, Women's Bureau, U.S. Department of Labor, 1958, p. 54.

shows. When income is related to education for full-time employees, men receive about 60 percent more than women in all educational levels, and men with four years or more of college receive over 83 percent higher income than women in this category, as Table 9.5 shows.

When income is compared on a racial basis it is clear that white women receive more than twice the income of nonwhite women. The wage differential between white and nonwhite men is somewhat less, but for both races

[18] *1958 Handbook on Women Workers*, p. 53.

TABLE 9.5.   Income and Education of Men and Women, 1956

| Years of School Completed | Median Income | | | |
| | Total Income Recipients | | Year-Round Full-Time Workers | |
	Women	Men	Women	Men
Total	$1,146	$3,608	$2,828	$4,462
College				
4 years or more	$3,050	$6,038	$3,809	$6,980
Less than 4 years	1,734	4,458	3,440	5,457
High school				
4 years	1,898	4,413	3,021	4,887
Less than 4 years	941	3,577	2,583	4,514
Elementary school				
8 years	957	3,229	2,408	4,035
Less than 8 years	724	2,012	1,811	3,120

SOURCE: *1958 Handbook on Women Workers*, Bulletin No. 266, Women's Bureau, U.S. Department of Labor, 1958, p. 54.

men receive much more than women. In 1956 the average white woman received $2179, the average white man $4260. For the nonwhite women the yearly income averaged only $970, while the average nonwhite men received $2396 (see Table 9.6).[19] Race thus is an even greater factor in discrimination than sex.

TABLE 9.6.   Wage or Salary Income of White and Nonwhite Women and Men, 1956 and 1939

| Group and Year | All Workers | |
	Women	Men
White		
1956	$2,179	$4,260
1939	676	1,112
Nonwhite		
1956	970	2,396
1939	246	460

SOURCE: *1958 Handbook on Women Workers*, Bulletin No. 266, Women's Bureau, U.S. Department of Labor, 1958, p. 55.

Studies made in 1956 in five manufacturing industries showed that women earned considerably less than men on an hourly basis, as shown in Table 9.7. In 1954 straight earnings in manufacturing industries were nearly one-third less—i.e., $51.20 per week for women for a forty-hour week and $72 per week for men. In the coat-and-suit industries in 1957 men averaged much more than women, according to Table 9.8. In retail trade in 1956 the same was true. In all retail trades women averaged $1.11 an hour and men $1.58.[20]

Discrimination Because of Male Attitudes

Professional women are faring better than formerly so far as teachers' salaries are concerned because wage scales are in effect.[21] Nevertheless

[19] *Ibid.*, p. 55.
[20] *Ibid.*, pp. 61–68.
[21] *Ibid.*, p. 72.

TABLE 9.7. Hourly Earnings of Women and Men in Five Manufacturing Industries, April, 1956

Industry	Number of Workers (in thousands)		Average Hourly Earnings		Percent Women Receiving—	
	Women	Men	Women	Men	Under $1.05	$1.50 and over
Food and kindred products	260	763	$1.35	$1.77	27	34
Apparel and related products	855	214	1.33	1.91	30	25
Furniture and fixtures	48	267	1.33	1.63	23	30
Leather and leather products	167	165	1.26	1.67	32	20
Textile-mill products	433	538	1.24	1.44	18	12

SOURCE: *1958 Handbook on Women Workers*, Bulletin No. 266, Women's Bureau, U.S. Department of Labor 1959, p. 61.

there is a tendency for men to be appointed to administrative positions even though there may be women who are better qualified. In colleges and universities relatively few women are heads of departments in institutions where faculties are predominantly men. Married women faculty members receive lower salaries in many colleges partly because their bargaining power is diminished because their husbands' jobs are in the same community.

The general reluctance and hostile attitudes men have against competing with women have made it difficult for the latter to follow their natural talents and professional inclinations. Women with a mechanical bent have had serious difficulty, for example, in securing admission to engineering schools.

Discrimination against women is thus far more serious in the professions than in industrial employment. On the other hand, women fill most of the

TABLE 9.8. Earnings of Women in Women's and Misses' Coat-and-Suit-Manufacturing Industry in 10 Major Areas, February, 1957

Area	Number of Women Production Workers	Average Hourly Earnings[a]		Percent of Women Receiving—	
		Women	Men	Less Than $1.20	$2.50 or More
Baltimore	603	$1.57	$2.08	18	6
Boston	193	1.74	2.70	15	4
Chicago	805	2.00	3.13	13	23
Kansas City	1,444	1.62	1.97	24	6
Los Angeles–Long Beach	2,352	1.85	3.19	11	16
Newark–Jersey City	5,477	1.87	2.57	12	15
New York City	10,206	2.22	2.95	4	29
Paterson	4,246	1.80	2.52	13	10
Philadelphia	469	1.77	2.82	16	13
San Francisco–Oakland	851	1.69	2.65	11	9

[a] Excludes premium pay for overtime and for work on week ends, holidays, and late shifts.

SOURCE: *1958 Handbook on Women Workers*, Bulletin No. 266, Women's Bureau, U.S. Department of Labor, p. 64.

jobs in certain occupational fields.[22] In industry they dominate the garment and textile trades, and they constitute 98 percent of the nurses, 94 percent of the typists and secretaries, and 80 percent of the waiters.

The learned professions have been more difficult to reconcile with women's role as homemaker and mother. Professional women have experienced many personal frustrations over their inability to secure deserved recognition or promotions in their work. Men obviously dislike to work under women and make it relatively certain that this will not happen.

In the professions of medicine and law, women experience serious discrimination although if they are exceptionally able they usually find an opportunity for study and practice. Most medical schools severely restrict their women applicants. American medical men as a group have been prejudiced against women in their field, whom they have disdainfully labeled "hen medics," and medical societies sometimes restrict their meetings to male members of the profession. The fact that only the superior women students have been permitted (in most instances) to study medicine has kept their performance high and has mitigated the prejudice to a certain degree. Some medical school deans allege that women medical students often marry and fail to complete their course and therefore constitute a major waste. It is an interesting fact that women constitute about 85 percent of the medical profession in Russia, and this was also true in czarist times. In Germany women constitute approximately one-third of the physicians. The prejudice against women in medicine is thus largely a cultural matter. Russians say, "Women have to care for the sick. Why shouldn't they know how?"

Women in law face much the same prejudice although certain modern Portias have made a notable contribution. A few outstanding women lawyers have become judges in the larger urban centers. Some of the hostility to women in the professions undoubtedly stems today more from men's desire for masculine association than from inherent belief in the inferiority of women.

Professional discrimination has not been directed against actresses and concert singers (who have often been glamorized by male admirers and employers alike). Actresses frequently receive very high salaries. The outstanding professional woman likewise may experience no great difficulties, but she nevertheless will face obstacles which relatively mediocre men never experience. In many instances a woman will have every qualification for a position except that she is not a man.

In the teaching field women outrank men markedly in elementary and secondary schools. Colleges and universities, however, have always been dominated by men. When women's colleges were founded, intellectual women were often employed as college teachers and frequently were presidents of women's colleges. Now that college education for women has become accepted, the proportion of men on the faculties of women's colleges has risen. The number of women on the faculties of coeducational institutions has meanwhile declined, particularly in the upper professional ranks. This discrimina-

[22] *1954 Handbook on Women Workers*, Women's Bureau U.S. Department of Labor, Washington, 1954, pp. 5–6.

tion against able and well-trained women is an especially frustrating mental hazard for women faculty members. Many college placement bureaus indicate that the job opportunities for college teaching are declining for women. The real reason for this, however, is that such a small percentage of highly qualified women is available. In a study conducted by the Research Division of the National Education Association in 1957, slightly less than 9 percent of those awarded Ph.D. degrees were women.[23] Since nearly all positions other than the rank of instructor require the Ph.D. degree this gives an essential reason for the low number of women professors.

Much of the difficulty women have in securing professorial positions is a matter of lack of training. If women expect to make a major contribution to academic life they will have to attend graduate schools and secure the re-

TABLE 9.9. Employment of Women College Graduates, Class of 1955

Employment and/or Educational Status	Number	Percent
Number reporting status	80,852	100
Employed only	57,923	71
Full time	55,464	68
Part time	2,459	3
Employed and studying further	7,078	9
Employed full time, studying part time	5,966	7
Employed part time, studying part time	485	1
Studying full time, employed part time	627	1
Studying only	6,816	8
Full time	6,428	8
Part time	388	a
Seeking work	2,916	4
Not seeking work	6,119	8

Total full-time jobs: 61,430
Total studying: 13,894; full time, 7,055

a Less than 1 percent.

SOURCE: *Employment After College, Report on Women Graduates, Class of 1955.* U.S. Department of Labor, 1956, Table III.

quired education. If they wish to play a larger part in higher education they will have to be adequately prepared. Unless the present trend toward early marriage among college women is reversed there is no likelihood that the number of women Ph.D.'s will increase.

The Employment of Women College Graduates

Although the majority of college women graduates marry within two years after they finish college many of these young women work until they have their first baby. In an effort to discover the patterns of work among recent college graduates the Women's Bureau of the Department of Labor sent a questionnaire to all college women graduates of the class of 1955 with reference to their employment and whether or not they were taking postgraduate work. The questionnaire was answered by 80,852 women. As Table 9.9 shows, 71 percent of this class was employed—68 percent full

[23] *Teacher Supply and Demand in Colleges and Universities,* National Education Association, Washington, 1957, p. 35.

time, 3 percent part time. Nine percent were employed and studying—7 percent studying part time and employed full time, 1 percent studying part time and employed part time, and 1 percent studying full time and employed part time.

Only 8 percent were studying full time (without employment) and less than 1 percent part time. In addition, 4 percent were seeking work and 8 percent were neither seeking work (nor studying). These figures indicate the significance of working or studying in order to secure work later. We can assume most women engage in postgraduate study for the purpose of qualifying for subsequent positions.

Of the group employed, one-fourth were interested in a career, one-fourth were indefinite in their plans, and one-half considered their work temporary activity.[24]

Other Adjustment Problems

Certain other problems complicate the role of the married woman working outside the home. One is the fact that men have the traditional and legal right to determine where the home shall be and many women have to give up their work when their husbands accept jobs in other cities. This often keeps women from getting ahead, but it is something which cannot be altered if the home and family life is to be maintained. Tensions and frustrations may result.

On the other hand, some corporations object to having the wives of executives hold jobs, partly for this reason and partly because they feel that such a situation reflects unfavorably on the corporation. An important man has social obligations to his firm which are more difficult to meet if the wife is employed. Questions with reference to the quality of the housekeeping and the amount of attention which can be given children also complicate the working woman's problem.[25]

It has been widely held, too, that the woman who works may affect her husband's ambition—that he will have less incentive to forge ahead in his work. The wife's income is not all added to the family budget in any event since she must spend more money for clothes and for her lunches, carfare, and the expense of any "baby-sitters" or domestic servants which her absence from home requires.

Minimum Wage and Equal Pay Legislation

A movement to extend equal pay for equal work without reference to sex grew during World War I when the National War Labor Board enforced the policy in war work. The progress in this direction is discouraging, however. By 1958 only seventeen states had enacted laws requiring equal pay for men and women when both are employed at comparable work. They are

[24] *Employment After College, Report on Women Graduates, Class of 1955*, U.S. Department of Labor, Washington, 1956, p. 15.

[25] Mary A. Hatch and David L. Hatch, "Problems of Married Working Women as Presented by Popular Magazines," *Social Forces, 37*:148–153 (December, 1958).

Alaska, Arkansas, California, Colorado, Connecticut, Illinois, Maine, Massachusetts, Michigan, Montana, New Hampshire, New Jersey, New York, Oregon, Pennsylvania, Rhode Island, and Washington.[26] By 1958 thirty-two states, the District of Columbia, and Puerto Rico had enacted minimum wage laws for women. These are Alaska, Arizona, Arkansas, California, Colorado, Connecticut, the District of Columbia, Hawaii, Idaho, Illinois, Kansas, Kentucky, Louisiana, Maine, Massachusetts, Minnesota, Nevada, New Hampshire, New Jersey, New Mexico, New York, North Dakota, Ohio, Oklahoma, Oregon, Pennsylvania, Rhode Island, South Dakota, Utah, Vermont, Washington, Wisconsin, Wyoming, and Puerto Rico.[27] Both minimum wage and equal pay laws tend to reduce the exploitation of women so far as wages are concerned. Nevertheless, there are still many evasions of the laws.

Services for Working Wives and Mothers

Commercial and welfare agencies have supplied commodities and services which, partially at least, meet the new social needs. Most clothing is now factory made. Relatively few women make all of their own or their children's clothing. Much food is now processed and ready for the table or requires only a short time for preparation. Canned goods, which have been on the market a long time, lessened the housewife's work. Now the frozen food industry has made it possible to have foods rivaling fresh foods with a minimum of effort. Frozen dinners which provide meat and two vegetables are available for individual service. These are a boon to the housewife for they can be heated quickly and provide a tasty meal. Such meals are too expensive for the low-paid woman worker but are within the range of the middle-class woman's budget.

Modern household equipment—electrical washers, vacuums, etc.—have made it possible for laundry and cleaning to be done with less effort. In many ways housekeeping chores have been lightened. It is nevertheless true that many working wives still have a heavy burden if they attempt to do all of the normal household tasks.

Redefinition of Women's Roles

Any redefining of the roles of the sexes raises questions. A major one is whether a man's success really depends on having his wife devote her whole time to creating a home and giving him encouragement and motivation to succeed. The remarkable contribution that American women make to community life on a volunteer basis, whether as hospital aides or Red Cross workers, in Community Chest drives or in promotion of endowment funds or symphony projects, makes it clear that upper-middle-class women have a reservoir of energy that can be channeled into socially useful achievements. Nobody thinks that such work is taking women out of the home, because they pursue civic work without pay on a part-time basis.

[26] *1958 Handbook on Women Workers,* pp. 118–119.
[27] *Ibid.,* p. 117.

Part-time work for married women might make it possible for a much larger group to utilize their professional training without jeopardizing their home life in any way. The fact that so many well-educated women work without pay is testimony to their creative energy. It is also probably a way in which men permit their wives to utilize their creative energy without diminishing their husbands' egos. Significantly, very few important studies on working women have been made in recent years.[28]

SELECTED BIBLIOGRAPHY

Brittain, Vera, *Lady into Woman,* The Macmillan Company, New York, 1953. Chap. 15 contains a challenging statement of the changed aspect of women's life organization under the title "The Human Revolution."

Canham, Erwin D. (ed.), *Woman Power,* National Man Power Council, Columbia University Press, New York, 1957. This is one of the best analyses of the current strength of women in the national man power.

Canham, Erwin D. (ed.), *Work in the Lives of Married Women,* National Man Power Council, Columbia University Press, New York, 1958. The entire book has much valuable material for the student who wishes a fuller discussion of the issues.

Ellis, Evelyn, "Social Psychological Correlates of Upward Social Mobility Among Unmarried Career Women," *American Sociological Review, 17:*558–563 (October, 1952). This is an interesting study of the reasons women strive toward social mobility.

Employment After College, Report on Women Graduates, Class of 1955, U.S. Department of Labor, Washington, 1956. A very interesting analysis of what modern women college graduates are doing a year after finishing college shows that a large share are both married and working.

Hatch, Mary A., and Hatch, David L., "Problems of Married Working Women as Presented by Popular Magazines," *Social Forces, 37:*148–153 (December, 1958). Some of the special problems of working married women are analyzed.

Komarovsky, Mirra, *Women in the Modern World,* Little, Brown and Company, Boston, 1953. An excellent analysis is made of the dilemma of the modern woman, particularly the educated woman.

Lundberg, Ferdinand, and Farnham, Marynia, *Modern Woman, The Lost Sex,* Harper & Brothers, New York, 1947. These authors take a somber attitude toward the modern woman.

1958 Handbook on Women Workers, Bulletin No. 266, Women's Bureau, U.S. Department of Labor, Washington, 1958. This publication (and ones which appear later) should be consulted for details about women's employment and the discriminations women encounter in wages, in the professions, etc.

Oettinger, Katherine Brownell, "Maternal Employment and Children," in Erwin D. Canham (ed.), *Work in the Lives of Married Women,* Columbia University Press, New York, 1958, pp. 133–150. The head of the Welfare Division of the United States Department of Health, Education, and Welfare presents a vivid picture of the working mother.

---

[28] Cf. *Employment After College, Report on Women Graduates, Class of 1955;* Canham, *op. cit.,* p. viii.

Pruette, Lorinne, *Women and Leisure,* E. P. Dutton and Company, Inc., New York, 1924. This book is a pungent analysis of the impact of the industrial revolution upon women's work.

Teacher Supply and Demand in Colleges and Universities, National Education Association, Washington, 1957. This study shows that the percentage of women teachers on a college level is declining, chiefly because so few women qualify for a Ph.D. degree.

CHAPTER 10

Children in Industry

The Problem of Child Labor

The shift from an agricultural and commercial society to an industrialized one has been one of the most important developments in modern times. It has modified many social relationships and broken others completely, as the members of an industrial society have been forced to adjust to new ways of life. We have examined some of the aspects of social disorganization as they have affected first men and then women in industry. Industrialism has also made a serious impact upon the status and role of children. In many ways the latter are the most vulnerable of all when they leave the shelter of their homes and enter the office, factory, field, or city street.

The opposition to the employment of women has stemmed from deep-seated prejudices of men and from the traditional attitudes that women's place is in the home. Relatively few groups have therefore openly objected to protecting women by law, despite the fact that approximately twenty million of them are now subject to the vicissitudes of gainful employment. The objection to child labor legislation, however, has been widespread, vociferous, and bitter. This has come from various sources, including farmers and the Roman Catholic clergy, as well as industrial and commercial groups which have profited by child labor. The farmers have fought child labor laws on the erroneous ground that such legislation would keep children from helping their parents on the farm. The Catholic clergy have objected on the ground that federal regulation threatens the authority of the family, which they consider paramount in this field.

As a result of these and other objections, children continue to be exploited in both industry and agriculture. This exploitation is greater than that suffered by women, chiefly because children are underaged, totally inexperienced, and without industrial unions to protect them. Children, up to now at least, do not bargain collectively and have no spokesmen to deal with employers. Women's and child workers' chief protection thus has been the collective conscience which is expressed by lawmakers. Lawmakers, on the other hand, are hounded notoriously by selfish economic interests.

Children are also the victims of their own shortsighted desire for becoming wage earners and of selfish and ignorant parents who are willing to sacrifice their children's future for their present economic contribution to the family.

The parents of child laborers are usually without much education themselves and see little value in keeping their children in school. Some parents are also ill and handicapped and see no other solution to family needs, but present-day public assistance funds and private charity organizations exist to meet just such problems. There is virtually no need for parents to be dependent upon children's wages today.

The Exploitation of Children in Perspective

We have, nevertheless, come a long way in protecting children from the handicapping and disorganizing aspects of unregulated child labor.[1] During the early part of the nineteenth century, New England mills employed children eight or nine years old, often for twelve or thirteen hours a day. Soon New Englanders recognized the danger that these children would grow up illiterate. In 1813, Connecticut required millowners to teach children the three R's. In 1836, Massachusetts enacted a law requiring all children under fifteen to receive education for at least three months a year. Other New England states enacted compulsory school laws and passed restrictions on children's working more than ten hours a day.

Outside of New England there was no great mass employment of children until the Civil War gave impetus to large-scale production.[2] Children then became an important part of the labor force, and after 1870 child labor expanded rapidly as a part of the toll of machine methods. As early as 1881, adult workers were aroused with reference to both the disorganization of the child laborer and the "unfair competition" which the children posed for adult labor. Children could operate many machines with facility. In that year, the newly founded American Federation of Labor urged the abolition of child labor. Not until considerably later, however, did the effort to restrain employers from exploiting young children gain momentum.

During the period from 1885 on, European immigrants flooded the country to participate in the vast industrial development. Industrialists sponsored immigration to promote an oversupply of labor, so that they might keep wages low for all labor and operate their businesses at higher profits. The children of such laborers had little alternative but to seek work in order to add their pittances to the family income. By 1900, 26 percent of the boys under fifteen and 10 percent of the girls were industrially employed.[3] Because there were virtually no enforced standards with reference to hours, wages, or conditions of work, the children suffered pitiable exploitation. Many socially minded persons became aroused, and in 1904 the National Child Labor Committee was organized. The latter was instrumental in influencing the creation of the federal Children's Bureau. This agency was first attached to the Department of Commerce in 1912, was transferred to the Department of Labor in 1913, became a special bureau of the

[1] Sol Markoff, "Youth and Work," *Children,* March–April, 1957, reprint.
[2] Lucy Manning, *Why Child Labor Laws?* Child Labor Series No. 1, Bureau of Labor Standards, U.S. Department of Labor, Washington, 1946, pp. 1–2.
[3] *Newsbriefs,* No. 11, The Twentieth Century Fund, New York, 1949.

Federal Security Agency in 1946, and with the creation of the Department of Health, Education, and Welfare in 1952 was attached to the Welfare Division. Meanwhile the Child Labor Division of the Children's Bureau has been retained by the Department of Labor.

Following World War I, the number of children employed in industry decreased sharply, largely because of the decline in industrial production, but partly because of the movement opposed to child labor, which culminated in the enactment of two federal laws governing child labor. Both were later declared unconstitutional, but the movement to restrict child labor continued. A child labor amendment was enacted by Congress in 1924, which thus far has been ratified by twenty-eight states. In consequence of the generally aroused opinion, the number of employed children from ten to fifteen decreased 46.7 percent between 1910 and 1920 and 37.1 percent between 1920 and 1930. Stated differently, 18.4 percent of children ten to fifteen were employed in 1910, 8.5 percent in 1920, and only 4.7 percent in 1930. The 37.1 percent decline in ten- to fifteen-year-old laborers in 1930 was much greater than that of workers from fifteen to seventeen, however, where the decline was only 13.6 percent.[4]

During the depression years of the thirties, the problem of the child laborer took a series of turns. Because of the vast number of unemployed breadwinners, many children left school to help support their families or themselves. Often these cases were not reported to any statistical bureau. There were other trends accompanying the employment of children during the depression. Children drifted to the less desirable, lower-paid, and generally unregulated industries. Many young persons were out of school because they could not afford clothes, books, and carfare. Their idleness was often personally disorganizing.

At the same time, social sentiment was mounting against child labor. The National Recovery Act was in force between 1933 and 1935, and prohibited (1) children under sixteen years of age from working in industry and (2) those between sixteen and eighteen from employment in the hazardous industries except where work permits were granted. Children were practically eliminated from the labor scene temporarily. The NRA was declared unconstitutional in 1935, and the number of children working soon mounted in consequence.

In 1937, however, the "Sugar Act," which prohibited children under fourteen from working in the beet fields, went into effect. Those from fourteen to sixteen were not allowed to work more than eight hours a day in the beet industry and were to receive the same wages as adults.[5] A revision of the law in 1940 severely penalized all beet growers hiring children by making them ineligible for marketing benefits. Children were virtually eliminated

[4] Cf. "Child Workers in the United States, 1930," *Monthly Labor Review, 35*:1334–1336 (December, 1932).

[5] Section 301 of the Sugar Act of 1937, *Public Laws*, No. 414, 75th Congress.

from one of the industries in which they were most seriously exploited.[6] Meanwhile the Fair Labor Standards Act of 1938, often designated the "Wage and Hour Act," prohibited the shipment in interstate or foreign commerce of *any* article produced under conditions of "oppressive child labor."

The Fair Labor Standards Act, as amended in 1957, sets sixteen years as the limit for any employment during school hours or for any time in agriculture and in manufacturing, mining, or processing occupations requiring duties in workrooms or factories and for power-driven machinery. Thirteen orders now prohibit employment in explosives, manufacturing, driving or helping on motor vehicles, coal mining, logging and sawmilling, operating power-driven woodworking machines, exposure to radioactive substances, operating hoisting apparatus or metal forming, punching, and shearing machines, mining in non-coal industries, work in slaughtering and meat packing and rendering plants and on power-driven bakery machinery—and other work considered particularly hazardous. In these industries children must be eighteen before they can be employed. They must also be eighteen before they can be employed as public messengers or as operators of vehicles.[7]

The Fair Labor Standards Act was declared constitutional in 1941 in the case of the *United States* vs. *Darby*. The right of the federal government to restrict child labor and to enforce standards was no longer to be questioned, so far as industries involved in interstate commerce were concerned. In the covered industries, child labor has very nearly disappeared, although certain violations continually occur. The Public Contracts Act also forbids child labor of boys under sixteen and girls under eighteen in the manufacture of goods under contract to the federal government.

During World War II, child labor laws were relaxed in order to increase the number of available workers in the factories and to meet the demands for labor on the home front. So much of the normal labor force was absorbed either in the armed services or in the production of war materials that there was a real difficulty in meeting essential civilian needs. Children were recruited on every hand, and in many instances were illegally employed under the coverage of existent state and federal laws.

Only a small percentage of these violations ever came to public attention; people winked at the hiring of children because there was often no other help available. Even so, the increases reported were an index to the general situation. In North Carolina in 1943, for example, there were fourteen times as many violations of the state child labor laws reported as in 1940, and in the first half of 1944 twenty-two times as many violations were reported as in the first half of 1940. In Illinois, less than forty establishments were found guilty of evading child labor laws from January through June in 1941, and more than 500 were guilty for the same period in 1944. Figures for violations

[6] Amendment Report No. 1977, Union Calendar No. 756, 76th Congress.
[7] *A Guide to Child Labor Provisions of the Fair Labor Standards Act,* Child Labor Bulletin No. 101, U.S. Department of Labor, Washington, 1958, pp. 2–3.

of the federal Fair Labor Standards Act rose to 8436 for the year ending June 30, 1944, in contrast to 1761 for the year ending June 30, 1941.[8]

Moreover, the *legal* standards for the employment of children were also relaxed. Over half of the states let down their restrictions on child labor during the war period, with reference to one or more provisions affecting children under eighteen. Three other states operated under laws allowing wartime emergency employment of children which had never been repealed following World War I.[9]

The Disorganizing Aspects of Child Labor

The disorganizing aspects of child labor may be classified briefly as the physical, mental, and moral hazards to which the child is exposed.

1. *Physical Hazards.* Teen-agers (who constitute most of the legally and illegally employed children today) are notoriously reckless and are especially subject to disabling personal injuries. Following World War II, it was found that workers under eighteen had one and a half times as many disabling accidents as those over eighteen.

2. *The Mental Handicaps of Early Employment.* Where compulsory educational standards are low and early child labor is permitted, children are deprived of the education necessary to appreciate art, literature, and science from which they would derive great mental satisfactions. They are also unable to compete as effectively in the economic world. As Table 10.1 shows, young persons who complete only the eighth grade or who do not finish high school consistently earn markedly less than those who finish high school and much less than those who finish college. Those who finish only elementary school have a slight lead over those with one to three years of high school at the time of early employment, however. The high school graduate immediately outstrips those with elementary schooling and with one to three years of high school. Earning capacity is geared to the years of education for all persons twenty years of age and older.

3. *Moral Dangers.* The moral dangers of early employment are chiefly those of association. They are particularly present in night work in the street trades, in contacts with illegal activities such as gambling, narcotic rings, and certain aspects of the entertainment world. Wherever children are exposed to vicious influences or criminal activities, they are bound to have their own life organization affected. Children cannot develop concepts of honesty, personal integrity, and social well-being when they are constantly associated with adults whose activities and life patterns are opposed to the generally accepted social values. A child employed at any labor which involves the subversion of social well-being to selfish interests is in danger of personal disorganization. He is learning to define situations selfishly and hedonistically,

---

[8] Ella Arvilla Merritt and Floy Hendricks, *Trend of Child Labor, 1940–1944,* Serial No. R 1743, reprint from *Monthly Labor Review,* April, 1945, p. 2.

[9] "Summary of Wartime Relaxations of State Laws Affecting the Employment of Minors Under 18" (mimeographed bulletin), Children's Bureau, U.S. Department of Labor, Washington, February 12, 1946, p. 1.

TABLE 10.1.   Median Income in 1958 of Males[a] 14 Years of Age and Over by Years of School Completed, by Age and Sex, for the U.S.

Years of School Completed	14 to 24 Years of Age	25 to 34 Years of Age	35 to 44 Years of Age	45 to 54 Years of Age	55 to 64 Years of Age	65 Years and Over
Total[b]	$1,010	$4,459	$4,924	$4,501	$3,968	$1,488
Elementary school						
Total	735	3,018	3,495	3,428	3,215	1,448
Less than 8 years[c]	722	2,522	2,860	2,694	2,661	1,289
8 years	747	3,526	4,149	4,065	3,792	1,729
High School						
Total	1,276	4,529	5,076	5,002	4,846	2,004
1 to 3 years	770	4,275	4,718	4,522	4,512	1,910
4 years	2,411	4,688	5,335	5,433	5,273	2,240
College						
Total	1,543	5,548	6,934	7,774	6,493	3,092
1 to 3 years	1,257	5,023	6,302	6,366	5,472	2,710
4 years or more						
Total	2,477	5,970	7,731	9,220	7,857	3,658
4 years	2,857	5,914	7,543	9,129	7,161	—
5 years or more	—	6,092	8,043	9,386	—	—
Median years of school completed	10.7	12.3	12.1	10.3	8.7	8.2

[a] Data not available for women.

[b] Includes persons not reporting years of school completed, not shown separately.

[c] Includes persons reporting no years of school completed, not shown separately.

SOURCE: Bureau of the Census, *Consumer Income, Current Population Reports*, Series P-60, No. 33 (January 15, 1960).

without reference to the values which the larger society respects and tries to impose on its members.

Children who do not have to assume economic burdens until they are older and have received a better education have an advantage over those who enter industry early. With the impressive gains made by protective legislation, many people have assumed that modern industry no longer imposes any of the threats to children that it formerly did. Unfortunately the situation is far from ideal. Although modern educational requirements and both federal and state labor legislation have given greater protection by extending minimum age and hour provisions and by restricting the types of work at which children may be employed, there are still many types of employment not covered by legislation.

Minimum Age Legislation

The basic minimum age for permitting children to work varies, as Table 10.2 shows. Nineteen states have a basic minimum of 16 years, but they vary in the age at which children may work outside of school hours. A number of states permit children to work at age 12 after school although the general trend is to 14 (except for street trades, discussed later on). Twenty-five states have a basic age of 14 for permitting children to work, and

TABLE 10.2. Minimum Age for Child Labor by State, with Minimums for Regular Work, for Outside School Hours, and for Hazardous Industries

State	Basic Minimum Age for Regular Work	Basic Minimum Age for Outside School Hours	Basic Minimum Age for Hazardous Industries
Alabama	16	14	16, 18, 21
Alaska	16	14	16, 18, 21
Arizona	14	14 (except 10 for boys and 18 for girls in street trades)	16 and 18
Arkansas	14	14 (except vacation periods)	16 and 18
California	15	14 (12 during summer vacation)	16
Colorado	14	No provision (except permit from school superintendent) 12 during vacation	16 and 18
Connecticut	16	14	16 and 18
Delaware	14	12	16 and 18
District of Columbia	14	14	16 and 18
Florida	16	12	16, 18, 21
Georgia	16	14 (12 and 13 for boys in groceries and retail)	16
Hawaii	16	14	16 and 18
Idaho	14	14	In one occupation—21 years
Illinois	16	14	16
Indiana	14	14	16, 18, 21
Iowa	14	14	16 (18 for girls only)
Kansas[a]	14	14	16 (21 in one industry)
Kentucky	16	16 (14 if a high school graduate or if mentally retarded)	16 and 18
Louisiana	16	16 (12 for a golf caddy)	16 and 18
Maine	16	15 during school	16 and 18
Maryland	16	14	16 and 18
Massachusetts	16	14	16 and 18
Michigan	14	14 (many exceptions)	18 (or approval by Commissioner of Labor)
Minnesota	14	14 (12 for street trades for boys, 18 for girls)	16
Mississippi	14	14	No provision
Missouri	14	12 for newsboys	14, 16, 18, 21
Montana	16	16 (except by certificate)	16
Nebraska	14	14 (certificate for some occupations between 14 and 16)	16

TABLE 10.2 (Continued)

State	Basic Minimum Age for Regular Work	Basic Minimum Age for Outside School Hours	Basic Minimum Age for Hazardous Industries
Nevada	14 (14 to 17 certificate required)	14 (boys 10 and girls 16 for newspaper)	No provision
New Hampshire	14	No provision	No provision
New Jersey	16	14 (12 for newsboys delivering papers, 18 for girls)	16 and 18
New Mexico	14	14	16 and 18
New York	16 (high school graduates 14)	14	16 and 18
North Carolina	16	14 (nonfactory)	16 and 18
North Dakota	14	14	16 and 18
Ohio	16 (except high school graduates and 14-year-olds incapable of benefiting from study)	14	16 and 18
Oklahoma	14	14	15, 16, 21
Oregon	14	14 (two weeks for 12-year-olds in summer vacation)	16 and 18
Pennsylvania	16	14	16 and 18
Puerto Rico	16	14 (12 in street trades, other restrictions for older persons)	16 and 18
Rhode Island	16	14	16 and 18
South Carolina	16	No restrictions	16
South Dakota	14	14	16
Tennessee	16	14	16 and 18
Texas	15	15 (special permission to 12 and over)	17
Utah	14	10 (in agriculture and as caddies)	14, 15, 16
Vermont	14	No provision	16
Virginia	16	14	16 and 18 (under 14 and 16 for boys and girls in restaurants)
Washington	14 (boys) 16 (girls)	14 and 15 (if attending continuation school)	16 and 18
West Virginia	16 (or eighth grade)	None	18
Wisconsin	14	12 and 14	16, 18, 21
Wyoming	None (except no employment during school)	None	16 and 18

[a] Law ambiguous.

SOURCE: Data furnished by the Bureau of Labor Standards, U.S. Department of Labor, July, 1959.

twenty-four have age 16. California alone has the age of 15 and Wyoming has no age limit at all, except that no child may be employed during school hours.

Even where the basic minimum is 16 children may usually be released when there is grave need for employment or where children are working as domestics or for their parents. In general the matter of a child's working is limited to those in gainful occupations.

Compulsory Education Laws

Compulsory education laws now generally require all children to attend school until they are 16 or older, as Table 10.3 shows. Five states (Nevada, New Mexico, North Dakota, Pennsylvania, and Wyoming) require students to attend school until they are 17 (unless they have finished high school), and four states—Ohio, Oklahoma, Oregon, and Utah—require attendance until 18. Colorado is the serious laggard, requiring attendance until only 14. All the remaining states require 16 years with the exception of Mississippi and South Carolina, which repealed their compulsory school laws over the desegregation issue. Mississippi had previously established 17 years as a minimum and South Carolina 16. Despite sentiment to the contrary it seems likely that these standards will be restored. Louisiana has also passed a proviso that the compulsory school law may be suspended where integration is ordered.[10]

All the states have provisions for suspending the law, usually because of extenuating circumstances in which the child's work is necessary for family support, or because the child is mentally incapable of profiting from further study or has achieved a certain level of education. Approximately 97 percent of the children under 16 and 81 percent of those 16 to 17 are in school. These percentages are very encouraging.[11]

Nevertheless there were 1.1 million children 14 to 17 not in school in 1958—most of them 16- to 17-year-olds. Slightly over half of those out of school were girls.[12] A large percentage were from rural areas, as Table 10.6 shows, with rural farm children's enrollment lagging behind that of rural nonfarm children. Since modern farming methods indicate that 65 percent of these young people will have to seek jobs off the farm they need all the education they can acquire.[13]

Tables 10.4 and 10.5 show, however, that there has been a great decline in the number of employed children not in school since 1940, when more than half of the employed 14- to 15-year-olds were not in school and three-fourths of the 16- to 17-year-olds who were working were not in school.

Several states permit younger children to work where there is certification

---

[10] Data furnished by the Bureau of Labor Standards, U.S. Department of Labor.

[11] *Young Workers Under 18, 1958 Supplement,* Leaflet No. 6, Bureau of Labor Standards, U.S. Department of Labor, Washington, 1959.

[12] *Ibid.*

[13] *Ibid.* Cf. also Chapter 20, "The Rural Community," for a discussion of farm population trends.

TABLE 10.3. Basic Minimum School Age by State

State	Basic Minimum School Age
Alabama	16
Alaska	16
Arizona	16
Arkansas	16
California	16
Colorado	14
Connecticut	16
Delaware	16
District of Columbia	16
Florida	16
Georgia	16
Hawaii	16
Idaho	16
Illinois	16
Indiana	16
Iowa	16
Kansas	16
Kentucky	16
Louisiana	16
Maine	16
Maryland	16
Massachusetts	16
Michigan	16
Minnesota	16
Mississippi	repealed (formerly 17)
Missouri	16
Montana	16
Nebraska	16
Nevada	17
New Hampshire	16
New Jersey	16
New Mexico	17
New York	16
North Carolina	16
North Dakota	17
Ohio	18
Oklahoma	18
Oregon	18
Pennsylvania	17
Puerto Rico	16
Rhode Island	16
South Carolina	repealed (formerly 16)
South Dakota	16
Tennessee	16
Texas	16
Utah	18
Vermont	16
Virginia	16
Washington	16
West Virginia	16
Wisconsin	16
Wyoming	17

SOURCE: Data furnished by Bureau of Labor Standards, U.S. Department of Labor, July, 1959.

TABLE 10.4. School Enrollment Status of Employed Youth
14 and 15 Years old: 1940, 1944–1958
(numbers in thousands)

Year	Total Employed Number	Percent	Enrolled in School Number	Percent	Not Enrolled in School Number	Percent
1940	290	100.0	130	44.8	160	55.2
1944	1,284	100.0	1,006	78.3	278	21.7
1945	a	—	a	—	a	—
1946	761	100.0	568	74.6	193	25.4
1947	692	100.0	494	71.4	198	28.6
1948	717	100.0	529	73.8	188	26.2
1949	701	100.0	553	78.9	148	21.1
1950	916	100.0	786	85.8	130	14.2
1951	762	100.0	658	86.4	104	13.6
1952	650	100.0	572	88.0	78	12.0
1953	655	100.0	571	87.3	84	12.7
1954	709	100.0	640	90.3	69	9.7
1955	827	100.0	754	91.2	73	8.8
1956	884	100.0	836	94.5	49	5.5
1957	894	100.0	854	95.5	40	4.5
1958	825	100.0	755	91.5	70	8.5

a Not available.

SOURCE: Table VIIIa, "Trend Tables on Youth Employment and School Enrollment, 1940, 1944–1958," Bureau of Labor Standards, U.S. Department of Labor, July, 1959 (mimeographed bulletin).

TABLE 10.5. School Enrollment Status of Employed Youth
16 and 17 Years Old: 1940, 1944–1958
(numbers in thousands)

Year	Total Employed Number	Percent	Enrolled in School Number	Percent	Not Enrolled in School Number	Percent
1940	770	100.0	180	23.4	590	76.6
1944	2,564	100.0	1,341	52.3	1,223	47.7
1945	a	—	a	—	a	—
1946	1,539	100.0	562	36.5	977	63.5
1947	1,554	100.0	611	39.3	943	60.7
1948	1,584	100.0	753	47.5	831	52.5
1949	1,370	100.0	648	47.3	722	52.7
1950	1,555	100.0	827	53.2	728	46.8
1951	1,582	100.0	948	59.9	634	40.1
1952	1,574	100.0	830	52.7	744	47.3
1953	1,347	100.0	710	52.7	636	47.3
1954	1,375	100.0	897	65.1	480	34.9
1955	1,522	100.0	968	63.6	554	36.4
1956	1,593	100.0	1,028	64.5	566	35.5
1957	1,571	100.0	1,098	69.9	473	30.1
1958	1,548	100.0	1,093	70.6	455	29.4

a Not available.

SOURCE: Table VIIIb, "Trend Tables on Youth Employment and School Enrollment, 1940, 1944–1958," Bureau of Labor Standards, U.S. Department of Labor, July, 1959 (mimeographed bulletin).

that the child is retarded and can no longer profit from further education. With half the states having a minimum working age of fourteen the situation seems to need improvement. On the other hand, child labor conditions have much improved because every state now has a compulsory school law.[14] The worst problems so far as hazards to children are concerned are now in the street trades, in messenger service, and in agriculture.

Child Workers in Agriculture

The Federal Fair Labor Standards Act now prohibits children under sixteen from working in agriculture during school hours. Since most agricultural commodities are "articles of interstate commerce" this is a logical extension in coverage. Children in agriculture often work very hard. They are also often exposed to hazards of dangerous machinery. Equally serious, they are kept out of school to work.

Technically farmers are forbidden to employ child labor under sixteen during school hours, but the federal law places no limit on work before and after school. Willful violation of this law is subject to a fine of $10,000, but it is impossible to employ enough federal agents to insure observance.

Most farms do not come within the provisions of the act, however, since children on farms are permitted to work for their parents. Only eight states and one territory and the District of Columbia provide minimum hours for working outside school hours and only fifteen states and the District of Columbia provide a minimum age for working during school hours.

Many states permit absence from school to help with harvesting of crops. Many completely exempt agriculture from the minimum age requirements for child labor.

Apparently most states exempt agricultural labor from the restricted list of industries under any child labor laws they have enacted, either: (1) from the traditional sentiments toward what is presumed to be the healthful, wholesome life on the farm, or (2) more especially from the fact that farmers are so well represented in state legislatures. These representatives of agriculture become highly concerned lest laws prevent farm children from helping with chores before and after school or helping generally with farm work on Saturdays and during summer vacation.

In the more prosperous rural states most rural children are enrolled in school. Rural enrollments are also improving elsewhere. In 1958 rural children out of school had decreased nearly 12 percent since 1951. Nevertheless the proportion of rural children not in school is significantly greater than that of urban children. Nearly three times as many rural children 14 to 15 years of age were out of school in rural areas, as Table 10.6 shows.[15]

[14] Data obtained from *State Child Labor Standards* Bulletin No. 158, U.S. Department of Labor, Washington, 1952, and later unpublished data furnished by the Bureau of Labor Standards, U.S. Department of Labor, in July, 1959.

[15] *Child Workers in Agriculture*, Leaflet No. 4, Bureau of Labor Standards, U.S. Department of Labor, Washington, 1959.

TABLE 10.6. School Enrollment by Age
Groups for Rural and Urban Children
in 1951 and 1958

| | Percent of Population Not Enrolled in School | | | |
| | October, 1958 | | October, 1951 | |
Age	Urban	Rural	Urban	Rural
10–13	0.4	1.0	0.4	2.2
14–15	2.2	6.1	2.3	13.7
16–17	18.3	24.8	20.8	36.2

SOURCE: *Child Workers in Agriculture*, Leaflet
No. 4, Bureau of Labor Standards, U.S. Department of Labor, 1959.

Migrant Farm Labor

Most farmers do not exploit their own children seriously, although
some parents in backward areas may not see the necessity for education.
The really serious rural child labor problem is that of the migrant child
laborer. In October, 1958, children working in agriculture constituted about
one-third of all workers 14 to 17 years of age. In July, 1957, a survey disclosed that there were around 500,000 youngsters between 10 and 15 working on farms for pay. At least one-third of these were working for 35 hours or
more a week.[16]

The children of migrant agricultural workers who move from one harvest
field to another suffer more serious handicaps than most child workers. In
1954 it was estimated that 150,000 children under eighteen accompanied
their parents. Of these, 50,000 children were themselves employed. In many
of the other cases they merely helped their parents. Often the whole family
works in the cotton fields, the fruit orchards, the potato fields, the cranberry
bogs, or on whatever crop needs gathering. In the Southwest many child
laborers come in illegally from Mexico.[17]

The curtailment of the migrant child's education is much more serious
than that of the rural farm child. A joint study made by the National Council
on Agricultural Life and the Department of Rural Education of the National
Education Association showed that migratory child laborers entered school
late and often withdrew a month or two early. The migratory children
covered were in Florida, Virginia, Texas, and Illinois, as Table 10.7 shows.
For Florida, 87.5 percent of the Negro child migrants had enrolled by November, whereas white children enrolled gradually from September to March.
In Texas, over 30 percent of both white and Negro children did not enroll
until January or later. Withdrawals are equally serious. The Florida white
migrants began withdrawing in April (although 80 percent of the Negroes
stayed until the end of school). In Texas, children withdrew in September

[16] *Ibid.*
[17] *1954 Annual Report of the Wage and Hour and Public Contracts Divisions*, U.S.
Department of Labor, Washington, 1955, p. 21.

TABLE 10.7.   Entries of Migrant Children by Months—1952–1953

| Date | Florida | | | | Virginia | | Texas | | Illinois | |
| | Negro | | White | | | | | | | |
	No.	%	No.	%	No.	%	No.	%	No.	%
Total	1079	100.0	120ᵃ	100.0	47	100.0	394	100.0	133	100.0
Opening of school	189	17.6	24	20.0	9	19.2	23	5.8	—	—
Remainder of September	83	7.7	4	3.3	24	51.1	47	11.9	2	1.5
October	304	28.2	14	11.7	10	21.2	52	13.2	—	—
November	367	34.0	28	23.3	3	6.4	73	18.5	—	—
December	41	3.8	14	11.7	—	—	68	17.3	—	—
January	47	4.4	8	6.7	—	—	91	23.1	—	—
February	10	.9	13	10.8	—	—	9	2.3	—	—
March	9	.8	15	12.5	—	—	5	1.3	—	—
April	5	.5	—	—	1	2.1	9	2.3	76	57.1
May	3	.3	—	—	—	—	16	4.1	55	41.4
Not recorded	21	1.8	—	—	—	—	1	.2	—	—

ᵃ Includes some double entries by same child.

SOURCE: Table 34 (derived from 1719 migrant pupil report cards) in Shirley E. Greene, *The Education of Migrant Children*, Department of Rural Education, National Education Association, Washington, 1954, p. 87. Quoted by permission.

and October to go to western Texas for cotton harvesting and did not re-enroll for several months.[18] Compulsory education laws apply only to resident children and not to migratory children.

Working Outside School Hours

Although compulsory school laws are relatively well enforced, many children work long hours outside school hours when minimum age restrictions are usually much lower, as the list of minimum age restrictions indicates. In Kentucky, Louisiana, and Montana, however, the minimum age is 16 and in Maine and Texas 15. In three states, Delaware, Florida, and Wisconsin, the minimum is 12 and worse yet, in Utah only 10. In six states, West Virginia, Colorado, South Carolina, Vermont, New Hampshire, and Wyoming, there is no restriction. The other 35 states and Puerto Rico all have a basic 14 years minimum for work outside school hours.

These provisions do not tell the whole story, however. Many states exempt specific types of work (in addition to agriculture). Georgia permits boys 12 and 13 to work in grocery and retail stores. Several states permit children 10 or 12 to work at street trades, although girls are usually required to be 16 or 18.

Street Trades

Street trades represent a special hazard for children, but 24 states have no regulations with reference to them, and Oklahoma merely prohibits girls under 16 from selling newspapers on the street. There has been little

[18] Shirley E. Greene, *The Education of Migrant Children*, Department of Rural Education, National Education Association, Washington, 1954, p. 87.

improvement in the regulation of street trades during the last ten years. The 26 states and the District of Columbia which regulate street trades do not offer much protection since boys 10, 11, and 12 years of age are permitted to sell papers in most of these states. Although the street trades include magazine sellers, peddlers, bootblacks, junk collectors, and others, the majority of street workers today are newsboys. The Fair Labor Standards Act covers any newspaper dealers who ship their papers to other states. This provides that all children must be 16 who are employed, except those aged 14 and 15 who may work after school.

In an effort to evade federal and state laws many newspapers have required the boys engaged in newspaper distribution to enter into contracts which make them "independent contractors" and then forced them to buy the papers outright and collect from the subscribers. This practice has been denounced by the federal authorities, but a state law seems to be required to circumvent the machinations of newspaper publishers. As Table 10.8 shows, most states offer very little local protection to newsboys or newsgirls. In 25 states there is no provision for regulating newspaper or street trades at night. In other states, boys are not regulated although girls are; in four states the minimum for newsboys is ten years. In Utah the minimum age is 10 for both boys and girls. Pennsylvania and California presume to regulate children who are employed but permit "independent contractors" to operate. Girls under 21 are not permitted to sell newspapers on the street in Pennsylvania. Small boys, however, in business for themselves are often on the street in Philadelphia and Pittsburgh at 11 or 12 P.M. selling newspapers. Quite aside from the moral hazards, these children do not get enough sleep. There is no valid reason for permitting children to work at such trades.

Entertainment

About two-thirds of the state child labor laws include provisions which apply to employment of children in legitimate theatrical productions, and usually in concerts as well. Sixteen states and the District of Columbia require special permits for theatrical performances. These are District of Columbia, California, Colorado, Delaware, Illinois, Louisiana, Maryland, Massachusetts, Michigan, Minnesota, New Mexico, New York, North Dakota, Ohio, Oregon, Rhode Island, and Virginia. No minimum age is set in any of these laws, however, except by the Minnesota law, where the minimum age is 10, and the District of Columbia, where it is 7. In New York a minimum age of 7 has been set administratively. Under thirteen of the seventeen laws, certain conditions must be met before any permit is issued. This usually means that the issuing officer must be satisfied that the conditions of employment are not detrimental to the health or morals of the child, that his education is not neglected, and that his supervision is adequate.

In some sixteen or eighteen other states, the laws that apply to general employment apply to children in public performances, either because such performances are specifically mentioned or because the provisions of the

TABLE 10.8. Regulations on Newspaper Selling at Night by State

State	Minimum Age	
	Boys	Girls
Alabama	12	18
Alaska	None	None
Arizona	10	16
Arkansas	None	None
California	10	18
	(contract work permitted)	
Colorado	None	10
Connecticut	None	None
Delaware	12	14
District of Columbia	12	18
Florida	10	16
Georgia	16	16
	(prohibited after 9 P.M.)	
Hawaii	None	None
Idaho	None	None
Illinois	None	None
Indiana	None	None
Iowa	11	18
Kansas	None	None
Kentucky	None	18
Louisiana	14	18
Maine	None	None
Maryland	12	18
Massachusetts	12	18
Michigan	None	None
Minnesota	12	18
Mississippi	None	None
Missouri	12	14
Montana	None	None
Nebraska	None	None
Nevada	None	None
New Hampshire	10	16
New Jersey	14	18
New Mexico	None	None
New York	14	18
North Carolina	14	18
North Dakota	None	None
Ohio	None	None
Oklahoma	None	18
Oregon	None	None
Pennsylvania	12—for independent contract (14, if employed)	21—for independent contract
Puerto Rico	12	18
	15— if in dangerous areas)	
Rhode Island	12	16
South Carolina	None	None
South Dakota	None	None
Tennessee	None	None
	(boys and girls—14, if during school hours)	
Texas	None	None
Utah	10	10
Vermont	None	None
Virginia	12	18
Washington	None	None
West Virginia	None	None
Wisconsin	13	18
Wyoming	None	None

laws are broad enough to include such employment. In some of these states, minimum ages of 14 or 16 are set. In others, night-work provisions applying to any gainful occupation after 6 P.M., 7 P.M., or 8 P.M. have in effect made a 16-year minimum for theatrical employment.

In addition to such provisions applying to legitimate stage performances, 32 states set a minimum age of 14, 16, or 18 for employment in singing and dancing, which means that in these states most vaudeville acts would be prohibited. California and New York (where the greatest number of children are involved) have very detailed requirements which must be met in order to permit the child to appear in a theatrical production. Many states, however, do not have much protection for children in entertainment other than night-work restrictions. Few if any children are now employed in night clubs because most states restrict the employment of children were liquor is served.

Child actors are only a small part of the children employed in the entertainment world. In 1947 the Bureau of Old Age and Survivors Insurance tabulated 193,700 young persons under 18 in amusement services, of whom 14,600 were under 14, 64,000 were 14 and 15, and 115,100 were 16 and 17 years of age. Such services include ushering in motion-picture and other theaters, selling soft drinks, candy, and popcorn, and acting as cashiers during afternoons after school or in the evening. They also include working at beach resorts, billiard halls, swimming pools and bowling alleys, and in the miscellaneous attractions of rodeos, country fairs, race tracks, ball parks, etc. Many of these amusement places are poorly regulated. In general wages are low, hours are long, and the children work so late they get insufficient sleep. Having little time to study, they may fail in school. In addition, they often are exposed to vicious persons among their customers.[19]

In recent years pin setting in bowling alleys has been recognized as one of the most hazardous occupations for young boys because they work chiefly at night (often until 11:30 P.M. or later). Many boys go to work at four and often miss their main (or evening) meal. They are too tired to do their school work; their health is impaired by lack of sleep and by living on candy and "cokes." The work is heavy; a boy often has to roll the sixteen-pound ball 500 times every two hours. If he works eight hours, he is bound to be exhausted. He is also subjected to injury from rolling balls and flying pins.[20]

Bowling alleys seldom keep employment records, and the youngsters compete with derelicts and drifters who may exert an objectionable influence. Bowling alleys are among the worst offenders of those who fail to conform to state and local child labor regulations. Most bowlers are respectable people. If they recognized the hazards of the pin-setters and refused to patronize alleys which did not enforce desirable standards, the problem could be solved very easily.[21]

[19] *They Work While You Play,* Bulletin No. 124, U.S. Department of Labor, Washington, 1950, pp. 9–16.

[20] Clara M. Beyer, "A Break for the Pin Boys," *Children,* September–October, 1954, reprint.

[21] *Ibid.*

Public Messenger Service and Night Work

Public messengers who work at night are exposed to the less desirable influences in every community because they must deliver messages to many businesses engaged in illegal and disorganizing activities. All the manifold enterprises of the underworld require the services of public messengers, just as do legitimate businesses and private individuals. At night the underworld operates more flagrantly than in the daytime, partly because the cover of darkness helps keep its activities hidden. For this reason, all but three states specifically forbid young persons to be employed at night.

Not all states mention messenger service specifically. In some states the prohibition is against all work after 6 P.M.; in others after 9 P.M.; and in still others after 10 P.M. The District of Columbia prohibits night work for boys 10 to 17 years of age after 10 P.M. and after midnight for those 18 to 21. Ten states restrict all persons under 18 from night work, ten states all those under 21, and one state all those under 16. North Carolina differs from the other states in restricting young persons as public messengers from 1 A.M. to 6 A.M. Since few messages are delivered at such an hour, this is not much of a restriction. Colorado exempts night work in the summertime. In any event, the prohibition of night work by implication at least includes messenger service, where it is not specifically exempted. Many states, however, permit young persons past 16 to deliver messages at night. New York and Pennsylvania, on the other hand, limit the delivery of messages after 10 P.M. and 8 P.M. respectively to persons over 21.

The children in messenger service for Western Union Telegraph Company might conceivably be thought to be involved in interstate commerce since messages cross state lines. The United States Supreme Court has ruled, however, that they do not come under the restriction of federal child labor regulations because they "do not produce and ship goods." Yet many deliver messages in the midst of city traffic where they encounter physical dangers, and messages delivered to gambling joints and other objectionable places carry moral danger, day or night.

Hazardous Industries

By 1959, all states except New Hampshire, Mississippi, and Nevada had special regulations restricting child labor in hazardous industries, with the ages varying from 16 to 18. South Carolina's law has the greatest coverage since no person under 16 is allowed to work in any factory, mine, or textile establishment.[22] Many of the states do not come up to the 18-year-old standard of the Fair Labor Practices Act, which covers a major share of the manufacturing and mining industries. The fact that states lag behind the federal government in protecting young persons is probably an index to the strength of local economic interests, in comparison to the interest of those concerned with the welfare of teen-age workers.

[22] Data furnished by the Bureau of Labor Standards, U.S. Department of Labor, July, 1959.

Conclusion

Child labor as a serious problem is on its way out in the United States, as this chapter should make clear. This fact will probably require extensive revision of our educational system in order to look after the interests of children who are slow learners and drop out of school.

Nevertheless there are areas in which child labor is still used. There is thus continuous need for vigilance in enforcing standards. The fact that compulsory education laws have solved a major share of the problem is itself an interesting commentary on the interrelated character of social institutions.

SELECTED BIBLIOGRAPHY

Abbott, Grace, *The Child and the State,* University of Chicago Press, Chicago, 1938, part IV, "Child Labor." This is one of the classic analyses of child labor prior to World War II.

Child Workers in Agriculture, Leaflet No. 4, Bureau of Labor Standards, U.S. Department of Labor, Washington, 1959. A brief review is given of the problem of children employed in agriculture.

Children. This magazine, issued every other month by the United States Children's Bureau, often contains articles on child labor.

Greene, Shirley E., *The Education of Migrant Children,* Department of Rural Education, National Education Association, Washington, 1954. This book gives a telling account of the problems of child migratory workers.

A Guide to Child Labor Provisions of the Fair Labor Standards Act, Child Labor Bulletin No. 101, U.S. Department of Labor, Washington, 1958. This bulletin presents a brief summary of the federal regulations of child labor.

Lumpkin, Katherine DuPre, and Douglas, Dorothy Wolff, *Child Workers in America,* Robert M. McBride Company, Inc., New York, 1937. This is an authoritative study of child labor during the thirties and earlier.

Markoff, Sol, "Youth and Work," *Children,* March–April, 1957, reprint. This gives an excellent discussion of the problem of agricultural child laborers.

State Child-Labor Standards, 1952 (and sporadically thereafter). This publication, issued by the Bureau of Labor Standards of the United States Department of Labor, contains a state-by-state analysis of child labor provisions. (Current data can be obtained on request.)

They Work While You Play, Bulletin No. 124, Bureau of Labor Standards, U.S. Department of Labor, Washington, 1950. This is a telling indictment of the hazards to children in entertainment enterprises.

Trend Tables on Youth Employment and School Enrollment, 1940, 1944–1958, Bureau of Labor Standards, U.S. Department of Labor, Washington, 1959. This shows the significant changes in the employment of children since 1940.

Young Workers Under 18, 1958 Supplement Leaflet No. 6, Bureau of Labor Standards, U.S. Department of Labor, Washington, 1959. This gives valuable information on current trends in child labor. It should be noted that the most current material is not generally available in books.

CHAPTER 11

The Mentally Disorganized

THE MENTALLY DEFECTIVE

Introduction

A sizable share of the persons who fail to adjust according to the definition of normal (as accepted by society) fall into the classification of mentally disorganized. This classification in turn is further divided into (1) the mentally deficient, and (2) the mentally ill (or mentally deranged).

The mentally deficient are often called *aments,* which means that they are lacking in intelligence. The mentally deranged are designated *dements;* that is, they are persons whose intelligence has deteriorated. Both may be regarded as disorganized, however. The mentally deficient individual ordinarily has not deteriorated or revolted against society. Rather, because of his lack of normal mentality his problem is essentially that of being unorganized. He fails to accept social definitions of what is suitable, expected, or compulsory social behavior largely because he is unable to comprehend the rules that govern social behavior. Much less does he understand the reasons for the existence of such rules. In fact, society does not try to enforce responsibility for obeying rules upon the mentally handicapped. Many feeble-minded children are potentially disorganized, and some undoubtedly will fall later into the classification of the mentally deranged or the delinquent and criminal groups.

Most of our scientific knowledge concerning mental disabilities has been developed out of practical necessity. Mentally retarded children are a serious problem in the schools. A major share of the intellectual understanding of feeble-mindedness has been limited, therefore, to the study of children of school age, although most of the feeble-minded grow up and attain adulthood. Relatively few children are regarded as mentally deranged or are segregated in institutions. Consequently, most of what we know about emotional disorders is limited to mentally deranged adults, whether young adults, middle-aged, or older persons. The belief exists that the assumption of adult responsibilities and the making of adult decisions entail stresses and strains which result in mental disorders. We have little knowledge or insight into how the stresses and strains of childhood produce subsequent disorders, except as they have been emphasized in psychoanalytic literature and techniques. There are thus still vast unexplored areas of emotional and mental disorders.

Both cultism on the part of psychiatrists and general disdain for psychiatry on the part of the majority of medical practitioners undoubtedly account for the cultural lag in this area of medical-psychological and sociological research.

Mental Disfunction and Life Adjustment

Persons lacking normal intelligence are more seriously handicapped today than in earlier times. Even in colonial times the majority of children did not know how to read. Yet they got along fairly well in a society which did not expect them to be literate. The public school did not exist and only parents who could afford to pay for their children's education sent them to school. (There were, of course, exceptional instances in which a wealthy man paid for the education of a bright poor child.) With compulsory education we have become much more conscious of the inequalities in ability and of the fact that some could not learn much under any circumstances.

Low-grade mental ability had been recognized long before the invention of intelligence tests, but it was not as great a handicap earlier as it is today. Successful life adjustment today virtually requires the ability to read newspapers, tax bills, road signs, and danger signals. In a simple primitive type of existence danger signs were more obvious. The waterfalls, the gorge, the wild beasts were dangers for which no abstract symbols were required. Social responsibilities in modern society are also much more complicated than in simpler societies. Hence the illiterate by social consensus do not "belong" or participate effectively in the complicated social order today.

We have already discussed, in Chapter 3, the adjustments adolescents are required to make to achieve adulthood. With these adjustments behind them, young adults take on the responsibilities of parenthood, child training, supporting a family, and maintaining a home. They must also accept responsibilities as citizens, as members of the PTA, as supporters of the church and charitable and civic organizations, and try to provide a suitable social environment for their children. Some adults cannot measure up to all the requirements and break under the strain. Others do very well until the children leave home to go to college or to set up their own households.

As the young people shift their emotional dependence and loyalties from their parents to their mates the parents have to make a major adjustment. Often this is hardest for the mother. Sometimes the father has his severest economic and business strains just as he begins to slip physically. Some men have a stroke. Other develop ulcers and still others have emotional disorders. Some decide to prove they "never felt younger" by having an affair or demanding a divorce.

As the years progress old age descends, and for many this spells both loss of mate and financial insecurity. Often old people eat ill-advisedly, chiefly because they have so little to spend for food. Chemical and nutritive changes occur as physical and mental functioning declines. Some persons become "senile" mentally, act "childish," and lose their powers to reason.[1] Some literally run off from their supervising relatives or nurses. All ages have their special mental problems. Those with a sound body, a good mind, and an adequate income need even more than these. They need emotional security, expressed by the interest and affection of someone who cares. Wise physicians have long recognized that what most persons in mental institutions need is a friend and kind, loving care.

When we discuss the mental disorders it is thus with a consciousness of the need to understand more than scholars know at present. The frontiers of research into mental functioning have been opened, but many areas are still unexplored. Yet, as Dr. Lemkau has pointed out, we know far more about the defective and disorganized than about the normal and the genius. We can observe physical abnormalities and measure intelligence (or lack of it). But measuring traits of character important in a satisfactory adjustment is much harder. Generosity, stick-to-itiveness, consideration for others, and responsibility are not so easy to define or measure accurately, even though we are all well aware of their existence.[2] Our basic concern here, however, will be with the abnormal, the mentally deficient and the mentally ill.

The Measurement of Intelligence

Although persons with low-grade mentality have been observed throughout history, it was not until various tests for measuring intelligence had been developed that we had our first objective device for comparing intellectual abilities. These tests have become fairly well standardized, and at the present time the feeble-minded are generally classified according to mental ability. The first significant work in the field was that of Dr. Binet and Dr. Simon in their psychological research at the Sorbonne. Through a series of tests which they devised, a standard basis was developed for determining normal mental ability for a given chronological age. This was in 1905. The next year the tests were first employed in America. After considerable experimentation with these and other tests, the Stanford Revision of the Binet-Simon test was perfected by Terman, who made the suitable changes required by differences in language and culture.

As all who are familiar with mental tests know, the basis of scoring the Binet-Simon test is simple. A person's mental age is established by the number of tests he completes successfully. His "intelligence quotient" is the ratio between his "mental" age and his "chronological" age.[3] A normal child aged ten will complete all the tests devised for the ten-year-old. His intelligence quotient, or "IQ," as it is popularly called, is thus 100. If he completes all the tests for a fourteen-year-old at the age of ten, his IQ is 140 and he rates as

[1] Paul V. Lemkau, *Mental Hygiene in Public Health*, McGraw-Hill Book Company, Inc., New York, 1955, chaps. XVI and XVII.

[2] *Ibid.*, p. 142.

[3] Lewis M. Terman, *The Measurement of Intelligence*, Houghton Mifflin Company, Boston, 1916, p. 53.

very superior. If his IQ is above 140 he is a near genius. If he rates below 70 he is generally considered definitely feeble-minded.

The feeble-minded, like the "normal," fall into several categories of deficiency. According to Terman's classification, the upper-grade feeble-minded with IQ's between 50 and 70 are designated as morons, subclassified as high-grade and low-grade morons. Between 20 and 50 they are designated as imbecile and below 20 as idiot, as in the tabulation below:[4]

IQ	Commonplace Classification
Above 140	"Near" genius or genius
120–140	Very superior intelligence
110–120	Superior intelligence
90–110	Normal, or average intelligence
80–90	Dull normal
70–80	Borderline (sometimes classified as dull, sometimes as feeble-minded)
Below 70	Definitely feeble-minded
60–70	High-grade moron
50–60	Low-grade moron
20–50	Imbecile
Below 20	Idiot

The idiot is thus the lowest ranking of the mentally handicapped and is forced to lead a relatively "vegetative" existence. The imbecile has a little more comprehension, whereas the moron can be trained to do useful work. All the feeble-minded require special care or supervision. The moron can profit from grammar school training, although he will never excel. Morons are often subdivided into low-grade and high-grade morons with IQ from 50 to 59 and 60–69 respectively. This classification has been developed and approved by the American Association for Mental Deficiency.[5]

The dull normal classification includes IQ's from 70 to 79 and the borderline from 80 to 89. Normal intelligence is generally classified as 90 to 109 with 100 as the average. Persons above 110 are superior, those above 120 very superior, and genius is generally classified as 140 or above, as given in Terman's table. The ratings as established by Terman's tests were initially held to remain constant throughout life.

Fluctuations in the IQ ratings have nevertheless occurred, attributed by Terman and Merrill chiefly to errors in administering.[6] More recently, Dr. David Wechsler has done considerable research on IQ ratings and has devised a scale which has eliminated the extreme classifications of genius and the subdivisions of feeble-minded. Wechsler's scale follows:

[4] *Ibid.,* pp. 65–104.

[5] *Statistical Manual for Use of Institutions for Mental Defectives,* National Association for Mental Health, Inc., New York, 1946.

[6] Lewis M. Terman and Maud A. Merrill, *Measuring Intelligence,* Houghton Mifflin Company, Boston, 1937, pp. 38–39.

IQ	Wechsler's Classification
128 and over	Very superior
120–127	Superior
111–119	Bright normal
91–110	Normal
80–90	Dull normal
66–79	Borderline
65 and below	Defective

For dealing with feeble-minded cases, some division is highly practical, however, and the classifications of idiot, imbecile, and moron are usually retained. Wechsler's cutting point of 65 as the upper limit of feeble-mindedness is sometimes applied,[7] but the National Association of Mental Health accepts Terman's classification.

Borderline and dull normal persons are not classified as feeble-minded. They are, however, handicapped and potentially dangerous both to themselves and to society because they often do not appear to be handicapped and are thus not detected. Borderline persons are often gullible and thus easily exploited. They are especially liable to be tricked into criminal activities or to be cheated out of their property. Frequently they lack sex inhibitions. Borderline girls in particular are apt to become sex offenders.

The presence of many dull normal or borderline children in the schools tends to undermine the quality of education for those of normal and superior intelligence. Compulsory school laws have required that dull normal and borderline children remain in school until they are sixteen or seventeen. This has created problems of educational organization and instruction which have often lowered the intellectual training of the superior students.

The mentally incompetent are more prone to personal disorganization than are persons of normal mental ability. They are a special source of social disorganization. On the other hand, normal intelligence (when not accompanied by moral training and a high sense of social responsibility) is also potentially dangerous. Men of high ability also become disorganized and make clever crooks, master minds for criminal gangs, or dictators who threaten the whole social structure.

The Extent of Feeble-Mindedness

No one really knows how many persons are feeble-minded because there has never been any complete census of mental defectives. Some have held that there are 4,500,000 mentally deficient in this country but experts in the field maintain that this is much too high a figure. They generally agree that about 2 percent of our school-age population is defective.[8] Tredgold estimates that less than 1 percent (8 per 1000) of the English population is mentally deficient and the same is probably more nearly true of the population

---

[7] David Wechsler, *The Measurement of Adult Intelligence,* The Williams and Wilkins Company, Baltimore, 1944, p. 40, Table 4.

[8] *White House Conference on Child Health and Protection, 1930,* New York, The Appleton-Century Company, 1931, p. 308.

in the United States. At least Wallin estimated so in 1924. Even I.Q. tests in Wallin's opinion are no sure index to mentality because intelligence is not a simple unity but a complex, heterogeneous condition. A study made by Wallin in 1949 showed that 65 percent of the retarded children in ungraded classes in eleven different areas came from the lower economic and social classes.[9] This is a significant fact and deserves intensive exploration. Lack of stimulation and motivation probably are important reasons for this differentiation but they have never been properly analyzed in relation to I.Q. ratings.

In 1956 there were 144,786 mental defectives and epileptics in the average daily resident population of public institutions.[10] In 1955 there were 156,479 cases in institutions or discharged from institutions. Of this total, 138,655 were mentally defective, 16,496 were epileptic, 967 were "others" (presumably cases pending diagnosis), and the remaining were not classified. During the year 15,392 cases were admitted, 14,043 of whom were feeble-minded, and 4682 such defectives were discharged. Meanwhile over 2000 died during the year.[11]

Epileptics may require special care because of the frequency or the severity of their attacks, but they are not necessarily feeble-minded, although some obviously are. Recent research has shown that epileptic children who have convulsions are retarded more frequently than normal children. Many mild cases of epilepsy have only momentary blank periods and are apparently not affected mentally. Younger epileptic children are more likely to be retarded than older ones, and those who have frequent attacks than those with mild attacks.[12] Medical treatment enables many to function normally.

Normal Children in Feeble-Minded Institutions

Unfortunately not all who are committed to institutions for the feeble-minded are mentally deficient. Commitments to institutions for the mentally deficient have been far from scientific in the past. Many institutions formerly admitted children as feeble-minded without any testing of their intelligence or any evidence of their mental incompetence except the complaint of the teachers, parents, or doctors, or the fact that they failed in school. Recent disclosures of normal children in schools for the feeble-minded have been shocking. When one of the present authors of this text was a member of the Kansas Public Welfare (Temporary) Commission during 1931–1933,[13] all the inmates (192 in number) at the Kansas Training School (for the feeble-

---

[9] J. E. W. Wallin, "Prevalence of Mental Retardates," *School and Society, 86:55–56* (February, 1958).

[10] *Patients in Mental Institutions 1956,* part I, "Public Institutions for Mental Defectives and Epileptics," Public Health Service, U.S. Department of Health, Education, and Welfare, Washington, 1959, p. 1–47. Cases were not classified in the 1956 census of institutions.

[11] *Patients in Mental Institutions, 1955,* part I, "Public Institutions for Mental Defectives and Epileptics," U.S. Department of Health, Education, and Welfare, Washington, 1958, p. 10.

[12] *Cyclopedia of Medicine,* Review Service, F. A. Davis Company, Philadelphia, 1956, pp. 575–594.

[13] Miss Elliott was a member of this commission.

minded) were given intelligence tests. To the consternation of state authorities, ten children of normal intelligence (two of whom were superior) and fourteen who were dull normal were discovered. There were nineteen additional who were borderline and seventeen with an IQ of between 65 and 69, all of whom could have profited from special academic education in the public schools. None of these children was receiving proper academic instruction.[14]

No one knows how many normal children (not to mention dull normal and borderline children who could profit from an education) have been routed to feeble-minded institutions in time past. Nor do we know how many feeble-minded are not given special care. Normal persons still are in such institutions today. It is a startling fact that children who failed in school—because they were bored or because they were upset emotionally—have been committed to institutions on the teacher's testimony as being "unable to learn."

Recent press notices told of an intelligent sixty-seven-year-old Iowan who had spent most of his life in what was formerly called the Iowa Home for Feeble-minded Children (now Glenwood State School). He was committed on October 15, 1898, by his mother because he "rolled his eyes" like Blind Boone, the pianist. The mother had been frightened by Blind Boone's peculiar habit of rolling his eyes when she heard him play before Mayo was born. She was pregnant at the time and attributed Mayo's peculiarity to this "prenatal influence." When a trained superintendent was appointed at Glenwood in 1957, he discovered that this patient had an IQ of 120. Furthermore, he found fifty other inmates with higher IQ's than some of the staff. Like many other such institutions, Glenwood School had been staffed by people without proper training for working with the mentally retarded. It has been estimated that there are probably 5000 normal persons in such institutions because of lack of proper admission procedures. This amounts to a virtual life sentence to oblivion.[15] The exposure to a non-stimulating environment must be distressing to a normal child. The fact that he is given so little education must also affect his mental ability adversely.

Types of Amentia

Specialists in the field of feeble-mindedness or amentia hold it is due either (1) to a defective germ plasm (or heredity) or (2) to environmental factors. Hereditary feeble-mindedness may be called primary amentia and that resulting from postnatal disease or accident secondary amentia. Dr. Tredgold claims that the great majority of feeble-minded inherit their mental condition because of abnormalities in the germ plasm. Most of those with inherited abnormalities are not severely handicapped but are the dullards—those who learn slowly in schools and in general fall into the lowest occupational groups. Relatively little clinical research has been conducted with

[14] *Report of the Public Welfare Temporary Commission, State of Kansas,* Topeka, January 15, 1933, pp. 136–137.
[15] Cf. Robert Wallace, "A Life-Time Thrown Away by a Mistake 59 Years Ago," *Life,* 44:121–122 (March 24, 1958).

reference to the upper realms of low-grade mentality; hence not much is known scientifically about the nervous structure of morons or borderline and dull normal cases. There has been extensive research on the lowest types of feeble-minded and these unquestionably have imperfections in their brain structure.[16] On the other hand, so many high-grade morons and borderline and dull normal cases have responded to intensive training in recent years that research both in educational techniques and in biochemistry will probably enable this group to improve markedly. Further study certainly would give us valuable insight into the causes of such malfunction of high-grade morons and the nature of dull normal and borderline intelligence. The analysis presented here refers primarily to the lower-grade mentally deficient and is derived from clinical research. We know a great deal scientifically about hereditary low-grade mental deficiency.

PRIMARY AMENTIAS

Primary amentias, because they are due to heredity, cannot be prevented by any known techniques except by elimination of the fetus.

Since the majority of the low-grade feeble-minded are the offspring of apparently normal persons, sterilization is no solution (as we discuss later on). Mild cases of feeble-mindedness do not have pronounced characteristics (as mentioned above), but severe types manifest distinctly differentiated and easily recognizable characteristics. The chief varieties of primary amentia are (1) mongolism, (2) microcephaly, (3) sclerotic amentia, and (4) amaurotic family idiocy.[17]

1. *Mongolism.* This is the term applied to a type of defectiveness in which the victim has a characteristic Mongolian eye slant with an accompanying strabismus. There are, however, many other features, including a squat, depressed nose, stumpy hands, wide gaps between toes, small round skull, etc. The majority of Mongols are imbeciles and only a small percentage live to adulthood. Treatment to date has not been beneficial.[18] It seems unfortunate that the disease has been given an ethnic name, for it has no relation to race.

2. *Microcephaly.* In microcephaly or "pin-headedness" the head is small and narrow with a marked recession of the frontal brain area and a flattening of the back of the brain. Microcephalics fall within all three levels of feeble-mindedness. Dwarfs may be also microcephalics, but some dwarfs are very intelligent and well developed. They are normal, but miniature. When microcephalics are defective their brain structure is markedly imperfect.[19]

3. *Sclerotic Amentia.* Sclerotic amentia is caused by a fibrous overgrowth on the brain and often accompanies epilepsy.

[16] Cf. A. F. Tredgold (assisted by R. F. Tredgold), *A Textbook of Mental Deficiency (Amentia)*, The Williams and Wilkins Company, Baltimore, 1952 (8th ed.), pp. 20–21 and 121–122. The data on the classification of mental deficiency are chiefly derived from this important work.

[17] *Ibid.*, pp. 214–215.

[18] *Ibid.*, pp. 218–219.

[19] *Ibid.*, pp. 223.

4. *Amaurotic Family Idiocy.* Amaurotic family idiocy is a hereditary condition present in infants in which there is progressive degeneration of the brain cells with accompanying blindness, muscular debility, wasting of the flesh, and finally death. Formerly it was believed to be a disease which occurred only among Jews.[20] It is apparently caused by inbreeding. As a disease of infancy it is primarily a Jewish disease, although it occurs among others. In the infantile form, the baby appears normal at birth, but at about three months of age displays marked weakness in the back and neck, which is accompanied by emaciation. Eyesight dims and the child eventually becomes totally blind while becoming weaker. Such children usually die before they are two years old but sometimes live until two and one-half. When the disease is of the *juvenile* form (that is, among children past infancy) amaurotic idiocy is more common among Gentiles than Jews. There is the same enfeeblement and emaciation with an arrest of mental development (which often amounts to a virtual dementia). Sight always becomes dim. A few amaurotic cases live until their twenties but none survive until thirty.[21]

Further types of primary amentia derived from other types of defective germ plasm occur which we cannot discuss in detail. Fortunately for the human race nature eliminates a large share of defective fetuses (which develop either from defective germ plasms or injury) through spontaneous abortion or "miscarriage." Studies made of several hundred fetuses at a famous medical research laboratory indicated that nearly all were defective. Unfortunately some of them develop to full term and thus institute a persistent and distressing problem because they never develop into adequate personalities.[22]

SECONDARY AMENTIA

Tredgold estimates that 20 percent of amentia is caused by non-heredity factors which affect the development and functioning of the nervous system. These may affect the child before birth, during birth, and after birth. A child may be a "congenital idiot" and still have come from normal germ plasm. Some physical accident which occurred during the mother's pregnancy, some diseased condition of the mother, or some chemical or nutritive problem during pregnancy may have damaged the fetus so as to affect the brain and nervous system adversely.[23]

The varieties of secondary amentia include four types: (1) traumatic, (2) infectious, (3) degenerative, and (4) deprivative. In addition to Tredgold's classification a fifth type due to toxic poisoning should also be included.

1. *Traumatic Feeble-Mindedness.* Traumatic feeble-mindedness (feeble-mindedness caused by injury) accounts for only 5 percent of all cases of mental deficiency. Such injuries are usually caused by blows on the head, whether

---

[20] *Ibid.,* pp. 229–230.
[21] Students who wish to pursue this topic are urged to consult Tredgold's text.
[22] A research specialist at the Mayo Clinic gave the authors this information.
[23] Tredgold, *op. cit.,* chap. XIV.

during the pregnancy, during birth, or as the result of severe falls of the child during infancy. To produce feeble-mindedness trauma must cause lesions in the brain. Blows on the head are also thought to cause some cases of epilepsy (which may or may not be accompanied by amentia). The largest number of brain injuries are received during birth and are a result of a difficult birth because of the size of the child's head. As a matter of fact, stillbirths are often due to severe brain hemorrhage.[24] Intercranial hemorrhage is common in premature babies, many of whom are mentally retarded. Some cases of traumatic amentia carry no outward sign. Other traumas result in some degree of paralysis, of which cerebral palsy is a well-known variety. Such traumatic paralysis is not always accompanied by amentia, but many cerebral palsy victims are retarded. The Rhesus (Rh) blood factor is apparently an important factor in certain other types of traumatic amentia. In these cases there is a severe jaundice at birth as well as brain damage.[25]

2. *Infectious Amentias.* Infections of the *meningitic* and *encephalitic* types cause about 11 percent of all traumatic brain injuries. *Tuberculosis, pneumonia,* and *streptococcic meningitis* are among the types of infection which may cause amentia. In times past these infections were likely to be fatal but with the new antibiotic drug treatment recovery often occurs. *Spinal meningitis* (due to meningococcus) and polio both may cause brain damage if not promptly treated. Sleeping sickness (*encephalitis lethargica*) is an inflammation of the brain which attacks all ages and may result in severe brain injury, even in later life. This damage may result in psychosis, but often there is mental deterioration without any delusions. Cases suffering from the disease often lose emotional control, however, and some become violent and unmanageable. Others may become behavior problems.[26]

Hydrocephalic amentia is caused by excess cerebrospinal fluid and usually results in a peculiar bulging enlargement of the skull with an inverted-pyramid or "top-heavy" look. This condition is apparently the result of brain infection. The pressure meanwhile tends to destroy brain tissue and the amentia results from this destruction.[27]

Syphilis is an infection responsible for some cases of feeble-mindedness. Earlier estimation of the incidence of syphilis among the feeble-minded ranged from very low to as much as 44 percent, a figure unquestionably exaggerated. Two American studies in which there was an actual count of such cases showed 3.4 percent in one feeble-minded institution to be syphilitic and 1.15 percent in another. The use of modern antibiotics has greatly reduced the incidence of syphilitic amentia in recent years.[28]

Rubella (or German measles) if contracted by the mother during pregnancy sometimes causes severe brain damage to the fetus. The disease itself

[24] *Ibid.,* pp. 248–260.
[25] *Ibid.,* pp. 260–261.
[26] *Ibid.,* pp. 264–267.
[27] *Ibid.,* pp. 268–271.
[28] Cited in *ibid.,* p. 274.

is a relatively mild infection and the reason for its having a serious effect on the fetus is not clearly understood. The danger to the fetus from rubella is not as great as is commonly believed, however.

In addition to the infections listed above, the so-called childhood diseases of measles, whooping cough, and mumps occasionally result in brain injury.[29]

Certain *poisons* cause brain lesions sufficient to produce severe amentia. It seems likely that their action resembles infections chemically. Lead is an especially dangerous poison to children and is a major reason for avoiding paint on children's beds and toys and dye in their clothing.[30] It is well known that children are prone to chew everything they can get in their mouths.

3. *Degenerative Amentia.* Certain amentias are the result of little-understood degenerative processes which occur during infancy and childhood. Sometimes a child's mental ability seems to deteriorate without cause. He fails to develop normally even though apparently normal at birth. Certain types of epilepsy are apparently due to degenerative processes rather than to hereditary conditions (although others are hereditary). *Schizophrenia amentia* is likewise a condition of childhood in which the child's mental development is arrested after a comparatively normal earlier development.[31] Some authorities hold that this may be emotional in origin but psychiatrists are not agreed.

4. *Deprivative Amentias.* Sometimes an environmental lack (in food, water, or other items) causes a marked decrease in mental ability. Cretinism is one of the most important varieties of deprivative amentia. Cretinism is apparently caused by metabolic disturbances which are thought to occur because of a lack of iodine in the water. Cretins appear normal at birth but fail to develop after they are six months or so old. The medical presumption is that the child receives enough thyroid from the mother during the prenatal and nursing period, but he later fails to grow, develops a puffy appearance, a slow pulse, low red cell blood count, and low temperature. He also becomes mentally torpid. If he is properly treated with thyroid, these symptoms disappear. If not treated, he suffers general impairment of all mental faculties.[32] Other endocrine amentias result from a malfunctioning pituitary and from thymus and adrenal disorders.[33]

Nutritional amentia is the result of lack of proper nutrition either prenatally or after birth. Children with this type of amentia are unusually weak and retarded. Richitic idiocy due to metabolic disturbances in absorbing calcium is one of the commonest forms.[34]

Isolation amentia is the type of mental retardation accompanying lack of

[29] "Report of the Committee on Growth and Development," part IV of *White House Conference on Child Health and Protection*, Appleton-Century-Crofts, Inc., New York, 1932, pp. 223–224.

[30] *Ibid.*

[31] Tredgold, *op. cit.*, pp. 277–287.

[32] *Ibid.*, pp. 289–295.

[33] *Ibid.*, pp. 295–296.

[34] *Ibid.*, pp. 297–298.

sight or hearing. Because the brain does not receive the sense stimuli (which is true for the normal child) the brain fails to develop. These sense deprivations are often initially caused by infectious diseases such as scarlet fever or congenital syphilis. Children reared in institutions often receive little personal attention and training and consequently grow up with very limited vocabulary and mental comprehension. They too have a deprivation type of amentia. Babies in orphanages, for example, often drink milk and orange juice, or eat cereal, meat, vegetables, and fruit without knowing a single name for items in their diet. They are isolated from (or deprived of) normal stimuli and have little power of communication.

Certain types of feeble-mindedness are hard to classify because they involve both inheritance and environmental influences. In general we know that a weak child may be affected more adversely by environmental factors than a child with a sound constitution. Tredgold's classification of amentias may thus seem a bit arbitrary, but it gives us a broad picture of the wide variety of types of mental disability and their etiology.[35]

Sterilization

Many people have urged the sterilization of the feeble-minded as a means of controlling feeble-mindedness. Sterilization, however, is not an effective means of eliminating the problem, for research shows that only 11 percent of the feeble-minded have feeble-minded parents.[36] Perfectly normal people may have some defective germ cells out of the millions which they produce, and occasionally these are the ones which produce the defective fetus. Most defective fetuses are eliminated through "spontaneous abortion," but some develop and live on in an ill-fated existence.

Many mental defectives are nonhereditary cases and are the result of accidents, glandular disfunction, and infectious and nutritional disorders. Because of the value we place on personality in modern society, these individuals represent a serious segment of the individually disorganized. Most of the cases of serious or low-grade defectiveness are institutionalized and form a sizable part of the forgotten children and men and women. That some normal children should be committed to institutions because of improper diagnosis is one of the tragedies of our times. These children's lives are in a very special sense disorganized.

The Emotional Factor in Feeble-Mindedness

Obviously the children who are retarded because of emotional factors are not as severely handicapped as those with serious brain injuries or those with hereditary defects. For the latter there is little hope. But for the seemingly dull children who fail in school because of emotional difficulties the prognosis may be hopeful. Effective psychiatric help or constructive effort on the part of teachers and social workers to get at the underlying causes of his intellectual apathy will do much to help the child. The real cause usually lies

[35] *Ibid.*, pp. 301–305.
[36] "Report of the Committee on Growth and Development," pp. 220–225.

with the parents (and frequently with the mother since she traditionally supplies so much of the child's emotional security).

It seems likely that there is an emotional factor in feeble-mindedness even where the child appears to have inherited his amentia. If a mother is mentally defective, she usually fails to give the child the attention, fondling, and love that a normal parent gives. She takes no pride in his accomplishments and gives him no stimulation to learn from books. Where there is no "rewards in smiles," the child has little impetus to learn.[37] Sarason's opinion is undoubtedly true. Mentally retarded persons make poor parents.

Although it was originally held that the IQ would remain constant if the tests were properly administered, it is a fact that many children who test low improve later. These children are ordinarily in the upper ranges of feeble-mindedness. Dr. Bernardine G. Schmidt, for example, worked with 254 school children designated as feeble-minded. She discovered that their IQ's were raised on the average of 25.3 points. Eighty percent of the children gained more than 30 points while one child actually scored 71 points higher. Dr. Schmidt had three groups of low-grade children who were given special help in reading and were also helped by training in special skills. Many of these children came from homes known to social agencies. The homes were also substandard emotionally, and it seems likely that the emotional factor was of real importance in their intelligence testing. In contrast to the improvement in the group given special help, 68 children in a control group with an average IQ of 60 actually declined in intelligence. These children were given no systematic help or "emotional bolstering" and their average IQ five years later was 56.4.[38]

A smaller study of seventeen children with IQ under 90, conducted by Nancy Staver, showed that these children had fears of mutilation and death. Fifteen of the mothers had a history of illness and they had projected their own fears on their children.[39]

Major Differences Between Feeble-Mindedness and Mental Illness

The mentally deranged ordinarily represent more complicated personality disorders than the feeble-minded because their mental abilities are distorted, they substitute the unreal for the real, and they are often highly emotional or hysterical. In fact, their reactions are so unlike normal reactions that in earlier periods they were often regarded as "possessed" by external, evil spirits to which their bodies had given hostage. The mentally ill today often imagine themselves to be someone else, as for example a great figure in history or some other powerful or rich person. This gives us a clue as to why

[37] Seymour B. Sarason, *Psychological Problems in Mental Deficiency*, Harper & Brothers, New York, 1949, pp. 157–163.

[38] Bernardine G. Schmidt, *Changes in Personal, Social, and Intellectual Behavior of Children Originally Classified as Feebleminded*, Psychological Monographs, Vol. 60, No. 281, American Psychological Association, Inc., Washington, 1946, pp. 30, 87, and 90–91.

[39] Nancy Staver, "The Child's Learning Difficulty as Related to the Emotional Problems of the Mother," *American Journal of Orthopsychiatry*, 23:131–140 (January, 1953).

TABLE 11.1. Expenditures of Public Institutions for Mental Defectives and Epileptics, by State: United States, 1956
(statistics based on reports from 97 of the 100 public institutions[a])

State[a]	Total Expenditures	Maintenance Expenditures					Additions, Improvements and Other Expenditures	Average Daily Resident-Patient Populations[b]
		Total	Salaries and Wages	Purchased Provisions	Fuel, Light, and Water	Other Maintenance		
Alabama	$ 938,457	$ 808,469	$ 618,448	$ 148,834	$ 41,187	—	$ 129,988	1,507
Arizona	826,591	391,810	247,479	78,174	13,420	52,737	434,781	316
California	17,890,433	13,712,997	10,677,991	1,708,050	384,227	942,729	4,177,436	8,527
Colorado	1,807,747	1,377,403	853,892	125,670	92,410	305,431	430,344	1,131
Connecticut	8,054,933	5,299,244	3,680,132	572,457	341,376	705,279	2,755,689	3,107
Delaware	851,203	739,492	434,296	92,391	50,420	162,385	111,711	522
District of Columbia	1,352,154	1,182,392	937,445	144,020	72,307	28,620	169,762	719
Florida	2,071,422	1,666,091	950,002	210,494	82,709	422,886	405,331	1,075
Georgia	1,361,839	814,243	374,425	148,911	67,615	223,292	547,596	830
Idaho	768,280	714,819	479,032	67,889	42,848	125,050	53,461	895
Illinois	8,586,326	8,314,142	4,564,181	1,853,574	458,598	1,437,789	272,184	10,240
Indiana	6,312,556	5,380,847	3,409,102	788,210	340,240	843,295	931,709	4,619
Iowa	3,457,730	2,918,620	1,964,338	488,361	174,481	291,440	539,110	3,416
Kansas	3,927,066	2,992,049	1,833,334	449,486	115,393	593,836	935,017	2,005
Louisiana	1,410,834	1,379,379	965,856	95,551	64,409	253,563	31,455	1,324
Maine	1,644,292	1,456,771	921,002	293,389	91,705	150,675	187,521	1,465
Maryland	3,445,355	3,188,413	1,958,301	404,149	194,819	631,144	256,942	2,026
Massachusetts	12,247,268	12,247,268	8,466,068	1,261,454	763,625	1,756,121	—	8,496
Michigan	22,271,686	15,032,625	11,900,342	1,511,324	518,528	1,102,431	7,239,061	9,611
Minnesota[c]	4,831,790	4,771,781	3,246,776	794,572	207,689	522,744	60,009	4,788
Mississippi	544,597	481,257	179,031	121,172	18,103	162,951	63,340	860
Missouri	2,700,562	1,928,677	1,262,365	243,934	96,112	326,266	771,885	2,357

State							
Montana	871,040	531,117	244,777	112,206	51,307	122,827	339,923	579
Nebraska	1,574,848	1,193,645	769,467	163,295	56,306	204,577	381,203	2,062
New Hampshire	778,144	770,141	516,184	99,500	62,171	92,286	8,003	791
New Jersey	7,921,123	5,472,062	3,732,391	613,159	361,207	765,305	2,449,061	4,761
New Mexico	142,898	121,677	66,674	13,335	8,001	33,667	21,221	137
New York	33,879,690	30,726,426	23,011,976	3,115,702	1,356,355	3,242,393	3,153,264	24,408
North Carolina	2,306,444	1,710,068	1,074,360	211,570	25,942	398,196	596,376	1,761
Ohio	9,666,513	7,934,522	5,627,202	1,217,304	358,405	731,611	1,731,991	7,554
Oklahoma	1,497,298	1,384,847	854,549	166,335	64,366	299,597	112,451	1,944
Oregon	2,018,255	1,985,922	1,323,173	201,810	63,046	397,893	32,333	1,845
Pennsylvania	8,912,728	8,835,931	6,012,795	1,284,795	500,350	1,037,991	76,797	8,749
Rhode Island	1,104,903	1,044,717	620,484	215,642	86,870	121,721	60,186	875
South Carolina	2,535,368	1,478,860	896,990	177,135	81,884	322,851	1,056,508	1,805
South Dakota	814,695	732,716	459,681	82,734	72,558	117,743	81,979	912
Tennessee	793,635	774,510	328,615	212,736	42,654	190,505	19,125	1,077
Texas	4,735,436	4,501,482	2,901,811	835,584	151,044	613,043	233,954	4,746
Utah	663,723	654,453	472,897	42,053	24,822	114,681	9,270	748
Vermont	549,255	529,580	313,451	42,306	8,832	164,991	19,675	537
Virginia	2,976,115	2,507,031	1,650,262	407,418	81,174	368,177	469,084	2,590
Washington	4,475,779	3,581,301	2,326,077	707,614	226,144	321,466	894,478	3,143
West Virginia	241,680	208,442	117,228	37,625	16,611	36,978	33,238	190
Wisconsin	5,217,211	4,805,174	3,516,271	493,612	170,102	625,189	412,037	3,229
Wyoming	900,864	567,275	335,634	81,104	24,945	125,592	333,589	507
United States Total[c]	$201,880,766	$168,850,688	$117,096,787	$22,136,640	$8,127,317	$21,489,944	$33,030,078	144,786

[a] Arkansas and Nevada do not have public institutions for the care of mental defectives and epileptics.
[b] Includes only population of institutions reporting expenditures.
[c] Data not available for one institution in each of the following States: Kentucky, Minnesota and North Dakota.

SOURCE: *Patients in Mental Institutions, 1956*, part I, "Public Institutions for Mental Defectives and Epileptics," Public Health Service, U.S. Department of Health, Education, and Welfare, 1959. p. I-47.

mental patients were formerly thought to be possessed. The mentally ill also often behave so queerly, so emotionally, and become so difficult to manage that it is easy to see they are "not acting like themselves." It has taken the medical profession a long time, however, to recognize that such personality changes are mental diseases which have a traceable etiology. Sometimes the disease has a physical cause (as we shall discuss later), but frequently its source lies in the stresses and strains of daily life. We have thus come to regard many mental diseases as emotional disorders because they are precipitated by emotional stress.

As the scientific study of mental disabilities developed, the classifications of amentia and dementia became less dichotomized than earlier. Psychologists used to hold that the feeble-minded lived in a simple mental world and were not subject to the stresses and strains which produced mental derangement. Today we know this is not true, for some feeble-minded become deranged. Again, some seemingly feeble-minded are not defective in brain structure but are retarded because they are unhappy and have been emotionally neglected.

Unadjustment Problems of the Mentally Deficient

The mentally deficient constitute a far greater social burden than the cost of institutional care (which is reserved chiefly for the worst cases). Many are supported by their families or the community. The feeble-minded also require special teaching in our schools and often retard the instruction for normal children. A large number become dependent or are never able to earn a living wage. Criminality was once considered a particular characteristic of the feeble-minded, but today criminologists doubt that any sizable proportion of crime is committed by the mentally defective.[40] Sex offenses are common among the mentally defective, as discussed in Chapter 6. Since these offenses are more common in the lower economic and social groups the fact of low status may be an important factor in both mental ability and behavior, as we have suggested.

Modern urban living makes it very difficult for the feeble-minded person. His problems are obviously less complicated in a rural or village environment. Most feeble-minded are considered more unorganized than disorganized. They are unable to look after their own needs or to participate effectively in family or community life.

That current research should point to emotional disturbance as a probable factor in mental functioning or seeming retardation should stimulate further study. The biochemical effect of emotional disturbance upon mental functioning deserves more intensive research. New trends in mental derangement research are proceeding along this line, too, as we discuss in the next chapter.

The feeble-minded have been socially neglected chiefly because society

---

[40] Elio D. Monachesi, "Some Personality Characteristics of Delinquents and Non Delinquents," *Journal of Criminal Law and Criminology,* 38:487–500 (January–February, 1948).

has taken a hopeless attitude toward them. The fact that the average expenditure for institutionalized mental defectives and epileptics was only $1394.40 annually in 1956 (this figure was derived from Table 11.1) is an index to what Albert Deutsch calls the purely custodial nature of the care given in most states.[41] If we keep these human beings alive they deserve to be treated with greater thought of helping them. Better training both for the slow learners in our schools and for those in our special institutions might enable many of them to lead a self-sufficient and fairly organized existence. And first of all, those admitted to the feeble-minded category must be more adequately screened. The careless classification of the normal as feeble-minded is a tragic commentary on the social definition of intelligence.

Present understanding indicates that the problem is social, medical, and educational. As a result of the recent research in mental deficiency, it is obvious that the old psychological truisms must be discarded, particularly those which maintain that the I.Q. is a stable entity. Leo Kanner has held that three categories of feeble-mindedness should be established: (1) absolute feeble-mindedness, (2) relative feeble-mindedness, and (3) apparent feeble-mindedness. The first would require custodial care, the second special education and vocational facilities, and the third adequate diagnosis and treatment of handicaps.[42] But further research may indicate that these classifications also must be revised. For despite the criticisms of Dr. Schmidt's study, there is reason to believe that many with low mental ratings will improve under proper stimulation.

SELECTED BIBLIOGRAPHY

Deutsch, Albert, *The Mentally Ill in America*, Columbia University Press, New York, 1949. This book gives a revelatory presentation of the treatment of the mentally deficient.

Lemkau, Paul V., *Mental Hygiene in Public Health*, McGraw-Hill Book Company, Inc., New York, 1955. Several chapters are devoted to mental hygiene in relation to mental deficiency. The material relating to older people is especially good.

Mental Health Statistics, Current Reports, Public Health Service, National Institute of Mental Health, Bethesda, Maryland. These annual reports will enable students and instructors to obtain the latest statistics on mental deficiency in public institutions.

Patients in Mental Institutions, 1955, part I, "Public Institutions for Mental Defectives and Epileptics," U.S. Department of Health, Education, and Welfare, Washington, 1958. This report contains a detailed analysis of the types of mental defectives in our institutions.

"Report of the Committee on Growth and Development," part IV, *White House Conference on Child Health and Protection*, Appleton-Century-Crofts, Inc.,

---

[41] Albert Deutsch, *The Mentally Ill in America*, Columbia University Press, New York, 1949, p. 380.

[42] Leo Kanner, "Feeblemindedness, Absolute, Relative and Apparent," *The Nervous Child*, 7:365–397 (October, 1948).

New York, 1932. The findings of the best-informed persons in the United States with reference to mental deficiency are summarized.

Sarason, Seymour B., *Psychological Problems in Mental Deficiency*, Harper & Brothers, New York, 1949. This book gives a summary of important trends in the study of the mentally deficient.

Schmidt, Bernardine G., *Changes in Personal, Social and Intellectual Behavior of Children Originally Classified as Feebleminded, Psychological Monographs*, Vol. 60, No. 281, American Psychological Association, Inc., Washington, 1946. This is an important (although controversial) contribution to the understanding of mental retardation and its relation to emotional deprivation.

Staver, Nancy, "The Child's Learning Difficulty as Relative to the Emotional Problems of the Mother," *American Journal of Orthopsychiatry, 23:*131–140 (January, 1953). This constitutes a small but important research into the effect of the emotional instability of the mother in relation to the child.

Terman, Lewis, *The Measurement of Intelligence*, Houghton Mifflin Company, Boston, 1916. This is the classic study on mental testing.

Tredgold, A. E. (assisted by R. F. Tredgold), *A Textbook of Mental Deficiency*, The Williams and Wilkins Company, Baltimore, 1952. This book covers the important medical research into the physical causes of mental deficiency.

Wechsler, David, *The Measurement of Adult Intelligence*, The Williams and Wilkins Company, Baltimore, 1944. This gives Dr. Wechsler's revision of the 1.2 ratings and is widely used for classifying adult intelligence.

CHAPTER 12

The Mentally Deranged

MENTAL ILLNESS AND PERSONAL DISORGANIZATION

In the process of development the individual must pass from the fetal stage into the outside world. He then develops through the growing process of infancy, childhood, and adolescence before he emerges as a full-grown and mature adult.[1] Some psychologists hold that relatively few people ever become truly mature. In folk parlance, women recognize the "little boy" in men's foibles and men are amused or amazed by the "childishness" of women. Nevertheless, most people become relatively mature and self-controlled as they take on the responsibility of a job, a profession, marriage, and parenthood. People who fail to become responsible adults are in fact unorganized or disorganized personalities even though they may be physically fit.

Some persons escape reality through mental illnesses because they are unable to adjust to the stresses and strains which life imposes. Other mental illnesses occur as the result of brain damage caused either by injuries such as concussions or by infections or poisons (the latter including alcohol and drugs). So far as the individuals are concerned, both those suffering from acute and chronic brain syndromes and those whose illness stems from emotional disturbances are disorganized and unable to assume any effective role in society. In a very real sense the mental illnesses which are induced by stresses and strains are an index to social disorganization since such illnesses are a response to what (for the emotionally disturbed) is a social order unfavorable to their effective functioning.

Mental illness thus has important sociological implications because of the number of persons who are incapacitated and the fact that much of it is the result of social stresses and strains. A major characteristic of mental patients is their inability to function effectively. In case of severe disorders such persons, popularly adjudged insane, are unable to function at all. Those who have milder neurotic disorders are unable to fulfill their roles in an effective and acceptable fashion. Even though they carry on in their work, marriage, or social relationships, they are a constant problem to themselves and to other persons.

[1] Cf. Paul V. Lemkau, *Mental Hygiene in Public Health,* McGraw-Hill Book Company, Inc., New York, 1955, part II, chaps. X–XV.

283

The Extent of Mental Illness

The extent of mental illness is only partially known. The United States Department of Health, Education, and Welfare issues statistical reports for civilian patients in public and private mental hospitals and in general hospitals with psychiatric facilities, but many cases are missed because reports are made on a voluntary basis. A large number of private and general hospitals and some state hospitals fail to cooperate. State reports on public hospitals are also published but many of these are non-comparable because each state compiles its data according to a locally devised plan. Some do not attempt to publish details with reference to the type of mental disease. Mental patients in veterans' hospitals are not included in the federal report. The picture is therefore far from complete. The United States Public Health Service estimated in 1946 that there were eight million Americans suffering from some form of mental disease.[2] The estimate included many neurotics and non-deranged individuals who seek medical care from their private physicians or ply themselves with patent medicines. These neurotics allegedly constitute a sizable share of the average physician's practice. Unfortunately the average medical practitioner does not "cure" them. They return again and again for prescriptions when they really need to develop interests outside themselves if they are to achieve mental health.

Such patients are not deranged; they merely "enjoy poor health"—and the only delusion they have is the belief that their problem is physical. It is true that their anxiety creates aches and pains, but their health problem is essentially mental and emotional. Any cure for their disorders lies in an understanding of their difficulties and reconstruction of their basic attitudes. What is more important, many persons with serious mental disorders are not receiving treatment because relatives or the patients themselves are not willing to seek it. For the extent of severe cases of mental derangement, the hospital figures give a fairly accurate picture. Most severely deranged persons are receiving treatment. But many mildly deranged are receiving no institutional treatment, and often such cases receive no extra-institutional care. Some receive care at home, others are on the waiting lists of hospitals, and still others are released to home care. According to Hollingshead and Redlich, only a fraction of the mentally ill are in hospitals.[3] Those who are receiving care they estimate to be divided percentagewise as follows:

Patients in	Percent
State hospitals	68.0
Veterans' hospitals	4.2
Public clinics of private hospitals	8.0
Private practice	19.0
Private hospitals	Less than 2 percent

SOURCE: August B. Hollingshead and Frederick C. Redlich, *Social Class and Mental Illness*, John Wiley and Sons, Inc., New York, 1958, pp. 146–155.

[2] *Patients in Mental Hospitals: 1946,* Bureau of the Census, U.S. Department of Commerce, Washington, 1948, p. 8.

[3] August B. Hollingshead and Frederick C. Redlich, *Social Class and Mental Illness,* John Wiley and Sons, Inc., New York, 1958, p. 5.

PATIENTS IN RESIDENCE IN PUBLIC MENTAL HOSPITALS

The number of patients as indicated by those in residence in public mental hospitals has declined somewhat in recent years. At the end of 1957 there were 548,431 such patients, in 1956 there were 551,390, and in 1955 there were 557,969.[4] This decline is a result of the increased discharge rate. On the other hand, the first admissions have increased. In 1955 there were 119,-321 first admissions, in 1956 there were 125,539, and in 1957 there were 129,688.[5]

The distribution of patients in public mental hospitals is striking. In 1957 (as chart 12.1 more or less shows) urban areas had the highest rates. New

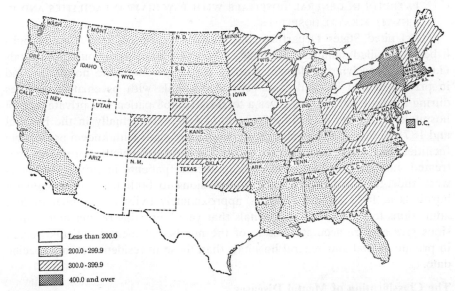

Less than 200.0
200.0 - 299.9
300.0 - 399.9
400.0 and over

CHART 12.1. Average Daily Resident Patients in Public Hospitals for Mental Disease per 100,000 Civilian Population, 1957. (Based on provisional data, subject to later revision.) (From *Mental Health Statistics, Current Reports,* Series MHB-H-3, U.S. Department of Health, Education, and Welfare, May, 1958, p. 1.)

York State had the highest rate—605.2 per 100,000 population—although Massachusetts, New Hampshire, Delaware, and the District of Columbia were not far behind. On the other hand, according to the map, Iowa, Texas, New Mexico, Arizona, Nevada, Idaho, Utah, and Wyoming had low rates— New Mexico the lowest of all with only 118.4 per 100,000.[6] These data seem to indicate that mental cases in urban areas are more likely to be hospitalized because hospitalization is more imperative. The complexity of city life makes the mental patient more dangerous both to himself and to others. City traffic,

[4] *Mental Health Statistics, Current Reports,* Series MHB-H-5, U.S. Department of Health, Education, and Welfare, Public Health Service, National Institute of Mental Health, May, 1958, pp. 2–5.
[5] *Ibid.,* pp. 6–7.
[6] *Ibid.*

congested living conditions in apartments, the confusion and hubbub of commercial and industrial activities all require a fair degree of mental and emotional stability. But we also have reason to believe that the competition and frustrations of daily living are more serious in highly populated areas. Density of population is only one factor. Iowa is more densely populated than the Dakotas but has a lower rate, for reasons that are not apparent.

In addition to the patients in residence, public mental hospitals also supervise patients released to family care or to other extramural care, and release rates are a factor in the hospitalization rate in some states. In 1955 nearly 90,000 received extramural care.

PATIENTS IN GENERAL HOSPITALS WITH PSYCHIATRIC FACILITIES AND IN PRIVATE MENTAL HOSPITALS

The United States Department of Health, Education, and Welfare published a detailed summary of statistics covering patients in public hospitals (i.e., those receiving prolonged care in public psychopathic hospitals) and in private mental hospitals and general hospitals with psychiatric facilities during the year 1955.[7] There was a total of 16,468 patients in private mental hospitals at the end of 1955, of whom 14,590 were actually in the hospital and 1878 were in extramural care. In general hospitals with known psychiatric facilities, 6459 were in residence. These figures give no picture of the number treated, however, since the majority of mental patients in private hospitals were short-term patients. The first admissions to both private and general hospitals in 1955 totaled 237,686, approximately twice the number of first admissions to public mental hospitals that year.[8] For this reason first admissions give a more accurate picture of the number of mental patients treated in private mental and general hospitals than those in residence at any specific date.

The Classification of Mental Diseases

Until recently mental illnesses were usually classified as physical, toxic, and functional. *Physical* (or organic) psychoses subsumed those due to brain injury or to physical degeneration (either because of senility or cerebral degeneration because of arteriosclerosis). The *toxic* psychoses included those due to physical disease or tumors attacking the brain tissue and those due to drugs or alcohol. The *functional* psychoses were those mental illnesses having no discoverable organic pathology. The functional psychoses were, in short, those precipitated by a failure to make a satisfactory social adjustment.[9]

A new nomenclature for mental disease was adopted in 1952 by the American Psychiatric Association and approved by the American Medical

---

[7] *Patients in Mental Institutions, 1955,* part II, "Public Hospitals for the Mentally Ill," and part III, "Private Hospitals for the Mentally Ill and General Hospitals with Psychiatric Facilities," U.S. Department of Health, Education, and Welfare, Washington, 1958.

[8] *Ibid.,* part II, p. 13.

[9] Edward A. Strecker, *Fundamentals of Psychiatry,* J. B. Lippincott Company, Philadelphia, 1947 (4th ed.), chap. III, "Classification of Mental Diseases."

Association.[10] This classification separates those with brain syndromes (that is, those whose mental aberrations are the result of brain injury, disease, or toxic condition) from those whose symptoms are purely psychotic or neurotic. The mentally ill patient is then defined as one who has a personality disorder, whatever the source of his illness. The individual is regarded as a unit,[11] and his disorder is accordingly defined by its manifestations. Mental illnesses thus are classified according to whether they are (1) brain syndromes (symptoms of brain disease or injury) with mental reaction, (2) psychotic disorders (which are essentially mental disorders with specific mental reactions), or (3) those of the psychoneurotic or neurotic type.[12]

The new mental disease nomenclature is a distinct improvement and classifies the symptoms according to both their etiology and their characteristic reactions. The term "brain syndromes" is substituted for "organic psychoses" and the syndromes are subdivided into acute and chronic brain syndromes with their particular reactions. The acute brain syndromes thus include alcohol intoxication, trauma, and "other." The chronic brain syndromes are those associated with

> Meningoencephalitic syphilis
> Other central nervous system syphilis
> Alcoholic intoxication
> Drug or poison intoxication (except alcohol)
> Trauma
> Cerebral arteriosclerosis
> Other circulatory disturbance
> Convulsive disorder
> Senile brain disease
> Other disturbances of metabolism, growth, and nutrition
> All other chronic brain syndromes

This classification is less rigid and recognizes the brain condition to be a symptom of the disease. Such disease is essentially a function of a physical disease or injury of the brain. Only those diseases which are essentially psychogenic in origin are now termed psychotic. The current classification of psychotic disorders includes involutional reaction, manic-depressive reaction, schizophrenic reaction, paranoid reaction, and "other." In addition, other functional non-psychotic and personality disorders are classified as mental illnesses. These include

> Psychophysiologic, autonomic, and visceral disorders
> Psychoneurotic reactions
> Total personality disorders

[10] *Patients in Mental Institutions, 1955,* part II, "Public Hospitals for the Mentally Ill," p. II–8.

[11] William C. Menninger, *Psychiatry, Its Evolution and Present Status,* Cornell University Press, Ithaca, 1948.

[12] *Patients in Mental Institutions, 1955,* part II, pp. II–48–54.

Transient situational personality disturbances
Mental deficiency
Undiagnosed mental disorder

In addition to these categories, certain patients are referred to mental hospitals because they are emotionally upset but these are diagnosed as "without mental disorder."

This new classification does not satisfy the Menningers, who recognize that classification tends to fasten names to patients when no true scientific entities exist. Dr. Karl A. Menninger also points out that classification of mental patients may contribute to their failure to recover if a classification is made in their (the patients') hearing. At the Menninger Clinic, the patient is therefore classified according to the new nomenclature only on discharge. Previous to that time he is placed in one of four categories of symptoms: (1) mild symptoms, (2) noticeable neurotic behavior, (3) episodic emotional scenes, and (4) severe disorganization of the whole personality.[13]

CHARACTERISTICS OF THE MAJOR TYPES OF MENTAL DISEASE

All mental patients who lose their orientation with reality are easily recognized when they hear imaginary voices, scream violently when there is no danger, or go into a deep melancholic state. The reasons for their acting in such a fashion are not always so obvious. Some persons with a brain injury may act very much the same as persons whose maladjusted behavior is the result of an emotional conflict or shock. An accurate diagnosis requires a medical background as well as psychiatric training.

Mental Illness Due to Brain Damage

Where the brain's function is disturbed either by infectious disease or by traumata, it is likely to be very serious because brain cells are often destroyed. Once destroyed, such cells never grow again. A variety of abnormal reactions may result. There may be *disorientation of place and time* so that the patient thinks he is in another place, or that the time is different from the actual time. Other patients may believe that two people or two places are identical (or more or less identical). This disorder is called *reduplication*. Still others may have *paraphasia*—that is, they recognize the object for what it is but refer to it by some other word. They may, for example, call the piano "potato." All of these reactions, whether *disorientation, reduplicative delusions,* or *paraphasia,* may follow head injury, brain hemorrhage, acute inflammation of the brain, or acute toxic states.[14]

Following brain damage, personal behavior often changes markedly. It is

[13] *Newsweek,* February 10, 1958, p. 76.
[14] Edwin A. Weinstein, E. C. Alvord, Jr., and David McK. Rioch, "Disorders Associated with Disturbance of Brain Function," *Mental Health in the United States, Annals of the American Academy of Political and Social Science, 286:*34–44 (March, 1953).

believed that the changes are manifestations of the personality's attempt to maintain its integrity. Five types of changes occur frequently, but these are believed to be different indications of similar anatomical lesions. They are as follows:

1. The patients in the first group deny that anything has happened to them. If paralyzed, the patient maintains that he cannot move because of laziness or gives some other unrealistic explanation. He may remain calm and bland, whereas he often was depressed or upset earlier.
2. A second group blame their condition on another person's evil doing. Someone has poisoned them, or willed that they be injured.
3. A third group explain their condition humorously. They are contrariwise often depressed, despite their humor.
4. A fourth group become childish. They often lack sex and other inhibitions, have feeding difficulties, etc.
5. A fifth group become drowsy, sleep a great deal, and are unresponsive to questions.

All patients with brain damage should be spared emotional and physical stress because they have both a lower resistance to emotional stresses and lower physical endurance. When brain damage is severe, hallucinations, delirium, stupor, or coma may occur. The vital centers (those controlling blood pressure, respiration, heart, etc.) are less often affected than the higher (or mental) centers. Some hold that the human organism unconsciously favors its vital organs in its attempt to survive. Where the vital organs are attacked death may result, although sometimes vital centers are affected transiently.[15] Cases of cerebral arteriosclerosis (the degeneration of arteries which results in either occlusion or rupture) and senility constitute 40 percent of the admissions to mental hospitals.[16]

SENILE BRAIN SYNDROMES

Senile brain deterioration is much like that which occurs in cerebral arteriosclerosis—since hardening of brain blood vessels occurs in both. Nutritional deficiency, particularly vitamin C deficiency, seems to be a factor in senile dementia. The digestive system does not function as effectively as it did earlier and old people, especially old people without much income, often eat very poorly balanced diets. Senile dementia takes many forms—from simple deterioration, decline in memory and intellectual capacity, to confusion, depression, agitation, paranoia, and presbyophrenia, in which the verbalizations are often disoriented and meaningless although there is surface alertness. Some persons also develop what is known as presenile dementia or "Alzheimer's disease" which occurs prematurely, sometimes as early as forty for women and by sixty for men. In this mental illness marked de-

---

[15] *Ibid.*
[16] *Ibid.*

terioration of the brain structure, loss of fiber, and enlargement of certain cells are evident.[17]

DAMAGE DUE TO DISEASE

Syphilis formerly was an important source of brain disorder in its tertiary stage. The brain cells and blood vessels are both attacked in this stage of the disease and the nervous manifestations include general paresis, locomotor ataxia, and meningovascular syphilis. Today the antibiotics have been so successful in treating syphilis that few cases are expected to reach the tertiary state.[18] *Encephalitis* is due to brain infection. It is caused by a number of neurotropic viruses and in certain instances may also be caused by mumps and measles.[19] *Cerebral palsy* is a blanket term covering a wide number of brain injuries. Injury to the brain before or during birth may cause cerebral palsy. Some cerebral palsy cases have no special mental disorders other than lack of coordination and difficulty of verbal expression. Some, however, seem to develop definitely psychotic difficulties.[20]

ALCOHOLISM AND DRUG ADDICTION

Alcoholism, narcotic addiction, or large doses of other drugs introduced into the blood stream may affect the brain either acutely or chronically if long continued. Alcoholism and narcotic addiction are in a sense habits, but they may also produce a diseased condition. Much alcoholism and drug addiction may be regarded as a psychopathic defense reaction against a painful world. The reactions may thus be dual. There may be an evidence of a neurotic, psychotic, or psychopathic disturbance, but these drugs also damage the nervous system and reduce the person's competence and his ability to organize his behavior effectively.[21] The true alcoholic is escaping reality by the euphoric effect of the alcohol, just as the psychotic is escaping by positing an unreal situation in his mind. Many alcoholics and drug addicts are thus below par mentally and emotionally.

The Psychotic and Neurotic Disorders

The mental illnesses due to trauma or infection are obviously related to damage or destruction of brain cells. Formerly these were classed as organic psychoses. The new nomenclature, as stated above, applies the term "psychotic disorders" only to those mental illnesses which are psychogenic (or emotional) in origin. As Tables 12.1, 12.2, and 12.3 show, these mental illnesses constitute the largest category of hospitalized mental patients. Modern psychiatry is careful to admit, however, that, even where emotional disturbances have precipitated the disease, there may be some alteration in brain structure.

Psychosomatic medicine recognizes that emotional upsets can cause physical disease just as physical illness and handicaps may cause emotional

---

[17] Edward A. Strecker, *Fundamentals of Psychiatry,* J. B. Lippincott Company, Philadelphia, 1952 (4th ed.), pp. 31–32.
[18] Weinstein *et al., op. cit.*
[19] *Ibid.*
[20] *Ibid.*
[21] *Ibid.*

TABLE 12.1. First Admissions to Private Mental Hospitals in U.S., 1955, According to Mental Disorder[a]

Type of Disorder	Total	Number of Patients Admitted
Total	**41,711**	**41,711**
I. *Brain Syndromes*		
Acute brain syndromes	1,257	
Alcoholic intoxication		773
All others		484
Chronic brain syndromes	5,475	
Meningoencephalitic syphilis		31
Other CNS syphilis		43
Alcoholic intoxication		514
Drug and other poison intoxication (except alcohol)		72
Trauma		109
Cerebral arteriosclerosis		2,312
Other circulation disturbance		182
Convulsive disorder		163
Senile brain disease		1,577
Other disturbances of metabolism, growth, nutrition		140
All other chronic brain syndromes		332
II. *Total Psychotic Disorders*	19,933	
Involutional psychotic reaction		4,022
Manic depressive reaction		3,103
Psychotic depressive reaction		2,675
Schizophrenic reactions		8,674
Paranoid reactions		1,085
Other		374
III. *Personality and Non-Psychotic Disorders*	15,046	
Psychophysiologic, autonomic, and visceral disorders		182
Psychoneurotic reactions		7,716
Total personality disorders		5,857
Transient situational personality disturbances		329
Mental deficiency		130
Mental disorder undiagnosed		489
Without mental disorder		343

[a] Based on reports from 211 of 309 known private hospitals. Does not include 4685 first admissions for whom information was lacking.

SOURCE: *Patients in Mental Institutions, 1955*, part III, "Private Hospitals for the Mentally Ill and General Hospitals with Psychiatric Facilities," U.S. Department of Health, Education, and Welfare, 1958, pp. 24–25.

reactions. It is well known, for example, that great anxiety may bring on attacks of arthritis and that stomach ulcers and cardiac ailments are related to tension. On the other hand, people who are seriously injured and as a result are maimed or badly handicapped afterwards may have difficulty in accepting their condition. People suffering bone injuries which cannot be mended "good as new" have to "learn to limp and like it" or suffer emotional distortions if they do not. Diseases which attack the central nervous system are especially conducive to irritable reactions.

TABLE 12.2. Mental Patients in Residence in Public Mental Hospitals by Type of Syndrome at the End of the Year 1955[a]

Type of Disorder	Total	Number of Patients in Residence
Total	**410,359**	**410,359**
I. *Brain Syndromes*		
Acute brain syndromes—alcoholic	2,950	1,510
All other conditions		1,440
Chronic brain syndromes associated with:	107,913	
Meningoencephalitic syphilis		18,761
Other CNS syphilis		2,659
Alcoholic intoxication		7,493
Drug or poison (except alcohol)		267
Traum		2,475
Cerebraal arteriosclerosis		31,860
Other circulatory disturbance		1,686
Convulsive disorders		11,328
Senile brain disease		22,305
Other disturbances of metabolism, growth, and nutrition		1,897
All other chronic brain syndromes		7,182
II. *Total Psychotic Disorders*	244,899	
Involutional psychotic reaction		11,012
Manic depressive reaction		25,326
Psychotic depressive reaction		1,078
Schizophrenic reactions		196,598
Paranoid reactions		7,054
Other		3,831
III. *Personality and Psychic Non Psychotic Disorders*	54,597	
Psychophysiologic, autonomic, and visceral disorders		276
Psychoneurotic reactions		3,897
Total personality disorders		9,950
Transient situational personality disturbances		690
Mental deficiency		34,999
Mental disorders undiagnosed		3,944
Without mental disorder		841

[a] Based on reports from 196 of 217 state hospitals and 47 of 48 county hospitals. Does not include 147,610 known unclassified cases.

SOURCE: *Patients in Mental Institutions, 1955*, part II, "Public Hospitals in the United States," U.S. Department of Health, Education, and Welfare, 1958, pp. 54–55.

The human personality is very complicated. Nevertheless it functions as a unit even though played upon by many diverse influences. Recent research indicates that definite physical and chemical alterations may occur when patients have been emotionally disturbed. A report given at the Association of American Physicians by a research team from the New York Hospital–Cornell Medical Center in New York concludes that pathological substances are present in the spinal fluid to an excessive degree in patients with known nerve diseases and with schizophrenia.[22] It seems likely that further research

[22] Robert K. Plumb, "Enzyme Linked to Schizophrenia," *New York Times,* May 7, 1958, p. 32, col. 1.

TABLE 12.3. Number of Patients Discharged in 1955 from General Hospitals with Psychiatric Facilities According to Mental Disorder[a]

Mental Disorder	Total	Number of Patients Discharged
Total	**153,521**	**153,521**
I. *Brain Syndromes*		
Acute brain syndromes	13,055	
Alcoholic intoxication		8,979
Convulsive disorder		543
All other conditions		3,533
Chronic brain syndromes	24,058	
Meningoencephalitic syphilis		279
Other CNS syphilis		265
Alcoholic intoxication		3,454
Trauma		681
Cerebral arteriosclerosis		8,407
Senile brain disease		5,442
Convulsive disorder		1,476
All other		4,054
II. *Total Psychotic Disorders*	52,817	
Involutional psychotic reaction		7,004
Manic depressive reactions		5,280
Psychotic depressive reactions		5,629
Schizophrenic reactions		29,298
Paranoid reactions		2,127
All other		3,479
III. *Neurotic and Psychoneurotic Reactions*	29,417	
Psychobiologic, autonomic, and visceral disorders		2,341
Psychoneurotic reactions		27,076
IV. *Personality Disorders*	24,085	
Personality pattern disturbance		6,089
Alcoholic intoxication		14,598
Drug addiction		1,794
All other		1,604
V. *Other Personality Problems*	10,089	
Transient situational personality disorders		3,049
Mental deficiency		1,413
Mental disorder undiagnosed		3,266
Without mental disorder		2,361

[a] Based on reports from 319 of 530 general hospitals.

SOURCE: *Patients in Mental Institutions, 1955*, part III, "Private Hospitals for the Mentally Ill and General Hospitals with Psychiatric Facilities," U.S. Department of Health, Education, and Welfare, 1958, pp. 38–39.

may disclose other indications of abnormal physical or chemical conditions among patients with functional psychoses.

As Dr. Howard A. Rusk has pointed out, we need to develop extensive research coordinating the metabolic, psychological, and social factors with chemical and pharmacological research on the effect of psychoactive drugs upon brain function.[23] Important findings are bound to be made.

[23] Howard A. Rusk, "Mental Health Gains, II," *New York Times,* May 11, 1958, p. 72, cols. 1 and 2. Cf. also R. A. Schermerhorn, "Needed Research in Social Psychiatry," *Social Problems, 1*:17–22 (July, 1953).

The major psychotic disorders are as follows:

INVOLUTIONAL PSYCHOTIC REACTIONS

Involutional melancholia formerly was classified as an organic psychosis. It occurs at a time of distinct biological changes both in sex functioning (particularly for women) and in metabolic adjustment. Hence it has often been regarded as caused by physical and chemical changes in the body. Most psychiatrists today, however, believe involutional melancholia to be psychogenic in origin, and the reclassification of mental disease places it with the psychotic disorders rather than with the brain syndromes.

The menopausal age for women and the age involving endocrine and other glandular adjustment for men is often marked by poor health, and involutional melancholia (when it occurs) seems to accompany these conditions. The onset of the disease is thus usually between forty and fifty for women and from fifty to sixty for men. Psychiatrists generally agree that it is the psychological adjustments men and women face at these ages, rather than the bodily changes per se, which are responsible for the melancholia.[24]

Schizophrenia is characteristically a disease of young people. Growing up and accepting adult responsibilities involves serious life adjustments and some young people cannot take on such responsibility. But those middle-aged or past must likewise face adjustments. As he approaches fifty every individual must recognize that his most active years are over. He must also expect to have waning strength and a decline in activity in the years ahead. Worse still, most people have to accept the fact that they will never realize many of their heart-set goals. Some will have lost jobs because of ill health, bad luck, widespread unemployment, or personal maladjustment. Others will have been injured in accidents. Still others will have tasted of success and accumulated money, only to find it has brought little real satisfaction.

Women who have devoted time and effort to bringing up their children often feel useless and discouraged after forty-five. Their children have grown up and "don't need them." When children leave home for college or to get married, the mother's major function is over. Wise women know that it is important to develop other interests and activities. Otherwise they may literally have nothing to live for and in consequence may fall prey to a psychotic disorder. If a mother has to face the fact that her child has turned out badly—or that he has decided upon a career or a marriage which she opposes—she may become very discouraged.

A few persons have a *series* of unfortunate experiences which precipitate the disease. Some have had only one crisis. One may have lost a beloved child; another may be suddenly widowed. Still another may have developed cancer. All of these persons will perhaps have difficulty in maintaining their emotional serenity if they have other special problems of health adjustment simultaneously.

Fortunately the prognosis for involutional melancholia is good, although the

[24] Samuel W. Hartwell, *Practical Psychiatry and Mental Hygiene,* McGraw-Hill Book Company, Inc., New York, 1947, pp. 222–223.

illness may last a year and a half or two years.[25] The major characteristics of the disease are depression and a sense of guilt because of a presumed failure. The delusions are usually of a somatic sort. Patients often worry about their health, imagine their blood is water, and become greatly concerned about their digestion and elimination.[26]

SCHIZOPHRENIC PSYCHOTIC REACTIONS

The schizophrenic patient is characteristically an adolescent, with all of the crucial problems to which adolescence is heir. As we pointed out in Chapter 3, the anxious adolescent is greatly concerned by his problems in assuming an adult role. If there is a significant failure to solve personal conflicts and adjust to social relationships, behavior in which there is progressive deterioration may occur. Why a person develops schizophrenic reactions instead of some other pathological behavior is a question which has never been answered. For some cases, we may well raise the question whether institutional treatment is not a factor in the schizophrenic's progressive regression. Hospital treatment itself may be conducive to regression, because the patient has so little opportunity for interesting activities or those which promote his self-esteem. The authoritarian discipline in a mental hospital may thus lead to (1) further withdrawal and (2) lack of interaction. Both of these reactions are characteristic of schizophrenia.[27] The dreary and sometimes brutal routine existence so graphically described by Albert Deutsch[28] must produce very adverse reactions on the hypersensitive minds of many mental patients.

Schizophrenic reactions of adults vary. There may be anxiety, accompanied by fantasy and hallucinations. There may be *catatonia,* in which the individual assumes a rigid position from which he does not move for days. It has been suggested that he may fear quite literally that any moving on his part will provoke some retaliation from the staff.[29]

MANIC-DEPRESSIVE PSYCHOTIC REACTIONS

The manic-depressive reactions were initially classified together because there was believed to be a cyclical vacillation from a depressed anxious state to one of excited optimistic and assertive behavior. The manic is still depressed, however. But by his manic behavior he helps to overcome his melancholy and anxiety. Thus the manic distracts himself. His behavior is in a sense an exaggerated variety of "whistling in the dark." Manic individuals are "snapping out" of their depression by asserting the opposite type of feelings.[30] The manic-depressive syndrome does not, however, always occur together or in sequence. Some persons withdraw into a depressed state without

[25] *Ibid.,* pp. 224–225.
[26] *Ibid.,* pp. 225–227.
[27] Edward J. Stainbrook, "The Schizophrenic Manic and Depressive Behavioral Reactions," in *Mental Health in the United States, Annals of the American Academy of Political and Social Science,* 286:45–54 (March, 1953).
[28] Deutsch, *op. cit.*
[29] Stainbrook, *op. cit.*
[30] *Ibid.*

a later manic phase, and vice versa. They are simply the psychologically depressed.

PARANOID PSYCHOTIC REACTIONS

Paranoidal reactions often complicate schizophrenic psychoses. The paranoid has delusions of power or grandeur which he projects onto other people. He imagines that they are trying to outbest him or connive against him. If a person fails to communicate effectively with his associates, this may intensify his belief that others are hostile or critical.[31]

The war taught us much about paranoidal reactions. They were particularly common among prisoners of war who developed a high degree of anxiety. Often they were unable because of a language barrier to communicate with their captors, and sometimes they could not talk at all with other prisoners. Aliens also have a high incidence of schizophrenic paranoia and this too is apparently related to inability to communicate their needs, wishes, and fears. They often become very suspicious and believe that others are trying to arrest them or deport them. Many such paranoids become intensely emotional and fearful.

The Neuroses

The neuroses are emotional illnesses in which there is either a pseudophysical ailment or an extreme nervous condition without any discoverable physical abnormality and without any severance of contact with reality. The neurotic does not imagine he is Napoleon nor does he have other systematic intellectual delusions. Instead he may develop functional physical illnesses or he may become an alcoholic or drug addict in order to escape the tensions in his daily life. His anxiety may also result in ineffective personal relationships, or it may take the form of indigestion, constipation, or sex frigidity. His real trouble is that he is maladapted to the life he is living.

The tensions and stresses of everyday life, whether they arise out of marital difficulties, the failure to achieve a much-hoped-for promotion, a loss of job, or some other disturbing experience, may set off neurotic behavior. Most people are able to adjust to problems of living without any extreme or long-enduring reactions. Whether or not a man (or woman) can accept a crisis situation relatively calmly depends partly (1) upon his heredity and constitutional make-up and partly (2) upon his early life experiences and how he has met pain and difficulties in the past.[32] If a boy has always been allowed to run away from reality while in grammar school, at a later date he may not be able to face an adult difficulty with equanimity. It is always easier to face reality if one has not developed a pattern for escaping it.

---

[31] Ibid.

[32] Ernest W. Burgess, "Social Factors in the Etiology and Prevention of Mental Disorders," Social Problems, 1:53–56 (October, 1953). Cf. also Arnold Rose, "Factors in Mental Breakdown in Combat," in Arnold Rose (ed.), Mental Health and Mental Disorder, W. W. Norton and Company, Inc., New York, 1955, pp. 291–313, especially p. 311.

If the individual feels guilty because of something he did to precipitate an unpleasant situation, he later may turn his hostility toward himself and become depressed. Instead of surveying the ways and means by which he may best solve his particular dilemma, he allows himself to be crushed and defeated, with accompanying hostile reactions.[33]

The hostilities of such individuals are not released as are those of the normal person, who learns to overlook the idiosyncracies and animosities of others. The normal person recognizes that parents are at times unreasonable or overcritical. They sometimes punish on an unwarranted basis—but they also love their children. Likewise relatives, friends, and husbands and wives have to learn to forgive each other for individual faults and petty outbursts of temper. They too can be expected to love again—if they are not mutually overcome by their expressed hostilities. The emotionally mature person realizes this, but the neurotic goes on to emphasize the negative in his work, friends, and social relationships.

Neuroses take a variety of forms. A common neurosis is *hysteria,* in which the emotional conflict is converted into a simulated disease of blindness, deafness, or paralysis. There may be *motor* symptoms such as spasms or *somatic* symptoms with nausea. Sometimes there is *amnesia,* and the patient may forget who he is or where he is. There may also be *obsessive compulsive reactions* so that the person has to repeat an unreasonable type of behavior —walk only on certain streets or stay in bed the same day each month.[34]

Psychopathic Personality Disorders

A psychopathic personality has been defined facetiously as "a person who is not insane but who behaves as though he were." Such persons are erratic and noncooperative, tend to be egocentric, and always behave to suit themselves, without any consideration for others. They have few loyalties. They "expect to be forgiven but have no capacity to forgive." They are often cruel and dishonest in their personal relationships. Many criminals are "egocentric psychopaths" and feel little remorse for their behavior.[35] Other psychopathic persons may be excitable and behave childishly with uncontrolled anger outbursts. Some sex offenders fall into this group of uninhibited persons.

Early Symptoms of Mental Illness

A little worry about the best solution to a given difficulty will not hurt anyone. Any crisis—whether a death in the family, an unexpected illness, an injury from an accident, being called into military service, the loss of a job, or disappointment in a friend—calls for intelligence and a rallying of one's internal and external resources. Fortunately most people, in popular

---

[33] Sol Wiener Ginsburg, "The Neuroses," *Mental Health in the United States, Annals of the American Academy of Political and Social Science,* 286:55–64 (March, 1953).
[34] Strecker, *op. cit.,* pp. 167–172.
[35] Hartwell, *op cit.,* pp. 331–332.

parlance, "can take it." Everyone has to live through emotionally upsetting experiences. Life is filled with them.

Some people have difficulty in shaking their anxieties and tensions, however, and others seem to create crises by their own emotional responses to situations. Such people become fearful and suspicious toward those with whom they are associated. They may even project their feelings on one or two persons and make them embody all their own ill feelings. These are the danger signals. The National Association for Mental Health has developed a little pamphlet for persons who have prolonged anxiety. A series of questions are presented as a guide to one's mental health. They include the following:

Do minor problems and disappointments throw you into a dither?
Do you find it difficult to get along with people and are people having trouble getting along with you?
Do the small pleasures of life fail to satisfy you?
Are you unable to stop thinking of your anxieties?
Do you fear people in situations that never used to trouble you?
Are you suspicious of people, mistrustful of your friends?
Do you have the feeling of being trapped?
Do you feel inadequate, suffer tortures of self-doubt?

If a person's answers are "yes" to most of these questions, he is given eleven things to do. These are listed below:

1. Talk it out with some trustworthy person in whom you can confide.
2. Escape for a while, with a brief trip.
3. Work off the anger which has arisen. Don't explode but use your energy constructively.
4. Give in occasionally, even when you are sure you are right.
5. Do something for others instead of worrying about yourself.
6. Take one thing at a time.
7. Shun the superman urge. Don't expect too much of yourself.
8. Go easy with your criticism. People who are really let down about themselves are the ones who feel let down by others' shortcomings.
9. Give the other fellow a break instead of trying to edge out your competitors. If the other person does not feel you are a threat, he stops being one.
10. Make yourself available. You are probably left out because you don't make the first move.
11. Schedule your recreation and be sure to take it. Throw yourself into a hobby in your hours off.

Taking such advice is not always easy for incipient mental cases. If any disturbed person finds it impossible to follow such advice, he should see a psychiatrist.

Mental Patients Receiving Treatment in Hospitals in 1955

In 1955 there were 76,915 first admissions to the 226 private mental hospitals and 160,771 first admissions to the 333 general hospitals with psychiatric facilities.[36] This was approximately twice the 119,321 first admissions to public mental hospitals. Public mental hospitals also had 54,442 readmissions, which included patients with a previous record (either private or public).

Most of the first admissions to public mental hospitals are for long-time care, whereas most patients in private institutions receive short-time care. Patients in residence in private mental hospitals totaled 14,590 at the end of 1955, and 6459 were in general hospitals with psychiatric facilities.[37] The majority of mental patients in private and general hospitals were thus short-term patients, whereas 557,969 patients were in residence in public mental hospitals.[38] The bulk of patients requiring prolonged care are thus confined in public institutions. These constitute most of the serious cases.

Improvements in Hospital Treatment

We have gone a long way since the first mental hospital in the United States was opened in Connecticut in 1821. Nevertheless much of the treatment in public hospitals is woefully inadequate and at times has been shamefully brutal. Many state hospitals have been staffed with physicians having little or no special training in mental disease and orderlies and their assistants have often been incompetent or cruel in dealing with their emotionally disturbed charges.

In recent years, particularly during and since World War II, mental hospitals have improved considerably. Albert Deutsch's book *The Shame of the States*[39] revealed shocking conditions in many state hospitals which he described in vivid detail. Some institutions he inspected were unbelievably medieval. Most were overcrowded and inexcusably dirty. Sometimes patients were kept in damp, dingy basements. Often they went weeks without diagnosis. Food was unbalanced. Even worse, the patients were often mistreated by the attendants. The public became aroused by these disclosures and psychiatrists themselves began to take greater interest in proper treatment.

The extensive problem of emotional disorders among our armed services during the war made the medical profession acutely conscious of the extent of psychiatric disorders. Between January, 1942, and June, 1945, 918,961 of the 15 million admissions to army hospitals were for neuropsychiatric services. Of these, 586,516 were for psychoneuroses (now generally called neuroses). An additional 256,134 were discharged from the army because of emotional disturbance.[40] This experience with disturbed soldiers unques-

[36] *Patients in Mental Institutions, 1955,* part III, p. 13. These were the hospitals for which there was information. Only 226 out of 309 known private mental hospitals reported, 333 of 530 known general hospitals with psychiatric facilities, 216 out of 217 prolonged-care public mental hospitals, and 47 out of 48 public psychiatric hospitals.

[37] *Ibid.,* p. 33.

[38] *Patients in Mental Institutions, 1955,* part II, pp. 12–13.

[39] Published by Harcourt, Brace and Company, New York, 1948.

[40] William C. Menninger, *Psychiatry in a Troubled World,* The Macmillan Company, New York, 1948, pp. 127–128.

tionably had an important impact upon mental hospitals and psychiatry. Dr. William C. Menninger of the famed Menninger Clinic of Topeka, Kansas, headed the psychiatric services in the army. When he returned to Kansas he and his brother helped to reorganize the Kansas State Mental Hospitals. They set up a training school for psychiatrists at the Menninger Foundation, which they created and which is administered as a part of the University of Kansas. The Menningers' influence has been far reaching. They not only revamped the treatment of the mentally ill in Kansas but are now training psychiatrists who work with patients in other states.

Great improvements have been developed by psychiatrists in many other states, but mental hospitals have far to go to equal the institutions that care for physical disorders.

Diagnosis of Civilian Mental Patients in Hospitals

An examination of Tables 12.1, 12.2, and 12.3 shows that the largest category of first admissions to private mental hospitals and general hospitals with psychiatric facilities (hereafter called general hospitals) during 1955 and of resident patients in public mental hospitals at the end of 1955 received treatment for psychotic disorders. Over half of the resident patients in public mental hospitals (244,899 out of 410,539), nearly half of the first admissions to private mental hospitals (19,933 out of 41,711), and approximately a third of the first admissions to general hospitals (52,817 out of 153,521) were psychotic.[41]

Despite the much larger number of total patients in public mental hospitals the combined cases of *involutional* melancholia in private and general hospitals (11,026) was about the same as in public mental hospitals (11,012). Since these cases usually receive short-term treatment they can more often afford private care than can most psychotic patients. On the other hand, the vast majority of manic depressives (a recurrent disorder) and schizophrenics are most likely to be confined in public mental hospitals.

The largest percentage of patients with brain syndromes were in public hospitals. Twenty-seven percent of patients (110,863 of a total of 410,539) in public mental hospitals had brain syndromes, 24 percent of the patients in general hospitals (37,113 of 153,521) had such symptoms, but only 16 percent (6732 out of 41,711) of the patients in private mental hospitals had brain symptoms. On the other hand, most of the cases of *acute* brain syndromes (13,055) were patients in general hospitals. Over half of these had acute alcoholic disturbances. The great majority of syphilitic brain syndrome cases are in public hospitals. This group has declined markedly since antibiotic drug treatment has come into use.

Neurotics and those suffering from various types of non-psychotic dis-

[41] For purposes of the present analysis, data on first admissions to private mental hospitals and general hospitals were used since the cases were mostly for short-term treatment and the total number of first admissions gives a much better picture of the cases treated.

orders are more apt to be treated in general hospitals than in either public or private mental hospitals presumably because they are admitted as medical patients. Over 42 percent of the mental cases in general hospitals (63,591 out of 153,521) were receiving treatment for neurotic disorders or personality disorders. Sixteen percent (6732 of 41,711) of the cases in private mental hospitals were neurotic or personality problems, as were about 13 percent (54,597 of 410,539) of the diagnosed patients in public mental hospitals.

SOCIAL FACTORS IN MENTAL ILLNESS

Social Strains in Modern Life

A major share of mental disorganization is the result of inability to adjust to the strains of modern life. Tensions in international relations, the struggle for material possessions, the problems of sexual maladjustment, the frustrations of the job, the aggressions engendered by competition, the migration which involves marked cultural adjustment, the pervasive attempt to rise in the social scale, the discrimination against minority groups, and the hidden memories of unhappy family relationships—these and many other factors combine to increase the difficulty of living in the age of the cold war and the intercontinental ballistic missile. In studying them, sociologists have contributed significantly to the new field of social psychiatry.[42]

Much mental disorganization is partially, at least, caused by frustration and anxiety. The modern social structure is so organized that many persons are unable to receive the love, recognition, prestige, acceptance, and security which they strongly desire. Such values are, for the most part, derived from interpersonal relationships. An individual must be loved, recognized, and accepted *by someone else*—whether it be husband, wife, parents, comrades, business associates, or friends. In other words, his mental organization depends upon successful communication with others, and their assurance that he is loved, admired, and cherished. At the same time, he may become overanxious either lest he be deprived of this assurance in the future or because he has been deprived of it in the past.[43]

Mental disorganization is thus a function of inadequate communication. The mentally deficient person is usually handicapped from birth in his ability to communicate with others. His personality never really develops. *The neurotic can communicate but his ability to communicate is impaired by unconscious anxiety. The psychotic withdraws from normal social contacts* and as a result lives in a "world of his own." All such cases, whether defective, neurotic, or psychotic, are isolated in one degree or another from their as-

---

[42] Cf. H. Warren Dunham, "Social Psychiatry," *American Sociological Review, 13:* 183–197 (April, 1948); Schermerhorn, *op. cit.*

[43] Harry Stack Sullivan, *The Interpersonal Theory of Psychiatry,* W. W. Norton and Company, Inc., New York, 1953, "Introduction."

sociates in the sense that they are unable to interact effectively. The feeble-minded are never truly organized, whereas the neurotic and psychotic are disorganized. In the psychotic's case, his interpersonal adjustments become truly intolerable.

Where the social environment fosters isolation, the mental disorganization rate tends to be high. Modern life is especially conducive to such isolation, whether in the community, on the job, or in other personal relationships. Among the factors in modern society that interfere with mental health in this sense are the growing pressures on the small businessman; the increasing anonymity of big business and industry; the growing decentralization of the family through the employment of married women; and the extension of automation, which cuts down contact between men on the job.[44] In the urban community most people no longer know their neighbors. City people move frequently and tend to retain old friendships without bothering about new ones.

Urban rates for mental disorder are much higher than rural rates. An analysis made of a large number of studies of urban and rural rates for all mental disorders and for classified psychoses showed urban rates markedly higher for all three categories. There are reasons for this. Urban life is conducive to both isolation and mobility. Obviously most mobile people are not mental cases. Nevertheless, a person who has deep roots in a community tends to have a stable personality.[45]

Alexander Leighton has pointed out the role of the social environment in fostering or undermining mental health, as the case may be. He lists the goals which normal individuals find necessary for mental health: "(1) physical security; (2) sexual satisfaction; (3) the expression of hostility; (4) the expression of love; (5) the securing of love; (6) the obtaining of recognition; (7) the expression of spontaneity; (8) orientation in regard to one's place in society and the place of others; (9) membership in a definite human group; (10) a sense of belonging to a moral order and of being right in what one does."[46]

It is self-evident that most of these goals cannot be achieved without satisfactory group relationships. Social disorganization, as we have discussed earlier, arises when group relationships are strained or broken. Well-organized individuals can meet the strain of mobility, broken relationships, and cultural change, but those less stable may develop symptoms of emotional disturbance. Any social situation that increases disorganized relationships thus fosters mental illness. The individual who is isolated from group contacts and is unable to love, to enjoy friendship, acceptance, and recognition may be in danger of mental disorganization. By the same token the

[44] Cf. Rose, *op. cit.,* pp. 99–101, and Jules Henry, "Cultural Change and Mental Health," *Mental Hygiene,* 41:323–326 (July, 1957).

[45] Melvin L. Kohn and John A. Clausen, "Social Isolation and Schizophrenia," *American Sociological Review,* 20:265–273 (June, 1955).

[46] Alexander H. Leighton, "Psychiatric Disorder and Social Environment," *Psychiatry,* 18:367–383 (November, 1955), pp. 375–376.

society that deprives many of its members of personal satisfactions will have a high rate of mental illness.[47]

In any society some people suffer more deprivations than others. That is, some are more favored with reference to income, racial background, ethnic status, class advantages, education, employment, occupational prestige, family stability, and exposure to dangers of war. These are a few of the differentials that distinguish the rate of mental disorganization among groups. Concern over personal handicaps seems to precipitate more mental illness than anxiety over the welfare of other people. Bereavement thus is more disorganizing than worry over relatives in danger. But in any event persons who participate fully in modern culture and have relatively few worries about income, prejudice, or lack of education appear to have a lower rate of mental illness than persons who are unable to enjoy the full fruits of our present civilization. Most of the studies made in social psychiatry are concerned with one or more of these differential factors.[48]

Work and Mental Illness

A person's work is often a source of strain both because of competition and because of the frustration of individual goals. So much significance is attached to income and good jobs in our society that the failure to achieve better pay or a more desirable job may produce mental illness. Some men and women are much disturbed when they see others given positions of responsibility, higher pay, and greater prestige. Consequently relationships with their superiors become increasingly unpleasant while their working hours are filled with frustration, anxiety, and unhappiness. The fault may be with the boss, who makes things so difficult for his subordinates that some develop neurotic reactions. Others learn to take major and minor irritations in their stride. Many of the most important and difficult life adjustments are those "on the job."[49] Physicians recognize this and often advise nervous, tense people to seek different employment.

Work is the source of other mental strains, one of the most important of which is job insecurity. For the industrially employed the hazards of unemployment are commonplace. Being unemployed is not only a financial disaster. It is a threat to one's esteem. For those sure of their job there may be no possibility of securing a more desirable one, or one they would prefer. Most persons have to recognize that they will never reach an executive position. Hollingshead and Redlich found a sense of frustration and despair common among the lower class in New Haven. These people "felt that their jobs were unsatisfactory; they worried about how long they would last, the nature of the work, that they did not pay enough to meet the needs of their

---

[47] Burgess, *op. cit.*

[48] E. Gartly Jaco, "Social Factors in Mental Disease in Texas," *Social Problems, 4:*322–328 (April, 1957).

[49] Cf. Robert Dubin, *The World of Work,* Prentice-Hall, Inc., Englewood Cliffs, N.J., 1958. This book discusses many of the emotional problems of work.

families, that there was no advancement, [and] that the job carried no status. . . ."[50]

For the average person, work is also the most conspicuous aspect of personal success or failure. Competition is the basis of work and money is the most tangible form of reward. Concern with money may become a neurotic complex, as people compete for it as the symbol of success. Some persons, obsessed with money and failing to secure as much as they want, become neurotically depressed. Money ceases to be a means to an end but becomes an end in itself. Psychiatrists report that the difficulties of many of their mental patients center about money.[51]

According to the norms of our society, an individual will rise in the social scale through his own activities. Failure to do so may bring mental strain, as the difference between achievement and expectations makes itself apparent to the individual, his family, and his associates. A study of schizophrenic patients disclosed less upward status mobility among them than among a control group of persons who were not mentally ill. Schizophrenics were not, in this study, "status achievers," and this fact may have a definite bearing upon their mental problems. Whether they have been unable to achieve status *because* of their schizophrenic tendencies or whether the latter resulted from their *failure* to move upward is not clear. In any case, persons who become schizophrenic are apparently found to a disproportionate degree among the "failures" in this world.[52]

Migration and Mental Illness

A number of studies show that migration is conducive to mental illness. Migration involves the physical departure of an individual from his cultural surroundings and the consequent necessity of adjusting to a new set of interpersonal relationships.[53] The immigrant who leaves the Old World and comes to the New is the most obvious example of migration. But the individual who leaves the country and comes to the metropolis is also migrating. In each case, the person quite literally breaks his former relationships and is forced to form new ones in a strange setting. Failure to make these adjustments satisfactorily may result in mental illness.[54]

This was made evident in a study of first admissions to New York hospitals over a three-year period. Here the admission rates for migrants was much higher than for non-migrants where the factors of age, sex, and color were controlled. Manic depressive, schizophrenic, and other psychoses

[50] August B. Hollingshead *et al.,* "Social Mobility and Mental Illness," *American Sociological Review, 19:*577–584 (October, 1954), p. 584.

[51] Stanley A. Leavy and Lawrence Z. Freedman, "Psychoneurosis and Economic Life," *Social Forces, 4:*55–67 (July, 1956).

[52] Mary H. Lystad, "Social Mobility Among Selected Groups of Schizophrenic Patients," *American Sociological Review, 22:*288–292 (June, 1957).

[53] William Peterson, "A General Typology of Migration," *American Sociological Review, 23:*256–266 (June, 1958).

[54] Migration and social disorganization are discussed in Chapter 25.

were found to be 20 percent higher for foreign-born females than for native white females. Admission rates for native-born migrants from other states were even higher, with a rate from 60 to 100 percent higher than for native-born New Yorkers. Among nonwhites (chiefly Negroes) the rate of first admissions was three times as high among migrants as among non-migrants. The necessity of adjusting to strange surroundings undoubtedly augments mental difficulties.[55]

Another study of mental patients, in New Haven, disclosed further relationships between migration and mental illness. A significant difference was discovered between the native-born and the foreign-born with respect to the emotional disorders, the illnesses of old age, and the organic illnesses. The figures do not necessarily represent the percentages of mental disease in the population of New Haven as a whole, but merely of those persons under the care of a psychiatrist. Many foreign-born persons are unwilling to seek mental assistance and hence may have been underrepresented in this study. But in terms of those who sought psychiatric treatment, the role of migration appears to be significant.[56]

Race, Ethnic Background, and Mental Illness

Mobility and migration may be augmented by many other factors that interfere with communication and isolate the individual from full participation. Differences in ethnic background, religion, and racial heritage thus retard assimilation and bar migrants from communication. Ethnic migrants may experience personality disorganization while racial minorities may have inadequate cultural participation from the beginning.[57] Prejudice may isolate the minority group member from intimate interaction with others, and this deprivation may in turn precipitate mental illness. As has been stated, "Sociocultural situations which interfere with the opportunity to interact with a fairly large number of different kinds of other people limit personality development and hence foster psychiatric disorder."[58]

A study made in the thirties of Negro and white rates of mental illness in Illinois showed the Negro rate of first admissions to be two and one-half times that of the white. Most of these Negroes migrated from the southern states in search of better opportunities.[59] In the large cities of the North, Negroes have also contributed disproportionately to the crime rates. The frustrations which they experienced in the North probably contributed to their high rate both of crime and of mental illness. In Alabama, on the

---

[55] Benjamin Malzberg and Everett Lee, *A Study of First Admissions to Hospitals for Mental Disease,* Social Science Research Council, New York, 1956, pp. 119–120.

[56] Bertram H. Roberts and Jerome K. Myers, "Religion, National Origin, Immigration, and Mental Illness," *American Journal of Psychiatry, 110*:759–764 (April, 1954).

[57] "The Effects of Segregation and the Consequences of Desegregation: A Social Science Statement," *Journal of Negro Education, 22*:68–76 (Winter, 1953).

[58] Leighton, *op. cit.,* p. 383.

[59] Joseph S. Jacob, "A Comparative Study of the Incidence of Insanity Among Negroes and Whites," *Bulletin of the University of Georgia, 37*:13–16 (1938).

other hand, the Negro rate of mental illness is approximately the same as that of the white. Negroes have an equally low (if not lower) status in Alabama than in Illinois. But their problems in Illinois are complicated by mobility, culture shock, and ambiguity of status.

A later study of first admissions to state mental hospitals in Ohio disclosed even more decisive racial differences. Negroes had much higher rates than whites, as a group, for syphilitic psychosis, alcoholic psychosis, and schizophrenia. Schizophrenia is the most prevalent form of psychotic illness and is closely related to social isolation. Because of his race, the Negro is cut off from effective communication with many aspects of American life. Negroes on first admission in Ohio ranked low in income, occupation, education, and socioeconomic status.[60]

Ethnic differences are themselves barriers to communication. In certain communities, persons of Italian descent are subject to discrimination; in other places doors are closed to those of Irish descent. In some areas Jews may be isolated from complete cultural participation. Membership in a minority ethnic group, in short, is often a "source of stress" for the individual, if he is held back occupationally, socially, and culturally.[61]

A recent study of mental illness in Texas throws additional light upon the problems of ethnic minorities. The Spanish-American group in that state form an important ethnic minority, whose members generally are not accepted by the native Anglo-Americans. Their adjustment problems are evidenced in a higher incidence of manic depressive and involutional psychoses than appears among native groups. On the other hand, the number of cases of schizophrenia (and a few other types of mental disorder) were considerably lower among the Spanish Americans.[62] The Spanish Americans apparently do not seek psychiatric treatment for the less violent forms of mental illness. The manic depressive and involutional forms are so serious, however, that some sort of treatment is necessary.

Ecological Aspects of Mental Illness

Mental illness is related to position in the social structure, as the discussion on occupation, mobility, ethnic group, and race has made clear. All affect the individual's position in our culture. The pioneer study of Faris and Dunham on the ecological aspects of mental illness pointed out the differential impact of urban neighborhoods on mental disease. These sociologists studied the distribution of mental disease in various parts of Chicago and found that schizophrenia cases were concentrated in the cheap rooming-house districts where homeless men lived. In the central business district and in the deteriorated Negro communities there was also a higher than

[60] Robert M. Frumkin, "Race and Major Mental Disorders: A Research Note," *Journal of Negro Education, 23:*97–98 (Winter, 1954).

[61] Paul Barrabee and Otto Von Mering, "Ethnic Variations in Mental Illness in Families with Psychotic Children," *Social Problems, 1:*48–53 (October, 1953), p. 50.

[62] Jaco, *op. cit.*

average rate. Social isolation was the most characteristic aspect of these areas, whether on basis of sex (for homeless men), ethnic, or immigrant isolation or racial isolation in the case of Negroes.[63]

Cases with manic depressive psychoses, on the other hand, were not concentrated but were scattered randomly throughout the city although they apparently came from better residential areas and higher-class levels than was true for schizophrenics.[64]

The fact of the ecological distribution of schizophrenia has been clearly established, even though the nature of the distribution may vary in industrial and political-type communities.[65] There is a lack of agreement as to why this distribution occurs. Some psychiatrists maintain that actual or potential schizophrenics "naturally" find their way to depressed urban areas and thus swell the rates in such sections. Others hold that the social isolation of individuals living in high-mobility neighborhoods makes it difficult for them to maintain communication, which in turn, results in schizophrenic symptoms. Still others believe that social isolation is an important factor in schizophrenia but are perplexed as to why some persons become mentally ill and others do not.[66] On the surface it would seem that the stronger the life organization of the individual the less likely he is to become mentally ill. There is need for more research in the effect of ecology on mental illness.

Social Class and Mental Illness

Social class, as indicated in the recent research of Hollingshead and Redlich, is probably more significantly related to mental illness than is ecology per se. Social class is a broad and inclusive concept which includes not merely the position of the individual in the social structure but such factors as occupation, income, education, cultural values, "way of life," family background, participation in outside groups, ethnic status, religious denomination, expectations of mobility, and self-identification.[67] Inasmuch as mental health involves the individual as a whole, class is perhaps the most important *single* variable in the etiology of mental illness.[68]

Hollingshead and Redlich's study was concerned with mental health of the various social classes in New Haven and they found a *significant inverse relationship* between social class and mental illness. That is, the lowest overall

[63] Robert E. L. Faris and H. Warren Dunham, *Mental Disorders in Urban Areas,* University of Chicago Press, Chicago, 1939, chap. 3.

[64] *Ibid.,* chap. 4. Also H. Warren Dunham, "Some Persistent Problems in the Epidemiology of Mental Disorders," *American Journal of Psychiatry, 109*:567–575 (February, 1953).

[65] Ivan Belknap and E. Gartly Jaco, "The Epidemiology of Mental Disorders in a Political-Type City, 1946–1952," *Interrelations Between the Social Environment and Psychiatric Disorders,* Milbank Memorial Fund, New York, 1953.

[66] John A. Clausen and Melvin L. Kohn, "The Ecological Approach in Social Psychiatry," *American Journal of Sociology, 60*:140–151 (September, 1954).

[67] Walter Goldschmidt, "Social Class in America—A Critical Review," *American Anthropologist, 52*:483–498 (October–December, 1950).

[68] Hollingshead and Redlich, *op. cit.*

mental illness rates were in the upper classes and the highest rates were in the lower classes. The farther down the inhabitants of New Haven descended in the social scale the higher the per capita rate of mental illness. The population of the city was divided into five classes—upper, upper-middle, middle, working, and lower. The classes were numbered from 1 to 5 with the upper class assigned to number 1, the lower class to number 5. The crude rate of mental illness per 100,000 population for each class was then adjusted for age and sex with the following results: Classes I and II, which were combined, had a rate of 553 per 100,000 of the population; Class III had a rate of 528 (the only distortion in the general curve); Class IV had a rate of 642 and Class V a rate of 1668 per 100,000 population, as Table 12.4 shows.[69]

TABLE 12.4. Incidence of Mental Illness
According to Class in New Haven

Class	Adjusted Rate of Mental Illness per 100,000
I and II	553
III	528
IV	665
V	1,668

SOURCE: August B. Hollingshead and Frederick C. Redlich, *Social Class and Mental Illness*, John Wiley and Sons, Inc., New York, 1958, p. 210.

TABLE 12.5. Incidence of Mental Illness According to Marital Status by Class in Comparison to Number of Marital Status in Population According to Class

Class	Percent of Cases	Percent of Class
Married Patients		
I–II	10.8	12.8
III	15.3	22.1
IV	42.3	48.9
V	31.6	16.3
Separated, Divorced, and Widowed Patients		
I–II	5.1	8.6
III	12.9	16.7
IV	35.7	48.6
V	46.3	26.1
Unmarried Patients		
I–II	6.4	9.9
III	12.7	17.9
IV	40.6	50.1
V	40.3	23.0

SOURCE: August B. Hollingshead and Frederick C. Redlich, *Social Class and Mental Illness*, John Wiley and Sons, Inc., New York, 1958, p. 203.

[69] *Ibid.*, p. 210.

TABLE 12.6.   Percentage of Mental Patients in
New Haven According to Race and Class

		White Patients	*Population*
Class	I–II	8.3	11.7
	III	14.2	20.8
	IV	41.1	50.1
	V	36.4	17.4
		Negro Patients	*Population*
Class	I–II	0.0	1.0
	III	6.3	4.0
	IV	14.6	36.9
	V	79.1	58.1

SOURCE: August B. Hollingshead and Frederick C.
Redlich, *Social Class and Mental Illness*, John Wiley and
Sons, Inc., New York, 1958, p. 202.

A further analysis of the rates of mental illness, according to marital status, showed the same general increase with a descent in class, except that the highest rate of mental illness for married persons was in Class IV and the next highest in Class V. For persons with broken family relationships (i.e., separated, widowed, divorced), the distribution followed the inverse relationship from highest to lowest class. The highest rate of mental illness among those with broken homes was thus found in the lowest class, the next highest in the working class, the next in the middle class, and the lowest rate in the upper-middle and upper. The two highest classes were lumped together for statistical purposes because of the comparatively small number in these groups.[70]

When these cases were analyzed according to race, the rates of mental illness followed the same general trend as in the married population, i.e., the highest rates were in Class IV and the next highest in Class V. The rate of mental illness was extremely high in Class V, but the majority of Negroes were in this class. At the same time, rates for Negroes in the middle class were comparatively low, thus further suggesting that class factors, rather than race as such, are important in causing mental illness. The majority of whites were in Class IV, and the greatest number of persons experiencing social stress were in this group.[71]

The Hollingshead and Redlich study thus indicates conclusively that position in the social structure tends to affect mental health. Economic stress, physical illness, family disorganization, and psychological frustration increase as one descends the social scale. The hazards to mental health are greater in the lower class, and schizophrenia is especially prevalent in this group. Neurotic illness seems to be more common among the middle and upper classes, at least as far as those seeking treatment is concerned. Treatment of neuroses involves communication between the patient and the

[70] *Ibid.*, p. 203.
[71] *Ibid.*, p. 202.

psychiatrist, and many lower-class neurotics are apparently either unwilling to seek medical care or unable to profit by it once they have it.[72]

War and Mental Illness

War is one of the most disorganizing aspects of modern society and imposes great strains upon both soldiers and civilians (particularly those civilians in combat areas). As mentioned earlier, approximately 6 percent (918,961) of the 15 million admissions to army hospitals from January, 1942, to June, 1945, were for psychoneurotic disorders.[73] Many of these men would not have been mentally ill under peacetime conditions but broke under the tremendous strains of danger, "of killing and being killed," and of the reversals in social values characteristic of war time. The great discipline required on the field of battle and in aerial warfare was more than some men could endure. Nevertheless the psychiatric division of the Medical Division of the Army found that a large number of those who collapsed emotionally during or after combat had had a previous history of ineffectiveness or nervous instability.

In some cases, the factors contributing to mental disorganization were complex, as may be illustrated in the case of a young pilot flying in formation who was ordered to fire at a target. He did so and hit the wing of a buddy's plane. Inasmuch as he was obeying orders, he was in no way legally culpable. But the fact that he might have moved his plane and thus avoided hitting his friend's plane continued to haunt him. Psychoanalysis revealed that the disturbed pilot was jealous of his friend and anxious to excel him. His friend flew out of formation, presumably because he was overcompetitive. Basic to the whole situation, however, was unconscious hostility.[74] Other studies have indicated that more neuroses and psychoses among the armed services were due to *unconscious* conflicts than to *conscious* strains.[75]

Among the civilian population exposed to enemy air raids many exhibited "temporary acute behavioral disorders," i.e., shock, extreme fright, loss of memory, and similar disfunctions. At the same time, the civilian populations of England, France, and Germany showed no marked increase in *chronic* mental disorders during or after World War II. Where severe and prolonged mental illness occurred psychiatrists have held that a predisposition to it was present before the traumatic experience. Persons who broke down under the shock of bombing and other dangers thus tended to have temperamental difficulties, unconscious conflicts, or other hostilities and inadequacies, dating back to early experience. After the shock of air raids, the majority were able to resume normal activities in a few hours, days, or perhaps weeks.[76]

[72] Jerome K. Myers and Leslie Schaffer, "Social Stratification and Psychiatric Practice: A Study of an Out-Patient Clinic," *American Sociological Review,* 19:307–310 (June, 1954).

[73] Menninger, *Psychiatry in a Troubled World*, pp. 126–127.

[74] Roy R. Grinker and John P. Spiegel, *Men Under Stress,* The Blakiston Company, Philadelphia, 1945, pp. 313–314.

[75] Cf., for example, Irving L. Janis, *Air War and Emotional Stress,* McGraw-Hill Book Company, Inc., New York, 1951, pp. 77–79.

[76] *Ibid.,* pp. 92–96.

Children, like adults, varied in their reaction to danger. In general, children reacted according to the degree of anxiety of their parents, but there was also evidence of marked "startle reactions" and severe fright at night as aftermaths of these experiences. Prolonged or chronic reactions were rare, but even so, many children cried in their sleep for a long time after a serious shock. Some undoubtledly suffered emotionally as the result of improper diet. Still others had emotional problems resulting from exposure to war conditions. A Dutch war orphan left homeless by German air raids and later adopted by an American psychiatrist was strongly aggressive toward her foster parents and for several months responded to their efforts to be kind by biting and kicking them. Her hostility was largely a matter of fear, resulting from her own shocking experience. Her psychiatrist foster father, however, finally resorted to kicking and biting her. Only then did she learn that to receive kindness she must merit kindness.[77]

Family and Mental Illness

The family has often been called the cradle of personality. The child's early experiences in the family involve the most important series of social contacts he is likely to have. During the formative years the child's relationships with his parents (especially his mother) carry strong emotional overtones. The mother provides the satisfaction for many of his basic needs —ranging from food to love. The extent to which these needs are supplied by the mother—and to a lesser degree by the father and the siblings—go far in determining the child's mental and emotional structure. We cannot go into this subject in detail, but some of the relationships between family experience and subsequent emotional adjustment should be indicated.[78]

The child is born into a group relationship that is already established. The emotional tone of this group is an important factor in the child's subsequent emotional adjustment. The child who perceives that his parents are in constant and bitter conflict is bound to be insecure. His own difficulties may take the form of juvenile delinquency, in which he unconsciously tries to punish his parents for what they have done to him. In a sense he is "rejecting" his parents, and he indicates his rejection by actions ranging from irritableness to the malicious destruction of property.[79]

The family probably has an even more direct impact upon mental health. A recent study was made of the life histories of 1000 military men referred to a mental hygiene clinic for emotional and mental problems. Both parents of men with severe psychoneuroses tended to be unstable nervously. On the other hand, the military men whose parents had good nervous stability were generally diagnosed as "without mental disease."[80]

---

[77] Case known to the authors.

[78] A. R. Mangus, "Family Impacts on Mental Health," *Marriage and Family Living,* *19:*256–262 (August, 1957).

[79] F. Ivan Nye, "The Rejected Parent and Delinquency," *Marriage and Family Living,* *18:*291–300 (November, 1956).

[80] Herman R. Lantz, "Nervous Stability of Parents as Reported in a Psychiatric Sample of One Thousand," *Marriage and Family Living, 20:*69–72 (February, 1958).

The emotionally disturbed parent is clearly inadequate to carry out parental responsibilities. He or she is often extremely self-centered, aggressive, hostile, or selfish. Such a parent is usually most concerned with satisfying his or her own emotional needs and may in fact exploit the child as a means of satisfying them. The parent thus may reject the child by punishment, or extreme coldness. Or the parent may attempt to overcome guilt feelings by showering the child with attention, presents, or solicitude. In any case the child suffers.[81]

Where the mother is neurotic or emotionally disturbed she may become overattached to her son or daughter, especially if her own marriage is less successful than she had anticipated.[82] She may unconsciously seek the emotional satisfactions from her son which she fails to receive from her husband. This is particularly likely if the son is an only child. Only sons often have great difficulty in breaking away from their mothers and assuming the adult responsibilities of marriage. Mother may unconsciously feign illness at the mere suggestion of an engagement. They may object to any career that takes the son away from home. Because they appeal to the deep-seated filial love, these mothers in effect exploit their sons emotionally. Many wartime neuroses and psychoses in the armed services were attributed to this emotional immaturity in the form of "Momism."[83]

Where daughters are the victims of such misplaced affection, the situation is equally difficult. In the small, modern, urban family, the mother is usually closer emotionally than the father to daughters, contrary to the suppositions of those adhering to Freudian Oedipus complex theory.[84] The overprotective mother may create all sorts of fears for her daughter—fear of sex, pregnancy, childbirth, and of men in general. In so doing, the mother is unconsciously projecting her hostility against her own marriage and is also trying to satisfy her own frustrated emotions through her daughter.[85]

Modern society exacts an unequal toll of its members. Some persons are more exposed than others to the stresses that produce or intensify mental disorganization. The stresses give rise to anxiety, which in turn interferes with communication. Members of the submerged classes often resent their lot. So, too, do minority groups or those who are continually transferring from one community to another. All of these conditions produce strain on personality organization. When there is great social disorganization such as

[81] *Ibid.*

[82] Lee G. Burchinal *et al.,* "Marriage Adjustment, Personality Characteristics of Parents and the Personality Adjustment of Their Children," *Marriage and Family Living, 19:*366–372 (November, 1957).

[83] Edward A. Strecker, *Their Mothers' Sons,* J. B. Lippincott Company, Philadelphia, 1951.

[84] Robert F. Winch, "Further Data and Observations on the Oedipus Hypothesis: The Consequence of an Inadequate Hypothesis," *American Sociological Review, 16:*784–795 (December, 1951).

[85] Cf. Edward A. Strecker, *Their Mothers' Daughters,* J. B. Lippincott Company, Philadelphia, 1956.

that entailed in modern warfare many persons are upset who would otherwise have had a satisfactory life. Despite the advances in technology and our prosperity and unrivaled standard of living, many persons never make a satisfactory life adjustment. In the words of Henry Thoreau, they continue to live in "quiet desperation." Mental illness is one type of personal disorganization resulting from such strain and anxiety.

SELECTED BIBLIOGRAPHY

Dubin, Robert, *The World of Work,* Prentice-Hall, Inc., Englewood Cliffs, N.J., 1958. In this book the author gives an excellent account of the stresses and strains which occur among workers on the job.

Faris, Robert E. L., and Dunham, H. Warren, *Mental Disorders in Urban Areas,* University of Chicago Press, Chicago, 1939. This was one of the first important studies in the relation between ecology and disease.

Grinker, Roy R., and Spiegel, John P., *Men Under Stress,* The Blakiston Company, Philadelphia, 1945. This book contains many case histories of men who "cracked up" under the strain of war.

Hollingshead, August B., and Redlich, Frederick C., *Social Class and Mental Illness,* John Wiley and Sons, Inc., New York, 1958. Awarded the MacIver prize for its outstanding contribution to sociology, this book involves a detailed and difficult analysis of the problem of class as it affects mental illness.

Lemkau, Paul V., *Mental Hygiene in Public Health,* McGraw-Hill Book Company, Inc., New York, 1955, part II. This book presents an excellent analysis of the role of mental hygiene in public health.

Malzberg, Benjamin, and Lee, Everett, *A Study of First Admissions to Hospitals for Mental Disease,* Social Science Research Council, New York, 1956. This book contains an important study on migration as a factor in mental illness.

Menninger, William C., *Psychiatry, Its Evolution and Present Status,* Cornell University Press, Ithaca, 1948. This book is one of the best analyses of the development and present functions of psychiatry.

Menninger, William C., *Psychiatry in a Troubled World,* The Macmillan Company, New York, 1948. The head of the Psychiatric Services of the United States Army during World War II gives a brilliant and sympathetic study of men who broke under emotional strain.

Mental Health Statistics, Current Reports, Series MHB-H-5, U.S. Department of Health, Education, and Welfare, Public Health Service, National Institute of Mental Health, Washington, May, 1958. These reports, which are available annually, should be consulted for the latest statistics on mental health.

Patients in Mental Institutions, 1955, part II, "Public Hospitals for the Mentally Ill," and part III, "Private Hospitals for the Mentally Ill and General Hospitals with Psychiatric Facilities," U.S. Department of Health, Education, and Welfare, Washington, 1958. These reports give complete details with reference to mental patients, their diagnosis, hospitalization, type of hospital, etc., for the year 1955.

Rose, Arnold (ed.), *Mental Health and Mental Disorder,* W. W. Norton and Company, Inc., New York, 1955. Prepared by a special committee of the Society for the Study of Social Problems, this volume has contributions by some of the ablest people in the field.

Strecker, Edward A., *Fundamentals of Psychiatry*, J. B. Lippincott Company, Philadelphia, 1947 (4th ed.). This is a very readable volume in psychiatry.

Strecker, Edward A., *Their Mothers' Daughters*, J. B. Lippincott Company, Philadelphia, 1956. This volume presents the emotional disorders rooted in daughters' overattachment to their mothers.

Strecker, Edward A., *Their Mothers' Sons*, J. B. Lippincott Company, Philadelphia, 1951. This is a popular presentation of the emotional problems arising from sons' overattachment to their mothers.

Sullivan, Harry Stack, *The Interpersonal Theory of Psychiatry*, W. W. Norton and Company, Inc., New York, 1953. One of the ablest psychiatrists in the United States presents his theory of emotional disorders.

CHAPTER 13

The Suicide

The Nature of Suicide

Suicide, said Durkheim, is the term applied to "all cases of death resulting directly or indirectly from a positive or negative act of the victim himself, which he knows will produce this result."[1] In Western society, suicide is the final and irreversible culmination of personal disorganization. It is the last stage in a series of progressive changes in attitude, from a blind and unthinking love of life to a desire to escape life and all that it means. In other societies, suicide has additional meanings; the individual may kill himself because the group expects him to do so and its ties are very strong. In the latter case, suicide may constitute an index of social *organization* and group cohesion. In our society, however, suicide indicates a *disorganization* of the ties that bind the members of the organized group together.

The number of persons who put an end to their lives in the United States varies from 15,000 to 20,000 each year, depending upon the state of the business cycle and the status of peace or war. Besides these "successful" suicides, an estimated 100,000 persons are "unsuccessful," inasmuch as they try to kill themselves but do not succeed.[2] In addition to the official suicides and recognized suicidal attempts, many suicides are never recorded as such. Among this number are those (1) who deliberately kill themselves (and sometimes others) in automobile accidents; (2) who fail to kill themselves on the first attempt, only to die several days, weeks, or months later, presumably from "natural" causes; and (3) who actually succeed in killing themselves in other ways but the fact is never officially admitted. The statistical data on suicide are thus unreliable and do not begin to indicate the total number of deaths caused by "a positive or negative act of the victim himself."[3]

An estimated 100,000 persons are thus so personally disorganized that they annually attempt suicide unsuccessfully. This fact constitutes a serious commentary on our society. For suicide is primarily a social phenomenon, and the majority of persons who commit suicide reflect the disorganization of the

---

[1] Emile Durkheim, *Suicide* (translated by John A. Spaulding and George Simpson), The Free Press, Glencoe, Ill., 1951, p. 44.

[2] Metropolitan Life Insurance Company, "Suicides That Fail," *Statistical Bulletin*, May, 1941.

[3] Cf. George Simpson, "Methodological Problems in Determining the Aetiology of Suicide," *American Sociological Review, 15*:658–663 (October, 1950).

society. The suicide has broken with the group under the most drastic circumstances. The causes of his act must be sought eventually in the society that formed his personality and that provided the framework within which he lived. The group has insufficient consensus to maintain the integrity of all of its members. In his study of suicide Durkheim has provided the classic analysis of those relationships between the individual and society that culminate in suicide.[4]

The Social Aspects of Suicide

Durkheim analyzes suicide under three general headings—the "altruistic," the "egoistic," and the "anomic." We may consider each of these types, with particular reference to the social factors.

1. *Altruistic Suicide.* Altruistic suicide occurs when the integration of the individual with the group is very close. This type is found among many primitive peoples, where social integration is strong. It is also found in more advanced societies, such as India and Japan, where the sense of social responsibility is highly developed. Under the pressure of the moral codes, persons who are old and enfeebled, women whose husbands are dead, and servants whose masters are deceased are expected to commit suicide. The force of the mores is such that it becomes the *duty* of such persons to kill themselves. The power of social control is so great that suicide is performed in an almost routine fashion by the person socially designated for this fate. "The weight of society," Durkheim held, "is thus brought to bear on him to lead him to destroy himself."[5] The act is imposed by the group to serve its own ends, rather than those of the individual.

The rate of altruistic suicide will thus vary with the integration of the society. Highly integrated societies may be expected to have a high rate of altruistic suicide, whereas those with a lower degree of integration will have a lower rate of such self-destruction, provided, of course, that altruistic suicide is in the mores in the first place. This general relationship is illustrated in a study of suicide and social structure in Ceylon. Wide variations were discovered in the suicide rates of various subcultures within the larger culture of Ceylon. Those subcultures that demonstrated the strongest integration had the highest rate of altruistic suicide. Suicide because of parental displeasure or following failure at examinations was common among young people in the strongly integrated subcultures, as contrasted with those in the subcultures having the weakest integration. In the subcultures with the highest suicide rates the ego belongs to the group, not to the individual. The claims of the group may be so strong as to result in suicide.[6]

2. *Egoistic Suicide.* Egoistic suicide occurs when the integration of the individual with the group is too loose and ill defined. "In this case," explains

[4] Durkheim, *op. cit.,* Book II, "Social Causes and Social Types." This general hypothesis has recently been examined and extended. Cf. Jack P. Gibbs and Walter T. Martin, "A Theory of Status Integration and Its Relationship to Suicide," *American Sociological Review,* 23:140–147 (April, 1958).

[5] Durkheim, *op. cit.,* p. 219.

[6] Jacqueline H. Straus and Murray A. Straus, "Suicide, Homicide, and Social Structure in Ceylon," *American Journal of Sociology,* 58:461–469 (March, 1953).

Durkheim, "the bond attaching man to life relaxes because that attaching him to society is itself slack. . . . The individual yields to the slightest shock of circumstance because the state of society has made him a ready prey to suicide."[7] Much of the suicide in modern society reflects this lack of integration. Consensus has broken down, leaving the individual isolated from many of the normal contacts of society. When the group is disorganized in this way, egoistic suicide becomes the predominant form of self-destruction. In Durkheim's words, "suicide varies inversely with the degree of integration of the social groups of which the individual forms a part."[8] Suicide is both a result of and an index to the relative degree of social disorganization in society.

Modern man has become partially emancipated from the duties of a closely integrated group life. He has lost important rights and privileges that are the prerogatives of such a life. The individual loses contact with the group, and the group loosens its hold upon its members. When the link binding the individual to society is thus weakened, the link binding him to life is similarly weakened. "Social man," Durkheim points out, "necessarily presupposes a society which he expresses and serves. If this dissolves, if we no longer feel it in existence and action about and above us, whatever is social in us is deprived of all objective foundation."[9] The conditions that emancipate the individual from primary group life may carry a corresponding emancipation from life itself. A disorganized society lays the foundation for that form of personal disorganization that terminates in egoistic suicide.

3. *Anomic Suicide.* The third type of suicide is called *anomic;* it results from a large-scale lack of social regulation of individual behavior. This type is closely related to egoistic suicide, but the emphasis in anomic suicide is upon the dissolution of the norms that bind society together. Social controls that have become internalized in the individual undergo a partial or complete disorganization, leaving him without the traditional sanctions so important to social health. In anomic suicide, the social order has lost its equilibrium following some upheaval or series of upheavals; the individual is often the loser. "Every disturbance of equilibrium," says Durkheim, "even though it achieves greater comfort and a heightening of general vitality, is an impulse to voluntary death."[10]

Anomic suicide may arise from a severe break in the social equilibrium, such as a business depression, an inflation, or a boom. The "will to live" among some persons is threatened by sudden changes in their way of life, whether an elevation or a decline in the social scale. For other persons, the mere existence in a dynamic society makes adjustment difficult. Such persons feel that they are unable to control their destiny in the face of impersonal forces of society.[11] This sense of *anomie* may become so strong that some

[7] Durkheim, *op. cit.*, pp. 214–215.

[8] *Ibid.*, p. 209; Gibbs and Martin, *op. cit.*

[9] *Ibid.*, p. 213.

[10] *Ibid.*, p. 246. This thesis is questioned by Andrew F. Henry and James F. Short, *Suicide and Homicide*, The Free Press, Glencoe, Ill., 1954, chap. 2.

[11] David Riesman *et al., The Lonely Crowd,* Doubleday Anchor Books, New York, 1953, chap. 12.

persons have the impression they are not "really" living. "The boredom of 'not living,' " therefore, "grows into a general loss of spontaneity that culminates in the inner deadness which precedes the physical death of the suicide."[12]

The Psychoanalytic Concept of Suicide

Suicide has been further clarified by the insights of the psychoanalysts. To them it is a final expression of self-contempt which turns into active self-hatred. Aggression is directed against the self, instead of against other persons. General expressions of aggression may range from insult to murder on one level and from group hostility to total war on another. The individual also directs his aggressive impulses against himself, and they may take the form of excessive anxiety, feelings of guilt, and other neurotic and psychotic manifestations. The self is ordinarily an object of love to the individual. It may also become an object of a hate so great that the end is self-destruction.[13]

The psychoanalysts are concerned with the factors deep in the psyche which cause the individual to take his own life. These internal factors determine whether or not a given individual will react in a suicidal fashion to external stresses. One of the most excruciating of these stresses, in this view, is the real or threatened loss of love. This does not merely mean love between romantic lovers or husbands and wives; even more, it involves various forms of affection, acceptance, and intimacy in interpersonal relations. When the individual feels that he is denied affection, he ordinarily turns his aggressions against those who seem to be denying him. In certain cases, however, he internalizes them and directs them against himself. Then he becomes a potential suicide.[14]

According to the Freudian hypothesis, the will to live is not the only basic urge present in human beings. Man also possesses, deep within his unconscious, an equally well-defined will to die. The drama of individual life may be considered in terms of the constant internecine war between these two powerful tendencies. Under certain circumstances, the will to die may overcome the will to live. The death wish may be so weak that it is only partially successful in overcoming the life wish. In this event, the individual may take his own life by slow and torturous stages—by drinking himself to death, by mutilating himself in an ingenious variety of ways, by suffering a series of painful voluntary accidents, or by various other extremes of antisocial behavior. The mental hospitals, the alcoholic wards, and in many cases the wards treating "ordinary" diseases and accidents are filled with persons who are making an end to themselves under the imperious bidding of the will to die. In extreme cases, the wish to die becomes so powerful that the individual

---

[12] Elwin H. Powell, "Occupation, Status, and Suicide: Toward a Redefinition of Anomie," *American Sociological Review, 23*:131–139 (April, 1958), p. 139.

[13] Karl A. Menninger, *Man Against Himself*, Harcourt, Brace and Company, New York, 1938.

[14] Don D. Jackson, "Suicide," *Scientific American, 191*:89–96 (November, 1954). Cf. Martin Gold, "Suicide, Homicide, and the Socialization of Aggression," *American Journal of Sociology, 63*:651–661 (May, 1958).

takes the most drastic step of all and commits suicide. Death triumphs over life.[15]

Suicide can be completely understood, Menninger contends, only as a highly complex form of death which involves three distinct elements: first, the wish to kill; second, the wish to be killed; and third, the wish to die. In other words, the suicide must first entertain murderous desires which may take overt form either upon himself or upon other persons. He must then direct these impulses directly upon his own person in the violent act of self-murder. Finally, he must truly wish to die, with all the force of his unconscious psychic drives. Only then can the suicide be consummated.[16]

The presence of the second wish, *the wish to be killed,* does not necessarily imply the concomitant presence of the third wish, *the wish to die.* Only in this way, Menninger maintains, can the pleadings of the person who has recently attempted suicide unsuccessfully and then earnestly entreats the doctor to save his life at all costs be explained. This paradoxical situation cannot be dismissed by the glib assumption that the would-be suicide has "changed his mind." Something more fundamental has happened. The patient may have entertained violent and murderous intentions upon himself. But at the same time he did not wish to surrender his life completely and whatever satisfaction he might find in this world. The one wish is active, the other is a passive resignation. The two often are not reconciled. In such cases, the suicide really does not want to die.[17]

The individual may thus look forward to the thought of dying without fully realizing its implications. He may derive unconscious pleasure from the prospect of forgetting his anxieties in the permanent sleep of death. He may unconsciously hope to gain the love of certain persons after he has committed suicide. He may think that he is placating his superego (unconscious conscience) by punishing himself through suicide.[18] For these and other reasons, he may entertain the fantasy of suicide and may even make a suicidal attempt. In this "partial suicide" he may be unconsciously attempting to eat his cake and have it too. He may desire the satisfaction that will allegedly come from punishing his conscience through the dramatic gesture of suicide. At the same time, he does not wish to give up completely the "joys" of life.[19]

Trends in Suicide

Suicide is a social phenomenon, with special reference to the relationships between the person and the group. It is also an individual phenomenon, in terms of the processes occurring within the psyche. We are primarily concerned with the social, rather than the psychoanalytic, implications of suicide,

[15] Menninger, *op. cit.*

[16] *Ibid.*, part II.

[17] *Ibid.*

[18] Otto Fenichel, *The Psychoanalytic Theory of Neurosis,* W. W. Norton and Company, Inc., New York, 1945, pp. 400–401.

[19] Mayer Fisch, "The Suicidal Gesture: A Study of 114 Military Patients Hospitalized Because of Abortive Suicide Attempts," *American Journal of Psychiatry, 111*:33–36 (July, 1954).

although insight into the human psyche unquestionably adds to our understanding of it. Before we deal with the various social factors that, in combination, bring about a tendency to suicide, we may briefly examine the trends in recent decades. Table 13.1 traces the trends in the number of suicides

TABLE 13.1. Trends in Number of Suicides and Crude
Death Rates per 100,000 for Suicide 1930-1957

Year	Number of Suicides	Crude Death Rate from Suicide per 100,000 Population
1930	18,551	15.7
1931	20,088	16.8
1932	20,927	17.4
1933	19,993	15.9
1934	18,828	14.9
1935	18,214	14.3
1936	18,294	14.3
1937	19,294	15.9
1938	19,802	15.3
1939	18,511	14.1
1940	18,907	14.3
1941	17,102	12.9
1942	16,117	12.0
1943	13,725	10.2
1944	13,231	10.0
1945	14,782	11.2
1946	16,152	11.5
1947	16,538	11.5
1948	16,354	11.2
1949	16,993	11.4
1950	17,145	11.4
1951	16,740	10.9
1952	16,030	10.3
1953	16,090	10.2
1954	16,356	10.1
1955	16,760	10.2
1956	16,727	10.0
1957	15,980 (est.)	9.4 (est.)

SOURCES: These data are taken from Department of Health, Education, and Welfare, Public Health Service, National Office of Vital Statistics, *Vital Statistics—Special Reports*, National Summaries, *Summary of Vital Statistics*, variously dated.

and the death rates per 100,000 of the population from suicide during the past three decades.

In the decades under consideration, the United States passed through a great depression, a world war, and a period of postwar inflation. The suicide rate varied according to these massive social changes. During the depression it rose to its highest figure in recent history, as millions of men and women were unemployed and destitute. During World War II the rate fell to a very low figure, as the nation faced an external threat against which many persons could direct their aggressions. The postwar inflation was marked by full employment, which had the effect of maintaining the suicide rate at a low level, even after wartime tensions were relaxed. Great crises have different effects upon the rate of self-destruction and the number of cases involved.

Personal disorganization ending in suicide is apparent in varying degrees in different segments of the population. Wide differences occur with respect to sex, religion, marital status, age, place of residence, economic condition, and other factors. Insecurity, frustration, and self-aggression differently affect different groups and individuals. The same combination of circumstances may induce a higher incidence of suicide in one group than in another. Even more striking differences in rates occur between individuals who are frustrated or upset.

Sex and Suicide

The first and most striking distinction in suicide rates in our society is that between men and women. More men than women kill themselves. The specific sex ratios vary somewhat according to race and nationality, but in general the ratio of men to women committing suicide is three or four to one in western Europe and America. Authorities ranging in time from Morselli to Dublin agree on this general observation with respect to past experience.[20] The most recent data confirm this ratio, which has continued with surprising stability for generations. In the year 1957 a total of 15,980 suicides were recorded in the United States, of which number 12,280 were white males and 3700 were white females. The rate per 100,000 of the white population was 15.7 for the male and 4.7 for the female. For the nonwhite population, the sexual difference was somewhat greater, with a rate of 5.5 per 100,000 for the male and only 1.4 for the female.[21] The rate of self-destruction is thus several times higher for men than for women.

This categorical statement must be qualified by pointing out that, whereas the rate of *successful* suicides is much higher for men, the rate of *unsuccessful* suicides is more nearly equal. Data on attempted suicides are obviously not as accurate as those for "successful" suicides, but the available information indicates that the number of women who try (but fail) to commit suicide is at least equal to and perhaps slightly larger than the number of men who make a similarly unsuccessful attempt. Reasons for this feminine "failure" are somewhat obscure, but they undoubtedly include the following: (1) The wish to die may be weaker in would-be suicides among women; (2) the means of suicide chosen by women are more accessible and less lethal than those chosen by men; (3) the means chosen by women (e.g., poisoning) tend to be less violent and disfiguring and are also less destructive to life; (4) the ma-

---

[20] Henry Morselli, *Suicide: An Essay on Comparative Moral Statistics,* Appleton-Century-Crofts, Inc., New York, 1882, p. 189; Louis I. Dublin, *To Be or Not to Be,* Harrison Smith and Robert Haas, Inc., New York, 1933, pp. 43–51.

[21] U.S. Department of Health, Education, and Welfare, Public Health Service, National Office of Vital Statistics, *Annual Summary for 1957—Part II,* "Estimated Numbers of Deaths and Death Rates for Selected Causes: United States," Vol. 6, No. 13 (August 27, 1958).

jority of women who attempt suicide are under thirty, at which age most suicides attempted by either sex are unsuccessful; (5) women deliberately choose non-lethal methods in order to win the sympathy of a lover or husband after they are revived.[22]

These factors may help to explain the comparative equality in numbers of unsuccessful suicides between men and women, but they still do not explain the differences in *successful* suicides. In this latter connection, various hypotheses have been advanced concerning men's inability to bear severe and sustained pain, their tendency to become unduly discouraged in the face of adversity, their incapacity to put up with the minor crises of life, and other psychological and physiological weaknesses of the "stronger" sex. The reasons seem to be cultural and social in character, however, rather than inherent in the genetic organization of the two sexes. The social attitudes developed by the role that each sex has traditionally played in Western civilization undoubtedly have an important effect in determining the suicide ratio.[23]

Men have traditionally been called upon to face the difficulties inherent in the struggle to make a living. Women share in these activities, it is true, but not to the same degree. Their lives are not so completely dependent upon worldly success. Self-sacrifice and resignation have been the lot of women, whereas ambition has been the motivating force in the lives of men. When this socially stimulated will to succeed is thwarted, men take their lives in bitter frustration. Until recently both the formal and the informal education of the sexes perpetuated the tradition of masculine aggression and feminine passivity. Perhaps these roles may become more equalized by the increasing participation of women in many of the traditional affairs of a man-made world. In such event, women may become subjected to the same variety of influences bringing about an extremity of personal disorganization. As yet, however, there is little evidence that the changing status of women has resulted in an increasing proportion of suicides.

Suicide and Family Disorganization

The personal disorganization arising from broken family ties is so serious that it often culminates in suicide. This fact is statistically demonstrable for European countries. Unfortunately, mortality statistics in the United States as a whole do not give the marital status of the suicide. Hence we can only infer a similar relationship in this country. However, such intensive studies as have been made here maintain the European ratios among the single, married, divorced, and widowed. The highest rate of self-destruction is found among the divorced, the next highest among the widowed, the next among the unmarried, and the lowest among the married.[24]

Durkheim has made an elaborate analysis of the causes for the high suicide

[22] Metropolitan Life Insurance Company, *op. cit.*

[23] Cf. Calvin F. Schmid and Maurice D. Van Arsdol, Jr., "Completed and Attempted Suicides: A Comparative Analysis," *American Sociological Review*, 20:273–283 (June, 1955).

[24] Morselli, *op. cit.*, pp. 226–239; Dublin, *op. cit.*, chap. 11, "Marital Status and Suicide."

rate among groups of "abnormal" marital status. The family, he contends, exerts a socializing and integrative influence upon its members, not because of any innate magic in the marriage state per se but because of the cohesive character of any closely knit social group. The family group is fully complete only with husband, wife, and children. Men who experience family pressures and subtle responsibilities are not so prone to commit suicide as others. The functional interrelationships of this intimate group are not easily broken. Habits are woven about the paterfamilias that militate against any reckless distaste for life.[25]

Conversely, an abrupt severance of these group relationships through separation, divorce, or death constitutes a crisis of the greatest magnitude in the life organization of one or both of the partners. This crisis is felt in direct proportion to the closeness of the original ties. The problems of the bereaved often reach a climax in complete personal breakdown and suicide. Loneliness, sex hunger, a thwarted craving for response and affection, anger, misanthropy, disorganized emotional tensions, venereal disease—all these and many other factors contribute to the demoralization and eventual suicide of the man or woman whose marriage has been violently dissolved either by death or by order of court.

"Bereavement" may occur before marriage, when the individual is jilted by a loved one. In a nation nourished on the romantic tradition, many suicides arise from the disappointment, disillusionment, and disruption of emotional relationships between the sexes before, during, or outside of marriage. The jilted lover cannot understand why the fates deny him the affection that burns so strongly in his heart. When this affection is not reciprocated, he may fully realize, perhaps for the first time, the inharmonious character of the universe. In a cold and implacable world there often seems to be no connection between the desire for love and its acceptance by another. The most important system of values in the personal life scheme may collapse under the impact of romantic difficulties, leaving to the bereaved the sole apparent solution of suicide.

Romantic frustration also accounts for many unsuccessful suicides. Some of these abortive attempts are initiated with serious intentions. Others are begun with the deliberate intention of failure, as the unhappy lover takes a non-lethal dose of poison, jumps into a shallow river, or turns on the gas when there is someone else in the house. The purpose of these macabre maneuvers is presumably to demonstrate extreme affection for, evoke sympathy from, or cause unhappiness to the unsatisfactory loved one. Women are the principal participants in these performances, although the rate of *successful* suicides (as we stated) runs approximately three to one for the males. Women whose romances have been frustrated may thus fail in their suicidal attempts because of lack of physical strength, unfamiliarity with many of the most deadly methods of self-destruction, or lack of a genuine wish to die. Whatever the

[25] Durkheim, *op. cit.*, Book II, chap. 3; Maurice Halbwachs, *Les Causes du Suicide,* Felix Alcan, Paris, 1930, chap. 8, "Le Suicide et la Famille."

combination of conscious or unconscious motives, these unhappy lovers will live to love another day.[26]

Religion and Suicide

Two factors in religious relationships and observances seem to affect the suicide rate. First, a widely accepted belief that self-murder is sinful and that the suicide will suffer a dire punishment reduces the rate. Second, strong religious bonds bring about a high degree of social organization and corresponding lack of the personal and social disorganization that results in suicide. Religion is thus a dual prophylactic against suicide.[27]

Christianity has condemned and disapproved of suicide since the days of the early church fathers.[28] Only the Creator, says the church, has the power to fix man's hour of death. One who cherishes a firm belief in the reality of a future life, replete with either rewards or punishments, is loath to depart from this world in a way that will jeopardize that future. A rigorous religious training from childhood will do much toward steeling even the most world-weary against self-murder. The person whose life organization is firmly integrated with the church will be more stable and less prone to suicide. The Catholic Church deprives the suicide of Christian burial. The orthodox Jewish law forbids burial to the suicide in the same cemetery with those who have met their death in a natural way.

The anti-suicidal prophylaxis of these religions is not, says Durkheim, to be primarily attributed either to the religious concepts themselves or to the sinfulness which many religions impute to self-destruction. It comes rather from the fact that a strong religious group constitutes a veritable society in itself, with many beliefs, traditions, and practices which are obligatory to the individual. The stronger these regulatory practices, the more closely integrated is the social group and the less liable are its individual members to become demoralized to the point of suicide. The Protestant church does not foster an internal cohesiveness of sufficient intensity to inoculate all its members effectively against suicide. In the orthodox Catholic and Jewish faiths, this solidarity is their most precious heritage.

These two great institutional structures have evolved definitions of almost every conceivable social situation. They furnish to their members a satisfying and definite set of collective representations, which are sufficient to most of them in the majority of situations. In the comparatively rare cases that these definitions are unsatisfactory, or when the communicant refuses to accept them, they have various socially therapeutic techniques to prevent complete personal disorganization.

From the time when Martin Luther nailed the theses to the door at Wittenberg, Protestantism has been an individualistic religion, relying on the person

[26] Metropolitan Life Insurance Company, "Why Do People Kill Themselves?" *Statistical Bulletin,* February, 1945.

[27] Durkheim, *op. cit.,* Book II, chap. 2; Halbwachs, *op. cit.,* chap. 9, "Le Suicide et la Religion"; cf. also Dublin, *op. cit.,* chap. 10, "Religious Affiliation and Suicide."

[28] Dublin, *op. cit.,* chap. 16, "The Attitude of the Christian Church Regarding Suicide."

to interpret the Scriptures as he sees fit and gain salvation as best he may. Success in business or in making his soul safe for another world may bring considerable pride of achievement. But failure to do either or both of these things may bring equally bitter remorse, repentance, and personal disorganization. The Protestant church has no confessional, an institutional device which is unquestionably effective in deterring many Catholics from suicide. Furthermore, Protestantism has traditionally encouraged free thinking and has sanctioned the open and candid examination of the revealed truths of dogmatic religion. While this process has been extremely helpful in the development of scientific investigation, it has often been disorganizing to the person whose faith was thus destroyed.

The different religious attitudes have many implications for the psychoanalytic conception of suicide. In the Catholic ideology, as noted, the individual is relieved of the most acute sense of guilt through the confessional and the other institutional rituals. The Catholic Church, furthermore, offers the mother image of the Virgin Mary as a symbol of mercy and forgiveness. The sinner can address himself to her in his extremity and she will intercede in his behalf with her Son. The Protestant ideology contains no such mechanisms to limit the sense of guilt of the individual who directs his aggressions against himself with possible suicidal intent. The Protestant sinner must face the wrath of God and his own conscience virtually unaided, with no merciful Mother to help him. The guilt arising from the realization of his illicit impulses may be so strong that he cannot face it alone. In such a dire extremity, suicide may seem the only way out.[29]

The suicide rate thus has been traditionally higher among Protestants than among Catholics or Jews. Statistics as to the religious affiliations of suicides are not available for the United States and we are again forced to confine our generalizations to the European countries. These data are themselves obsolete because they describe the conditions prior to World War I or at best those existing between wars. Before World War I, there was an unmistakable ranking of Protestant, Catholic, and Jewish suicides in the order of decreasing frequency. What the situation is after years of war, occupation, and mass slaughter among Protestants, Catholics, and Jews alike, no man can say. With millions of persons lost in the hecatombs of the Nazi extermination camps, the suicide rate among various religious groups during World War II will never be known.[30]

Even before the unparalleled slaughter of World War II the suicide rate among the Jews had begun to show a substantial increase. In the decades between the wars, the Jewish trading classes were severely shaken by the waves of inflation that swept over Europe. The Jews also were predominantly urban in residence and the secularism of the metropolis affected their former solidarity. Judaism itself was declining as an integrative and stabilizing force.

[29] Simpson, *op. cit.*, pp. 661–662.
[30] Cf. Elie A. Cohen, *Human Behavior in the Concentration Camp*, W. W. Norton and Company, Inc., New York, 1953.

The anti-Semitism that was used as a political device to crush liberal movements also had its effect upon the problems of the Jews and the increase in their rate of self-destruction. Taken together, the increase in Jewish suicide even before their systematic extermination by the Nazis paints a tragic picture of social disorganization. The bonds of a religious and cultural group were dissolved under the combined pressures of social change and organized prejudice.

Urbanism and Suicide

As civilization becomes increasingly complex and more people crowd together in cities, the natural supposition is that suicide will increase. In general, this appears to be the case, although the relationship between urbanism and suicide is not a simple one of cause and effect.[31] The suicide rate in urban communities is generally higher than in rural areas, although even this relationship may be changing.[32] The rate has increased over the past century, as this country has become more urbanized. But we cannot draw the corollary conclusion that urbanization automatically increases suicide. Furthermore, suicide does not increase directly with the size of the city; certain secondary cities rank above the principal cities. Rates are affected by special forces operating at different intensity in different regions rather than by the mere size of the urban population.[33]

The causes of suicide are complex, as are the causes for any other social phenomenon. Many factors combine to cause one particular individual (and not another) to divert his aggressions upon himself in the form of suicide. Many of the well-known and oft-repeated distinctions between rural and urban life help to explain the higher rate of suicide in the urban community. Social disorganization is, in general, greater in the city than in the country. Many primary relationships break down in the city, and many urban dwellers fail to find satisfaction in secondary associations.[34]

The role of urbanism in suicide has been extensively explored by Sorokin and Zimmerman. They find that "community of tradition, feeling, belief, interest, and intimacy in the relationships" tend to be lacking in the metropolitan environment. In addition to this impairment of consensus, social mobility is greater; social interaction is subject to more violent disturbances; crisis situations are more common. The greater choice of behavior in the city presents problems to the person who lacks the ability to direct himself. In a simpler society, the mores make most of his choices for him, but in the city the burden is placed upon him alone.[35]

[31] Dublin, op. cit., chap. 3, "Urban and Rural Rates."

[32] W. Widick Schroeder and J. Allan Beegle, "Suicide: An Instance of High Rural Rates," Rural Sociology, 18:45–52 (March, 1953).

[33] Austin L. Porterfield, "Indices of Suicide and Homicide by States and Cities: Some Southern-Non-Southern Contrasts with Implications for Research," American Sociological Review, 14:481–490 (August, 1949).

[34] Cf. Floyd Dotson, "Patterns of Voluntary Association Among Urban Working-Class Families," American Sociological Review, 16:687–693 (October, 1951).

[35] Pitirim A. Sorokin and Carle C. Zimmerman, Principles of Rural-Urban Sociology, Henry Holt and Company, Inc., New York, 1929, chap. 7, "Rural-Urban Suicides."

These differentials may be equalized in the future, not so much because of a decrease in suicide rates in the city but because of an increase in those in the country. Rural districts are gradually becoming urbanized; social mobility in the nation is increasing; and many elements of cohesion in the village and open country are disappearing. An indication of these trends is given in a study of rural-urban suicide in Michigan, where the suicide rates for rural males were almost twice as high as those for urban males.[36] These data indicate that differences in age and nativity were not responsible for the high rates of rural, as compared to urban, suicide. Explanations for this disparity involve two related considerations: (1) the conflict between rural and urban values, as urban values become more widely disseminated and rural persons become correspondingly disorganized; and (2) the occupation of the rural male suicides, whose jobs were characteristic of urban groups, even though they (the suicides) lived in rural areas. As the rural areas become more markedly urban, the situation in Michigan may become more widespread.[37]

Economic Aspects of Suicide

Economic factors play an important part in determining the trends in suicide. There is a positive correlation between suicide and business. There is a negative correlation between suicide and the swings in the business cycle. As the business cycle turns down, the number of suicides goes up. Better business conditions are associated with a decline in the number and rate of suicide. The suicide rate rose from a "normal" figure of 12.8 per 100,000 population in 1926 to a high of 17.4 in 1932, at the depth of the Great Depression. The upturn in business activity and national confidence beginning in 1933 was accompanied by a drop in the suicide rate to 15.9 in that year and to 14.3 in 1936.[38] World War II introduced other complicating factors into the general situation, but the high level of postwar business activity was undoubtedly partly responsible for the comparatively low rate of 11.5 in 1947. The early years of the 1950's were marked by a continuing high rate of business activity, and the suicide rate declined to 9.4 per 100,000 for 1957.[39]

We may classify economic suicides under three headings. These categories are not mutually exclusive and they involve considerable overlapping. Nevertheless, they help to clarify the economic ramifications of suicide, especially in terms of the differences in attitudes of the various groups. These categories comprise the egoistic and the anomic types of Durkheim, depending upon whether we stress the individual detachment from the group (egoistic) or the breakdown in the equilibrium of society as a whole (anomic).

1. *Loss of Status.* Among the most spectacular victims of self-inflicted death are presidents of large corporations, financiers, and persons in other

[36] Schroeder and Beegle, *op. cit.*

[37] *Ibid.*, pp. 51–52.

[38] U.S. Department of Health, Education, and Welfare, Public Health Service, National Office of Vital Statistics, *United States: Summary of Vital Statistics, 1945, Vital Statistics—Special Reports*, Vol. 26, No. 1 (April 4, 1947), Tables N and O.

[39] U.S. Department of Health, Education, and Welfare, Public Health Service, National Office of Vital Statistics, *Leading Causes of Death, Vital Statistics—Special Reports*, National Summaries, Vol. 46, No. 8 (June 28, 1957), Table 1.

fiduciary positions who have violated their trust and have been unable to face the penalty. Dramatic suicides of large-scale swindlers are examples of such persons who kill themselves rather than suffer the consequences of their wholesale betrayal of public confidence. The loss of status is too much to bear. The thought that the former president of the First National Bank of Blanktown is in danger of serving sentence as a common thief—he who was once the pillar of righteousness and sound business dealings in the community—is often too bitter a pill for the ex-president to swallow. Such criminal defaults may remain hidden for a long time in a business boom, but they come to light in times of acute depression. To the ruined and disgraced culprit, suicide seems the only way out.[40]

Even where there are no criminal implications, times of financial panic bring suicides among the very wealthy. These persons are not so much victims of poverty and want as they are sufferers from a general crisis situation, which involves their own loss of social status. Their descent in the economic scale is not so catastrophic as to render them penniless or even poverty-stricken, as that state is ordinarily understood. Nevertheless, the prospect of drastic curtailment of their scale of life, with the consequent lowered social status, is often defined as the complete collapse of their social world. Suicide is often the result of this despair.

2. *Loss of Comfort.*   Businessmen, large and small, bankrupt by the fall in commodity prices, security values, and general business volume, form a second and middle class of depression-fostered suicides. This class is closely related to the first in many respects, but the difference in attitude between the two groups sets them off from each other. The first group consists of those persons of superior economic and social status who are deprived of their elevated position by economic factors. The rank and file of business and professional men, on the other hand, clearly never aspire to such a position, whether it be the presidency of a huge national corporation or that of the only bank in a small town. The second class have a different conception of their role in the group, growing out of their relatively humbler economic position.

This type of suicide may also be laid directly to the capitalistic ethic, since the role that the person plays is a function of his business acumen and cash income. Business failure is accompanied by a loss of self-confidence, a feeling that life is a dismal fiasco, and a corresponding desire to seek release from this humiliation in death. Accompanying the belief in the importance of money is the equally powerful worship of the things that money can buy. Physical comfort, measured by material possessions and "conspicuous consumption," becomes the *summum bonum.* The deprivation of these creature comforts, and the equally bitter knowledge that it is no longer possible to buy them, may stifle much of the significance of life itself. When these pecuniary values collapse, in many cases there is nothing to live for.

3. *Loss of Security.*   We may consider briefly the third victim of self-destruction induced or augmented by economic reverses—the unemployed,

[40] Cf. Donald R. Cressey, *Other People's Money,* The Free Press, Glencoe, Ill., 1953. This is a study of the social psychology of embezzlement.

destitute, starving man or woman. Skilled and unskilled workers, anxious to practice their craft or give their physical strength, may be forced to choose between slow starvation and suicide, particularly when they are not legal residents of the town in which they find themselves. In such cases, suicide does not result from fear of punishment, loss of social status, or unwillingness to retrench in the scale of living. Rather is it the result of unemployment, of grinding poverty, of homelessness, of the loss of basic economic and social security.

There is therefore a relationship between economic factors and suicide, but it is not always simple. Economic security and high status are not enough to keep the individual from directing his aggressive impulses against himself. In one study of social class, indeed, it was found that middle- and upper-class persons tend to direct their aggressions against themselves to a greater extent than do lower-class persons. The latter have a sense of inferiority and insecurity and direct their aggressions against others. The aggressive impulses of the middle class ordinarily take the form of anxiety and feelings of guilt, whereby the self is minimized and made to feel inferior. In other cases, however, this tendency may be a contributory factor in suicide.[41]

Many persons who are economically secure and occupy positions of high economic status nevertheless commit suicide. Such status is widely presumed to be the principal goal of our society, the end toward which most persons are consistently directed and the attainment of which should therefore bring stability of personality. Economic ends by themselves, however, do not appear to bring peace of mind; economic success is no guarantee of immunity against the self-aggression that may terminate in suicide. Economic uncertainties and deprivations are often among the factors that combine to bring about suicide, but economic security is not enough to insure the emotional security which every man seeks.[42]

War and Suicide

Depression is one type of mass crisis for modern man. Total war is another. Both produce disruptions in the social equilibrium, but their effect upon the suicide rate is very different. Depression increases the suicide rate. War decreases it. War creates a social situation in which the individual becomes more closely integrated with the group and hence is less willing to leave it. The cohesive force of nationalism is so strong that he is lifted out of himself in time of national danger, and his will to live is correspondingly strengthened. As Durkheim points out, "Great social disturbances and great popular wars rouse collective sentiments, stimulate partisan spirit and patriotism, political and national faith . . . and . . . at least temporarily cause a stronger integration of society."[43]

---

[41] Samuel Z. Klausner, "Social Class and Self-Control," *Journal of Social Psychology,* 38:201–205 (November, 1953).
[42] Simpson, *op. cit.,* p. 662. Cf. Henry and Short, *op. cit.,* chap. 2.
[43] Durkheim, *op. cit.,* p. 208.

The decline in the suicide rate in the United States during World War II was an impressive testimony to this phenomenon. In the year 1940, the nation had its final full year of peace and the suicide rate was 14.3 per 100,000 population. In 1941, the rate fell to 12.9, in 1942 to 12, in 1943 to 10.2, and in 1944 to an unprecedented low of 10 per 100,000 population. In the first six months of 1945, the rate continued to decline. The war in Europe ended in May of 1945, and the war in the Pacific ended in August of the same year. The suicide rate began to rise almost immediately after the end of the war in Europe and continued to rise throughout the remainder of 1945.[44] The rate for the United States for 1945 was 11.2, for 1946 it was 11.5, and for 1947 it was also 11.5.[45] The wartime decline in suicides has several explanations.

1. *Psychological Factors.* Commenting further upon the effect of war upon suicide, Durkheim says that "the salutary influence . . . is due not to the crisis but to the struggles it occasions. As they force men to close ranks and confront the common danger, the individual thinks less of himself and more of the common cause."[46] The welfare of the nation temporarily transcends any individual difficulties. The result is a strong feeling of consensus and integration.[47] In a complex modern society, many persons feel isolated from the group and lose their sense of belonging. The intensity of the national spirit during total war brings these individuals back into society, where they are encouraged to contribute their part to the national effort.[48]

2. *Economic Factors.* Economic factors reducing the wartime suicide rate are the inflation, full employment, and business boom that often accompany the war. The United States was fortunate during World War II in this respect, inasmuch as it was able to fight the war and maintain a boom at the same time. In the period from July 1, 1940, to July 1, 1945, the federal government expended a total of $323 billion, largely upon the preparation for and conduct of World War II.[49] The expenditures raised the national income to unprecedented heights and reduced unemployment to the record low figure of 630,000 in October, 1944.[50] Economic security was (temporarily) assured for every person willing and able to work. Jobs were available at high rates of pay.

[44] Metropolitan Life Insurance Company, "Postwar Increase in Suicide," *Statistical Bulletin,* April, 1946.

[45] U.S. Department of Health, Education, and Welfare, National Office of Vital Statistics, *Deaths and Death Rates for Selected Causes: 1947, Vital Statistics—Special Reports,* National Summaries, Vol. 31, No. 4 (July 11, 1949), Tables 1 and 2.

[46] Durkheim, *op. cit.,* p. 208.

[47] Cf. Walter Lunden, "Suicides in France, 1910–43," *American Journal of Sociology,* 52:321–334 (January, 1947).

[48] Francis E. Merrill, *Social Problems on the Home Front,* Harper & Brothers, New York, 1948, pp. 226–228.

[49] Statement of Daniel W. Bell, Under Secretary of the Treasury, in an address before the Association of Stock Exchange Firms, quoted in the *New York Times,* November 25, 1945.

[50] Bureau of the Census, *Monthly Report on the Labor Force, Population: MRLF,* August 15, 1945.

Workers were upgraded into positions of greater skill and responsibility. Suicides declined in the face of this activity.[51]

3. *Battle Factors.* A third reason for the wartime decline in suicide reflects what, for want of a better term, might be called "battle" factors. The mobilization of modern war removes several million men from the civilian population who might ordinarily be expected to swell the suicide figures. An indeterminate number of these mobilized civilians may, in effect, commit suicide in battle by needlessly exposing themselves to enemy action. The motivation for such behavior may be both conscious and unconscious. The soldier who is killed in this way may or may not be aware beforehand that he is deliberately seeking death. We recall that Durkheim defined suicide as any death "resulting directly or indirectly from a positive or negative act of the victim himself, which he knows will produce this result."[52] The soldier who deliberately finds death in battle "knows" either consciously or unconsciously that he wishes to die. His act is thus a true suicide.[53]

Suicide and Mental Disease

Personal disorganization, as we have seen, may culminate in mental disease. The patient may spend his time nursing delusions of grandeur. He may brood his life away in deep and hopeless melancholia. He may become mentally ill in other ways but still never lay violent hands upon himself or others. He may, however, take the final tragic flight from life and kill himself. In this sense, suicide is the denouement of personal disorganization. Some persons who take this step are clearly psychotic. But by no means all are deranged. There is a common belief that *all* suicides are insane, at least temporarily. This is not true. The majority of suicides are not psychotic in any scientific sense of that term.[54]

The most rational man may, under certain circumstances, take his own life. He does not have to be "insane" to do so. Many non-suicidal persons are unable to understand how, in rational cold blood, an individual can fire a bullet into his brain or jump from the upper floor of an office building. These victims of alleged insanity do not manifest any of the scientific aspects of mental disease. They do not suffer from "delusions, hallucinations, degeneracy of mental capacity, or uncontrolled emotional states." Most suicides, in short, are perfectly sane, but they are unquestionably examples of extreme personal disorganization.[55]

Certain specific mental disorders, however, are apparently related to suicide. These include melancholia, acute paranoia, senile dementia, dementia praecox, dementia paralytica, and chronic alcoholism.[56] The psychosis is not,

[51] Metropolitan Life Insurance Company, "Suicides Decline to New Low Level," *Statistical Bulletin,* July, 1944.

[52] Durkheim, *op. cit.,* p. 44.

[53] Simpson, *op. cit.,* p. 662.

[54] Ruth Shonle Cavan, *Suicide,* University of Chicago Press, Chicago, 1928, p. 112 n.

[55] *Ibid.,* p. 112.

[56] *Ibid.,* pp. 117 ff.

in the majority of cases, the sole cause for the suicide. Some external crisis must be added to the psychosis, and together they may bring about the suicidal act. To the psychotic, as to the normal person, suicide may seem the only means of escape. Despite the presence of mental illness in many suicides, we must therefore conclude that they represent but a fraction (albeit a large one) of the total number.[57] "Thus," concludes Durkheim, "no psychopathic state bears a regular and indisputable relation to suicide. A society does not depend for its number of suicides on those persons who are mentally ill."[58]

Miscellaneous Contributory Factors

Other elements may, singly or in combination, bring about or accentuate the final break in the bonds that hold the individual to society. Some of these factors (old age and disease) reflect physiological changes that may decrease the will to live. Others (arrest, alcohol, and change of location) impinge from the outside upon a life organization already progressively weakened.

1. *Old Age.* As people grow older, the stresses and strains of life begin to tell more severely upon them. The suicide rate increases with age, from a negligible figure in the years below twenty to a rate of 36.7 per 100,000 of the population in the years 45–64 in 1955. In the age group 15–24 years the rate was 2; in the group 25–44 years it rose to 5.7; and in the age group 45–64 years it was 36.7.[59] The reasons for the increase include the following: (a) The degenerative diseases take an increasing toll in the later years of life, and suicide is often a response to this fact. (b) Suicide among the aged may be increased by their knowledge that, in any event, death from "natural" causes is not far off. (c) The aged in our society have no functional roles to perform and are therefore a prey to feelings of loneliness, neglect, and insecurity.[60]

2. *Physical Disease.* Closely related to old age in motivating suicide is the factor of incurable disease. Many believe that this is one circumstance under which suicide may be condoned, but such an attitude is not universally held. Be that as it may, a large number of persons are so disturbed by their physical condition that they commit suicide. In other cases, severe illness causes a break in the life organization that, although not necessarily fatal, is still as demoralizing as severe pain. Interruption in activities hitherto considered vital may bring about suicide from sheer boredom or exasperation. The individual who has been warned that he must give up an active life because of a heart condition may find his existence savorless. In these and other ways, physical disease may cause the individual to end a life that no longer seems worth the pain and the trouble.

[57] *Ibid.,* p. 122.

[58] Durkheim, *op. cit.,* p. 81.

[59] *Vital Statistics Special Reports, 1955,* Vol. 46, No. 8, U.S. Department of Health, Education, and Welfare, Public Health Service, National Office of Vital Statistics, pp. 240–243.

[60] Simpson, *op. cit.,* p. 660.

3. *Arrest.* The social environment may induce suicide. Arrest is one of the conditions under which some persons commit suicide, even when their crime is not a serious one, out of a mixture of fear and shame. Others may be threatened with execution or life imprisonment and may derive a grisly satisfaction from cheating the gallows, the electric chair, or the penitentiary. In these and related cases, the arrest may not in itself be the principal motivating factor but may be merely the culmination of a series of frustrations which are finally directed against the self. The emotional condition of the suicide, in other words, cannot be understood completely in terms of the immediate situation but must be traced back through his life history. The event that actually sets off the "suicide potential" may be comparatively trivial.[61]

4. *Alcohol.* The excessive use of alcohol is listed among the contributory causes of suicide in all of the European compilations.[62] The effect of alcohol upon the life organization is not measured accurately by the number of persons who kill themselves while drunk or immediately after. The disorganization process is more subtle and is manifested in the personality disorganization of the clinical alcoholic.[63] The actual death may be attributed to some other cause or causes, although alcohol has been the dominant factor in producing the suicide potential. Frustration and insecurity may bring about the neurotic condition characteristic of clinical alcoholism. This latter condition does not ordinarily take the spectacular form of suicide. The self-destruction may be less violent, as the individual vents his aggressive impulses upon himself by the slower process of alcoholic disorganization. The eventual death of the alcoholic will be listed as arising from "natural" causes and not as suicide, but the unconscious impulses toward self-destruction may be the same.

5. *Change of Location.* Suicide attributed to change of social surroundings is part of the larger process of disorganization that gives rise to egoistic suicide. The world of the individual has been subjected to a violent change as he leaves one social setting and enters another. Suicide through change of location is part of the delayed "culture shock" to which the immigrant is subject. The suicide rate among the foreign born in this country, for example, is higher than among the native born, according to such data as are available.

Suicides among the foreign born apparently do not occur during the first years of foreign residence, a time that would seem most productive of violent disturbances in the life organization. The period of greatest personal disorganization occurs when the children of the foreign born are growing up and the "culture clash" between the generations is at its height. Many foreign-born residents commit suicide in their fear lest both they and their children lose their cultural autonomy and become forced to live a quasi-marginal existence on the fringe of American society.[64]

---

[61] *Ibid.*
[62] Cf. Morselli, *op. cit.,* pp. 288 ff.
[63] Chapter 7, "The Alcoholic," *supra.*
[64] Cavan, *op. cit.,* pp. 276–279.

The Ecology of Suicide

The position of the individual in the social system is an important factor in his life. Hence it might be expected that suicide would follow the ecological structure of the city, with a high rate in the areas showing a concentration of other forms of social disorganization. Suicide would thus be another index of the persons with weak and unstable life organizations who gravitate to the areas of hobohemia, the slum, and the other areas of high mobility. Suicide would represent the extremity of personal failure, lack of adjustment, and social disorganization. This general hypothesis is borne out in two early ecological studies of suicide. It is questioned by a later study.

The two early studies on the ecological aspects of suicide were those of Cavan of Chicago and Schmid of Seattle.[65] Suicides were found to cluster in the same ecological areas with other forms of social disorganization. In Chicago they were concentrated in four general areas: (a) the central business district and its immediate vicinity, where many of the dingy hotels and homeless men are found; (b) the near North Side, an area of high mobility and unattached men and women who live in dreary hall bedrooms; (c) the near South Side, where most of the commercialized vice is located; (d) the West Madison Street area, which is the hobohemia, the "main stem" of the homeless man.[66] In Seattle, suicides were concentrated in a single area near the center of the city, where other forms of social disorganization were similarly clustered.[67] Allowing for the differences in size, the concentration of suicides in the areas of high mobility of the two cities was approximately the same.

These studies demonstrate a close relationship between suicide, mobility, and social disorganization. The downtown area of Seattle, adjacent to the railroad and steamship terminals, receives those persons whose vocations involve constant movement—the homeless man, the prostitute, the adventurer, and the criminal.[68] In Chicago the same elements characterized both suicide and mobility. Suicide areas corresponded to such diverse indices of mobility and disorganization as lodging houses, pawnshops, deaths from alcoholism, use of drugs, disorderly hotels, cabarets, vice resorts, and venereal disease infection. Anonymity is a final factor in the picture of disorganization and suicide found in these areas of high mobility. After registering under an assumed name and destroying all marks of identification, a man may snuff out his life and no one is ever the wiser.[69]

This general relationship between suicide and social disorganization is questioned by a recent series of studies conducted in several southern cities, notably in Fort Worth, Texas.[70] Porterfield found that there is a differential,

---

[65] *Ibid.;* Calvin F. Schmid, *Suicides in Seattle, 1914 to 1925. An Ecological and Behavioristic Study,* University of Washington Press, Seattle, 1928. Cf. also Schmid and Van Arsdol, *op. cit.*

[66] Cavan, *op. cit.,* p. 81.

[67] Schmid, *op. cit.,* chap. 2, "The Ecology of Suicide."

[68] Schmid and Van Arsdol, *op. cit.*

[69] Schmid, *op. cit.,* pp. 16–21.

rather than a direct, relationship between suicide and certain types of social disorganization. Divorce, alcoholism, and suicide show a tendency to vary in the *same* direction, whereas depressed economic status, homicide, and suicide vary in the *opposite* direction. That is, cities with high rates of divorce and alcoholism show high rates of suicide, whereas cities with high rates of depressed economic status and homicide show low rates of suicide. These differences are also apparent within the same city.[71]

In the ecological areas of Fort Worth the same differential relationship between suicide and other forms of social disorganization was found. Suicide thus appears to be functionally related to *some* types of social disorganization but not *others*. In Fort Worth the areas with high suicide rates are high in social status and percentage of native whites and low in crime rates. Conversely, areas with low suicide rates are high in crime and percentage of persons living under depressed social conditions. Suicide appears to be a special type of social disorganization, with a pattern largely independent of the other manifestations of this process. Suicide is found in areas where the other conventional indices of social disorganization are lacking. These distributions do not fit in with the ecological patterns previously found in Chicago and Seattle. The Fort Worth data seem to indicate that the ecological relationship between suicide and *all* forms of social disorganization is not as direct as had been previously supposed.[72]

The variations in suicide rates between cities and between ecological areas within the same city may be partially explained in terms of social structure and social relationships. Porterfield concludes that population groups whose relationships are essentially primary (i.e., dealing with other persons) may show a high tendency to homicide and a low tendency to suicide. The underprivileged population of the average southern city, especially the Negro group, stresses primary and interpersonal relationships and hence resorts less frequently to suicide. The Negro may be less concerned with economic motivation as evidence of status than is the average white man. In the more privileged sections of the city the white man may direct his aggressions against himself (suicide), whereas the underprivileged Negro may direct his aggressions against others (homicide). Thus areas with high indices of social disorganization may have a low frequency of suicide. The personal disorganization that ends in suicide may have a different etiology from that which ends in homicide and other forms of social disorganization.[73] The lower Negro suicide rate is also partly attributable to his greater fear of death.

[70] Austin L. Porterfield, "Indices of Suicide and Homicide by States and Cities: Some Southern-Non-Southern Contrasts with Implications for Research," *American Sociological Review, 14*:481–490 (August, 1949); Austin L. Porterfield, "Suicide and Crime in the Social Structure of an Urban Setting: Fort Worth, 1930–1950," *American Sociological Review, 17*:341–349 (June, 1952); Austin L. Porterfield, "Suicide and Crime in Folk and Secular Society," *American Journal of Sociology, 57*:331–338 (January, 1952).

[71] Porterfield, "Suicide and Crime in the Social Structure of an Urban Setting: Fort Worth, 1930–1950, *op. cit.*"

[72] *Ibid.*

[73] *Ibid.* See also Henry and Short, *op. cit.,* chap. 2.

SELECTED BIBLIOGRAPHY

Cavan, Ruth Shonle, *Suicide,* University of Chicago Press, Chicago, 1928. This is a comprehensive statement of the many ramifications of the suicide problem, including a sociopsychological analysis of the genesis of suicidal attitudes.

Durkheim, Emile, *Suicide* (translated by John A. Spaulding and George Simpson), The Free Press, Glencoe, Ill., 1951. This is the classic sociological study of suicide, now translated into English for the first time. Durkheim examines suicide as a *sociological* phenomenon, in terms of the degree and kind of integration in a given society.

Gibbs, Jack P., and Martin, Walter T., "A Theory of Status Integration and Its Relationship to Suicide," *American Sociological Review, 23:*140–147 (April, 1958). This article extends the basic analysis of Durkheim and develops the general proposition that "The suicide rate of a population varies inversely with the stability and durability of social relationships within that population."

Henry, Andrew F., and Short, James F., *Suicide and Homicide,* The Free Press, Glencoe, Ill., 1954. In this significant study, the authors examine Durkheim's central hypothesis in the light of recent statistical data. The central hypothesis of the present study is that "suicide varies negatively and homicide positively with the extent of external restraint over behavior."

Jackson, Don D., "Suicide," *Scientific American, 191:*88–96 (November, 1954). In this psychoanalytic analysis of suicide, the author states that "suicide usually is the result of a conditioned personality and a triggering external stress." The stress in many instances, he suggests, may be traced to the loss of love in interpersonal relations.

Menninger, Karl A., *Man Against Himself,* Harcourt, Brace and Company, New York, 1938. This is a lucid statement, illustrated by case histories from the author's wide clinical experience, of the orthodox Freudian concept of suicide.

Porterfield, Austin L., "Suicide and Crime in Folk and Secular Society," *American Journal of Sociology, 57:*331–338 (January, 1952). This is one of a series of articles in which the author reported on the relationships between suicide and various forms of social disorganization.

Powell, Elwin H., "Occupation, Status, and Suicide: Toward a Redefinition of Anomie," *American Sociological Review, 23:*131–139 (April, 1958). The argument of this important sociological analysis is that "occupation provides function and determines the individual's social status which is an index to his conceptual system. The conceptual system is the source of anomie, which is a primary variable in suicide. Therefore, suicide is correlated with occupation."

Schmid, Calvin F., and Van Arsdol, Maurice D., Jr., "Completed and Attempted Suicides: A Comparative Analysis," *American Sociological Review, 20:*273–283 (June, 1955). This paper is perhaps the only source of knowledge of the distribution and social characteristics of *completed* and *attempted* suicides "for the same population, area and period." Data are presented from Seattle on age and sex differentials, marital status, occupation, and methods for completed and attempted suicides.

Schneidman, Edwin S., and Farberow, Norman L. (eds.), *Clues to Suicide,* McGraw-Hill Book Company, Inc., New York, 1957. This book is a "series of essays on various theoretical and practical aspects of suicide." It is edited by two sociologists and its contributors include scientists who have dealt with suicide from the psychiatric, military, and psychological points of view.

PART THREE

Family Disorganization

CHAPTER 14

Family Disorganization

The Family and Society

The family, composed of husband, wife, and children, is the basic biological and social unit in our society. The modern family is the nuclear family rather than the larger kith and kin group. As such it is the most important small group—the subsystem of our larger society.[1] The family is thus an intimate primary group, instituted because of the need for affection of husband and wife. In the great majority of cases the family begins when two persons "fall in love" and they hope to live happily ever after. Most people marry in the hope of finding permanent happiness with a member of the opposite sex.[2] Needless to say, this happiness is not always forthcoming, and the group formed on this hope may be broken. Family disorganization is thus the weakening, breakdown, or dissolution of the small group comprising the nuclear family.

Family disorganization is closely related to the disorganization in the larger society. The attitudes, values, and norms of the family members reflect the culture, which is derived from the interaction of the members of the larger society. This interaction occurs along economic, political, religious, recreational, and welfare lines. The individual husbands and wives assume roles in the larger society, as well as in the small subsystem of the family. The success of the marriage is thus affected by how they fulfill their roles in the society. Conflicting norms and values in the larger world are reflected in how marriage partners evaluate each other, hence are important factors in determining the number of marriages that fail.

There are many variants of the family group. In our society the possible forms include the childless family; the widowed family; the illegitimate family, composed of unmarried mother and child; the divorced family, with divorced mother and child; and the "normal" family of father, mother, and children. The Bureau of the Census is the source for much of our statistical information on the family and defines it as "a group of two or more persons

[1] Talcott Parsons and Robert F. Bales, *Family, Socialization, and Interaction Process*, The Free Press, Glencoe, Ill., 1955, p. 19.

[2] Robert F. Winch, *Mate-Selection: A Study of Complementary Needs*, Harper & Brothers, New York, 1958, chap. 1.

residing together who are related by blood, marriage, or adoption. . . ."[3]
All of the family forms are included in this definition. Excluded is the large
or extended family unit, composed of uncles, aunts, grandparents, and in-laws
who are not living under the same roof (i.e., "residing together"). Both for
statistical and for common-sense purposes, therefore, the nuclear family is
viewed as a small group of persons living together.[4]

In its parent-child relationship, the family is a natural phenomenon upon
which all organized society has rested. Whether in preliterate or civilized societies, the structure of the family owes its existence to both organic urges
and social needs. The most obvious needs are the sexual impulse and the
sustenance and socialization of the offspring. The needs both of the parents
and of the offspring are modified by cultural forces and these account for the
variations of the family in different societies.[5] The need for affectionate response is thus generally identified with the sexual impulse, although the
fact that commercialized sexual barter exists indicates that sex and affection
are not necessarily synonymous. In the modern, middle-class family sexual
satisfaction is regarded as important for the wife as well as the husband.[6]

The helplessness of the infant and the importance of learned (as distinguished from instinctive) behavior in human beings account for the second basic need fulfilled by the family. For the first twelve years or so of
his life the child is dependent upon other persons for physical survival. In the
family, furthermore, the child has his first induction into interpersonal interaction. In these relationships he learns the prevailing patterns of social behavior.[7] The mother's inferior physical strength and her comparative incapacity during pregnancy and childbirth both foster the protective role of the
husband. This role has declined somewhat at the present time because the
welfare state has taken over many protective functions in lower-class families.

The family is thus an important agent of social control. Many of the
group norms are learned in the family, and so are the definitions of suitable
behavior. The folkways, mores, and institutional controls that regulate courtship, marriage, and the public and private roles of husband and wife are
largely learned in the family. In addition, the acceptance of the norms of behavior in the larger society—such as those dealing with the church, the state,

---

[3] Bureau of the Census, *Population Characteristics, Marital Status, Economic Status,
and Family Status: March 1957, Current Population Reports,* Series P-20, No. 81
(March 19, 1958), p. 2.

[4] Parsons and Bales, *op. cit.,* pp. 299–300. For a study of the nuclear family, see
Robert D. Hess and Gerald Handel, *Family Worlds: A Psychosocial Approach to Family
Life,* University of Chicago Press, Chicago, 1959.

[5] For an authoritative discussion of the variations, see George P. Murdock, *Social
Structure,* The Macmillan Company, New York, 1949.

[6] Ernest W. Burgess and Paul Wallin, *Engagement and Marriage,* J. B. Lippincott
Company, Philadelphia, 1953, chap. 20.

[7] Glenn R. Hawkes, "The Child in the Family," *Marriage and Family Living, 19:46–
51* (February, 1957).

and the business structure—are acquired in the same way. Norms connected with the family are so firmly embedded in the culture that their violation is very disorganizing to the society. Divorce, desertion, delinquency, and other aspects of social disorganization relating to the family are viewed as pressing social problems, with many implications both for individuals and for society as a whole.

The Family and Social Change

The family is an integral part of the larger society. The members occupy statuses and assume roles in other groups whose activities carry them far afield from the intimate family group. The statuses and roles are constantly changing, just as the institutions and associations themselves change. The development of material culture, the rate of invention and technological innovation, the improved facilities for transportation and communication, and the widespread industrialization and urbanization are all familiar agents of change.[8] In combination, these factors have weakened many of the previously accepted patterns of family life including those accepted within the memory of living men.[9]

Out of these interrelated impersonal forces, a new type of family life is emerging. The interplay of social, economic, political, technological, and philosophical factors has given rise to new attitudes, values, and norms that have affected the family (as well as every other institution). The type of family that afforded a satisfactory basis for life in the Middle Ages leaves something to be desired in the second half of the twentieth century. The home and village economy has changed to the urban factory system. Belief in the absolute wisdom of the early fathers of the church is for many persons no longer tenable. Also, added understanding of the motivations of human conduct has altered traditional views of the functions of marriage and human personality. From all this a hedonistic philosophy has emerged which sets great store by happiness for its own sake. This, too, has further altered the structure and functions of the family.[10]

Whenever economic, political, social, moral, philosophical, or religious changes affect the lives of individuals, the family registers the changes like a social barometer. Either as parents or as children, most people live in close contact with their kinship groups. Situations that affect the group relationships of individuals in the larger society clearly affect the most intimate relationships of all in the family. The functioning of the economic system influences the family wage. The changed status of women alters the pattern of family authority.[11] The mass media of communication have undermined

---

[8] Cf. Ronald Lippitt et al., *The Dynamics of Planned Change,* Harcourt, Brace and Company, New York, 1958, chap. 1.

[9] Ernest W. Burgess, "The Family in a Changing Society," *American Journal of Sociology, 53:*417–422 (May, 1948).

[10] Nelson N. Foote, "Love," *Psychiatry, 16:*245–251 (August, 1953).

[11] Helen M. Hacker, "The New Burdens of Masculinity," *Marriage and Family Living, 19:*227–233 (August, 1957).

much of the authority of parents over their children.[12] The decline in religious authority has modified the philosophy of family life. In an era that emphasizes material comfort and social welfare, problems of any future "hereafter" lose some of their importance.

New attitudes toward marriage and new standards of family life are thus replacing some of the older conceptions. Attitudes such as "the father is head of the family" and "woman's place is in the home" provided the basis for former family life, and their dissolution threatens the organization of the group to a certain extent. Old controls are obsolete and many of them have vanished, but there are no new ones to take their place. Men and women must go on living while trying to solve their problems. Trial and error must precede any satisfactory adjustment. Perplexed by situations for which there is no easy solution, people have experimented in the hope of finding a satisfactory basis for marriage under modern conditions.

Few of these experimenters or their critics realize the extent to which marriage is enmeshed in a rapidly changing situation. Young people are often adjudged selfish because they seek release from a marriage that has failed to live up to their expectations. In reality, they have merely accepted the romantic and pleasure-seeking philosophy that pervades contemporary American society.[13] In addition, they have faced the crises of World War II and the postwar years. They have also been encouraged to go into debt to buy a house, automobile, television set, deep freeze, and the rest of the symbols of the good life. When recession brings unemployment and loss of income, many of these symbols become burdens rather than satisfactions. Frequently they produce tensions. When this is true it is no wonder that marriage bonds often become loosened.

The Nature of Family Organization

The unity of any group requires a similarity of attitudes and values among the various members. The family is no exception. Group organization is closely related to cohesiveness, which is defined as "the forces which are acting on the members to stay in a group . . . the attraction of membership in a group for its members."[14] The effectiveness of any group from family to friendship group thus depends first of all upon its ability to continue as such. When a family is disorganized because of conflicting interests, it naturally ceases to perform its functions as a family. In a broader sense, society functions as long as large numbers of persons continue to interact in groups. When that interaction is impaired, there is social disorganization.

The family was defined long ago as a "unity of interacting personalities."[15]

---

[12] David Riesman *et al., The Lonely Crowd,* Doubleday Anchor Books, New York, 1953.

[13] Charles W. Hobart, "Disillusionment in Marriage, and Romanticism," *Marriage and Family Living,* 20:156–162 (May, 1958).

[14] Kurt W. Back, "Influence Through Social Communication," *Journal of Abnormal and Social Psychology,* 46:9–23 (January, 1951), p. 9.

[15] Ernest W. Burgess, "The Family as a Unity of Interacting Personalities," *The Family,* 7:3–9 (March, 1926).

In the effective family great importance lies in its unity. When unity is present, the family is organized; when unity is lacking, family disorganization has begun. The breakdown of unity may take the form of domestic discord, which renders harmonious interaction difficult, although an open break in the formal unity of the group may never occur. Tensions may take the extreme form of desertion or divorce. If this happens, family disorganization is complete, both sociologically and legally. The members must knit up the tangled skein of their lives under new and different circumstances.[16]

The family is initially formed because it meets certain psychological, emotional, or social needs of its members. The degree of organization in the family is related to the extent to which the group continues to meet these needs. When two or more persons become friends, they seek appreciation, acceptance, and participation. When two persons enter marriage, which is followed in most cases by a family, their needs are more complicated. They are largely motivated by "love"—itself a complex sentiment involving such background factors as (1) the relationship of each person to his (or her) parents, (2) each person's image of an ideal mate,[17] and (3) his emotional needs for a mate who will dominate him, care for him, or build his ego, as the case may be.[18]

Other and somewhat more obvious factors combine to bring persons together in marriage. The status of being married often carries considerable prestige, and many persons are anxious to gain this status. Others may seek prestige by marrying a particular individual, partly because they are "in love" and partly because the other is handsome, beautiful, or rich. Social position, family background, and occupational prestige are other motivating factors that cause people to marry. Just as the group is formed in answer to a variety of conscious and unconscious needs, so it may be weakened when these needs are not met. Both family organization and family disorganization are thus related to the satisfaction of needs.[19]

Family organization may be further characterized by certain general factors that give unity to this group:

1. *Objectives.* The organized family possesses an essential unity of objectives. Its adult members have similar attitudes on most of the important aspects of their joint activities. This similarity of objectives is related to such mutual problems as the care, discipline, and education of the children, the allocation of major items in the family budget, the location of the home, the employment of the wife, and the question of sex relations. When the marriage group is formed, each person brings his own value system to the relationship.

---

[16] William J. Goode, *After Divorce*, The Free Press, Glencoe, Ill., 1956.

[17] Anselm Strauss, "The Ideal and Chosen Mate," *American Sociological Review,* 52:204–208 (November, 1946).

[18] Robert F. Winch and Thomas and Virginia Ktsanes, "The Theory of Complementary Needs in Mate-Selection: An Analytic and Descriptive Study," *American Sociological Review, 19*:241–249 (June, 1954).

[19] Fred L. Strodtbeck, "Husband-Wife Interaction over Revealed Differences," *American Sociological Review, 16*:468–473 (August, 1951).

The subsequent interaction will determine the degree of unity of these value systems (i.e., the objectives). As Keeley points out, unity tends to be highest in those marriages "where the interaction is of a cooperative, shared sort; where the marriage is longest; where the most basic values are involved; where the values are mutually functional to the behavior of both husband and wife; where the couple has similar socioeconomic backgrounds; [and] where the role-taking ability of the couple is high. . . ."[20]

2. *Individuality.* In even the most perfectly functioning family each member has a distinct personality. Complete harmony between individual ambition and family welfare is therefore difficult. Nevertheless, in the organized family the members subordinate many of their interests to the group welfare. In an organized society, each member is faced with a number of role patterns, which set the standard for his (or her) behavior as a husband or wife. In our society the husband is generally expected to be breadwinner, chief disciplinarian of the children, and companion to his sons. The wife is expected to be homemaker, provider of affection, and family representative in many community activities. Certain aspects of these roles must be learned by the spouses in the course of family interaction. Marriage involves the reciprocal responses of husbands and wives. Each must be somewhat "domesticated," as it were, in the performance of his or her family roles. Family organization is related to the extent to which each spouse functions adequately in these roles.[21]

3. *Interests.* The members of the traditional family had substantially similar interests in most respects, since their lives were largely spent in the same social milieu. In religious practices, education, recreation, and economic activities, the members usually participated as a unit. Such identification is clearly impossible in modern urban society, where family members develop different interests by virtue of their roles in various secondary groups. A family that is too highly fragmented by divergent interests has difficulty in performing any common activities. Locke's study of happily married couples as contrasted with those divorced showed that the former had a larger number of interests in common, ranging from friends to recreational preferences. This does not mean that *all* forms of common interests automatically produced family organization. Churchgoing, listening to the radio, reading, sports, and music were found to be organizing interests. Drinking, dancing, and card-playing were common interests of divorced couples and hence related to family disorganization.[22]

4. *Needs.* A further factor in family organization is the satisfaction of emotional needs. Marriages in which certain mutual needs are satisfied are generally characterized by a high degree of organization. Marriage, as stated,

[20] Benjamin J. Keeley, "Value Convergence and Marital Relations," *Marriage and Family Living, 17:*342–345 (November, 1955), p. 345.

[21] Leland H. Stott, "The Problem of Evaluating Family Success," *Marriage and Family Living, 13:*149–153 (Fall, 1951).

[22] Harvey J. Locke, *Predicting Adjustment in Marriage,* Henry Holt and Company, Inc., New York, 1951, pp. 256–262.

provides need satisfaction, including such varied needs as those for sexual release and for dominance by another person. Some needs are organic (sex); others are learned (romantic love). The need for sexual release is usually a very conscious and imperious one, especially for the male. His further need for a dominant, motherly wife may be largely unconscious. Some needs are complementary, in the sense that each spouse gratifies a reciprocal need in the other. The husband who needs a motherly and protective wife thus satisfies his own needs when he marries such a woman. If his wife has a complementary need to mother and protect someone, she too is gratified by the interaction. These requirements are very different, but they complement each other, in that each provides a form of emotional gratification the other wants.[23]

Individual families differ in the degree to which they fulfill needs, as well as in the other criteria of family organization.[24] Perfectly organized families so far as needs are concerned are rare, even as completely disorganized families are the exception rather than the rule. Most families muddle through. Their interaction is marked by occasional bickerings and tensions, but they still continue to function as organized units. For some, however, the tensions become so great that one or both members do not wish to continue as a group. Some of the tensions grow out of the divergent personalities of the spouses. Others grow out of precipitate social crises. Thus World War II abruptly severed millions of families, many of which never were reunited. There are many factors which threaten family stability.

The Nature of Family Disorganization

In the broadest sense, family disorganization includes any weakness, maladjustment, or dissolution of the ties binding members of this group together. Family disorganization may thus comprise not only the tensions between husband and wife but those arising between parents and children and those between siblings. Parent-child tensions often present serious problems of adjustment and may result in permanent individual difficulties. These tensions do not, however, ordinarily threaten the family group unless they entail conflicts between the parents. Rifts between husband and wife are more serious than those involving parents and children. Even if children reject their parents—or vice versa—the marriage usually survives.[25]

The conjugal relationship between husband and wife is the central bond uniting the family in our society. When this bond is broken, the family is broken. Family disorganization is social disorganization in the most literal sense, for it is the breakdown of the primary group. In desertion, death, and divorce, a central human relationship is severed and with it a functioning group. This relationship is reciprocal, in that it involves the role of each per-

[23] Winch, *op. cit.,* p. 93.
[24] Cf. Luther T. Jansen, "Measuring Family Solidarity," *American Sociological Review,* 17:727–733 (December, 1952).
[25] F. Ivan Nye, "The Rejected Parent and Delinquency," *Marriage and Family Living,* 18:291–297 (November, 1956).

son in relation to the other. The husband is expected to act in a certain way toward the wife, and she in turn is expected to perform certain actions toward him. Family disorganization is the weakening and disruption of these role patterns.[26]

Many persons think of family disorganization primarily in terms of such manifestations as separation, desertion, divorce, failure to support, and physical violence.[27] These actions are important in themselves, but they do not encompass the full story. They are the external forms of a more basic disorganization of the role patterns and other interpersonal relationships in the marriage group. In many cases, indeed, the legal fiction of organized group life may be maintained even when interpersonal contacts are at a minimum. Some families continue to live together because of religious beliefs which forbid divorce. In others, economic motives may cause the wife to endure a marriage from which conjugal affection has long since fled. The large-scale employment of women in recent decades has doubtless decreased this combination of economic dependence and loveless marriage, but the unhappy unbroken marriage still exists.

Many discordant spouses shrink from divorce because of the (real or imagined) welfare of the children. There is a traditional viewpoint that children are better off with their own parents, no matter how quarrelsome, vindictive, and hostile the latter may be. Recent evidence suggests that this assumption may have to be revised. Nye's study showed that in many such cases children living with a mother who loved them were better adjusted than those living with both parents who wrangled bitterly and continually. In other instances, the child may be "relieved of a parent unable or unwilling to play the role of parent, and, if the remaining parent remarries, may receive one who can and will play the role satisfactorily."[28]

In other families, the outward shell of family integration may be maintained while affectional and/or sexual needs are satisfied elsewhere. This pattern has long been tacitly accepted in many European countries, where the norms demand permanent monogamy but permit extramarital experience for the husband. The extent of such behavior in our own society is unknown, although Kinsey has estimated that approximately one-half of all married men have extramarital relations at some time during their marriage.[29] These extramarital adventures do not necessarily mean the family is disorganized. They may merely indicate a search for variety. The Kinsey data, nevertheless, indicate the extent to which sexual norms are more honored in the breach than the observance.

[26] A. R. Mangus, "Role Theory and Marriage Counseling," *Social Forces, 35*:200–209 (March, 1957).

[27] Cf. Reuben Hill, "Social Stresses on the Family: 1. Generic Features of Families Under Stress," *Social Casework, 39*:139–150 (February–March, 1958).

[28] F. Ivan Nye, "Child Adjustment in Broken and in Unhappy Unbroken Homes," *Marriage and Family Living, 19*:356–361 (November, 1957).

[29] Alfred C. Kinsey *et al., Sexual Behavior in the Human Male,* W. B. Saunders Company, Philadelphia, 1948, p. 585.

Many men and women thus tolerate their marriage when most of the presumed essentials of conjugal affection are lacking. In these cases marriage is far from achieving the vital purposes of family life. At the same time, we must realize that every family has conflicts, frustrations, and tensions and hence must overcome both minor and major crises. Each man and woman enters marriage with different ideas and attitudes born out of his or her experience. It is not surprising that personality traits, role expectations, and value patterns of one may occasionally irritate the other. Only by integrating attitudes and role performances can satisfactory family organization be achieved.[30]

The prolonged intimacy of married life requires a mutual give-and-take by both partners. It also requires an acceptance of traditional marital roles (at least to a certain degree) so that each will know what to expect of the other.[31] Thus most women submerge their formal identity by adopting their husband's name. Most men automatically assume the economic burden of the family and consider their role of provider their chief function. Many women accept masculine authority on basic family decisions, even though they (the women) may question the ultimate wisdom of their spouses. Husbands have the legal right to the final decision in establishing a residence. They often assume the major authority in questions of family finance, and in disciplining the children.

In recent years, however, there has been a notable increase in the number of wives who share such authority. Equalitarian roles seem to be increasing—especially in such fields as "child-rearing, decision-making, and recreation"[32] —doubtless in answer to the increasing employment of women, the growing number of women in higher education,[33] and the gradual abolition of legal inequalities of women. At the same time, women still tend to defer to their husbands' judgments and men continue to cling to their authoritative prerogatives. Both traditional roles arise from the acceptance of the patriarchal point of view, which is still strong in the culture.

When the traditional patterns conflict too strongly with actual experience, the organization of the family is disturbed. In adjusting to new situations, husbands and wives find themselves doing things they are not "supposed" to do. New inventions, standards of living, and educational opportunities require adjustments in timeworn behavior patterns. Old situations yield to the new, and former values are weakened by new practices. In this way, certain aspects of the social structure lose their earlier significance. This may be "progress," but it also involves social disorganization. Group patterns are broken by new activity.

[30] Cf. Alver H. Jacobson, "Conflict of Attitudes Toward the Roles of the Husband and Wife in Marriage," *American Sociological Review,* 17:146–150 (April, 1952).

[31] A. R. Mangus, "Family Impacts on Mental Health," *Marriage and Family Living,* 19:256–262 (August, 1957).

[32] William G. Dyer, "The Institutionalization of Equalitarian Family Norms," *Marriage and Family Living, 20:*53–58 (February, 1958).

[33] Paul C. Glick and Hugh Carter, "Marriage Patterns and Educational Level," *American Sociological Review, 23:*294–300 (June, 1958).

If a woman is making a necessary economic contribution to the family, for example, it is idle to prate about her place being in the home. In the spring of 1957, the number of *working couples* reached a record total of 10,800,000, or 28 percent of the estimated 38,900,000 married couples in the country.[34] In this impressive number of cases, the place of the woman was obviously *not* in the home, no matter what the traditional norms held to the contrary. A wife who is as well educated as her husband will likewise look to him as a comrade rather than as a lord and master. Such challenges to the traditional standards represent an increased democracy, but they also cause problems of adjustment.[35]

The revolt against the old order is often expressed in half-crystallized attitudes. Women themselves are not always certain what they want. They may wish to have their cake and eat it too. On the one hand, they want higher education and a professional career after college. On the other hand, they want marriage and a family after a few years of business or professional experience.[36] They want to combine professional and domestic roles, often without realizing that homemaking and motherhood are full-time jobs. The author of one study thus regretfully concluded that "there is a certain inconsistency, lack of definiteness, and lack of realism about expectations for adult roles among a significant proportion of women college students."[37]

Family Disorganization and Social Structure

Family disorganization is also related to changes in the structure of society. Status and role in marriage are rapidly shifting, as husbands and wives assume new social positions and play new parts both in the larger society and in the family.[38] The traditional family pattern evolved slowly during the centuries when social change was at a minimum. The younger generation usually accepted the expectations of the elders without question. In contemporary society, however, many persons are unable to live up to their roles. Through no fault of their own, young husbands and wives cannot do what they are expected to do. Life situations are so altered that many role patterns no longer apply. Yet these same patterns are the only guide for the individual to his own behavior or that of his spouse. Patterned behavior is thus partially broken down and a situation of social disorganization arises.

Marital roles are the product of previous social interaction, and they direct present interaction. Behavior of present-day husbands and wives is directed in part by the expectations of an earlier day. Marital roles are literally social

[34] Bureau of the Census, *Labor Force, Family Characteristics of Working Wives: March 1957, Current Population Reports,* Series P-50, No. 81 (March, 1958), Table 1.
[35] Nelson N. Foote, "Changes in American Marriage Patterns and the Role of Women," *Eugenics Quarterly, 1:*254–260 (December, 1954).
[36] Harold T. Christensen and Marilynn M. Swihart, "Postgraduation Role Preferences of Senior Women in College," *Marriage and Family Living, 18:*52–57 (February, 1956).
[37] Arnold M. Rose, "The Adequacy of Women's Expectations for Adult Roles," *Social Forces, 30:*69–77 (October, 1951).
[38] Talcott Parsons, "The Social Structure of the Family," chap. 10 in Ruth N. Anshen (ed.), *The Family: Its Function and Destiny,* Harper & Brothers, New York, 1949.

products and assume a certain ideal character in the culture. They indicate the way spouses are supposed to act—what a "good" husband and "good" wife are supposed to do and how they are supposed to feel. These expectations call for responses which formerly applied but are not suitable to present conditions. Confusion thus arises on such matters as whether the wife shall be gainfully employed, who shall manage the finances, and who shall discipline the children. Family rights and duties used to be clearly defined, but today the ambiguity is such that many persons are never quite sure what their roles actually are.[39]

It is the wife, generally speaking, who faces the major confusion in status and role,[40] not because of any temperamental weakness or genetic incapacity of women but merely because their role behavior has changed more drastically than that of men. The husband is still largely controlled by his role as chief provider. The wife has no such clear-cut continuity of role. She continues to act as housekeeper and mother. But beyond that her behavior has become extremely complex. As indicated, she is often gainfully employed, participates increasingly in higher education, and bears fewer children than before. In addition to her traditional roles, she is also expected to be companion, counselor, practical nurse, chauffeur, and mistress—activities that are difficult to combine in one person.[41]

The modern, educated, middle-class, urban wife is thus confronted with several difficult role situations.

1. *Multiplicity of Roles.* With the variety of roles open to her—many of them mutually contradictory—it is no wonder that the wife cannot merely choose one and follow it through. The traditional family structure was based upon a comparatively few feminine roles, on which there was virtual agreement. Today occupational, professional, and class groups stress different roles for the wife. Business groups emphasize the wife's companion and partner roles. Lower-class groups stress the mother and earner roles. In many families, the wife is expected to play all these roles at once. What roles she decides to assume may increase the difficulty of adjustment.[42]

2. *Dissatisfaction with Roles.* Higher education has increased the number of wives qualified in every way (except by custom) to assume an equal role with their husbands in business, the professions, and the home. The number of opportunities open to the modern wife are so large that many wives express dissatisfaction with their roles as housekeeper and mother. According to Kirkpatrick, "Many a capable wife, with talents fully equal to those of her husband, has gone neurotic living her years as a housewife in envy of the woman

---

[39] Leonard S. Cottrell, Jr., "The Adjustment of the Individual to his Age and Sex Roles," *American Sociological Review*, 7:617–620 (October, 1942).

[40] John P. Spiegel, "New Perspectives in the Study of the Family," *Marriage and Family Living*, 16:4–12 (February, 1954).

[41] Mirra Komarovsky, "Cultural Contradictions and Sex Roles," *American Journal of Sociology*, 52:184–189 (November, 1946).

[42] Mirra Komarovsky, *Women in the Modern World*, Little, Brown, and Company, Boston, 1953, chap. 4, "The Homemaker and Her Problems."

who is a marriage partner."[43] Such dissatisfaction was rare in an earlier day, when vocational opportunities for women were limited and the choice of roles was limited.

3. *Conflict of Roles.* In families where the traditional role patterns remain strong, conflict may arise when the wife attempts to assume a role not consistent with them. Many husbands object to any assumption of authority by their wives in fields which they (the husbands) consider their own. These conflicts often stem from the gainful employment of the wife. The problems related to this role may depend essentially upon the attitude of the husband. If he accepts his wife's employment gracefully, the adjustment problems are minimized. If he strenuously objects to this role, the problems are intensified.[44] The husband may also believe that his wife's jurisdiction ends with the kitchen and should not extend to major decisions. When such role conflicts persist, family disorganization may be imminent.

4. *Definition of Roles.* New definitions of status and role for the wife thus involve a corresponding adjustment for the husband. These definitions may involve a threat to his ego. Role patterns that remained virtually unchanged for centuries were based upon the legal, social, and economic authority of the male. As the wife has assumed greater power, many of the old patterns have become strained. Both husbands and wives may have difficulty in agreeing on their new roles, for the patterns have not been fully accepted in all of their implications. Each spouse must improvise some aspects of his or her role, with no sure pattern for guidance. Such improvisation may be challenging, but it is also difficult. The possibilities of failure are great.

The Changing Functions of the Family

The disorganization of the family may also be viewed in terms of its loss of function. The functions of any institution are the activities which its members perform in connection with their roles. The traditional family was a multifunctional institution and had various economic, protective, educational, religious, recreational, biological, affectional, and status functions. The historical family was aided in their performance by the dictums of the church. The self-sufficiency of the historical family meant that its members acted in all of these capacities. This multifunctional pattern no longer exists, except in an attenuated form in the farm family. Social change has shifted functions from the family to other institutions, and in many respects the contemporary family is a mere shadow of its former self.[45]

The *economic* function, for example, has diminished in importance because the family is no longer a major unit of production. With the exception

[43] Clifford Kirkpatrick, "The Measurement of Ethical Inconsistency in Marriage," *International Journal of Ethics, 46:*444–460 (July, 1936), p. 447.

[44] Artie Gianopulos and Howard E. Mitchell, "Marital Disagreement in Working Wife Marriages as a Function of Husband's Attitude Toward Wife's Employment," *Marriage and Family Living, 19:*373–378 (November, 1957).

[45] The classic statement of this hypothesis was given by William F. Ogburn and Clark Tibbitts in "The Family and Its Functions," *Recent Social Trends,* McGraw-Hill Book Company, Inc., New York, 1933, chap. 13.

of the farm family, few families form a complete economic group. The consumption side of the economic function remains with the family, but most of its productive aspects have been removed. Other trends have placed the burden of formal education almost entirely upon the community, and the family has largely lost its *educational* function except for the child's early years. The modern church school has taken over most of the religious training and has correspondingly minimized the *religious* function of the family. The state has assumed authority for protecting the welfare of its citizens from the cradle to the grave. At one end of the life span, the state has increased its protective role over the child; at the other end, programs of old age assistance have further decreased the *protective* function of the family toward those in their declining years.

Certain traditional functions have been partly assumed by other institutions or associations. Commercial recreation has become so powerful as to eliminate almost completely the *recreational* function of the family, especially in the urban centers. The *status-giving* function is in a state of flux and has not been replaced by any corresponding agency. In an earlier day, status was largely determined by birth. Position in the community was in large measure the result of one's membership in a particular family. Today much of the emphasis is upon the individual and his achievements rather than upon his membership within a family group. This trend is democratic, but it also represents a decline in a traditional function.

We may well ask at this point what the family is still good for. What functions does it continue to perform that enable it to remain as the basic institutional pattern? The chief value of the contemporary family appears to lie in three functions which no other institution can perform: the *biological, socialization,* and *affectional* functions. As the others have declined in importance, these three have assumed increasing importance.

1. *The Biological Function.* The biological function refers to the role of the family in providing the socially acceptable relationship within which children are conceived and born. The biological function is the means whereby society is recruited by the addition of new members. It is the most crucial of all functions, for without it the family and the society would obviously wither away and die. This function has fluctuated in recent decades, with the crude birth rate (i.e., the number of births per 1000 of the population) reaching a low of 16.6 in 1933 and a high of 26.6 in 1947. The birth rate continued high throughout the mid-1950's, with a rate of 25.3 in 1957.[46] There is no question of either the importance or the continuance of the family's biological function.

2. *The Socialization Function.* Socialization is the process by which personality in the child is acquired through social interaction. The chief agency in this interaction is the family, and the early contacts of the child are almost

---

[46] Continuing information on the biological function is furnished by the Department of Health, Education, and Welfare, National Office of Vital Statistics, *Monthly Vital Statistics Bulletin,* Washington, published monthly, and various special reports.

exclusively with members of this group. Each society must teach the child to be a responsible member, and does so principally through the family. Here the child learns the accepted social norms, attitudes, values, and behavior patterns, and his behavior becomes predictable to other members of the society. Language, sex patterns, religious beliefs, table manners, and the rest of the varied cultural elements are thus handed on through the family.[47]

3. *The Affectional Function.* The third continuing function of the family is the provision it gives for intimate and affectionate emotional response. This includes satisfaction for sexual impulses but involves much more: sympathetic understanding, gratification of the ego, emotional security, and the sense of being loved and appreciated. The affectional function also entails conjugal affection, the feeling of love and appreciation between spouses which is derived from many years of sympathetic interaction. Where conjugal affection exists the husband and wife respect each other's personalities and are, in effect, the best friend each has ever had.

The affectional function in the contemporary family nevertheless carries an implicit hazard for its stable organization. It is important in bringing the family together, as the man and woman "fall in love" with someone who promises to fulfill their needs for affection. By its very nature, however, this emphasis introduces an instability into the marital relationship, especially when invested with the romantic expectations of modern society. When persons fail to find the happiness in marriage which they have been led to expect, they often assume that they have made an unfortunate choice and accordingly seek a divorce. With all its manifold delights, affection is a two-edged sword. Neither party can promise to love another person twenty years hence exactly as he does at marriage. Attitudes and personalities change. Marriage needs more than romantic affection to insure its permanence.

The Process of Family Disorganization

Many persons insist that the family is not what it used to be. They are perfectly correct. The family has changed in a number of ways, some of which we have already pointed out. Husbands and wives no longer maintain many of their traditional statuses. Nor do they assume their traditional roles in the same fashion. This trend is viewed differently in terms of different value judgments. It is deplored by those who consider the old family structure the only possible or desirable one. Such persons believe that the husband should retain his authority, the wife should stay at home, and the children should be seen and not heard. In their nostalgia for the good old days, these critics fail ro realize that the traditional family was neither democratic nor equalitarian. They forget, too, that democratic individualism cannot be affirmed in business, industry, and education and denied in the family.[48]

When people speak wistfully or bitterly (as the case may be) about "the

---

[47] Talcott Parsons, *The Social System,* The Free Press, Glencoe, Ill., 1951, chap. 6.
[48] William L. Kolb, "Sociologically Established Family Norms and Democratic Values," *Social Forces,* 26:451–456 (May, 1948).

decline of the family," they are thus referring to the decline of a particular type of family, not the family *as such*. The traditional, multifunctional, patriarchal, and agrarian family is clearly changing, and being succeeded by a new, equalitarian, democratic, and urban family. A new family structure is emerging, with new statuses and roles for its members.[49] Human beings may be expected to occupy these statuses and assume these roles for the foreseeable future. The family life may be changed but the family will continue to exist.

The acceptance of the changed family is not easy, for the traditional family is invested with powerful value judgments. This traditional family is held as the ideal and any change is viewed as a social problem. Values defining the traditional family are embedded in the personality structures of large numbers of persons and any threat to these values is perceived as a threat to the person who holds them. The individual becomes anxious when his values are threatened; when the threat involves millions of individuals, we have a serious social problem. Social disorganization (i.e., the breakdown of the traditional family) is thus defined as a social problem (i.e., the threat to a basic social value).[50]

Adherence to this attitude is by no means universal, for an increasing number of persons view the decline of the traditional family with equanimity, if not with outright approval. These persons maintain that the former family was discriminatory, unjust, and stultifying to half of the participants—namely, the women. Women were treated as inferior beings who performed necessary functions but who were nevertheless second-class citizens in many important respects. In short, women were essentially a minority group within a patriarchal family structure.[51] This minority group status is changing in employment, education, and politics, and the modification disorganizes many of the old relationships based upon previous status. The *existence* of these structural changes is widely admitted; their *acceptance* in terms of changed family structure is still subject to wide variation.

The structural changes occasioned by alterations in women's status have been accompanied by a new attitude toward divorce. For better or worse, divorce has gained a new respectability. In recent years approximately 380,-000 couples annually have come to the parting of the ways.[52] The attitude toward divorce is itself a reflection of changing norms of family life. Marriage is no longer regarded as a means of grace but as an end in itself. The end in this case is personal happiness. Insofar as each marriage is productive of such

[49] Cf. E. Gartly Jaco and Ivan Belknap, "Is a New Family Form Emerging in the Urban Fringe?" *American Sociologican Review, 18:*551–557 (October, 1953).

[50] Francis E. Merrill, "The Self and the Other: An Emerging Field of Social Problems," *Social Problems, 4:*200–207 (January, 1957).

[51] Helen M. Hacker, "Women as a Minority Group," *Social Forces, 30:*60–69 (October, 1951).

[52] *Marriages and Divorces, Vital Statistics—Special Reports,* National Office of Vital Statistics, Department of Health, Education, and Welfare, Vol. 48, No. 3 (April 9, 1958), Table A.

happiness, it is considered satisfactory. When happiness is not forthcoming—whether from boredom or active conflict—many persons believe that the marriage has failed to realize its central purpose.[53]

Recognition of this fact should not be construed as a plea for more and better divorces. It is merely a candid acknowledgment of widespread social change. This new attitude toward divorce has been accompanied by the insistence that marriage should promote the well-being of men and women both individually and collectively. It is part of a broader emphasis upon secularism in Western society, wherein this life is considered more important than any rewards in a future existence. Secularism is marked by receptivity toward change, especially in the basic institutional relationships.[54] Business, industry, politics, education, religion, and recreation have all been marked by a growing secularism. Since individuals participate actively in these institutions their family life is bound to reflect this basic shift in the social climate.

Divorce is thus an admission of the failure of a hedonistic and secular venture. When interpersonal tensions eventuate in divorce, there is a breakdown of hopes and anticipations, as well as the legal bonds of marriage. Separation, desertion, and divorce are final stages of the disorganization process, rather than "causes" of the process itself. With divorce the breakdown is given legal recognition. Desertion and separation are often links in the events leading up to divorce. In some instances they are virtually semi-divorces in the sense that the break is final, even though it is not recognized by law. The tensions and conflicts that cause desertion are for the most part those that cause a couple to seek divorce.

Family disorganization is therefore social disorganization in a very literal sense. The family is a small and tightly knit group that is held together by marriage. When the social relationships binding the married pair are broken, the group itself is broken. The disorganization of the group in one sense reflects the reverse of the motivations that brought it together. Persons marry in order to satisfy basic personal needs. In divorce and other forms of disorganization, the family members may have concluded that: (1) the needs that brought them together have diminished; (2) the needs are still there, but they cannot be satisfied with this particular spouse; (3) the needs continue to exist, but they cannot be satisfied with *any* spouse.

Approximately three-quarters of all divorced men and two-thirds of all divorced women ultimately remarry.[55] Hence we may assume that most of these persons have reached conclusion (2) above; they continue to have faith in marriage as a solution to their personal needs, but they believe they can satisfy their needs better with some other partner. The rate of remarriage indicates that marriage is in no danger of disappearance. Persons who divorce and remarry have not lost faith in marriage but have merely concluded that *this*

[53] Burgess and Wallin, *op. cit.,* chap. 15, "Measuring Marital Success."

[54] Howard Becker, "Sacred and Secular Societies," *Social Forces,* 28:361–376 (May, 1950).

[55] Paul C. Glick, *American Families,* John Wiley and Sons, Inc., New York, 1957, pp. 139–140.

particular marriage does not satisfy their needs. The impermanence of a substantial minority of families is regarded as a social problem. But divorce does not threaten the continuance of the family as such, as we discuss in later chapters.

In its broader aspects, social disorganization is often so intangible that it is difficult for the average person to see or comprehend that it exists. The disorganization of an individual family, however, is very real and tangible. A functioning marriage group has been replaced by two or more isolated individuals.[56] The members go on living, sometimes more satisfactorily and sometimes less so than before the divorce. But a primary group has been broken. A series of intimate and personal relationships has ceased to exist.[57] For those who belonged to this particular group, life will require many adjustments.

SELECTED BIBLIOGRAPHY

Glick, Paul C., *American Families,* John Wiley and Sons, Inc., New York, 1957. This important monograph is based upon official statistics, principally from the Bureau of the Census, dealing with various aspects of the American family. As such, it is indispensable to an understanding of the family.

Goode, William J., *After Divorce,* The Free Press, Glencoe, Ill., 1956. Although the principal theme of this study is the series of adjustments *after* divorce, the author offers many significant insights into the nature, process, and causes of family disorganization itself.

Hobart, Charles W., "Disillusionment in Marriage, and Romanticism," *Marriage and Family Living, 20:*156–162 (May, 1958). An important psychological factor in contemporary family disorganization is romantic infatuation prior to marriage. This empirical study examines some of the relationships between frustrated romanticism and disillusionment with family life.

Kolb, William L., "Sociologically Established Family Norms and Democratic Values," *Social Forces, 26:*451–456 (May, 1948). This is a penetrating analysis of the value structure of the family in a democratic, equalitarian, and secular society.

Locke, Harvey J., *Predicting Adjustment in Marriage,* Henry Holt and Company, Inc., New York, 1951. A sample of happily married couples is contrasted with one of divorced couples, with a view to determining the nature of family organization and disorganization.

Mangus, A. R., "Family Impacts on Mental Health," *Marriage and Family Living, 19:*256–262 (August, 1957). In this and another article entitled "Role Theory and Marriage Counseling," *Social Forces, 35:*200–209 (March, 1957), the author explores the nature of marital roles and their relationship to the organiza-

Marriages and Divorces, Vital Statistics—Special Reports, National Office of Vital Statistics, Department of Health, Education, and Welfare, Washington, published periodically. These compilations are the basic statistical source for the major trends in the formation and disorganization of families in the United States.

[56] George C. Homans, *The Human Group,* Harcourt, Brace and Company, New York, 1950, p. 457.
[57] Goode, *op. cit.,* chap. 1.

tion and disorganization of the family. This is an important theoretical contribution to the understanding of marital interaction.

Merrill, Francis E., *Courtship and Marriage,* Henry Holt and Company, Inc., New York, 1959 (rev. ed.). This text is a sociological and cultural analysis of courtship, marriage, and divorce problems. A detailed summary of research is an important feature of the book.

Merrill, Francis E., "The Self and the Other: An Emerging Field of Social Problems," *Social Problems,* 4:200–207 (January, 1957). This article examines some of the implications of self-other relationships to social problems. One of the central elements in family organization and disorganization is the pattern of self-other relationships between the spouses.

Parsons, Talcott, and Bales, Robert F., *Family, Socialization, and Interaction Process,* The Free Press, Glencoe, Ill., 1955. The family is here viewed as a small social system that operates within the framework of the larger society. The personalities of the members reflect the society as a whole, but the small group of the individual family is also a distinct social unit.

Thomas, William I., and Znaniecki, Florian, *The Polish Peasant in Europe and America,* Alfred A. Knopf, Inc., New York, 1927, Vol. II, pp. 1134–1170. These selected pages contain the classic analysis of the concept of social disorganization in terms of conflicting patterns of attitudes and values.

CHAPTER 15

Family Tensions

The Concept of Family Tensions

Family tensions as discussed in this chapter are limited to conflicts between husband and wife. As such they either threaten the stability of the marriage or result in its eventual disorganization. There are, of course, other family tensions—between parent and children, between siblings, and between in-laws and members of the larger kith and kin group. Sometimes these other tensions cause conflicts between husband and wife. Our concern here is only with the hostilities between the marriage partners.

Family tensions constitute the real, as distinguished from the legal, causes for family disorganization. Many tomes have been written attributing family disorganization to vast and impersonal social forces, such as the industrial revolution, the increasing secularization of society, and the growing urbanization of the population. These factors are important in promoting family instability but the immediate break in any individual family is caused by tensions between husband and wife. Their cumulative effect is such that a shared existence becomes intolerable to one or both and a breakdown in the family organization occurs.

There is, however, nothing contradictory in ascribing family disorganization on the one hand to the industrial revolution and on the other to tensions between the contracting parties. There have always been men and women who found their marriage ties burdensome and their family life unhappy. A changed economic, social, legal, and moral order has merely facilitated the release from such bonds. Although marriage is a legal status it is a very personal relationship, in which the wishes, desires, and attitudes of the spouses have become more important than the institutional structure. The nature of tensions and the way they contribute to the disorganization of the individual family have become correspondingly important.[1]

The disorganization process in marriage takes the form of a more or less continuous conflict in attitudes that strains the ties holding the couple together. The accompanying tensions have certain general characteristics: (1) Common objectives gradually disappear and individual aims become

[1] Ernest W. Burgess and Harvey J. Locke, *The Family: From Institution to Companionship*, American Book Company, New York, 1953 (rev. ed.), chap. 1.

more important than family aims; (2) cooperative effort begins to slow down; (3) mutual services are withheld between husband and wife; (4) interpersonal relationships are no longer coordinated; (5) interaction between the pair group and other groups is altered; (6) emotional attitudes of husband and wife become antagonistic or indifferent.[2]

Any classification of family tensions is thus an arbitrary attempt to categorize the factors that precipitate clashes between the spouses. Family disorganization is the result of a combination of factors rather than one specific factor. Marriage involves two complex and diverse personalities, and marital tensions reflect their differences. Each spouse embodies different patterns of traits within his personality, and each reacts to the patterns in the other. Marriage is a way of life that involves a sharing of life, friends, property, income, attitudes, goals, ideals, and ambitions. Hence the tensions that break down the family group reflect both the personalities of the spouses and the interaction between them.

Professor Baber maintains that the causes of divorces (or family tensions) are the same as the causes of quarreling and of unhappy marriages. He thus regards Terman's study *Psychological Factors in Marital Happiness* as actually a study of the reasons for family conflict. Terman's study showed that husbands had fifty-seven grievances against their wives and wives had fifty-three against their husbands. Those which were considered the nine most serious grievances by each spouse are listed in Table 15.1. There were many addi-

TABLE 15.1. Grievances of Husbands and Wives
(792 couples)

Husbands	Order of Seriousness	Wives
Wife nags him	1	Husband selfish and inconsiderate
Wife not affectionate	2	Husband unsuccessful in business
Wife selfish and inconsiderate	3	Husband untruthful
Wife complains too much	4	Husband complains too much
Wife interferes with hobbies	5	Husband does not show affection
Wife slovenly	6	Husband does not talk things over
Wife quick tempered	7	Husband "touchy"
Wife conceited	8	Husband disinterested in children
Wife insincere	9	Husband disinterested in home

tional grievances, however: husbands objected to their wives because they tried to improve them, were too talkative, lazy, extravagant, poor cooks, too old, etc. Wives, on the other hand, objected seriously to the husbands' being rude, to the husbands' relatives, table manners, being too much interested in business, being late to meals, etc.[3]

[2] E. T. Kreuger, "A Study of Marriage Incompatibility," *The Family*, 9:53–60 (April, 1928).

[3] R. E. Baber, *Marriage and the Family*, McGraw-Hill Book Company, Inc., 1939, p. 423.

In general, family tensions may be classified as *personal* or as *social*. Personal tensions arise primarily from the personality structures of the spouses. Social tensions are situational in origin and arise out of the social setting in which the marriage functions. Personal tensions thus include those stemming from the individual's social values, behavior patterns, and sexual relationships. Social tensions include those arising from the position of the married couple in the social structure, such as class status, economic condition, occupation, employment of the wife, and unemployment of the husband.

While we may analyze these tensions separately it would be more or less impossible to find them existing separately in any given family. The social values of a person reflect his religious background; behavior patterns are related to class status; and problems relating to sex are closely connected with social position. We may think of these tensions as constituting a rough continuum, with such personal elements as temperament at one end and such situational elements as unemployment at the other. Without exception, however, all of these tensions affect the interpersonal relationships of the couple. Tensions of all kinds—from unpleasant table manners to religious conflicts—focus upon the two persons whose interaction determines whether or not the marriage will survive.[4]

Temperamental Factors

Temperament may be defined as the combination of genetic qualities in the individual that determine his emotional reactions. Temperamental qualities appear to be largely innate. Although they may be controlled, they cannot be eliminated. The person who reacts quickly and angrily can learn to control his outward expression of emotion but not his inward indignation. Aristotle made the classic grouping of temperaments—the sanguine (cheerful), choleric (hot-tempered), melancholic (gloomy), and phlegmatic (sluggish). Jung gives a more recent classification. He maintains that there are three general types of temperament, each consisting of two opposites: (1) In the first category are the familiar introvert and extrovert, i.e., the individual who is drawn inward toward himself or outward toward others. (2) The second category consists of persons who perceive largely through the senses and those who perceive primarily through intuition. (3) The third category consists of those who form judgments on the basis of rational thought and those whose judgments are based largely upon feeling.[5]

Terman and his associates emphasized the importance of temperamental factors. They conclude that certain temperamental factors are basic to marital happiness and outweigh many of the social factors emphasized by sociologists. Unhappy couples are characterized by such temperamental traits as: "to be touchy and grouchy; to lose their tempers easily; to fight to get their own way; to be critical of others; to be careless of others' feelings; to chafe under dis-

[4] Cf. Reuben Hill, "Social Stresses on the Family: 1. Generic Features of Families Under Stress," *Social Casework,* 39:139–150 (February–March, 1958).

[5] Horace Gray, "Psychological Types in Married People," *Journal of Social Psychology,* 29:189–200 (May, 1949).

cipline or to rebel against orders; to show any dislike that they happen to feel; to be easily affected by praise or blame; to lack self-confidence; . . . to be often in a state of excitement; and to alternate between happiness and sadness without apparent cause."[6]

Locke found that the choleric person, as might be expected, is likely to make an unsatisfactory marital adjustment. The spouse who recovered quickly from anger, however, made a better adjustment than the one who was slower to do so.[7]

The relationship between temperament and marital tensions is often more subtle. Men and women enter marriage in an attempt (largely unconscious) to satisfy a variety of deep psychological needs, many of which are temperamental. Marriage is the most approved institution for the satisfaction of these needs, and the individual enters marriage with strong expectations of satisfying them. The strength of the expectations may have an important bearing upon the success of the marriage. Men who wish to be dominated thus gain satisfaction from women who wish to dominate. Tensions arise, on the other hand, when domineering men marry domineering women. In such cases, personal needs *conflict* rather than *complement* each other.[8]

Burgess and Wallin hold that compatibility of personality, of which temperament is an important component, is more important for the husband than the wife. The wife apparently accepts the necessity of adjusting to a greater degree than the husband. She makes more of an effort to work out a satisfactory adjustment than he does. When she meets with temperamental differences, she tries to get along with her husband, whereas he is more likely to give up in despair. Marriage appears (on balance) to be more important to the wife and she is willing to try harder to make it work. When temperamental difficulties are so overpowering that even she is unwilling to make the effort, the marriage is in serious trouble.[9]

Social Values

Agreement on social values is basic to any group and particularly important in marriage. Each marriage partner has his or her own values, the things he or she considers important.[10] Seldom do they agree completely; hence most marriages are bound to be marked by varying degrees of agreement and disagreement. Couples may differ on their preferences regarding

[6] Lewis M. Terman *et al., Psychological Factors in Marital Happiness,* McGraw-Hill Book Company, Inc., New York, 1938, p. 369.

[7] Harvey J. Locke, *Predicting Adjustment in Marriage,* Henry Holt and Company, Inc., New York, 1951, p. 204.

[8] Robert F. Winch, *Mate-Selection: A Study of Complementary Needs,* Harper & Brothers, New York, 1958.

[9] Ernest W. Burgess and Paul Wallin, *Engagement and Marriage,* J. B. Lippincott Company, Philadelphia, 1953, pp. 436–437.

[10] Benjamin J. Keeley, "Value Convergence and Marital Relations," *Marriage and Family Living, 17:*342–345 (November, 1955). Cf. also Florence R. Kluckhohn, "Family Diagnosis: 1. Variations in the Basic Values of Family Systems," *Social Casework, 39:*63–72 (February–March, 1958).

such matters as handling money, recreation, religion, demonstrations of affection, relationships to their in-laws, and table manners.[11]

Social values involve a great variety of behavior patterns. One important value is the marriage itself. In fact, the attitude toward the marriage as a value is often the deciding factor in its success. For some persons, marriage is their most important single value, and they will do everything they can to adjust satisfactorily. For others, the marriage is not as important as their personal happiness, comfort, or success. If the motivation to continue is strong, the couple can surmount difficulties that would disorganize another marriage. If the motivation is comparatively weak, the marriage will dissolve easily under the stress of tensions.[12]

Willingness to adapt to the values of the spouse is thus an important element in easing family tensions. Two persons cannot have exactly the same system of values. Hence each must adapt to the other, without at the same time completely sacrificing his own integrity. Adaptability is not a single trait but a group of traits, some of which can be learned. Adaptability can be increased "in the degree to which [the spouse] is able to develop further his capacity for empathy (i.e., feeling with others), to become more flexible in his marital and other relations, to take advantage of situations which intensify motivation to adapt, and to learn and put into practice knowledge and skills desirable for marriage."[13] Spouses lacking in any or all of these abilities may find that marital tensions generate rapidly over disparities in social values.

The values of married couples also involve persons outside the marriage. Locke measured the importance of other persons as values in terms of "sociability" and "conventionality." The first included such criteria as making friends easily, membership in organizations, concern with what others may think, and a sense of humor. Conventionality was measured in terms of whether the marriage took place in a church, whether the couple attended Sunday School before marriage, and whether they went to church after marriage. Locke's definition of conventionality is clearly religious in focus, but he found that agreement on religious values was positively related to marital adjustment. Lack of agreement on these values was associated with marital maladjustment.[14]

Differences in religious belief are a further source of marital tensions. These tensions arise from marriages between persons of different faiths. Matters of religious dogma are usually not as disturbing as controversy over the religious education of children, the use of contraception, and attitudes toward divorce. The amount of *potential* tension appears to be increasing because of the growing number of mixed marriages involving Catholics and non-Catholics. Such marriages are sanctioned by the church only after the non-Catholic

---

[11] Locke, *op. cit.*, p. 85.
[12] Burgess and Wallin, *op. cit.*, chap. 19, "Adaptability."
[13] *Ibid.*, p. 654.
[14] Locke, *op. cit.*, chap. 11.

future spouse signs an antenuptial agreement. In this document the non-Catholic agrees (1) that the marriage shall be dissolved only by death, (2) that the children shall be baptized and educated in the Catholic faith, and (3) that the official Catholic policy regarding "artificial" methods of contraception shall be observed.[15]

After the agreement is duly signed, the Catholic Church will permit the marriage to be performed by a priest. The marriage is then accepted under canon (i.e., church) law. The church nevertheless discourages such marriages. Mixed marriages, according to estimates by Catholic sociologists, constitute more than 30 percent of all Catholic marriages.[16] Marital tensions often arise in such marriages, even though the antenuptial agreement has been duly signed. Many persons do not anticipate the difficulties over problems of this sort. They sign the agreement in perfectly good faith but later find that they cannot abide by it. The birth of a child may change the attitude of the non-Catholic spouse, who may be unwilling to rear a child in a faith to which he or she does not subscribe. Tensions are greater when the non-Catholic mate has a strong religious faith.[17]

Tensions are apt to be especially strong when the wife is a Protestant or Jew. The close relationship between mother and child means that the child is likely to subscribe to the faith of the mother, who if she is a devout Protestant may object to rearing her child in an alien faith. Difficulties are not so frequent when the husband is a Protestant, since the wife can bring up the children in her own faith. Divorce rates thus tend to be higher in marriages where the husband is Catholic and the wife Protestant. In a study made by Monahan and Kephart, 21 percent of such marriages ended in divorce, as compared to 7 percent of those in which the husband was a Protestant and the wife a Catholic.[18]

Where no nuptial agreement is signed the church does not sanction the marriage. Family dissolution is even greater in this case. Since the church holds that there has been no real marriage, remarriage is often permitted.

Behavior Patterns

Behavior patterns are methods of response learned by the individual in a particular social setting. Since behavior patterns are learned, they theoretically can be modified. In practice, however, they have often become so ingrained in the personality at time of marriage that they are hard to change later. In the field of marital tensions, behavior patterns range in importance and complexity from personal habits to complex response patterns. In the

[15] "Marriage—Mixed," *The Catholic Encyclopedia,* Encyclopedia Press, Inc., New York, 1910.

[16] John L. Thomas, "The Factor of Religion in the Selection of Marriage Mates," *American Sociological Review, 16:*487–491 (August, 1951).

[17] Judson T. Landis, "Marriages of Mixed and Non-Mixed Religious Faith," *American Sociological Review, 14:*401–407 (June, 1949).

[18] *Ibid.,* p. 403. Cf. Thomas P. Monahan and William M. Kephart, "Divorce and Desertion by Religious and Mixed-Religious Groups," *American Journal of Sociology, 59:*454–465 (March, 1954).

first category are social manners, personal hygiene, and conversational usages. In the second are child-rearing practices, ways of making decisions, and the treatment of other persons.

The most obvious behavior patterns fall under the heading of "manners," "etiquette," and "politeness." These often become symbolic factors in marital tensions but are seldom deep-seated causes in their own right. Wives who divorce their husbands for "offensive table manners" are probably responding to a comparatively unimportant form of behavior that *stands for* a complex combination of tensions. A wife may likewise sincerely believe that she dislikes her husband because he takes his shoes off after dinner. But her feelings may actually be caused by sexual tensions, conflicts over money, or differences in class background.[19] Marital tensions involve two personalities and reflect all the conscious and unconscious differences between them. Abhorred behavior patterns are often the symbol of larger and more deep-seated hostilities.[20]

Behavior patterns may also include real as well as symbolic sources of marital tensions. One such real source is the pattern of authority, which is absorbed in the parental family experience. In the contemporary American family there are several types of authority patterns: (1) families controlled by the mother; (2) families controlled by the father; (3) families that are jointly controlled, with both husband and wife having a hand in democratic decisions. Each person acquires his own conception of authority from his early family experience and carries this pattern into his own marriage. Tensions may arise when the patterns of the parental families are incompatible or conflicting.[21]

The husband may have grown up in a family where the father was dominant and the mother submissive. His wife, on the other hand, may have lived in a family where the authority was largely vested in the wife and the husband played a submissive role. Each person incorporated a different pattern of family authority into his personality and brought a different set of role expectations to the marriage. The husband expected the wife to be submissive while the wife expected the same behavior from him. Both were disappointed and marital tensions resulted.[22]

Tensions do not inevitably arise from conflicting role expectations in the realm of authority, however. Adaptability is possible and is important if adjustment is to be made. Burgess and Wallin list some of the ways by which authority tensions may be reduced: (1) *suggestion*—the subordinate person may suggest a solution to a given problem and then persuade the dominant

[19] Clark E. Vincent, "Social and Interpersonal Sources of Symptomatic Frigidity," *Marriage and Family Living, 18:*355–360 (November, 1956).

[20] Harriet E. Mowrer, *Personality Adjustment and Domestic Discord,* American Book Company, New York, 1935, pp. 219–220.

[21] Hazel L. Ingersoll, "A Study of the Transmission of Authority Patterns in the Family," *Genetic Psychology Monographs, 38:*225–302 (1948).

[22] *Ibid.,* pp. 256–258. Cf. also Luther T. Jansen, "Measuring Family Solidarity," *American Sociological Review, 17:*727–733 (August, 1952).

spouse that the idea came from him (or her); (2) *division*—the responsibility may be deliberately divided, with one spouse making the decisions on household matters and the other taking charge of business matters; (3) *preparation*—the subordinate person may prepare the ground for a request before it is actually made, and in this way decrease the surprise and an otherwise negative reaction of the other; (4) *emotionalism*—weeping and other emotional appeals may help weaker members to gain their ends, although this device may merely irritate the dominant member and make him more disagreeable than ever.[23]

Response Tensions

Response tensions arise because one or both partners fail to receive or give as much affection as had been anticipated. The search for love in its various forms is a central reason for marriage in our society. Marriage is the relationship in which romance is presumed to flourish. When love declines or is lacking marriage becomes a difficult relationship. Courtship is conducted under exceptionally pleasant, exciting, and "romantic" conditions, and the transition to the everyday relationships of marriage may be disillusioning.[24] Romantic attraction flourishes under conditions of strangeness and sexual inhibition. When sexual tensions are released in marriage, romanticism gradually fades away. A certain amount of personal strangeness and sexual restraint is apparently necessary for romantic love.[25]

Sexual tensions are related to romantic frustrations, but they are not synonymous. Sexual tensions are the unresolved conflicts relating to the performance of the sexual act. Both men and women (especially the former) enter marriage anticipating satisfactory sexual experience, which often fails to be achieved. It should be made clear, however, that sexual incompatibility is not the only, or even the most important, cause of marital tensions. Family disorganization arises from a variety of tensions, of which sex is only one. Satisfactory sexual relations may symbolize other aspects of the marriage. Adjustment or maladjustment often appears as either sexual harmony or frustration.[26]

Terman and his associates made one of the first studies of sexual tensions. They concluded that sexual factors did not constitute the major determinant of marital success. In fact sexual factors that were previously assumed to be important showed little or no correlation with marital adjustment. Among these factors were "reported and preferred frequency of intercourse, estimated duration of intercourse, . . . methods of contraception used, distrust

---

[23] Burgess and Wallin, *op. cit.,* pp. 644–648.

[24] Charles W. Hobart, "Disillusionment in Marriage, and Romanticism," *Marriage and Family Living, 20:*156–162 (May, 1958).

[25] Robert O. Blood, Jr., "Romance and Premarital Intercourse—Incompatibles?" *Marriage and Family Living, 14:*105–108 (May, 1952).

[26] Burgess and Wallin, *op. cit.,* chap. 20, "The Sex Factor in Marriage." This is one of the most balanced discussions in the literature.

of contraceptives, fear of pregnancy, . . . wife's history of sex shock, rhythm in wife's sexual desire. . . ."[27]

In a later study Terman explored the role of sexual tensions further with reference to "orgasm adequacy" of the wife. This was defined as her ability to experience orgasm "usually" or "always." "Orgasm inadequacy" was the ability to have orgasm only "sometimes" or "never." Terman concluded that orgasm adequacy was significant but not basic to successful marital adjustment. This conclusion, according to Terman, "is supported by the slight relationship between wife's orgasm adequacy and the incidence of divorce or separation . . . , and by the fact that the percentage of divorce among inadequate wives does not differ significantly from the percentage among adequate wives."[28]

On the other hand, the Kinsey reports consider sexual satisfaction important for the wife's adjustment. The marital relationship is a form of social interaction, in which each person takes the other into account and responds accordingly. Attainment of orgasm is important for the wife, according to Kinsey, and hence for the husband and the relationship itself. In many middle-class marriages the husband may regard failure to bring about orgasm in the wife as a failure on his part, which in turn may interfere with his own sexual role. In marital interaction the behavior of the husband is a stimulus to the behavior of the wife and vice versa. Hence her reaction to the sexual act is important to the couple's sexual adjustment.[29]

The most extensive research in this field has been done by Burgess and Wallin, who concluded that sexual adjustment is more important to the husband than to the wife. Husbands with low scores on marital success in general thus had a greater probability of low scores on sexual adjustment than was true for the wives. Sexual gratification was something the husband expected in marriage and he was disappointed when he failed to obtain it. For the wives, sexual gratification was often merely an additional satisfaction in an otherwise successful marriage. If the marriage was otherwise happy they were not unhappy without it.[30]

These findings reveal that wives who are otherwise happy may derive pleasure from the sexual relationship because it *symbolizes* a good relationship with their husbands. The level of sexual expectation of the husband is, however, considerably higher. Men enter marriage with the expectation of frequent and gratifying sexual intercourse. Hence they have more chance of disappointment than women, whose expectations are not so high. As Burgess and Wallin stated, "There is much more margin for the worsening than there is for the improving of the sexual adjustment of husbands. The opposite appears to

---

[27] Terman *et al., op. cit.,* p. 373.

[28] Lewis M. Terman *et al.,* "Correlation of Orgasm Adequacy in a Group of 556 Wives," *Journal of Psychology,* 32:115–172 (October, 1951).

[29] Alfred C. Kinsey *et al., Sexual Behavior in the Human Female,* W. B. Saunders Company, Philadelphia, 1953, p. 373.

[30] Burgess and Wallin, *op. cit.,* pp. 676–697.

be true of the sexual adjustment of wives."[31] Sexual tensions are thus both more common and more significant for the husband than for the wife. This is probably the major explanation for extramarital excursions of men.

Relations with In-Laws

The contemporary American family assumes that the married couple will function independently from the rest of society, especially from their parents. This expectation is often frustrated by the parents of one or both spouses. The young people may be forced to live with their parents or otherwise be obliged to spend a great deal of time with them. The small conjugal family is so tightly knit that it is often hard for parents and children alike to break these ties and for the young people to form an adult group of their own. Emotions are so deeply embedded in the personality that both parties may find it difficult to start an independent group.[32]

Marital tensions relating to in-laws are part of the folklore in virtually all societies. Many primitive peoples, indeed, have a "mother-in-law taboo," which expressly forbids the mother-in-law and son-in-law to speak or even to cross each other's paths. Mother-in-law jokes in our own culture offer additional evidence of this folk wisdom. An important part of marital adjustment, however, still involves relations with in-laws. The husband must adjust to his wife's parents and she to his. In addition, each must work out a satisfactory relationship to his own parents.[33]

One of the hardest lessons that parents must learn is to avoid interfering with the marital problems of their children. Parents have ambitions and desires for their children's happiness, and they often insist upon imposing their opinions upon the reluctant children. Parents may resent conduct of the son-in-law or daughter-in-law because they feel that their own child is the victim of an unfair relationship. They may insist that the daughter-in-law is too extravagant, that she is uncooperative, or that she is unsuited to her task as mother. In many ways, unsought advice of the older generation may cause tensions in the marriage of their children.

A crucial aspect of this problem is the comparative success with which the child is emancipated emotionally from his parents. Winch maintains that it is more difficult for the son to emancipate himself because of the strong tie uniting mother and son. In American middle-class society there is thus "a tendency for (a) the mother to be the preferred parent, (b) the son to be the preferred child, and (c) for the mother-son relationship to be the strongest of the four parent-child relationships."[34] The son's task is further complicated by

---

[31] *Ibid.*, p. 695.

[32] Cf. Marvin B. Sussman, "The Help Pattern in the Middle-Class Family," *American Sociological Review, 18*:22–28 (February, 1953).

[33] Cf. Paul Wallin and Howard M. Vollmer, "Marital Happiness of Parents and Their Children's Attitudes to Them," *American Sociological Review, 18*:424–431 (August, 1953).

[34] Robert F. Winch, *The Modern Family*, Henry Holt and Company, Inc., New York, 1952, p. 299.

the fact that he is *supposed* to break more completely with his family than is his wife.[35]

Komarovsky believes, however, that the girl has the greater difficulty in emancipation from her parental family. The role of the boy, she holds, allows him to stay away from home, come in late, and otherwise act independently of his parents. The girl is supposed to stay home, help with the housework, and generally maintain a closer tie with her family. The boy also has greater freedom in his adolescent love affairs, whereas the girl is supervised more closely in her dating and other relationships with the opposite sex. Thus "the differential training of boys and girls in anticipation of adult sex roles has had, as an unintentional by-product, a closer identification of the girl with her family and her greater responsibility for family support."[36]

Irrespective of who has the greater difficulty of liberation, it is clear that this emancipation is an important factor in marital tensions. The loving son may be unable to shift from the role of son to that of husband, and his mother may have even more trouble in adjusting to this change. The daughter may also have trouble in changing from daughter to wife, although for different reasons. The emotional attachment in our society is generally stronger between mother and child than between father and child. Hence the mother-in-law rather than the father-in-law is a greater source of tension, both for the son and for the daughter.[37]

Marital Roles

The individual's conception of his role in marriage is also important in determining its relative success or failure. Husband and wife come into marriage with a system of self-other patterns which they have developed in their earlier experience, notably in their parental families. They attempt to carry over these roles into their married life and in the process may generate family tensions. The spoiled daughter who idolizes her father may try to assume the same attitudes toward her husband in her marriage and expect him to assume her father's role. The only son of an adoring mother may fail to receive the same response from his wife as he did from his mother. Each spouse is frustrated in his or her attempt to carry the role he had in his parental family with him into his marriage.[38]

The husband thus expects to be the chief provider for his wife and family. He expects his wife to take care of the home, rear the children, and be his affectionate companion. The wife presumes her husband will be kind and thoughtful and help out occasionally around the house. Her disappointment

[35] Robert F. Winch, "Further Data and Observations on the Oedipus Hypothesis: The Consequence of an Inadequate Hypothesis," *American Sociological Review,* 16:784–795 (December, 1951).

[36] Mirra Komarovsky, "Functional Analysis of Sex Roles," *American Sociological Review, 15:*508–516 (August, 1950), p. 514.

[37] Burgess and Wallin, *op. cit.,* p. 605.

[38] Robert S. Ort, "A Study of Role Conflicts as Related to Happiness in Marriage," *Journal of Abnormal and Social Psychology,* 45:691–699 (October, 1950).

may become acute when he fails to act as she anticipated. She may have built up this conception from her experience with her own father. After she has been married for a few months, however, she perceives her husband as cold, suspicious, and distant—in short, as a *role-frustrating,* rather than a *role-fulfilling,* partner. If the husband fails to perceive in his wife the qualities he has expected, he, too, feels frustrated and marital tensions increase.[39] Marital tensions thus reflect "the degree to which the role expectations that one partner has of the other are congruent with the other's own role expectations."[40]

Such failure may in turn generate aggression toward the marriage partner. John is frustrated in his need for the motherly warmth he expected in his wife. Mary is equally frustrated because she needs a strong, dominant man to make basic decisions for her. In each case, the spouse may not be fully aware of the nature of his need or the reasons for his frustration. He merely knows that he is disappointed and angry because things have not worked out the way he anticipated. In marital interaction, hostility on the part of one partner generates a similar feeling in the other. A vicious circle of tensions may thus be engendered without either one's recognizing the true source of his feelings.

Social roles cause marital tensions in a more general sense. The socially defined marital roles are the stereotyped versions of the "good husband" and the "good wife" and hence have a strong motivating effect upon behavior. Most people try to assume these roles as they understand them. Difficulties may arise from the fact that the roles are inherently incompatible with urban life and so become *impossible* to perform. Traditional conceptions of roles evolved in an agricultural society when the family structure was very different from our own. But these roles are still part of the cultural heritage and men and women are expected to assume them.[41]

Nevertheless there is confusion in present-day marital roles. As Mirra Komarovsky perceptively points out, "Our culture is full of contradictions and inconsistencies with regard to women's roles, . . . new social goals have emerged without the parallel development of social machinery for their attainment, . . . norms persist which are no longer functionally appropriate to the social situations, . . . behavior patterns useful at some stage become dysfunctional at another. . . ."[42]

Social Class

Tensions may arise because of the class position of the two mates prior to marriage or because of occupational status, income level, employ-

---

[39] A. R. Mangus, "Family Impacts on Mental Health," *Marriage and Family Living,* 19:256–262 (August, 1957).

[40] *Ibid.*

[41] Leonard S. Cottrell, Jr., "The Adjustment of the Individual to His Age and Sex Roles," *American Sociological Review,* 7:617–620 (October, 1942).

[42] Komarovsky, *op. cit.,* p. 508.

ment of the wife, and unemployment of the husband. Conflict situations occurring on this level inevitably involve the personalities of the partners.[43]

"By defining the people with whom an individual may have intimate social
relationships," says Allison Davis, "our social class system narrows his learning and training environment."[44] Social class partially sets the stage for marital
adjustment and maladjustment. Class status is important during the person's
formative years in the parental family, as his personality is molded by his environment. Status is also important when he starts his own family. Position
in the social level determines many of the tensions to which the marriage is
exposed. When men and women of *different* class backgrounds marry, other
tensions may arise. We may survey briefly some of the family tensions that
are characteristic of different social levels.[45]

1. *Upper Class.* The upper class is generally divided into two categories
—the "established" upper class and the "new" upper class. The first is the old,
wealthy, and educated group in the community; the second comprises newly
rich persons lacking in family background, who may have more wealth than
the old families. The established upper class usually insists upon marriage
within its own social level. Thus many of the tensions that divide other families
(e.g., religious, ethnic, and cultural differences) are comparatively rare. The
established upper-class family has its "normal" quota of *personal* tensions
arising from personality difficulties, but many *social* tensions are controlled
or eliminated altogether. This family exerts strong pressure upon its members
to conform to family and class codes and (above all) not to marry "beneath"
their class.

The "new" upper class experiences many tensions because of its recent rise
in the social scale. This group may be torn by tensions stemming from acute
alcoholism, emotional insecurity, conspicuous consumption, quarrels between members, and personal aggression against spouses and children. The
head of the family is often highly aggressive and owes his economic success
to this fact. He cannot carry his aggressions home and expect his wife and
children to obey his every whim. The assurance of status of the established
upper-class family is conspicuously lacking in the newly "arrived" family.
Their children often have too much money, too many cars, and too much freedom in an effort to prove their status.

2. *Middle Class.* The middle class is characteristically motivated by the
desire for upward mobility, and this may become a major source of tensions
between its members. Some middle-class families are able to achieve higher
status, but many more do well to stay where they are. A difference between

[43] August B. Hollingshead, "Cultural Factors in the Selection of Marriage Mates,"
*American Sociological Review, 15:*619–627 (October, 1950).

[44] Allison Davis, "Child Rearing in the Class Structure of American Society," in *The
Family in Democratic Society,* Columbia University Press, New York, 1949, p. 69.

[45] The following is adapted from August B. Hollingshead, "Class Differences in Family
Stability," *Annals of the American Academy of Political and Social Science, 272:*39–46
(November, 1950).

aspiration and achievement may bring about frustration and tensions.[46] Interpersonal relationships are the principal form of tensions among this large segment of the population. Temperamental incompatibilities, differences in social values, and frustrations of sexual expectations are among the factors giving rise to marital tensions among middle-class families. Differences between parents and children are a further source of tensions. Children are often educated for upward mobility and in this process feel ashamed of their parents. The children may be educated for goals which their parents do not comprehend.

3. *Working Class.* The working class subsumes the millions of families whose principal breadwinner works with his hands. Such families are especially subject to tensions related to economic insecurity. The average weekly income of many highly skilled members of the working class is larger, to be sure, than that of many middle-class, white-collar families. Their economic security is not so great, however, because work stoppages are common in industry. A large percentage of working-class wives are gainfully employed outside the home and encounter difficulties in caring for their children as a result. Housing facilities of the working-class family are often inadequate. Crowding may thus add to their group tensions.

Family disorganization from all causes (e.g., death, desertion, divorce, separation) increases as we descend the class scale. We shall discuss this aspect in detail in Chapter 17. The working-class family is "prematurely" broken in approximately twice as many cases as is the middle-class family. The "family cycle" of birth, rearing the children, marriage of the children, and old age is often broken in the working class,[47] which suffers from hazards arising from its position in the social structure. The stable family is the ideal in the working class, but this ideal is often lost through unemployment, separation, and premature death of the breadwinner.[48]

4. *Lower Class.* The line between the working class and the lower class is difficult to draw, inasmuch as many families are marginal to either group. In its "typical" form, the lower class includes the underprivileged worker who works at underpaid, dirty, unskilled, and manual labor. His employment is often intermittent, and he has long periods of unemployment. During these periods he lives as best he can, sometimes on public relief and sometimes on his relatives or friends. Instability in lower-class families is very high, with an estimated 50–60 percent failing to complete the family cycle because of various forms of disorganization.[49]

[46] Earl L. Koos, "Class Differences in Family Reactions to Crisis," *Marriage and Family Living,* 12:77–78 (Summer, 1950). The broader implications of this situation are explored by Vance Packard in *The Status Seekers,* David McKay Company, Inc., New York, 1959.

[47] Paul C. Glick, *American Families,* John Wiley and Sons, Inc., New York, 1957, chap. 3.

[48] Hollingshead, "Class Differences in Family Stability," p. 44.

[49] *Ibid.* For a further analysis of the personal and family problems of the different social classes, see August B. Hollingshead and Frederick C. Redlich, *Social Class and Mental Illness,* John Wiley and Sons, Inc., New York, 1958.

The way of life of the lower-class family also gives rise to strong personal aggressions. Although economically insecure, the working-class family spends heavily on "nonessentials" and goes into debt to do so. Adult members are often aggressive toward each other and the husband may strike the wife in anger. The children are disciplined by physical punishment. They are also exposed to bodily aggression from other children. Such tensions are rare in the middle-class family. The lower-class conflicts are more or less unique to their class level.[50]

Serious tensions are more or less bound to arise when persons of different class levels marry. The subculture of each social class is in some respects a world of its own, and persons grow up with different standards on matters ranging from manners to sex behavior. Wives who expect certain niceties of "good manners" are thus outraged when their husbands pick their teeth at the table. A woman who has been reared in an upper-middle-class home shrinks when her husband strikes a child. College-educated husbands wince when their lower-middle-class wives make grammatical blunders before company. Religious observances, eating customs, and recreational habits all vary in the different classes. These too may cause or intensify marital tensions.

Class difficulties are often expressed in sexual relations. The response relationship is, as we stated earlier, a complex behavior pattern, which symbolizes many other forms of family maladjustment. In marriages between upper-middle-class wives and lower-middle-class husbands, the wife may be disgusted by the sexual advances of her husband and think him crude and vulgar. Where the woman marries a man of a higher social level, she may be the one who seems "crude and vulgar" to her more "refined" spouse. The wife may be ashamed of her spontaneous sexual advances and retreat into a restrained gentility, in which neither she nor her husband can enter fully into the sexual relationship. Persons from different class backgrounds thus interpret behavior of their mates differently.[51]

Economic Tensions

The category of economic tensions obviously covers a wide variety of subdivisions, most of which may be safely assumed to be further sources of irritation. There are economic tensions due to sheer poverty, unemployment, and patterns of spending the income. Some tensions are created by the nature of modern industrial organization, so far as men in executive positions are concerned. Other more personal problems resulting from the financial dependence of the wife or those arising when the wife follows a career or when both husband and wife are working also create tensions.

Sheer poverty is often a factor in family tensions.[52] The husband may be unable to provide for his family's support and deserts his family from a sense

[50] Davis, *op. cit.;* Arnold W. Green, "The Middle-Class Male Child and Neurosis," *American Sociological Review, 11:*31–41 (February, 1946).

[51] Vincent, *op. cit.,* pp. 355–356.

[52] Jay L. Roney, "Special Stresses on Low-Income Families," *Social Casework, 39:*150–156 (February–March, 1958).

of guilt. The wife may chide him for not "being any good" or she may obtain work herself without proper provision for the children. In any event, as we discuss in the next chapter, divorce rates are now highest in the lower-class occupational levels.[53] Desertion is primarily a lower-class phenomenon, although desertions occur occasionally on all levels. Sufficient income is essential for effective family organization.[54]

Unemployment created innumerable family tensions during the depression. Married persons often separated because they could not keep up a home. These families swelled the divorce rates during the war, chiefly because they could not afford a divorce earlier. Unemployment apparently augments other tensions. Many of the unfortunate behavior patterns of alcoholism, bitter quarreling, and physical violence may be a result of unstable employment and a man's lack of work.[55]

Spending the family income was found by Landis to be the second most difficult field of adjustment. The majority (56 percent) of the couples in his study claimed that their economic adjustment had been "adequate" from the beginning, but a substantial minority reported that, even after ten or twenty years, they had not worked out a mutually agreeable system.[56] Differences over economic matters may symbolize temperamental differences. The wife may be a hopeful person who believes in spending up to the limit (or beyond) of the family income, whereas the husband is temperamentally inclined to save his money for future satisfactions.[57]

Business stresses are most likely to occur in the upper income brackets. In many respects executives' wives suffer most from the way corporation policies invade the privacy of a man's home and family life. Ethel Ward McLemore delivered a telling speech before a conference of businessmen and educators at Babson Institute for Business Administration on May 20, 1955, in which she pointed out how selling and promoting industrial success have been pushed to the extent that they are destroying the fabric of family life. Mrs. McLemore maintained that a man's personality, principles, profession, and human dignity are being sacrificed to a company pattern; that giving gifts, entertaining, Sunday leisure, even church membership is taken over or altered to fit company demands. This situation is accompanied by the mother's assumption of major parental duties and supervision of the children. Most of the family social life revolves around the company interests and company "contacts." Mrs. McLemore believes that the stresses and strains of business life are creating

[53] William J. Goode, "Economic Factors and Marital Stability," *American Sociological Review, 16*:802–812 (December, 1951).

[54] Allison Davis, "The Motivation of the Underprivileged Worker," chap. 5 in William F. Whyte (ed.), *Industry and Society,* McGraw-Hill Book Company, Inc., New York, 1946.

[55] *Ibid.,* pp. 803–804.

[56] Judson T. Landis, "Length of Time Required to Achieve Adjustment in Marriage," *American Sociological Review, 11*:666–677 (December, 1946).

[57] Louis Schneider and Sverre Lysgaard, "The Deferred Gratification Pattern: A Preliminary Study," *American Sociological Review, 18*:142–149 (April, 1953).

many emotional disturbances in family life.[58] Sometimes a man's success in business is determined by how far his wife cooperates as a "corporation" or "organization" wife.

The employment of the wife is a possible source of tension. Most working wives are employed so that they may provide for vital family needs or help their children through college. In general these women are not working primarily for love of their work but to eke out the family budget. Consequently their employment would seem to promote the family's well-being and should not cause great resentment on the part of the husband. Locke's study supports this conclusion for he found the wife's employment unrelated to her marital adjustment or that of her husband. But he did find that divorced men were more likely to disapprove of the wife's employment than men whose marriage was successful.

Tension resulting from the *economic independence of the wife* is of special interest to college students, since college men and women frequently enter marriages in which the wife works at least for a while after marriage. The college woman who has had special training and has tasted of success in her field frequently finds herself loath to give up her work when she marries. More than that, she may regard her work as a "cause" and continue her endeavors because she feels that she represents a movement identified with the welfare of her sex.

Moreover, as recent figures indicate, the working wife represents more than half of the labor force.[59] Even so, she presents a number of possible sources of family difficulties. Men have acquiesced in large measure to the new freedom which women enjoy. But many husbands, particularly those who married during the twenties or earlier, have never entirely divested themselves of the notion that it is the husband's duty to support his wife and that a woman cannot create a suitable home and make any major economic contribution at the same time. Even women who have had excellent training often forfeit any chance for professional success at the time of marriage. If a woman can render valuable volunteer service to her community without accepting fees, most husbands do not object. Take the case of Mrs. Glenn, for example. She is the wife of a prominent surgeon in a middle western city and is an unusually fine musician, accomplished in both piano and organ. Before her marriage she studied abroad and was the youngest member of the faculty of a leading conservatory. After her marriage she wanted very much to continue teaching. Her husband objected strenuously, however, maintaining that it would "ruin his practice." He told her he was willing for her to serve a leading church as organist (without pay) and to appear in guest recitals before the Tuesday Musical Club. After many students beseeched her for instruction, she convinced her husband that "it would do no harm for her to give a few lessons."

[58] Ethel Ward McLemore, "Restoring Stability to the Family," *Vital Speeches, 21:* 1330–1334 (July 1, 1955).

[59] Cf. Chapter 9, "Women in Industry."

He was willing to "allow" her the privilege of teaching on Tuesday mornings from nine to twelve. Because she realized that her husband feels intensely on the subject she reluctantly accepted his arbitrary ruling.

Women with professional training tend to marry men of the same profession today, whereas earlier many did not marry. Such occupational propinquity would seem ideally to provide for the identity and interests seemingly essential to a successful marriage. Just as the professional man's best friends are usually in the same field, so the sharing of the same interests by men and women would seem to have its advantages. Olive Schreiner held that "a certain mental camaraderie and community of impersonal interests is imperative . . . if the union is to remain a living and growing reality."[60] Actually, however, there are striking instances in which such happy predictions have not worked out, particularly when the wife is the markedly superior of the two partners. Where husband and wife are both musicians or actors there have been particularly high divorce rates. If the wife's capacity is recognized as superior to her husband's, her spouse seldom enjoys playing the inferior role. Professional jealousy rather than cooperative effort may thus characterize the marriage partnership.

The professional woman may see economic independence as the goal of her sex. The monotonous aspect of housework, the mechanical drudgery which the routine of cooking, cleaning, and keeping a house in order entails may impress her as beneath the dignity of a trained mind. Actually, of course, every sort of work is to a certain degree monotonous, depending upon the creative intelligence and enthusiasm applied to the task. Doubtless in many instances the professionally trained woman is capable of making so valuable a contribution as to warrant her keeping on with her work following marriage. For a great many others, however, such work is considered in the light of an "expression of personality," or an "outlet for creative ability." It is rather confused reasoning which assumes that a badly written poem or mechanical clerical job possesses creative possibilities surpassing those of an intelligent homemaker. Running a home effectively and bringing up a family require intelligence and administrative ability and should be a source of "recognition."

On the other hand, any successfully adjusted person should have interests which extend beyond his particular means of earning a livelihood. Likewise a successful housewife must work out some adequate coordination of her interests within and outside the home. But she must also recognize that there can be no more important or permanent work than the care and training of children. The affectionate care which the mother gives her child cannot be replaced by any sort of impersonal institutionalized treatment. Likewise, most of her contribution can never be reduced to purely economic terms.

As a corollary of the tension which may grow out of the economic independence of wives, the enforced economic dependence of the majority of married women is often irksome. The woman who has had a successful profes-

---

[60] Olive Schreiner, *Women and Labor,* Frederick A. Stokes Company, New York, 1911, p. 294.

sional career or held a good business position before marriage may find economic dependence a thorn in the flesh. In addition she may find it necessary to reduce her whole range of expenditures to fit the scale of her husband's purse. Petty economies so important to balancing the budget may be unduly irritating and lead to friction.

On the other hand, in the current generation of young couples both husband and wife may work, with the fullest sort of cooperative relationship. Many young couples can marry earlier because the wife has a job while her husband is in a professional school or finishing his college training. Such an arrangement frequently means that the husband must assume certain domestic duties and responsibilities. Since maids are seldom available he may have to assist with the housework to the extent of cooking and wielding the dust mop. In the hurried rush and tear which office regime demands, countless sources of irritation may arise when the wife is dashing out of the house to the same 7:45 express as her husband. The quiet, orderly existence of the "ideal" home becomes impossible under such circumstances. The necessary rearrangement of values in the marriage may be at once possible and the source of other equally desirable values. Husbands and wives in this situation often find they have a common desire to stay at home evenings. They may even develop a real sharing of domestic duties.

If there are children the problems are more complicated. Young children need affectionate attention which nurses and baby-sitters seldom supply. Unless the mother's earning power is relatively high the difference in family income will be slight if she pays for the help and spends a great deal more for clothes. Where the mother is low-paid her children are often neglected, but here the economic pressure may make her working outside the home imperative. Greater provision for child-care services in the community might reduce these problems.

A recent study by Artie Gianopulos and Howard E. Mitchell concluded that the husband's attitude was the most important factor in determining whether tensions arose from the employment of the wife. The hypothesis advanced in this study was that "the attitude of the husband toward the wife's working is a critical factor in determining both the volume of conflict reported by spouses, as well as the consistency with which spouses perceive what they are in conflict about."[61] In general, this hypothesis was demonstrated in three types of marital situations: (1) those in which the wife worked and the husband disapproved, (2) those in which the wife worked and the husband approved, and (3) those in which the wife did not work.[62]

Several areas of marital behavior were established, including the domestic-economic, the cultural, the interpersonal, and the parental-social. Husbands who disapproved of their wives' employment had more items of conflict in

[61] Artie Gianopulos and Howard E. Mitchell, "Marital Disagreement in Working Wife Marriages as a Function of Husband's Attitude Toward Wife's Employment," *Marriage and Family Living,* 19:373–378 (November, 1957).
[62] *Ibid.*

each of these areas than did those who approved. Disapproval was centered in the "domestic-economic" field, which included household management, spending the family income, sharing tasks about the home, and relations with children. All of these activities are related to the traditional role of the wife, which was in some husbands' opinion slighted by her gainful employment. When the husband understands and sympathizes with his wife's motives in seeking employment, many of the related difficulties can be solved. If this sympathy is not forthcoming, the problems of the wife's employment may unbalance the family equation.[63]

Many husbands still feel, however, that the employment of their wives interferes with their other marital roles in ways which they (the husbands) consider more important. Disgruntled spouses claim that their working wives fail to keep the house clean, neglect the children, and lack sufficient interest in affectional relationships. Tensions in other phases of family interaction may thus be caused or intensified by the employment of the wife. Some capable and energetic wives can play all the domestic roles adequately and still keep a job. Others, however, find that the demands of the job are so great that they neglect their other duties. Many couples therefore believe that the added income does not compensate for the problems entailed.

The tensions which we have examined are the real, as distinguished from the legal, causes of family disorganization.[64] Husbands and wives dissolve their marriages because of tensions arising between them rather than because of the formal legal provisions for divorce. Divorce, however, is the legally sanctioned method of severing family relationships and will be discussed in the next two chapters. As social attitudes change, divorce provisions are altered, and in two states incompatibility is now a permissible ground for divorce. The state has an interest in maintaining a stable family structure and hence tends to be rigid about grounds for divorce.

SELECTED BIBLIOGRAPHY

Burgess, Ernest W., and Wallin, Paul, *Engagement and Marriage,* J. B. Lippincott Company, Philadelphia, 1953. This book contains a wealth of empirical data on the various situations that give rise to marital tensions. The treatment of sexual tensions is especially subtle.

Gianopulos, Artie, and Mitchell, Howard E., "Marital Disagreement in Working Wife Marriages as a Function of Husband's Attitude Toward Wife's Employment," *Marriage and Family Living, 19:*373–378 (November, 1957). An important variable in the success or failure of marriages in which the wife works is the attitude of the husband toward the wife's employment. Where the attitude is generally favorable, tensions tend to be minimized; where unfavorable, the opposite is the case.

Goode, William J., "Economic Factors and Marital Stability," *American Sociological Review, 16:*802–812 (December, 1951). This thoughtful article effectively

---

[63] *Ibid.*

[64] Harry C. Harmsworth and Mhyra S. Minnis, "Non-Statutory Causes of Divorce: The Lawyer's Point of View," *Marriage and Family Living, 17:*316–321 (November, 1955).

disposes of the myth that the lower-class family is universally marked by stability, affection, and cohesion. The rate of family disorganization from all causes actually *increases* as one descends the socioeconomic scale.

Hollingshead, August B., "Class Differences in Family Stability," *Annals of the American Academy of Political and Social Science, 272:*39–46 (November, 1950). Each of the major social levels has its own problems of family tensions. In general, however, the tensions increase in both number and severity as one goes from the upper, through the middle, to the working and lower classes.

Landis, Judson T., "Length of Time Required to Achieve Adjustment in Marriage," *American Sociological Review, 11:*666–677 (December, 1946). In this ingenious study, the causes of family tensions are viewed in relation to the time necessary to surmount them. The sources of greatest difficulty in adjustment were found to be first sex and second money.

Mangus, A. R., "Family Impacts on Mental Health," *Marriage and Family Living, 19:*256–262 (August, 1957). This is a suggestive analysis of family disorganization in terms of the roles which the spouses bring to the marriage. Tensions are apt to arise when there is a basic lack of congruence (agreement) between the role expectations of husband and wife regarding their own and each other's behavior.

Terman, Lewis M., *et al., Psychological Factors in Marital Happiness,* McGraw-Hill Book Company, Inc., New York, 1938. Written more than two decades ago, this is still an important psychological contribution to marital happiness and marital tensions. The emphasis is upon the personalities of the spouses and the extent to which these qualities make for harmony or disorganization.

Vincent, Clark E., "Social and Interpersonal Sources of Symptomatic Frigidity," *Marriage and Family Living, 18:*355–360 (November, 1956). Sexual tensions in marriage may result from differences in social class background of the spouses. A "frigid" wife may be reacting to the (to her) uncouth advances of a lower-class husband rather than to any "biological" factors in her own personality structure.

Wallin, Paul, and Vollmer, Howard M., "Marital Happiness of Parents and Their Children's Attitudes to Them," *American Sociological Review, 18:*424–431 (August, 1953). This article explores some of the complex relationships between the atmosphere of the parental home, the attachment of the child to each parent, and the happiness (or unhappiness) of the children in their own subsequent marriages.

Winch, Robert F., *Mate-Selection: A Study of Complementary Needs,* Harper & Brothers, New York, 1958. This important monograph offers new insights into many phases of marital relationships—among them the possible increase in marital tensions when complementary emotional needs of the spouses are *not* met. When both spouses have a strong need to dominate, for example, the result may be greater tensions between them.

CHAPTER 16

Desertion and Divorce

The Nature of Desertion

Some couples whose lives are torn by family tensions maintain their formal and legal solidarity for reasons of religious faith, pride, prestige, family pressures, or inertia. For others life together does not go on.

Desertion and divorce are the final tragic denouements of family disorganization. They are open indications of a rift in the family organization, avowals of a breakdown in the marital bond, and evidence of a desire to escape the onus of marriage ties. Divorce is a legal status, indicating a dissolved marriage relationship. Desertion, if permanent, is an unofficial indication of the same thing, but it is at the same time a penal offense. A man can be sent to prison for deserting his family.

Desertion is also a frequently cited legal reason for divorce, but in such cases the "desertion" is often a subterfuge or legal fiction. Many persons sue on the grounds of desertion when the real reason is incompatibility or infidelity. The only desertion involved is that either the husband or the wife has moved out. What has really happened is that they have separated. Husbands or wives who have been truly deserted sometimes do not sue for divorce because of the fact. Some feel ashamed and stigmatized and prefer not to give publicity to their private affairs. In any case, such a family is irretrievably broken.

Desertion, as the term is ordinarily employed, means the irresponsible departure from the home of either husband or wife, leaving the family to fend for itself. Most true deserters are men and apparently most are from the lower economic groups. Fewer upper-middle-class or upper-class men neglect their families. S. Howard Patterson's study in Philadelphia a good many years ago indicated that unskilled laborers deserted less frequently, however, than skilled and semiskilled laborers.[1] For class reasons deserted wives frequently are handicapped both by lack of legal knowledge and by lack of financial means for obtaining a divorce. This is especially the case in Negro desertion. In consequence, we have no way of knowing the exact extent of desertion, whereas divorce statistics are available for most states and for the country as a whole.

[1] S. Howard Patterson, "Family Desertion and Non-Support," *Journal of Delinquency*, 7:249–282, 299–333 (September and November, 1922).

Extent of Desertion

Although there are no accurate figures for desertion, according to a Bureau of the Census release for 1957 there were 791,000 men and 1,146,-000 women listed as "separated." These figures did not include married persons living apart for several months because of the employment situation. They included the legally separated, those living apart expecting to get a divorce, and the permanently or temporarily estranged.[2] Obviously men do not admit separation as frequently as women.

Negro women are much more likely to be separated than white women. The same study showed 8 percent of all nonwhite (chiefly Negro) women to be separated from their husbands, in contrast to 1.9 percent of all married women. Negro women are much more apt to be living in irregular[3] and common-law marriages than other women. Desertion of Negro women is an index to the generally less stable marriages among Negroes and is unquestionably affected by their prevailing low economic and social status as a whole.

Roman Catholics, on the other hand, have a desertion rate estimated to be around 40 percent higher than that of the general population. Monahan and Kephart believe this is the case because divorce is not acceptable to members of the Catholic faith. Hence when marriage becomes intolerable one party may simply walk out.[4]

Although desertion occurs more frequently in the lower class, there are some deserting fathers in the middle and upper classes, as Thomas P. Monahan's study of deserting fathers against whom court orders were issued in Philadelphia shows. In that city 30 percent of the fathers implicated were white-collar workers.[5] It is well known, however, that a disproportionate share of the deserters haled into court are those who have relatively good incomes and can therefore be expected to pay.

Types of Desertion

In general, there are two types of desertion, permanent and temporary. The permanent desertion has often been characterized as "the poor man's divorce." It makes the social break for those to whom divorce is impossible. The cost of a divorce is seldom less than $100, a sum which makes legal recognition of broken marital relations out of the question for a large number of persons. Desertion is also a recognized ground for divorce, as stated, and eventually the deserted husband or wife may start legal proceedings. Actually, the deserting spouse may have socially or at least psychologically valid reasons for escaping his marital ties.

[2] Bureau of the Census, *Population Characteristics, Marital Status, Economic Status, and Family Status: March 1957, Current Population Reports,* Series P-20, No. 81 (March 19, 1958) Table 1.

[3] *Ibid.,* Table 2.

[4] Thomas P. Monahan and William M. Kephart, "Divorce and Deserton by Religious and Mixed-Religious Groups," *American Journal of Sociology,* 59:454–465 (March, 1954).

[5] Thomas P. Monahan, "Family Fugitives," *Marriage and Family Living,* 20:146–151 (May, 1958).

The temporary, or short-time, desertion, often called the "poor man's vacation," may likewise be indicative of a low family wage. The man of comfortable income can afford a holiday in the Rockies, a fishing trip to the north woods, or perhaps a three-months sojourn in Europe and thus escape an irksome environment. He recognizes the psychological and physical restoration which comes from new scenes and new faces. Both husband and wife are often refreshed by an occasional vacation from each other. Indeed, some would have us believe that monotony is the single greatest cause of marital unhappiness and that "a sabbatical year for marriage" might well be the solution to many of the family's personal tensions.[6]

To the poor man, an absence from home is possible only if he evades the responsibility of providing shoes and groceries for the children. The wear and tear of the daily grind in the factory brings with it the need for a change of scenery. The arrival of a new baby may drive him to distraction. Taking to the road may seem the only possible way out. Social workers frequently report cases of husbands who desert their wives during childbirth. Three or four weeks later they may return to take up their burden again just as inevitably as they departed. The local public assistance agency usually takes care of the family in the interim. Although personal tensions are unquestionably aggravating factors in such cases, the problem seems to possess a peculiar economic aspect. Low income as such, however, is not the whole story. When the wages are cut off, as in the case of unemployment, desertions tend to fall off.[7] In the complete absence of income, the acute need for sympathy is probably greater than any urge for a new environment.

Eubank made a detailed classification of deserters within five categories some forty years ago.[8]

1. *The Spurious Deserter.* Not a deserter in the true sense, the spurious deserter merely leaves his family in order to escape some financial responsibility or to secure charitable relief. He knows that an empty coalbin and barren pantry shelves will call forth relief from the welfare agency.

2. *The Gradual Deserter.* The gradual deserter develops more or less unconsciously because of necessary absence from home. He is forced to stay away from home by reason of his occupation, or because he is an immigrant away from his family and native land. New interests absorb his attention and he gradually grows away from his family. He may never return or send for them. It is this type of deserter who is hardest to locate and hardest to compel to meet his responsibilities.[9]

[6] Samuel H. Adams, "A Sabbatical Year for Marriage," *Harper's Magazine, 156*:94–100 (December, 1927).

[7] Cf. Samuel A. Stouffer and Paul F. Lazarsfeld, *Research Memorandum on the Family in the Depression,* Social Science Research Council, New York, 1937, pp. 72–74.

[8] Earle E. Eubank, *A Study of Family Desertion,* Department of Public Welfare, Chicago, 1916, pp. 37–49.

[9] Formerly the International Migration Service was called upon to investigate instances of husbands and wives who had spouses and children in other countries. Because of no adequate international legislation, moral suasion rather than legal compulsion must usually be relied upon to secure support for such dependents.

3. *The Intermittent Husband.* Under a third category is included the chronic periodic deserter who leaves home at somewhat regular intervals. When domestic difficulties develop, men seem to be more likely to walk out than to "find relief in tears and upbraidings." When the scene has quieted down, they return. The intermittent category also includes the "peculiar periodic deserter" who deserts when a new baby is born. There may be many explanations of this type, but apparently a significant reason for deserting is the fact of the crisis itself and an unwillingness to undergo the mental strain of enduring his wife's travail.

4. *The Ill-Advised-Marriage Type.* Following a hastily arranged or ill-suited marriage, the husband may find the relationship completely distasteful and desert shortly after the marriage. Generally these desertions are permanent and may likewise amount to "the poor man's divorce."

5. *The Last-Resort Type.* The last-resort type makes a complete break with his wife and family only after having made successive attempts at readjustment. In desperation he decides that it is no use trying to go on. His desertion is a definite and final termination of the unsatisfactory relationship.

6. *The Symbolic Deserter.* On the basis of Harriet Mowrer's analysis, we may add another category to this classification—the symbolic deserter. The desertion is the symbol of the psychological conflict taking place in the individual. The overt act serves as an escape mechanism. Such a deserter may be moved by the simple desire to escape marital responsibilities. He may also threaten to leave home unless he is given more attention and prestige as an indispensable member of the family.[10]

Social Disorganization and Desertion

Many of the consequences of desertion are similar to those of divorce, for the family may be permanently dissolved. Desertion, however, presents a few special problems. Emotionally the wife and children often suffer much more severely than in the case of divorce, for desertion entails a humiliating rejection of the spouse. It also carries with it lack of certainty. Will the husband return? Is it possible he has met death unnoticed or unnotified? These and countless other questions plague the deserted wife. The children feel especially hurt by a father or mother who cares so little about them as to leave them without support. What to tell young children about their father often perplexes the mother. For children are cruel to each other and taunt the one who cannot explain where his father is.

The wife and mother in the family often finds herself in serious economic straits. She is not eligible for a widow's pension and alimony obviously is lacking. Frequently she must be entirely dependent upon public support. She may secure work outside the home, in which event her children are left unsupervised during the hours before and after school. Out of this situation slack school attendance, delinquency, and neglect may arise. The children in turn

[10] Harriet R. Mowrer, *Personality Adjustment and Domestic Discord,* American Book Company, New York, 1935, p. 221.

are often absorbed into industry at an early age, with their education and future earning power cut short. Should the worthless father be the intermittent type of deserter, his occasional returns may be an unwholesome added influence. The children may develop a completely distorted notion of normal family life and be seriously damaged by the unfortunate behavior pattern set before them. The wife may become pregnant during an intermittent visit, only to be subsequently deserted, with all the problems created by an unwanted child and another mouth to feed.

If the husband goes for good, his departure may signal a more favorable outlook for the family. If he has been a drunken ne'er-do-well who was seldom employed, his absence from the home may well relieve both psychological and economic tensions. In such situations the husband's problem becomes more crucial and may easily eventuate in complete personal demoralization. Freed from the normal restraining influence of the primary group, he swells the ranks of the drifting, homeless men. Passing from bad to worse, he sleeps in the flophouse when he has a dime, but both literally and psychologically he is often to be found in the gutter. The painful memories or shattered ideals of the divorced husband may be partially dispelled by the social sanction which the legal proceedings have accorded his status. For the deserter there can be only a blunted social conscience, an evasion of obligations, and a disregard for any responsibility for dependents. Accompanying this disregard for social values, a high degree of personal demoralization must be expected.

Where a reconciliation is possible this may be the most practical solution to the problem. The couple's disinclination to preserve the marriage, however, may mean the state must assume responsibility for the children. One of the saddest aspects of desertion is the children who suffer from such neglect. The present aid to dependent children is largely concerned with meeting their needs. Most of the children in orphanages are orphans only in the sense that their parents have neglected them. The children of desertion are often seriously disturbed emotionally because they are so humiliated by the experience. Many appear backward mentally, as we have discussed in Chapter 11, because they receive little or no affection in the institution. We are only beginning to recognize how the "sins of the parents" are visited on the child. From such buffeted and unhappy children are recruited many of our major problems of delinquency and crime, as well as general problems of adult adjustment.

The social importance of providing support for deserted families is obvious. Unless the child has some support the extent of the social disorganization may be very serious, as Saul Kaplan points out. Many children would be forced to leave school and be poorly prepared for adult life. Some would be on the verge of starvation and subject to delinquent behavior, such as thieving, because their extreme poverty would be a great stimulus to steal.[11] Because this problem is not greatly different from that of defaulting divorced and separated husbands, the whole topic is treated together later in the chapter.

[11] Saul Kaplan, *Support from Absent Fathers in Aid to Dependent Children, Social Security Bulletin*, 21:3–13 (February, 1958).

DIVORCE

The Nature of Divorce

So long as marriage is regulated by the state, any release from the bonds of matrimony must be determined according to conditions laid down by the state. Divorce in our society is the final and legal termination of marriage. During the Middle Ages and until relatively recently in England, the power to sever marriage ties was vested in the church, and then only in special and restricted instances. But at that time the church was literally vested with legal authority in other matters. The position of the church on the formation and dissolution of marriage has formed the cultral background for later regulation by the state. The religious point of view still colors attitudes toward family and marriage in many ways. Meanwhile, so far as the conservative religious groups are concerned, canons of the church still regulate marriage patterns and any dissolution of marriage which is permitted.

Divorce is nearly always a tragedy, for it generally means blighted faith, broken troth, and severe disillusionment. Sometimes one party wants a divorce in order to marry another person. This leaves the other mate to feel that he or she has been judged and found wanting, that he or she has failed to pass the test of a successful and cooperative spouse. In a sense one mate is rejecting another when both parties do not want the divorce. This makes the divorce process an emotional upheaval for the rejected person, who often may care deeply for the other. The rejected mate may also feel crushed and humiliated because his pride is hurt. In any event, divorce is more than a legal problem. It is often an acute personal experience.

Because marriage has proved so unstable in modern society, many critics of manners and morals have blamed divorce for the current problems of family disorganization. This is fallacious reasoning. Divorces occur after the family is disorganized, when one or both parties have a strong desire to dissolve their relationship. They do not occur in happy, well-adjusted families. In other words, divorce merely gives a legal status to a marriage already disrupted. On the other hand, there are many unsatisfactory and unhappy marriages not terminated by divorce. People who dislike and irritate each other often keep up the semblance of a marriage for one reason or another. Factors as diverse as religious belief, pressure from in-laws, small children who need care, inability of the wife to make her own living, and fear of loss of prestige may deter couples from suing for divorce. Sometimes the spouse is mentally ill and such a ground is not permitted in the particular state.

Divorce can never be reckoned "as a strictly private affair," however, as may be the case in a broken engagement. For despite the personal angles of the divorcees' problems, widespread divorce is generally considered *"prima facie* prejudicial to public interest." This is because society as a whole— whether we are speaking of the community, the state, or the nation—has a stake in successful family life and the acceptance of the mature responsibilities of marriage by its adult members. Wholesome, stable family life is desirable in the first place because it is conducive to effective living and therefore to effective citizenship. Equally important, if not more so, is the community's concern for responsible parenthood and adequate care and training for the children, which is nowhere well supplied outside the family system.

The history of divorce represents the long struggle of people to subdue their passions and regulate their domestic relations to the best interest of the parties immediately involved and the group as a whole. Sometimes social interests and personal advantage have been in conflict, and often social interests have overshadowed the personal indignities which rigid divorce laws have involved. It is equally true that commercialized, profit-seeking divorce legislation is subversive to social ends. Human decency demands that we recognize the fallibility of human judgment and allow the possibility of retrieving a mistake, even though that mistake be the choice of a life mate. But it is difficult to accomplish this without sacrificing either the dignity of marriage or the sovereignty of the state as the severing agency.

Divorce from a Historical Perspective

As a social phenomenon, divorce must have been in existence as long as socially regulated marriage. The earliest known legal forms of divorce regulation are found in the Code of Hammurabi, which was drawn up around 2300 to 2250 B.C. According to this code, marriage was virtually a purchase arrangement in which the bride enjoyed a status little better than that of a chattel. The husband might divorce his wife at will without assigning any cause. Indeed, in some ways the status of the concubine was superior to that of the wife, for the concubine had certain pecuniary guaranties against a purely arbitrary dismissal. On the other hand, certain factors affected the status of the divorced wife of Babylon. If she were an adulteress she might be bound to her accomplice and tossed into the water.[12]

Among the early Hebrews, divorce was a masculine prerogative. This was established by the scriptural injunction in Deuteronomy 24:1–2 to the effect that "when a man hath taken a wife, and married her, and it come to pass that she find no favour in his eyes, because he hath found some uncleanness in her, then let him write her a bill of divorcement, and give it in her hand, and send her out of his house. And when she is departed out of his house, she may go and be another man's wife." This right to divorce his wife at pleasure was accepted among all Jews until the eleventh century.

Under the earliest Roman law, on the day of marriage the bride was transferred from her father's to her husband's authority. The husband had complete right to renounce his marital relationships and obligations if he so desired, but he was subject to certain restrictions. A wife might not be repudiated without the forfeit of property, unless she were guilty of adultery or drinking wine. When the Roman law was codified into the Twelve Tables, divorce for both

[12] Cf. Hyacinthe Ringrose, *Marriage and Divorce Laws of the World,* Musson-Draper, London, 1911, pp. 11–13.

husbands and wives was allowed to terminate the relation upon securing a bill of divorcement. The state imposed certain pecuniary restrictions, however, and if a husband were guilty of adultery he was required to return his wife's dowry immediately. If the offense were less serious, six months was allowed for the restitution.[13]

After the advent of Christianity, Roman law was considerably mitigated by Christian influences. Divorce by mutual consent, however, continued until the second half of the fourth century. When Constantine adopted the Christian faith, he tried to restrict divorce by pecuniary penalties except for certain reasons. Divorce was allowed to the husband in case his wife committed murder, prepared poison, or acted as a procuress. Similarly, the wife might divorce her husband for murder, preparation of poison, or rifling of tombs.[14]

In A.D. 449, Theodosius II and Valentinian III enacted provisions to the effect that either the husband or the wife might secure a divorce for treason, adultery, murder, forgery, rifling of tombs, stealing from churches, robbery, cattle stealing, attempt to murder, or beating. A wife could also secure divorce in case her husband brought lewd women into her house, but she was not allowed to remarry until after five years had elapsed. The husband, on the other hand, could divorce his wife for dining, against his wishes, with any man not a relative, for staying out nights, or for attending public entertainments contrary to his orders. This was in "Christian" Rome.[15] It is thus clear that Christianity did not immediately impose a rigid marriage code.[16] Justinian attempted to abolish divorce by mutual consent by requiring the loss of all property in such instances. The wife was permitted to divorce her husband if he made an attack upon her life, urged her to prostitution, falsely accused her of adultery, were treasonous or impotent, or brought a vicious woman into her home. For the husband, seven grounds were allowed—adultery, plots against him, treason, attending dinners and dances with other men, absence from home at night unless visiting her parents, going to the theater, impotence, and abortion.[17]

Christian Teachings on Divorce

We have made this brief excursion into the history of divorce because the three major roots of Euro-American marriage and divorce legislation are generally conceded to be in the canons of the Jewish and Christian religion, Roman law, and Teutonic custom.[18] The influence of the Christian church upon the marriage status has unquestionably been to conserve the permanent monogamic family. Although no detailed analysis of the marriage estate by Jesus is extant, his teachings with reference to marriage are basically rooted

---

[13] *Encyclopaedia Britannica,* New York, 14th ed., Vol. VII, p. 454.

[14] Joseph McCabe, *The Influence of the Church on Marriage and Divorce,* C. A. Watts and Company, Ltd., London, 1916, pp. 71–72.

[15] *Ibid.,* pp. 73–74.

[16] *Ibid.,* p. 74.

[17] *Ibid.,* p. 75.

[18] John Dewey and James H. Tufts, *Ethics,* Henry Holt and Company, Inc., New York, 1908, p. 574.

in the fact of sex itself.[19] His longest pronouncement on the subject is as follows: "Have ye not read, that He who made them at the beginning made them male and female?" He says, further: "For this cause shall a man leave father and mother, and shall cleave to his wife: and they twain shall be one flesh. Wherefore they are no more twain, but one flesh. What therefore God hath joined together, let no man put asunder."

Jesus was voicing this opinion at a time when Jewish divorce scandals were running riot. His sentiments were in direct contradiction to practices among his compatriots. Whereupon they questioned him, "Why did Moses then command to give a writing of divorcement, and to put her away?" And he said, "Moses, because of the hardness of your hearts suffered you to put away your wives; but from the beginning it was not so."[20] How the last phrase should be interpreted is a much mooted point. Lichtenberger holds that Jesus was speaking of a principle and not a historic fact.[21] Jesus, however, qualified his statement by saying that any man who put away his wife except for fornication was guilty of adultery, and that whoever married the woman so put aside also committed adultery.[22] Nevertheless he recognized the impracticability of his point of view as an absolute basis for establishing human relations, for he himself said: "All men cannot receive this saying, save they to whom it is given."[23] With penetrating psychological insight, Jesus recognized that the difference between the thought and the act was not great, and that "Whosoever looketh at a woman to lust after her hath committed adultery in his heart."

St. Paul and the early church fathers have had much more influence in the development of the church doctrine on marriage and divorce than did Christ. St. Paul was only mildly enthusiastic about the marriage estate. He was definitely of the opinion that woman was man's inferior and that sex was essentially impure. The ideal life was the single life. Yet he was willing to concede, "If they cannot contain, let them marry. For it is better to marry than to burn."[24] As for those who had entered into marriage, he maintained, "Let not the wife depart from her husband, but and if she depart, let her remain unmarried, or be reconciled to her husband and let not the husband put away his wife." Further, "If any brother hath a wife that believeth not, and she be pleased to dwell with him, let him not put her away. And the woman which hath an husband that believeth not, and if he be pleased to dwell with her, let her not leave him. For the unbelieving husband is sanctified by the wife, and the unbelieving wife is sanctified by the husband: else were your children unclean; but now are they holy."[25]

[19] Cf. James P. Lichtenberger, *Divorce: A Social Interpretation,* McGraw-Hill Book Company, Inc., New York, 1931, p. 50.

[20] Matthew 19:4–8.

[21] Lichtenberger, *op. cit.,* p. 52.

[22] Matthew 19:9.

[23] Matthew 19:11.

[24] I Corinthians 7:9.

[25] I Corinthians 7:12–14.

One statement of St. Paul has raised a controversy which has never been satisfactorily settled. What did he mean by his pronouncement: "But if the unbelieving depart, let him depart. A brother or a sister is not under bondage in such cases; but God hath called us to peace."[26] Whether or not under such circumstances divorce and remarriage might be justified by the church has often been debated but never definitely settled. This passage has generally been construed as the "Pauline privilege of desertion,"[27] although the Catholic Church has allowed divorce and second marriage to a Christian separated from a nonbeliever on this authority but has maintained there was no true marriage in the first instance. Protestants have gone further and claimed that malicious desertion entitles divorce whether the deserter be a nonbeliever or not.[28]

Leaders in the early church did not always agree on whether or not divorce might be allowed. The earliest formal position on divorce which the church took as an organization was the canon accepted at the Council of Carthage in A.D. 407. This incorporated the doctrine of St. Augustine, who held unreservedly to the idea that marriage was a sacrament and hence indissoluble. Decrees of nullity in case the marriage had never been consummated were, however, allowed at an early date, as well as in case of impediments, including fraud, force, serious mistake, impuberty, impotence, a previous marriage, a vow of chastity, difference of religion, and consanguinity.[29] Even where the marriage had been consummated, if the impediments made the marriage illegal the nullity decree was granted. The status of the children, however, was not affected. In such instances a later marriage was possible, although new evidence might reverse the decree.[30] After the division of the church into the Eastern (Greek Orthodox) and Roman Catholic bodies (A.D. 843) the Greek Church condoned divorce for adultery, and more recently for other offenses. In Russia the Orthodox Church allows a second marriage for both parties after a period of penance. In other branches of the Greek Orthodox faith, only "innocent" parties may remarry.[31]

Changing Conceptions of Divorce

During medieval times the organized church became a powerful political influence. Canon law regulated divorce throughout Europe from the twelfth century until the Reformation, and in Roman Catholic countries until much later. So far as Roman Catholics are concerned, the canon law is still in effect and the canons are legally enacted in the State law in some countries.

---

[26] I Corinthians 7:15.

[27] Cf. Theodore D. Woolsey, *Essay on Divorce and Divorce Legislation,* Charles Scribner's Sons, New York, 1869, pp. 75–85.

[28] *Ibid.,* p. 77.

[29] *Ibid.,* p. 119.

[30] *Ibid.,* pp. 123–124. These early canons of the church have been incorporated in civil legislation with reference to divorce throughout Western civilization and show the impact of the church upon such legislation.

[31] Cf. James Hastings (ed.), *Encyclopaedia of Religion and Ethics,* Charles Scribner's Sons, New York, 1914, Vol. VI, p. 434.

Scotland revolted against the Roman dictum in 1573 and made desertion as well as adultery ground for divorce.[32]

When Luther precipitated the Protestant Reformation and rejected the Catholic teaching of the sacramental nature of marriage, he paved the way for western civil marriage. Nevertheless, Luther never completely divested himself of a belief in its sacramental character. Neither have Protestant churches ever entirely relinquished the idea. Although Luther took an aggressive stand for the regulation of marriage by the state, he maintained at the same time that marriage was a symbol of the "greatest, holiest, worthiest, noblest thing that has ever been or can be—the union of the divine and human nature in Christ."[33]

Holland passed the first permissive civil-contract marriage law in 1580. England under Cromwell first made civil marriage obligatory in 1653, but with the overthrow of the Cromwellian regime the law became inoperative. In 1753, civil marriage was reestablished, but the church continued to grant divorces *a mensa et toro*. Prior to 1857, absolute divorces in England were granted only by act of Parliament, whereas ecclesiastical courts had the right of granting divorces *a mensa et toro*.

In 1857, jurisdiction in divorce was transferred to the civil authorities by the Matrimonial Causes Act, which went into effect on January 1, 1858. This act provided that a man could divorce his wife for adultery, whereas a wife could divorce her adulterous husband only if there were an additional complaint of cruelty, desertion for two or more years, bigamy, incest, rape, or unnatural offenses. By act of 1860, divorces were denied in case the petitioner was guilty of connivance, collusion, or misconduct. Moreover, if the deserting husband were abroad no suit could be instituted. Not until 1937 was the English law changed to permit divorce on additional grounds. As further revised in 1950, the English Matrimonial Causes Act now provides that divorces may be granted on grounds of adultery following marriage, desertion for three years, cruelty such as to injure mind and body, and insanity for five years. The wife also may secure a divorce from her husband in case he is guilty of sex perversions.

Current Religious Attitudes Toward Divorce

Technically speaking, the Roman Catholic Church objects to absolute divorce. In certain circumstances a divorce is permitted, but in no such case does the Roman Catholic Church permit remarriage for divorced members. Nevertheless many Roman Catholics have their marriages annulled by church authorities. They may then secure a legal divorce and subsequently remarry with the blessing of the church where both parties to the second marriage are Roman Catholics. Protestants therefore are inclined to regard the statement by the Roman Church that there has been no divorced person remarried by

[32] James Bryce, *Marriage and Divorce,* Oxford University Press, New York, 1901, p. 48.

[33] Heinrich Leopold von Strampf, *Dr. Luther, Ueber die Ehe,* p. 205, cited by Lichtenberger, *op. cit.,* p. 93.

the Catholic Church as a legal fiction. Many annulments would not have been granted by legal authorities since the parties had lived in normal conjugal relationship for several years. In these instances one of the marriage partners has been a non-Catholic and the marriage was performed outside the church. The church has held, therefore, that from its point of view no true marriage ever existed. When priests of the church have performed the ceremony in a mixed marriage, however, no such annulment is possible.

The Church of England holds as rigidly as the Roman Church to the doctrine of indissolubility of marriage and frowns upon remarriage of a divorced person by its clergy. The Protestant Episcopal (American branch of the Anglican) Church now permits the remarriage of the "innocent" party one year after the divorce takes place, if the divorce is approved by the bishop of the diocese in which it was granted. An Episcopal clergyman cannot be divorced and retain his position as a priest of the church. The majority of other Protestant churches permit the remarriage of divorced persons with varying restrictions. Generally speaking, however, there has never been any enthusiasm on the part of Protestant churches for divorce.

Judaism, like Christianity, is divided, although only three ways. There is (1) the Orthodox Jewish group with its age-old traditional practices, (2) the Reform (or Liberal) Jewish group and (3) the Conservatives, who are halfway between. For all of these groups no marriage between a Jew and a non-Jew can take place under Jewish law. Civil marriage between Jewish and non-Jewish persons is recognized to a varying extent and is accepted to a greater degree by the Reform Jews than by the Orthodox and Conservatives. If the non-Jewish party to a marriage accepts Judaism, the marriage is no longer considered mixed. A person can become a Jew either by birth or by choice; in the latter case he is accepted by a court of three after a period of instruction. Any rabbi may officiate at a marriage of a Jew by birth and a Jew by conversion. There is some variation between the three (Reform, Conservative, and Orthodox) groups in the ritual required in the process of conversion. Marriage between a Jew and an unconverted person is called "mixed marriage," whereas marriage between a Jew and a converted Jew is called "intermarriage."

Members of the Jewish faith view marriage as a religious process (much as the Christians do). The Orthodox and Conservative Jews hold that the breaking of marriage, or divorce, must also be a religious process. For these two divisions of Judaism, therefore, no person who merely has a civil divorce is really divorced. This point of view is in essence a legal fiction much like the Roman Catholic position. The difficulty with this attitude is increased by the fact that, according to Jewish law, only a husband can grant a divorce. It is he who gives the wife the bill of divorcement, just as in Biblical times. A Jewish wife thus cannot divorce her husband.

This superior right of the husband created no serious difficulty during the Middle Ages, when Jewish communities were virtually autonomous. At that time, when the wife had a serious grievance against her husband she could complain to the rabbi or the Jewish court, who in turn could order the man to give his wife a divorce. Today, however, the authority of religious courts has largely faded away. In case of a civil divorce, the former husband can be autocratic if he wishes. He can absolutely prevent his former wife from marrying again under Jewish law, since she is not divorced until he divorces her. The Conservative Jewish group has tried to mitigate this present-day dilemma of the former husband's vested authority. They are now introducing a new form of marriage contract in which both parties promise to bring their problems to a rabbinical court should their marriage fail. Thus, if they are to be divorced, arrangements can be easily made for them to get a Jewish divorce also. The Reform Jews have gone much farther and have taken a more "radical" stand. Reform Jews accept the civil divorce as fully valid. Therefore, anyone divorced by the civil courts is deemed divorced in Reform Judaism and the rabbi will remarry either party without any further requirements except the dictates of his own conscience.

The Reform solution serves to mitigate another analogous problem. Traditional Jewish law does not provide release from marriage on presumption of death if a man disappears for a long period. There must be evidence of people who saw him die. An Enoch Arden situation thus cannot occur under Jewish law. Consequently, despite the hundreds of thousands of Jewish men who were liquidated under Hitler or who otherwise disappeared in recent international upheavals, there are hundreds of thousands of women who cannot remarry. These women are certain their husbands are dead but cannot establish the fact. The Jewish law still holds that there is no legal evidence that the husband has died. Since the husband alone can give the wife a divorce, it cannot be secured by either the Conservative or Orthodox woman in such a case.[34]

Types of Divorce Decree

There are two major types of legal divorce: (1) absolute divorce (*a vinculo matrimonii*), which effects a full and complete dissolution of marital rights and obligations and leaves both parties in the status of single persons; (2) partial divorce or legal separation (divorce *a mensa et toro*), which does not dissolve the marriage but merely gives legal status to the "separation from bed and board" until such time as the husband and wife agree to take up residence together. The latter arrangement ordinarily carries some provision for the separate support of the wife. Separate maintenances are seldom satisfactory, since the fiction of marriage is preserved while the husband has no wife and the wife is without a husband. The arrangement effectively prevents remarriage of either party and hence is acceptable to the Roman Catholic Church and all other groups which frown on remarriage. Whether or not this type of separation ever serves any valid purpose is highly questionable from

---

[34] Statement made by Dr. Solomon B. Freehof to Mabel A. Elliott. Dr. Freehof, one of the outstanding Jewish scholars in the United States, is rabbi at Rodef Sholem Temple (Reform Synagogue), Pittsburgh. See also Solomon B. Freehof, *Reform Jewish Practice,* Hebrew Union College Press, Cincinnati, 1944, pp. 98–110.

a sociological viewpoint. Any protection which an innocent party may hope to derive from the arrangement could better be secured by absolute divorce.[35]

Slightly over half the states grant partial divorces. The dubious aspects in such divorces are nevertheless apparent. The spouses are no longer truly husband and wife and yet cannot remarry. Some authorities claim that such divorces actually promote illicit behavior since they make it impossible for persons so divorced to marry. Women sometimes ask for legal separation in order to prevent their husbands from marrying, sometimes from religious and sometimes from punitive motives. Practices in the various states range from express prohibition of such legal separations in Florida to the granting of legal separation as the first stage of all divorces (except in case of adultery and conviction for crime) in Louisiana. Statistics for partial divorces are not separated from the absolute divorce statistics in many states.

The Extent of Divorce

The extent of divorce may be indicated partially by the number of divorced persons in our population and by the annual divorce rates. In 1956 it was estimated that there were 926,000 men and 1,492,000 women who were divorced in the United States. These figures do not include all the people who had been divorced, since approximately three-fourths of the divorced men and two-thirds of the divorced women eventually remarry.[36] These figures indicate that men must remarry sooner than women, however.

The annual divorce rates vary. In the year 1948 the number of divorces granted reached 408,000, an all-time high. Later, as Table 16.1 shows, the rate varied between 377,000 and 382,000 during the years 1954 to 1957. The divorce rate is thus fairly predictable although it was considerably higher

TABLE 16.1.   Divorces and Divorce Rates: United States, Each Division and State, 1954–1957

(By place of occurrence. Includes reported annulments. Rates per 1000 estimated midyear population in each area.)

Area	Number				Rate			
	1957	1956	1955	1954	1957	1956	1955	1954
United States	381,000	382,000	377,000	379,000	2.2	2.3	2.3	2.4
New England	12,572	—	12,993[a]	—	1.3	—	1.3[a]	—
Maine	1,906	1,926	1,960	2,093	2.0	2.1	2.1	2.3
New Hampshire	1,039	1,059	1,076	1,067	1.8	1.9	1.9	1.9
Vermont	526	527	533	542	1.4	1.4	1.5	1.4
Massachusetts	5,523	—	5,892[a]	5,835[a]	1.1	—	1.2[a]	1.2[a]
Rhode Island	933	913	827	—	1.1	1.1	1.0	—
Connecticut	2,645	2,617	2,705	2,876	1.2	1.2	1.2	1.3
Middle Atlantic	—	—	—	—	—	—	—	—
New York	—	—	—	—	—	—	—	—
New Jersey	4,665	4,891	4,844	4,609	0.8	0.9	0.9	0.9
Pennsylvania	10,859	11,533	11,160	11,698	1.0	1.1	1.0	1.1

[35] Helen I. Clarke, *Social Legislation,* Appleton-Century-Crofts, Inc., New York, 1940, pp. 139–140.

[36] Paul C. Glick, *American Families,* John Wiley and Sons, Inc., New York, 1957, pp. 139–140.

TABLE 16.1 (*Continued*)
(By place of occurrence. Includes reported annulments. Rates per 1000 estimated midyear population in each area.)

Area	Number				Rate			
	1957	1956	1955	1954	1957	1956	1955	1954
East North Central	—	—	—	—	—	—	—	—
Ohio	22,730	21,344	22,259	21,665	2.5	2.4	2.5	2.4
Indiana[a]	—	12,026	11,317	11,856	—	2.7	2.6	2.8
Illinois	—	—	—	—	—	—	—	—
Michigan	15,442	16,228	17,676[b]	16,281[b]	2.0	2.1	2.4[b]	2.3[b]
Wisconsin	4,375	4,488	4,720	4,887	1.1	1.2	1.3	1.3
West North Central[b]	27,121	28,312	29,286	30,210	1.8	1.9	2.0	2.1
Minnesota	3,778	3,948	3,804	4,029	1.1	1.2	1.2	1.3
Iowa	4,134	4,850	5,195	5,217	1.5	1.8	1.9	2.0
Missouri[b]	10,861	10,993	11,351	11,705	2.6	2.6	2.7	2.8
North Dakota	545	488	543	554	0.8	0.8	0.8	0.9
South Dakota	622	850	868	954	0.9	1.2	1.3	1.4
Nebraska	2,204	2,284[c]	2,424	2,427	1.5	1.6[c]	1.7	1.8
Kansas	4,977	4,899	5,101	5,324	2.4	2.3	2.5	2.6
South Atlantic	—	—	—	—	—	—	—	—
Delaware	682	598	509	655	1.6	1.4	1.3	1.8
Maryland	5,632	5,490	5,422	5,111	1.9	1.9	2.0	2.0
District of Columbia	1,911	1,092	1,085	1,140	2.3	1.4	1.3	1.3
Virginia	6,675	7,133	7,116	7,262	1.7	1.9	2.0	2.1
West Virginia	—	—	—	—	—	—	—	—
North Carolina	—	—	—	—	—	—	—	—
South Carolina	2,788	2,731	2,700[b]	2,425[b]	1.2	1.2	1.2[b]	1.1[b]
Georgia[b]	8,798	7,751	7,547	7,041	2.3	2.1	2.1	1.9
Florida	18,744	20,238	19,999	19,387	4.5	5.1	5.5	5.7
East South Central	—	—	—	—	—	—	—	—
Kentucky	—	—	—	—	—	—	—	—
Tennessee	8,602	8,410	8,342	7,866	2.5	2.5	2.5	2.3
Alabama	10,925[b]	10,469	9,721	8,916	3.5[b]	3.4	3.2	2.9
Mississippi	4,974	5,027	4,845	5,001	2.3	2.3	2.3	2.3
West South Central	—	—	—	—	—	—	—	—
Arkansas	5,500[b]	4,973	5,113[b]	7,917[b]	3.1[b]	2.8	2.9[b]	4.4[b]
Louisiana	—	—	—	—	—	—	—	—
Oklahoma	12,233[a]	12,439[a]	12,521[b]	12,846[a]	5.4[a]	5.6[a]	5.7[b]	5.9[a]
Texas[b]	34,871	33,831	34,921	36,000	3.8	3.8	4.0	4.3
Mountain[a]	29,597	30,410	27,635	28,906	4.7	5.0	4.6	5.1
Montana	2,004	1,985	1,909	1,966	3.0	3.0	3.0	3.2
Idaho	2,360	2,214	2,414	2,523	3.7	3.5	4.0	4.2
Wyoming	1,148	1,145[b]	1,127	1,185[b]	3.6	3.6[b]	3.6	4.0[b]
Colorado[a]	5,100	5,800	4,900	4,300	3.1	3.6	3.1	2.9
New Mexico[a]	3,065	2,337	2,140	2,500	3.8	3.0	2.7	3.3
Arizona	5,328[b]	5,571	3,526	4,790[a]	4.9[b]	5.5	3.4	5.2[a]
Utah	1,343	2,217	2,060	2,140	1.6	2.7	2.6	2.8
Nevada	9,249	9,141	9,559	9,502	35.3	36.0	39.0	44.8
Pacific	62,024	56,939[a]	56,544[a]	56,544[a]	3.4	3.2[a]	3.3[a]	3.4[a]
Washington	12,764	8,641[a]	8,787[a]	8,321[a]	4.7	3.2[a]	3.4[a]	3.3[a]
Oregon	5,261	5,827	6,158	6,130	3.0	3.4	3.6	3.7
California	43,999	42,471	41,599	42,093	3.2	3.2	3.2	3.4

a Data estimated.
b Data incomplete.
c Includes 16 decrees of separate maintenance.

SOURCE: National Office of Vital Statistics, *Marriage and Divorces, 1957, Vital Statistics—Special Reports*, Vol. 50, No. 7, August 29, 1959, p. 189.

during World War II. Despite our relatively high divorce rate it is obvious that the majority of marriages survive.

Interlocutory Decrees

An interlocutory divorce is one which does not become final until a waiting period has elapsed. In Louisiana no final decrees are given except for adultery and conviction of a crime. All other divorces are initially legal separations. One year must elapse before a final hearing may be held. If no reconciliation is in effect, a decree may be granted but it does not become final until one year later in the case of the party in whose favor the divorce was drawn and not for a year and sixty days in the case of the party against whom the suit is entered.[37] In California decrees are also called interlocutory and final and all divorces are interlocutory for one year. If no reconciliation has taken place a final decree may be granted either on the motion of either party or on the court's motion.[38]

In many other states a waiting period is required before remarriage but this does not always restrict remarriage since divorced parties often marry in other states. Restrictions on the right to remarry vary from thirty days in Georgia, to end of the court term in New Hampshire, to one year in Arizona and Wisconsin. Kansas, Minnesota, Nebraska, Oklahoma, and the District of Columbia require six months. Vermont requires six months for the plaintiff and two years for the guilty party. Indiana restricts remarriage only in case notices are published to the effect that the party may not marry for two years. Utah, New York, and New Jersey require a three-months waiting period. Rhode Island requires thirty days after six months, Virginia four months, West Virginia sixty days, and Puerto Rico one month. South Carolina provides that three months must elapse between filing of suit and granting of decree.[39]

The purpose in all interlocutory decrees or waiting periods is to provide a cooling-off period and a chance for reconciliation.

Real Versus Legal Reasons for Divorce

The real reasons for divorce are those tensions and irritations which make it impossible for a man and woman to "get along" within the bonds of matrimony. These reasons were discussed at length in a previous chapter. When the two appear before the particular tribunal which is to decide whether or not they shall be released, however, their pleas frequently bear little relation to the marital problems involved. If the only legal ground for absolute divorce is adultery, that charge often will be made whether or not the defendant is guilty. In other cases, the husband and wife may make a mutual agreement to separate, but the decree will be entered on the ground of desertion.

In general the decree is sought on the least incriminating terms—even though the spouse may be guilty of more reprehensible conduct. A curious

[37] Martindale-Hubbell, *Law Directory,* Vol. IV, *Digest of Laws,* 1959.
[38] *Ibid.*
[39] *Ibid.*

vestige of chivalry persists in divorce court procedure. Even though the husband is often the one who insists upon breaking the marriage tie, he usually chooses to have the charges made by his wife. Social prejudice still places a woman in an unfavorable light if her husband initiates the suit. Society may also condemn him if he accuses an "innocent" wife of unseemly conduct. Hence only in case of a grave breach of the mores—such as adultery, attack on life, or actual, as well as legal, desertion—do we find dissatisfied husbands humiliating their wives by initiating proceedings.

In the eyes of the law, it is practically impossible for a married couple to come to the parting of the ways and agree to a "friendly" divorce. Such an arrangement is deemed "collusion." As Louis Harris points out, "According to our modern divorce courts this is considered several degrees worse than murder." Even though the lives of both parties may be ultimately ruined by continuing in an impossible situation, they cannot secure a divorce by honestly admitting the reasons for their unhappiness. Nevertheless, there often is a tacit collusion.[40] Consequently, a large share of testimony offered at divorce hearings would not bear investigation and is frequently nothing more or less than perjury. Divorce judges are generally cognizant of this, but they have learned that no legal suasion can enforce the marriage status on unwilling parties. This winking at perjured testimony may seem to lower the dignity of the court and of marriage. Judges are, however, generally agreed that such perjury is a lesser evil than requiring men and women to commit adultery or such other offenses as are technically necessary to secure the divorce decree.[41]

Legal Grounds for Divorce

Because of our peculiar system of federal and state government, the United States has the most confusing system of divorce legislation in the world. Until 1949, South Carolina did not allow divorce on any ground. After amending their state constitution in March, 1949, the South Carolina legislature adopted provisions for divorce on the grounds of adultery, desertion, cruelty, and habitual drunkenness.[42] With that law the last stronghold of complete rigidity in marriage vows was ended in the United States. New York is now the only state which makes adultery the sole reason for absolute divorce. Desertion as valid ground is differently defined in the various states, and a wide range of grounds is accepted by some and not by others. Fabricated residence requirements are notoriously common in Virginia. Although Reno is considered the divorce capital of the country, presence in the community is actually required. Grounds for divorce in some states are grounds for nullity in others and are disallowed in either case in still others.

Part of the difficulty which the state encounters in enforcing regulations admittedly lies in this lack of adequate definition of the situation. When is a marriage valid? Should we humanize the divorce statutes of our eastern

[40] Cf. Louis Harris, *Love, Marriage and Divorce in History and Law,* The Stratford Company, Boston, 1930, p. 99.

[41] *Ibid.,* p. 100.

[42] Cf. *Acts and Joint Resolutions, South Carolina,* 1949, Statute No. 137, pp. 216–220.

states? Are conditions in various sections of the country so different as to warrant such a wide variance in divorce regulations? Is a uniform divorce law the solution to the difficulty? Our analysis makes no claim to the definitive answer. The diversity in social backgrounds, the heterogeneous population groups, the conflict between modern statutes and the old common-law interpretations, the differences in the political power of the Roman Catholic Church, and the confusion attendant upon the new status of women are a few of the reasons why a common definition of the marriage situation is difficult to attain.[43] Although the specific divorce legislation may indicate public attitudes in the various states, it is no accurate gauge of either marital conditions or sex morality. Illegitimacy was in fact highest in the country in South Carolina during the long period in which no divorce was allowed in that state.

Since marriage and the family are so intimately related to the welfare of the individual and the social group, the state has every right to impose regulations. There will always be a lag, however, between ideals and practices in reference to marriage, since social conditions change so much more rapidly than the law. Eventually it is to be hoped that marriage and divorce legislation will offer some real insight into the psychosocial phases of marital maladjustment. Many of our legal categories for divorce are abstract juridicial entities far removed from the fragile stuff out of which marriage is made. Let us review these legal grounds as summarized in Table 16.2.[44]

1. *Adultery.* Adultery is the voluntary sexual intercourse of a married man or woman with a person other than the offender's wife or husband. Adultery is the almost universally acceptable ground for a divorce in all countries where divorce is permitted. The law generally recognizes that the act, to be regarded as valid reason for divorce, must be voluntary and willful. That is, neither party may be insane, or acting in the belief that the legal spouse is dead.[45] In all cases the co-respondent may appear and contest the proceedings if he or she desires. Separation at the time of the alleged adultery is no defense, and connivance in adulterous conduct is considered a bar to divorce. However, it is a well-known fact that collusion enters into a large share of divorces granted on these charges. In New York, where adultery is the only cause allowed,[46] many allegations of adultery are accepted on very scanty evidence.

In establishing the fact of infidelity in most states, evidence of opportunity must be accompanied by convincing evidence of will to commit such an act. Entering a house of ill fame, venereal disease contracted after marriage, clandestine correspondence with a paramour are accepted as evidence. Unless confessions are corroborated by further evidence they are not enough, since

[43] Cf. Anthony M. Turano, "The Conflict in Divorce Laws," *American Mercury 17:* 459–462 (August, 1929).

[44] Cf. Martindale-Hubbell, *op. cit.,* for divorce provisions of the several states. Divorce laws for this book were all checked in Martindale-Hubbell's *Law Directory.*

[45] Clarke, *op. cit.,* p. 120.

[46] New York allows a dissolution of marriage after an absence of five years where the missing party is not located, and divorce *a mensa et toro* for cruelty and abandonment.

TABLE 16.2. Grounds for Divorce: By States, 1959

States and Possessions	Adultery	Bigamy	Conviction for crime	Cruelty	Desertion	Drug addiction	Drunkenness	Impotence	Incompatibility	Insanity	Neglect	Nonsupport	Separation	Venereal Disease	Wife pregnant by another	Other Grounds
Alabama	X		X	X	X	X	X	X		X[a]		X	X		X	Crime against nature, violence
Alaska	X		X	X	X		X	X	X	X[b]	X	X				Felony before marriage
Arizona	X		X	X	X		X	X				X	X			
Arkansas	X		X	X	X	X	X	X		X[b]		X	X		X	Personal indignities
California	X		X	X	X		X			X[b]	X	X				
Colorado	X		X	X	X	X	X	X		X[a]	X	X				Divorce in another state
Connecticut	X		X	X	X		X			X[a]		X				Any violation of conjugal rights; Fraudulent contract; 7 years' absence (unheard of)
Delaware	X	X	X	X	X		X			X[a]		X				Complainant under age at time of marriage and marriage not confirmed after reaching age

	Prohibited degree of relationship	Ungovernable temper	Divorce in any other state	Prohibited degree of relationship	Force, menace, duress, or fraud	Mental incapacity at marriage	Leprosy, mental suffering	Attempt on life		Fraudulent contract	Loathsome disease, uniting with religious sect forbidding cohabitation	Force, fraud, or duress	Danger to life and limb of wife	Public degradation, attempt on life	Fugitive from justice	Libel	Anything rendering marriage null and void
District of Columbia	X																
Florida	X	X	X														
Georgia	X			X					X^a		X	X					
Hawaii	X			X	X		X		X^b	X	X						
Idaho	X			X	X	X	X		X^b	X	X						
Illinois	X			X				X		X	X						
Indiana	X			X	X	X	X		X^a	X	X						
Iowa	X		X^d	X	X	X	X			X	X						
Kansas	X	X	X	X	X	X	X		X^a	X	X			X			
Kentucky	X		X	X	X	X	X		X^a	X				X			
Louisiana	X			X						X		X	X		X		
Maine	X			X	X		X			X	X			X	X		
Maryland	X	X		X	X		X	X^e		X	X			X			X

TABLE 16.2. Grounds for Divorce: By States, 1959 (*Continued*)

States and Possessions	Adultery	Bigamy	Conviction for crime	Cruelty	Desertion	Drug addiction	Drunkenness	Impotence	Incompatibility	Insanity	Neglect	Nonsupport	Separation	Venereal Disease	Wife pregnant by another	Other Grounds
Massachusetts	X		X	X	X	X	X	X				X	X			
Michigan	X		X^e	X	X		X	X				X				To any person who has secured a divorce in another state
Minnesota	X	X	X	X	X		X	X		X^a			X			Court separation or decree for 2 years
Mississippi	X	X	X	X	X	X	X	X		X					X	Consanguinity of prohibited degree / Insanity at time of marriage unknown to spouse
Missouri	X		X	X	X		X	X			X	X			X	Personal indignities, vagrancy of husband
Montana	X		X	X	X	X	X			X^a	X	X				Grievous mental suffering, false charges against chastity, repeated threat of violence
Nebraska	X		X	X	X	X	X	X		X^a	X	X	X			
Nevada	X		X	X	X		X	X		X^f	X	X	X			

398

State	Treatment injurious to life or health	Absence unheard of 3 years	Wife living 10 years in another state without consent, alien leaves wife for 2 years, no thought of returning	Member religious sect forbidding marriage	Failure of husband to support according to means	Marriage may be declared dissolved if spouse absent unheard of for 5 years (legally dead)	Legal separation for adultery, cruelty, abandonment, nonsupport	Crime against nature	Huntington's Chorea, paresis, or epileptic insanity	Fraudulent contract, securing divorce without state, trying to secure release from duties	Fraudulent contract, procurement of divorce in other state, trying to secure release from duties	Indignities	Incapability of procreation	Indignities, fraud, force, coercion	Prohibited consanguinity	Attempt to corrupt sons	Attempt to prostitute daughters	Proposal to prostitute wife
New Hampshire	X	X	X				X	X										
New Jersey	X		X	X														
New Mexico	X	X	X	X	X		X		X	X	X							
New York	X					X												
North Carolina	X		X				X	X^a	X		X							
North Dakota	X	X	X		X		X	X^a	X	X	X							
Ohio	X	X	X	X	X		X		X	X	X							
Oklahoma	X	X	X		X		X	X^a	X	X	X							
Oregon	X	X	X		X		X	X^b			X							
Pennsylvania	X	X	X		X		X				X	X						
Puerto Rico	X	X	X		X		X	X^a	X		X				X^a			

TABLE 16.2. Grounds for Divorce: By States, 1959 (*Continued*)

States and Possessions	Adultery	Bigamy	Conviction for crime	Cruelty	Desertion	Drug addiction	Drunkenness	Impotence	Incompatibility	Insanity	Neglect	Nonsupport	Separation	Venereal Disease	Wife pregnant by another	Other Grounds
Rhode Island	X			X	X	X	X	X				X	X			Where marriage originally voidable or spouse civilly dead because of criminal conduct
South Carolina	X			X	X	X	X									Any gross violation of marriage covenant
South Dakota	X		X	X	X		X			X[a]	X	X				
Tennessee	X	X	X	X	X		X	X				X	X		X	Attempt on life of other Refusal of wife to accompany husband to Tennessee
Texas	X		X	X	X		X			X[a]			X			Testimony for conviction of crime must not be by spouse

400

		Absence 7 years, never heard from	Fugitive from justice	Sodomy or buggery	Previous sentence to penitentiary unknown to spouse at time of marriage	Prostitution unknown to husband at time of marriage	Personal indignities	Force or fraud where no cohabitation	Under legal age	Reasonable apprehension of bodily hurt	Conviction of crime prior to marriage and unknown	Vagrancy, intolerable indignities
Utah	X	X	X	X		X	X	X	X		X	X
Vermont	X	X	X	Xᵇ	X	X	X	Xᵃ	X		X	X
Virginia	X	X	X	X		X			X			X
Virgin Islands	X	X	X	X		X	X	X				
Washington	X	X	X	X	Xᶠ	X	X	X	X		X	X
West Virginia	X	X	X	X	X	X			X		X	X
Wisconsin	X	X	X	X	X	X			X		X	X
Wyoming	X	X	X	X	Xᶠ	X	X	X	X		X	X

401

ᵃ 5 years.
ᵇ 3 years.
ᶜ At time of marriage.
ᵈ Unless he has illegitimate child at time of marriage.
ᵉ May be automatic.
ᶠ 2 years.
ᵍ 7 years.
ʰ Vermont permits intolerable severity, which would seem to be cruelty and is entered as such.

SOURCE: Chart compiled by Mabel A. Elliott from summaries of legislation in Martindale-Hubbell, *Law Directory*, Vol. IV, *Digest of Laws*, 1959.

they may be inspired by collusion. Testimony of persons of questionable character is without weight unless further established.[47]

Adultery is a ground for divorce in all states and territories of the United States as Table 16.2 shows, but ranks fifth among the alleged legal grounds. A number of states specifically stipulate that adultery is a ground only when unforgiven or not condoned, however. One state requires that the suit for divorce on such a ground be within three years after the adulterous conduct occurred. In several states the guilty party may not marry his accomplice.

2. *Bigamy.* A bigamous marriage is in itself illegal; hence all such marriages are strictly speaking null and void. Even so, eleven states permit divorce on this ground, presumably to protect the status of a woman (or man) who has innocently contracted such a marriage unknowingly and may have had children by such a union. Otherwise the position of the innocent party would be that of an adulterer. To establish bigamy, the previous marriage must be proved valid. In case of previous divorce, bigamy may be established only if the decree was granted by a court which had no jurisdiction. The husband or wife who has disappeared or has not been heard of for five or more years is generally regarded as legally dead. The spouse cannot be held criminally liable in case of remarriage. Bigamy involves proof of cohabitation, either through marriage certificate and license or by oral testimony of the one solemnizing the ceremony.[48]

3. *Cruelty.* Cruelty ranks third among the most frequently permitted grounds for divorce, but first among the alleged grounds for which divorces are sought. As Table 16.2 shows, the Virgin Islands and Puerto Rico and all states except Maryland, New York, North Carolina, Virginia, and the District of Columbia permit divorce on this ground. The states differ in their definitions of cruelty, however. Some states permit divorce for physical cruelty or conduct endangering health or life only. Others permit divorce for mental cruelty or for anything which causes great mental suffering on the part of the plaintiff. Vermont specifies "intolerable severity," which may be presumed to be a variety of cruelty although some authorities do not classify it as such. Several states also permit divorce for ungovernable temper, which would seem to be a form of mental cruelty, if the defendant indulged in severe tongue-lashings.[49] Petulance without some apprehension of physical harm is not enough, however, nor is mere discourtesy.[50]

4. *Habitual Drunkenness.* Habitual drunkenness is ground for divorce in forty-three states and in Puerto Rico and the Virgin Islands. The period of drunkenness varies. Iowa stipulates that the drunkenness must occur after the marriage, Illinois that the drunkenness must exist over a period of two years. Several states provide that habitual drunkenness must exist for a year, whereas others merely indicate that habitual drunkenness is a legal ground for divorce.

[47] Clarke, *op. cit.*, p. 120.

[48] Cf. Frank H. Keezer, *A Treatise on the Law of Marriage and Divorce,* The Bobbs-Merrill Company, Inc., Indianapolis, 1959 (3rd ed.).

[49] Martindale-Hubbell, *op. cit.*

[50] Clarke, *op. cit.*, pp. 121–122.

The term "habitual" implies, however, that the drunkenness must have extended over a considerable period.[51]

5. *Drug Addiction.* Drug addiction is specified as grounds for divorce in eleven states and Puerto Rico. Usually drug addiction is an extension of the ground covering drunkenness or intoxication.[52]

6. *Desertion.* Desertion applies as ground for absolute divorce in all states except North Carolina and New York. Limited divorce or legal separation in New York may be obtained after unavailing search for the absent spouse for five years. Desertion as ground for divorce may be defined as the willful and voluntary separation of one party from the other without justification or the other's consent, and with no intention of returning to the domestic hearth. To be adequate justification for divorce, the desertion must be willful, continuous, and with the idea of permanence. Mere refusal of sexual intercourse is not generally considered desertion, although such refusal without good cause has been considered so in a few jurisdictions and has been defined by statute as desertion in a few states.[53]

If the misconduct of the husband or wife forces the other person to leave, the injured party is entitled to divorce on ground of constructive desertion. Petty disagreements over trivial matters are not, however, sufficient to justify deserting one's partner, nor again does separation by mutual consent constitute legal desertion. If either the husband or the wife in good faith attempts unsuccessfully to secure a reconciliation, the court may allow the plea of desertion. Generally speaking, the husband has the "legal and moral right" to establish residence. If the wife refuses to follow him to another locality, she is guilty of desertion.

The ethics of the desertion principle are not in any sense consistent. Cases of forced marriages performed to prevent bastardy or to legitimatize offspring are sometimes accompanied by an agreement not to live together. In such cases the wife later may be entitled to divorce on the ground of desertion. In case a man causes his wife to leave home because of his own misconduct, he is still liable for her support, although he has the right to determine where she shall make her necessary expenditures. Failure to support, as such, is not desertion, but may give additional evidence in a desertion charge.[54] If a woman has been driven out because of her husband's misconduct, publication of notice to the effect that he will not pay for any expenses his wife may incur has no legal effect whatsoever. He is still liable for her support.

7. *Impotence.* Impotence is the physical incapacity of either party to consummate the marriage and is generally a ground either for divorce or for rendering the contract void. To be valid ground for divorce, impotence must exist prior to the marriage and must be of a permanent nature, rendering sexual intercourse impossible. Thirty-six states and Puerto Rico and the Vir-

[51] Martindale-Hubbell, *op. cit.*
[52] *Ibid.*
[53] Martindale-Hubbell, *op. cit.* Cf. Clarke, *op. cit.,* p. 123.
[54] Clarke, *op. cit.,* p. 124.

gin Islands provide impotence as a ground for divorce.[55] Although barrenness was ground for divorce in earlier times, sterility in itself is not considered sufficient legal ground for divorce at present in most states.[56] It is a ground in Pennsylvania.

8. *Insanity.* Insanity is universally recognized in Western society by both church and state as an impediment to marriage. As ground for divorce, however, insanity has been accepted only relatively recently but the present trend is definitely toward recognizing it as a ground. Thirty states and Puerto Rico and the Virgin Islands now make insanity grounds for divorce, while one state, Pennsylvania, permits the divorce of insane persons on the same grounds as other persons if such grounds exist, but not for insanity per se. In Georgia, the person from whom a divorce is sought must have been insane at the time of marriage. In the other twenty-nine states, the insanity must occur after marriage, be considered incurable, and have persisted for a period of years. The most common provision is that such insanity must have existed for five years, during which time the person must have been confined to an institution. Puerto Rico stipulates a duration of seven years. Three western states permit divorce for insanity after only two years' confinement in a mental hospital.[57] Should the recent research in medical treatment of mental illness prove successful (see Chapter 12), this ground obviously may be altered.

Many religious leaders and other conservative people object to divorce on grounds of insanity for both religious and humane reasons. They believe that the insane person is the victim of a tragedy and hold that the spouse should not be exempted from marital responsibilities for an insane spouse any more than in case of tuberculosis or cancer. Others maintain that marriage is basically a spiritual union and that if the mind is deteriorated the personality change makes the marriage essentially void or nonexistent. Most of the states permitting divorce for insanity require husbands securing such a divorce to assume full responsibility for the insane person's support. Some also require burial expenses in case of death.

9. *Loathsome Disease.* Only three states permit divorce for loathsome disease. Illinois specifies that divorce may be granted if the guilty spouse has venereal disease. Kentucky permits divorce for loathsome disease, which presumably includes venereal disease, while Hawaii permits divorce for leprosy. It is safe to say that venereal disease is sometimes used as evidence of adultery in other states where the disease itself is not a ground.

10. *Prohibited Degree of Relationship.* All states render marriages null and void where proscribed degree of consanguinity exists. Four states, Florida, Georgia, Mississippi, and Pennsylvania, also permit divorce on such a ground, presumably to protect the status of innocent parties and their children where marriages have been made unwittingly. Maryland also permits di-

---

[55] Martindale-Hubbell, *op. cit.*
[56] Clarke, *op. cit.*
[57] Martindale-Hubbell, *op. cit.*

vorce for this reason, since divorces may be obtained in Maryland for "any reason which renders the marriage null and void."

11. *Pregnancy by Another at Time of Marriage.* Husbands may secure divorces in fourteen states if their wives were pregnant by another man unknown to them at time of marriage. These are Alabama, Arizona, Georgia, Iowa, Kansas, Kentucky, Mississippi, Missouri, New Mexico, North Carolina, Oklahoma, Tennessee, Virginia, and Wyoming. Of this group, Iowa limits the right of the husband to secure a divorce for such a pregnancy if he has an illegitimate child at the time of his marriage. Adultery or some other allegation may be made in other states where divorce for pregnancy of the wife by another is not specifically permitted. In at least one state, a divorce for unchaste conduct unknown at time of marriage is a ground.

12. *Personal Indignities.* A number of states, including Arkansas, Missouri, Pennsylvania, Washington, and Wyoming, provide that personal indignities are grounds for divorce. This charge is broad enough to include a wide variety of inexcusable conduct. An outraged Pennslyvania husband recently brought suit against his wife for divorce on such a ground. When asked to name the indignities, he alleged the following offenses on the part of his wife: "(1) bragging about affairs with other men, (2) making the family residence headquarters of female drinking orgies, (3) misrepresentation of her age and concealment of a previous marriage, and setting a bull mastiff on him when he tried to return home."[58] More often personal indignities are alleged with reference to sex practices which the plaintiff regards as unnatural or offensive.

13. *Miscellaneous Grounds.* Crime against nature (which may be defined further either as sodomy or as homosexuality) is a ground for divorce in Alabama, North Carolina, and Virginia. Homosexuality is, however, virtually everywhere considered grounds for release from marriage bonds. It may be considered as a variety of cruelty, as impotence, as a personal indignity, as a fraudulent contract, as a circumstance rendering the marriage null and void, or as a gross violation of the marriage covenant. The true homosexual is not interested in marriage as such and the state tries in every way to protect the innocent victim from fraud in these cases. Puerto Rico goes a step farther with reference to defining what many states have recognized more silently and provides that divorce may be granted in case the spouse attempts to corrupt sons or prostitute daughters or wife. Some states provide as a ground the spouse's having obtained a divorce in another state.

14. *Incompatibility.* Incompatibility is unquestionably a basic reason for divorce in most instances, but such a ground is permitted in only three states, Alaska, New Mexico, and Oklahoma, and in the Virgin Islands. Incompatibility is a blanket term covering conflict and tensions which make it difficult or impossible for a given couple to get along. Such a ground is in a sense contrary to the generally accepted legal assumption that a divorce can be granted only to an innocent party because of the serious misconduct of the spouse who is the defendant in the divorce suit. Incompatibility imputes a mutuality

[58] *Pittsburgh Post-Gazette,* August 4, 1955, p. 16.

in the desire for release from marriage bonds, and any such collusion makes divorce technically null and void in most jurisdictions.

15. *Nonsupport.* Nonsupport is a statutory ground for divorce in thirty-three states while neglect is a ground in seventeen states. Nonsupport may also be considered a special variety of cruelty if the husband is well and able to support his wife; hence by interpretation it is a ground in most states. On the other hand, if the wife has independent means or is self-supporting, this may be considered insufficient grounds. When a husband is ill or physically disabled, the wife may not secure a divorce for nonsupport.[59]

16. *Fraud, Duress, and Mistake.* Any gross deception or misrepresentation on the part of either contracting party may render the marriage voidable. In a few states fraud, duress, or mistake is also a ground for divorce. This is true in Connecticut, Ohio, and Oklahoma. A marriage cannot be annuled, however, for the husband's false representations as to his character or the extent of his property. A man who represents his former wife as dead, whereas in fact he was divorced, is not considered sufficiently culpable to warrant a divorce on such ground. For persons holding serious scruples about marrying a divorcee, this may nevertheless result in termination of the union. In case the wife is pregnant by a man other than her husband at time of marriage and conceals the fact from her husband, such fraud is sufficient ground for divorce. If the husband has had premarital sex relations with his wife, however, he is not entitled to divorce, even though she be pregnant by another man. In this case the law assumes that he must have been apprised of her character and should have been on his guard.[60]

Generally speaking, marriages performed under *duress* are null and void unless afterward ratified by assent or voluntary cohabitation. Most states make duress ground for divorce. On the other hand, marriage in which the husband is virtually compelled to marry the girl or suffer punishment for seduction is not considered legal duress.[61]

Mistake as ground for nullity or divorce is allowed only if there has been a positive mistake as to identity. As one court has expressed it, "Nothing would be more dangerous than to allow those who have agreed to take each other in terms 'for better or worse,' to be permitted to say that one of the parties is worse than expected."[62] Actually, of course, most divorces occur for exactly that reason.

Divorce Procedure

Divorce procedure involves the so-called innocent party's suing a spouse in civil court and alleging serious misbehavior by the defendant with evidence and witnesses to support the allegations. Since there is seldom a situation in which one party is wholly to blame for marital tensions, the pro-

[59] Clarke, *op. cit.,* pp. 280–288.
[60] *Ibid.,* pp. 103–105.
[61] *Ibid.*
[62] *Long vs. Long,* 77 N. Car. 304, 1877.

cedure which attaches blame to one party of itself often increases the antagonism between husband and wife.

Theoretically divorces are granted only for serious faults that render the marriage intolerable. The divorce complainants often make allegations against their estranged spouses which the latter resent as unfounded. Such accusations are likely to anger, crush, or humiliate the defendant. Judge Paul W. Alexander of Toledo suggests that the divorce court (like the juvenile court) should be organized to help embattled spouses, instead of penalizing them. For estranged spouses often need treatment more than anything else.[63] In the future, Judge Alexander's idea may well be adopted, and social case work procedures may take the place of the outworn adversary type of divorce court trial.

Annulment

In addition to provisions for divorce, the various states also dissolve marriages by annulment. A decree of annulment means that no marriage ever legally occurred between the parties, that no property rights are involved, and that, unless there are express statutes to the contrary, any children born from the union are illegitimate. As our analyses of the legal grounds for divorce show, divorces are obtained in some states on grounds which would be legal basis for establishing nullity in others. There is no uniformity as to the reasons recognized by the various states. Bigamy, for example, is ground for divorce in some states, renders a marriage null and void in a number of others, and in still others is ground for annulment.[64]

Alimony

Alimony is a legal allowance granted to the wife (and occasionally to the husband) when living apart from him (or her) after the divorce has been granted. Such an allowance presumably corresponds to the type of support which would have been the wife's (or husband's) if the marriage relation had been continued. Initially alimony was considered in the nature of a penalty, and the federal government has only recently been willing to accept alimony deductions from income taxes as "support" rather than considering them as fines. Since legal divorce *ipso facto* presumes some fault on the part of the defendant, the wife still retains the right to the support which her husband assumed at marriage—if she is granted the decree.[65]

Temporary alimony, or *alimony pendente lite,* is an allowance granted the wife while the divorce suit is pending. It is generally allowed whether or not she wins the suit on the presumption of her innocence. Every state, with the exception of Tennessee, has made some legal provisions for temporary alimony to the wife. In 1935, Illinois passed a law which provided for tem-

[63] Paul W. Alexander, "Let's Get the Embattled Spouses Out of the Trenches," *Law and Contemporary Problems, 18:*98–106 (Winter, 1953).

[64] Clarke, *op. cit.,* pp. 105–106.

[65] Clarke, *op. cit.,* "Today alimony, strictly speaking, is an enforcement of the husband's obligation to support the wife." *Ibid.,* p. 133.

porary alimony to be granted the husband. Temporary alimony usually continues during the period of litigation and ceases with the final judgment or upon the death of either party.[66] In general, counsel fees and all such costs are paid by the husband.

When *permanent alimony* is awarded, the needs of the children and the wife's conduct are factors in determining its amount. The size of the husband's estate, the existence of any other provision for the wife's support, and her own means of support, if any, are all taken into account in establishing the amount to be paid. The actual determination of the alimony is left to the discretion of the court in every state but Georgia, where the jury may fix the amount.[67] In Pennsylvania a wife who has no children cannot be awarded alimony.[68]

A change in domestic arrangements, such as the marriage of the ex-wife or the decreased earning power of the husband, may cause the court to revise the alimony decree. In case of the reconciliation and remarriage of the estranged persons, the alimony ceases. If the wife marries someone else, the alimony is generally rescinded except for such portion as may be used for the support of minor children. If the husband remarries, however, his obligation for the support of his former wife still remains, in some instances with grave injustice to himself. If a woman has refused to live with her husband and has divorced him on trivial grounds, she may be able to exert a more powerful control over him than before the divorce occurred. Many divorced husbands believe themselves to be tied for life financially to a woman who has failed to abide by her marriage contract.

Despite the fact that wives frequently do not ask for alimony, the rate varies from state to state. In 1943 approximately 50 percent of women plaintiffs in divorce cases in Wisconsin asked for alimony, in contrast to 20 percent of those in Oklahoma and only 11 percent of those in Florida.[69] Where children are involved or where women have never been employed outside the home, some sort of financial provision should be made. Women who have never held paid jobs often have a difficult time securing work. Children need assistance until they are able to earn for themselves, and in many families this means until they are through college. At the least, it means providing support through the compulsory education period and if possible until the children finish high school. Sometimes a wife resolves never to take a cent of money from her estranged husband when this actually imposes an insufferable burden on herself.

The state is interested in the well-being of both wife and children and should make certain that suitable financial arrangements are made. On the other hand, some unscrupulous women marry with a view to later divorce and the award of a sizable alimony. In a few spectacular cases such women

[66] *Ibid.,* p. 135.
[67] *Ibid.,* p. 134.
[68] Martindale-Hubbell, *op. cit.*
[69] Public Health Service, *Vital Statistics—Special Reports,* Vol. 17, No. 25, U.S. Department of Health, Education, and Welfare (June 9, 1943).

may secure enormous financial settlements. The collection of alimony for the majority of divorcées is, however, no easy matter. Ex-husbands often default on alimony payments; part of the relief load in every city stems from support of children whose fathers fail to make their alimony payments, as we discuss later.

The alimony-paying husband may also have a bleak outlook. If he contributes enough to support his wife he may never be able to remarry. In consequence, many husbands fail to pay alimony or to keep gentlemen's agreements where the support problem is settled out of court. Some states penalize defaulting alimony payers and even send ex-husbands to jail. Imprisonment for debt is unconstitutional, but imprisonment of a defaulting husband is interpreted as contempt of court rather than jailing for debt.[70] The recent attempts of federal and state authorities to enforce support of children may lead to further legislation on alimony.

To pay or not to pay alimony thus has many facets. The mother and children may suffer personal disorganization from lack of income. So may the father if alimony imposes a crushing burden. One should not lavish too much sympathy on the way the wealthy ex-husband is exploited. His plight is not especially serious. But the low-wage earner who tries to support two establishments is in a difficult position. In the eyes of the estranged wife or an outraged public, this may be "what he deserves," but the husband may react by evading the law. He may also become completely disorganized.

Desertion, Divorce, and Nonsupport

One of the most serious angles of family breakdown by desertion, separation, and divorce is thus the failure of the normal breadwinner to contribute to his family's support. In general an "honorable" middle- or upper-class man—even when separated or divorced—makes an attempt to support his wife and children. The vast majority of deserters do not, and the taxpayer must support the children where the deserting father fails to contribute to his family's support and the mother is unable to do so. Consequently many states have made failure of the father to support his family a penal offense, as mentioned earlier. This has not proved very successful because deserting husbands often leave the state. Even where they remain accessible social workers are often reluctant to bring charges. In fact social workers have generally maintained that bringing charges makes the father more belligerent and that if he is sent to jail no support will be forthcoming anyway.

Mothers seldom desert their children, but when they do judges condemn them bitterly because the children are often left cold, hungry, and otherwise neglected. Such mothers are held to be lacking in mother-love and often arouse great antagonism. Actually they may simply be as tired and discouraged as any father who walks out.

The American Bar Association has taken a rigid view with reference to

---

[70] Cf. Ray E. Baber, *Marriage and the Family*, McGraw-Hill Book Company, Inc., New York, 1939, p. 484.

fathers and sponsored the Uniform Enforcement of Support Act, which has now been adopted by all fifty states, Puerto Rico, and the District of Columbia although the provisions vary slightly from one state to another.[71] This act provides that each state must enforce court orders for support upon fathers within the state when such orders have been made by judges on the complaint of spouse or social agency in another state.

The seriousness of this problem is evident in the fact that 323,600 families (involving 836,200 children in which the father was estranged and absent) received aid to dependent children during 1955 under provisions of the Social Security Act. These families represented 53.2 percent of all families and 50.3 percent of all children receiving such aid.[72]

In consequence of the agitation on the part of the American Bar Association, journalists, editors, and the general public became convinced that far too many fathers were absconding and forcing the taxpayers to assume an unwarranted burden. Implementation of the legislation requiring courts in all states to institute proceedings against a father who had left his family in another state was not easy, however.

Therefore, in 1950 Congress adopted a new provision of the Social Security Act which went into effect on July 1, 1952. It required public assistance agencies to notify the local law enforcement agencies whenever aid to dependent children was granted because a parent deserted.[73] This presumably was to enable the Uniform Enforcement of Support Law to swing into action and to secure greater support from deserting fathers.

Three years later (in 1955) the Federal Bureau of Public Assistance in cooperation with state bureaus of public assistance made a survey of the support received from absent fathers in such cases. In the summer of 1955 the data on the 323,600 families with 836,200 children (referred to above) were analyzed. In 185,500 of the families the father's marriage was broken by divorce, separation, and desertion. In the remaining cases the father had never married the mother.[74] Data for only 162,400 of the legitimate fathers were analyzed (because cases in Nevada and California had to be excluded). Of the 162,400 fathers only 18.3 percent made a contribution, 81.1 percent made no contribution, and in 0.6 percent the contribution, if any, was unknown.[75] Most of the fathers (76.8 percent) who contributed to the support of the family were divorced or separated, whereas only 22 percent of the fathers who had deliberately deserted their families contributed. The whereabouts of the divorced and separated fathers was more apt to be known than that of the deserting fathers and they were more likely to live in the jurisdiction of the court issuing the orders. Whether more fathers would contribute if

[71] See Martindale-Hubbell, *op. cit.,* for these laws.
[72] Kaplan, *op. cit.*
[73] U.S.C.A., Sec. 602 (a) (10), 1952.
[74] The unmarried mother's plight is discussed in Chapter 6.
[75] Kaplan, *op. cit.*

greater effort were made to locate them cannot be stated. They might well do so, but the expense and effort would in many instances outweigh any contribution.[76] Where the previously married fathers (either divorced or separated) contributed, the amounts were usually small. Approximately half contributed less than $50 a month and only 11.3 percent contributed $100 or more. The small amounts paid to the families are partly a function of the father's economic instability. Divorced men are known to receive less income than married men. About half the number of men receiving a divorce remarry within three years after securing a divorce. With new family obligations it is difficult for them to contribute to their first family.

The high percentage of deserted families in the group is partly accounted for by the fact that children who are orphaned or whose father has died receive aid under provisions of the old age and survivors' insurance provisions of the Social Security Act. Nevertheless there was an absolute increase of 50 percent in the families requiring assistance because of the father's estrangement during the period from 1948 to 1955. The estranged fathers whose marriage had been broken by desertion, divorce, and separation constituted 57.3 percent of all the "ADC" families. The remaining 42.7 percent were never married to the mothers. The unmarried mothers receiving aid to dependent children rose 91 percent during the 1948–1955 period. Those receiving such aid are a reflection of the large increase in illegitimacy.

Implementation of the Enforcement of Support Act has not been encouraging. Nearly two-thirds (62.4 percent) of the fathers under court order to support the child failed to do so. On the other hand, only 35.2 percent of those who made voluntary agreements failed to contribute. In general, court proceedings tend to increase the hostility between parents, but where the father violates an agreement there is nothing else to do but bring suit.[77]

Less than a sixth of the fathers who separated from the mothers in the study had made agreements and these appear to be the most responsible fathers in the group. As time elapses, however, fathers whether under court order or under agreement tend to contribute less and less. If the father lives in the same jurisdiction as the court where the order is made he is more likely to contribute than if he is at a distance where enforcement is more difficult.[78]

Of the fathers who were outright deserters and assumed no responsibility, place of residence was known in only 30.1 percent of the cases, only 24.3 percent were subject to agreement or court order, and only 9.5 percent contributed to the family's support.[79]

Percentagewise, Negro fathers are much more generally "absent" than white fathers, for 40.9 percent of the fathers in the study were nonwhite (mostly Negro) whereas Negroes constitute around 10 percent of the popula-

[76] *Ibid.*
[77] *Ibid.*
[78] *Ibid.*
[79] *Ibid.*

tion as a whole. Nonwhite absent fathers also contribute less often (14 percent) as contrasted to white fathers (21.3 percent). Nonwhite fathers also seldom are under court order or agreement to support their children.[80]

Relatively few absent fathers return to their families. In fact only 1820 of the 162,400 fathers were known to have returned home. An additional 1073 cases were closed because of the increased support from the father. About two-fifths of the returning fathers were apparently intermittent deserters.[81]

The security which federal and state aid provides for divorced, separated, and deserted families mitigates some of the worst effects of insufficient income which plague so many divorced and deserted families.[82] There is apparently no rule which judges apply with reference to support orders. Some judges investigate a case, others depend upon hunches as to what a man can afford. Some court orders are too high, others too low. Those which are too high are likely to remain unpaid. The aid to dependent children assistance is undoubtedly rendering an important service to needy children. Nevertheless, there are probably cases in which the father's irresponsibility is enhanced by the existence of the law. He knows the state will not let his child suffer seriously for lack of support, at least not for long.[83]

SELECTED BIBLIOGRAPHY

The bibliography on desertion and divorce is given at the end of Chapter 17.

---

[80] *Ibid.*
[81] *Ibid.*
[82] *Ibid.*
[83] Henry H. Foster, Jr., *Dependent Children and the Law,* reprint from *University of Pittsburgh Law Review,* Spring, 1957, pp. 579–606.

CHAPTER 17

Divorce: Patterns and Trends

Divorce, Church, and the State

The Roman Catholic Church has always taken a rigid stand against divorce and enforces a divorce canon in which it endeavors to incorporate Christ's teachings to the effect that no man should put away his wife except for adultery, and (with reference to the indissolubility of marriage) "What God has joined together, let no man put asunder." Marriage is therefore believed to be a sacrament which cannot be set aside by earthly powers if once performed by a Catholic priest. The Catholic Church obviously recognizes that some marriages are unhappy and that marriage partners often cause their mates much distress and suffering. When this happens it is regarded as part of the cross a Christian must bear and his religion should give him grace sufficient to meet his difficulties. When and if the burden becomes intolerable the church will permit legal separation (divorce *a mensa et toro*) but will not authorize remarriage. In Italy, Spain, and Portugal the population is nearly all Roman Catholic; the Roman Catholic Church is officially the state church and the church's divorce canon is the state law of divorce. No one may secure an absolute divorce or remarry in these countries, as is also true in certain South American countries to be discussed later on.

Elsewhere the Roman Catholic Church has powerful suasive power over its members (even though the law may permit divorce). In some European states Catholics were previously restricted by law from remarrying even though non-Catholics might secure divorce. In any event faithful members of the church are not divorced.

France, despite its Catholic background, has more liberal divorce provisions than other Latin countries. Even so, French judges are required to attempt to reconcile the couple. If the defendant does not appear, a decree by default may be granted after a waiting period of eight months. In such cases the woman to whom a decree is rendered must wait 300 days before remarrying unless she had borne a child (and presumably is permitted to wed the father). There is a strong tradition toward maintaining the family in France.

The Church of England has been in essential agreement with the Roman Catholic Church so far as its divorce canon is concerned. The remarriage of

413

divorced persons (even of the innocent party) is thus frowned upon by the Anglican Church. This was made very evident in the thwarted romance of Princess Margaret and Group Captain Peter Townsend, a divorcee and a commoner. Nevertheless where the British courts have permitted a divorce, remarriage is left up to the conscience of the officiating clergyman, although any marriage of a divorced person is officially disapproved.

Before 1857 there was no divorce in England except by act of Parliament. The law enacted that year permitted divorce to the husband on ground of his wife's adultery, whereas a wife might secure a divorce only for adultery plus cruelty on the part of her husband. These provisions kept divorces to a very low number and remained unaltered until 1937, when the highly publicized divorce of Wallis Simpson (on what many believed were "trumped-up" grounds) and her subsequent marriage to the former King of England were factors in the modification of the British law. Today divorce may be obtained in England for adultery, desertion for three years, cruelty such as to injure mind and body, and insanity for five years. The wife may also secure a divorce if her husband practices sex perversions.[1]

Germany since World War II has expurgated all anti-Semitic provisions for divorce which were in force under Hitler. Divorce is permitted for adultery, violation of marital obligations, desertion, insanity for three years, and venereal disease (where the latter two grounds are "morally justified"). Germany, like many American states, does not permit divorce, however, if the alleged grounds have been condoned by the marriage partner. The idea of guilt is taken seriously by Germans and both parties may on occasion be declared guilty. If a wife has a moral lapse after the divorce is granted she is required to have her maiden name restored.[2]

The Scandinavian countries are almost completely Protestant and have the most lenient divorce provisions of continental western Europe. Thus in Denmark, Norway, and Sweden divorce by mutual consent may be obtained. The procedure requires both parties to consult with their pastor or a proper governmental official, who is obliged to try to work out a reconciliation. Failing this, a divorce following a specific waiting period may be granted. In Sweden the couple must wait for one year, in Denmark one year and a half, and in Norway three years. Divorces are also granted for other more orthodox reasons in these countries, including adultery, six months' absence, insanity for three years, life imprisonment, neglect of domestic duties, and venereal disease. Divorce may also be granted by royal prerogative for grave reasons.[3]

The Russian Revolution abolished the establishment of the church, and

---

[1] Martindale-Hubbell, *Law Directory,* Vol. IV. *Digest of Laws,* 1959. (This directory is alphabetized, but not paginated.)

[2] *Official Gazette of the Control Council for Germany,* No. 4 (Berlin 28, 1946), Law 16, "Marriage Law," pp. 77–94.

[3] Martindale-Hubbell, *op cit.* Cf. also Mabel A. Elliott, "The Scope and Meaning of Divorce," chap. XXII in Howard Becker and Reuben Hill (eds.), *Family, Marriage, and Parenthood,* D. C. Heath and Company, Boston, 1955, pp. 668–708.

the Communist constitution and government are avowedly atheistic, as we discuss in Chapter 30. During the early days of the newly constituted USSR less than half the marriages were legally solemnized, and divorce could be secured by either party merely by asking for it. It was not even necessary to apply for the divorce in person. One could obtain it by mailing a post card to the Marriage and Divorce Bureau. During the twenties and early thirties divorce rates in Russia were the highest in the world. Support of children was rigidly enforced, however, and a man could be required to contribute from 25 to 35 percent of his earnings for his children's care. Obviously he could not afford many divorces. Eventually the officials recognized that stable family life was important to the state and in 1935 a governmental campaign began to induce all couples to register their marriage (if they were living together). Officials were also required to try to dissuade applicants from getting a divorce. In 1937 rigid grounds for divorce were adopted, but in 1944 all grounds for divorce were abolished, as were all common-law marriages (or marriage by cohabitation). The Edict of July 8, 1944, now in force, requires that divorces be granted only for serious reasons after examination of the truth of the arguments. The decision is made on the merits of the individual case. The procedure is complicated and expensive, which acts as a further deterrent. The application for a divorce is first made to the people's court, which tries to reconcile the couple. If it cannot do so the case is referred to the Regional Court, which conducts an investigation and tries to reconcile the couple. Failing this, it gives its judgment on a divorce but the case may be appealed to the Superior Court. Ordinarily all questions of alimony, custody of children, division of property, etc., are decided by the Regional Court. The Soviet government has thus become very conservative about family and divorce matters.[4] It also frowns severely on illicit sex relations and is trying to promote a moral life without any assistance from religious teaching.[5]

In South America, despite the nominal adherence to Roman Catholicism, fourteen countries now permit divorce for a wide variety of reasons (most have seventeen grounds). In several countries, including Costa Rica, Nicaragua, Bolivia, and Uruguay, divorce is possible on grounds of mutual consent after separation for a specified period. On the other hand, Chile, Brazil, Argentina, and Paraguay still permit no absolute divorce, although legal separation is permitted for grave reasons. Many persons in these states obtain migratory divorces in other countries, and in some states (including Brazil) concubinage is legal. In this relationship the children are legitimate but have no rights of inheritance. Concubinage is, however, a ground for divorce in Nicaragua.

In Mexico each state within the republic has a separate divorce law. In the federal district of Mexico seventeen reasons are permitted and definite

[4] W. W. Kulski, *The Soviet Regime,* Syracuse University Press, Syracuse, 1959, pp. 189–191.
[5] Cf. Chapter 30, pp. 710, 727.

grounds must be alleged. In Chihuahua no residence is required and divorce by mail is permitted for a fee of $60. In urban Mexico women conform much more consistently to the teachings of the Roman Catholic Church than do men, and a woman seldom seeks a divorce. So far as the peasantry is concerned, those of Indian descent have often hesitated to have their marriage performed according to rules of church or state and prefer to be married according to tribal rituals.[6]

Because Mexican divorces are very easy for Americans to secure (sometimes without the knowledge of the spouse) some American states have refused to recognize them. Such divorces are a part of the aftermath of the political revolution in Mexico and represent a significant decline in the church's authority. They also indicate a tawdry commercialization of divorce. Divorce by mail is also essentially undemocratic since one spouse may act without the knowledge of the other.

In Canada divorce laws are still much like those which existed earlier in England. In four provinces, Quebec, Yukon, Newfoundland, and the Northwest Territory, divorce is possible only by act of Parliament, and then ordinarily only for adultery. Nova Scotia permits divorce for adultery and cruelty and otherwise by act of Parliament. In the other Canadian provinces adultery is the major reason for divorce although other sex offenses are permitted grounds in some jurisdictions. British Columbia and Manitoba permit divorce only for adultery. In Alberta sodomy, rape, and bestiality are further grounds. Saskatchewan permits divorce for sexual malpractices of the husband. In New Brunswick frigidity and impotence are additional reasons. In Prince Edward Island the latter two offenses and consanguinity are grounds.[7] Canada, as a pioneer Dominion, is still less liberal than the mother country with reference to divorce.

In the United States we have deviated widely from the divorce rules applicable during our colonial status, although retaining the basic English common law in most of our civil procedures. Reasons for these differences have never been carefully explored.

Religious influences in the United States have been varied. The Church of England, the Presbyterian Church, the Quakers, the Puritans, and the Catholics all affected colonial divorce legislation. The Lutherans became influential soon after the American Revolution, and the many subsequent divisions of Protestantism have permitted further deviations from the earlier more rigid norm. Only in South Carolina (which had no divorce provisions at all until 1949), in the District of Columbia (which has recently extended its provisions from adultery to include several other grounds), and in New York State has the influence of the Roman Catholic Church and other conservative religious groups been sufficient to keep the grounds restricted to adultery. Today New York is the only state limiting divorce to this ground. Even though divorces are often granted for alleged rather than real

[6] Cf. Elliott, *op. cit.*
[7] Martindale-Hubbell, *op. cit.*

reasons, as we have mentioned, lawmakers tend to regard the grounds as the bona fide bases on which marriage ties may be severed. Adultery is the universally recognized basis for severing marriage ties in the United States, but only a small proportion of divorces are now granted for this reason.

Current Trends in Divorce Legislation and Procedure in the United States

Many people believe that the United States has "easy" divorce laws. This is not exactly true. As a glance at Table 16.2 will reveal, there is great similarity in the divorce provisions of the various states. Admissible grounds have been gradually extended in nearly all states except New York. Most of the grounds still involve serious breaches of marriage or serious misconduct, however. They are an attempt on the part of legislators to meet the problems of marital conflict realistically.

Recent developments in divorce legislation include the adoption of a divorce statute by South Carolina in 1949 which permits divorce for adultery, desertion for a period of one year, physical cruelty, and habitual drunkenness. The District of Columbia extended its divorce grounds from adultery to conviction of crime, desertion, and separation.

Conviction of crime, insanity, separation, and mutual consent are all relatively new grounds. Conviction of crime has been very widely adopted and is an admissible ground in forty-six jurisdictions. Insanity enduring over varying lengths of time is a ground in thirty states, Puerto Rico, and the Virgin Islands. Separation is now permitted as a ground in at least twenty-two states. This ground may be considered an evidence of more lenient tendency since the marriage partners may agree to separate and secure a divorce later, which is almost tantamount to divorce by mutual consent—not permitted in most states because it is regarded as "collusion." Only New Mexico (which was first to adopt such a provision), Alaska, Oklahoma, and the Virgin Islands permit divorce by mutual consent.

The trend toward a waiting period is distinctly conservative, however, as mentioned earlier in Chapter 16. Such a waiting period tends (1) to discourage hasty divorce, (2) to promote reconciliation, (3) to afford opportunity for preventing fraud or collusion, and (4) to prevent hasty remarriage.[8]

The chief leniency in American divorce is in the short residence requirements in a few states and the general tendency of judges to accept testimony without any attempt at verification. Reno, Nevada, has long been a mecca for those wanting a quick divorce. It requires only six weeks' residence but insists on the physical presence of the plaintiff for that time. Utah and the Virgin Islands have the same residence requirements. Wyoming requires sixty days and Florida and Arkansas grant divorces after ninety days' residence. Florida, Arkansas, and Nevada have done more to commercialize divorce than other states, however. Florida as a favorite vacation spot pro-

[8] Chester G. Vernier, *American Family Laws*, Vol. II, *Divorce and Separation*, Stanford University Press, Stanford, 1932, p. 152.

vides a pleasant sojourn while sitting out the residence requirement. Arkansas exploits its divorce attraction in connection with its Hot Springs resort. Reno has the best-organized facilities for securing a divorce as painlessly as possible. Divorces are usually granted to the plaintiff with virtually no attempt to ascertain the facts. Many states consequently raise questions from time to time about the validity of the plaintiff's residence in these states and frequently refuse to accept such divorces as valid when test cases are made.[9] On the other hand, migratory divorce has certain advantages and provides a safety valve for intolerable marriages from which there is no legitimate escape at home. It is especially useful for persons in New York State and a few other places with rigid restrictions. South Carolinians formerly sought divorce in neighboring states or in Reno. They often used to set up a fictitious residence by the device of mailing their laundry to Georgia and securing a divorce from that state. A person was held to live where he had his laundry done.

Any decent person can find objections to the divorce mills, but where there is no possibility of reconciliation divorce is often the lesser of possible evils. Illegitimacy rates and illicit sexual liaisons are always common where divorce restrictions are severe. The Roman and Anglican churches have always claimed that marriage is a spiritual union, but neither has been willing to recognize any spiritual basis for allowing egress from unfortunate marriage.

Migratory divorces are not a very desirable solution to marital conflict because the problems of alimony and support for children are difficult to enforce, as we discussed in Chapter 16. Custody of children is also hard to enforce where the granting court never sees the parties to the divorce again. Hence migratory divorce often creates problems which are never satisfactorily solved.

Trends in the Divorce Rate

During World War II there was a sharp upturn in divorce rates, as Table 17.1 shows. The number of divorces increased from 264,000 in 1940 to 400,000 in 1944. The rates had been increasing slowly but consistently ever since the first statistics were gathered in 1867, however (except for a brief period during the depression).[10] Following World War II the rates went up even more sharply during the years 1945 to 1947, reaching a peak of 610,000 in 1946.

During the depression years (1930–1940) the temporary decline in divorces occurred primarily because many people could not afford to pay the legal fees involved. It was also held by some that couples were drawn together because of the difficult times they had to face, but this is debatable. Many marriages failed because they foundered on economic rocks. They were not legally severed until the war years restored work, prosperity, and

[9] Morris Ploscowe, *The Truth About Divorce,* Hawthorn Books, Inc., New York, 1955, pp. 151–161.

[10] Congress had actually initiated the policy of gathering divorce data with an idea of keeping down a dangerous trend.

TABLE 17.1. Divorces and Crude Divorce Rates: United States, 1867–1957 (rates per 1000 estimated midyear population, for all years except 1940 and 1950;[a] divorces estimated for years 1907–1915, 1917–1921, 1933–1948[b])

Year	Estimated Midyear Population	Divorces[c] Number	Rate	Year	Estimated Midyear Population	Divorces Number	Rate
1957	170,293,000	381,000	2.2	1911	93,867,814	89,219	1.0
1956	167,259,000	382,000	2.3	1910	92,406,536	83,045	0.9
1955	164,303,000	377,000	2.3	1909	90,491,525	79,671	0.9
1954	161,183,000	379,000	2.4	1908	88,708,976	76,852	0.9
1953	158,320,000	390,000	2.5	1907	87,000,271	76,571	0.9
1952	155,761,000	392,000	2.5	1906	85,436,556	72,062	0.8
1951	153,384,000	381,000	2.5	1905	83,819,666	67,976	0.8
1950	150,697,361	385,144	2.6	1904	82,164,974	66,199	0.8
1949	148,665,000	397,000	2.7	1903	80,632,152	64,925	0.8
1948	146,093,000	408,000	2.8	1902	79,160,196	61,480	0.8
1947	143,414,000	483,000	3.4	1901	77,585,128	60,984	0.8
1946	141,235,000	610,000	4.3	1900	76,094,134	55,751	0.7
1945	139,585,518	485,000	3.5	1899	74,798,612	51,437	0.7
1944	138,083,449	400,000	2.9	1898	73,493,926	47,849	0.7
1943	136,497,049	359,000	2.6	1897	72,189,240	44,699	0.6
1942	134,664,924	321,000	2.4	1896	70,884,554	42,937	0.6
1941	133,202,873	293,000	2.2	1895	69,579,868	40,387	0.6
1940	131,970,224	264,000	2.0	1894	68,275,182	37,568	0.6
1939	130,879,718	251,000	1.9	1893	66,970,496	37,468	0.6
1938	129,824,939	244,000	1.9	1892	65,665,810	36,579	0.6
1937	128,824,829	249,000	1.9	1891	64,361,124	35,540	0.6
1936	128,053,180	236,000	1.8	1890	63,056,438	33,461	0.5
1935	127,250,232	218,000	1.7	1889	61,775,121	31,735	0.5
1934	126,373,773	204,000	1.6	1888	60,495,927	28,669	0.5
1933	125,578,763	165,000	1.3	1887	59,216,733	27,919	0.5
1932	124,840,471	164,241	1.3	1886	57,937,540	25,535	0.4
1931	124,039,648	188,003	1.5	1885	56,658,347	23,472	0.4
1930	123,076,741	195,961	1.6	1884	55,379,154	22,994	0.4
1929	121,769,939	205,876	1.7	1883	54,099,961	23,198	0.4
1928	120,501,115	200,176	1.7	1882	52,820,768	22,112	0.4
1927	119,038,062	196,292	1.6	1881	51,541,575	20,762	0.4
1926	117,399,225	184,678	1.6	1880	50,262,382	19,663	0.4
1925	115,831,963	175,449	1.5	1879	49,208,194	17,083	0.3
1924	114,113,463	170,952	1.5	1878	48,174,461	16,089	0.3
1923	111,949,945	165,096	1.5	1877	47,140,727	15,687	0.3
1922	110,054,778	148,815	1.4	1876	46,106,994	14,800	0.3
1921	108,541,489	159,580	1.5	1875	45,073,260	14,212	0.3
1920	106,466,420	170,505	1.6	1874	44,039,527	13,989	0.3
1919	105,062,747	141,527	1.3	1873	43,005,794	13,156	0.3
1918	104,549,886	116,254	1.1	1872	41,972,060	12,390	0.3
1917	103,413,743	121,564	1.2	1871	40,938,327	11,586	0.3
1916	101,965,984	114,000	1.1	1870	39,904,593	10,962	0.3
1915	100,549,013	104,298	1.0	1869	39,050,729	10,939	0.3
1914	99,117,567	100,584	1.0	1868	38,213,216	10,150	0.3
1913	97,226,814	91,307	0.9	1867	37,375,703	9,937	0.3
1912	95,331,300	94,318	1.0				

[a] 1940 and 1950 population based on April 1 population.

[b] 1957 divorces estimated for Illinois, Indiana, Kentucky, Louisiana, New York, North Carolina, and West Virginia.

[c] 1940–1946 rates include armed forces overseas population.

SOURCES: Taken partly from Table I, *Marriages and Divorces, United States and Each State, and Alaska, Hawaii, Puerto Rico, and the Virgin Islands, 1957, Vital Statistics—Special Reports*, Vol. 50, No. 7 (June 5, 1959), p. 187 and from Table IX, *Provisional Marriage and Divorce Statistics, United States, 1948, Vital Statistics—Special Reports*, Vol. 31, No. 16 (November 4, 1949), p. 229.

capacity to pay for the divorce. The high divorce rate during the latter part of the war was undoubtedly a result primarily of the hastily contracted "romantic" and ill-advised marriages earlier in the war. Many young people married persons they scarcely knew in their almost frantic desire for emotional security in the midst of wartime stress. Soldiers were married and returned to the front after a week-end honeymoon. When they came home the war bride often had no understanding of her husband's war experience and was wholly unprepared for his maturity and the alteration in his values. At best the two were often strangers. The young wife, on the other hand, may have faced motherhood alone. For the soldier-father it was often difficult to take up life with a wife he scarcely knew and a baby he had never seen. At times he felt like an intruder. Worse still, the prolonged separations sometimes meant that the husbands and wives entered into extramarital liaisons. Some fell in love. Others merely became promiscuous. A small number of women married for their husbands' allotment checks and a few of these zealous ladies married several times and were routed to federal prisons. Sometimes men married foreign women in the war areas. Some of these marriages had little chance of survival considering the social and cultural disparities involved. Some long wartime engagements culminated in marriage at the end of the war, without consideration of the alterations in personality of the partners.

Many thus married hastily on return from the army without weighing the factors which make for success in marriage. For some who had engaged in illicit affairs in the war theater a family breakdown at home was inevitable. Some families met the various crises imposed by war separations admirably, but usually because they had already met and survived previous crises. Although the officials in the army permitted men furloughs for home visits they never worked out any program for promoting family welfare as such.[11]

After 1947 divorce rates declined sharply. Despite the great increase in our population the number of divorces granted was 381,000 in 1957 and 382,000 in 1956 with a percentage decrease in rate for each year. Whether the current trend downward will continue is difficult to predict. Whether the lower rate indicates more responsible attitudes or the more favorable economic and social milieu in which families are functioning today none can say. We can only "wait and see" at this juncture.

The Legal Grounds for Which Divorces Are Granted

Legal grounds for which divorces were granted were available for only twenty-seven states in 1957. As Table 17.2 shows, only 2193 or 1.54 percent of the 143,812 divorces were granted in those states for adultery. More divorces (2404 or 1.67 percent) were granted for drunkenness than for adultery. Cruelty was the major alleged ground, charged in 71,298 or

---

[11] Reuben Hill, *Families Under Stress,* Harper & Brothers, New York, 1949, pp. 317–320 and 360–361.

nearly one-half of the divorce cases. But obviously almost any reason can be construed as a variety of cruelty. Desertion ranked second and accounted for 28,504 cases or 19.1 percent. The third ranking charge was much lower with 4614 and involved only 2.9 percent of the total cases.

In some states, however, a special charge accounted for many more cases than did some of the widely accepted grounds. In Missouri and Ohio together, over 27,000 cases (nearly as many as the total number of desertion cases) were charged with indignities and the dual charges of "gross neglect and cruelty" or "gross neglect and neglect of duty."

Certain widely permitted grounds were seldom used, and obviously would not be alleged where the ground was not the real reason. These included insanity, fraud, and drunkenness. Only 98 of the 143,812 divorces were granted for insanity, which indicates that most spouses do not secure release from marriage vows when their partner is mentally ill. Although separation is a ground currently permitted in twenty two states, Puerto Rico is the only jurisdiction where this ground is significant. Nearly half the divorces in Puerto Rico are for separation.

These data on legal grounds make it clear that most people do not "air their dirty linen in public" and the spouses tend to get a divorce for the least embarrassing reasons unless they are incensed. When the wife is guilty of adultery the husband may be so outraged as to make the allegation openly. In general most people prefer not to ventilate family scandals, and often the defendant never appears to answer charges. Sometimes the husband fights a divorce suit against him when he feels he has been wronged or when he wants custody of the children. But unless the wife is of a notoriously bad character judges are prone to award custody to the wife even where the husband presses the suit for divorce.

Marriages with Persons from Outside the State

Marriages with foreigners have been recognized as especially liable to divorce because of the danger of cultural conflict between the mates. The same thing appears to be true where mates come from different and non-contiguous states. Thomas P. Monahan has analyzed the divorces in Iowa between natives of the state and between Iowans and persons from non-contiguous states. He concludes that marriages between persons living in the state are more durable than those between Iowans and residents from non-contiguous or distant states.[12] Several reasons would seem to account for this. Many young people derive considerable ballast in their newly married status from being able to return occasionally to the parental home. Parents can help their married children understand that a certain amount of tension and maladjustment is normal in marriage and that "given-and-take" is essential in all satisfactory marriages.

[12] Thomas P. Monahan, "The Duration of Marriage to Divorce: Second Marriages and Migratory Types," *Marriage and Family Living, 21*:134–138 (May, 1959).

TABLE 17.2. Divorces and Annulments by Legal Grounds for Decree for 27 States and Puerto Rico and Virgin Islands, 1957 (by place of occurence)

Area	Total	Legal Grounds for Decree[a]											
		Adultery	Bigamy	Conviction of crime	Cruelty	Desertion	Drunkenness	Fraud	Insanity	Nonsupport	Under age	Other[b]	Not stated
Total, 27 states and Puerto Rico and Virgin Islands	143,812	2,193	487	791	71,298	28,504	2,404	511	98	4,164	90	30,658	2,614
Divorces	142,206	2,190	131	790	71,259	28,493	2,399	63	83	4,161	1	30,361	2,275
Annulments	1,606	3	356	1	39	11	5	448	15	3	89	297	339
Alabama[c]	10,925	407	16	14	5,437	4,575	293	—	17	52	4	53	57
Alaska	552	3	—	4	85	29	4	—	—	3	—	421	3
Connecticut	2,645	70	—	10	1,791	592	95	9	18	—	—	37	23
Delaware	682	45	13	2	157	402	31	—	1	—	—	29	2
Florida	18,744	130	81	—	13,189	4,095	761	53	7	—	5	352	71
Georgia	8,798	28	4	32	4,926	1,532	270	36	12	37	5	49	1,867
Hawaii[e]	1,182	6	9	4	51	147	—	3	2	79	6	881	—
Idaho	2,360	9	1	23	2,000	127	20	7	4	25	7	2	136
Iowa	4,134	33	23	80	3,713	215	48	3	2	3	—	5	2
Kansas	4,977	16	10	27	3,471	405	8	23	9	985	—	22	1
Maine	1,906	6	—	—	1,645	108	38	—	—	92	—	1	16
Michigan	15,442	14	—	30	13,851	811	43	100	—	446	—	119	28
Mississippi	4,974	235	9	25	2,405	1,911	293	—	2	—	—	41	53
Missouri[c]	10,861	76	7	69	106	1,352	95	96	—	102	—	8,950	104
Montana	2,004	7	2	22	1,627	169	3	—	2	57	9	10	—
Nebraska	2,204	37	37	7	1,441	156	312	18	4	178	13	1	—
New Hampshire	1,039	44	8	5	768	163	14	11	—	16	8	2	—

	C1	C2	C3	C4	C5	C6	C7	C8	C9	C10	C11	C12
New Jersey	4,665	491	48	—	829	3,169	—	128	—	—	—	—
North Dakota	545	1	5	5	378	63	5	3	1	24	55	—
Ohio	22,730	117	50	186	1,652	973	—	—	—	—	19,734	18
Oregon	5,261	5	—	41	4,640	405	11	4	6	1	19	129
South Dakota	622	3	4	3	502	64	10	5	4	24	2	1
Tennessee	8,602	150	34	81	5,258	987	47	5	1	1,994	42	9
Utah	1,343	—	21	5	1,098	28	5	6	1	36	44	94
Vermont	526	10	—	2	294	12	—	—	5	75	125	3
Virginia	6,675	258	107	113	6,138	—	—	9	2	—	27	—
Wyoming	1,148	1	7	9	52	120	2	—	1	17	937	—
Puerto Rico[d]	5,040	233	—	4	978	1,356	2	—	2	—	2,465	—
Virgin Islands	117	8	—	—	—	22	—	—	—	—	87	—

[a] Specified legal grounds closely related to those shown are grouped as follows: Adultery includes "infidelity." Bigamy includes "bigamy (illegal marriage)." Conviction of crime includes "conviction of crime (penitentiary)," "conviction of felony," "felony," and "imprisonment." Cruelty includes "cruel and inhumane treatment," "extreme cruelty," "physical cruelty," and "violence." Desertion includes "constructive desertion" and "willful desertion." Drunkenness includes "habitual intemperance," "habitual drunkenness," "intemperance," and "intoxication." Fraud includes "fraud or misrepresentation of facts when married," "fraudulent contract," and "license obtained fraudulently." Insanity includes "insanity at time of marriage," "mental incapacity," "unsound mind," and "incurable." Under age includes "marriage under age of consent" and "not legal age."

[b] Divorces and annulments by specified legal grounds included in this group are shown separately below where the number granted on these grounds formed 10 percent or more of the total number occurring in the area:

Missouri:	Indignities	8,950
Ohio:	Gross neglect and extreme cruelty	8,565
	Gross neglect and neglect of duty	10,363
Vermont:	Living apart 3 years	125
Wyoming:	Indignities	890
Alaska:	Incompatibility	412
Hawaii:	Grievous mental suffering	372
Puerto Rico:	Separated for more than 3 years	2,464
Virgin Islands:	Incompatibility of temperament	87

[c] Data incomplete.

[d] Excludes annulments.

SOURCE: National Office of Vital Statistics, Divorces and Annulments, Detailed Statistics for Reporting Areas, Vital Statistics—Special Reports, Vol. 50, No. 11 (August 19, 1959), Table 2.

Person to Whom Divorce Is Granted

Most divorces are granted to women. In 1932 women received 73.5 percent of the divorces and in 1950 they received 72.2 percent.[13] The high percentage is thus constant. This is an interesting fact because it is well known that many men ask their wives for the divorce. Nevertheless such men usually wish to preserve some degree of chivalry and do not subject their wives to stigma. The wife still suffers more socially than the husband from being the defendant in a divorce trial. Where a wife grossly outrages the

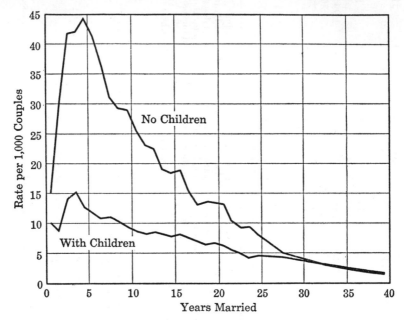

CHART 17.1. Divorce Rate for Married Couples With and Without Children Under 18 Years of Age, First 40 Years of Marriage, United States, 1948. (Used by permission of author and publisher from Paul H. Jacobson, "Differentials in Divorce by Duration of Marriage and Size of Family," *American Sociological Review, 15*:235–244 [April, 1950].)

man's sense of decency by commiting adultery or deserting small children he is usually less reluctant to bring suit. If the husband does not wish to remarry he is not likely to bring suit particularly if he has children. Divorce often means the father has little further contact with his children. Unless they are interested in remarriage men are less apt to initiate divorce proceedings, partly we may assume because they can escape an unhappy marriage through their work and find many satisfactions outside of marriage.

Although divorces are granted more often to couples without children, children can no longer be considered a major deterrent to divorce, as Dr.

[13] Public Health Service, *Statistics on Divorces and Annulments, Specified States, 1950, Vital Statistics—Special Reports* (December 9, 1952), p. 68.

Paul H. Jacobson of the Metropolitan Life Insurance Company has pointed out. He maintains that children are no longer an important factor in preventing divorce except during the first five years of marriage. His detailed analysis of divorce statistics for 1948 shows that the divorce rate for persons married five years or less is nearly three times higher for childless couples than for those with children. This disparity in rate declines rapidly, however, with an increase in the duration of the marriage, as Chart 17.1 shows. For persons married sixteen to twenty years the divorce rate was approximately twice as high for childless couples as for those with children under eighteen. After twenty-five years of marriage the rates approached each other rapidly and after thirty years they were identical. Dr. Jacobson is of the opinion, however, that divorce is probably less likely in families with two and three children than in those with only one child. He also holds that childlessness is not necessarily associated with divorce. On the other hand, both divorce and childlessness may be due to tensions between the married couple.[14]

Age at Marriage, Divorce, and Separation

Women who marry early have a very high divorce and separation rate. In fact those who marry under 18 have a much higher divorce rate than those who marry only a few years later. This is indicated by the number of young women first marrying at various age levels between 1940 and 1949 who have remarried. (Few women in the early age groups are widowed; hence we can assume that nearly all of these remarried women were divorced.) As the figures below show, the rate of those remarrying who were first married under 18 was nearly twice the rate of those marrying between 18 and 19 and approximately three times that of those marrying between 22 and 24. For those marrying after the age of 25 the stability of marriage is nearly as high as that for women marrying at 30 or over.

Ages of Women Marrying from 1940 to 1949	*Percentage Who Married More Than Once*
14–17 years	21.9
18 and 19 years	13.4
20 and 21 years	8.6
22–24 years	6.5
25–29 years	5.8
30 years and over	5.3

SOURCES: Data taken from Bureau of the Census, *Current Population Reports*, Series P-20, No. 67, and unpublished census data as summarized in Paul C. Glick, *American Families*, John Wiley and Sons, Inc., New York, 1957, p. 112.

Relatively few boys are married during their teens, and when they marry their marriages are equally unstable. In 1950 the male population 14 to 17 years old was chiefly single, but over half of the male teen-agers not single

[14] Paul H. Jacobson, "Differentials in Divorce by Duration of Marriage and Size of Family," *American Sociological Review*, 15:235–244 (April, 1950).

were involved in broken marriages as the following figures show. Obviously very young male marriages are highly unstable, but they are also uncommon. Probably most very young marriages are forced marriages, which are generally believed to be unstable. No recent studies are available on this subject, however.

Total Number Males 14 to 17 Years, 1950	Total Single Males 14 to 17 Years, 1950	Total Once Married	Total Living with Wife	Males Once Married 14 to 17 Years, 1950			
				Separated	Other (Not Living with Wife)	Widowed	Divorced
4,293,480	4,247,760	45,720	22,320	4,110	11,220	4,440	3,630

SOURCE: Data derived from Bureau of the Census, *United States Census of Population 1950*, Special Report P-E, No. 20, 1953, Table 1, pp. 2D-16.

Sex Ratio and Divorce Rates

Although data are incomplete, there appears to be some relation between the proportions of the sexes in the population and the divorce rate, as Table 17.3 shows. Where there are more native-born white males than

TABLE 17.3.   A Comparison of Sex Ratios and Divorce

Section of Country	Males per 100 Females Native White	Divorce Rates per 1000 in 1957
Northeastern states	96.4	1.3
Middle Atlantic states	95.9	Less than 1 (estimated)
East north central states	98.5	Not estimated
West north central states	99.6	1.8
South Atlantic states	99.2	Not estimated
East south central states	99.3	Over 2.5 for states given
West south central states	100.3	Over 3.1 for states given
Mountain states	103.5	4.7
Pacific states	99.9	3.4
Washington	104.6	4.7
Oregon	102.2	3.0
California	98.4	3.2

SOURCES: *Statistical Abstract of the United States, 1959*, p. 31, for sex ratios, and *Marriages and Divorces, United States and Each State, and Alaska, Hawaii, Puerto Rico, and the Virgin Islands (U.S.), 1957, Vital Statistics—Special Reports*, Vol. 50, No. 7 (June 5, 1959), p. 189.

females divorce provisions tend to be more lenient, as in the mountain states and the west south central and Pacific coast states, than where the number of females exceeds that of the males. According to 1957 figures, shown in Table 16.1, Nevada is the state with the highest rate, but this is almost wholly explained by the special provisions for migratory divorce (as mentioned elsewhere). Nevada's rate is 35.3 per 1000 population, which in nearly seven times as high as the Oklahoma rate of 5.4 per 1000. Arizona ranks next with 4.9 per 1000 and Washington follows with 4.7. All of the mountain states have a high rate except Utah. In Utah the high percentage of Mormons in the population probably accounts for the low rate. Mormons apparently have a highly stable family life which is reinforced by religious belief.

Working Wives and Divorce

There is no exact information as to whether working wives are more likely to be divorced than those who are wholly dependent economically on their husbands. Probably working wives have a higher rate because a woman who can support herself does not have to endure an intolerable marriage. But even if working wives did secure a disproportionate number of divorces, it would not mean that work per se was a factor in the divorce. It might indicate rather that the economic problems of the family were serious. We have information, on the other hand, which indicates that more remarried women were in the labor force during the period 1948–1957 (except for 1953–1954) than women who were first married. These data seem to give presumptive evidence that the previously divorced, who constitute a major share of the remarried, worked before they were divorced. Paul C. Glick of the Bureau of the Census says it seems likely that married women who get a divorce have more work experience and are more capable of self-support than those who become separated but do not get a divorce. Certainly more divorced women have a higher income than married, widowed, or separated women, although single women have higher incomes than do married, divorced, or widowed women.[15] Sometimes of course the fact that the wife is working is a serious reason for the marital conflict. Sometimes there are serious problems involving slighted housekeeping and the neglect of children when the wife works outside the home. Studies indicate that the greatest conflicts about a wife's working arise when the husband disapproves of her being employed.[16] This in turn may be reflected in the work history of divorcees.

The fact that divorced women are better able to take care of themselves financially than separated, widowed, or married women may be one reason for the declining alimony awards. Men likewise may be less hesitant to ask for a divorce where the wife is obviously competent to look after herself.

Divorce and Education

The exact relation between education and divorce is not clear. We have more information about the education of divorced women than of divorced men. During the years 1948 to 1950 divorce was higher among all women and among white women who had dropped out of high school and college than among those who had less education. It was lowest among those who finished college and next lowest among those who finished high

[15] Paul C. Glick, *American Families,* John Wiley and Sons, Inc., New York, 1957, pp. 157–158.
[16] Artie Gianopulos and Howard E. Mitchell, "Marital Disagreement in Working Wife Marriages as a Function of Husband's Attitude Toward Wife's Employment," *Marriage and Family Living, 19:*373–378 (November, 1957).

school. These facts led Dr. Glick to suggest that persistence in finishing an educational goal may affect persistence in marriage, because persistence is a character trait. Separation rates are four times as high for nonwhite women as for white women and divorce rates are much higher for nonwhite college graduates than for white college graduates. In fact nonwhite college graduates have the highest divorce rate of all nonwhite educational levels. Separation rates are also high for nonwhite college graduates.[17]

College education per se is thus no prophylaxis for divorce although white women college graduates have the lowest rate among women of various educational achievements. Obtaining a degree thus seems to be correlated somewhat with a lower divorce rate. There is also some slight presumptive evidence of the stabilizing effect of college training, as shown in some other figures with reference to both men and women. In 1957, 3.9 percent of the widowed and divorced males over twenty-five years of age had completed four years of college, in contrast to 9.5 percent of the married. Slightly fewer, 3.4 percent, of the widowed and divorced females over twenty-five years of age in contrast to 5.2 percent of the married had completed four years of college. This again seems to give some evidence that proportionately fewer college-trained persons secure divorces.[18] Whether their training has been a definite factor in preventing divorce is hard to establish. Those who complete college may possess more of the personality factors which promote success in marriage. A class and economic factor is also involved. There is evidence, however, that higher education is associated to a greater extent with permanent marriage than with tendency to obtain divorce.

The presumptive influence of education on stability of marriage is further indicated by negative relation between increase in educational achievement and the number of remarriages. Of the men who remarried between 1947 and 1954, 33.6 percent had seven years or less education, 37 percent had eight years, 19.1 had one to three years of high school, 16.9 percent had one to three years of college, and 12.5 percent finished college. Much the same ratio applied to women's remarriage although more women remarried in the lower educational achievement group and few among the college graduates. Only 8.6 percent of the women who remarried had a college degree, while there were 42.7 percent with seven years' education or less, 36.1 percent with eight years, 23.2 percent with one to three years of high school, 13.7 percent who were high school graduates and 14.9 percent who had one to three years of college.[19] More than 70 percent of the men who remarried did not go beyond the eighth grade and over 78 percent of the women failed to go further. Since approximately 75 percent of those remarrying have been divorced (including about 10 percent who have been both divorced and widowed) and 25 percent have been widowed only,[20] it is hard to establish

[17] Glick, *op. cit.*, pp. 153–154.
[18] *Statistical Abstract of the United States, 1959*, p. 109.
[19] Computations derived from Table 99 in Glick, *op. cit.*, p. 147.
[20] *Ibid.*, p. 143.

any exact relation to educational status and remarriage. Nevertheless a disproportionate number of divorced persons have low educational achievements. This trend is not likely to continue to be so pronounced since the majority of young people today have some high school training. It will be interesting to see whether later studies will indicate a drop in divorce with higher educational achievements.

Occupational Level, Divorce, and Desertion

We have known for a long time that family instability was highest in the lowest social and economic stratum while rigid enforcement of marital vows apparently has always been greatest in the middle and upper classes. During the early part of the twentieth century this instability of the poor man's marriage was shown chiefly in the high desertion rate, frequently noted in social work literature. Income and living scales of the working class were much lower proportionately during the first decades than they are today. Most unskilled workingmen were too poor to consider a divorce. The only available statistical analysis of divorces with reference to occupational level until recently was that published by the Bureau of the Census in 1909 covering occupations of persons granted divorce for the years 1867–1906. In this large-scale study the highest rates were among traveling men, actors, musicians, physicians, and stenographers, all persons with many contacts with the opposite sex. Bankers, lawyers, plumbers, butchers, professors, servants, and merchants ranked next. Manufacturers, clergymen, carpenters, miners, mechanics, farmers, and farm laborers ranked lowest.[21]

H. Ashley Weeks' study in 1943 of the differential divorce rates among school children's families in Spokane, Washington, was the first to indicate that divorce rates in the various occupations had changed. Weeks found that the rate was lowest among professional groups and rose gradually with decline in occupational status, with the highest rate occurring among unskilled laborers.[22] The unskilled laborers' rate, however, was only slightly higher than that of the professional groups. These data were confirmed by several subsequent studies including an analysis by the Bureau of the Census of a random sample of 25,000 in 1949. The latter study also showed that the greatest "proneness to divorce" was among lower occupational levels—with the highest rate among service workers, laborers (except farm and mine), and semiskilled workers.[23] These studies led William J. Goode to compute an occupational "proneness to divorce" index by dividing "other marital status" percent by the "married wife present" percent, and he found that service workers had the highest proneness to divorce, with all types of workers ranking higher than clerical and sales, proprietors, and profes-

[21] Bureau of the Census, *Marriage and Divorce 1887–1906,* Bulletin 96, 1909, pp. 46–51.

[22] H. Ashley Weeks, "Differential Divorce Rates by Occupations," *Social Forces, 21:* 334–337 (March, 1943).

[23] *Population Characteristics, Current Population Reports,* Series P-20, no. 23 (March 4, 1949), p. 17.

sional.[24] The latter had the lowest. Both Weeks' and Goode's studies covered divorce rate of parents, however, and neglected the fact that 60 percent of divorcees are childless. A further study by Kephart of 1434 random divorce cases in Philadelphia for males in 1937–1950 showed the same general rank of divorce rates with the exception of labor service males.[25] They varied proportionately, however. Professional men and proprietors had less than a proportionate percentage of divorces so far as ratio in relation to their number was considered. Clerical workers, salesmen, and skilled workers had a higher than proportionate percentage. And the semiskilled also had a higher than proportionate rate. Labor service workers were underrepresented.

Kephart also examined the desertion rates of cases brought into court on

TABLE 17.4. Ratio of Divorces per 1000 Employed Males in Iowa (divorce data for 1953, employment data for 1950)

Professionals	3.4	4.4
Owners-officials		2.9
Clerks	5.9	4.5
Salesmen		6.9
Craftsmen		7.8
Operatives		8.3
Service workers	18.7	5.9
Laborers		26.9
Farm owners	1.5	1.7
Farm laborers		.9

SOURCE: Table 1, Thomas P. Monahan, "Divorce by Occupational Level," *Marriage and Family Living, 17*: 322–324 (November, 1955).

an occupational basis in Philadelphia and found a high number in the upper occupational groups. Kephart seemed to believe that this finding disproved the opinion that desertion is primarily a lower-class-family phenomenon. A later study made by Saul Kaplan for the Public Assistance Division of the United States Department of Health, Education, and Welfare makes it abundantly clear, however, that the men referred to court for desertion tend to be only those from whom some possibility of securing support is possible. A large number of deserters are impossible to locate, and many others have no visible means for supporting their dependents. Middle-class women who are deserted are much more likely to bring support charges against deserting husbands. Social workers likewise are much more likely to refer cases where there is some possibility of obtaining support.[26] Court-

[24] William J. Goode, "Economic Factors and Marital Stability," *American Sociological Review, 16*:802–812 (December, 1951).

[25] William M. Kephart, "Occupational Level and Marital Disruption," *American Sociological Review, 20*:456–465 (August, 1955).

[26] Saul Kaplan, "Support from Absent Fathers in Aid to Dependent Children," *Social Security Bulletin, 21*:3–13 (February, 1958). This is referred to in detail in Chapter 16.

reported cases of desertion are thus no index of desertion rates according to occupational level.

Monahan's study of the occupational level of persons to whom divorces were granted in Iowa[27] meanwhile confirms the present trend of higher divorce rates in the lower occupational levels. Monahan found that the lowest percentage of divorce was granted to clerks; professional men ranked next; owners and officials next; salesmen next. Craftsmen, operatives, and laborers had much higher rates. A larger percentage was granted to farm owners than to professions, but farm laborers had the lowest percentage of all, as Table 17.4 shows.

TABLE 17.5.   Percentage of Iowa Males in Occupational Group with Percentage of Divorced Males in Each Group

	Percentage of Employed Iowa Males in Occupational Group	Percentage of Divorced Males in Iowa Occupational Group
Professionals	5.4	4.0
Owners-officials	9.8	4.8
Clerks	4.6	3.5
Salesmen	6.1	7.1
Craftsmen	14.7	19.3
Operatives	13.8	19.3
Service workers	4.1	4.0
Laborers	6.4	29.0
Farm owners	26.3 } 35	7.7 } 9
Farm laborers	8.1	1.3

SOURCE: Derived from Table 1, Thomas P. Monahan, "Divorce by Occupational Level," *Marriage and Family Living*, 17: 322–324 (November, 1955).

A more satisfactory basis for comparing divorce rates by occupational level is to consider the ratio of divorces with reference to the number of persons in the occupational levels. Monahan computed this, as shown in Table 17.5. In the nonfarm population professional men had slightly less than their proportionate share of divorces and owner-officials had markedly less. Clerks' rates by this rating were not much less than professional rates. For all other urban groups except service workers the rate was disproportionately high— and for laborers almost five times a proportionate percentage for their number.

Farmers, on the other hand, constituted 35 percent of the population and had 9 percent of divorces, which means they had only one-fourth of the divorces in proportion to their number. Farm divorce rates thus deserve further analysis. Iowa farmers are on the whole wealthy. Nearly the whole state ranks in the upper 20 percent of the farm incomes of the nation. The low divorce rate of farm owners is partly a function of their standard of living.

[27] Thomas P. Monahan, "Divorce by Occupational Level," *Marriage and Family Living*, 17:322–324 (November, 1955).

They have fewer economic tensions. But farm divorces are low everywhere and the low rate may in part reflect rural culture.

Many farmers and their wives whose marriages endure are probably no more compatible than city people who seek divorces. The farmer and his wife have fewer personal contacts with attractive members of the opposite sex. The dissatisfied farm wife often has no skills other than as a housewife and would hesitate to leave her husband. She would probably have a hard time making a living for herself. On the other hand, the wife may have inherited the farm from her father and there is no inducement for her to leave. Much of the farmer's conservatism about divorce is probably based on common sense.

The low divorce rate among farm laborers also bears further interpretation. Relatively few farm laborers in Iowa are married. They are single men who live with the farm owner's household. Farmers seldom marry until they are able to operate a farm by themselves; hence the farm laborers as such are bound to have a low divorce rate. A detailed analysis of marital status of all occupational groups in relation to divorce would give us a truer picture of the occupational factor in divorce. If married farm laborers were considered they might have a much higher divorce rate.

Whatever the occupational level, divorces represent a final break in the family organization, so far as the marriage is concerned. The divorce does not erase family relationship for children and it often creates difficult adjustments for the former mates. These we discuss in the next chapter.

SELECTED BIBLIOGRAPHY

Divorces and Annulments, Detailed Statistics for Reporting Areas, Vital Statistics —Special Reports, National Office of Vital Statistics (annual reports). These reports give annual national statistics and should be consulted to keep textual material up to date.

Elliott, Mabel A., "Divorce Legislation and Family Instability," *Annals of the American Academy of Political and Social Science, 272*:134–147 (November, 1950). This article discusses the significance of changes and trends in divorce legislation in the United States, Great Britain, Europe, Mexico, and South American countries. Divorce rates are related to legislation, but desertion, illegitimacy, and other evidences of family instability appear to be frequent where divorce laws are stringent.

Elliott, Mabel A., "The Scope and Meaning of Divorce," in Howard Becker and Reuben Hill (eds.), *Family Marriage and Parenthood,* D. C. Heath and Company, Boston, 1955, pp. 668–708. This article also presents an analysis of divorce trends in the United States and abroad.

Foster, Henry H., Jr., *Dependent Children and the Law,* reprint from *University of Pittsburgh Law Review,* Spring, 1957, pp. 579–606. An excellent analysis is given from a legal point of view of Allegheny County cases of nonsupport brought to court under the aid to dependent children provisions.

Gianopulos, Artie, and Mitchell, Howard E., "Marital Disagreement in Working Wife Marriages as a Function of Husband's Attitude Toward Wife's Employment," *Marriage and Family Living, 19*:373–378 (November, 1957). This study shows that the husband's attitude toward his wife's working is the major factor in whether or not her working produces conflict.

Glick, Paul C., *American Families,* John Wiley and Sons, Inc., New York, 1957. This is a research sociologist's detailed analysis of census data on the American family and gives much valuable resource material on age, education, working wives, etc. and divorce rate.

Goode, William J., "Economic Factors and Marital Stability," *American Sociological Review, 16*:802–812 (December, 1951). This study shows the proneness to divorce among couples according to occupational level.

Hill, Reuben, *Families Under Stress,* Harper & Brothers, New York, 1949. This research project shows how families in Iowa met the stresses of the wartime era.

Kaplan, Saul, "Support from Absent Fathers in Aid to Dependent Children," *Social Security Bulletin, 21*:3–13 (February, 1958). This is a very important study of desertion of fathers involving a statistical analysis of all the desertion cases in which state and federal relief was given under aid to dependent children grants. Most fathers were found to be of low economic status or fathers of illegitimate children.

Merrill, Francis E., *Courtship and Marriage,* Henry Holt and Company, Inc., New York, 1959. A recent text summarizes most of the available materials on desertion, divorce, and post-divorce problems.

Monahan, Thomas P., "Divorce by Occupational Level," *Marriage and Family Living, 17*:322–324 (November, 1955). This analysis shows the comparatively low rate of divorce among professional men and farmers and higher rates in lower urban occupational levels.

Monahan, Thomas P., "The Duration of Marriage to Divorce: Second Marriages and Migratory Types," *Marriage and Family Living, 21*:134–138 (May, 1959). The factor of migration of one mate to the state in which married and its impact on divorce is analyzed.

Monahan, Thomas P., and Kephart, William M., "Divorce and Desertion by Religious and Mixed-Religious Groups," *American Journal of Sociology, 59*: 454–465 (March, 1954). This study shows that desertion is more common among Roman Catholic men than other religious groups (presumably because divorce is not permissible).

Ploscowe, Morris, *The Truth About Divorce,* Hawthorn Books, Inc., New York, 1955. A well-known New York judge discusses the real and legal aspects of divorce.

Weeks, H. Ashley, "Differential Divorce Rates by Occupations," *Social Forces, 21*:334–337 (March, 1943). This was the first study to indicate a high divorce rate among the working class.

CHAPTER 18

After Divorce

Disorganization After Divorce

Disorganization does not end with divorce. The dissolution of the marriage contract is the final outcome of a long process of family disorganization. But it is final to the participants only in the sense that it represents a formal break in a previously intimate relationship. Life for both must go on. The husband must adjust his emotional life, his personal habits, his business and social life. The wife must make all of these adjustments, and in addition she often must provide for her support. If there are children, their lives must continue in new and strange social surroundings. Divorce is the end of the marriage; for its individual participants, however, it merely represents a change from one status to another. The roles associated with the new status are often difficult.[1]

The disorganization of divorced persons is augmented by the adverse social definitions which are attached to divorce. A certain degree of moral turpitude is often automatically and gratuitously attributed to the principals, on the ground that one or both must have committed an immoral or at least an undesirable act. Many persons still view divorce as a deliberate flouting of permanent monogamy by two spouses acting with a perverse free will. Some divorces come under this indictment but the majority do not. Such indictments of divorce are a residual from the time when adultery was the sole or major reason for divorce. As a result of this attitude, divorced persons often have a feeling of guilt, either conscious or unconscious, which complicates their reactions to other persons and to themselves. When the divorced person is viewed suspiciously by righteous (and self-righteous) persons, his personal maladjustment is bound to increase.[2]

The adverse definition of divorce obscures the problem in another sense. The assumption is that disorganization after divorce is the result of the divorce and not of factors in the prior relationship. Waller and Hill point out that "much of the apparent cost of divorce inheres not in divorce itself but

[1] The most extensive study of the post-divorce situation is given by William J. Goode, *After Divorce*, The Free Press, Glencoe, Ill., 1956. This book combines an intensive investigation of a sample of divorced women with a general analysis of the role of divorce in our society.

[2] Cf. Morris L. Ernst and David Loth, *For Better or Worse*, Harper & Brothers, New York, 1951.

in the unhappy marriage which precedes divorce, and in the peculiar conditioning of the individuals in their parental families which renders them liable to unhappy marriage and divorce."[3] The divorce process is a shattering experience in itself, and the dissolution of a relationship as intimate as marriage is difficult for the participants. At the same time, many of the disorganizing elements had their foundation during the years of marriage and even before. The personality difficulty may have existed long before the divorce and may have been a factor in precipitating the crisis. "The costs of divorce are great," conclude Waller and Hill, "but probably they are less than those of remaining in a genuinely unhappy marriage."[4]

The time element is another factor in weighing divorce against an unhappy marriage. The bonds of matrimony are cumulative, and a seemingly unhappy couple may grow closer through the years from sheer habit. One or two years of marriage involve a different pattern of relationships from that in a marriage lasting ten or fifteen years. The crisis may be less severe in a short marriage because the habit patterns have not become deeply incorporated in the personalities of the spouses. In marriages that have continued for a long time, the habits may be so strong that it is more disorganizing to break the marriage than to continue it.[5]

Divorce involves a basic change in status and role. Persons with a strong, well-integrated life organization may survive the change with comparative ease. Persons with less integrated personalities or those who care too deeply will not take it so easily. They cannot adjust immediately (or perhaps ever) to their new status. Nor does society provide much assistance. There are no norms covering the behavior of divorced persons or the behavior of others toward them. The social structure is based upon the conception of permanent monogamy, and any other arrangement is not anticipated.

This ambiguity of roles is apparent in a number of instances. (1) There are no norms for the behavior of relatives or friends during the dissolution of the marriage. The financial arrangements, social relationships, and emotional problems of the spouses are not covered by patterned social expectations, as is true in death and bereavement. (2) The spouse who leaves the home often has literally no place to go. There is no moral obligation for his (or her) family to take him back, as many primitive societies do under the same circumstances. He is therefore on his own, at least as far as formal role expectations are concerned.[6] (3) In the matter of name, the wife is in an ambiguous position. Despite the fact that she is no longer married, she usually retains her husband's name. Children keep their father's name, even if their mother returns to her own parental family, thus further complicating the kinship status. (4) The role behavior of the former spouses is even less clear.

[3] Willard Waller, *The Family: A Dynamic Interpretation* (revised by Reuben Hill), The Dryden Press, Inc., New York, 1951, p. 538.

[4] *Ibid.*

[5] *Ibid.*

[6] Goode, *op. cit.*, pp. 12–15.

Neither is exactly "single," although he or she is not married. Their emotional behavior is open to further ambiguity. They do not know whether they "should" be happy or sad, relieved or depressed, hopeful or resigned. (5) Finally, there is much uncertainty as to how the parties should go about forming a new marital relationship. When should the ex-wife start going out with other men; what should the attitude of her parents be toward prospective suitors; and how should the children (if any) be prepared for such a change in their lives? In short, divorce disorganizes the traditional pattern of roles in the conjugal family. An adequate pattern of new roles has not yet been evolved.[7]

The Number of the Divorced

Post-divorce adjustments are many and complicated. In March, 1958, there were an estimated 1,458,000 women and 1,028,000 men in the civilian population who had been divorced and had not remarried. These figures represented 2.3 percent of all females and 1.8 percent of all males over fourteen years of age.[8] This impressive total, however, does not fully reflect the scope of post-divorce adjustment. Only persons officially counted as divorced are included—i.e., those who admitted their status to the census ennumerator. An indeterminate number were doubtless unwilling to list themselves in this category because of the continuing prejudice against divorce. If the truth were known, many of those recorded as "unmarried" or "widowed" would swell the total of the divorced.

In addition, the census enumerated some 1,342,000 women and 865,000 men as "separated" from their mates. This category, which includes "those with legal separations, those living apart with intentions of obtaining a divorce, and other persons permanently or temporarily estranged from their spouses because of marital discord," comprises an estimated 2.1 percent of the women and 1.5 percent of the men in the United States over fourteen years of age. As an index to marital disorganization, these figures are almost as significant as those for divorce.[9]

The above figures represent the number of men and women who *at any one time* are in the process of adjustment following divorce or separation. They do not include the millions who have been previously divorced and are now remarried. In the decade 1940–1950, an estimated 4,000,000 marriages were ended by divorce. The majority of the men and women involved were subsequently remarried and hence are not listed as either divorced or separated. Remarriage is the most popular "solution" to the problem of divorce. Approximately two-thirds of all divorced women and three-quarters of all divorced men ultimately remarry, usually within five years after the divorce.

---

[7] *Ibid.*

[8] Bureau of the Census, *Population Characteristics, Marital Status and Family Status: March 1958, Current Population Reports,* Series P-20, No. 87 (November 14, 1958), Table 1.

[9] *Ibid.*

The median length of time between the divorce and the subsequent re-marriage of both men and women is 2.7 years.[10]

Approximately one out of every five marriages is therefore a remarriage.[11] In the majority of remarriages one or both mates have been previously divorced. One study by the Bureau of the Census disclosed that one-quarter of all brides in the age group 25 to 29 years were divorcées. In the age group 35 to 44 years, previously divorced women comprised approximately one-half of those marrying. Divorced women represented about one-third of all brides in their early fifties. For the grooms, about one-eighth of the age group 25 to 29 had been previously divorced and about half of those marrying at age 40 to 49.[12]

The trends in remarriage may be viewed in still another way. In a recent period (1947–1954), approximately 62 percent of the remarriages involved men and women who had been previously divorced and 25 percent those who had been widowed. Of the remaining 13 percent of the remarriages, between 1 and 2 percent had been divorced more than once but never widowed, 6 percent had been divorced and widowed once, and 4 percent had been previously married more than twice, including at least once following divorce. For a small percentage (between 1 and 2) there was no report. More than three-fifths of all remarriages thus involve persons who have undergone at least one divorce experience.[13]

We do not imply that all, or even a large proportion, of these millions of divorced persons are or have been seriously disorganized by their experience.[14] In many cases their personal lives have been greatly improved, stabilized, and generally made more tranquil following their divorce. Some emerge stronger than before. Many find complete personal reorganization about their new marriage.[15] Others, however, are unable to adjust to their changed status. The high divorce rate means that a sizable number of people face personal disorganization. A change in status and role of this magnitude presents countless difficulties.[16]

Divorce and Crisis

Divorce is both a cumulative and a precipitate crisis for the participants. It is *cumulative* in that tensions accumulate, piling irritation upon irritation, humiliation upon humiliation, and anger upon anger. What Waller

[10] Paul C. Glick, *American Families,* John Wiley and Sons, Inc., New York, 1957, pp. 138–139.

[11] See Jessie Bernard, *Remarriage, A Study of Marriage,* The Dryden Press, Inc., New York, 1956.

[12] Metropolitan Life Insurance Company, "Current Pattern of Marriage and Remarriage," *Statistical Bulletin,* June, 1953.

[13] Glick, *op. cit.,* p. 143.

[14] Harvey J. Locke and William J. Klausner, "Marital Adjustment of Divorced Persons in Subsequent Marriages," *Sociology and Social Research,* 33:97–101 (November–December, 1948).

[15] Goode, *op. cit.,* chap. 22.

[16] Bernard, *op. cit.,* chap. 11.

and Hill call "the tempo of bitterness" steadily increases, as the mutual affection of the spouses disintegrates.[17] It is *precipitate* in that the final break may come as a sudden shock to one or both spouses. The emotional peak of the crisis is often reached at the point of final separation, rather than when the divorce decree is granted. This latter occurrence is often an anticlimax.[18]

The decision to break the marital relationship is seldom reached simultaneously. One spouse or the other takes the initiative in the events leading up to the final break. In our marital pattern, the husband more often than the wife is the one who wishes to break the relationship. The forces drawing the husband out of the home are stronger than those acting upon the wife. The husband is ordinarily away from home more, is more likely to become involved with other women, and is more apt to neglect his family for reasons ranging from drinking with men companions to excessive preoccupation with business. As a result, says Goode, "Although the wife will have fairly serious charges to make against her husband, we believe that in our generation it is more often the husband who first wishes to escape from the marriage."[19]

The process of final alienation may therefore be long and wearing for both parties. Group relationships are internalized in their personalities. The reluctant one must be convinced that the decision is irrevocable. The latter may continue to protest, write despairing letters, beg "forgiveness," and generally proclaim to the four winds (and any available friends) his or her undying affection. Each decision during the alienation process represents an additional emotional strain. Despite the prevailing conception that Americans hurry to the divorce court at the first serious disagreement, the evidence is otherwise. Most couples do not break their marriages so easily. The average final divorce action in the sample studied by Goode followed two years of agonizing reappraisal of the marriage.[20]

The crisis situation is not finished when the marriage has been dissolved.[21] New decisions must be made and new relationships must be faced and integrated. The preliminary attempts at readjustment tend to occur along the lines of former behavior patterns, but these are seldom successful. Often an entirely new life organization must be worked out, taking into consideration all of the factors in the changed situation. The preliminary period of numbness, restlessness, and uneasy search for immediate solutions does not last forever. Sooner or later, specific problems of reorganization arise. The divorced person quickly finds that something must be done about a number of things.[22]

[17] Waller, *op. cit.*, pp. 521–523.
[18] Goode, *op. cit.*, p. 187.
[19] *Ibid.*, p. 135.
[20] *Ibid.*, p. 137.
[21] Willard Waller, *The Old Love and the New,* Liveright Publishing Corporation, New York, 1930, chap. 2, "Transition Pains."
[22] Cf. Thomas D. Eliot, "Handling Family Strains and Shocks," chap. 21 in Howard Becker and Reuben Hill (eds.), *Family, Marriage, and Parenthood,* D. C. Heath and Company, Boston, 1948.

Some persons pretend that divorce does not constitute a crisis after all. They try to act as if their change in status and role after divorce were an unpleasant but unavoidable experience that must be borne as graciously as possible. Outwardly they treat this situation, in the happy phrase of Burgess and Locke, as "similar to the observable relationships between the same type of persons in an automobile accident."[23] These participants in divorce do not rant or curse their fate. They are "friendly, courteous, and considerate" in their dealings with each other. The arrangements for the divorce are conducted in a well-bred fashion, with no overt evidence of bad feeling. Both parties maintain the fiction that they want the divorce, even if they do not. Underneath this serene exterior, however, they may be undergoing a severe crisis.[24]

The crisis attending divorce naturally varies with the circumstances and the personalities involved. The shock is often less intense when the estranged mates have been spatially separated for some time, or when they have lived together for months or years without conjugal relations. Divorces following forced marriages do not constitute crises in the same sense as do those of persons who married for love. The previously divorced may regard the experience more casually than those undergoing it for the first time. These exceptions do not, however, invalidate the general conception of divorce in terms of crisis and personal disorganization. In our society, divorce is a bitter and disillusioning experience for most people.[25]

Divorce and Sexual Adjustment

The problem of sexual adjustment is perhaps the most elemental one facing the divorced person. The dynamic nature of sexual tensions makes this adjustment difficult. The definition of sexual behavior in our society invests any expression outside of marriage with strong social disapproval. The sexual activity of married life unites both social and physiological aspects. When both of these forces are interrupted by divorce, the person faces a crisis. A pattern of intimate social relationships has been abruptly broken, and social disorganization, temporary or permanent, of a very literal kind has occurred. Various types of reorganization may be attempted. Rigid sexual repression may be practiced. The divorced person may become deeply interested in another love object, whether it be work, children, or another member of the opposite sex. Substitute sex relationships may be sought which offer physical release and little more.[26]

The research of Kinsey and his colleagues has thrown some light upon the sexual adjustment of the divorced person. Apparently the male resumes an

[23] Ernest W. Burgess and Harvey J. Locke, *The Family,* American Book Company, New York, 1945, p. 638.

[24] *Ibid.,* pp. 638–639.

[25] For a variety of brief case histories of the various types of crises faced by divorced persons, see David G. Wittels, "The Post Reports on Divorce," *Saturday Evening Post,* Vol. 220 (January, February, 1950).

[26] Cf. Ernst and Loth, *op. cit.,* chap. 4, "Sex."

active sex life (after a lapse of time) in much the same form as before he was divorced. A small (although fairly conclusive) sample in the Kinsey study indicates that from 80 to 85 percent of the total sexual outlet of divorced males consists of heterosexual intercourse. This percentage is as high as that for the male who is still married.[27] Despite our society's strong disapproval of the extramarital expression of sexual behavior, the divorced male apparently continues to be sexually active after his divorce.[28]

The divorced woman is faced with different problems of sexual adjustment. If she engages in an illicit love affair, she runs the risk of pregnancy outside the protective sanctuary of marriage. The traditional double standard of sexual morality tends to prohibit women of any (or no) marital status from actively seeking outside expression of the sexual impulse. Women who do seek such expression find that their behavior is judged more severely than that of men. For these and other reasons, the post-divorce sexual adjustment of the divorced[29] woman apparently does not follow the same pattern as that of the man. Kinsey states that the divorced female often has no heterosexual contacts whatsoever and may go for years without such experience. The sexual impulses of women are presumably less demanding than those of men and less easily aroused by symbolic stimuli. This combination of social and psychological factors may account for the difference in behavior.[30]

Whatever her actual behavior, the divorced woman is subjected to a variety of insulting proposals because of her ambiguous status. The very word "divorcée" is still synonymous with "scarlet woman" to many persons. No matter how virtuous she may be, the divorcée is considered fair game by the amateur Casanovas in the community. That some divorcées *do* exemplify the popular concept does not make the situation any easier for the majority who do not, and whose adjustment is not helped by a considerable segment of the male population.[31]

The crisis of divorce does not of itself change the personalities of the spouses or the habitual responses they have evolved during their marriage. Hence their sexual adjustment (or lack of it) may take a diversity of forms. "The nature of these reactions," state Ernst and Loth, "seems to be governed in great measure by the sexual adjustment which the couple had made, whether one or both had formed a more desirable sexual attachment and how much their sexual problems worried them."[32] The role of sex in their

[27] Alfred C. Kinsey *et al., Sexual Behavior in the Human Male,* W. B. Saunders Company, Philadelphia, 1948, pp. 294–296.

[28] In the Kinsey enumeration there is no breakdown between "widowed" and "divorced" males. Both are listed as "postmarital." It is reasonable to assume, however, that the rate of heterosexual intercourse is higher among divorced men than among widowers. Hence the 80–85 percent estimate for the divorced man is probably conservative.

[29] Kinsey does not distinguish in this enumeration between "widowed" and "divorced" women, thus following his practice for the male.

[30] Alfred C. Kinsey *et al., Sexual Behavior in the Human Female,* W. B. Saunders Company, Philadelphia, 1953, chap. 16.

[31] Goode, *op. cit.,* pp. 213–214.

[32] Ernst and Loth, *op. cit.,* p. 67.

marriage, the importance attached to it, and their own personal qualities are among the factors determining their subsequent sexual adjustment.[33] Whatever the character of this adjustment, however, it presents an immediate and sometimes explosive problem to the divorced person.

Divorce and the Injured Ego

The central social value in the life of every person is his own self. We derive our conception of ourselves largely (although not wholly) from the attitudes held by others toward us. These attitudes are inferred by the process of taking the role of the other and viewing oneself with his eyes.[34] The child is particularly dependent upon the self-judgments which he attributes to others, notably his parents. As he grows older and his social self becomes more integrated, he is less directly dependent upon the attitudes of others. At no time in his life, however, does he become completely independent of them. Failure to be favorably considered by others brings about insecurity of his ego. Divorce combines many of the elements that contribute to such insecurity.

It is important, therefore, for the individual to have a favorable attitude toward himself, so that he may be worthy of his own affection. Without some element of self-affection his life would be completely worthless. This element is *not* synonymous with conceit or selfishness; it is more fundamental than these.[35] Divorce impairs the self-feeling in several ways. (1) The failure to make a success of marriage, regardless of the "fault" of the spouse, is a serious reflection upon the self. (2) Friends may take sides and blame one mate for the failure of the marriage, thus contributing to the injured ego-feeling of the "guilty" one. (3) The residual social attitude toward divorce, with its implication of failure and even deliberate moral turpitude, still further undermines the ego of the divorced person.

Many divorces, as we have mentioned, are obtained over the active or tacit opposition of one party. Such a situation is damaging to the ego of the person who has been (in his own mind) weighed and found wanting in the marital balance. The appreciation so necessary to the self is not forthcoming from perhaps the sole person in the world who, at one time, provided it. When this recognition is withheld to the extent of the other's seeking to dissolve the marital relationship, the ego structure of the rejected one may suffer an irreparable blow. The experience may be intensified by the recriminations that often accompany the divorce process.[36]

The rejected spouse may be driven to extreme lengths to restore his faith in himself. The taxi dance hall gains a number of its patrons from divorced men,

[33] Cf. Harvey J. Locke, *Predicting Adjustment in Marriage,* Henry Holt and Company, Inc., New York, 1951, chap. 7, "Sexual Behavior."

[34] George Herbert Mead, *Mind, Self and Society* (edited by Charles W. Morris), University of Chicago Press, Chicago, 1934.

[35] Therese Benedek, *Insight and Personality Adjustment,* The Ronald Press Company, New York, 1946, chap. 1.

[36] Cf. Paul Sayre, "Divorce for the Unworthy: Specific Grounds for Divorce," *Law and Contemporary Problems, 18:*26–32 (Winter, 1953).

who are seeking to regain their shattered self-respect by proving that they are still personable males. The same motives may send men to the bartered society of prostitutes. This self-delusion is all the more transparent since the taxi dancer and the prostitute alike are compelled to accept all comers, no matter how unattractive.[37] In the society of these paid companions the divorced man may regain a questionable modicum of self-feeling.

The injured ego of the divorced person may make him sensitive to real or fancied slights, snubs, or other alleged reflections on his new status. This status *is* comparatively new in our society, in the sense that divorce has been common for only a few generations. The divorcee must work out his own adjustments because the mores have not yet prescribed accepted roles. Hence he tends to be self-conscious with other persons, for he is never sure how he will be accepted in his new role. He is, in a very real way, a social pioneer, inasmuch as he must improvise his role as he goes along, with little precedent to guide him. The social habits of and toward him are not yet established, and he must formulate new patterns of behavior which may run counter to the traditional patterns. A mild paranoid reaction may accompany this continued insecurity, as the divorcee is unable to adjust to his changed status.[38]

The ambiguous status of the divorced person may force him to rebuild his ego-feeling in still other ways. His former mate may resort to invidious assertions concerning his physical, mental, or moral characteristics. Each mate may turn against the other in an unconscious effort to destroy the idealization formerly given the relationship.[39] If the divorce is granted on the basis of palpable transgression, the injured party may derive compensation for his own deflated ego. He may have the comfortable feeling that he has done everything possible to salvage the marriage. He may gain further masochistic satisfaction by publicly playing the role of the injured party, even though he may be aware that he is actually far from "blameless" in the failure of the marriage.

Other compensatory devices may include a misanthropic attitude toward the other sex, with particular emphasis upon the former spouse. Work may take the place of the old love, and the divorced person may console himself for his marital failure by conspicuous success in business or professional activity. The divorced person has a strong emotional need for self-justification. In these and other ways, he may strive to rebuild the delicate structure of the self.

Divorce and Habit

In a classic chapter in his *Principles of Psychology*, William James discussed the formation of habit in the individual, comparing this process to the weaving and reweaving of myriads of tiny threads into a powerful and virtually unbreakable cable. In *Human Nature and Conduct*, John Dewey

[37] Paul G. Cressey, *The Taxi-Dance Hall*, University of Chicago Press, Chicago, 1932, pp. 117–118.

[38] Cf. Eliot, *op. cit.*, pp. 628–630.

[39] Waller, *The Family*, pp. 521–523.

likewise emphasized the importance of habit in individual and social relationships. Dewey thus pointed out that the individual not only *has* habits but in a very real sense *is* his habits. The truth of these remarks is forcibly brought to the attention of the divorced person when his marriage is violently broken. In this relationship, habits have arisen about the most powerful emotions in the personality. When the habits are broken, the individual loses something of himself.[40]

During their common life, husband and wife have perforce adapted themselves to many common routines. These patterns are built into the personality, especially in marriages that continue for years. There is an element of habituation even in the periodicity with which a married couple has sex relations. Many other activities of married life become routinized, even such details as frying the bacon or buttering the toast. When the marriage is broken, these routines seek, in almost anthropomorphic fashion, their customary expression. The erstwhile mates are unable to abandon their marital habits immediately after the divorce decree has been signed. These habits are themselves.[41]

The failure to adjust to the abrupt disruption of habit brings frustration, unrest, and dissatisfaction. Each mate has been forcibly deprived of reciprocal patterns that were easy because they were habitual. No two married persons are completely incompatible in every respect, and many divorced couples are compatible in a number of ways. Divorced husbands and wives may miss such chores as picking up the other's clothes, emptying the garbage, and closing the window in the morning—duties which were formerly accepted as part of the household routine.

The life of every individual, both in and out of marriage, is partially composed of a series of more or less complex acts, many of which are habitual and hence comparatively effortless. Marriage is a *conjugal* affair, which means that it stresses the relationships between two persons. In an extraordinary variety of these reciprocal acts, each spouse has come to expect certain responses from the other. In the cumulative crisis leading to the divorce, the mutual expectations have been gradually broken. A surprising number of them, however, survive the legal disruption of the marriage.

The readjustment following divorce is, in a sense, a process of breaking old habits and forming new ones and cannot be accomplished overnight. Part of this adjustment occurs on a conscious level, and an attitude of cooperation is helpful. Much of it, however, goes forward on an unconscious level, as new habits are gradually established about new persons and situations. When the old habits are first broken, it may seem that life will be impossible without them. A few take this attitude literally and commit suicide. The majority carry on until the process of readjustment is complete and a new life organization has been worked out. New habits slowly emerge to take the place of the old.[42]

[40] *Ibid.,* pp. 552–553.
[41] *Ibid.*
[42] Waller, *The Family,* pp. 552–559.

Divorce and Social Relationships

A variety of complications occur in the social relationships of husband and wife after divorce, which may result in frustration and insecurity. As we have noted, the life of the divorced person is complicated by the new role which he or she is called upon to play. His relationships to other persons, both those who are aware of his changed status and those who are not, become subtly altered by this new pattern. As Waller points out, the role of the divorcee is not a figment of his own imagination but a very real thing, which must be treated as a social fact. It must be accepted. It cannot be ignored.[43]

The divorced person is immediately faced with gossip in all of its malicious forms. Tongues will wag, no matter how innocent he or she may be of moral turpitude. The small town has from time immemorial been the happy hunting ground for the gossip, but the corrosive influence of barbed tongues is felt in the metropolitan community as well. Any primary group experiences the influence of gossip, which often operates on the principle that the divorcee is guilty until he has been proved innocent. Even in the latter case, certain reservations concerning the moral status of one or both of the participants are entertained by a segment of the community. The age-old prejudices against divorce do not easily die. The "innocent" are branded with the "guilty."

The group relations of the divorced person are often disrupted. Friends tend to take sides, and each ex-mate is cut off from some of the groups with which he was formerly connected. There is thus inevitably a pruning of friendships. The resultant confusion represents social disorganization in the sense of breaking previous group relationships. The wife, the husband, and the zealous friends are all, in their fashion, compelled to limit their social horizons. The difficulties are intensified because of the high emotional tensions. In extreme cases, one of the divorced persons may be left virtually friendless and be forced to rebuild his entire social world. This process requires a personal autonomy that few people have. Lacking it, and cut off from the stabilizing influence of primary groups, the personality may become disorganized.[44]

In other circumstances, the process of reorganization may not be so devastating. The former wife may merely shift her circle of friends and, in Goode's words, begin the process of "once more finding her own identity as a person and being accepted as a person who is eligible to be a spouse."[45] This sort of adjustment appears to be comparatively easy for some, extremely difficult for others. Social mobility in our society is high, and the mobility of the divorced person is higher than the average. The divorced person tends to leave his former social milieu where his marriage has failed and seek out an environment where a new status may be assumed and a new role played.[46]

This situation illustrates the dynamic aspects of a flexible and secular

[43] Waller, *The Old Love and the New*, p. 200.
[44] *Ibid.*, pp. 212–214.
[45] Goode, *op. cit.*, p. 241.
[46] *Ibid.*, pp. 241–242.

society. Social groups are continually breaking down and others are arising about new persons with different needs. The divorcee experiences one form of social disorganization with the dissolution of his marriage. He goes through another with many of his former friends. At the same time, life must go on. He meets new people, forms new interpersonal relations, and reintegrates his life about a new pattern. Especially among young people, this reorganization goes on until the ex-husband and ex-wife assume another status, that of husband and wife in a new marriage.[47]

Such a solution does not always follow. Some divorced persons are unable to initiate the relationships that will carry them into another and presumably more satisfactory marriage. Others initiate but never complete these relationships. In the meantime, there are additional difficulties, depending upon the nature of the community, the religious affiliations of the divorced persons, and their occupational and professional roles. In some social settings the divorcee is under compulsion (or thinks he is) to conceal his marital status. Preferment, promotion, and even his job may hinge on maintaining the secret of his broken marriage. The increasing frequency of divorce has eliminated much of this prejudice. In certain professional roles, however, the status of being divorced still carries overtones of social disapproval.

Divorce and Economic Roles

Machiavelli long ago remarked that men could with more equanimity lose their fathers than their patrimony. Certainly many of the bitterest hatreds between persons who have lived together intimately are related to the subject of money. In the conjugal family system, the divorced wife cannot automatically return to her own family and expect unquestioning acceptance and support. Specific financial arrangement must be made, either through alimony, separate maintenance, or the efforts of the wife.[48]

Whatever the arrangements, the economic factor is important at all stages as a source of recrimination. Husbands complain of the alleged extravagance of their present wives or the alimony they must pay their former wives. Wives complain of the niggardliness of their present husbands or the penuriousness of their ex-husbands. Wives often resent the economies they must undergo or the work they must undertake to support themselves. Judson T. Landis found in his study of adjustment in marriage that money constituted the second most difficult field (sex being the first).[49] In a pecuniary economy, money symbolizes many temperamental, personality, and sexual differences between a husband and wife. Some of these difficulties are carried over into divorce.

Masculine occupations and professions are frequently dependent upon the good will of other persons, ranging from a relatively small group of

[47] *Ibid.*, chaps. 18–19.
[48] See *ibid.*, chap. 16, "Postdivorce Economic Activities."
[49] Judson T. Landis, "Length of Time Required to Achieve Adjustment in Marriage," *American Sociological Review*, 11:666–677 (December, 1946).

clients or patients to the entire country. Status may be seriously jeopardized by a divorce, especially by one savoring of scandal. Public opinion is especially censorious toward members of the ministry and the academic professions. There is a wide variety in such opinion, depending upon the type of profession, the mores of the community, and the circumstances attending the divorce. Where there has been open transgression of the mores, the career of the man may be ruined. When the wife bears the onus for the divorce, public opinion may be more lenient toward the husband, with fewer attendant economic hazards.[50]

Alimony presents a problem for some husbands, although the majority of divorces do not entail this obligation. Recent data are not available for the country as a whole, but a study of all divorces in Illinois between 1940 and 1950 provides a presumably representative sample. Ninety-three percent of the 302,000 divorces granted in this decade did *not* involve alimony, though 42 percent of the decrees involved children. In the majority of cases (86 percent), custody of the children was awarded to the mother, although she did not receive alimony. Most wives prefer to be financially independent of their erstwhile husbands, even when this means working to support the children.[51]

The support of the wife and children after divorce is thus largely left to the wife. The majority of divorced women, especially those who are young and able-bodied, enter the labor force. In an earlier year (1947), there was an estimated total of 1,140,000 divorced women in the population, of whom 792,000 or 69.5 percent were gainfully employed. This figure may be compared with the 28.3 percent of the widows who were gainfully employed, and it reflects the ability of the divorced woman to support herself, even when she has dependent children.[52]

In recent years, the Bureau of the Census has not distinguished between the employment status of widows and divorced women but has combined them in a single category. In March, 1958, statistics for the labor force included 3,604,000 widowed *and* divorced women. This figure represented 37.9 percent of the 9,505,000 women in these two categories in the total population. The proportion of divorced women in the labor force presumably did not substantially change between 1947 and 1956. Approximately seven in every ten divorced women were gainfully employed.[53]

Children of Divorce

Children are accustomed to look to their parents for affection and security. The sudden disruption of this primary group relationship is a shock

[50] Waller, *The Old Love and the New*, pp. 233–237.

[51] The Law School, The University of Chicago, *Conference on Divorce: February 29, 1952*, Conference Series No. 9, p. 4.

[52] Bureau of the Census, *Population Characteristics, Characteristics of Single, Married, Widowed, and Divorced Persons in 1947*, Current Population Reports, Series P-20, No. 10 (February 6, 1948), Table 9.

[53] Bureau of the Census, *Labor Force, Marital and Family Characteristics of Workers: March 1958*, Current Population Reports, Series P-50, No. 87 (January, 1959), Table A.

to the child's developing personality. He has come to rely upon his parents for his attitudes, his values, and the emotional overtones that color his personality. When his emotional security and family ties are disturbed by divorce, the child often does not know which way to turn. His world has come tumbling down about his ears.[54]

A semblance of the previous security is often restored by the subsequent remarriage of one or both parents. But the new home seldom can take the place of the old. For those children old enough to know both their own parents, the stepfather or stepmother may always be fundamentally a stranger, lacking the wisdom, omnipotence, and affection that clung like an aura to the old parent. For the average child of divorce, the intangible aspects of family solidarity have gone out of his life. Even so, many children apparently make a completely satisfactory adjustment to their new status. But the uncertainty of the divorce situation may condition their entire personality. They have lost the sense of belonging to a stable group, composed of parents who will care for them and love them without question or qualification.[55]

This deprivation of security is manifested in the personal disorganization of children from broken homes. Juvenile delinquency, adolescent crime, youthful sex offenses, and immature vagabondage all may be partially traced to irregular family life. Some homes are broken by death and desertion, as well as divorce, but the problems in the latter case are even more complex. A strong personal sense of guilt often troubles the children of divorce because their parents have somehow transgressed the mores. Hence the child of divorce must wrestle with a moral problem which the bereaved child never faces. In unconscious compensation for the alleged transgressions of his parents, the child may engage in delinquent or antisocial behavior.[56]

Divorce does not disorganize children in all cultures. The basic family unit in the Western world is the conjugal group, composed of husband, wife, and children. When the husband-wife relationship is dissolved, the family no longer exists. In other cultures, the *consanguine* family is based primarily upon blood kinship, rather than marriage. In case of divorce, the children remain with the mother's or father's family and consequently experience no drastic interruption in their way of life. The children of divorce are ordinarily able to maintain permanent relationships with adults, who will perform the role of the missing parent. Uncles and aunts act as substitute fathers and mothers, and the continuity of the basic family relationship remains substantially unbroken. In this way, children are spared much of the personal disorganization accompanying the rupture of the conjugal family in Western society.[57]

[54] Kingsley Davis, "Sociological and Statistical Analysis," *Law and Contemporary Problems,* 10:700–720 (Summer, 1944).

[55] James S. Plant, "The Psychiatrist Views Children of Divorced Parents," *Law and Contemporary Problems,* 10:807–818 (Summer, 1944).

[56] Cf. Raphael Lemkin, "Orphans of Living Parents: A Comparative Legal and Sociological View," *Law and Contemporary Problems,* 10:834–854 (Summer, 1944).

[57] Davis, *op. cit.,* pp. 701–703.

Personal disorganization of the child may not result *entirely* from the divorce of his parents. It may also be the partial product of their unhappy marriage, which is not the same thing. That is, the child may suffer from the fact that his parents were unhappily married, rather than because they were ultimately divorced. The happiness of children seems to be closely related to the marital happiness (or lack of happiness) of their parents.[58] The crisis of divorce unquestionably increases the insecurity of many children and hence adds to their difficulties. In families where divorce never takes place, however, children may still be unloved, rejected, insecure, and unhappy.[59] One cannot attribute *all* of the difficulties of the child of divorce to divorce itself. Some of them may arise from unhappy marriage.[60]

This general hypothesis is further explored by Goode. The structural position of the family (i.e., whether the husband and wife are living under the same roof) may not be as important to the child as other and less tangible factors. Among the latter are warmth, love, and understanding, rather than the factors of "broken" and "unbroken" homes. A bickering, discordant, and hate-ridden home may be worse for the child than a home with one loving parent. In view of the traditional value judgments concerning the importance of family stability, this approach opens new vistas in the problem of children of divorce.[61]

Goode examines some of these considerations in the sample of divorced women in his study. Many variables appear in assessing the role of the child of divorce, in addition to the fact of divorce itself. There are, for example, questions as to the age of the child and whether he had known his father well or only vaguely. Relationships with the father subsequent to divorce are another variable—notably, how often the child saw his father, under what circumstances, and for how long. Still other factors are related to the child's feelings toward his father before the divorce—whether he loved him deeply, was indifferent to him, actively hated him, or identified completely with his mother. Considering all of these factors, Goode concludes that "in almost all these cases the mothers believed that their children had better lives as divorced children than they would have had as children in marital conflict."[62]

In each of the above divorces, the relationships binding the child to both parents and to the functioning group of the family were broken. Social disorganization was thus present, although the nature of the broken relationships varied. In some cases, close ties existed between the child and both parents; in others, they were largely between mother and child, with the father even then an outsider. The net result of the disorganization of the marital group

---

[58] Cf. Paul Wallin and Howard M. Vollmer, "Marital Happiness of Parents and Their Children's Attitudes to Them," *American Sociological Review*, 18:424–431 (August, 1953).

[59] Roswell H. Johnson, "Suppressed, Delayed, Damaging and Avoided Divorces," *Law and Contemporary Problems*, 18:72–97 (Winter, 1953), pp. 76–77.

[60] Waller, *The Family*, pp. 542–543.

[61] Goode, *op. cit.*, chap. 21, "The Children of Divorce."

[62] *Ibid.*, pp. 329–330.

may in the long run be desirable for the child. The damage to his emerging personality may have been done long before the formal separation. Whatever the ultimate consequences and value judgments, however, a network of interpersonal relationships has been broken.

Adjustment of the Child

Certain specific problems arise about the child of divorce in our society. On some of them we have considerable factual information; on others very little. We may indicate several aspects of the overall situation.

1. *The Scope of the Problem.* Approximately 347,000 children are involved in their parents' divorces each year. An estimated 377,000 divorces involved some 347,000 children under 18 years of age in 1955. The "ratio" of children to divorces was approximately 87 per 100. This does not mean that 87 percent of *all* divorces had children, but that a considerable minority of divorces affected more than one child.[63] The trend has been toward a slow increase in the percentage of divorces involving children.[64] Before World War II, an estimated two out of three divorces were childless; immediately after the war, this ratio changed to approximately three out of five with no children; in the middle 1950's, about one-half of all divorces had no children. The present situation is summarized as follows: "In more than one-half of the cases . . . , no children were reported; in more than one-fifth of the cases (22.8 percent) 1 child was reported; and in one-fourth, 2 children or more were reported."[65]

The estimated figure of 347,000 refers to the number of children *in any one year* whose family relations (such as they are) are broken by divorce. The total number of children whose parents have *ever* been divorced is of course much larger. Some evidence of this latter number is offered by the Bureau of the Census, which in April, 1955, estimated that 1,118,000 children under eighteen were living with a parent who had been divorced. Of this number, 122,000 were living with their fathers and 996,000 with their mothers.[66]

Contrary to widespread popular assumption, therefore, the presence of children does *not* appear to be a preventive against divorce. The fact that an even larger percentage of divorces do not involve children reflects the heavy concentration of divorces in the early years of marriage, before children have been born in any case. Furthermore, the presence of children among the great majority of desertion and nonsupport cases in the family welfare agencies indicates that men who are bent on breaking their family relationships are

---

[63] *Divorce and Annulments: Detailed Statistics for Reporting Areas, 1955, Vital Statistics—Special Reports,* National Office of Vital Statistics, U.S. Department of Health, Education, and Welfare, Vol. 46, No. 4 (April 9, 1957), p. 95.

[64] Paul H. Jacobson, "Differentials in Divorce by Duration of Marriage and Size of Family," *American Sociological Review,* 15:235–244 (April, 1950).

[65] *Divorce and Annulments: Detailed Statistics for Reporting Areas, 1955, op. cit.,* p. 95.

[66] *Population Characteristics, Household and Family Characteristics: April 1955 and 1954, Current Population Reports,* Bureau of the Census, Series P-20, No. 67 (May 2, 1956), Table 11.

not deterred by children. Thomas Monahan is of the opinion that "Marital stability . . . may have no general relationship to childbearing."[67]

2. *The Problem of Custody.* One of the most pressing concerns prior to the divorce—and often for many years thereafter—is the custody of the child. In the majority of cases, as we have stated, custody is given to the mother. Under these conditions, the implications for the personality of the child may be far-reaching. He must live in an incomplete family group, at least until his mother remarries. Each parent has his or her own role patterns to inculcate in the child, and this instruction is obviously impossible in a home headed by the mother alone. Try as she will, she cannot assume *both* parental roles. Furthermore, the child learns from both parents many of the roles which he will have in adult life. This role guidance is manifestly impossible when the father is absent.[68]

The problem of custody is officially settled by the judge. When the case comes to court, it is his duty to award the custody of the child (or children) to one or the other parent. Some judges recognize the momentous nature of their decision and make every effort to choose wisely. They weigh a variety of factors in the balance, ranging from the preference of the child to the financial condition of the parents.[69]

Other judges are not so careful. The obstacles to intensive investigation are formidable. The number of cases is too great, especially in the large cities. Divorce courts rarely have social workers at their disposal; hence any investigation by the judges tends to be informal and haphazard. Some judges prefer to remain strictly legalistic so as to forestall any possible criticism. In the end most judges award the children to the mother, unless she is notoriously unfit.

In the state of Illinois, in a recent ten-year period, the mother was awarded custody in 86 percent of the cases, the father in 9 percent, with the decision "reserved" in 5 percent. Approximately 90 percent of the cases were uncontested, and the judge had very little opportunity to hear anything more than proof of grounds for the decree. In 93 percent of the cases the mother waived alimony. She then asked for the custody and support of the children, was declared by her witnesses to be a fit and proper person to care for the children, and assured the court that she could manage. Sometimes she actually would be able to manage; often she would not. It is difficult for a judge to be a Solomon, yet the stuff of human personality is hanging in the balance.[70]

3. *The Problem of Allegiance.* When the custody of the children is finally arranged (sometimes after prolonged dispute), the question is still far

[67] Thomas P. Monahan, "Is Childlessness Related to Family Stability?" *American Sociological Review, 20:*446–456 (August, 1955), p. 456.

[68] Goode, *op. cit.,* pp. 308–310.

[69] Carl A. Weinman, "The Trial Judge Awards Custody," *Law and Contemporary Problems, 10:*721–736 (Summer, 1944), pp. 734–735.

[70] Edwin A. Robson, "The Law and Practice of Divorce: The Judge's Point of View," The Law School, The University of Chicago, *Conference on Divorce: February 29, 1952,* Conference Series No. 9, pp. 4–5.

from settled.[71] The parents may work out an arrangement permitting the child to live with his mother most of the year and spend the rest of the time with his father. The child thus lives in an incomplete family and has the society of one of his parents only at irregular intervals, but his new world is marked by conflicts between them. The child of divorced parents may find out early in life that his parents are weak and petty, as each tries to wean him away from the other. In the midst of this figurative (and often literal) pulling and hauling, the child's emotional security may be undermined.[72]

In these internecine struggles, a boy may take sides with his mother and develop a bitter hatred for his father. Many divorced mothers deliberately foster this alienation because of their own need for affection and justification.[73] They attempt to bind their sons to them with cords of sympathy. Relations between divorced mothers and their daughters may involve an estrangement if the latter cast their sympathies with their fathers. Children of both sexes are often closer to their mother than to their father.[74] In unhappy marriages, there is a strong tendency for both boys *and* girls to identify with their mothers rather than their fathers. Because of her closer contact, the mother is in a better position to influence the children and evoke sympathetic identification while the father is correspondingly devalued.[75]

4. *The Problem of Group Adjustment.* The difficulties of the child of divorce may be carried over into the play group. Children are strong conformists and any abnormality or deviation from the customary pattern is viewed with suspicion. The child who lives with only one of his parents is often rejected by his playmates. Other children have *both* a mother and a father. He may come to believe that his own parents are less capable, intelligent, or forbearing than those of other children. In the small, conjugal family, the child looks to his parents for guidance, affection, and esteem. The child of divorce may be denied these gratifications. His role in the group may change and his status with his fellows suffer accordingly.[76]

The emotional maladjustments of childhood may continue into later life. The imprint of these early experiences upon the personality of the child is so strong that years after the divorce the basic insecurity may persist. College administrators have long been aware of the emotional difficulties of the child of divorce. Often he has no standard but the uncertain example of his parents. His psyche has received a severe shock, one that endures for many years. Hence, grown older he may be prone to many of the symptoms of personal disorganization peculiar to college boys—drinking heavily, over-

[71] John W. Bronson, "Custody on Appeal," *Law and Contemporary Problems, 10:* 737–746 (Summer, 1944).

[72] Cf. Ernst and Loth, *op. cit.,* pp. 153–159.

[73] Goode, *op. cit.,* pp. 315–316.

[74] Robert F. Winch, "Further Data and Observations on the Oedipus Hypothesis: The Consequence of an Inadequate Hypothesis," *American Sociological Review, 16:*784–795 (December, 1951).

[75] Wallin and Vollmer, *op. cit.,* pp. 430–431.

[76] Ernest R. Mowrer, "Divorce and Readjustment," *Annals of the American Academy of Political and Social Science, 160:*191–196 (March, 1932).

cutting classes, and generally indicating a strong, if temporary, tendency to personality disorganization.

Another aspect of group maladjustment may persist into the married lives of children of divorce. In view of their parents' marital disaster, the children may develop an understandable cynicism toward marriage as a stable relationship. They themselves may marry with the attitude that the marriage can be terminated by either party on a comparatively slight pretext. The mores of divorce are thus perpetuated from one generation to the next. The disorganization of one family begets the disorganization of the next. The normal difficulties of marital adjustment may be augmented by a disillusion with marriage itself, which has arisen from the experience of divorced parents.[77]

A final aspect of group adjustment (or maladjustment) may appear when the parents remarry and the additional complexities of stepparents and half brothers and sisters arise. A bewildering variety of roles faces the child, for which his prior experience has offered little guidance. Strange adults, brothers, and sisters are suddenly introduced into his life, and he may find the situation bewildering. When both parents remarry and have had younger children by their new spouses, the child of the first marriage may find himself without either a spiritual or a physical home. His parents are absorbed in their new children. With the memory of his own father or mother still strong, he may resent the affectionate advances of his mother's new husband or his father's new wife, no matter how well intentioned they may be. From such complex group situations, personal maladjustment is an unpleasant possibility.[78]

SELECTED BIBLIOGRAPHY

Bernard, Jessie, *Remarriage: A Study of Marriage,* The Dryden Press, Inc., New York, 1956. This illuminating study of divorce and remarriage combines a general statement of the problem with an intensive investigation by the author of a selected group of persons who have experienced these changes in status.

Conference on Divorce, The Law School, The University of Chicago, Chicago, 1952. This symposium on the legal problems of divorce is indicative of the increased interest in the field by the legal profession.

Davis, Kingsley, "Sociological and Statistical Analysis," *Law and Contemporary Problems, 10:*700–720 (Summer, 1944). This is an earlier symposium (see above), in which law and behavioral science combined to present an analysis of the children of divorce. In a significant sociological introduction, Kingsley Davis places the problem in its structural and cultural perspective.

Ernst, Morris L., and Loth, David, *For Better or Worse,* Harper & Brothers, New York, 1951. The senior author of this popularly written treatise is a lawyer with extensive experience in the adjustments (and lack of adjustments) following divorce. In the final chapter, the authors offer some suggestions for minimizing the personal disorganization accompanying divorce.

[77] Cf. Paul Popenoe and Donna Wicks, "Marital Happiness in Two Generations," *Mental Hygiene, 21:*218–223 (April, 1937).

[78] For a discussion of fictional portrayals of these and related situations, cf. James H. Barnett and Rhoda Gruen, "Recent American Divorce Novels, 1938–1945," *Social Forces, 26:*322–327 (March, 1948).

Goode, William J., *After Divorce*, The Free Press, Glencoe, Ill., 1956. This is the most complete and thoughtful study of the problems of divorce currently available. The book consists of two types of subject matter: (1) an *intensive* analysis of 425 divorced urban mothers, living in metropolitan Detroit; (2) an *extensive* analysis of the meaning of divorce and the adjustments to it arising from the institutional structure of American society.

Johnson, Roswell H., "Suppressed, Delayed, Damaging and Avoided Divorces," *Law and Contemporary Problems, 18*:72–97 (Winter, 1953). The thesis of this article is that all divorces should not be viewed in equal terms by the legal authorities. Some divorces should be hastened and others should not be allowed to happen at all.

Locke, Harvey J., *Predicting Adjustment in Marriage*, Henry Holt and Company, Inc., New York, 1951. The general purpose of this thoughtful study is to "contribute to an understanding of human adjustment through an analysis of factors associated with marital adjustment and maladjustment." More specifically, it is "a comparison of . . . examples of divorced and happily married persons in a single county of Indiana."

Plant, James S., "The Psychiatrist Views Children of Divorced Parents," *Law and Contemporary Problems, 10*:807–818 (Summer, 1944). The insecurities, inadequacies, and frustrations of the child of divorced parents are the related themes of this article.

Waller, Willard, *The Family: A Dynamic Interpretation* (Revised by Reuben Hill), The Dryden Press, Inc., New York, 1951. The original edition of this thoughtful analysis was written by the late Willard Waller. The present edition was revised by Reuben Hill. Part Six deals with family disorganization, and there is a keen awareness of the implications of divorce for the person who has undergone this change of status.

Waller, Willard, *The Old Love and the New*, Liveright Publishing Corporation, New York, 1930. This is a penetrating sociological interpretation of the changes in status and role after divorce. The study is based upon a limited number of case histories taken three decades ago, and many of the adjustment problems of the divorcee have changed since that time.

PART FOUR

Community and National Disorganization

CHAPTER 19

Community Disorganization

The Nature of the Community

Social disorganization is the decline, breakdown, and dissolution of the interpersonal relationships binding human beings together in groups. This process is essentially the same with the individual, the family, or the other social systems that make up the larger society. In each case, we are merely looking at the disorganization of the group from a different point of view.

Previous chapters have emphasized the manifestations of social disorganization as they affect individuals and family groups although we have also dealt briefly with the extent of the problems entailed. In this section our emphasis shifts to the community aspects of disorganization, both rural and urban. We are also concerned with some of the persistent general problems of social disorganization arising out of crime, unemployment, mobility, migration, discrimination, and segregation as they affect the nation as a whole. In this chapter and most of the chapters in part four we are primarily interested in general aspects of urban disorganization. Two chapters, however, deal with rural disorganization. The chapters covering crime, mobility, migration, discrimination, and segregation are national in their focus and scope. These particular problems are aspects of the social disorganization of our nation as a whole.

The community involves two related aspects, the *geographical* and the *psychological*.[1] In a geographical sense, the community is a contiguous distribution of people and institutions. In a sociopsychological sense, it may be regarded in terms of the psychological elements that make it a living entity. The latter approach stresses the factors that bring about and break down consensus. The community is a complex social system with both a physical locus and a sociopsychological consensus. In a functional sense, these elements combine to produce the community in action.

The community as described by Park and Burgess is a cluster of spatially intimate social units, a "constellation of institutions."[2] Wirth suggests that the

---

[1] A recent survey of the literature on the community lists some 94 different definitions. Cf. George A. Hillery, Jr., "Definitions of Community: Areas of Agreement," *Rural Sociology, 20*:111–123 (June, 1955).

[2] Robert E. Park and Ernest W. Burgess, *Introduction to the Science of Sociology*, University of Chicago Press, Chicago, 1924, p. 493.

community is characterized by "a territorial base, distribution in space of men, institutions, and activities, close living together on the basis of kinship and organic interdependence, and a common life based upon the mutual correspondence of interests. . . ."[3] Blackwell views the community as "a locus for a set of basic, interacting institutions through the functioning of which a majority of the residents find it possible to meet their needs and have developed something of a sense of togetherness, with a consequent potential ability to act together as an entity."[4]

In the Yankee City studies, the community was broadly defined as "a body of people having a common organization or common interests and living in the same place under the same laws and regulations."[5] In a more restricted, structural sense, the community denotes "a number of people sharing certain interests, sentiments, behavior, and objects in common by virtue of belonging to a social group."[6] The members of the groups engage in ordered and reciprocal relationships, and these constitute the social structure of the community. The members of different social classes interact in terms of different patterns of social relationships.[7]

The community has been the basis of organized social existence since before the dawn of history. The development of agriculture in Neolithic times first made a settled existence possible; the community therefore dates from perhaps 10,000–15,000 years before the present era. During much of this early period, growth was slow and the average community remained small. It was not until about 5000 B.C. that the cultural base had developed sufficiently for the "true" city to emerge. Even today in many parts of the world urban life is still virtually unknown and the small rural village is the characteristic form of human community.[8]

In the development of the United States, several patterns of community living have arisen. (1) *The New England town* was one of the earliest forms of the American community, and it followed essentially the pattern brought by the Puritans from England. (2) *The Southern county* rather than the town is still the basis for community living and psychological identification in the South. (3) *The Main Street service center* of the Middle West began as a crossroads center for supplying the basic commodities to the surrounding farms. It has continued in this role as a distribution point. (4) *The mill town* arose about one or more mills or industrial plants and has continued in this functional relationship. (5) *The metropolitan conglomeration* has become

[3] Louis Wirth, "The Scope and Problems of the Community," *Publication of the American Sociological Society,* 27:61–73 (May, 1933).

[4] Gordon W. Blackwell, "A Theoretical Framework for Sociological Research in Community Organization," *Social Forces, 33:*57–64 (October, 1954), p. 58.

[5] W. Lloyd Warner and Paul S. Lunt, *The Social Life of a Modern Community,* Yale University Press, New Haven, 1941, p. 16.

[6] *Ibid.*

[7] August B. Hollingshead, "Community Research: Development and Present Condition," *American Sociological Review, 13:*136–156 (April, 1948).

[8] Kingsley Davis, "The Origin and Growth of Urbanization in the World," *American Journal of Sociology, 60:*429–437 (March, 1955).

a national and even a world center for a variety of specialized functions and services.[9]

In our subsequent investigation of community disorganization, the community will be regarded as a center of social interaction, rather than as a strictly physical or geographical entity. Such an approach follows that of Arensberg. "Community study," as he says, "is that method in which a problem (or problems) in the nature, interconnections, or dynamics of behavior and attitudes is explored against or within the surround of other behavior and attitudes of the individuals making up the life of a particular community. It is a naturalistic, comparative method."[10] In this sense, social interaction transcends the local scene and becomes one aspect of the interaction of the larger society.

Our discussion of community disorganization will be concerned with general processes rather than with specific communities. In some respects, social interaction differs among communities according to size, spatial organization, growth and decline, functional specialization, and regional location.[11] In other respects, however, the interaction is very similar. In the modern dynamic and interdependent society, arbitrary distinctions between communities in terms of size or any other criteria are both inadequate and misleading. Some forms of social interaction are more common in one type of community than in another. Certain groups (e.g., voluntary associations) are somewhat more characteristic of the metropolitan community than of the small town. But in a deeper sense the similarities are greater than the differences.[12] Our interest is in social disorganization wherever it occurs.

The Ecology of the Community

The community is, in one sense, a cluster or constellation of related institutions occupying adjacent locations in space, as we have mentioned. Human beings are spatially located with reference to other human beings, institutions, and social systems. This distribution is a basic factor in the interpersonal relations of the individual and the functioning of the institution. Social interaction occurs within spatial limits. The study of these factors, the "spatial and sustenance relationships of people and institutions," is known as human ecology.[13]

Our interest in human ecology stems from the light which it throws upon the disorganization of social groups. The *place* of the individual in the com-

[9] Conrad M. Arensberg, "American Communities," *American Anthropologist, 57:* 1143–1162 (December, 1955).

[10] Conrad M. Arensberg, "The Community-Study Method," *American Journal of Sociology, 60:*109–124 (September, 1954), p. 110. This approach to the community is followed in a significant textbook: Irvin T. Sanders, *The Community: An Introduction to a Social System,* The Ronald Press Company, New York, 1958.

[11] Otis D. Duncan and Albert J. Reiss, Jr., *Social Characteristics of Urban and Rural Communities, 1950,* John Wiley and Sons, Inc., New York, 1956, chap. 1.

[12] Horace Miner, "The Folk-Urban Continuum," *American Sociological Review, 17:* 529–537 (October, 1952).

[13] James A. Quinn, *Human Ecology,* Prentice-Hall, Inc., New York, 1950.

munity has an important bearing upon his group interaction. A change in locus brings about a corresponding modification in relationships. Changes are continually occurring in a dynamic society, both on the community and on the national level. The functions of the different areas are constantly altered, with new ethnic and racial groups invading the positions formerly occupied by other groups and new institutions taking the place of old ones in the restless matrix of the community. Human ecology, being concerned with these dynamic and functional matters, may therefore be formally defined as "a study of the spatial and temporal relations of human beings as affected by the selective, distributive, and accommodative forces of the environment."[14]

Social interaction takes place within a physical setting. Competition for economic status brings about social mobility, as the individual moves within the community and from one community to another.[15] At one and the same time, he is conflicting, accommodating, assimilating, and (above all) communicating with others in a restless and dynamic modern society. As these ecological processes occur, they bring about both social organization and social disorganization. Group relationships holding people together are continually forming and dissolving under the impact of interaction.[16]

The concept of position has implications both for individual and for community disorganization. A man's place in the social structure, for example, has a definite bearing upon his social and mental health. This situation has been explored in a series of studies at Yale.[17] The general hypothesis is that position is related to the incidence, forms, and treatment of psychiatric disorders. The incidence of schizophrenia, for example, is disproportionately high in the lower classes, with more than two and one-half times as many cases in the lowest class as might be expected. In summary, the authors state that "there are definite connections between particular types of social environments in which people live, as measured by the social class concept, and the emergence of particular kinds of psychiatric disorders. . . ."[18]

Sudden changes in the ecological pattern of a community may cause other forms of social disorganization. The introduction of one group or function into an area formerly occupied by another group or function may disorganize many group relationships. Negro invasion of an area formerly occupied by whites has traditionally been an explosive situation, although there is evidence

[14] Roderick D. McKenzie, "The Ecological Approach to the Study of the Human Community," in Robert E. Park, Ernest W. Burgess, and Roderick D. McKenzie (eds.), *The City,* University of Chicago Press, Chicago, 1925, pp. 63–64.

[15] Robert E. L. Faris, "Ecological Factors in Human Behavior," chap. 24 in James McV. Hunt (ed.), *Personality and the Behavior Disorders,* The Ronald Press Company, New York, 1944, Vol. 2, pp. 736–738.

[16] E. Gordon Ericksen, *Urban Behavior,* The Macmillan Company, New York, 1954.

[17] August B. Hollingshead and Frederick G. Redlich, "Social Stratification and Psychiatric Disorders," *American Sociological Review, 18:*163–169 (April, 1953).

[18] *Ibid.,* p. 169. See also August B. Hollingshead and Frederick C. Redlich, "Schizophrenia and Social Structure," *American Journal of Psychiatry, 110:*695–701 (March, 1954). These studies are brought together in August B. Hollingshead and Frederick C. Redlich, *Social Class and Mental Illness,* John Wiley and Sons, Inc., New York, 1958.

that this form of social disorganization is declining to some degree.[19] The invasion of Puerto Ricans into a section in New York City once held by other racial and/or ethnic groups gives rise to other types of community disorganization.

The arbitrary segregation of one group is an ecological process which produces attitudes of frustration, insecurity, and aggression in the minority group, forced to live in an undesirable area. An extensive study of residential segregation in the decade 1940–1950 disclosed that this process had *increased* in the majority of the cities of the country, both north and south, despite the legislation and public sentiment against it.[20] Of a total of 185 cities, segregation had increased in 129, decreased in 52, and remained the same in 4.

Other forms of population movement have ecological repercussions, both in the local community and on the national scene. The rapid drift of population from the rural areas to the urban centers is one of the most far-reaching of these changes. Millions of people have been suddenly removed from the close primary relationships of the rural community to the secondary relationships of the large city. The mass migrations of millions of Europeans have also precipitated social disorganization. These movements involve changes in geographical location, spatial contact, interpersonal relationships, and cultural contact. We shall consider them in later chapters.[21]

The ecological approach thus contributes to the understanding of the community. Contrary to the thought of some of its early exponents, however, this point of view is not the only, or even the principal, tool for understanding. Ecological position gives the setting within which social interaction occurs. But human beings are also symbol-using persons, and interaction takes place on the symbolic level. Social organization and disorganization involve group relationships, which are dependent upon symbolic communication.[22] The position of the individual or the group *conditions,* rather than *determines,* this interaction. In a sense, then, ecological factors "set the stage for man, the actor."[23] Social disorganization is primarily concerned with the actor rather than the stage.

The Nature of Community Disorganization

Community organization is dependent upon cooperation and consensus. There is, of course, no such thing as complete cooperation or complete

[19] Arnold M. Rose *et al.,* "Neighborhood Reactions to Isolated Negro Residents: An Alternative to Invasion and Succession," *American Sociological Review,* 18:497–507 (October, 1953).

[20] Donald O. Cowgill, "Trends in Residential Segregation of Nonwhites in American Cities, 1940–1950," *American Sociological Review,* 21:43–47 (February, 1956). See also Otis D. Duncan and Stanley Lieberson, "Ethnic Segregation and Assimilation," *American Journal of Sociology,* 64:364–374 (January, 1959).

[21] See Chapter 24, "Mobility," and Chapter 25, "Migration."

[22] Jurgen Ruesch, "Synopsis of the Theory of Human Communication," *Psychiatry,* 16:215–243 (August, 1953).

[23] Louis Wirth, "Human Ecology," *American Journal of Sociology,* 50:483–488 (May, 1945), p. 488.

consensus, and both are subject to wide variations. Every community has some tensions and conflicts and some groups and institutions in the process of disorganization. The more dynamic the community, the more rapidly the social structure is built up and broken down. In the modern urban community, consensus on any matter is generally partial. Since men are more concerned with their private interests than with those of the community, areas in which consensus is possible are limited.[24]

The disorganizing aspects of urban community life are partially caused by the impersonal process of social change. A certain amount of social disorganization is inevitable and "normal" in the dynamic community. Industrial encroachment upon residential areas, the mobility of the population, the segregation of racial and ethnic minority groups, and the breakdown of neighborhood consensus—these and other factors are implicit in the growth of the modern city. Social disorganization, whether temporary or permanent, is the price of a dynamic society. Only in a static society can perfect consensus be approached.

From a cultural standpoint, the above dynamic processes break down patterns of traditional and expected relationships. Such disorganization is evident in the relationships between immigrants and native-born groups. Disparities in culture create barriers to assimilation. These barriers make for maladjustment in the incoming group, which occupies a marginal cultural status. Nationality groups fight to maintain their religious and cultural patterns but in so doing arouse hostile attitudes on the part of the native population groups. The struggle for status goes on for generations, long after assimilation seems complete. Community and national consensus under these circumstances is difficult to achieve and even more difficult to retain.[25]

Community organization is closely related to the political situation. Politics is one of the few fields in which most members of the modern community share vital interests. Taxation, good government, law enforcement, crime prevention, and social welfare are important aspects of community organization and disorganization. Despite the central importance of the political process, many persons do not think of local government as their concern. They pay more attention to their own jobs and amusements than to the public welfare. If the community were completely organized, there would be little difference between individual and social welfare. In the modern community, the best that can be expected is a pale approximation of this consensus.[26]

In their first survey of Middletown, the Lynds found that the average citizen had only a minimum of personal responsibility for the community and was more or less indifferent to its corporate purposes. Political corruption

---

[24] Cf. William I. Thomas and Florian Znaniecki, *The Polish Peasant in Europe and America,* Alfred A. Knopf, Inc., New York, 1927, Vol. II, pp. 1171–1173.

[25] Seymour M. Lipset, "The Sources of the 'Radical Right,' " chap. 7 in Daniel Bell (ed.), *The New American Right,* Criterion Books, New York, 1955.

[26] Charles P. Taft, "What Is the Civic Conscience?" *Annals of the American Academy of Political and Social Science,* 280:142–148 (March, 1952).

was condoned as long as the taxpayer did not believe that his own rights suffered.[27] When the Lynds revisited Middletown ten years later, the same apathy was apparent. Inquiries as to the modifications (if any) in the political structure were met with this pithy statement: "Whatever changes you may find elsewhere in Middletown, you will find that our politics and government are still the same crooked old shell game."[28]

More recently, a study of a community known as Easterntown revealed much the same unconcern. The salary scale for local officials was so low that few men of ability ran for office. The community was run honestly and there was little corruption, but the administration was reactionary and maintained only routine community services. New and vital functions were not accepted because they would raise the tax rate. Education was neglected; teachers' salaries were kept low; new school buildings were not built. The periodic efforts made by civic organizations to interest the citizens in their community were doomed from the start. The problem was not so much one of community disorganization as a lack of involvement in community affairs.[29]

The disorganization of the community is a complex process involving the partial or complete breakdown of the groups, institutions, and voluntary associations whose combined activities make up community interaction. This process has been measured by indexes to various aspects of formal group life: population, health, social welfare, education, housing, recreation, and combinations of these. In this sense, community disorganization is a function of the efficiency of the groups that express orderly social interaction. A community that ranks low in all or a majority of these indexes is one in which social organization is inadequate.[30]

Community disorganization may also be approached in terms of different forms of social disorganization for which the community maintains some responsibility. Among the aspects of direct community concern are ". . . unsocial juvenile behavior (delinquency, truancy, etc.); separation of children from their own homes through placement by agency according to a definite plan (in foster homes, institutions, homes of relatives or friends); crimes indicative of family disorganization (non-support, neglect, abuse); structural evidence of family disorganization (divorce, separation); major crimes; and commitment to mental institutions."[31]

The organization of the community may also be measured in a more general sense—for example, by the comparative success of Community Chest

[27] Robert S. Lynd and Helen M. Lynd, *Middletown,* Harcourt, Brace and Company, New York, 1929, p. 413.

[28] Robert S. Lynd and Helen M. Lynd, *Middletown in Transition,* Harcourt, Brace and Company, New York, 1937, p. 319.

[29] Arnold M. Rose, "Communication and Participation in a Small City as Viewed by Its Leaders," *International Journal of Opinion and Attitude Research,* 5:367–390 (Fall, 1951), pp. 387–389.

[30] Edward J. Baur, "Statistical Indexes of the Social Aspects of Communities," *Social Forces, 33:*64–75 (October, 1954).

[31] Bradley Buell, "Preventing and Controlling Disordered Behavior," *Mental Hygiene, 39:*365–375 (July, 1955), p. 373.

campaigns.[32] The most ambitious general attempt at measurement has been made by Robert C. Angell in a comprehensive study of the integration of American cities. In his view the social integration of a city is reflected in (1) the degree of community support of schools, libraries, and recreational facilities; (2) the proportion of native whites to nonwhites; (3) the proportion of mothers gainfully employed; and (4) the disparity of income between social classes.[33]

A tendency toward community disintegration (disorganization), then, would be signified by lack of community support for schools or recreational facilities. Education and recreation are strong organizing forces. A high proportion of minority racial or ethnic groups would further indicate the inability of the community to function effectively, for conflict, discrimination, and social tensions are likely to be present. In summarizing his findings, Angell concludes that moral integration in any group is "the degree to which there is a set of common ends and values toward which all the members are oriented and in terms of which the life of the group is organized."[34] The absence of such integration gives rise to social disorganization.

Participation in Community Interaction

Failure to participate in the "communal" life of the community is another aspect of social disorganization.[35] Lack of participation is particularly evident in the metropolitan center, where the person's only community ties often are those of his job. Under such conditions, community activities are often optional, and the family may prefer not to take stronger roots than is absolutely necessary. In many urban areas, neighborliness is almost nonexistent; each person has only the slightest interest in the activities of his fellow citizens. The social role of the church is decreasing in importance as the communicants turn toward commercialized recreation and other forms of leisure-time activities.

Community interaction is also at a minimum in the new mass-produced suburbs of the large cities. These "communities" have grown up since World War II, and they consist in scores (and sometimes hundreds) of identical or nearly identical houses or garden apartments. These suburbs are so new that they have not had time to develop any community institutions with roots. The population is largely composed of young, middle-class couples who are highly mobile in two senses—physically and socially. Many of these families stay only a year or so before moving on to another city and another suburb. Their status is discussed in the chapter on mobility. Here we merely indicate

---

[32] C. Arnold Anderson, "Community Chest Campaigns as an Index of Community Integration," *Social Forces, 33:*76–81 (October, 1954).

[33] Robert C. Angell, "The Moral Integration of American Cities," *American Journal of Sociology, 57:*1–140 (July, 1951) (special supplement). Also Robert C. Angell, *Free Society and Moral Crisis,* University of Michigan Press, Ann Arbor, 1958.

[34] Angell, "The Moral Integration of American Cities," p. 115.

[35] Stuart A. Queen, "Social Participation in Relation to Social Disorganization," *American Sociological Review, 14:*251–257 (April, 1949).

that the lack of participation is such that "the new suburb is a community only in the sense that it is an aggregate of buildings. . . ."[36]

Participation in the urban community is largely related to social class. In general, membership in voluntary associations increases with income and social status. Persons in the middle and upper classes are more active in political, cultural, and civic groups than those in the lower classes.[37] The latter have slight affiliation with voluntary associations and spend much of their leisure time with their kinship groups. A study of working-class people in New Haven found that "approximately two-fifths of the husbands and wives . . . had no intimate friends outside the family and kin groups."[38] Working-class participation outside of family groups was largely confined to religious and union groups. Even participation on this level was not as high as some would have expected.

The conception of America as a nation of "joiners" is therefore limited. Participation is mostly confined to the middle and upper classes, and these groups dominate the organizational life of the community.[39] Men of the working class do not feel at home here, nor do their wives. Barriers of education, ethnic group, and social status are very strong, and the average lower-class person hesitates to mingle with those whose backgrounds differ from his own. Ability to participate is learned behavior, and the proper roles are not learned by lower-class persons because they seldom have the opportunity. The middle-class person, on the other hand, joins many community groups because they are an aid to his own upward mobility.[40]

The implications of this differential participation for community disorganization are not entirely clear. Some students maintain that the middle class is the most highly qualified by ability, education, status, and training to assume leadership in community activities. But the community is not truly organized if a considerable proportion of the population does not participate in civic affairs. The middle class has no monopoly on the abilities vital to community organization. Lack of participation by the working classes leaves a significant segment unrepresented in community matters.[41]

Mobility and Community Disorganization

Mobility is of primary importance in community disorganization. The degree of mobility in the community is an index of the consensus between the

---

[36] Sidonie M. Gruenberg, "The Challenge of the New Suburbs," *Marriage and Family Living,* 17:133–137 (May, 1955), p. 134.

[37] Mirra Komarovsky, "The Voluntary Associations of Urban Dwellers," *American Sociological Review,* 11:686–698 (December, 1946).

[38] Floyd Dotson, "Patterns of Voluntary Association Among Urban Working-Class Families," *American Sociological Review,* 16:657–693 (October, 1951), p. 693.

[39] Leonard Reissman, "Class, Leisure, and Social Participation," *American Sociological Review,* 19:76–84 (February, 1954).

[40] John M. Foskett, "Social Structure and Social Participation," *American Sociological Review,* 20:431–438 (August, 1955).

[41] Reissman, *op. cit.,* pp. 83–84.

members. Hence mobility has been called the "pulse of the community." Mobility influences the interpersonal relations of human beings by limiting their continuous social interaction. The mobile individual has difficulty integrating with other persons in formal group relationships.[42] When he leaves one community and goes to another, many of his group relationships are broken. Each individual, whether child or adult, establishes group relationships in a settled community setting. Mobility disrupts these ties and, in a literal sense, brings about social disorganization.

In general, social mobility is greater in large cities than in smaller communities. This differential results from the following factors: (1) The *division of labor* is greater and specialization is more advanced in large industrial centers. More specialized occupations mean that people move about in search of new jobs, either within the metropolitan community itself or from one such community to another. (2) *Urban growth* encourages mobility. Large cities have grown faster than the rest of the country and consequently more positions are available than in smaller and more stable communities. These positions are filled in part by movement from the farms and small towns. (3) *Birth rates* are lower in cities. During the growth of the large cities (except for a period following World War II), the latter did not reproduce themselves. The gap in the urban birth rates—especially among the middle- and upper-middle-class groups—has been partially offset by migrants from smaller communities.[43]

Persons who are constantly moving from place to place have no roots. They have difficulty in identifying themselves with local community institutions and lack the sense of "belonging" that is so important to citizenship. Thus in a mobile community many of the people are "strangers" both to each other and to the norms and values of the community.[44] Some persons develop a progressive alienation from society because they cannot identify themselves with its problems, either in the community or on the broader level of the national society. As the Lynds say, the result of this process is "the marked impairment of those elements in social organization in a democratic culture which depend heavily upon the individual's feeling himself to be rooted in the subsoil of neighborhood and community and therefore personally committed to participating in terms of *its* problems and *its* future."[45]

The nature of economic activity in the metropolitan community likewise makes this identification difficult to attain. Men and women frequently live far from their work and must spend considerable time each day traveling back and forth. The Bureau of the Census has recently gathered some information on the pace of this daily mobility. Approximately one-seventh of

[42] Peter M. Blau, "Social Mobility and Interpersonal Relations," *American Sociological Review*, 21:290–295 (June, 1956).

[43] Seymour M. Lipset, "Social Mobility and Urbanization," *Rural Sociology*, 20:220–228 (September–December, 1955), pp. 226–227.

[44] Rudolf Heberle, "A Note on Riesman's *The Lonely Crowd*," *American Journal of Sociology*, 62:34–36 (July, 1956).

[45] Lynd and Lynd, *Middletown in Transition*, p. 188.

all workers live and work in a different county. This fraction (14.1 percent) does not include those who commute from a suburb to a central city in the same county. In New York City, approximately 61.5 percent of all workers live and work in the same borough; 34.5 percent live in one borough and work in another; and approximately 5.0 percent live in the city and work outside it.[46]

On a national scale, mobility is measured by change of residence over a one-year period. In the year ending March, 1958, approximately one out of every five persons (19.8 percent) was not living in the same house he had lived in the year before. A total of 33,000,000 persons had changed their residence during the year. Of this number, 22,000,000 (13.1 percent) lived in a different house in the same county, and 11,000,000 (6.7 percent) were living in a different county.[47] Such mobility means that many group relationships are constantly broken and are difficult to replace.[48]

Mobility may either produce or accelerate social disorganization in the community. There is a close correlation between mobility and dependency; for instance, it is harder for a stranger to get a job. The geographical distribution of youthful offenders also corresponds to indices of high mobility. In the urban community, commercialized vice and mobility are closely related. Prostitution flourishes because of the mobile and anonymous persons who comprise its patrons. In certain forms of mental illness, mobility seems to be both a cause and an effect. That is, persons with some types of mental disorganization concentrate in high-mobility areas. They may live there initially or they may be drawn there by the nature of their interpersonal difficulties.

Family disorganization is also related to mobility. Divorce rates are high among families continually on the move. Mobility has a disorganizing effect upon the group relationships of children. When they are continually withdrawn from school and forced to adjust to new teachers and new educational systems, their schooling may be fragmentary and inefficient. Children of transients and migratory casual laborers often get no schooling at all. These related aspects of social mobility and social disorganization are considered in more detail elsewhere. We merely indicate here that stable group relationships are interrupted and fragmented by mobility.

The Community and Social Institutions

The disorganization of the community is an index to the efficiency of its major institutional structures. In his analysis of social norms, Sumner long ago offered the classic definition of a social institution: it is *a concept*

[46] Bureau of the Census, *Population Characteristics, County of Work and County of Residence: September, 1954, Current Population Reports,* Series P-20, No. 60 (August 17, 1955).

[47] Bureau of the Census, *Population Characteristics, Mobility of the Population of the United States: March 1957 to 1958, Current Population Reports,* Series P-20, No. 85 (October 13, 1958), Table 1.

[48] Donald J. Bogue, "The Quantitative Study of Social Dynamics and Social Change," *American Journal of Sociology,* 57:565–568 (May, 1952).

plus a structure.[49] An institution is thus an idea plus a mechanism for its implementation. In Sumner's words, "the structure is the framework or apparatus or perhaps only a number of functionaries set to cooperate in prescribed ways at a certain conjuncture."[50] The idea of education is to transmit accumulated knowledge to the younger generation. The structure of education includes such diverse items as curriculums, teachers, laboratories, classrooms, accrediting agencies, libraries, and diplomas.

Numerous sociologists since Sumner have written on social institutions, but Chapin has made one of the most significant contributions. Social institutions arise out of repeated groupings of interacting human individuals in response to elemental needs or drives. Out of these needs a structure is developed which combines four related "type parts." The resulting configuration possesses relative rigidity and persistence of form and tends to function as a unit.[51] The type parts of institutional structure are (1) attitudes or behavior patterns, (2) symbolic culture traits or symbols, (3) utilitarian culture traits or property, (4) codes of oral or written specifications. The type parts may be illustrated in the family. (1) Underlying attitudes and behavior patterns are love, affection, loyalty, and respect. (2) The marriage ring, family crest, and heirlooms are symbolic traits. (3) The home and furniture are utilitarian traits. (4) The marriage license, the marriage certificate, family practices, and genealogy are oral and written codes.

Local institutions are nucleated, usually about something tangible such as property. Family life takes place chiefly within the walls of the home. Governmental activities are carried on within the county, state, and federal buildings. Worship takes place in the church. The term "institution" is also sometimes applied to more general cultural phenomena such as art, law, ethics, science, and language. These Chapin calls general or diffused social institutions. We say art and language are institutions, but neither is a nucleated functioning of individuals in the sense that a family or a bank is.

But diffused culture patterns exert an extremely important effect upon community functioning. Science may change the fate of nations both in war and in peace. The ethics of a nation will determine what is permissible in international relationships as well as in local communities. Legal systems limit or promote efficiency in community functioning. In the local social institution the material and the nonmaterial culture interpenetrate.

Institutions become routinized and standardized forms of response to recurrent social situations. The more venerable and successful an institution is, the more its activities become incrusted with age and tradition. Rituals and ceremonies play an increasingly important part in institutional practice and often become ends in themselves rather than means to any vital community end. Sometimes institutions lose touch with life, whether they are

---

[49] William Graham Sumner, *Folkways,* Ginn and Company, Boston, 1906, p. 53.
[50] *Ibid.*
[51] Cf. F. Stuart Chapin, *Contemporary American Institutions,* Harper & Brothers, New York, 1935, chap. 2.

the tiny churches of a rural community or the national government of a country. When this process of formalism sets in, atrophy has begun. It becomes increasingly difficult to infuse new life into the institutional structure.

There is a close relationship between formalism and institutional disorganization, even though at first glance the two conditions appear to be at opposite poles of the social process. Members of the institution may outwardly be held in check by the formal norms of institutional control. But mentally they are in revolt. In the French Revolution of 1789 and the Russian Revolution of 1917, governments possessing great apparent stability were overcome by new and powerful forces. Such formalistic and despotic institutional structures were ripe for revolution because they had not kept pace with the changing times. Consensus had long since vanished.

Social Institutions and Social Change

Social institutions do more than meet current group needs. They also preserve the social heritage and transmit it from one generation to the next. Institutions resist changes which threaten their position in the social structure. Creeds, constitutions, charters, methods, policies, ideologies, norms, and values are accepted as eternal verities rather than as working instruments for meeting human needs. People look upon institutional change with considerable uneasiness, particularly when their traditional symbols are called into question. As the Lynds have commented, "This resistance to change tends to be maintained long after the demands of inner coherence and smooth functioning of individual and culture demand more forthright adaptation."[52]

Conservatism is a spontaneous reaction against the psychological impact of social change. Individual habit patterns are channelized along a particular line of response, and people oppose change because it involves a readjustment of these patterns. Change in this sense is a form of individual disorganization, as psychological patterns are broken down. The individual fails to weigh the pros and cons rationally but instead reacts impulsively and often aggressively to change or the suggestion of it. He may even reject innovations which would be to his own advantage. Small wage earners reject proposals for social insurance. Local communities may refuse to cooperate in federal housing projects because of ideological objections. This human propensity has long been recognized. The Declaration of Independence states that ". . . all experience hath shewn that mankind are more disposed to suffer while evils are sufferable, than to right themselves by abolishing the forms to which they are accustomed."

Resistance to social change does not occur entirely on an irrational level. Much resistance is conscious and deliberate on the part of persons who have a stake in the existing structure. They resist change because they are unwilling to relinquish power or privilege. They represent a vested interest, which Veblen characterized as "a marketable right to get something for

[52] Lynd and Lynd, *Middletown in Transition,* p. xvi.

nothing."[53] Vested interests comprise "immaterial wealth, intangible assets" which accrue to persons by virtue of their position in a particular institution or group of institutions. In this sense, vested interests include "landlords and other persons classed as 'gentry,' the clergy, the crown . . . and its agents, civil and military."[54]

The most impressive form of vested interest is today found among the very wealthy who are in strategic positions in one or more large corporations. Their position gives them inside information, large expense accounts, bonuses, and other forms of special favors. These men are in no sense "idle rich"; they are extremely busy increasing their wealth and power by such activities as "promoting and managing, directing, and speculating." In certain cases they strenuously resist social change because they fear it will undermine their commanding influence. In other cases, however, they adapt themselves to social change and benefit by it. In the economic sphere, at least, the role of the vested interests has changed since Veblen's day.[55]

The activity of the vested interests is also illustrated in the local community, where individuals, cliques, and organized interest groups can be seen in relationship to the use of *power*. These vested interests, in Mills' expressive phrase, "possess more than do others of whatever there is locally to possess."[56] They usually own the local newspaper, the radio station, and the other media of mass communication. They control the banks and the principal sources of financial power. They are prominent in the ownership and management of the local industries. Their wives and daughters have their pictures in the local paper. Their children often perpetuate their power by marrying each other.[57]

These local vested interests operate through personal friendships, interlocking directorates, and family ties. Many come from the "old" families that have had wealth and power for several generations. In some cases, members of "new" families gain entry into the charmed circles by demonstrating their financial power. They may be unsure of their status, and they aspire to greater security when their children have been accepted into the local elite. Most citizens of the local community never think of questioning the authority of the elite groups. The less powerful are often more zealous in their support of conservative principles than their wealthy fellow citizens. The occasional nonconformist is silenced in various ways, ranging from informal pressure to threats, intimidation, and possible economic and social reprisal. The usual reaction to suggestions of change takes the form of "fear, pessimism, and silence."[58]

[53] Thorstein Veblen, *The Vested Interests and the State of the Industrial Arts*, B. W. Huebsch, New York, 1919, p. 100.

[54] *Ibid.*, p. 162.

[55] C. Wright Mills, *The Power Elite*, Oxford University Press, New York, 1956, chap. 5, "The Very Rich."

[56] *Ibid.*, p. 30.

[57] *Ibid.*

[58] Floyd Hunter, *Community Power Structure*, University of North Carolina Press, Chapel Hill, 1953, chap. 9.

Conflict and Community Disorganization

Conflict is a basic element in community disorganization. It may arise between groups, institutions, cliques, factions, or classes. Every community has some element of conflict. Human desires are virtually limitless, whereas the means of satisfying them are limited. In the struggle for scarce goals men will always come into conflict, both individually and through organized groups. Because social conflict emphasizes the differences between groups and minimizes their similarities, it is always a disorganizing force. One group may have its consensus increased in a conflict situation, but conflicting groups in a community break down harmonious social relationships.[59]

A variety of elements can set off one group from another. Much of our subsequent analysis of community and national disorganization deals with the divisive impact of conflict. Political conflict often destroys the perspective of voters. Individuals become so loyal to their party that they forget their responsibility to the community. Basic to this process is the local corruption of one or both of the major political parties. Revenue from graft, crime, and vice may be important in keeping the party in power.

Community conflict may also arise from religious differences. The town may be divided between Catholics and Protestants. Religious institutions may be in conflict over matters that are apparently remote from religious doctrine as such. The controversy may center on medical practice, birth control, divorce, censorship of books and movies, or the use of public funds for sectarian services. These conflicts are likely to be especially acute in the field of education. Among the educational issues that often generate religious controversy are religious observances in the public schools, appointments of representatives of the different religious groups to the school board, and instruction in marriage and the family, sexual reproduction, and contraception.[60]

Religious tensions may also exist between the different Protestant denominations. The Baptists, Methodists, Congregationalists, and Episcopalians are often at odds over doctrinal or educational issues. Conflict on this level is especially apparent in rural communities and small towns in the South and Middle West, where the dominant religious ideology is still Protestant. Social class and religious affiliation are closely related; middle- and upper-middle-class persons tend to belong to the older and more conservative Protestant denominations and lower-class persons are identified with the newer and more evangelical sects.

Other community conflicts may occur between youth and age, conservatives and liberals, the educated and the uneducated.[61] In one industrial community (New Haven, Connecticut), the combined impact of all of these

[59] Georg Simmel, *Conflict* and *The Web of Group-Affiliations* (translated by Kurt H. Wolff and Reinhard Bendix), The Free Press, Glencoe, Ill., 1955, chap. 1.

[60] Leo Pfeffer, "Issues That Divide," *Journal of Social Issues*, 12:21–39 (Third Quarter, 1956). This entire issue of the *Journal* is devoted to religious conflict.

[61] Samuel A. Stouffer, *Communism, Conformity, and Civil Liberties*, Doubleday and Company, Inc., New York, 1955.

factors upon the social organization was graphically illustrated in a study made to discover the role of women's voluntary associations in the social structure. Participation in these organizations was based upon group differences. Hence an important (although by no means the only) effect of the organizations was to accentuate community tensions. This study thus offers an oblique measure of the nature and forms of community disorganization arising from group conflict.[62]

1. *Racial Cleavage.*   The sharpest line of community cleavage among voluntary associations was based upon race. The biological fact of skin pigmentation separated human beings from each other in a variety of interpersonal relations, ranging from marriage to political action. In the sample of 177 voluntary associations, approximately 90 percent were racially exclusive.

2. *Religious Cleavage.*   The next most important aspect of cleavage was based upon religion. The study revealed that 76 percent of the community organizations were religiously exclusive. Protestants, Catholics, and Jews comprised the tripartite division of major religious groups, only 24 percent of which permitted interreligious membership.

3. *Ethnic Cleavage.*   The third form of community cleavage reflected ethnic (i.e., national and/or cultural) differences. Approximately 50 percent of the voluntary organizations showed such differentiation. Among the stated ethnic categories were "old" American, "recent" American (i.e., native born of foreign-born parents), and Italian, Swedish, and Polish. Cultural factors were thus still important in setting one group off from another, even after the "melting pot" had presumably done its work.

4. *Social Prestige Cleavage.*   The fourth aspect of community cleavage evidenced in New Haven was social prestige. In contrast to the other three, social prestige was not in itself a clear-cut factor but operated within the other three types. For example, social prestige was a factor in different associations based upon race. Membership in all-white organizations was in turn limited by prestige factors. Likewise, religious organizations reflected prestige differences, as did organizations based upon ethnic differences.[63]

This study of women's voluntary associations indicates the extent to which social groups portray cleavages and cleavages within cleavages. More precisely, the study shows that "within the basic pattern of racial cleavage, religion may become a divisive element; that, within the religiously separated organizational groupings, ethnic differences become significant; and that, within racial, religious, or ethnic divisions, social prestige may create still further subdivisions."[64] In American society several important differences form the focal points about which arise a variety of conflicting groups.

The disorganization of the community is a complex and impersonal

---

[62] Mhyra S. Minnis, "Cleavage in Women's Organizations: A Reflection of the Social Structure of a City," *American Sociological Review,* 18:47–53 (February, 1953).

[63] *Ibid.,* pp. 48–51.

[64] *Ibid.,* p. 53.

operation depending more upon social processes than upon personalities per se. It results from the dynamic and heterogeneous nature of American society. Differences in value systems between groups and classes are both cause and effect of this dynamic quality. Conflicts between racial, religious, ethnic, and class groups produce tensions that weaken the social structure. Elements in the power structure may also obstruct community organization, when those in power disagree on basic values. Since community organization takes place through groups, institutions, and associations, the breakdown of the relationships holding these groups together is the process of community disorganization.[65]

SELECTED BIBLIOGRAPHY

Angell, Robert C., "The Moral Integration of American Cities," *American Journal of Sociology, 57:*1–140 (July, 1951), Special Supplement. This monograph reports on a series of studies of the factors making for community organization and disorganization.

Arensberg, Conrad M., "American Communities," *American Anthropologist, 57:* 1143–1162 (December, 1955). By the same author, "The Community-Study Method," *American Journal of Sociology, 60:*109–124 (September, 1954). These articles are important contributions to the study of the community. In the first article, the author outlines certain typical patterns assumed by the community. In the second, he indicates his philosophy of community study as an analysis of social interaction rather than of individual communities.

Duncan, Otis D., and Reiss, Albert J., Jr., *Social Characteristics of Urban and Rural Communities, 1950,* John Wiley and Sons, Inc., New York, 1956. This monograph analyzes a mass of detailed information originally gathered by the Bureau of the Census and relating to the American community. It is the definitive statistical study of such matters as the size of the community, its spatial organization, community growth and decline, and the functional specialization of communities.

Hillery, George A., Jr., "Definitions of Community: Areas of Agreement," *Rural Sociology, 20:*111–123 (June, 1955). Various definitions of the community are analyzed in this article, in which the author selects certain elements that are typical of all the definitions. The emphasis is primarily, although not entirely, upon the rural community.

Hollingshead, August B., "Community Research: Development and Present Condition," *American Sociological Review, 13:*136–156 (April, 1948). This article traces the development of sociological research in the community and indicates the major trends in this expanding field.

Hunter, Floyd, *Community Power Structure,* University of North Carolina Press, Chapel Hill, 1953. The power relationships in a single community are the theme of this monograph, in which individuals, cliques, and organized interest groups are examined.

Lynd, Robert S., and Lynd, Helen M., *Middletown,* Harcourt, Brace and Company, New York, 1929. By the same authors, *Middletown in Transition,* Harcourt, Brace and Company, New York, 1937. These two volumes comprise the

[65] Blackwell, *op. cit.,* p. 64.

most famous community study ever made in the United States. The first analysis was conducted in the 1920's and the second approximately ten years later, after a decade of boom and depression.

Mills, C. Wright, *The Power Elite*, Oxford University Press, New York, 1956. Chapter 2 of this hard-hitting book is devoted to the power structure of the local community, with its leading families, its centers of dominance, and its class alignments. The increasing centralization of the country has meant that the local elite is no longer as powerful as it was.

Reissman, Leonard, "Class, Leisure, and Social Participation," *American Sociological Review*, 19:76–84 (February, 1954). Community organization is viewed in terms of social class participation in the voluntary associations.

Sanders, Irvin T., *The Community: An Introduction to a Social System*, The Ronald Press Company, New York, 1958. The central thesis of this textbook is that "a community, like a group, is essentially a system of social interaction." The author examines various aspects of the community in this interactional frame of reference.

Thomas, William I., and Znaniecki, Florian, *The Polish Peasant in Europe and America*, Alfred A. Knopf, Inc., New York, 1927 (two vols.). In Vol. II, part I, of this sociological classic, there is a chapter entitled "Disorganization of the Community" which has served as the theoretical foundation for much of the subsequent research in this field.

Warner, W. Lloyd, and Lunt, Paul S., *The Social Life of a Modern Community*, Yale University Press, New Haven, 1941. This is the first of a series of monographs depicting the life of a community called "Yankee City." The authors were particularly interested in the social structure of the community, in terms of the alignments of social class.

CHAPTER 20

The Rural Community
The Agricultural Revolution

Social Change and the Farm

Most individual and social disorganization occurs in urban communities. There are fewer disorganized individuals, fewer divorces, fewer slums, and relatively less social disorganization in the rural areas where social controls are more personal and no one can hide behind the anonymity which characterizes city life. Farm life, in fact, virtually requires a stable and orderly existence if the farm work is carried on successfully. Of course, community disruptions and dislocations have occurred in farm areas. There have been agricultural depressions and disturbing rural social changes. The introduction of the reaper and binder, the sulky plow, and other horse-drawn machinery which provided a seat for the farmer also increased the amount of land one man could cultivate. When the farmer no longer had to trudge behind the plow or to mow with a scythe, farming made its most notable advance since the scythe's advent around 500 B.C. Horse-drawn machinery was revolutionary in taking the drudgery out of farming.

Today we are in the midst of another agricultural revolution—this one of far greater proportions. The current revolution has been occasioned both by scientific seed and soil experimentation and by the various inventions which have resulted in the mechanization of agricultural production. As a consequence there have been dislocations in population and altered needs for the services supplied by the small towns and villages. In the fertile productive areas, communities have prospered, whereas communities where the land is of marginal productivity have been unable to compete. Many rural areas have been unable to provide adequate educational, medical, and religious institutions to serve the rural population. The villages and small towns which have provided a marketing place for farm produce as well as services and commodities for the farmer's consumption have also felt the impact of social change on the farm. The rural community is important to city dwellers, for our whole country is enmeshed in a rural hinterland. The metropolitan areas and the larger and smaller cities are all dependent upon rural production for their bread, meat, vegetables, fruit, and milk.

Our cultural roots as a nation are also essentially rural despite the rela-

475

tively high degree of urbanization. Our folkways and mores, our laws and institutions have all arisen from a rural matrix.[1] Our way of life has recently been altered but from colonial days until the end of the nineteenth century the whole country was basically rural.[2] In 1790 nearly 95 percent of the population lived on farms or in rural towns and villages. Many cities with their bustling industrial activity soon arose but the farmers who settled on the land were responsible in a very important sense for the development of the country. As late as 1900, 60.3 percent of the population lived on farms or in small towns and villages. By 1950 more of the rural population was nonfarm than farm population, with 41 percent of the population living in rural areas, i.e., in places under 2500, as Table 20.1 shows.

The bulk of our people thus live in towns and cities, and the rural communities face serious problems of community disorganization. Cultural change, scientific research, and a conflict of interests have all played a part in the disruption of rural communities. Much of our country is, however, still essentially rural. The degree of ruralness varies. The southern states had the largest rural population as an area, but many of the mountain and middle western states were more than half rural in 1950. In the northeastern part of the country, most of the people live in nonrural areas. Statistics are therefore misleading when we think of this country as preponderantly urban. Cities have grown larger and larger but most of the land is still sparsely settled and devoted to agricultural pursuits.

What Is a Rural Community?

Before we attempt to analyze the tremendous changes which have produced rural disorganization and the extent of this disorganization, we should first define what we mean by the rural community. Strictly speaking, even the metropolis has a rural hinterland, which tends to merge almost imperceptibly with the outskirts of the suburbs and occasionally with the city limits. Long Island with its great estates and truck farms is surprisingly rural although close to New York. Likewise the open country near Chicago, Minneapolis, Philadelphia, or San Francisco is rural but not typically or essentially rural because it is adjacent to and served by the institutions and facilities available in the city. On the other hand, not all open-country residents are engaged in agriculture. Today many people live in the open country, in rural settlements or villages and towns under 2500 population, and work in larger towns and cities. These people constitute the rural "nonfarm" population. Nonfarm rural dwellers do not live where they work or work where they live, and in consequence they are only partially identified with either community. In a sense these people may contribute to the social disorganization of both communities. They vote where they sleep but often do not participate significantly in the civic and social institutions.

[1] Roscoe Pound, *Criminal Justice in America,* Henry Holt and Company, Inc., New York, 1940, chap. IV.

[2] Howard Odum, *The Way of the South,* The Macmillan Company, New York, 1947, p. 81.

The rural nonfarmers are thus "in" but not "of" the country. They often retain identifications with city institutions such as sending their children to city schools and attending city churches. Many of them live in the commercially developed housing projects which surround our large cities. Three-fifths of these places are unincorporated and depend upon commercial interests (including banks which own the mortgages) to see that public utilities and institutions—schools, churches, and banks—and shopping facilities are available. These new rural-urban fringes of urban areas constitute a social phenomenon that deserves detailed sociological analysis. They are not truly rural but rather spilled-over urban populations which have arisen with the expansion of cities.[3] They are nevertheless related to rural community disorganization for within the rural-urban fringe population are many of the young people who left the farm and village for the opportunities in the city. Our major concern in this chapter, however, lies with the agricultural community and the rural villages and small towns under 2500 in population which serve the farmers' needs.

Rural Community Disorganization

Many rural communities, whether in upper, middle, or low income levels, have been seriously disorganized by the profound and disruptive changes which federal legislation, agricultural science, and modern invention have brought about. These in turn have set in motion a far-reaching series of changes which have affected the economic and social structure both on the farm and in the small town serving the farmer's basic needs. Today farming is becoming a great industry rather than a way of life. The alterations and dislocations in agricultural economy resemble in many ways those which occurred with large-scale industry and the advent of the factory system. The disorganizing processes are so extensive that it is often difficult to decide what is cause and what is effect. The farm population and agricultural village and town are in a state of crisis because of the interrelated factors which have produced the agricultural revolution.

Rural disorganization differs from urban disorganization in having less "organized disorganization" than do larger towns and cities. Social controls are more effective in the country where everyone knows his neighbor and his neighbor's business. Consequently there is relatively little organized crime or vice in the country. Nor do the problems of political corruption exist as they do in the city. Rural disorganization is more often the function of poverty and ignorance and the inadequacy of the social institutions which serve rural needs.

It is thus the low-income areas in which rural disorganization is most severe. Obviously not all rural disorganization is a matter of economics and finance. Some is related to isolated ruralness per se, where the rural dwellers have no access to villages, towns, and cities and there is a lack of adequate

---

[3] Otis Dudley Duncan and Albert J. Reiss, *Social Character of Urban and Rural Communities,* John Wiley and Sons, Inc., New York, 1958, pp. 117–119.

TABLE 20.1. Percent of Population Living in Places of Specified Size[a] Each State, 1950 and 1900

State	1950 250,000 or More	1950 100,000 to 250,000	1950 25,000 to 100,000	1950 2,500 to 25,000	1950 Under 2,500	1900 250,000 or More	1900 100,000 to 250,000	1900 25,000 to 100,000	1900 2,500 to 25,000	1900 Under 2,500
United States	23.1	6.4	12.3	17.2	41.0	14.4	4.3	7.3	13.7	60.3
New England	8.6	17.9	28.0	19.9	25.7	10.0	9.1	22.4	27.1	31.4
Maine	—	—	16.4	24.6	59.0	—	—	7.2	26.3	66.5
New Hampshire	—	—	27.3	29.2	43.5	—	—	13.8	32.9	53.3
Vermont	—	—	8.8	27.7	63.6	—	—	—	22.1	77.9
Massachusetts	17.1	17.3	31.3	22.2	12.1	20.0	8.0	30.4	27.6	14.0
Rhode Island	—	31.4	38.3	18.8	11.6	—	41.0	15.7	31.6	11.7
Connecticut	—	30.1	25.2	8.8	35.9	—	11.9	24.5	23.5	40.1
Middle Atlantic	40.7	5.3	11.3	17.7	24.9	35.0	6.9	8.5	14.9	34.8
New York	59.4	4.1	6.9	9.8	19.8	52.1	3.7	5.5	11.6	27.1
New Jersey	15.3	10.4	24.5	29.3	20.4	—	29.6	18.5	22.4	29.4
Pennsylvania	26.2	4.5	11.5	23.6	34.2	25.6	3.7	9.0	16.4	45.3
East North Central	29.3	4.9	14.6	16.9	34.3	18.6	2.7	5.9	18.0	54.8
Ohio	29.9	6.7	12.8	17.0	33.6	17.0	6.2	5.8	19.0	51.9
Indiana	10.9	13.0	15.5	17.0	43.6	—	6.7	7.0	20.5	65.7
Illinois	41.6	1.3	13.6	18.0	25.5	35.2	—	4.5	14.5	45.7
Michigan	29.0	5.3	14.6	15.4	35.7	11.8	—	7.5	20.0	60.7
Wisconsin	18.6	—	20.5	16.4	44.5	13.8	—	5.7	18.7	61.8
West North Central	17.1	4.4	9.6	19.4	50.1	5.6	7.1	4.3	11.5	71.5
Minnesota	27.9	3.5	2.8	19.7	46.1	—	20.9	3.0	10.2	65.9
Iowa	—	6.8	21.6	18.5	53.1	—	—	9.8	15.9	74.4
Missouri	33.2	—	8.0	16.7	42.1	18.5	8.6	.8	8.4	63.7
North Dakota	—	—	10.5	16.1	73.4	—	—	—	7.3	92.7
South Dakota	—	—	12.0	21.2	66.9	—	—	—	10.2	89.8
Nebraska	18.9	15.6	7.5	19.4	54.2	—	9.6	6.2	7.9	76.3
Kansas	—	—	7.3	24.5	52.6	—	—	5.8	16.6	77.6
South Atlantic	9.8	7.2	11.5	13.9	57.5	7.5	—	4.9	8.9	78.6
Delaware	—	34.7	—	11.8	53.5	—	—	41.4	5.0	53.6

Maryland	50.2	6.9	—	—	42.8	45.6	9.0	4.9	—	40.5
Dist. of Columbia	—	—	—	—	100.0	—	—	—	—	100.0
Virginia	81.7	11.2	7.1	—	—	59.7	10.1	12.7	17.5	—
West Virginia	86.9	9.0	4.1	—	—	68.1	15.2	16.7	—	—
North Carolina	90.1	9.9	—	—	—	69.5	14.9	12.3	3.3	—
South Carolina	87.2	8.6	4.2	—	—	71.2	16.9	11.9	—	—
Georgia	84.4	7.3	8.3	—	—	59.9	17.3	9.7	3.5	9.6
Florida	79.7	14.9	5.4	—	—	43.5	18.1	17.5	20.9	—
East South Central	*85.0*	*6.3*	*4.6*	*4.1*	—	*64.5*	*13.6*	*6.6*	*5.8*	*9.5*
Kentucky	78.2	7.7	4.5	9.5	—	66.5	12.5	8.4	—	12.5
Tennessee	83.8	4.0	7.1	5.1	—	61.6	11.5	1.8	13.1	12.0
Alabama	88.1	6.0	5.9	—	—	59.9	16.5	5.3	7.7	10.6
Mississippi	92.3	7.7	—	—	—	72.4	14.3	13.3	—	—
West South Central	*83.8*	*8.1*	*3.7*	—	*4.4*	*47.0*	*20.8*	*8.5*	*7.9*	*15.7*
Arkansas	91.5	5.6	2.9	—	—	67.7	18.7	8.3	5.4	—
Louisiana	73.5	5.7	—	—	20.8	49.2	14.6	5.5	9.4	21.3
Oklahoma	92.6	7.4	—	—	—	50.4	24.4	6.0	19.1	—
Texas	82.9	10.4	6.7	—	—	40.2	22.4	10.3	4.8	22.3
Mountain	*67.7*	*17.6*	*6.7*	*8.0*	—	*51.2*	*22.7*	*12.2*	*5.7*	*8.2*
Montana	65.3	22.2	12.5	—	—	57.2	25.1	17.6	—	—
Idaho	93.8	6.2	—	—	—	60.2	29.5	10.3	—	—
Wyoming	71.2	28.8	—	—	—	50.2	38.8	11.0	—	—
Colorado	51.7	18.3	5.2	24.8	—	42.6	17.7	8.2	—	31.4
New Mexico	86.0	14.0	—	—	—	53.8	24.1	22.1	14.3	—
Arizona	84.1	15.9	—	—	—	63.5	16.2	6.1	26.4	—
Utah	61.9	18.8	19.3	—	—	40.1	21.0	12.5	—	—
Nevada	83.0	17.0	—	—	—	47.5	32.2	20.3	—	—
Pacific	*53.6*	*13.8*	*14.1*	*4.2*	*14.2*	*37.1*	*15.2*	*11.7*	*4.6*	*31.5*
Washington	59.2	10.9	30.0	—	—	46.4	13.7	7.4	12.8	19.7
Oregon	67.8	10.3	21.9	—	—	51.9	18.4	5.2	—	24.6
California	47.7	15.8	6.5	6.9	23.1	32.9	15.0	13.6	3.4	35.1

a Classified according to the definition of urban places used in the 1940 Census. Places under 2500 include rural areas. Source of basic data: U.S. Bureau of the Census, *Number of Inhabitants, 1950*, Series P-A.

SOURCE: Metropolitan Life Insurance Company, "Most Americans Live in Small Communities," *Statistical Bulletin*, April, 1952.

institutional resources for that reason. Extreme ruralness and low income level often coincide, and these areas fail seriously in providing desirable standards for schools, churches, and medical facilities.

The Agricultural Revolution

The most important factor in the shifts in rural population and rural economy is unquestionably the agricultural revolution. During the twentieth century the production of crops and livestock has been revolutionized by a variety of cultural and social changes, by inventions, and by scientific research, as mentioned above. We cannot discuss them all in detail, but the changes which have made the most impact upon the farmer's way of life are (1) the automotive mechanization of farm operations including preparation of the soil, planting, cultivation, and harvesting; (2) scientific research and the subsequent introduction of scientific methods of improving crop yields and livestock (for both meat and dairy purposes); (3) the building of hard-surfaced all-weather highways; (4) the consolidation of schools; (5) the "rurbanization" of rural areas; (6) the declining farm population; (7) tenancy; (8) federal subsidies to farmers; and (9) the changing rural class structure. These factors are themselves interrelated and there are many other factors which have produced disruptions in the rural community which we cannot discuss. These nine have been responsible, however, for a major share of the tremendous alterations in farm life.

The Mechanization of Agriculture

The most important single factor in changing farm life has been the mechanization of agricultural production by automotive farm implements. This change has taken much of the romance as well as the drudgery out of farm life and has greatly reduced the need for farm labor as well. The farmer no longer drives a team behind a plow, and even the memory of the farmer using a hoe or cutting a swath with his scythe with a paean of praise to his Maker has vanished. Today the farmer sits on the seat of a powerful tractor, which pulls a plow, a corn planter, a wheat or clover seeder. He later makes hay sitting on a machine which cuts and bales the hay in one operation. Similarly he cuts and threshes his grain with another single machine, the "combine." This grain is transferred to cribs by automotive elevators and if the farmer does not own the land, he may weigh his and his landlord's share of the grain accurately on the farm scales.

It costs a large sum of money to stock a farm with such machinery. In addition, the farmer must own a truck to transport his products to market, an electrical or gasoline pump to insure water for his livestock, an automobile to transport his family, and a large variety of small tools. Most small farms have thus become unprofitable to operate. No farmer can afford all this expensive machinery if he operates 100 to 120 acres. Even the former standard 160 acres for the family farm in the Middle West is no longer a suitable unit for farming. A farmer now needs larger acreage to make his investment in machinery pay. As a result, the farmers who are making money are large-scale farmers, whether they operate family commercial farms or corporation-owned farms. With the mechanization of agriculture, farming has thus become a commercial enterprise, with increased capital assets. The average farm was worth about $36,000 in 1958 (and this included part-time and subsistence farms). Total farm assets were valued at $177 billion and capital requirements are likely to increase.[4]

Unfortunately more than half the farm operators (59 percent) are subsistence or part-time farmers who supply only 9 percent of the farm output.[5] Meanwhile successful farming has become big business, with significant economic rewards to the farmer who operates land enough to make his investment pay. This means that competent farmers are buying out less successful farmers. A major reason for the decline in farm population is thus a result of an increase in the average farm acreage. Machinery makes it possible for the farmer to work longer hours as well as to cultivate a larger area. With powerful searchlights, he can even operate his tractor-drawn machinery at night. He can in fact cultivate two or three times as much land without help as his father formerly could with several hired farm hands during the planting and harvesting seasons.

Modern agricultural mechanization has also promoted specialization in agricultural production. During an earlier period many farmers spent considerable time raising vegetables and curing meat for their own consumption and developed skills in storing them for winter use. Such self-sufficiency is disappearing today. Prosperous farmers often raise only a small (or no) part of the vegetables or food consumed by the family.

Few well-to-do farmers, for example, raise their own potatoes unless they are potato farmers. Fewer still cure their own meat. Much less do they take corn and wheat to be ground into meal and flour. In the middle western states of Illinois and Iowa, the farmer's major crops are now corn and soybeans, which are sold to village grain merchants, shipped to the Chicago market, or fed to cattle and hogs.

In western Kansas and the Dakotas, the major crop is wheat. There farmers often do not even raise a spring garden of lettuce and radishes. Their major concern in their vast operations is with the field crop, not with supplying food for the family table. Such large-scale agricultural production is often much more profitable than earlier farm operations but it reduces many of the previous satisfactions of farm life. The farmer's wife has more leisure today. But there is no enticing aroma from the jam kettle in the farm kitchen, for she selects her jam at the supermarket. Seldom too is there any delight in freshly baked bread, or in crocks of yellow cream in the spring house. Churning day or baking day is a thing of the past on the average farm. The

---

[4] Earl I. Butz, "The New Look in Agriculture," *Banking*, 50:86, 88, 90 (January, 1958).

[5] *Ibid.*

farmer's wife today spends more time shopping than formerly, and she also spends more time participating in civic affairs. The ledger entries are obviously not all on the debit side.

Improvement of Agricultural Science

Equally significant changes have been wrought in agriculture through the scientific research which has resulted in improved seed and improved crops. Hybrid seed corn, for example, has more than doubled the corn yield per acre. Experiment with sprays has reduced the destruction of crops through disease. With better seed, better preparation of soil, and better pest control, the farmer has made not two but often three or four blades of wheat grow where only one grew before. The federal government has aided this development through its extensive program of soil building by refunding part of the cost of improving soil fertility.

Good Roads

Not only has mechanical invention altered farm machinery and made large-scale farming practicable, but the invention of the automobile has destroyed the farm's isolation. The automobile was the forerunner of agricultural mechanization. As soon as farmers began to use automobiles extensively, all-weather roads became imperative. Today most farming areas have some form of gravel or hard-surfaced roads, and most areas have easy access to paved state and national highways. Good roads are clearly of major importance to the farmer in permitting him to market his crops and livestock without reference to the weather.

Good roads have, on the other hand, altered the nature of rural community organization. They have made possible consolidated schools and closed the one-room district schools in many areas. Much of this is good. But hard-surfaced roads have also altered the patterning of rural social relationships. Farmers no longer depend upon the Grange or their neighbors for their social activities. They find their recreation at the nearby town's movies. And they drive long distances to resorts, to state parks, and to cities. Here they may shop and enjoy some of the cultural advantages of the urban center.

Consolidated Schools

The changes in rural schools are discussed in detail later on. Consolidated schools are to a large extent responsible for the "rurbanization" of farmers' children and should therefore be mentioned here. In consolidated schools they come in contact with many nonrural children and with non-farm-oriented stimuli. Farm children feel a great incentive to keep up with the village or town children and to participate in the same type of leisure-time activities. The rural child thus becomes more sophisticated than when he goes to a one-room school. The school curriculum is generally broader and widens the student's interest. Consequently, he often becomes interested in a nonfarm vocation or profession; when the farmer's children attended rural schools, a much smaller percentage went on to high school and college. The consolidated school also profoundly affects the farm child's standard of living. He wants and expects to have everything his own age group thinks essential.

Today compulsory education has greatly increased the number of farm children who attend high school. More and more farm young people have been exposed to good books and good music. Through radio programs, TV, and the movies, they have received a taste of the theater. Teachers in rural high schools have urged them to go to college or there has been a self-initiated stimulus. Thus the number of rural young people who go to college has been markedly increased. Many agricultural college graduates actually return to the farm. But a great many rural young people who are graduated from college or university prepare for the professions and settle in larger towns and cities. Often it is the most intelligent students who leave the farm.[6]

"Rurbanization" of Rural Areas

The farmers' and their children's increased contact with town and city life has changed rural life. With consolidation of schools and the compulsory education laws which operate in all but two states, rural young people are for the most part attending high school. In prosperous farming areas a large share attend college. In certain states, such as Iowa and Illinois, a great many farmers read the city newspapers. They also hear the same radio broadcasts as their city cousins. They respond to the same mass stimuli, including the same advertisements. Today the average farm has electricity with the same sort of refrigeration, television, and lighting that city people enjoy. Consequently, as Earl I. Butz has said, the "city limit sign now designates only a tax boundary." The way of life is much the same whether one lives in a rural or an urban area.[7]

Farm Tenancy

Farm tenancy was a problem before the agricultural revolution. It still complicates every aspect of the farm problem. The turnover of farm tenants is high. This in turn tends to affect farm income and soil fertility as well as any civic participation or basic interest by tenants in community institutions.[8]

Mobile tenants often farm by methods which exhaust or "mine" the soil because they wish to obtain as high income with as little outlay as possible. If a farmer has a one-, two-, or three-year lease, he often hesitates to invest in fertilizers or other soil builders. He also is not inclined to make fence and building repairs since he will not profit much from them. When a farmer

[6] Carroll D. Clark and Noel P. Gist, "Intelligence as a Factor in Occupational Choice," *American Sociological Review,* 3:683–684 (October, 1938).

[7] Butz, *op. cit.* Cf. also J. H. Kolb and Edmund de S. Brunner, *A Study of Rural Society,* Houghton Mifflin Company, Boston, 1952 (4th ed.), p. 277.

[8] "Extracts from the Iowa Farm Tenancy Committee," cited by Luigi G. Ligutti and John C. Rawe, *Rural Roads to Security,* Bruce Publishing Company, Milwaukee, 1940.

remains on a farm for a brief period, the value of the farm itself is likely to deteriorate.[9]

Tenancy, as the term is employed in the southern states, includes "share tenants" and "sharecroppers." These people are not tenants in the same way farm renters in the North are. The sharecroppers are actually farm laborers or farm hands. T. Lynn Smith holds that the share tenants and sharecroppers should not be called tenants at all.[10] They have no rights in the land except those specified by the landlord and they have no lease as is customary in the northern states. Share tenants and sharecroppers merely agree to produce and pick a given crop or farm a particular plot of ground. Their economic position is comparable to that of wage field hands, except that the latter do not ordinarily stay on the land after the crop is harvested. Renters, on the other hand, are farm operators and are generally permitted to make the decisions as to which crops are planted, and how they are cultivated and fertilized, etc.[11]

Tenancy and Rural Disorganization

Property deterioration is only one of the disorganizing aspects of high turnover in tenants. Rural institutions all suffer. The first of March is a common moving time for farm tenants and this means that children of tenants often have their schooling disrupted. Sometimes they miss several weeks of school. In any event their education suffers because courses are given in a different sequence in the new school—so that they "miss fractions in arithmetic" or a particular segment of American history. Churches also suffer seriously in areas where tenancy is high, as is discussed later.

With all its drawbacks tenancy has increased markedly during the last few decades, largely because owners have died and the heirs have moved to the city or small town. Tenancy is common both in high- and in low-income areas. Seven of the ten states with the highest percentage of tenant-operated farms in 1950 were southern, as Table 20.2 indicates. Tenancy is also an important aspect of farming in Iowa and Illinois, which are two of the most prosperous farm states. Iowa is almost wholly in the upper-fifth level of farm incomes. These statistics are not completely satisfactory since the tenant figures for southern states include the sharecropper, who differs from tenants who are farm operators, as mentioned above.[12]

In the South often both farm tenant operators and croppers fall in the low-level income group with croppers falling lower than tenant operators. Living conditions are poor; some ramshackle houses have "windows without glass, leaking roofs, flimsy walls, and no plumbing at all."[13] The highly mobile tenant

---

[9] See Rainer Schickele, *Farm Tenure in Iowa,* Iowa AES Bulletin 356, Ames, 1937, p. 262 (cited by T. Lynn Smith).

[10] T. Lynn Smith, *The Sociology of Rural Life,* Harper & Brothers, New York, 1947, pp. 280–285.

[11] *Ibid.*

[12] Wilson Gee, *The Social Economics of Agriculture,* The Macmillan Company, New York, 1954, p. 195.

[13] Cf. Odum, *op. cit.,* p. 280. Rural poverty is improving somewhat in the South.

farmer has no incentive to spend any money on the farm. His low income and perennial debt keep him perpetually discouraged.[14]

Even in prosperous farming areas there is a tendency for the farm to run down unless it is supervised by an efficient farm manager. Despite its drawbacks, farm tenancy as such should not be considered prima-facie evidence

TABLE 20.2. Percentage of Farm
Tenancy of Ten States with
Highest Percentages of
Farm Tenants in 1950

Mississippi	51.6
South Carolina	45.3
Georgia	42.8
Alabama	41.4
Louisiana	39.6
Nebraska	38.6
North Carolina	38.3
Iowa	38.2
Arkansas	37.6
Illinois	34.6

SOURCE: Data derived from Table
11 in Wilson Gee, *The Social Economics of Agriculture*, The Macmillan
Company, New York, 1954, p. 190.

of rural disorganization. So long as property is inherited, farm tenancy will exist as a means of preserving family holdings and transmitting property from one generation to another.[15] Furthermore, farm tenancy provides an income to the farm owner who reaches an age at which he can no longer work the farm.

Tenancy also has advantages for the farm operator for it relieves him of the burden of capital risk. There are many other aspects to farm tenancy, including the exploitation of tenants and the allegedly deteriorating effects of absentee landownership.[16] It is not necessarily correct, however, that the landowner is concerned only with income from the farm to the detriment of the farm itself or that the farm tenant is always a pitiful person struggling to eke out a living. Nor is the latter necessarily given to exploiting the soil disastrously in order to produce a higher income, after which he will move on to another farm to "mine" in similar fashion.

Many of the problems related to farm tenancy deserve detailed research rather than dogmatic denunciation.[17] Nevertheless it is self-evident that renters are not likely to be as actively concerned in building up community institutions or in making rural neighborhoods a good place to live in as is the farm owner. Much could be done meanwhile to improve the relation between

[14] *Ibid.*
[15] Otis Durant Duncan, "A Sociological Approach to Farm Tenancy Research," *Rural Sociology*, 5:285–291 (September, 1940).
[16] *Ibid.*
[17] *Ibid.*

landlord and tenant: increasing the length of leases, compensating for improvements made by the tenant, and arbitrating disputes between landlord and tenant.[18]

The Declining Farm Population

The declining farm population is both a cause and an effect of the dislocations in the agricultural industry, as well as a significant change in itself. As an effect, the loss of farm population is obviously related to the mechanization of farming, which made it possible for one man to do the work of several men. The increased yields of agriculture because of scientific advances likewise resulted in greater production and reduced manpower needs. Consequently there have been fewer jobs for agricultural laborers or "farm hands." Wages for farm labor have always been near the bottom of the wage scale and farm hands have thus been stimulated to seek employment elsewhere. Since farm laborers ordinarily receive board and room as well as wages, the dollar wages are not an entirely fair basis for comparison, but the hourly wages of farm workers have been very low.

The farm population has also declined for other reasons, which Gladys K. Bowles has summarized as follows: (1) the economic opportunities in urban, village, or small-town employment; (2) the educational advantages (either for the young person migrating or for the children in case of married men); (3) marital opportunities; (4) retirement for older farmers; (5) service in the armed forces (which may or may not result in a permanent shift of residence); and (6) other satisfactions derived from urban life.[19]

The gradual decrease in the farm population actually began about 1910, but migration from the rural farm to the nonfarm areas was not high until after World War I. During the decade 1920–1930 there was a net loss of approximately 6.1 million persons in the farm population. These people had moved off the farm and were still alive in an urban or village community in 1930. (We do not know exactly how many died among those who retired from the farm.) During the depression decade of 1930–1940 farmers had less incentive to move and the rate of migration declined, but there was still a net loss of 3.5 million in the farm population. Jobs were difficult to find in both the cities and smaller centers. In fact, there was actually an increase in the number who left the urban areas for the farm during this period. But between 1940 and 1950 a new trek to the city began; the net loss in the farm population was 8.6 million persons.[20] Part of this population shift began with the draft of farm boys into military service, but the trend has continued.

Despite the mobility of farmers, their movement has not been as great as that of residents in towns and cities. In the period from April, 1956, to April, 1957, only 13.9 percent of farmers moved, most of them presumably

---

[18] *"Extracts from the Iowa Farm Tenancy Committee,"* op. cit.

[19] Gladys K. Bowles, "Migration Patterns of the Rural-Farm Population, Thirteen Economic Regions of the United States, 1940—1950," *Rural Sociology,* 22:1–11 (March, 1957).

[20] *Ibid.*

tenant farmers. Most farmers also moved within the same county, only 4.8 percent going to a different county. This 4.8 percent included the 1.8 percent of farmers who moved to counties in other states or outside the United States, as well as those moving from one county to another in the same state. In any event many of those moving from county to county or state to state are not trekking to the city.[21]

Since 1950 the decline in farm population has continued not only percentagewise but in actual numbers. In 1950, 25,058,000 people or 16 percent of the population lived on farms, as indicated by Table 20.3. By 1958 our

TABLE 20.3. Population of the United States, Including
Armed Forces Overseas, and Farm Population:
April, 1950 to 1958

Year	Total Population Including Armed Forces Overseas	Farm Population Number of Persons	Percent of Total Population
1958	173,435,000	20,827,000	12.0
1957	170,510,000	20,396,000	12.0
1956	167,498,000	22,257,000	13.3
1955	164,619,000	22,158,000	13.5
1954	161,761,000	21,890,000	13.5
1953	159,012,000	22,679,000	14.3
1952	156,421,000	24,283,000	15.5
1951	153,691,000	24,160,000	15.7
1950	151,132,000	25,058,000	16.6

SOURCE: *Farm Population, Estimates of the Farm Population of the United States, April 1950 to 1956*, Bureau of the Census, U.S. Department of Commerce, and Agricultural Marketing Service, U.S. Department of Agriculture, Series Census–AMS (P-27), No. 25 (August 8, 1958), p. 1.

total population had increased by some 22,000,000, but the farm population was only 20,827,000 (or 12 percent of the total population). As Table 20.4 shows, the most striking decline in the farm population was in the age groups from 20 to 24 and 25 to 44, or the young and early middle-aged adults. In 1958 there were a half-million fewer persons aged 20 to 24 on the farm and 1,622,000 less in the group 25 to 44. These figures as analyzed further in Table 20.4 show that the adult labor force for these two age groups declined approximately 2,100,000 in eight years. For the group 45 years of age and over, the decline was less marked. It is thus the young adult farmer who is moving to the city. The older "established" farmers are staying on the farms.

The decrease in the number of farmers is a part of the social disruption inherent in the growth in size of farms and the displacement of agricultural workers occasioned by the mechanization of agriculture. The decline in farm population has in itself produced further disorganization, however, by

[21] Bureau of the Census, *Population Characteristics, Mobility of the Population in the United States, April 1956 to April 1957, Current Population Reports*, Series P-20, No. 82 (July 21, 1958), p. 1.

reducing the need for personal services in the adjoining villages and urban centers. Likewise the number of people who can be counted upon either to support community institutions or to profit from the institutions' functions has declined.

The loss of the farm population to larger towns and cities creates many

TABLE 20.4.   Estimated Civilian Population Living on Farms, by Age and Sex: April, 1958 and 1950

Age	1958			1950		
	Total	Male	Female	Total	Male	Female
All ages	20,827,000	10,809,000	10,018,000	25,058,000	13,039,000	12,019,000
Under 14 years	6,558,000	3,428,000	3,130,000	7,597,000	3,969,000	3,628,000
14 years and over	14,269,000	7,381,000	6,888,000	17,461,000	9,070,000	8,391,000
14 to 17 years	1,861,000	971,000	890,000	1,994,000	1,064,000	930,000
18 and 19 years	646,000	340,000	305,000	820,000	436,000	384,000
20 to 24 years	1,064,000	598,000	466,000	1,596,000	819,000	777,000
25 to 44 years	4,420,000	2,129,000	2,290,000	6,042,000	2,976,000	3,066,000
45 to 64 years	4,438,000	2,338,000	2,100,000	4,927,000	2,626,000	2,301,000
65 years and over	1,840,000	1,006,000	835,000	2,082,000	1,149,000	933,000

SOURCE: *Farm Population, Estimates of the Farm Population of the United States, April 1950 to 1958,* Bureau of the Census, U.S. Department of Commerce, and Agricultural Marketing Service, U.S. Department of Agriculture, Series Census–AMS (P-27), No. 25 (August 8, 1958), p. 2.

interrelated problems. The farming areas suffer from the declining institutions and from the increased per capita cost of maintaining them. Small towns and villages which have been the marketing and service centers for farmers suffer economically because there is less demand for groceries, clothing, haircuts, and other personal services. Clerks and bookkeepers face unemployment. Compared to the farmer's problems, the plight of the salaried persons living in small rural towns is often very serious. With declining sales, employers cannot pay decent wages. Yet to meet the demand of farm trade, stores have to keep open so the farmer can make his purchases after he is through in the fields. Wage rates are often less than the legal rate and there is no pay for overtime. The wage earner in the rural town is the forgotten man of the agricultural revolution.[22]

These small-town wage earners also move on to swell the ranks of industry in larger towns and cities and complicate the unemployment hazards of the labor force. In many ways the successive changes set in motion by the revolution in agriculture resemble those occasioned over 300 years ago by the rise of the town economy and the shift from farming to sheep raising in England. Then the farmers migrated to the towns and precipitated the crisis

[22] Carl T. Rowan, *Grow or Die,* reprint from *Minneapolis Morning Tribune,* February, 1958 (eighth of a series).

which led to imprisonment for debt, workhouses, and the Elizabethan poor laws. Our present insight and understanding will undoubtedly prevent any such serious developments, but even so the results of these population shifts are far-reaching.

Federal Subsidies for Farmers

Part of the agricultural revolution has been brought about by the subsidies granted farmers. Subsidies began during the 1930's when the American farmers suffered so seriously from the decline in farm prices. Many farmer-operators at that time were buying their farms on long-time mortgages and were unable to meet their payments at the bank. The foreclosure of mortgages was ruinous not only to the farmers. Hundreds of banks also failed because banks had over-loaned on farm land in the 1920's immediately preceding the stock market decline of 1929. The depression lasted until war production revived the American economy during World War II.

Farm prices sank so low during the thirties that the plight of the farmer became a national issue. As a result, the federal government undertook the stabilization of farm prices by guaranteeing a fixed price to all farmers who cooperated with a program which involved a restriction of acreage planted, a restriction in livestock output, and a program of soil building. This whole procedure restored a reasonable price to farm products and gave the farmers some much needed cash in depressed areas. The plan was justified on the same basis that the restrictive tariff benefits and the subsidies to special industries have been justified. Unquestionably the subsidies helped to lift agriculture from a seriously depressed state.

Since World War II the farm subsidies have been continued in order to maintain a stable agricultural output and to insure the production of food-stuffs so essential to the well-being of the nation. Such controls have many ramifications and have caused considerable criticism which we cannot discuss here. The controls have operated in many areas to increase production (even where acreage has been restricted) and have been of the most benefit to farmers on the best land.[23]

The Changing Class Structure Among Farmers

Wealth, education, and family background have always given upper-class rank to individual American farmers. We have an excellent example in the status of George Washington as a wealthy farmer, general, and "father of his country." The social distance between the farm hand and the farmer's family was not ordinarily great (particularly in pioneer times) except in the South, where a caste system was imposed on Negro workers. In the North, a farm hand sometimes married the farmer's daughter and later took over the farm's operation.

Today a wide gap separates the migrant farm hand from the farm owner.

[23] Students interested in the pros and cons of the farm subsidies question should read the conflicting viewpoints in editorial opinion in the *Wall Street Journal* in contrast to articles in the *Farm Journal, Wallace's Farmer,* and *Successful Farming.*

The farm hand finds it increasingly difficult to rise in the rural social structure.[24] At best he can seldom hope to become more than a struggling tenant.
In fact, rural society in the United States has become highly stratified. Wealthy
and comfortably fixed farmers tend to visualize their problem much as
bankers and industrialists envision the problems of industrial production.
Both are concerned with an adequate return on invested capital.

Despite the increase in farm acreage mentioned earlier, farm ownership has
also gone up since World War II, partly because of the government ("G.I.")
loans made available to young farmers who had served in the military forces.
With this increase in ownership there has been a concomitant decrease of
both sharecroppers and renters.[25] In 1950 there were 5,382,162 farms, as
contrasted to 5,859,169 farms in 1945, and 6,096,799 farms in 1940.[26] The
number of farm owners who operated their land, on the other hand, reached
its highest point since 1900 in 1950, when 57.4 percent of the farm operators
owned their land and an additional 15.3 percent were part-owners.[27] The
federal government's aid to struggling tenant farmers through the Federal
Security Association has also enabled some of them to become farm owners.
By and large, however, the federal farm program has widened the gap between successful and marginal farmers.

Purchasing a farm involves a large outlay, not only for the farm itself, but
for the necessary machinery to operate it. A study of family commercial farms
in Indiana showed that the machinery costs for farms ran from $26 to $340
per acre, depending upon whether the farmer produced grain, ran a livestock
farm, or ran a dairy farm. The latter required the most expensive machinery.
Such farms involve a high degree of economic risk.[28]

One reason for the precarious condition of farming is that neither farmers
nor government officials have been able to gear production to a price schedule
which will insure a reasonable profit. Except for certain well-organized
agriculturists (including fruit growers and dairy farmers), farmers have not
been able to produce for established prices, as have many corporations,
among which price fixing is widely practiced. Fruit growers' exchanges have
limited prices by restricting the marketing of produce, and milk producers
have usually operated under prices established by state commissions. Most
farm prices are established by the grain and livestock markets in large cities
according to the bids of those who deal in commodities and livestock under a
system of so-called free competition.[29] These now operate under federal

[24] Charles P. Loomis and J. Allan Beegle, *Rural Sociology,* Prentice-Hall, Inc., Englewood Cliffs, N.J., 1957, p. 192.

[25] Alvin L. Bernard, "Cultural Changes in American Rural Life," in *Rural Education a
Forward Look,* Yearbook, 1955, Department of Rural Education, National Education Association of the United States, Washington, 1955, pp. 306–311.

[26] *Statistical Abstract of the United States, 1952,* pp. 581–582.

[27] *Ibid.*

[28] Lawrence E. Kreider, "Farm Equipment Investment," *Banking, 51:*82–84 (July,
1958).

[29] *Leonard H. Schoff, A National Agricultural Policy,* Harper & Brothers, New York,
1950, pp. 138–139.

regulations, but prices are usually unrelated to the cost of production or the capital invested.

Farm production is therefore taking on more and more of an industrial complexion. Contracting is also becoming highly important in coordinating farm production with food processing and canning firms. This has been one way that farmers have been able to operate without reference to prices on the open market. It eliminates risk and is one plan which bankers favor.[30] Although scientific planning is becoming more common, the vast majority of farmers are still using seed of unknown origin, purity, or germination qualities.[31] Part of the farmer's inefficiency has undoubtedly been lack of suitable education. Intelligence and education are just as essential for good farming as they are for success in other lines of work. Until recently educational standards in rural areas, particularly in the South, were very low and this condition is closely related to the problem of marginal farming.[32]

Farmers' Organizations and the Class Structure

As might be supposed, it is the successful commercial farmers who have been most articulate. These men have become very powerful politically through organized groups and the farm bloc in Congress. The most important of the farm organizations are the Farm Bureau, the Grange, and the Farmers' Union.

1. *The Farm Bureau.* The Farm Bureau, which is most highly organized in the prosperous midwest corn belt, is closely associated with the United States Department of Agriculture and the extension services of the state Agricultural colleges.[33] It is powerful because it tends to represent the interests of farmers in the upper-level income group. The Farm Bureau has been an important part of the powerful farm bloc, which has demanded the same sort of governmental protection and assistance received by the major industries through tariffs and special subsidies to basic and infant industries. The Farm Bureau's interests thus are in a sense in conflict with those of the marginal farmers, who have little influence with the Department of Agriculture or the state agricultural colleges.

The Farm Bureau has also aimed to promote "the good life" for farmers. It has fostered organizations for farm women and developed work with young people, notably in the 4-H groups, which aim to promote permanent interest in farm life by encouraging the raising of livestock and developing skills in homemaking, cooking, and dressmaking. The women's groups strive to improve family life in everything connected with homemaking on the farm. They hold demonstrations on such matters as gardening, canning and freezing food, interior decorating, and nutrition.

[30] G. B. Wood, "County Bankers Face the Challenge of Agri-business," *Banking, 50:* 82–84, 123 (January, 1958).

[31] Mary B. Leach, "News for Country Bankers," *Banking, 51:*81 (July, 1958).

[32] *Rural Development Program,* Second Annual Report of the Secretary of Agriculture, Washington, September, 1957, p. 9.

[33] Loomis and Beegle, *op. cit.,* pp. 306–307.

2. *The National Grange.* The National Grange, which is a secret organization of farmers, is strongest in New England and the eastern states although it has considerable influence in some western states. It is technically a fraternal organization rather than an upper-class farm group, and it tends to stress the values of the rural way of life. Membership can be denied by negative votes and certain rituals are observed at its meetings. The Grange is less powerful than the Farm Bureau because it has no relation to official agricultural agencies. It has been very successful in promoting an *esprit de corps* among its members and has been more interested in the small farmer than has the Farm Bureau.

3. *The National Farmers' Union.* In order to foster effective rural living, the Farmers' Union has actively promoted better rural schools, better rural health, more recreational facilities, and full employment for farm families. To accomplish full employment, the Union has proposed the consolidation of the small-acreage farms into farms which can yield an acceptable standard of living. But it also demands that large holdings be divided into family-size farms.[34]

How far such a self-inaugurated movement can stay the tide of large-scale mechanized agriculture is questionable. The small farmer simply cannot afford the machinery to produce effectively in competition with the larger farm operator. Only by some form of cooperative sharing of machinery is the small farmer likely to survive. Primarily concerned with the low-income farmer, the Farmers' Union has opposed the proposals to retire marginal farmers. This organization maintains that it is the large-scale farmer and the absentee landlord who have driven the small farmer off the land and destroyed the values of rural living.

Because of its more radical stand on agricultural issues, the National Farmers' Union has frequently been at the storm center of the conflict between rural and urban interests. In fact, it has often represented "embattled" farmers. The Farmers' Union has demanded government loans for the small farmer. It has also promoted cooperatives and has actively opposed the corporation farm. As a result, large corporation-owned farms have been outlawed in at least two states. The Union has been especially articulate against "speculators," corporations, absentee landlords, and "suitcase" farmers (who move out from town every spring and move back as soon as their single crop is harvested).[35]

Farmers' cooperatives are also strong in certain areas where they have promoted marketing and purchasing associations in order to provide greater income to farmers.

All of these farm organizations have aimed at the farmer's economic well-being and the better interpretation of his problems. They have all tried fairly successfully to influence legislation, and most of the representatives and

---

[34] Earle Hitch, *Rebuilding Rural America,* Harper & Brothers, New York, 1950, chap. XXV, "The League of Embattled Farmers."

[35] Cf. Burton W. Kreitlow, *Rural Education, Community Backgrounds,* Harper & Brothers, New York, 1957, p. 273.

senators in agricultural states are active in support of farm programs. The farmers' organizations also serve another function. In some communities they have given farmers their only organized social outlet aside from the church and school.[36]

Farm Laborers

Farm labor tends to be the lowest paid of all labor, as we mentioned earlier. The lowest pay is in the southern states, where there are the most workers. In October, 1954, for example, the rate was less than 40 cents an hour in South Carolina and 45 cents an hour in Georgia and Mississippi, whereas the wages of a factory worker in the southern states averaged $1.81 an hour.[37]

The majority of farm laborers are unorganized and have little voice in determining wage scales or conditions of work except in the areas of agriculture affected by interstate commerce and covered by the Federal Wage and Hour Bill. Even where farm workers are technically covered by this law, federal officials are virtually helpless. It is almost impossible to enforce federal regulations upon a small-scale farmer who employs one or two farm hands for a week or a month. Rates of pay for farm hands tend to rise with other wages. But in general there can be no effective control when the period of work is so short and the farm operator is hiring in a buyer's market. On the other hand, demand for seasonal farm help is often acute during the short harvesting period. Sometimes, therefore, the farmer must pay high wages or see his crops perish.

Another seldom discussed but serious problem is that of the displaced farm laborer who cannot translate his skills to work on the assembly line. The average farmer has acquired a variety of skills in agriculture. He is, in fact, literally required to be a Jack-of-all-trades. He must know how to judge soil and its need for fertilizers; he must be able to operate complicated farm machinery; he must be something of a mechanic in order to make minor repairs. He must know how to build fence which will resist the onslaught of his neighbor's cattle. He must know "the time for sowing and the time for reaping." He must know how to store his grain, how to control pests, how to maintain sanitation. He must be familiar with animal husbandry and be something of a veterinarian. He must understand the vagaries of farm prices and farm marketing—for wise marketing will greatly enhance his income.

These skills are acquired slowly and sometimes almost unconsciously, for the farm boy learns a great deal from observation and tutelage when he is still a schoolboy. Yet very few of these skills can be transferred to a city job. Consequently the farm laborer who seeks employment in a factory often has to start in the lowest wage category. He may be clumsy at the new tasks because they are so different. The monotony of repetitious factory labor is often overwhelming to the farmer accustomed to the variety of tasks which farming

---

[36] Loomis and Beegle, *op. cit.*, pp. 310–312.
[37] Seymour Brandwein, "U.S. Farm Workers Are Paid the Least," *American Federationist, 62*:27 (January, 1955).

imposes. There is thus a great social loss entailed because the farmer cannot transfer his vocational training.

The Level of Living Among American Farmers

The level at which rural people live is obviously related to their income. American farmers live better in prosperous agricultural areas than do the majority of town and city residents. There are certain rural areas, however, where the level of living is high so far as income is concerned but which are so sparsely settled that the local communities are unable to support satisfactory health, education, and welfare institutions.

The level of living varies markedly in different parts of the country, but the very low level is chiefly characteristic of the southern states. As Chart 20.1 shows, the counties ranking in the lowest and the next to lowest fifths in 1954 were concentrated there. The Agricultural Marketing Service has conducted a series of detailed studies of the level of living in 3035 of the 3070 counties in the United States for the years 1945, 1950, and 1954.[38] The levels themselves were determined by standards of consumption which included whether farmers had electricity, telephones, and automobiles. The assumption was that electricity was an index to the use of electrical conveniences. Where all three were present there was a general tendency for farms to be mechanized and for the size of farms to be larger in 1954 than in 1950.[39]

The highest level of farm living in 1954 was in California, New Jersey, Iowa, and Connecticut. Iowa, primarily an agricultural state, fell almost entirely in the upper-fifth level of living. Equally high in rank was the upper half of Illinois and virtually all of New Jersey, Massachusetts, Connecticut, Rhode Island, and Long Island. The largest territory with an upper-fifth living level was in California but a sizable area in that state also ranked in the middle fifth and the lowest fifth. There were considerable areas of upper level of farm living in many other states. The highest areas crossed the corn belt states of Ohio, Indiana, Illinois, Iowa, Nebraska, and Kansas, and included the southern part of Minnesota and Wisconsin, as well as isolated sections of Texas, Oregon, Washington, and other states.

On the other hand, the low-level counties were also widely scattered in the North, West and East although the most serious level was in the southern states.[40] In general the farmers in high level-of-living counties owned automobiles and could easily take advantage of health, recreation, and library facilities in nearby towns and cities. The high level-of-living areas do not coincide exactly with high income areas but tend to do so.

Low-Income-Level Counties

Despite recent prosperity in agriculture some sections of the country have a seriously low income. As Chart 20.2 indicates, the areas in which the

[38] Certain isolated counties in New Mexico and Arizona were omitted from the study.
[39] Margaret Jarman Hagood, Gladys K. Bowles, and Robert R. Morris, *Farm Operator Level of Living Indexes for Counties of the United States, 1945, 1950, and 1954,* Agricultural Marketing Service, U.S. Department of Agriculture, Statistical Bulletin No. 204, Washington, 1957, pp. 1–2.
[40] *Ibid.,* p. 8.

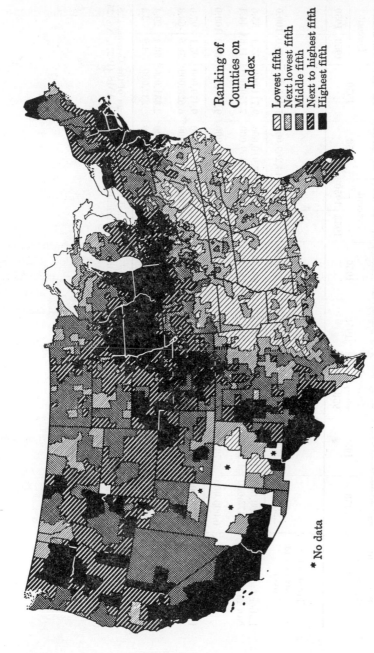

CHART 20.1. Farm-Operator Family Level-of-Living Indexes, 1954. (From *Farm Operator Family Level-of-Living Indexes for Counties of the United States, 1945, 1950, and 1954,* U.S. Department of Agriculture, Statistical Bulletin No. 204, March, 1957, p. 17.)

TABLE 20.5. Employment Status of the Civilian Population 14 Years Old and Over Living on Farms, by Sex: April, 1958 and 1950

Employment Status and Industry	Male				Female				Total			
	1958	1950	Percent		1958	1950	Percent		1958	1950	Percent	
			1958	1950			1958	1950			1958	1950
Total, 14 years and over	7,381,000	9,070,000	100.0	100.0	6,888,000	8,391,000	100.0	100.0	14,269,000	17,461,000	100.0	100.0
Labor force	6,008,000	7,787,000	81.4	85.9	1,903,000	1,924,000	27.6	22.9	7,910,000	9,711,000	55.4	55.6
Not in labor force	1,373,000	1,283,000	18.6	14.1	4,985,000	6,467,000	72.4	77.1	6,359,000	7,750,000	44.6	44.4
Labor force	6,008,000	7,787,000	100.0	100.0	1,903,000	1,924,000	100.0	100.0	7,910,000	9,711,000	100.0	100.0
Employed	5,728,000	7,628,000	95.3	98.0	1,792,000	1,851,000	94.2	96.2	7,520,000	9,479,000	95.1	97.6
Agriculture	3,777,000	5,732,000	62.9	73.6	703,000	896,000	36.9	46.6	4,480,000	6,628,000	56.6	68.3
Nonagricultural industries	1,951,000	1,896,000	32.5	24.3	1,089,000	955,000	57.2	49.6	3,040,000	2,851,000	38.4	29.4
Unemployed	279,000	159,000	4.6	2.0	111,000	73,000	5.8	3.8	391,000	232,000	4.9	2.4

SOURCE: *Farm Population, Estimates of the Farm Population of the United States, April 1950 to 1958*, Bureau of the Census, U.S. Department of Commerce, and Agricultural Marketing Service, U.S. Department of Agriculture, Series Census–AMS (P-27), No. 25 (August 8, 1958), p. 2.

farm family income is under $1000 are concentrated in the southern and southwestern states. Here the level of living is in the lowest fifth of the nation and the farm production is low. Cutover land in counties in northern Minnesota, Wisconsin, and Michigan has a substantial (rather than serious) problem of low income and low level of living.

Virtually the whole area in the southern states has low income, low level of living, or low productivity. Much of Pennsylvania has a moderately serious problem, as is true of counties in the southern sections of Ohio, Indiana, and Illinois. Many of these counties are also included in the 101

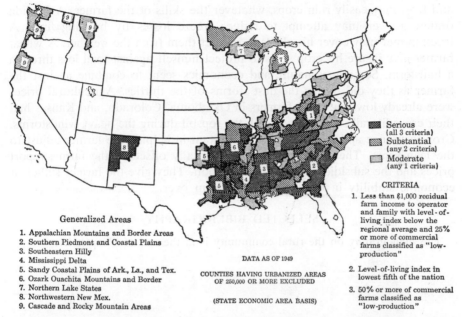

Serious
(all 3 criteria)

Substantial
(any 2 criteria)

Moderate
(any 1 criteria)

Generalized Areas

1. Appalachian Mountains and Border Areas
2. Southern Piedmont and Coastal Plains
3. Southeastern Hilly
4. Mississippi Delta
5. Sandy Coastal Plains of Ark., La., and Tex.
6. Ozark Ouachita Mountains and Border
7. Northern Lake States
8. Northwestern New Mex.
9. Cascade and Rocky Mountain Areas

DATA AS OF 1949

COUNTIES HAVING URBANIZED AREAS
OF 250,000 OR MORE EXCLUDED

(STATE ECONOMIC AREA BASIS)

CRITERIA

1. Less than $1,000 residual farm income to operator and family with level-of-living index below the regional average and 25% or more of commercial farms classified as "low-production"

2. Level-of-living index in lowest fifth of the nation

3. 50% or more of commercial farms classified as "low-production"

CHART 20.2.   Low-Income and Level-of-Living Areas in Agriculture. (From *Farm Operator Family Level-of-Living Indexes for Counties of the United States, 1945, 1950, and 1954,* U.S. Department of Agriculture, Statistical Bulletin No. 204, March, 1957, p. 21.)

most rural counties, which are discussed in a later section on rural schools.[41] Extreme ruralness, low income, and low level of living tend thus to characterize the same areas. Rural disorganization (like urban disorganization) has many facets.

Level of Living and Rural Community Disorganization

Obviously not all rural disorganization is a matter of level of living. As we have seen there is considerable social disorganization in high-income rural areas where farms are increasing in size and a smaller number of workers is required to operate the farms. Part of the trek to the city has been from

[41] See Chapter 21.

prosperous areas. A decline in population seriously affects the support of institutions. Rural communities may also be unable to maintain effective social institutions to serve the needs of their people because of their sheer ruralness. It is hard for a small population to provide adequate institutions. Nevertheless it is the economic base of the community and the prevailing level of living of the citizens that in the long run determine the ability to support good hospitals, good schools, and good churches. Where income is low, the institutions serving the community are usually inadequate and substandard.

Even in high-income rural areas, farmers face unusual hazards because their crops are dependent upon the weather. Heavy rains and floods, freezes and frost may easily ruin crops, whatever the skills of the farmer. A Florida orange grower may attempt to reduce freeze losses by building fires. A truck farmer may cover his plants to protect them from the weather. A wheat farmer may insure his crop so as to protect himself against total loss through a hailstorm. Sometimes nature and economics seem to combine against the farmer as they did during the dust storms of the thirties. Agricultural prices were already low, but some farmers in Oklahoma, Colorado, and Kansas had their crops literally blown away with the topsoil during the heavy windstorms. Crop insurance and bank loans are important in helping the farmer adjust to the lean years. These hazards are also partially offset by the farm support prices and the subsidies paid for conservation. They give the farmer sufficient economic stability in bad years to tide him over.

SELECTED BIBLIOGRAPHY

The bibliography on the rural community is at the end of Chapter 21.

CHAPTER 21

The Rural Community
Institutional Disorganization and Change

Rural Institutional Disorganization
The changes in agricultural methods and the shifts in rural population have had a profound impact on the institutions serving farmers' needs. Many of the rural institutions affected were in villages and smaller towns; some, like the rural church and rural school were in the open country. These are rapidly vanishing and rural communities are becoming "rurbanized," as we mentioned. Some of the decline in rural institutions has made for major changes in the rural way of life. In numerous instances rural institutions lag far behind those available in urban centers. This fact also has an impact on the rural community because many people desert the farm as much for better opportunities for health, education and recreation as they do to escape farm work. For the present-day well-to-do farmer, life is not greatly different from life in the city. Rural institutions meanwhile are falling behind in fulfilling vital needs of rural people in many areas.[1]

The Closing of Country Banks
One of the results of urban industrial and commercial expansion has been the decline of locally owned banks in villages and small towns. Generally this has been a matter of country banks' selling out to larger banking corporations in nearby towns and cities. An analysis of the figures for the period December 31, 1951, through December 31, 1957, supplied by the Federal Deposit Insurance Corporation showed that nearly 400 banks in places under 2500 population were merged or absorbed by nearby city banks.[2]

Although locally owned village banks were absorbed or merged throughout the country, the trend was most pronounced in New York, Pennsylvania, Ohio, Michigan, and Indiana (all states with a large industrial population in

---

[1] J. H. Kolb and Edmund de S. Brunner, *A Study of Rural Society,* Houghton Mifflin Company, Boston (4th ed.), 1952, chaps. XVIII–XXII. These chapters give an excellent detailed analysis of rural institutions.

[2] The names of banks absorbed or merged and the places where they were located were supplied by the Federal Deposit Insurance Corporation. These were checked with census data by Miss Elliott to determine the size of places where banks were sold or closed.

the East and Midwest), and in California, Oregon, and Washington on the west coast. As Table 21.1 indicates, there were 52 banks merged or absorbed in New York State, 49 in Pennsylvania, 32 in Ohio, 26 in Michigan, and 10 in Indiana. On the west coast, 12 country banks were merged or absorbed in Oregon, 19 in Washington, and 20 in California. On the other hand, no com-

TABLE 21.1. Country Banks Absorbed or Merged with City Banks, 1951–1957

State	Number of Banks Absorbed or Merged
New York	52
Pennsylvania	49
Ohio	32
Michigan	26
Indiana	10
California	20
Oregon	12
Washington	19

SOURCE: Data computed by Miss Elliott from reports of the Federal Deposit Insurance Corporation, 1951–1957.

parable trend occurred in Illinois and Massachusetts, despite their great urban population, because of laws forbidding such changes.

The absorption of rural banks by their sister city institutions is thus another index to the commercial character of present-day rural life. The relationship between the farmer and the banker is becoming increasingly impersonal. Where the village bank is locally owned, the banker usually knows his customers personally. The farmer's ability as a farmer and his habits of saving and spending constitute his "credit risk." When the rural bank is a part of a large city corporation, the small farmer must depend upon his financial standing to secure commercial loans. The Farm Home Administration (formerly the Farm Security Association) has developed a special loan service at low interest rates in recent years to meet the special financial needs of small farmers who cannot secure bank loans.[3]

The Rural Development Program

Because of the acute problems of the farmers in low-income and low level-of-living areas, President Eisenhower asked Congress in 1954 to sponsor a broad program of rural redevelopment in these sections.[4] The Department of Agriculture was later authorized to develop a program aimed both to help such farmers and to retire marginal land. To accomplish this, in turn, the Department of Agriculture launched a major research program (with the assistance of many private organizations) to determine the needs of farmers. The report recommended four main goals for these areas: (1) more efficient

[3] Lowry Nelson, *Rural Sociology,* American Book Company, New York, 1948, p. 481.
[4] *Progress in the Rural Development Program,* First Annual Report of the Secretary of Agriculture, Washington, September, 1956, pp. 2–3.

farming, (2) balanced industrial and business development, (3) improved levels of health, education, and family welfare, and (4) heightened participation in religious and civic life.[5] To achieve these goals, a committee composed of the under secretaries of the Departments of Interior, Commerce, Labor, Health, Education, and Welfare, and a number of other government officials and rural specialists was organized under the chairmanship of Under-Secretary of Agriculture True D. Morse.

THE 102 PILOT COUNTIES

The National Rural Redevelopment Committee has worked with state and local rural development committees and by 1958 had 102 "pilot" county projects in thirty states organized. (See Table 21.2.) Sixty-five of the counties

TABLE 21.2. Comparison of Rural Development Program Pilot Counties and Areas with Total Counties of the United States as to Income, Infant Mortality, and Selected Health Resources

Item	102 Counties involved in Rural Development Program	3067 Counties of United States
1. Per capita income, estimated, 1956	$1,232	$1,681
2. Infant mortality rates (deaths under 1 year of age per 1,000 live births), 1954	31.0	26.6
3. Number of counties included in areas covered by full-time organized public health services, 1956	89	2209
4. Per capita expenditures for full-time organized public health services in areas having such services, 1956		
Total from all sources	$ .70	$ 1.20
Total from local sources	.34	.88
Total from state sources	.27	.25
Total from federal sources	.09	.07
5. Health department personnel per 100,000 population in areas served by full-time organized public health services, 1956		
Physicians	.7	.9
Public health nurses	5.9	8.5
Sanitation personnel	2.9	5.2
6. Beds in general and allied special hospitals per 1,000 population, 1956		
Total beds	2.5	4.1
Acceptable beds	2.1	3.7
7. Private dental, medical, and nursing personnel per 100,000 population, 1950		
Physicians and surgeons	58	127
Dentists	23	50
Professional nurses	110	264
Practical nurses	47	90

SOURCE: *Health Improvement Activity in Rural Development Program Counties,* Second Progress Report, published jointly by the Agricultural Marketing Service, U.S. Department of Agriculture, and the Public Health Service, U.S. Department of Health, Education, and Welfare, March, 1958, p. 5.

[5] *Ibid.,* p. 3.

were separate counties and the rest were adjoining counties concentrated in four areas.[6]

The Rural Development Program's task is conceived as that of improving farming techniques where possible. If there is no likelihood of improvement, it aims to augment income by additional employment either for the farmer or for members of his family. Sometimes the wife is helped to secure an industrial job in a neighboring town. Sometimes the project is concerned with building better roads so the children can go to consolidated schools. Occasionally electrification is made possible by stimulating a power company to extend its service. Or again, a safe water supply is insured by digging wells.

Specialists from agricultural colleges have been enlisted in soil improvement. Income has sometimes been supplemented by planting special crops. For example, in Hardin County, Tennessee, farmers greatly increased their income by raising pimiento peppers. In Sawyer County, Wisconsin, they have begun raising wild rice and in Lewis County, West Virginia, wool-producing sheep. In certain areas, new industries related to agriculture have been established, such as vegetable canning factories and sorghum mills. In Alabama, better marketing facilities for the berry crop were developed. In North Carolina, women have made clothes at home for sale in local stores. These are a few of the many ways in which ingenious plans have been developed to add to the farmer's income and raise his level of living.

In general the plan has involved a balancing of agriculture with industry.[7] To finance this program there has been a yearly appropriation of $15,000-000 for loans while the expenses of administering have been an additional several million dollars each year.[8] Despite certain obvious achievements of the program, it has been widely criticized as a movement to get farmers off the land. Economically it is sound because the lowest-income farmers cannot otherwise maintain a desirable level of living. That the program involves much disorganization is also apparent. For these farmers there are many difficult adjustments to be made.

Farm subsidies meanwhile have not resulted in the decline in agricultural production which was anticipated. Because the farm subsidy program has required a restriction in acreage and the planting of certain lands to soil-building crops rather than those produced for market, a lower output was predicted. Unfortunately things did not work out this way. Agricultural research increased the productivity of seed, fertilizers increased the productivity of the soil, and farmers generally produced larger crops than before despite acreage restriction. Some persons thought that the mechanization which resulted in a decline in the farm population would also reduce surplus crops, but obviously it did not. Stabilizing agriculture by some sort of subsidy

[6] Cf. *Rural Development Program,* Second Annual Report of the Secretary of Agriculture, Washington, September, 1957, p. 111.

[7] *Ibid.,* pp. 2–4.

[8] *Ibid.,* p. 26.

would seem to be as defensible as supporting any basic industry, but the problem of large surpluses is still unsolved.

The Retirement of Marginal Land

Some experts maintain that the only solution to the farm problem is to retire marginal land. To do this one expert, Lauren Soth, holds that the government must help farmers get off the land into nonagricultural pursuits by subsidizing them temporarily.[9] This he would accomplish by offering farmers a cash payment to enable them to move to a city and get started at a new type of work. In an earlier day, the federal government through the Homestead Act and the sale of public lands for minimum fees literally subsidized the people who moved from towns and cities to the farm. Now many farmers are no longer needed because of increased production and mechanized planting, cultivation, and harvesting. This is no fault of the farmer. Soth therefore holds that it is unreasonable to ask the farm population to bear the whole burden of adjustment.[10] These disruptive changes have been occasioned by scientific and technological changes and have affected the lives of millions of rural people in a dramatic and disorganizing fashion.

Some students of rural sociology believe there are other ways out. Dr. Ralph Borsodi, for example, has tried to develop a satisfying way of life for small farmers at his School of Living in Suffern, New York. He believes that such farmers could create a desirable way of life by processing their own food, milling their own flour and corn meal, and raising their own poultry, meat, fruit, and vegetables. If a farmer did not buy food in the market at enormous prices it would be possible for him to live on much less. He might also weave his own textiles as a means of promoting a self-sufficient existence.[11]

Industrialization of Rural Areas

Another trend which has marked the decline in rural farm population is the industrialization of rural areas. The farmers who have been crowded off the land, whether marginal or non-marginal, have to seek work elsewhere. Many have migrated to the outer rims of the metropolitan areas. Here they maintain a more or less rural residence while working in mills and factories.

Meanwhile there has been another movement of city people to the rural rim of the cities, well exemplified in Pittsburgh, which has dropped in population during the last decade while Allegheny County (in which Pittsburgh is located) has gained markedly. Surrounding counties whose population is a part of the great metropolitan industrial area of Pittsburgh have also increased. Much of the farming and woodland areas has been taken over by industrial contractors who have built homes for a wide variety of people. The latter include the upper middle class (both business and professional), who

[9] Lauren Soth, *Farm Trouble*, Princeton University Press, Princeton, 1957, p. 137.
[10] *Ibid.*, p. 133.
[11] Cf. Luigi G. Ligutti and John C. Rawe, *Rural Roads to Security*, Bruce Publishing Company, Milwaukee, 1940, especially chap. XII and pp. 313–315.

buy the homes with luxury features and four bedrooms, the middle class, and the industrial workers, who desire more modest but completely modern homes.

Many of these communities have no real government outside of the township officers, but the real estate and mortgage holding companies enforce a relatively high standard of sanitation and orderliness. Schools and churches have been established with surprising promptness to satisfy the newcomers' educational and spiritual needs. The commercially built homes are virtually all sold on a money-down and time-payment basis to persons who are interested in keeping up the place and making the community a desirable one in which to live.

Shopping centers have spawned to meet the needs of this new suburbia with, however, little regulation as to zoning or types of building. The income level of this rural nonfarm community is relatively high. Nevertheless the members of the new community are a highly mobile group. Many are also economically mobile and will move on as they move up the income ladder. A few are minor executives in great industrial corporations and are likely to be transferred to other cities as promotions come.

The new communities located in various directions from the city are virtually all the planned commercial ventures of industrial builders whose major aim is to sell at a profit rather than to build up a permanent community. Indirectly, of course, they will profit if the community standards are kept high. Many of the normal institutional controls are either unorganized or inoperative in these rural nonfarm areas. Here is a new and virtually unexplored area for sociological research; it seems likely that such communities hastily conceived and hastily built will face special types of social disorganization.

Many industrial plants are also now located outside cities, partly to save taxes. Heavy industry—steel mills and automobile plants—is found in the industrial suburbs of Pittsburgh, Akron, Chicago, Detroit, and elsewhere. These industrial suburbs are often part and parcel of the greater community in every sense except that they have a separate local government and a separate tax structure.

On the other hand, many light industry suburbs are located in small outlying communities where they can have pleasant buildings and surroundings. This is true, for example, of a number of research laboratories and pharmaceutical manufacturers. In such cases workers may live in the open country or in rural housing developments from which they commute to the factory or laboratory.

Rural Institutions

The failure of open country village and small-town institutions to serve the needs of the rural population is another major aspect of rural community disorganization. The most notable rural institutional inadequacies are those of (1) the churches, (2) the health facilities, and (3) the schools. Other institutional inadequacies also exist, including ineffective economic institutions such as banks (mentioned earlier) and merchandising facilities, which are declining in small towns. The farmer often has to go farther than formerly to buy everything except groceries. There are no detailed studies of the decline in rural economic institutions, however.

The Rural Church

The National Council of Churches has no accurate statistics on the number of churches in the open country and in places under 2500 for the nation as a whole.[12] Nor do most of the national bodies of the separate denominations keep any reliable statistics on rural churches. Social institutions, despite their rural roots, apparently become as urbanized as their leaders. This appears to be true of the modern church, whose leaders are nearly all located in the larger cities. Some of the largest denominations are chiefly urban in their membership. Many of the different church denominations do not accept the current census and sociological division of rural and urban as "places under 2500" and "2500 and above." The Methodists and Presbyterians, for example, classify all churches in places under 10,000 as "town and country." The Lutherans, on the other hand, use 25,000 as the dividing line,[13] which means that they classify many small-city churches as rural.

It is a sad fact that the personal ambition of the clergy to become leaders in city churches is partly responsible for the rural church's dilemma. Rural churches also suffer from lack of financial support either in getting started or for maintaining existing institutions.

Official statistics for church members are without any classification as to rural and urban. According to the *World Almanac* for 1958 over 62 percent of the population belonged to some church. This was an increase of more than 14 percent over the previous year. This 62 percent includes *all* baptized Roman Catholics but only those formally received into the church in Protestant denominations.[14] Many people apparently consider themselves religious who are not officially listed as church members, however. According to an estimate made by the Bureau of the Census in March, 1957, 96 percent of the population over fourteen years of age reported themselves as identified with a religious group. This included 79 million who classified themselves as Protestants. Of the Protestants, 23.5 million regarded themselves as Baptists, 16.7 million as Methodists, 8.4 million as Lutherans, and 6.7 million as Presbyterians. The remaining Protestants professed identification with smaller denominational bodies. Roman Catholics who identified themselves as such numbered 30.7 million. The Jews over fourteen years of age totaled 3.9 million. Only 3.2 million people held that they had no religion.[15]

---

[12] Richard O. Comfort, Executive Director, Department of the Town and Country Church, National Council of Churches of Christ, correspondence dated September 12, 1958.

[13] *Ibid.*

[14] *The World Almanac and Book of Facts, 1958,* New York World-Telegram Corporation, New York, 1958, p. 711.

[15] Bureau of the Census, *Religion Reported by Civilian Population of the United States: March, 1957, Current Population Reports,* Series P-20, No. 79 (February 8, 1958), p. 1.

According to this estimate, if 96 percent of the farm population believe they belong to religious groups we could say that approximately 12,698,240 persons (over fourteen years of age) were identified with specific religious groups. The percentage of active church members obviously is much less than this for both rural and urban areas, but these census figures indicate how important our religious heritage is, even to the nonchurch members. The American people obviously believe in the church even where they do not support it, and even when it does not serve their religious needs in any specific way.

PART-TIME RURAL CHURCHES

The rural churches are often unable to support a full-time pastor. Where churches are located in the open country, they often have services only once or twice a month. Sometimes they have no minister at all, but may share a minister with a church in a nearby community. Only churches located in villages tend to have full-time ministers and some village churches share their ministers with another village church. This is true, for example, of the Episcopal churches in many villages and small towns.

The same trend is evidenced in a recent survey made of rural churches in Missouri by the University of Missouri Agricultural Experiment Station in which 505 churches in 99 out of 1230 rural townships in the state were studied. These townships (which were scattered throughout the state) had no community with 2500 or more in population.[16] Open-country church services were found to be notably less frequent than those in villages and small towns. Regular services were held every Sunday in only 42 percent of the 505 Missouri rural churches in the study. Approximately one-third (32.8 percent) had service twice a month and slightly over one-fifth (21.8 percent) had service only once a month. On the other hand, 86.7 percent of the churches in the larger villages had full-time services but only 57.3 percent of the small village churches had full-time service. The open-country churches had regular Sunday services in slightly less than one-third of the cases (32.3 percent).[17]

The percentage of active church members is obviously much less than the total membership, whether rural or urban. The 505 rural churches in the Missouri study, however, had a high active membership. The percentage of participating members was 45.4 percent of the population while the membership constituted 48.7 percent of the population. Most cities' churches have a higher percentage of nonparticipating members.[18]

THE CLOSING OF RURAL CHURCHES

With the decline in rural population, it is natural that some rural churches should close. We do not know exactly how many have closed in recent years,

---

[16] Milton Coughenor and Lawrence M. Hepple, *The Church in Rural Missouri: Part II, Religious Groups in Missouri,* University of Missouri, College of Agriculture Experiment Station, Bulletin 633 B, 1957, pp. 42–44.

[17] *Ibid.,* p. 78.

[18] *Ibid.,* p. 60.

but Richard O. Comfort of the National Council of Churches of Christ estimates that around 1000 have been closing annually for the last ten or fifteen years.[19]

Roman Catholic rural parishes often do better than non-Catholic parishes in retaining their membership. C. J. Nuesse's study of a midwestern rural Catholic parish shows, for example, a significant increase in membership from 1912 to 1949. Nevertheless there were defections occasioned by mixed marriage and children of mixed marriage, and lapses both in religious observance and in payment of church dues. This parish grew without the diversity of appeal of recreational clubs or Sunday school through which many Protestant members are recruited.[20]

Part of the decline in the rural church takes place because farmers belong to churches in a small town or village. With the advent of the automobile and good roads, the farmer can easily attend services a few miles away. Many such churches now draw a large share of their members from the surrounding rural area. Some farmers prefer to go to village or small-town churches where the service is more interesting. However, when an open-country church is closed, the farmer does not always attend church in a nearby village. Closing a rural church involves more hazards than attend the consolidation of a rural school district with a village center because children are required to go to school. Farmers do not have to go to church and often feel no especial loyalty to a village church, especially if it is of a different denomination or is a union church.

The divisiveness of denominational bodies in rural areas also means that many communities cannot provide effective church services. A number of studies of open-country and village churches made in the 1940's in places with under 500 people showed they were usually trying to support too many churches. In Iowa, for example, a study of thirty-five small communities showed they were trying to support 194 churches.[21] In certain areas, however, virtually all the residents are Amish, United Brethren, or Roman Catholic. In such places the church is a true community expression of religious interest. Closing rural churches thus is not bad of itself. Many union churches have been able to operate successfully because they have had more members and better financial support than when the community was divided among too many churches. But where sectarianism runs high many people drop off in church attendance when their church is closed.

In certain communities, meanwhile, there has been a salutary increase in the number of rural churches holding half-time or regular Sunday services. An

[19] Richard O. Comfort, correspondence, September 12, 1958. The estimate is probably a little high.

[20] C. J. Nuesse, "Membership Trends in a Rural Catholic Parish," *Rural Sociology*, 22:123–130 (June, 1957).

[21] H. Paul Douglass, "Some Protestant Churches in Rural America: A Summary and Interpretation," in *Town and Country Church*, January, 1950, p. 7, cited by Wilson Gee in *The Social Economics of Agriculture*, The Macmillan Company, 1954 (3rd ed.), p. 559.

earlier survey in Missouri indicated 47 percent of the rural churches were "quarter-time" in 1934 (in contrast to 21.08 percent in the 1952 study), and 21.8 percent were half-time in 1934 in contrast to 45.4 percent in 1952. Only 11.1 percent of open-country churches were full-time in 1934 in contrast to 32.3 percent in 1952. Full-time churches in small villages increased from 22.4 to 57.3 percent and in the larger villages 86.7 percent were full-time, as mentioned above. Since many rural churches have been closed it may be that the surviving rural churches were strengthened as a result.[22]

ATTENDANCE AT RURAL CHURCH SERVICES AND THE RURAL CLASS STRUCTURE

According to William H. Sewell's study in Oklahoma, rural church attendance was apparently highest among the wealthy farm families and decreased with each successive level in economic status. His analysis included the church attendance and membership of 800 farm families. These families were divided into four levels of living standard, 200 in each group, and the percentages were as given in Table 21.3.[23]

TABLE 21.3.   Church Membership and Attendance of 800 Oklahoma Farm Families by Economic Level

Membership and Attendance	Economic Level			
	Richest	Upper Middle	Lower Middle	Lowest
Husband church member	74.0	53.0	41.0	23.5
Husband attends church	77.9	65.3	54.5	40.5
Wife church member	88.0	72.4	57.5	33.0
Wife attends church	85.9	74.5	58.5	43.0

REGIONALISM AND THE RURAL CHURCH

The rural South (including the nine states of Virginia, North and South Carolina, Georgia, Mississippi, Alabama, Louisiana, Tennessee, and Kentucky) remains a stronghold of Protestantism. But even here many churches are declining because of financial inability to support a regular minister. Consequently many churches hold services only once or twice a month. In areas where tenancy is high the church suffers severely from the lack of financial support. This is true in the southwest section of Oklahoma, as well as in Missouri, Arkansas, and Texas. In the Northwest, the rural population is dispersed because of the size of the farms or ranches and there are also notable tensions between farmers and the town and city populations. All of these factors seem to affect church attendance. In the Middle West—including Iowa, Illinois, Wisconsin, Indiana, Ohio, and Michigan—there are more rural church memberships, but these are chiefly in the small-town and village churches. Kansas, Nebraska, and northern Oklahoma also rank high in rural

[22] Coughenor and Hepple, op. cit., p. 79.
[23] William H. Sewell, The Construction and Standardization of a Scale for the Measurement of the Socio-Economic Status of Oklahoma Farm Families, Stillwater, Oklahoma, AES Technical Bulletin No. 9, April, 1940, Table 3, pp. 29–30. (The table is quoted by permission of the author.)

church memberships and there are some new and well-functioning churches in the open country in these areas. In the Mountain States, the isolation of much of the rural population is not conducive to churchgoing. On the Pacific coast, a large percentage of the population of both town and country do not belong to a church.[24] This area is closer to the frontier and church attendance has always been lower in the more recently organized community.

Rural Health Institutions

HEALTH NEEDS IN THE RURAL COMMUNITY

The inadequacy of rural health facilities is of special concern. In fact, the lack of adequate medical and public health facilities is crucial in many rural areas. People are prone to believe that living in the country—with its fresh vegetables and milk, sunshine and uncontaminated air—is bound to be healthier than living in town. This is not true. American farm boys drafted into military service for World War II had the highest rejection rate for physical defects.[25] The rejection rate of farm youth eighteen and nineteen years old was 41.1 percent, in contrast to an average rate of slightly over 25 percent for the nation.[26] Maternal and infant death rates have also been high in the most rural states.[27]

Many of our farming areas and rural villages are without any medical facilities. Rural counties frequently have no physician or dentist, and in approximately 1000 counties (nearly one-third of the nation) there are no hospitals of any sort. In addition there are often no nurses and no special health facilities such as physical therapists and X-ray technicians. The distances that people must travel to consult a physician or conversely the distances the physician must travel to see patients contribute further to the lack of medical care. The low farm incomes in the low-income-level counties and the poor roads in certain areas are also basic factors in rural health hazards. Lack of health education is probably even more important. Where rural educational achievement is low, particularly in farm areas where the income is low, many do not understand the elementary facts of sanitation and suitable diet.[28]

HEALTH HAZARDS IN RURAL AREAS

Some people may well hesitate to live on the farm because of actual health hazards. Water supply, sewage disposal, and milk supply for the most part are virtually unregulated. A survey of rural public health services in forty-four different counties in all sections of the country in 1930 made it plain that farmers had few of the benefits of public health regulation in these three vital concerns. Only in the western states was there any significant attempt to

[24] Gee, *op. cit.*, pp. 546–548.
[25] *Ibid.*
[26] Edmund deS. Brunner and Wilbur C. Hallenbeck, *American Society: Urban and Rural Patterns,* Harper & Brothers, New York, 1955, p. 453.
[27] Laverne Burchfield, *Our Rural Communities,* Public Administration Services, Chicago, 1947, chap. V, "Medical Care and Health Services."
[28] *Ibid.*

control rural drinking water. Supervision of the milk and water supply consumed on the farm simply did not exist.[29] The health of the farm family depends largely on the interest of the individual farmer and his wife for the safety of their family's health, and most of the standards are self-imposed. In all parts of the country unapproved privies exceeded sanitary privies nearly 5 to 1. Nevertheless, health education and a rising standard of living have greatly improved the provisions for sanitary privies, for sewage disposal and dairy cow inspection in many areas in recent years.

School health programs have done much to educate children. They in turn have enlightened their parents on health matters, ranging from suitable diet and sanitation to health safeguards.[30] Certain southern states, notably Georgia and Alabama, have made great improvements which were initiated by educating rural school children. In Bullock County, Georgia, for example, a school educational program reduced the incidence of hookworm among school children from 60 to 27.7 percent in three and one-half years.[31]

THE CLASS STRUCTURE AND MEDICAL CARE

It should not be supposed that medical care is adequate in all northern rural communities. Health needs are still partially met according to ability to pay in all sections of the country. A survey of the rural village "Regionville" and its surrounding farm community in New York State showed that social class was closely associated both with illness and with treatment. Class I, "the successful people of Regionville," included business and professional people. There were 51 households in Class I, 29 of which lived in the village and 22 outside. Class II included 335 households, 186 of which were within the village, 149 outside (of which 131 were farm families). The villagers in Class II were wage earners who were able to live acceptably on their wages. The farmers in Class II had a higher average income on the whole than the wage earners. Class III was composed of unskilled or "unsteady" wage earners and farmers with lower incomes. There were 128 households in Class III, 82 of whom lived in the village and 46 in rural areas. The farmers in Class III all lived on less valuable land than the other farmers.[32]

The lowest income group in Regionville had the most illness, and the number of disabling illnesses increased with each decline in social class. In class I there was an average of 1.35 disabling illnesses per year per person, in Class II an average of 1.56, and in Class III an average of 2.16. With reference to treatment for illnesses, only 18 percent of Class II reported disabling illnesses which received no treatment, whereas 33.3 percent of Class I and 33.0 percent of Class III received no treatment. The percentage of long disabling illnesses was much greater, however, in Classes II and III than in

[29] Allen W. Freeman, *A Study of Rural Health Service,* The Commonwealth Fund, New York, 1933.

[30] George A. Works and Simon O. Lesser, *Rural America Today,* University of Chicago Press, Chicago, 1942, pp. 201–202.

[31] *Ibid.*

[32] Earl L. Koos, *The Health of Regionville,* Columbia University Press, New York, 1954, pp. 18–22.

Class I.[33] Non-disabling illnesses were also greater in Classes II and III than in Class I as Table 21.4 shows.

Whether or not one had a family physician in Regionville likewise depended upon social (and economic) class. In Class I, 82.4 percent and in Class II 73.5 percent of the households had a family physician. This was a sizable

TABLE 21.4. Percentage of Disabling and Non-Disabling Diseases in Regionville by Class

Type of Illness	Class I	Class II	Class III
Disabling	1.35	1.56	2.16
Non-disabling	1.05	1.16	1.49

SOURCE: Earl L. Koos, *The Health of Regionville*, Columbia University Press, New York, 1954, p. 51.

majority. In Class III, on the other hand, only 36.5 percent had a regular family doctor.[34] More persons in Class III (17.6 percent) consulted a druggist for advice in contrast to 8.6 percent of Class II and none at all of Class I. Chiropractors were also more frequently employed by members of Class III[35] than by members of Classes I and II.[36]

REGIONAL VARIATIONS IN RURAL HEALTH STANDARDS

1. *Rural Physician Ratios.* Southern rural areas on the whole are the most seriously handicapped. In 1950 New York as a state had the highest physician-population ratio with 206 physicians per 100,000 population and 135 in its semirural counties, while Mississippi had the lowest with 63 physicians per 100,000 for the entire state and only 39 per 100,000 in the isolated rural counties. Alabama had 70 physicians per 100,000 for the state as a whole, and 37 for isolated rural areas. Georgia and Kentucky both had 83 physicians to 100,000 population for the state as a whole and 39 for the rural counties. Tennessee had 94 physicians to 100,000 population for the state as a whole and only 36 for the rural areas. Louisiana also had a very low physician ratio for the rural population, 38 per 100,000. Utah was the only nonsouthern state with a comparable ratio of 37 for the rural counties. On a statewide basis, Utah had 116 physicians per 100,000. Other states having a low physician ratio for rural areas were North Dakota (40), New Mexico (41), South Dakota (41), Arkansas (43), Ohio (44), Florida (45), Virginia (47), and West Virginia (48). Massachusetts has the highest ratio pf physicians in rural areas of the state with 124 (which is more than the state average in 33 states). Massachusetts is not typically rural, however, since much of its rural population is nonfarm. California ranked next with 87, followed by Nevada with 79, Iowa with 73, and Kansas with 71.[37] The ratio in Nevada

[33] *Ibid.*, pp. 42–49.
[34] *Ibid.*, p. 59.
[35] *Ibid.*, p. 91.
[36] *Ibid.*, p. 107.
[37] Cf. Table D, *Health Manpower Source Book*, sec. IV, "County Data," Public Health Service, U.S. Department of Health, Education, and Welfare, Washington, 1954, p. 23. (There were no completely rural counties in New York State.)

is probably less satisfactory than in Iowa and Kansas because distances to a doctor are often so great.

2. *Hospital Facilities.* Even more striking than the disparity in the available physicians is the difference in general hospital facilities available. Here again the southern states and especially their rural sections have the fewest facilities. In 1945 the U.S. Public Health Service made a study of the national hospital facilities in 126 primary health centers where existing hospitals and hospital potentialities were presumed sufficient to provide for a surrounding region. Of these 126 regions, 17 were in the Northeast, 38 in the north central section, 52 in the South, and 19 in the West. In the Northeast only 1 region had less than three beds per 1000 population. In the north central states 9 regions were under this ratio, and in the West 1 region was under this minimum. In the South, on the other hand, 33 regions had less than three beds per 1000. The distribution of physicians followed a similar pattern. Of the 23 regions with less than 75 physicians per 100,000, 18 were in the South.[38]

These lacks inevitably mean that many rural people, particularly those in the South, do not receive the medical care they need, especially if they cannot pay for it. Others will not receive medical care even when their condition is critical because the distance from adequate care is so great. The high death rate of Negro mothers in the rural South and the paucity of medical care in certain rural and mountainous districts are evidences of the need for socially financed medical care in such areas.

The low-income-level rural areas thus have the highest number of other deficiencies. Health facilities are inadequate. No public agencies provide medical services for those who are unable to pay, as they do in most cities. There are whole counties without a dentist and doctor. The low-income pilot areas have approximately half as adequate medical service per 100,000 population as the average for all counties in the country.[39]

Rural Educational Institutions

Many critics of our educational system believe that all public schools fail to give training adequate for modern times. This is an educational issue beyond the compass of the present book. The inadequacy of the rural schools in many areas is not a controversial matter, however. Rural education has suffered perennially from poor teachers, one-room schools, inadequate funds, and poor attendance. In some states the problem is augmented by poverty, in others by "ruralness" itself. Some people leave the farm primarily to secure a better education for their children.

The draining off of the superior farm population is itself disorganizing to the best interests of the community. On the other hand, poorly educated rural people also swell the numbers of those who leave the farm for work in the city. The fact that the industrial cities recruit many workers from rural areas

[38] *Ibid.,* p. 27.
[39] *Rural Development Program,* Second Annual Report of the Secretary of Agriculture, Washington, September, 1957, p. 24.

means that such communities suffer from the poorly educated segment of the rural migrants.

THE RURAL TEACHERS

The most disconcerting statistics with reference to rural teachers is that two-thirds of the 70,000 substandard and emergency teachers employed in 1954 were teaching in rural schools.[40] Recruitment of teachers for rural schools is hampered by the conditions and responsibilities imposed upon the teachers. In one-room schools, in particular, teachers often have to do janitor service, i.e., clean the schoolhouse and tend the fire (including carrying in the fuel from an outside storage house). Some teachers report they have to haul drinking water and either supervise or cook and serve lunches to the pupils.

In addition, rural teachers often can find no suitable place to live. However, many rural teachers today are married and live at home. In fact they often drive an average of 4.6 miles to the school. There are still numerous living problems for the single teacher. In 1951, one out of four rural teachers reported that they lived without sanitary plumbing or a bathtub. One out of three lived where there was no telephone. Worse yet, rural teachers' salaries are still about one-third less than those of urban teachers. Yet the rural teacher is virtually required to own an automobile if he or she does not "board" with a farm family. With rural salaries so low, it is small wonder that rural schools do not attract many superior teachers.[41]

RURAL SCHOOL ATTENDANCE

Too many rural children are not receiving the benefit they might derive from existing rural school facilities. According to figures published in 1958, there were 17,959,000 rural children aged 5 to 17. Of these, 1,621,000 were not in school. The largest share of the latter, 1,067,000, were of grade school age. As Table 21.5 shows, there were almost twice as many rural nonfarm children as farm children 5 to 13 years old, but the number not enrolled was much greater among farm children. On the other hand, the disparity between

TABLE 21.5. Rural School Age Population Classified According to Rural Nonfarm and Rural Farm Enrollment

Age	Rural Nonfarm		Rural Farm		Total Rural	
	Total Population	Enrollment in School	Total Population	Enrollment in School	Total Population	Enrollment in School
5–13	8,656,000	8,023,000	4,816,000	4,382,000	13,472,000	12,405,000
14–17	2,639,000	2,326,000	1,848,000	1,607,000	4,487,000	3,933,000
5–17	11,295,000	10,349,000	6,664,000	5,989,000	17,959,000	16,338,000

SOURCE: U.S. Census Bureau, Series P-20, No. 80, February 13, 1958.

[40] Morris S. Wallace, "The Meaning of Equal Opportunity for Rural Youth," in *The Preparation, Certification, and Recruitment to Serve Rural People,* Department of Rural Education, National Education Association, Washington, 1955, pp. 1–21.

[41] *Ibid.*

the school attendance of the 14- to 17-year-olds—roughly the high school group—was not so great. Rural high school attendance is going up. Even so, there are too many rural children not in school. Some of them are in the migratory farm labor group discussed in connection with child labor in Chapter 10.

THE ONE-TEACHER SCHOOL

The most serious rural handicap in education is the one-teacher school. Here the same person has to teach several grades and can give little time to any one grade level. In fact, the vast majority of teachers in such schools give *all* the instruction. Surprisingly, the highest number of these schools is in the north central states where the rural income is relatively high. There has fortunately been a great decline in the one-teacher school during the twentieth century. In 1917–1918, 70.8 percent of the schools in the country were one-teacher schools. By 1947–1948 one-teacher schools were down to 44 percent.[42]

The decrease in both the number of one-room schools and the number of school districts has been equally rapid in recent years. In 1953–1954 there were approximately 155,000 public schools, but during the period 1952–1954 the number of administrative units had been reduced 11 percent. This means that many school districts (chiefly rural) were consolidated, and a general improvement in educational standards took place.[43] Nevertheless there were 110,875 one-teacher elementary schools and 25,637 one-teacher secondary schools in 1953–1954.[44] In extremely isolated areas the one-room school is still needed; where this is true, however, rural education must suffer.

SCHOOLS IN THE 101 MOST RURAL COUNTIES

In order to find out how ruralness itself contributes to the inadequacies of rural schools, the U.S. Office of Education surveyed the educational situation in the 101 most rural counties in 1955–1956.[45] This is not the same group as the 102 pilot counties in the Rural Development Program, although some counties appear in both groups. It is significant, however, that the southern states have both the lowest-income-level areas and the highest degree of ruralness.

These very rural counties were not confined to the South, however, but were distributed in twenty-four states and included all sections of the country except the far western, the middle eastern, and the New England states. The latter were not included either because they were too industrial or because

[42] Cf. Walter H. Gaumnitz and David T. Blose, *The One Teacher School—Its Midcentury Status,* U.S. Office of Education, 1950, p. 21, cited by Gee, *op. cit.,* p. 583.

[43] *Statistical Summary of Education, 1953–1954,* U.S. Department of Health, Education, and Welfare, Washington, 1957, p. 3.

[44] *Statistics of State School Systems,* Office of Education, U.S. Department of Health, Education, and Welfare, Washington, 1956, p. 40.

[45] "Preliminary Statistics of Rural County School Systems 1955–1956," photostatic report of typewritten copy of study made by Walter Gaumnitz, Emmanuel Reiser, Stanton Craigie, Mary Anne Harvey, *et al.,* of the U.S. Office of Education, 1958, p. 3. (Courtesy of Dr. Mapheus Smith.)

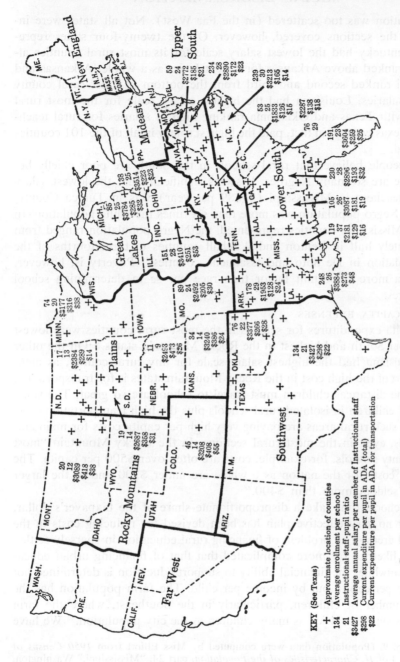

KEY (See Texas)

+   Approximate location of counties
134   Average enrollment per school
21   Instructional staff-pupil ratio
$3427   Average annual salary per member of Instructional staff
$298   Current expenditure per pupil in ADA (total)
$22   Current expenditure per pupil in ADA (for transportation)

CHART 21.1. Location and Major Personnel and Fiscal Indexes of the Selected 101 Rural Counties by States. (From *Preliminary Statistics of Rural County School Systems 1955–1956*, U.S. Office of Education Circular No. 529, 1958, p. 4.)

the population was too scattered (in the Far West). Not all states were included in the sections covered, however. Of the twenty-four states represented, Kentucky had the lowest salary scale for its most rural counties although it ranked above Arkansas for state salaries as a whole. Arkansas and Mississippi ranked second and third from the bottom of most rural county teachers' salaries. Louisiana had the highest salary scale for the most rural counties, with Texas and Oklahoma ranking high in salaries for rural teachers. One Texas county, in fact, paid the highest salary in all of the 101 counties represented.

Many people believe that rural schools in the South are poor chiefly because there are so many Negroes. It seems significant that the lowest salary scale for teachers in Mississippi ($1889 per year) was in Tunica County, where the Negro population was more than six times the white population. In the other Mississippi counties represented, the Negro population ranged from approximately half in Benton and Walthall counties to three-fourths of the total population in De Soto and Issaquena counties.[46] Poverty is, however, probably a more important factor than race per se in determining school expenditures.

PER CAPITA EXPENSES

Per capita expenditures for schools in the most rural counties were lowest in the upper South and highest in the Rocky Mountain states.[47] On the other hand, Louisiana had the highest salary scale for any rural county, as mentioned. Part of the high cost in the Rocky Mountain states is for transportation because the distances children must travel to school are so great. The small number of children in isolated rural schools plus the high transportation costs mean that such rural areas are paying very high per capita costs for maintaining schools, even in the most rural sections. In the Rocky Mountain "most rural" county schools, for example, costs are often over $500 per capita. The per capita costs for the nation as a whole are under $300 and in the larger cities are seldom more than $400.[48]

Rural schools thus take a disproportionate share of the taxpayer's dollar, and so far no very effective plan has been devised for reducing costs in the most rural areas. The problem of financing rural education in sparsely settled regions is likewise far more complicated that that of financing urban education.[49] Meanwhile, the financial ability to support education is determined not by income per capita but by income per child. The farm population has the greatest number of children, particularly in the Southeast, where the farm population supports twice as many children as the city population.[50] We have

---

[46] Ibid., p. 9. (Population data were computed by Miss Elliott from 1950 Census of Population, Vol. II, Characteristics of the Population, part 24, "Mississippi," Washington, 1952, pp. 24–110 and 24–114.)

[47] Ibid., p. 14.

[48] Ibid., pp. 13–14.

[49] Ibid., p. 14.

[50] Douglas Ensminger, "The Rural School and Education," in Carl C. Taylor et al., Rural Life in the United States, Alfred A. Knopf, Inc., New York, 1949, pp. 92–115.

far to go in order to give rural children as good schools as are available to city children.

The Cultural Satisfactions of City Life

"Nowhere to go" and "nothing to do" are the perennial complaints of rural young people both on farms and in small towns and villages. Even to attend a movie, it is usually necessary to travel from the village center to a town of 5000 or more population. Since a higher percentage of farmers have automobiles than is true of villagers, farm children may attend movies as often as village children, if not more often.

High schools in villages and small towns try to promote recreational activities through their various athletic events, plays, glee clubs, and choruses. Any thoroughgoing program for promoting interest in drama, painting, literature, and music, however, is usually lacking. State universities and agricultural colleges might do much to give country boys and girls and their parents some appreciation of painting, folk dancing, music, and handicrafts through their extension divisions.

Part of the trek to the city obviously is not related to the lack of demand for farm labor. For years a sizable amount of the growth of cities has been due to the number of persons born and reared on farms, chiefly young people, who have sought the cultural advantages of city life. Before the agricultural revolution more young women than young men left the farm, chiefly because there was little chance for the young women to earn their living in rural areas except as "hired girls" working for neighbors or as rural teachers. But young men also left the farms and villages, and an important number of successful business and professional men in cities belong in this group. Both the men and the women usually had a zeal for education. Many came from well-to-do homes and their parents were able to finance a high school and college education.

The farm boy or girl who attends college is very likely to seek out the city, not merely for the job opportunities but because of a desire to hear good music, to see art exhibits, to attend the theater, and to hear an occasional lecture. Here, too, is access to the great libraries. Those who go into business also seek out the city, where they can have some of its cultural advantages. As Carl T. Rowan has said, it is not only the agricultural revolution which has increased the urban population. There has also been a "cultural revolution."[51]

Conclusion

The disorganization inherent in both the mechanization of agriculture and the reallocation of a sizable share of the farm population does not mean that agriculture is a declining industry. On the contrary, science has greatly increased agricultural production in the United States. Meanwhile farm ma-

[51] Carl T. Rowan, *Grow or Die,* reprint from *Minneapolis Morning Tribune,* February, 1958 (sixth and eighth of a series). This series gives an illuminating picture of the farm problem in the Northwest.

chinery has become very expensive and it requires a high capital outlay for the successful farmer to carry on his operations. In consequence many farms of relatively low productivity are no longer capable of producing a decent living for their operators. Such farmers are being driven from the land while the life of those who remain on the farm has been increasingly urbanized. More and more rural institutions have been transferred to villages and towns, but rural religious, health, and educational facilities are on the whole inadequate when compared with either desirable or urban standards. The impact of the agricultural revolution also means that such institutions serve smaller populations than previously. There are many maladjustments in present-day rural life. Farming is in a state of transition from a family enterprize to a commercialized industry.

SELECTED BIBLIOGRAPHY

Bernard, Alvin L., "Cultural Changes in American Rural Life," in *Rural Education: A Forward Look,* Yearbook, 1955, Department of Rural Education, National Education Association, Washington, 1955, pp. 306–311. The cultural changes which have come about in American rural life are well analyzed.

Bowles, Gladys K., "Migration Patterns of Rural-Farm Population, Thirteen Economic Regions of the United States, 1940–1950," *Rural Sociology, 22:*1–11 (March, 1957). This is an excellent analysis of the changes in the rural population during the decade 1940–1950.

Bureau of the Census, *Population Characteristics, Mobility of the Population in the United States, April 1956 to April 1957, Current Population Reports,* Series P-20, No. 82 (July 21, 1958). This report shows the trends in population shift from rural to urban areas.

Duncan, Otis Dudley, and Reiss, Albert J., *Social Character of Urban and Rural Communities,* John Wiley and Sons, Inc., New York, 1958. An excellent analysis is made of census data relating to the social characteristics of the rural and urban populations.

Duncan, Otis Durant, "A Sociological Approach to Farm Tenancy Research," *Rural Sociology, 5:*285–291 (September, 1940). Farm tenancy is not always associated with rural disorganization (as this article indicates). Farm ownership and retirement property inheritance often make tenancy more or less inevitable.

Gaumnitz, Walter, Reiser, Emmanuel, Craigie, Stanton, Harvey, Mary Anne, *et al.,* *Statistics of Rural County Systems 1955–1956,* U.S. Office of Education, Washington, 1958. Rural educational institutions and their problems are particularly well analyzed.

Gee, Wilson, *The Social Economics of Agriculture,* The Macmillan Company, New York, 1954. This is one of the best texts in rural sociology.

Health Manpower Source Book, Sec. IV, "County Data," Public Health Service, U.S. Department of Health, Education, and Welfare, Washington, 1954. This important health survey shows health needs to be greatest in the low-income and most rural counties.

Kolb, J. H., and Brunner, Edmund deS., *A Study of Rural Society,* Houghton Mifflin Company, Boston, 1952. This book contains some especially good chapters on rural institutions.

Loomis, Charles P., and Beegle, J. Allan, *Rural Sociology,* Prentice-Hall, Inc., Englewood Cliffs, N.J., 1957. In this recent text in rural sociology the material on the rural class structure is particularly good.

Rural Development Program, Second Annual Report of the Secretary of Agriculture, Washington, September, 1957. This and subsequent reports should be consulted for information with reference to the government's program for the rural people in low-income areas.

Schickele, Rainer, *Farm Tenure in Iowa,* Iowa AES Bulletin 356, Ames, 1937. This bulletin gives an excellent picture of the farm tenant problem during the thirties in Iowa.

Smith, T. Lynn, *The Sociology of Rural Life,* Harper & Brothers, New York, 1947. This book has some excellent material on the sharecropper's problem.

Soth, Lauren, *Farm Trouble,* Princeton University Press, Princeton, 1957. This book contains an interesting proposal for helping farmers get off marginal land.

Wood, G. B., "County Bankers Face the Challenge of Agri-business," *Banking,* 50:82–84, 123 (January, 1958). This article shows the importance of bank financing and the need for helping farmers eliminate risks by coordinating their production with the processing of agricultural products.

CHAPTER 22

Political Corruption

The Nature of Political Corruption

Modern political corruption is part of the larger process of social disorganization. The institutions of a preindustrial society have partially broken down under the impact of social change. The traditional forms of democratic local government were established in a society where social mobility was limited, the population was homogeneous, and the majority of citizens was interested in the central social and political problems. The consensus of the community could find adequate expression through the mechanisms of local government in an earlier day, but this is becoming increasingly difficult. In addition to symbolizing the breakdown of a traditional social order, political corruption augments other elements of social disorganization.[1]

Political corruption in a technical sense is the willful exploitation of political office or opportunity for personal gain. Corruption involves an unlawful act (or failure to act) and a tangible or intangible benefit. The corrupt individual defines the situation in terms of personal aggrandizement, rather than community service. The machinery of government is manipulated in the interests of predatory groups. Politicians, criminals, and businessmen employ the resources of the community for their own ends, rather than for those of the general welfare. The civic conscience has changed under the impact of social disorganization. The political structure both reflects and causes this ethical change.[2]

Political corruption is an expression of a breakdown in community attitudes and structures. Corruption is not confined to political figures, who may, indeed, have higher ethical standards than many persons not actively engaged in government.[3] Many business and professional leaders, smugly entrenched behind an impregnable barrier of civic virtue, exhibit the same attitudes toward the welfare of the community as do their less respected fellow citizens. The individual who dodges his local taxes is in effect contributing to this general attitude of political irresponsibility. Political corruption is in a sense

[1] Robert E. L. Faris, *Social Disorganization,* The Ronald Press Company, New York, 1948, p. 369.

[2] Charles P. Taft, "What Is the Civic Conscience?" *Annals of the American Academy of Political and Social Science, 280:*142–148 (March, 1952).

[3] William H. Young, "Governors, Mayors, and Community Ethics," *Annals of the American Academy of Political and Social Science, 280:*47–50 (March, 1952).

a product of the mores of an acquisitive society, where financial values are predominant and the pragmatic sanction of behavior lies in its pecuniary success.[4]

The institutional studies of F. Stuart Chapin throw additional light upon the nature of political corruption. He suggests that the local political structure may be viewed as a group of related institutions of varying degrees of legality. These institutions fall into three categories: (1) the traditional legal institutions which comprise the formal structure of local government; (2) the quasi-legal institutions which comprise the hierarchy of political parties, recognized by law but skirting the fringes of legality in their activities; (3) the extralegal institutions forming the invisible government of the city. The most important of these are the predatory business groups, the corrupt politicians, the grafting policemen, the vice and gambling interests, the racketeers, and the criminals.[5]

The elements in the extralegal institutions are the "natural" products of certain elements in human behavior. The process by which personality arises out of social interaction brings about certain difficulties. The majority of persons profess codes and sanctions which they zealously support publicly but often conveniently forget. The personalities of these people are not fully integrated about a central pattern of social values. They are often easily manipulated by a few determined and highly integrated men, whose personality structures are based upon corrupt and antisocial values. The institutions of the underworld, which provide the resources for the corrupt political organization, are patronized by many of the unintegrated members of the general public. The symbiosis of crime, vice, and political corruption is thus supported by the appetites of those members of the general public who are, in the words of Mark Antony, "honorable men." The political boss, the powerful racketeer, and the commercialized vice operator exploit the habits of these unintegrated persons.[6]

It has been suggested that in political corruption the difficulty is not one of social *disorganization* but rather of social *organization*. This position maintains that we can hardly speak of social disorganization in connection with the tightly organized institutional structure of the underworld and marginal upperworld. Commenting upon the nature of these structures, Whyte indicates that "in every group there . . . [is] a hierarchical structure of social relations binding the individuals to one another and . . . the groups . . . [are] also hierarchically related to one another."[7] This "hierarchical structure" is the organization which, in furtherance of its purposes, is so efficient. Such organizations have grown up to answer the political and social needs of large groups

[4] Peter H. Odegard, "Corruption: Political: United States," *Encyclopaedia of the Social Sciences,* The Macmillan Company, New York, 1934.

[5] F. Stuart Chapin, *Contemporary American Institutions,* Harper & Brothers, New York, 1935, chaps. 3 and 4.

[6] *Ibid.,* pp. 43–47.

[7] William F. Whyte, *Street Corner Society,* University of Chicago Press, Chicago, 1955 (rev. ed.), p. viii.

of people in the metropolitan centers. Nevertheless, it is the disorganization of the traditional sociopolitical structures which has provided the need for these new structures.

Political Corruption and Social Structure

Political corruption may be observed in the relationship between the political machine and the social structure. The continued existence of the machine indicates that it performs a function (or group of functions) which contemporary society needs and which is not performed by any other institution or combination of institutions. As originally conceived by the framers of the Constitution, the system of the separation of governmental powers was established so that no one individual or group could be vested with concentrated political power. As a consequence of this policy, governmental authority is so dispersed and limited by legal restrictions that no one can act on a complaint. This situation is especially prevalent in municipal government, where political corruption has operated most effectively.[8]

The modern urban community generates many tensions and needs that must be met in some fashion if organized social life is to continue. Tensions remain at a minimum in a simple, homogeneous community, where the citizens can take a responsible role in civic activities and where the problems themselves are comparatively simple. Constitutional government works fairly well under these conditions. But not in the modern metropolis. Here minority groups struggle for acculturation and political power; organized vice and crime satisfy the sexual and related tensions of the citizens; and "legitimate" businesses of various types seek monopolistic concentration. The machine provides extralegal satisfaction of this variety of needs. As Merton states the situation, ". . . the functional deficiencies of the official structure generate an alternative (unofficial) structure to fulfill existing needs somewhat more effectively."[9] These needs may be listed as follows:

1. *The Needs of Underprivileged Groups.* The first unofficial function of the machine is to fulfill some of the more pressing needs of the underprivileged groups in the large city, especially those groups whose members have but recently come to this country. "In our prevailingly impersonal society," as Merton says, "the machine, through its local agents, fulfills the important social *function of humanizing and personalizing all manner of assistance* to those in need."[10] In the early days of the present century, the flood of immigration provided a constant supply of clients for this unofficial welfare agency as personified by the political boss. The latter offered at least a minimum of help to the newcomer, with no questions asked and with no stipulation except his support and that of his friends and his family at the polls. Today public welfare services have changed the nature of the needs of the

---

[8] The following is adapted from Robert K. Merton, "Manifest and Latent Functions," Chap. 1 in *Social Theory and Social Structure,* The Free Press, Glencoe, Ill., 1949.

[9] *Ibid.,* p. 73.

[10] *Ibid.*

underprivileged in many respects. But poor people still need many things which the machine can supply (after a fashion).

2. *The Needs of "Overprivileged" Groups.* The overpriviliged groups comprise the various business organizations that seek special favors from the local government. They include such legitimate enterprises as public utility, transportation, contracting, and other concerns to which the elimination or control of competition is the primary consideration. The heads of these large business enterprises find it more satisfactory to deal with a single powerful person (i.e., the boss) than with a number of elected public officials whose powers are strictly limited by statute. The boss is in a position to make the crucial decisions and, even more important, can enforce them throughout the intricate bureaucracy of the city government. His word in these matters is "law," even though there is obviously no legal basis for his decisions. He serves as a liaison officer between the business community and the political world. His services are therefore in great demand by many of the same business enterprises whose leaders publicly deplore his existence. Without reference to considerations of public and private morality, the political machine with the boss at its head performs a function that is otherwise lacking in the modern city.

3. *The Needs of "Illegitimate" Groups.* The large city is also the center of important concentrations of "illegitimate" businesses—vice, crime, gambling, and rackets. Their services are in demand by numerous persons, who are willing to pay large sums because these activities exist outside the law. The "illegitimate" businesses are extremely profitable. They are thus able to pay handsomely for freedom from molestation by the legally elected authorities, whose duty it is to enforce the laws against them. The men who operate illegal enterprises are even more anxious than those who operate within the law to have a single person or small group of persons to whom they can go for protection. The vice lords and racket kings are just as interested in monopoly as the traction lords and utilities kings, although for different reasons. In each case, the political machine provides the structure for the satisfaction of this need for monopolistic control.

4. *The Needs of Minority Groups.* The fourth type of subgroup served by the political machine is the minority group, whose members have a strong motivation for upward mobility in a society where such movement is often denied them. The personnel of minority groups is often much the same as that of the underprivileged groups, but the needs are somewhat different. The earlier case involved the need for survival and for basic necessities. The present case refers to the need for movement upward in the socioeconomic scale by many of these same individuals.[11] The underprivileged groups are limited to manual labor, at least initially, and upward mobility by this means alone is difficult. Many of the minority groups, however, have gained control of the political machinery and have thereby opened the channels to higher status

[11] The implications of this situation are explored in Daniel Bell (ed.), *The New American Right,* Criterion Books, New York, 1955.

through the accumulation of money and power. The political abilities of the Irish are proverbial, and their aptitude for politics has been duplicated by the Italians and the Poles in many urban centers. In a society that defines status largely in terms of pecuniary attainment, the machine has provided the means for advancement for large numbers of minority group members whose movement through "respectable" channels would have been more difficult.[12]

Political Corruption in American Culture

Political corruption and organized crime are related aspects of American society. Many traditional culture patterns encourage corrupt and criminal behavior. Much of the heritage of the frontier is lawless. The early Americans often took the law into their own hands.[13] The clash of cultures in the metropolitan centers has added to the confused attitude toward the law. Many city residents are both poor and ignorant and can thus be easily manipulated. Relationships in the urban community are so complex that they are often difficult to understand, especially if one is unfamiliar with the elements of the culture that make for lawful behavior. The cultural heterogeneity of the large city is thus an added factor in the disorganization of local government.

This cultural situation likewise affects the practical working of the political system. It is difficult for constructive social opinion to exist in a community where racial and ethnic heritages are not reconciled. Until the process of assimilation has been completed, cultural values will tend to remain stronger than community values. In a slum area of a large eastern city, for example, Italian-Americans are not allowed to participate fully in many aspects of American society. Despite their most strenuous efforts, they remain unassimilated because of the barrier of prejudice.[14]

The political organization attempts to capitalize on resentments of minority groups and exploit them for its own advantage. Some of the most corrupt local machines still operate in areas that are occupied by underprivileged minority groups. Negro, Puerto Rican, Mexican, and (in certain areas) Italian neighborhoods remain the strongholds of the corrupt machine. The hostilities and frustrations of such groups are used to further selfish political ends. In these communities the organization can deliver a block of votes to any candidate it chooses.[15]

The spoils system in municipal and national government is another cultural influence promoting corruption. Contrary to the prevailing impression, the system of turning supporters of the losing party out of office did not originate with Andrew Jackson. That stalwart frontiersman merely employed this system

---

[12] Cf. Whyte, *op. cit.*, chap. 6, "Politics and the Social Structure."

[13] Mabel A. Elliott, "Crime and the Frontier Mores," *American Sociological Review,* 9:185–192 (April, 1944).

[14] Whyte, *op. cit.*, pp. 272–273.

[15] Lawrence H. Fuchs, "Some Political Aspects of Immigration," *Law and Contemporary Problems,* 21:270–283 (Spring, 1956).

more openly than had any of his predecessors in the White House. The spoils system is far older than Jackson. As a close student of the problem points out, "Patronage came to this country with the settlers in Colonial times."[16] It has since been adapted with native genius to the American scene. But Americans did not invent it.[17]

Through the machinery of the spoils system, a considerable segment of the structure of government has become a political football. Responsible city, state, and national officials are removed periodically for no other reason than a change in political control. This system is subversive of any tradition of public service, whether in a small municipality or in the national government. A political victory sets in motion efforts to circumvent the civil service system, as was evidenced after the Republican victory in 1952.

The close connection between big business and politics is another cultural influence making for political corruption. This alliance has been ventilated by novelist[18] and political scientist[19] alike, and it was a striking characteristic of the large city a generation ago. The great corporate interests of the urban community—the banks, the railroads, the big manufacturing concerns, the contractors, and the public utilities—were frequently collaborators with the corrupt political interests. These business groups were seeking special favors from the local government, in the form of franchises, tax reductions, and other privileges, and it behooved them to influence the government in their favor. In return for special privilege, the corporate interests furnished financial backing for the machine both during and between elections.

This situation has changed in recent years. The attention of the businessmen has largely shifted from the local to the national government. On the local scene, business is no longer seeking so many new privileges, but wishes to retain those it already has. Legislation is occasionally introduced at the local level to *deprive* business interests of certain privileges, such as special tax exemptions, which they regard as their just due. In this case, business mobilizes the resources of the political machine in its fight against the proposed legislation. The increased centralization of government in Washington, however, has meant that numerous activities formerly performed locally are now a function of the federal government. Hence the relationship between business and local government in many fields is no longer as close as it used to be. As Whyte maintains, big business as the supporter of the machine has been succeeded by the rackets.[20]

[16] C. J. Friedrich, "The Rise and Decline of the Spoils Tradition," *Annals of the American Academy of Political and Social Science, 189:*10–16 (January, 1937).

[17] Cf. Estes Kefauver, "Past and Present Standards of Public Ethics in America: Are We Improving?" *Annals of the American Academy of Political and Social Science, 280:* 1–8 (March, 1952).

[18] Theodore Dreiser, *The Financier,* Harper & Brothers, New York, 1912; Theodore Dreiser, *The Titan,* John Lane Company, New York, 1914.

[19] Carroll H. Wooddy, *The Case of Frank L. Smith,* University of Chicago Press, Chicago, 1931.

[20] Whyte, *op. cit.,* p. 200.

Political-Criminal Symbiosis

The corrupt politician not only assists the gangster and the racketeer. The process of political symbiosis is reciprocal and the criminal elements further the cause of their political allies in many ways. In fact, the success of certain political organizations and politicians is a matter of vital interest to the racketeer, for his freedom from molestation by the authorities, as well as his continued enjoyment of special privilege, depends upon their election. Hence the racketeer needs no urging to become an ardent political worker. In the slum areas of the large cities, elections often assume the characteristics of a war between rival political factions. Each group mobilizes its underworld supporters, and there is often bitter feeling between them. Each side is convinced that if they do not steal the election the other side will. The end justifies the means.[21]

Fraudulent practices tend to center in those areas where the minority population is numerous and comparatively unassimilated and where gangs and racketeers work in close collaboration with the local political organization. On election day, the rival groups enlist their most enthusiastic and efficient supporters. Jobs are assigned on the basis of social differentiation. The men who are involved in vote frauds (i.e., voting several times) are in the lowest level of the hierarchy, for their activities are considered unethical even by the other members of the organization. On a somewhat higher level are those in charge of the work in the precincts. Above the precinct captains are those in charge of several precincts. The local boss is at the top of the hierarchy. These workers are by no means all criminals, but the symbiotic relationship between legitimate political workers and the strong-arm criminal elements is often very close.[22]

In an earlier period, the election activities of the criminal and quasi-criminal elements were more flagrant. Landesco described some of the practices employed a generation ago by the criminal colleagues of the corrupt politicians.[23] He separated the vote frauds practiced into three main categories:

1. Irregular practices of election officials. These activities include the padding of registration books; the failure to send notices to legal voters who are known to be hostile to the machine; the substitution of machine personnel for regularly constituted election officials; the falsification, transference, and substitution of ballots and tally sheets; and a host of other irregularities.
2. Irregular activities of party workers. These include devices to increase machine registration among those whose votes can be bought; the stuffing of ballot boxes; irregular voting of all kinds; the kidnaping of rival workers; and even the murder of party workers of opposing factions.

---

[21] *Ibid.,* p. 240.

[22] *Ibid.*

[23] John Landesco, "Organized Crime in Chicago," *Illinois Crime Survey,* Illinois Association for Criminal Justice, Chicago, 1929, pp. 1017–1021.

3. Irregular legal proceedings after elections. These may take the form of demanding recounts for the purpose of discrediting the opposing faction; opposition to legitimate investigations into illegal election practices; and the quashing of indictments upon a technicality.[24]

In recent years, the election activities of the machine and its criminal supporters have become less violent. There is less recourse to open physical intimidation at the polls. "Repeating" may still occur on a large scale, however, if the party in power controls the election board which supervises elections in large urban centers. The person who is appointed to the board by a political boss will ordinarily repay this favor by appointing friends of the machine to strategic positions at the polls as inspectors, clerks, and wardens. In these and other ways, the contemporary election practices of the machine are more subtle than were those of the early machine organizations.[25]

The collaboration of the political machine and the criminal interests may have become less flagrant because of the exposure of their activities. The Kefauver television investigation of the relationships between local government and racketeers threw the blinding spotlight of national publicity upon these activities in a number of cities.[26] The newspapers, the radio, and the mass circulation magazines have likewise done their share in exposing graft and corruption. These efforts have increased public knowledge of corruption and aroused public opinion.[27]

The Institutionalization of Political Corruption

It is inevitable that long-continued political behavior of this character should become institutionalized. Mechanisms have grown up more or less spontaneously for the perpetuation of the ideals, the attitudes, the values, and the techniques of these politically interested persons. Political parties themselves are in a real sense institutions. They are concepts which have acquired well-developed structures. Even more pertinent examples are certain lodges, clubs, and halls in the large city—social organizations that arise about the twin concepts of money and power, acquire and train a body of faithful functionaries, and gradually take on all the characteristics of social institutions.[28]

The most obvious example of the institutionalization of corrupt political behavior is Tammany Hall. This organization has been a formidable figure in the political life of New York City for more than a century. It has survived reform movements and crusades of all kinds on the part of the embattled citizens of our largest city. It has relinquished its formal control in one elec-

[24] *Ibid.* Cf. also Whyte, *op. cit.*, chap. 6, "Politics and the Social Structure."
[25] Sidney M. Shalett, "They Put the Arm on the Vote Thieves," *Saturday Evening Post*, 229:43 ff. (February 23, 1957).
[26] A. T. Klots, "Trial by Television: Kefauver Committee," *Harper's Magazine*, 203: 90–94 (October, 1951).
[27] Cabell Phillips, "Exit the Boss, Enter the Leader," *New York Times Magazine*, April 15, 1956.
[28] William Graham Sumner, *Folkways*, Ginn and Company, Boston, 1906, pp. 53–54.

tion, only to be triumphantly returned to office and power by a tidal wave of votes in the next. The Tammany philosophy harbors no illusions concerning the altruistic nature of human beings. It operates on the cynical principal that most men are working for their own interest most of the time. Money and recognition are the pillars of the Tammany hierarchy.

Any classification of this or any similar institution as either "moral" or "immoral," "good" or "bad" is futile. The fact that such institutions continue to exist in the hurly-burly of urban politics seems to bestow upon them the pragmatic sanction of survival. Whatever the city, whatever the political party, a certain number of men will apparently engage in unethical behavior, provided they are able to do so without running more than a nominal risk of punishment. In this situation, we have an explanation (although not a justification) for the existence of the corrupt political machines that arose under similar conditions in different cities. In ethical terms, political corruption is undesirable. In scientific terms, it is a manifestation of various social forces in the urban community.

"The traditional municipal machine," says a close student of politics, "was a party organization, dominated by one or more bosses, which controlled the entire political process by means of physical force, economic sanctions, social pressures, and political favoritism."[29] The machine was (and is) built upon the principle of primary group control. The political leader does a favor for a constituent and the latter responds by giving his vote or other service in return. The organization with the most extensive and efficient network of such interpersonal obligations is the most successful.[30]

This pattern of political organization has been repeated, with local variations, in almost every large city in the United States at one time or another. The political complexion of the dominant machine—whether Democratic or Republican—varies with the community and the times. During the twenty years of Democratic hegemony from 1932 to 1952, most of the dominant urban organizations were Democratic, although many local differences existed. The influence of the party organization pervades every aspect of the community. Business, recreation, transportation, welfare, taxation, and education are among the phases of community life that are touched, directly or indirectly, by the machine.

The heyday of the political machine has doubtless passed, as economic, social, and political changes have modified the environment in which it formerly flourished. Individual machines will continue to operate for decades, hanging desperately to the remnants of their former glory. But the trend is against them. The yearly influx of hundreds of thousands of immigrants into the large cities has virtually ceased. The machine has thus been deprived of many of its most loyal supporters. The nation is gradually growing more homogeneous, and the local machine will accordingly lose much of its appeal

[29] Roy V. Peel, "New Machines for Old: Decline of the Bosses," *Nation,* 177:188–190 (September 5, 1953).
[30] Whyte, *op. cit.,* pp. 240–252.

to minority groups. More people are taking an active and informed interest in local government and this participation will eventually curtail the influence of the machine. The courts are being removed from politics in many cities, a trend that will still further undermine the power of the machine.[31]

The extension of the welfare function of the government has likewise fostered the decline of the machine. The old-fashioned organization was a kind of unofficial welfare agency, which periodically dispensed baskets of coal and Christmas turkeys to deserving constituents. The emergence of the welfare state—with unemployment insurance, old age pensions, aid to widows with dependent children, and maternity benefits—has deprived the machine of much of its hold over underprivileged voters. Because these welfare functions are centralized in the federal government they are largely removed from local control. The administration of welfare services is directed by specially trained persons, whose loyalties are vested in the public welfare rather than in politics.[32]

The slow decline of the machine has thus reflected a combination of factors: (1) the decline in patronage available to the local organization, as more jobs are placed under civil service and otherwise restricted; (2) the rise of the public services for social welfare provided officially by city, state, and national governments; (3) the increased power of organized labor, so that individual workers need no longer look to the machine for help; (4) the flight of millions of voters from the central cities to the suburbs, which decreases the power of the urban machines; (5) the higher level of education of the population, which means that the average individual is less dependent upon an all-powerful political machine; (6) extension of the mass communication media—newspapers, magazines, radio, and television—which inform the voters on public issues in general and those of their own community in particular.[33]

The Role of the Boss

We have already mentioned the boss. He is one of the most picturesque efflorescences of the political process in the urban community. It is he who, on the one hand, receives upon his broad and capable shoulders the vituperation of the clergy, reform politicians, and citizens vitally concerned with the public welfare.[34] On the other hand, he thrusts into his capacious pockets the graft, "honest" or otherwise, that results from the various irregularities for which he is so heartily condemned. The names of these party stalwarts have gone down through the history of American municipal government as symbols of the disorganization of the urban community through political malfeasance.

[31] Fiorello H. La Guardia, "Bosses Are Bunk," *Atlantic Monthly,* 180:21–24 (July, 1947).

[32] Edith Abbott, "Public Welfare and Politics," *Social Service Review,* 10:395–412 (September, 1936).

[33] Phillips, *op. cit.*

[34] For a controversy on the role of the boss, cf. Edward J. Flynn, "Bosses and Machines," *Atlantic Monthly,* 179:34–40 (May, 1947); La Guardia, *op. cit.*

The names of Tweed, Croker, and Plunkitt can be matched by those figures who are undermining political institutions today.

Instead of being a man of mystery, the boss is not essentially different from many captains of industry who carry out their activities under the protecting cloak of prestige. Both are concerned with getting things done, and neither is especially concerned whether the means are within the law or not. As Lincoln Steffens learned early in his career, there is often no essential difference between a political and a financial boss in either motives or methods.[35]

One of the more genial examples of the genus boss is George Washington Plunkitt, the boss of Tammany Hall during the early years of the twentieth century. He is credited with formulating the classic distinction between "honest" and "dishonest" graft. His differentiation, smacking strongly of casuistry, is somewhat as follows: "Dishonest" graft is derived from such activities as gambling, crime, and prostitution. It is in reality "protection money" paid to politicians by proprietors of illegal resorts in exchange for protection from prosecution. "Honest" graft, on the other hand, may be summed up in essence by Plunkitt's favorite expression: "I seen my opportunities and I took 'em." From one standpoint, it is merely profit from "inside" information concerning such matters as the location of certain civic improvements or other appropriations for municipal purposes. The "honest" grafter buys land near a proposed public park and sells it at an advanced price when news of the city's proposal is announced. Boss Plunkitt looked on such operations as legitimate business transactions and considered any emoluments so derived as the just reward for superior business foresight. In short, money made in this way is "honest" graft.[36]

Such jovial self-justifications as Boss Plunkitt's are plausible enough not only to deceive large numbers of the electorate but also to serve as soothing rationalizations to the individuals who indulge in them. One difficulty in dealing with these borderline violations of political ethics is that they are so closely akin to certain operations formerly conducted by leading citizens. To all intents and purposes, there was no practical difference between the highly profitable activities of Boss Plunkitt and those of the persons who invested in securities on the basis of just such confidential advance information. These influential individuals may well have been expected to condone such efforts at "honest graft" among leading politicians when they themselves were similarly involved.[37]

As one who was strikingly successful in his conflict against the entrenched power of the Tammany machine, the late Mayor Fiorello La Guardia made

---

[35] *The Autobiography of Lincoln Steffens,* Harcourt, Brace and Company, New York, 1931, p. 235.

[36] W. I. Riordan, *Plunkitt of Tammany Hall,* McClure, Phillips, and Company, New York, 1905, pp. 3–4. Another influential leader of Tammany Hall, Richard Croker, took pains to deny any acceptance of "dishonest graft" during his overlordship. Cf. Steffens, *op. cit.,* p. 238. Cf. also discussion in next chapter, pp. 554–556.

[37] Cf. Charles E. Merriam, *Chicago; A More Intimate View of Urban Politics,* The Macmillan Company, New York, 1929, pp. 61 ff.

some especially pertinent remarks on the subject of bosses and machines. Shortly before he died, this doughty champion of good government stated categorically that there is no such thing as a "good" boss. "If he is good," said La Guardia, "he is not a political boss; and if he is a political boss, he's no good." Although the boss and all he represents have been a fixture in the urban community for more than a century, there is no record that he ever rendered any signal patriotic or civic service, watched solicitously over the taxpayer's money, or appointed only able and competent men to office. On the contrary, as La Guardia maintained, "The history of political bosses is a sordid story."[38]

The Nature of Graft

One of the most important aspects of community disorganization through political corruption is the phenomenon of graft. Graft is a comprehensive term covering a variety of irregularities. These may range from a cigar accepted by a policeman who has overlooked a minor traffic violation to a swindle that costs a city millions of dollars. Graft involves the abuse of power in dealing with the resources of the government in the interests of private profit. In this sense, graft is merely a particular phase of corruption.

Any public act may be considered from two points of view in order to ascertain whether or not graft is involved. First, if the act entails a specific abuse of power it is a definite instance of graft. The criteria which define abuse of power may be legal, customary, or ethical. Second, if a definite profit is involved, the act is an example of graft. The profit may be either pecuniary or in the nature of special favors granted to the dispenser of the graft.

Community organization is threatened by the corrupt activities arising from graft. The police force, from the patrolman on the beat to the commissioner in the city hall, may become the tool of antisocial elements. The criminal and the racketeer flourish unmolested. The common citizen acquires a cynical disregard for the principles of city government in general and for his own city government in particular. He remains away from the polls at election time with the mental reservation that his own vote will have a negligible effect in ridding the city of its corrupt politicians.

Bribery and graft have long been a lucrative mechanism for reconciling moral traditions with actual practices. Laws are placed on the statute books against gambling, racketeering, and prostitution. The laws are consonant with the mores of the society, which conceives these forms of behavior as morally wrong. The laws against the vices, however, are seldom strictly enforced. Men have always been able to enjoy forbidden pleasures, provided they were willing to pay for them.[39] These payments have been made with bribes and the puritanical codes ignored. The vice interests and the corrupt politicians thus align themselves against many of the "better" elements of the community. The better elements do not present a united front; some of them

[38] La Guardia, *op. cit.*, p. 21.
[39] Cf. Chapin, *op. cit.*, chaps. 3–4.

are overtly or tacitly opposed to the enforcement of the laws. The racketeers and the vice interests have the financial resources with which to bribe officials to overlook violations of the legal codes dealing with the vices.[40]

Graft and Business

Political corruption finds its way into legitimate business by devious routes. The party in control has the power to purchase materials and services for the maintenance of city operations and to contract for new public works. This affords a favorite instrument for graft, and the abuse is carried on with varying degrees of subtlety, depending upon the power of the entrenched organization and the temper of the citizenry. Where the purchasing agent of the city has complete autonomy, it is not uncommon for him to demand a percentage of the total cost of any project or contract which he awards. In certain cases the law stipulates that contracts under a certain amount do not require open competitive bidding. Large illegal contracts may be awarded by dividing the total remuneration for the contract into a number of small vouchers and paying them to the favored firms who have been awarded the contract without the formality of open bidding.

Where a semblance of competitive bidding cannot be avoided, various methods are in vogue to discourage the unfavored firms. Specifications may be so worded that only one company has the equipment to meet the requirements. Patented articles may be demanded, under the full knowledge that the favored company is the sole owner of the patent. Specifications may be so worded that no company can possibly fulfill them. The firms outside the circle of graft may be so discouraged by these rigorous requirements as to withdraw their bids. Those on the inside, who know that they will not be expected to fulfill the letter of the requirements, offer their bids and are awarded the contracts.

Corrupt officials may also be so lax in enforcing contracts that a favored firm can introduce shoddy materials and make an inordinate profit. On the other hand, companies who are not in the charmed circle of corruption but who have been given the contract regardless of the enmity of certain powerful officials may find that the specifications are enforced so rigidly as to make their fulfillment virtually impossible.

Dummy corporations are another favorite device of corrupt officials to conceal their depredations upon the public treasury. These bogus companies act as middlemen between the city and the manufacturers of the basic commodities. They are fraudulently awarded a contract by the city to supply certain articles or services. They purchase these articles from the manufacturers at the lowest possible price and then resell them to the city at a handsome profit, without risking a penny. The amount of the profit depends upon their cupidity and shrewdness. There is no other limit.[41]

[40] Cf. Joseph F. Dinneen, "The Anatomy of Graft," *Harper's Magazine*, 205:38–46 (July, 1952).

[41] Cf. John T. Flynn, *Graft in Business*, Vanguard Press, New York, 1931.

Graft and the Police

According to Whyte, "the primary function of the police department [in Cornerville] is not the enforcement of the law but the regulation of illegal activities."[42] The police work closely with the underworld here, especially with the gambling and racketeering interests. In many districts of the city, the police are under conflicting social pressures. Remote pressures come from the good people of the city, who have incorporated their moral norms into the law and expect the law to be enforced. The more intimate pressures come from the people of the slum area, who are either financially interested in vice and racketeering or not unsympathetic to it. In terms of his own personal background, the average policeman is closer to the people of the slum than to the upper class, and he tends to think in terms of his own group. The racketeers encourage this attitude by offering him financial inducements to enforce the vice laws with considerable laxity.[43]

"Law enforcement," Whyte says, "has a direct effect upon Cornerville people, whereas it only indirectly affects the 'good people' of the city. Under these circumstances the smoothest course for the officer is to conform to the social organization with which he is in direct contact and at the same time try to give the impression to the outside world that he is enforcing the law."[44] Every slum section of every large city is obviously not a Cornerville nor is every policeman a grafter or potential grafter. Nevertheless, such behavior is fairly common. The symbiotic relationship between criminals and police is evidence that in certain communities these elements of disorganization do exist.

In the past, the police often served as intermediaries in the payment of graft between the vice lords and the politicians. There has been, however, a significant change in recent years, due to the increasing size of underworld operations and their corresponding change in business methods. The individual policeman formerly collected the graft personally from the various vice resorts and gambling operations in his district. He then relayed these funds to the political hierarchy. This was an essentially wasteful method and it has been widely modified. Under more efficient modern practice, graft is paid to a central political organization by the heads of the vice syndicates. In this way, a comparatively few persons are in a position to become enormously wealthy through their control of some vantage point in the pattern of corruption. The average patrolman, on the other hand, is correspondingly several stages removed from the "big money."[45]

Because of the tremendous power of the vested interests of vice and corruption, the honest police official has a difficult task to maintain honesty in his force. The commissioner of police is politically appointed and subject to re-

---

[42] Whyte, *op. cit.*, p. 138.
[43] *Ibid.*
[44] *Ibid.*
[45] V. O. Key, Jr., "Police Graft," *American Journal of Sociology*, 40:624–636 (March, 1935).

moval by the mayor. Since his tenure is precarious, it is hard for him to enforce standards of honesty in the permanent force, even if he is so inclined. The officers and men are often more subservient to a politician than to their own transitory superiors. In addition, the police official must be eternally on his guard or he may be hoodwinked by the dishonest members of his force who try to advance their own interests by thwarting his best efforts.

In many urban communities, open violation of the liquor, gambling, and prostitution ordinances is ignored by the police if the owners of the disorderly resorts have paid sufficient "protection." An overzealous patrolman who reports a glaring violation of the law may find to his sorrow that the violation has been committed with the full knowledge and consent of his superiors. If he arrests the wrong person, he may find himself patrolling a beat in the lonely areas on the outskirts of the city. If he protests to his superiors and demands an investigation, his efforts and those of the reform elements in the community will be stymied. It is an unwritten law that no policeman will testify against a colleague. Under such circumstances "the policeman's lot," to quote Gilbert and Sullivan, "is not a happy one."

Political corruption is thus the manifestation of certain "natural" forces in society. In American society many groups have strong needs that cannot be (or at least have not been) provided for by the legal political structure. Illegal structures have therefore arisen to supplement the legal machinery of government. These structures, rather than the individuals who temporarily comprise them, are the chief causes of political corruption. As Lincoln Steffens pointed out, it is not the individual but the system of privilege that causes political corruption.[46]

The moral values of the middle class are strongly opposed to the machine. Morality, however, is not enough. It must be supplemented by understanding. The opposition of the middle class must be directed against the illegal structure rather than the individual participants. It is more difficult to change the structure than to elect a new set of municipal officials. Yet only by altering the structure is it possible to build a system of local government that will operate with a minimum of corruption under modern conditions. As Merton has said, "any attempt to eliminate an existing social structure without providing adequate alternative structures for fulfilling the functions previously fulfilled by the abolished organization is doomed to failure."[47] The needs previously filled by the machine must be filled by legal institutional structures if reform is to be more than mere social ritual.

SELECTED BIBLIOGRAPHY

Annals of the American Academy of Political and Social Science, Vol. 280 (March, 1952). This issue of the *Annals* examines the entire problem of municipal government, with examples of social organization and social disorganization drawn from a variety of communities.

[46] Steffens, *op. cit.,* p. 407.
[47] Merton, *op. cit.,* p. 79.

Bell, Daniel (ed.), *The New American Right,* Criterion Books, New York, 1955. This symposium deals with some of the political implications, on the local and national levels, of the heterogeneous composition of the American people. The search for status by immigrant minority groups is one of the recurring themes of the book.

Fuchs, Lawrence H., "Some Political Aspects of Immigration," *Law and Contemporary Problems, 21:*270–283 (Spring, 1956). Throughout the past century, successive waves of ethnic and racial minority groups have provided much of the mass popular support for the corrupt political machines of the urban community.

Gosnell, Harold F., *Machine Politics: Chicago Model,* University of Chicago Press, Chicago, 1937. The techniques of getting out the vote are described in this volume, which deals with the relationships between the political machine and the social structure of the city.

Kefauver, Estes, "Past and Present Standards of Public Ethics in America: Are We Improving?" *Annals of the American Academy of Political and Social Science, 280:*1–8 (March, 1952). A leading political figure who, as a senator, had extensive experience in exposing political corruption and crime on the municipal level gives his views concerning the status of public ethics.

Merton, Robert K., *Social Theory and Social Structure,* The Free Press, Glencoe, Ill., 1949, chap. 1, "Manifest and Latent Functions." The political machine is here analyzed in terms of its role in providing extralegal satisfactions for needs which are not satisfied by legal institutions.

Odegard, Peter H., "Corruption: Political: United States," *Encyclopaedia of the Social Sciences,* The Macmillan Company, New York, 1934. This analysis deals with political corruption as the "natural" product of the historical and social development of American society.

Steffens, Lincoln, *The Autobiography of Lincoln Steffens,* Harcourt, Brace and Company, New York, 1931. The "greatest reporter of our time" analyzes the broad trends in American society that have given rise to social disorganization through political corruption. The author was personally active in exposing corrupt political practices in the early years of the present century.

Taft, Charles P., "What Is the Civic Conscience?" *Annals of the American Academy of Political and Social Science, 280:*142–148 (March, 1952). A civic leader who has been active in the campaign for good government states his conception of the current status of the civic conscience.

Whyte, William F., *Street Corner Society,* University of Chicago Press, Chicago, 1955 (rev. ed.). This report on lower-class urban life and politics in a large eastern city was made by a participant-observer, who presents a significant analysis of the political structure as it operated in the years immediately prior to World War II.

CHAPTER 23

Crime and the Community

The crime rate is a major index to community disorganization because it is a measure of the degree to which the citizens fail to live up to the community's moral requirements. Crimes are sometimes defined as negative mores. They are violations of the moral values of the group which are forbidden and punished by law. They are types of conduct which are considered offenses against the general welfare, and persons convicted of crime tend thus to be stigmatized by the conviction as well as by any punishment which may be exacted. The community with a high crime rate is likewise one in which a sizable share of the citizens flout the important social values. On the other hand, the community itself is to a large degree responsible for the crime rate. For the citizens in the community permit conditions to exist which generate crime and tolerate crime, and in turn the community becomes disorganized by crime. This disorganization is measured by the extent to which life and property are not safe and political corruption is rife, while the losses sustained by crime undermine the general well-being. Statistics indicate that crime rates have been rising consistently although there are limits to this interpretation, as discussed in Chapter 5. Crime statistics are now analyzed on a somewhat different basis from that used before 1957. But 1957 rates showed a rise over previous years and rates for 1958 indicated a 7.4 percent rise over 1957 as the discussion of the crime index in Chapter 5, makes clear.

Costs of Crime

Costs of crime are also an index to social and community disorganization insofar as they represent a definite impact upon the material well-being of the citizens. Statistics are not available for the country as a whole, but economic crimes in 405 cities with a population over 25,000 accounted for losses of $265,700,000 (of which $143,300,000 was recovered). Most of the recovery was for automobiles, however. These figures covered roughly cities with only 30 percent of the population and hence are no index to the total economic costs.[1]

Many losses from crime are not reported, particularly those derived from

---

[1] *Uniform Crime Reports for the United States, 1958,* Federal Bureau of Investigation, U.S. Department of Justice, Washington, 1959, p. 75.

the activities of corrupt politicians and organized crime. These losses cannot be estimated because there are no available records. The amounts undoubtedly run into far more than those of the small-time criminal, however.

The noneconomic losses can be measured only partially in the lives lost in murder, the stigma and emotional distress occasioned by rape, the distorted values of those engaged in crime. There is no gauge for estimating the in-

TABLE 23.1.   Value of Property Stolen and Value of Property Recovered, by Type of Property, 1958

(405 cities over 25,000; total population 61,228,835)

Type of Property	Value of Property		Percent Recovered
	Stolen	Recovered	
Total	**$265,700,000**	**$143,300,000**	**53.9**
Currency, notes, etc.	31,700,000	3,800,000	12.0
Jewelry and precious metals	23,200,000	2,200,000	9.5
Furs	7,600,000	400,000	5.3
Clothing	12,200,000	1,100,000	9.0
Locally stolen automobiles	134,900,000	124,400,000	92.2
Miscellaneous	56,100,000	11,400,000	20.3

SOURCE: *Uniform Crime Reports for the United States, 1958,* Federal Bureau of Investigation, U.S. Department of Justice, 1959, p. 3.

fluence of criminals upon their homes and upon the community's well-being. Similarly the extent to which dishonesty is accepted and the degree to which lack of integrity has undermined our institutions can only be roughly measured in an occasional exposé. We have reason to believe, however, that organized crime and political corruption are taking a heavy toll.

Causes of Crime

Even though the community may be held responsible for crime there is no simple explanation for its existence. Crime covers a wide variety of behavior and it would defy reason to assume that stealing from a store, robbing a bank, committing rape, driving while drunk, and committing murder were all to be traced to one cause. Motivations for crime are surely as complicated as for other types of behavior. Nevertheless there are certain distinctive aspects of American culture which explain particular tendencies in American crime. The community is to a major degree involved in all these considerations.

The peculiar characteristics of the American way of life give us a perspective on why our crime rate is so high. These include (1) our puritanical crime laws, (2) our unintegrated Negro population, (3) the clash between our Nordic Protestant norm-setting population and the later southern and eastern European Catholic immigrants, (4) the constitutional right of Americans to bear arms, (5) our love of freedom, (6) our frontier heritage,

(7) class differentials in the treatment of offenders in our social organization,[2] (8) the nature of the modern social organization, (9) norms of behavior and social values. Our crime rates are affected, too, by our criminal law, by those who make a business of crime, and by the corruption and incompetency in the administration of criminal justice. They are also very probably influenced significantly by honest misguided efforts of citizens but for these we have no satisfactory data.

1. *Puritanical American Crime Laws.* Part of the American crime rate is a function of the peculiarly puritanical character of our crime laws. In addition to punishing the crimes which are universally considered serious offenses, Americans punish behavior which is more or less condoned in many nations. We thus punish prostitution and drunkenness, which other nations regard as vices and the church in these countries regards as sins. The largest category of arrests in the United States in 1958, for example (38.8 percent), was for drunkenness. This included 908,957 out of the total 2,340,004 persons arrested.[3] In Europe drunkenness is not an offense in most countries. In Germany, for example, a person might be locked up if he were in physical danger because of his intoxicated state, but drunkenness itself is not a crime unless one is "dead drunk." Likewise there are no liquor taxes in Germany. It is tea and coffee which are taxed.

Prostitution is one of the offenses for which women are most frequently arrested in the United States. If this offense is added to disorderly conduct and vagrancy arrests (which are euphemistic terms for prostitution) it constitutes the second most important female crime. Prostitution (although carrying a stigma of ill repute) is seldom punished in Europe. Even in England prostitutes are permitted to ply their trade openly so long as they are not "offensive." In the United States known prostitutes are often arrested merely because they are on the street, particularly after dark. It is even difficult for a prostitute known to the police to go on a legitimate errand at night.[4] In Europe prostitution is more or less accepted as a necessary evil although there have been numerous attempts at times to restrict it.

Gambling is a crime in the United States but is widely permitted in Europe. Monaco's major economic enterprise is gambling, as is well known. France raises welfare funds with a national lottery, and the Irish sweepstakes are internationally promoted. In the United States 61,546 people were arrested for gambling in 1958, over three-fourths of whom were Negroes.[5] The numbers game (or policy racket, as it is sometimes called) is an especially widespread gambling offense.

Today professional gamblers are required to pay a federal tax although their activities are illegal. This is an obvious attempt of Congress to tax the

---

[2] Mabel A. Elliott, "Perspective on the American Crime Problem," *Social Problems,* 5:184–193 (Winter, 1957–1958).

[3] *Uniform Crime Reports, 1958,* p. 96.

[4] *Ibid.;* cf. also Mabel A. Elliott, *Crime in Modern Society,* Harper & Brothers, New York, 1952, p. 205.

[5] *Uniform Crime Reports, 1958,* p. 97.

offense out of existence by bringing the culprits to light. The number of persons arrested for gambling has meanwhile increased 400 percent since 1950. Part of this increase has been the result of increased vigilance of local police following the Senate investigations conducted by the Kefauver senatorial committee during 1950 and 1951 and the subsequent legislation.

2. *Our Unintegrated Negro Population.* A second important major factor in our crime rate is undoubtedly our unintegrated Negro population. The fact of the high Negro crime rate has been badly interpreted and sometimes offered as a basic reason for not integrating Negroes within our population and for denying them their civil rights. Actually the high crime rate would appear to be a more valid reason for ending their segregation. Negroes contribute heavily both to what are regarded universally as very serious crimes and to our puritanically defined offenses. There are many reasons for Negro crime, but we can be reasonably sure that the subculture in which Negroes are forced to live is to a major degree responsible for their high rate. A much larger percentage of Negroes than white persons are in the lower economic and social strata, and as a group Negroes have a much lower educational achievement than is true for white people.

It is also frequently alleged that the high rate exists because Negroes are more likely to be arrested and punished for crimes because of racial prejudice, but this is only partly true. Negroes actually commit many serious crimes. A large number of these are offenses against Negroes which are never reported, and a considerable share of known serious Negro crimes never are punished in areas where Negroes are not allowed to "clutter up" the white man's courts. A study of serious crimes committed in Houston, Texas, some years ago illustrated this very point.[6]

Statistics for arrests show that despite these unreported crimes Negroes commit a disproportionate share of serious and violent crimes for which any citizen would be arrested—if known. Negroes constitute slightly less than 10 percent of our population, but in 1958 they were arrested for approximately 62 percent of the murder and nonnegligent manslaughter cases, as Table 23.2 shows. They also constituted over half of those arrested for possessing or carrying weapons without a license. They were involved in over half of the arrests for robbery, almost two-thirds of those for aggravated assault, slightly more than 30 percent of the arrests for larceny, approximately 48 percent of those for forcible rape, and over 45 percent of those for prostitution. They also constituted 57 percent of those arrested on narcotics charges and over 75 percent of those arrested for gambling.[7] These are considered serious offenses and arrests are usually made either on sworn warrants or when "caught in the act."

Even so, prejudice is probably an important factor, since the second-class

[6] John D. Bowles, "Comparative Analysis of 100 Negro Offenders and 100 White Offenders Brought Before the Court of Harris County, State of Texas," Master's thesis, University of Kansas Library, 1933.

[7] *Uniform Crime Reports, 1958,* p. 97. (Percentages computed by Miss Elliott.)

citizenship to which so many Negroes are condemned has its roots in prejudice, and this segregated status very likely leads to their high crime rates. The
housing in most urban Negro districts is appalling, as we discuss later in
Chapter 28 and these deteriorated areas harbor many other undesirable in-

TABLE 23.2. Arrests by Race, 1958, 1,586 Cities Over 2,500, Total Population 52,329,497

Offense Charged	Total	Race					
		White	Negro	Indian	Chi-nese	Japa-nese	All Others
Total	2,340,004	1,583,070	696,209	43,126	1,252	296	16,051
Criminal homicide:							
(a) Murder and non-negligent man-slaughter	2,303	840	1,427	8	2	2	24
(b) Manslaughter by negligence	1,166	904	245	7	2	—	8
Robbery	14,968	6,732	8,034	72	7	—	123
Aggravated assault	25,824	9,073	16,389	75	5	2	280
Other assaults	82,454	45,840	35,733	311	26	4	540
Burglary—breaking or entering	61,045	41,754	18,623	343	27	1	297
Larceny—theft	118,325	80,292	36,642	678	57	13	643
Auto theft	30,240	23,691	6,135	227	31	7	149
Embezzlement and fraud	19,489	15,618	3,782	48	1	2	38
Stolen property; buying, receiving, etc.	5,504	3,666	1,765	23	1	—	49
Forgery and counterfeiting	11,317	9,580	1,653	52	9	3	20
Forcible rape	3,680	1,821	1,797	9	—	—	53
Prostitution and commercialized vice	17,482	9,194	7,885	110	20	7	266
Other sex offenses (includes statutory rape)	24,517	17,079	7,058	105	14	8	253
Narcotic drug laws	9,863	3,807	5,740	17	34	4	261
Weapons, carrying, possessing, etc.	18,611	8,678	9,693	56	13	4	167
Offenses against family and children	23,701	15,118	8,378	71	7	—	127
Liquor laws	52,707	34,158	17,877	453	21	10	188
Driving while intoxicated	102,219	84,640	16,068	1,008	16	16	471
Disorderly conduct	281,997	161,721	115,171	2,301	83	17	2,704
Drunkenness	908,957	673,894	195,051	33,017	297	128	6,570
Vagrancy	88,351	64,665	20,950	1,929	97	24	686
Gambling	61,546	13,820	46,767	3	341	8	607
Suspicion	96,740	63,231	32,711	579	42	10	167
All other offenses	276,998	193,254	80,635	1,624	99	26	1,360

SOURCE: *Uniform Crime Reports, 1958,* Federal Bureau of Investigation, U.S. Department of Justice, 1959, p. 97.

fluences. Segregation also generates much of the bitterness and frustration which are responsible for countless violent crimes. Part of the explanation undoubtedly lies in the sordid economic and social environment with its accepted patterns of criminal conduct. Where Negroes constitute the bulk of the population, as in Mississippi, reported crime rates are less.[8]

Nevertheless we cannot say with true scientific accuracy why Negroes commit more serious and violent crimes than white people of relatively similar economic and social status. Psychiatric and psychological research in the area of Negro crime is largely lacking. On the other hand, we know that crime is very low among the upper-class well-educated Negroes. Upper-class Negroes try hard to enforce respectable standards of conduct.

Dr. Franklin Frasier, the eminent Negro sociologist, has maintained that upper-class and highly educated Negroes pay no attention to the problems of less favorably situated Negroes.[9] This is unfortunate because it creates resentment on the part of Negroes who feel their own race is uninterested in their problems and has deserted them.

Do lack of education and lack of identification with the norms and values of middle-class American society account for the high Negro crime rate? It seems likely that this is true and that it is the segregated subculture in which lower-class Negroes live which is basically responsible for their high crime rate. Dr. Hans von Hentig has maintained, however, that the high Negro murder rate is a function of the distorted sex ratio.[10] There are more Negro women than men because of the high death rate of Negro men, particularly those under thirty-five.

In 1950 there were only 92.6 nonwhite males 15 to 39 years of age for every 100 females.[11] Jealousy derived from scarcity of men Dr. von Hentig believes to be a major factor in Negro murder—but this has not been proved. There are undoubtedly other factors. The whole problem of Negro crime has many ramifications which only a cooperating team of sociologists, psychologists, biologists, and physicians can penetrate effectively. It should be a challenge to the best-trained researchers of both races, since it is a problem which affects us all. Certainly there is need for our educated Negroes to take an active part in the research.

The Indian population also contributes a disproportionate number of offenders, mostly for drunkenness. Over 10 percent of the Indian population is involved in arrests. The high Indian crime rate also represents a maladjusted minority group situation. However, Indians do not bulk large in our total rate.

3. *Culture Conflict.* Another major factor in our crime rate has been the cultural conflict between "old stock" American Nordic Protestants and the

---

[8] Austin L. Porterfield and Robert H. Talbert, *Crime, Suicide and Social Well-Being,* Leo Potishman Foundation, Fort Worth, 1948, p. 38.

[9] E. Franklin Frazier, *Black Bourgeoisie,* The Free Press, Glencoe, Ill., 1957, p. 235.

[10] Hans von Hentig, "The Criminality of the Negro," *Journal of Criminal Law and Criminology, 30*:662–680 (January–February, 1940).

[11] *1950 United States Census of the Population,* U.S. Department of Commerce, Washington, 1953, No. 1, pp. 76–77.

population of southern and eastern European Roman Catholic derivation. Many studies have also shown that those of the Mediterranean and eastern European stock have contributed far more crimes than recent immigrants from northern Europe. Courtland C. Van Vechten's study in 1941 indicated, however, that older foreign-born men had a very low crime rate and were more law-abiding than the native born. It was the *young* foreign-born men who got in trouble and these had a considerably higher rate than our native-born young men.[12] Youth is a major factor in crime in all countries, but where there is cultural adjustment in addition crime rates are apparently likely to be higher. Crime rates of selected foreign-born groups were studied in 1930 by the National Commission on Law Observance and Enforcement. While there was variation from city to city, certain groups (Italian, Greek, and Slavic immigrants) had the highest crime rates of any population groups. Thus there were 3057 Czechoslovakians out of every 10,000 of this nationality arrested in Akron, Ohio, that year, and 1366 out of every 10,000 Italians. In Jersey City 1579 Greeks out of 10,000 were arrested, as was true of 1278 Greeks in Cincinnati. On the other hand, only 4 out of 10,000 British were arrested in Cincinnati and only 49 in Akron.[13] Of course the southeastern Europeans were often handicapped by poverty, but it seems obvious that cultural conflict conditioned the tendency to be arrested. The fact that we were living under prohibition laws at the time undoubtedly increased the crime rate. Offenses against the Volstead Act were high during this period. Some persons who were natives of countries where drinking liquor and wines was a culture trait were more or less bound to break the law in America.[14] The vast majority of southern and eastern Europeans were law-abiding even so, but these disparities in crime rates are undoubtedly related to difficulties in adjusting to a new culture.

4. *The Right to Bear Arms.* Our constitutional right to bear arms accounts for many crimes. This particular right appears to be an anachronism held over from colonial and pioneer society when dangers from Indians and the wild animals on the frontier may have seemed to justify it. The Constitution was enacted shortly after the American Revolution and some persons undoubtedly believed that an armed citizenry was a defense against a tyrannical government. No other civilized country permits ordinary civilians to carry arms. The possession of arms is largely responsible for our adult crimes of violence: murders, especially those among Negroes, occur over seemingly minor problems; many emotional explosions would not result in murder if there were no revolvers, rifles, or shotguns available. If the American public wishes to reduce crimes of violence a constitutional amendment is in order

[12] Courtland C. Van Vechten, "The Criminality of the Foreign Born," *Journal of Criminal Law and Criminology, 32:*139–147 (July–August, 1941).

[13] Cf. Table 2–A, *Report on Crime and the Foreign Born* (Report 10), National Commission on Law Observance and Enforcement, Washington, 1931, p. 101.

[14] Elliott, *Crime in Modern Society,* pp. 289–297.

prohibiting the unregulated manufacture of guns of all sorts and the sale of such weapons to civilians. We see fit to restrict fireworks because of the danger. Firearms appear to be a far more serious source of death, injury, and crime.

5. *Our Frontier Heritage.* Another important cultural aspect of the crime problem is love of freedom, which is part of our frontier heritage. The colonies were still pioneer territories when they revolted against the tyranny of the mother country, and Americans have always believed in as little governmental regulation as possible although the trend has been toward increasing regulation in recent years. The vast open spaces and sparsely settled land made possible a high degree of freedom from restraint in pioneer times. The backwoods country of America was invaded before any institutions of law and order were established, and even when territorial governments were established only a minimum of restraint was imposed. Most of those who opened up the West were interested in abiding by the generally accepted rules and regulations relating to private property and concepts of honor and decency. But even during the colonial period a lawless, adventurous element had sought out the frontier. Outlaws from Virginia escaped to the less settled areas in North Carolina. Later these and others pushed over the mountains to the West. Following the revolution the Northwest Territory was opened up.

The Louisiana purchase later stimulated settlement beyond the Mississippi and soon the Middle West became a relatively peaceful cooperative community. Farther west in the plains and mountain states was the "wild West" where some men came honestly to wrest a fortune from the silver and gold mines or to raise cattle in the Great Plains. But here too came the outlaw, the escaped convict, and the desperado. Stagecoach robberies and holdups at the end of the cattle trail became legendary. Some of these gunmen took on the character of quasi heroes, but they were deadly enemies of those who were interested in peaceful pursuits. The lynch law of the frontier (both in North Carolina and among the "vigilantes" of the West) became the organized protest of decent men trying to enforce their conceptions of the "common law" upon the western settlements.

Eventually the orderly processes of governmental control were established, legislatures were elected and there was no need for citizens to "take the law in their own hands." Likewise the free lands (or those which sold for a dollar and a quarter an acre) were exhausted. There was no longer an opportunity for any who chose to stake a claim and wrest a living from the soil. With the closing of the frontier came urban expansion. In the industrial cities native born and immigrants were offered a chance to make a living in factory or mill, while others sought employment in the development of the mining industry. With this new life freedom was restricted. Injustices occurred on the labor scene. With the exhaustion of free lands the dissatisfied urban worker could not turn to the soil for a living nor could he move on because living conditions were distasteful. As Frederick L. Turner has said, with the closing of the frontier Americans turned from the land to the law for security.[15] In this, of course, Europe offered us many examples. But out of the new situation created by large-scale industrial employment a great variety of restraining laws were enacted in the United States.

The new laws have created a new set of crimes while restraining undesirable business practices and extending the rights and welfare of workers. Tax laws have produced crimes of tax evasion. Conspiracy laws have been expanded to include restraint of trade and to forbid monopolistic practices and price fixing. A whole new category of what Sutherland has called the "white collar criminal" has thus emerged.[16] Americans chafe at the restriction these laws impose. Many businessmen who violate such laws consider the *laws* wrong (and *not* their conduct). Hence instead of repealing laws (where they seem inoperable) we challenge them in the courts. Our law schools train lawyers in the art of finding loopholes in the law and thus "protect the citizen against the law-makers."

We thus have Americans acting upon the curious belief that they can "pick and choose" which laws they will obey instead of trying to obtain the repeal of unsatisfactory laws. Industrial corporations in particular have opposed the new laws, especially those purporting to help the masses. The supporters of the new legislation have been denounced as "do-gooders," as though doing good were a naïve and grievous thing. The lawless conduct of wealthy and respected citizens has many facets but it shows a striking lack of concern for human welfare which has much in common with that of the outlaw on the frontier. Meanwhile we are fast becoming a welfare state and so have created much confusion in social values and a vague definition of antisocial conduct.

We also are taking another new direction. Powerful government officials in recent years have often sought to prevent individuals who were accused of affiliation with Communists from asserting their constitutional rights. The invocation of the Fifth Amendment, which provides that no one can be required to testify against himself, has been considered literal evidence of guilt. We are on the verge of a new area, but it seems likely that our freedoms will be further restricted if fear of Communism continues. Here is another perspective on the problem of freedom and crime which needs further exploration.[17]

7. *Class Differentials in Treatment of Offenders.* We are led to believe that there are important differentials in punishing offenders against the law. For obvious reasons middle-class and upper-class people commit fewer per-

[15] Frederick L. Turner, *The Frontier in American History,* Henry Holt and Company, Inc., New York, 1920, p. 32. Cf. also Mabel A. Elliott, "Crime and the Frontier Mores," *American Sociological Review,* 9:185–192 (April, 1944). (Most of this discussion of the frontier is derived from Miss Elliott's article.)

[16] Cf. Edwin H. Sutherland, *White Collar Crime,* The Dryden Press, Inc., New York, 1949, for a detailed discussion.

[17] This section has been largely derived from Mabel A. Elliott, "Perspective on the American Crime Problem," *Social Problems,* 5:184–193 (Winter, 1957–1958).

sonal thefts. Nevertheless, recent research has destroyed the validity formerly attached to the belief that the upper middle class and upper economic and social groups are much more law-abiding than other groups. The researches of Porterfield,[18] Sutherland,[19] and others have been discussed in Chapters 4 and 5. Differences in class status, furthermore, have a marked effect upon the degree to which those who commit offenses are punished. The upper middle and upper classes protect themselves against the full measure of the law and thus tend to retain the respect of the community. Upper-class lawbreakers do not usually offend the sensibilities of the group to the same extent as do lower-class offenders. Many of the recent laws enacted for the purpose of regulating modern industry have met with organized resistance on the part of big business. As we have pointed out in the chapter on "The Adult Offender," Sutherland maintains that criminal conduct is commonplace among major industrial leaders. Even when laws are enforced, there has been a differential implementation of them on a class basis. As Sutherland points out, 71 percent of the decisions in which the antitrust law was invoked against trade unions during the years 1890–1929 were made under the jurisdiction of criminal courts. For the same period, only 27 percent of the decisions against industrial organizations were cases in which the offense was designated as a criminal evasion of the law.[20]

The businessman has respect in the community because of his wealth and because he has supplied essential needs or desirable services from a social point of view. Lower-class persons who offend the law have no such status in the community. The gangster has no social status at all. He has exploited human frailties for a price or has extorted large sums because he has been able to execute his threats violently if his requests were not met. Nevertheless, the ethics of the market place have furnished certain patterns for the practices of the underworld. The phrase "business is business" has covered many dubious operations. Even so, members of the upper middle class believe fundamentally in the validity of law and order, even when they break their own laws. They have not always recognized that only when all groups accept the responsibility entailed in good citizenship may we expect greater acceptance of the validity of the laws when applied to lower-class offenders.

Criminal laws embody social values of the society as a whole, whereas lawbreaking represents one phase of social practice. Values and practices have never conformed in any complete sense in any social organization. So long as human beings carry within themselves the ambivalent emotions of love and hate, of respect and enmity, of desire for power and for community well-being, crime will continue to be a community problem. But part of our crime prob-

---

[18] Austin L. Porterfield, *Youth in Trouble,* Leo Potishman Foundation, Fort Worth, 1946.

[19] Cf. Sutherland, *op. cit.,* and James S. Wallerstein and Clement J. Wyle, *Our Law Abiding Law Breakers,* reprint from *Probation,* April, 1947.

[20] Edwin H. Sutherland, "The White Collar Criminal," in Vernon C. Branham and Samuel B. Kutash (ed.), *Encyclopedia of Criminology,* Philosophical Library, New York, 1949, pp. 511–515.

lem has unexplored reaches because of the tendency of the powerful groups to protect their own interests, rather than those of society. In consequence, crime as a community problem is very different from what many people have been led to believe. It is chiefly the petty offender who is caught and punished by our legal system. More important as a disorganizing factor in community life is the lawlessness promoted by the organized crime of the underworld and the equally organized illegal activities of many forms of business enterprise.[21]

8. *Crime and Modern Social Organization.* Crime as such has increased markedly in the United States partly because we have become more and more urban and so are exposed to a growing variety of relationships and stimuli. Only some 12 percent are now deriving their living from the soil. Another 12 percent are rural nonfarm residents, essentially urban in their lifework and in their orientation. They merely live farther "from the madding crowd." Urbanization creates countless complexities in living. There are many more laws governing human behavior in cities than in the open country. Urbanization has also placed a great emphasis upon material well-being; disparities in income and purchasing power probably create more envy between the classes in the city than in the country. Poor rural neighborhoods tend to share a common poverty although crime rates have gone up in the country. Those living in city slums often live only a few blocks from wealthy neighborhoods. In Chicago the Gold Coast presses close to the North Side slums. In New York the fashionable East River Drive, Beekman Hill, and Sutton Place are only two blocks away from deteriorated areas. So it is with many other sections of the city. A much greater proportion of the convicted criminals come from the slums than from other urban areas.

Meanwhile the rural areas are becoming urbanized as the result of the explosion of urban populations into the outer rim of our cities. It is also true that rural people are participating in urban culture in far greater number than ever before. Virtually all rural children go to movies in urban areas and attend school in cities or small towns. Rural crime rates are rising, but interestingly enough, they decrease as the distance of the rural area from a large urban center increases. Sutherland found that crime rates decreased significantly in concentric circles drawn around several centers of population.[22]

An important reason why crime is higher in the city lies in the fact of the opportunity for crime. There are more victims to rob, burglarize, rape, or murder. There are more available items to steal in stores, public buildings, and homes. More persons are in the streets to injure by careless driving. How much the particular victim invites crimes has never been established, but obviously swindlers, burglars, robbers, rapists, *et al.* seek out victims and know the peculiar frailties of children, women, old people, and immigrants.[23]

[21] Harry Elmer Barnes and Negley K. Teeters, *New Horizons of Criminology,* Prentice-Hall, Inc., Englewood Cliffs, N.J., 1959 (3rd ed.), chaps. II and III.

[22] Edwin H. Sutherland, *Principles of Criminology,* J. C. Lippincott and Company, Philadelphia, 1947, pp. 44–45 and 135–138.

[23] Cf. Hans von Hentig, *The Criminal and His Victim,* Yale University Press, New Haven, 1948, for a detailed discussion of this.

Modern merchandising policies make it easy for thieves to steal because goods can be so easily taken from counters and shelves, particularly in department stores, variety stores, and especially supermarkets, where the customer helps himself.

Modern businesses, on the other hand, have developed many ways of successfully defrauding the public. Articles are advertised as possessing unusual qualities devised to increase beauty, improve automobile power, prevent tooth decay, or improve health. These items are often worthless and are withdrawn from the market before any action by the government can take place. All of these businesses violate the trust of gullible persons and are actually engaged in criminal conduct.

Sometimes persons exploit the trust of others, gaining entrance to homes by claiming to be service men, plumbers, telephone repair men, etc. They then proceed to rob the apartment and sometimes tie up or kill their victims. Such offenses are more common in apartment houses and dormitories than elsewhere because the victim does not control the services and does not know whether the service has been ordered or not. Thieves also are on the lookout for parties and may invade the bedrooms where guests lay valuable wraps and purses. In large social functions among the upper social groups thieves in evening clothes may crash the party and take jewels of the unsuspecting guests and hostess.[24] The impersonality of city life and the fact that so many people are coming and going makes it easy for the criminal to escape notice. Despite the great need for police and night watchmen relatively few urban residential districts have much police service.

9. *Norms of Behavior and Social Values.* Many Europeans think that Americans are wholly materialistic. During the last decade of the nineteenth century and the period between 1900 and World War I immigrants were often lured to this country as a land of economic opportunity where a poor boy could make a million. They were then rudely shocked to find that their backbreaking toil in the steel mills and mines was poorly paid and life was a matter of grinding poverty. It should not be surprising that some who could never expect to achieve riches honestly were tempted to make easy money illicitly. A few notorious gangsters like Lucky Luciano and Frank Costello apparently came here because of the opportunities to build a crime syndicate.

Some people in earlier generations had been able by dint of hard work and intelligence to make sizable fortunes honestly through the exploitation of natural resources. Countless others had achieved a comfortable middle-class status by patient effort. The American people as a whole have a standard of living higher than that of any other nation. But this does not mean that Americans value material goods more than honesty, integrity, and decency and relative freedom for the individual. Our people have been reluctant, however, to discuss their basic values. Thus, our government has even sponsored a radio program, beamed from West Berlin and aimed at the Soviet Union

[24] Richard R. Korn and Lloyd W. McCorkle, *Criminology and Penology,* Henry Holt and Company, Inc., New York, 1959, pp. 134–137.

and her east European satellites, which has emphasized the number of automobiles, bathtubs, and shiny new gadgets American citizens possess. We have done a very poor job of educating some of the eastern and southern European immigrants with reference to our spiritual values. Belief in the value of human life, human liberty, and freedom from tyranny are the basic tenets of our democracy. We enjoy a high standard of living partly because our citizens have great motivation as "equals" in a common political structure.

Disorganized Areas and Crime

Most studies of the community and crime have analyzed the community in which the offender was reared. Slum areas with their deteriorated and crowded homes have thus been held to be breeding places for criminality, for delinquency and crime cases tend to be concentrated here. At least this is true for the cases which crowd our courts. The studies of Clifford R. Shaw, Henry D. McKay, and others have confirmed this conclusion. The slum area has relatively few effective means of social control over its members.[25] Unfortunately lawbreaking is apparently common among persons from middleclass and upper-class areas, as we have discussed in Chapters 4 and 5. Nevertheless, there are reasons why persons who live in the slums have a high crime rate. They are nearly always from the lower economic and social strata and have more stimulation to obtain by illegal means the material goods which are otherwise denied them. Here many illicit activities, such as the narcotic trade and houses of prostitution, are centered. Here are the gangster hide-outs. The Negro population is also usually concentrated in slum areas.

In the Hill district in Pittsburgh, for example, crime and delinquency rates are high. Some of the thieving and a large proportion of the murders in Pittsburgh are actually committed in the area. A comparative study of both police-referred and parent-referred delinquency cases in Pittsburgh showed a high concentration in the Hill area.[26] Most of the Negro cases were in this section, and in a large share of them the mother in the family was working and the children were left to fend for themselves. In any event people who live in slum areas, whether children or adults, are subject to many external pressures toward nonconformity to the standards of the larger community. Life is harder and cheaper in the slum. Slum neighbors tend to report neighbors and the neighbors' children for misconduct. Middle-class neighbors seldom commit crimes against neighbors and where their children misbehave the cases are not often reported to authorities.

On the other hand, a large share of the criminal activities of the slum-dwelling offenders are committed outside their home neighborhoods where possibilities for economic reward are greater. Nevertheless, many slum dwell-

[25] Cf. Clifford R. Shaw and Henry D. McKay, *Juvenile Delinquency and Urban Areas*, University of Chicago Press, Chicago, 1942, chap. XX.

[26] Cf. Marcia Glazer and Barbara Wietrzynski, "A Comparative Study of Parent-Referred and Police-Referred Cases of the Allegheny County Juvenile Court, Disposed January 1 through June 30, 1954," unpublished MS., Chatham College Library. (Tutorial project supervised by Miss Elliott.)

ers do not come into conflict with the law. Some persons hold that it is the defective family relationships of the slum dwellers and not the community standards that affect the high delinquency rate. This is the conclusion of William and Joan McCord in their re-evaluation of the Somerville-Cambridge study. They recognize, however, that children in good neighborhoods are less "criminal" even when their home situation is unfavorable.[27] Which is more important, the outside social environment or the home, is a debate that has not thus far been settled. The poor and incompetent and those who cannot compete effectively because of race tend to gravitate to the slums. Family disorganization is very high among these groups, too, as our discussion of divorce and desertion in Chapter 16 makes clear. Conduct standards seem to be affected by neighborhood standards and vice versa.

The Professional Criminal and Organized Crime

Most criminals who come in contact with the law are only incidentally criminal. Even though their criminality is socially disorganizing they do not make it their lifework. Certain offenders, the professional criminals, and those whose major activities are absorbed in organized crime derive their primary income from activities which disorganize the community. These people make a profession of undermining the enforcement of law and operating large business enterprises on a thoroughly dishonest basis. They flout the moral and social values of the community and derive enormous economic returns by fleecing personal victims (if they are professional criminals) and the general public (if they are "organized" criminals). Because the latter operate by conniving with corrupt officials, the true extent of their cost to the community is seldom known. But it must be much greater than that of the relatively small-time property offenders.

1. *The Professional Criminal.* Anyone who makes crime his lifework is a professional criminal. If successful, he often becomes very skilled in his chosen work. Thus we have the professional thief, the confidence man, and the swindler as major types of professional criminals. Such men may be lone operators or operate with a small cooperating group. Not all professional criminals can be considered organized criminals, even though they share their profits with the group with whom they work.

The professional criminal who operates on a limited basis tends to confine his activities to thieving, the receiving of stolen goods, and swindling. Sometimes the profits are very high, but there is no attempt to estimate this type of illicit business. Swindlers get a line on gullible people with available cash and persuade them that a secret tip or a bonanza scheme will enable them to increase their money many-fold. Such professionals use well-established patterns for extracting money from naïve people. Thus a wealthy farmer may be persuaded that he can double or triple his money on "a sure-to-win investment." Usually two people operate in getting a third person fleeced of his funds.

[27] Cf. William and Joan McCord, *Origins of Crime,* Columbia University Press, New York, 1959, especially pp. 166–172.

Sometimes the victim puts up money to prove his integrity and is asked to go on some errand. When he returns his money and the swindler are gone.[28]

A small-town Pennsylvania physician recently lost $84,000 through the persuasiveness of a "con" man. David W. Mawrer maintains that professional men are notoriously gullible, presumably because of their lack of business experience. Widows who have a fair inheritance but have never had any business experience are also fair game.[29] The only reason such people are taken in by swindlers, however, is that they too are motivated by a desire to make unreasonable returns on their money. The victims of swindling thus share in the guilt and often fail to report their losses for this reason. Swindlers usually plan a quick getaway and many are never located.

2. *Organized Crime.* The persons engaged in organized crime are those conducting the big business in criminal enterprise mentioned earlier. They have no articles of incorporation and receive no charter authorizing their illicit enterprises. Nevertheless, they could not exist without some cooperation on the part of politicians and especially of the police. In order to operate, organized crime must have protection. This is secured by paying bribes to officials (especially to police), by making political contributions, and by offering officials a share of the profits. "Unholy" alliances exist between organized crime and corrupt politicians. Some of the methods of modern businessmen, for that matter, are not greatly different from those of organized crime so far as securing special political favors is concerned. Many members of state legislatures have been hired as retainers by large corporations. They support legislation which favors these companies and work diligently against anything which might hurt their business. Thus insurance agents become legislators to defeat teachers' pensions bills. Representatives of physicians in Congress may try to forestall medical insurance. Such legislators are virtual lobbyists although they purportedly represent the people's interest.

Many of the activities of organized crime are similar to those of the professional thief or swindler. The organized criminals merely operate a vast enterprise from which they derive enormous returns. In the 1930's Martin Mooney held that organized crime had more than twice the combined yearly incomes of General Motors, United States Steel, the Hearst newspapers, the Radio Corporation of America, the National City Bank, and "twenty-five other powerful business enterprises in the country."[30]

When swindlers work with a syndicate they are part of an organized crime activity. Extensive swindling enterprises are set up to lure a wide variety of gullible investors who are interested in "making big money quick," just as the victims of lone operators are lured. Some of these are fly-by-night corporations which disappear before they can be indicted by the courts.

[28] Cf. John C. R. McDonald, *Crime Is a Business,* Stanford University Press, Stanford, 1939, pp. 12–16.

[29] David W. Mawrer, *The Big Con,* The Bobbs-Merrill Company, Inc., Indianapolis, 1940, pp. 111–115.

[30] Martin Mooney, *Crime, Incorporated,* McGraw-Hill Book Company, Inc., New York, 1935, p. 7.

Racketeering is a special variety of organized crime in which the victims are exploited under threat of violence or for a share in the illegal profits.[31] During the 1930's many "respectable" businessmen contributed to the racketeers' coffers by paying tributes to gangsters. They were literally required to pay a certain sum every month or their place of business would be blown up. The cutthroat methods of racketeers are not new. Many were borrowed from the pirates and highwaymen of an earlier era. Some are much like the ruthless methods of competitive industry before present-day regulations were enacted.

Organized crime reached new proportions in the United States during the prohibition era. When the Volstead Act made the sale of beverages with more than 3.2 percent alcoholic content illegal, bootlegging became a very active criminal enterprise. Bootlegging (the illegal sale of liquor) involved a wide variety of coordinated activities, ranging from secret engagements with ships at sea by small "rumrunning" boats (which avoided the coast guards) to the management of fleets of trucks to carry the liquor overland under the armed guard of gangsters. Meanwhile many distilleries and breweries operated illegally within this country. The bootleggers supplied their wares to speakeasies, which carried on their business with the assistance of police protection and connivance of patrons throughout the country. The rewards of bootleggers ran into many millions. Meanwhile, efforts to prosecute bootleggers swamped our legal machinery.[32]

The vast empire of Al Capone in Chicago was never wholly exposed but it was well known that he controlled an intricate network of prostitution, bootlegging, and gambling. The ledger for Capone's profits on gambling alone showed that these amounted to $600,000 for a three-year period. It was the discovery of this ledger that led to Capone's eleven-year sentence to a federal prison for income tax evasion.[33] Other notorious names included Frank Nitti, John Dillinger, and Legs Diamond. These men lived in great style, often in the best sections of the city if they were able to secure a residence there.

During the thirties, rackets included such diverse activities as pinball games, policy or numbers rackets, race track gambling, gambling establishments (with cards or dice), counterfeiting, narcotics distribution, and slot machine operation.[34] Many of these still flourish. The juke box industry is dominated by a group of Chicago gangsters and is one of the current lucrative rackets.[35] Gangsters provided the violence and armed threats for racketeers during the heyday of prohibition and many still serve as bodyguards for organized criminals.

Today many racketeers have invaded legitimate industries. Frank Cos-

[31] *Ibid.,* chap. III.

[32] *Report on the Cost of Crime,* Report No. 12 of the National Commission on Law Observance and Enforcement, Washington, 1931, pp. 106–114, and 129.

[33] Cf. Alan Hynd, *The Giant Killers,* Robert M. McBride Company, Inc., New York, 1945, for a detailed account of Capone's "empire."

[34] Mooney, *op. cit.,* chap. III.

[35] Virgil W. Peterson, *A Report on Chicago Crimes for 1958,* Chicago Crime Commission, 1959, pp. 36–37.

tello, one of the most notorious of the organized criminals in New York, testified before the Kefauver investigating committee that he was then operating only in legitimate industries. (Formerly he had been interested in a wide variety of rackets ranging from commerce in kewpie dolls to pinball games and slot machines.)[36]

Government-financed building operations (aimed at relieving the housing shortage following World War II) provided a special opportunity for organized crime to slip in unsuspected. The czars of organized crime entered into construction contracts on a "cost plus" basis, i.e., plus a particular percentage. Costs were determined on the basis of honest estimates for sturdy materials, heavy walls, and high-grade plumbing. The buildings were often erected with flimsy materials, however, with both rentals and percentages based on the heavier costs. Sometimes costs were merely padded.[37]

Many of the organized criminals who engaged in bootlegging during the war now dominate certain liquor interests (since they own and operate the same businesses legally now). Much of the wholesale and retail distribution of liquor (where it is not sold in state stores) is controlled by former gangster organizations.[38]

Criminal Law and Crime

Some maintain that criminal law itself creates crime. This view is valid only in the sense that the law defines crime. When new categories of conduct are forbidden, the nature of crime changes and the list of probable offenders is thereby increased. Sometimes the laws run so counter to human behavior that they are difficult to enforce and seem to contribute to the whole picture of crime and community disorganization. Prohibition in the United States is a case in point. And as mentioned, our tendency to forbid a greater variety of conduct accounts for much of the difference between American and European crime rates.

Some legalists, as, for example, John H. Wigmore, hold that the law restrains the multitude even though it may not restrain those who break it.[39] This judgment is not demonstrably true. As John Waite points out, when Richard Bruno Hauptmann was executed for kidnaping the Lindbergh baby, kidnaping increased.[40] Laws against thieving and murder have existed as long as recorded history.[41]

These old and universally condemned crimes were originally avenged by

---

[36] *Investigation of Organized Crime in Interstate Commerce,* Hearings Before the Special Committee to Investigate Organized Crime in Interstate Commerce, U.S. Senate, 81st Congress, Washington, 1950, part 2, pp. 125–130.

[37] Cf. Elliott, *Crime in Modern Society,* pp. 150–151.

[38] *Investigation of Organized Crime in Interstate Commerce,* part 4, "Missouri," pp. 313–324.

[39] John H. Wigmore, *The Illinois Crime Survey,* Illinois Association for Criminal Justice, Chicago, 1929, sec. I, chap. XIV.

[40] John Barker Waite, "The Legal Approach to Crime and Correction," *Law and Contemporary Problems, 23:*594 (Winter, 1958).

[41] Chilperic Edwards, *The Hammurabi Code,* Watts, London, 1904, chap. IV.

the victim and his family. Only offenses which upset the whole group, such as evasion of hunting rules, witchcraft, and black magic, were socially punished. With the beginnings of civilization man began to see that personal wrongs hurt the group of which he was a part. These included murder, thieving, rape, mayhem, perjury, etc., and were incorporated in detail in the Code of Hammurabi and later in the Mosaic code in the Old Testament.[42] Because of their religious condemnation the reprehensible character of these crimes is reinforced by notions of sin.

Crimes of this nature are therefore generally accepted as the truly serious crimes even by those who commit them. Religious condemnation gives them an evil connotation. The Mosaic code was written almost word for word into the German penal code and was the basis of much of the English common law. In the Massachusetts Bay Colony a proper Biblical reference was appended to every law to indicate its divine authority. The Pilgrim Fathers too depended chiefly on the Old Testament.[43]

Today the newer and modern crimes are defined by the legislators who are without any religious halo. Legislators tend to be members of upper-middle-class society and represent a middle-class morality. Most of the new crimes involve evasion of taxes, neglect of responsibility for dependents, violation of rules affecting labor conditions, and ignoring of regulations which seek to decrease the dangers inherent in modern living. The legislators express concern for social welfare. They also extend social responsibility both for individuals and for corporations in areas of conduct which were previously less restricted. Consequently many persons do not regard the new offenses so seriously as they did the older crimes. Some people break the laws deliberately while ignorant people may break them unknowingly.

LAW ENFORCEMENT OFFICIALS AND THE MACHINERY OF JUSTICE

If laws were enforced honestly, rigidly, and efficiently, they might very well curb crime. Unfortunately our political structure is often shot through with corruption, while the police, courts, and institutions and agencies for dealing with criminals are often ineffective even where there is no corruption. Methods of operation are generally established on habit rather than on any scientific basis and hence have little relation to preventing subsequent crimes by the offender.

Corruption and Inefficient Administration and Crime

There are many aspects of community life which prevent a more effective control of crime. Some are inherent in the nature of our political institutions—in the ineffectiveness of political authorities, police, courts, and

[42] As found in Exodus 20 and 23, the entire book of Deuteronomy, and Leviticus 17 and 26, all a part of the Pentateuch.
[43] James Leyburn, *Frontier Folkways*, Yale University Press, New Haven, 1935, p. 23.

the prison system, as well as probation and parole agencies. Others are inherent in public opinion itself.

CORRUPTION OF POLITICAL INSTITUTIONS

We have already discussed corruption of political institutions in Chapter 22. Political corruption not only *promotes* crime; political corruption *is* crime. Undermining the public welfare for the advantage of the few, taking the people's money for illicit purposes, or padding the public payrolls is robbery, by whatever name it is disguised. When corrupt political officials are caught, they are criminally indicted. If adjudged solely on the seriousness of their offense, they would receive the full penalty of the law. This seldom happens, for even the courtroom feels the strength of the politician's power. Yet it is the corrupt politicians who make other crimes possible. Without the collusion between corrupt politicians and criminals, as indicated in the preceding chapter, organized crime would be drastically reduced.

Almost any large city in America could, at some time in its history, furnish examples of such collusion. During the decade of the thirties, for instance, Kansas City enjoyed the unenviable reputation of being perhaps the most politically corrupt and crime-ridden city in America. It attracted nation-wide attention. Earlier, New York, Chicago, and Philadelphia were dominated by corrupt political organizations. Under Mayor La Guardia New York made great strides toward eliminating corruption in local politics. Chicago has elected a reform mayor in recent years. But the power of the criminal-political collusion is not completely broken.

The tremendous size of our great metropolitan centers makes it difficult for decent citizens to be informed or to maintain the constant vigilance which good government requires. Frank Costello is known to have been a kingpin, not merely in organized crime but in New York City politics. He exerted major control in electing William O'Dwyer mayor of New York and Thomas A. Aurelio judge of the New York State Supreme Court. A recent exposé of political corruption in New York shows that staggering amounts are being spent in gambling (much of it openly) and that political officials were engaged in systematic "pay-offs."

Thus Cook and Gleason charge that "for a little fee" fire inspectors will not enforce certain building codes and that contractors pay off the police in order that their trucks may deliver construction materials without securing thirty to forty summonses a day.[44] The "Manhattantown" slum clearance project lined the pockets of the promoters without the erection of any building. Organized crime has obviously wedged itself into New York's public-financed housing under Title No. 1. Federal audits disclosed the amazing payment of funds for audits to members of the corporation which was handling the construction. They also paid themselves salaries and fees for "managing the site" as well as placing insurance contracts, and fees for coal, fuel oil, and mainte-

---

[44] Fred J. Cook and Gene Gleason, "The Shame of New York," *The Nation*, October 31, 1959, part 9, pp. 306–313 (special issue).

nance within their own group. Other scandals have been uncovered in building projects in Harlem, Greenwich Village, and elsewhere within New York City.[45]

In some communities, collusion between politicians and the underworld is more extensive than in others. In Chicago, the political relationships with crime were notorious under the regime of "Big Bill" Thompson. In New York, policemen received protection money from gangsters during an earlier period. In recent years the old Tammany Hall has again returned to power. Harry Gross allegedly paid out $1,000,000 for police protection in Brooklyn in 1950. There were probably even higher pay-offs in Manhattan, the Bronx, and elsewhere. One Philadelphia gambling ring likewise paid an annual bribe of $2,000,000, according to the Kefauver hearings.[46]

Why do the local citizens permit such conditions to exist? Many Americans obviously do not live up to the democratic ideals which they extol. As Will Rogers said many years ago, in reference to the attempt to defeat the corrupt political machine in Chicago: "They are trying to beat Bill Thompson with the better-element vote. The trouble with Chicago is there ain't enough better element."

Great cities are not alone in providing outrageous evidences of political corruption. Often such activities occur in small towns and suburbs. School boards in small cities may favor the brick factory of a board member, as in a community known to the authors. Prostitution and vice may flourish in an industrial suburb. No matter what the size of the community, democracy cannot keep out crime without active vigilance on the part of citizens and officials alike.

The police are an important link in criminal justice in every community. Unfortunately the intellectual caliber of the police is seldom very high. Many policemen are apparently appointed because they are physically strong rather than mentally alert. There have been no recent surveys of the mental ability of police, but those conducted earlier indicated that they were rather generally of low-grade intelligence. Often the police employ lawless methods (including the "third degree") or prolonged and brutal interviews, make false arrests, including arrests on suspicion, and tap wires to secure evidence (another illegal practice). Many police believe that they "have to break the law to secure justice."[47] Lawlessness on the part of law enforcement officers is particularly unfortunate for it creates disrespect for the law. Where police are corrupt the situation is much worse since justice becomes a mockery and the police are literally "aiders and abettors" of crime. Police who have professional training also presumably have greater inhibitions against corruption. Obviously there are honest policemen in all ranks from foot patrol to superintendent. But it is a problem to insure such honesty.

Lack of competency on the part of the police may be as great a hazard to

---

[45] *Ibid.*, parts 6 and 7, pp. 284–300.
[46] *Ibid.*, p. 308.
[47] Elliott, *Crime in Modern Society*, chap. XVII, "The Police."

the community as corrupt police. True police protection cannot be assured without police who have adequate intelligence and education. A policeman also needs to be physically strong. He should be acquainted with the places where crimes tend to be committed. He should be trained in police techniques and criminology. Relatively few police possess such qualifications. Wichita, Kansas, Milwaukee, Wisconsin, Berkeley, California, and Evanston, Illinois, are among the communities which have made notable achievements in this direction.[48] Because police salary scales are rather low it is often hard to get adequately trained men for any except the supervisory jobs.

Adequate policing meanwhile is important to community well-being. Competent and prompt investigation of reported crimes is essential if offenders are to be apprehended. Adequate patrol, particularly in areas where crimes are likely to occur and at hours when crimes are likely to be committed, is important. If night watchmen and more regular police were on duty during the hours from 2 to 4 A.M., household burglaries would be greatly reduced. These are the hours when houses are apt to be entered. More purse snatching also occurs at night. It would seem sensible to have the best policing done at night, but ordinarily this is not the case. In most cities the late shift, from 11 P.M. to 7 A.M., is considered the least attractive and assigned to the newest recruits.[49]

CRIMINAL PROCEDURES

As a democracy America is committed to the welfare of its individual members. The right to a trial by jury, the requirement of a warrant in order to search any premises, the stipulation that no man shall be twice in jeopardy of his life for the same offense, freedom from cruel and unusual punishment, and placing the burden of proof of misconduct on the state are all provisions of our Constitution. They do not *ipso facto* mean that justice is always accomplished, however. Technicalities in an indictment may result in its being quashed. Evidence which establishes an individual's guilt may be inadmissible and this sometimes enables an obviously guilty man to escape justice.[50]

There are many other ways in which a miscarriage of justice may occur. The indictment may grow out of false testimony or mistaken identity. It is often difficult for people to recall the criminal's looks, what he wore, or other details used in establishing identity. Police may resort to pitiless questioning. Sometimes they use brute force and secure confessions because the individual is physically or psychologically exhausted.[51] On the other hand, clever crooks may plant evidence so that it points to the guilt of an innocent person. Sometimes detectives and reporters jump to conclusions and accuse a person whose innocence would be obvious if the case were pursued further. Sometimes there is virtual establishment of guilt of the innocent by newspapers and incompetent police. Cook and Gleason report an important instance in the

[48] *Ibid.*, pp. 461–463.
[49] *Ibid.*, p. 459.
[50] *Ibid.*, pp. 540–541.
[51] Cf. Korn and McCorkle, *op. cit.*, pp. 87–97.

brutal slaying of a Staten Island doctor and his wife in 1958 in which their eight-year-old son was virtually accused of the murder, both by police and by the newspapers. This cruel charge was made before an examination of the victims, yet a sober consideration of the child's testimony should have been enough to absolve him.[52]

The Disposition of the Convicted Offenders

The community's disapproval of the criminal is expressed by convicting him. He may then be placed on probation if the judge believes his previous conduct warrants it. Otherwise the judge must sentence him to prison (unless he is given the death penalty). How the judge makes this decision he is not required to indicate in American jurisprudence. In certain European countries he must give his reasons. In all states except California the judge must assign either a definite sentence or a sentence within definite limits. These restrictions on sentences are incorporated in state laws with reference to specific crimes presumably to prevent unusual or cruel sentence (in accordance with the Constitution's provisions). The sentence is somehow supposed to sum up the reprehensibility of the convict's conduct.

PROBATION

If the offender is placed on probation he needs wise counsel and assistance. He should have help in securing a job, and be guided in his family and community relations. Leisure-time activities must also be provided. Otherwise the probationer may easily get into trouble again. Probation officers are often poorly trained and usually have more cases than they can properly supervise. Probation is widely used in some states and seldom employed in others.[53] The *Attorney General's Survey of Release Procedures* indicated that 61 percent of the 19,256 probationers in sixteen states had no further record.[54] Detailed follow-up studies indicate that probationers do not make as good an adjustment as these figures indicate. The Gluecks, for example, found that nearly all (92.4 percent) eventually failed at least part of the time.[55] Many factors make it difficult for the criminal to adjust, including his return to his old home and his old associates.

A study made of the disposition of 100 unselected alleged female first offenders disposed by the Allegheny County Criminal Court (50 of whom were sent to the workhouse and 50 of whom were placed on probation) showed very little indication of sound reasoning back of the decisions. Twelve of these so-called first offenders were not first offenders at all. Pre-sentence investigations were not made routinely and the judges apparently disposed of the cases without much consideration of the offender's personality or background. Contrary to expectations, they sentenced more younger women to the work-

---

[52] Cook and Gleason, *op. cit.*, pp. 313–330.

[53] *Attorney General's Survey of Release Procedures*, Vol. II, *Probation*, U. S. Department of Justice, Washington, pp. 9–10.

[54] *Ibid.*, pp. 335–337.

[55] Sheldon and Eleanor Glueck, *Criminal Careers in Retrospect*, The Commonwealth Fund, New York, 1943, p. 151.

house and placed more of the older women on probation. In the crowded court dockets in Pittsburgh there is little time for evaluating cases.[56] This is very likely true in most of the criminal courts in the country.

The state and the community both have a vital interest in the offender's rehabilitation. This present sentencing practices in no way provide. Modern sentencing is absurdly unscientific. No judge is in a position to diagnose the behavior difficulties of the prisoner at the bar—nor is the legislator who writes the law defining penal sentences.

IMPRISONMENT

If the offender is sentenced to prison the community (or state) must provide a secure place for him and assume responsibility for his food, clothing, cleanliness, health, labor, recreation, and religious expression. Sometimes suitable educational and vocational training is provided. Personnel must be provided for looking after every single detail of these services in addition to the persons who assume responsibility for the custody of the prisoners.

When the convict is sentenced to prison most states require either a definite sentence or an indeterminate sentence within prescribed limits in order to prevent "cruel and unusual punishments." In California young persons under twenty-three (who are not subject to the death penalty or life imprisonment) are sentenced to the California Youth Authority and all adult convicts (who are not disqualified for various reasons) are sentenced to the California Adult Authority. These authorities study the offenders from all angles at the diagnostic centers and then transfer them to the institutions which are presumably best suited to their needs. In cases of first offenders, the inmates' sentences are frequently reviewed and decreased or increased depending upon the individual's progress. Such adjustments are not made for habitual offenders, who have to serve a period within the limits of the indeterminate sentence. In California other new types of penal practice also have been put into practice including extensive facilities for psychological testing, psychiatric examinations, and social investigations. On the basis of these and other findings, prisoners go through a "classification" program. That is, a plan for the prisoner's treatment is worked out on the basis of what is known about him and what activities and work schedules can be utilized to his advantage. Many other states have now adopted these services although they do not have as complete control over a man's stay in prison as the California authorities. The best prisons also brief the prisoner on the available facilities within the prison which can help him during his incarceration.[57] Timing would seem to be as important in rehabilitative treatment as it is in medical treatment. Too much bed rest is bad for certain surgical patients. Similarly, too long a prison sentence may contribute to a man's permanent maladjustment. As it is, we know that around 60 percent of our prisoners will commit as serious crimes after they are released as those for which they are now serving sentence.

[56] Joan E. V. Anderson, "A Study of 100 (Alleged) Women First Offenders Brought Before the Allegheny County Criminal Court," unpublished MS.

[57] New Developments in The Admission-Orientation Program," *Progress Report,* 3:4–16 (January, 1949) (published by the Federal Bureau of Prisons, Washington).

Penal treatment is hampered meanwhile because the community is torn between a desire to punish and a desire to enable the prisoner to become a socially responsible and well-adjusted civilian.[58] This is the community's dilemma with reference to crime and its treatment. Our present penal methods are producing recidivists. Until community opinion is committed to a research program which will study the rehabilitative effect of various programs and make experiments in the light of the knowledge derived, we can expect little progress in dealing with offenders.

PAROLE

Parole as the term is now employed is the release of the prisoner before his sentence has expired under the supervision of a parole officer. Virtually all criminologists and penologists recognize that prisoners need help in adjusting to normal life outside the prison. The public unfortunately often thinks of parole as leniency—but most states extend parole only to the prisoner whose behavior and circumstances indicate that they will be reasonably safe in permitting him to be released. Most prisoners would fare better if they were released under some sort of supervision and had someone to consult when confronted with difficulties. This is what parole aims to give.

There has been much research with reference to the factors contributing to parole success. The Gluecks hold that six items are the most valid prognostically: (1) industrial record prior to commitment, (2) previous reformatory or delinquency records (the fewer the better), (3) the number of prior arrests before commitment (those with none have the best prognosis), (4) prior penal experience (those without such record make the best adjustment), (5) economic responsibility of the offender for support of dependents (one who has previously assumed such support makes a better adjustment), (6) mental normality (those with abnormal mental characteristics make the worst adjustment).[59]

These factors were isolated from a group of twenty-two items previously considered important by Ernest W. Burgess[60] which included greater details about the offender, his offense, parental and marital status, community, age, etc. These items were recognized as being of unequal weight. More recently a study of inmates' "hunches" was made by Lloyd E. Ohlin and Richard A. Lawrence in Illinois and they concluded that the scores of a prisoner's predictable success and predictions made by intelligent selected prisoners in estimating their fellow inmates' success were identical.[61] This study gives us ground for thinking that common-sense evaluations may be as accurate for predicting success on parole as more elaborate devices.

[58] Cf. Korn and McCorkle, *op. cit.,* pp. 593–598. Cf. also Mabel A. Elliott, *Conflicting Theories in Statutory Penal Law,* University of Chicago Press, Chicago, 1931, especially chaps. I, II, and XIII.

[59] Sheldon and Eleanor Glueck, *Five Hundred Criminal Careers,* Harvard University Press, Cambridge, 1930, pp. 283–284.

[60] Ernest W. Burgess, "Factors Determining Success or Failure on Parole," in Andrew A. Bruce, Ernest W. Burgess, Albert J. Harno, and John Landesco, *The Workings of the Indeterminate Sentence and the Parole System in Illinois,* Parole Board of Illinois, Springfield, 1928, chap. XXX.

[61] Lloyd E. Ohlin, *Selection for Parole,* Russell Sage Foundation, New York, 1951, p. 69.

Success on parole has not been very satisfactory although an Alabama study indicated success in 89.1 percent of the cases.[62] There is a question, however, whether parolees can be considered successful if no offenses are committed before the sentence expires, and whether these prisoners were permanently successful. A study made in Pennsylvania during 1947–1948 showed that 67.8 percent of the men who were paroled during 1926–1933 were successful.[63] Unfortunately, powerful prisoners who have corrupt allies in politics are often able to get an early release. These men usually return to their previous pursuits. Parole should be divorced from politics if abuse of parole is to be eliminated.[64]

Meanwhile many parole officers lack the requisite training to be good parole officers and often their task of supervision is beyond accomplishment. Virtually all authorities say no parole officer can supervise more than fifty persons. He is often required to supervise several hundred.

There are many reasons why our penal institutions are not more successful. Lack of community concern has much to do with backward penal policies, just as it is responsible for political corruption and the breeding places of crime. Criminal science has far to go before it can become truly rehabilitative. Nevertheless, penal authorities are functioning in much the same way as the farmer who said he was not farming as well as he knew how. The political basis of personnel appointments and the maladministration in our prisons as well as in our probation and parole agencies (because of lack of training and lack of personnel) complicate any attempts to reform the offender. We need to conduct further research but we could easily improve penal agencies on the basis of what we already know. Most communities are apathetic about released criminals and do little to help them become acceptable citizens. This attitude itself is a factor in the increasing crime rate.

In a number of communities a local citizens' organization has taken a constructive role in working with police and the courts to keep down crime. The Chicago Crime Commission, for example, is composed of leading citizens including professionally trained criminologists. While it has in no sense abolished the crime problem, the increase in crime rate in Chicago has been considerably less than the national average.[65] The problem of crime prevention is beyond the scope of this chapter but it is vitally related to community organization.

SELECTED BIBLIOGRAPHY

Barnes, Harry Elmer, and Teeters, Negley K., *New Horizons of Criminology*, Prentice-Hall, Inc., Englewood Cliffs, N.J., 1959 (3rd ed.). This book contains

[62] Mary Ruth Graham, *These Came Back*, Bureau of Public Administration, University of Alabama Press, University, 1946, p. 103. The Gluecks' studies contradict this.

[63] Leon T. Stern, "Popular or Scientific Evaluation of Parole," *National Probation and Parole Association Yearbook 1948*, New York, 1949, pp. 55–70.

[64] Cf. Martin Mooney, *The Parole Scandal*, Lymanhouse, Los Angeles, 1939, for a disclosure of parole "evils." Obviously not all paroles are like these.

[65] Cf. Peterson, *op. cit.*, p. 3.

some of the best material on organized crime and its impact on the American community structure.

Elliott, Mabel A., *Conflicting Theories in Statutory Penal Law,* University of Chicago Press, Chicago, 1931. An analysis of the conflicting theories which make the administration of criminal procedures and penal institutions very complicated is given in this book.

Elliott, Mabel A., "Crime and the Frontier Mores," *American Sociological Review,* 9:185–192 (April, 1944). This article analyzes the lack of institutional controls and the lusty crimes of frontier days.

Elliott, Mabel A., *Crime in Modern Society,* Harper & Brothers, New York, 1952. Several chapters in this book relate to the community and cultural aspects of crime.

Elliott, Mabel A., "Delinquent Behavior of People," *Phylon,* 5:242–251 (Third Quarter, 1949). The special relation of American culture to the crime rate is discussed.

Elliott, Mabel A., "Perspective on the American Crime Problem," *Social Problems,* 5:184–193 (Winter, 1957–1958). The cultural reasons for the disparity between American and European crime rates are examined.

Hentig, Hans von, *The Criminal and His Victim,* Yale University Press, New Haven, 1948. This analysis of the role of the victim in producing crime offers original and important insights into crime.

Investigations of Organized Crime in Interstate Commerce, Hearings Before the Special Committee to Investigate Crime in Interstate Commerce, U.S. Senate, 81st Congress, Washington, 1950, Reports I–XIX. These hearings contain some of the most shocking revelations of the degree to which organized crimes operate in urban American communities. The reports led to many local attempts to deal with the criminals. They offer much information which has never been analyzed in detail.

Korn, Richard R., and McCorkle, Lloyd W., *Criminology and Penology,* Henry Holt and Company, Inc., New York, 1959. A new text offers fresh insights into the community and group aspects of crime.

Mooney, Martin, *Crime, Incorporated,* McGraw-Hill Book Company, Inc., New York, 1935. This is an exposé of the extensive racketeering during the depression.

Peterson, Virgil W., *A Report on Chicago Crime for 1958,* Chicago Crime Commission, 1959. This report shows how a citizens' agency works in trying to keep down crime in a great metropolitan area.

Porterfield, Austin L., and Talbert, Robert H., *Crime, Suicide and Social Well-Being,* Leo Potishman Foundation, Fort Worth, 1948. Race and crime are shown to be partly related to "mixing of the populations."

Prohibition Enforcement, Official Records of the National Commission on Law Observance and Enforcement, Vol. I, Washington, 1931. The pros and cons of the prohibition issue and its relation to the crime rate are presented.

Sutherland, Edwin H., *White Collar Crime,* The Dryden Press, Inc., New York, 1949. This book is an important contribution on the lawlessness in respected American business enterprises.

Turner, Frederick L., *The Frontier in American History,* Henry Holt and Company, Inc., New York, 1920. This is the classic analysis of the impact of the frontier in our cultural heritage.

CHAPTER 24

Mobility

The Concept of Social Mobility

The tendency of animals to move about over the surface of the earth is one of their distinctive characteristics. Man is the most mobile of all creatures. The nature of man's social life is partially determined by the restlessness that drives him from place to place. In the words of Park and Burgess, society is "made up of individuals spatially separated, territorially distributed, and capable of independent locomotion."[1] Neither its individual components nor society itself can be dissociated from the fundamental assumption of human mobility. Mobility involves changes in position that bring about new contacts and stimulations. It may therefore be defined as spatial change involving new mental contacts.[2]

Mere routine movement of a fixed and changeless character does not constitute social mobility. There must be a change of stimulus as well as a response to the new stimulus before simple physical movement becomes social mobility. Mobility involves psychological as well as physical change—new ideas, experiences, and outlooks. Mental contact and communication are the important considerations in mobility, as they are in society itself. Human mobility possesses the dual aspect of physical and mental movement.[3]

The distinction between physical mobility and psychological mobility is in part only conceptual, inasmuch as they are two aspects of the same situation. It is impossible for a normal human being to move from place to place (or even exist) without experiencing some new sensation, however slight. A society characterized by a high degree of mobility differs from one in which mobility is at a minimum. Persons who move as part of their way of life develop different habits and customs from those of people who remain physically stable. Mobility is a striking characteristic of present-day American society.[4]

Social mobility may also be considered in terms of changes in social status. The concept of status related to tenure of residence has long been a familiar

[1] Robert E. Park and Ernest W. Burgess, *Introduction to the Science of Sociology,* University of Chicago Press, Chicago, 1924, p. 508.

[2] Pitirim A. Sorokin, *Social Mobility,* Harper & Brothers, New York, 1927.

[3] Cf. Ronald Freedman and Amos H. Hawley, "Education and Occupation of Migrants in the Depression," *American Journal of Sociology,* 56:161–166 (September, 1950).

[4] Cf. Sidney Goldstein, "Repeated Migration as a Factor in High Mobility Rates," *America Sociological Review,* 19:536–541 (October, 1954).

criterion of social mobility. This approach may be expanded to include such areas as marital, family, and fertility status; educational attainment; employment status; social class; income level; health status; church affiliation; and type of housing and home ownership. The person may change his status in one or more of these respects, and each such change constitutes a form of social mobility. An individual who undergoes several status changes within a given period—such as place of residence, marital situation, church affiliation, and type of housing—is by definition a mobile person. One who retains his statuses in these and other respects is a stable person. By the same token, a society in which a large number of people are mobile with respect to status is a highly mobile one. Social mobility in this sense is the very stuff of social change.[5]

Social mobility is a permanent characteristic of contemporary society. The institutional structure, however, is not adequately organized to deal with it. Stability is defined as the norm, and any departures therefrom are viewed as abnormal and undesirable. Hence our society has preferred to ignore the presence of large numbers of unattached and (at least temporarily) homeless persons. The adjustments of these persons are rendered more difficult by the failure of society to provide for them. Many are forced to make inadequate housing arrangements, whether in private families (not their own), lodging houses, shelters, or flophouses. Not all unattached persons are penniless; many of them can afford to pay a reasonable amount for living quarters. Despite this fact, however, the available arrangements tend to increase the isolation that often accompanies a life of unusual mobility. The problem is one of cultural lag. Society still considers the status of being unattached "either a temporary or an unusual condition." For perhaps 10 percent of the population this status is relatively common.[6]

Social mobility and the adjustments of the mobile population present a number of significant ramifications. We are concerned here, however, with social mobility as both a *cause of* and an *index to* social disorganization. Modern transportation and communication have made our society the most mobile the world has ever seen. Although mobility and disorganization are not inevitably concomitant, a highly mobile society is one in which traditional group patterns break down. Consequently, it behooves us to examine closely this symptom of a dynamic society. Here, as elsewhere, we find that personal and social disorganization are different aspects of the same process.

Current Status of Social Mobility

More than 33,000,000 residents of the United States change their place of residence at least once every year. Of this number, approximately 22,000,000 confine their movements to the same county, whereas 11,000,000

[5] Donald J. Bogue, "The Quantitative Study of Social Dynamics and Social Change," *American Journal of Sociology, 57:*565–568 (May, 1952).

[6] Arnold M. Rose, "Living Arrangements of Unattached Persons," *American Sociological Review, 12:*429–435 (August, 1947).

move from one county to another, as shown in Table 24.1. America is the most mobile nation the world has every seen. Movement is virtually a way of life. The physical stability of most European countries has never been known here. In this country approximately nine out of every ten persons over the age of one year have moved at least once in their lifetimes. The one person in ten who has lived in the same house since birth is generally under eighteen years of age. Counting the adult population (i.e., those over eighteen), only 2 percent have lived in the same house all their lives.[7]

Mobility varies with age. The most mobile segment of the population is composed of young adults; 42.6 percent of those from twenty to twenty-four years of age moved at least once during the year 1957–1958. After this high rate, there was a steady decline in rate of mobility in the remaining age groups. Persons in the labor force are more mobile than the very young or the very old. The unemployed are more mobile than the employed. Males are more mobile than females, and whites move more often (and longer distances) than nonwhites.[8] In terms of residence, the rural nonfarm population is the most mobile, with 22.8 percent of this group moving at least once. The percentage of mobile persons among the urban population was 19.7, whereas that of the rural farm population was only 14.4.[9]

The role of occupation is indicated by the mobility rates of the various occupational groups in an earlier study. The lowest rate was found among farmers and farm managers, with only 8 percent of this group moving within a year. Managers, officials, and proprietors have a rate of 15 percent, which was somewhat below that for professional persons (16.9 percent) and for operatives (19.6 percent). The highest mobility rate for any occupational group was that of farm laborers, with 26.8 percent in this category.[10] We shall consider the problems of this group later in the chapter, inasmuch as migratory farm laborers present special problems.

The mobility of the depression years of the 1930's was widely viewed as a hectic symptom of a disorganized society, whose structure was undergoing at the least a severe shock and at the most a possible collapse. The mobility of the postwar years, on the other hand, was viewed as a healthy indication of a vigorous society which was adjusting to changes in production. Such mobility symbolizes a new kind of society—a society that is secular rather than sacred and is increasingly based upon impersonal and secondary relationships instead of personal and primary ones. Traditional norms and values for the most part arose in a social structure based upon physical stability. Many of these values lose their force when the original conditions no longer apply.

[7] Bureau of the Census, *Population Characteristics, Mobility of the Population of the United States: March 1957 to 1958, Current Population Reports,* Series P-20, No. 85 (October 13, 1958).

[8] *Ibid.,* Table 3.

[9] *Ibid.,* Table 2.

[10] Bureau of the Census, *Population Characteristics, Mobility of the Population of the United States: April 1950 to April 1951, Current Population Reports,* Series P-20, No. 39 (July 14, 1952), Table 9. Many farmers have since left the farm. Cf. Chapters 20 and 21.

TABLE 24.1. Mobility Status and Type of Mobility of the Civilian Population, 1957–1958

Period, Color, and Sex	Total Civilian Population	Same House (Nonmovers)	Different House in the United States (Movers)						Abroad at Beginning of Period
			Total	Same County	Different County (Migrants)			
					Total	Within a State	Between States	
March 1957 to 1958								
Both sexes, total	167,604,000	133,501,000	33,263,000	22,023,000	11,240,000	5,656,000	5,584,000	840,000
White	149,206,000	119,770,000	28,656,000	18,383,000	10,273,000	5,233,000	5,040,000	780,000
Nonwhite	18,398,000	13,731,000	4,607,000	3,640,000	967,000	423,000	544,000	60,000
Male, total	82,117,000	64,920,000	16,664,000	10,884,000	5,780,000	2,898,000	2,882,000	533,000
White	73,214,000	58,295,000	14,424,000	9,165,000	5,259,000	2,651,000	2,608,000	495,000
Nonwhite	8,903,000	6,625,000	2,240,000	1,719,000	521,000	247,000	274,000	38,000
Female, total	85,487,000	68,581,000	16,599,000	11,139,000	5,460,000	2,758,000	2,702,000	307,000
White	75,992,000	61,475,000	14,232,000	9,218,000	5,014,000	2,582,000	2,432,000	285,000
Nonwhite	9,495,000	7,106,000	2,367,000	1,921,000	446,000	176,000	270,000	22,000
Percent Distribution								
Both sexes, total	100.0	79.7	19.8	13.1	6.7	3.4	3.3	0.5
White	100.0	80.3	19.2	12.3	6.9	3.5	3.4	0.5
Nonwhite	100.0	74.6	25.1	19.8	5.3	2.3	3.0	0.3
Male, total	100.0	79.1	20.3	13.3	7.0	3.5	3.5	0.6
White	100.0	79.6	19.7	12.5	7.2	3.6	3.6	0.7
Nonwhite	100.0	74.4	25.2	19.3	5.9	2.8	3.1	0.4
Female, total	100.0	80.2	19.4	13.0	6.4	3.2	3.2	0.4
White	100.0	80.9	18.7	12.1	6.6	3.4	3.2	0.4
Nonwhite	100.0	74.9	24.9	20.2	4.7	1.9	2.8	0.2

SOURCE: Bureau of the Census, *Population Characteristics, Mobility of the Population of the United States: March 1957 to 1958, Current Population Reports,* Series P-20, No. 85 (October 13, 1958), Table 1.

The New Mobility

This new mobility has an important impact upon interpersonal relationships. Mobility has been remarkably constant since the movement of population leveled off following World War II. In the year 1957–1958, approximately one out of every five (19.8 percent) people moved their residence at least once, either in the same county (13.1 percent) or to a different county (6.7 percent). These moves, as noted, involved a total of approximately 33,000,000 persons one year of age and older.[11]

This is social dynamics with a vengeance. The movement of 33,000,000 persons into and out of thousands of local neighborhoods and communities means that countless groups are continually forming and dissolving as the result of a changing membership. Children are entering and leaving play groups, teen-agers are joining and quitting high school cliques, and adults are forming and taking leave of friendship groups of varying degrees of casualness and intimacy. Statuses are subject to a bewildering change as millions transfer their interpersonal relationships over a twelve-month period. Social organization and disorganization, in the literal sense of making and breaking interpersonal ties, is occurring at the most rapid rate in history.

This dynamic process of mobility is not uniform, however. In general, the large metropolitan community is more mobile than the smaller community. The division of labor in the large city means that employment opportunities are greater and that more people move in search of better jobs. The movement to the large cities from the rest of the country is continuous, as individuals come in search of greater economic opportunities, recreational resources, and freedom from primary group restraints. The birth rate in the large city, especially in the classes with the highest economic and social status, has been so low that these groups have not (until recently) reproduced themselves. Persons moving to the city from small towns and rural communities have partially filled this demographic gap.[12]

The process of organization and disorganization may be differentiated in other terms. Persons in rural nonfarm areas are, as noted, more mobile than those who live in either rural farm or urban areas. The West is more mobile than the other regions, with the Northeast the least mobile. Nonwhites move more frequently than whites, although the latter tend to travel longer distances. Residents of standard metropolitan areas change residence oftener than those in other areas. Wage and salary workers move more than either the self-employed and the unpaid family workers. In the heterogeneous population of the United States there are a variety of intergroup differences in mobility.[13]

No generalization can be made, therefore, concerning the new mobility

[11] Bureau of the Census, *Mobility of the Population of the United States: March 1957 to 1958*, Table 1.

[12] Seymour M. Lipset, "Social Mobility and Urbanization," *Rural Sociology*, 20:220–228 (September–December, 1955).

[13] *Ibid.*

which is equally valid for all classes, occupations, regions, residential groups, races, and age groups. Continued high mobility is likely (along with other factors) to have profound effects upon American society and these effects will be related to social organization and disorganization. Interpersonal relationships will not be as stable and enduring as those of an earlier society. Scores of millions of persons will continue to be "strangers" in their community and the group relationships which they form will be less permanent than those of another day.[14]

The stranger is one whose background is unknown to other persons and who is himself unfamiliar with the group norms and values. The newcomer tries to adjust to group expectations as he sees them. He tries, that is, to *conform* to the overt behavior patterns and be as conventional as possible. In a community where the average individual lives for a long time (and his family has lived for a longer time) he can (to a certain extent, at least) be himself and be permitted minor eccentricities. In the mobile American society nonconformities are often avoided because each person wishes to be accepted by the other members of the community. In sections where the majority of people are strangers, the element of overt conformity is correspondingly high. This fact may partially explain the emphasis upon conformity and the intolerance of nonconformity in modern American society.[15]

Vertical Mobility

We are primarily concerned with *horizontal* mobility in this chapter, and we have observed the trends in movement from place to place. There is also much vertical mobility, i.e., movement upward or downward in the class structure. People often rise in the status system by moving from place to place, especially when they work for a large corporation and gradually move up in the bureaucratic hierarchy. As they do so, they are mobile in both senses. They find it difficult to put down strong roots when they live in a dormitory suburb for two years and then move on to another. Because they put down no roots mobile individuals face a dilemma in their interpersonal relations. From it stem many of their attitudes and much of their conduct.[16]

Other factors, notably the cold war, are also instrumental in the drive toward conformity, but the fact of mobility is clearly there. The vertically mobile person is dependent upon others for advancement. He therefore strives to follow the conventional norms and finds emotional security in insisting that others do likewise. The horizontally mobile person, especially the middle-class "striver," is also careful to observe the accepted patterns of the community.[17]

[14] Rudolf Heberle, "A Note on Riesman's 'The Lonely Crowd,'" *American Journal of Sociology,* 62:34–36 (July, 1956).

[15] Cf. Samuel A. Stouffer, *Communism, Conformity, and Civil Liberties,* Doubleday and Company, Inc., New York, 1955.

[16] Peter M. Blau, "Social Mobility and Interpersonal Relations," *American Sociological Review,* 21:290–295 (June, 1956).

[17] Heberle, *op. cit.,* p. 36.

Appearances are important to all members of the family, but especially to the children, whose status depends upon conformity to the patterns of the other-directed peer group. In the middle-class suburbs, many families are on their way up the ladder of success. In their climb, they move from New York to Chicago to Detroit to Los Angeles and back again to New York. At each stage they are dependent upon the good will of others. On this essentially rootless existence, their status depends upon conformity.[18]

The new mobility is also strikingly noticeable in the "factory-made suburbs" that have arisen since World War II in the metropolitan areas outside the large cities.[19] These new suburbs differ from the older ones, which housed the elite and the middle class. The new suburbs have sprung full-blown from the drawing boards of architects and the imaginations of real estate promoters. They provide comfortable housing for young families, but they are characterized by a stultifying conformity.

Such suburbs are largely occupied by two generations—parents and young children. There is no "older generation." The children do not know their grandparents, and they play with other children who are similarly rootless. The extended family system is virtually nonexistent in the new society.[20] Many of the young married people are in fact vaguely ashamed of their own parents. The latter are often first-generation immigrants who settled in the slums of the large cities from which their children are now fleeing. The way of life of the new suburbs means that many people are not so much *disorganized* as *unorganized,* in the sense that their participation in settled community relationships (e.g., church, school, business) is marginal. The group ties which automatically arise in a more stable society are largely absent.[21]

Such existence involves a new way of life in another sense. The continuity marking a community that has grown in more organic fashion is unknown. Everybody is a newcomer and the children grow up in an impermanent and transient environment. There are few traditions, and the supermarket is often the only meaningful institution. Parents and children alike live in an atmosphere where the fashions in behavior are made by the mass media and everyone is encouraged to think alike. Symbols of status are consumer durable goods, and the type of family automobile serves as an "index" to the family. The majority of residents do not become involved with the community because they expect to move away in a year or so.[22]

The new mobility is inevitably viewed in terms of the value judgments of an earlier day. The norms of our society reflect a rural and comparatively

[18] David Riesman *et al., The Lonely Crowd,* Doubleday Anchor Books, New York, 1953.
[19] Sidonie M. Gruenberg, "The Challenge of the New Suburbs," *Marriage and Family Living,* 17:133–137 (May, 1955).
[20] Cf. E. Gartly Jaco and Ivan Belknap, "Is a New Family Form Emerging in the Urban Fringe?" *American Sociological Review,* 18:551–557 (October, 1953).
[21] Gruenberg, *op. cit.,* pp. 134–135.
[22] William H. Whyte, Jr., *The Organization Man,* Simon and Schuster, Inc., New York, 1956, part VII, especially chaps. 21–22.

settled community life, despite the strong impact of the frontier. Norms of courtship, marriage, sex relationships, religious participation, social inter- course, and the rest have traditionally been those of the farm and small town. For many older persons, therefore, the new way of life as typified in the factory-made suburbs represents a change for the worse, entailing all manner of social problems. Younger persons, on the whole, welcome the emancipa- tion from primary controls and the freedom to rise in the status scale exempli- fied by the new mobility.

The Homeless Population

The participants in the new mobility just discussed have homes, even though they may move fairly often. They experience certain minor difficul- ties as a result of their moves from one packaged suburb to another. They undergo the disorganization and reorganization of many group relationships. But their lives remain comparatively stable, whether they live in the housing developments of Long Island, in the suburbs of Chicago, or in the sprawling outskirts of Los Angeles. Many other people, however, are not so fortunate. They have no homes, material possessions, or settled place in any commu- nity. They are the real sufferers from extreme social mobility. They are the homeless population.

The homeless population is the product of factors that are basically eco- nomic in origin. America was settled by a people eager for economic advance- ment, who pushed westward in search of material reward. The decades be- tween the two world wars were marked by increasing numbers of persons who left home in search of better economic opportunities—or any opportunities at all. Most of those who cut themselves loose completely from the primary ties of home and community did so because of their depressed economic condition or because they were unemployed. Other factors such as drink, sexual maladjustment, family difficulties, personal inadequacy, and wander- lust are also instrumental, singly or collectively, in causing the mobility of the homeless. But economic motives are primary in these movements.[23]

The homeless population is composed of those for whom mobility has be- come a way of life. The Great Depression of the 1930's changed the com- position of the homeless population, as large numbers of boys, girls, and fami- lies were forced to take to the road in search of employment.[24] These groups were more vulnerable to the difficulties of a mobile way of life than were the unattached adult males of an earlier hobo generation. In the years following the depression, most of the members of these mobile groups came to rest, established permanent homes, and abandoned life on the road. At any one time, however, large numbers of individuals and families continue to be with- out a settled residence.

[23] Daniel O. Price, "Some Socio-Economic Factors in Internal Migration," *Social Forces*, 29:409–415 (May, 1951).
[24] Ronald Freedman and Amos H. Hawley, "Migration and Occupational Mobility in the Depression," *American Journal of Sociology*, 55:171–177 (December, 1949).

1. *The Migratory-Casual Worker.*   The migratory-casual worker is one who works and wanders. His mobility is partly voluntary. He performs a necessary function in the economic system, for he builds the dams, harvests the wheat, picks and packs the fruit, cuts the timber, and maintains the right of way on the railroads. His work is unskilled, irregular, seasonal, and often carried on far from the centers of population. Ordinarily he receives little more than a bare subsistence for his labors. He is, in short, "a wanderer . . . [and] follows a way of life which bars him from membership in any community."[25]

The largest single group of migratory-casual laborers is that of the farm laborers, who work seasonally and move from farm to farm and region to region as they harvest, pick, cut, and pack the perishable crops. These agricultural migrants have been described as people "who temporarily leave their home community and move to other communities beyond commuting distance. They may move once, twice, or ten times a year. They may travel 200 miles or 2,000 miles. They may work for one employer or many employers."[26]

The number of migratory agricultural workers in America varies widely throughout the year. In the winter months it is estimated at approximately 200,000. At the peak of the summer and early fall seasons, it is estimated to rise to approximately 800,000 domestic workers, in addition to an estimated 200,000 foreign workers, most of whom are Mexicans. Here we have around a million persons whose life for part of every year is deprived of settled group relationships.[27]

The migrations of agricultural workers follow three main streams: (a) *Eastern.* One large group stays on the east coast and moves slowly northward, starting in Florida and moving up the Atlantic coast as the season advances. This group reaches New York State in the late summer and early fall and then returns to Florida, to spend the winter. (b) *Texas.* A second large group starts in South Texas and moves across Texas and into the mountain and plains states as the different crops ripen. Some of this group go into the Great Lakes states to harvest fruits, vegetables, and sugar beets. (c) *California.* The third major group originates in California and tends to stay within the boundaries of that state. The diversification of crops in California is such that many migrant workers can find employment all the year around without leaving the state. A minority continue up the coast to Washington, Oregon, and Idaho.[28]

Employment of migrant farm labor is largely centered in a dozen states. At the peak of employment in 1956, the numbers of migrants employed in the first twelve states were as follows: Texas, 112,880; California, 62,900; Michi-

[25] Theodore Caplow, *The Sociology of Work,* University of Minnesota Press, Minneapolis, 1954, p. 91.

[26] William Mirengoff, "Migratory Farm Labor Population," in *Proceedings of Consultation on Migratory Farm Labor,* under the auspices of U.S. Department of Labor, Washington, 1957, p. 28.

[27] *Ibid.,* p. 106, Table 1.

[28] *Ibid.,* pp. 32–33.

gan, 48,234; New York, 29,360; Arizona, 22,320; Florida, 21,288; Oregon, 20,411; New Jersey, 16,207; Washington, 12,906; Wisconsin, 12,869; Kansas, 12,500; and Virginia, 11,400.[29] This number included American and Puerto Rican workers. The exact number of Mexican workers is unknown, for the majority enter and leave the country illegally and hence are not officially counted. They probably amount to 200,000, as noted.

Migrant farm workers live precariously on the fringe of the social and economic structure. The nature of their work means that they cannot bargain collectively with employers but must take what is offered. The Fair Labor Standards Act specifically exempts agricultural workers from both the minimum and overtime wage requirements.[30] Consequently the annual wage of the migratory farm worker is among the lowest of wages for all occupational groups.

In one sample of farm workers on the Atlantic coast the average wage per day was $4.99; the average number of days worked per year was 182; and the average individual earnings per year totaled $908. With more than one person per household working, the average annual earnings per household were $1733.[31] This figure compares miserably with the average (median) family income in 1956 of $4800.[32] The earnings of the migratory farm worker are measured in terms of the "household," which is a more inclusive term than "family," since a household may contain more than one family. Hence the annual earnings of $1733 for the migratory farm *household* are even more meager as compared to the $4800 for the average *family*.

The migratory farm population is composed of men, women, and children. Most of them move as individuals, but many migrate as family units. In one study based upon a national sample in 1954, some 75 percent of those over fourteen years of age were men and 25 percent were women.[33]

An indeterminate number had young children with them, and the latter were exposed to the disorganizing influences associated with mobility. The children who migrate suffer from interrupted schooling, or sometimes have no formal schooling at all. Health hazards are present, and nourishment, sanitation, and medical care are often lacking.[34] This is discussed in Chapter 10, "Children in Industry."

The migratory farm worker leads a marginal existence from several viewpoints. His mobile life keeps him outside ordered group life. His children cannot go to school or participate in a continuous play group. His economic status is low because of the unskilled character of his job, the lack of collective bar-

[29] *Proceedings of Consultation on Migratory Farm Labor,* p. 107, Table 2.
[30] Beatrice McConnell, "Protection of Agricultural Workers Under Labor Laws," in *Proceedings of Consultation on Migratory Farm Labor,* pp. 84–88.
[31] *Proceedings of Consultation on Migratory Farm Labor,* p. 105.
[32] Bureau of the Census, *Consumer Income, Family Income Up 8 Percent Since 1955,* Current Population Reports, Series P-60, No. 26 (September 9, 1957).
[33] *Proceedings . . . on Migratory Farm Labor,* p. 104.
[34] Sheridan T. Maitland, "Number and Characteristics of Migratory Farm Workers," in *Proceedings of Consultation on Migratory Farm Labor,* pp. 39–40.

gaining power, and the complete absence of governmental protection. In addition, the migratory worker is deprived of many welfare provisions because he is not a legal resident of any community. Residence requirements range from three months to five years. They are established by townships, counties, and states and restrict local governments from giving assistance to needy migrants, even though the assistance comes from the federal government.[35] Some communities provide emergency relief, however.

2. *The Tramp.* The tramp is a nonworking migrant. Largely or completely foot-loose, he wanders from place to place with no fixed destination. His aimless peregrinations have become a vocation. He tries to conform to the laws of the community sufficiently to stay out of jail. But community traditions have little meaning for him. He is on his way, but he does not know (or care) where he is going. He has few group relationships and these are usually casual and secondary. He may, it is true, work out a life organization of a sort.[36] He may even say that the pleasures of settled group life have no allure for him. But any casting-up of the balance sheet indicates that he has lost more than he has gained.

3. *The Transient.* The transient is a product of unemployment. He has either lost or quit his job and is traveling in search of another. He is not a migratory-casual worker, for he is seeking a permanent job. Neither is he a tramp, for he actively wants work. The transient is a self-respecting individual who is unable to find work in his local community and is looking for it elsewhere. He may be a mechanic whose factory has closed or moved away; a shopkeeper who has gone bankrupt; a skilled laborer laid off after years of steady work; or a farmer whose farm has blown away in a dust storm. In an earlier generation, such people would have found a new home in the West. With the passing of the frontier, they are obliged to wander about the country in search of work.

During the depression of the 1930's, the problem of transiency reached an acute stage. Widespread unemployment forced millions of men, women, and children to take to the road looking for work. The large number of migratory-casual workers was augmented by hundreds of thousands of men with a stable work history who left home rather than accept relief.[37] In addition, large numbers of girls, women, and whole families abandoned the primary contacts of a settled community life.[38] The transient population during this period included both the mobile labor group and millions of unemployed.

The desperate struggle for survival of the transient family was vividly portrayed by John Steinbeck in his novel *The Grapes of Wrath*.[39] The collec-

[35] Marguerite Windhauser, "Residence Requirements," in *Proceedings . . . on Migratory Farm Labor,* pp. 90–93.

[36] Robert E. Park, "The Mind of the Hobo," in Robert E. Park (ed.), *The City,* University of Chicago Press, Chicago, 1925.

[37] John N. Webb, *The Transient Unemployed,* Works Progress Administration, Division of Social Research, Research Monograph III, Washington, 1935.

[38] John N. Webb and Malcolm Brown, *Migrant Families,* Works Progress Administration, Division of Social Research, Research Monograph No. 18, Washington, 1938.

[39] John Steinbeck, *The Grapes of Wrath,* The Viking Press, New York, 1939.

tive hero of the novel is the Joad family, hard-working people whose fore-fathers plowed the fields of Oklahoma. Like thousands of other families, the Joads were forced off their land by large-scale agriculture and were obliged to leave the soil that had nourished their ancestors for generations. Lured by handbills promising lucrative employment in the sunny valleys of California, the Joads loaded their possessions and children into their automobile. When they reached California, their hopes of the good life were rudely shattered. Thousands of persons in similar circumstances had come before them and had forced wages below the subsistence level. They lived in crowded work camps in poverty and squalor.

The transient unemployed are in a far better position today than were the Joads two decades ago. Employment is still at a high level, working conditions are better, and the hopelessness of the depression has been succeeded by faith in the future of America. Despite these changes, the transient faces problems, especially if his mobility is prolonged. In many cases, his situation is like that of the migratory-casual worker, for he and his family are deprived of stable institutional relationships during their mobility. Schooling for the children is irregular, health conditions are unsatisfactory, and job opportunities are often uncertain.

The extent of this transient mobility is indicated by the Bureau of the Census. In March, 1956, 261,000 *unemployed* male migrants were listed in a sample survey of the population as a whole. Of this number, 118,000 were seeking work within a state and 143,000 had traveled from one state to another. The unemployed *female* migrant population that year numbered 123,000, of whom 61,000 moved within a state and 62,000 from one state to another. When these figures are compared with the 43,175,000 males and 19,905,000 females that *are* employed, the transient unemployed constitute a small number.[40] But the fact that almost 400,000 men and women were on the road seeking employment during a period of unprecedented prosperity and presumably full employment indicates that the problem of transiency is still an important one.

Mobility and Social Disorganization

One of the reasons we are interested in social mobility is that it breaks group relationships if it is of an extreme form. This breaking of group relationships causes many of the problems of a mobile and secular society. Cooley long ago called attention to the close dependence of the individual upon the primary group. Standards of right and wrong are largely derived from one's family. When persons shift rapidly from place to place they lose much of this primary contact. Victims of extreme mobility become spiritually nomadic and hence morally remote from the very groups with which they have traditionally been most closely associated.[41] The individual who moves from group to

[40] Bureau of the Census, *Population Characteristics, Mobility of the Population of the United States: March 1955 to 1956, Current Population Reports,* Series P-20, No. 73 (March 12, 1957), Table 4.

[41] Charles Horton Cooley, *Social Process,* Charles Scribner's Sons, New York, 1922, p. 180.

group and status to status becomes increasingly isolated from the continuous social control which is implicit in a settled society.

Constrained by few of the ties that have bound men together in Western culture, the mobile individual may lose his sense of social responsibility and welcome a break in the "cake of custom." But when many individuals lose their ties with a settled society, the entire social structure may be undermined. The extreme mobility of the postwar years in Europe, with millions of persons permanently separated from their homes, is a case in point.[42] Individuals normally are affected and controlled by a stable pattern of group expectations. All this is lost when they flee their homes. Under such conditions, the web of organized relationships that constitutes society tends to break down.[43]

Personal disorganization is apparently a concomitant of extreme mobility, and often a result of the same process. A study of mental and personality disorders in Baltimore indicated that the mobile population there furnished more than its share of psychoses, neuroses, psychopathic personalities, and other types of personality disorder among adults and children.[44] Normal persons may be forced by circumstances beyond their control into a life of extreme mobility, which may result in the disorganization of their personalities.

On the other hand, persons with a marked tendency to personality deviation may not be able to adjust themselves to any fixed environment and therefore may move about excessively. Mobility itself thus appears to be both a cause and an effect of inordinate movement. Persons who move after short intervals from one residence to another within a city have a higher rate of personal disorganization than newcomers from other communities. The rate of mobility within the city, seems to be more important than a change of environment from one city to another.[45]

The Homeless Man

The relationship between mobility and social disorganization is illustrated by the homeless man, whose way of life cuts him off from many of the settled contacts of the normal person. The homeless man epitomizes the sociological impact of the break in the ties that bind the individual to the organized group. In a study of the relationship between alcohol and homelessness, the concept of "undersocialization" is applied to the permanently mobile members of our society. In the words of this study, undersocialized persons are, in general, "deprived of the opportunity of sharing experiences with others, of belonging to social groups and participating in social activities."[46] The home-

---

[42] Cf. Eugene M. Kulischer, "Displaced Persons in the Modern World," *Annals of the American Academy of Political and Social Science,* 262:166–177 (March, 1949).

[43] Sorokin, *op. cit.,* pp. 515–528.

[44] Christopher Tietze, Paul V. Lemkau, and Marcia Cooper, "Personality Disorder and Spatial Mobility," *American Journal of Sociology,* 48:29–39 (July, 1942), p. 39.

[45] *Ibid.* Cf. also E. Gartly Jaco, "The Social Isolation Hypothesis and Schizophrenia," *American Sociological Review,* 19:567–577 (October, 1954).

[46] Robert Straus, "Alcohol and the Homeless Man," *Quarterly Journal of Studies on Alcohol,* 7:360–404 (December, 1946), p. 363.

less man is such an individual. He has failed, for one reason or other, to adjust to the normal expectations of the stable group.

The process of socialization starts at birth and continues through life, although at a reduced rate in the later years. We do not know the nature of the qualities that cause the incipiently homeless man to reject socialization, just as we do not know the qualities that cause the ordinary person to accept this process. Early group influences play an important part in socialization, but they are not all-important. Many persons from substantially the same group milieu develop at different rates in the complex process of socialization.

As a result of insufficient socialization, the homeless man is deprived of "certain important personal satisfactions, such as affection, prestige, the feeling of security, the rewarding aspects of identifying with others, and the like."[47] These satisfactions arise from continued association with others, and the person who lacks them experiences a corresponding lack in his personality. The personality of the homeless man reflects the major institutional deprivations that have resulted in his undersocialization.[48]

1. *Marriage and the Family*. The social relationships of marriage and the institutional patterns of the family comprise the most intimate form of socialization. The sexual drives of the male find institutionalized gratification in marriage. The person participates in the various relationships of the community through the family. Men who have never established family ties or have broken ties once established are deprived of a powerful socializing agency. A high percentage of homeless men are not married.

2. *Parental Home*. The individual experiences his first socialization in the parental home. Hence some of the qualities that afterward cause him to become homeless are doubtless established in the parental family. Complete data on this aspect of the early lives of homeless men were not available, but many had a record of a parental family that was either unstable or broken. As a result, the home was unable to provide the emotional satisfactions so necessary to the development of personality. Many of the homeless men in the study took to the road when they were young and have been following it ever since.

3. *Education*. The school is another agency in socialization. The homeless men in the Straus study showed a degree of education roughly comparable to that of the general population. At the same time, there was a high incidence of men who had failed to complete a particular educational goal— whether graduation from grade school, high school, or college. This characteristic is expressive of failure to follow through with other projects when once started. In the institutional fields of marriage, the family, occupation, and education, the homeless men were insufficiently motivated to carry through their projects to completion.[49]

---

[47] *Ibid.*

[48] The following is adapted from Straus, *op. cit.* This study was primarily directed at the role of alcohol in the lives of homeless men. In the course of the study, however, Straus discovered certain pertinent facts about mobility as such.

[49] *Ibid.*, pp. 387–389.

4. *Occupational Status.* The occupational status of the homeless man is by definition low, inasmuch as the nature of his activity precludes permanent or lucrative activity. The majority (81 percent) of the men in the study had gone down in occupational status since they had increased their mobility. In this way they had cut themselves off from another form of permanent socialization. The tenure of their occupational status, furthermore, was very short, as they moved from one casual job to another. As the homeless men grew older, the tenure of their jobs grew shorter, and their undersocialization became correspondingly more pronounced.[50]

5. *Alcoholism.* The personal disorganization of the homeless man tends to take the form of excessive drinking. Alcoholism may be both a cause and an effect of homelessness. Men who are addicted to alcohol may have their group relationships so disorganized that it is easy to take to the road to escape further responsibility. Men who have taken to the road for other reasons often find that their mobile life inclines them to excessive drinking. The cycle of undersocialization thus becomes a vicious one, as the individual becomes increasingly cut off from normal group relationships.[51]

The End of the Road

The time comes when the homeless man reaches the end of the road. He may become progressively disorganized by years of living without family, friends, or a permanent home. He may be prematurely aged by active dissipation, culminating in alcoholism. He may, in the "natural" course of events, become so infirm that he can no longer earn a living on the road or in the city. Whatever the circumstances, the homeless man finally reaches a stage when his life organization is broken, his ties are long since dissolved, and he can look forward to nothing but a succession of drunken days and nights before death comes in an alley, a gutter, or a cheap hotel. Long before that time comes, the homeless man has hit Skid Row.

Skid Row is the term which has come to apply to an area that caters to the needs of homeless men for shelter, support, and sustenance. In the middle of the last century, Seattle had a street known as Skid Road, down which logs were "skidded" from the nearby forest to a sawmill at the edge of the water. Along this road, itinerant timber laborers and other mobile workers and nonworkers congregated. Saloons, brothels, and cheap hotels arose to care for their most pressing needs. Every large city has such a constellation of institutions. Chicago has its West Madison Street; New York its Bowery; San Francisco its Mission Street; and Los Angeles its East Fifth Street. The original Skid Road has been changed to Skid Row, but the function remains the same.[52]

Skid Row is also known to sociologists as Hobohemia. This graphic title

[50] *Ibid.,* pp. 389–393.
[51] *Ibid.,* pp. 396–399. Cf. also Robert Straus and Raymond G. McCarthy, "Nonaddictive Pathological Drinking Patterns of Homeless Men," *Quarterly Journal of Studies on Alcohol,* 12:601–611 (December, 1951).
[52] "Hallelujah Time for Bums," *Time,* 70:16, 33 (October 14, 1957).

was first used by Nels Anderson, who wrote the initial definitive study of the homeless man. Hobohemia is an unplanned area where a group of institutional patterns have evolved to meet the specialized needs of those men who "have resigned from society."[53] Among these patterns are "flophouses, cheap restaurants, ten-cent saloons, pawnshops, burlesque shows, all-night movies, second-hand stores, fundamentalist missions . . . , recruiting offices, jungles, park benches, and barber shops. . . ."[54] During the past fifty years these institutions have met the needs of such varied clients as lumberjacks, railroad workers, wheat harvesters, fruit pickers, boys running away from home, transient unemployed, soldiers on leave, and men on old age pensions in the brave new world of the welfare state. The individuals change, but the patterns of Hobohemia remain.[55]

The homeless men may band together with others for survival and support, but for the most part it is every man for himself. This does not mean that complete anarchy rules on Skid Row. Patterns of group expectations evolve here as elsewhere and the individual does well to follow them. If he has been given part of a bottle of wine, he is under strong obligation to return the favor. A man who treats another to a meal or a flop expects the same when the other is in funds. A man may help another stay out of reach of the police, and he expects reciprocal action. Temporary groups may be formed, with one man seeking new clothes, another specializing in begging, and a third seeking shelter at charitable and religious organizations. A basic reciprocity, therefore, obtains on Skid Row, and the lone individual violates these norms at his peril.[56]

Some transient workers passing through town on their way to a new job are also to be found on Skid Row. Others have come in from the lumber camps, fruit ranches, and wheat fields to live on their wages until spring. These men consider themselves responsible workers. They do not think that their life organization is in any sense broken. Although technically unemployed, they are not unemployable. For them, Skid Row is merely a convenient way station between jobs.[57]

Later—when age, infirmity, and the other occupational hazards have caught up with them—these transients are likely to become permanent residents of Skid Row. They then will be unemployables, "the superannuated, the physically and mentally handicapped, . . . [the] alcoholics, . . . the illiterates, the emotionally unstable. . . ."[58] Through inclination, infirmity, or both, they will never again hold a steady job. Many will never again take to the road in search of even seasonal employment. They no longer plan to re-

---

[53] Quoted from a statement by Wilbert L. Hindman, Chairman of the Los Angeles Welfare Planning Committee on Skid Row, in *ibid.*, p. 33.

[54] Caplow, *op. cit.*, p. 91.

[55] *Ibid.*, pp. 91–92.

[56] Joan K. Jackson and Ralph Connor, "The Skid Road Alcoholic," *Quarterly Journal of Studies on Alcohol,* 14:468–486 (September, 1953), pp. 473–479.

[57] *Ibid.*, pp. 470–473.

[58] Caplow, *op. cit.*, p. 93.

turn next year to the wheat fields or the orange groves. When a man becomes a permanent resident of Skid Row he has hit bottom. He looks forward no farther than the next meal, the next flop, or the next drink.

These men thus live on the fringe of society. Some rely on the Evangelical Protestant missions for food and shelter. The latter try to rehabilitate them by a combination of religion and physical aid. Some homeless men—or "mission stiffs," as they are called—huddle in the barren rooms of these missions, where they are required to listen to a sermon before they receive any food. Other missions make their religious services voluntary. Most of the men are completely cynical about their "religious" participation and accept the sermon as the price they must pay for a meal and a means of keeping soul and body together.[59]

When the newcomer first comes to Skid Row he must familiarize himself with its particular institutional setting. He must learn the location of the missions, the attitudes of their leaders, how the police look upon homeless men, where the best places to eat are, what sections are the best for begging—and other bits of local folklore. He may enter into cautious relationships with other homeless men, but these contacts are limited to specific purposes. Most of these men are unwilling or unable to maintain permanent group relationships in the outside world. They have no intention of entering into any new entangling alliances on Skid Row. They do not trust each other—probably for good reason.[60]

Drinking on Skid Row

The most important single value of many permanent residents of Skid Row is alcohol. Not all the men are clinical alcoholics, but the great majority drink more or less excessively. Drinking in fact is related to social status on Skid Row. A rough gradation exists in terms of the type of beverage consumed. At the top of the status ladder are those who are sufficiently affluent to drink whisky at so much per shot. Beer drinkers come next, and many in this category are able to reinforce their beer with an occasional shot of whisky. At a considerably lower level are the "winos," who drink fortified wine by the bottle. This beverage gives the consumer the maximum amount of alcoholic content per unit cost. The winos are looked down upon by most of the inhabitants of Skid Row; the term is a derogatory one which the person seldom applies to himself. Winos have a bad smell, "wine sores" on their bodies, and a generally squalid appearance. At the very bottom are the men who drink nonbeverage alcohol, which they laboriously strain through handkerchiefs to eliminate some of the major impurities. These "rubby-dubs" (from rubbing alcohol) are usually solitary men, beyond the pale even of Skid Row and rejected by the group. They live their brief lives in an alcoholic stupor.[61]

[59] Jackson and Connor, *op. cit.*, p. 476.

[60] *Ibid.*, pp. 473–479. Cf. W. Jack Peterson and Milton A. Maxwell, "The Skid Row 'Wino,' " *Social Problems*, 5:308–316 (Spring, 1958).

[61] Jackson and Connor, *op. cit.*, p. 470.

Alcohol is a symptom, rather than a cause, of much of the personal disorganization on Skid Row. Straus and McCarthy classify approximately half of their sample of 444 homeless men as heavy uncontrolled drinkers (i.e., addictive alcoholics), and the other half as either moderate or heavy controlled drinkers. A few (47) men indicated that they were nondrinkers.[62] Most of the homeless men on Skid Row clearly drink more than they "should," and alcohol breaks down their ability for normal group relationships. A substantial minority, however, drink because they *want* to, because alcohol plays an important role in their personal adjustment. The rest drink because they must, whenever and whatever they can.

Mobility was unquestionably a major factor in the initial disorganization of these men. Because of their complete rootlessness their disorganization is reinforced by their escape through alcohol. In early times when mobility was not so great many of the failures and misfits became beggars on the streets and public squares.

Most individuals who move from place to place are not so disorganized by mobility as the men on Skid Row. Nevertheless, the constant uprooting of great numbers of people upsets their group relationships and the social controls which an earlier society imposed on its members. Many of the strains and stresses in family life and many of the problems of institutional disorganization arise from that mobility.

SELECTED BIBLIOGRAPHY

Anderson, Nels, *The Hobo,* University of Chicago Press, Chicago, 1923. For many years this was the standard sociological study of the homeless man. The drastic changes in the mobile population during the depression of the 1930's and World War II were accompanied by changes in the social structure. Despite these qualifications, many of the insights on the role of the homeless man are still valuable.

Blau, Peter M., "Social Mobility and Interpersonal Relations," *American Sociological Review, 21:*290–295 (June, 1956). Although this article is primarily concerned with vertical rather than horizontal mobility, many of the suggestions on interpersonal relations are valid for internal migration as well.

Bogue, Donald J., "The Quantitative Study of Social Dynamics and Social Change," *American Journal of Sociology, 57:*565–568 (May, 1952). This is an interesting attempt to measure social mobility in terms of changes in status, including such areas as marital, family, and fertility status; educational attainment; church affiliation; and type of housing and home ownership.

Bureau of the Census, *Population Characteristics, Mobility of the Population of the United States, Current Population Reports,* Series P-20, published periodically. The Bureau of the Census makes available at frequent intervals the results of its continuing sampling of the mobility of the American people.

Caplow, Theodore, *The Sociology of Work,* University of Minnesota Press, Minneapolis, 1954. Chapter 4 of this book deals with social mobility in its various manifestations.

[62] Straus and McCarthy, *op. cit.,* p. 606.

Gruenberg, Sidonie M., "The Challenge of the New Suburbs," *Marriage and Family Living*, *17*:133–137 (May, 1955). The new, mass-produced suburbs which have sprung up all over the country are expressly made for mobile and rootless young persons, who will make many more moves before they eventually settle down.

Merrill, Francis E., *Social Problems on the Home Front*, Harper & Brothers, New York, 1948. Chapter 1 of this monograph discusses the role of social mobility in bringing about and accentuating the social changes accompanying World War II.

Migrant Labor, A Human Problem, Report and Recommendations, Federal Interagency Committee on Migrant Labor, U.S. Department of Labor, Washington, 1947. This is an official study of the problems arising from migrant labor in the period immediately after World War II.

Sorokin, Pitirim A., *Social Mobility*, Harper & Brothers, New York, 1927. Although written some three decades ago, this book is still the most authoritative study of the theory of social mobility.

Straus, Robert, "Alcohol and the Homeless Man," *Quarterly Journal of Studies on Alcohol*, *7*:360–404 (December, 1946). The relationships between alcohol and the homeless man are here viewed in terms of the concept of *undersocialization*.

CHAPTER 25

Migration

The Concept of Migration

Since long before the dawn of history human beings have wandered from place to place in hordes, families, clans, and tribes. Migration has played an important role in the development of society.[1] There is a significant difference, however, between early migrations and those of modern times in terms of the number of persons and the purposes that have motivated them. The ancient migrations involved entire societies that carried their culture with them. Social disorganization was largely absent, for the social structure was solidly maintained. Individuals and families retained the familiar aspects of their culture and the continuity of group life was seldom threatened.

Not so in modern times. Migration has become an individual or (at best) a family enterprise, rather than an organized group movement. Many millions of persons have migrated to the United States, but they have for the most part been individually motivated. They have come to this country as individuals and families, not as clans, tribes, or nations. It is largely for this reason that social disorganization has resulted. Modern migrants can neither bring their culture with them nor participate in a familiar culture when they arrive. They must give up much that is familiar and adjust to a different set of social definitions. In the present chapter we shall consider some of the relationships between this break in the "cake of custom" and social disorganization.[2]

Culture conflict is fundamental to the disorganization of the migrant and of the society into which he enters. Culture conflict is especially apparent in the large city, where there is a large immigrant population. The heterogeneity of American culture is such that the immigrant is forced to play a number of conflicting roles. He may be victimized by the clashing heritages of the several groups in which he claims membership.[3]

Culture conflict is especially apparent among the children of the foreign

[1] William Peterson, "A General Typology of Migration," *American Sociological Review*, 23:256–266 (June, 1958).

[2] For an overall account of immigration to the United States in the postwar world, see Hugh Carter (ed.), "Reappraising Our Immigration Policy," *Annals of the American Academy of Political and Social Science*, Vol. 262 (March, 1949) (special issue).

[3] Louis Wirth, "Culture Conflict and Delinquency," *Social Forces*, 9:484–492 (June, 1931).

born. With ties both within and without the parental family, the second generation is torn between two patterns of behavior, two sets of definitions. In an earlier period, the sociologist was concerned with the adjustments of the immigrants themselves, who had come to this country to make their way in the new world. This older generation is rapidly dying off and is not being re- placed by new immigrants because of our present restrictions. For the children and grandchildren of the original migrants, however, the struggle for adjustment still goes on. Ethnic problems have not been completely solved by the assimilation of the first generation. They are still apparent in the lives of millions of children and grandchildren of the foreign born.[4]

The culture conflict of the immigrant has also been examined in terms of the aspects of the culture to which he is exposed. Many phases of social disorganization among immigrants and their children may result from "isola- tion from the private culture of America and contact with the public culture of America."[5] The public culture involves the most chaotic aspects of American life. The immigrant sees the new country through the secondary media of the press, political corruption, business activity, and other phases where ethical standards are often not high. The standards of public culture are, in part, those of "misrepresentation, sharp practices, graft, grasping competition, and disregard of human beings."[6] These are the definitions of the market place, where shady and quasi-legal dealings are excused under the protecting cloak of the marketing mentality.[7]

American private culture, on the other hand, is that of the primary group and reflects the intimate phases of family life and primary morality. This culture is largely unknown to the immigrant. He lives in a different world and is cut off from the private culture by the barriers of unfamiliarity, language difficulties, and prejudice. Whatever contact he has with it is gained through newspapers, motion pictures, and other forms of mass communication. The sympathetic relationships so necessary to complete assimilation are lacking. The immigrant gains a distorted conception of American culture. His children are likewise exposed to the public culture and try to adapt their expectations and behavior accordingly. The immigrant thus has little insight into the basic ideals of Americans.

The problems of assimilation have been considered in a new light in recent years. The traditional approach to the adjustment of the immigrant was in terms of the "melting pot," wherein all newcomers to this country were, sooner or later, magically fused into a common, static, and uniform culture. This concept has given way to that of "cultural pluralism," which "recognizes the ethnic diversity of our population and takes cognizance of the time ele-

[4] Samuel Koenig, "Second- and Third-Generation Americans," chap. 21 in Francis J. Brown and Joseph S. Roucek (eds.), *One America*, Prentice-Hall, Inc., New York, 1945.

[5] E. H. Sutherland, "Social Process in Behavior Problems," in Emory S. Bogardus (ed.), *Social Problems and Social Processes*, University of Chicago Press, Chicago, 1933, p. 54.

[6] *Ibid*.

[7] Erich Fromm, *Man for Himself*, Rinehart and Company, Inc., New York, 1947.

ment in processes of assimilation."[8] The recipient culture is viewed as heterogeneous and variegated, with different contributions from the various ethnic groups. This point of view denies that American culture is stable and fixed for all time in a common pattern established by the early Anglo-Saxon colonists. American culture is rather seen as dynamic, with constant change as the different culture traits are brought into the main pattern. The culture patterns of the various immigrant groups thus contribute to the overall pattern and therefore should be cherished.[9]

The recognition of the role of different ethnic contributions in the pattern of American culture is an important step in understanding the adjustment or maladjustment of the immigrant. The concept of cultural pluralism, however, is confined to a comparatively small segment of the population, consisting primarily of those persons with knowledge, understanding, and sophistication in the cultural disciplines. The mass of the people do not react in an enlightened fashion to the strangers within our gates. Their value judgments are still based upon certain alleged cultural uniformities, handed down for generations, while their concepts of American values are more ideal than the actuality. Meanwhile, the prejudice arising from the immigrant's strangeness and inability to conform to prevailing cultural norms continues to militate against his adjustment. Whatever the enlightened and humanitarian insights of the specialist, the man on the street still reacts emotionally to manifest differences in culture.[10]

The Marginal Man

The concept of the "marginal man" throws additional light upon the disorganization of the migrant and of the society to which he comes. The conflict of cultures is most acute in the marginal man and he is exposed to the schizophrenic influences of his status. The marginal man has been defined as "a cultural hybrid, a man living and sharing intimately in the cultural life and traditions of two distinct peoples; never quite willing to break, even if he were permitted to do so, with his past and his traditions and not quite accepted, because of racial prejudice, in the new society in which he now sought to find a place . . . a man on the margin of two cultures and two societies, which never completely interpenetrated and fused."[11]

Culture conflict thus marks the marginal man.[12] He may or may not be biologically marginal (e.g., of mixed racial stock), but in any case he is

[8] Clyde V. Kiser, "Cultural Pluralism," *Annals of the American Academy of Political and Social Science, 262*:117–130 (March, 1949), p. 129.

[9] John H. Burma, "Some Cultural Aspects of Immigration: Its Impact, Especially on Our Arts and Sciences," *Law and Contemporary Problems, 21*:284–298 (Spring, 1956).

[10] Cf. David I. Golovensky, "The Marginal Man Concept: An Analysis and Critique," *Social Forces, 30*:333–339 (March, 1952).

[11] Robert E. Park, "Human Migration and the Marginal Man," *American Journal of Sociology, 33*:881–893 (May, 1928), p. 892. Park uses "racial" to mean ethnic.

[12] The most extensive study of the marginal man has been made by Everett V. Stonequist, *The Marginal Man*, Charles Scribner's Sons, New York, 1937.

culturally so. His marginal situation is the result of migrating from one cultural group to another. The process by which the United States has grown through the migration of tens of millions of culturally heterogeneous persons has created perhaps the most massive and prolonged example of marginality in history. The cycle of the marginal man—from his first shock of contact with American life to his gradual adjustment to the new culture—has been enacted in millions of individual lives. Many aspects of social disorganization have been either initiated or intensified by the presence of large numbers of persons who (through no fault of their own) have been marginal to the prevailing culture pattern. Yet our culture is the product of millions of such persons. Each has brought his contribution to the overall pattern, but he has also inadvertently added to the heterogeneity of this pattern in the process.[13]

The natural history of the marginal man has three related stages. (1) The culturally marginal person is initially ignorant of his own status because his differences have not been specifically defined for him. In addition, he ordinarily does not have enough insight to understand the extent of his differences from other persons in the new environment. (2) When he learns, often painfully, of his strangeness, he enters the second or crisis stage. He must then redefine himself in terms of the new situation, which means he must adjust his conception of himself as well as his role in the group. At this stage, he may suffer shock and become permanently disorganized. (3) The third stage is dependent upon the facility with which the crisis is met or rationalized. If the marginal man makes a successful redefinition, he may gradually overcome his status. If he is unsuccessful, he may relegate himself permanently to marginality and intensify his personal disorganization.[14]

If the immigrant is mature when he enters the new society, he may have great difficulty in adjusting to its culture. His children experience the marginal status even more directly, since they are caught *between* the old-world culture (represented by their parents) and that of the new world (represented by the play group, the school, and the other cultural elements). Social isolation may accompany these cultural differences and the immigrant and his children may feel that they do not fully belong to the United States. Their language, religion, and cultural traits mark them as different. Since these qualities are intimately related to the personality, the latter may suffer when behavior patterns are scorned.[15]

The marginal man is denied the opportunity to play a significant role in certain groups. His personality may be stultified accordingly. His status is often uncertain and his conception of his role or roles equally so. Thousands of isolated persons, brooding in the ethnic areas of the large cities, live an

[13] Cf. Francis J. Brown, "Backgrounds of American Heterogeneity," chap. 2 in Brown and Roucek, *op. cit.*

[14] Stonequist, *op. cit.*, chap. 5, "The Life-Cycle of the Marginal Man."

[15] Nathan Glazer, "The Integration of American Immigrants," *Law and Contemporary Problems*, 21:256–269 (Spring, 1956). See also Otis Durant Duncan and Stanley Liberson, "Ethnic Segregation and Assimilation," *American Journal of Sociology*, 64:364–374 (January, 1959).

unhappy existence between two worlds, the one they left and the one that refuses to accept them completely.[16]

The concept of the marginal man has been criticized in recent years. Green believes this concept to be too vague and difficult to validate in specific research, inasmuch as it assumes that the external conflict of the marginal group is echoed in the individual psyche. He further questions the assumption that the children of the foreign born always identify with their parents and hence suffer the emotional ambivalence of a marginal status.[17] Golovensky holds that cultural pluralism in America reduces the adjustment pattern with various cultural strains. Thus the Pole or the Jew can identify himself with the Polish or Jewish elements in American culture and hence have no feeling of his own marginality. In this sense, "Americanism is not a product but a process; it is not a being but a becoming. Therefore, it is not a conflict between native and foreign elements of a cultural amalgam but an interplay of cultural ingredients in perpetual interaction."[18]

Green's contention—that the concept of the marginal man is difficult to quantify—is a valid one, although it would seem to be no more difficult than many concepts resting upon the complex basis of personality. Golovensky's concept of cultural pluralism is also valid, although it would appear to be an ideal, rather than an actual, situation. Rightly or wrongly, value judgments as to the desirability of one culture over another remain important elements in the immigrant's adjustment. In this sense, the situation of marginality is a fact, however unpalatable. Value judgments become factors in the rejection and maladjustment of the marginal man.

Trends in American Immigration

With this conceptual framework, we may examine the trends in American immigration.[19] In the hundred years between 1830 and 1930, approximately 38,000,000 persons migrated to the United States. Immigration reached its height during the early years of the present century, when more than a million persons entered the country annually. Following World War I, there was still a large yearly influx, with more than 800,000 arriving in 1921. This flood of new arrivals was arrested by the Restriction Act of 1924, and immigration was immediately reduced to a small percentage of the previous influx. During the depression of the 1930's, immigration was temporarily reversed and for several years the nation actually lost population through emigration. From 1932 to 1935, more alien residents left the country

[16] Stonequist, *op. cit.*, chap. 10, "Maladjustment and Adjustment."

[17] Arnold W. Green, "A Re-Examination of the Marginal Man Concept," *Social Forces*, 26:167–171 (December, 1947).

[18] Golovensky, *op. cit.*, p. 337.

[19] Cf. Carl Wittke, "Immigration Policy Prior to World War I," *Annals of the American Academy of Political and Social Science*, 262:5–14 (March, 1949); Edward P. Hutchinson, "Immigration Policy Since World War I," *Annals of the American Academy of Political and Social Science*, 262:15–21 (March, 1949); John Higham, "American Immigration Policy in Historical Perspective," *Law and Contemporary Problems*, 21:213–235 (Spring, 1956).

to take up residence elsewhere than were admitted for permanent residence here. As indicated in Table 25.1, the tide began to turn again in 1936 and continued to rise for the next decade, although it was not until after the war in 1946 that there was a net increase of more than 90,000 persons through immigration.[20]

During the period from 1945 to 1956 there was a marked increase in aliens

TABLE 25.1.   Immigrant and Emigrant Aliens, 1931–1956

Year	Immigrant Aliens Admitted	Emigrant Aliens Departed	Net Increase or Decrease
1931	97,139	61,882	35,257
1932	35,576	103,295	−67,719
1933	23,068	80,081	−57,013
1934	29,470	39,771	−10,301
1935	34,956	38,834	−3,878
1936	36,329	35,817	512
1937	50,244	26,736	23,508
1938	67,895	25,210	42,685
1939	82,998	26,651	56,347
1940	70,756	21,461	49,295
1941	51,776	17,115	34,661
1942	28,781	7,363	21,418
1943	23,725	5,107	18,618
1944	28,551	5,669	22,882
1945	38,119	7,442	30,677
1946	108,721	18,143	90,578
1947	147,292	22,501	124,791
1948	170,570	20,875	149,695
1949	188,317	24,586	163,731
1950	249,187	27,598	221,589
1951	205,717	26,174	179,543
1952	265,520	21,880	243,640
1953	170,434	24,256	146,178
1954	208,177	30,665	177,512
1955	237,790	31,245	206,545
1956	321,625	22,824	298,801

SOURCES: The figures from 1931 to 1946 are taken from Department of Justice, Immigration and Naturalization Service, *Annual Reports*. The figures from 1946 to 1956 are taken from Bureau of the Census, *Statistical Abstract of the United States, 1957*, 1957, Table 106, p. 92.

admitted to the United States. The annual increase ranged from a low of 38,119 in 1945 to a high of 321,625 in 1956. These trends are shown in Chart 25.1.

Immediately following World War II, total immigration was increased by approximately 120,000 wives and children of servicemen who married overseas. In the years 1950 to 1956, thousands of refugees swelled the total. Many entered under the Refugee Relief Act, which allowed 209,000 quota-exempt

[20] Adena M. Rich, "Current Immigration Problems," *Social Service Review*, 21:85–106 (March, 1947).

admissions between 1953 and 1956. Puerto Ricans have also averaged close to 40,000 annually in recent years. The latest group of refugee immigrants have been the Hungarians, of whom some 32,000 entered the country in the first six months after their ill-starred insurrection of November, 1956.[21]

Despite these recent increases, the long-term trend in immigration has been downward since the Restriction Act of 1924.[22] In 1930, there were

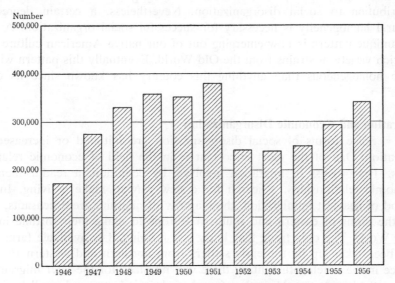

CHART 25.1. Annual Population Increase from Civilian Migration, United States, 1946–1956. (From Metropolitan Life Insurance Company, "Current Pattern of Immigration," *Statistical Bulletin,* April, 1957.)

13,983,000 foreign-born persons in the United States; in 1940 the number had shrunk to 11,419,000 and in 1950 to 10,184,000. The ratio of the foreign born to the native population has also declined, with the foreign born constituting 22.7 percent of the population in 1930, only 9.7 percent in 1940, and 6.6 percent in 1950.[23] Today, most of the foreign born are adults and represent an aging group. Their death rate is consequently high and will continue to increase as they grow older. The number of the foreign born admitted to this country each year is far smaller than the number who die.[24]

These demographic trends point to certain social considerations. The cultural heterogeneity that characterized this country for many decades is dis-

[21] Metropolitan Life Insurance Company, "Current Pattern of Immigration," *Statistical Bulletin,* April, 1957.

[22] Dudley Kirk and Earl Huyck, "Overseas Migration from Europe Since World War II," *American Sociological Review, 19:447–456* (August, 1954).

[23] Bureau of the Census, United States Census of Population, 1950, *General Characteristics: U.S. Summary,* Washington, 1952, Table 35.

[24] Metropolitan Life Insurance Company, "The Passing of Our Foreign Born," *Statistical Bulletin,* June, 1945.

appearing, as generations of native-born children and grandchildren of the foreign born are reared in the American way of life. The variety of cultures that formerly existed in the metropolitan areas was often greater than the native pattern could absorb effectively. Many phases of social disorganization—from political corruption to juvenile delinquency—were affected by this diversity of conflicting patterns. In the long run the positive contribution of the immigrant groups has been incalculably greater than their unwitting contribution to social disorganization. Nevertheless, a certain degree of cultural homogeneity is necessary for successful social organization. A new and unique pattern is now emerging out of our native American culture and the rich variety of strains from the Old World. Eventually this pattern will be more homogeneous than anything this country has known since its early days.[25]

Migration and Economic Disorganization

Some forms of social disorganization are initiated or increased by migration. One of the most important is in the field of economic relationships. The process of migration involves, by definition, a readjustment of economic relationships, a search for a new way to make a living. In the period of heaviest immigration, the majority of migrants were peasants, who left the farms of eastern and southern Europe to make their fortune in the New World. The only trade they knew was farming. The available farm land had been taken up by the early settlers from northern and western Europe. Hence in the nineteenth century there was no place for the later migrants to go but the large cities. Here they found work in industry and small business. This new way of life lacked security, and unemployment was a constant threat. In Europe the farmer, even though a tenant, had considerable stability. He knew at least for one year in advance where he would live and what he would be doing. His chance of acquiring wealth was slight, but he was always assured of food, shelter, and employment.[26]

Not so for the immigrant in America.[27] He was ordinarily one of the most marginal members of the labor force, the first (white) man to be fired and the last hired. The work he has perforce done in this country has been markedly different from what he did in the old country. The peasant has become an industrial worker. No matter how conscientious he was, he might lose his job at the whim of a foreman or the turn of the business cycle. He was encouraged to go into debt through installment purchases, only to lose his automobile and television set at the first lapse of payments. His economic life has often been literally from hand to mouth.[28]

---

[25] Maurice R. Davie, "Our Vanishing Minorities," chap. 27 in Brown and Roucek *op. cit.*

[26] William I. Thomas and Florian Znaniecki, *The Polish Peasant in Europe and America,* Alfred A. Knopf, Inc., New York, 1927, Vol. II, pp. 1692–1702.

[27] Joseph J. Spengler, "Some Economic Aspects of Immigration into the United States," *Law and Contemporary Problems, 21:*236–255 (Spring, 1956).

[28] Cf. A. Ross Eckler and Jack Zlotnick, "Immigration and the Labor Force," *Annals of the American Academy of Political and Social Science, 262:*92–101 (March, 1949).

During the depression of the 1930's the immigrant's economic situation was complicated by the widespread unemployment. There was opposition to extending relief to the alien and even to the foreign-born citizen. Many persons maintained that aliens had no right to support from the local community, the state, or the federal government. Despite the efforts of the national administration to prevent such discrimination against aliens, it was a practice in many local communities. Americans were willing to accept the brawn and muscle of the immigrant as long as he was needed to develop our national resources, build our cities, and throw our railroads across the Great Plains. But they objected to supporting the immigrant when out of work.[29]

The immigrant has had other difficulties. He has traditionally been the object of prejudice, hostility, and suspicion on the part of the native born. He has been forced to live in the most disagreeable sections of the city and to rear his children in slums. He has been offered the most unpleasant and degrading jobs and has been depicted as taking the bread out of the mouth of the native-born worker. In recent years, he has been suspected at times of unorthodox political beliefs, if not downright subversion. Certain industries discriminate against or discharge workers who have not become citizens. Discrimination in a variety of forms has been the lot of the immigrant.[30]

When the immigrant was a trained professional worker he was subjected to to difficulties of another sort. In some states, aliens have been barred by law from practicing medicine, law, architecture, or teaching—all professions requiring many years of expensive preparation. Skilled foreign-born doctors have been forbidden to practice medicine on the ground that the profession was already overcrowded or that their training was inadequate. The first of these allegations is demonstrably false, since there is a recognized shortage of doctors. The second is more valid, for the training of physicians in some foreign countries is not as complete as in our own. Nevertheless, alien doctors willing and able to take additional training have been effectively discouraged from doing so by the stipulations of state legislation.[31]

The economic adjustment of the immigrant since World War II has been, on the whole, easier than in earlier periods. The United States has enjoyed a period of prosperity and full employment, and jobs have been comparatively easy to find. There has also been more sympathy for the postwar migrant because he was, in most cases, fleeing from Communism or its threat. The large industrial cities were able to absorb these latest immigrants with comparatively little difficulty. In the year 1952, nearly three-fifths of the immigrants settled in cities of 100,000 or over. Here the economic problems of

[29] Cf. R. Clyde White and Mary K. White, *Research Memorandum on Social Aspects of Relief Policies in the Depression,* Social Science Research Council, New York, 1937; Donald Young, *Research Memorandum on Minority Peoples in the Depression,* Social Science Research Council, New York, 1937.

[30] Henry Pratt Fairchild, "Public Opinion on Immigration," *Annals of the American Academy of Political and Social Science, 262:*185–192 (March, 1949).

[31] Marie Ginsburg, "Adjustment of the Professional Refugee," *Annals of the American Academy of Political and Social Science, 203:*155–161 (May, 1939).

assimilation were minimized by the unprecedented level of economic activity.[32]

Migration and Social Disorganization

1. *Religious Disorganization.* The breakdown in group relationships suffered by the immigrant extends into his institutional affiliations. Religion is one. Religious affiliations are more effective when families are members of the same churches, or when the church is a community institution. In a simple environment, religion and the rest of the social structure are inextricably related. When primary contacts are replaced by secondary ones and the intimacy of the small peasant village is replaced by the complex structure of the city, religious ties are likely to be weakened. The church often loses it hold upon the immigrant in his new environment.

The prejudice against some religious groups is an added factor in the disorganization of this central institution, as we discuss in Chapter 27. We should mention here, however, that prejudice is a disorganizing force in religious institutions. From the point of view of the religious authorities, assimilation is often synonymous with disorganization. Renunciation of the old faith may involve a deep emotional conflict, but continued participation in a foreign nationality-related church may partially disbar the immigrant from full participation in the new life. The marginal position of the immigrant may be thus intensified by the affiliation with a Polish church or a Hungarian church, for example.[33]

Religion plays a dual role in the adjustment of the immigrant. For the church acts both as an integrative and as a disorganizing force. Religion holds the immigrant group together and provides a powerful emotional and institutional buffer against the shocks of the new life. At the same time, religious differences comprise the basis for intolerance and thus may unwittingly hinder the process of adjustment. Religious and other ethnic agencies constitute an obstacle to assimilation, if assimilation entails the loss of cultural identity and the unconditional acceptance of the new patterns. If assimilation is a matter of cultural pluralism, the nationality-oriented institutions may *contribute* to the American way of life. The religious institutions thus have an ambivalent role.[34]

2. *Family Disorganization.* The family is another institution that is disorganized by migration. The solidarity of the large kith and kin family of the Old World ultimately collapses in the New World. There is no place in the metropolitan community for the extended, peasant type of family organization. The ties that bind the group under rural conditions dissolve in the urban

---

[32] Kirk and Huyck, *op. cit.,* p. 449.

[33] Cf. Willard Johnson, "Religion and Minority Peoples," chap. 24 in Brown and Roucek, *op. cit.*

[34] Y. J. Chyz and Read Lewis, "Agencies Organized by Nationality Groups in the United States," *Annals of the American Academy of Political and Social Science, 262:* 148–158 (March, 1949).

slum. The patriarchal power of the father cannot survive these changes for more than one generation. The children insist on being emancipated and remove themselves from the dominance of the father. This process is part of the acquisition of the American way of life and the patriarchal family is a casualty.

When the breadwinner comes to this country in search of work he may leave his family behind. This was often true in earlier times. Despite good intentions, many migrants never got around to sending for their families and eventually lost sight of them altogether. In other cases, the members of the family were not permitted to leave the old country when the husband was ready to send for them. The quota laws have operated with arbitrary disregard for family considerations. The exigencies of war created other serious problems of family disorganization. Consular records were destroyed, affidavits of support were required, and other bureaucratic procedures compounded the difficulties which many immigrant families suffered during the war and postwar years.[35]

Family disorganization reached its most severe form with the refugee. Whereas the family separation of the voluntary immigrant was self-induced, that of the refugee was the bitter fruit of persecution, imprisonment, and death. As Davie points out, "Among refugees it is *usual* to be separated, husband from wife, children from parents; it is *unusual* for a whole family to be together."[36] The migration immediately before and after World War II was marked by the most extensive family separation in history. During the war, the International Red Cross in Geneva received some 17,000,000 individual requests for information concerning members of separated families.[37] This frequently could not be supplied. Many a person will never know whether his wife, son, daughter, mother, father, brother, or sister is still alive. Those who have gained the sanctuary of America are haunted by the fate of their loved ones abroad. In fact refugees often feel a devastating sense of guilt because they have escaped and their loved ones have not.[38]

3. *Individual Disorganization.* Migration tends to break down the institutional structures of the family, the church, and the economic organization. Definitions formerly held sacred lose their cohesive force in the new social milieu. Many of the informal social controls no longer bind the group together. Life loses some of its meaning when the old values have been lost or tarnished. The process of individual disorganization is complex and involves countless variables. The data do not conclusively indicate the full impact of immigration upon the individual. Nevertheless, there are a number of observable personality changes which accompany immigration. We shall mention two forms of disorganization.

[35] Rich, *op. cit.,* p. 103.
[36] Maurice R. Davie, *Refugees in America,* Harper & Brothers, New York, 1947, p. 145.
[37] *Ibid.*
[38] *Ibid.,* pp. 145–146.

a. There appears to be a close relationship between certain functional *mental disorders* and the cultural origins of the individual.[39] In a study made of mental patients who were under treatment in New Haven the differences between the rates of mental illness found among the foreign born and among those of native birth were significant. The findings disclosed that "There is a significant difference in the distribution of native- and foreign-born with a higher proportion of foreign-born in the total psychiatric population and in the diagnostic categories of affective disorder, illnesses of senescence, and the organic illnesses. . . . In the remaining diagnostic categories there are no significant differences between the native- and foreign-born."[40] In terms of the various nationality groups, it was found that the Italians were high in affective disorders and the illnesses of senescence, the Irish in alcoholism and drug addiction, northwest Europeans in senescent difficulties, and the Poles and Russians in affective disorders and schizophrenia.[41]

These data are merely suggestive and not necessarily conclusive concerning the specific role of immigration in mental disease. The survey does not purport to be a study of the true prevalence of mental disease in the population but is limited to those persons under treatment by a psychiatrist. This last factor is significant, since there are differences between religious and nationality groups concerning their recognition of, and willingness to be treated psychiatrically for, mental illness. The Jewish religion recognizes no conflict between its teachings and the theory and practice of psychoanalysis. The Catholic religion has opposed psychoanalysis in the treatment of its members. Difference in religious attitude may account for the high rate of Jewish persons under treatment for psychoneuroses and the total absence of Irish persons under treatment for the same disorders.[42]

b. *Suicide,* as we mention in Chapter 13, has been classified by Durkheim in three categories. Suicides arise from (1) too close an integration between the individual and the group (altruistic suicide); (2) the isolation of the individual from the group (egoistic suicide); (3) a decrease in the cohesion of the larger society (suicide *anomique*).[43] The immigrant appears to be drawn to the two latter types of suicide. He may suffer isolation from his former primary groups or he may become personally disorganized when the society itself is undergoing rapid and disintegrating changes. Since data are

[39] Cf. August B. Hollingshead and Frederick C. Redlich, "Social Stratification and Schizophrenia," *American Sociological Review, 19*:302–306 (June, 1954); Jerome K. Myers and Leslie Schaffer, "Social Stratification and Psychiatric Practice: A Study of an Out-Patient Clinic," *American Sociological Review, 19*:307–310 (June, 1954); August B. Hollingshead and Frederick C. Redlich, "Schizophrenia and Social Structure," *American Journal of Psychiatry, 110*:695–701 (March, 1954).

[40] Bertram H. Roberts and Jerome K. Myers, "Religion, National Origin, Immigration, and Mental Illness," *American Journal of Psychiatry, 110*:759–764 (April, 1954), p. 761.

[41] *Ibid.* Cf. also Paul Barrabee and Otto Von Mering, "Ethnic Variations in Mental Stress in Families with Psychotic Children," *Social Problems, 1*:48–53 (October, 1953).

[42] Roberts and Myers, *op. cit.,* p. 762.

[43] Emile Durkheim, *Suicide,* (translated by John A. Spaulding and George Simpson), The Free Press, Glencoe, Ill., 1951.

not available, we cannot establish the relationships between migration and suicide on a national scale. Such fragmentary evidence as exists suggests a disproportionately high suicide rate among the foreign born.[44]

Suicide apparently does not often occur during the first years of foreign residence, although this is a time that superficially might seem to be most characterized by stresses and strains. Individual disorganization among peacetime migrants seems rather to occur when their children are growing up. The culture conflict is then most acute between the generations. The foreign born may believe that they have lost their own cultural autonomy while their children are destined to lead a marginal existence on the fringe of American society. Suicide appears to be one reaction to this subtle disorganization of the family group.[45]

Culture conflict is intensified in times of persecution, extermination, and war. The refugee fortunate enough to reach the United States with his health and resources intact may know that his family was carried away to extermination camps in Europe. The atrocities perpetrated upon the Jewish people during World War II, when some 6,000,000 European Jews were exterminated by the Nazis, undoubtedly increased the suicide rate among the survivors who managed to reach this country. Jews who had long been residents in the United States often heard of the death of their parents or other close relatives in Europe. Such information probably swelled the Jewish suicide rate. Jewish religious teachings formerly served as a preventive against suicide. This influence was diminished markedly by the persecutions of World War II.

The Refugee

For centuries man's inhumanity to man has forced minority groups to migrate to new lands. Many of the migrants from central and eastern Europe who settled in America were inspired by the desire to escape the persecutions inflicted upon them in the Old World.

The recent social and political upheavals have intensified such flights. The widespread social disorganization which both attended and followed World War I increased the pressure upon millions of persons to abandon their ancestral homes and set out for another land. World War II added millions of refugees to those already wandering miserably without a home. Many of these men, women, and children have become "nansen"—people without a country. Refugees without a homeland are issued "Nansen" passports. War, revolution, political persecution, ethnic intolerance, and class hatred have disorganized age-old culture patterns, dissolved traditional community relationships, and broken family ties.[46]

[44] Adolph D. Frenay, *The Suicide Problem in the United States*, Richard G. Badger, Boston, 1926, p. 136.

[45] Ruth Shonle Cavan, *Suicide*, University of Chicago Press, Chicago, 1928, pp. 276–279.

[46] Richard Robbins, "The Refugee Status: Challenge and Response," *Law and Contemporary Problems*, 21:311–333 (Spring, 1956).

The refugee is a person who does not leave his home voluntarily but is obliged to flee because of persecution or the threat of persecution on account of his race, religion, ethnic group, or political beliefs. He is ordinarily not concerned with economic betterment. He is fleeing for his own life and that of his family. Often he has no choice as to his time of departure, the circumstances under which he leaves, or his ultimate or proximate destination. His leave-taking is precipitate and he may be able to take nothing with him but the clothes on his back and such knowledge and skills as he possesses. He is usually deprived of any protection by his native state, since his hatred or fear of political leaders is the basic reason for his flight. He is a stateless man, a modern wanderer, a twentieth-century outcast.[47]

The refugee fortunate enough to reach America is thus a very special kind of immigrant. The earlier immigrants usually came at their own volition. They were chiefly peasants, laborers, and artisans, whereas the refugees are predominantly of the business, professional, and intellectual classes. Many refugees are well educated, with university and advanced professional training. Their educational background is in striking contrast to that of the immigrants, who usually had little schooling.[48]

The earlier immigrants had little or no training in foreign languages, were usually parochial in their interests, and entered the main stream of American life slowly. The refugee is often a linguist, has broad international interests, and tends to enter the intellectual life in America very rapidly. Refugees usually take out naturalization papers as soon as possible, whereas other immigrants tend to be naturalized slowly. Many earlier immigrants remained aliens for decades, through either ignorance or inertia. The refugee thus presents far less difficulty in personal adjustment than the immigrant.[49]

The Displaced Person

At the end of World War II, some 20,000,000 Europeans were living under a foreign government. The majority of these homeless persons were in Germany, where they had been deported by the Nazis to perform the many civilian functions required by a nation involved in total war. In the months following the ending of hostilities, these Russians, Poles, Czechs, Frenchmen, Belgians, Dutch, Norwegians, and others gradually found their way home. Many had been believed to be dead. On arriving home they faced further difficulties. Often their homes had been destroyed and their families were dead or had been dispersed without their knowledge. They themselves were sometimes permanently shattered in health by the physical and emotional experiences to which they had been subjected.[50]

---

[47] Davie, *Refugees in America,* pp. 2–3. Cf. also Maurice R. Davie and Samuel Koenig, "Adjustment of Refugees to American Life," *Annals of the American Academy of Political and Social Science,* 262:159–165 (March, 1949).

[48] Davie, *Refugees in America,* pp. 45–46.

[49] Robbins, *op. cit.,* pp. 314–316.

[50] Fred K. Hoehler, *Europe's Homeless Millions,* Foreign Policy Association, New York, 1947, chap. 1.

For approximately a million prisoners in Germany after the termination of hostilities there was no prospect of returning to their homes. They were the last refugees of World War II, those who had fled their homelands in eastern Europe. Some of them had sympathized or collaborated with the Nazis during the occupation and hence were anathema to the Communist governments that had assumed power after the end of the war. The majority, however, were persons with only slight political orientation. Whatever their reasons for moving, they had no place to go.[51]

These displaced persons comprised a wide variety of nationality and religious groups. Poles were the largest group, with 572,920. The Latvians constituted 97,830, the Lithuanians 60,500, the Yugoslavians 51,530, and the Estonians 31,910. Additional numbers came from Czechoslovakia, Italy, Greece, Holland, France, and Belgium, although the great majority were from eastern Europe. So far as religious affiliation was concerned, the ratio was 80 percent Christian and 20 percent Jewish, with Polish Roman Catholics representing the largest single religious group.

Occupationally speaking, the majority of displaced persons were agricultural workers, but a large number of professional men, skilled artisans, and shop-keepers were among the group. These people were not the shiftless and feckless population of a continent but men and women who had decided to leave their country rather than submit to a dictatorship of which they disapproved. For this reason, after the war was over they were called the "hard core of non-repatriatables."[52]

The displaced persons were displaced in other ways than geographically. "These individuals," said one authority, "were displaced not only physically, but socially and economically as well, their problems more serious and varied than those of any large group of migrants in history."[53] Political, economic, social, and individual insecurity was their lot, and they had little but their own perseverance to help them through the bleak postwar years. In the four-and-one-half-year period ending in 1952, the International Refugee Organization resettled 1,038,750 refugees in some 48 countries. The United States by special legislation accepted about 400,000 through the Displaced Persons Commission. These "D.P.'s," as they were called, were fitted into American society during a period of postwar prosperity and full employment.[54]

Nevertheless migration for some of these became a source of social disorganization. The group ties of the refugees have usually been broken violently and abruptly. The disorganization resulting from religious and political persecution is ordinarily greater than that of the earlier immigrant

[51] Cf. William S. Bernard, "Not Sympathy, but Action," *Survey Graphic, 36:*133–137 (February, 1947).

[52] *Ibid.,* Table 1. Cf. also Eugene M. Kulischer, "Displaced Persons in the Modern World," *Annals of the American Academy of Political and Social Science, 262:*166–177 (March, 1949).

[53] Hoehler, *op. cit.,* p. 9.

[54] *Whom We Shall Welcome,* Report of the President's Commission on Immigration and Naturalization, Washington, 1953, p. 58.

who sought a new home in the New World. In any form of migration, however, relationships are broken and the primary group is threatened with dissolution.

Migration and Status Striving

Migration has left an indelible imprint upon American society. We have considered many of the adjustments an immigrant has to make to American culture, in fields ranging from the economic to the religious. For most immigrants these adjustments have long since been made, for better or worse, and large-scale immigration is now a thing of the past. The millions who came to these shores from 1900 to 1920 are in their declining years or have died. Their grandchildren are third-generation Americans and in many ways are more vociferously American than those from old American stock.

These third-generation men and women comprise a substantial segment of the population in the United States today and their ideology has an important influence upon the contemporary political and social scene. It was subtly determined (or at least modified) by the migration of their forebears half a century ago. The early attempt at cultural assimilation of the first and second generation has been replaced by an overwhelming desire to get ahead. In Mead's words, ". . . these 'third-generation' Americans . . . are always moving, always readjusting, always hoping to buy a better car and a better radio. . . ."[55] Such goals are not confined to the children and grandchildren of the foreign born, for Americans of all ethnic backgrounds, "old" and "new," share them. Many third-generation Americans may have over emphasized them, however; they take them more seriously than do older Americans, who do not believe that economic status is the only symbol of the American way of life.[56]

In a nation blessed with peace and plenty, the problems of social disorganization would appear to be as slight as a dynamic society permits.[57] The grandchildren, especially, of the foreign-born who came to this country in the last great waves of immigration have prospered, raised their material standard of living beyond their wildest dreams, and educated their children for white-collar jobs and the professions. The latter have, in many cases, celebrated their emancipation from their Old World heritage by moving from the city into the expanding metropolitan suburbs. But their emancipation is still incomplete. The third generation is still anxious about its status.[58]

This anxiety appears to be an important factor in the intolerance of many "new" American families. Despite increased prosperity, economic security, and other material advantages, these families still have deep-seated doubts

[55] Margaret Mead, *And Keep Your Powder Dry,* William Morrow and Company, Inc., New York, 1942, p. 39.

[56] This thesis is explored in the various essays assembled in Daniel Bell (ed.), *The New American Right,* Criterion Books, New York, 1955.

[57] Francis E. Merrill, "Social Character and Social Problems," *Social Problems, 3:7–12* (July, 1955).

[58] David Riesman and Nathan Glazer, "The Intellectuals and the Discontented Classes," chap. 3 in Bell, *op. cit.*

over their "belonging" to that American society which their ancestors worked so hard to reach. As one observer puts it, "The problems raised by the tasks of keeping the family together, disciplining children for the American race for success, trying to conform to unfamiliar standards, *protecting economic and social status won at the cost of much sacrifice,* holding the respect of children who grow American more rapidly than their parents, have thrown heavy burdens on the internal relationships of many new American families."[59]

By social status we mean the relative position in the social structure held by individuals and groups, as is discussed in Chapter 1. Status may vary in degree, and persons with particular ethnic, religious, social, educational, or economic qualifications have higher status than others.[60] In the United States, the status of the immigrant has been low—lowest generally among the most recent ethnic, racial, or religious group. Anglo-Saxon Protestant groups have, on the whole, the highest status because they were the first to settle in this country. Other ethnic groups—Irish, Germans, Scandinavians, Italians, Poles, and southwestern Europeans, for example—have held low status initially but have gradually risen in the scale as they have acquired wealth, education, and power.

This rise has not merely involved individual members of low-status groups; it has also characterized entire segments of the population as they have participated in the unprecedented prosperity following World War II. But despite their rise in material level, the new Americans do not yet feel completely certain of their status. Their new nationality is still not something they can take for granted but must be affirmed, to themselves and to others. Many of them continually try to demonstrate that they are as "American" as anyone else, that they accept the democratic ideology completely, and that the discrimination against their parents and grandparents is now a thing of the past.[61]

In their efforts to demonstrate their status, many of the new Americans therefore exhibit a superconformity to what they consider American ideals. This in turn involves a strong intolerance of nonconformity, whether religious, economic, or political.

In many cases minority-group immigrants become intolerant as they attempt to identify themselves with "Americanism" as they conceive it. At the same time, they reject any behavior which differs from their own conception of the American way of life. Minority immigration status is still closely related to lower-class and lower-educational background, elements which are themselves related to intolerance.[62]

---

[59] Richard Hofstadter, "The Pseudo-Conservative Revolt," chap. 2 in Bell, *op. cit.,* p. 46. (Our italics.)

[60] Gerhard E. Lenski, "Status Crystallization: A Non-Vertical Dimension of Social Status," *American Sociological Review, 19:*405–413 (August, 1954). For a revealing popular analysis of this general problem, see Vance Packard, *The Status Seekers,* David McKay Company, Inc., New York, 1959.

[61] Mead, *op. cit.,* p. 53.

[62] Cf. Samuel A. Stouffer, *Communism, Conformity, and Civil Liberties,* Doubleday and Company, Inc., New York, 1955.

In trying to identify themselves with American ideals, immigrant groups have often drifted into support of what has been called "the new American right" or the "radical right." This group is very heterogeneous in composition, but its members have in common many beliefs which are opposed to the traditional American belief in freedom, equality, and tolerance. "This group," says Lipset, "is characterized as radical because it desires to make far-reaching changes in American institutions, and because it seeks to eliminate from American political life those persons and institutions which threaten either its values, or its economic interests."[63]

The radical right is a force making for social disorganization because it seeks to break down culture patterns resting at the very basis of the American way of life. Among these patterns are the right of assembly, the right to petition against grievances, the right of free association, the right to travel, and the right of free speech. The radical right has made a number of deliberate attempts to abrogate these and other freedoms, while acting in the name of "Americanism" and against the totalitarian enemy of Communism.[64]

This movement has been facilitated by the continued crisis of the cold war. The United States is threatened on a world-wide scale by the Communist world. Many of the status insecurities of the third-generation Americans are heightened by these international pressures. The radical right, however, sees the enemy not only as Communism but also as liberals, New Dealers, government officials, labor leaders, free-thinkers, and all others who do not conform to its version of the American ideology. Personal insecurities are projected into the outside world, and the slightest nonconformity is seen as equivalent to disloyalty.

The impact of immigration upon the society and culture of America has thus produced significant change. Social disorganization accompanying migration formerly was indicated in the rates of delinquency, crime, ill health, poverty, mental disease, family disorganization, and the like. Each new immigrant group suffered high rates in comparison with the other and more fully assimilated groups. This disadvantage, however, has been only temporary. As each minority group has become successively integrated into the society, the extent of traditional forms of social disorganization within it has gradually declined. Differences between most ethnic minorities and the "older" Americans are becoming negligible. Social disorganization on this differential level, therefore, is in process of ultimate disappearance.[65]

On another and more complex level, however, the problem is not so simple. Emotional differences between groups of Americans continue to exist. Irish-Americans, German-Americans, Polish-Americans, and Italian-Americans hold emotional ties with their homelands, with especial reference to the

---

[63] Seymour M. Lipset, "The Sources of the 'Radical Right,'" chap. 7 in Bell, op. cit., p. 166.

[64] Cf. Lawrence H. Fuchs, "Some Political Aspects of Immigration," Law and Contemporary Problems, 21:270–283 (Spring, 1956).

[65] Glazer, op. cit., pp. 258–261.

foreign policies of these countries. National consensus is sometimes strained by tensions engendered by such ethnic differences, and the divergences are exploited by men who would deliberately break down the traditional foundations of the American way of life. Social disorganization thus continues to be a legacy of cultural heterogeneity.

SELECTED BIBLIOGRAPHY

Bell, Daniel (ed.), *The New American Right,* Criterion Books, New York, 1955. The articles in this book deal with different aspects of the "new American right," which has attempted in recent years to turn the clock back on various traditional freedoms. One of the constituents of this heterogeneous group is the third-generation immigrant, whose striving for status often takes the form of superconformity and intolerance.

Carter, Hugh (ed.), "Reappraising Our Immigration Policy," *Annals of the American Academy of Political and Social Science,* Vol. 262 (March, 1949) (special issue): A group of experts on the various aspects of immigration and related issues have contributed to this special issue of the *Annals,* which constitutes one of the most authoritative appraisals of this problem in recent years.

Davie, Maurice R., *Refugees in America,* Harper & Brothers, New York, 1947. The adjustment of the postwar refugee to America and America's adjustment to him are different in many respects from the problems of the earlier immigrant.

Glazer, Nathan, "The Integration of American Immigrants," *Law and Contemporary Problems, 21*:256–269 (Spring, 1956). This thoughtful article considers the problems of integration, ranging from the traditional problems of crime, delinquency, mental illness, and the like to the more subtle considerations of political action and cultural integration.

Handlin, Oscar, *The Uprooted,* Little, Brown and Company, Boston, 1951. This study of immigration, written by a social historian, indicates the breakdown of interpersonal relationships suffered by the generations of peasants who left their homeland for the New World.

Kirk, Dudley, and Huyck, Earl, "Overseas Migration from Europe Since World War II," *American Sociological Review, 19*:447–456 (August, 1954). This is an analysis of the mass migration (involving some 5,000,000 persons) from Europe to various parts of the New World in the period 1946–1952, immediately after World War II.

Law and Contemporary Problems, "Immigration," Vol. 21 (Spring, 1956) (special issue). This is a recent and authoritative statement of the contemporary problems of immigration. Included in the symposium are articles dealing with the historical aspects, economic implications, political aspects, influence upon the "higher culture," and political repercussions of immigration as they involve the third, fourth, and even fifth generations of ethnic minority groups in this country.

Packard, Vance, *The Status Seekers,* David McKay Company, Inc., New York, 1959. This popularly written treatise examines the widespread implications of status in American life, in terms of both native-born and foreign-born groups. Problems of status are seen to bedevil the majority of persons in this country, despite the traditional assumption that class differences do not exist.

Park, Robert E., "Human Migration and the Marginal Man," *American Journal of Sociology,* 33:881–893 (May, 1928). In this article, Park presented the original statement of the concept of the marginal man, which has been an important tool in the subsequent analysis of immigration.

Peterson, William, "A General Typology of Migration," *American Sociological Review,* 23:256–266 (June, 1958). The author of this article indicates five broad classes of migration—"primitive, forced, impelled, free, and mass" migration.

Thomas, William I., and Znaniecki, Florian, *The Polish Peasant in Europe and America,* Alfred A. Knopf, Inc., New York, 1927 (two vols.). This is the most impressive sociological study of immigration in the literature. The principal source is a voluminous mass of letters and life histories of Polish immigrants. The several introductions and methodological notes interspersed throughout these volumes are landmarks in the study of social psychology and social disorganization.

CHAPTER 26

Unemployment

The Great Depression

During the 1930's the Great Depression produced the most serious and sustained unemployment this country has ever known. An estimated 14,000,000 persons were out of work in 1932 at the depth of the depression. Despite a few upturns in industry it was not until the United States entered World War II that unemployment became negligible. The depression was obviously no purely American phenomenon but was rather a part of the world-wide economic dislocations. It had its inception (in part, at least) in the post-World War I economy of Europe, which no longer provided a market for the surplus of agricultural and manufactured goods supplied by American farmers and industrialists.

There was some serious unemployment immediately after World War I during the early twenties in the United States but this was followed by a subsequent "boom" recovery. The boom was succeeded by the stock market crash of 1929, which led to the ruin of many large corporations and swept away many little businesses as well. Farmers were wiped out by the decline in prices. Meanwhile unemployment became cumulative, for buying power decreased with every person thrown out of work. Communities often were unable to feed and clothe the hungry because so many persons were in dire need that local resources were taxed beyond their capacity.

When state and local efforts failed to provide for the needs of the vast numbers of unemployed, the federal government made a series of attempts to deal with the problem. Initially the federal government provided "emergency relief." Work projects and public works were later organized to provide idle workers with something to do. There were a few instances of improvements in business but with the outbreak of World War II in Europe our unemployment increased. Shortly before the United States entered the war around 10,000,000 persons were still out of work.[1]

Unemployment and Social Disorganization

The disruptive aspects of widespread and long-continued unemployment over a period of ten years are hard for the present generation of college

[1] William Green, "Editorial," *The American Federationist,* 48:16 (August, 1940).

students to comprehend. Many of their parents, however, can recall the terrifying proportions of the prolonged inability to obtain work during the Great Depression.[2] The 14,000,000 people unemployed at the worst point in the depression were out of work when the population was much lower than it is today. During the peak of unemployment in the early thirties industry was operating at about half of its total productive capacity. Farmers had plenty to do but were nevertheless in a desperate financial situation with wheat selling under 50 cents a bushel and corn for 31 cents.[3] Farms were lost because farmers could not pay the mortgages. Particularly in the Middle West, banks in turn failed because they had over-loaned on the mortgages.

Merchants could no longer sell the clothes on the racks or the cloth on the shelves. Support for churches and schools declined and teachers received large salary cuts. In Chicago teachers were paid with scrip instead of money for two years. They could cash this scrip only at a discount or in exchange for purchases. In a Kansas community known to the authors every teacher from the superintendent down was paid $50 a month. Grocers failed because they extended credit to their hungry customers. Men roamed the country looking vainly for work, as did teen-age boys and girls. Even in the learned professions there was often no opportunity. Only in social work was there an increased demand for trained people.[4]

Hopes, fortunes, and professional ambitions were destroyed by lack of income and business failures. Many businessmen committed suicide because they could not face their changed financial status. Children and adults suffered from lack of an adequate diet.[5] Eventually the federal government extended emergency relief to the states. Later a program locally sponsored and federally financed (dubiously called Works Progress Administration) put people to work at "made" work. This was called "boondoggling" because the value of the work was often questionable. The saving of men obviously was the first consideration and the program accomplished this by making them feel they had earned their income. Later an organized program of public works under the PWA employed many men at the public construction of roads, buildings and dams, and the much debated Tennessee Valley Authority.

The unemployment problem was never solved by such measures, however. They merely kept the economy going. It was not until our entry into World War II that the labor force was virtually all recruited for (1) the tremendous production of war matériel and (2) the construction of housing for men inducted into the army and the population which shifted to war production

[2] E. Wight Bakke, *The Unemployed Worker,* Yale University Press, New Haven, 1940, for a good picture of the depression.

[3] Frederick Lewis Allen, *The Big Change,* Harper & Brothers, New York, 1952, pp. 147–149.

[4] See Walter M. Kotschnig, *Unemployment in the Learned Professions,* Oxford University Press, London, 1937, for a survey of unemployment among graduates of colleges and universities and in the professions.

[5] Cf. Marion Elderton, *Case Studies of Unemployment,* National Federation of Settlements, University of Pennsylvania Press, Philadelphia, 1931, pp. 1–49.

centers. Many women heretofore unemployed went to work in various defense projects. Most of the young men went into the armed services and the unemployed decreased to around 100,000.

In the decade and a half following the end of World War II unemployment has reared its head several times. The number of unemployed and the disorganization entailed has been very much less, however, than during the depressed thirties. Nevertheless, each of the so-called recessions has lowered the buying power of those unemployed and has had a serious impact on the communities where unemployment rates have been high. The inability to secure work disorganizes the community in many ways. Economic crimes tend to increase, support for churches and schools goes down, and merchants fail in business. Even the health of large numbers of people may be involved if they cannot pay the rent and provide for an adequate diet. Much of the disorganizing aspect of the contemporary unemployment problem is fortunately mitigated by the provisions for unemployment compensation and for public assistance when the unemployment coverage expires.

Post-World War II Recessions

After the United States entered World War II unemployment was kept to a minimum by government contracts for armament and war matériel. The average number of weekly unemployment checks in 1944 was 79,000 and most of the checks were for persons temporarily out of a job. When the war was over many dire predictions were made that 8,000,000 persons would be unemployed.[6] But because of the large demand for consumer goods and the enormous expenditures for defense, armament, and men in military service overseas, no such serious problem has occurred.

There have been three serious dips in employment, however, in what have been called postwar "recessions." These were in 1948–1950, 1953–1955, and 1958–1959, as Chart 26.1 indicates. The recession occurring in 1958–1959 was the severest. During its peak in 1958 the number of unemployed rose above 5,000,000 and continued to hover around that figure for months.[7] This was 7.5 percent of the labor force.[8] Even though conditions seemed to improve, 4.9 percent of the labor force was unemployed in June, 1959.[9] The serious nature of the 1958–1959 recession is further indicated by the fact that all told 14,100,000 persons were unemployed and looking for work at some time during 1958. Unemployment at any one time thus does not indicate the extent of unemployment during the year.

On the more favorable side of the unemployment problem we should recognize (1) that the economy is absorbing an ever increasing number of workers and (2) that those who were employed at some time during the year

[6] *Monthly Labor Review*, 60:1237 (June, 1945).

[7] Bureau of the Census, *Labor Force, Annual Report of the Labor Force, 1958, Current Population Reports*, Series P-50, No. 89 (June, 1959), p. 1.

[8] *Ibid.*, p. 10.

[9] Bureau of the Census, *Labor Force, Monthly Report on the Labor Force, Current Population Reports*, Series P-57, No. 204 (June 30, 1959), p. 1.

1958 totaled 77,117,000.[10] Some of these were students working during vacation. There were also persons with jobs for the Christmas trade and workers employed at seasonal jobs. The average number of persons employed throughout the year 1958 was only 64,000,000, in contrast to a 65,000,000 average for 1957.[11]

In the recession of 1948–1950 unemployment was temporarily more acute

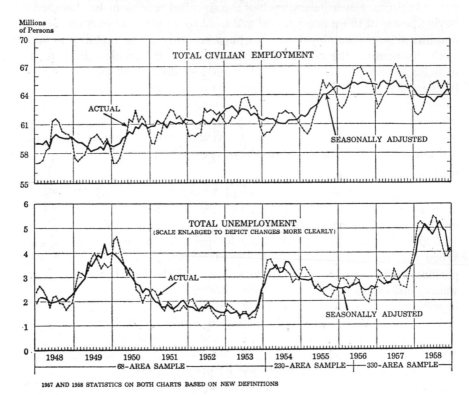

CHART 26.1. Trends in Employment and Unemployment, Actual and Seasonally Adjusted, January, 1947, Through 1958. (From *Annual Report on the Labor Force, 1958, Current Population Reports,* Series P-50, No. 89, June, 1959, p. 2.)

than in the other two recessions when the unemployment rate was 7.8 (Table 26.1), but this was complicated by major strikes. The 1959 recession also continued through the summer and was augmented by the steel strike. The 1953–1955 recession was less serious than the other two, but nevertheless the unemployment rate was slightly over 6 percent during September, 1954. Since all of these recessions happened in a little over ten years, unemployment of around 5 percent of the population must be regarded as more or less a

[10] Bureau of the Census, *Labor Force, Work Experience of the Population in 1958, Current Population Reports,* Series P-50, No. 91 (June 30, 1959), p. 1.

[11] *Annual Report of the Labor Force, 1958,* p. 1.

TABLE 26.1. Seasonally Adjusted Rate of Unemployment in Three Postwar Recessions (percent of civilian labor force who were unemployed; adjusted for comparability with definitions adopted in January, 1957)

Phase of Unemployment Cycle	1957 to 1958 Month	Rate	1953 to 1955 Month	Rate	1948 to 1950 Month	Rate
Low point in unemployment just prior to recession	July 1957	4.2	Aug. 1953	2.6	Oct. 1948	3.7
Rise in unemployment to recession peak	Aug. 1957	4.3	Sept. 1953	2.9	Nov. 1948	4.0
	Sept. 1957	4.5	Oct. 1953	3.1	Dec. 1948	4.2
	Oct. 1957	4.7	Nov. 1953	3.5	Jan. 1949	4.5
	Nov. 1957	4.9	Dec. 1953	4.5	Feb. 1949	4.7
	Dec. 1957	5.0	Jan. 1954	4.8	March 1949	4.9
	Jan. 1958	5.8	Feb. 1954	5.3	April 1949	5.2
	Feb. 1958	6.7	March 1954	5.7	May 1949	6.2
	March 1958	7.0	April 1954	5.8	June 1949	5.9
	April 1958	7.5	May 1954	6.0	July 1949	6.4
					Aug. 1949	6.7
Stability in unemployment except for minor fluctuations	May 1958	7.2	June 1954	5.4[a]	Sept. 1949	6.5
	June 1958	6.8[a]	July 1954	5.7	Oct. 1949	7.8[b]
	July 1958	7.3	Aug. 1954	6.0	Nov. 1949	6.7
	Aug. 1958	7.6	Sept. 1954	6.1	Dec. 1949	6.8
					Jan. 1950	6.7
Recovery in unemployment	Sept. 1958	7.2	Oct. 1954	5.7	Feb. 1950	6.4
	Oct. 1958	7.1	Nov. 1954	5.4	March 1950	6.3
	Nov. 1958	5.9	Dec. 1954	5.0	April 1950	5.8
	Dec. 1958	6.1	Jan. 1955	4.9	May 1950	5.7

[a] Reflects problem of seasonally adjusting unemployment in summer of recession years.
[b] Rate exaggerated by secondary effects of occurrence of major strikes.

SOURCE: Bureau of the Census, *Current Population Reports, Annual Report of the Labor Force, 1958*, Series P-50, No. 89, (June, 1959) p. 10.

perennial problem. For a sizable group of people, lack of economic security is thus a constant threat.

The Causes of Unemployment

Classical economists have tried to explain the problem of unemployment as essentially a function of demand and supply. They argue that if more goods are demanded employment would increase. If fewer goods are consumed employment declines until the supply is consumed. This, however, is more an exercise in logic than a true explanation. Actually there can be no simple explanation of unemployment because so many factors affect the labor market. A number of these forces are impersonal. Overproduction, lack of coordinated planning, technological improvements, automation, and stock market speculation with its inevitable "boom and bust" have all contributed to unemployment.

Personal factors may also prevent employment. Physical incapacities, lack of education and skills, personality characteristics, age, and sex may limit the job opportunities for particular people. Even knowing the right people may on occasion help a person secure or hold a job. The son or daughter of an important person, whether the latter is president of the United States or of an industrial corporation, bank, or college will have greater job opportunities than an equally able person with less influential contacts.

The major "causes" of unemployment, however, are dislocations in the economic structure, which tend to become cumulative. That is, *unemployment produces unemployment*. When men are laid off they no longer have regular income, although unemployment insurance may enable them to pay for the most essential items of food and shelter. This in turn means that fewer goods are sold. When large numbers are out of work clerks and service employees as well as factory workers will be laid off because it is no longer profitable to employ them. Where a depression is long continued only a sudden and critical need for extensive new goods and services will "get men back to work" without coordinated planning.

IMPERSONAL FACTORS

1. *Cyclical Unemployment.* The interrelated aspects of overproduction, declining demand, and the shutdown of factories are a part of cyclical unemployment. Some economists in the past have maintained that monopoly control of industry is responsible for these periodic declines in industry.[12] Others have held that they are essentially caused by the decline in foreign markets and the high tariffs which prevent interchange of goods.[13] (This view is particularly stressed with reference to the Great Depression.) John Maynard Keynes, Alvin H. Hansen, and others have maintained that these are not the main causes. The real reason lies, says Keynes and those who accept his point of view, in an upset in the balance of savings over investment. A good or "boom" period is generated when investments exceed savings. A slump or depression occurs when savings exceed investment and the wariness of the solvent contributes to their undoing.[14]

2. *Technological Unemployment.* Much modern unemployment has been due to the reduction of man power necessary to produce a finished article. Throughout the whole course of economic development since the industrial revolution, man has been forced to adjust himself to the processes

[12] Roland W. Bartlett, *Security for the People,* Wilcox and Follett Company, Chicago, 1949, pp. 6–9.

[13] Cf. David Cushman Coyle, *Roads to a New America,* Little, Brown and Company, Boston, 1938, p. 178.

[14] See Alvin H. Hansen, *Economic Policy and Full Employment,* McGraw-Hill Book Company, Inc., New York, 1947, for a detailed discussion of unemployment and an essentially Keynesian explanation. See also John Maynard Keynes, *The General Theory of Employment, Interest and Money,* Harcourt, Brace and Company, New York, 1936, and John Maynard Keynes, "An Economic Analysis of Unemployment," in *Unemployment as a World Problem,* Harris Foundation Lectures, 1931, University of Chicago Press, Chicago, 1932, pp. 18–22.

of machine production. Every increase in mechanical skill has had its debit as well as its credit side. Modern machine production has multiplied the number of commodities consumed by the average man and increased his share of food, clothes, and services. This has meant a constantly rising standard of material comfort and a concomitant increase in the consumption of luxury goods. At the same time, industry has diminished the average man's economic security, since every advance in technology has meant a displacement of human labor. Indeed, some manufacturing processes have become so perfected as to be virtually automatic.

Technological unemployment is not new. The men who produced copper tools upset the flint industries of the Stone Age. Science merely makes for more rapid changes, more complicated displacements. Monetary values have become social values, and they, too, are disturbed by man's inventiveness. Chemical research has also upset many industries. Nylon, dacron, and other synthetics have caused severe repercussions in the Japanese silk market. New chemical fertilizers have greatly increased farm yields per acre. But new inventions do more than merely displace labor. They create poverty, which results from the destruction of old investments and therefore restricts the market for new productions. A vicious circle is produced. Technological unemployment thus augments the business cycle in many ways. In the long run, technological improvements may increase employment in related service industries. Nevertheless, continued improvements in mechanical devices mean that employment opportunities have to increase proportionately or there will be an added residue of unemployment.

3. *Automation.* Automation is a special aspect of technological development which has made it possible for machines to carry on amazingly intricate operations at the push of a button. Automation has displaced many operators of varying degrees of skill, although it has also created new opportunities for advanced technical skills and has greatly increased productivity. We have already discussed (in Chapter 20) how far the new coordinated agricultural machines have reduced the need for farm labor. The automobile industry was down some 400,000 workers in 1959, judging from the membership in the auto workers' union. Before the great steel strike of 1959 several hundred thousand men had been laid off in that industry with no hope of being called back because of automation.[15] Office mechanization, particularly in the bookkeeping and computation areas, has likewise reduced office help—often as much as two-thirds. In the long run opportunities for professional skills may be increased and opportunities to use these services may be expanded.[16] The overall effect of automation is indicated by the fact that there was a decline of 2,000,000 in the number of workers employed in manufacturing production between 1953 and 1959, but an increase of over a third of a million non-

[15] Anonymous, "Lasting Unemployment," *The New Republic, 140:*4–5 (April 20, 1959).

[16] Charles E. Silberman and Sanford S. Parker, "How the United States Can Get 50 Per Cent Richer," *Fortune, 59:*107–111 and ff. (March, 1959).

production workers.[17] Automation apparently creates a demand for more supervisors as well as for persons with special education and skill.

4. *Seasonal Unemployment.* Certain occupations are by their nature seasonal. Farm labor and the building trades are the most notable of these. In agriculture the seasonal aspects of planting and harvesting are obvious. Despite the mechanization of agriculture there is great need for seasonal labor in picking certain types of fruit and vegetables by hand and in hoeing and weeding, even though chemicals have aided in weed control.[18] Because of the seasonal aspect of much farm labor, farm workers tend to be both hard up and out of work for months at a time. In 1957, for example, farm workers who worked 25 days or more averaged only 125 days, and since farm workers usually work 6 days a week this mean that they worked approximately 21 out of the 52 weeks. These workers also worked 19 days at nonfarm work.[19] Farm laborers thus suffer from serious underemployment.

The building trades, particularly in outside work, are often stopped by cold or rainy weather, and unemployment tends to run high in winter. Periods of seasonal demand affect the garment industry, the silver industry (which has its peak selling in June and December), and even the sale of soap and house-cleaning items, which is higher in spring and fall. Careful planning for seasonal demands has reduced part but not all of the unemployment in these industries.

5. *Unemployment Because of Strikes.* From the worker's point of view, a strike called by his union may be nearly as serious as involuntary unemployment so far as lack of work and wage loss are concerned. In the steel strike of 1959, for example, the steel workers lost $20,000,000 the first two weeks.[20] Today relief (and sometimes unemployment compensation as well) is available to strikers. Nevertheless, living costs are cut to the minimum and many workers experience very serious reduction in living standards. Sometimes there is real suffering from the lack of income while labor and management fail to agree on wages and conditions of work.

PERSONAL FACTORS

Fluctuations in demand thus determine the ups and downs of employment. But *personal* factors may make it impossible for certain persons to get a job, the most important of which are summarized below:

1. *Lack of Education and Skill.* Certain people fail to get the jobs to which they aspire because they lack education and skill. Skill is not, however, the only factor in job retention. Foremen and supervisors, for example, are

[17] Stanley H. Ruttenberg, "Economic and Social Implications" (of technological advance), *Monthly Labor Review,* 82:164–165 (February, 1959).

[18] Varden Fuller, "Farm Labor, Supply, Policies, Practices," *Monthly Labor Review,* 82:518–523 (May, 1959).

[19] Cf. *The Hired Farm Working Force of 1957: A Progress Report,* Agricultural Marketing Service, U.S. Department of Agriculture, Washington, September, 1958, p. 4.

[20] Alfred P. Klausler, "Steel Town Frustration," *Christian Century,* 76:920–921 (August 12, 1959).

more likely to be kept on the job full-time than are highly skilled rank-and-file workers.[21]

2. *Age.* The very young who have never had a job and persons sixty-five or over have the greatest difficulty in getting a job. Young persons who have never been employed have no established record or skill, and older persons often are unable physically to keep up with the demands of the job.

Figures for 1958 showed that young men aged twenty to thirty-four had a much higher unemployment rate than older persons. This reflects the fact that many senior job holders are protected in their jobs by seniority clauses in the union contracts. Nevertheless, middle-aged workers—once unemployed —often have a more difficult time gaining a foothold in industry than younger unemployed persons.[22] In general, industries prefer to pay retirement and unemployment benefits to persons with years of possible service ahead. A high percentage of professional people, on the other hand, work after they are sixty-five.[23] Persons with well-established reputations in the professional field are not as likely to retire except in the teaching profession, where compulsory retirement ages are often in effect. Many people are well able to earn a livelihood beyond age sixty-five and there is a social loss when their productive skills are not utilized. Unemployed older people often decline mentally and emotionally because they have no serious interest in life. Most persons sixty-five and over who have been industrially employed are now eligible for retirement benefits. Many do not seek further employment.[24]

For most persons past sixty-five lack of employment means a serious decline in income. This is sometimes partly offset by unemployment insurance but usually by old age assistance. Neither provides a desirable standard of living for those who have heretofore had an income which covered all the necessities and some of the comforts and luxuries. Nevertheless the economic plight of the aged has greatly improved since the Social Security Act was adopted in 1935. Many aged were previously forced to live in the county poorhouse, which was provided by the community through county taxes.

Unemployment brings many other adjustments to old people in addition to problems of support. For men in particular the lack of routine activity is difficult to face. The average retired man is not an intellectual and does not enjoy visiting libraries and art galleries. Old men often become bored and restless without something interesting to fill their hours. The adjustment is often difficult for the wife—and not only because of the low household budget imposed by reduced income. Her routine is also upset and instead of enjoying the companionship made possible by her husband's enforced leisure she has to reorganize her activities because her husband is "home all the time." For

---

[21] *Work Experience of the Population in 1958*, p. 3.

[22] *Ibid.*, p. 5.

[23] Cf. Metropolitan Life Insurance Company, "What Our Older People Do," *Statistical Bulletin*, February, 1954.

[24] *Ibid.*, p. 6.

persons without family ties and living on a minimum budget life is often still more drab. Homeless old men living alone may resort to a diet of milk and corn flakes. For old women living on an old age assistance check the outlook is also difficult. It is often hard to find funds to buy a new pair of hose, much less a dress or coat. Present old age insurance and public assistance provisions have taken some of the terror out of old age, but life is by no means easy for old people.

The American people have made it more difficult for the aged than is generally true in western Europe. There professional people (including teachers) have much greater job opportunities in later life than they are allowed in the United States. They also receive better income when retired. Members of university faculties in Germany, for example, receive full pay on retirement. Even in wealthy families older people usually live with their children when widowed. In France the grandparents are usually assigned positions of real responsibility. If they are on old age stipends from the government such money goes much further when spent in a family than by one person living alone.

3. *The Unemployable.* Certain people cannot fill jobs because they are mentally, emotionally, or physically incompetent. Persons with definite mental deficiency cannot ordinarily obtain jobs which require judgment or sustained reasoning although they may perform certain routine tasks very well. Those who are emotionally unstable may become serious personality problems even though they are not truly disturbed or disoriented. People who are "hard to get along with," who explode in temper tantrums, have difficulty in obtaining and retaining jobs for which their skills and abilities might otherwise make them suitable. Many of these make up the men and women who are continually looking for work.

People with serious physical handicaps also have problems in securing employment. The extensive rehabilitation work sponsored by public and private agencies has resulted in the employment of many competent people with physical handicaps. The federal government has led the way in making it possible for the handicapped to obtain jobs commensurate with their ability. They must work within their handicaps, and this generally means that they can perform better at white-collar jobs than in those involving heavy work.

4. *The Physically Ill and Injured.* A sizable number of persons are temporarily or permanently unemployed because of illness or injuries. Approximately 4,300,000 workers lost time without pay because of illness in 1958. This was 500,000 less than in 1957, when influenza rates were higher. Public administration workers had the lowest illness, but most workers in this category are eligible for sick leave pay. More blue-collar workers lose time from illness than do white-collar employees, and the loss of wages is higher proportionately. It is also significant that nonwhite workers in all categories but laborers lose more time from illness than white workers. Over 13 percent of nonwhite household employees lose one or more weeks of work, in contrast to 4.8 percent of white household employees.

In 1958 there were 75,000 workers who suffered permanent injuries and more than 1,700,000 who were disabled for a day or more. (In addition, approximately 13,300 died from accidents on the job.) As Table 26.2 shows, more workers are hurt in the logging industry than in anything else; sanitation departments have the next highest injury rate, often because of cuts from broken glass in garbage. Coal mines rank third, sawmills fourth, and the various heavy industries and construction work make up most of those with

TABLE 26.2. Work Injury Experience in Selected Industries,[a] 1957

Industry	Disabling Injuries per 1,000,000 Employee-Hours Worked	Deaths per 1,000 Disabling Injuries
Logging	62.3	9
Sanitation departments, state and local	53.6	1
Coal mines	44.2	27
Sawmills and planing mills	40.4	4
Roofing and sheet metal work	39.8	[b]
Highway and street construction	34.8	11
Metal mines	33.0	14[c]
General building contractors	32.4	4
Structural clay products	32.2	2
Warehousing and storage	31.4	2
Structural steel erection and ornamental iron work	31.0	25
Nonmetal mines	26.9	11
Heavy construction, except highway and street	26.6	19
Ship building and repairing	17.3	9
Crude petroleum and natural gas extraction	16.4	11[c]
Electric light and power	5.5	29
Petroleum refining	5.3	13[c]
Blast furnaces and steel mills	4.0	21
Industrial organic chemicals	3.5	17

[a] Selected because of a relatively high frequency rate or a comparatively high ratio of deaths to injuries. The term "injury" includes occupational disease.

[b] Less than 1 per 1,000.

[c] Includes permanent-total impairments.

SOURCE: Metropolitan Life Insurance Company, *Statistical Bulletin*, May, 1959, from data derived from *Injury Rates by Industry, 1957*, Bureau of Labor Statistics, U.S. Department of Labor, from data given by companies reporting to the Bureau.

very high rates. Death rates, on the other hand, are highest in the electrical industry, coal mining, and heavy structural steel construction. Steel mills and industrial chemicals have relatively low accident rates at present but they do have high death rates. The dangers in these industries are obvious because of the hazards of explosions or intense heat. Actually many more are injured at home than on the job, but these injuries also kept people from work. The average disability for 1956 varied in the different industries. In petroleum and coal industries the average time lost by the injured was 139 days. In private electric and gas utilities it was 165 days, and in public electric and gas utilities 132 days. Firemen injured on the job had 121 days of average disability.[25]

The Occupational Hazards in Unemployment

Of 63,848,000 persons who were employed in industry in 1958, 18.6 percent had some unemployment. An estimated 40.6 percent of those unemployed had two or more periods of unemployment, as Table 26.3 shows.

1. *Agricultural and Extractive Industries.* Unemployment among farm laborers has been particularly serious since World War II because of the great increase in mechanized sowing and harvesting of crops. This is discussed in Chapter 20, but it should be noted here that during periods of seasonal employment many less are actually employed because machinery has displaced man power in agriculture. Unless the trend of agricultural production is altered markedly there is likely to be a further decrease in job opportunities for agricultural workers.

Agricultural workers also lose time traveling from job to job. In order to obtain their low incomes many agricultural laborers migrate from one harvest area to another. In the western wheat fields, workers start in Texas, go on to Oklahoma and Kansas, and then move farther north and west to the Dakotas, Wyoming, and Montana. Men working in wheat fields go singly. In picking fruits and vegetables whole families are likely to migrate and find work together. On the Pacific coast, the workers push north as the crops ripen. These partially employed workers and their families often live in unsuitable and unsanitary housing. Children are kept out of school. The families have inadequate diets and virtually no medical care. Meanwhile unemployment insurance has been extended in recent years to farm workers, which has been a significant step toward alleviating their serious economic plight.[26]

Unemployment also tends to be chronic in coal mining regions and in the railroad centers where electrification and the use of Diesel engines have lowered the demand for railroad employment. Where there is a mass exodus of an industry (as, for example, in the case of the textile mills which have moved from New England to Southern states), there is also a labor surplus. The unemployed in eleven chronically depressed areas in Pennsylvania collected from 28 to 38 percent of the total unemployment compensation paid in the state during 1953 to 1956. The same sort of situation applied in Kentucky and was undoubtedly true of other depressed areas in the country.[27]

2. *Nonagricultural Industries.* In the nonagricultural industries layoffs generally occur because there is a decline in the demand for the finished product or inability to purchase commodities because of lowered buying power. Thus the 1958 recession occasioned extensive layoffs in "hard goods" manufacturing, especially in the automobile industry, where 48.8 percent of

---

[25] Cf. Metropolitan Life Insurance Company, *Statistical Bulletin,* May, 1959, and *Statistical Abstract of the United States, 1958,* p. 234.

[26] Fuller, *op. cit.*

[27] Gerald G. Somers, "Problems in Unemployment Insurance," *Monthly Labor Review,* 82:245–248 (March, 1959).

the workers were unemployed during part of the year. But 26.6 percent of all hard industries suffered some unemployment. This cutback in the hard goods industry was much higher than in the 1948–1950 and 1953–1955 recessions. Workers employed in construction were almost as hard hit as automobile workers, with 43.1 percent out of work at some time.

Persons in food manufacturing industries suffered a lower cutback, with 20.6 percent unemployed. Textile mills had 23.2 percent of their workers laid off, while garment manufacturers had a greater percentage (34.9 percent), as Table 26.3 shows. Over a fifth of the transportation workers not employed by railroads were laid off, and 14.7 percent of railroad workers suffered from unemployment. Of those unemployed in 1958, 45 percent were unemployed for fifteen weeks or more. For most of these persons there was a real dent in their annual income.[28] Merchant seamen also have considerable unemployment. In the period July 1, 1956–June 30, 1957, the average seaman worked 243 days, but over a twelfth worked only 120 days and nearly a third worked less than 210 days. More than a third worked more than 300 days.[29]

Employment in the entertainment world is also irregular. Actors, singers, and dancers are frequently out of work. Only 28 percent had full-time employment in 1958.[30] Often a play closes early. Only persons who are "names" have much security in the theater. A pianist may have sudden acclaim after years of mild notices. With its provisions for home entertainment television also made serious inroads upon the job opportunities for persons engaged in the entertainment business.

Household workers had an unemployment rate of 13.3 percent and persons in the entertainment world were unemployed 18.4 percent of the time. Persons in welfare and religious work, in education, and in public administration had the lowest unemployment.[31] Since the general welfare depends on their more or less continuous service, unemployment tends to be low. In fact, most schools and social agencies could profitably use more employees, if budgets permitted.

The Duration of Unemployment

The duration of unemployment is a measure of the seriousness of the problem. Of those unemployed in 1958, 20 percent had a difficult time securing a job and were unemployed for twenty-seven weeks or more, as Table 26.3 shows. Almost the same percentage (19.3) were without a job from one to four weeks; a similar percentage (19.2) from five to ten; and a third from eleven to twenty-six weeks.[32] For those unemployed for more than

[28] Bureau of the Census, *Labor Force, Work Experience of the Population in 1958, Current Population Reports,* Series P-50 No. 91 (June 30, 1959), p. 1.

[29] Anonymous, "Earnings and Employment of American Seamen in 1957" (a study conducted by the Bureau of Labor Statistics), *Monthly Labor Review,* 82:33–40 (January, 1959).

[30] *Work Experience of the Population in 1958,* p. 3.

[31] *Ibid.*

[32] *Ibid.,* p. 23.

TABLE 26.3. Extent of Unemployment by Industry: Wage
(Percent not shown where

Industry of Longest Job in 1958	Total Wage and Salary Workers (thousands)	Total with Unemployment or Layoffs	
		Number (thousands)	Percent of Total Wage and Salary Workers
Total	**63,848**	**11,897**	**18.6**
Agriculture	2,771	647	23.3
Nonagricultural industries	61,077	11,250	18.4
Forestry and fisheries	118	33	—
Mining	650	183	28.2
Construction	4,277	1,844	43.1
Manufacturing	17,864	4,236	23.7
Durable goods	10,034	2,674	26.6
Lumber and wood products, except furniture	658	235	35.7
Furniture and fixtures	394	130	33.0
Stone, clay, and glass products	505	127	25.1
Primary metal industries	1,123	304	27.1
Fabricated metal products	1,195	264	22.1
Machinery, except electrical	1,575	364	23.1
Electrical machinery	1,278	253	19.8
Transportation equipment	2,364	752	31.8
Automobiles	1,033	504	48.8
Other transportation equipment	1,331	248	18.6
Other durable goods	942	245	26.0
Nondurable goods	7,830	1,562	19.9
Food and kindred products	1,697	349	20.6
Textile mill products	1,088	252	23.2
Apparel and other fabricated textile products	1,288	450	34.9
Printing, publishing, and allied industries	1,238	107	8.6
Chemicals and allied products	964	128	13.3
Other nondurable goods	1,555	276	17.7
Transportation, communication, and other public utilities	4,657	666	14.3
Railroads and railway express service	1,118	164	14.7
Other transportation	1,692	371	21.9
Telecommunications	844	47	5.6
Other public utilities	1,003	84	8.4
Trade	12,638	2,073	16.4
Wholesale trade	2,381	333	14.0
Retail trade	10,257	1,740	17.0
Service industries	17,530	2,001	11.4
Finance, insurance, and real estate	2,568	257	10.0
Business and repair services	1,359	223	16.4
Private households	3,507	467	13.3
Personal services, except private household	1,913	350	18.3
Entertainment and recreation services	792	146	18.4
Medical and other health services	2,445	215	8.8
Welfare and religious services	717	42	5.9
Educational services	3,432	194	5.7
Other professional services	797	107	13.4
Public administration	3,343	214	6.4

SOURCE: Bureau of the Census, *Labor Force, Work Experience of the Population in 1958, Cur-*

Salary and Workers by Longest Job in 1958, for the United States
base is less than 150,000)

| | Percent Distribution of Workers with Unemployment or Layoffs in 1958 | | | | | | Percent of Total Unemployed with 2 or More Spells of Unemployment |
| Total | Year-Round Workers Who Lost 1 or 2 Weeks | Part-Year Workers by Weeks of Unemployment | | | | | |
		1 to 4 Weeks	5 to 10 Weeks	11 to 14 Weeks	15 to 26 Weeks	27 Weeks or More	
100.0	9.2	19.3	19.2	11.9	20.6	19.9	40.9
100.0	6.0	13.8	15.1	10.5	22.9	31.7	59.5
100.0	9.4	19.6	19.4	11.9	20.5	19.2	39.8
—	—	—	—	—	—	—	—
100.0	8.7	8.2	24.6	15.8	17.5	25.1	39.9
100.0	6.3	13.5	19.8	13.9	26.2	20.1	57.1
100.0	11.5	18.2	19.5	12.0	19.9	18.9	36.0
100.0	11.4	17.9	18.4	10.8	20.8	20.8	35.2
100.0	13.2	18.3	21.7	9.4	23.4	14.0	58.3
—	—	—	—	—	—	—	—
100.0	12.8	14.5	14.8	11.2	26.0	20.7	32.9
100.0	10.6	15.5	22.3	15.2	23.1	13.3	34.5
100.0	12.9	19.8	17.6	11.8	16.8	21.2	32.1
100.0	13.8	17.8	14.6	10.7	17.8	25.3	28.9
100.0	8.1	20.3	20.6	7.6	20.9	22.5	35.4
100.0	6.5	22.6	19.2	6.9	19.0	25.6	34.7
100.0	11.3	15.7	23.4	8.9	24.6	16.1	36.7
100.0	12.7	15.9	15.1	14.7	20.0	21.6	30.6
100.0	11.7	18.8	21.4	14.0	18.2	15.7	37.5
100.0	10.0	19.2	17.5	16.6	18.3	18.3	43.3
100.0	7.5	17.5	22.6	14.3	18.3	19.8	29.4
100.0	9.3	19.3	26.0	13.6	19.8	12.0	44.9
—	—	—	—	—	—	—	—
100.0	18.8	21.0	21.4	12.7	15.2	10.9	29.0
100.0	10.1	16.7	16.4	9.9	24.6	22.4	40.1
100.0	7.9	6.1	9.8	9.8	32.9	33.5	34.8
100.0	10.8	16.2	20.8	11.3	22.1	18.9	44.7
—	—	—	—	—	—	—	—
100.0	8.1	25.0	19.2	10.0	19.0	18.7	36.0
100.0	7.5	24.3	23.1	8.7	19.8	16.5	36.0
100.0	8.2	25.1	18.5	10.3	18.8	19.1	36.0
100.0	9.3	24.3	19.8	11.7	16.9	17.9	36.5
100.0	11.3	31.5	26.1	9.3	13.2	8.6	22.6
100.0	5.4	16.1	18.4	12.6	26.5	21.1	45.3
100.0	10.1	19.7	19.5	12.2	16.1	22.5	52.7
100.0	10.0	21.7	19.7	10.3	16.9	21.4	38.0
100.0	—	—	—	—	—	—	—
100.0	10.2	28.4	18.1	13.0	14.9	15.3	27.4
—	—	—	—	—	—	—	—
100.0	10.3	32.0	16.5	13.4	18.0	9.8	23.2
—	—	—	—	—	—	—	—
100.0	5.6	21.0	18.2	17.8	19.6	17.8	31.3

rent Population Reports, Series P-50 (June 30, 1959), p. 22.

fifteen weeks, the situation is often serious because unemployment insurance is insufficient to meet many pressing needs. During the postwar recessions unemployment has not lasted as long as it did in the 1930's, and the suffering has been less intense. Nevertheless it is very difficult to be without regular wages. Many wage earners have made purchases on time payments and they often lose all they have invested because of inability to complete their payments. The loss of wages thus spirals into even greater losses.

Unemployment as a Community Problem

So far as Western civilization is concerned, unemployment long has been a community problem in a local and national sense. Attempts to deal with it have been confined to the local, state, and national resources. But these attempts have heretofore been on an alleviating basis rather than with the idea of preventing unemployment. When the problem has been relatively slight, each local community has usually tried to "look after its own." When communities have been unable to meet the problem because the number in need of relief exhausted local resources, state governments have usually come to their rescue. In the depression of the thirties, local and state resources became inadequate and the nation as a whole began to develop a community consciousness on the problem. This was first manifest in the Federal Emergency Relief Administration in 1933 and 1934. By 1935, social thinking had crystallized into the need for meeting the various angles of the problem. The Social Security Act adopted that year provided constructive measures for reducing the hazards of unemployment and for providing public assistance to increase allotments which the various states were giving to persons unable to support themselves. The Social Security Act created a nation-wide community with reference to dealing with the relief problem.

Unemployment, however, is an economic phenomenon which is not contained within national boundaries. Just as the industrial expansion under capitalistic production has depended upon world markets, likewise employment has depended upon the strength of those markets. The simplest of observations should make this plain. Europe with its millions of population, Canada with its sparsely settled expanses, and the United States with its great industrial development all experienced the same type of economic dislocations. Many businessmen and politicians initially failed to recognize the interrelatedness of the national economy and the world's economic problems.

The Unemployment Act of 1946

Memory of the dislocations and distress of the depression haunted the hearts and minds of every person over thirty as the United States emerged as victor from World War II in the midst of great prosperity. Resolved that the boom would not result in overinvestment, overexpansion, and inevitable depression, Congress passed the Unemployment Act of 1946. This act declared that a national policy should be established to promote free enterprise and economic opportunities, self-employment and the promotion of maximum employment, and production and purchasing power. The act provided that the President submit an Economic Report to each session of Congress and as many supplementary reports as he deemed necessary. To this end a Council of Economic Advisers was created to advise the President, gather data, appraise activities, and promote policies which would avoid economic fluctuations.[33] In other words, Congress was asking for the best economic advice as to ways and means for promoting full employment and high production without creating a situation which would end in a cyclical decline and depression.

Thus wage increases have been fostered and high wartime taxes have been retained to reduce the possibility of excessive investment and expansion. For the first time in our history, Congress has promoted economic planning to avert economic crises. Meanwhile, the implementation of the Marshall Plan for relief to distressed European nations who needed assistance in order to restore their means of production has created foreign markets for our goods and kept our production high. These plans have many implications which we cannot discuss here. From a sociological point of view, such planning in advance represents an important new direction in social thinking.

Government Spending to Promote Employment

Today both major political parties have recognized the need for preventing unemployment from becoming widespread. Government spending to promote employment since 1945 has, however, been largely in the defense industries and in the production of goods and services for the armed forces whether at home or stationed overseas. During the fifties over half of all federal expenditures were made for defense purposes.[34] It seems obvious that our economy can never be truly stable until it operates on full production which is geared to peaceful purposes rather than to defense. The mere possibility of an improvement in the "cold war" between the USSR and the United States was enough to bring a decline in the stocks of companies with defense contracts after Khrushchev was invited to visit the United States in August, 1959.[35]

But since defense goods have no value unless there is need for defense, any decrease in such production is bound to bring about dislocations in the economic structure. Thus the prosperity in the post-World War II period is in a large degree attributable to governmental orders and defense production. This means that our economy is essentially socialistic insofar as its prosperity is concerned, since it is financed by governmental spending. Most economists recognize this but are unwilling to explore its implications in terms of potential

[33] *United States Statutes at Large,* 79th Congress, 2nd Session, 1946, Vol. 60, *Public Laws,* chap. 33, Public Law 304.

[34] John K. Galbraith, *The Affluent Society,* Houghton Mifflin Company, Boston, 1958, p. 312.

[35] *Time,* 74:82–83 (August 17, 1959).

unemployment should the government spending cease. It seems incredible that so inherent a danger should be so widely ignored.[36]

Galbraith, however, gives the problem important space in his book *The Affluent Society*. He maintains that we should release tax funds now used for defense production for civilian services. This would make possible improvements in our schools, roads, and other welfare institutions. It would also make possible a desirable balance in production for private consumption and needed public services. Galbraith points out, however, that most industrialists regard production for public service as an immoral and confiscatory way to spend taxes.[37]

The Social Security Act

The Social Security Act of 1935 was a significant attempt to solve the human problems arising from lack of support, especially the lack of support of dependents. This act and its subsequent amendments have reduced the most serious aspects of mass unemployment in the United States. The act provides for a cooperative program of insurance between industries, the various states, and the federal government. The three cooperate in raising funds which are used to offset the financial and personal hazards created by lack of income. These hazards cover a variety of situations for which the funds provide some means of support.

1. *Unemployment Insurance.* The act (as revised in 1959) levies a payroll tax on all employers with four or more employees (and in some states with fewer than four) in the covered industries. (Certain charitable and religious workers are not covered.) The fund provides insurance for persons who lose their jobs under specified conditions but is for a limited period ranging from twenty to thirty weeks. After this insurance expires, public assistance (or relief) is available if necessary. The maximum benefits vary from $26 to $59 a week in the various states and twelve states make provision for allowances for dependents. When persons are laid off or are released from work pending reemployment, most workers are covered by this insurance. Agricultural workers, domestic servants, and self-employed persons (formerly not covered) are now eligible for unemployment insurance. Federal civilian workers, ex-servicemen and veterans, and railway employees are covered under special programs which were in force when the Social Security Act was first enacted.[38]

2. *Old Age, Survivors, and Disability Insurance.* Old age insurance pays retirement benefits to covered employed persons when they reach sixty-five and over, to their wives sixty-two or over, and to their survivors and depend-

---

[36] Raymond T. Bye, for example, dismisses this very important consideration with one sentence. Cf. Raymond T. Bye, *Principles of Economics,* Appleton-Century-Crofts, Inc., New York, 1956 (5th ed.), p. 262.

[37] Galbraith, *op. cit.,* chap. XVIII.

[38] *A Brief Explanation of the Social Security Act,* Social Security Administration, U.S. Department of Health, Education, and Welfare, Washington, March, 1959, pp. 6–14.

ents in case of death. Nearly all people gainfully employed are now covered by this plan. Federal civilian employees and railway workers as mentioned are covered by older retirement plans, but in certain cases railway workers may be eligible for both railway retirement payments and old age insurance. Doctors, state and local government employees, and those in a few nonprofit organizations are not covered. Persons disabled between the ages of fifty and sixty-five are also covered by the provisions of old age insurance.[39]

The amounts paid each retired worker vary according to the taxed incomes he previously received. Incomes up to $4800 were taxed for the first time in 1958. Initially the highest wages taxed were $3600, later raised to $4200 and then to $4800. The highest insurance available by 1959 (based on $4800 income) was $127 a month to the single retired worker and $190.50 for husband and wife. The lowest retirement stipend was $33 a month. Dependent children received additional amounts.[40] The retirement benefit is not supposed, generally speaking, to be enough to support retired people but is considered a stimulant and supplement to savings.

3. *Federal Public Assistance.* For (a) persons over sixty-five who are unable to work and have no unemployment insurance, (b) children whose parents are unable to support them, and (c) the blind and the totally disabled, special assistance is given to the states. This assistance is for monthly payments to such needy persons according to a variety of matching programs as summarized below:

a. *Old age assistance* is for persons too old to work. The federal government pays four-fifths of $30 per month and from 50 to 65 percent of additional amounts up to $65 a month—the remaining amounts paid by the states. In states where income is low the federal government pays a higher proportion of the assistance to old persons.[41]

b. *Aid to dependent children* is available for children whose parents cannot or do not support them. The federal government pays from $17 to $30 a month (depending upon age). It pays $14 of $17 and from 50 to 65 percent of the amounts from $17 to $30.[42]

c. *Aid to the blind* is usually more generous than aid to other needy persons who are either wholly or partly unemployed, perhaps because blindness arouses great sympathy. The amounts and types of benefit vary from state to state, but blind persons are permitted to earn $50 a month and still be eligible for assistance.[43]

d. *Aid to the totally disabled* is provided by each state. Needy persons over eighteen who are permanently and totally disabled (whether physically or mentally) and consequently unable to support themselves are eligible.

[39] *Ibid.,* pp. 14–15.
[40] *Ibid.,* p. 23.
[41] *Ibid.,* p. 38.
[42] *Ibid.,* pp. 42–43. Cf. Chapter 16 of the present volume for a discussion of fathers who do not support their children.
[43] *Ibid.*

Amounts of aid vary, for rehabilitation and physical restoration are stressed. Persons partially disabled are also assisted in most states.[44]

e. *Maternal and child services* vary from state to state, but the amounts are not as rigidly defined as for most types of assistance. Crippled children are provided with a variety of rehabilitation services and medical and surgical treatment, if needed. Homeless, dependent, and neglected children are given aid, and funds are also available for protective services for children in danger of becoming delinquent.[45] These services are essentially an extension of unemployment insurance since mothers are paid to stay at home to look after their children instead of seeking work so as to support them.

Long-Time Aspects of Unemployment

To summarize the present situation: our nation appears to face a continuous 5 percent unemployment rate (even with our extensive government spending for defense) if there are no special programs to take up the slack.[46] Any future projections of the extent of unemployment are concerned with imponderables. There is, however, the anomalous threat of extensive unemployment if the tensions between the East and the West, and in particular between the United States and the USSR, are relaxed, as we mentioned earlier. Since our post-World War II prosperity and employment rates have been largely based upon government spending for defense we shall have to have some intelligent and extensive spending for peacetime needs if a serious collapse of the economic structure is to be averted. If we could plan to spend amounts for peaceful uses comparable to those for defense, many improvements in housing, in roads, in schools, in art galleries, and in music would follow. Investors generally object to such welfare spending beyond restricted "relief" needs because there is no monetary income from the capital expended.[47]

Our government will probably never again revert to the theory of laissez-faire economics or to unregulated capitalism. How far we shall go in becoming a welfare state is hard to predict *but we are partially a welfare state now,* despite the protestations from major segments of the body politic and from industry. We have a policy of monetary and fiscal stabilization, a progressive income tax, and a social security program which prevents our unemployment problem from becoming as serious as it would otherwise be.[48] Social planning and government spending will be essential to achieve continued full employment.

---

[44] *Ibid.* For the complete details of the Social Security Act as revised see *Compilation of Social Security Laws,* 1959 (and successive years), Social Security Administration, Washington.

[45] *Ibid.,* p. 46.

[46] News item, *The American Federationist,* 6:20 (May–June, 1959).

[47] Galbraith, *op. cit.,* chap. XIX, "The Investment Balance."

[48] See Paul T. Homan, Albert Gailord Hart, and Arnold W. Sametz, *The Economic Order,* Harcourt, Brace and Company, New York, 1958, chap. XXXIII, for a clarifying discussion on "liberal socialism" and the welfare state.

SELECTED BIBLIOGRAPHY

Allen, Frederick Lewis, *The Big Change,* Harper & Brothers, New York, 1952. This book is a very effective description of the problems of the depression and the changes made by our social security program.

American Federationist (current issues). This official journal of the AFL-CIO gives up-to-date analyses of the problem and extent of unemployment.

Bakke, E. Wight, *The Unemployed Worker,* Yale University Press, New Haven, 1940. This is one of the best surveys of the humiliation and suffering of great segments of our population during the Great Depression.

Bartlett, Roland W., *Security for the People,* Wilcox and Follett Company, Chicago, 1949. A discussion of the role of monopoly in producing economic crises points up the need for a government program for promoting security.

A Brief Explanation of the Social Security Act, Social Security Administration, U.S. Department of Health, Education, and Welfare, Washington, March, 1959. The details of the Social Security Act as amended through 1958 are briefly given.

Bye, Raymond T., *Principles of Economics,* Appleton-Century-Crofts, Inc., New York, 1956 (5th ed.). This standard text gives an excellent statement of the classical explanation of the ups and downs of the business cycle.

Galbraith, John K., *The Affluent Society,* Houghton Mifflin Company, Boston, 1958. This book gives a cogently reasoned analysis of the productive capacity of modern industry and the need for government spending both to promote full employment and to enhance living for all through improved public services.

Hansen, Alvin H., *The American Economy,* McGraw-Hill Book Company, Inc., New York, 1957. Data which Hansen believes confirm the essential validity of the Keynes doctrine are presented.

Hansen, Alvin H., *Economic Policy and Full Employment,* McGraw-Hill Book Company, Inc., New York, 1947. In this book Hansen clarifies the Keynes doctrine of unemployment.

Keynes, John Maynard, *The General Theory of Employment, Interest and Money,* Harcourt, Brace and Company, 1936. This book has had a profound effect on economic thinking in maintaining that wider saving of money to the point that savings exceed investment will depress prices and ruin business with resultant unemployment.

Monthly Labor Review (current issues). This monthly publication of the U.S. Department of Labor provides excellent analyses of current unemployment problems from careful, unbiased reviews of primary data. It is indispensable for keeping up to date in a way that no textbook can possibly provide because of the time element.

Monthly Report on the Labor Force, Current Population Reports, Series P-57. This Bureau of the Census series published up to June 30, 1959, provides excellent material for understanding unemployment since the depression in particular. Labor force data are now available from the Bureau of Labor Statistics.

Social Security Administration, *Compilation of Social Security Laws,* Government Printing Office, Washington, 1959. This gives the Social Security Act of 1935 as amended in 1939, 1946, 1950, 1952, 1954, 1956, 1957, and 1958, with the provisions of the Internal Revenue Code and the employment taxes which facilitate the social security insurance provided by the act.

Work Experience of the Population in 1958, Labor Force, Current Population Re-

ports, Series P-50, No. 91, June 30, 1959. An excellent analysis of primary data by the staff of the Bureau of the Census, this series has been discontinued. Students and faculty should consult labor force information now issued by the Bureau of Labor Statistics, U.S. Department of Labor.

Yoder, Dale, *Manpower Economic and Labor Problems,* McGraw-Hill Book Company, Inc., New York, 1950. This book presents important data on the perennial problem of unemployment.

CHAPTER 27

Religious Minorities

Social Disorganization and the Melting Pot

We have discussed the absorption of the various cultural and ethnic groups within our native population in the chapter on migration. While certain nationality groups have tried to maintain their cultural identity in this country, nearly all have been successfully merged with the overall American cultural complex. Most immigrants have wanted to become Americans. This cooperative fusion of cultures has been without precedent in modern society. In no other country have peoples of different origins wished so fervently to be identified as members of another culture. Commager has attributed this conversion of many alien stocks "to a spirit of Brotherhood, transcending class, race, religion, a feeling that all dwellers within these states are partners in a common enterprise. . . ."[1] This spirit of brotherhood is a basic value in America. It is a product of the common sharing of the problems of frontier living and of hewing a civilization out of a wilderness. Serious cultural tensions have existed at times, but these have often been between the older American stock and the more recently arrived immigrants, whose cultural differences and lesser economic status were distinctly to their disadvantage.

Many economic tensions have likewise arisen between transported European peasant laborers and "Yankee" American capital. Nevertheless, the tensions were mitigated by the educational efforts of the public school and the intercultural projects of the YMCA, the YWCA, and the social settlement. These and other agencies helped the newcomers in their adjustment problems in the new land. Life for most first-generation immigrants was hard in America. But their children and their children's children have been absorbed into the American pattern so completely that there is little to distinguish the ideals and values of the child of Polish stock from those of a descendant of the Scotch-Irish settlers of the eighteenth and early nineteenth centuries. The melting pot has made "of all nations one people" chiefly because their sons and daughters wanted so earnestly to become Americans.

In two respects, however, our melting pot has not produced mutual tolerance

[1] Henry S. Commager, *The Growth of the American Republic*, Oxford University Press, New York, 1937, Vol. II, pp. 591–592. Cf. E. A. Benians, *Race and Nation in the United States*, Cambridge University Press, Cambridge, 1946.

and acceptance. We refer to religious and racial prejudice and discrimination. Two religious groups, the Roman Catholics and the Jews, have for very different reasons been victims of prejudice and discrimination. One racial group, the Negro, has been subject to much more serious restrictions. As the result of the caste system in the South the Negroes have been forced to accept second-class citizenship—yet they constitute one-tenth of the total population. The problems of religious and racial discrimination are among the most important social and ethical problems of American society.[2]

Many people thus consider the Negro problem the most serious single dilemma of our democracy.[3] Religious differences are presumably more amenable to education and resolution because they can be modified by cultural approaches. Prejudice against the Catholic and the Jew is not based upon biological factors, although this basis is sometimes alleged in the case of the Jew. The Negro, however, has visible biological characteristics which cannot be modified. The modification must instead be in the attitudes toward the Negro race as a symbol of inferiority.

We shall therefore examine the reasons for prejudice (which are mostly rationalized justifications rather than facts) and the particular manifestations (or types of discrimination) that such prejudice takes. The existence of prejudice is an index to social disorganization and the breakdown of consensus of a democratic society. Prejudice and discrimination lead to social disorganization because they produce conflict and prevent individuals from effective participation in the social organization. They are also indices to existing disorganization, as our discussion will make clear.

The Nature of Prejudice and Discrimination

The terms "prejudice," "discrimination," and "segregation" are often confused. They are related but not similar. *Prejudice* is a pattern of hostile attitudes by which an individual is placed in a particular category and judged accordingly. *Discrimination* refers to overt acts committed against individuals and minority groups because of the prejudice of the dominant majority. *Segregation* is a special form of discrimination whereby the minority group is denied access to such institutional facilities of the larger society as schools, hotels, restaurants, recreational facilities, and transportation.

Prejudice is thus a state of mind, whereas discrimination and segregation are specific acts or series of acts. Prejudice is the root of discrimination and segregation and provides much (but not all) of the motivating force. A factory owner, for example, may be prejudiced against Negroes but may still hire them because he needs their labor. Another factory owner may refuse to hire Negroes at all and may thus practice discrimination as well as

---

[2] Louis Wirth, "The Unfinished Business of American Democracy," *Annals of the American Academy of Political and Social Science 244:*1–9 (March, 1946).

[3] Cf. Gunnar M. Myrdal, *An American Dilemma,* Harper & Brothers, New York, 1944.

feel prejudice. Discrimination is, in effect, an *acting out* of prejudice, with a resulting impact upon social interaction.[4]

Some persons also confuse "race," "religious," and "ethnic" prejudice. *Race* is a biological term and *races* (in the plural) are "populations which differ in the frequencies of some gene or genes."[5] Negroes are a race and prejudice against them is race prejudice. Prejudice against Jews, however, is *not* race prejudice, although it is often so called. The Jews are not a race in any scientific sense. They are an ethnic division of the Caucasian race, which has been marked for over two thousand years by distinct religious and cultural characteristics. The distinctive qualities of Jews are religious, familial, cultural, and educational, *not* racial in the genetic sense. The Jews are a minority primarily because of their social or cultural, rather than their "racial," qualities.[6]

Catholic Prejudice in America

In an earlier period, Roman Catholics in the United States were often a repressed and frustrated minority. They were victims of vicious attacks, legal discriminations, and political maneuvers. Protestant clergymen often preached anti-Catholic sermons in the name of promoting Christianity, and many Catholics still feel insecure in what is dominantly a Protestant culture. Statistically speaking, Catholics are still a minority. But their number has increased so rapidly with the influx of southern European immigrants that they are now the most powerful Christian group in America, even though there are nearly twice as many Protestants. There were 36,023,977 Catholics and 68,165,701 Protestants in the United States (including Hawaii and Alaska) in 1958.[7] In addition, a large number of people consider themselves Protestant, athough they are not active church members.

Protestants lack strength because they represent so many divisions and diversities of faith in their 226 sects and denominations.[8] The strength of the Catholics lies in their unity, their hierarchical organization, and their obedience to principles laid down by the ranking priesthood and the papal offices. In consequence, Catholics have achieved such a strong political status that they have effectively blocked state and federal legislation which they have believed to be antithetical to their religious beliefs. They have thus been largely responsible for (1) preventing the ratification of the Child Labor Amendment, (2) blocking the passage of more liberal divorce laws in New York and other states, and (3) prohibiting the dissemination of birth control

[4] Gordon W. Allport, *The Nature of Prejudice*, Addison-Wesley Publishing Company, Inc., Cambridge, 1954, pp. 14–15.

[5] L. C. Dunn and Th. Dobzhansky, *Heredity, Race and Society*, New American Library, New York, 1952 (rev. ed.), p. 118.

[6] Allport, *op. cit.*, pp. 119–125.

[7] *World Almanac and Book of Facts, 1959,* New York World-Telegram Corporation, New York, 1959, pp. 711–712.

[8] *Ibid.*

materials through the mails. They also have taken a firm stand in favor of extending civil rights to Negroes.

Many prejudices still exist against Catholics, especially in those sections of the country where the Catholic population is comparatively small. Prior to 1960 a Catholic candidate for President was held to have little chance for election though several Catholic governors, notably in Pennsylvania, California, and Maine had been elected. The Ku Klux Klan has periodically rallied anti-Catholic, as well as anti-Negro, forces. In recent years, Catholics have done much to create favorable attitudes toward their church by emphasizing the essential points of the Christian faith in which all Christians more or less agree, and by cooperating in the efforts of the National Conference of Christians and Jews to end bigotry and establish tolerance. Scholarly Catholics have been successful, meanwhile, in creating favor among upper-class and educated groups, and a sizable number of influential Protestants have been converted to the Catholic faith. Catholic clergymen have broadcast sermons over national radio hookups emphasizing the Catholic point of view. Others with literary facility have written best-selling religious books which have been read by Protestant and Catholic alike.

Certainly the most active aspects of Protestant-Catholic religious conflict have subsided. On the other hand, Catholicism is sometimes defined as a threat to the established religious values of Protestant-dominated America, insofar as Catholics have sought federal aid for their educational projects and have affected (directly and indirectly) the curriculums and reading materials of public schools and colleges. In certain respects, these points of view represent differences in basic values. The lack of consensus on these matters is symptomatic of different definitions of the situation.

In general, discrimination against the Catholics is slight at the present time. Catholics are not segregated residentially, kept out of country clubs, opposed by professional groups, or accused of bad manners. In their European nationality groups, outside of Nordic countries, Catholics have long been dominant and have not been reared in an atmosphere of persecution, repression, and conflict. Hence they have not developed many of the frustrations and insecurities of the Jew or the Negro.

Jewish Prejudice in America

The exact number of Jews cannot be stated with any complete accuracy. The estimated number of Jews was 5,261,550 in the United States in 1958, according to the *American Jewish Year Book*.[9] The religious survey conducted by the Census Bureau in 1958 indicated that there were approximately 5,039,000,[10] a number based on projections from a partial census. This included 3,868,000 Jews over 14, and 1,107,000 children under 14 and 64,000 with one Jewish parent. The *American Jewish Year Book*

[9] *The American Jewish Year Book,* American Jewish Committee, New York, 1959, p. 18.

[10] Bureau of the Census, *Provisional Estimates of the Population of the United States, Current Population Reports,* Series P-25, No. 189 (July 1, 1958), p. 1.

holds, however, that there were 5000 Jewish children in orphanages and 30,000 Jews in the armed services.[11] Other sources indicated that there must be an additional 200,000 because a certain number of Jews concentrated in urban areas were not accounted for. Today half the American Jews are concentrated in New York City and constitute the largest Jewish group in any city. Because of Hitler's maniacal extermination of the Jews, around 6,000,-000 perished under his regime. There are now approximately 12,000,000 Jews altogether, of whom 2,000,000 live in the Soviet Union, 1,780,000 in Israel, 1,452,350 in the various countries in Europe, and the rest scattered in Africa, Asia, Australia, and South America.[12]

Because Jews have *attempted* to maintain their cultural identity they have often not been assimilated completely into the American pattern. But as long as there were only a handful of Jews in this country there seems to have been little prejudice. The first Jews came to America in 1633 to engage in trade and commerce. They performed a valuable and important function in developing trade relations with other countries. Most were from Spain and Portugal. During the revolution of 1848, a sizable number of German Jews came to this country.[13] It was not until 1880 and thereafter, however, that the great Jewish migrations from Eastern Europe began. Both political and economic reasons motivated this movement, and thousands of Jews fled from Russia and Poland before the pogroms of the czars. Many of these refugees were skilled in the needle trades and were soon absorbed in the garment industries. Most of the needleworkers settled in New York to make it the great center of this industry and the largest Jewish city in the world.

With their skills, their talents, and their interest in education, the arts, and industry, the Jews achieved distinction and came to dominate many fields. Anti-Semitic prejudice arose correspondingly in various quarters. It was not serious, however, until after World War I, when the Jews had become conspicuous in certain cities. To the uncritical, the Jew posed an easy explanation for the social and economic insecurity then threatening the nation.

The dislocations in the economy imposed by World War I and the rapid shutting down of war industries entailed numerous social repercussions. All the problems inherent in rapid urbanization had been enhanced by war production. The crowded housing, threatening depression, and unemployment of the period added to these aspects of social disorganization. There were mass hatreds aroused by the war, fears generated by the Russian Revolution, and the pressures toward national exclusiveness which any national crisis produces. Many persons needed a scapegoat and the Jew had long served this purpose in Europe. The flame was fanned by the alleged disclosures of the so-called *Protocols of the Elders of Zion,* which were then widely believed and accepted.

[11] *The American Jewish Year Book,* 1959, p. 4.
[12] *Ibid.,* pp. 121–125.
[13] Cf. Anita Libman Lebeson, *Jewish Pioneers in America 1492–1848,* Brentano's, New York, 1931.

The Protocols of the Elders of Zion

These forged "documents" were one of the most notorious political schemes on record for promoting anti-Semitism and had been developed by Russian secret police to help the Czar in his ruthless pogroms against the Jews. The Protocols were first published and circulated in 1905 but were known to have been produced sometime between 1895 and 1900. They purported to be a series of lectures which showed that the existing social disorganization, the breakdown of standards of conduct, terrorism, the increasing national debt, and the rise of international banking (allegedly involved) were all part of a deliberately conceived Jewish plot to gain dominance over the whole world.[14]

These so-called "documents" were released in Europe at the end of World War I in 1918. Previously the Balfour Declaration had enabled the Zionists to secure a national home in Palestine in 1917 (as a prelude to the present state of Israel). Many Jews had been active in the meetings at Versailles in the execution of the peace treaties. They had also been active in Communist Putsches in Germany and Hungary. President Wilson's closest adviser was a Jew. Consequently many people were willing to believe that there was not only a Jewish plot to enforce secret rule of the world but that it was also Communistic.

Copies of the Protocols were widely circulated by the White Russians who fled to Europe, many of them presumably acting in good faith. In 1919 a German translation was made which apparently did much to foster the rise of Hitler and the Nazi persecution of the Jews. They were also widely circulated in England and were published in the United States in Henry Ford's newspaper the *Dearborn Independent*. (Henry Ford later issued an apology for this error.)

In August, 1921, a correspondent of the *London Times* discovered the Protocols to be a forgery. They were found to have been to a large extent lifted (to the extent of 1400 of the 2500 lines) from a satire written by a French Gentile lawyer, Maurice Joly, entitled *Dialogue en Enfers entre Montesquieu and Machiavel* (*Dialogue in Hell Between Montesquieu and Machiavelli*). Throughout the book the forgers had substituted the "Elders of Zion" for Napoleon. Where the Protocols were not taken bodily from the French satire they were developed in similar vein, but with a special Russian appeal. Since the Jewish press was very important at that time in Europe, any phrases in the original referring to the press were changed to read the Jewish press. Postwar Europe was torn by political upheavals and it was easy for anxious people to accept the Protocols as truth. In addition, their authenticity was vouched for in the name of a nonexistent British publisher. One of the most ridiculous of the allegations stated that the plot had been initiated by King Solomon with the assistance of 1,921,960 fellow plotters![15]

[14] James Parkes, *An Enemy of the People: Anti-Semitism*, Penguin Books, New York, 1946, chap. II, "The Protocols of the Elders of Zion."
[15] *Ibid.*

That the Protocols were believed then and are still believed by many uninformed persons is a commentary on human gullibility. They were to a large degree responsible for focusing resentment on the Jews and hastened the spread of vicious anti-Semitism throughout the world.

It would be a mistake, however, to say there was no European Jewish question. As Hannah Arendt has made clear, it was the Jewish question which precipitated the rise of Hitler and World War II. The great Jewish banking house of Rothschild with its five international branches along with other international bankers had financed the crowns of Europe and the shaky nation-states whose rivalries eventuated in World War I. These bankers had no political ambitions. Their role was to loan money. In so doing, they owed no political allegiance, although they were the financial advisers to kings.

These banking houses emerged virtually unscathed (because of their international alliance) from World War I and the subsequent economic ruin which affected so much of central Europe. Wealthy sons of members of the financial corporations turned to the professions. Following World War I European Jews were fast assuming an important role in the cultural life of the great European cities. The fact that the Jewish people were without strong national ties and largely "unassimilated" in central and eastern Europe added fuel to the fire. And it is true that certain intellectual nonreligious Jews worked in behalf of the Communist movement. For these unreligious Jews the classless atheistic ideology of the Communists offered a chance for assimilation and identification with political and social life. But to say that the Jews as a body were engaged in a plot to rule the world was both ridiculous and palpably untrue. That the rising Jewish populations of Europe were in part unassimilated is a fact which was variously and viciously interpreted. Eventually it led to the destruction of European Jewry under Hitler. Anti-Semitism was thus a major factor in precipitating totalitarianism in Germany.[16] Earlier the Jewish question had rocked France in the Dreyfus affair. In this case Dreyfus, an army officer, was accused of treason and the charges were apparently anti-Semitic in origin.

Organized Anti-Semitism in the United States

Organized anti-Semitism is the attempt to arouse and enforce discriminatory practices. Organized anti-Semitism had begun on a large scale in Europe during the nineteenth century before the advent of the Protocols. The latter merely intensified the existing movement. In Russia, Poland, Austria, and Germany various reactionary groups utilized prejudice against the Jews for political reasons. The old landed aristocracy was afraid of the development of trade and the capitalism which threatened their power (despite the fact that most of the trading, merchandising, and capitalist developments were in the hands of non-Jews). It was easy for political manipulators to

---

[16] Hannah Arendt, *The Origins of Totalitarianism,* Meridian Books, New York, 1958 (2nd ed.), chaps. I–IV. As Miss Arendt says, anti-Semitism was an outrage to common sense—but it was also a powerful and consuming movement.

label these new developments as "Jewish" for their purposes because certain individual Jews were very successful.[17] With the distribution and spread of propaganda by the Protocols in this country many anti-Semitic organizations arose. As our post-World War I economic dislocations devolved into the long-continued depression anti-Semitism rose by leaps and bounds.

During the period 1933–1941, some 121 known anti-Semitic organizations arose for the avowed or implicit purpose of spreading propaganda among the American people against the Jews. Many of these organizations had direct links with the Nazi government and were thus directly in the pay of a foreign power. The majority of the 121 organizations were comparatively unimportant, but several had an elaborate, nation-wide structure supplied with apparently unlimited funds. Among these was the German-American Bund, composed chiefly of German-Americans whose sentimental ties to the fatherland included the anti-Semitism long latent in central Europe. The Silver Shirts was an organization made up largely of native American, lower-middle-class persons whose fears of alleged Jewish financial domination were cleverly exploited. The National Union for Social Justice was launched by Father Charles E. Coughlin, partly as a vehicle to attack the New Deal and partly as an apparent personal bid for power. In the course of his vitriolic attacks on the Jews, Father Coughlin repeated some of Dr. Goebbels' speeches almost verbatim. The Defenders of the Christian Faith, under the Rev. Gerald B. Winrod, tried mobilizing fundamentalist Protestant hatred against the Jews on the grounds of the alleged similarity between the Jewish ideology and Communism.[18]

These and many similar organizations during this stormy decade appealed to various segments of the American people—to different economic groups and religious faiths and to people of different social and economic backgrounds. All of the perpetrators of these propaganda campaigns had one thing in common, namely, their conscious or unconscious fear of social change as it might affect their own personal lives. The bulk of the membership of the organizations comprised the lower middle class, people believing that they had much to lose in the way of status because of the increasing power of organized labor and the rise of the "welfare state." There were leaders in industry, government, and the professions, however, who also occasionally voiced prejudices similar to those of the organized groups. The threat of Communism was for many of these persons identified with the Jews on the one hand and the New Deal on the other. Jews were denounced in the same breath as international bankers and Communists. In this, the arguments of the anti-Semites reached a *reductio ad absurdum*. Jews were denounced both as Communists working for the overthrow of the capitalistic system and as international bankers who profited by the same system.

Certain organized anti-Semitic groups are still functioning and making

---

[17] Parkes, *op. cit.*, p. 5.
[18] Donald S. Strong, *Organized Anti-Semitism in America,* American Council on Public Affairs, Washington, 1941, pp. 14–16.

hostile attacks on Jews. They are responsible to a large degree for the irrational beliefs and hostile attitudes which are spread by many individuals who do not realize either the falsity or the origin of such beliefs and attitudes. Among the groups spreading anti-Semitic doctrines are the American Nationalists, headed by Gerald L. K. Smith, the revived Ku Klux Klan, the National Economic Council, the White Citizens Councils, the Christian Nationalists, the Christian Educational Association, and the Constitutional Education League. Although allegedly organized to promote and maintain segregation the White Citizens Councils are patently anti-Semitic. The present role of the Klan as expressed by Imperial Wizard Eldon L. Edwards is to attack "Catholics, Jews, Communists, Negroes and Northern agitators for menacing the White heritage." In keeping with this vow the Klan has terrorized Negroes, burned crosses at the homes of prominent desegregationists, and bombed synagogues in the South.[19]

Some of the above organizations harbor reputable individuals but they nevertheless appeal to religious prejudice and anti-Semitism. Joseph P. Kamp, head of the Constitutional Education League refused to reveal its membership to a Congressional committee and went to jail for contempt of Congress. This league has frequently held that reputable Jews were members of a "Communist Conspiracy." The list of hatemongers is a long one. The most absurd and invidious of the movements have been the anti-Semitic political campaigns. In one southern state a candidate for governor stated that citizens must be informed of the "Communist-Jewish Conspiracy now bent on destroying the White Race and White Christian Civilization. . . ."[20] The Constitution party revived in 1957 has again given wide credence to the false Protocols of the Elders of Zion.[21]

Patterns of Anti-Semitic Discrimination in the United States

As one of the best Jewish scholars has pointed out, Jews today regard most anti-Semitism in America as relatively mild. In recent years Jews have been active in the desegregation of Negroes while also bending their energies toward investigating why anti-Semites behave as they do and trying to cure them. Meanwhile there have been no clear-cut and penetrating analyses of the extent and depth of the problem.[22] Scientific research in the area is difficult because researchers are either Jewish or non-Jewish and hence unconsciously may interpret the problem from their particular perspectives. Nevertheless, anti-Semitism still exists, despite the fact that the American Jew has made a significant contribution to virtually every area of American life.

Most organized anti-Semitism in the United States is what Halpern calls the

[19] *Bigotry in Action,* American Jewish Committee, New York, 1958 (pamphlet), pp. 2–13.
[20] *Ibid.,* pp. 14–17.
[21] *Ibid.,* p. 19.
[22] Ben Halpern, "America Is Different," in Marshall Sklare (ed.), *The Jews, Social Patterns of an American Group,* The Free Press, Glencoe, Ill., 1958, pp. 23–39.

"lunatic fringe" variety,[23] because Jews have been active in espousing civil rights for Negroes. Violent anti-Semitism broke out during 1957–1958, when synagogues were bombed in seven southern communities, namely, Charleston, Miami, Nashville, Jacksonville, Birmingham, and Atlanta. There was also slight damage to a synagogue in Peoria, Illinois, although this was thought to be the work of a crank. Altogether, eighty such bombings occurred after the United States Supreme Court ordered public schools desegregated in May, 1954. Here the desegregation issue was thus the flame that kindled anti-Semitism.

The various organized anti-Semitic groups in the South have recently revived the Communist and world conspiracy theme of the false Protocols of the Elders of Zion. They have made many other fanatical statements in literature which they have circulated surreptitiously. The violence, while alarming, was condemned by President Eisenhower, public officials, and newspaper editors. In Atlanta, prompt work resulted in bringing the person suspected of wrecking the Jewish Temple in that city to trial.[24]

Strong racist movements are likely to condemn any groups or individuals which oppose their efforts, but most of the southern people are unquestionably opposed to this violence. The major forms of anti-Semitic discrimination are not violent, as the following discussion makes clear.

Rationalized Reasons for Prejudice

Although the forged Protocols set off some of the anti-Semitism in post-World War I Europe and in America, basic reasons for the prejudice and discrimination were widespread social disorganization and mass insecurity. Nevertheless, logical explanations must always be adduced to assuage guilt feelings and to justify what would otherwise be regarded as unethical conduct. Such rationalizations represent unreasonable interpretations placed upon certain facts. The most important rationalizations are based upon interpretations of religious, cultural, and endogamous practices of the Jewish people and certain alleged unpleasant personal characteristics. The latter are doubtless true in a few instances but in no sense do they characterize the Jewish people any more than they do offensive persons in other groups. Yet these are the "reasons" most prejudiced people give to justify anti-Semitic behavior. They are summarized below:

1. *Religious Factors.* Religious beliefs have been a primary source and justification for much anti-Semitism on the part of both Moslems and Christians. The Christians have been especially culpable. Some Christian anti-Semitism may have been initiated by the persecutions to which early Christians themselves were subjected. In banding together for their own protection, they perforce rejected all "who did not believe in the true Christ." Because the Jews rejected Jesus and his teachings and delivered him to the Roman

[23] Ben Halpern, *The American Jew,* Theodor Herzl Foundation, New York, 1956, p. 16.
[24] *The American Jewish Year Book, 1959,* pp. 44–47.

rulers of Palestine for trial, Christians have widely held that the Jews killed Christ. Technically the Romans killed Christ. Today most Jewish scholars and rabbis recognize Jesus as one of their greatest teachers and prophets but disavow him as the Christ or Messiah.

To the Christians, Christ may have been a "stumbling block" to the Jews, as St. Paul said. But the mistreatment of successive generations of Jews for their forefathers' rejection of him is the quintessence of un-Christianity. For Christianity is itself an outgrowth of Judaism and many of the ethical pronouncements of Jesus were derived from the later prophets of the Old Testament. Modern theologians recognize that Christianity is deeply rooted in Judaism. Jews and Christians thus share a common heritage although they have opposing views on some matters.

2. *Cultural Factors.* The Jewish culture as such tends to set off the Jewish people, who themselves recognize that being a Jew is more than merely adhering to certain religious beliefs and practices. The Jews represent a culture with a long history and a people who have preserved a high degree of biological exclusiveness. Their cultural pattern is distinctive and it involves the Hebrew (as well as the Yiddish) language, special dietary habits, family patterns, and special rhythms of holidays and workdays which are more or less their exclusive heritage.

These habits set them off from other people insofar as Jews maintain their orthodox traditions. These differences give rise to fears and suspicion on the part of unsophisticated persons not sharing in the same practices. Jewish culinary habits, for example, may be distasteful to persons unaccustomed to such cooking. In fact, the single tendency of Jews to season cooked meats and vegetables with garlic is often cited as reason enough for keeping Jews out of apartment houses. The older Orthodox Jewish men dressed distinctively. They wore shawls, and the Orthodox rabbis still wear beards, which make them look strange to the non-Jewish population. Conformity rather than diversity has been a (somewhat) unconscious standard by which Americans have accepted other peoples.

3. *Endogamous Factors.* Endogamy is the tendency to marry within a particular group. The Jews have long attempted to maintain their group integrity by frowning upon intermarriage with non-Jews, although this practice is increasingly widespread. Intermarriage is regarded with disfavor by Orthodox Jews, for endogamy has been one of the principal methods of keeping the group together during the long centuries of wandering and persecution. The liberal Jewish groups do not oppose intermarriage as seriously as do the Orthodox, and much of this barrier to assimilation is breaking down.

4. *Personal Factors.* A fourth rationalization or explanation for anti-Semitism is the allegedly offensive personal behavior of Jews. Disagreeable personal traits are obviously found in persons of all religions, races, and creeds and are not the exclusive characteristic of any group. Some of the frustration and insecurity among the Jews undoubtedly manifests itself in occasional aggressive and offensive behavior, just as any group may tend to

compensate for its inferior status in ways considered unpleasant by others. The element of prejudgment in all prejudice, however, attributes these obnoxious traits to *all* Jews and assumes that such behavior is inherent in their "racial" heritage. This is nonsense. Behavior patterns are the responses to definite social situations and are not inherent in the germ plasm of any individual or group.

The Social Structure and Prejudice

Rationalizations for anti-Semitic behavior cannot be justified by any ethical or democratic principle. The social structure in which an individual lives and the factors which affect his status are undoubtedly more important in producing prejudiced attitudes and the resulting discriminatory practices than are the rationalizations per se.

There have been many researches by social scientists, psychologists, and anthropologists (to mention a few) as to why a person becomes prejudiced. We may profitably review the most important of these theories briefly. The various authorities do not fully agree, but taken together their conclusions give a picture of how the social structure is involved in producing prejudice.[25]

1. *Biological Differences.* The oldest and most obvious explanation of prejudice is based upon the fact of biological differences. The individual in the dominant group is presumably prejudiced against any who differ in physical traits from him. This argument loses much of its validity when we realize that *all* biological differences do not evoke fear and prejudice, but only *certain* differences. The biological traits of the Negro and those allegedly pertaining to the Jew are the objects of prejudice only because the individual has been taught to regard them as such. The explanation of the prejudice must be pushed at least one step farther back.

2. *Economic Competition.* Prejudice has also been attributed to economic competition. This theory maintains that the individual is prejudiced against another group if he comes into economic competition with it. There is considerable justification for this point of view, inasmuch as the most violent prejudice against the Negro in the South comes from the poor-white and lower-middle-class groups which are most directly menaced by free Negro labor. Prejudice against the Jew thus may presumably be attributed to the sharp competition offered by Jewish merchants and traders. Similar activity on the part of Yankee traders, however, is considered a mark of superior acumen and regarded with commendation. The Marxist doctrine of the class struggle emphasizes this approach, which is unquestionably important but is by no means the only factor in arousing prejudice.[26]

3. *Frustration-Aggression.* A third theory of prejudice attributes it to aggression arising from frustration. The theory is that frustration tends to produce aggression and that the continued frustrations of the poor whites in the

[25] Cf. Arnold and Caroline Rose, *America Divided,* Alfred A. Knopf, Inc., New York, 1948, chap. 10. Much of the following discussion is based on the Roses' data.

[26] Cf. Oliver C. Cox, *Caste, Class, and Race,* Doubleday and Company, Inc., New York, 1948.

rural South and the lower middle class in the urban North are largely responsible for anti-Negro and anti-Semitic prejudice respectively. The anger of the frustrated and depressed classes must be directed against some objects other than the accepted social institutions, or revolution or some other form of violent social disorganization may ensue. The Negro and the Jew are thus the scapegoats for the aggressions of the repressed groups in the social structure. Although it is by no means certain that frustration inevitably leads to aggression, this explanation offers significant insight into the social forces producing the veiled (and often unveiled) hatreds that take the form of prejudice.[27]

4. *Rural-Urban Conflicts.* The traditional fear and hostility of the rural dweller for the urban person and for the environment which he represents afford another explanation for anti-Semitic prejudice. The Jew has been associated with the city for centuries and has acquired much of the attendant intellectualism, impersonality, and mobility of the city dweller. Many of the relationships of the traditional social order, especially in the United States, are those of the country and small town and are based upon primary relationships, personal contacts, and relative stability of residence. The Jew may thus be the symbol for the change and disorganization associated with the city and hence may be viewed with suspicion and distrust.[28]

5. *Social Neurosis.* Another explanation of prejudice, with especial reference to anti-Semitism, is that prejudiced behavior constitutes a social neurosis, with the same compulsive and irrational characteristics that an individual neurosis has.[29] The anti-Semite is thus "compelled" by the nature of his maladjustment to hate the Jews because this is the only way he can rid himself of his own inner insecurities. The anti-Semite is as completely irrational as the true neurotic when he maintains in one and the same breath that Jews are Communists and international bankers, aggressive and ingratiating, weak and strong, clannish and intrusive, oversexed and impotent, successful and low class, omniscient and defenseless, and possess still other sets of completely antithetical characteristics.[30] Many of the rationalizations of anti-Semitism, as we have indicated, simply do not make sense. The important consideration, according to this theory, is not the logic of the prejudice but the function served by the mass neurosis.

6. *Value Conflicts.* Gunnar Myrdal's theory of prejudice is based upon the contradiction between discrimination and the democratic creed. The treatment of the Negro and the Jew in the United States patently violates the American creed and the values Americans profess. The prejudice against

---

[27] Cf. John Dollard, *Caste and Class in a Southern Town,* Yale University Press, New Haven, 1937; John Dollard *et al., Frustration and Aggression,* Yale University Press, New Haven, 1939.

[28] Rose, *op. cit.,* p. 288.

[29] Read Bain, "Sociopathy of Anti-Semitism," *Sociometry,* 6:460–464 (1943), cited in *ibid.,* p. 295.

[30] Nathan W. Ackerman and Marie Jahoda, "Toward a Dynamic Interpretation of Anti-Semitic Attitudes," *American Journal of Orthopsychiatry, 18:*163–173 (January, 1948).

the Negro is thus in a sense an explanation for the treatment accorded him in the South. The white Southerner could not deliberately and continuously violate the values of the American creed without resorting to some rationalized explanation based on the allegedly innate inferiority of the Negro. These attitudes are incorporated in the culture and form its principal ideological foundation. Despite the integration of this pattern of rationalizations into the caste structure of the South, some persons hold that prejudice and discrimination produce inner conflicts on both the conscious and the subconscious levels. Prejudice thus lays a heavy toll upon those who hold it as well as those who experience its direct impact.[31]

All of these factors contribute in some degree to religious and racial prejudice and to the social disorganization characteristic of the social milieu in which prejudice occurs. It is in the midst of many threatening factors that the prejudiced personality develops.

The Prejudiced Personality

Some persons are mildly prejudiced merely because they have unwittingly absorbed prejudices from their cultural environment. They express such sentiments through ignorance. People who are definitely bitter, hostile, and quasi-professional hatemongers, however, are disorganized personalities. They are the spokesmen for organized anti-Semitism. They actively resent the Jew and his skills, his intellectual gifts, and his economic achievements. Consequently they are aroused by fears that Jews will obtain dominance by securing the highest recognition, the best jobs, and the most money.

Racists, on the other hand, fear the advance and domination of the Negro. In order to explain their prejudices such persons often ascribe a long series of faults to those whom they would discriminate against. All people have faults, but the reasons for prejudice are more significantly to be found in the mind and hostilities of the prejudiced. The basic "causes" of prejudice, therefore, should be sought in the majority group rather than in the minority group. The reasons for prejudice lie in the experience of the whites, Protestants, and Christians, not in the alleged qualities of the Negroes, Catholics, and Jews. Bitterly prejudiced persons are essentially authoritarian personalities. They usually possess some or all of the following characteristics, which have been assigned to prejudiced persons by sociologists, psychologists, anthropologists, psychiatrists, and others:

1. *Insecurity*. The outstanding characteristic of the prejudiced person is his insecurity, his sense of not belonging or of failure to achieve his goal, and his subsequent feeling of social isolation. He is often not conscious of this feeling, but it is nevertheless apparent in the hatred which he feels for minority groups who do not belong either.

2. *Compulsive Conformity*. One index of personal insecurity is the individual's desire to conform to the outward manifestations of society. The prejudiced person wishes to be like everyone else—to join the same organi-

---

[31] Myrdal, *op. cit.*

zations, believe the same truths, and above all to love and hate the same things. He seizes upon the latent prejudice in his social milieu and becomes a fanatical anti-Semite or Negrophobe in an unconscious attempt to be like the others.

3. *Stereotyped Thinking.* As might be expected, the prejudiced person tends to be a stereotyped, rather than an original, thinker. This means that he thinks in stereotypes, slogans, clichés, and catch phrases to a greater extent than the nonprejudiced. Prejudice itself is a pattern of stereotyped attitudes which many individuals accept without question.

4. *Social Aggression.* The prejudiced person tends to be socially aggressive toward minority groups, displaying his feelings at all times and with little or no provocation. The bitter anti-Semite will thus often go out of his way to insult or provoke a Jew, while at the same time claiming that the victim started the aggression. By projecting his aggression on minority groups, the anti-Semite tries to forget his own feelings of insecurity and anxiety.

5. *Lack of Insight.* The prejudiced person has little insight into his own personality and fails to understand that he is attributing his own undesirable traits to other persons. The anti-Semite fails to "take the role of the other" toward himself, to look at himself as others do, and hence is unable to understand his own conduct. In extreme cases a lack of insight denotes neurotic or psychotic conduct and, as we have indicated, prejudice as a mass phenomenon has many of the characteristics of a neurosis.[32]

The prejudiced person is thus unconsciously projecting his fears and anxiety on other people because he feels weak, threatened, and insecure. Prejudice appears to occur at times of social crises, following wars, and during widespread epidemics. In times of relative stability there has been little expression of violent or fanatical prejudice.[33] The prejudiced person and the victim of his prejudice are both aspects of social disorganization. Most prejudiced persons are at present more active in anti-Negro and pro-segregation movements than against the Jews, but there is always a possibility that a serious social crisis will reinflame the anti-Semites.

Social Discrimination[34]

If social discrimination had no extensions beyond limiting Jewish social contacts to Jews and Gentiles to Gentiles, some people might not think it too serious. Actually such discrimination goes much farther since membership in social clubs and organizations is often a basis for industrial and political advancement. Similarly, a large share of the power structure of com-

[32] Adapted from Rose, *op. cit.*, chap. 10; Ernest Simmel (ed.), *Anti-Semitism: A Social Disease*, International Universities Press, New York, 1946, pp. 96–124; Ackerman and Jahoda, *op. cit.* Cf. also Eugene Hartley, *Problems in Prejudice*, King's Crown Press, New York, 1946; Suzanne Reichard, "Rorschach Study of Prejudiced Personality," *American Journal of Orthopsychiatry*, 18:280–286 (April, 1948).

[33] Samuel Lowy, *Cooperation, Tolerance and Prejudice*, Routledge and Kegan Paul, Ltd., London, 1948, p. 140.

[34] Cf. John Slawson, *Social Discrimination, The Last Barrier*, American Jewish Committee, New York, 1955, for further implications on this topic.

munity control is shaped in the informal contacts of businessmen at their private clubs and after business hours. The social discrimination inherent in restricted private clubs, whether leading men's clubs, country clubs, or college fraternities, as well as in the restricted clientele of exclusive resort hotels thus keeps many able and civic-minded Jews from participating in civic and economic as well as social affairs.[35] On the other hand, certain elite college and university clubs are open to Jews by virtue of their college or university affiliation.

Resort hotels have been the most serious open-to-the-public institutions restricting Jewish guests. These hotels often advertise "selected clientele," "restricted clientele" or even "Gentiles only." Some establishments have gone so far as to advertise "Christians only," thus belying any true Christian character. This constant humiliation to which Jews are subjected often creates extremely difficult personal situations. A deep sense of insecurity, of being unwanted, is an unpleasant part of the heritage of the Jew.

Since resort hotels are open to public patronage there would seem to be no legitimate basis upon which social discrimination could be enforced so long as the patrons behave with decorum and pay their bills. Nevertheless, many persons are excluded because their surnames are Jewish. Reservation clerks who are not certain may question a person as to his church affiliation and then say, "I don't think you will be happy here." Some surnames, particularly the German, may or may not be Jewish; this practice is therefore often as embarrassing to Christians as to Jews. Jewish people of taste and refinement and with sufficient means to pay for pleasant accommodations are continually harassed by "No vacancy" replies, when they know very well that Gentile friends have no difficulty in securing rooms. In recent years many Jewish resorts of high caliber have been developed which partly offset such problems.

Housing and Real Estate Restrictions

In many cities certain neighborhoods maintain restrictions by "gentlemen's agreements" not to sell to any Jewish or Negro buyer. In upper- and upper-middle-class neighborhoods these restrictions apply chiefly to Jews. In Pittsburgh, for example, the largest real estate firm owning and operating a series of so-called luxury apartments, has consistently refused to rent to Jewish clients. In the same city, on the other hand, Jewish firms have built a series of high-grade apartments which have been open to Jewish and non-Jewish residents alike with a dominant proportion of Jewish clients. Jewish people are also the predominant residents in a high-grade upper-middle-class section of the city in which special kosher meat and grocery stores cater to Jewish dietary requirements. A number of synagogues are located in this area and Jewish people have no difficulty in obtaining good housing. They may have difficulty in buying or renting where they would like to in certain other areas. Nevertheless, such restrictions are breaking down. Several Jew-

---

[35] N. C. Belth, *The Private Club and the Power Structure in the Dimensions of Social Discrimination,* Anti-Defamation League, New York, no date (pamphlet), pp. 5–9.

ish families have purchased or built fine homes on Woodland Road in Pittsburgh, the most exclusive residential district within the city.

In some cities, and especially in particular suburbs, there are still organized efforts to keep Jews from coming in. La Jolla, California, and Bronxville, New York, are examples. Bronxville, an upper- and upper-middle-class suburb of New York City, is known to real estate men as the "holy square mile." Real estate people will not sell to Jews; they tell them they will be happier elsewhere.[36] All other suburbs to the north of New York City are open to Jews, however.

Educational Discrimination

Formerly many Jewish students had serious difficulties in obtaining entrance to the Ivy League universities and the more exclusive "Big Seven" women's colleges. As a result of agitation, however, a larger percentage of Jews have been admitted in recent years. Most authorities believe that college admission policies have relaxed notably although no complete studies of educational discrimination have been made within the last decade.

Jews have had a strong tradition for scholarship, and a much higher percentage of Jews than non-Jews attend college. In 1954 it was estimated that Jewish students constituted 8 percent of total college students, whereas only 3 percent of the population is Jewish.[37] Moreover, a much higher percentage of Jewish students finish their college and preparatory training than is true of non-Jewish students. A survey of 1633 institutions resulted in replies from 1534 colleges and universities, which constituted a 94 percent return. This survey accounted for 2,140,331 students, of whom 9 percent were Jewish. Apparently, then, Jews are receiving three times as much service from institutions of higher learning as non-Jews. Many administrative officers therefore insist that there are no just grounds for Jewish complaints.

The admissions policies of the exclusive schools, however, have caused most of the protests.[38] Jews object to being excluded because they are Jews. The number of Jewish students in men's colleges dropped from 10.2 percent of the total enrollment in 1935 to 4.6 percent in 1946; the number of Jewish women in women's colleges dropped from 11.8 to 8.4 percent.[39] The chief complaint has been in the difficulty in obtaining entrance to professional schools. The percentage of Jewish students in professional schools dropped from 9 percent of the total in 1935 to 7 percent in 1946. In the profession of medicine, specifically, the proportion of Jewish students dropped from 15.9 to 12.7 percent during these years in 67 out of 89 medical schools. Dentistry students dropped from 28.2 to 18.9 percent. There was also a precipitate

---

[36] Harry Gersh, "Gentlemen's Agreement in Bronxville," *Commentary*, 27:109–116 (February, 1959). Cf. Charles Abrams, *Forbidden Neighbors*, Harper & Brothers, New York, 1955, for a comprehensive study of housing discrimination.

[37] Natalie F. Joffe, *The American Jewish Family*, National Council of Jewish Women, New York, 1954, p. 12.

[38] *The American Jewish Year Book, 1948–1949*, Vol. L, p. 768.

[39] *Ibid.*

drop of Jewish law students from 25.8 to 11.1 percent among the 77 law schools (of a total of 160) reporting.

These earlier figures were admittedly incomplete. Some 700 institutions have since stopped reporting religious affiliation because they no longer include this information on the students' records. Northwestern University is the latest of the great educational institutions to drop religious preference requests on its application blanks. In general, Jewish authorities maintain that the chief discrimination today is in the postgraduate schools of medicine, law, and engineering.[40] Here the prejudice seems to be rooted in the members of the profession as much as it is in the educational institutions.

The charge that there has been serious discrimination against the Jews in American colleges and universities was not sustained by the study completed in July, 1959, in New York State. This showed little if any discrimination against accepting Jewish students who were in the top quarter of their high school class. Questionnaires were sent out by the American Jewish Congress in cooperation with the New York State Department of Education to 4441 high school graduates of such rank. Replies were received from 1235 graduates, who were distributed with a fair degree of proportion to the population of various parts of the state. Religiouswise the proportion of Jews replying was higher than that of non-Jews, 37.1 percent (whereas the population of the state is approximately 15 percent Jewish); 30.8 percent of the replies were from Protestants, 29.1 percent from Catholics, and 3.0 percent indicated they were either nonreligious or belonged to other religious faiths.

The Jewish students had filed 3.1 applications on the average as compared to 2.4 by the Protestants and 2.3 by the Catholics. More Jewish students also applied to Ivy League institutions—38.4 percent as contrasted to 26.8 percent of the Protestants and 8.9 percent of the Catholics. The returns showed that 67.6 percent of the Jews applying were accepted by Ivy League institutions in comparison to 73.5 percent of the Protestants and 56.3 percent of the Catholics. When the rate of acceptance of applications (rather than that of applicants) was analyzed, it was found that 72.2 percent of the Jewish and 73.3 percent of the Protestants were successful. On the other hand, only 59.5 percent of Catholics were accepted. If any discrimination was practiced it would seem to be against Catholics, but this is not as serious as it seems because many indicated a first choice for Catholic institutions. So far as Jews were concerned, their acceptance and that of Protestants was almost exactly the same in both Ivy League and non-Ivy League institutions, i.e., 72.2 percent and 73.3 percent respectively.[41]

The majority of Jewish students are concentrated in New York City, New England, the middle Atlantic and east north central states, and Chicago.

[40] Cf. Benjamin R. Epstein, *The Cold Program* (tr. by Max L. Berges), Jewish Publication Society of America, Philadelphia, 1939, for a detailed account of such practices in the western world.

[41] "A Survey of the Experiences of 1235 New York State High School Graduates in Seeking Admission to College," American Jewish Congress, New York, July, 1959, pp. 1–18 (mimeographed).

Most of them go to tax-supported colleges and universities in their local environment, where there is less likelihood of discrimination. State universities in recent years have accepted few students from other states unless they were "children of alumni," because they were already overcrowded by "G.I.'s." Part of the discrimination against Jews may have occurred because of the enormous increase in college registration from young men and women under the "G.I. Bill of Rights." Private colleges reserve the right to include total personality qualifications in their admission requirements and can refuse to admit anyone for "personality" reasons.

In certain areas Jewish students bulk large in the enrollments. They constitute the majority of students in New York City colleges (public and private alike). Though figures are lacking, the majority of college and university students in institutions controlled by the Board of Higher Education of New York City are Jewish. Earlier a study made public by the American Council of Education showed Jewish students of the first high school quintile, that is, those ranking in the first 20 percent of high school students, had the greatest difficulty in securing admission to college. And these Jewish students were children of college-bred professional and business men.[42]

That Jewish students have greater *innate* intellectual capacity than non-Jewish students seems unlikely, although no control studies have ever been published on this topic. At the same time, Jewish students unquestionably have demonstrated their high scholastic ability. It is possible that as a group they have a willingness to work harder at their academic studies in order to gain an acceptable place in the social structure. The respect for learning, furthermore, is strong in the Jewish culture pattern. Jews have a long history of scholarly achievement. Many Gentile students are quite content to devote themselves to extracurricular activities in order to achieve a good "social rating." Jewish students realize that their principal hope for admission to professional schools usually depends upon high scholastic rating, since they still face certain prejudices.

Economic Discriminations

The economic position of the vast majority of American Jews is now middle class with a definite weighting toward the upper-middle-class rating. Some, of course, are economically upper class. Surveys made between 1948 and 1953 of the local Jewish communities in fourteen cities[43] showed that the proportion engaged in nonmanual occupations ranged from 75 to 96 percent. Even in New York City with its large Jewish population two-thirds of those gainfully employed are working in white-collar jobs.[44]

[42] "Council Announces Results of College Admissions Study," *Key Reporter,* Summer, 1949, p. 769.

[43] These included Camden, N.J., Charleston, S.C., Gary, Ind., Indianapolis, Ind., Los Angeles, Calif., Miami, Fla., Nashville, Tenn., New Orleans, La., Newark, N.J., the suburbs of Newark (considered as a separate community), Passaic, N.J., Port Chester, N.Y., Trenton, N.J., and Utica, N.Y.

[44] Nathan Glazer, "The American Jew and the Attainment of Middle Class Rank (Some Trends and Explanations)," in Sklare, *op. cit.,* pp. 138–146.

In three of the cities surveyed, New Orleans, Trenton, and Passaic, information was available for those professionally employed during the period 1935–1945. In New Orleans the number of professionally engaged Jews increased from 15 to 21 percent of the total and in Trenton from 12 to 19 percent. In Passaic there was no change. With the rise in the number of professionally trained there was a decline in the number engaged as clerks and salesmen from 36.5 percent to 27 percent.[45]

Even when American Jews are manual workers they are characterized by such middle-class values as thrift, foresight, moderation, and an emphasis upon learning. In their recreational habits working-class Jews of the 1930's were likely to participate in middle-class leisure-time activities: athletic games, swimming, playing tennis or golf, or attending concerts and lectures.[46]

Actual employment discrimination against Jews is obviously declining. A sampling of discrimination by employment agencies in 1930 indicated that 95 percent of the job orders were closed to Jews. A sample survey of employment restrictions made in the San Francisco area in 1956 by the Institute of Industrial Relations in California reported that only 22 percent of 340 major industries discriminated against Jews. This situation is probably typical of other sections. At least twelve states have now enacted fair employment practices acts and the trend will increase.

A major share of existing anti-Semitism in industry is more subtle. It often takes the form of denying promotions to Jews for jobs in the upper echelons for which they are well qualified.[47] The prejudice that keeps qualified Jews from entering postgraduate schools also prevents their advance in these fields. Nevertheless, the Jewish people have made notable contributions in the professions. In medicine, they have distinguished themselves in medical research, as the names of Dr. Jonas Salk of polio vaccine fame and Selman A. Waksman, who developed streptomycin, indicate.

We cannot recount here the long list of Jews who have made a notable place in industry or have attained high economic status in other fields. The Jewish people dominate the entertainment world of theater, radio, movies, and TV; the fur and garment industries; and the department store field. They head some of our finest orchestras. They have been successful in politics, as is witnessed by Governor Ribicoff of Connecticut and Anne X. Alpern, who is Attorney General of Pennsylvania. In proportion to their numbers Jews have had marked success in the economic and professional arena despite the existing discriminations.

Religious Discrimination

Discrimination by Christians against Jews, although diminished, still exists. Christians (scarcely deserving the name) are responsible for most of the social and economic discriminations against Jews in America. Such

---

[45] *Ibid.*
[46] *Ibid.*
[47] Benjamin R. Epstein, *Antisemitism in the United States: A Current Appraisal,* reprint from *The New Leader,* May 29, 1957, pp. 6–7. (Pamphlet.)

discrimination is both un-Christian and a continual factor in community disorganization. Attempts have been made in recent years, however, to emphasize the similarities in Christian and Jewish teachings as well as their common roots. Christian and Jewish theologians now speak of the Judeo-Christian ethic as an evidence of their shared beliefs. Much of this understanding has been the result of the activities of the National Conference of Christians and Jews, which came into being in an effort to promote friendly relationships between Protestants, Catholics, and Jews.

Officially there is no discrimination in the United States today against Jewish religious worship, religious practices, or observance of holidays. But because this is a dominantly Christian country there are certain laws restricting business activities on Sunday; Christmas and Good Friday are generally recognized as holidays by government and business organizations. Many Jewish merchants who observe the orthodox Sabbath on Saturday have objected strenuously to Sunday closing laws on grounds of discrimination.

In a sense it is true that religious discrimination is basic to all other types of discrimination. Many Jews believe that all tensions between Jewish and Christian groups are essentially religious. Christians and Jews realize that Jewish conversion to Christianity would eliminate the Jewish problem, but to the Jew this would be anathema.[48] Yet Theodor Herzl, founder of the Zionist movement, was of the opinion that there are only two alternatives by which the Jews may resolve their essential problem: one is to seek a homeland in what is now modern Israel; the second is to be assimilated. Many American Jews have not taken Zionism too seriously nor are they too concerned whether or not they shall assimilate or risk arousing anti-Semitism.[49] Many are actually irreligious.

Modern religious Jews are today divided into three groups: (1) the *Orthodox,* who strive to retain ancient rituals and practices, and all their cultural habits as well; (2) the *Reform Jews,* who have incorporated many of the forms and practices of Western culture into their religious worship and way of life; and (3) the *Conservatives,* who attempt to take a compromise position. For the Reform Jews in America and for many of the other, America, not Israel, is their homeland. At the same time, they wish to maintain their essential identity. This Reform group is willing to worship on Sunday if need be, and to shed many dietary and other habits considered unessential to their religious and ethical concepts. For the Orthodox Jews Western culture creates many problems. This is one of the reasons that we have many "self-imposed ghettos" or Jewish neighborhoods in American cities. For here Jewish butchers and grocers are accessible so that a kosher diet may be maintained, as mentioned above. Kosher restaurants provide for those eating out and synagogues are near by for daily prayer. The Reform Jew who seeks greater identification with his non-Jewish fellow citizens is inevitably partly "assimilated."

[48] Halpern, *The American Jew,* especially pp. 71–73.
[49] Halpern, "America Is Different," in Sklare, *op. cit.,* pp. 37–39.

That there should be *any* religious discrimination in the United States is often perplexing to the Jew. It is difficult for him to understand that the American conception of religious freedom was initially (and still is to a certain extent) a restricted freedom. For although the Constitution of the United States guarantees religious freedom and stipulates that there shall be no established church, the states have generally promoted the Christian religion.[50] What the Founding Fathers intended was that no particular sect of *Christianity* should be established *as a church* because of the diversity of our Christian sects.

Patrick Henry introduced a law providing state support for the Christian religion in 1784 (which was later defeated). Georgia followed by guaranteeing religious freedom in 1789 and Pennsylvania and South Carolina in 1790. But many states did not go this far until the middle of the nineteeth century.[51] Many states still support laws which enhance Christian teaching. This nation is essentially Christian in its values and orientation. The laws on Sunday closing and the restriction of business on Sunday contribute to what the Jew considers his dilemma in pursuing his own religious principles and the observance of his Sabbath but conform to majority opinion.

Judaism Today—A Summary

Compared with the unbelievable massacre of Jews by the Nazis, any anti-Semitism in the United States today pales into insignificance. European Jewry was virtually destroyed during Hitler's regime, and this destruction has altered the whole focus of the Jewish problem. American Jews now constitute the largest national body of Jews; it and the Israeli form the two main constituents of present-day Judaism. It is true that slightly more Jews live in the USSR than are now in Israel, but many of these are Marxists and are irreligious in their orientation. They hope to be assimilated within a classless, nonreligious society. The Marxists say, therefore, that there is no Jewish problem in the Soviet Union, whereas Orthodox Jews fear for their obliteration as a group under Communism.

The creation of the Jewish state of Israel meanwhile has fulfilled the hopes of Theodor Herzl and other Zionists who first worked for its achievement. Herzl, a Viennese journalist, wrote his impassioned plea for a Jewish homeland in 1896 (in *Der Judenstaat*) and was active in organizing the Zionist movement in 1897. In 1917 the Balfour Proclamation opened Palestine to the Jews, but not until after the awful slaughter of Jews under Hitler and the close of World War II was the state of Israel finally established.[52]

For the Jews who have found refuge, work, and a good life in Israel, the Jewish problem may seem to be settled. Most American Jews of the non-Zionist persuasion, however, have become so identified with American values

[50] Leo Schall, "The Jews in the United States—A Survey," Brooklyn Jewish Center, 1955, p. 9 (mimeographed).

[51] *Ibid.*

[52] Rufus Learsi, *The Jews in America,* World Publishing Company, Cleveland, 1954, pp. 176–182.

that they have no desire to seek a homeland in Israel. Their "homeland" is America.[53] Their gifts and contributions to American culture are evident. The larger body of Americans recognize their talents and skills and do not in any political sense persecute the Jews today. Nevertheless, Jews are still not admitted to full participation in American social and economic life. The fact that the American Jewish population has remained relatively constant while the non-Jewish population has increased significantly in the last two decades is an indication that considerable assimilation of the Jew is taking place. Is this the only answer to discrimination? Or can there be greater toleration and cooperation in America?

SELECTED BIBLIOGRAPHY

Abrams, Charles, *Forbidden Neighbors,* Harper & Brothers, New York, 1955. This book is a comprehensive study of discrimination in housing in the United States.

Ackerman, Nathan W., and Jahoda, Marie, "Toward a Dynamic Interpretation of Anti-Semitic Attitudes," *American Journal of Orthopsychiatry, 18:*163–173 (January, 1948). This article analyzes the neurotic aspects of anti-Semitism.

Allport, Gordon W., *The Nature of Prejudice,* Addison-Wesley Publishing Company, Cambridge, 1954. This is one of the best definitive analyses of the nature of prejudice from an objective viewpoint.

The American Jewish Year Book. This annual report presents current data and statistics on all important Jewish organizations and Jewish problems.

Annals of the American Academy of Political and Social Science, Vol. 244 (March, 1946). This entire volume is devoted to the subject of prejudice.

Anonymous, *Bigotry in Action,* American Jewish Committee, New York, 1958 (pamphlet). An excellent condensation is given of the activities of current anti-Semitic organizations.

Arendt, Hannah, *The Origins of Totalitarianism,* Meridian Books, New York, 1958 (2nd ed.), chaps. I–IV. This is a brilliant and detailed statement of the relation between the Jewish question in Europe and the rise of totalitarianism.

Cox, Oliver C., *Caste, Class, and Race,* Doubleday and Company, Inc., New York, 1948. The Marxian doctrine is applied to racial prejudice.

Dollard, John, *Frustration and Aggression,* Yale University Press, New Haven, 1939. The theory that prejudice is the result of the aggressive behavior of repressed persons is presented. Prejudice is thus a veiled or unveiled hatred.

Halpern, Ben, *The American Jew,* Theodor Herzl Foundation, New York, 1956. The ideas and aims of Zionism as well as problems of contemporary discrimination are excellently stated.

Learsi, Rufus, *The Jews in America: A History,* World Publishing Company, Cleveland, 1954. This gives an excellent history of Jews in the United States, their present achievements and problems.

Lebeson, Anita Libman, *Jewish Pioneers in America 1492–1848,* Brentano's, New York, 1931. This book is a valuable history of early Jewish migrations to America.

[53] Halpern, "America Is Different," in Sklare, *op. cit.*

Parkes, James, *An Enemy of the People: Anti-Semitism*, Penguin Books, Inc., New York, 1946. The dangerous aspects of anti-Semitism and the extent of organized prejudice in the Western world are well discussed. This book contains the forged "Protocols of the Elders of Zion."

Rose, Arnold and Caroline, *America Divided*, Alfred A. Knopf, Inc., New York, 1948. The alleged and real reasons for anti-Semitism are analyzed.

Sklare, Marshall (ed.), *The Jews, Social Patterns of an American Group*, The Free Press, Glencoe, Ill., 1958. This volume contains 33 analyses of various aspects of Jewish problems and patterns of living by outstanding scholars.

Slawson, John, *Social Discrimination, The Last Barrier*, American Jewish Committee, New York, 1955 (pamphlet). This little pamphlet makes clear that social discriminations against Jews, while declining, are still serious in most communities.

CHAPTER 28

Racial Minorities

Race: A Definition

Race is always with us. Hence it is probably the most serious continuous internal source of tensions in the United States. Economic cycles have their ups and downs, and crime rates vary with social disorganization. But race involves a permanent and visible division of humanity to which long-established patterns of prejudice are attached. Race is the term applied to the four major divisions of human population and refers to the differences in skin color (or pigmentation), head shape (or cephalic index), nose shape, stature, structure of the hair, and other features. The most distinctive aspect of race is skin color, although there are many variations of pigmentation within each race. Thus we commonly call the Caucasoid race the white race; the Negroid race the black race; the Mongoloid race the yellow race; and the Australoid race the brown—with full recognition that there are many variations and overlappings.

Racial differentiations have caused much conflict and led to many unscientific conclusions about racial superiority and inferiority. Some anthropologists accordingly have held that we should abandon the term and call these broad classifications of humanity ethnic groups. Ethnic groups are generally defined as groups with a common culture, and this proposal would therefore seem to have little practical value. Race has been a badly abused word because of the absurd and emotionalized interpretation placed upon the fact of racial differences. Biologists and anthropologists believe racial differences have developed partially from biological isolation but are largely the products of natural selection. We know very little about the actual reasons for such biological differences except that skin color is an adaptation to climate. The heavy pigmentation of the dark-skinned peoples is a definite protection against the tropical sun. The fair skin of the Nordic makes it possible for him to absorb more of the northern sun's rays.[1]

Differences in skin color lead to irrational fears and serious discriminatory treatment. This fact can be explained partly by "strangeness" with all the fears and attractions that "being different" occasions. Much of present-day racial discrimination is cultural, however, for it involves the individual's absorption

[1] M. F. Ashley Montagu, *Man's Most Dangerous Myth*, Harper & Brothers, New York, 1952 (3rd ed.), chap. III.

of attitudes which are a part of the structure of the society in which he lives.[2] This is true in all sections of the United States. Racial discrimination against the Negro has been most serious in the southern states, whereas discrimination and prejudice against the Oriental has been most severe on the Pacific coast.

The fact of race differences at the same time has been a factor in promoting sex attraction and racial hybridization. One of the major scandals of our own southern history during slavery was the high degree of racial miscegenation. A sizable number of slaves were children of their masters, and some of the "best blood of the South" runs in the veins of the American Negro. As Arthur W. Calhoun has well said, no system of exploitation ever respects the virtue of women of the subject class.[3] The noted psychiatrist Dr. Herman K. Adler stated that part of the racial hostility pattern in the South lies in the very fact of the Negro's sex attraction. In any event, wherever races have migrated into territory dominated by another racial group, there has been racial intermixture, whether in China, the South Seas, Africa, or America. A sizable number of intermarriages between American soldiers and Orientals have occurred in the last fifteen years.

The Small Minority Groups

The major race problem in the United States is obviously that of the Negro. The seriousness of this problem should not allow us to close our eyes, however, to the problems of the small minority groups, particularly the American Indians, the Mexican Indians, the Chinese and Japanese. The individual member of a small minority may have just as acute discrimination problems as the Negro does.

According to the United States Census Bureau, there were approximately 19,269,000 nonwhites in our dominantly white population in 1958. Of these, over 17,000,000 were Negro. Other nonwhite races were not analyzed for 1958 but in 1950 there were 117,629 Chinese, 141,768 Japanese, and 343,410 American Indians.[4] A smattering of Mexican Indians, Koreans, Puerto Rican Negroes, South Pacific Polynesians, and others made up the rest. At various times in our history American Indians, Chinese, and Japanese have been the source of intense hostility and unreasonable fear.

1. *The American Indian.* Of all the small minority groups, the American Indian has had the greatest grievances and on the whole the least success in gaining recognition of his plight. White colonizers fought the Indians who

---

[2] Louis Wirth, "The Unfinished Business of American Democracy," *Annals of the American Academy of Political and Social Science, 244*:1–9 (March, 1946).

[3] Arthur W. Calhoun, *A Social History of the American Family,* Barnes and Noble, Inc., New York, 1945 (3 vols. in 1). Vol. II, chap. III, of this work gives a detailed discussion of Negro-white sexual association and miscegenation.

[4] Bureau of the Census, *Racial Composition of the Population, for the United States by States: 1950,* Advance Reports, Series PC-14, No. 13 (July, 1953), p. 3; *Estimates of the Population of the United States by Age, Color, and Sex, July 1, 1956 to 1958,* and *Population Estimates, Current Population Reports,* Series P-25, No. 193 (February 13, 1959), p. 5.

opposed their settlements and western expansion. Eventually the white man drove most of them out of their territory and forced them to accept life on a reservation as wards of the government. During the 450 years since Europeans invaded America, the Indians have maintained the identity and integrity of their individual tribes by what John Collier calls a "delaying action." Most tribes have refused to adopt the Anglo-American culture and have adhered with simple tenacity to their tribal folkways and mores.

The history of the American treatment of the Indian is a serious stain on our national escutcheon. We have not only deprived the Indian of his heritage but failed to give him any reasonable *quid pro quo*. Even where we have had treaty agreements, the Indians have usually been deprived of their lands and any privileges previously extended them. The Indian's struggle to regain his liberty and be accepted as an American citizen cannot be recounted here in detail. But it was not until 1924 that the American Indian became a citizen. Even then, Arizona and New Mexico refused to permit him to vote until 1948 when the United States Supreme Court held it unconstitutional to disenfranchise Indians.

Many Indians, especially those in the Southwest, have been very poor. The recent opening of uranium mining in the Southwest has greatly enhanced the economic position of the Navaho, however, and a number of the Oklahoma Indians have holdings in oil. For most Indians life has been very hard. The majority have no spokesman to make the American people conscious of the poverty and injustice which are their lot.

The federal government, meanwhile, has altered its policy. In some instances treaties have been further abrogated and the Indian's culture and way of life are being pressed, according to John Collier, "toward a kind of social, cultural, and spiritual genocide."[5] His viewpoint, however, ignores the question as to whether the Indian should seek to live by his old tribal culture in the twentieth century. We have poured millions of dollars into foreign aid for the purpose of helping "backward" peoples in other countries. Why not help the American Indians to become acculturated to the American way of life? Many educated Indians have become fully acculturated whereas others have resisted any assimilation. Whether or not to retain the old way of life is unquestionably the focus of conflict between old and new generations of Indians. Apparently there will be no immediate consensus. Meanwhile the federal government has greatly improved the educational and health program for Indians, has aided in the Indians' economic development through improving their agricultural production and craft work, has extended their civil rights, and has permitted local and state government to deal directly with the Indian groups.[6]

2. *The Mexican and Mexican Indians.* Some of the Mexicans who live in the southwestern states are of pure or relatively pure upper-class Spanish

[5] John Collier, "The United States Indian," in Joseph Gittler (ed.), *Understanding Minority Groups,* John Wiley and Sons, Inc., New York, 1956, chap. III.
[6] Theodore H. Haas, "Commentary," in Gittler, *op. cit.,* pp. 51–57.

stock. They have lived in virtual cultural isolation on ranches or settlements ever since California and the Southwest were annexed by the United States. The majority of Mexicans, however, have some Indian blood.

The number of Mexican laborers who have come to this country is variously estimated, because so many have crossed into the United States illegally. The Census Bureau estimates that there are 424,726 foreign-born Mexicans and 1,570,740 Spanish-speaking people. The National Resources Planning Board in 1938 estimated that there were 3,000,000 persons of Mexican or Spanish-speaking ancestry in the United States; some think this is a more reliable number.[7] The Mexicans have been an economically and socially subordinate group, and the native white population in the Southwest has often reacted toward them in a discriminatory fashion. In many places the Mexican is segregated and cut off from full participation in the community life.

3. *The Oriental Minorities.* The Oriental minorities in the United States consist roughly of 400,000 people of whom the Japanese and Chinese are the only important groups in size.[8] None of the Oriental groups is large because their immigration is and has been so severely restricted. The first important group of Chinese to come to the United States were laborers imported to build the Union Pacific Railroad. Shortly after this project was completed, anti-Chinese sentiment became strong on the Pacific coast, and Congress passed the Chinese Exclusion Act of 1882.

The Japanese were not excluded until later when their major competition in Pacific Coast agriculture led President Roosevelt to negotiate a "gentlemen's agreement" in 1908. The immigration laws were drastically revised during the twenties and the Japanese were excluded by the Immigration Law of 1924, which applied to all Asiatics. Today under the McCarran-Walter Act of 1953, a quota of 100 is allowed all Oriental national groups except the Chinese and Japanese. The Chinese now have a quota of 105 and the Japanese 185.[9] The spouses and children of persons admitted are also permitted to enter the country. Certain groups, such as students, teachers, scholars, writers, and business and professional men, are also allowed to come in under temporary visas.

Racial bars are stern insofar as the quota of Orientals is concerned. The McCarran-Walter Act, however, abolished one seriously resented discrimination, namely, the racial bar to naturalization. Today alien Orientals may become citizens. Previously only those born in the United States could be naturalized. The new immigration provisions also limit 50 percent of the quota to persons of "higher education, specialized experience or exceptional ability." This provision has led to certain criticism, even though it means

[7] Bureau of the Census, *Persons of Spanish Surname 1950, United States Census of Population,* Special Report P-E, No. 3C, 1953, pp. 6–7. Cf. also R. A. Schermerhorn, *These Our People,* D. C. Heath and Company, Boston, 1949, p. 176.

[8] *Racial Composition of the Population, for the United States by States: 1950,* p. 3.

[9] *World Almanac and Book of Facts, 1959,* New York World-Telegram Corporation, New York, 1959, p. 644.

that at least half of the Chinese and Japanese entering this country are of unusual ability.

a. *The Japanese* became very unpopular in the West during the post-World War I period largely because of their economic competition. This was an important factor in the exclusion of Asiatics in 1924. The law also barred alien Japanese from becoming citizens. There were around 127,000 Japanese in this country at the time of the Japanese attack on Pearl Harbor in 1941, of whom 57,000 were aliens. The Japanese on the west coast were then subjected to insult and discrimination. The mass hysteria was shared by citizens, military leaders, the President, and Congress and led to the evacuation of the native born and alien Japanese from the west coast without any attempt to discover whether they were loyal citizens. The Japanese were forced to settle in virtual detention camps in the mountain states area, often at great personal loss.[10] Male Japanese, citizens and aliens alike, however, were allowed to join the armed forces after processing for loyalty. The aliens were required to forswear allegiance to their native country. One of the relocation camps became a center of revolt, and a violent outbreak occurred. The military leaders who were to a large degree responsible for the evacuation insisted that there was not time to differentiate between the loyal and disloyal Japanese. This was a great mistake. The nation would have had an equally difficult time processing native and alien Germans. It is obvious that race prejudice led to much greater fear and discrimination in the case of the Japanese. After the war the United States government tried to compensate the Japanese for the losses they sustained, although compensation was only partly accomplished.[11] By 1950, 80 percent of the Japanese in this country were again living on the west coast. Sixty percent of them were in California—presumably because it meant "home" to them, despite their unpleasant experience. Some 7500 of the younger people remained in the Chicago vicinity and 2300 in the New York area.

The aftermath of this brutal treatment of the Japanese is summarized in two volumes by Dorothy S. Thomas and her assistants, *The Spoilage*[12] and *The Salvage*.[13] The first volume refers to those who "sat out" the war in what were virtually concentration camps. Some revolted; some renounced their citizenship; and some became definitely disorganized. Others were permitted to move out of the camps and seek relocation in the Middle West and the East. Nearly half of the males in this group were able to achieve a college education (as compared to 25 percent of the whites in the area). The number of Japanese women receiving a college education was also proportionately twice that of native white women.

[10] George E. Simpson and Milton Yinger, *Racial and Cultural Minorities*, Harper & Brothers, New York, 1958, p. 133.

[11] *Ibid.*

[12] Dorothy Swaine Thomas and Richard Nishimoto, *The Spoilage*, University of California Press, Berkeley, 1946.

[13] Dorothy Swaine Thomas and James Sakoda, *The Salvage*, University of California Press, Berkeley, 1952.

Prejudice against the Japanese remains high on the west coast. This is illustrated in the underrepresentation of Japanese in professional and proprietary occupations. Almost 30 percent of both Japanese and whites have had college training in the Los Angeles and San Francisco areas. There are, however, many less Japanese employed at a professional level, and far more are working at unskilled labor (percentagewise) than is true for whites. In the Middle West and East the distributions are more favorable to the Japanese.[14]

b. *The Chinese* are small in number and suffer a corresponding psychological discrimination in their tiny quota. The treatment of Chinese has markedly improved, however, particularly on the west coast. The discrimination was previously much more intense there than elsewhere and the move to exclude Chinese originated there. Those Chinese permitted to remain on the quota and those who are occasionally stranded and permitted to remain suffer certain discriminations economically and socially.

There is great difficulty in getting a job commensurate with training. Rose Hum Lee tells of a Chinese social scientist was was forced to take a job as an electrician and another who supported himself raising chickens.[15] Very few Chinese are hired by corporations and even when they are there is little chance for promotion. In China, in contrast, the university-trained person has great opportunity. Housing is likewise a problem in this country. Graduate students who may have belonged to the elite in China or Formosa have difficulty in securing housing. Professionally trained persons who remain in this country have similar difficulties.[16]

THE NEGRO

The Negro's special problems are our major concern in this chapter. The Negro is by far our largest minority group. Obviously he has come a long way since slavery, but he has never achieved in any complete sense the constitutional rights guaranteed him by the Thirteenth, Fourteenth and Fifteenth amendments. Many Negroes have secured a good education and become professional members of our society without achieving any true acceptance. Nor have they been allowed to participate fully in civic affairs or in our cultural and social life. Nevertheless, the Negro has made such notable achievements in this direction within recent years that the possibility of his increasing acceptance is imminent. This is an era of transition from the status of a second-class citizen to that of a fully participating member of the body politic.

So much has happened in the last decade that we cannot cover all of the trends. Military segregation in the armed services has been eliminated, so we

[14] The material in this section is largely drawn from Dorothy Swaine Thomas' article, "The Japanese American," in Gittler, *op. cit.*, pp. 84–108.

[15] Rose Hum Lee, "The Stranded Chinese in the United States," *Phylon, 19:*180–194 (August, 1958).

[16] C. K. Yang, interview, September 28, 1959.

shall not discuss that previous thorn in the Negro soldier's flesh. Public transportation has been partially desegregated. In most other areas the Negro has made notable progress, partly because of (1) the National Association for the Advancement of Colored People's continual attack on discrimination and (2) the quiet educational leadership of the Urban League. These two organizations have made it their goal to transform the lot of the Negro, but they have had much assistance from white educators, writers, legislators, ministers, lawyers, and members of the Supreme Court.

The Negro has thus pricked the conscience of white America, particularly with reference to his educational and housing needs. These have dominated his major efforts in recent years and shall be our major concern here. Other areas of discrimination will receive attention once the Negro child has an opportunity to be taught as well as a white child and has a right to live in a decent and attractive place. The latest developments in these other problem areas will also be covered briefly.

EDUCATIONAL DISCRIMINATION

College and University Discrimination

The attempt to overcome educational discrimination is upsetting many traditions in the South. For a long time the educated leaders in the Negro's fight to end discrimination have recognized that better educational facilities were of key importance to securing all other rights. This is probably a major reason for the resistance. An educated minority will be far more effective in gaining acceptance and much better able to achieve economic and other opportunities. They will also be in a far better position to assert themselves at the polls. The initial attack on educational discrimination came at the college and university level.

Although a large number of public and private Negro colleges and universities purported to serve the Negro's demand for higher education, most of them ranked very low in the caliber of their faculty and in their libraries and laboratory facilities. Evaluating organizations say that nearly all Negro institutions of higher learning offer inferior instruction although they have recently improved. Even in the better Negro institutions only a fraction of the faculty have a Ph.D. degree. A survey conducted after World War II showed the median percentage of Ph.D.'s for faculties in American colleges (and this included the poorest) was 35 percent, whereas in Negro colleges the percentage was only 16.[17] Achievement tests administered to Negro students in Negro colleges show that they rank far below white college students of similar rank. Most of this difference is a matter of training.[18] Northern state institutions have long been open to competent Negro students, as have many of the

[17] Donald C. Thompson, "Career Patterns of Teachers in Negro Colleges," *Social Forces, 36:*270–276 (March, 1958).

[18] E. Franklin Frazier, *The Negro in the United States,* The Macmillan Company, New York, 1949, chap. XVII.

best private colleges and universities. But relatively few Negroes have been enrolled.

Most southern states meanwhile have pursued a determined policy of keeping the Negro out of both their tax-supported and their private institutions of higher learning. In order to open these doors to the Negro, the NAACP has initiated many lawsuits against the various southern state universities refusing admission to Negroes. The first test case, that of *Lloyd Gaines* vs. *the University of Missouri,* was carried to the United States Supreme Court in 1938. The Court then ruled that a Negro could insist upon entrance to the state university if no equal training was provided in a separate institution. Mr. Gaines had applied for admission to the School of Journalism. In consequence, the state of Missouri set up a separate school at considerable expense.

This, however, was not what the Negroes were striving for. They wished to be admitted to regular state universities on an equal basis. Consequently, when Ada Fisher gained admission on a segregated basis to the University of Oklahoma after a U.S. Supreme Court decision in 1947, she refused to enroll although certain other Negro students availed themselves of the opportunity. Later a Negro student was allowed to register at the University of Arkansas Medical School on a segregated basis, but the segregation was not enforced because it was too much bother.

Public sentiment changed rapidly following these decisions, and the Universities of Kentucky, Delaware, Maryland, and West Virginia instituted the policy of admitting Negroes to graduate and professional schools. In the meantime, on June 5, 1950, two important decisions were rendered by the U.S. Supreme Court which struck at the heart of segregated education. In the one, the Court ruled that the University of Texas Law School must admit Heman M. Sweatt instead of requiring him to attend an inferior law school set up for Negroes at Houston. In the other case, the Court ruled that the University of Oklahoma could not require Negro graduate students to sit apart from white students or enforce other varieties of segregation against them. These two decisions as was expected have had a far-reaching impact on discriminatory practices in other institutions.[19]

After these decisions Kentucky, Virginia, Louisiana, and Texas state universities and ten private southern universities opened their graduate schools to Negroes. With the Supreme Court decision in 1954 that all segregation was unconstitutional many state and private institutions have desegregated.[20] By 1956 Negroes were enrolled in 105 of 206 tax-supported colleges and universities, 55 of 188 Protestant colleges, and 35 of 45 Catholic institutions in the South.[21] Segregation is still maintained in the public uni-

[19] *New York Times,* June 6, 1950, pp. 1, 18. Students should consult current issues of *The Crisis* for recent changes in the educational status of Negroes.

[20] This decision is discussed more fully in the next section since it primarily affected public schools. By extension it obviously applies to institutions of higher learning.

[21] Don Shoemaker (ed.), *With all Deliberate Speed,* Harper & Brothers, New York, 1957, p. 166.

versities of Mississippi, South Carolina, Georgia, and Alabama. The University of Alabama has been ordered to open its doors to Negro students and Miss Autherine Lucy was enrolled as a student there for three "turbulent" days in 1956. Her stay created a virtual riot and the Board of Trustees asked her to withdraw for fear of further violence. Miss Lucy made charges of conspiracy against the university and she was then expelled summarily by the Board.[22]

With the integration decree all tax-supported Negro colleges were required to open their doors to whites. By 1957 a thousand white students had enrolled in former Negro institutions.[23] Meanwhile the Universities of Arkansas, Delaware, Kentucky, Louisville, Maryland, Missouri, North Carolina, Oklahoma, Tennessee, Texas, and Virginia are integrated, along with a long list of state colleges and junior colleges.[24] Admission has not brought full social acceptance in all of these institutions, but a notable achievement has taken place.

Public Schools

The second step in achieving educational integration was an attack on the elementary and high school levels of the public schools. Many of the early attempts to secure integration were made in the border and north of the border states. Often desegregation came voluntarily and with no difficulty from local school boards. In the southern states and most of the border states separate schools were universal at mid-century. Five different lawsuits were therefore brought locally in behalf of Negro students who wished to gain admission to white schools. These suits were in Topeka, Kansas; Clarendon County, South Carolina; Prince Edward County, Virginia; Wilmington, Delaware; and the District of Columbia. Following a series of lower court decisions the cases were appealed to the United States Supreme Court in 1952. Two hearings were held, one in June and one in December of 1953.[25]

Then came the historic decision of May 17, 1954. The United States Supreme Court rendered the decision that the "separate but equal" doctrine under which segregated school systems had been maintained was unconstitutional and an infringement of the Fourteenth Amendment. The desegregation of schools in seventeen southern states and certain sections of other states was therefore ordered "with all deliberate speed."[26] The southern schools up to then had operated under an extension of the *Plessy* vs. *Ferguson* decision in 1896. The latter had applied to segregated railroad transportation for Negroes and the 1954 decision held it invalid when applied to schools.[27]

The Supreme Court decision was made after an earnest attempt to discover the disparities in Negro and white schools. Educators, psychologists,

[22] *Ibid.*, pp. 166–169.
[23] *Ibid.*, p. 175.
[24] *Ibid.*, p. 123.
[25] *Ibid.*, pp. 3–4.
[26] Cf. Herbert Hill and Jack Greenberg, *Citizens Guide to Desegregation*, Beacon Press, Boston, 1955, chap. X, "The Supreme Court Decisions."
[27] *Ibid.*, p. 9.

psychiatrists, and social scientists were called in to give expert testimony.[28] When the momentous decision of May 17, 1954, was made, 40 percent of all public school pupils lived in areas where segregation was mandatory. Seventeen states (Arkansas, Alabama, Delaware, Florida, Georgia, Kentucky, Louisiana, Maryland, Mississippi, Missouri, North Carolina, Oklahoma, South Carolina, Tennessee, Texas, Virginia, and West Virginia) and the District of Columbia imposed segregation by law. In addition, four states (Arizona, Kansas, Wyoming, and New Mexico) permitted local option on whether or not schools should be segregated.[29]

Progress in Desegregation

The result of the Supreme Court order to integrate with all deliberate speed has been to retard speed deliberately in most of the southern states.[30] Nevertheless, some of the hardest resisting communities have made a beginning. In Little Rock, Arkansas, high schools were opened again (after being closed a year) on August 12, 1959, with one Negro boy enrolled in Central High School and three Negroes in Hall High. Technical High School in the same city opened with all white students and Horace Mann High School with all Negroes.

Much the same pattern has applied in North Carolina, with token integration in five high schools. One high school opened its doors to fifteen children of Negro Marine Corps personnel. Nashville, Tennessee, has adopted a plan of gradual integration grade by grade. Delaware has done the same. Texas has practically no integration outside the western section of the state where few Negroes live. Most of Oklahoma, on the other hand, has desegregated; by August, 1959, 238 of the 271 school districts admitted both races to their schools. Florida's only gesture in integration by August, 1959, was the admission of four Negro students in an elementary school in Miami. In October of 1959, however, 461 Negro children were admitted to white schools. Louisiana had no mixed schools in 1959 but was under court orders to develop a plan in 1960. South Carolina, Georgia, Virginia, and Alabama, meanwhile, passed legislation that required their public schools to be closed should segregation be forced. Virginia has more or less relented and now has token integration.[31] While the Georgia law was still in effect Atlanta received a federal court order to integrate by 1960. This was later deferred to 1961. In the states of Mississippi, Alabama, and South Carolina there had been no move whatsoever toward desegregation by the spring of 1960.[32]

The whole matter of desegregation has been variously met by cooperation, reluctance, hostility, or an adamant opposition in different parts of the South.

[28] *Ibid.,* chap. VII and VIII.

[29] *New York Times,* May 18, 1954, sec. C, p. 18.

[30] Helen Fuller, "Deliberate, Yes—Speed, No," *The New Republic, 140:*10–14 (March 16, 1959).

[31] Shoemaker, *op. cit.,* pp. 28–29. Consult newspapers and magazines for current achievements.

[32] Cf. *U.S. News and World Report, 47:*38–40 (August 24, 1959) for early developments.

That most of the South would hesitate to make a move to desegregate is to be expected, sociologically speaking. It is always difficult to uproot practices long embedded in the mores. This was apparently in the mind of the Supreme Court justices on May 31, 1955, when they remanded an appeal of a segregated case to the lower court and fastened responsibilities for the achievement of desegregation on lower courts and on local school authorities. Butler A. Jones, a well-known Negro sociologist, believes it will take another decade for the upper southern states to integrate and that the deep South will not complete integration before a decade and a half unless the United States Supreme Court orders a speeding up. The fact that Negroes are gaining an increasing political leverage in the South may hasten the process.[33] Despite the widespread delays two of the most notable of the city-wide integration plans were successfully carried through in Washington and St. Louis shortly after the Supreme Court ruling, as described below.

1. *St. Louis.* St. Louis has made one of the most effective adjustments to the Supreme Court decision of May 17, 1954. This may seem surprising because St. Louis is essentially southern in attitudes and patterns of thinking. It is furthermore the largest city in the former slave-owning state of Missouri. Part of the reason for the early success in integration in St. Louis stems from the good relations previously established between the races. The swimming pools in the parks were opened to Negroes in 1949. This precipitated a temporary crisis and the pools were closed for a year. The next year, however, they were opened permanently to both groups.

During the early forties, the churches began to include both races in their membership. In 1947 all Catholic churches were desegregated. The Catholic Church also initiated desegregation in 1947 in all of its elementary and secondary schools by order of the Archbishop. Some 700 parents of children enrolled in parochial schools protested and threatened suit. When told they must acquiesce or be excommunicated they appealed to the Apostolic Delegate from the Vatican in Washington. The Apostolic Delegate called for the group to dissolve and they obeyed. The Catholics subsequently demonstrated that desegregation would work.

The labor unions and the press in St. Louis also supported the desegregation move. Both the School Board and the teachers had likewise been earnestly concerned about integration before the Supreme Court decision. The National Conference of Christians and Jews financed a series of Intergroup Education summer projects for teachers which were sponsored by the American Council on Education. Intergroup youth projects were also encouraged. All this was effective background for carrying out the Court decision locally.

The School Board thus was able to develop a master plan for accomplishing desegregation in a year's time. In September, 1954, all teachers colleges and special schools for the handicapped were desegregated. By February 1, 1955, all adult education courses and all high schools except the technical school

[33] Butler A. Jones, "The Case Is Remanded," *Social Problems*, 7:27–33 (Summer, 1959).

were integrated. By September, 1955, integration was put in operation in all other schools. St. Louis is thus an object lesson in how fast integration can take place when the community attitudes are favorable.[34]

2. *Washington, D.C.* Washington has also developed a careful and efficient plan for integrating the schools within a short time. The nation's capital has long been notorious for failing to meet the basic needs of the Negro. Housing for Negroes is especially poor, and economic opportunities are very limited because there are few jobs available except those of service workers. Furthermore, the Negro has no civic rights within the city. The white citizens also lack the vote but a major reason for this is that white citizens have been afraid the Negroes would achieve political power.

Schools had always been segregated in Washington but the superintendent of schools anticipated the desegregation decision several years in advance. Television instruction in the classroom was initiated in March, 1952, with Negro and white teachers in the same program. When the Supreme Court decision came, on May 17, 1954, the Board of Education had a plan for action ready. When school opened on September 13, 1954, Negro and white children were enrolled in 116 (73 percent) of the city's schools, with Negro and white teachers instructing in 37 (23 percent) of the schools. By November 4, 123 schools were integrated.

Naturally there were some protests. Poor learners were thrown into classes with those of superior ability and achievement medians were temporarily below national standards. Many Negro homes were so substandard culturally that this posed a serious reason for the Negro children's retardation. The Board of Education attacked the problem, with increased facilities for subnormal children on the elementary and junior high levels. The low school achievement of Negro children in Washington is unquestionably related to the poverty, social deprivation, and unstable home conditions which characterize so many Negro families. Desegregation of the Washington schools will expose many of these children to middle-class values and for some it will stimulate a desire to achieve these values. Desegregated schools will thus result in a better education for all Negroes including the slow learners. No school program can offset the disadvantages of low moral and economic status, but it can help the child take an important step in the right direction.[35]

Disorganization and Desegregation

The Court decision of May 17, 1954, was followed by confusion, rebellion, and disorganization as well as by attempts at integration! Eleven states (Alabama, Arkansas, Florida, Georgia, Louisiana, Mississippi, North Carolina, South Carolina, Tennessee, Texas, and Virginia) have tried either by legislation or by court actions to restrict or stop altogether any attempt to

[34] Bonita H. Valien, *The St. Louis Story,* Anti-Defamation League, New York, 1956 (pamphlet).

[35] Carl F. Hansen, *Miracle of Social Adjustment, Desegregation in the Washington, D.C., Schools,* Anti-Defamation League, New York, 1957 (pamphlet).

carry out the order of the Supreme Court.[36] As mentioned, four states initiated movements to close their public schools altogether and support private schools. Little Rock, Arkansas, Clinton, Tennessee, and other communities were temporarily in a state of strife, while White Citizens Councils in other states tried to lead a peaceable but effective opposition to prevent any integration. The White Citizens Councils have tried to use economic and other pressures against Negroes seeking to enter their children in previously all-white schools. In Alabama the NAACP has been outlawed, and inflammatory attitudes against this organization exist rather generally in the deep South. Jewish organizations, notably the Anti-Defamation League of B'nai B'rith, have been active in support of desegregation. Hence anti-Semitism has arisen in various communities and a series of synagogues have been bombed (as mentioned in Chapter 27).

Despite the aroused public feeling many white citizens have recognized that the desegregation order was based upon the Negro's just rights. The price of halting desegregation is too great for continued opposition. Southerners have found that the white citizens do not have the resources to provide adequate schools for their children on a private basis in any immediate future. The racial tension thus has merged into a conflict over whether *any* children are to have an education if integration is denied to the Negro.[37] Meanwhile the present method of employing judicial decision both to determine the rate of desegregation and to pass judgment when Negroes sue for their right to desegregated education is a very technical and expensive method to bring about desegregation of the schools. But desegregation is sure to come.

Ben W. Palmer, prominent Minneapolis lawyer, suggests that the decision which stands as law could be much more appropriately implemented by an administrative body or council created to undertake the task. Such a practice has a long-time precedent in both English and American law. In the United States we have the Interstate Commerce Commission (since 1887), the Federal Trade Commission (since 1914), the Federal Communications Commission (since 1934), the Civil Aeronautics Board (since 1938), the Atomic Energy Commission (since 1946), and the Civil Rights Commission (since 1957). A National Integration Committee or Commission might be empowered to appoint local integrational committees which would operate under its supervision and with its assistance and that of hired experts. The Commission would have power to enforce its decisions with appeal to the courts on questions of law. As Mr. Palmer recognizes, this is not a perfect solution, but it would provide a workable method instead of the present situation, which depends upon litigation and court action with all of the inevitable confusion and delay.[38]

[36] Shoemaker, *op. cit.,* pp. 102–103, and 114.
[37] Editorial, "Schools Open in Turmoil," *Christian Century,* 76:987–988 (September 2, 1959).
[38] Ben W. Palmer, "We Need Integration Councils," *America,* 101:652–653 (August 29, 1959).

The Girard College Case

Spurred by the Supreme Court decision that public schools must desegregate, the NAACP made an attempt to force Girard College in Philadelphia to open its doors to Negro boys. Girard College, which is a secondary technical boarding school for poor boys, was established by the will of Stephen Girard, a wealthy Philadelphia banker. Girard College has one of the largest endowments of any educational institution in the country— some $98,000,000. According to Girard's will the school was to be administered by the city of Philadelphia. The NAACP sponsored a suit against the city to secure the admission of Negro boys to the public-administered college. The Philadelphia County Orphan's Court tried the case and held that the Board of Directors of City Trusts (which supervised the college) had the right to exclude Negroes from a private college. The case was subsequently sustained by the Pennsylvania Supreme Court and then was carried to the United States Supreme Court, which remanded it to the Pennsylvania Supreme Court. This court sent back the case to the Orphan's Court. The United States Supreme Court had held that a state agency such as the Board of Directors of City Trusts could not deny Negro boys admission under the Fourteenth Amendment. The Orphan's Court, however, did not order admission of Negro students.[39] Instead it altered the basis for administering the college and appointed private trustees. The court decided it could best carry out the will of Girard by the latter course. The city of Philadelphia and the Negro litigants both contested this action, but the transfer to private trustees was ordered sustained both by the Pennsylvania and by the United States Supreme Courts.

The case has several important implications. First, it established that any public administration of racially restricted institutions is unconstitutional.[40] But by permitting the college to continue operation by transferring the administration from a public to a private agency the case also more or less firmly established the right of private schools to determine their own admission policy.[41] This means that Negro students cannot demand entrance to private institutions.

HOUSING DISCRIMINATION

Housing discrimination against the Negro occurs on several levels. One is the segregated basis of housing which has forced Negroes to live in certain areas. Because of segregation, Negroes crowd into all-Negro areas. Overcrowding has been serious especially in northern cities where the influx of southern Negroes has greatly increased the Negro population. Price discrimination is another problem for the Negro. Often he must pay exorbitant

---

[39] See Arthur S. Miller, *Racial Discrimination and Private Education,* University of North Carolina Press, Chapel Hill, 1957, for a discussion of this.

[40] Milton M. Gordon, "The Girard Case: Resolution and Social Significance," *Social Problems, 7:15–27* (Summer, 1959).

[41] *Ibid.*

rent for substandard housing. Even where Negroes have sufficient money to buy a house they often have had to pay a premium to induce the owner to sell to them. It has also been difficult for Negroes to find building space in new suburban developments. Negroes thus have three strikes against them when they look for a place to live.

Segregated Housing

Segregated housing tends to combine all or most of these discriminatory practices and was declared an infringement of the Fourteenth Amendment and therefore illegal by the United States Supreme Court in 1917.[42] This decision, however, has been more often honored in the breach than in the observance. Segregated housing is, generally speaking, much more institutionalized in the North than in the South.[43] During slavery Negroes usually lived in small houses at the back of the "big" house. This pattern of small Negro homes in the better residential areas has persisted in many southern cities.

In the North, Negroes have usually crowded into certain districts; as they invaded, white residents moved out. Housing became congested, with larger homes cut up into numerous apartments. The neighborhoods deteriorated quickly because landlords refused to make repairs. In other areas cheap, flimsy, ramshackle, substandard houses were erected. Both types of neighborhoods were overcrowded and soon became dirty, unsanitary slums.

This dismal type of Negro housing can be found in New York, Philadelphia, Pittsburgh, Chicago, and numerous other northern cities, large and small. In many such areas there are no parks, and no place for the children to play except the streets. Other undesirable factors complicate the problems of Negro slum life. Criminal groups, narcotic rings, and prostitution often seek out such areas because depressed groups are less likely to report illicit activities to the police.

The concentration of Negroes into substandard areas has characterized the segregated housing situation. A study was made in 1949–1955 by the Human Relations Commission of Pittsburgh of 44,666 occupied dwellings, of which 7472 were occupied by Negroes. Over half of the Negro families in the study lived in housing with no central heating and in unsanitary and deteriorating condition. One-third had inadequate bathing and toilet facilities. Overcrowding was less serious, but one-fourth of the houses were overcrowded. Negroes lived in 42 percent of all the substandard dwellings and 59 percent of those described as slums.[44] These situations were some of the problems which the Urban Redevelopment Program in Pittsburgh sought to improve. There had been a large influx of Negroes into this city and a 30 percent increase during the period 1950 to 1957.

The heaviest concentration of Negroes was in the Lower Hill district al-

[42] Simpson and Yinger, *op. cit.,* p. 488.

[43] Frank F. Lee, "A Cross Institutional Comparison of Northern and Southern Race Relations," *Social Forces, 42*:185–191 (January, 1958).

[44] Herbert A. Aurbach, *The Status of Housing of Negroes in Pittsburgh,* Mayor's Commission on Human Relations, Pittsburgh, 1958, pp. 2 and 15.

though relatively concentrated Negro areas also exist in the Homewood-Brushton area and the East Liberty section of the city. The worst housing is in the Hill district. The Lower Hill district is being torn down and families have consequently been moved out, many into public housing, others into privately owned buildings. The Upper Hill is now almost entirely Negro. Many houses have been broken up into multiple housing units to accommodate families from the Lower Hill who had nowhere else to go.[45] The survey of the various Negro areas showed that a few white persons lived in the same blocks in which 92 percent of the Pittsburgh Negroes lived. On the other hand, 27 percent of the whites lived in the same block with a Negro person (although in certain instances the latter was a servant).[46]

In New York City's Borough of Manhattan the Negro housing problem has been intensified by the influx of Puerto Ricans (many of whom are Negro) in the Harlem area. Here the disgraceful crowding and bad housing has been accompanied by serious teen-age tensions and a great increase in violence among juveniles. Other problems in this area involve language and cultural adjustments far exceeding those of Negroes who move north from the southern states.

So far as segregation is concerned, Chicago has the greatest problem. Nearly 1,000,000 Negroes live in Chicago, with 500,000 of them concentrated in the "black belt." This area has extended southward from 20th Street and has taken over what was formerly a desirable middle-class area in the vicinity of the University of Chicago. Because of extreme overcrowding the deterioration has become increasingly serious since 1950. The Negro population is growing by about 32,000 each year (14,000 by excess of births over deaths and 18,000 by migration from the South). By 1965 Negroes are expected to constitute 25 percent of the population of Chicago. In communities suburban to Chicago the increase in Negro population has been less spectacular and will probably constitute around 6.4 percent of the population by 1965.[47]

In Chicago, as elsewhere, the nonwhite population increased without any proportionate increase in housing units available. Between 1940 and 1950 the Negro population increased 80.5 percent, while the number of dwellings occupied by Negroes increased 72.3 percent. Meanwhile white-occupied units increased. Thus over half (53 percent) of the Negro housing was substandard or dilapidated, while only 15 percent of the white housing was so classified.[48]

Deterioration has often characterized low-rental Negro housing both in the North and in the South. More northern segregated Negro areas have had a

---

[45] *Ibid.,* p. 3.

[46] *Ibid.,* p. 11. This was formerly an all-white area.

[47] "Urban Renewal and the Negro in Chicago," A Report by the Chicago Urban League Community Services Department, Chicago, July 31, 1958, pp. 4 and 10 (mimeographed).

[48] Otis Dudley Duncan and Beverly Duncan, *The Negro Population of Chicago,* University of Chicago Press, Chicago, 1957, pp. 77–79.

serious problem of overcrowding, however, because of the large numbers of Negroes coming north. This has meant that relatives moved in with relatives or friends moved in with friends because of lack of available space. The consequent overcrowding has brought rapid deterioration and attendant problems of health and sanitation. In most cities the expense of rebuilding and clearance has been more than local public and private resources could finance. Federal housing legislation has made an attempt to meet this serious social need.

Public Housing

Public housing was first initiated by the Federal Enabling Act of 1937 during the depression. The purpose of the act was to supply decent urban housing for lower-income groups and persons on relief which could not be financed by private capital. This act provided for the creation of the National Public Housing Authority and was extended by important amendments in 1949 and successive amendments since that date. It now operates under the title of the Public Housing Authority.

This federal act provides much of the money for building public housing open to Negroes in both the South and the North. It specifically refrains, however, from stipulating that such housing shall involve any racial integration or nondiscriminatory regulations. This omission was a recognized concession to the southern bloc in Congress. The administrative regulations as set up by the national Public Housing Authority office in Washington recommend that such funds be used on a nondiscriminatory basis. It is left to the local communities to work out the methods for interpreting how nondiscrimination shall be observed. By 1957, local ordinances and state legislation with nondiscriminatory clauses had been enacted in twenty-one states and the District of Columbia. The states were Arizona, California, Colorado, Connecticut, Delaware, Illinois, Indiana, Maryland, Massachusetts, Michigan, Minnesota, Missouri, Nebraska, New Jersey, New York, Ohio, Oregon, Pennsylvania, Rhode Island, Washington, and Wisconsin.[49]

Many variations in interpretation appear. In some cities public housing has been administered on an "open-occupancy" basis—with tenants accepted on a "first come, first served" basis. In general, however, it has been hard to secure integrated housing if the Negro tenants exceeded from 40 to 60 percent. White tenants are not willing to be the minority tenants. Some apartments have therefore operated on a planned basis—admitting a certain number of each race. In some neighborhoods several buildings have been erected around one court, with segregated buildings but an "integrated project." The specific plan is determined by the local authority but the trend since the war has been toward integrated buildings.[50]

---

[49] *Nondiscrimination Clauses in Regard to Public Housing, Private Housing, and Urban Redevelopment Undertakings* (prepared by the Racial Relations Service and the Office of the General Counsel), Housing and Home Finance Agency, Washington, October, 1957, pp. 1–64.

[50] Alfred Tronzo of the Pittsburgh Housing Authority, interview, October 6, 1959.

Urban Redevelopment

The Urban Redevelopment Law was adopted by Congress in 1945 (Public Law 991, Act of 1945) and subsequently amended in 1949, 1954, and since. This law specifically provides that any housing erected on lands acquired under an urban redevelopment authority be administered without reference to "race, creed or color." The Urban Redevelopment Authority receives federal assistance in buying and clearing land in deteriorated areas. It then transfers the land to private developers, who must accept the non-discriminatory clause in order to secure the contract and federal assistance in the construction.

In Pittsburgh, where an extensive redevelopment program is under way, private corporations expect to erect a luxury apartment in the old Hill district which will be administered on an open-occupancy basis.[51] This is a new venture in interracial luxury housing. Local renewal or redevelopment authorities operate under state laws or local ordinances. Such legislation provides for the administration of urban renewal projects according to the provisions of the federal law. California, Connecticut, Illinois, Massachusetts, Michigan, Minnesota, New Jersey, New York, Oregon, Pennsylvania, and Washington have adopted state urban development laws, but many cities in other states have adopted local ordinances permitting such operation.[52]

New York in 1948 and Pittsburgh in 1959 enacted local ordinances which outlawed racial discrimination in private housing, both in buying and in renting. These two cities have made the first liberal extensions of housing policy in the United States. Other cities will undoubtedly follow suit.

Racially Integrated Housing in Practice

Because integrated housing is such a new venture there has been great interest and considerable research in how such experiments have turned out. Many Negro leaders have believed that racial hostility would decrease if white and nonwhite could live in the same areas or the same apartment houses. Integrated neighborhoods and integrated housing are too new, however, to warrant any such authoritative conclusions. Some of the research seems to indicate relative success in acceptance of integration; other studies have not been so optimistic. Sentiments and attitudes are hard to change and an occasional unpleasant experience may be given undue weight in any evaluation. As a matter of fact, formal action has often been ahead of the general level of community thinking about race. Leaders in civic affairs, in the courts, and in political office have recognized that discrimination is both illegal and untenable on any ethical grounds but the rank and file have not.

Many of the discriminations against Negroes moving into white neighborhoods have been enforced by restrictive covenants in which neighbors and

[51] Theodore L. Hazlett, Counsel for the Urban Redevelopment Program, Pittsburgh, interview, October 6, 1959. Cf. also B. T. McGraw, "The Housing Act of 1954 and Implications for Minorities," *Phylon, 16*:171 (April, 1955).

[52] *Nondiscrimination Clauses in Regard to Public Housing, Private Housing, and Urban Redevelopment Undertakings, op. cit.*

real estate men agreed not to sell or rent to Negroes. In 1948 the United States Supreme Court held that such restrictions may be entered into voluntarily. They cannot be legally enforced, however, if a co-signer changes his mind. This decision has broken down widespread tendencies to segregate neighborhoods by such covenants.

Actions speak louder than words, but the recent trends in public housing are probably more an incorporation of the public's conscience than they are a matter of wholehearted public approval. The leaders have acted because they knew it was right in an area which public opinion has acceded gingerly at best. It will take time for public attitudes to catch up with what conscience tells them is right. But, as Norman Mailer has said, it is the actions of men and not their sentiments which make history.[53] Urban redevelopment is making social history while men are catching up in their attitudes.

How do the neighbors act when a Negro moves into an all-white area? In times past, in the North there has usually been marked hostility and a general exodus of the white population. In such cases the first Negroes to move in are usually persons of professional rank and relatively high income who have paid a premium to induce the white owners to sell. On the other hand, many white owners in desirable neighborhoods have informal non-written agreement to prevent Negroes from buying in their neighborhoods. Real estate people have also fought such invasions by insisting that property values would fall. Banks have often refused to lend money to white people buying property in an area where Negroes were moving in.

This pattern is changing slowly, partly because of the public housing legislation, which has made people more aware of the difficulties and indignities heaped upon Negroes. Several studies shed light on this problem. Ellsworth E. Rosen and Arnold Nicholson give an interesting account of how the white residents helped build better race relations when a Negro family moved in. They also describe the process of overcoming the pattern of real estate values going down and white persons moving out. Where Negroes possess the same educational background and cultural values they believe this can usually be accomplished.[54] Other studies have been made of such ventures in a number of cities. Among them are one by Arnold Rose in Minneapolis, one by C. R. Jones in Baltimore, Davis McEntire's study in San Francisco, and Henry G. Stetler's study in the state of Connecticut.[55]

All of these studies more or less agree that only upper-class Negroes of

---

[53] Quotation from *Advertisements for Myself* in "The Literary Sampler," *Saturday Review*, 42:21 (October 10, 1959).

[54] Ellsworth E. Rosen and Arnold Nicholson, "When a Negro Moves Next Door," *Saturday Evening Post*, 231:32–33 ff. (April 4, 1959).

[55] Arnold Rose, "Neighborhood Reactions to Isolated Negro Residents: An Alternative to Invasion and Succession," *American Sociological Review*, 18:497–507 (October, 1953); C. R. Jones, "Invasion and Racial Attitudes; a Study of Housing in a Border City," *Social Forces*, 27:285–290 (March, 1949); Davis McEntire, "A Study of Racial Attitudes in Neighborhoods Infiltrated by Non-Whites," School of Social Welfare, University of California, Berkeley, December, 1954 (mimeographed); and Henry G. Stetler, *Private Interracial Neighborhoods in Connecticut*, Commission on Civil Rights, Hartford, 1957.

relatively high education and income wish to move into all-white neighborhoods. Here they have usually purchased property. They have met opposition and have often had to pay considerably more for their property than white purchasers would have. In Stetler's study (which covered the whole state of Connecticut) however, Negro workers constituted about half those moving into white neighborhoods. Most of the Negroes studied (with the exception of those in Stetler's study) had lived in their previous communities for ten years or so and acquired sufficient capital to move to a better location.

The Pittsburgh Study

A recent study was made in Pittsburgh covering 25 upper-class Negro families who moved into what were previously all-white middle-class neighborhoods. This study aimed to discover (1) the Negroes' adjustment problem, (2) the hostile reactions which they had to meet, and (3) the expressed attitudes of their white neighbors. All of the Negro families qualifying for the study were known to the Urban League. Some in the original list lived too far from the city to be interviewed, although one in an adjacent county was included. Some had moved away from the city and a few could not be located. The 25 studied cases included all but two or three of the known Negroes then living in white neighborhoods in the Pittsburgh metropolitan area.

Interviews were conducted with all of the Negro families and with 2 of their close neighbors. Where possible, one next-door neighbor and another person in the same block were interviewed. Some families lived in rural nonfarm areas where there were no blocks and here the nearest neighbors were interviewed. Nine of the neighborhoods were within the city limits and 2 others were in well-built-up adjacent areas. Hence 11 were essentially urban. Six were in suburban neighborhoods with considerable space about the homes and 8 were "rural nonfarm" communities scattered on a country road. In 7 of the urban neighborhoods Negroes had lived on adjacent streets; hence aquiring a Negro neighbor on the particular street was not surprising. One of the significant findings of the study was that the Negroes' social and economic status was markedly higher than that of their white neighbors. More of the Negroes had a better education and more were professionally trained than was true for the whites. The Negroes also had considerably higher incomes and had bought, built, or rented houses higher in value than the average in the neighborhood.[56] Only 2 rented their homes; 12 built and 11 purchased them. They thus belonged to the upper-class Negro group, which corresponds roughly in living standards, education, and income with middle-class professional white people.

As for the problems they encountered, 7 of the Negro families reported great difficulty in securing either the house or a permit to build a house. The

[56] Elizabeth Heim, "A Study of the Adjustment Problems of Negro Families Who Have Settled in White Neighborhoods in the Pittsburgh Area, and the Attitudes of Their White Neighbors," unpublished MS., Chatham College Library, 1959, pp. 19 and 27. (This tutorial project was supervised by Miss Elliott and was made in cooperation with the Urban League.)

others had had less or no difficulty. So far as attitudes were concerned, only 13 percent of the 46 white persons for which there were expressed opinions were pleased when the Negro family first moved in; 48 percent said they were indifferent; 30 percent were annoyed, while the attitudes of 9 percent were classed as "very annoyed."[57]

Where the whites approved of their Negro neighbors they generally said that it was because it was fairer to the Negroes and "helped solve the race problem." Negroes were more likely to think that the whites could derive advantages from living in the same neighborhood with them than was true of the whites. The latter were more apt to believe the advantages were almost wholly for the Negro, even where the whites approved of the Negro's living in the area.[58] Even though the white persons recognized that their Negro neighbors were well educated and persons with good incomes, many expressed reluctance at having their children, especially if they were teenagers, have too much contact. In terms of religion, the Jewish neighbors (only 6) were all favorable to the Negroes. More Catholics were prejudiced than Protestants,[59] although this reaction was inconsistent with the stand of the Catholic hierarchy in favor of abolishing prejudicial treatment.

White persons were found to change their attitudes somewhat after the Negroes had moved in and lived there for a while. The expressed white attitudes were inconsistent. Forty-two percent said they were now glad to have the Negro in the neighborhood but only 6 percent said they would be pleased to have another Negro move into the area. All but 2 of the Negroes believed there were advantages to living in interracial areas. Only 14 of the 50 whites (28 percent) approved of integrated neighborhoods, 18 percent approved conditionally, 10 percent were neutral, and 46 percent were opposed.[60]

Negroes believed generally that there were distinct advantages to living in such an area since "the neighborhood was better" and "there was a better class of people." In general, the better-educated white persons and those in white-collar jobs had a more friendly and positive attitude to the Negroes than did the whites of lower educational and occupational status. But where there was hostility at the beginning, the majority of white people eventually came to accept and like their Negro neighbors. The white people who had known Negroes earlier also gave greater indication of favorable attitudes than those who had never had any such association.

Contacts between white and Negro are unquestionably essential if Negroes and whites are to know each other well. Seventy percent of the Negroes and 30 percent of the whites interviewed said they had had some interracial contacts in their home. This disparity in the percentages may indicate that the Negroes had contacts with white persons other than those interviewed. It may indicate, too, that there is a different interpretation of what "contacts" are.

[57] *Ibid.*, p. 65.
[58] *Ibid.*, pp. 69–71.
[59] *Ibid.*, pp. 81–82.
[60] *Ibid.*, p. 91.

The Negroes were more likely to approve interracial contacts than the whites. Since the Negroes were better educated than the whites their education may have affected this characteristic. The better-educated white persons had more favorable attitudes toward the Negro.[61] Where there were children, the children usually played together and the parents' contacts often increased for this reason.

Integration in Public Housing

Not all integrated housing projects have been completely successful, as was to be expected. A study conducted by Daniel M. Wilner, Rosabelle P. Walkley, and Stuart W. Cook compared two groups of white persons, one living in a housing project with integrated buildings and the other in a project with a segregated building across the court from a building occupied by Negroes. Four projects were included in the study, two in industrial cities in New England with a population of 150,000 and two in larger cities, one of 600,000 population and one of 2,000,000 in a middle Atlantic state.[62]

The researchers in this study assumed that white persons who lived in an integrated building would be more favorable toward integration than those who lived in segregated buildings across the court from Negroes. They discovered that more white persons who lived in segregated buildings across the court from Negroes expressed themselves as in favor of living in integrated buildings. On the other hand, more white persons who lived in integrated buildings recommended living in segregated buildings. Those living in segregated buildings also expressed more esteem for Negroes, and more of those living in the segregated buildings expressed satisfaction with where they lived.[63] Many factors affect racial attitudes. Some people may resent their Negro or white neighbors and fear loss of status when living in an integrated project. Both races may have prior hostilities toward each other which have to be overcome before they become friends in an integrated project.[64] Cultural differences or habits may be less irritating when living in separate buildings although some white persons in *integrated* buildings lived farther from Negroes than those living in *separate* buildings. Habits of neatness in keeping halls, basements, and incinerator rooms clean often affect attitudes of apartment neighbors toward each other.

Some Negroes who move out of run-down and slum neighborhoods into public housing projects may thus need special training in the amenities of community living in large apartment houses. Some white people also need to be trained in such social considerations. Public housing officials conceivably could spend a little thought and effort in helping their clients to become good neighbors, particularly when they have moved out of the slums. Habit patterns may vary somewhat on a racial basis and both races could profit from

[61] *Ibid.,* p. 94.
[62] Daniel M. Wilner, Rosabelle P. Walkley, and Stuart W. Cook, *Human Relations in Interracial Housing,* University of Minnesota Press, Minneapolis, 1955, p. 15.
[63] *Ibid.,* p. 149.
[64] *Ibid.,* p. 151.

more understanding of what is to be expected. Where integrated housing has been particularly successful the Negroes and whites have had relatively the same educational background and standards. Many of the Negro adults who have moved from the South have not had as good educational backgrounds as the whites because of the inadequacies of Negro education in the South.

Southern housing for Negroes is often much better than northern. This is to the Southerner's great credit. Because Negroes have often lived in better residential areas there is not so great a tendency to allow such neighborhoods to decline. New housing projects there are of a superior sort. Those in Atlanta, for example, include very desirable housing near the Negro colleges and university. Many wealthy Negroes live in Atlanta, and a recent suburban development for Negroes there contains a large number of homes in the $40,000 to $60,000 class and above. Good architecture, spacious grounds, and planting make this a handsome area.[65]

Public Accommodations

One of the most serious problems of Negroes is finding a desirable place to eat and sleep while traveling. Until recently most good hotels and motels refused to accept Negro patrons. Today the situation is changing, partly as the result of changed attitudes toward housing. Twenty-two states have enacted laws requiring hotels to accept Negro patrons. In some states, including Colorado, Connecticut, Massachusetts, Montana, Nebraska, New Jersey, New York, Oregon, Rhode Island, Vermont, and Washington, public accommodations have been extended to cover all types of public facilities. Several states have desegregated swimming pools. A number of southern cities have extended public recreational facilities to Negroes (which will be discussed in the section on recreation). Nebraska apparently has the best enforcement of the law. Any patron denied available service may call the police, who will aid him in obtaining services.[66]

In general, however, the operation of the laws in most states is not very effective. Negroes are told that no rooms are available or are required to pay a premium price; food service is delayed and the food served is poor. Nevertheless, good hotels in Atlantic City, Washington, D.C., and elsewhere accept Negro patrons and provide good service.[67] In Pennsylvania restaurants operating under franchise on the turnpike have recently extended service to Negroes in the dining rooms. Previously they were required to stand at a counter.

ECONOMIC DISCRIMINATION

The Negro obviously had no employment problem under slavery. With all the social, economic, and political disruptions following emancipation, his

[65] William B. Hartsfield, excerpts from testimony, "A Veteran Mayor Talks of Another Race Problem," *U.S. News and World Report,* 46:108–109 (May 4, 1959).

[66] Gaines T. Bradford, Acting Director, Urban League of Pittsburgh, interview, September 28, 1959.

[67] Simpson and Yinger, *op. cit.,* p. 486.

difficulty in making a living has been greater than before. During slave days his master usually gave him ample food, shelter, and medical care—if only to protect his investment. Following the Civil War, the Negro was forced into the lowest economic level because of his social status and widespread fears on the part of both northern and southern white workers that they might be supplanted. White workingmen objected not only to working with Negroes but also to Negroes' receiving the same pay. In fact, much of the economic discrimination against the Negro stems from the fears and prejudices of the white laborer.

As a consequence of the attitude of white laborers, the Negro's economic position remained virtually static until the second decade of the twentieth century. Then the dislocations in industry created by the demand for war workers during World War I resulted in a mass migration of Negroes to northern cities. This internal effect of the war was an initial step in the industrialization of the Negro worker and an important factor in his subsequent demands for equal wages and job opportunities. During this period he gained a toe hold in industry. Negro women in particular had their first chance to obtain jobs in types of work other than laundry work and domestic service. They were employed in various textile, food, clothing, millinery, shoe, and other light industries. In the South there were also increased opportunities for employment of Negroes but chiefly in the low-skilled industries.[68]

Many unions still discriminate against Negroes. These include railway clerks, railway trainmen, railway telegraphers, pulp workers, carpenters, paper makers, electrical workers, and certain local unions. When admitted to the merged AFL-CIO IN 1957 the Brotherhood of Railroad Trainmen promised to deal with the matter of admitting Negroes in its convention for 1958. Instead the convention was put off until 1962. The fact that many Negroes are unskilled or semiskilled is a reason often cited for keeping them out. White men, on the other hand, often acquire skill on the job. Prejudice among white workers has been one of the serious aspects of racial discrimination. Local unions reflect local sentiment because laborers are a part of the community. Some locals have cooperated with White Citizens Councils. The outlawing of segregated local unions has been suggested as a method of improving racial practices, rather than the expulsion of a whole union.[69]

World War II crystallized the racial issues in employment. The manifest absurdity of fighting for democracy abroad while denying it to the Negro at home finally resulted in improving the position of this group. Numerous directives were issued by the War Production Board and other agencies to no avail. Negro resentment against the racial restrictions imposed by personnel policies in war industries mounted and a March-on-Washington Committee

[68] Cf. Horace R. Cayton and George R. Mitchell, *Black Workers in the New Unions,* University of North Carolina Press, Chapel Hill, 1939, for an extensive discussion on this topic.

[69] Paul Jacobs, "The Negro Worker Asserts His Rights," *The Reporter,* 21:16–21 (July 23, 1959).

was planned in 1941. One hundred thousand Negroes were organized to march to the White House. It was then that President Roosevelt issued his famous Executive Order 8802, proclaiming that all defense industries and governmental departments should take measures to administer their programs without discrimination. Following this, a Fair Employment Practices Committee was set up to carry out the order. Local attitudes were still hard to overcome, but notable increases in Negro employment took place within a year. By 1944 Negroes were widely employed with marked increases in their wage scales. The FEPC expired in 1946, but by this time 100 local councils had been established in the various states to work on state legislation to eliminate discrimination in the employment of minority groups. By 1947 four states—New York, New Jersey, Massachusetts, and Connecticut— had enacted bills requiring all industries to hire persons from all racial and religious groups on an indiscriminate basis. Ten additional states now have their own FEPC laws, namely, Alaska, Colorado, Michigan, Minnesota, New Mexico, Oregon, Pennsylvania, Rhode Island, Washington, and Wisconsin. Two other states, Kansas and Indiana, also have enacted laws, but they are nonenforceable as now drawn.[70]

Economic discrimination has decreased on the whole because of the Negro's much greater opportunities for employment. In the federal government, applications no longer indicate race and many jobs are now filled from written applications. A general policy of nondiscrimination also prevails in the federal government although relatively few of the higher-salaried positions and headships of bureaus and divisions go to Negroes. We have a Negro delegate to the United Nations, Ralph Bunche, and this is a highly rated position. The educational level of Negroes has increased so markedly in recent years that more and more positions will be available because of eligibility. Nevertheless, it is still hard for a Negro to be appointed in many areas.

Differential Incomes According to Race

Negro wages tend to be much lower than those of white persons, although wages in union-covered industries are the same for all groups in the same job category. Most Negroes do not belong to unions, nor do many Negroes have income other than wages. In 1949 the median Negro wage was only $952.[71] In contrast, the average family in the United States had an income of $4440 in 1950.[72] Wages for both groups have since increased but there is still a significant differential between Negro and white wages. In 1957, the median income for white families and single individuals living alone was $5166. For nonwhite families and single individuals living alone the median income was $2764.[73] Part of these differences unquestionably exist because so many more Negroes are working at unskilled or semiskilled jobs. When

[70] Gaines T. Bradford, interview, September 28, 1959.
[71] Bureau of the Census, *Statistical Abstract of the United States, 1959,* p. 30.
[72] *Ibid.,* p. 317.
[73] *Ibid.,* p. 318.

unemployment occurs Negroes still bear more than their fair share of the burden. In March, 1959, for example, there were 609,000 nonwhite males and 2,362,000 white males unemployed. That is, nearly 25 percent of the male unemployed were colored, whereas proportionately only 10 percent should be. The proportion of unemployed colored women was over 25 percent.[74]

In terms of occupation, the proportion of Negro professional workers has increased, while the number of farmers and farm managers has decreased, in the last decade. Farm laboring groups and farm foremen have also decreased, reflecting the Negro's increasing trek to the city. The number of Negro laborers and service workers has meanwhile gone up, but the number of Negro factory workers has remained relatively constant. A large share of Negroes are still relatively unskilled.[75]

OTHER TYPES OF DISCRIMINATION

Segregation on Public Carriers

"Jim Crowism" or segregation on trains and buses was almost completely enforced in southern states prior to June 3, 1946. On that date the United States Supreme Court reversed the decision of the circuit court in Middlesex County, Virginia (which had also been upheld by the Supreme Court of Appeals of Virginia), with reference to the conviction of a Negro woman who had refused to move to a rear seat of an interstate bus. A Virginia statute required this segregation of passengers, but the U.S. Supreme Court declared that it interfered with the operation of commerce. Since that time there have been notable improvements in the practices of interstate bus and train transportation for Negroes, so far as segregation is concerned. In Virginia, for example, higher courts have reversed their verdicts and several cases in North Carolina have been settled out of court. Negroes of quiet, refined appearance had very little difficulty in securing Pullman car reservations in the South, although many railroads still pursued a policy of segregation on day coaches prior to the important ruling on June 5, 1950.

On this date the practice of seating Negro passengers at separate tables set aside and curtained off from other passengers was declared a violation of the Interstate Commerce Act. This decision reverses an earlier ruling by the Interstate Commerce Commission that segregation on railroads does not violate any law, in absence of a federal law, so long as the railroad provides Negroes with service in reserved dining cars and provides them with transportation.[76]

Local bus segregation meanwhile has been the source of much agitation in Montgomery, Alabama, and elsewhere. In Montgomery, the effort of Negroes

[74] *Ibid.*, p. 219.
[75] *Ibid.*
[76] *New York Times,* June 6, 1950, pp. 1, 18. Cf. also *The Negro Handbook, 1949,* The Macmillan Company, New York, 1949, pp. 64–70.

to end segregation on buses led to a bitter fight culminating in a United States Supreme Court decision in December, 1956. In 1957, a district court declared segregated buses illegal in Miami. Some twenty cities have since quietly desegregated, but Birmingham, Alabama, and a few other cities have renewed efforts to enforce segregation.[77]

Health Discrimination

Health and length of life have increased markedly for the nonwhite population just as they have for whites. Even so, death rates are still much higher per 1000 population for nonwhites (chiefly Negro) for all age categories. Male and female white infants under one year had a death rate of 26.3 and 20.0 per 1000 respectively in 1956, whereas male and female nonwhite babies under one year had a rate of 47.1 and 37.6 respectively. Death rates fell off greatly the next year for Negro infants but were twice as high for nonwhite as for white. Nonwhite children's rates likewise declined somewhat although still higher than white. After twenty years of age death rates were increased but nonwhite rates were twice as high as for whites in their twenties and thirties. In fact all through the adult years up to sixty-five death rates for colored persons were considerably higher. For women in their early fifties rates were three times as high for nonwhite women as for white women.[78] By the same token, most of the death rates from specific diseases are much higher among Negroes than whites.[79]

It is well known that health is related to income, which in turn is a major factor in early medical treatment and adequate diagnosis. Income also is an important factor in diet, and many Negroes do not eat properly because they cannot afford to do so. In many areas hospital facilities for Negroes are completely inadequate. Certain diseases have also been very high among Negroes, notably venereal disease, but the current program for venereal disease control is helping reduce that health hazard (see Chapter 6).

Recreational Discrimination

Recreational discrimination is of special concern to students of social disorganization. The lack of opportunities for wholesome leisure-time activities means that Negroes—especially young people—tend to participate in the less desirable variety, which always seem to be available. For the boys this is often street-corner society, a crap game, or a furtive visit to the forbidden tavern. The commercial recreational facilities in the segregated districts where lower-class Negroes live are often veritable dives. Many of these places are engaged in illegal activities such as selling narcotics and are a direct stimulus to delinquent conduct. Recreation is not the solution to the juvenile delin-

---

[77] Simpson and Yinger, *op. cit.*, pp. 483–484.

[78] *Statistical Abstract of the United States, 1959*, p. 60.

[79] National Office of Vital Statistics, *Death Rates for Selected Causes by Age, Color and Sex, United States and Each State, 1949–1951, Vital Statistics—Special Reports*, Vol. 49, Nos. 1–57, Washington, 1959.

quency problem. Nevertheless, lack of suitable recreational facilities undoubtedly is a factor in the alarming juvenile delinquency rate among Negroes.

Recreational discrimination has diminished in recent years so far as the use of public facilities is concerned. One important trend is the lack of discrimination in popular sports. The Fourth Circuit Court of Appeals in Richmond, Virginia, revised a previous decision of the Federal District Court in Baltimore which had permitted segregated facilities. Public parks and playgrounds in Nashville were desegregated in February, 1956. In Fort Lauderdale, Florida, municipal golf courses were opened to Negroes by court order in 1957. Meanwhile, Pennsylvania courts have ruled that privately owned pools open to the public (i.e., those commercially operated) must extend their facilities to Negroes.

In the last few years many legitimate theaters and concert halls have likewise extended their services to Negroes. The National Theatre in Washington was closed because New York actors refused to open a play while segregation was in force. This theater was finally opened to Negroes and other theaters in Washington are now open to the general public.[80]

Private clubs (white clubs, that is) are generally closed to Negroes. The West Side Tennis Club in Forest Hills, New York, has, however, abolished racial discrimination as the result of a furor over Ralph Bunche's son's application for membership.[81]

A second type of recreational segregation applies where Negroes are allowed restricted privileges within a specific commercial establishment. Many theaters, for example, have permitted Negroes to sit only in the highest balcony, often dubbed "nigger heaven" in popular parlance. Pools may be open to Negroes for certain hours on certain days of the week. Excursion boats may provide special Negro quarters on lower decks. Certain hotels will allow Negroes attending scientific meetings or conventions of learned societies to eat in the dining rooms only during "annual banquets" or during the time the conference lasts.

Because of these restrictions against the Negro he tends to find most of his social outlet in his church, in visiting relatives and friends, and in his own clubs and lodges. He lets off steam in religious revivals and finds conviviality in church suppers and in the various clubs and social organizations connected with the church.[82] He builds up his ego in the ceremonies and rituals of his lodge, where he may aspire to be the Grand Potentate. In an effort to offset his social frustrations in his leisure activities he may indulge in conspicuous consumption, beyond reason so far as his income is concerned, and drive an expensive car, buy expensive liquor, or wear flashy clothes. Because all the Negroes are segregated, white Americans themselves have little opportunity

---

[80] Carl T. Rowan, *Go South to Sorrow*, Random House, New York, 1957, p. 228.

[81] *Newsweek, 54*:23–24 (July 20, 1959).

[82] Hortense Powdermaker, *After Freedom*, The Viking Press, Inc., New York, 1939, chap. 13, "The Secular Role of the Church."

for really understanding the Negro. The latter, on the other hand, tends to idealize the white race and exaggerate his own liabilities in comparison.[83]

Civil Discrimination

One of the perennial complaints of the Negro has been the denial of his right to vote through a series of eligibility rules in the South. These include (1) denying the vote to persons whose grandfathers could not vote (now outlawed by Supreme Court decision); (2) making all important political decisions in the primaries, which used to be limited to white voters, (3) the poll tax; and (4) more recently, a series of character qualifications. White primaries were outlawed by the United States Supreme Court in 1944 and the number of Negroes on the voting rolls has steadily increased since that date. In 1958 there were 1,321,731 registered Negro voters in eleven southern states where the Negro vote was previously negligible. This is about one-fourth of the potential Negro vote in these states.[84]

With the Negro's trek to the city the Negro population in southern urban centers has increased, as has the Negro's interest in the vote. The poll tax, which earlier prevented so many Negroes from voting, now exists in only five states, Alabama, Arkansas, Mississippi, Texas, and Virginia. Even in these states the fact that Negroes now draw wages means that the tax has lost some of its deterring power, since they can afford to pay the fee.[85]

The literary test and new laws restricting the vote to persons of "good character" who have never committed certain crimes is a widespread pattern for excluding Negroes from voting. Many Negroes have committed petty thefts and many have committed adultery. These are effective bars to voting where character qualifications are enforced, since Negroes are required to answer rigid questions. The same basis for excluding voters is obviously not employed with the whites.[86] This has become a major political issue.

The Southerner's greatest fear of the Negro voter is in those counties where Negroes outnumber whites. There are twenty-nine counties in the South where no Negroes are even registered although the population is over 50 percent Negro. These counties are largely rural, where Negro educational standards are lowest and Negro fear of white violence is greatest. The southern Negro needs political education to understand the meaning of voting. Some Negro city churches have helped instruct him. In the estimation of Ralph McGill the Negro tends (like the white citizen) to vote in accordance with his interests. Having been exploited by his fellow Negroes as well as by white persons, and aspiring to be accepted by the American community, he will not vote for a Negro merely because he is a Negro.[87] If white politicians offer the Negro a fair deal, the latter will respond. Earl Long's atti-

---

[83] Frazier, *op. cit.*, p. 678.
[84] Ralph McGill, "If the Southern Negro Got the Vote," *New York Times Magazine*, June 21, 1959, pp. 5, 22.
[85] Fuller, *op. cit.*
[86] *Ibid.*
[87] McGill, *op. cit.*

tude has thus been one of practical cynicism. He has denounced and insulted Negroes publicly but has secured their support by welfare spending in their benefit.[88]

Crime and the Negro

A special aspect of civil discrimination is involved in the Negro's differential crime rate. Negro crime is discussed in Chapter 23; hence the treatment here will be brief. Negroes actually commit many serious crimes. The charge that they are more apt to be arrested and punished for minor offenses is therefore only partially true.

Negroes commit far more murders and aggravated assaults than white persons although there are ten times as many whites as Negroes. They also commit more petty larceny, but recent national figures exclude the count of stolen items under $50 in value. Narcotic charges for this one-tenth of the population also exceed those made against whites. More Negroes than white persons are arrested for carrying arms. Negro rape cases total almost as many as those for the white population. Negro gambling arrests are three times as high as white arrests (partly because of the widespread "playing the numbers" among Negroes). In many other categories Negro crime rates are completely disproportionate to the number of the Negro population.[89]

Most of the recounted offenses are serious and the criminal (if caught) would be arrested irrespective of race. Many Negro offenders are not punished as severely as a white man might be. Negro murderers often receive a light sentence. A Negro shot a white automobile salesman in Pittsburgh because he (the Negro) objected to having the time payments on his car cover interest. He alleged that the additional $15 required was not a part of the contract. In this case the Negro was convicted of murder and sentenced to two years in prison. Other Negro murderers in Pittsburgh have received low sentences. Such light sentences are also common in certain sections of the South. In some areas, indeed, Negroes are seldom punished because they "clutter up the white men's courts."

The significant consideration here is that crime as an index of social disorganization is particularly prevalent among Negroes. This is largely a function of the widespread disadvantage and discrimination to which the Negro is subjected. He is continually frustrated by economic, social, educational, religious, and other discrimination. He is a part of our society but unable to participate fully in it. Many of the social values of our culture therefore have less meaning to him. Why not steal if wages and job opportunities are denied? Why not escape the dirt and grime of the slum through drink or narcotics? Nor is it surprising that the Negroes' frustrations often are expressed by violence or other criminal conduct.

[88] William L. Rivers, "The Long Long Trail Awinding," *The Reporter, 21*:30–33 (July 23, 1959).

[89] *Uniform Crime Reports, 1958,* Annual Report, Federal Bureau of Investigation, U.S. Department of Justice, Washington, September, 1959, p. 97.

Religious Discrimination

Race discrimination is antithetical to the religious teachings of the Christian church (whether Catholic or Protestant) and likewise to those of the Jewish faith. The Catholic Church took the first emphatic historical stand against racism shortly after the discovery of America when Pope Paul III condemned the Spanish cruelty toward and enslaving of the Indians. In his treatise *De Indis* Francisco de Vittoria, the Dominican, asserted that all black- and yellow-skinned people "are men like Europeans."[90] The concept of Christian brotherhood leaves no place for discriminatory treatment.

Even though Spanish Catholics may have initiated racial discrimination in the West Indies, the Protestant Church, particularly in the South, has tolerated segregation. Its members have also promoted discriminatory practices. The Catholic church has never done this and today has taken a decisive stand against segregation. Since Catholics are constrained to follow the pronouncements of the clergy, there has been much less open opposition to desegregation by Catholics. Because of the many divisions of Protestants it has been difficult to establish a Protestant protest to current discrimination. The South has been predominantly Protestant, and many church members and some of the clergy have absorbed the prejudiced attitudes embedded in southern social structure. Many Protestant clergymen, however, are taking a courageous stand against discriminatory practices. There have been numerous instances in which they have been asked to resign for doing so.

Throughout the South Negroes are welcome to attend Catholic services, but relatively few Protestants churches have taken so decisive a stand; but Protestant clergy are generally more advanced theologically than their parishioners. Even in the North the clergy are generally very conservative on the race question. A survey was conducted among 822 Methodist ministers in the Indiana and 139 in the Lexington Conferences by the Bureau of Social and Religious Research of Garrett Biblical Institute. The questionnaire was answered by 663 of the Indiana ministers and 65 from the Lexington Conference. Asked whether they would encourage Negroes to affiliate with their church if members opposed, 353 (53.2 percent) said they would; 169 (25.5 percent) said they would encourage Negroes to attend but not to join; 85 (12.8 percent) said they would encourage them to attend a church of their own race; 56 (8.5 percent) did not reply. Significantly, the younger men (under forty-five) were more likely to be in favor of integration than the older men. Sociologically speaking, this is to be expected because their prejudices are less ingrained.[91]

The failure of many avowed Christians to accept the principle of brotherhood in race relations has had many far-flung repercussions. The Dutch Reformed Church in Africa has favored the apartheid movement, even though

[90] See Yves M. J. Congar, M.P., *The Catholic Church and the Race Question,* UNESCO, Paris, 1953, for a discussion of this.

[91] Alan K. Waltz and Robert L. Wilson, "Ministers' Attitudes Toward Integration," *Phylon, 19:*195–198 (August, 1958).

certain Church of England clergy have taken a courageous stand against it. The Mau Mau movement had much of its source in the fact that the church leaders were willing to enforce discrimination.[92] In this country 75,000 self-styled Negro Muslims (unidentified with the Moslems) have arisen. They belligerently oppose Christianity because it is the religion of the white man, who opposes the rights of the Negro. This sect is an explosive facet of the race problem on the religious front.[93]

The Right Rev. Robert R. Brown, Episcopal Bishop of the Little Rock Diocese, holds that the religious segregation struggle is a symbol of the struggle between pulpit and pew. The various Protestant, Catholic, and Jewish clergy have tried to foster integration, but have had little support from their congregations.[94] A large proportion of clergymen are thus facing a difficult problem in getting their parishes to face up to the unethical character of segregation practices. Some clergymen have had to witness protest meetings of their denomination of a "Save the Church from Integration" character in which the latter tried to indicate that they were official church organizations. At the same time virtually all the national bodies of the larger Protestant denominations have condemned racial discrimination in and out of the church. Many churches and their ministers are truly in agony over this problem.[95]

Meanwhile it should be remembered that the initial steps toward religious segregation were taken by the Negroes themselves under slavery. They wanted to hold their church services "in their own way," where they could pray, shout, or sing as they felt moved. The Negro Baptists first broke off in 1776 and the Negro Methodists shortly after the Revolution. Whether organized or not, the Negroes' separate meetings became a fact during slavery.[96] The southern whites did not impose the separation then although many have come to think that there is now something sacrosanct about keeping religious groups separate on the color line.

The religious issues raised by segregation are essentially moral and not theological. What the Negro wants is to be accepted, to be free and equal. The political leaders of the post-Civil War period virtually forced the Congress to adopt civil rights legislation and the Thirteenth, Fourteenth, and Fifteenth amendments. There has not been any full support to achieving the rights laid down in these provisions even in the North. Many Union soldiers who fought and bled during the war over slavery were prejudiced against the Negro. During the period 1865 to 1868 Negroes were denied the right to vote in eight northern states. The prejudice was, of course, even greater in the South because the Negroes' new status had been thrust upon them. Conse-

[92] The Church and Race Relations in Africa and Asia (An N.B.C. Radio Discussion), University of Chicago Roundtable, No. 855, Chicago, August 10, 1954.

[93] "The Black Supremacists," Time, 74:24–25 (August 10, 1959).

[94] Cf. review of Bishop Brown's book, Bigger Than Little Rock, Seabury Press, 1959, by Harry Golden in "Perseverance Against Violence," The Nation, 188:456–457 (May 16, 1959).

[95] Thomas Reeves, "Methodist Layman's Union Victim," Christian Century, 76:995 (September 2, 1959). Cf. also Ralph McGill, "The Agony of the Southern Minister," New York Times Magazine, September 27, 1959, pp. 16 and 57 ff.

[96] Frazier, op. cit., chap. XIV.

quently the southern states contrived in ingenious ways to prevent the Negro from achieving his new rights even though they were guaranteed by constitutional amendment. At times the United States Supreme Court has been equally ingenious in negating these rights by such compromising decisions as that involved in extending "separate but equal" facilities.[97] C. Vann Woodward holds that the Union fought the Civil War on "borrowed moral capital." Only recently have we begun to realize that in freeing the Negro we also committed ourselves to his equality and the right to opportunities. The recognition of our moral debt has come slowly.

The Intermarriage Issue

Certain Southerners claim that their opposition to the Negroes' advance has rested largely on a fear of sexual intimacy. If the Negro could have increased equality without intimacy the southern white citizen would not bring up his recurrent theme of "mongrelization." Nor would he presumably raise his continually repeated question "Would you want your daughter to marry a Negro?" The fear of intermarriage is thus basic to the Southerner's objection to mixed dancing and eating and to integrated education.

If there could be increased equality without intimacy integration would be less disturbing to the whites.[98] In the North, however, most public schools have always been integrated save those serving school districts which are wholly or chiefly Negro. Little intermarriage has taken place. There are a number of angles to the Southerner's fear of intermarriage. Many southern white men have illicit affairs with Negro women. "Mongrelization" is thus not exactly new in the South. This is the white man's guilt, not the Negro's. What the white man may really fear is having an irate Negro father demand that he marry his daughter.

Discrimination and Social Disorganization

Racial discrimination is currently the most important domestic problem facing the United States. Both in numbers of persons involved and in manifold repercussions upon virtually all phases of our social life, racial tensions cause or accentuate more social disorganization than any other single factor. In the continuing process of interaction within American society, all Americans (white and black alike) are directly or indirectly affected by racial prejudice, discrimination, and segregation. We have examined some of the principal aspects of this problem, particularly those of education and housing. We have also indicated (in considerably less detail) some of the other ways in which 10 percent of our citizens are denied equal opportunity to participate in the American society. Groups can function adequately only when the great majority of their members participate in their activities. Discrimination impairs or threatens social participation.

The efficient action of social groups also requires a high degree of consensus

[97] C. Vann Woodward, "Equality, America's Deferred Commitment," *The American Scholar*, 27:459–472 (Autumn, 1958).

[98] Laura H. Rhyne and Charles R. Foster, "Integrated Yet Isolated," *Commonweal*, 70:535–536 (September 25, 1959).

(agreement upon basic values and willingness to act upon these values). Prejudice and discrimination on a large scale seriously limit the values of freedom, opportunity, and equality that form the basis of democratic society. If the Negro does not have a fair chance for an equal education, if he is denied equality in housing, recreation, religion, and civil rights, and if he cannot use his abilities and skills to equal advantage in making a living, then the disparity between values and performance interferes with the functioning of the group. If a society professes one set of values and practices another, the resulting gap between creed and deed produces a basic cynicism that further threatens social solidarity. Prejudice and discrimination are, in final analysis, problems of group values and group morality.

Individual and social disorganization are, as we have indicated, different aspects of the same process. This relationship is clearly indicated in the personality of the Negro. Delinquency, crime, family disorganization, ill health, and (often) a violent self-hatred are facets of personal disorganization. Such disorganization is not limited to the Negro. The white man has his share of personal, family, and community disorganization that stems, partly at least, from his own prejudice and discrimination. Much of the ignorance, poverty, intolerance, and violence that mark life in parts of the rural South can be attributed to the low educational standards, the inefficient use of manpower, and the bitterness that has been a function of the conflict between the races. Part of this is due to poverty, per se.

The white man may or may not, as some psychiatrists allege, suffer from unconscious guilt feelings because of his discrimination against the Negro. There is no question, however, that many white men suffer from more tangible personal problems which have arisen out of the intolerance and suspicion in which he, as well as the Negro, has lived for more than a century. Social disorganization is intensified by ignorance and the two are closely related to prejudice. There is thus a vicious circle of discrimination. Social interaction is a reciprocal process. Segregation is a two-edged sword that cuts both ways.[99]

There is another aspect of social disorganization that has been accentuated by racial prejudice and discrimination. This is the position of the United States in the society of nations. In the current struggle for the minds of millions of men and women throughout the world, American treatment of racial minorities is the most important propaganda weapon the enemies and lukewarm friends of democracy have. Most of the "uncommitted" peoples of the world have dark skins. It is often hard for them to accept our sincerity when we profess democratic values and at the same time deny the Negro an equal participation in American life. The United States cannot purport to stand for democratic values if the American people do not accept them for all their members. If these values are disregarded and denied the status of the United States is lowered accordingly.

[99] Milton M. Gordon and John P. Roche, "Segregation—Two-Edged Sword," *New York Times Magazine,* April 25, 1954.

SELECTED BIBLIOGRAPHY

Blaustein, Albert P., and Ferguson, Clarence Clyde, *Desegregation and the Law,* Rutgers University Press, New Brunswick, 1957. An analysis of the legal problems related to desegregation is presented.

Brown, F. J., and Roucek, J. C. (eds.), *One America,* Prentice-Hall, Inc., New York, 1945. An excellent symposium discusses the various racial, cultural, and national groups which make up America.

The Crisis, Official Publication of the NAACP. Students are urged to read current issues of this for news about discrimination.

Frazier, E. Franklin, *The Negro in the United States,* The Macmillan Company, New York, 1949. This is one of the best books on the history and problems of the Negro.

Hansen, Carl F., *Miracle of Social Adjustment,* Desegregation of the Washington, D.C., Schools, Anti-Defamation League, New York, 1957. This gives a picture of how Washington made a rapid change to integrated schools.

Hill, Herbert, and Greenberg, Jack, *Citizens Guide to De-Segregation,* Beacon Press, Boston, 1955. The authors study the events and facts leading to the Supreme Court decision against segregation in the schools.

Miller, Arthur S., *Racial Discrimination and Private Education. A Legal Analysis,* University of North Carolina Press, Chapel Hill, 1957. The legal attempts to desegregate private education are investigated.

Montagu, M. F. Ashley, *Man's Most Dangerous Myth,* Harper & Brothers, New York, 1952. An able discussion of the nonsense about racial superiority and inferiority is presented.

Myrdal, Gunnar, *An American Dilemma,* Harper & Brothers, New York, 1944. The author gives a sympathetic treatment of the Negro problem and the American dilemma of inconsistency in withholding democratic rights from its largest minority group.

Phylon, A Quarterly of Race and Culture. This journal has many valuable articles on current Negro problems.

Schermerhorn, R. A., *These Our People,* D. C. Heath and Company, Boston, 1949. The problems of cultural conflict in America are given excellent treatment.

Shoemaker, Don (ed.), *With All Deliberate Speed,* Harper & Brothers, New York, 1957. This is an objective account, from the point of view of a series of southern observers, of the compliance and noncompliance with the Supreme Court's ruling on segregation.

Simpson, George E., and Yinger, J. Milton, *Racial and Cultural Minorities,* Harper & Brothers, New York, 1958 (rev. ed.). This is a detailed analysis of prejudice and discrimination in the United States.

"Urban Renewal and the Negro in Chicago," A Report by the Chicago Urban League Community Services Department, Chicago, 1938 (mimeographed). Here is an excellent picture of the serious problem of Negro housing in Chicago and plans for its improvement.

Valien, Bonita H., *The St. Louis Story,* Anti-Defamation League, New York, 1956. A detailed account of St. Louis' early achievement of desegregation in the schools is given.

PART FIVE

International Disorganization

CHAPTER 29

Revolution

Revolution and Social Disorganization

We are living in an age of world revolution. The goals of this revolution vary as between nations, classes, and religions. In the Communist world, there is a fervent conviction that the world is moving toward the Marxist goals of socialism and the dictatorship of the proletariat. In the free world, the vast majority believe that the wave of the future is moving toward the continued spread of industrial techniques, the gradual emancipation of colonial peoples, and the eventual triumph of democratic freedoms. The goals of these worlds may differ widely, but agreement upon the fact of revolutionary change (however defined) is widespread. The Communist bloc thus views these drastic forms of social change with eager anticipation, as presaging the emergence of a new and better social order. The free nations are filled with fear and insecurity at the prospect of violent dislocations in the internal structures of large areas. The *fact* of revolution, however, remains.[1]

Revolution, totalitarianism, and war are social movements growing out of social disorganization on a supernational scale. In varying degrees, they are the results of a breakdown in world consensus and involve different forms of social disorganization, all of which have world-wide implications. Such colossal dislocations in the social structure as the French, Russian, and Chinese revolutions have caused repercussions far from Paris, Petrograd, and Peking. These changes have raised ghosts which generations have failed to exorcise. The twentieth century is a century of revolution, totalitarianism, and total war.[2]

Revolution is social disorganization in its most literal sense. The pattern of relationships binding a large functioning group (the national state) is broken down, partially under its own weight and partially by the efforts of the revolutionary leaders, the "elite."[3] The political ties that formerly held the people together are disrupted and the government temporarily ceases to be an adequately functioning entity. The basic consensus of the society is broken. So-

[1] Harold D. Lasswell, *The World Revolution of Our Time,* Hoover Institute Studies, Stanford University Press, Stanford, 1951, p. 1.

[2] Raymond Aron, *The Century of Total War,* Doubleday and Company, Inc., New York, 1954.

[3] Philip Selznick, *The Organizational Weapon: A Study of Bolshevik Strategy and Tactics,* McGraw-Hill Book Company, Inc., New York, 1952.

cial and moral codes disintegrate. The informal assumptions of the people that bind the social structure together are likewise temporarily dissolved. In a complete revolution, all of the major institutions undergo drastic changes. The state, the church, the school, and the family are so closely interrelated that a change in one is reflected in all the others.[4]

Revolution is thus one of the most radical forms of social change in recent history. The societies of Russia, India, and China have altered during the memory of living man. In Russia and China, the changes have been violent, whereas in India they have been comparatively peaceful. The Chinese Revolution is still in process. Group standards, attitudes, values, and habits are being altered under the efforts of the monolithic Communist party. The Chinese culture, which had been comparatively static for centuries, has suddenly become dynamic.

The upheavals in China have been in the general interest of the Revolution, inasmuch as they have disorganized relationships characteristic of the old society. These changes, once in motion, cannot be arbitrarily curtailed at the convenience of the Communist government. Revolutions have a way of continuing to their logical conclusion, in a manner completely unanticipated. As expressed by a Chinese scholar, "By challenging old traditions, by overcoming resistance to change, and by demanding widespread participation in various mass organizations, the Communists are setting in motion new forces which may in the end prove bigger and more powerful than communism itself."[5]

Revolution in the modern world is thus taking place in the midst of other sweeping social changes. Society is becoming less rural and agrarian and more urban and industrial, as we have discussed. Until relatively recently Europe and Asia were characterized by feudal social organization, with highly developed class stratification and attitudes of subordination and superordination. Life was organized about rural and village doings, and social status was largely ascribed (i.e., given at birth) rather than achieved (i.e., earned).[6] Social mobility, both horizontal and vertical, was comparatively limited, and the average individual lived and died within the same network of traditional relationships. The societies of eastern Europe, Russia, China, India, and the Near East were all organized about such a system, with local variations, before the rise of industrialism.[7]

This order has largely broken down. Changes have occurred at different

[4] Rex D. Hopper, "The Revolutionary Process," *Social Forces, 28*:270–279 (March, 1950).

[5] Theodore Hsi-En Chen, "The Marxist Remolding of Chinese Society," *American Journal of Sociology, 58*:340–346 (January, 1953), p. 346.

[6] Ralph Linton, *The Study of Man,* Appleton-Century-Crofts, Inc., New York, 1936, p. 157.

[7] Arthur K. Davis, "Conflict Between Major Social Systems: The Soviet-American Case," *Social Forces, 30*:29–36 (October, 1951). See also Daniel Lerner, *The Passing of Traditional Society,* The Free Press, Glencoe, Ill., 1958.

rates, but the fact of change itself is unmistakable. This shift in social organization constitutes a social revolution, whether or not a new government assumes power. The Communist parties of the world have attempted to move into the power vacuum left by the decline of feudalism. They have been able, therefore, to *exploit* situations that were already intrinsically revolutionary, such as those convulsing the vast continent of Asia. The situations would, in large measure, have existed whether or not organized Communism had ever appeared. These basic changes have arisen from a combination of economic, industrial, and social factors that are largely unrelated to organized political pressure.[8]

In underdeveloped areas, the forces of revolution are broadly based in the changing social structure. Meanwhile the totalitarian and the democratic powers are competing for the direction of the revolutionary forces, which are advancing like a prairie fire.[9] This struggle for the attitudes and allegiances of half the world is often misunderstood by the democratic nations, who tend to assume that revolutionary changes in the social structure are synonymous with the establishment of Communist dictatorships. Neither the Communist powers nor the democratic nations are able to *cause* these great social changes, with their accompanying modifications in the lives of hundreds of millions of persons. At most the two great antagonists in the cold war can only divert the revolutionary movements into their respective camps. The major weapons in this struggle are not bombs and tanks. They are rather ideas, values, and examples.[10]

The value judgments concerning revolution naturally vary from class to class and from one historical period to another.[11] The persons who are in a position to lose their status view revolution with horror. For those who "have nothing to lose but their chains," revolution may portend a new day. The evaluation of revolution requires historical perspective. The French and American revolutions are now generally regarded as desirable in terms of their ultimate effects, if not in their contemporary manifestations. The Daughters of the American Revolution view that event in retrospect as eminently desirable, an attitude which they obviously do not hold concerning the contemporary Russian and Chinese revolutions. The particular definition of a revolution is an index to the value judgments of the class and the time.[12]

[8] Cf. Philip E. Mosely, "Soviet Policy and the Revolutions in Asia," *Annals of the American Academy of Political and Social Science, 276*:91–98 (July, 1951).

[9] Cf. Hans Gerth and C. Wright Mills, *Character and Social Structure,* Harcourt, Brace and Company, New York, 1953, pp. 441–450, "Revolution and Counterrevolution."

[10] Davis, *op. cit.* Cf. also Juliusz Katz-Suchy, "National Liberation and Social Progress in Asia," *Annals of the American Academy of Political and Social Science, 276*:48–59 (July, 1951).

[11] R. R. Palmer, "Reflections on the French Revolution," *Political Science Quarterly, 67*:64–80 (March, 1952).

[12] Crane Brinton, *The Anatomy of Revolution,* Prentice-Hall, Inc., New York, 1952, pp. 2–3.

The Nature of Revolution

Considerable confusion exists as to the exact nature of revolution. The term has been applied to social and political upheavals as varied as the spasmodic "elections" in certain Central American countries and the complex series of events such as the Reformation or the industrial revolution. In sociological terms, revolution is a transvaluation of attitudes and values toward the existing social structure. These changes involve widespread social disorganization, both before and after the actual shift in the center of political power.[13]

There are at least four different (although related) conceptions of revolution. Thus a revolution is regarded:

1. As a purely political phenomenon, involving a change in the location of sovereignty. The shift in power from one military clique to another in a country controlled by the army would constitute a revolution in this sense.
2. As a shift in the composition of the elites, whereby one group holding power is replaced by another *type* of group. An elite composed of businessmen, for example, may be replaced by one whose members come from the military class.[14]
3. As a sweeping social change in any single segment of the social structure, whether religious, economic, political, or industrial. The Reformation was such a change in the religious structure, and the introduction of the mobile internal-combustion engine was a "revolutionary" change in transportation.
4. As a basic change in attitudes toward the central institutions of a society. In terms of this definition, many of the economic, political, and social upheavals often regarded as revolutions are merely the external manifestations of a change in social attitudes.

The conception of revolution as a change in social attitudes is the one followed in this book. Social disorganization is thus the breakdown of the group, brought about in large part by changes in social attitudes. Revolution is the culmination of a long series of social changes which affect the attitudes of the masses. These attitudes must be affected before any significant revolutionary change takes place. Without such a deep psychological modification, revolution becomes mere rebellion, insurrection, or revolt.

The importance of basic modifications in attitudes is attested by Thomas and Znaniecki. In their words, the first prerequisite to revolution is "a demand for new values for a whole group, community, class, nation." The second essential feature is the conscious and deliberate abolition of a traditional social system. Accompanying this social unheaval, a significant change in institutional relationships occurs. Heretofore individual revolt has been stifled or sublimated by such traditional institutional forms as religion and

---

[13] Hopper, *op. cit.,* pp. 270–271.
[14] Harold D. Lasswell *et al., The Comparative Study of Elites,* Hoover Institute Studies, Stanford University Press, Stanford, 1952.

the class structure. Revolution sweeps aside these ancient and powerful barriers.[15]

Sorokin has expanded the concept of revolutionary attitudes in his researches into the "internal disturbances" that periodically threaten to destroy the consensus of nations. He maintains that the most important element in the genesis of a revolution is a fundamental unsettlement in the goals and values of a particular society. In his view "the main and indispensable condition for an eruption of internal disturbances is that the social system or the cultural system or both shall be unsettled." If the people truly accept existing conditions they will undergo poverty, starvation, and defeat in battle. If this framework of social attitudes is disorganized, the members of the society have lost the chief stabilizing influence. Their definitions of right and wrong are no longer rigidly maintained and they are ready to break their age-old connections with the traditional social order.[16]

A deliberate change of attitudes is apparent in the Chinese Revolution, where the Communists have carefully attempted to modify many of the attitudes that had been present in the culture of China. As a student of the Chinese Revolution has stated, "The Communists in China are not only introducing a new political regime and a new economic order; they have set out to remake Chinese society and *to change the attitudes and psychology of the people*."[17] These revolutionary attitudes involve such traditional relationships as the status of women, the relations between the sexes, the structure of the family, class relations, and government control. In these and many other ways, the ancient Chinese social structure is being transformed by drastic and violent revolutionary change within a generation.[18]

Revolution and Social Tensions

Revolution involves a change in social attitudes toward the central values of a society. A discussion of the causes of revolution should therefore stress the genesis of revolutionary tendencies to act. These attitudes are generated by repressive forces in the social structure, which may be "real" or "imaginary," in the sense that they may or may not be apparent to impartial observers. If large numbers of the people believe that the repressions are real, however, they are real to them. The economic conditions in eighteenth-century France were, for example, better than in most of Europe. Robespierre and others (although suffering no privation themselves) nevertheless were able to persuade the French masses that their economic lot was desperate.[19]

The outbreak of the revolution occurs when the cumulative repressions of

---

[15] William I. Thomas and Florian Znaniecki, *The Polish Peasant in Europe and America*, Alfred A. Knopf, Inc., New York, 1927, Vol. II, chap. 5, "Revolutionary Attitudes."

[16] Pitirim A. Sorokin, *Social and Cultural Dynamics*, American Book Company, New York, 1937, Vol. III, p. 499.

[17] Hsi-En Chen, *op. cit.*, p. 340. (Our italics.)

[18] *Ibid.*

[19] Brinton, *op. cit.*, pp. 30–38.

the people (real or imagined) have brought about a high degree of psychological tension.[20] The institutions of prerevolutionary society are said to repress or restrict the expression of the wishes for security, new experience, response, and recognition.[21] Or the repression is viewed in terms of reflexes and instincts.[22] Irrespective of terminology, the fact of repression is important in generating revolutionary changes in attitudes.

Repressive forces alone, however, are not sufficient to engender revolution. Certain positive forces must also be present before the masses are moved to action.[23] These compulsive forces include: (1) *widespread provocation*—discontent with the *status quo,* and provocative action by the government crystallizes a desire for action; (2) *public opinion*—individual resentment must be sufficiently general to stir up collective resentment if group action is to occur; (3) *program of reform*—revolutionary action must be based upon a program of reform that promises to alleviate the major abuses; (4) *trusted leadership* —leadership may or may not exist before the outbreak of the revolution, but it must arise soon after if the masses are to be enlisted in collective action; (5) *weakness of conservatives*—if the ruling classes are strong, it is axiomatic that they cannot be overthrown. (Lenin, the Bolshevik leader, recognized this fact. "A revolution occurs," he said, "when the upper classes cannot and the lower classes will not continue the old system.")[24]

1. *Economic Tensions.* It is widely believed (a) that economic factors are the primary cause of revolution; and (b) that the lower the level of living in a country, the greater the possibility of such action. The relationship is not so simple. In all societies that have undergone a revolution, there have unquestionably been many persons living at submarginal economic levels, who had no stake in maintaining the economic system, and who were faced with stark hunger. In the days before the French Revolution, Queen Marie Antoinette is said to have asked naïvely why the hungry Frenchmen who had no bread did not eat cake. Many families in Moscow had not eaten a full meal for months preceding the Russian Revolution.[25] When a man is hungry, the existing institutions lose any hallowed importance with which they have been vested earlier. Economic tensions are unquestionably instrumental in arousing revolutionary attitudes.

The nations that have undergone the great revolutions of modern times have not, however, been those with the lowest living scales. The American colonies, prerevolutionary France, and even czarist Russia were, compara-

[20] Leon Trotsky, *The History of the Russian Revolution,* Simon and Schuster, Inc., New York, 1932, Vol. I, p. 76.

[21] L. P. Edwards, *The Natural History of Revolution,* University of Chicago Press, Chicago, 1927, pp. 3–4.

[22] Pitirim A. Sorokin, *The Sociology of Revolution,* J. B. Lippincott Company, Philadelphia, 1925, chap. 17.

[23] Adapted from Louis Gottschalk, "Causes of Revolution," *American Journal of Sociology,* 50:1–8 (July, 1944).

[24] *Ibid.,* p. 8.

[25] William H. Chamberlin, *The Russian Revolution,* The Macmillan Company, New York, 1935, Vol. I, p. 262.

tively speaking, in a favorable economic position in comparison with that in many other contemporary countries. Furthermore, these revolutionary nations were on the upgrade economically and the scale of living was rising.[26] The economic tensions that precipitated these revolutions arose largely between persons who had already tasted some of the joys of ownership and the existing government. The peasants and petty bourgeoisie who own some property look with hungry eyes upon the large estates of the nobility, the rich, and the clergy. The actual fighting in the streets may be done by the penniless proletariat, but the revolution is often sparked by the middle classes. Economic tensions are thus clearly present, not so much in the form of actual distress "but rather a feeling on the part of some of the chief enterprising groups that their opportunities for getting on in this world are unduly limited by political arrangements."[27] There is no question, however, that the Russian peasant's economic status was low.

2. *Security Tensions.* A second tension producing revolutionary attitudes arises from physical insecurity. The individual may be threatened with loss of life and the nation with military disaster. In time of war, each person of military age is faced with the possibility of death, injury, or imprisonment. The collective excitement of nationalism is strong and often carries the individual along in its sacrificial fervor, so that he may willingly face the prospect of death in battle for the fatherland. Eventually, however, millions of men begin to lose any desire to immolate themselves for the king, emperor, or ruling class. The nation itself may face the possibility of extinction as an autonomous political group.[28]

In a further discussion of social values, Lasswell speaks of "shared well-being" as an important pattern of group expectations. Where there is such well-being "the motives and circumstances leading to suicide, murder, war, and civil violence are reduced or eliminated."[29] Casualties in war, both military and civilian; casualties by revolution, revolt, or insurrection; number of men under arms and specializing in violence; proportion of the national income spent on violence or the preparation for violence; and war scares between the great powers all reduce hope for social well-being.[30]

War, on the other hand, may serve as an antidote for revolution, and many rulers have purposely involved their countries in a war in order to bolster their own regimes. The previous mass aggressions or hostilities are directed outward against the foreign foe instead of inward against the government. But this dangerous adventure must be successful. If it fails, revolution is hastened. Many revolutions have followed defeat in foreign war. Bulgaria, Turkey, Germany, Austria, Hungary, and Russia all underwent revolutions of varying degrees of severity after their defeat in World War I. France ushered in the

[26] Brinton, *op. cit.*, pp. 33–35.
[27] *Ibid.*, p. 36.
[28] Edwards, *op. cit.*, p. 48.
[29] Lasswell, *The World Revolution of Our Time*, p. 24.
[30] *Ibid.*, pp. 24–25.

Third Republic by a revolution following her humiliation by Germany in 1870.[31] The Russian Revolution was precipitated by the unfavorable progress of World War I. "Land, bread, and peace" became the rallying cry of the Bolsheviks in their successful attempt to overthrow the provisional government. The most important of these slogans was "peace."

3. *Freedom Tensions.* A third type of prerevolutionary tension results from shackling the freedom of the individual. The concept of liberty has long been the battle cry for revolution. It will continue to stir men to revolution, in their hope that a change in government will strike off the chains that restrain them. In times past, the threat to freedom has taken different forms. Martial law, *lettres de cachet,* unfair trials, terrorism of security police, deportation, arbitrary and unlawful imprisonment—all have been the instruments of a moribund ruling class desperately attempting to postpone the day when it must give up its power.

The slogan of "Liberty, equality, and fraternity" that rang in the streets of Paris was a clarion call to lovers of freedom the world over to cast off their bonds. The colonial patriots who picked off the British from behind the New England stone fences were animated by a desire for freedom from foreign economic and political domination. The revolutionary crowds that thronged the streets of Petrograd and Moscow thrilled to their newly found freedom from the rule of the Czar. The fact that one form of repression is often exchanged for another and even more unpleasant variety is not evident until later. In the totalitarian revolutions of the twentieth century individual freedom has come to be characterized as a "bourgeois superstition."[32]

4. *Stratification Tensions.* A further type of tension arises from a rigid form of social stratification. A strong system of class or caste by definition represses the abilities and skills of persons not fortunate enough to be born in the upper strata. When no vertical mobility is possible, pressures for an overthrow of the system itself eventually will slowly but surely accumulate. Under the old regime, there is a denial of equal opportunity to receive recognition commensurate with talent. Such a situation represents a negation of the social value that Lasswell has called "shared respect": the giving and receiving of affirmations of the worth of the individual both as a human being and because he possesses certain unique and valuable qualities.[33] Repressions of this value are inherent in the social structure of the old order. Men of ability in the lower classes cannot escape such repressions without destroying the structure itself.[34]

In a prerevolutionary society, privilege has thus become so entrenched in the social structure that many men cannot find adequate expression for their latent powers. The system creates a body of malcontents, who know that they and their children are doomed to oblivion under the existing social organiza-

---

[31] Sorokin, *Social and Cultural Dynamics,* Vol. III, pp. 489–490.
[32] Brinton, *op. cit.,* pp. 289–293, "A Paradox of Revolution."
[33] Lasswell, *The World Revolution of Our Time,* p. 20.
[34] Sorokin, *The Sociology of Revolution,* pp. 381–382.

tion. The lack of vertical mobility may ultimately give rise to revolution, just as steam that keeps building up and has no outlet will eventually cause an explosion. Revolutionary propaganda demands the "circulation of the elites," i.e., recruiting the personnel of leadership from the ablest members of the society.[35] In a social structure with a high degree of emphasis on "career open to talents," the circulation of the elites is efficient. In a structure where such circulation is rendered difficult or impossible, revolution may be furthered.[36] It is the relatively underprivileged elites who foment and carry through the revolution.

The Natural History of Revolution

Revolution at the same time is a form of collective behavior and as such exhibits certain uniformities. These are apparent whether we are considering the English, French, American, Russian, or Chinese Revolution. Under certain conditions, human beings tend to act collectively in accordance with certain general sequences, which can be investigated by scientific methods. These sequences are subject to variations that reflect differences in culture, social structure, and historical development. Nevertheless, all revolutions tend to follow rather clearly discernible stages. The isolation and investigation of these sequences is the task of the sociologist, as distinguished from the historian, who is concerned with a unique series of events. The typical stages in collective behavior that together constitute the *natural history* of revolution[37] include the following:

1. *Preliminary Unrest.* The first stage in the natural history of revolution is one of vague and inchoate unrest. The people sense that something is wrong but they do not know what to do about it. An increase in social mobility occurs, which is at once a symptom of social disorganization and a cause for further disorganization. Large numbers of men are cut off from their basic institutional relationships and are deprived of some of the formal and informal social controls of an ordered society. This mobility heightens the rate of vice, crime, and other indices of social disorganization. Social change is on the way, whether the people know it or not.[38]

This preliminary stage is marked by mass excitement and restlessness, which has both individual and collective manifestations. The interaction assumes the characteristics of a "milling" process. The members of the society interact symbolically in public gathering places and enhance the feeling of unrest. As a result the "Mass" is formed, which is characterized by the following features: "first, the people . . . come from all walks and levels of life; second, the mass is made up of anonymous persons, responding to common

[35] Cf. Gaetano Mosca, *The Ruling Class,* McGraw-Hill Book Company, Inc., New York, 1939.

[36] Lasswell *et al., The Comparative Study of Elites,* chap. II, "The Elite Concept."

[37] The natural history approach to the study of revolution was first developed by L. P. Edwards, *The Natural History of Revolution,* followed by Crane Brinton, *The Anatomy of Revolution,* and further explored sociologically by Rex D. Hopper, "The Revolutionary Process," *Social Forces,* 28:270–279 (March, 1950).

[38] Edwards, *op. cit.,* chap. 3, "Preliminary Symptoms of Unrest."

influences but unknown to each other; third, because they are unknown to each other, there is little interaction . . . between the members . . . ; fourth, there is little or no organization on the level of mass behavior."[39]

2. *Defection of the Intellectuals.* The intellectuals are the persons who mold public opinion and hold the attention of large special publics. They are "the authors, the editors, the lecturers, the artists, the teachers, the priests, the preachers."[40] The members of these groups were earlier in complete sympathy with the values of the social structure. But with social change the intellectuals transfer their allegiance from the old order to the new. In the process, they release a veritable flood of "subversive" literature in the form of newspapers, pamphlets, brochures, books. Some lead mass meetings. Many of their speeches and published works are the comparatively innocuous reactions of the parlor intellectuals that flourished before the French and Russian revolutions.[41]

As the revolution approaches and social disorganization becomes more pronounced, the intellectuals become more vociferous in their denunciations of the existing order. Violent attacks are made upon the way of life of the upper classes and the institutions for which they stand. No individual or institution is spared. Many of the best journalists, pamphleteers, and editors join in the crusade and add to the collective dissatisfaction. Some intellectuals are merely deserting a lost cause and are acting as opportunists to further their own interests. Others are sincerely voicing their cherished hopes of a better social order. In either event, the existing regime is deprived of its ablest intellectual defenders. It thus suffers a body blow.[42]

3. *Emergence of the Social Myth.* The third stage in the natural history of revolution is the emergence of "the social myth."[43] The social myth embodies a vision, an ideal, and a vaguely defined but very real hope for the future. The French and American revolutions abounded in slogans which incorporated the social myth of individual freedom. Both the French social philosophers and Jefferson proclaimed the existence of certain inalienable rights which were recognized by all men. They thus furnished the intellectual foundation for the slogan of "Life, liberty, and the pursuit of happiness."[44] Basic to the social myth is a passionate hope for freedom from the oppression of the old order.

This stage in the revolution is marked by the formation of political symbols. The symbols have a strong psychological influence upon the masses and motivate them to revolutionary action. The new myth is interpreted through such symbols as democracy, liberty, the dictatorship of the proletariat, socialism, and the nation. The essential characteristic of a symbol is that it stands

[39] Hopper, *op. cit.,* p. 272.

[40] Edwards, *op. cit.,* p. 38.

[41] Sorokin, *The Sociology of Revolution,* pp. 41–42.

[42] For a stimulating discussion of the transfer of allegiance of the intellectuals, see Brinton, *op. cit.,* pp. 42–53, "The Desertion of the Intellectuals."

[43] Georges Sorel, *Reflections on Violence* (translated), B. W. Huebsch, New York, 1912.

[44] Palmer, *op. cit.*

for something else. A symbol may be a word, a phrase, or an object heavily weighted with emotion. In the minds of the people, each symbol stands for a complex set of hopes, fears, and aspirations. The reaction to symbols tends to be emotional rather than rational, and the individual in the prerevolutionary society focuses his hopes upon the symbols of the emerging myth. In this sense, the symbol is a stimulus to collective action toward the realization of the revolutionary myth.[45]

4. *The Outbreak of Revolution.* The fourth stage is marked by the actual outbreak of the revolution. This event often occurs in dramatic and unmistakable fashion. Thus the masses stormed the Bastille in Paris, attacked the Winter Palace in Petrograd, and celebrated the Boston Tea Party. These actions are all highly symbolic, inasmuch as they involve deliberate violence directed against buildings, institutions, or laws that symbolize the old regime. The Bastille was the prison for political offenders under the monarchy. It stood, therefore, in the popular mind for the abuses perpetrated by the monarchy and the ruling classes, despite the fact that only a handful of offenders were actually incarcerated in the building. The Boston Tea Party symbolized, in another way, the defiance of British authority and thus dramatized the issue of taxation without representation. When the masses sense that the authorities have been openly defied, they are quick to press on to further revolutionary triumphs.[46]

5. *The Rule of the Liberals.* For an indefinite period after the collapse of the old regime, power is held by the liberals and moderate reformers, who attempt to conciliate both factions, the extremists and the conservatives. In the early days of the revolution, the extreme revolutionists are not sufficiently strong to seige power or to combat openly the liberal coalition. During this period most of the revolutionary leaders are either exiled or imprisoned. In both the French and Russian revolutions the left wing did not gain power until a provisional government failed to placate the extremists—those who wanted a return to the old order and those who wanted a complete revolutionary change. The moderates are forced on the defensive and end by pleasing neither the exponents nor the opponents of the old regime.[47]

The rule of the liberals is thus ordinarily doomed. They are confronted with such handicaps as armed invasion by countries supporting the old regime, internal rebellion by the extreme factions, political inexperience, and the emergence of the new myth sponsored by the revolutionary party.[48] The length of the tenure of the liberals is determined by their political and military strength, the organization of the radicals, and outside events. In the Russian Revolution, the "normal" revolutionary sequence was complicated by the war. The coalition government of Kerensky wished to carry on the war to the bitter end, aided by the armed intervention of the Allies. The Bolsheviks

[45] Harold D. Lasswell *et al., The Comparative Study of Symbols,* Hoover Institute Studies, Stanford University Press, Stanford, 1952, chap. I, "Political Symbols."

[46] Brinton, *op. cit.,* chap. 3, "First Stages of Revolution."

[47] *Ibid.,* chap. 5, "The Rule of the Moderates."

[48] Hopper, *op. cit.,* pp. 275–276.

read the temper of the people more clearly. The workers, soldiers, peasants, and bourgeoisie wanted peace. The Bolsheviks promised peace and seized the power.[49]

6. *The Seizure of Power.* Radicalism succeeds liberalism. The revolutionists have organized and carried through their successful conspiracy. The leaders have capitalized upon the revolutionary upsurge among the people and have ridden the wave of the future. The party is small in numbers but highly disciplined, resourceful, ruthless, and dedicated. We cannot consider here all of the steps whereby the successful *coup d'état* (i.e., seizure of power) occurs. This action is planned and directed by a small and fanatical group of men who know what they want and are prepared to go to any lengths to get it. The concept of "dual power" is often the basis for the seizure of power; that is, a system of *unofficial* (dual) government arises along with the official (legitimate) government, which it ultimately overthrows. The unofficial government of the workers' and soldiers' soviets in Russia thus succeeded in overthrowing the official government of the moderates. The Jacobin clubs in France took over from the liberals who came before them.[50]

The techniques of the *coup d'état* have been perfected since the Russian Revolution. It is no longer necessary for the democratic government to be completely destroyed before a new totalitarian state can be erected on its ruins. The system of dual power merely extends to the control of certain agencies of the democratic government. The Communists enter the army, the police, and agencies of public information and thus dominate the effective machinery of government. The seizure of power in Czechoslovakia in February, 1948, is a classic example. The Communists had so infiltrated the centers of power that they were able to assume control of the legitimate government with comparative ease. The outward form of government remained substantially the same, but the basis of sovereignty underwent a drastic shift. In this sense, the nation experienced a true revolution.[51]

7. *The Reign of Terror.* The successful seizure of power by the radicals is often followed by the Reign of Terror. This is a period of war against foreign armies, as well as civil war against the exponents of the old regime. During the period of the Terror there is also an attempted counterrevolution, when the dispossessed classes seek to reverse the trend of revolution. The Terror represents an attempt by the revolutionists to prevent this contingency. Hence the period is not so much one of random disorganization as it is one of the calculated use of fear. The primary purpose of the Terror is to terrify. Recalcitrants are frightened into line by the stress on the unpleasant consequences to those who do not comply with the new rule.[52]

Brinton characterizes this "neutralization of opposition elements"[53] as follows: (a) The habit of violence has been inculcated in the masses and it is

---

[49] Brinton, *op. cit.*, pp. 159–162, "The Failure of the Moderates."

[50] Selznick, *op. cit.*, chap. 6, "Dual Power and the Coup d'Etat."

[51] *Ibid.*, pp. 264–274.

[52] Edwards, *op. cit.*, chap. 8, "The Reign of Terror"; also Chamberlin, *op. cit.*, Vol. I, chap. 23, "Terror, Red and White."

[53] Selznick, *op. cit.*, p. 236. The phrase is Selznick's.

accentuated by the Terror. (b) The pressure of foreign and civil war speeds up the centralization of government and provides the psychological atmosphere for the Terror. (c) The machinery of government is new and the formal controls during the Terror do not always operate with maximum efficiency. (d) The Terror is a time of economic crisis, when the necessities of life are in short supply and production is at a standstill. (e) The class antagonisms of the revolution are accentuated during the Terror. (Thus Jacobins guillotined aristocrats, Bolsheviks shot White Russians, and peasants pursued landlords.) (f) The revolutionary leaders are feeling their power during the Terror, and this period is one of learning and adjustment for them. (g) The intensity of revolutionary faith reaches fanatical heights during the Terror. It is this faith that gives to the Terror its combination of "spiritual fury, of exaltation, of devotion and self-sacrifice, of cruelty, madness, and high-grade humbug."[54]

9. *The Institutionalization of Revolution.* The final stage in the natural history of revolution is the institutionalization of the new myth. The men who have led the revolution consolidate and legalize their power. The groups that once opposed the government now *are* the government. Attitudes toward the basic institutions must be reconciled with the goals of the new regime. The institutionalization of revolution has been described as "the process by which collective behavior which begins outside formal offices and without formal rules, engaged in by unconventional groups of people, in unexpected situations, or in ways contrary to use and wont, develop [sic] formal offices, organized groups, defined situations, and a new body of sanctioned use and wont."[55] The behavior of the masses has run the gamut from the spontaneous agitation of those who were discontented with the *status quo,* through the organized and unorganized excesses of the revolution, to the comparative stability of the postrevolutionary period.

This is also the period of reaction, when the average person is tired of privations, wars, and excesses of zeal and wishes to be let alone to pursue his ordinary life. This is the period of Thermidor, which was the name applied to the time of reaction after the French Revolution, when men attempted to forget the Revolution in the pursuit of pleasure. Thermidor is also marked by the amnesty of political prisoners, the removal of repressions, the return of the organized church, and the emphasis upon social reorganization instead of social disorganization. This does not mean that change has come full cycle and things are the same as before. It means that the revolution has temporarily slowed down in order to take stock of itself and consolidate its position.[56]

Social Disorganization During Revolution

Revolution exemplifies one type of social disorganization in its most complete sense. The traditional relationships that bind the national state together under an accepted system of power are wholly or partially broken. A

---

[54] Brinton, *op. cit.,* pp. 218–225. The quotation appears on p. 223.
[55] Hopper, *op. cit.,* p. 278.
[56] Brinton, *op. cit.,* chap. 8, "Thermidor."

large social organization that was formerly functioning (after a fashion, at least) has suddenly ceased to exist. Many institutional ties are violently disrupted in the process.[57] The groups that are most closely identified with the dominant power status of the old regime tend to ignore the social disorganization that gives rise to revolution. These groups are very conscious of the social disorganization following the implementation of the new regime. A complete picture of revolution should include both forms.

1. *Revolution and Property Rights.* Revolution disorganizes the system of property rights in a society. The early stages are marked by wholesale "appropriations" of the property of the former possessing classes. From the standpoint of the old regime, complete anarchy exists. Many of the thefts are deplored by the responsible leaders of the revolution, but the criminal and quasi-criminal elements cannot resist the temptation. Under the first exhilarating freedom from constraint, the various classes steal from each other—the poor from the rich, the workman from the employer, and the peasant from the landlord. The traditional restraints based upon respect for property rights are temporarily nullified.[58]

The progress of the revolution ultimately results in state control of much of the property formerly owned by private persons or institutions. Stealing declines precipitately, for men are shot for stealing from the state. The new rights of the state are guarded even more zealously than were the personal rights of the old regime. The revolution creates a new privileged class, whose members may not own property themselves but who have access to many of the advantages of property. The system of stratification based upon property is one of the first elements in the social structure to change. The change may or may not be permanent. The propertied classes ultimately assumed many of their former rights after the French Revolution. They have not been able to do so in Russia. It remains to be seen whether or not the property relationships in China have undergone a temporary or permanent change.[59]

2. *Revolution and the Sex Mores.* Previous standards of sex morality are also disorganized during and immediately after a revolution. Some persons deliberately flout traditional sexual controls to show their disrespect for the old order. Others take advantage of the temporary relaxation in control to indulge in sexual behavior that would normally be forbidden by mores and laws alike. There have been many descriptions, some undoubtedly exaggerated, of the sexual excesses carried on under the aegis of the "Goddess of Liberty" during the French Revolution. In the height of the revolutionary enthusiasm, marriage was condemned as an institution fit only for timid poltroons.[60]

In the early days of the Russian Revolution, many young persons aban-

[57] Rudolf Heberle, *Social Movements,* Appleton-Century-Crofts, Inc., New York, 1951, pp. 372–377.

[58] Sorokin, *The Sociology of Revolution,* pp. 58–64.

[59] Cf. Harold R. Isaacs, "The Blind Alley of Totalitarianism," *Annals of the American Academy of Political and Social Science, 276:*81–90 (July, 1951).

[60] Sorokin, *The Sociology of Revolution,* pp. 93–97.

doned conventional moral standards and openly lived together without state license or religious ceremony. For a time, divorce was obtainable by mailing a post-card request to the Marriage Bureau, and abortion was legalized.[61] In recent years, however, there has been a movement away from revolutionary laxity and a return to stricter family ties.

The Chinese Revolution exhibits an interesting departure from the usual revolutionary pattern with regard to sex relations. An effort is apparently being made to minimize the importance of sex, in the ultimate interest of greater revolutionary fervor. Love is officially regarded as bourgeois in origin, and the enjoyment of sexual relationships for their own sake is considered inimical to political solidarity. The attitude is one of militant puritanism, and young people contemplating marriage are encouraged to plight their troth on a basis of political affinity, rather than upon the outlawed attractions of romantic or sexual love. Women are supposed to take their places beside their men in office, farm, and factory, rather than to live as "parasitic" wives who capitalize upon their sexual attractions. The new society of China, like that of the imaginary totalitarian state of George Orwell, is symbolized by women in overalls, not in evening clothes or bathing suits.[62]

3. *Revolution and the Church.* The church is one of the most powerful institutions of a stable society. Hence it is one of the first to come in conflict with a revolutionary regime. The established church, both in eighteenth-century France and in twentieth-century Russia, supported the old order because it was an integral part of that order. It is for this principal reason that any revolutionary party must reckon with the power of the church. Religious and doctrinal considerations, as ordinarily defined, are not the most important factors in this conflict; matters of property, temporal power, education, and social control are paramount. Two ways of life, two forms of control, two powerful institutions are face to face. The power of one must eventually be broken.[63]

The role of the church enforcing old social norms explains in large part the systematic attempt of revolutionary regimes to discourage and eventually destroy organized religion. The disciples of Voltaire were determined to wipe out forever the institution of the church. The Communists attempt to limit the power of Christianity and substitute devotion to the totalitarian state for worship of the gentle Christ. It is a commonplace that revolution itself (more strictly, the revolutionary myth) has become the religion of its devotees.

The revolution thus introduces a new morality, based on secular rather than religious values. In Communist China a double standard of morality is officially taught that is frankly presumed to promote the welfare of the state. There is one standard of morality for the friends and another for the enemies

---

[61] This matter is discussed more fully in Chapter 17.

[62] Hsi-En Chen, *op. cit.*, pp. 342–344. Cf. also George Orwell's *1984* for his account of the totalitarian state of the future.

[63] Brinton, *op. cit.*, pp. 237–242.

of the new regime. The individual is encouraged to love all those who are co-operating with the Revolution. He is encouraged to hate those who are defined as opponents of the Revolution.[64]

4. *Revolution and Human Life.* In commenting upon the initial impact of the Russian Revolution, Chamberlin summarized the situation in a single sentence: "Human life was very cheap in those years." This attitude toward human life is perhaps the most terrible self-indictment of revolution. The years of upheaval following the Russian Revolution were marked by civil war, terror, and wholesale murder. Thousands of men, women, and children were shot down in cold blood by the partisans of both the Reds and the Whites. Innocent merchants were assassinated by the Red secret police on the mere suspicion that they were not wholeheartedly sympathetic to the new regime. Simple peasants were massacred by the White armies if they were suspected of revolutionary sympathies. In such times, man is indeed a wolf to his fellows —*homo homini lupus.*[65]

The men on both sides of the barricades justify this behavior as a necessary, albeit unpleasant, means to a desirable end. Trotsky explains how the Bolshevik philosophy justifies murder as a last resort. Revolution cannot survive, he maintains, if its proponents are too liberal in their treatment of opponents. The more difficult the struggle to overthrow the vested interests, the more drastic the subsequent revolutionary dictatorship must be. According to Trotsky, temporizing is in the end more painful than severe and immediate action.[66] Under such circumstances, human life is unimportant before the myth of the revolution. Gentle country lawyers become fiends in human form. The Paris populace went to executions as to an exciting form of amusement.

The disregard for human life during times of revolution may also be explained by the nature and source of the hatreds released at this time. Many of these hatreds have been generated by the same repressive forces that brought on the revolution—namely, the oppression which the upper classes inflicted consciously or unconsciously upon the lower. When the existing social structure is destroyed, slaves turn upon masters, serfs upon landlords, soldiers upon officers, workers upon owners, and the uneducated upon the educated. In so doing, these groups often wreak vengeance for their own past sufferings upon groups that have had no part in those sufferings. Cruelty begets reciprocal action by the immediate victims. The innocent suffer with the guilty. In this vicious circle, hatred and murder feed upon each other.[67]

Within a given nation revolution is thus a form of social disorganization on a national scale. The breakdown of the social structure is related to revolution in two senses: (1) in the events leading up to (i.e., "causing") the revolution; (2) in the events following (i.e., "resulting from") the revolution. In

[64] Hsi-En Chen, *op. cit.,* p. 341.
[65] Chamberlin, *op. cit..* Vol. I, chap. 36, "The Revolution and Daily Life."
[66] Trotsky, *op. cit.,* Vol. I, p. 236.
[67] Chamberlin, *op. cit.,* Vol. II, pp. 356–357.

each case, statuses are violently modified, roles are changed, and the cultural patterns holding people together in organized groups undergo various stresses and strains. In the modern world, revolution tends to eventuate in the totalitarian state, whether Fascist or Communist. Indeed, the purpose of many (but not all) contemporary revolutionary movements, however much their proponents may protest their "democratic" intentions, is to bring about some form of totalitarian power structure.

World Revolution and America

There is also a world-wide aspect to modern revolutions, totalitarianism, and war.[68] Two world wars and the shadow of a third have placed an indelible stamp on the twentieth century. World Wars I and II ended in revolution and totalitarianism. The Russian Revolution was of a new type, spearheaded by the militant proletariat. Past revolutions have been essentially middle-class in character, even though the bourgeoisie often enlisted the help of the lower classes in their collective enterprise. Proletarian revolution, engineered by professional revolutionaries and aided by the presence of the Red Army, has changed the power structure of eastern Europe since World War II. The subsequent breakdown of the old social order is another example of social disorganization par excellence.[69]

In the Far East, as we have indicated, revolutions of a different type followed World War II. Millions of natives rose against the white colonial powers. These revolutions were accompanied by a strong wave of nationalism, as the native peoples were fired with the desire for independence from the political, economic, and social hegemony of the Western powers. One form of revolutionary movement gained the freedom of the vast subcontinent of India. Another brought the breakdown of the traditional relationships between the Dutch and the people of Indonesia. In China, the Revolution was a struggle between peasants and landlords, workmen and property owners, with the lower classes seizing power through civil war.[70]

The peoples of the Near East and Africa have also heard the siren call of revolution and nationalism. Conflict with the great colonial powers of England and France has arisen in the lands bordering upon the Mediterranean. Egypt, Syria, Morocco, Tunis, and Algeria have been among the countries experiencing political and social revolution, sometimes with civil war, sometimes with undeclared guerrilla war, and sometimes with comparatively little bloodshed. The democratic nations of the West have been in an ambiguous position in relation to these powerful social movements. The traditions of freedom and self-determination are sympathetic to the nationalistic aspirations of

[68] Arnold Toynbee, "New Vistas for the Historian," *Saturday Review, 39*:7–8 (January 7, 1956).

[69] Vera M. Dean, "Revolution in Three Acts," *Foreign Policy Bulletin, 35*:52–55 (December 15, 1955).

[70] See F. F. Liu, *A Military History of Modern China, 1929–1949,* Princeton University Press, Princeton, 1956. Chap. 19 of this book contains an account of the defeat of the Nationalist armies by the Communists.

former colonial peoples. At the same time, the economic interests in the Western nations (notably in oil) have been fearful of the loss of their valuable properties.

These nascent revolutions in the underdeveloped countries have been aided and abetted by international Communism, when it has served the purposes of the Kremlin to support them. The Western nations have been reluctant, at the same time, to admit the validity of the nationalistic hopes of the restless peoples. In some cases, the Western nations have supported the feudal regimes which have subjugated the peoples of the Near East. The forces of international Communism have shrewdly capitalized upon the nationalistic hopes of depressed peoples but have frequently diverted the momentum for their (the Communists') own purposes. The future course of the cold war will, in large measure, be determined by the attitude of the two major conflicting forces—the totalitarian and the democratic—toward these nationalistic movements. As one authority puts it, the crucial consideration is "which side can most promptly and effectively help to complete the uncompleted revolutions of Asia and Africa, [and] the Middle East. . . ."[71]

In the midst of this turmoil of revolution, counterrevolution, and nationalistic war, the English-speaking nations have been singularly free from the violence that has accompanied social change in other parts of the world. Change has been rapid in both Great Britain and America, but it has occurred peacefully. The United States has greatly extended the functions and responsibilities of government in recent decades. The depression of the 1930's and World War II produced the most radical series of social changes of any comparable period in our history. These modifications took place through legislative and administrative processes and in accordance with democratic principles.[72]

Other nations and peoples have not been so fortunate, either now or in the past. The day of violent revolution and counterrevolution is not over. These examples of social disorganization are immediate realities for hundreds of millions of persons throughout the world. They are not details recounted in the history books but living experiences. In the next chapter, we shall deal with the results of these revolutionary changes, totalitarianism, with particular reference to Communism and Fascism.

SELECTED BIBLIOGRAPHY

Aron, Raymond, *The Century of Total War,* Doubleday and Company, Inc., New York, 1954. The present century is wracked by revolution, totalitarianism, and war. In this book a leading French writer discusses the world situation in the decade of the 1950's.

Barber, Elinor G., *The Bourgeoisie in 18th Century France,* Princeton University Press, Princeton, 1955. In this analysis of the structure of prerevolutionary

---

[71] Dean. *op. cit.,* p. 55.

[72] Stuart M. Chapman, "The Right of Revolution and the Rights of Man," *Yale Review,* *43:*576–588 (June, 1954).

France the author contends that the frustration of the status aspirations of the bourgeoisie was an important factor leading to the Revolution.

Brinton, Crane, *The Anatomy of Revolution,* Prentice-Hall, Inc., New York, 1952 (rev. ed.). This is a popular discussion by a noted historian of the "natural history" of revolution (see below), replete with historical insights into the nature of the revolutionary process.

Dean, Vera M., "Revolution in Three Acts," *Foreign Policy Bulletin, 35:52–55* (December 15, 1955). The author of this article discusses the principal forms of revolution in recent decades, ranging from the totalitarian movements of Communism and Fascism to the nationalistic revolutions which are at present convulsing the Near East, the Far East, and Africa.

Edwards, L. P., *The Natural History of Revolution,* University of Chicago Press, Chicago, 1927. In this study of the major revolutions of modern history the author outlines the typical stages in the natural history of these movements and suggests that, despite local variations, they nevertheless follow a definite sociological pattern.

Heberle, Rudolf, *Social Movements,* Appleton-Century-Crofts, Inc., New York, 1951. In this analysis of collective behavior, revolutionary movements are examined in their social settings, with particular reference to the major social movements of the modern world. This is an excellent sociological introduction to social movements, of which revolution is one of the most violent examples.

Hopper, Rex D., "The Revolutionary Process," *Social Forces, 28:270–279* (March, 1950). This article is a significant brief contribution to the sociological theory of revolution, based upon the natural history approach.

Lasswell, Harold D., *et al., The World Revolution of Our Time,* Hoover Institute Studies, Stanford University Press, Stanford, 1951. The twentieth century is the age of world revolution(s). Whether considered individually (e.g., Russian, Chinese) or collectively (e.g., in the history of the modern world), revolution is a central theme of the modern age.

Selznick, Philip, *The Organizational Weapon,* McGraw-Hill Book Company, Inc., New York, 1952. The subtitle of this book is "A Study of Bolshevik Strategy and Tactics," which indicates the subject matter. This is a significant contribution to the theory and tactics of modern revolution.

Trotsky, Leon, *The History of the Russian Revolution,* Simon and Schuster, Inc., New York, 1932. The first great revolution of the twentieth century is described by one of its leaders and principal participants. The author was hardly an impartial observer of these great events, but his (admitted) bias does not nullify the value of the book to a student of social change.

CHAPTER 30

Totalitarianism

Revolution and Totalitarianism

    The revolutionary political methods and type of police state which developed after the seizure of power by the Communists in Russia, the Nazis in Germany, and the Fascists in Italy shook the political structure of the civilized world. Democratic nations have become less democratic themselves in attempting to hold the line against the spread of totalitarianism. The Second World War witnessed the Communist and democratic nations uniting in the great conflict which enveloped the Northern Hemisphere and extended into Africa and the South Pacific. After the capitalist and Communist "democracies" achieved a common victory over the Nazis and Fascists the ideological struggle took a new direction. The United States and the USSR have emerged as the two great powers. Their political and economic ideals are in a mortal struggle for survival in a cold war which keeps the two nations in perilous balance. A large share of the fiscal expenditures of the United States has gone into atomic research, into building military installations and bombing bases, and into maintaining the armed services abroad. Russia has likewise spent large sums on atomic research and has taken over the countries on her eastern border as satellites. She has also aided China and other Asiatic countries in implementing Communist revolutions. Fascism extended its boundaries into Spain, Portugal, and Argentina under Peron's government as well as in other smaller South American countries. Because the totalitarian regimes have made such profound alterations in the social structure of modern society, an examination of the nature and implications of totalitarianism has great significance to the sociologist. Under our very eyes social change is being rapidly implemented, and the class structure of society is being profoundly altered. The social values and institutions of the modern world have been questioned, reassessed, and given greater or lesser importance by the Central Committee and the Presidium of the Supreme Soviet, in whom the authority of the Russian government is vested.

    The general tone of the rigid controls of the Soviet government has softened somewhat in recent years, and any interpretation of what final form Communism will take is problematical. In the extensive literature covering the Soviet regime there is a mass of evidence which indicates the disruptive character of Communism both in the Soviet Union and beyond its borders.

At the same time there are equally impressive data on the material achievements of the Russian economy, the remarkable development of higher education, and the outstanding scientific achievements in atomic research, nuclear physics and astrophysics, and the exploration of outer space. It is a striking fact, as Golob points out, that the best recent analyses of the Soviet regime are objective. There are relatively few books today which present an emotionally biased and outright condemnation of Communism.[1] This is not true for Nazism. Most analyses conclude that the aims and methods of Nazism were an outrage both to human sensibilities and to human intelligence. Meanwhile there has been a milder condemnation of Fascism as it took shape in Italy, Spain, and Portugal.

Our aim in this chapter is to be objective. We shall thus hope to make clear that the shift from a malfunctioning autocratic monarchical government in Russia to the present regime was brutal, disruptive, and disorganizing to the most prized values of Western society. If tyranny is declining it is also true, as Dr. Hocking has said, that "the USSR has inherited a mandate . . . for world revolution,"[2] even where the people are disposed to resist one. At the same time there is some indication "that the ingredient of tyranny still present in spots is on the way out."[3] If so, there is hope. But if more and more nations are involved in violent revolution, totalitarianism will paint a recurrent picture of the disorganization described in this chapter.

Totalitarianism: A Definition

Totalitarianism may be defined as the absolute and authoritarian method or methods by which a revolutionary political organization takes over a government. The new government is thus authoritarian. Totalitarianism aims to take over the power quickly and involves total or absolute control over those governed. As exemplified in German Nazism and Soviet Communism, it vests absolute power in the titular head of the government. Theoretically this was shared in the Soviet Union by the Presidium, which was identical with the Central Committee of the Communist Party. To a lesser degree, Italian Fascism was also totalitarian.

The authority of the titular head of a totalitarian regime is supported and undergirded by an elaborate bureaucratic organization which regulates the economy, the institutional services, including those of health, education, and welfare, housing, marriage and family duties, the courts, and the penal system. The bureaucratic network extends to the remotest village, and many local and provincial authorities wield important powers. Nevertheless, the final and decisive authority is vested in the dictator (or premier) and the chairman of the Central Committee in the case of the Soviet Union (where the chairman of the Central Committee and the premier are the same person). Likewise Hitler in Germany and Mussolini in Italy were vested with absolute power.

[1] Eugene O. Golob, *The Isms*, Harper & Brothers, New York, 1954, pp. 535–538.
[2] William E. Hocking, *Strength of Men and Nations*, Harper & Brothers, New York, 1959, pp. 127–128.
[3] *Ibid.*, p. 47.

Under totalitarianism the decisions of the leader possess the authority of law. Law by decree thus negates any constitutional rules or provisions for preserving the rights and privileges of citizens if the leader holds that a decree is necessary for promoting the interests of the existing order. Tyranny and dictatorships are nothing new in human history. The modern tyranny of totalitarianism, however, is based on a highly bureaucratized system of power in which members of a powerful elite group serve as lieutenants or "cadres" in carrying out the program outlined by the state.

The Common Characteristics of Totalitarianism

All totalitarian dictatorships, whether Fascist or Communists, possess certain identifiable characteristics. As outlined by Friedrich and Brzezinski,[4] these are summarized below with brief explanations. The explanations, however, are only partly derived from Friedrich and Brzezinski.

1. *An Official Ideology.* The ideology aims at providing all members of the supporting society with a comprehensive theory of government and a projection of things to come. It tends to take on a prophetic, messianic character and to be vested with a religious quality.

2. *A Single Mass Party.* This party is led by one man, the dictator, and an organized group of the elite. The latter are regarded as specially competent to promote the aims of the new dictatorship and to give unquestioned acceptance to its ideology. Sometimes the party is superior to the government, but it may be merely inextricably intertwined in the government.

3. *A System of Terroristic Police Control.* This is exemplified in the Gestapo in Germany and the former OGPU and present NKVD in the Soviet Union. The activities of the totalitarian police are characteristically directed, not merely against obvious "enemies" of the regime, but against special classes. (These are illustrated by the liquidation of the Jews and the attack on the Poles by the Nazis, and by the attack on the clergy, the capitalists, and old intelligentsia in Russia.)

4. *An Effective Propaganda Machine.* The propaganda machine is achieved by virtually complete control over mass communication by the party and its cadres. This includes control over the press, radio, TV, and motion pictures. Dramatic production also must be in harmony with the party line. All clergy were intimidated in Germany and Russia and all tax funds for the support of the church in Russia were cut off. Since churches had long been supported by taxes this provided an effective way to close them since there was no plan for voluntary support.

5. *Control over Armed Weapons.* There is virtually complete control over the manufacture and use of arms or other weapons which could be used against the government. This effectively prevents a people's uprising against a tyrannical government.

[4] Carl T. Friedrich and Zbigniew K. Brzezinski, *Totalitarian Dictatorship and Autocracy,* Harvard University Press, Cambridge, 1956, pp. 9–10.

6. *A Centrally Controlled and Directed Operation of the Entire Economy.*
In Fascism, Nazism, and Communism the structure of the government is
identified with the economy. The workers and peasants presumably have
some voice in determining the operation of local factories, farms, or organized
services. In both Nazism and Fascism the cabinet of the central government
was theoretically representative of the various industries. In Italy the Fascist
government in 1938 included twenty-two corporations classified into three
groups: six in agricultural and related industries, ten in manufacturing industries, and six in professional, recreational, and service industries. Members
of the armed services, police, judges, professors, and state employees or agents
of the Ministries of Interior, Foreign Affairs, and Colonies were forbidden to
organize.[5]

The Nazi economic structure was organized into five "estates": the Labor
Front, the Estate of Trade and Industry, the Estate of Crafts, the Estate of
Agriculture, and the Cultural Estate.[6] Their representatives in the government were supposed to advance the interests of each group. Actually they
were the means of instructing the various industries as to the specific tasks
which were to be carried out and, as Friedrich and Brzezinski state, the
particular structure of the government was not important. It was the autocratic decree of the dictator (influenced sometimes by the elite, sometimes by
an autonomous decision) which determined the course of the ship of state.[7]

In the Soviet Union the Council of People's Ministries provides likewise
for a minister for the various industries, but the Communist Central Committee is the real seat of authority, with major power vested in the premier, who
is also the chairman of the Central Committee, as mentioned. Many members
of the Central Committee are also members of the Council of People's
Ministries. The Soviet Union maintains the illusion of representative government, however, through the Supreme Soviet of the nation. This organization
consists of two large bodies: the Soviet of the Union (with from 600 to 700
members), which is composed of local representatives elected from each
electoral district of 300,000 people; and the Soviet of Nationalities, which is
composed of deputies elected from each "national" subdivision of the Soviet
Union and has some 1300 members.[8] The representative bodies actually
have little power. They meet briefly twice a year, primarily to affirm the decisions of the Central Committee. The representatives are elected on a one-party
ballot. Elections are in the nature of a national festival or celebration since
there is no contest for office.[9]

[5] William N. Loucks and J. Weldon Hoot, *Comparative Economic Systems*, Harper &
Brothers, New York, 1948 (rev. ed.), p. 668.
[6] Karl Loewenstein, *Hitler's Germany*, The Macmillan Company, New York, 1939,
pp. 137–154.
[7] Friedrich and Brzezinski, *op. cit.*, p. 18.
[8] Loucks and Hoot, *op. cit.*, p. 581.
[9] W. W. Kulski, *The Soviet Regime*, Syracuse University Press, Syracuse, 1959 (rev.
ed.), p. 74.

The structure of totalitarian governments thus has relatively little importance. The constitutional rights are not enforced by such restraints as are imposed upon the legislative, executive, and judicial branches of a democracy. So long as totalitarianism is in force, the judiciary is a part of the administrative hierarchy free to condemn only according to the dictator's or the supporting bureaucracy's policy.[10]

Dynamics of Totalitarianism

In every instance totalitarianism has developed and maintained its autocratic rule by (1) arousing a fanatical and irrational support of the masses by a systematic control of communication and (2) brutally eliminating anyone who opposed the new regime.

1. *Irrational Support of the Masses.* One of the most striking aspects of totalitarianism is the enthusiasm which the party is able to inspire in the mass of citizens. The social disorganization, economic distress, and tottering governments from which all totalitarian movements emerge are terrifying and confusing experiences to the majority of citizens. The authority and new direction of the leader or dictator are important in inspiring new hope, a belief that there is a Utopia to be achieved. All of this gives the leader a certain messianic character and the whole totalitarian movement takes on a quasi-religious quality. Hitler, known as *Der Führer* (the leader), Mussolini, known best as *Il Duce,* and Lenin, the infallible interpreter of Marx, were not merely heroes; they were saviors leading their adherents into a promised land.[11] Hitler continually exhorted people to believe him because *"Der Führer* knows best." Mussolini demanded that his followers "Believe, obey, fight," while Lenin became the virtual saint of Marxism by pledging the workers a future state in which they would be supreme. Khrushchev in fact refers to the principles of the Communist party as "holy Leninist principles."[12]

2. *The Elite.* The totalitarian movements are also alike in creating an elite group to implement the new regime. In the Soviet Union the alleged goal has been democratic but it has been bent on securing a government *for* the people, not *by* them. The Communist party thus purports to know what the worker wants and what he needs and because of its vested authority imposes its will on all the citizens in order to secure this. The totalitarian movement's tactics which thus seek to benefit the masses are based upon a fundamental belief in the superiority of the elite. It is they who must guide the people to an understanding of what is best for them.

3. *Rigid Control of Means of Communication.* Modern mass means of instantaneous radio, telephonic, and television communication give unlimited

[10] Friedrich and Brzezinski, *op. cit.,* pp. 18–19.
[11] Friedrich and Brzezinski, *op. cit.*
[12] Nikita S. Khrushchev, "Secret Speech Concerning the Cult of the Individual," delivered at the Twentieth Congress of the Communist Party of the Soviet Union, February 25, 1956, in *The Anti Stalin Campaign and International Communism* (edited by the Russian Institute of Columbia University), Columbia University Press, New York, 1956, p. 20.

opportunity to indoctrinate the people. These media are generally employed to reenforce party edicts and to indicate the party line on current affairs. Broadcasts are rigidly censored to keep out anything which might be conceived as opposed to those in power. Thus Hitler conducted his campaign against the "Polish atrocities" as a justification for starting World War II. Mussolini employed radio announcing units on the streets to bring special messages to the people. How to keep broadcasts from democratic countries from reaching the people led to all manner of policing radios. In Germany people were forbidden to listen to British broadcasts, although many defied the order. Since World War II the Soviet Union has developed an effective "jamming" device which prevents the reception of foreign broadcasts. This has been directed particularly at the "Voice of America," which has tried to reach the Russian people and tell them about the values and advantages in the American democratic system. Since the Soviets believe these broadcasts are aimed at undermining their system it is easy to understand why they do not wish their citizens to hear them.

4. *The Press.* Totalitarian governments likewise control the press, both in order to launch progovernment propaganda and as a device for preventing the circulation of true information about Western democracies. Many subtle lies were circulated in the form of news stories in Hitler's Germany. The defects in the political structure of the United States are frequently "blown up" in a disproportionate fashion today in the USSR; thus it is held that there is no democracy in a country which denies the Negro his political rights, and pictures of slum areas in American cities are displayed as an index to the housing standards in America. The Soviet press is the voice of the Central Committee.

5. *The Church.* Totalitarianism particularly in Nazi Germany and Russia has relentlessly punished the clergy for teachings antithetical to the state.[13] In Fascist Italy Mussolini made a cynical compromise with the Vatican. Hitler attacked the church rather obviously because the Christian doctrine of "loving your enemies" was the opposite of the methods employed by the Nazis to eliminate their enemies. In this the Communists hold the same point of view. "Loving your enemies" according to Communist doctrine is tantamount to "loving evil"! To the Communist there is no comprehension that one can love the individual while deploring his evil ways.

In consequence the Nazis and Communists both made war on the church although initially the Nazis rejected the Communists' atheistic philosophy (as a part of their general rejection of Communism). The Nazis and Fascists were less open in their anti-Christian attacks, but the Communists launched a bold attempt to liquidate the Russian Orthodox Church because Communism is *avowedly atheistic*. All church property and church schools and seminaries passed over to ownership of the state. Many priests (those who raised their voice against such action) were executed and some of the churches were converted into Anti-Religious Museums in an effort to convince the people

[13] See Friedrich and Brzezinski, *op. cit.*, chap. XXIII, for a detailed discussion of totalitarianism and the churches.

of the outmoded, unscientific, and in some instances vicious nature of the church. A few churches were permitted to remain open, but all of their former means of support through taxes was withdrawn. In consequence the churches in Russia were very poor after the Revolution. In the Thirties the few remaining churches were well attended but the bulk of the congregation were older people, who had not been as thoroughly indoctrinated as the young people. Older people were usually considered hopeless and the major attempt to indoctrinate was directed toward those twenty-four years of age or younger.[14] As a further effort to divorce the people from the church, marriage was secularized.

During World War II, however, the clergy both in Germany and in the Soviet Union supported their national governments. Meanwhile a group of "German Christians" had developed in Germany who tried to reconcile the Nazi ideology with the Christian faith. This move outraged the Protestant clergy, who organized in protest. The Catholic Church also subsequently took a stand against its previous attempt to compromise on political issues.[15] There was therefore widespread retaliation against the church in Germany, which was relaxed only because of the war effort of the clergy.

In Russia the softened approach to religion during World War II was in part at least a gesture toward the United States and Great Britain as their wartime "Christian" allies although the Russian church also gave widespread support to the Soviet effort to drive out the Nazis. This tolerance has continued. Today new churches are built occasionally by the Soviet Union after proper applications have been filed, but there is no financial support and most of the young people never enter a church. The current official attitude of Khrushchev and the Central Committee is that "religion is a matter of conscience." Even so, no clergyman can oppose the party line or official action; hence the church cannot protest atheistic propaganda. Anyone who is not a Communist may belong to a church but he cannot engage in Christian education if more than three persons are present. There are no Sunday schools, no parochial schools, no religious young people's organizations or evangelistic meetings. One can merely attend a church service or a choir rehearsal.[16]

It should be stated in passing that Communism today wants party members and the Soviet people as a whole to lead a good life and to observe a strict moral code.[17] During the early days of the Revolution this was not true. There were many sexual excesses. The clergy meanwhile have accepted their attenuated role apparently as a part of the trial of being Christians. The church's main emphasis is therefore on the inner life and the life eternal. It functions by taking no issue with the government.[18] This may be a response to the

---

[14] This information was given to Miss Elliott by Soviet officials on a visit to the Soviet Union.

[15] Friedrich and Brzezinski, *op. cit.,* p. 255.

[16] Marcus Bach, *God and the Soviets,* Thomas Y. Crowell Company, New York, 1958, p. 199.

[17] *Ibid.,* p. 110.

[18] *Ibid.,* chap. III.

stepped-up antireligious "educational" campaign which the Central Committee has promoted since 1954.[19]

6. *The Surveillance of the Police State.* The surveillance of the totalitarian police state makes it very difficult for individuals or groups to dissent from authoritarian decrees. Any suspect individual is constantly watched and often summarily dispatched to prison or the firing squad on little if any valid evidence. During the Nazi regime countless people simply disappeared and their fate was never known to friends or relatives. In Russia the liquidation of the nobility and the educated class was carried on without any evidence at all of their illegal or antisocial conduct. Many had not even made any open avowal of opposition. They were eliminated because they were members of a hated privileged class.

The passport system for native citizens was instituted by the Soviets as a special aspect of the police state. All urban residents in the Soviet Union must carry a passport, which does possess certain advantages of identification. The name, date of birth, sex, military status, residence, marital status, date of employment, and date of arrival in a community are all stamped in the passport. The rigid enforcement of passport rules is one of the ways in which the individual is severely regimented in the USSR. All his comings and goings must be known.

Thus the passport in a real sense circumscribes the freedom of the individual for he cannot leave home without it. The Soviet government regards the passport as essential to the protection of the public order and to state security.[20] Many European states (Germany, for example) likewise require all strangers to register with the police, if they stay more than a few days. The Russians also regard the passport as protection against fleeing criminals or escaped prisoners. (The latter are not granted passports). Again, passports are considered an aid to the preservation of morals. No couple can register at a hotel as man and wife if their passports do not record their marriage. The major reason for exacting passports of native-born citizens is, however, political. It is a matter of being able to check quickly on the identity of an individual and his purpose in being in a particular place.

All publications, newspapers, and radio scripts are subject to censorship and all printing presses are controlled by the state. All meetings must be licensed in advance; hence "freedom of association" is obviously limited. All voluntary associations must apply to the Presidium of the Supreme Soviet for authorization and the associations' objectives must correspond with those of the state. Farmers' cooperatives or collective farms and fishermen are not permitted to have national or territorial unions (presumably because of fear that they might acquire political power). Industrial cooperatives may have local unions but no national, regional, or district meetings.[21] Farmers in Russia as elsewhere are notably individualistic and the government is taking no risk.

[19] Friedrich and Brzezinski, *op. cit.,* pp. 253–254.
[20] Kulski, *op. cit.,* p. 413.
[21] *Ibid.,* pp. 146–147.

Meanwhile any association which is formed to promote nonconformist ideas is considered counterrevolutionary. Only where such counterrevolutionary activities are considered relatively harmless is there any clemency.[22]

THE ROOTS OF TOTALITARIANISM

Revolutionary Movements in the Nineteenth Century

There have been many attempts to explain why such a brutal and terrifying phenomenon of twentieth-century Western culture as totalitarianism should have occurred. Certain scholars have tried to fasten responsibility to a single reason for such a reversal in democratic trends. Obviously, however, there was no one cause for these organized attempts to alter the basic democratic institutions and social values. It is of course true from the sociological point of view that social disorganization and social change precipitated the Communist seizure of power in Russia, Hitler's rise to power in Germany, and Mussolini's March on Rome.

Yet the roots of totalitarianism go much deeper than the social disorganization occasioned by tottering monarchies, upset economic structures, and the cynical disillusionment following the Versailles Treaty, although these are often alleged to be the "causes" of totalitarianism. The roots of totalitarianism were entwined in the political and economic ferment which had disturbed the crowns of Europe for more than 150 years. The Marxian practice of making a person suspect and therefore guilty because he belonged to the privileged class is the counterpart of the rule enforced during the French Revolution's Reign of Terror under Robespierre's leadership.

The notion that the will of the people (translated by Marx to the interests of the working class) must be imposed by those who see it correctly (i.e., by the elite) is likewise inherent in Rousseau's doctrine of the social contract. As Rousseau expressed this, ". . . the people always desire good, but left to themselves they do not always know where the good lies."[23] Rousseau's "Legislator" therefore had to shape the young nation with the assistance of laws revealed to his superior wisdom.[24] Thus the general will of the people is an imposed will which by its nature negates the slow lumbering legislative processes of the Western democracy. The doctrine of Rousseau also prepared the way for the dictatorship of the proletariat in the shape of an elite. Robespierre and his aide Saint-Just developed the dynamic quality of the idea in the dictatorship of the Jacobins during the French Revolution. These men reduced the matter of achieving an equalitarian state to a set of intellectual rationalizations or deductions which have been called scientism. Precisely the same argument has provided the present-day Communists with a similar reason for calling the principles of Communism "scientific."[25] The logic of Com-

---

[22] *Ibid.*, p. 149.

[23] Cited by J. F. Talman, *The Rise of Totalitarian Democracy*, Beacon Press, Boston, 1952, pp. 47–48.

[24] *Ibid.*, p. 49.

[25] *Ibid.*, parts I and II, has an excellent discussion of this.

munism, coldly reasoned from broad generalizations, gives it its claim to be scientific. Its actual implementation in the Soviet Union, like that of the Jacobins' ideology, was a matter of improvisation. When the Soviet plan (which was presumed to work) appeared to be failing, a new plan was quickly put into operation.[26] Thus Robespierre may well be called the prototype of Stalin. In order for people to be equal they must think alike, act alike, and accept a common thesis, according to totalitarian doctrine. Free communication in France was curtailed by Robespierre and he intended to enforce this censorship until other nations "became as France."[27] Even the "Iron Curtain" was thus a part of the revolutionary scheme in France although it was not so designated.

Pan-Slavism and Pan-Germanism

In 1870, as Talman points out, the French role as the political Messiah of Western Europe died out. But the French revolutionary spirit spread eastward to Russia where Pan-Slavism had already fostered a messianic complex in the Russian people.[28] The Russians believed their political destiny was to unite all Slavs and they had been revolting in a series of uprisings against the oppressive Russian monarchy for many years. This belief in their destiny was further augmented by the Russian Orthodox Church's conception of its role as the only true church and the conviction that the real seat of the church was in Russia and not in Rome.[29]

Hannah Arendt believes Pan-Slavism was the major factor in the Russian Communist Revolution and that Pan-Germanism was equally potent in fomenting Nazism. Both movements had their intellectual proponents. Pan-Slavism was an intellectual movement in czarist Russia and Pan-Germanism a student-oriented movement which was originated by one man, Georg von Schoenerer, in Austria.[30] Both movements were imperialistic in their philosophy and were promoted by the desire of organized groups to expand in order to unite peoples of similar ethnic origin. They represented what Miss Arendt calls a "tribal nationalism." Both in Russia and in Austria-Hungary nation and state were separate entities in which the state imposed its rule on diverse nations. For the rest of Europe, on the other hand, the state and the nation were identified as "nation-states" (as a result of the political developments following the French Revolution).

These same Pan movements developed a special mystique, the claim to being a divinely chosen people, as contrasted to the Judeo-Christian idea of man as created by God in the mythical, generic sense. In Christian nations,

[26] *Ibid.*, pp. 66–77.

[27] *Ibid.*, pp. 132–148.

[28] *Ibid.*, pp. 252–253.

[29] Cf. in this connection Alexei S. Khomyakov and Ivan S. Aksakov, "Slavophil and Orthodox Russia," in Hans Kohn (ed.), *The Mind of Modern Russia*, Rutgers University Press, New Brunswick, 1955, pp. 104–108, and Georgii P. Fedotov, "Russia and Freedom," in *ibid.*, pp. 257–281.

[30] Hannah Arendt, *The Origins of Totalitarianism* (translated by Therese Pol), Meridian Books, New York, 1958 (2nd ed.), p. 238.

therefore, men were held to be possessed of certain natural God-given equal rights (which may be defined as the political rights of man). We cannot go into the history of the Pan movements here, but some knowledge of the Pan-Slav and the Pan-German ideology is essential to understanding the fervor with which Nazism and Communism were supported by the masses. Both gave the sense of historical destiny to the adherents of these extremes of totalitarianism.

These two peoples—the Germans and the Russians—were thus able to acquire a sense of mission. The Communists have followed to a marked degree the blueprints of the Pan-Slavs in extending their empire while retaining the Pan-Slav's love for the limitless power of bureaucracy as it had been previously exerted by the czarist government. The Communists did not have to justify arbitrary power. It was part of their heritage. The Pan-German Nazism, originating as it did in Austria, likewise retained the law of decree of the Austro-Hungarian monarchy when it took over Germany and extended its empire to neighboring states.[31] The collapse of Germany and of the Austro-Hungarian monarchy after World War I provided the opportunity for the spread of Pan-Germanism. The decline of the Russian monarchy made the later seizure of power by the Communists relatively easy.

Anti-Semitism

The waning of the nation-states which made it possible for the Pan movements to assume important dimensions was accompanied by the rise of modern anti-Semitism. This is one of the most striking facts in the background of totalitarianism. The weakening of the European monarchies (or the nation-states) was apparently largely responsible for the simultaneous decline of the Jew in international and national affairs. We have already discussed the influence of the Jewish financial advisers and bankers in the courts of Europe and the marked rise of anti-Semitism following World War I. Both modern anti-Semitism and the emancipation of the Jews from noncitizenship had their beginnings in France. During the French Revolution Robespierre objected strenuously both to the Jews' desire to be a culturally autonomous group and to their leading an isolated (or ghetto) existence. He therefore made the Jewish people citizens of France with full political equality. Jews as a "nation within a nation" were not allowed to exist[32] because Robespierre feared such an arrangement. Following the French Revolution the Jews in eastern and central Europe were likewise politically emancipated by the rising nation-states during the nineteenth century.

The nation-states unfortunately did not provide any true equality for the masses of people as the French revolutionists had hoped. Instead class status was an important aspect of the individual European's social condition up to World War I. In Germany the members of the aristocracy were even privileged before the law, but in all countries an individual's position in society

[31] *Ibid.,* chap. VII, "Continental Imperialism, the Pan Movements."
[32] *Ibid.,* pp. 11–12.

depended almost wholly on his birth. The only exception was in the case of the Jews, who lived almost wholly outside the European social system. As Miss Arendt says, the Jews were "neither workers, middle class people, landowners or peasants,"[33] although economically they were often well-off.

Miss Arendt maintains that modern anti-Semitism stems largely from the fact that so many Jews were wealthy after World War I. Many Jews were able to survive the financial ruin of nations occasioned by the war and to do so because of their international connections. Jewish international bankers who were the financial advisers to crumbling monarchical states often did not ally themselves with the states. They loaned money as an economic service, not because they were national patriots. The anti-Semitic movement was already organized, however, as an outgrowth of resentment of their nonassimilated status by an upper- and middle-class group, with the noblemen for protagonists and the howling mob of petty bourgeoisie for chorus, as Friedrich Engels said.[34]

Anti-Semitism had in fact reached serious proportions during the latter part of the nineteenth century when leaders in the movement tried to enlist the conservative leaders in the Catholic Church in France and Austria and the Protestant Church in Germany—some of whom capitulated. Anti-Semitic parties were organized which made no secret of their purpose and aim to eliminate the Jews. They also aimed to eliminate the nation-states because they held that Jews were the power behind these states. The anti-Semitic parties were the "parties above all parties," i.e., international in character.[35]

The first international Anti-Semitic Congress was held in Dresden in 1882 with 3000 delegates. It was partly precipitated by the financial scandals involved in the construction of the Panama Canal, in which Jewish bankers were involved with the French government. By the end of the century the excitement over the swindles had died down, but anti-Semitism again reared its ugly head in the famous Dreyfus affair in 1894. In this case, Dreyfus, an officer of the French General Staff, was convicted of espionage and sentenced to deportation on Devil's Island for life. Many people believed there was an anti-Semitic plot against Dreyfus and the case was widely debated. Consequently Dreyfus' sentence was reduced to ten years. After two years in prison he was pardoned and later, in 1906, acquitted of all charges.

The Dreyfus affair and the later anti-Semitic movement both gained much of their furor from the circulation of the "Protocols of the Elders of Zion." This document contained the alleged Jewish plot to conquer the world which we have discussed in Chapter 27. It was circulated to an even greater extent following the end of World War I and was widely believed by the masses. That it was an outrage to common sense seemed to be in its favor. In the confusion and distress imposed by tottering empires and economic ruin people believed the unbelievable. Out of this anti-Semitic movement Nazism was un-

[33] *Ibid.*, pp. 12–13.
[34] *Ibid.*, p. 37.
[35] *Ibid.*, pp. 37–38.

questionably sparked. And out of the latter movement grew the systematic extermination of European Jews.

The Slavic peoples of Russia were also on Hitler's list for elimination. They are non-Teutonic and therefore inferior, according to his Aryan prejudice. Within Germany the Communists, the Social Democrats, the racially impure (i.e., the partly Jewish), and the churches were also "the people's enemies."[36] Anti-Semitism was thus more than anti-Semitic; it was anti-Christian and anti-human. For the outrageous destruction of human beings on the basis of religious and ethnic origin involves all that is antithetical to Christian teachings and humane beliefs.

Atheism

Some have held that anti-Semitism is a basic characteristic of the totalitarian personality. This is obviously not necessarily true. Communists in power have not been anti-Semitic to any significant degree except during Stalin's regime.[37] Any anti-Semitism in recent years in Russia has been primarily against Jewish desire for representation as a nation. No religion is promoted in Russia. Even so, the Jewish religion is tolerated and that is all that can be said for Communistic treatment of any religion. Karl Marx, the founder of the Soviet Communistic theory, was anti-Semitic, however. He was born of Jewish German parents who became Christians when he was a small boy and he was reared in the Christian faith. Subsequently he became an atheist, however, and his atheistic principles were implemented by Lenin in the Communist doctrine followed by the USSR.

Lenin, like Marx, was also a Jew, but an atheist. Nevertheless, both Marx and his followers accept the Christian ideal of the brotherhood of man. But in rejecting the religious aspect of Christianity, Communism has no compunction against employing brutal and un-Christian methods in creating its new regime. In final analysis anti-Semitism is easily merged in totalitarianism's atheism, which permits brutal liquidation of all who disagree with its aims or block its plans. The individual has no worth per se.

Although Karl Marx himself was violently anti-Semitic, this has not been well known (outside of Jewish circles) because his attacks on the Jews have been expurgated from most of the English translations of his writings. The vitriolic character of his anti-Semitism is clear in the little book *World Without Jews,* published in this country in 1959. It contains a series of three of Marx's essays on Bruno Bauer's books *The Jewish Question*[38] and *The Capacity of Today's Jews and Christians to Become Free.*[39] In these books Bauer states that the "Jew has the privilege of being a Jew" and thus has rights that the Christian does not have. He then asks why the Jew should demand emancipation from the Christian state. Bauer contends that the Jew

---

[36] *Ibid.*
[37] Cf. Dagobert D. Runes, "Introduction," in Karl Marx, *World Without Jews,* Philosophical Library, Inc., New York, 1959, pp. i-xii.
[38] Published in Braunschweig, 1843.
[39] Published in Zurich and Winterthur, 1843.

wants the state to give up its prejudice but that he, the Jew, does not wish to give up *his* prejudice. The Christian state cannot emancipate the Jew from his religion and Bauer therefore contends that the Jew is asking the impossible.[40]

Marx believed that Christianity was ethically superior to Judaism but that both should be shed like snakeskins. He therefore replied to Bauer's question of how Jews could expect to be emancipated by maintaining that they could be emancipated only "by the emancipation of society from Jewry"![41] This means, of course, that Judaism should disappear. Marx made a number of very bitter attacks on the Jews in this connection, saying they were wholly materialistic in their religion. He raised and answered two questions: "What is the object of the Jew's worship in this world? Usury. What is his worldly God? Money."[42]

One must remember that Jews were the most important international bankers at the time he was writing. But Marx went on to say, ". . . *Emancipation from usury, that is from practical, real Judaism would constitute the emancipation of our time.*"[43] Marx as the father of Communism was thus an important source of the anti-Semitism which became such a significant factor in the political movements of the 1880's and 1890's. Marx's doctrine of the need for emancipating the world from Jews plus the alleged plot of the Jews for world mastery furnished Hitler with part of his platform for their annihilation. Runes claims that Colonel Nasser today (as Khrushchev's ally) is distributing the nefarious "Protocols of the Elders of Zion" in Egypt.[44]

When Khrushchev was in the United States in September, 1959, he stated that Jews had religious freedom in the Soviet Union. This is true in that they have as much as any religious group. Jewish people reply that they have no political rights, that they cannot be members of the Supreme Soviet or serve as officers of the army and navy. They also maintain that Stalin threatened to deport all Jews to the Marshlands of Biro-Bidjan in Siberia.[45] Had the Jews been willing to go to this desolate area, conceivably they could have been a nation. The Soviet Union recognizes no representation except on a territorial basis. *There is no religious representation in the Supreme Soviet.* Nor can any avowed Christian (of whom there are many more than Jews) hold any office in the Soviet Union. The Communists also object to the Zionist movement because it advances the political control of the Jewish religion. When religious groups ask for political representation they are seeking what both Marxian doctrine and the present government oppose in the nature of their philosophy of state! It could even be interpreted as treasonous.

[40] Marx, *op. cit.,* pp. 1–2. (It should be remembered that Marx was writing during the period in which the Christian church was the state religion and the king served by "divine right.")

[41] *Ibid.,* p. 45.

[42] *Ibid.,* p. 37.

[43] *Ibid.,* pp. 36–37. (Our italics.)

[44] Runes, *op. cit.,* pp. vii-viii.

[45] *Ibid.,* p. vi.

In the academies of science, in museums and libraries where there is little or no chance of promoting their special interests Jews are permitted positions without discrimination. They are not permitted to print Hebrew calendars, or to publish in Yiddish or Hebrew. They may, however, publish in Russian.[46] Christians have no special language in Russia. This fact apparently enhances the Communist argument that no group should have a special language unless it is a territorial group.

Atheism rather than anti-Semitism is thus a basic characteristic of both Nazism and Communism. With the acceptance of an ideology hostile to religion, it was possible for Hitler, Lenin, and later Stalin to justify intellectually the systematic purges of all persons who they believed stood in the way of achieving their respective goals. Part of the goal of Nazism was to exterminate the Jews. The goal of Communism is to achieve the good life for the worker through a unified state by eliminating any person who (from the dictator's point of view) stands in the way. This attempt to achieve good ends by immoral means has been a disillusioning process to many of the intellectuals who once supported Communism but have since deserted its ranks.[47]

The Moral Crisis of Sensate Culture

The atheism which is a part of Communism Sorokin believes to be inherent in what he calls our sensate culture. He maintains that the most important aspect of all the social changes that precipitated totalitarianism was the moral crisis, in which we are still enmeshed and which is inherent in the decline of the sensate (or materialistic) culture. Western culture, both in America and in Europe, is in an extraordinary crisis, Sorokin thinks, and in the process of disintegrating.[48] It has become increasingly sensate since 1300, with a consequent deterioration of spiritual values, as manifest in forms of art, empirical systems of philosophy, scientific discovery, and technical invention. With the emphasis upon material culture, spiritual values decline and all contractual relationships suffer.

To Sorokin neither revolution, totalitarianism, nor war is to be explained in itself. These things are rather indices and symptoms of a decaying *sensate* culture. Cultures fluctuate between (1) those which are idealistic and which have spiritual values (as was true of the Middle Ages) and (2) the culture which has dominated the last 600 years and is basically concerned only with the physical, the empirical, the secular and utilitarian.[49] Sorokin believes that we are now sloughing off this dominantly sensate culture and that the present crisis is part of the pains of transition.[50] The disintegration of a sensate culture occurs according to a relatively precise pattern. First there is the crisis, then

[46] Philip Ben, "Jewish Life Today in the Soviet Union," *The New Republic, 140*:11–12 (February 9, 1959).

[47] Cf. Richard Crossman (ed.), *The God That Failed,* Harper & Brothers, New York, 1949.

[48] Pitirim A. Sorokin's book *The Crisis of Our Age,* E. P. Dutton and Company, Inc., New York, 1945, discusses this in detail.

[49] *Ibid.,* pp. 17–23.

[50] *Ibid.,* chap. VI.

the ordeal, the catharsis, the charisma (or healing grace), and the resurrection (or revitalized social order).[51] Sorokin's theory of totalitarianism is thus somewhat theological, but he has built up a sizable amount of empirical (or "sensate") data to corroborate it.

Escape from Freedom

To Eric Fromm, on the other hand, Nazism was essentially a psychological problem and the hold it had over the Germans can be understood only in psychological terms. The Germans were tired and without hope following their defeat and the post-World War I depression and Nazism appealed to them because of its authoritarian nature. The dictator has a fanatical urge for power. The persons who submit to the authority of Fascism or Nazism (Fromm insists) find some security and escape from responsibility in being united with millions of others who share the same feelings. The authoritarian ideology which glorifies the leader and the Nazi practices is thus a neurotic symptom of the group. This has a function for the group comparable to that of an individual's neurotic symptom by which he escapes unbearable psychological conditions. Life then becomes possible even though the solution is not a happy one.[52] The escape from freedom does not bring true happiness because it is contrary to the growing desire for freedom which, in Fromm's estimation, is "the necessary result of the process of individuation and the growth of culture."[53]

It is true that Hitler was supported by mass enthusiasm. But he and his confreres including the Storm Troopers also employed all manner of psychological devices to stir up enthusiasm. Nazi mass meetings were held for the purpose of promoting hypersuggestibility. Teaching was controlled, as we shall discuss. Lies, and especially the "Big Lie," were widely disseminated to promote cooperative behavior. And terror was used as a major device for inducing conformity, as we have mentioned.

Escape from freedom is a partial psychiatric explanation for Nazism. But is not the whole truth, for it ignores the factor of fear. Hitler was a master strategist in the use of fear and struck people where it hurt them most. Those who were "politically unreliable" were fired from their jobs. Those who took stern issue with the Nazi atrocities were routed to prison or concentration camp or had to flee the country. Those of relatively high position were often placed under the strain of having their parents put to death if they did not capitulate. Many people lacked the courage of their convictions because they were afraid. Fear made the German people vulnerable to the outrages of Nazism.

Suggestibility

Part of the explanation for the success of any totalitarian movement is the fact of mass psychology, implemented by the various controls of com-

[51] *Ibid.*, pp. 321–325.
[52] See Eric Fromm, *Escape from Freedom,* Rinehart and Company, Inc., New York, 1941, pp. 209–210.
[53] *Ibid.*, p. 239.

munication as discussed later. Nazism rose amidst the economic and political collapse in Germany, which the Weimar Republic was helpless to overcome. Yet the German people were as skillful and competent as they had ever been. Hitler and his advisers saw correctly that the real wealth of the people lay in their productive power, not in their monetary system. This is one of the few truths incorporated in the Nazi ideology.[54] By identifying the economic structure with the state, by rigidly planning the economy, and by developing a strong military structure Hitler restored the Germany economy. He gave the people purchasing power, even though their money was worth little in international exchange.

Hitler also built up an army to "save them from Communism," which absorbed the unemployed males and put people to work. The mode of greeting was changed from *"Grüss Gott"* or *"Guten Morgen"* to *"Heil Hitler."* The discouraged and defeated unemployed had jobs and Hitler became their hero. The troops marched in the streets, singing, as a further means of enlisting emotional support. The shocking anti-Semitism, the unbelievable distortion of truth, the brutal methods against those who dissented were accepted by the masses in much the same way that lynching mobs are induced to violence. They were safe as long as they cooperated and they lost any sense of individual responsibility for heinous crimes committed by the whole group at the instigation of a leader.

That the fanaticism of the masses was deliberately cultivated by *Der Führer* and his elite group, the masses did not realize. That the defeated Germans were to become the rulers of the world expanded the ego of the most lowly. It also fired the zeal of some persons who were better educated. Even some clergymen were at first inclined to cooperate, but the moral and ethical depravity of Nazism eventually brought many of these to protest. Certain intellectuals, notably the university professors, pursued their research and teaching by "keeping still" on political issues. Those who did not were imprisoned or liquidated.

A truly objective analysis of the far reaches of the collective behavior of the Nazis is yet to be written. But the organization of German young people in the Youth Movement, the deliberate distortion of education, the control of the press, the constant repetition of slogans, of lies, and of anti-Semitic propaganda, and the use of deceit are object lessons in how to overcome socially accepted principles of decency or concern for the fundamental dignity of man. The gullibility of human beings is a fearful weapon in the hands of the unscrupulous.

In the case of Communism, Lenin similarly justified the liquidation of the "enemies of the people," i.e., those in the upper classes and old aristocracy. A few upper-class members became adherents of the new order—but these were often so distrusted that they eventually were deported to labor camps

[54] See Frank Munk, *The Legacy of Nazism,* The Macmillan Company, New York, 1943, for a detailed analysis of the economics of Nazism.

or shot. The intrigue and liquidation of the revolutionary phase of Communism under Lenin did not decline when Stalin came to power. For dictators in any totalitarian government tend to become obsessed with their power. Most of the old aristocracy was out of the way under Stalin, but the ruthlessness of the Communist state increased. In its initial stages the goals of Communism, especially that of the brotherhood of man, were ends for which the brutal means was condoned.

The roots of totalitarianism are thus complex; they are historical and cultural; they are also psychological. People are led to believe in ideas which are contrary both to good sense and to human decency. They are led to behave contrary to all established convictions with reference to human rights. Why? It is not easy to explain. The old struggle between good and evil which has concerned the philosophers since time immemorial is obviously involved. Does behaving in an evil fashion have a special fascination for the mob? How can mass murder and the complete abnegation of humane values contribute to the cult of the individual which Khrushchev has so forcefully accused Stalin of promoting in his famous secret speech to the Central Committee?[55] Hitler believed that evil doing had a morbid attraction for the masses. The fanaticism of the Nazis in Germany and the leftist revolutionists in Russia seems to indicate that he was right.[56] It is also a strange fact that Stalin trusted Hitler and refused to believe his own associates when they warned him that the Germans were preparing to invade the Soviet Union.[57]

SOCIAL DISORGANIZATION IN INSTITUTIONS AND SOCIAL VALUES

There is no question that important achievements were made in Italy and Germany under Fascism in the field of science, in the development of economic productivity, in improved standards of living. The Soviet Union has likewise made marked gains and the Communist scientific achievements in the field of astrophysics have astounded the Western world. But the curtailment of the civil rights and freedoms of man under the political controls of totalitarianism is one of the most serious examples of disorganization in the human purposes underlying political institutions.

These aspects of social disorganization include the political restrictions on human liberty and freedom, the brutal methods condoned for achieving the ends of the state, the distortion and censorship of truth which has affected both general information and education and made it impossible for the people to know the nature of life outside the boundaries of the police state. The purposes of education have often been subverted to the ends of propaganda and political goals. Religious institutions which have been the major source of

---

[55] Khrushchev, *op. cit.*, pp. 1–89.
[56] Arendt, *op. cit.*, p. 307.
[57] Khrushchev, *op. cit.*, pp. 43–45.

ethical principles in Western civilization have likewise been seriously under-mined. These are only a few of the aspects of "organized disorganization" which occur under a state which has unlimited power.

Human Freedoms

The liberation of the human spirit has been inherent in the political philosophy of the Western democracies. That they have not succeeded in giv-ing all classes of people the same degree of freedom is evidenced in the dis-parities in education and social and economic status of the individual, as well as the particular opportunities he may have. Our democracies are by no means ideal states, but they have been the most effective human strivings to-ward the common welfare to date. In totalitarian governments the individual is subjected to the tyrannical power of the state, allegedly to eliminate the enemies of the new order and to make it possible for the government to carry on its program. Under totalitarianism the individual has no guaranteed free-doms to protect him from the excesses of legislation, the tyrannical exercise of power by the dictators, or unrestricted judicial authority.

All totalitarian governments have set up constitutions theoretically giving the individual certain rights, but policies of the dictators are able to set aside any rights which citizens may presume to have. Thus Hitler instituted the law of decree, and in Italy Mussolini took over a large share of the portfolios in his cabinet. In a very real sense, indeed, Mussolini *was the cabinet*. In both Fascist countries, human liberty became a very limited matter, while the state became an end in itself.

In the Soviet Union, the Central Committee passed a resolution assuring Soviet citizens various rights. Among them were the "right to labor, educa-tion, leisure, participation in state affairs, freedom of speech, and of the press, freedom of conscience and also a real opportunity for the free development of personal abilities and other democratic rights and freedoms for all members of society without exception."[58] The resolution added, however, that "the essence of democracy is not in formal appearances but in whether the political power really serves and reflects the will and interest of the majority of the people, the interests of the working people."[59]

The Constitution (Article 125) further provides the right to hold mass meetings, as well as street processions and demonstrations. All such activities must be specifically authorized by permission in advance and all organizations must be approved by the Presidium of the Soviet State. The government can also dissolve any organization when its objectives are considered inimical to the state.[60] Article 124 of the Constitution likewise provides for freedom of conscience and religious worship, as well as freedom of antireligious propa-ganda. Because official Communist doctrine is avowedly atheistic the state

[58] "Resolution of the Central Committee of the Communist Party of the Soviet Union, June 30, 1956," published by *Pravda,* Moscow, on July 2, 1956, in *The Anti Stalin Campaign and International Communism,* p. 296.
[59] *Ibid.*
[60] Kulski, *op. cit.,* pp. 146–147.

thus authorizes the antireligious propaganda but does not permit religious propaganda, as we have mentioned before.[61]

Freedom of Occupation and Enterprise

Freedom of enterprise and of occupational choice is a relative matter even in the Western world. Intelligence, family position, economic status, and particular environment all limit whether or not an individual will be able to pursue the long years of study which the professions require or to preside over a business. Family background and parental as well as individual ambition are also factors in occupational choice. We have a great deal of choice, even so, and there has always been a sizable degree of social mobility in the United States. A large share of the leaders in industry and finance, as well as in the professions, have come from a rural background. This is particularly true in the South and Midwest, where much of the wealth is rural. In our most productive agricultural areas, farm income and educational standards are high and rural children can rise on the occupational ladder.

Despite great increases in educational opportunity in the Soviet Union, the present-day peasant cannot decide for himself that he will seek work in the city, or as a young man (or woman) attend a university. In fact, the Soviet peasant cannot go to a city or town for more than five days because he has no passport. Since the peasant has to market his produce and purchase necessary items, he is allowed this five-day privilege. He cannot transfer to another collective farm without permission. If there is need for industrial workers in some special field, he may be recruited or in a rare instance he may be permitted further education.

Dehumanization Through Brutality

The dehumanizing effects of brutality are hard to measure. The tactics of the Communists have often been brutal, however, even in the eyes of Communists! Khrushchev, in his amazing secret speech on February 25, 1956, to the Twentieth Congress of the Communist Party of the Soviet Union in Moscow, condemned unmercifully Stalin's ruthless liquidations of both the masses and the Communists themselves. Khrushchev, in fact, accused Stalin of originating the concept of "enemy of the people" and permitting the execution of such "enemies" *without any proof of guilt.* He also accused Stalin of obtaining confessions through physical pressure and of ordering mass arrests and deportations and executions without trial.[62]

During the period when the Revolution was taking place, liquidation of the "exploiting classes" was justified according to Communist philosophy (popularly called the "party line"), but Stalin had regular party members shot. According to Khrushchev, 98 of the 139 members and candidates for the Central Committee (70 percent) were shot. Even the secret police assigned to murder Kirov and others were later shot in order to cover up the conspiracy against Kirov, whom Khrushchev says was an innocent man. Khrushchev re-

[61] *Ibid.,* pp. 151–152.
[62] Khrushchev, *op. cit.,* pp. 12–15.

counted many other instances in which important members of the elite were liquidated in the wave of arrests in 1937–1939. All told, thousands of innocent members of the party died as a result of false charges which were brought against them.[63]

Under Lenin there had of course been many liquidations of the "enemies of the people." At the outset of the Revolution Lenin eliminated the nobility and educated classes, as stated earlier. These people were suspect not because of any evidences of illegal or antisocial behavior, or even any open avowal of opposition, but because they were members of the privileged class.[64] And when Stalin carried out the collectivization of the peasants, between five and ten million kulaks perished. Some were killed outright but millions died from starvation because the Soviet government would not send food into areas where the peasants had refused to cooperate.[65] Stalin's tremendous urge for power, as Khrushchev said, led him to exterminate not merely his enemies but also his friends.[66] Absolute power, no matter how fanatically supported at first, is bound to be rejected by the masses eventually. As Lincoln said, "You cannot fool all the people all of the time." There is a point when reason penetrates fanaticism and the suggestibility of the people declines. Apparently this has resulted in a certain relaxing of brutality in the USSR today.

Nazi brutalities under Hitler were probably greater in number of outright killings because of Hitler's avowed extermination policy toward the Jews. In the Auschwitz concentration camp alone, an alleged 2,500,000 people were killed in the gas chambers; another 500,000 died from disease and starvation. Some Jews were subjected to cruel experiments with poison, freezing in water, or pressure chambers. All told, 6,000,000 Jews perished as the result of Hitler's ruthless policy (4,000,000 in extermination centers), most of whom were buried in mass graves.[67]

Members of the civilian population also were killed by the Germans in occupied countries. Many French people were executed, although the exact number is not known. In Czechoslovakia and Russia, the Germans' slaughter of Slavs as well as Jews was common. Hitler held that Slavs must perish to make room for the Germans. These unbelievable brutalities were all part of a policy of systematic annihilation of civilians which had no military justification.[68] In comparison, the deaths inflicted under Mussolini's dictatorship

---

[63] Ibid., pp. 20–40.

[64] William H. Chamberlin, The Russian Revolution, The Macmillan Company, New York, 1935, Vol. I, pp. 356–357.

[65] Lin Yutang, The Secret Name, Farrar, Straus and Cudahy, Inc., New York, 1958, p. 130.

[66] Khrushchev, op. cit., This amazing document recounts numerous instances in which Stalin had persons who considered themselves his aides and friends shot.

[67] "Nazi Conspiracy and Aggression," Opinion and Judgment, Office of the United States Counsel for Prosecution of Axis Criminality, Government Printing Office, Washington, 1947, in Alan P. Grimes and Robert D. Horwitz, Modern Political Ideologies, Oxford University Press, New York, 1959, pp. 460–462.

[68] Ibid., pp. 455–458.

were negligible. There was no important anti-Semitism in Italy and the sentences carried out—while relatively ruthless—involved only seven death sentences in the years 1926 to 1932. Some 257 suffered sentences of more than ten years; 1360 had lesser sentences and a large number were exiled. What is more astonishing, 12,000 were tried and found innocent, which was unthinkable under either Hitler or Stalin.[69] In contrast, merely to be arrested in Russia was virtually a sign of guilt, while Jews arrested in Germany were generally denied the dignity of a trial.

Political Corruption

Lord Acton's oft-quoted theory that "power tends to corrupt and absolute power tends to corrupt absolutely" has ample verification in the outrages to human sensibilities which occurred under Hitler and Stalin. The enormity of Hitler's crime against humanity was well expressed in the testimony of the defendant at the Nuremburg trials when he stated, "A thousand years will pass and this guilt of Germany will not be erased."[70]

Stalin's gluttony for power has likewise been condemned by Khrushchev as "the cult of the individual." In establishing his case Khrushchev recounted numerous instances when Stalin would not listen to members of the Central Committee when they referred to conditions in the provinces. And during World War II Stalin often refused to take expert military advice, with the needless loss of thousands of lives. Stalin in fact became an almost complete dictator who seldom paid any attention to the advice of the Central Committee. Meanwhile his sense of power and self-adulation increased. He refused to listen to Churchill when the latter warned of an impending German attack on the Soviet Union. He also insisted on writing a history of the Communist party in the Soviet Union and his own biography, in both of which he was given fulsome praise.[71] This "mania for greatness" made Stalin make one-man decisions and distrust his closest advisers. On the other hand, Stalin trusted Beria, who was notoriously corrupt and personally responsible for the liquidation of thousands of persons. Corruption thus breeds corruption, as Khrushchev's testimony indicates.[72]

Peron, as Fascist dictator of the Argentine Republic, is another example of corruption under totalitarianism. The Fascist government which Peron headed was never so brutal as its European prototypes, however. Peron's corruption was primarily financial and moral. Compared to Hitler or Stalin, Peron was a mild dictator. Anyone who expressed contempt for the Peron government could be imprisoned from six months to a year; if contempt was expressed for an important government official, including the President, the punishment might be up to three years; against lesser officials the punishment ranged from two months to two years. Treason was punished by the death penalty or life

[69] E. Kohn-Bramstedt, *Dictatorship and Political Police: The Technique of Control by Fear*, London, 1945, pp. 51 ff., cited by Arendt, *op. cit.*, p. 309.
[70] "Nazi Conspiracy and Aggression," p. 459.
[71] Khrushchev, *op. cit.*, pp. 70–76.
[72] *Ibid.*, pp. 65–69.

imprisonment, and political prisoners were often tortured with electrical devices. In Peron's Argentina "liberty was not allowed to undermine liberty."[73] Any political system which does not permit criticism by the citizens is likely to fall into corruption, however, because the exercise of power is intoxicating to those wielding it. The price of good government, is as we all know, eternal vigilance. In a democracy constitutional controls and public opinion tend to limit power.

The Distortion of Truth

By the systematic use of propaganda, by censorship, and by deliberate use of deceit totalitarian governments are able to build up concepts of their relative superiority to other governments and the belief that only within their country is life good. The goals of the people are held therefore to be the only ones intelligent and truth-loving people can accept.

The perversion of education to the purposes of political propaganda likewise has been one of the most important ways in which truth has been distorted. In the Soviet Union the Marxist philosophy has been maintained chiefly by this means. Much of the educational program is inevitably enlightening in language, mathematics, and science. Nevertheless many courses involve political indoctrination. History and the social sciences are taught according to the Marxian line, and it is difficult for the student to realize that he is being indoctrinated. At the same time, the Russian schools are unquestionably producing outstanding experts in technology and science. But the subjects to be studied and their priority of preference are partly at least determined by the need in the particular fields.[74]

In Nazi Germany children in grade school were taught in their readers to hate French children. Many subject-matter courses were introduced on race, family sociology, and colonial policies which were aimed primarily at securing mass support for government policies. Teachers under totalitarian regimes thus take on the role of indoctrinators rather than teachers of truth. Even where they may object personally to certain brutalities, other angles of propaganda may seem wholly acceptable to them. The German argument for "return of their colonies" gained wide acceptance through the constant reiteration of this theme in history, economics, and geography classes.

Scholars and scientists have often paid lip service to the totalitarian systems in Germany and Russia. In many instances scientists appear to have survived because they became interested in trivia, on the one hand, or in abstract mathematics and physics, on the other. There are no Marxian laws of mathematics or nuclear fission. In these areas scientific achievement has been remarkable, for outer space is outside the dogma of Communism. Perhaps some of the recent magnificent achievements of the Russians may be at-

---

[73] G. I. Blanksten, *Peron's Argentina,* University of Chicago Press, Chicago, 1952, pp. 174–185. We cannot go into detail about the spread of totalitarianism in South America. For further information consult Edward Tomlinson, *Battle for the Hemisphere,* Charles Scribner's Sons, New York, 1947.

[74] Friedrich and Brzezinski, *op. cit.,* p. 124.

tributed to the fact that it takes no mental equivocation to "expound the truth" in these areas.

How long totalitarian restrictions can last is of course a question. In the case of Russia, the great increase in the number of persons receiving a secondary and university education means that they will inevitably begin to question the validity of many of the premises of a police state. An increasing number of people are surely aware of the inconsistencies in Communist propaganda. The expressed material goal of the Russian Communists (for over thirty years) has been to equal and surpass the United States. It is absurd for the Communists to decry the American standard of living if they are trying to reach such a standard themselves. Likewise the stimulus to expend great effort while living on a low standard will eventually evoke little response if the hoped-for rewards never come in sight. Current demands of the Russian people for peace and for a greater variety of consumer goods are in themselves evidence of the people's concern for the rewards promised them by Communism.

The Family

Initially the family was under serious attack in Russia, largely because the church dominated conceptions of family law and morality. Divorces could be had practically for the asking and there was widespread sex experimentation. In Germany there was similar disavowal of the rules of chastity and marriage fidelity, and women were urged to produce children for the Fatherland. Today, under the change implemented by laws in 1937 and 1944 in the USSR, divorces are granted only for serious reasons. Sex immorality is definitely frowned upon. The previous attack on bourgeois morality is a thing of the past so far as the family is concerned. (Many facets of family organization and divorce are discussed in Part Three, "Family Disorganization," hence are not presented in detail here.)

The Attack on the Church

The church is the conserver of the highest social values and ethical principles within a culture, even though it may on occasion fail to keep up with social change. By affiliation with the church many persons are constrained to order their lives with greater concern for love and kindness to their families, friends, and fellow men. Without the institution of the church many people would be far more selfish and less restricted in their antisocial tendencies. We have had ample evidence in our own country of the lawlessness on the frontier, in which there was, as has been said, "no Sunday west of Bismarck, no God west of Cheyenne."

According to Braden, the attack of Communism against Christianity has been more devastating than any other wave of indifference or attack upon the church. This is largely because (1) the antireligious emphasis is held necessary to achieve the aim of Communism, even though its professed aim is to achieve a good life (which is also a part of the goal of Christianity); (2) Communism in turn has become essentially a secular religion with tremendous emotional drives; (3) and Communism has organized itself into a highly disciplined party which controls both its members and the large mass of citizens in an almost absolute fashion.[75]

The major aim of Communism, theoretically at least, is the good life for all. This grew out of a deep desire for social justice best exemplified in the famous slogan "From each according to his ability, to each according to his need." But to achieve this goal everything is subject to "serving the interests of the working people" according to the interpretation of the party leaders and the Soviet state. The law of the Soviet state expressly requires that "all citizens, institutions, and officials observe all Soviet laws precisely and without protest."[76] Furthermore, counterrevolutionary propaganda is strictly forbidden. This inevitably includes religious propaganda since religion opposes the official atheistic policy of the Soviet government and the Communist party. The lack of belief in religion has made it possible for the Communists to accept the brutal use of physical force.[77]

Future Trends in Totalitarianism

We would not be fair if we did not indicate the present strength of Communism. As Ebenstein has pointed out, widening the base from which the elite is recruited is probably its most important strength.[78] This insures an ever increasing group of leaders. In western Europe and to a lesser degree in the United States the elite (i.e., the leaders in government, the army, business, science, and the arts) have come from the upper and middle classes. A sizable share have come from the upper-middle class. There has always been the poor boy who made good but he has been the exception. There has been little opportunity for the superior members of the lower class to rise to positions of leadership. In Russia the present leaders all appear to be persons of exceptional ability as well as physical stamina and they were nearly all recruited from the working class.

Rapid industrialization is a second source of totalitarian strength and power. Russia by supreme effort has raised itself from a backward economy to one which rivals the United States. The rate of industrial increase has in recent years exceeded our own and within the next ten years the Soviet Union expects "to equal and surpass America." The Russians also expect to reduce their work week from forty-six to forty hours. Whether they are able to equal our standard of living in this short time is questionable. There is no question, however, that the Russian economy has improved at a remarkable rate.[79]

In atomic research Russia has caught up with and surpassed the United

[75] Charles S. Braden, *Communism and World Religions,* Harper & Brothers, New York, 1953, p. 236.

[76] A. Ya. Vyshinsky, *The Law of the Soviet State,* p. 640, quoted by Kulski, *op. cit.,* pp. 143–144.

[77] Sorokin, *The Crisis of Our Age,* pp. 205–206.

[78] William Ebenstein, *Today's Isms,* Prentice-Hall, Inc., Englewood Cliffs, N.J., (2nd ed.), pp. 23–54.

[79] *Ibid.,* pp. 56–59.

States. In the area of outer space aeronautics Russia's achievements have startled the scientific world. In their quest for knowledge and techniques in the most intricate aspects of astrophysics the Russians have indisputably out-distanced Western scientists. This fact has given great prestige to Russian research laboratories and to their highly disciplined educational program.

A fourth demonstrated strength of the USSR is the military power which enabled it to annex a rim of European countries during World War II and to dominate a group of satellite countries in Europe and Asia. During and after World War II parts of Rumania, East Prussia, eastern Czechoslovakia, eastern Poland, and Finland were annexed along with all of Estonia, Latvia, Lithu-ania, Tannu Tuva, and certain Japanese possessions. Following World War II Albania, Bulgaria, Czechoslovakia, East Germany and East Berlin, Hungary, Poland, Rumania, and outer Mongolia have become "satellite" nations.

China too has been aided and abetted in her pursuit of Communist goals by the Russians although China has insisted upon a certain autonomy in setting up her own goals.[80] China meanwhile dominates North Korea, North Viet-nam, and Tibet while Communism is spreading in Laos and in other Asiatic countries. There is also a strong move to extend Communism in South America.[81] Over 900,000,000 people, one-third of the human race, are now living under a Communist political structure. The notion that Communism is weak and likely to fold up is thus so much nonsense. Communism is on the move. As sociologists we must be concerned with what this entails for human society. Up to now Communism has been disorganizing because it has dis-rupted the contemporary institutions and perverted the truth and other values in order to gain acceptance among the people under its control.

The weakness of totalitarianism is the disorganization which it imposes. What directions totalitarianism may take in the future is difficult to say. Under Khrushchev there has been a definite trend to less brutality and less liquida-tion of the Soviet nationals, as we have discussed. Will the police state, as Marx promised, "wither away"? It seems likely that the education of so many superior children to their highest capacity will have a further liberating and softening effect on brutal controls. Sulzberger[82] and others have held that there has been a "Great Thaw" in the hostilities between the East and the West which may result in a reversal of certain trends. The visit of Premier Khrushchev to the United States in 1959 was heralded as one constructive step to lessen tensions. If the Western powers fail to cooperate in a disarma-ment program the Communists will have fuel for their propaganda that the

[80] Ebenstein considers China a satellite, but recent developments indicate China's de-termination to set up Communism in its own way. Cf. *ibid.*, pp. 59–62.

[81] Because of space limitations we cannot discuss South American political ferment but both Communism and Fascist forces have been struggling for extension there, and Peron's government was a Fascist regime, as mentioned earlier.

[82] Cyrus L. Sulzberger, *The Big Thaw,* Harper & Brothers, New York, 1954, discusses this topic in detail. Cf. also Hocking, *op. cit.*

capitalist nations are planning military aggression. Lack of trust and lack of consensus will inevitably plague the Western powers' attitudes toward the USSR. The Communists claim that history is on their side and that they will inevitably win. This the Western powers propose to prevent. If there is no compromise we shall, as Sorokin says, "fight totalitarianism with totalitarianism." For war itself always involves regimentation of national groups, as the discussion in the next chapter makes clear.

Meanwhile our country is rapidly becoming a welfare state. Capitalism is rigidly controlled in the United States and the stock of our large corporations though often concentrated is also widely distributed. Income is redistributed through the tax structure; the wealthiest Americans must pay 91 percent of their income to the government. Workers now have an effective voice in our political and economic structure. Will Communism and controlled capitalism converge further? This is a question we cannot answer at this time.

Many of the changes which have thus transpired in the United States have been resisted by persons who would divert the inevitable uncertainties and insecurities to their own ends. The underlying sentiment which has been mobilized as the "new American right" is an influence working for social disorganization because it has literally attempted to break down the traditional freedoms that have been the foundation of American life: the right of assembly, free speech, free petition, and free association. Acting in the name of "Americanism," the new American right has made various efforts to sabotage these freedoms and divert national patriotism into channels that would literally "subvert" the traditions of this country.[83]

By and large, however, social change has been accepted in the United States, irrespective of class, religion, or ethnic group. It has not been ushered in by the rattle of small-arms fire or the roar of revolutionary crowds at the barricades. The American workingman has remained as basically conservative as the other groups, in striking contrast to the situation in many Western countries. The working class in this country has sought a larger share of the national income, but without any major modification of the traditional social structure. The "American dream" of unlimited possibilities for personal advancement is still the dominant ideology of all classes in America and will doubtless continue to be for a long time to come.[84]

Totalitarianism nevertheless has a dynamism that forces it to seek expansion, either in ideological or in territorial form, at the expense of other nations and peoples. The Fascist drive toward dynamic expansion led to World War II. The Communist drive toward ideological expansion, with or without recourse to armed force, has led to the cold war. A third world war is something all nations,[85] Communist and democratic, wish to avoid.

[83] Seymour M. Lipset, "The Sources of the 'Radical Right,'" chap. 7 in Daniel Bell (ed.), *The New American Right*, Criterion Books, New York, 1955.

[84] W. Lloyd Warner and James C. Abegglen, *Big Business Leaders in America*, Harper & Brothers, New York, 1955.

[85] Arnold J. Toynbee, "New Vistas for the Historian," *Saturday Review*, 39:7–8 (January 7, 1956).

SELECTED BIBLIOGRAPHY

Arendt, Hannah, *The Origins of Totalitarianism* (translated by Therese Pol), Meridian Books, New York, 1958 (2nd ed.). This book by a distinguished German writer presents a carefully documented analysis of the importance of anti-Semitism and of the Pan-Slav and Pan-German movements in precipitating totalitarianism in Germany and in Russia. The author also discusses the little-known fact that Marx was bitterly anti-Semitic.

Bach, Marcus, *God and the Soviets,* Thomas Y. Crowell Company, New York, 1958. This book presents a vivid picture of the restrictions imposed upon religious activity (while religion is also "tolerated") in Russia. There are interesting sidelights on the Soviet attempt to enforce high moral standards without any religious support.

Blanksten, G. I., *Peron's Argentina,* University of Chicago Press, Chicago, 1952. An excellent account is given of the political corruption (particularly the financial and moral corruption) under the Peron administration in Argentina.

Braden, Charles S., *Communism and World Religions,* Harper & Brothers, New York, 1953. The threat which Communism poses for the Christian and other religions is carefully analyzed.

Ebenstein, William, *Today's Isms,* Prentice-Hall, Inc., Englewood Cliffs, N.J., 1958, (2nd ed.). This book gives a summary of the characteristics of Communism, Fascism, socialism, and capitalism with the "strengths and weaknesses" of each. The interpretation leans to the conservative.

Friedrich, Carl J., and Brzezinski, Zbigniew, *Totalitarian Dictatorships and Autocracy,* Harvard University Press, Cambridge, 1956. This is one of the best analyses of the general characteristics of the totalitarian dictatorships.

Fromm, Eric, *Escape from Freedom,* Rinehart and Company, Inc., New York, 1941. The well-known psychoanalyst maintains that totalitarianism is due to a drive for power on the part of the dictator and a desire to escape responsibility on the part of the masses who follow him.

Golob, Eugene O., *The Isms,* Harper & Brothers, New York, 1954. The author gives a calm appraisal of the "isms" with some hope that the most brutal aspects of Communism may be on the way out.

Grimes, Alan P., and Horwitz, Robert D., *Modern Political Ideologies,* Oxford University Press, New York, 1959. This book has an excellent set of readings including valuable material on the judgment of the United States Counsel for Persecution of Axis Criminality.

Hocking, William E., *Strength of Men and Nations,* Harper & Brothers, New York, 1959. A careful attempt is made to analyze the possibilities for coexisting with the USSR.

Khrushchev, Nikita S., "Secret Speech Concerning the Cult of the Individual" delivered at the Twentieth Congress of the Communist Part of the Soviet Union, February 25, 1956, in *The Anti Stalin Campaign and International Communism* (edited by the Russian Institute, Columbia University), Columbia University Press, New York, 1956. This is one of the most amazing documents available on the brutal liquidations of Soviet nationals including members of the Communist party and the Central Committee under Stalin's regime.

Kohn, Hans (ed.), *The Mind of Modern Russia,* Rutgers University Press, New Brunswick, 1955. This book presents in translation a series of essays written by outstanding Russian scholars and theologians. It gives unusual insight into the fanatic religious beliefs of the Russian Orthodox and the strength of the Pan-Slavic movement of the nineteenth century.

Kulski, W. W., *The Soviet Regime,* Syracuse University Press, Syracuse, 1959 (3rd ed.). This book has the best factual data available in one volume with reference to the Soviet regime. The discussion is unemotional although conservative in orientation.

Lin Yutang, *The Secret Name,* Farrar, Straus and Cudahy, Inc., New York, 1958. A very interesting and factual analysis of the disorganization under Communism in Europe and Asia is given by a distinguished Chinese writer.

Sorokin, Pitirim A., *The Crisis of Our Age,* E. P. Dutton and Company, Inc., New York, 1945. In this book (which is a published series of lectures) Sorokin summarizes his detailed studies on the long-term trends in culture. Our present crisis is held to have occurred at the end of some 600 years of "sensate" culture.

Talman, J. F., *The Rise of Totalitarian Democracy,* Beacon Press, Boston, 1952. This is probably the best available analysis of the eighteenth- and nineteenth-century roots of modern totalitarianism. Talman is a noted Jewish scholar at the University of Jerusalem.

CHAPTER 31

War

War and Social Disorganization

War is social disorganization in its most violent form. War is the formal disruption of the relationships that bind nations together in (uneasy) peacetime harmony. War disturbs world harmony, international trade, the free exchange of ideas, and the communication between peoples that is so vital to human relationships in the twentieth century. The forces of democracy, Christianity, and science which serve, each in its own way, to unite men in a common and reciprocal bond are devastated by war as by no other human catastrophe.

The United Nations Organization has not yet become organized into a truly stable relationship, nor was the League of Nations. Hence we cannot say that war disorganizes an international structure when the latter does not fully exist. Nevertheless, war destroys whatever stability previously existed between the nations in conflict. Meanwhile, war and its attendant hatreds constitute the strongest barrier against the eventual appearance of a peaceful grouping of the peoples of the world.[1] The First World War set Western civilization back generations in its slow and tortuous progress toward a better collective life. The Second World War was even more catastrophic in its effects upon world harmony. This conflict ended with the nations of the world aligned in two armed camps.[2]

War not only disorganizes international relations; it also demoralizes individuals, destroys families, and disrupts communities. It is true that certain aspects of war lead to an increase in national consensus, as public opinion is mobilized against the outside aggressor. But the disorganizing effects of total war far overshadow whatever temporary national enthusiasm is engendered by the emergency. The disruptive impact of World War II upon the peoples of the belligerent nations will last for generations. The destruction of property, the devastation of land, and the loss of human life were all so great

---

[1] Arnold J. Toynbee, "New Vistas for the Historian," *Saturday Review,* 39:7–8 (January 7, 1956).
[2] Harold D. Lasswell, "World Organization and Society," chap. 6 in Daniel Lerner and Harold D. Lasswell (eds.), *The Policy Sciences,* Stanford University Press, Stanford, 1951.

that they are literally beyond comprehension. We can only touch briefly upon the many group relationships that were wholly or partially destroyed by World War II.

War often appears to be a final stage of world disorganization, in which revolution and totalitarianism are both preliminary stages. But revolution and totalitarianism are also the aftermath of war. The flow of history is constant, and it is difficult to say whether certain events are primarily the results of prior incidents or the antecedents of things to come. Fascism and Communism arose from the dislocations following World War I. But in its bid for world power, Fascism directly provoked World War II. Now the advance of Communism threatens to be the most important factor in precipitating a possible World War III.

Revolution is a drastic change in the social structure of a single country, which may invoke Fascism as a counterforce against actual or alleged revolutionary action. Fascism is sometimes imposed following the implicit threat of revolution, as was true in Germany and Italy. But Fascism either leads to war or is a constant threat of war, as the dictator attempts to bolster his domestic power by menacing gestures against other and (presumably) less powerful nations.[3] War shifts the scene of disorganization from the national to the international front.

War is no longer a conflict between professional soldiers, who conduct it as an intricate and comparatively bloodless game, with little threat to the structure of the belligerent nations. Modern war has become a death struggle between nations, or coalitions of nations, in which every man, woman, and child is directly or indirectly involved. There were few persons in the modern world who did not experience in some degree the impact of World War II. With the threat of the atomic and the hydrogen bomb hanging over the peoples of the world, the world is finally reaching its ultimate potential power of social disorganization. A full-scale nuclear war would mean the destruction of modern civilization.[4]

War has thus become total war. The twentieth century will go down in history as the century of total war.[5] The development of science, the industrialization of nations, the rise of the conscript army, and the crushing economic burden have combined to take war out of the hands of the diplomats and soldiers and entrust it to the nation as a whole. Total war has been dehumanized and has become an impersonal struggle in which the balance is shifted not so much by personal courage as by steel output, technological advancement, and bureaucratic rationalization. In fact, "Whole nations are becoming targets. Material abundance has completely altered the stakes of

[3] Stuart W. Chapman, "The Right of Revolution and the Rights of Man," *Yale Review, 43:576–588* (June, 1954).

[4] Cf. David F. Cavers, "The Economic Consequences of Atomic Attack," *Annals of the American Academy of Political and Social Science, 290:27–34* (November, 1953).

[5] Raymond Aron, *The Century of Total War* (translated), Doubleday and Company, Inc., New York, 1954.

diplomacy; the stakes now are all or nothing; total war, perhaps total death, is the alternative to peace."[6]

The techniques of total war have increased the social disorganization of armed conflict. Some of these techniques are the result of the totalitarian state's belief that the end justifies the means. Other techniques have been made possible by the increase in the destructive power of modern weapons. The mass deportation of civilian workers, the terrorism inflicted upon the citizens of occupied countries, the expulsion of entire peoples from their homes, the wholesale murder of ethnic groups, the tortures of the secret police, the guerrilla warfare of resistance movements, the savage reprisals upon the resisting populations, the strategic bombing of entire industrial areas— these are among the techniques of total war that were developed or perfected during World War II. Any wars in the future will utilize some or all of these techniques. We cannot expect to turn the clock back to the limited wars of an earlier day.[7]

War and Social Change

Modern war takes place in a dynamic society, where social change is already occurring at an unprecedented speed. Total war speeds up the rapidity of social change and consequently intensifies the disorganization of group relationships. New culture traits are being rapidly introduced into modern society in "normal" times, but the pace is greatly accelerated by total war. When World War II occurred the nations had not completely recovered from the changes set in motion by World War I. The depression had further intensified the rate at which changes were introduced into the societies of the democracies and the dictatorships alike. Inventions had raised the specter of technological unemployment, in addition to the other changes which they had introduced into a modern industrial society.

The wartime emergency increased the emphasis upon technological innovation.[8] Mammoth bomber plants were constructed, giant shipyards arose almost overnight, and whole secret cities were established to conduct the nuclear fission research which culminated in the atomic bomb. Economic institutions changed along with technology, as the entire industrial resources of the warring nations were converted to war production. Millions of civilian workers moved to new cities and new regions to man the war industries. Communities doubled and tripled in size, with all the difficulties entailed in crowded living and mobile populations. All of these changes disrupted organized group relationships.

The social changes on the home front took a variety of additional forms.

[6] John U. Nef, *War and Human Progress,* Harvard University Press, Cambridge, 1950, pp. 372–373.

[7] Aron, *op. cit.,* p. 43.

[8] Bernard Brodie, "New Techniques of War and National Policies," in William F. Ogburn (ed.), *Technology and International Relations,* University of Chicago Press, Chicago, 1949.

A rapidly changing society is also a disorganized society, for men cannot construct new group ties as fast as the old ones are broken.

In the sociological frame of reference, wartime social change represents population migration; social mobility; the evolution of new technologies and new industries; the rush of population to the congested centers of war industry; the unprecedented increase in the labor force from tapping new strata of the population; the imposition of new social controls upon industry and the consumer; the increased number of broken families, some broken permanently by death or desertion, others temporarily by absence in the armed forces; housing problems, as thousands of families move from farm to trailer or tenement in a war boom town; family tensions, as the wage-earning wife for the first time asserts her independence; ill-advised war marriages, as boys and girls marry during a ten-day furlough; juvenile delinquency in the war centers; prostitution and sexual promiscuity as thousands of adolescent girls follow the glamour of the uniform to the camp towns and embarkation centers; racial tensions in population centers where the races come together under the frustrating circumstances of total war; religious and cultural conflict as accumulated tensions are directed toward the alien group at hand instead of the distant enemy—these are some of the aspects of social change as intensified by total war.[9]

To a certain degree, however, war produces a tightening of the bonds of group solidarity with a consequent temporary increase in social organization. The external danger to the nation strengthens many of the ties of the individual to the group. This process was illustrated by the sharp decrease in suicide during World War II, as many tensions and frustrations were directed against the external enemy instead of against the self. The attack upon venereal disease as a military problem enlisted the combined efforts of many groups in the fight against prostitution, so that this form of social disorganization was virtually eliminated in many areas. Certain (but by no means all) racial and religious antagonisms were temporarily alleviated through joint national cooperation in a common cause. In a few selected areas of human relationships the social changes set in motion by World War II thus promoted the national consensus. These organizing forces, however, were offset many times by the forces of social disorganization released by total war.

The role of social change in World War II in this country was a selective one. In short,

World War II thus made a dynamic society more dynamic, increased the rate of change in an already rapidly changing society, and intensified many of the social problems deriving from the disparity in the rate of change between the various segments of this society. The normal processes of social change characteristic of our society were stimulated by the impact of the war. Many of the social problems arising from wartime maladjustments were thus much the same as those apparent in peacetime, with their severity enhanced by accelerated wartime change.[10]

[9] Francis E. Merrill, *Social Problems on the Home Front,* Harper & Brothers, New York, 1948, pp. 2–3.
[10] *Ibid.,* p. 10.

Causes of War

Modern war seldom comes suddenly. The extensive preparations necessary for total war mean that the national economy must be centralized and rationalized toward the common goal. This process takes time. The first overt act of aggression may, it is true, occur with all the speed of bombers and guided missiles. But the very nature of total war means that it must be preceded by a long period of industrial mobilization. World War II has been followed by the cold war, where the line between peace and war was drawn only in terms of the methods employed by the great powers, not in terms of the ultimate goals sought by them. In the cold war the means have been limited, in the sense that neither side resorts to all-out conflict. The ultimate ends of world power, however, are unlimited.[11] Under such conditions, the nation is (in theory, at least) prepared for war at any time, and the interceptor planes guarding the large cities are manned twenty-four hours a day.

Modern war is a function of modern society, with its mass tensions, insecurities, ideological rivalries, and social disorganization. War is a manifestation of disorganized international relationships. The more complex the structure of the belligerent units, the greater the number of factors that combine to bring about a state of war between them. We can consider only the most significant factors that produce war in the twentieth century.[12]

1. *Nationalism.* Exaggerated and chauvinistic nationalism leads to war. This pattern of attitudes and values is a part of the ethnocentrism of national groups, which causes them to regard their culture as superior to that of all other nations. In addition, they often wish to impose their culture upon other nations by force. Failure to appreciate the culture of other peoples and the tendency to ridicule this culture contribute to international hostilities. This attitude reached its final expression in the racism of the Nazis, in which the Germans were self-glorified as a superior race, whose domination of Europe would be a boon to mankind.[13] Slogans, myths, and collective representations enhance this sense of superiority. Supernationalism of this kind may lead to war.[14]

2. *Economic Factors.* The struggle to secure an adequate share of economic goods, the search for markets, the competition for raw materials, and the conflict for colonies are among the economic factors that contribute to modern war. The struggle for power between the great industrial nations is a realistic struggle for oil, uranium, food, and markets. This does not mean, however, that economic drives culminating in imperialist expansion are the *most important* causes of modern war. This Communist concept of imperialism has been considerably modified recently. The years leading up to World

[11] Aron, *op. cit.*, chap. 9, "The Conventions of the Cold War."

[12] Cf. L. L. Bernard, *War and Its Causes,* Henry Holt and Company, Inc., New York, 1944.

[13] Ruth Benedict, *Race: Science and Politics,* The Viking Press, Inc., New York, 1945 (rev. ed.).

[14] Cf. Quincy Wright, *A Study of War,* University of Chicago Press, Chicago, 1942, chap. 27, "Nationalism and War."

War I were years of prosperity in the capitalist countries. Neither World War I nor World War II was precipitated directly by a conflict over colonies.[15]

3. *Population Pressure.* Population pressure is a factor in modern war. Nations which are stifled by a rapidly increasing population feel the urge to expand at the expense of other nations. Density of population alone, however, is not in itself a cause of war. India has not resorted to war to solve its population problems. Communist China entered the Korean War for reasons other than the desire for more room for its teeming people. Density of population *plus* a warlike culture affords an excuse for aggression. Germany, Italy, and Japan faced the problem of overpopulation, which they used to justify their embarking upon World War II. Dictators encourage the increase of population to create a war machine and at the same time deplore the limited resources of their nations.[16]

4. *Technology.* Technological advance is a factor in promoting war. Modern technology requires large capital investments, unlimited supplies of natural resources, and unrestricted markets. The new technology has thus advanced nationalism and helped to organize the modern world for destruction and war. The diversion of technological resources into the production of nuclear weapons is the most spectacular case in point.[17]

5. *Propaganda.* Without the popular will to fight, none of the other factors by themselves could induce war. Wars are no longer fought by mercenaries, and the citizen soldier must be taught to fight. Some persons maintain that the tendency to war is instinctive.[18] This is erroneous. Men would never go to war if they had not been conditioned to do so. The individual would never risk his life, liberty, and property if it were not for the attitudes inculcated by those in power. In order to get men to fight they must be indoctrinated by propaganda, which is directed both toward the citizens at home and toward those of other nations. The real reasons for the war are obscured by emotional appeals.[19]

6. *Ideologies.* Ideologies are the complex patterns of beliefs and values that are supported by a given society. The most dynamic ideologies of our day are nationalism, democracy, Communism, and Fascism. Nations and peoples have embraced these ideologies and have gone to war in support of them. World War I was in many ways the last of the great wars between nations. World War II was conceived (by Great Britain, France, the United States, and the USSR) as an ideological conflict in defense of democracy against a militant Fascism. The masses on both sides may not understand the implications of their ideological beliefs, but they are willing to die for them.

[15] Aron, *op. cit.,* chap. 3, "The Leninist Myth of Imperialism."

[16] Cf. Bernard, *op. cit.,* chap. 14, "Population Pressure as a Cause of War."

[17] Harold D. Lasswell *et al., The Comparative Study of Elites,* Hoover Institute Studies, Stanford University Press, Stanford, 1952, pp. 14–15.

[18] Cf. Wright, *op. cit.,* chap. 33, "Human Nature and War."

[19] *Ibid.,* chap. 30, "Public Opinion and War."

Like the religious wars of an earlier day, ideological war takes on a bitterness that can arise only from a sense of being right.[20]

7. *Internal Tensions.* Serious internal tensions constitute another cause of war. They may reflect such factors as a low scale of living, fear of the police, frustration of sexual impulses, and inability to achieve emotional satisfactions. These tensions may be channelized against an internal enemy, as the Nazis directed them against the Jews. Totalitarian tensions may also be directed against an external enemy, and the result may be aggressive war. Tensions exist in democratic societies, too, where they constitute explosive forces that may find their outlet in agitation for war. The fears of the American people during the early years of the cold war arose partly from the possibility of atomic attack by the Soviet Union and partly from the reality of the Korean War. Consequently there was strong and widespread opposition to international Communism.[21]

8. *War.* Each nation defines the causes of war in terms of its own national or ideological interests. These interests persist even after destructive and exhausting wars. Nations naturally do not regard each other as friends for a long time after they have engaged in mortal combat. The peace between the first two world wars proved to be merely an interlude during which hatreds and national animosities persisted. World War II was accompanied by enemy occupation, resistance movements, guerrilla warfare, wholesale deportation, summary execution of hostages, torture of subject peoples, and the deliberate extermination of millions of innocent men and women. The scars of World War II will linger on for generations. In a very real sense, therefore, war is itself a cause of war.[22]

Wars were formerly fought for limited objectives and involved limited means. Total war is fought for the total destruction of the enemy—his army, industrial capacity, cities, technology, economic resources, and civilian population. Under modern conditions, no one ever really "wins" a war. No one nation or group of nations derives a net national benefit from war. The threat of nuclear warfare makes this situation even more clear. Social disorganization has increased along with technological and industrial capacity to make war.[23] The application of technology to new weapons has enhanced the destructive possibilities of war.[24] Modern industrialism has made the entire society a potential military machine.

Our chief concern here is with the social disorganization occasioned when groups and institutions are disrupted by total conflict. There is a major impact

[20] Bernard, *op. cit.,* chap. 7, "The Ideologies of War."

[21] Arthur K. Davis, "Conflict Between Major Social Systems: The Soviet-American Case," *Social Forces, 30:*29–36 (October, 1951).

[22] Cf. Thomas D. Eliot, "A Criminological Approach to the Social Control of International Aggressions," *American Journal of Sociology, 58:*513–518 (March, 1953).

[23] Nef, *op. cit.,* chap. 18, "The Material Road to Total War," especially pp. 368 ff.

[24] Hanson W. Baldwin, "The New Face of War," *Bulletin of the Atomic Scientists, 12:* 153–158 (May, 1956).

of war upon human lives, both military and civilian. The economic costs of war are inestimable. War is the most voracious consumer of goods and services the world has ever seen. War destroys the spiritual values of Christian nations and has a disintegrating effect upon the mores. Family disorganization is multiplied many fold, in terms of separation, death, and divorce. Finally, war disrupts and disorganizes the basic institutions of the school, the church, and the state. Ordinary social life is based upon an intricate and intangible web of functioning relationships, many of which are disorganized by total war.

War and Human Life

"World War II," it has been conservatively stated, "was by far the most destructive in human history in terms of loss of life, both military and civilian, and of damage to social and economic institutions."[25] The most important human value is life itself. The loss of life, among both soldiers and civilians, far overshadowed any other loss in terms of social disorganization. Each soldier killed in battle and each civilian bombed or murdered belonged to several social groups. Every individual death either destroyed or appreciably weakened every group of which he was a member. The marriage group was destroyed by the death of the husband. The family group was shattered by the death of a son or father. Businesses, churches, clubs, scientific organizations were vitally affected both by the death of their leaders and by the extensive losses of their members. The social ramifications of the loss of human life were incalculable. Never before had so many social groups been broken so finally. Never before had so many marital, family, community, religious, economic, and educational groups been disorganized by the death of one or more of their members. World War II entailed social disorganization on a scale heretofore never known.

1. *Military Deaths.* Approximately 10,000,000 persons were killed in military action or died of wounds during World War II. The exact number of military deaths will never be known. Losses for the Axis powers are estimated at 5,500,000 and for the Allied nations totaled approximately 4,500,000. Germany suffered the largest number of military deaths, with an estimated 3,250,000. The other two Axis powers, Japan and Italy, lost 1,500,000 and 200,000 respectively.[26]

On the Allied side, Russia suffered by far the largest number of military deaths, with an estimated 3,000,000, which was approximately two-thirds of the total combat deaths sustained by the Allies. The British Empire lost an estimated 400,000, and the United States had approximately 325,000 men killed in combat or dead of battle wounds. The European allies lost a total of 450,000 men killed in combat, with France showing the highest total of military dead. An estimated 167,000 Frenchmen were killed in battle, while

[25] Metropolitan Life Insurance Company, "Military Deaths in World War II," *Statistical Bulletin,* January, 1946.
[26] *Ibid.*

an additional 100,000 civilians were executed by the Germans during the occupation. Many of the latter were members of the underground forces fighting the Germans. Poland lost an estimated 125,000 men in combat, while Military deaths of Yugoslavs totaled around 75,000 (not counting the civilians executed by the Germans). The 10,000,000 total deaths from all military causes during World War II may be compared with the 8,000,000 lost in World War I.[27]

In the Korean War, the United States lost an estimated total of 32,000 men killed in action or dead of wounds. This number includes an authenticated 24,000 battle deaths, plus most of the 9000 men originally listed as missing. The great majority of the latter (perhaps more than nine-tenths) may be presumed dead, making the total dead about 32,000. The Korean conflict lasted almost three years, from June 25, 1950, to June 12, 1953. Based upon the total number of men under arms in the Korean War, the battle death rate was 3.5 per 1000 per year. The rate per 1000 men under arms was 8.9 per year during World War II. The Marine Corps suffered the highest battle death rate of any service in both conflicts; in the Korean War, the rate for the Marine Corps was 7.1, as compared to 6.3 for the Army, 0.5 for the Air Force, and 0.2 for the Navy.[28]

2. *Civilian Deaths.* World War II was the most destructive war in history upon the civilian population. Bombings, executions of people in occupied countries, and the deliberate extermination of entire ethnic and religious groups (genocide) caused an estimated civilian toll of 12,000,000 killed and possibly twice that number maimed. Poland alone lost an estimated 6,000,000 dead, largely civilians, through the executions and organized extermination of the Jews and others who resisted the Nazis.[29]

Nothing in history can be remotely compared to these modern outrages. Barbarian hordes have conquered Europe from time to time in historical memory, but the methods of the Mongols were as nothing when compared to those of the Nazis.[30] In the USSR around 9,000,000 civilians were said to have perished.

War and Economic Factors

The economic cost incurred in the prosecution of World War II and the destruction resulting from it both reached astonomical proportions. Whether a nation is committed to a philosophy of private property or to one of state ownership, the physical aspects of property are the foundation of the social structure. People receive their support through the productive use of physical property, whether land, buildings, or machinery. Massive destruc-

[27] *Ibid.*

[28] Metropolitan Life Insurance Company, "United States War Losses in Korea," *Statistical Bulletin,* June, 1953.

[29] Emil Lengyel, "The Wreck of Europe," *Annals of the American Academy of Political and Social Science, 257:*13–22 (May, 1948). The mass extermination of the Jews is treated in the preceding chapter.

[30] Cf. Sheldon Glueck, *War Criminals: Their Prosecution and Punishment,* Alfred A. Knopf, Inc., New York, 1944.

tion of property marked World War II, which was the last of the old-fashioned, pre-atomic world wars. Should a third world war occur, the destructive potential derived from nuclear fission threatens a far greater devastation.[31]

1. *Destruction of Property*.   The value of the physical property destroyed during World War II was conservatively estimated at $230 billion. The largest share of this destruction occurred in Europe. Some of it resulted from the hostile action of the enemy, some from the bombing of the occupied country by the Allies. Still further desolation was occasioned by the embattled people's destroying their own property. The highly industrialized countries of western Europe were so ravaged by these combined forces of destruction that their productive capacities were reduced to 20 or 30 percent of the prewar output. Torn both by occupation and war, France was reduced in industrial productivity to 20 percent of prewar capacity at the time of its liberation in 1944.[32] We cannot estimate the extent of the physical destruction in Poland and the Soviet Union but it was much greater.

2. *Expenditures for War*.   The other major economic loss of World War II was the amount of goods and services expended for the unproductive purposes of war which might have been used in the productive purposes of peace. Estimates here can only be very general, for the expenditures for war cannot be accurately differentiated from the general running expenses of government. It has been calculated that the belligerent nations spent $1154 billion for war purposes. The United States spent $317 billion, Germany $272 billion, and Italy, one of the poorest of the belligerents, $94 billion.[33] Some of these expenditures were financed by taxation. Most entailed debts, however, and the nations will be paying for the great conflict for generations to come. A large share of wartime expenditures went into nonproductive items —guns, planes, tanks, and bombs—which were vital in winning the war. They also lowered the scale of living of the people.[34]

3. *Expenditures for the Cold War*.   These extraordinary wartime expenditures have continued in the postwar years because of the rising pressures of the "cold war." Such expenditures have a profound effect upon the national economy. The last decade was marked by a succession of multi-billion-dollar budgets for military expenditures, which have resulted in a rise in the price level with an inflationary effect upon the national economy. Thus the value of insurance policies, savings banks deposits, government and corporation bonds, and savings for old age or retirement have been partially destroyed by the decrease in the value of the dollar. There has also been an increase in the concentration of industry, occasioned by the policy of awarding defense contracts to a comparatively small number of industrial giants,

[31] Hans J. Morgenthau, "Has Atomic War Really Become Impossible?" *Bulletin of the Atomic Scientists,* 12:7–9 (January, 1956).

[32] Economic Cooperation Administration, *European Recovery Program, France: Country Study,* Washington, 1949, p. 1.

[33] Lengyel, *op. cit.*

[34] Cf. *European Recovery and American Aid,* Report of the President's Committee on Foreign Aid, Washington, 1947.

which already dominated their respective fields. Certain small industries may not survive. The economy is geared to producing instruments of war with little emphasis on those industries that make consumer goods and are not readily converted to war production. There has also been a tendency to economize upon domestic expenditures for welfare purposes, rather than to bring about savings in military expenditures.[35]

The economic implications of total war in a nuclear age are suggested by an ingenious attempt to estimate the cost of a third world war lasting for five years for the United States.[36] This estimate provides for a gradually increasing output of military equipment and supplies. It does not contain any guess as to the economic losses to this country from possible atomic and hydrogen attack.[37] In terms of the total federal budget in a future war, there would be an overall expenditure of some $2809 *billion* over a five-year period, or approximately $500 billion per year. This figure would include the normal costs of operating the federal government, but the bulk of the expenditures would be for military purposes. The amount of productive energy thus (theoretically) diverted from the fruitful activities of peace to the unproductive activities of total war is beyond the scope of the imagination.[38]

War and Spiritual Factors

A third disorganizing aspect of World War II was its effect upon the moral and spiritual standards of victor and vanquished alike. The Nazis introduced a new international immorality when they maintained that the end justifies every means in the ultimate interest of the totalitarian state. This morality has been continued by the power politics of the Communist states during the cold war. War against the totalitarian states is thus viewed as a Christian conflict, despite the Christian prohibitions against violence and bloodshed.[39]

Such contradictions between warring nations are by no means new. The unprecedented increase in the power of war to kill large numbers of persons has merely focused attention upon these logical difficulties. The postwar years have seen a growth of the cult of violence, whereby violence is justified for its own sake,[40] both on and off the battlefield.[41]

The successful prosecution of the war by the Allied powers forced them to engage in the large-scale bombing of civilian populations. This culminated in the use of the atomic bomb. The ethical implications of atomic bombing

---

[35] Robert A. Brady, "Defense Expenditures and the National Economy," *Annals of the American Academy of Political and Social Science*, 283:42–54 (September, 1952).

[36] Michael Albery, "The Cost of Wars," *Political Science Quarterly*, 67:267–282 (June, 1952).

[37] Cavers, *op. cit.*

[38] Albery, *op. cit.*, pp. 279–282.

[39] Cf. Karl Barth, *The Church and the War*, The Macmillan Company, New York, 1944, chap. 2, "The Role of the Church in Wartime."

[40] Nef, *op. cit.*, pp. 404–410.

[41] See, for example, Marvin Spiegelman, Carl Terwilliger, and Franklin Fearing, "The Content of Comic Strips: A Study of a Mass Medium of Communication," *Journal of Social Psychology*, 35:37–57 (February, 1952).

by nations acting in the name of Christian ethics have been widely discussed.[42] Such questions cannot be answered categorically, for they depend upon different social values. Military expediency, national policy, and religious conceptions are all intermingled in these spiritual questions. This diversity of moral definitions is itself a characteristic of a disorganized and revolutionary society.[43] Cynicism is bound to result.

The impact of two world wars within living memory has left the people of Europe confused and uncertain about traditional spiritual values. The Christian virtues of love, compassion, humility, and gentleness have often received short shrift in a world where might was right. The Christian morality has been largely discarded in the relationships between nations, if not between individuals. This substitution of a national morality for the morality of Christianity did not, of course, begin with World War II. Its immediate roots lie in the emerging cult of the nation-state during the nineteenth century. The ethical implications of this emergence are epitomized in the words of Cavour, who led the Italian people to national independence. "If we did for ourselves what we do for our country," he remarked, "what rascals we would be."[44] The individual is thus presumed to be relieved of many of the moral obligations of Christianity when acting in the interests of his country. "War," in other words, "became a moral equivalent for ethics and religion."[45]

The social disorganization accompanying World War II was, furthermore, so great that many controls have been hard to reestablish. Centuries of close communal living gave the average European a respect for legal and moral restraints. In a few brief years, much respect was wiped out. The black market was one example of such spiritual confusion. In some cases, the operation and patronage of the black market became a patriotic duty for the peoples of the occupied countries, for this was one way of circumventing the enemy. In the postwar struggle for survival, many continued such practices, with the conviction that they were still acting in a world that no longer recognized any law but the survival of the fittest.[46]

A further spiritual casualty of total war is "that provided by the love of beauty, tangible as well as intangible, in constructions of every kind, from a piece of cloth to a building, from a letter to a book."[47] In order to survive a total war, a nation must mobilize all its resources, spiritual as well as material. There is very little energy left over for the creation and enjoyment of beauty. Whether hot or cold, the practical and utilitarian considerations of war are such that delight in the arts is relegated to a secondary position. The practice

[42] Cf. Wayne A. R. Leys, "Human Values in the Atomic Age," *Annals of the American Academy of Political and Social Science, 290*:127–133 (November, 1953).

[43] Arnold J. Toynbee, "Has Christianity a Future?" in Ruth N. Anshen (ed.), *Beyond Victory,* Harcourt, Brace and Company, New York, 1943.

[44] Quoted by Peter Viereck, "The Revolution in Values: Roots of the European Catastrophe, 1870–1952," *Political Science Quarterly, 67*:339–356 (September, 1952), p. 343.

[45] Nef, *op. cit.,* p. 409.

[46] Preparatory Commission of the International Welfare Group, *Report of the Effects of War on Displaced Children,* prepared for the International Congress on Mental Health, London, August, 1949.

[47] Nef, *op. cit.,* p. 390.

of art becomes more esoteric, since the artist receives less acceptance from a society whose resources are directed toward prosecuting or preparing for war. The artist is looked upon as a nonproductive citizen, who contributes nothing to the garrison state, and whose activities may even detract from military goals.[48]

War and the Mores

War has a disruptive effect upon the mores by breaking down traditional and long-range considerations and substituting short-term and hedonistic responses to situations. War produces new situations to which the individual must adapt himself as best he can. The old patterns are not suitable to the new behavior and the person perforce acts in ways not sanctioned by the mores. In this way, the moral sanctions binding groups together are broken by the war situation. Large numbers of persons are no longer constrained by the controls implicit in the mores. Whether as civilians or soldiers, they follow their desires of the moment; many traditional norms have no further validity since death is always imminent. This process is, of course, relative, and most of the people in wartime still live according to most of the mores. But there is a perceptible weakening of the social control exerted by these most traditional of all patterns of group expectations.[49]

The decline in the mores is evidenced in wartime changes in sexual behavior. The wartime increase in sexual promiscuity is indicative of the general collapse in the taboos which govern peacetime society since sex mores have been the most emphasized.[50] The breakdown in social relationships during total war decreases the strength of the moral codes. These controls are exerted by the family, the church, and the neighborhood group, all of which experience a decline in influence. Family relationships are weakened by separation, mobility, employment in war industry, and the death of one or more members. The local community group is weakened by many of the same factors, as millions of persons break their home ties and move to other areas where they are strangers.[51] These wartime migrants are marginal in their new environment and hence are subject to fewer restraining pressures. In the United States, the dissolutions of the local group were peaceful, in the sense that they did not directly involve the violence of war and enemy occupation. In Europe, the local group was often suddenly and violently disrupted by deportation, execution, and mass destruction.

War and the Family

The social structure undergoes a series of tremendous alterations under the impact of war. No other form of social movement (except revolution) produces so many changes. As the central social institution, the family

[48] *Ibid.*

[49] Willard Waller (ed.), *War in the Twentieth Century,* The Dryden Press, Inc., New York, 1940, pp. 484–492.

[50] Cf. "Sex Delinquency Among Girls," *Journal of Social Hygiene,* 29:492–501 (November, 1943).

[51] Cf. Peter M. Blau, "Social Mobility and Interpersonal Relations," *American Sociological Review,* 21:290–295 (June, 1956).

is the most immediate institutional casualty of total war. Our statistical information is scanty concerning the family disorganization in Europe, which was infinitely more devastating than that which the American family experienced. In many European countries whole families were completely wiped out, some by military deaths but the majority by mass extermination. Under such conditions, the family which had *not* lost one or more of its members was the exception, rather than the rule. Young and old alike vanished into the Nazi gas chambers or were killed by the Fascist execution squads. In emphasizing the family disorganization which occurred in America, therefore, we are not attempting to minimize that in Europe. We are merely considering the American scene (1) because more data are available and (2) because the interest of the student is greater in his own society.

1. *Separation.* World War II produced the largest (temporary) disorganization of the American family that the nation has ever experienced. Between three and four million families were separated for varying periods during the war, some because of employment in distant war industries but the majority by service in the armed forces. Such prolonged separations were something new in the experience of the American family. The family is based upon the conjugal unit of husband and wife and cannot function effectively when they are separated. Most separated families resumed their interrupted relationship after the war and thus suffered no permanently disorganizing effects. But many families could not effect a unity after long years of living apart. Husband and wife were often unable to resume their marital arrangement after spending the initial years of marriage under wartime circumstances.[52]

2. *Death.* In a "normal" peacetime year, almost half a million families are broken by the death of the husband. In a representative year, for example, 449,000 husbands died, leaving that number of widows and 239,100 dependent children.[53] Figures on the number of married men among the 325,000 American dead in World War II are not exactly known, but they are estimated at more than 50,000. In June, 1945, some 50,000 war widows were receiving death benefits, a number sizably augmented by the casualties sustained in the closing months of the war.[54] The average age at death of the men killed in World War II was 24.5 years, with approximately half of all the deaths concentrated in the age group 20–24 years.[55] Most of the married men in the various age groups were not inducted; hence the number of marriages broken by death in the armed forces was comparatively small.

3. *Divorce.* War also increases the disorganization of the family through divorce, as discussed in Chapter 17. We do not need to recapitulate the figures

[52] Reuben Hill, *Families Under Stress,* Harper & Brothers, New York, 1949.

[53] Metropolitan Life Insurance Company, "Lower Mortality Promotes Family Stability," *Statistical Bulletin,* May, 1951.

[54] "Effects of War Casualties on Economic Responsibilities of Women," *Monthly Labor Review,* 62:181–186 (February, 1946).

[55] Metropolitan Life Insurance Company, "Age at Death in World War II," *Statistical Bulletin,* January, 1947.

here. Suffice it to say that divorce reached an all-time high as a direct consequence of the war and wartime marriages.[56]

Divorce rates showed a similar increase in many of the countries of western Europe. Summarizing the world-wide impact of the war, the statisticians of the Metropolitan Life Insurance Company state, "Despite the fact that millions of men in the armed forces were out of reach of civilian judicial processes, and despite national crises which should have diverted thoughts from domestic affairs, the divorce rate continued to rise the world over during the greater part of World War II."[57] The impact of the war on the family stemmed largely from the physical separation of three to four million married couples in the United States and many millions more in Europe.

In most countries the divorce rates remained substantially above their prewar levels, which indicated that the disorganization brought about by war and social change is a far-reaching phenomenon. In France and England the prewar divorce rate was low because of religious and legal factors; the postwar plateau was, nevertheless, considerably higher. In England and Wales, the liberalization of the divorce law occurred in 1938, immediately before the outbreak of the war. The postwar (1950) rate for these members of the United Kingdom was approximately *seven times* that of prewar years.[58]

War and Social Institutions

Total war also disorganizes the other social institutions. The life of any institution is based upon a series of reciprocal behavior patterns, which its members have acquired and practiced in their institutional life. In the school, for example, students and teachers acquire certain institutional and reciprocal roles, which comprise the educational process. Likewise, the church, the state, and the other institutional groups have their prescribed patterns of behavior, all of which are interrupted and changed by total war.[59]

The most complete institutional disorganization in World War II naturally occurred in areas marked by active combat (France, Poland, and Russia). Here the members of the community were completely occupied merely in keeping alive and conducting the minimum of institutional relationships. Other types of institutional disorganization characterized nations occupied by the enemy (Denmark, Belgium, Holland). Still others occurred in nations which were not occupied but were nevertheless within range of enemy air action (Great Britain). The geographical isolation and consequent freedom from attack and occupation of the United States meant that we experienced

[56] U.S. Department of Health, Education, and Welfare, National Office of Vital Statistics, *Marriage and Divorce Statistics, United States, 1946, Vital Statistics—Special Reports,* Vol. 27, No. 10 (October 24, 1947). Cf. Table 17.1 for a comparison of the divorce rates in 1946 and 1947 with trends before and after World War II.

[57] Metropolitan Life Insurance Company, "World-Wide Increase in Divorce," *Statistical Bulletin,* April, 1949.

[58] Metropolitan Life Insurance Company, "Postwar Divorce Rates Here and Abroad," *Statistical Bulletin,* June, 1952. Rates for postwar divorce in the United States are given in Chapter 17.

[59] Waller, *op. cit.,* pp. 482–484.

less institutional disruption than the belligerent countries. But the disorganization of institutional relationships in this country was, even so, very serious. Total war affects the total institutional life of a nation.

1. *The School.* Educational institutions are among the first to experience the impact of total war. In the battle zones, schools are completely suspended and the children fend for themselves as best they can. Educational institutions are subject to dislocations of varying degrees of severity in other countries. In England during World War II hundreds of thousands of children were evacuated from London early in the war. In the United States, the mobility of population interrupted the school lives of millions of children. Some children went without any schooling at all, and others were forced to attend school at odd hours, in inadequate quarters, and with insufficiently trained teachers. Many normal educational activities were curtailed, as the children were enrolled in salvage work, Red Cross campaigns, and similar operations related to the prosecution of the war. These are necessary and desirable in wartime, but they interfere with the normal activities of the school.[60]

The schools in the occupied countries were drastically and deliberately disorganized by the Nazis, who were determined to stamp out liberalism and nationalism and substitute the authoritarianism and racism of National Socialism. Pursuant to this general purpose, the Nazis resorted to "the murder of teachers, artists, scientists, and intellectual leaders; the burning of books; the pillaging and mutilation of works of art; the rifling of archives; and the theft of scientific apparatus."[61] In their efforts to direct the ideological development of the young people of France, Belgium, the Netherlands, Norway, Czechoslovakia, and the rest of the occupied countries, the Nazis converted the educational institutions, from kindergarten to university, into agencies for the dissemination of propaganda. Nothing was left undone either physically or psychologically which would help to pervert the concept and practice of education in the occupied countries.[62]

In the United States, the most serious form of disorganized educational relationship occasioned by the war was the decline in attendance. The United States Office of Education reported a decrease of approximately one million pupils enrolled in the nation's high schools in the school year 1943–1944, as compared to the school year 1940–1941. The enlistment or induction of high school students accounted for part of this decrease, but the largest part was occasioned by those who left school to work in war industries or (more often) in service industries as waitresses or filling station attendants. Many of these young people never returned to school, and the war deprived them of their right to an education.[63]

[60] *Understanding Juvenile Delinquency,* Children's Bureau Publication No. 300, Washington, 1943, p. 19.

[61] Federal Security Agency, U.S. Office of Education, *Education Under Enemy Occupation,* Washington, 1945, p. 1.

[62] *Ibid.*

[63] Ella A. Merritt and Floy Hendricks, "Trend of Child Labor, 1940–44," *Monthly Labor Review,* 60:756–775 (April, 1945).

2. *The Church.* The church is basically concerned with the vital realm of spiritual values. We have already considered some of the spiritual implications of total war to a Christian culture. During World War I both the Allies and the Central Powers prayed to the same Divine Power for victory, each nation secure in the belief that its own national aims were sanctioned by the Almighty. In World War II, the Nazis tacitly rejected Christianity as their central spiritual force and substituted the worship of the party, the state, and *Der Führer.* Many German clergymen worked for the government during the war, however. The conflict between Christian nations was not as pronounced as in the first war. The Allies could reasonably maintain that they were fighting in defense of Christian principles against a power which had rejected all the ethical and spiritual values of Christian culture and substituted the incarnation of brutal force.[64]

The church in wartime is always an instrument of national morale. It is an agency of spiritual assistance for those whose loved ones are in danger or have already made the supreme sacrifice. Clergymen of all faiths take their places in the armed forces as chaplains, where they do what they can to comfort the soldier in his hour of trial. The clergy who stay at home contribute to the civilian war effort and thus serve the national cause. The institution of the church, furthermore, is closely related to the other institutions through the interlocking roles of its communicants. In this way, "the same body of men, often the very same persons, who as church members deeply influence religious affairs, as politicians, business men, labor leaders or scholars guide also the political and economic destinies of their nations."[65] The fortunes of the church are thus inextricably intertwined with those of the national state.

The ultimate effect of modern war upon the status of institutional religion is difficult to assess. Some maintain that wartime disregard for many of the elements of the Christian tradition decreased the institutional power of religion in the Western world. Others insist that the catastrophic experience of total war has increased the religious attitudes of millions of persons and consequently strengthened the church. On balance, there appears to have been a definite increase in religious feeling in the period of the two world wars. The recent figures for those professing religion in the United States indicate a great upsurge of religious interest.[66]

3. *The State.* "War," according to a brilliant essayist in World War I, "is the health of the state."[67] By this he meant that the moral fervor of war in-

[64] For an extensive historical discussion of the effects of war upon religion, see Salo W. Baron, "Impact of Wars on Religion," *Political Science Quarterly,* 67:534–572 (December, 1952).

[65] *Ibid.,* p. 569.

[66] Bureau of the Census, *Religion Reported by Civilian Population of the United States: March, 1957, Current Population Reports,* Series P-20, No. 79 (February 8, 1958), p. 1.

[67] Randolph Bourne, "Unfinished Fragment on the State," in *Untimely Papers,* B. W. Huebach, New York, 1919.

creases the power of the state over its citizens and centralizes the control of the government. This increase in power is apparent in all nations during the early years of war and is generally true of nations that win a war. It does *not* apply to states that lose a war, for this situation may precipitate a revolution and a shift in power. During the war itself, however, the institutional power of the state is greatly enhanced. Total war mobilizes the energies of all the people toward the successful prosecution of the conflict. The life of the nation is at stake, and the individual tends to identify himself with the nation. The power of the government over the individual increases, as all other institutions are likewise directed toward the single goal of victory. Total war thus increases the power of the total state.[68]

The most obvious example of the total power of the state in wartime is the ability to draft men for combat and possible death. In contrast to the time when warfare was conducted largely by professional soldiers, modern war has become a democratic enterprise. All men of military age are, in theory, admitted to the complete equality of serving in the armed forces and possibly giving their lives. In other words, "The identification of violence with virtue, with the willingness to make a gratuitous sacrifice of one's life, made it possible not merely to restore the prestige of fighting under conditions of industrialism and mass slaughter, but to extend that prestige to all, to make it as democratic as the suffrage."[69]

The increased power of the wartime state also affects the civilian population, as consumer goods are rationed, prices are controlled, and compulsory savings plans are introduced. Labor organizations come more thoroughly under the direction of the government, for labor is a basic commodity in an industrial war. Cooperation is usually achieved by voluntary means, since most members of labor organizations are eager to contribute to the war effort. In cases of recalcitrant organizations, emergency war powers are evoked against the right to strike. Shifts in power within the institutional framework of the state itself are also apparent, as the executive branch assumes more control at the expense of the legislative and judicial. The general trend of government is in the direction of greater centralized authority, as the nation is mobilized into a single fighting unit.[70]

"Wars," it has been said, "begin in the minds of men."[71] Total war thus involves the total psychological mobilization of the nation. Differences of opinion on ideological and political matters are discarded as dangerous luxuries in wartime. The nation is mobilized against the external threat, and internal unorthodoxy receives slight toleration. The advocacy of an unpopular political belief may lead to imprisonment for citizens and deportation for

[68] Aron, *op. cit.*, chap. 4, "War and the Total State."
[69] Nef, *op. cit.*, p. 409.
[70] *Ibid.*, chap. 18, "The Material Road to Total War."
[71] This statement occurs in the preamble of the constitution of the United Nations Educational, Scientific, and Cultural Organization, commonly known as Unesco. For further discussion see Otto Klineberg, *Tensions Affecting International Understanding,* Social Science Research Council, Bulletin No. 62, New York, 1950.

aliens. Freedom of discussion is considered dangerous to the monolithic conformity deemed necessary for success in total war. The end is viewed as the safety of the state, and many new means are considered acceptable to that end. One of these is the increased power of the state over the minds of its people.[72]

Social Disorganization and the Cold War

We are now living in a period of "cold war." This graphic phrase was coined by Prime Minister Winston Churchill immediately after the end of World War II. In these words he dramatized the bipolarization of the postwar world. The cold war is a continued state of acute hostility in which two major groups of powers combat each other by every means short of open war. "The cold war," remarks Aron, "is a limited war—limited, however, not as to the stakes, but as to the means employed by the belligerents."[73] The means include the cessation of trade, propaganda, espionage, sabotage, "accidental" attacks upon enemy aircraft, belligerent pronouncements, crushing expenditures for "defense," and the official inculcation of hostile attitudes toward the enemy. The cold war is both the cause and the effect of the general tendency to bipolarization of power between the United States and the USSR since World War II. Some nations have attempted to maintain a precarious neutrality between these camps, but as international tensions have increased, such a role has become more and more difficult.[74]

There is a close relationship between bipolarity and the threat of war. As Lasswell points out, "Bipolarity is a function of a continuing high level of expected war. One basic characteristic of world culture is the expectation of violence, defined as the expectation that, whether one likes it or not, wars are viewed as likely."[75] When the peoples of the bipolar groups view war as inevitable, or at least likely, the danger of war is increased. Social attitudes are tendencies to act, and the stronger the tendencies the greater the possibility of action. Each side supports values which it is not prepared to yield, even at the risk of war.[76] If the world is to become one in which permanent peace is possible, the expectation of violence must be counterbalanced by other expectations.[77]

Meanwhile, the peoples of the world are tired and fearful of war. The leaders of both hostile camps are likewise fearful of the destructive possibilities of atomic war. Both the United States and the USSR would suffer overwhelming losses in the event of an all-out conflict. Great losses would also be sustained

[72] Nef. *op. cit.*, chap. 19, "The Intellectual Road to Total War."

[73] Aron, *op. cit.*, p. 171.

[74] Byron L. Fox, "International Cultural Relations," *American Sociological Review*, 15:489–495 (August, 1950).

[75] Harold D. Lasswell *et al.*, *The World Revolution of Our Time*, Hoover Institute Studies, Stanford University Press, Stanford, 1951, p. 33.

[76] Cf. Hans Gerth and C. Wright Mills, *Character and Social Structure*, Harcourt, Brace and Company, New York, 1953, pp. 472–480, "Character Structure in a Polarized World."

[77] Lasswell *et al.*, *The World Revolution of Our Time*, p. 33.

by the other nations aligned on each side. Khrushchev has implored the powerful nations to embark on a program of peace and freedom. Meanwhile, Eisenhower has carried a similar message to the peoples of the Mediterranean and Near East. An effective pact to eliminate war can come, however, only when the distrust and hostility between Communism and democracy are overcome. The struggle is not over.

"War," as John Nef says, "is now even less a separate problem than in earlier times; it is part of the total problem of modern civilization."[78] The problem must be solved if modern civilization is to survive. This does not mean that World War III would wipe out all of the men, women, and children in Europe and America, let alone those living in some of the more "backward" areas of the world. It *does* mean that a full-scale nuclear war would set the civilized world back incalculably in its cultural development. The drift toward another total war can be met only by the gradual evolution of some common basis of understanding between the antagonists of the bipolar world. This understanding would not be confined to the nations of the Western world, but would extend to the emerging nations of the Eastern world as well. For better or for worse, we are all members of one world. In a nuclear age, we shall eventually survive or perish together.[79]

We come now to the end of our road. This book opens on a note of social change and closes on the same note. Social change brings social disorganization, as the relationships that bind the group are strained and broken. Social change brings transformations in attitudes and values, and the old certainties tend to lose their force in a dynamic and anxious world. The individual changes with the roles which he is obliged to assume in a fluid social structure. The average person is only partially aware of the nature of the forces that affect so vitally his personal status and role. He is, however, uneasy as he tries to understand the vast repercussions of revolution, totalitarianism, and war upon his personal life.

A liberal education attempts to provide some understanding of the forces that are remaking the world before our eyes. These forces are complex. This book has merely hinted at some of them. We have tried, however, to open the way to a greater comprehension of the breakdown of the old patterns and the evolution of the new. A new world can be aided by an understanding of the changes taking place in the structure and functions of the old. If the reader has gained any additional insight into the world in which he lives and the changes taking place in it, this book will have served its purpose.

SELECTED BIBLIOGRAPHY

Aron, Raymond, *The Century of Total War,* Doubleday and Company, Inc., New York, 1954. The twentieth century has experienced the two greatest wars in history. Man will continue to live under the threat of a third world war. The

[78] Nef. *op. cit.,* p. 414.
[79] Toynbee, *op. cit.*

present century has also seen the emergence of total war, the implications of which are the subject of this perceptive analysis by a French sociologist.

Baldwin, Hanson W., "The New Face of War," *Bulletin of the Atomic Scientists, 12:*153–158 (May, 1956). In this article a leading writer on military affairs gives a dispassionate analysis of the changes that have occurred since World War II in the tactics and strategy of war. He is especially concerned with the technological changes that have brought nuclear weapons, guided missiles, new biological and chemical weapons, radioactive dusts and gases, and ships and submarines powered with nuclear reactors.

Bernard, L. L., *War and Its Causes,* Henry Holt and Company, Inc., New York, 1944. This volume deals thoughtfully and extensively with the causes of modern war and indicates the extreme complexity of international conflict in an age of total war.

Klineberg, Otto, *Tensions Affecting International Understanding,* Social Science Research Council, Bulletin No. 62, New York, 1950. This monograph explores the implications of the statement that wars begin in the minds of men. The author is a well-known psychologist who has been active in the studies conducted by the United Nations Educational, Scientific, and Cultural Organization.

Lasswell, Harold D., *et al., The World Revolution of Our Time,* Hoover Institute Studies, Stanford University Press, Stanford, 1951. This is the first of a series of perceptive studies conducted by the Hoover Institute into the massive cycle of war and revolution that marks our time.

Merrill, Francis E., *Social Problems on the Home Front,* Harper & Brothers, New York, 1948. This is a study of the trends in certain selected aspects of individual and social disorganization that were intensified, modified, or temporarily alleviated by the social changes of World War II. The book deals largely with the American scene, which is the "home front" of the title.

Morgenthau, Hans J., "Has Atomic War Really Become Impossible?" *Bulletin of the Atomic Scientists, 12:*7–9 (January, 1956). The answer given to this rhetorical question is "no." In his discussion of the "atomic stalemate," the author maintains that nuclear warfare has become infinitely grave but not impossible.

Nef, John U., *War and Human Progress,* Harvard University Press, Cambridge, 1950. The author directs his analysis to the hypothesis, often expressed, that war encourages many forms of progress, notably in technology and industry. He concludes that, on balance, this is not true and that war is more destructive than constructive in these fields.

Shils, Edward A., "Security and Science Sacrificed to Loyalty," *Bulletin of the Atomic Scientists, 11:*106–109 (April, 1955). The free exchange of scientific information has been one of the casualties of the cold war, even in fields only remotely connected with military security. This article explores some of the implications of the situation.

Wright, Quincy A., *A Study of War,* University of Chicago Press, Chicago, 1942 (2 vols.). This monumental work deals primarily with the historical, legal, and juridical aspects of war. In these terms, it is probably the most extensive treatise now available.

INDEXES

Index of Names

757

Index of Subjects

Abatement laws and prostitution, 171
Abortions, among married women, 165; among single women, 165
Accommodation, as a social process, 7; definition of, 7; inevitability of, 7
Actresses, lack of prejudice against working, 240
Adolescence, 53, 54, 87; adjustments of, 54, 266; criminality and, 127; juvenile delinquency and, 76
Adult offenders, 101–150; age increase and decline in offenses of, 101; anthropometric studies of, 131; army men compared in intelligence to, 136; as victims of circumstances, 149; body types and, 131; emotional factors affecting, 137–138; endocrine gland theory concerning, 130–131; foreign born among, 132–133, 542; lack of sense of responsibility of, 142; lower-class status of, 149; mental deficiency and, 135–136; mesomorphs among, 131; methods of dealing with, 49; Negro and white compared as, 139–140; personality profiles of, 138–140; physical characteristics of, 130–131; predominance of men among, 128–129; rejection of social values by, 101; sex offenders among, 136
    See also Adults, as criminals; Crime; Criminals; Negro crimes
Adultery, as grounds for divorce, 384, 385, 386, 387, 388, 414; as legal ground for divorce, 395, 396–401; definition of, 395; evidence for, 395, 402
Adults, adjustments of: to children, 266, to responsibilities, 266, to stresses and strains, 266; as criminals, 59; roles of, 54–55; responsibilities of, 266
    See also Adult offenders
Affection, sex in relation to, 340
Age, of marriage and divorce risk, 425; proportion of criminal offenses and, 101–102
Aged, the, 55

Agreement on social values, importance to marriage of, 360–361
Agricultural revolution, changing rural class structure and, 489–491; consolidation of schools and, 482–483; declining rural population and, 486–487; federal subsidies to farmers and, 489; hard-surfaced roads and, 482; mechanization of agriculture and, 475, 480–482; "rurbanization" of rural areas and, 483; scientific agriculture and, 475, 482; tenancy and, 483–484; varieties of: with horse-drawn machinery, 475, with scientific agriculture and mechanization, 475, with scythe, 475
Agricultural science, increased yields resulting from, 482
Agricultural society, shift to industrial society of, 246
Agricultural workers, *see* Farm laborers
Agriculture, 30; increased production in, 517
Aid to dependent children, extent of deserted children covered in, 382, 410–412
Akron, Ohio, 542
Alabama, 392, 396, 405, 485, 510, 511, 656; child labor provisions of, 252; mental illness of Negro residents of, 305–306; minimum school age in, 255; prisoners, 140; regulations on newspaper selling at night, 261
Alaska, 108, 243, 396, 405, 417; child labor provisions of, 252; minimum school age in, 255; regulations on newspaper selling at night, 261
Albania, 729
Alberta, Canada, 416
Alcohol, as a substitute for personal contacts, 187; as a disorganizer of personalities, 185; brain syndromes and, 196; depressant effect of, 193; emotional satisfactions of, 187; extent of consumption of, 184; fatigue and, 194; intoxica-

sin and, 553; psychiatry's conflict with, 104–105; restraint of nonlawbreakers by, 552; social values and, 545

Criminal procedures, indictments, 556; jury trials, 556; mistaken identity and, 556; technicalities, 556; "trials by newspaper," 557

Criminal science, greater research needed in, 560

Criminal types, Ferri's theory of, 114; Garofalo's theory of, 114; Lombroso's theory of, 114

Criminality, adult, 101; age and, 124–125; cultural and environmental factors in, 142–148; decrease of with increase in age, 125–126; divorce and, 143–144; economic factors in, 144–146; education and, 139, 140; emotional disturbances and, 143; habitual character of, 127–128; learned aspect of, 121; marital status and: of men, 142, of women, 143–144; median ages and, 126; multiple factors in, 123–124; puberty and, 126; selective factors in, 122–124; unemployment and, 145; work history and, 148; youth and, 124–125

Criminals, 521; Christian attitude toward, 63; in conflict with society, 106–107; limited knowledge concerning, 116; lower-class status and, 117; moral turpitude and, 105; professional, 549; white-collar class, 117

See also Adult offenders

Crippled and handicapped children, medical and rehabilitation services for, 620

Crisis, definition of, 35–36; different varieties of, 37–38; entire society and, 37; examples of, 36; individual cumulative type, 56; individual precipitate type, 56; psychological reactions to, 35; recognized aspect of modern life, 35; social disorganization and, 35–36; stages of, 35; types of situations and, 35; war and, 37

Cromwellian civil marriage, 388

Cruelty as legal ground for divorce, 396–401, 402

Cultural and ethnic groups, absorption of, 623

Cultural conflict, and social disorganization as exemplified in juvenile delinquency and political corruption, 588; as factor in crime, 541–542; as factor in divorce, 421; disorganizing aspects of, 584–585; intensified periods of, 593; value judgments and, 585

Cultural contradictions, women's role and, 368

Cultural heterogeneity, as factor in social disorganization, 599; decrease in, 587

Cultural lag, general nature of, 30; social disorganization and, 30–31

Cultural minorities, 99

Cultural revolution and rural migration to city, 517

Culture, American, 475–476, 547–548

Culture change, differential rates in, 30; diffusion and, 29; disorganization and, 29; invention and, 29

Culture shock, 584; suicide rates and, 333

Custody of children, judges' attitude toward, 421

Cut-over land, 495

Czechoslovakia, 724, 729, 748

Czechs, 594

Dark skin, climatic reasons for, 646

Daughters and break with parental family, 367

Death wish, *see* Will to die

Deaths in wartime, 740–741

Defenders of the Christian Faith, 630

Defense, expenditures since World War II, 742–743; spending: economic hazards in reducing, 618, full employment and, 617–618, substitute for, 618

Delaware, 392, 396, 663; child labor outside school hours, 259; child labor provisions of, 252; mental illness rates in, 285; minimum school age in, 255; regulations on newspaper selling at night, 261; restrictions on theatrical performances, 260

See also Illegitimacy

Delinquency, *see* Juvenile delinquency

Delinquency areas, Boston, Mass., 93; Birmingham, Ala., 93; Columbus, Ohio, 93; Denver, Colo., 93; Omaha, Neb., 93; Richmond, Va., 93

Delinquency patterning in cities, 99

Delinquent attitudes, 32

Delinquent children, backgrounds of: boys, 78–79, girls, 157–158; offenses of: boys, 73–74, girls, 157–158; sex offenses of, 74

See also Juvenile delinquents

Dements, 265

Desegregation, Catholic churches and, 657; disorganization and, 658–659; in Negro educational institutions, 655; in public schools, 656–658; in universities and colleges, 655; lawsuits, 655; possibilities for implementing, 659; public recreational facilities: in North, 674, in Washington, D.C., 674, with restrictions, 674; social disorganization and, 31; time requirements for, 657

Deserting fathers, 410–412

Deserting mothers, 409

police referred cases, 75; recidivism among, 63; referrals to court, 74–75; society's responsibility for, 66; stigmatizing of, 63

See also Juvenile delinquency

Kansas, 243, 392, 393, 397, 405, 511, 512, 571; child labor provisions of, 252; minimum school age in, 255; regulations on newspaper selling at night, 261

Kansas City, 96

Kansas Public Welfare (Temporary) Commission, 270

Kansas Training School, 270

Kentucky, 243, 392, 397, 404, 405, 511; child labor outside school hours, 259; child labor provisions of, 252; minimum school age in, 255; regulations on newspaper selling at night, 261

Khrushchev, 717, 721, 723, 725, 729, 752; secret speech to the Twentieth Congress of the Communist Party of the Soviet Union, 721, 723–724

Kinsey reports, 153–156; criticisms of, 156–157; moral implications of, 156; response to, 156–157

See also Sex behavior, studies of

Kirov, 723

Korean War, 738, 739; delinquency and, 94

Ku Klux Klan, 631

La Jolla, Calif., 639

Labor, goals of, 224; political power of, 224; social welfare and, 224

Labor organizations, hostility of toward women, 236; legislation against, 218; public opinion toward, 223; violence and, 223

Laborers, see Workers

"Land, bread, and peace," 692

Laos, 729

Latvia, 729

Law, women in, 240

Legal and moral restraints, destruction of by war, 744–745

Legal separation, as a first step in absolute divorce, 391; dubious social aspects of, 391; Roman Catholic acceptance of, 390–391

See also Interlocutory divorce decrees

Leisure, delinquency and, 89

Lenin, 720, 721, 724

Les Misérables, 96

Level of living among farmers, highest ranking states, 494; low in southern states, 494

Liberal education, 752

Licensing of voluntary organizations in Russia, 711

Life organization, see Individual life organization

Liquidation of peoples, during Lenin's regime, 723; during Hitler's regime, 723; during Stalin's regime, 723–724; of Jews, Marx's part in, 717; of nobility and educated classes in Soviet Union, 711; of regular party members, 723; without proof of guilt, 723

Lithuania, 729

Little Rock, Ark., 659

Loathsome disease, as a legal ground for divorce, 396–401, 404; as evidence of adultery, 404

Logging as prohibited industry for women, 234

London, 748

"Lonely Crowd, The," David Riesman's theory of, 59

Long Island, N.Y., 569

Los Angeles, Calif., 569

Louisiana, 149, 243, 391, 392, 393, 397, 415, 511, 656; child labor outside school hours, 259; child labor provisions of, 252; minimum school age in, 254–255; regulations on newspaper selling at night, 261; restrictions on theatrical performances, 260

Lower class, 27; family patterns of, 370–371; high rate of mental illness among, 57, 307–310; highest rate of family disorganization among, 370–371; largely unrepresented in community affairs, 465; social relations of, 465

Luther, Martin, civil marriage and, 388

Luxury values, relation to delinquency of, 93

McCarran-Walter Act of 1953, 650

Machine, definition of, 211; disorganizing impact on social order of, 211

McNaghten Case, 104

Maine, 243, 391, 397; child labor outside school hours, 259; child labor provisions of, 252; minimum school age of, 255; regulations on newspaper selling at night, 261

Management and labor conflict, causes of, 217

Manic-depressive psychoses, characteristics of, 295; depressed state and, 295; public hospital treatment of, 300

Manitoba, 416

Marginal farmers, inability to earn a decent living, 518

Marginal land, need for retirement of, 503; plans for developing: fees to help farmers

Date Due